CLYMER®

EVINRUDE/JOHNSON

2-STROKE OUTBOARD SHOP MANUAL

2-70 HP • 1995-2003 (Includes Jet Drive Models)

The world's finest publisher of mechanical how-to manuals

PRIMEDIA
Information Data Products

P.O. Box 12901, Overland Park, KS 66282-2901

Copyright ©2005 PRIMEDIA Business Magazines and Media Inc.

FIRST EDITION
First Printing December, 1998
Second Printing December, 2001
Third Printing August, 2003
SECOND EDITION
First Printing February, 2005

Printed in U.S.A.

CLYMER and colophon are registered trademarks of PRIMEDIA Business Magazines and Media Inc.

ISBN: 0-89287-929-7

Library of Congress: 2004116856

TECHNICAL ILLUSTRATIONS: Michael St. Clair, Robert Caldwell and Steve Amos.

TECHNICAL PHOTOGRAPHY: Scott Johnson. Assistance provided by: D&D Bay Marina, Beaver Dam, Wisconsin.

PRODUCTION: Dylan Goodwin.

TOOLS AND EQUIPMENT: Chapter Two tools courtesy of Thorsen Tool, Dallas, Texas. Chapter Two test equipment courtesy of Dixson, Inc., Grand Junction, Colorado.

COVER: Photo courtesy of Outboard Marine Corporation, Waukegan, Illinois.

CLYMER®

Publisher Shawn Etheridge

EDITORIAL

Managing Editor
James Grooms

Associate Editor
Tom Beazley
Lee Buell

Technical Writers
Jay Bogart
Michael Morlan
George Parise
Mark Rolling
Ed Scott
Ron Wright

Editorial Production Manager
Dylan Goodwin

Senior Production Editor
Greg Araujo

Production Editors
Holly Messinger
Darin Watson

Associate Production Editors
Susan Hartington
Julie Jantzer-Ward
Justin Marciniak

Technical Illustrators
Steve Amos
Errol McCarthy
Mitzi McCarthy
Bob Meyer

MARKETING/SALES AND ADMINISTRATION

Marketing Director
Rod Cain

Manager, Promotions and Packaging
Elda Starke

Advertising & Promotions Coordinator
Melissa Abbott

Marketing Coordinator
Chris Gregory

Art Director
Chris Paxton

Associate Art Director
Jennifer Knight

Sales Managers
Dutch Sadler, Marine
Matt Tusken, Motorcycles

Business Manager
Ron Rogers

Customer Service Manager
Terri Cannon

Customer Service Representatives
Shawna Davis
Courtney Hollars
Susan Kohlmeyer
Jennifer Lassiter
April LeBlond
Luis Lebron

Warehouse & Inventory Manager
Leah Hicks

PRIMEDIA
Business Magazines & Media
P.O. Box 12901, Overland Park, KS 66282-2901 • 800-262-1954 • 913-967-1719

The following books and guides are published by PRIMEDIA Business Directories & Books.

More information available at *primediabooks.com*

Contents

CHAPTER FIVE

SYNCHRONIZATION AND LINKAGE ADJUSTMENTS. 196

CHAPTER SIX

FUEL SYSTEM 243

CHAPTER SEVEN

IGNITION AND ELECTRICAL SYSTEMS. 305

CHAPTER EIGHT

POWER HEAD. 366

CHAPTER NINE
LOWER GEARCASE AND JET DRIVE UNITS **485**

CHAPTER TEN
TRIM AND TILT SYSTEMS **589**

CHAPTER ELEVEN
OIL INJECTION SYSTEMS **661**

CHAPTER TWELVE
ROPE STARTERS AND REMOTE CONTROLS **693**

INDEX **725**

WIRING DIAGRAMS **728**

Quick Reference Data

COMMON ENGINE SPECIFICATIONS

System	Specification
Fuel	
Recommended fuel	87 (or higher) pump posted octane (AKI[1]), containing no alcohol or oxygenates
Minimum requirements	87 (or higher) pump posted octane (AKI[1]), containing no more than 10% ethanol or 5% methanol
Unacceptable fuel	Any fuel with more than 10% ethanol or 5% methanol
Recommended fuel additives	OMC 2+4 Fuel Conditioner (dealer stock item) OMC Carbon Guard (dealer stock item)
Oil	
Recommended oil	Evinrude/Johnson TCW-3, 2-cycle outboard oil
Minimum requirements	NMMA approved TCW-3, 2-cycle outboard oil
Fuel to oil ratio	
Non-oil injected models	
After break-in	50:1
During break-in[2]	25:1
Oil injected models	
After break-in	Not applicable
During break-in[2]	50:1
Gear lubricant	
Recommended lubricant	OMC Ultra HPF Gear Lube or equivalent
Alternate lubricant	OMC Hi-Vis Gear Lube or equivalent
Battery (minimum ratings)	
Marine cranking amps (MCA)	465
Cold cranking amps (CCA)	360
Reserve capacity	90 minutes

1. See Chapter Four.
2. See Chapter Four for break-in procedures.

RECOMMENDED LUBRICANTS, SEALANTS AND ADHESIVES

	Part No.
Lubricants	
OMC Ultra HPF gear lube	(dealer stock item)
OMC Power trim/tilt and steering fluid	174997
OMC EP/wheel bearing grease	(dealer stock item)
OMC Moly lube	175356
OMC Triple guard grease	(dealer stock item)
OMC Needle bearing assembly grease	378642
OMC Starter pinion (bendix) lubricant	337016
OMC DPL light-duty penetrating lubricant	771171
OMC 6-in-1 heavy-duty penetrating lubricant	771159
OMC Anti-corrosion spray	771172
Sealants	
OMC RTV black silicone sealant	263753
OMC Gasket sealing compound	508235
OMC Black neoprene dip	909570
OMC Pipe sealant with Teflon	910048
OMC Gel Seal II (anaerobic sealant)	324073
3M Marine sealant 101 (polysulfide [OMC or locally available])	506852
Gasoila (varnish type fuel system sealant)	200763
	(continued)

RECOMMENDED LUBRICANTS, SEALANTS AND ADHESIVES (continued)

	Part No.
Adhesives	
OMC Type M adhesive	318535
Scotch grip 1300 adhesive (OMC or locally available)	982551
OMC Locquic primer	772032
OMC HT400 adhesive (high strength and temperature)	500424
OMC Ultra Lock threadlocking adhesive (high strength)	500422
OMC Nut Lock threadlocking adhesive (medium strength)	500418
OMC Screw Lock threadlocking adhesive (low strength)	500416
Miscellaneous	
OMC Engine degreaser	771164
OMC Electrical (dielectric) grease	503243
Heat sink compound (thermal joint compound)	322170
OMC Gel Seal and gasket remover (aerosol)	771050
OMC Gel Seal and gasket remover (liquid)	500415

RECOMMENDED CHAMPION SPARK PLUGS*

Model	Standard (alternate)	Extended idle operation
2, 3.3 and 3.5 hp	QL87YC (L87YC)	Not applicable
3 hp, 4 hp and 4 Deluxe	QL86C (L86C)	L90C
6 and 8 hp	QL86C (L86)	QL82YC
9.9 and 15 hp	QL82C (no alternate)	QL86C
18 Jet	QL82C (no alternate)	Not applicable
20-30 hp (two-cylinder)	QL82C (QL77JC4)	Not applicable
25 and 30 hp (three-cylinder)	QL86C (L86)	QL82YC
40 hp and 28 jet	QL78YC (no alternate)	Not applicable
48, 50 hp (two-cylinder) and 35 jet	QL78YC (no alternate)	QL82C
50 hp (three-cylinder)	QL78YC (no alternate)	QL82C
60 and 70 hp	QL78YC (no alternate)	Not applicable
65 hp (commercial)	QL78YC (no alternate)	QL82C

*On 1998-2003 models, use the spark plug type printed on emission control decal (affixed onto the engine).

GEARCASE GEAR RATIO AND APPROXIMATE LUBRICANT CAPACITY

Outboard model	Gear ratio	Tooth count	Lubricant capacity
2 and 3.3 hp	1.85:1	13.24	3 oz. (89 ml)
3.5 hp	1.85:1	13:24	2.7 oz. (80 ml)
3 and 4 hp	2.08:1	12:25	2.7 oz (80 ml)
4 Deluxe and 6-8 hp	2:23:1	13:29	11 oz. (325 ml)
9.9 and 15 hp	2.42:1	12:29	9 oz. (266 ml)
20, 25, 30 and 35 hp	2.15:1	13:28	11 oz. (325 ml)
28 Special	1.75:1	12:21	8 oz. (237 ml)
40-50 hp (two-cylinder)	2.42:1	12:29	16.4 oz. (485 ml)
50-70 hp (three-cylinder)	2.42:1	12:29	22 oz. (651 ml)
18-35 jet models	Not applicable	–	–

TEST WHEEL (PROPELLER) RECOMMENDATIONS

Model	OMC part No.	Minimum test rpm
2 hp	115208 (standard propeller)	4500
3.3 and 3.5 hp	115306	5000
3 and 4 hp	317738	4400
4 Deluxe	390123	5100
6 hp	390239	4800
8 hp	390239	5300
9.9 hp	340177	4900
15 hp	340177	5700
20-30 hp (two-cylinder)		
20 hp	386891	4550
25 hp	434505	4800
28 Special	398948	4800
30 hp	434505	5400
25 hp (three-cylinder)		
1995	434505	4400
1996-2003	434505	4200
35 hp (three-cylinder)	434505	5000
40-50 hp (two-cylinder)		
40 hp	432968	4900
48 and 50 hp	432968	5200
50-70 hp (three-cylinder)		
50 hp	386665	4600
60 hp	386665	5000
70 hp	386665	5700
18-35 jet models	Not applicable	Not applicable

STANDARD TORQUE VALUES—AMERICAN FASTENERS

Screw or nut size	in.-lb.	ft.-lb.	N•m
6	7-10	–	0.8-1.1
8	15-22	–	1.7-2.5
10	25-35	–	2.8-4.0
12	35-40	–	4.0-4.5
1/4	60-84	–	6.8-9.5
5/16	120-144	10-12	13.6-16.3
3/8	216-240	18-20	24.4-27.1
7/16	–	28-30	38.0-40.7
1/2	–	50	67.8

STANDARD TORQUE VALUES—METRIC FASTENERS

Screw or nut size	in.-lb.	ft.-lb.	N•m
M3	15-22	–	1.7-2.5
M4	24-36	–	2.7-4.1
M5	36-60	–	4.1-6.8
M6	84-106	–	9.5-12.0
M6 (Taptite)	108-132	9-11	12.2-14.9
M8	180-204	15-17	20.3-23.0
M10	–	26-28	35.3-38.0
M12	–	35	47.5
M14	–	60	81.3

CLYMER®

EVINRUDE/JOHNSON

2-STROKE OUTBOARD SHOP MANUAL

2-70 HP • 1995-2003 (Includes Jet Drive Models)

Introduction

This Clymer shop manual covers service and repair of all 1995-2003 model year 2-70 hp Evinrude and Johnson outboard motors designed for recreational use. Coverage is also provided for 18-35 jet drive models. Commercial, sail and 4-stroke models are not covered in this manual.

Step-by-step instructions and hundreds of illustrations guide you through tasks ranging from routine maintenance to complete overhaul.

This manual can be used by anyone from a first time owner to a professional technician. Easy-to-read type, detailed drawings and clear photographs give you all the information needed to do the procedure correctly.

Having a well-maintained outboard engine will increase your enjoyment of your boat as well as ensuring your safety offshore. Keep this shop manual handy and use it often. Performing routine, preventive maintenance will save you time and money by helping to prevent premature failure and unnecessary repairs.

Chapter One

General Information

This detailed, comprehensive manual contains complete information covering maintenance, repair and overhaul. Hundreds of photos and drawings guide you throughout every procedure.

Troubleshooting, tune-up, maintenance and repair are not difficult if you know what tools and equipment to use and what to do. Anyone not afraid to get their hands dirty, of average intelligence and with some mechanical ability can perform most of the procedures in this manual. See Chapter Two for more information on tools and techniques.

A shop manual is a reference. You want to be able to find information quickly. Clymer books are designed with you in mind. All chapters are thumb tabbed and important items are indexed at the end of the manual. All procedures, tables, photos and instructions in this manual assume the reader may be working on the machine or using the manual for the first time.

Keep the manual in a handy place in your toolbox or boat. It will help you to better understand how your boat runs, lower repair and maintenance costs and generally increase your enjoyment of your boat.

MANUAL ORGANIZATION

This chapter provides general information useful to boat owners and marine mechanics.

Chapter Two discusses the tools and techniques for preventative maintenance, troubleshooting and repair.

Chapter Three provides troubleshooting and testing procedures for all systems and individual components.

Following chapters describe specific systems, providing disassembly, inspection, assembly and adjustment procedures in simple step-by-step form. Specifications concerning a specific system are included at the end of the appropriate chapter.

NOTES, CAUTIONS AND WARNINGS

The terms NOTE, CAUTION and WARNING have specific meanings in this manual. A NOTE provides additional information to make a step or procedure easier or more clear. Disregarding a NOTE could cause inconvenience, but would not cause damage or personal injury.

A CAUTION emphasizes areas where equipment damage could cause permanent mechanical damage; however, personal injury is unlikely.

A WARNING emphasizes areas where personal injury or even death could result from negligence. Mechanical damage may also occur. WARNINGS *must* be taken seriously. In some cases, serious injury or death has resulted from disregarding similar warnings.

TORQUE SPECIFICATIONS

Torque specifications throughout this manual are given in foot-pounds (ft.-lb.), inch-pounds (in.-lb.) and newton meters (N•m.). Newton meters are being adopted in place of meter-kilograms (mkg) in accordance with the International Modernized Metric System. Existing torque wrenches calibrated in meter-kilograms can be used by performing a simple conversion: move the decimal point one place to the right. For example, 4.7 mkg = 47 N•m. This conversion is accurate enough for most mechanical operations even though the exact mathematical conversion is 3.5 mkg = 34.3 N•m.

ENGINE OPERATION

All marine engines, whether two or four-stroke, gasoline or diesel, operate on the Otto cycle of intake, compression, power and exhaust phases.

Two-Stroke Cycle

A two-stroke engine requires one crankshaft revolution (two strokes of the piston) to complete the Otto cycle. All engines covered in this manual are a two-stroke design. **Figure 1** shows gasoline two-stroke engine operation.

Four-Stroke Cycle

A four-stroke engine requires two crankshaft revolutions (four strokes of the piston) to complete the Otto cycle. **Figure 2** shows gasoline four-stroke engine operation.

FASTENERS

The material and design of the various fasteners used on marine equipment are carefully thought out and designed. Fastener design determines the type of tool required to work with the fastener. Fastener material is carefully selected to decrease the possibility of physical failure or corrosion. See *Galvanic Corrosion* in this chapter for information on marine materials.

Nuts, bolts and screws are manufactured in a wide range of thread patterns. To join a nut and bolt, the diameter of the bolt and the diameter of the hole in the nut must be the same. It is just as important that the threads are compatible.

The easiest way to determine if fastener threads are compatible is to turn the nut on the bolt, or bolt into its threaded opening, using fingers only. Be sure both pieces are clean. If much force is required, check the thread condition on each fastener. If the thread condition is good but the fasteners jam, the threads are not compatible.

Four important specifications describe the thread:

1. Diameter.
2. Threads per inch.
3. Thread pattern.

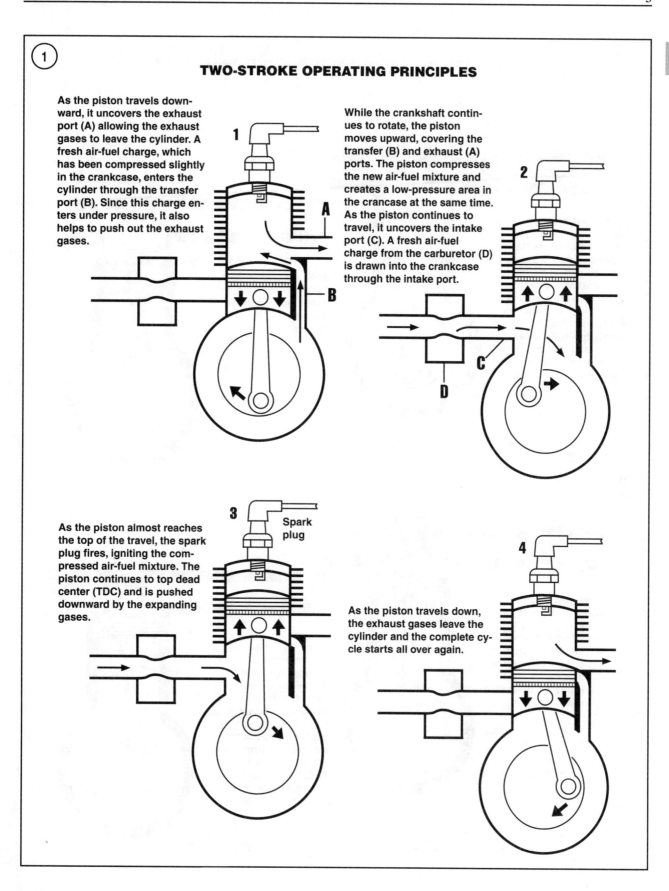

1

TWO-STROKE OPERATING PRINCIPLES

1 As the piston travels downward, it uncovers the exhaust port (A) allowing the exhaust gases to leave the cylinder. A fresh air-fuel charge, which has been compressed slightly in the crankcase, enters the cylinder through the transfer port (B). Since this charge enters under pressure, it also helps to push out the exhaust gases.

2 While the crankshaft continues to rotate, the piston moves upward, covering the transfer (B) and exhaust (A) ports. The piston compresses the new air-fuel mixture and creates a low-pressure area in the crancase at the same time. As the piston continues to travel, it uncovers the intake port (C). A fresh air-fuel charge from the carburetor (D) is drawn into the crankcase through the intake port.

3 As the piston almost reaches the top of the travel, the spark plug fires, igniting the compressed air-fuel mixture. The piston continues to top dead center (TDC) and is pushed downward by the expanding gases.

Spark plug

4 As the piston travels down, the exhaust gases leave the cylinder and the complete cycle starts all over again.

② **FOUR-STROKE GASOLINE OPERATING PRINCIPLES**

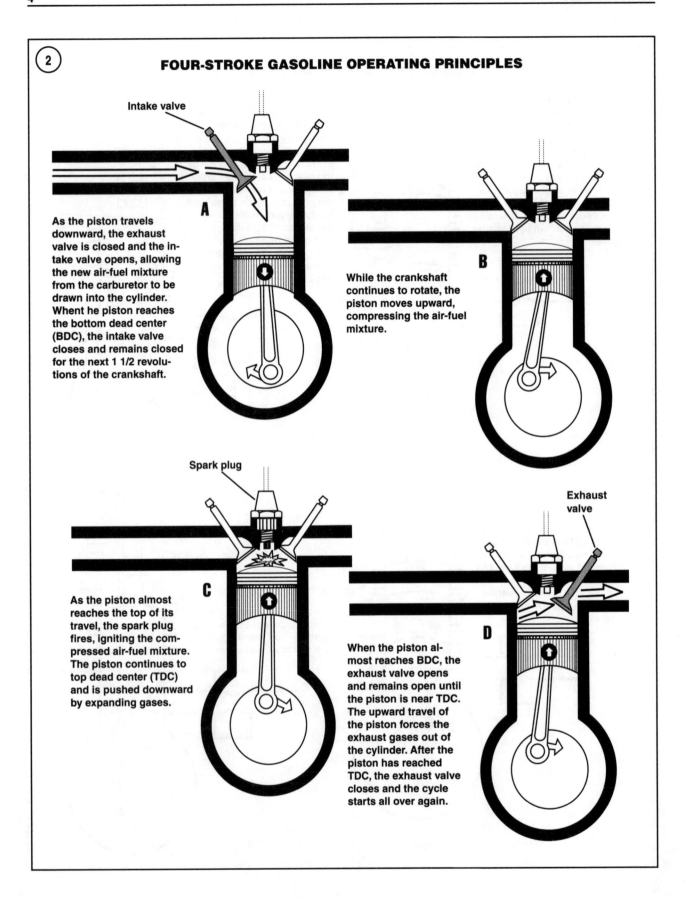

Intake valve

A

As the piston travels downward, the exhaust valve is closed and the intake valve opens, allowing the new air-fuel mixture from the carburetor to be drawn into the cylinder. Whent he piston reaches the bottom dead center (BDC), the intake valve closes and remains closed for the next 1 1/2 revolutions of the crankshaft.

B

While the crankshaft continues to rotate, the piston moves upward, compressing the air-fuel mixture.

Spark plug

C

As the piston almost reaches the top of its travel, the spark plug fires, igniting the compressed air-fuel mixture. The piston continues to top dead center (TDC) and is pushed downward by expanding gases.

Exhaust valve

D

When the piston almost reaches BDC, the exhaust valve opens and remains open until the piston is near TDC. The upward travel of the piston forces the exhaust gases out of the cylinder. After the piston has reached TDC, the exhaust valve closes and the cycle starts all over again.

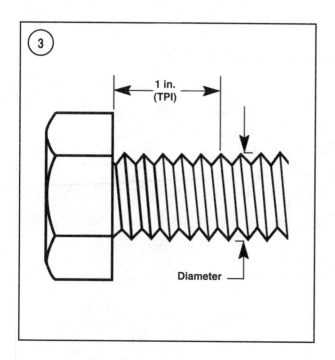

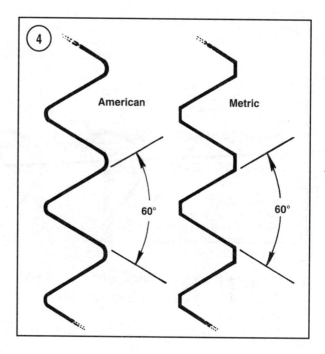

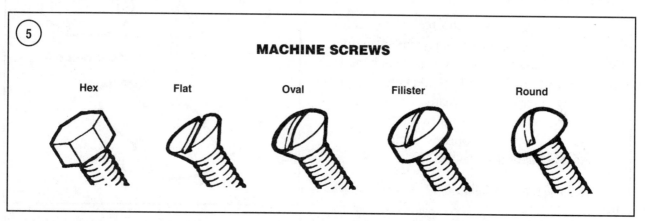

4. Thread direction

Figure 3 shows the first two specifications. Thread pattern is more subtle. Italian and British standards exist, but the most commonly used by marine equipment manufactures are American standard and metric standard. The root and top of the thread are cut differently as shown in **Figure 4**.

Most threads are cut so the fastener must be turned clockwise to tighten it. These are called right-hand threads. Some fasteners have left-hand threads; they must be turned counterclockwise to tighten. Left-hand threads are used in locations where normal rotation of the equipment would tend to loosen a right-hand threaded fastener. Assume all fasteners use right-hand threads unless the instructions specify otherwise.

Machine Screws

There are many different types of machine screws (**Figure 5**). Most are designed to protrude above the secured surface (rounded head) or be slightly recessed below the surface (flat head). In some applications the screw head is recessed well below the fastened sur-

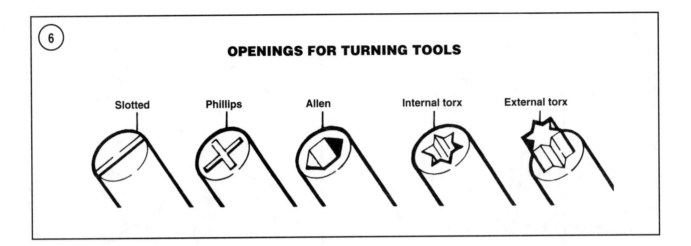

face. **Figure 6** shows a number of screw heads requiring different types of turning tools.

Bolts

Commonly called bolts, the technical name for this fastener is cap screw. They are normally described by diameter, threads per inch and length. For example, 1/4-20 × 1 indicates a bolt 1/4 in. in diameter with 20 threads per inch, 1 in. long. The measurement across two flats of the bolt head indicates the proper wrench size required to turn the bolt.

Nuts

Nuts are manufactured in a variety of types and sizes. Most are hexagonal (six-sides) and fit on bolts, screws and studs with the same diameter and threads per inch.

Figure 7 shows several types of nuts. The common nut is usually used with some type of lockwasher. Self-locking nuts have a nylon insert that helps prevent the nut from loosening; no lockwasher is required. Wing nuts are designed for fast removal by hand. Wing nuts are used for convenience in non-critical locations.

To indicate the size of a nut, manufactures specify the diameter of the opening and the threads per inch. This is similar to a bolt specifi-

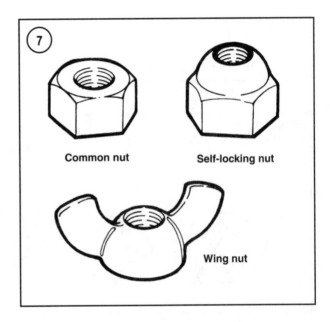

cation, but without the length dimension. The measurement across two flats of the nut indicates the wrench size required to turn the nut.

Washers

There are two basic types of washers: flat washers and lockwashers. A flat washer is a simple disc with a hole that fits the screw or bolt. Lockwashers are designed to prevent a fastener from working loose due to vibration, expansion and contraction. **Figure 8** shows several types of lockwashers. Note that flat washers are often

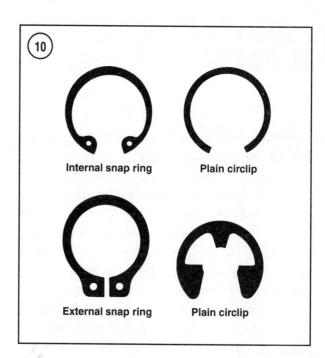

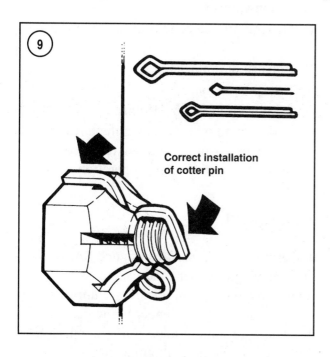

Correct installation
of cotter pin

used between a lockwasher and a fastener to provide a smooth bearing surface. This allows the fastener to be turned easily with a tool.

Cotter Pins

In certain applications, a fastener must be secured so it cannot possibly loosen. The propeller nut on some marine drive systems is one such ap-

plication. For this purpose, a cotter pin (**Figure 9**) and slotted or castellated nut is often used. To use a cotter pin, first make sure the pin fits snugly, but not too tight. Then, align a slot in the fastener with the hole in the bolt or axle. Insert the cotter pin through the nut and bolt or propeller shaft and bend the ends over to secure the cotter pin tightly. If the holes do not align, tighten the nut just enough to obtain the proper alignment. Unless specifically instructed to do so, never loosen the fastener to align the slot and hole. Because the cotter pin is weakened after installation and removal, never reuse a cotter pin. Cotter pins are available in several styles, lengths and diameters. Measure cotter pin length from the bottom of its head to the tip of its shortest prong.

Snap Rings

Snap rings (**Figure 10**) can be an internal or external design. They are used to retain components on shafts (external type) or inside openings (internal type). Snap rings can be reused if they are not distorted during removal. In some applications, snap rings of varying thickness (selective fit) can be selected to position or control end play of parts assemblies.

LUBRICANTS

Periodic lubrication helps ensure long service life for any type of equipment. It is especially important with marine equipment because it is exposed to salt, brackish or polluted water and other harsh environments. The type of lubricant used is just as important as the lubrication service itself, although in an emergency, the wrong type of lubricant is better than none at all. The following paragraphs describe the types of lubricants most often used on marine equipment. Be sure to follow the equipment manufacture's recommendations for the lubricant types.

Generally, all liquid lubricants are called *oil*. They may be mineral-based (including petroleum bases), natural-based (vegetable and animal bases), synthetic-based or emulsions (mixtures). *Grease* is lubricating oil that has a thickening compound added. The resulting material then usually enhanced with anticorrosion, antioxidant and extreme pressure (EP) additives. Grease is often classified by the type of thickener added; lithium and calcium soap are the most commonly used.

Two-stroke Engine Oil

Lubrication for a two-stroke engine is provided by oil mixed with the incoming air/fuel mixture. Some of the oil mist settles out in the crankcase, lubricating the crankshaft, bearings and lower end of the connecting rod. The rest of the oil enters the combustion chamber to lubricate the piston, rings and the cylinder wall. This oil is then burned along with the air/fuel mixture during the combustion process.

Engine oil must have several special qualities to work well in a two-stroke engine. It must mix easily and stay in suspension in gasoline.

When burned, it cannot leave behind excessive deposits. It must also withstand the high operating temperature associated with two-stroke engines.

The National Marine Manufacturer's Association (NMMA) has set standards for oil used in two-stroke, water-cooled engines. This is the NMMA TC-W (two-cycle, water-cooled) grade. It indicates the oil's performance in the following areas:

1. Lubrication (preventing wear and scuffing).
2. Spark plug fouling.
3. Piston ring sticking.
4. Preignition.
5. Piston varnish.
6. General engine condition (including deposits).
7. Exhaust port blockage.
8. Rust prevention.
9. Mixing ability with gasoline.

In addition to oil grade, manufactures specify the ratio of gasoline and oil required during break-in and normal engine operation.

Gearcase Oil

Gearcase lubricants are assigned SAE viscosity numbers under the same system as four-stroke engine oil. Gearcase lubricant falls into the SAE 72-250 range. Some gearcase lubricants are multigrade. For example, SAE 80-90 is a common multigrade gear lubricant.

Three types of marine gearcase lubricants are generally available; SAE 90 hypoid gearcase lubricant is designed for older manual-shift units; type C gearcase lubricant contains additives designed for the electric shift mechanisms; high-viscosity gearcase lubricant is a heavier oil designed to withstand the shock loads of high performance engines or units subjected to severe duty use. Always use the gearcase lubricant specified by the manufacturer.

Grease

Greases are graded by the National Lubricating Grease Institute (NLGI). Greases are graded by number according to the consistency of the grease. These ratings range from No. 000 to No. 6, with No. 6 being the most solid. A typical multipurpose grease is NLGI No. 2. For specific applications, equipment manufactures may require grease with an additive such as molybdenum disulfide (MOS^2).

GASKET SEALANT

Gasket sealant is used instead of preformed gaskets on some applications, or as a gasket dressing on others. Three types of gasket sealant are commonly used: gasket sealing compound, room temperature vulcanizing (RTV) and anaerobic. Because these materials have different sealing properties, they cannot be used interchangeably.

Gasket Sealing Compound

This nonhardening liquid is used primarily as a gasket dressing. Gasket sealing compound is available in tubes or brush top containers. When exposed to air or heat it forms a rubber-like coating. The coating fills in small imperfections in gasket and sealing surfaces. Do not use gasket sealing compound that is old, has began to solidify or has darkened in color.

Applying Gasket Sealing Compound

Carefully scrape residual gasket material, corrosion deposits or paint from the mating surfaces. Use a blunt scraper and work carefully to avoid damaging the mating surfaces. Use quick drying solvent and a clean shop towel and wipe oil or other contaminants from the surfaces. Wipe or blow loose material or contaminants

from the gasket. Brush a light coating on the mating surfaces and both sides of the gasket. Do not apply more compound than needed. Excess compound will be squeezed out as the surfaces mate and may contaminate other components. Do not allow compound into bolt or alignment pin holes

A hydraulic lock can occur as the bolt or pin compresses the compound, resulting in incorrect bolt torque.

RTV Sealant

This is a silicone gel supplied in tubes. Moisture in the air causes RTV to cure. Always place the cap on the tube as soon as possible if using RTV. RTV has a shelf life of approximately one year and will not cure properly after the shelf life expires. Check the expiration date on the tube and keep partially used tubes tightly sealed. RTV can generally fill gaps up to 1/4 in. (6.3 mm) and works well on slightly flexible surfaces.

Applying RTV Sealant

Carefully scrape all residual sealant and paint from the mating surfaces. Use a blunt scraper and work carefully to avoid damaging the mating surfaces. The mating surfaces must be absolutely free of gasket material, sealant, dirt, oil grease or other contamination. Lacquer thinner, acetone, isopropyl alcohol or similar solvents work well to clean the surfaces. Avoid using solvents with an oil, wax or petroleum base as they are not compatible with RTV compounds. Remove all sealant from bolt or alignment pin holes.

Apply RTV sealant in a continuous bead 0.08-0.12 in. (2-3 mm) thick. Circle all mounting bolt or alignment pin holes unless otherwise specified. Do not allow RTV sealant into bolt holes or other openings. A hydraulic lock can

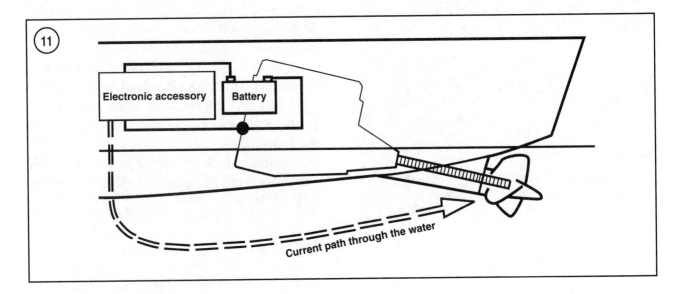

occur as the bolt or pin compresses the sealant, resulting in incorrect bolt torque. Tighten the mounting fasteners within 10 minutes after application.

Anaerobic Sealant

This is a gel supplied in tubes. It cures only in the absence of air, as when squeezed tightly between two machined mating surfaces. For this reason, it will not spoil if the cap is left off the tube. Do not use anaerobic sealant if one of the surfaces is flexible. Anaerobic sealant is able to fill gaps up to 0.030 in. (0.8 mm) and generally works best on rigid, machined flanges or surfaces.

Applying Anaerobic Sealant

Carefully scrape all residual sealant from the mating surfaces. Use a blunt scraper and work carefully to avoid damaging the mating surfaces. The mating surfaces must be absolutely free of gasket material, sealant, dirt, oil grease or other contamination. Lacquer thinner, acetone, isopropyl alcohol or similar solvents work well to clean the surfaces. Avoid using solvents with

an oil, wax or petroleum base as they are not compatible with anaerobic compounds. Clean a sealant from the bolt or alignment pin holes. Apply anaerobic sealant in a 0.04 in. (1 mm) thick continuous bead onto one of the surfaces. Circle all bolt and alignment pin openings. Do not apply sealant into bolt holes or other openings. A hydraulic lock can occur as the bolt or pin compresses the sealant, resulting in incorrect bolt torque. Tighten the mounting fasteners within 10 minutes after application.

GALVANIC CORROSION

A chemical reaction occurs whenever two different types of metal are joined by an electrical conductor and immersed in an electrolytic solution such as water. Electrons transfer from one metal to the other through the electrolyte and return through the conductor.

The hardware on a boat is made of many different types of metal. The boat hull acts as a conductor between the metals. Even if the hull is wooden or fiberglass, the slightest film of water (electrolyte) on the hull provides conductivity. This combination creates a good environment for electron flow (**Figure 11**). Unfortunately, this electron flow results in galvanic corrosion of the metal involved, causing one of the metals to be corroded or eroded away. The amount of electron flow, and therefore the amount of corrosion, depends on several factors:

1. The types of metal involved.
2. The efficiency of the conductor.
3. The strength of the electrolyte.

Metals

The chemical composition of the metal used in marine equipment has a significant effect on the amount and speed of galvanic corrosion. Certain metals are more resistant to corrosion than others. These electrically negative metals are commonly called *noble*; they act as the cathode in any reaction. Metals that are more subject to corrosion are electrically positive; they act as the anode in a reaction. The more *noble* metals include titanium, 18-8 stainless steel and nickel. Less *noble* metals include zinc, aluminum and magnesium. Galvanic corrosion becomes more severe as the difference in electrical potential between the two metals increases.

In some cases, galvanic corrosion can occur within a single piece of metal. For example, brass is a mixture of zinc and copper, and, when immersed in an electrolyte, the zinc portion of the mixture will corrode away as a galvanic re-action occurs between the zinc and copper particles.

Conductors

The hull of the boat often acts as the conductor between different types of metal. Marine equipment, such as the drive unit can act as the conductor. Large masses of metal, firmly connected together, are more efficient conductors than water. Rubber mountings and vinyl-based paint can act as insulators between pieces of metal.

Electrolyte

The water in which a boat operates acts as the electrolyte for the corrosion process. The more efficient a conductor is, the more severe and rapid the corrosion will be.

Cold, clean freshwater is the poorest electrolyte. Pollutants increase conductivity; therefore, brackish or saltwater is an efficient electrolyte. This is one of the reasons that most manufacturers recommend a freshwater flush after operating in polluted, brackish or saltwater.

Protection From Galvanic Corrosion

Because of the environment in which marine equipment must operate, it is practically impossible to totally prevent galvanic corrosion. However, there are several ways in which the process can be slowed. After taking these precautions, the next step is to *fool* the process into occurring only where you want it to occur. This is the role of sacrificial anodes and impressed current systems.

Slowing Corrosion

Some simple precautions can help reduce the amount of corrosion taking place outside the hull. These precautions are not substitutes for the corrosion protection methods discussed under *Sacrificial Anodes* and *Impressed Current Systems* in this chapter, but they can help these methods reduce corrosion.

Use fasteners made of metal more noble than the parts they secure. If corrosion occurs, the parts they secure may suffer but the fasteners are protected. The larger secured parts are more able to withstand the loss of material. Also major problems could arise if the fasteners corrode to the point of failure.

Keep all painted surfaces in good condition. If paint is scraped off and bare metal exposed, corrosion rapidly increases. Use a vinyl- or plastic-based paint, which acts as an electrical insulator.

Be careful when applying metal-based antifouling paint to the boat. Do not apply antifouling paint to metal parts of the boat or the drive unit. If applied to metal surfaces, this type of paint reacts with the metal and results in corrosion between the metal and the layer of paint. Maintain a minimum 1 in. (25 mm) border between the painted surface and any metal parts. Organic-based paints are available for use on metal surfaces.

Where a corrosion protection device is used, remember that it must be immersed in the electrolyte along with the boat to provide any protection. If you raise the gearcase out of the water with the boat docked, any anodes on the gearcase may be removed from the corrosion process rendering them ineffective. Never paint or apply any coating to anodes or other protection devices. Paint or other coatings insulate them from the corrosion process.

Any change in the boat's equipment, such as the installation of a new stainless steel propeller, changes the electrical potential and may cause increased corrosion. Always consider this when adding equipment or changing exposed materials. Install additional anodes or other protection equipment as required ensuring the corrosion protection system is up to the task. The expense to repair corrosion damage usually far exceeds that of additional corrosion protection.

Sacrificial Anodes

Sacrificial anodes are specially designed to do nothing but corrode. Properly fastening such pieces to the boat causes them to act as the anode in any galvanic reaction that occurs; any other metal in the reaction acts as the cathode and is not damaged.

Anodes are usually made or zinc, a far from a noble material. Some anodes are manufactured of an aluminum and indium alloy. This alloy is less noble than the aluminum alloy in drive system components, providing the desired sacrificial properties. The aluminum and indium alloy is more resistant to oxide coating than zinc anodes. Oxide coating occurs as the anode material reacts with oxygen in the water. An oxide coating will insulate the anode, dramatically reducing corrosion protection.

Anodes must be used properly to be effective. Simply fastening anodes to the boat in random locations will not do the job.

First determine how much anode surface is required to adequately protect the equipment's surface area. A good starting point is provided by the Military Specification MIL-A-818001, which states that one square inch of new anode protects either:

1. 800 square inches of freshly painted steel.
2. 250 square inches of bare steel or bare aluminum alloy.
3. 100 square inches of copper or copper alloy.

This rule is valid for a boat at rest. If underway, additional anode area is required to protect the same surface area.

The anode must be in good electrical contact with the metal that it protects. If possible, attach an anode to all metal surfaces requiring protection.

Good quality anodes have inserts around the fastener holes that are made of a more noble material. Otherwise, the anode could erode away around the fastener hole, allowing the anode to loosen or possibly fall off, thereby loosing needed protection.

Impressed Current System

An impressed current system can be added to any boat. The system generally consists of the anode, controller and reference electrode. The anode in this system is coated with a very noble

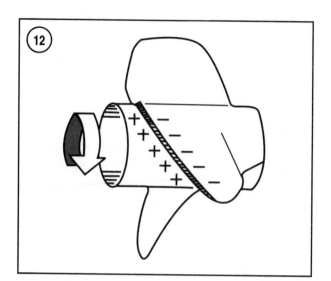

metal, such as platinum, so that it is almost corrosion-free and can last almost indefinitely. The reference electrode, under the boat's waterline, allows the control module to monitor the potential for corrosion. If the module senses that corrosion is occurring, it applies positive battery voltage to the anode. Current then flows from the anode to all other metal component, regardless of how noble or non-noble these components may be. Essentially, the electrical current from the battery counteracts the galvanic reaction to dramatically reduce corrosion damage.

Only a small amount of current is needed to counteract corrosion. Using input from the sensor, the control module provides only the amount of current needed to suppress galvanic corrosion. Most systems consume a maximum of 0.2 Ah at full demand. Under normal conditions, these systems can provide protection for 8-12 weeks without recharging the battery. Remember that this system must have constant connection to the battery. Often the battery supply to the system is connected to a battery switching device causing the operator to inadvertently shut off the system while docked.

An impressed current system is more expensive to install than sacrificial anodes but, considering the low maintenance requirements and the superior protection it provides, the long term cost may be lower.

PROPELLERS

The propeller is the final link between the boat's drive system and the water. A perfectly maintained engine and hull are useless if the propeller is the wrong type, is damaged or is deteriorated. Although propeller selection for a specific application is beyond the scope of this manual, the following provides the basic information needed to make an informed decision. The professional at a reputable marine dealership is the best source for a propeller recommendation.

How a Propeller Works

As the curved blades of a propeller rotate through the water, a high-pressure area forms on one side of the blade and a low-pressure area forms on the other side of the blade (**Figure 12**). The propeller moves toward the low-pressure area, carrying the boat with it.

Propeller Parts

Although a propeller is usually a one-piece unit, it is made of several different parts (**Figure 13**). Variations in the design of these parts make different propellers suitable for different applications.

The blade tip is the point of the blade furthest from the center of the propeller hub or propeller shaft bore. The blade tip separates the leading edge from the trailing edge.

The leading edge is the edge of the blade nearest the boat. During forward operation, this is the area of the blade that first cuts through the water.

The trailing edge is the surface of the blade furthest from the boat. During reverse operation,

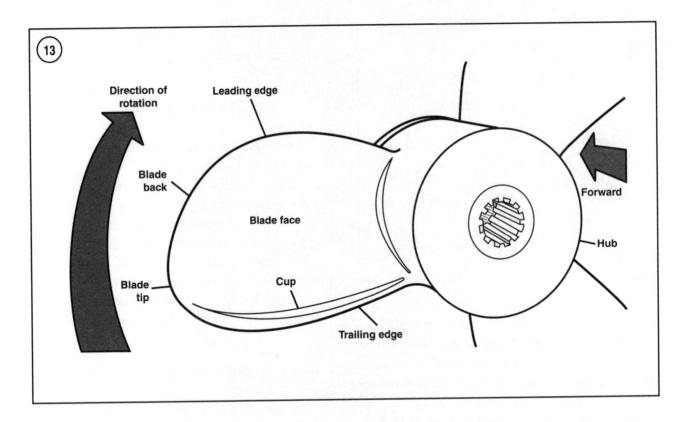

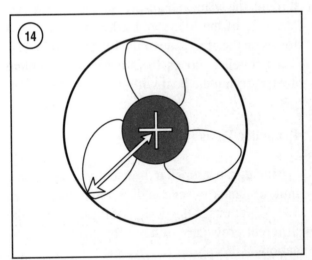

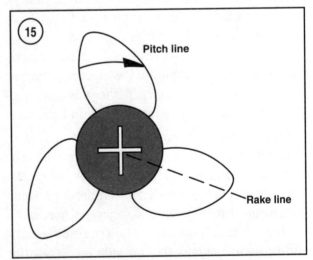

this is the area of the blade that first cuts through the water.

The blade face is the surface of the blade that faces away from the boat. During forward operation, high-pressure forms on this side of the blade.

The blade back is the surface of the blade that faces toward the boat. During forward gear operation, low-pressure forms on this side of the blade.

The cup is a small curve or lip on the trailing edge of the blade. Cupped propeller blades generally perform better than non-cupped propeller blades.

The hub is the center portion of the propeller. It connects the blades to the propeller shaft. On most drive systems, engine exhaust is routed through the hub; in this case, the hub is made up of an outer and inner portion, connected by ribs.

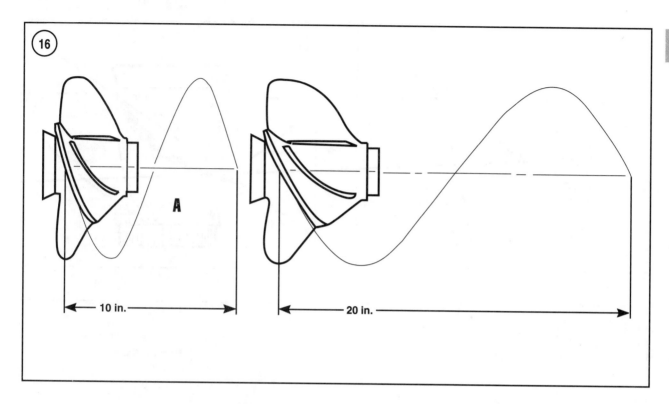

The diffuser ring is used on though-hub exhaust models to prevent exhaust gasses from entering the blade area.

Propeller Design

Changes in length, angle, thickness and material of propeller parts make different propellers suitable for different applications.

Diameter

Propeller diameter is the distance from the center of the hub to the blade tip, multiplied by two. Essentially it is the diameter of the circle formed by the blade tips during propeller rotation (**Figure 14**).

Pitch and rake

Propeller pitch and rake describe the placement of the blades in relation to the hub (**Figure 15**).

Pitch describes the theoretical distance the propeller would travel in one revolution. In A, **Figure 16**, the propeller would travel 10 inches in one revolution. In B, **Figure 16**, the propeller would travel 20 inches in one revolution. This distance is only theoretical; during operation, the propeller achieves only 75-85% of its pitch. Slip rate describes the difference in actual travel relative to the pitch. Lighter, faster boats typically achieve a lower slip rate than heavier, slower boats.

Propeller blades can be constructed with constant pitch (**Figure 17**) or progressive pitch (**Figure 18**). On a progressive propeller, the pitch starts low at the leading edge and increases toward the trailing edge. The propeller pitch specification is the average of the pitch across the entire blade. Propellers with progressive pitch usually provide better overall performance than constant pitch propellers.

Blade rake is specified in degrees and is measured along a line from the center of the hub to the blade tip. A blade that is perpendicular to the

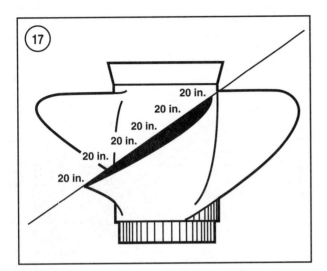

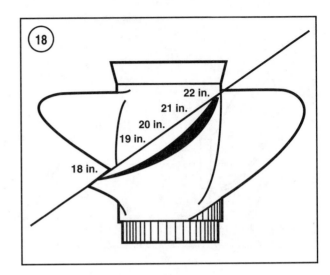

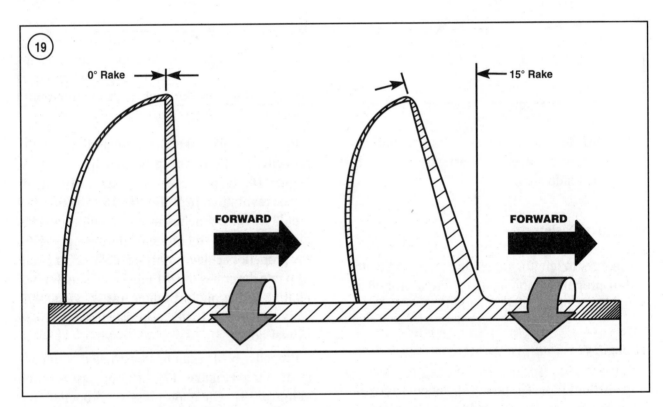

hub (**Figure 19**) has 0° rake. A blade that is angled from perpendicular (**Figure 19**) has a rake
expressed by its difference from perpendicular.
Most propellers have rakes ranging from 0-20°.
Lighter faster boats generally perform better
with propeller with a greater amount of rake.
Heavier, slower boats generally perform better
using a propeller with less rake.

Blade thickness

Blade thickness in not uniform at all points
along the blade. For efficiency, blades are as thin
a possible at all points while retaining enough
strength to move the boat. Blades are thicker
where they meet the hub and thinner at the blade
tips (**Figure 20**). This is necessary to support the

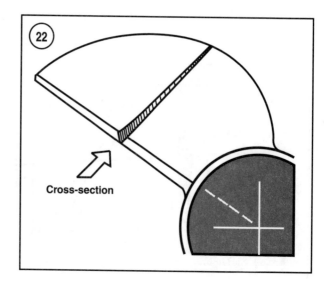

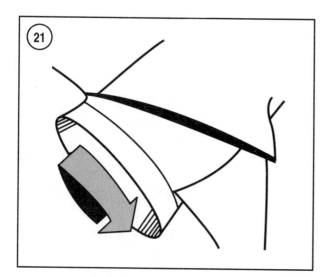

Cross-section

shaped cross-section (**Figure 22**). The leading edge is very thin and the blade thickness increases toward the trailing edge, where it is thickest. If a propeller such as this is run totally submerged, it is very inefficient.

Number of blades

The number of blades used on a propeller is a compromise between efficiency and vibration. A one-bladed propeller would the most efficient, but it would create an unacceptable amount of vibration. As blades are added, efficiency decreases, but so does vibration. Most propellers have three or four blades, representing the most practical trade-off between efficiency and vibration.

Material

Propeller materials are chosen for strength, corrosion resistance and economy. Stainless steel, aluminum, plastic and bronze are the most commonly used materials. Bronze is quite strong but rather expensive. Stainless steel is more common than bronze because of its combination of strength and lower cost. Aluminum alloy and plastic materials are the least expensive

heavier loads at the hub section of the blade. Overall blade thickness is dependent on the strength of the material used.

When cut along a line from the leading edge to the trailing edge in the central portion of the blade (**Figure 21**), the propeller blade resembles and airplane wing. The blade face, where high-pressure exists during forward rotation, is almost flat. The blade back, where low-pressure exists during forward rotation, is curved, with the thinnest portions at the edges and the thickest portion at the center.

Propellers that run only partially submerged, as in racing applications, may have a wedge

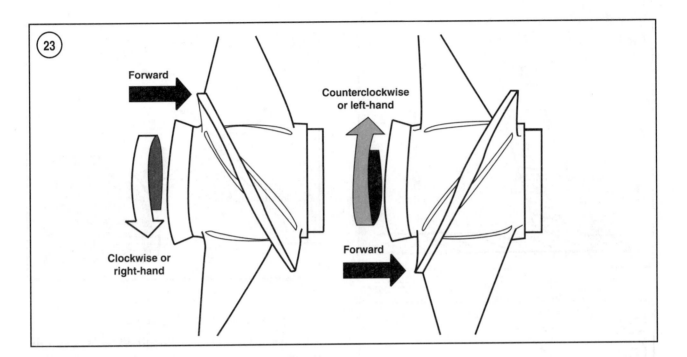

but usually lack the strength of stainless steel. Plastic propellers are more suited for lower horsepower applications.

Direction of rotation

Propellers are made for both right-hand and left hand rotations although right-hand is the most commonly used. As viewed from the rear of the boat while in forward gear, a right-hand propeller turns clockwise and a left-hand propeller turns counterclockwise. Off the boat, the direction of rotation is determined by observing the angle of the blades (**Figure 23**). A right-hand propeller's blade slant from the upper left to the lower right; a left-hand propeller's blades are opposite.

Cavitation and Ventilation

Cavitation and ventilation are *not* interchangeable terms; they refer to two distinct problems encountered during propeller operation.

To help understand cavitation, consider the relationship between pressure and the boiling point of water. At sea level, water boils at 212° F (100° C). As pressure increases, such as within an engine cooling system, the boiling point of the water increases—it boils at a temperature higher than 212° F (100° C). The opposite is also true. As pressure decreases, water boils at a temperature lower than 212° F (100° C). It the pressure drops low enough, water will boil at normal room temperature.

During normal propeller operation, low pressure forms on the blade back. Normally the pressure does not drop low enough for boiling to occur. However, poor propeller design, damaged blades or using the wrong propeller can cause unusually low pressure on the blade surface (**Figure 24**). If the pressure drops low enough, boiling occurs and bubbles form on the blade surfaces. As the boiling water moves to a higher pressure area of the blade, the boiling ceases and the bubbles collapse. The collapsing bubbles release energy that erodes the surface of the propeller blade.

Corroded surfaces, physical damage or even marine growth combined with high-speed operation can cause low pressure and cavitation on gearcase surfaces. In such cases, low pressure

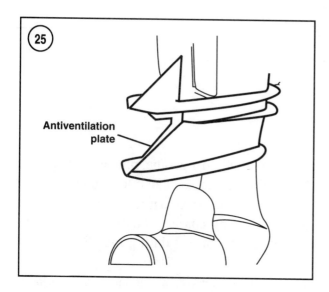

Bubbles condensing

Cavitation

Antiventilation plate

forms as water flows over a protrusion or rough surface. The boiling water forms bubbles that collapse as they move to a higher pressure area toward the rear of the surface imperfection.

This entire process of pressure drop, boiling and bubble collapse is called *cavitation*. The ensuing damage is called *cavitation burn*. Cavitation is caused by a decrease in pressure, not an increase in temperature.

Ventilation is not as complex a process as cavitation. Ventilation refers to air entering the blade area, either from above the water surface or from a though-hub exhaust system. As the blades meet the air, the propeller momentarily looses it bite with the water and subsequently loses most of its thrust. An added complication is that the propeller and engine over-rev, causing very low pressure on the blade back and massive cavitation.

Most marine drive systems have a plate (**Figure 25**) above the propeller designed to prevent surface air from entering the blade area. This plate is correctly called an *anti-ventilation plate*, although it is often incorrectly called an *anticavitation plate*.

Most propellers have a flared section at the rear of the propeller called a diffuser ring. This feature forms a barrier, and extends the exhaust passage far enough aft to prevent the exhaust gases from ventilating the propeller.

A close fit of the propeller to the gearcase is necessary to keep exhaust gasses from exiting and ventilating the propeller. Using the wrong propeller attaching hardware can position the propeller too far aft, preventing a close fit. The wrong hardware can also allow the propeller to rub heavily against the gearcase, causing rapid wear to both components. Wear or damage to these surfaces will allow the propeller to ventilate.

Chapter Two

Tools and Techniques

This chapter describes the common tools required for marine engine repair and troubleshooting. Techniques that make the work easier and more effective are also described. Some of the procedures in this book require special skills or expertise; it some cases it is better to entrust the job to a specialist or qualified dealership.

SAFETY FIRST

Professional mechanics can work for years and never suffer a serious injury. Avoiding injury is as simple as following a few rules and using common sense. Ignoring the rules can of often does lead to physical injury and/or damaged equipment.

1. Never use gasoline as a cleaning solvent.

2. Never smoke or use a torch near flammable liquids, such as cleaning solvent. Dirty or solvent soaked shop towels are extremely flammable. If working in a garage, remember that most home gas appliances have pilot lights.

3. Never smoke or use a torch in an area where a battery is being charged. Highly explosive hydrogen gas is formed during the charging process.

4. Use the proper size wrench to avoid damaged fasteners and bodily injury.

5. If loosening a tight or stuck fastener, consider what could happen if the wrench slips. Protect yourself accordingly.

6. Keep the work area clean, uncluttered and well lighted.

7. Wear safety goggles while using any type of tool. This is especially important when drilling, grinding or using a cold chisel.

8. Never use worn or damaged tools.

9. Keep a Coast Guard approved fire extinguisher handy. Ensure it is rated for gasoline (Class B) and electrical (Class C) fires.

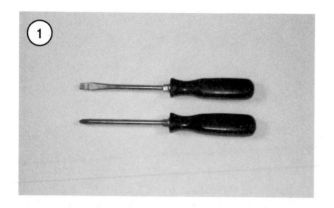

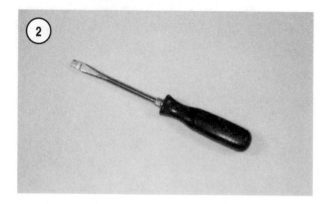

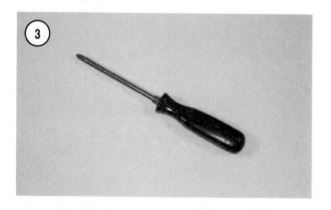

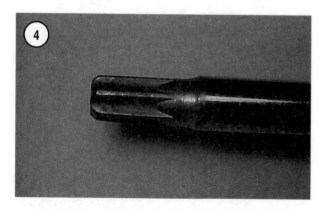

2

BASIC HAND TOOLS

A number of tools are required to maintain and repair a marine engine. Most of these tools are also used for home and automobile repair. Some tools are made especially for working on marine engines; these tools can be purchased from a marine dealership. Having the required tools always makes the job easier and more effective.

Keep the tools clean and in a suitable box. Keep them organized with related tools stored together. After using a tool, wipe it clean using a shop towel.

The following tools are required to perform virtually any repair job. Each tool is described and the recommended size given for starting a tool collection. Additional tools and some duplication may be added as you become more familiar with the equipment. You may need all U.S. standard tools, all metric size tools or a mixture of both.

Screwdrivers

A screwdriver (**Figure 1**) is a very basic tool, but if used improperly can do more damage than good. The slot on a screw has a definite dimension and shape. Always select a screwdriver that conforms to the shape of the screw. Use a small screwdriver for small screws and a large one for large screws or the screw head are damaged.

Three types of screwdrivers are commonly required: a slotted (flat-blade) screwdriver (**Figure 2**), Phillips screwdriver (**Figure 3**) and Torx screwdriver (**Figure 4**).

Screwdrivers are available in sets, which often include an assortment of slotted Phillips and Torx blades. If you buy them individually, buy at least the following:

    a. Slotted screwdriver—5/16 × 6 in. blade.

    b. Slotted screwdriver—3/8 × 12 in. blade.

    c. Phillips screwdriver—No. 2 tip, 6 in. blade.

d. Phillips screwdriver—No. 3 tip, 6 in. blade.

e. Torx screwdriver—T15 tip, 6 in. blade.

f. Torx screwdriver—T20 tip, 6 in. blade.

g. Torx screwdriver—T25 tip, 6 in. blade.

Use screwdrivers only for driving screws. Never use a screwdriver for prying or chiseling. Do not attempt to remove a Phillips, Torx or Allen head screw with a slotted screwdriver; you can damage the screw head so that even the proper tool is unable to remove it.

Keep the tip of a slotted screwdriver in good condition. Carefully grind the tip to the proper size and taper if it is worn or damaged. The sides of the blade must be parallel and the blade tip must be flat. Replace a Phillips or Torx screwdriver if its tip is worn or damaged.

Pliers

Pliers come in a wide range of types and sizes. Pliers are useful for cutting, gripping, bending and crimping. Never use pliers to cut hardened objects or turn bolts or nuts. **Figure 5** shows several types of pliers.

Each type of pliers has a specialized function. General-purpose pliers are mainly used for gripping and bending. Locking pliers are used for gripping objects very tightly, like a vise. Use needlenose pliers to grip or bend small objects. Adjustable or slip-joint pliers (**Figure 6**) can be adjusted to grip various sized objects; the jaws remain parallel for gripping objects such as pipe or tubing. There are many more types of pliers. The ones described here are the most common.

Box-end and Open-end Wrenches

Box-end and open-end wrenches (**Figure 7**) are available in sets in a variety of sizes. The number stamped near the end of the wrench refers to the distance between two parallel flats on the hex head bolt or nut.

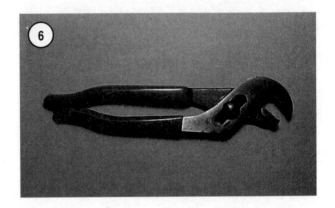

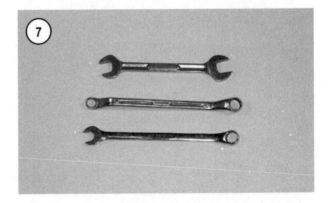

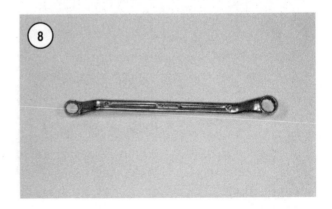

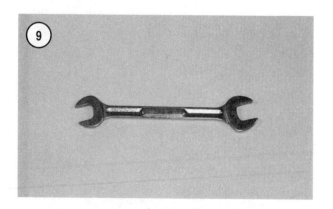

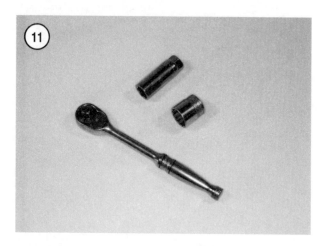

superior holding power; the 12-point allow a shorter swing if working in tight quarters.

Use an open-end wrench if a box-end wrench cannot be positioned over the nut or bolt. To prevent damage to the fastener, avoid using and open-end wrench if a large amount of tightening or loosening toque is required.

A combination wrench has both a box-end and open-end. Both ends are the same size.

Adjustable Wrenches

An adjustable wrench (**Figure 10**) can be adjusted to fit virtually any nut or bolt head. However, it can loosen and slip from the nut or bolt, causing damage to the nut and possible physical injury. Use an adjustable wrench only if a proper size open-end or box-end wrench in not available. Avoid using an adjustable wrench if a large amount of tightening or loosening torque is required.

Adjustable wrenches come in sized ranging from 4-18 in. overall length. A 6 or 8 in. size is recommended as an all-purpose wrench.

Socket Wrenches

A socket wrench (**Figure 11**) is generally faster, safer and more convenient to use than a common wrench. Sockets, which attach to a suitable handle, are available with six-point or 12-point openings and use 1/4, 3/8, and 1/2 in. drive sizes. The drive size corresponds to the square hole that mates with the ratchet or flex handle.

Torque Wrench

A torque wrench (**Figure 12**) is used with a socket to measure how tight a nut or bolt is installed. They come in a wide price range and in 1/4, 3/8, and 1/2 in. drive sizes. The drive size

Box-end wrenches (**Figure 8**) provide a better grip on the nut and are stronger than open end wrenches. An open-end wrench (**Figure 9**) grips the nut on only two flats. Unless it fits well, it may slip and round off the points on the nut. A box-end wrench grips all six flats. Box-end wrenches are available with six-point or 12 point openings. The six-point opening provides

corresponds to the square hole that mates with the socket.

A typical 1/4 in. drive torque wrench measures in in.-lb. increments, and has a range of 20-150 in.-lb. (2.2-17 Nm,). A typical 3/8 or ½ in. torque measures in ft.-lb. increments, and has a range of 10-150 ft.-lb. (14-203 Nm.).

Impact Driver

An impact driver (**Figure 13**) makes removal of tight fasteners easy and reduces damage to bolts and screws. Interchangeable bits allow use on a variety of fasteners.

Snap Ring Pliers

Snap ring pliers are required to remove snap rings. Snap ring pliers (**Figure 14**) usually come with different size tips; many designs can be switched to handle internal or external type snap rings.

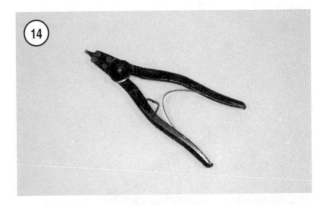

Hammers

Various types of hammers (**Figure 15**) are available to accommodate a number of applications. Use a ball-peen hammer to strike another tool, such as a punch or chisel. Use a soft-face hammer to strike a metal object without damaging it.

Never use a metal-faced hammer on engine and drive system components as severe damage will occur. You can always produce the same amount of force with a soft-faced hammer.

Always wear eye protection when using hammers. Make sure the hammer is in good condition and that the handle is not cracked. Select the correct hammer for the job and always strike the object squarely. Do not use the handle or the side of the hammer head to stroke an object.

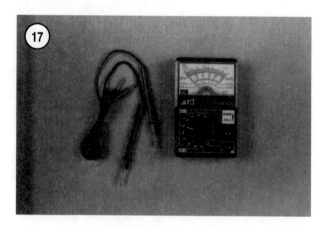

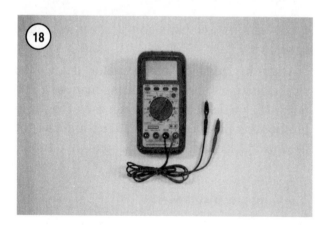

Feeler Gauges

This tool has either flat or wire measuring gauges (**Figure 16**). Use wire gauges to measure spark plug gap; use flat gauges for other measurements. A nonmagnetic (brass) gauge may be specified if working around magnetized components.

Other Special Tools

Many of the maintenance and repair procedures require special tools. Most of the necessary tools are available from a marine dealership or from tool suppliers. Instructions for their use and the manufacture's part number are included in the appropriate chapter.

Purchase the required tools from a local marine dealership or tool supplier. A qualified machinist, often at a lower price, can make some tools locally. Many marine dealerships and rental outlets will rent some of the required tools. Avoid using makeshift tools. Their use may result in damaged parts that cost far more than the recommended tool.

TEST EQUIPMENT

This section describes equipment used to perform testing, adjustments and measurements on marine engines. Most of these tools are available from a local marine dealership or automotive parts store.

Multimeter

This instrument is invaluable for electrical troubleshooting and service. It combines a voltmeter, ohmmeter and an ammeter in one unit. It is often called a VOM.

Two types of mutimeter are available, analog and digital. Analog meters (**Figure 17**) have a moving needle with marked bands on the meter face indicating the volt, ohm and amperage scales. An analog meter must be calibrated each time the scale is changed.

A digital meter (**Figure 18**) is ideally suited for electrical troubleshooting because it is easy to read and more accurate than an analog meter. Most models are auto-ranging, have automatic polarity compensation and internal overload protection circuits.

Either type of meter is suitable for most electrical testing described in this manual. An analog meter is better suited for testing pulsing voltage signals such as those produced by the ignition system. A digital meter is better suited for testing very low resistance or voltage reading (less than 1 volt or 1 ohm). The test procedure will indicate if a specific type of meter is required.

The ignition system produces electrical pulses that are too short in duration for accurate measurement with a using a conventional multimeter. Use a meter with peak-volt reading ca pability to test the ignition system. This type of meter captures the peak voltage reached during an electrical pulse.

Scale selection, meter specifications and test connections vary by the manufacturer and model of the meter. Thoroughly read the instructions supplied with the meter before performing any test. The meter and certain electrical components on the engine can be damaged if tested incorrectly. Have the test performed by a qualified professional if you are unfamiliar with the testing or general meter usage. The expense to replace damaged equipment can far exceed the cost of having the test performed by a professional.

Strobe Timing Light

This instrument is necessary for dynamic tuning (setting ignition timing while the engine is running). By flashing a light at the precise instant the spark plug fires, the position of the timing mark can be seen. The flashing light makes a moving mark appear to stand still next to a stationary mark.

Timing lights (**Figure 19**) range from inexpensive models with a neon bulb to expensive models with a xenon bulb, built in tachometer and timing advance compensator. A built in tachometer is very useful as most ignition timing

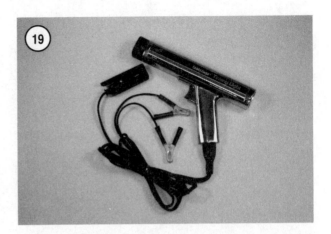

specifications are based on a specific engine speed.

A timing advance compensator delays the strobe enough to bring the timing mark to a certain place on the scale. Although useful for troubleshooting purposes, this feature should not be used to check or adjust the base ignition timing.

Tachometer/Dwell Meter

A portable tachometer (**Figure 20**) is needed to tune and test most marine engines. Ignition timing and carburetor adjustments must be performed at a specified engine speed. Tachometers are available with either an analog or digital display.

The fuel/air mixture must be adjusted with the engine running at idle speed. If using an analog

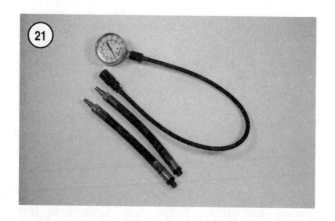

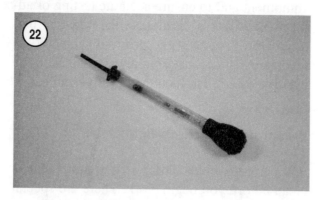

vide accurate measurement at all speeds without the need to change the range or scale. Many of these use an inductive pickup to receive the signal from the ignition system.

A dwell meter is often incorporated into the tachometer to allow testing and/or adjustments to engines with a breaker point ignition system.

Compression Gauge

This tool (**Figure 21**) measures the amount of pressure created in the combustion chamber during the compression stroke. Compression indicates the general engine condition making it one of the most useful troubleshooting tools.

The easiest type to use has screw-in adapters that fit the spark plug holes. Rubber tipped, press-in type gauges are also available. This type must be held firmly in the spark plug hole to prevent leakage and inaccurate test results..

Hydrometer

Use a hydrometer to measure specific gravity in the battery. Specific gravity is the density of the battery electrolyte as compared to pure water and indicates the battery's state of charge. Choose a hydrometer (**Figure 22**) with automatic temperature compensation; otherwise the electrolyte temperature must be measured during charging to determine the actual specific gravity.

tachometer, choose one with a low range of 0-1000 rpm or 0-2000 rpm range and a high range of 0-6000 rpm. The high range setting is needed for testing purposes but lacks the accuracy needed at lower speeds. At lower speeds the meter must be capable of detecting changes of 25 rpm or less.

Digital tachometers are generally easier to use than most analog type tachometers. They pro-

Precision Measuring Tools

Various tools are required to make precision measurements. A dial indicator (**Figure 23**), for example, is used to determine piston position in the cylinder, runout and end play of shafts and assemblies. It is also used to measure free movement between the gear teeth (backlash) in the drive unit.

Venier calipers (**Figure 24**), micrometers (**Figure 25**) and other precision tools are used to measure the size of parts, such as the piston.

Precision measuring equipment must be stored, handled and used carefully or it will not remain accurate.

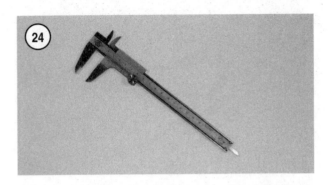

SERVICE HINTS

Most of the service procedures in this manual are straightforward and can be performed by anyone reasonably handy with tools. It is suggested, however, that you consider your skills and available tools and equipment before attempting a repair involving major disassembly of the engine or drive unit.

Some operations, for example, require the use of a press. Other operations require precision measurement. Have the procedure or measurements performed by a professional if you do not have access to the correct equipment or are unfamiliar with its use.

Special Battery Precautions

Disconnecting or connecting the battery can create a spike or surge of current throughout the electrical system. This spike or surge can damage certain components of the charging system. Always verify the ignition switch is in the OFF position before connecting or disconnecting the battery or changing the selection on a battery switch.

Always disconnect both battery cables and remove the battery from the boat for charging. If the battery cables are connected, the charger may induce a damaging spike or surge of current into the electrical system. During charging, batteries produce explosive and corrosive gasses. These gases can cause corrosion in the battery compartment and creates an extremely hazardous condition.

Disconnect the cables from the battery prior to testing, adjusting or repairing many of the systems or components on the engine. This is nec-

essary for safety, to prevent damage to test equipment and to ensure accurate testing or adjustment. Always disconnect the negative battery cable first, then the positive cable. When reconnecting the battery, always connect the positive cable first, then the negative cable.

Preparation for Disassembly

Repairs go much faster if the equipment is clean before you begin work. There are special cleaners such as Gunk or Bel-Ray Degreaser, for cleaning the engine and related components. Just spray or brush on the cleaning solution, let it stand, then rinse with a garden hose.

Use pressurized water to remove marine growth and corrosion or mineral deposits from external components such as the gearcase, drive shaft housing and clamp brackets. Avoid directing pressurized water directly as seals or gaskets; pressurized water can flow past seal and gasket surfaces and contaminate lubricating fluids.

> *WARNING*
> *Never use gasoline as a cleaning agent. It presents an extreme fire hazard. Always work in a well-ventilated area if using cleaning solvent. Keep a coast Guard approved fire extinguisher, rated for gasoline fires, readily accessible in the work area.*

Much of the labor charged for a job performed at a dealership is usually for removal and disas-

sembly of other parts to access defective parts or assemblies. It is frequently possible to perform most of the disassembly then take the defective part or assembly to the dealership for repair.

If you decide to perform the job yourself, read the appropriate section in this manual, in its entirety. Study the illustrations and text until you fully understand what is involved to complete the job. Make arrangements to purchase or rent all required special tools and equipment before starting.

Disassembly Precautions

During disassembly, keep a few general precautions in mind. Force is rarely needed to get things apart. If parts fit tightly, such as a bearing on a shaft, there is usually a tool designed to separate them. Never use a screwdriver to separate parts with a machined mating surface, such as the cylinder head or manifold. The surfaces will be damaged and leak.

Make diagrams or take instant photographs wherever similar-appearing parts are found. Often, disassembled parts are left for several days or longer before resuming work. You may not remember where everything came from, or carefully arranged parts may become disturbed.

Cover all openings after removing parts to keep contamination or other parts from entering.

Tag all similar internal parts for location and mounting direction. Reinstall all internal components in the same location and mounting direction as removed. Record the thickness and

mounting location of any shims as they are removed. Place small bolts and parts in plastic sandwich bags. Seal and label the bags with masking tape.

Tag all wires, hoses and connections and make a sketch of the routing. Never rely on memory alone; it may be several days or longer before you resume work.

Protect all painted surfaces from physical damage. Never allow gasoline or cleaning solvent on these surfaces.

Assembly Precautions

No parts, except those assembled with a press fit, require unusual force during assembly. If a part is hard to remove or install, find out why before proceeding.

When assembling parts, start all fasteners, then tighten evenly in an alternating or crossing pattern unless a specific tightening sequence or procedure is given.

When assembling parts, be sure all shims, spacers and washers are installed in the same position and location as removed.

Whenever a rotating part butts against a stationary part, look for a shim or washer. Use new gaskets, seals and O-rings if there is any doubt about the conditions of the used ones. Unless otherwise specified, a thin coating of oil on gaskets may help them seal more effectively. Use heavy grease to hold small parts in place if they tend to fall out during assembly.

Use emery cloth and oil to remove high spots from piston surfaces. Use a dull screwdriver to remove carbon deposits from the cylinder head, ports and piston crown. *Do not* scratch or gouge these surfaces. Wipe the surfaces clean with a *clean* shop towel when finished.

If the carburetor must be repaired, completely disassemble it and soak all metal parts in a commercial carburetor cleaner. Never soak gaskets and rubber or plastic parts in these cleaners.

Clean rubber or plastic parts in warm soapy water. Never use a wire to clean jets and small passages because they are easily damaged. Use compressed air to blow debris from all passages in the carburetor body.

Take your time and do the job right. Break-in procedure for a newly rebuilt engine or drive is the same as for a new one. Use the recommended break-in oil and follow the instructions provided in the appropriate chapter.

SPECIAL TIPS

Because of the extreme demands placed on marine equipment, several points must be kept in mind when performing service and repair. The following are general suggestions that may improve the overall life of the machine and help avoid costly failure.

1. Unless otherwise specified, apply a thread-locking compound, such as Loctite Threadlocker, to all bolts and nuts, even if secured with a lockwasher. Use only the specified grade of threadlocking compound. A screw or bolt lost from an engine cover or bearing retainer could easily cause serious and expensive damage before the loss is noticed. When applying threadlocking compound, use only enough to lightly coat the threads. If too much is used, it can work its way down the threads and contaminate seals or bearings.

2. If self-locking fasteners are used, replace them with new ones. Do not install standard fasteners in place of self-locking ones.

3. Use caution when using air tools to remove stainless steel nuts or bolts. The heat generated during rapid spinning easily damages the threads of stainless steel fasteners. To prevent thread damage, apply penetrating oil as a cooling agent and loosen or tighten them slowly.

4. Use a wide chisel to straighten the tab of a fold-over type lockwasher. Such a tool provides a better contact surface than a screwdriver or pry bar, making straightening easier. During installa-

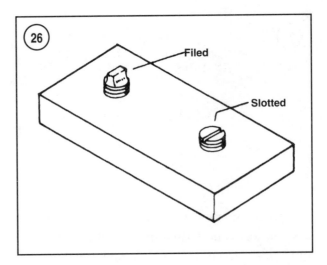

tion, use a new fold-over type lockwasher. If a new lockwasher is not available, fold over a tab on the washer that has not been previously used. Reusing the same tab may cause the washer to break, resulting in a loss of locking ability and a loose piece of metal adrift in the engine. When folding the tab into position, carefully pry it toward the flat on the bolt or nut. Use a pair or plies to bend the tab against the fastener. Do not use a punch and hammer to drive the tab into position. The resulting fold may be too sharp, weakening the washer and increasing its chance of failure.

5. Use only the specified replacement parts if replacing a missing or damaged bolt, screw or nut. Many fasteners are specially hardened for the application.

6. Install only the specified gaskets. Unless specified otherwise, install them without sealant. Many gaskets are made with a material that swells when it contacts oil. Gasket sealer prevents them from swelling as intended and can result in oil leakage. Most gaskets must be a specific thickness. Installing a gasket that is too thin or too thick in a critical area could cause expensive damage.

7. Make sure all shims and washers are reinstalled in the same location and position. Whenever a rotating part contacts a stationary part, look for a shim or washer.

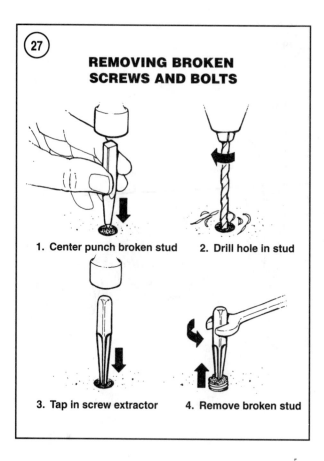

REMOVING BROKEN SCREWS AND BOLTS

1. Center punch broken stud

2. Drill hole in stud

3. Tap in screw extractor

4. Remove broken stud

MECHANICS TECHNIQUES

Marine engines are subjected to conditions very different from most engines. They are repeatedly subjected to a corrosive environment followed by periods of non-use for weeks or longer. Such use invites corrosion damage to fasteners, causing difficulty or breakage during removal. This section provides information that is useful for removing stuck or broken fasteners and repairing damaged threads.

Removing Stuck Fasteners

When a nut or bolt corrodes and cannot be removed, several methods may be used to loosen it. First, apply penetrating oil, such as Liquid Wrench or WD-40. Apply it liberally to the threads and allow it to penetrate for 10-15 minutes. Tap the fastener several times with a small

hammer; however, do not hit it hard enough to cause damage. Reapply the penetrating oil if necessary.

For stuck screws, apply penetrating oil as described, then insert a screwdriver in the slot. Tap the top of the screwdriver with a hammer. This looses the corrosion in the threads allowing it to turn. If the screw head is too damaged to use a screwdriver, grip the head with locking pliers and twist the screw from the assembly.

A Phillips, Allen or Torx screwdriver may start to slip in the screw during removal. If slippage occurs, stop immediately and apply a dab of course valve lapping compound onto the tip of the screwdriver. Valve lapping compound or a special screw removal compound is available from most hardware and automotive parts stores. Insert the driver into the screw and apply downward pressure while turning. The gritty material in the compound improves the grip on the screw, allowing more rotational force before slippage occurs. Keep the compound away from any other engine components. It is very abrasive and can cause rapid wear if applied onto moving or sliding surfaces.

Avoid applying heat unless specifically instructed because it may melt, warp or remove the temper from parts.

Removing Broken Bolts or Screws

The head of bolt or screw may unexpectedly twist off during removal. Several methods are available for removing the remaining portion of the bolt or screw.

If a large portion of the bolt or screw projects out, try gripping it with locking pliers. If the projecting portion is too small, file it to fit a wrench or cut a slot in it to fit a screwdriver (**Figure 26**). If the head breaks off flush or cannot be turned with a screwdriver or wrench, use a screw extractor (**Figure 27**). To do this, center punch the remaining portion of the screw or bolt. Select the proper size of extractor for the size of the fastener. Using the drill size specified on the extractor, drill a hole into the fastener. Do not drill deeper than the remaining fastener. Carefully tap the extractor into the hole and back the remnant out using a wrench on the extractor.

Remedying Stripped Threads

Occasionally, threads are stripped through carelessness or impact damage. Often the threads can be repaired by running a tap (for internal threads on nuts) or die (for external threads on bolts) through threads (**Figure 28**).

To clean or repair spark plug threads, use a spark plug tap. If an internal thread is damaged, it may be necessary to install a Helicoil or some other type of thread insert. Follow the manufacturer's instructions when installing their insert.

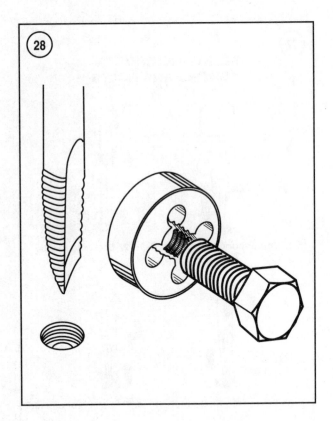

Chapter Three

Troubleshooting

Troubleshooting is the process of testing individual systems with the express purpose of isolating good systems from the defective or nonfunctional system(s). When a system is identified as defective, troubleshooting continues with testing of the individual components from the suspect system. It is very important to perform only one test procedure at a time, otherwise it will be difficult, if not impossible, to determine the condition of each individual component. Occasionally a component in a system cannot be stand-alone tested. In this case, other components are tested and eliminated until the suspect component is identified as defective by the process of elimination. The two most important rules of troubleshooting are to test systems before components and to be methodical. Haphazardly jumping from one system or component to another may eventually solve the problem, but time and effort will be wasted. Use the various system diagrams provided in this manual to identify all components in a system. Test each component in a rational order to determine which component has caused the system's failure.

The troubleshooting process generally begins when an unusual symptom (decrease in performance or unsatisfactory operating characteristic) is noticed. The next step is to define the symptom as accurately as possible. Key points to consider are:

1. Did the problem occur suddenly or gradually?

2. Is there a specific engine speed or load at which the problem occurs?

3. Does the weather (extreme hot or cold) or engine temperature affect the symptom?

4. Has any service work been recently performed?

5. Has the unit recently come out of storage?

6. Has the fuel supplier or fuel grade been recently changed?

7. Is the manufacturer's recommended oil being used?

8. Have any accessories been added to the boat or engine?

Once the symptom is adequately defined, attempt to duplicate the problem. Check the easy, simple areas first such as failure to prime the fuel system, attach the safety lanyard or an incorrect starting procedure.

Before beginning any troubleshooting procedure, perform a thorough visual inspection of the unit. Pay special attention to the condition of the battery cable connections (at both ends), all electrical harness connectors and terminals, fuel quantity, quality and supply. Look for indications of engine overheating, evidence of leaks (fuel, oil and water) and mechanical integrity (loose fasteners, cracked or broken castings). Learning to recognize visual defects is a skill that comes from self-discipline and patience. Take your time and look closely. Use your hands to touch, feel and wiggle components.

Be realistic about your capabilities, especially if working from a home garage or driveway. Avoid situations where a major disassembly has been hastily performed and you feel compelled to continue in a predicament that is well beyond your qualifications. Service departments tend to charge heavily to reassemble an engine that comes into the shop in several boxes, while some will refuse to take on such a job.

Proper lubrication, maintenance and engine tune-up as described in Chapter Four will reduce the necessity for troubleshooting. However, because of the harsh and demanding environment in which the outboard motor operates, troubleshooting at some point in the motor's serviceable life is inevitable.

This chapter concentrates on the actual troubleshooting procedure. Once the defective component is identified, refer to the appropriate chapter for removal and replacement procedures. Refer to the *Quick Reference Data* section at the front of the manual for tables containing common engine specifications, standard torque values, spark plug recommendations, and recommended test equipment, tool and fixture manufacturers and suppliers.

Tables 1-4 list recommended test equipment and tools, wire color codes and battery cable recommendations. **Tables 5-8** cover typical symptoms and solutions for the starting, charging, ignition and fuel systems. **Tables 9-15** list specifications (or identify) for the starting, charging and ignition systems. All tables are located at the end of the chapter.

SERVICE PRECAUTIONS— 1998-2003 MODEL YEAR ENGINES

The EPA (Environmental Protection Agency) certifies emission output for all 1998-2003 models. Certified models have an EPA certification plate mounted near the model identification plate on the engine midsection.

All repairs or service procedures must be performed exactly as specified to ensure the engine will continue to comply with EPA requirements. For the same reason, all replacement parts must meet or exceed the manufacturer's specifications.

If in doubt as to whether a repair or service procedure will adversely affect the engine's ability to maintain EPA compliance, contact an Evinrude or Johnson dealership, before beginning the repair or procedure.

SAFETY PRECAUTIONS

Wear approved eye protection (**Figure 1**) at all times. Especially when machinery is in operation and hammers are being used. Wear approved ear protection during all running tests and in the presence of noisy machinery. Keep loose clothing tucked in and long hair tied back and secured. Refer to the *Safety First* section in Chapter 2 for additional safety guidelines.

When making or breaking any electrical connection, always disconnect the negative battery cable. When performing tests that require cranking the engine without starting, disconnect and ground the spark plug leads to prevent accidental starting and sparks.

Securely cap or plug all disconnected fuel lines to prevent fuel discharge when the motor is cranked or the primer bulb is squeezed.

Thoroughly read all manufacturer's instructions and safety sheets and note all test equipment and special tools that are required.

Do not substitute parts unless you know they meet or exceed the original manufacturer's specifications.

Never run an outboard motor without an adequate water supply. Never run an outboard motor at wide-open throttle without an adequate load. Do not exceed 3000 rpm in neutral (no load).

Safely performing on-water tests requires 2 people—one person to operate the boat, the other to monitor the gauges or test instruments. All personnel must remain seated inside the boat at all times. It is not acceptable to lean over the transom while the boat is under way. Use extensions to allow all gauges and meters to be located in the normal seating area.

Test Wheels (Propellers)

OMC recommends using the specified test wheel (propeller) for test procedures that require the engine to be run under load. The correct test wheel will suitably load the engine while producing a minimal amount of thrust. A test wheel can be used in a test tank, with the boat on a trailer (backed into the water) or with the boat launched and tied to a dock.

Test wheels are available from OMC Genuine Parts and are listed in the *Quick Reference Data* section at the front of this manual. The test wheel is also used to determine if the engine is producing its rated power. A minimum test

speed is listed for each engine in the *Quick Reference Data* section. If the engine can reach or exceed the specified minimum test speed with the specified test wheel installed, the engine is producing its rated power. The gearcase must be submerged in water to at least its normal operating depth, and it must be shifted into FORWARD gear for this test.

A suitable test propeller can also be made by modifying (turning down) the diameter of a standard low pitch aluminum propeller until the recommended wide-open throttle speed can be obtained with the motor in a test tank (smaller motors) or on a trailer, backed into the water (larger engines). Because considerable thrust is produced by this

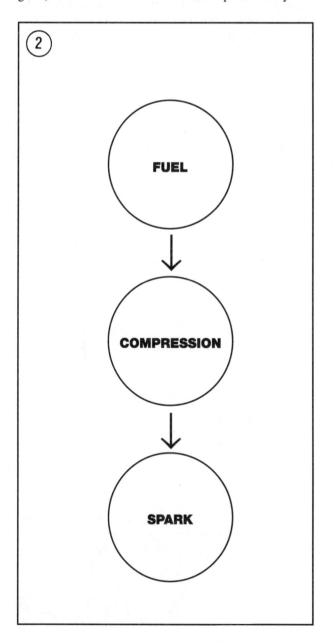

type of test propeller, be careful when tying the boat to a dock. Some docks may not be able to withstand the load.

Propeller repair stations can provide the modification service. Normally, approximately 1/3 to 1/2 of the blades will be removed. However, it is far better to remove too little, than too much. It may take several tries to achieve the correct full throttle speed, but once achieved, no further modifications are required. Many propeller repair stations have experience with this type of modification and may be able to recommend a starting point.

Test wheels and/or propellers allow simple tracking of engine performance. The full-throttle test speed of an engine fitted with the correct test wheel or correctly modified propeller can be tracked (recorded) from season to season. It is not unusual for a new or rebuilt engine to show a slight increase in test propeller speed as complete break-in is achieved. The engine will generally hold this speed over its normal service life. As the engine begins to wear out, the test wheel (propeller) speed will show a gradual decrease.

OPERATING REQUIREMENTS

All two-stroke engines require three basic conditions to run properly: The correct air and fuel mixture from the carburetor, crankcase and combustion chamber compression and adequate spark delivered to the spark plug at the correct time. When troubleshooting, it is helpful to remember: fuel, compression and spark (**Figure 2**). If any of these are lacking the motor will not run. First, verify the mechanical integrity of the engine by performing a compression test (Chapter Four). Once compression has been verified, test the ignition system with an air gap spark tester and then finally focus your attention on the fuel system. Troubleshooting in this order will provide the quickest results.

If the motor has been sitting for any length of time and refuses to start, check the condition of the battery first to make sure it is adequately charged, then inspect the battery cable connections at the battery and the engine. Examine the fuel delivery system. This includes the fuel tank, fuel pump, fuel lines, fuel filters and carburetor(s). Rust or corrosion may have formed in the tank, restricting fuel flow. Gasoline deposits may have gummed up carburetor jets and air passages. Gasoline tends to lose its potency after standing for long periods. Condensation may contaminate the fuel with water. Connect a portable tank containing fresh fuel mix to help isolate the problem. Do not drain the old gasoline unless you are sure it is at fault. Always dispose of old gasoline in accordance with EPA regulations.

Starting Difficulties

Occasionally, an outboard motor will be plagued by hard starting and generally poor performance (especially at low speeds) for which there seems to be no good cause. Fuel and ignition systems test satisfactorily and a compression test indicates that the combustion chamber (piston, rings, cylinder walls and head gasket) is in good condition.

What has not been tested is crankcase sealing. A two-stroke engine cannot function unless the crankcase is adequately sealed. As the piston travels downward, the crankcase must pressurize and push the air/fuel mixture into the combustion chamber as the intake ports are uncovered. Conversely, as the piston travels upward, the crankcase must create a vacuum to pull the air/fuel mixture into the crankcase from the carburetor in preparation for the next stroke. Refer to Chapter Two for operational diagrams of a typical two-stroke engine.

Leaks in the crankcase cause the air/fuel charge to leak into the atmosphere under crankcase compression. During the intake cycle, crankcase leakage will cause air from the atmosphere to be drawn into the crankcase, diluting the air/fuel charge. The net result is inadequate fuel in the combustion chamber. On multiple cylinder engines, each crankcase must be sealed from all other crankcases. Internal leakage will allow the air/fuel charge to leak to another cylinder's crankcase, rather than travel to the correct combustion chamber.

The function of the lower piston ring on most two-stroke engines is crankcase compression. It is difficult to test this ring. Compression tests typically test the upper (compression) ring, not the lower ring. A classic symptom of lower ring failure is the inability to idle at the recommended idle speed. An engine with this condition will run good at higher speeds, but will slowly die when idle is attempted.

External crankcase leakage can be identified with a visual inspection for fuel residue leaking from the crankcase parting line, upper and lower crankshaft seals, reed valves and the intake manifold. Pressure leaking from the crankcase can be quickly identified with a soap and water solution. Air leaking into the crankcase can be found by applying oil to the suspected sealing area. The oil will be drawn into the crankcase at the point of the leak.

Internal leakage is difficult to identify. If there are fittings on each crankcase for a fuel pump, primer or recirculation system, a fuel pressure/vacuum gauge can be attached. As the engine is cranked, a repeating pressure/vacuum cycle must be observed on the gauge. The pressure reading must be substantially higher than the vacuum reading. All cylinders must read basically the same. If this is not possible, the fuel and ignition system must be tested, and as a final resort, the engine disassembled and internally inspected.

TEST AND REPAIR EQUIPMENT

Voltage

Voltage is the pressure in an electrical circuit. The more pressure, the more work that can be done. Voltage can be visualized as water pressure in a garden hose. The more pressure, the further the water can be sprayed. You can have water present in the hose, but without pressure, you cannot accomplish anything. If the water pressure is too high, the hose will burst. When voltage is excessive it will leak past insulation and arc to ground. Voltage is always measured with a voltmeter in a simple parallel connection. The connection of a voltmeter directly to the negative and positive terminals of a battery is an example of a parallel

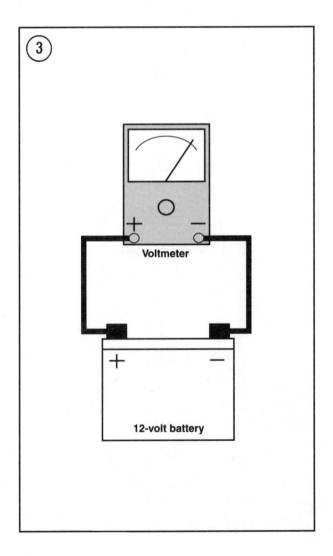

Voltmeter

12-volt battery

connection (**Figure 3**). Nothing has to be disconnected to make a parallel connection. Just as a water pressure gauge simply has a tap into a hose or pipe, a voltmeter is an electrical pressure gauge that taps into the electrical circuit.

DC Voltage

DC voltage is direct current voltage, meaning that the electricity always flows in one direction only. All circuits associated with the battery are DC circuits.

AC Voltage

AC voltage is alternating current, which means that the current flows in one direction momentarily then switches to the opposite direction. The frequency at which AC voltage changes direction is referred to as frequency or Hertz. Household wiring is 115 volts AC and typically 60 hertz (the average value of electrical pressure is 115 volts and the electricity changes direction 60 times per second). In typical outboard motor applications, the charging system's stator output is AC voltage. In larger, inboard pow-

ered applications, AC voltage is typically created by a dedicated AC generator (genset) that powers high load devices such as air-conditioning and appliances. Shore power is also AC voltage. Standard AC voltmeters take an average reading of the fluctuating voltage signal. RMS (root mean square) AC voltmeters use a different mathematical formula to determine the value of the voltage signal. RMS meters must only be used where specified, since the difference in readings between a standard AC meter and a RMS AC meter will be significant.

Peak Voltage

This type of measurement of AC voltage samples the absolute peak or highest value of the fluctuating AC voltage signal. Peak readings are substantially higher than standard or RMS AC values and are typically used when testing marine CD (capacitor discharge) ignition systems. Other manufacturers may refer to this as a DVA voltage reading. DVA stands for direct voltage adaptor, which has been used (by other manufacturers) to adapt a standard AC multimeter to measure peak AC voltage.

Failure to use a meter with a Peak (DVA) scale can cause good ignition components to be incorrectly diagnosed as bad. OMC specifically recommends one of the following peak voltage meters: the Stevens Instruments CD-77 or the Merc-O-Tronic 781. If any other meter is used, it must provide equivalent readings to these meters. See **Figure 4** for a typical multimeter with a Peak (DVA) scale.

Amperes

Amperes (amps) are referred to as current. Current is the actual flow of electricity in a circuit. Current can be visualized as water flowing from a garden hose. There can be pressure in the hose, but if we do not let it flow, no work can be done. The higher the flow of current, the more work that can be done. However, if too much current flows through a wire, the wire will overheat and melt. Melted wires are caused by excessive current, not excessive volts. Amps are measured with an ammeter in a simple series connection. The connection of an ammeter requires the disconnection of a circuit and the splicing of the ammeter into the circuit. Just as a water flow-meter must have the water flow through it in order to measure the flow, an ammeter is an electrical flow-meter that must have all of the current flow through it. Always use an ammeter that can read higher than the anticipated current flow. Always connect the red lead of the ammeter to where the electricity is coming from (electrical source) and the black lead of the

ammeter to where the electricity is going (electrical load).
See **Figure 5**.

Many digital multimeters can use inductive or clamp-on
ammeter probes (**Figure 6**). These probes read the magnetic field strength created by the current flowing through
a wire. No electrical connection is required, simply slip the
probe over the lead.

A simple form of ammeter is the direct reading inductive
ammeter (**Figure 7**). These meters directly read the magnetic field strength created by the current flowing through
a wire. No electrical connection is required, simply slip the
meter over the lead so the lead is located in the channel or
groove located on the rear of the meter. See **Figure 7**.

Watts

Watts (W) are the measurement units for power in an
electrical circuit. Watts rate the ability to do electrical
work. The easiest formula for calculating watts is to take
the system voltage times the amps flowing (12-volt system
times 10 amp alternator = 120 watt maximum load). You
can easily reverse-calculate amp load by dividing watts by
voltage. For example, a 12 watt radio (divided by 12-volt
system voltage) uses 1 amp of current. When calculating
load on a charging system, remember that you cannot carry
more load than the system is rated for or the battery will
constantly discharge.

Ohms

Ohms (Ω) are the measurement units for resistance in an
electrical circuit. Resistance causes a reduction in current
flow and a reduction (or drop) in voltage. Visualized as a
kink in a garden hose, which would cause less water
(current) to flow, it would also cause less pressure (volts)
to be available downstream from the kink. Ohms are measured with ohmmeters that are self-powered. Ohmmeters
send a small amount of electricity into a circuit and measure how hard they have to push to return the electricity to
the meter. An ohmmeter must only be used on a circuit or
component that is isolated (disconnected from any other
circuit or component) and has no voltage present. Ohmmeters are technically connected in series. For additional
information on measuring ohms, refer to *Ohmmeter guidelines* located later in this chapter

Voltage Drop Test

Since resistance causes voltage to drop, resistance can
be measured on an active circuit with a voltmeter. This is
the voltage drop test. Basically, a voltage drop test deter-

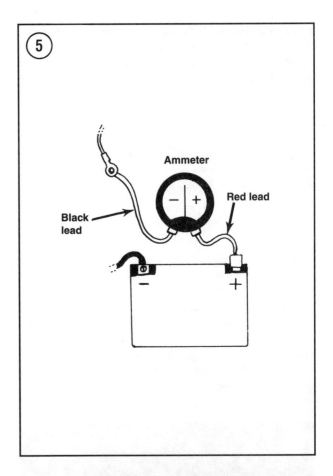

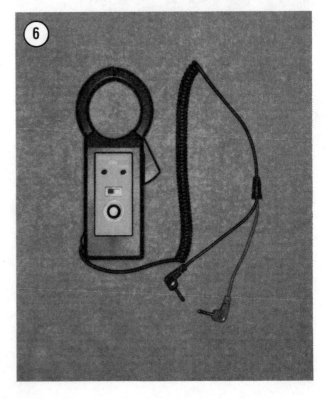

mines the difference between the voltage at the beginning of a circuit from the voltage at the end of the circuit, while the circuit is being operated. If the circuit has no resistance, there will be no voltage drop (the meter will read zero volts). The more resistance the circuit has, the higher the voltmeter reading will be. Generally, a voltage drop reading of one or more volts is considered unsatisfactory. The chief advantage to the voltage drop test over an ohmmeter resistance test is that the circuit is tested while under operation. It is important to remember that a zero reading on a voltage drop test is good, while a reading of battery voltage indicates an open circuit.

The voltage drop test provides an excellent means of testing solenoids (relays), battery cables and high current electrical leads (both positive and negative). As with the ammeter, always connect the red lead of the voltmeter to

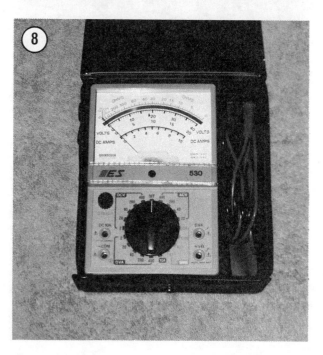

where the electricity is coming from (electrical source) and the black lead of the voltmeter to where the electricity is going (electrical load).

Multipliers

When using an analog multimeter to measure ohms, the scale choices are typically labeled R × 1, R × 10, R × 100 and so on. These are resistance scale multipliers. R × 100 means the meter reading should be multiplied by 100. If the needle indicated a reading of 75 ohms while set to the R × 100 scale, the actual resistance reading would be 75 × 100 or 7500 ohms. It is important to note and remember the scale multiplier when using an analog ohmmeter.

Other multipliers commonly used for volts, ohms and amps scales are: mega- (M), kilo- (k), milli- (m) and micro- (%). Mega (M) is a 1,000,000 multiplier, 75 mega-ohms (or 75 M-ohms) would be 75 million ohms. Kilo (k) is a 1,000 multiplier, 75 kilo-volts (or 75 k-volts) would be 75 thousand volts. Milli (m) is a 0.001 multiplier, 75 milli-volts (or 75 m-volts) would be 0.075 volts or 75 thousandths of a volt. Micro (%) is a 0.000001 multiplier, 75 micro-amps (or 75 %-amps) would be 0.000075 amps or 75 millionths of an amp.

Diodes

Diodes are one-way electrical check valves. A series of diodes used to change AC current to DC current is called a rectifier. Single diodes used to prevent reverse flow of electricity are typically called blocking diodes. Diodes can be tested with an analog meter set to any ohmmeter scale other than *low* or with a digital multimeter set to the diode test scale. A diode tested with an analog ohmmeter will indicate a relatively low reading in one polarity and a relatively high reading in the opposite polarity. A diode tested with a digital multimeter will read a voltage drop of approximately 0.4-0.9 volts in one polarity and an open circuit (typically OL or OUCH) in the opposite polarity.

Analog Multimeters

When using an analog meter (**Figure 8**) to read ohms, the meter must be re-calibrated (zeroed) each time the scale or range is changed. Normally the ohmmeter leads are connected for calibration, however some meters require the leads to be apart for calibration when using the low ohms scale. Always follow the manufacturer's instructions for calibration. When checking for *shorts to ground* calibrate on the highest scale available. When checking diodes, calibrate on the R × 10 scale or higher. If the ohmmeter is so equipped, never use the *low* scale to test a diode or short to ground. When checking for a specific resistance value, calibrate the ohmmeter on a scale that allows reading the specification as near the middle of the meter movement as possible. Analog meters allow easy visual identification of erratic or fluctuating readings.

Digital Multimeters

The digital multimeter is rapidly gaining popularity in the marine industry after many years of acceptance in the automotive industry. Digital displays are easy and clear to read. Most digital meters are auto-ranging, which means that they automatically shift to the scale most appropriate for displaying the value being read. However, the technician must be careful to read the scale correctly. Refer to *Multipliers* located previously in this chapter.

Fluctuating readings can be frustrating to read as the display will change several times a second. Quality digital multimeters typically have a bar graph located below the digital number display. The bar graph allows easy interpretation of fluctuating readings, similar to an analog meter. The scale range and multiplier (if applicable) will be displayed alongside the actual reading.

Most quality digital meters have a special diode test scale that measures the voltage drop of the diode, instead of the resistance. Do not attempt to use the digital multimeter's ohms scale to test diodes, as the readings will be inconsistent. The digital multimeter is protected by internal fuses that are usually uncommon sizes. Buy several spare fuses at the time of purchase.

Adapters are available for temperature readings, inductive ammeter readings and many other functions. **Figure 9** shows a digital multimeter in a protective case with several adapters.

Ohmmeter Guidelines

When using an analog or digital multimeter to measure ohms, it is important to remember two key points:

1. *Continuity*—Indicated by a 0 (zero) or very low (near zero) reading. Continuity means that electricity can flow and is best visualized as a solid wire. This condition is also referred to as a *closed circuit*.

2. *No continuity*—Indicated by an infinity (∞) or very high (near infinity) reading. No continuity means that electricity cannot flow and is best visualized as a broken wire. This condition is also referred to as an *open circuit*. A digital multimeter will typically read OL or OUCH to indicate no continuity. Always consult the manufacturer's instructions for your multimeter.

Resistance (Ohmmeter) Tests

The resistance values specified in the following test procedures are based on tests performed at room temperature. Actual resistance readings obtained during testing will generally be slightly higher if checked on hot components, and lower if checked on very cold components. In addition, resistance readings may vary depending on the manufacturer of the ohmmeter. Therefore, use discretion when failing any component that is only slightly out of specification. Many ohmmeters have difficulty reading

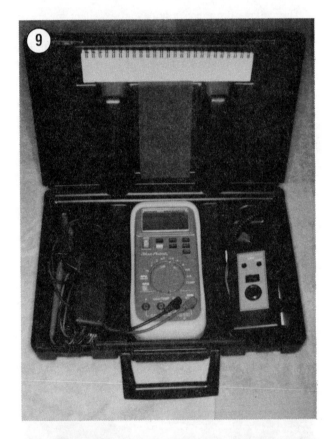

less than 1 ohm accurately. If this is the case, specifications of less than 1 ohm generally appear as a very low (continuity) reading.

Test Lamp

The test lamp is a useful tool for simple troubleshooting, such as starter circuits. A test lamp must not be used on electronic circuits, such as modern ignition and fuel injection circuits. The current draw of the test lamp can damage delicate electronic circuits. A test lamp also must not be used where specific voltage values are being sought. Before beginning any troubleshooting with a test lamp, connect the test lamp directly to the battery and observe the brightness of the bulb. You must reference the rest of your readings against this test. If the bulb does not glow as brightly as when it was connected directly to the battery, a problem is indicated.

A test lamp can be used to check ground circuits by connecting the test lamp lead directly to the positive (+) battery terminal. When the test lamp probe is connected to a good ground circuit, the lamp will glow brightly.

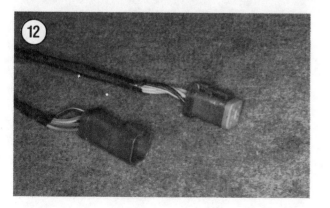

Electrical Repairs

Check all electrical connections for corrosion, mechanical damage, heat damage and loose connections. Clean and repair all connections as necessary. All wire splices or connector repairs must be made with waterproof marine grade connectors and heat shrink tubing. Marine and industrial suppliers are good sources for quality electrical repair equipment.

Four distinct types of connectors are used on engines covered in this manual. Refer to Chapter Seven for complete connector service.

1. *Bullet connectors*—The bullet connector (**Figure 10**) is a common connector used widely in the industry. The bullet connectors used on Evinrude/Johnson engines use vinyl sleeves with several internal sealing ribs to seal the sleeve to the lead as tightly as possible. Replacement male and female connectors, and their appropriate sleeves are listed in the manufacturer's parts catalog. The connectors are crimped in place using standard crimping pliers, such as OMC part No. 500906. Make sure the correct vinyl sleeve (male or female) is slid in place over the lead before crimping the connector in place.

2. *Amphenol connectors*—Amphenol connectors have been widely used on Evinrude/Johnson engines since 1978. Amphenol connectors are identified by their round, dark, rubber connector bodies. Often a wire locking clip (or wire bail) is used to keep the connector from vibrating apart. A disconnected Amphenol connector and its wire bail are shown in **Figure 11**. Replacement connector body part numbers are listed in the manufacturer's parts catalog. The four service tools required to service the connectors are listed in **Table 1**.

> *CAUTION*
> *Always lubricate Amphenol connectors with isopropyl alcohol when connecting or disconnecting the bodies and/or replacing pins. The water-resistant molded seals in the bodies will be irreparably damaged if no lubricant is used.*

3. *Deutsch connectors*—OMC began using Deutsch connectors (**Figure 12**) when the modular wiring system (MWS) was introduced on remote control models beginning with the 1996 (ED) model year. The modular wiring harness is designed to allow flexible, uncomplicated rigging with exceptional durability. These connectors are considered totally waterproof when correctly installed and serviced. Deutsch style connectors are easily identified by their hard plastic bodies, orange locking wedges and orange silicone elastomer seals. An external locking tab

prevents the connectors from vibrating apart and must be manually released before the connectors can be separated. Each terminal pin is locked into the connector body with its own individual internal locking tab. Connector bodies are available in two-four, six and eight pin configurations, with all configurations using the same male and female terminal pins, part No. 514679 (male) and part No. 514680 (female). Replacement connector body, locking wedge and seal part numbers are listed in the manufacturer's parts catalog. Two service tools (a connector service tool and crimping pliers) and a connector repair kit are listed in **Table 1**.

> *CAUTION*
> *Always lubricate the seals of Deutsch connectors with OMC Electrical Grease when reconnecting the bodies and/or replacing the pins. If the locking wedge has been removed, the connector body cavity (for the wedge) must be filled with OMC Electrical Grease to within 1/32 in. (0.8 mm) of the wedge to connector body mating surface.*

4. *Packard connectors*—While the Packard connector (**Figure 13**, typical) is used extensively in the automotive industry, its use is somewhat limited on Evinrude/Johnson engines. This connector is only used to connect an engine harness directly to an electrical or ignition component and is not used to connect a harness to another.

> *CAUTION*
> *Always lubricate the seals of Packard connectors with OMC Electrical Grease when reconnecting the bodies or replacing the pin(s), body or seal(s).*

There are 2 styles of Packard connector used on engines covered in this manual. The first style is easily identified by a flat arrangement of the terminal pins (in a straight row), the large U-shaped locking tab and the ribbed replaceable seals (one sealing the leads to the body and the other sealing the body to the component). This connector is used in four and five-pin configurations on the ignition module of the 25-35 hp (three-cylinder) engines as shown in **Figure 13**.

To replace the body or the lead-to-body seal, all terminal pins must be removed and cut from their leads. The pins must be individually unlocked by inserting a suitable terminal tool (from an automotive tool supplier) into the rear of the body after the lead-to-body seal is slid out and away from the body. Make sure the leads are routed through the new seal and/or connector body before crimping new terminal pins to the leads. After crimping pull the leads

(and pins) into the connector body until they lock in place. This is a *pull-to-lock* connector.

The second style of Packard connector is a six-pin configuration used on the ignition module of the 3 and 4 hp (except 4 Deluxe) models. This connector is easily identified by the two stacked rows of terminal pins (three each row). Each pin has its own individual rear seal, while a common ribbed seal is used to seal the connector body to the component. Illustrations of this connector are located in the appropriate ignition system section.

To replace the body (or the lead-to-body seals), the terminal pins must be individually unlocked by inserting a suitable terminal tool (such as a paper clip) into the front of the body and depressing the locking tab. The pin and lead may then be pulled out the rear of the body. Before reinserting the pin, lead and seal into the body, be sure to bend each pin's locking tab up slightly, to ensure a positive lock. Then push each lead (and pin) into the body until it locks in place. This is a *push-to-lock* connector.

WIRING HARNESSES

While many variations of wiring harnesses, switches, warning systems and controls are available, they will fall into one of the following general categories.

1995 (EO) Models

Prior to 1996, the engine wiring harness was connected to the remote control (boat) wiring harness with a large, red, ten-pin rubber plug. If the engine was equipped with trim and tilt, an additional five-pin Amphenol connector was used for the trim/tilt circuits. Bullet connectors were used to connect the oil tank's low oil sending unit to the engine harness. A dedicated safety lanyard switch is mounted in the control box or in the boats dash. The motor will only run when the lanyard is installed.

This system is referred to as the *Traditional Wiring Harness* in this manual. Refer to **Table 2** for the color codes used on traditional wiring harnesses.

1996-2003 (ED-ST) Models

Beginning with the 1996 (ED) model year, a new system called the modular wiring system (MWS) was incorporated. The MWS system was designed to be used with an OMC System Check engine monitoring gauge. The system check gauge (**Figure 14**) has four light emitting diodes (LEDs) that allow the operator to easily identify whether:

a. The engine is overheating.
b. The engine is not receiving oil.
c. The oil tank's oil level is low.

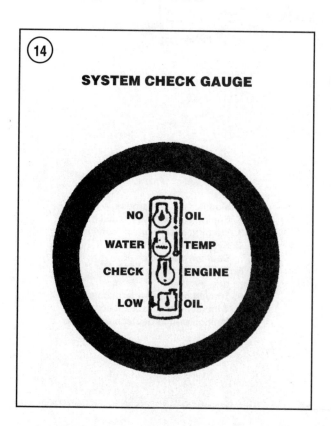

14

SYSTEM CHECK GAUGE

NO OIL
WATER TEMP
CHECK ENGINE
LOW OIL

The check engine light is not used by 70 hp and smaller motors. Several styles of OMC tachometers are available with the System Check gauge integrated into the tachometer. If a System Check gauge is not used, an audible driver module (part No. 176458) must be installed in its place. The module will sound the warning horn if any of the previously mentioned problems arise, but will not differentiate the exact cause of the warning signal.

The MWS main harness (**Figure 15**) uses 3 Deutsch connectors to connect the boat (remote control) harness to the engine harness and a single Deutsch connector to connect the remote oil tank to the engine harness. At the remote control end, a series of Deutsch connectors is used to connect the boat harness to the remote control (or ignition switch) harness, the warning horn, the System Check gauge (or audible driver module) and a trim/tilt switch (if equipped). Ring terminals are provided for the trim/tilt gauge, a conventional tachometer, switched battery positive (B+) and a black ground lead. Refer to **Table 3** for the color codes used on the MWS harness.

> *NOTE*
> *Deutsch connectors and special modular wiring system (MWS) harnesses are used on the 1996 (ED) and newer, 40-70 hp tiller handle models. These models are fully compatible with the System Check warning system.*

The safety lanyard switch is now incorporated into the ignition switch. Pulling the lanyard causes the ignition switch to mechanically rotate to the OFF or STOP position. It is not necessary for the lanyard to be installed for the motor to run. If the operator is ejected from the boat (with the lanyard), this design allows any remaining occupants in the boat to restart the engine and rescue the operator. The dedicated switch and associated wiring has been eliminated.

> *WARNING*
> *It is the operator's responsibility to make sure the lanyard is installed on the ignition switch and connected to the operator before beginning operation.*

STARTING SYSTEM

Description

Evinrude and Johnson 9.9 hp and larger models may be equipped with electric start systems. The starter motor is mounted vertically on the engine. When battery current is supplied to the starter motor, its pinion gear is thrust

3

upward to engage the teeth on the engine flywheel (**Figure 16**, typical). Once the engine starts, the pinion gear disengages from the flywheel. This process is similar to that used to crank an automotive engine.

The starting system requires a fully charged battery to provide the large amount of electrical current necessary to

operate the starter motor. Electric start models are equipped with an alternator to charge the battery during operation.

Models equipped with remote control use an electric starting system consisting of the battery, starter switch, neutral safety switch, starter solenoid, starter motor (and

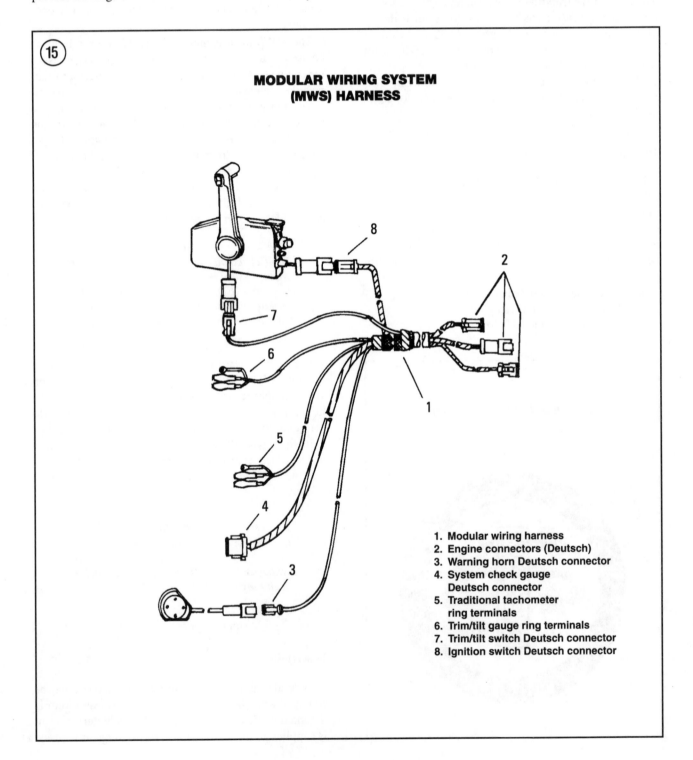

MODULAR WIRING SYSTEM (MWS) HARNESS

1. Modular wiring harness
2. Engine connectors (Deutsch)
3. Warning horn Deutsch connector
4. System check gauge Deutsch connector
5. Traditional tachometer ring terminals
6. Trim/tilt gauge ring terminals
7. Trim/tilt switch Deutsch connector
8. Ignition switch Deutsch connector

starter drive) and related wiring. See **Figure 17**. The neutral safety switch allows starter engagement only when the gear shift is in the NEUTRAL position. The neutral safety switch is mounted in the remote control box. A 20 amp fuse is used to protect the remote control key switch circuits. The fuse is located on the engine, between the starter solenoid and the main harness connector.

Engaging the starter switch allows current to flow through the neutral safety switch to the starter solenoid coil windings, causing the solenoid contacts to close. This permits current to flow directly from the battery, through the solenoid to the starter motor.

Solenoid design will vary, but all solenoids will use two large terminal studs (battery positive and starter cables) and two small terminal studs (black and yellow/red primary leads).

Because tiller handle models do not use a remote control box, the start button (or ignition switch) is mounted on the engine's lower cowl. The major components of this electric starting system are very similar to the remote control

3

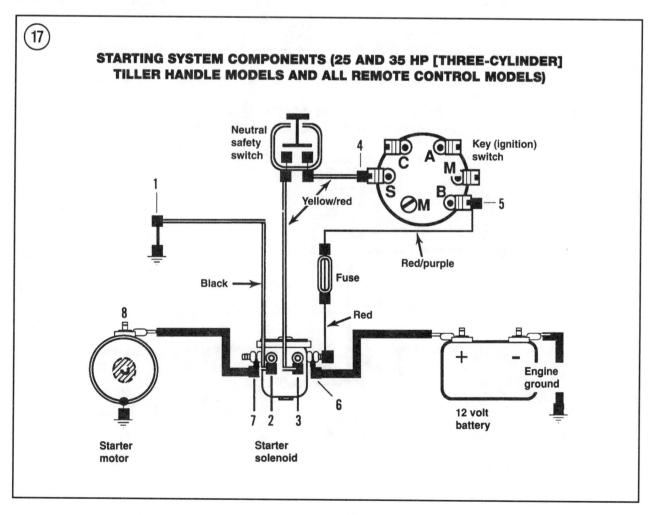

STARTING SYSTEM COMPONENTS (25 AND 35 HP [THREE-CYLINDER] TILLER HANDLE MODELS AND ALL REMOTE CONTROL MODELS)

models described previously, with the following exceptions:

1. *9.9 and 15 hp models*—There is no starter solenoid, neutral safety switch or 20 amp fuse. Depressing the starter button allows current to flow directly from the battery to the starter motor. See **Figure 18**. A mechanical linkage prevents the starter button from being depressed when the shift lever is in FORWARD or REVERSE gear.

2. *20-30 hp (two-cylinder)*—There is no 20 amp fuse. The neutral safety switch is mounted on the engine and controls the ground side of the starter solenoid windings. A starter push-button switch controls the positive side of the starter solenoid windings. The engine cannot start in gear when the neutral safety switch is functioning correctly. See **Figure 19**.

> *NOTE*
> *The wiring harness on 1996 (ED) and newer models uses Deutsch connectors as described previously under **Wiring harnesses**. For simplicity, the Deutsch connectors are not shown in the following diagrams.*

3. *25 and 35 hp (three-cylinder) models*—There is a 20 amp fuse. The neutral safety switch is mounted on the

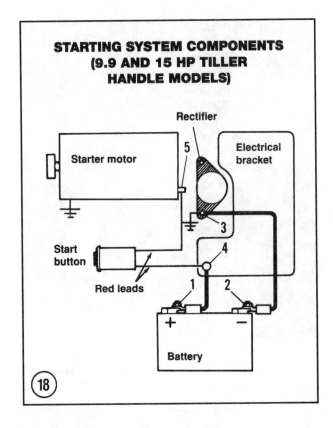

STARTING SYSTEM COMPONENTS (9.9 AND 15 HP TILLER HANDLE MODELS)

18

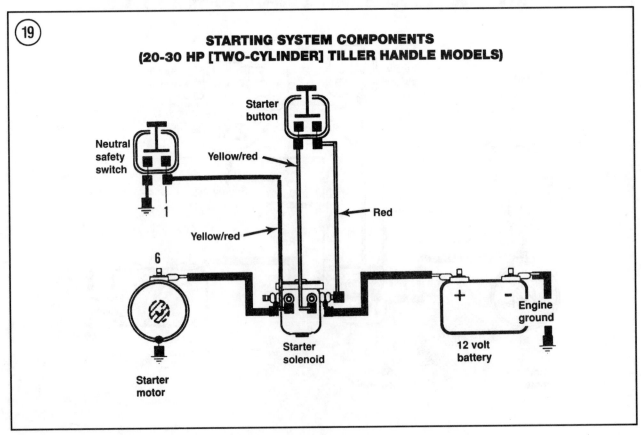

19

STARTING SYSTEM COMPONENTS (20-30 HP [TWO-CYLINDER] TILLER HANDLE MODELS)

engine and a standard rotary ignition switch is used. The starter solenoid is mounted directly to the bottom of the starter motor and is connected to the starter motor with a flat metal strap. The engine cannot start in gear if the neutral safety switch is functioning correctly. The wiring diagram is the same as the remote control models (**Figure 17**), with the exception of the starter solenoid-to-starter motor flat metal strap replacing the cable used on remote control models.

4. *40-70 hp models*—There is a 20 amp fuse, but no neutral safety switch. An ignition switch is used in conjunction with a starter button switch. The starter motor will only engage when the starter button is pushed and the ignition switch is in the ON or RUN position. See **Figure 20**. A mechanical linkage prevents the starter button from being depressed when the shift lever is in FORWARD or REVERSE gear.

> *CAUTION*
> *To prevent starter damage from overheating, do not operate the starter motor continu-*

ously for more than 30 seconds. Allow the motor to cool for at least 2 minutes between attempts to start the engine.

Troubleshooting Preparation

If the following procedures do not locate the problem, refer to **Table 5** for additional information. Before troubleshooting the starting circuit, be sure of the following:

  a. The battery is fully charged.
  b. The shift control lever is in the NEUTRAL position.
  c. All electrical connections are clean and tight. The battery cable connections must be secured with hex nuts and corrosion resistant lock washers. Do not use wing nuts to secure the battery cables to the battery.
  d. The wiring harness is in good condition, with no worn or frayed insulation.
  e. The fuse protecting the starter switch is not blown (remote control models and applicable tiller handle models).

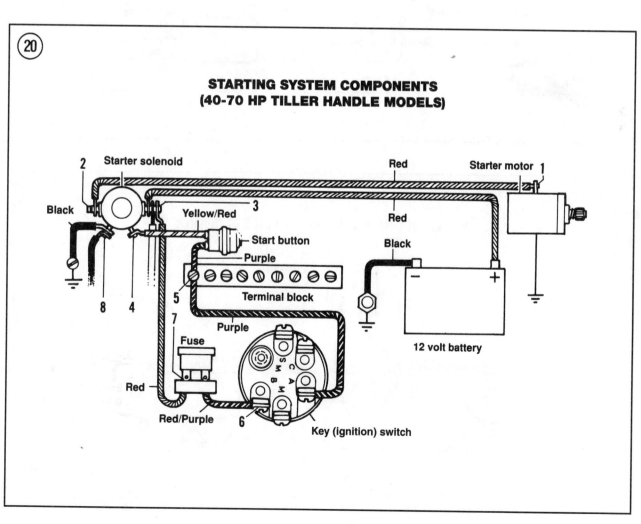

(20)

**STARTING SYSTEM COMPONENTS
(40-70 HP TILLER HANDLE MODELS)**

Starter solenoid

Red   Starter motor 1

2

Black

Yellow/Red
3

Start button
Purple

Terminal block

8   4   5

Red

Black

7

Purple

Fuse

Red

Red/Purple   6

Key (ignition) switch

12 volt battery

f. The power head and gearcase are not the problem (mechanical failure).

CAUTION
Unless otherwise noted, all voltage or test lamp tests must be performed with the leads connected and the connection or terminals exposed to accommodate test lead connection.

Starter Motor Turns Slowly

1. Make sure the battery is in acceptable condition and fully charged.
2. Inspect all electrical connections for looseness or corrosion. Clean and tighten as necessary.
3. Check for the proper size and length of battery cables. Refer to **Table 4** for recommended minimum cable gauge sizes and lengths. Replace cables that are undersize or

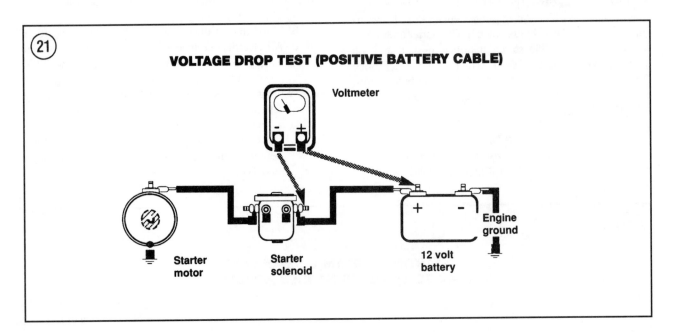

㉑

VOLTAGE DROP TEST (POSITIVE BATTERY CABLE)

Voltmeter

Starter motor

Starter solenoid

12 volt battery

Engine ground

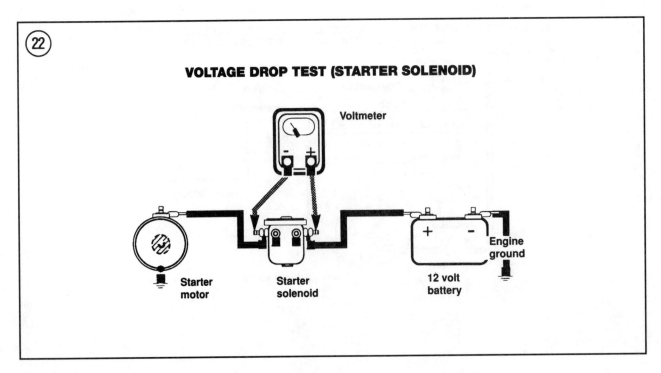

㉒

VOLTAGE DROP TEST (STARTER SOLENOID)

Voltmeter

Starter motor

Starter solenoid

12 volt battery

Engine ground

relocate the battery to shorten the distance between the battery and starter solenoid.

4. Disconnect and ground the spark plug leads to the engine to prevent accidental starting. Turn the flywheel clockwise by hand and check for mechanical binding. If mechanical binding is evident, remove the lower gearcase to determine if the binding is in the power head or the lower gearcase. If no binding is evident, continue to Step 5.

5. *All models except 9.9 and 15 hp tiller handle models—* Perform the starting system voltage drop test as described in the next section.

6. Check the starter motor no-load current draw and no-load speed as described in this chapter.

7. Reconnect the spark plug leads when finished with the troubleshooting procedure.

Starting system voltage drop test

As described in the beginning of this chapter, resistance causes voltage to drop. Excessive resistance in the battery cables, starter solenoid and starter cable can restrict the voltage to the starter, causing the starter motor to turn slowly. Slow cranking speeds cause low ignition system output and subsequent hard starting.

Use the following procedure to determine if any of the cables or the starter solenoid is the source of an excessive voltage drop. If the problem is intermittent, try gently pulling, bending and flexing the cables and connections during the test. Sudden voltmeter fluctuations indicate a poor connection has been located.

Remember that a voltage drop test is measuring the difference in voltage from the beginning of a circuit or component to the end of the circuit or component. If there is resistance in the circuit, the voltage at the end of the circuit will be less than the voltage at the beginning. The circuit must be active to take a voltage drop reading (in this case the starter must be engaged). A voltmeter reading of 0 (zero) means that no resistance is present in the test circuit. A reading of battery voltage means that the circuit is completely open (battery voltage going in and nothing coming out).

Refer to **Figures 21-24** for this procedure. Clean, tighten, repair or replace any cable or solenoid with excessive voltage drop.

1. Disconnect and ground the spark plug leads to the engine to prevent accidental starting.

2. Connect the positive (red) voltmeter lead to the positive battery terminal and the negative (black) voltmeter lead to the positive solenoid terminal as shown in **Figure 21**.

3. Engage the electric starter and observe the meter. If the meter indicates more than 0.3 volt, the positive battery cable has excessive resitance. Clean the connections, repair the terminal ends or replace the positive battery cable.

CAUTION
Do not connect the positive voltmeter lead in Step 4 until after the engine begins cranking. The open solenoid will read battery voltage

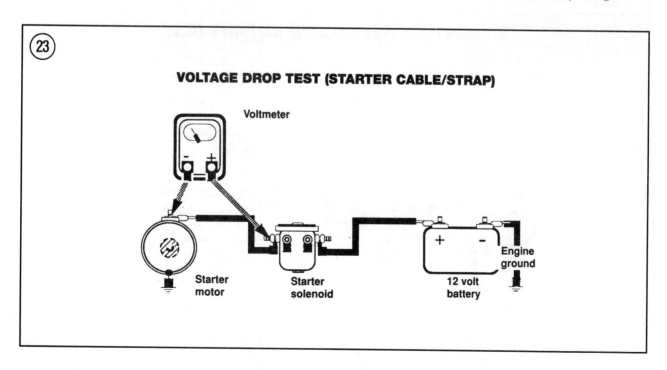

VOLTAGE DROP TEST (STARTER CABLE/STRAP)

Voltmeter

Starter motor

Starter solenoid

12 volt battery

Engine ground

and could damage the voltmeter if set to a very low volt scale. In addition, disconnect the voltmeter before stopping cranking.

4. Connect the *negative* voltmeter lead to the starter side of the solenoid as shown in **Figure 22**. Engage the electric starter. While the engine is cranking, touch the positive voltmeter lead to the battery cable positive solenoid terminal as shown in **Figure 22**. Note the meter reading, then remove the positive voltmeter lead and discontinue cranking. If the meter indicates more than 0.2 volt, the starter solenoid has excessive internal resistance and must be replaced.

5. Connect the positive voltmeter lead to the starter side of the solenoid and the negative voltmeter lead to the starter motor terminal as shown in **Figure 23**. Engage the electric starter and observe the meter. If the meter indicates more than 0.2 volt, there is excessive resistance in the starter motor cable (or strap). Clean the connections, repair the terminal ends or replace the starter motor cable (or strap).

6. Connect the positive voltmeter lead to the engine end of the negative battery cable and the negative voltmeter lead to the negative battery terminal as shown in **Figure 24**. Engage the electric starter and observe the meter. If the meter indicates more than 0.3 volt, there is excessive resistance in the battery negative cable. Clean the connections, repair the terminal ends or replace the negative battery cable.

7. Reconnect the spark plug leads when finished.

Starter Motor Does Not Turn

A test lamp or voltmeter are both acceptable tools for troubleshooting the starter circuit. If using a voltmeter, all test readings must be within 1 volt of battery voltage. A reading of 1 volt or more below battery voltage indicates problem (excessive resistance) with the circuit being tested. If using a test lamp, first connect the test lamp directly to the battery and observe the brightness of the bulb. You must reference the rest of your readings against this test. If the bulb does not glow as brightly as when it was connected directly to the battery, a problem (excessive resistance) is indicated.

CAUTION
Disconnect and ground the spark plug leads to the engine to prevent accidental starting during all test procedures. Make sure the shift control lever is in the NEUTRAL position.

25 and 35 hp (three-cylinder) tiller handle models and all remote control models

Refer to **Figure 25** for this procedure. Refer to the back of the manual for individual model wiring diagrams.

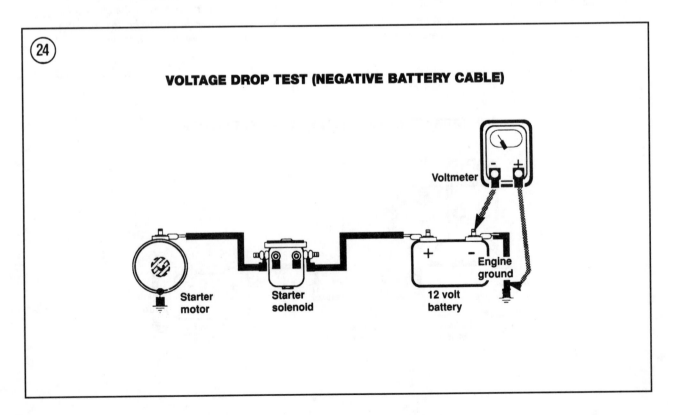

(24)

VOLTAGE DROP TEST (NEGATIVE BATTERY CABLE)

Voltmeter

Starter motor

Starter solenoid

12 volt battery

Engine ground

CAUTION
Disconnect and ground the spark plug leads to the engine to prevent accidental starting during all test procedures. Make sure the shift lever is in the NEUTRAL position.

1. Connect the test lamp lead to the *positive* terminal of the battery and touch the test lamp probe to metal anywhere on the engine block. The test lamp must light. If the lamp does not light or is dim, the battery ground cable connections are loose or corroded, or there is an open circuit in the battery ground cable. Clean and tighten the connections or replace the battery cable as required.

2. Connect the test lamp lead to a good engine ground and connect the test lamp probe to the starter solenoid input terminal (1, **Figure 25**). The test lamp must light. If the lamp does not light or is very dim, the battery cable connections are loose or corroded, or there is an open circuit in the cable between the battery and the solenoid. Clean and tighten the connections or replace the battery cable as required.

3. Remove the 20 amp fuse and connect the test lamp probe to the input side of the fuse holder (2, **Figure 25**). If the lamp does not light, repair or replace the red lead between the starter solenoid and the fuse holder.

4A. *25 and 35 hp (three-cylinder) tiller handle models—* Inspect the 20 amp fuse. Install a known good fuse into the fuse holder. Unplug the six-pin Amphenol or Deutsch connector between the ignition switch and the main engine harness. Connect the test light probe to pin E or pin No. 5 (red/purple lead) of the engine harness connector. If the test

3

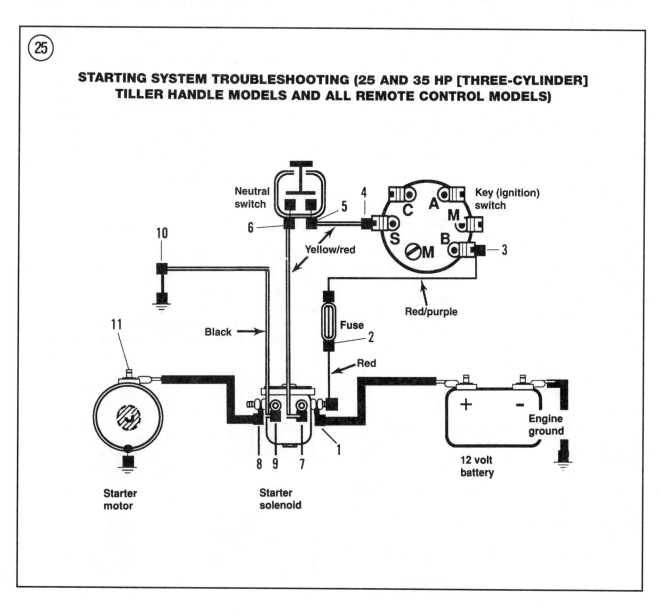

STARTING SYSTEM TROUBLESHOOTING (25 AND 35 HP [THREE-CYLINDER] TILLER HANDLE MODELS AND ALL REMOTE CONTROL MODELS)

lamp does not light, repair or replace the red/purple lead between the fuse holder and the six-pin engine harness connector.

4B. *Remote control models with traditional harnesses*—Inspect the 20 amp fuse. Install a known good fuse into the fuse holder. Unplug the large, red, 10-pin main harness connector and connect the test light probe to red/purple pin (1, **Figure 26**) of the main engine harness connector. If the test lamp does not light, repair or replace the red/purple lead between the fuse holder and the main engine harness connector.

4C. *Remote control models with MWS harnesses*—Inspect the 20 amp fuse. Install a known good fuse into the fuse holder. Unplug the six-pin Deutsch main harness connector and connect the test light probe to pin No. 5 (red/purple lead) of the engine harness connector. If the test lamp does not light, repair or replace the red/purple lead between the fuse holder and the six-pin Deutsch engine harness connector.

5A. *25 and 35 hp (three-cylinder) tiller handle models*—Reconnect the six-pin Amphenol or Deutsch connector and gain access to the rear of the ignition switch. Connect the test lamp probe to the ignition switch terminal B (red/purple lead). See 3, **Figure 25**. If the test lamp does not light, repair or replace the red/purple lead between pin E or pin No. 5 of the six-pin connector and the ignition switch terminal B.

5B. *Remote control models with traditional harnesses*—Reconnect the 10-pin main harness connector and gain access to the ignition switch on the dash or in the remote control box. Connect the test lamp probe to the ignition switch terminal B (red/purple lead). See 3, **Figure 25**. If the lamp does not light, repair or replace the red/purple lead between the red/purple pin of the main boat harness connector and the ignition switch terminal B. See **Figure 26** for pin location on the engine side of the main harness connector. Make sure the correct terminal is located on the boat harness side of the connector.

5C. *Remote control models with MWS harnesses*—Reconnect the six-pin Deutsch connector and gain access to the rear of the ignition switch on the dash or in the remote control box. Connect the test lamp probe to the ignition switch terminal B (red/purple lead). See 3, **Figure 25**. If the lamp does not light, repair or replace the red/purple lead between pin No. 5 of the six-pin Deutsch boat harness connector and the ignition switch terminal B.

6. Connect the test lamp probe to the ignition switch terminal S (4, **Figure 25**). With the ignition switch turned to the START position observe the test lamp. If the test lamp does not light, replace the ignition switch.

7A. *Remote control models*—Remove the cover from the remote control box and connect the test lamp probe to the ignition switch side of the neutral safety switch (5, **Figure 25**). With the ignition switch turned to the START position, observe the test lamp. If the test lamp does not light, repair or replace the lead between the neutral safety switch and the ignition switch.

7B. *25 and 35 hp (three-cylinder) tiller handle models*—Connect the test lamp probe to the ignition switch side of the neutral safety switch (5, **Figure 25**). With the ignition switch turned to the START position, observe the test lamp. If the test lamp does not light, repair or replace the yellow/red lead between the neutral safety switch and the ignition switch.

8. Move the test lamp probe to the solenoid side of the neutral safety switch (6, **Figure 25**). With the ignition switch turned to the START position, observe the test lamp. If the test lamp does not light, make sure the shift control is still in neutral and retest. Replace the neutral safety switch if the lamp does not light.

NOTE
On 25 and 35 hp (three-cylinder) tiller handle models, the neutral safety circuit (yellow/red lead) begins at the ignition switch and travels to the six-pin Amphenol (pin C) or Deutsch (pin No. 3) connector. It then loops back into the six-pin Amphenol (pin F) or Deutsch (pin No. 6) connector and onto the neutral safety switch. From the neutral safety switch, the circuit makes a final pass through the six-pin Amphenol (pin B) or Deutsch (pin No. 2) connector, then continues directly to the starter solenoid.

9. Connect the test lamp probe to the yellow/red terminal on the starter solenoid (7, **Figure 25**). With the ignition

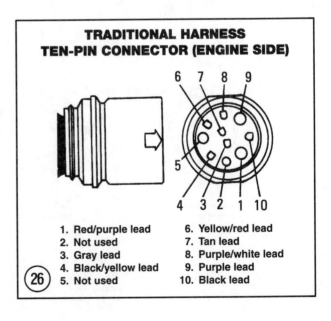

TRADITIONAL HARNESS TEN-PIN CONNECTOR (ENGINE SIDE)

1. Red/purple lead
2. Not used
3. Gray lead
4. Black/yellow lead
5. Not used
6. Yellow/red lead
7. Tan lead
8. Purple/white lead
9. Purple lead
10. Black lead

26

switch turned to the START position, observe the test lamp. If the test lamp does not light, repair or replace the yellow/red lead between the neutral safety switch and the starter solenoid. This includes the main harness connector.

10. Connect the test lamp probe to the starter solenoid terminal leading to the starter motor (8, **Figure 25**). With the ignition switch turned to the START position, observe the test lamp. If the test lamp does not light, connect the test lamp lead to the *positive* battery terminal and connect the test lamp probe to the small black (ground) terminal of the starter solenoid (9, **Figure 25**). If the test lamp does not light, repair or replace the ground lead between the starter solenoid and the engine block (10, **Figure 25**). If the test lamp lights only during the ground lead test, replace the starter solenoid.

11. Connect the test lamp lead to a good engine ground. Connect the test lamp probe to the starter motor terminal (11, **Figure 25**). With the ignition switch turned to the START position observe the test lamp. If the test lamp does not light, repair or replace the cable between the starter solenoid and the starter motor. If the test lamp lights, proceed to Step 13.

12. Remove the starter and inspect for paint or corrosion on the mounting bolts and bosses. If paint or corrosion is found, clean the mounting bolts and bosses and reinstall the starter and test starter engagement. If the starter still will not engage, remove the starter for replacement or repair.

13. Reconnect the spark plug leads when finished.

9.9 and 15 hp tiller handle models

Refer to **Figure 27** for this procedure. Refer to the back of the manual for complete engine wiring diagrams. The negative battery cable connects to the engine at one of the rectifier mounting screws (1, **Figure 27**).

> *CAUTION*
> *Disconnect and ground the spark plug leads to the engine to prevent accidental starting during this test. Make sure the shift lever is in the NEUTRAL position.*

1. Connect the test lamp lead to the *positive* terminal of the battery and touch the test lamp probe to metal anywhere on the engine block. The test lamp must light. If the lamp does not light or is dim, the battery ground cable connections are loose or corroded, or there is an open circuit in the battery ground cable. Clean and tighten the connections (including 1, **Figure 27**) or replace the battery cable as required.

2. Connect test lamp lead to a good engine ground. Then connect the test lamp probe to the battery cable terminal stud (2, **Figure 27**). The test lamp must light. If the lamp does not light or is very dim, the battery cable connections are loose or corroded, or there is an open in the cable between the battery and the stud. Clean and tighten the connections (including 2, **Figure 27**) or replace the battery cable as required.

3. Connect the test lamp probe to the starter motor terminal (3, **Figure 27**). Depress the starter switch and observe the test lamp. If the test lamp does not light, replace the push-button starter switch and cable assembly. If the test lamp lights, remove the starter and inspect for paint or corrosion on the mounting bolts and bosses. If paint or corrosion is found, clean the mounting bolts and bosses and reinstall the starter and test starter engagement. If the

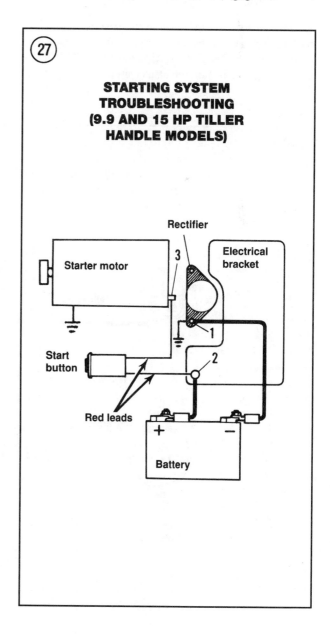

(27)

STARTING SYSTEM TROUBLESHOOTING (9.9 AND 15 HP TILLER HANDLE MODELS)

starter still will not engage, remove the starter for replacement or repair.

4. Reconnect the spark plug leads when finished.

20-30 hp (two-cylinder) tiller handle models

Refer to **Figure 28** for this procedure. Refer to the back of the manual for complete engine wiring diagrams.

> *CAUTION*
> *Disconnect and ground the spark plug leads to the engine to prevent accidental starting during all test procedures. Make sure the shift lever is in the NEUTRAL position.*

1. Connect the test lamp lead to the *positive* terminal of the battery and touch the test lamp probe to metal anywhere on the engine block. The test lamp must light. If the lamp does not light or is dim, the battery ground cable connections are loose or corroded, or there is an open circuit in the battery ground cable. Clean and tighten the connections or replace the battery cable as required.

2. Connect the test lamp lead to a good engine ground and connect the test lamp probe to the starter solenoid input terminal (1, **Figure 28**). The test lamp must light. If the lamp does not light or is very dim, the battery cable connections are loose or corroded, or there is an open in the cable between the battery and the solenoid. Clean and tighten the connections or replace the battery cable as required.

3. Connect the test lamp probe to the starter solenoid yellow/red terminal (2, **Figure 28**). Make sure that this is the terminal that is connected to the starter switch and not the neutral safety switch. With the starter switch depressed, observe the test lamp. If the test lamp does not light, replace the push-button starter switch and leads as an assembly.

4. Connect the test lamp probe to the starter solenoid yellow/red terminal (3, **Figure 28**). Make sure that this is the terminal that is connected to the neutral safety switch and not the starter switch. With the starter switch de-

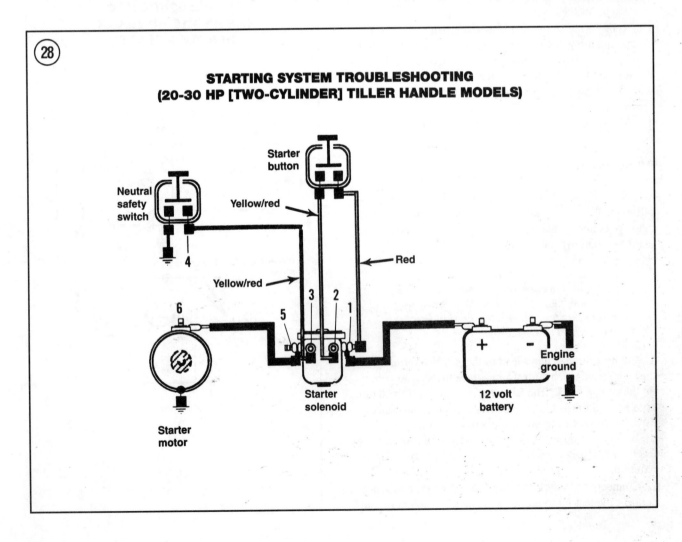

STARTING SYSTEM TROUBLESHOOTING
(20-30 HP [TWO-CYLINDER] TILLER HANDLE MODELS)

3

pressed, observe the test lamp. If the test lamp does not light, replace the starter solenoid.

5. Connect the test lamp probe to the neutral safety switch yellow/red terminal (4, **Figure 28**). With the starter switch depressed, observe the test lamp. If the test lamp does not light, the yellow/red lead has an open circuit. Repair or replace the yellow/red lead as necessary.

6. Connect the test lamp probe to the starter solenoid terminal leading to the starter motor (5, **Figure 28**). With the starter switch depressed, observe the test lamp. If the test lamp lights, proceed to Step 8. If the test lamp does not light, proceed to Step 7.

7. Disconnect the yellow/red lead (4, **Figure 28**) from the neutral safety switch and hold the lead to one of the switch's mounting screws. While holding the lead against a mounting screw, repeat Step 6. If the test lamp now lights, replace the neutral safety switch. If the test lamp still does not light, replace the starter solenoid.

8. Connect the test lamp probe to the starter motor terminal (6, **Figure 28**). With the starter switch depressed, observe the test lamp. If the test lamp does not light, repair

or replace the cable between the starter solenoid and the starter motor. If the test lamp lights, remove the starter and inspect for paint or corrosion on the mounting bolts and bosses. If paint or corrosion is found, clean the mounting bolts and bosses and reinstall the starter and test starter engagement. If the starter still will not engage, remove the starter for replacement or repair.

9. Reconnect the spark plug leads when finished.

40-70 hp tiller handle models

Refer to **Figure 29** for this procedure. Refer to the back of the manual for wiring diagrams.

CAUTION
Disconnect and ground the spark plug leads to the engine to prevent accidental starting during this test. Make sure the shift lever is in the NEUTRAL position.

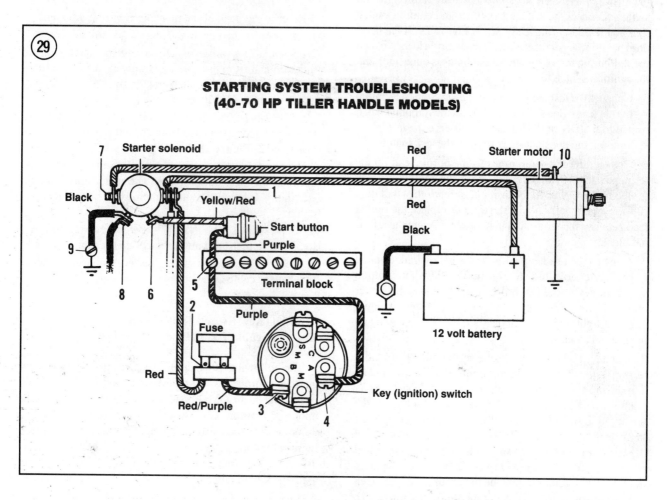

**STARTING SYSTEM TROUBLESHOOTING
(40-70 HP TILLER HANDLE MODELS)**

1. Connect the test lamp lead to the *positive* terminal of the battery and touch the test lamp probe to metal anywhere on the engine block. The test lamp must light. If the lamp does not light or is dim, the battery ground cable connections are loose or corroded, or there is an open circuit in the battery ground cable. Clean and tighten the connections or replace the battery cable as required.

2. Connect the test lamp lead to a good engine ground and connect the test lamp probe to the starter solenoid input terminal (1, **Figure 29**). The test lamp must light. If the lamp does not light or is very dim, the battery cable connections are loose or corroded, or there is an open in the cable between the battery and the solenoid. Clean and tighten the connections or replace the battery cable as required.

3. Remove the 20 amp fuse and connect the test lamp probe to the input side of the fuse holder (2, **Figure 29**). If the lamp does not light, repair or replace the red lead between the starter solenoid and the fuse holder.

4. Inspect the 20 amp fuse. Install a known good fuse into the fuse holder. Gain access to the rear of the ignition switch. Connect the test lamp probe to the ignition switch terminal B (red/purple lead). See 3, **Figure 29**. If the lamp does not light, repair or replace the red/purple lead between the red/purple pin of the main boat harness connector and the ignition switch terminal B.

5. Connect the test lamp probe to the key switch terminal A (purple lead). See 4, **Figure 29**. With the ignition switch turned to the ON or RUN position, observe the test lamp. If the test lamp does not light, replace the key switch.

6. Connect the test lamp probe to the purple lead on the terminal strip (5, **Figure 29**). With the ignition switch turned to the ON or RUN position, observe the test lamp. If the test lamp does not light, repair or replace the purple lead between the ignition switch terminal A and the terminal block.

7. Connect the test lamp probe to the yellow/red terminal of the starter solenoid (6, **Figure 29**). With the ignition switch turned to the ON or RUN position *and* the starter button depressed, observe the test lamp. If the test lamp does not light, replace the push-button starter switch and leads as an assembly.

8. Connect the test lamp probe to the starter solenoid terminal leading to the starter motor (7, **Figure 29**). With the ignition switch turned to the ON or RUN position *and* the starter button depressed, observe the test lamp. If the test lamp does not light, connect the test lamp lead to the *positive* battery terminal and connect the test lamp probe to the small black (ground) terminal of the starter solenoid (8, **Figure 29**). If the test lamp does not light, repair or replace the ground lead between the starter solenoid and the engine block (9, **Figure 29**).

If the test lamp lights only during the ground lead test, replace the starter solenoid.

9. Connect the test lamp lead to a good engine ground. Connect the test lamp probe to the starter motor terminal (10, **Figure 29**). With the ignition switch turned to the ON or RUN position *and* the starter button depressed, observe the test lamp. If the test lamp does not light, repair or replace the cable between the starter solenoid and the starter motor. If the test lamp lights, proceed to Step 10.

10. Remove the starter and inspect for paint or corrosion on the mounting bolts and bosses. If paint or corrosion is found, clean the mounting bolts and bosses and reinstall the starter and test starter engagement. If the starter still will not engage, remove the starter for replacement or repair.

11. Reconnect the spark plug leads when finished.

Push Button Starter Switch Test (9.9-30 hp Tiller Handle Models)

Refer to the back of the manual for wiring diagrams.

1. Disconnect the negative battery cable from the battery.

2A. *9.9 and 15 hp models*—Disconnect the start button red ring terminal from the positive battery cable terminal stud (2, **Figure 27**) and the other ring terminal from the starter motor terminal (3, **Figure 27**).

2B. *20-30 hp (two-cylinder) models*—Disconnect the start button red and yellow/red leads from the starter solenoid. See 1 and 2, **Figure 28**.

3. Connect an ohmmeter calibrated on the R × 1 scale, between the start button leads. The meter must read no continuity. Replace the start button if any other reading is noted.

4. Depress the start button. The meter must read continuity. Replace the start button if any other reading is noted.

5. Reconnect all leads when finished. Connect the negative battery cable last.

Ignition (Key) Switch Test (Remote Control and Applicable Tiller Handle Models)

The following procedure tests the ignition switch on models equipped with an OMC prewired remote control assembly or an OMC boat wiring harness with a dash-mounted ignition (key) switch. Most aftermarket prewired remote controls and boat wiring harnesses use the same wire color codes, key switch functions and terminal identification, but this test may not be valid on all models equipped with aftermarket controls and electrical harnesses.

This procedure also covers the ignition switches used on 25 and 35 hp (three-cylinder) and 40-70 hp, tiller handle, electric-start models.

On remote control-equipped models, the ignition switch and main wiring harness can be quickly tested at the boat side of the main engine harness connector, eliminating the need to disassemble the control box or remove the key switch from the dash panel. To identify the correct terminal pins (for the boat end of the connector) on a traditional wiring harness, refer to **Figure 30**. On models equipped with the modular wiring system (MWS) and Deutsch connectors, the color codes of the leads and their corresponding pin location in the connector body is self-evident.

On a traditional harness (using a dedicated safety lanyard switch), the safety lanyard must be installed on the safety lanyard switch in order to perform the tests at the engine's main harness connector. The safety lanyard switch is connected between the black/yellow and black leads of the ignition switch (both M terminals). If the lanyard is removed, an ohmmeter connected across the black/yellow and black pins of the main harness connector must show continuity, regardless of the ignition switch position. If the lanyard is installed and the switch is functioning correctly, the ignition switch will test as described in the following procedure.

If you decide to test at the engine harness connector on a remote control model, connect the ohmmeter to the appropriate pins based on the wire color codes called out in the following text. Testing at the engine harness connector will not isolate a bad wiring harness from the key switch. If the switch and harness fails the test procedure (at the main harness connector), the key switch will have to be disconnected and retested to verify that the main harness is not the problem. To test the key switch alone, follow the procedure as written.

NOTE
On ring terminal style switches, generally used on 1995 (EO) models, the black/yellow lead must be connected to the terminal that is elevated and points rearward (not toward the side like the rest of the remaining terminals).

Use an ohmmeter calibrated on the $R \times 1$ scale to test the key switch circuits. Refer to **Figure 31** for this procedure.

1. Disconnect the negative battery cable from the battery.

2. Gain access to the key switch and disconnect the leads from the key switch terminals. Note the color code and terminal markings of aftermarket switches.

3. Connect one lead of the ohmmeter to the ignition switch B terminal (red/purple lead) and the other ohmmeter lead to the A terminal (purple lead). When the switch is in the OFF position, no continuity must be noted.

4. Turn the switch to the ON or RUN position. The ohmmeter must indicate continuity.

5. Turn the switch to the START or CRANK position. The ohmmeter must indicate continuity.

6. Connect one lead of the ohmmeter to the B terminal (red/purple lead) and the other ohmmeter lead to the S terminal (yellow/red lead). When the switch is in the OFF position, no continuity must be noted.

3

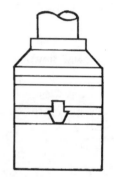

**TRADITIONAL HARNESS
TEN-PIN CONNECTOR (BOAT SIDE)**

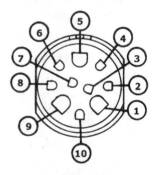

1. Red/purple lead
2. Not used
3. Gray lead
4. Black/yellow lead
5. Not used
6. Yellow/red lead
7. Tan lead
8. Purple/white lead
9. Purple lead
10. Black lead

7. Turn the switch to the START or CRANK position. The ohmmeter must indicate continuity.

8. Turn the switch to the OFF or STOP position. Connect one ohmmeter lead to an M terminal (black/yellow lead) and the other ohmmeter lead to the other M terminal (black lead). See **Figure 31**. The ohmmeter must indicate continuity.

9. While noting the meter, turn the switch to the ON (RUN) and START (CRANK) positions. The ohmmeter must read no continuity in both positions.

10. Turn the switch to the OFF or STOP position. Connect one ohmmeter lead to the B terminal (red/purple lead) and the other ohmmeter lead to the C terminal (purple/white lead). The ohmmeter must read no continuity.

11. Turn the switch to the ON or RUN position. The ohmmeter must read no continuity. Press in on the key to engage the CHOKE or PRIME position. The ohmmeter must read continuity in the CHOKE or PRIME position.

12. Turn the switch to the START or CRANK position. The ohmmeter must read no continuity. Press in on the key to engage the CHOKE or PRIME position. The ohmmeter must read continuity in the CHOKE or PRIME position.

13. Replace the ignition (key) switch if it does not perform as specified.

14. Reconnect all leads when finished. Connect the negative battery cable last.

Ignition (Key) Switch Leakage Test

Under some conditions, it is possible for the ignition switch to allow the high voltage present in the stop circuit (black/yellow) lead to leak to the other terminals in the key switch, but not show up during the ohmmeter test. To test for leakage, obtain a condenser tester and proceed as follows:

1. Disconnect the negative battery cable from the battery.

2. Gain access to the key switch and disconnect the leads from the key switch terminals. Note the color code and terminal markings of after-market switches.

3. Calibrate the condenser tester to check for condenser leakage. Follow its manufacturer's instructions.

4. Connect the black lead of the condenser tester to the M terminal that the black/yellow lead connects to (**Figure 31**). Make sure the ignition switch is in the OFF or STOP position.

5. Alternately connect the red lead of the condenser tester to each of the remaining ignition switch terminals (A, B, C and S) except the other M terminal and test each terminal for leakage. No leakage must be noted at each of the A, B, C and S terminals when the switch is in the OFF or STOP position.

6. Turn the switch to the ON or RUN position. Connect the red lead of the condenser tester to the remaining M

(black or black/white lead) terminal. Test this terminal for leakage. No leakage must be noted between the 2 M terminals when the switch is in the ON or RUN position.

7. Replace the ignition (key) switch if it does not perform as specified.

8. Reconnect all leads when finished. Connect the negative battery cable last.

Neutral Safety Switch Tests

The purpose of the neutral safety switch is to allow starter engagement *only* when the shift lever (gearcase) is in the NEUTRAL position. The starter must not engage

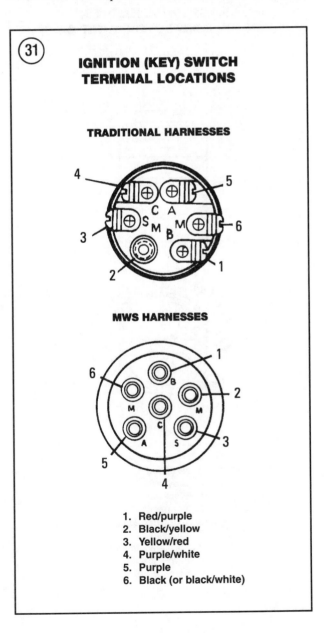

IGNITION (KEY) SWITCH TERMINAL LOCATIONS

TRADITIONAL HARNESSES

MWS HARNESSES

1. **Red/purple**
2. **Black/yellow**
3. **Yellow/red**
4. **Purple/white**
5. **Purple**
6. **Black (or black/white)**

when the shift lever (gearcase) is in either the FORWARD or REVERSE position.

Tiller handle models equipped with a neutral safety switch require adjustment of the switch to ensure proper operation. See Chapter Seven. The switch must be adjusted any time it has been removed or replaced, or if improper operation is noted.

Remote control models require remote control shift cable adjustment to ensure proper operation. See Chapter Twelve for shift cable adjustments. The shift cable must be adjusted anytime it, the gearcase or the control box has

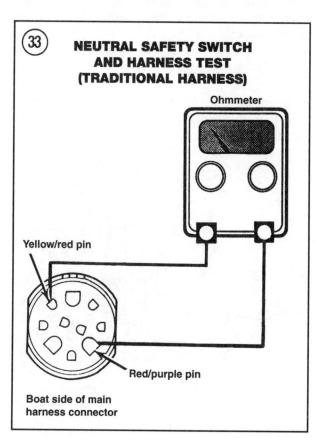

③③ NEUTRAL SAFETY SWITCH AND HARNESS TEST (TRADITIONAL HARNESS)

Ohmmeter

Yellow/red pin

Red/purple pin

Boat side of main harness connector

been removed, repaired or replaced, or if improper operation is noted.

Remote control models (boat harness and switch test)

> *CAUTION*
> *Moving the shift lever into FORWARD or REVERSE gear with the engine not running can damage the control box, shift cable and gearcase. Have an assistant rotate the propeller when it is necessary to shift the gearcase with the engine not running.*

The neutral safety switch is located in the control box. If the engine will crank with the control lever in the NEUTRAL position, but will not crank with the control lever in the FORWARD or REVERSE position, the neutral safety switch is functioning correctly.

To quickly test the switch and boat harness using an ohmmeter, proceed as follows:

1. Disconnect the negative battery cable from the battery and position the remote control shift lever into the NEUTRAL position.

2A. *Traditional harnesses*—Disconnect the large, red, 10-pin main harness connector from the engine.

2B. *Modular wiring system (MWS) harnesses*—Remove the connector box cover and disconnect the six-pin Deutsch main harness connector from the engine. See **Figure 32**, typical.

3A. *Traditional harnesses*—Connect an ohmmeter, calibrated on the R × 1 scale, to the boat side of the main harness connector as shown in **Figure 33**.

3B. *MWS harnesses*—Connect an ohmmeter, calibrated on the R × 1 scale, to the yellow/red (pin No. 2) and red/purple (pin No. 5) terminals of the main harness connector (boat side).

4. Turn the ignition (key) switch to the START position while noting the meter reading. The meter must indicate continuity.

5. While an assistant is rotating the propeller, position the shift lever in the FORWARD gear position.

6. Turn the ignition (key) switch to the START position while noting the meter reading. The meter must indicate no continuity.

7. While an assistant is rotating the propeller, position the shift lever in the REVERSE gear position.

8. Turn the ignition (key) switch to the START position while noting the meter reading. The meter must indicate no continuity.

9. If the test results are not as specified, either the boat wiring harness or the neutral safety switch are defective. Test the isolated neutral safety switch as described in the

next section. If the switch tests are satisfactory, there is an open circuit or high resistance in the boat harness yellow/red or red/purple leads. Repair or replace the harness as necessary.

10. Reconnect all leads when finished. Connect the negative battery cable last.

Remote control models (isolated switch test)

To test only the neutral safety switch, proceed as follows:

1. Disconnect the negative battery cable from the battery and position the remote control shift lever in the NEUTRAL position.
2. Open the control box to gain access to the switch.
3. Disconnect both yellow/red leads from the switch.
4. Connect an ohmmeter calibrated on the R × 1 scale to the switch terminals.

> *NOTE*
> *The switch must be depressed in NEUTRAL and extended in FORWARD and REVERSE.*

5. Depress the switch while noting the meter reading. The ohmmeter must indicate continuity.
6. Release (extend) the switch while noting the meter reading. The ohmmeter must indicate no continuity.
7. Replace the switch if it does not perform as specified.
8. Reconnect all leads when finished. Connect the negative battery cable last.

Tiller handle models (20-35 hp)

> *CAUTION*
> *Moving the shift lever into FORWARD or REVERSE gear while the engine is not running can damage the shift linkage and gearcase. Rotate the propeller if it is necessary to shift the gearcase while the engine is not running.*

On these models, a neutral safety switch is located on the engine, next to the shift linkage. On all other tiller handle models, mechanical linkage is used to prevent the starter button from being depressed while the shift linkage is in FORWARD or REVERSE gear. Refer to Chapter Seven for neutral safety switch and mechanical linkage adjustment procedures.

If the engine will crank with the control lever in the NEUTRAL position, but will not crank with the control lever in the FORWARD or REVERSE position, the neutral safety switch is functioning correctly.

To test the neutral safety switch using an ohmmeter, proceed as follows:

1. Disconnect the negative battery cable from the battery and position the shift lever in the NEUTRAL position.
2A. *20-30 hp (two-cylinder) models*—Disconnect the yellow/red lead from the neutral safety switch.
2B. *25 and 35 hp (three-cylinder) models*—Disconnect the six-pin Amphenol or Deutsch ignition switch connector from the engine harness connector.
3. Calibrate an ohmmeter on the R × 1 scale.
4A. *20-30 hp (two-cylinder) models*—Connect one lead of the ohmmeter to the neutral safety switch terminal and the other ohmmeter lead to a good engine ground. See **Figure 34**.
4B. *25 and 35 hp (three-cylinder) models*—Connect the ohmmeter to pins B (No. 2) and F (No. 6) of the six-pin Amphenol or Deutsch ignition switch connector.
5. With the shift lever in the NEUTRAL position, note the meter reading. The meter must indicate continuity.
6. While rotating the propeller, move the shift lever into the FORWARD gear position. Note the meter reading. The meter must indicate no continuity.
7. While rotating the propeller, move the shift lever into the REVERSE gear position. Note the meter reading. The meter must indicate no continuity.
8A. *20-30 hp (two-cylinder)*—If the switch does not perform as specified, refer to Chapter Seven and adjust the switch. Retest the switch function after adjustment. If the switch still does not perform as specified, replace the switch as described in Chapter Seven.
8B. *25 and 35 hp (three-cylinder) models*—Replace the switch if it does not perform as specified.

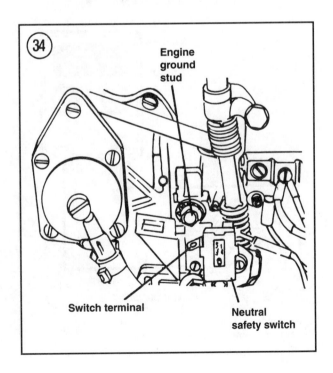

(34) Engine ground stud

Switch terminal

Neutral safety switch

9. Reconnect all leads when finished. Connect the negative battery cable last.

Starter Solenoid Bench Test

NOTE
All engine wiring harness leads must be disconnected from the solenoid for this test.

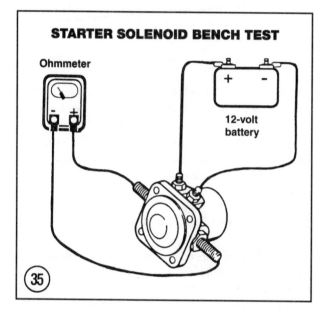

STARTER SOLENOID BENCH TEST

Solenoid style varies, but all solenoids have two large terminal studs and two small terminal studs. Refer to **Figure 35** for this procedure.
1. Disconnect the negative battery cable from the battery.
2. Disconnect all leads from the solenoid terminal studs. If necessary, remove the solenoid from the engine.
3. Connect an ohmmeter (calibrated on the R × 1 scale) to the two large terminal studs as shown in **Figure 35**, typical. The ohmmeter must indicate no continuity. Replace the solenoid if any other reading is noted.
4. Attach a 12-volt battery (with suitable jumper leads) to the two small terminal studs as shown in **Figure 35**, typical (polarity is not important). An audible click will be heard as (if) the solenoid engages. The ohmmeter must now indicate continuity. Replace the solenoid if any other reading is noted.
5. Reconnect all leads when finished. Connect the negative battery cable last.

Starter Motor No-Load Current Draw Test

If starter system troubleshooting indicates that additional starter motor tests are necessary, use the starter. no-load current draw test as an indicator of internal starter condition. A clamp-on or inductive ammeter, if available, is simplest to use as no electrical connections are required. Make sure that the ammeter being used can read higher than the anticipated highest amp reading (**Table 9**).

The starter motor speed must be measured during the no-load current draw test. A vibration tachometer, such as the Frahm Reed Tachometer can be used for this test. Simply hold the tachometer against the starter frame while the starter is running to measure its speed. A stroboscopic tachometer may also be used, but remember to make a reference mark on the starter drive (pinion gear) before beginning the test. Another option is to use a tachometer designed for model airplane engines, available from most hobby shops. This type of tachometer is simply held against the end of the starter drive to measure the speed.
1. Remove the starter motor assembly from the power head (Chapter Seven). Securely fasten the starter motor in a vise or other suitable holding fixture. Do not damage the starter motor by crushing it in the vise.
2. Obtain a fully charged battery with a minimum rating of 500 cold cranking amps (CCA), 650 marine cranking amps (MCA) or 60 ampere-hours. The battery must be in good condition for the test results to be accurate.
3. Connect a suitable voltmeter to the battery as shown in **Figure 36**.

CAUTION
*Make sure the ammeter used in the next step is of sufficient capacity to measure the expected amperage draw (**Table 9**) with an*

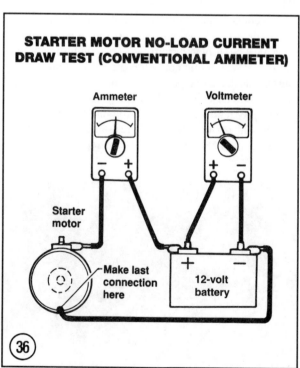

STARTER MOTOR NO-LOAD CURRENT DRAW TEST (CONVENTIONAL AMMETER)

adequate safety margin. For example, if the expected amperage draw is 30 amps, use a 50 amp or larger ammeter.

4A. *Conventional Ammeter*—Using heavy gauge battery cables or jumper cables, connect a conventional ammeter in series with the positive battery cable and the starter motor terminal (**Figure 36**). Then connect another heavy gauge battery cable or jumper cable to the negative battery terminal, but do not connect this cable to the starter at this time.

4B. *Inductive or Clamp-on Ammeter*—Using heavy gauge battery cables or jumper cables, connect the positive battery terminal to the starter motor terminal. Then install the clamp-on or inductive ammeter over this cable. Then connect another heavy gauge battery cable or jumper cable to the negative battery terminal, but do not connect this cable to the starter at this time. Use **Figure 36** as a reference.

WARNING
*Make the last battery connection to the starter frame in Step 4. **Do not** create any sparks at or near the battery or a serious explosion could occur.*

NOTE
*The battery must maintain at least 12.0-12.4 volts during the test. If the voltage falls below this range, yet the current draw does not exceed specification (**Table 9**), the battery is defective or not of sufficient capacity for the test.*

5. When ready to perform the no-load test, prepare a tachometer for the rpm measurement, then quickly and firmly connect the remaining cable to the starter motor frame (**Figure 36**). Note the amperage, voltage and rpm readings, then disconnect the jumper cable from the starter motor frame.

6. If the motor does not perform to specifications (**Table 9**), the motor must be repaired or replaced. See Chapter Seven. Refer to **Table 5** for additional starter motor symptoms and remedies.

AC (ALTERNATING CURRENT) LIGHTING COIL

Manual start models (4 Deluxe through 40 hp) can be equipped with an AC lighting coil kit. The lighting coil is located under the flywheel and is basically a standard stator coil without a rectifier or rectifier/regulator. The output of the AC lighting coil is directly proportional to engine speed.

A typical application of the AC lighting coil is to power the running lights on small boats, where the weight of a battery is not desired. The running lights are wired directly to the two or three yellow (yellow, yellow/gray [and yellow/blue]) lighting coil wires. The faster the motor is run, the brighter the lights.

If any one light fails as an open circuit, all of the lights on that circuit will go out. If any light fails as a short circuit, the remaining lights (on that circuit) will burn brighter and fail prematurely as they absorb the extra electricity. The load of the light bulbs must be matched to the output of the AC lighting coil. If the load is too great, the lights will be dim. If the load is too small, the lights will burn out at high speeds.

The output is generally rated in watts, which is the rating for electrical power. Watts (W) can be calculated by multiplying the amps times the voltage (usually 12-15 volts). For example, a four amp AC lighting coil can carry approximately a 60 watt load (4 amps × 15 volts = 60 watts).

Always follow the instructions provided with the kit when wiring the lights and determining the quantity and size of light bulbs to be used.

Troubleshooting AC Lighting Coil Systems

1. Verify that there are no open or short circuits in the leads going to the running lights or AC accessory. Inspect all of the bulbs in the lighting system. Any one bulb blowing open will cause all of the remaining bulbs (on that circuit) to go out from the open circuit.

2. The connections at the engine are generally bullet connectors or an OMC two-pin locking connector. All connections must be insulated from each other and from ground, and if the AC lighting coil wires are not being used, they must be insulated (capped or sleeved) from each other and the ground. Disconnect all lighting coil leads (yellow, yellow/gray [and yellow/blue]) from the appropriate connectors and perform the stator resistance and shorts-to-ground tests as described in the following steps.

3A. *9.9 and 15 hp models*—To test the stator resistance, calibrate an ohmmeter on the lowest scale possible and proceed as follows:

    a. Connect the ohmmeter black lead to the stator yellow bullet connector, then connect the red ohmmeter lead to the stator yellow/gray bullet connector. The meter must read 0.80-0.90 ohm.

    b. Move the red ohmmeter lead to the stator yellow/blue bullet connector. The meter must read 0.80-0.90 ohm.

    c. Move the ohmmeter black lead to the stator yellow/gray bullet connector. The meter must now read 1.5-1.7 ohms.

    d. Replace the AC lighting coil (stator) if the readings are not as specified.

3B. *25 and 35 hp (three-cylinder) models*—To test the stator resistance, calibrate an ohmmeter on the lowest scale possible. Connect the ohmmeter to the yellow and yellow/gray stator leads and note the meter reading. The reading must be 1.38-1.68 ohms. Replace the AC lighting coil (stator) if the reading is not within specification.

3C. *All other models*—Perform the following ohmmeter tests:

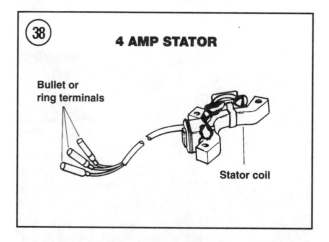

4 AMP STATOR

Bullet or ring terminals

Stator coil

    a. Connect the ohmmeter black lead to the stator yellow/gray bullet connector, then connect the red ohmmeter lead to the stator yellow bullet connector. The meter must read 0.81-0.91 ohm.

    b. Move the red ohmmeter lead to the stator yellow/blue bullet connector. The meter must now read 1.19-1.23 ohms.

    c. Replace the AC lighting coil if the readings are not as specified.

4. To perform a stator short to ground test, calibrate an ohmmeter on the highest scale available. Connect one ohmmeter lead to a clean engine ground. If the stator is removed, connect the ohmmeter to the stator's metal laminations (mounting screw bore). Connect the other ohmmeter lead to the stator yellow lead. The meter must read no continuity. If any other reading is noted, inspect the yellow lead for damaged insulation and repair if possible. If the lead is not damaged, replace the AC lighting coil (stator). Repeat this step for the stator yellow/gray (and yellow/blue) leads. All stator leads must indicate no continuity to ground.

5. Reconnect all leads when finished.

BATTERY CHARGING SYSTEM

Description

An alternator charging system is standard on all electric start models and optional on most rope start models. The job of the charging system is to keep the battery fully charged and supply current to run accessories. Charging systems can be divided into two basic designs: 4 and 5 amp unregulated systems and 12 amp regulated systems. Refer to **Table 10** for charging system identification and stator ohmmeter specifications and **Table 11** for charging system output specifications.

All systems use permanent magnets mounted in the flywheel (**Figure 37**) and a stator coil winding mounted to the power head. As the flywheel rotates, the magnetic fields in the flywheel pass through the stator coil windings, inducing AC (alternating current). The stator windings are a separate component on the 4 amp system (**Figure 38**), or an integral part of the stator assembly (also containing ignition system windings) on 5 and 12 amp systems. Unregulated systems use a rectifier to change the AC current to DC (direct current). See **Figure 39**, typical. The output from an unregulated charging system is directly proportional to engine speed. Because an unregulated system has the potential to overcharge the battery during long periods of wide-open throttle operation, a maintenance-free battery is not recommended. Overcharging a battery causes the electrolyte level to drop, leading to premature battery failure. Vented batteries that allow refilling of the electrolyte (as needed) provide longer service life.

Regulated systems use the same type of flywheel magnets and stator coil windings as the unregulated system, with a rectifier/regulator used instead of a rectifier. The rectifier portion of the rectifier/regulator changes the AC current to DC current, while the regulator portion monitors system voltage and controls the charging system output accordingly.

Batteries that are maintained at 13-15 volts will stay fully charged without excessive venting. The regulator controls the output of the charging system to keep system voltage at approximately 14.5 volts. The large red lead of the rectifier/regulator is DC output and also functions as the sensing terminal, allowing the regulator to monitor system voltage. A purple lead is used to supply key-switched battery positive voltage to turn the rectifier/regulator on and off with engine operation. Cast-in cooling fins are used to dissipate the heat that is generated from operation. See **Figure 40**.

Another function of the charging system is to provide the signal for the tachometer. The tachometer simply counts AC voltage pulses coming out of the stator before the AC voltage is rectified to DC. Therefore, tachometer failure is related to the charging system, not the ignition system. The tachometer connects to stator yellow/gray lead on unregulated systems, or the rectifier/regulator gray lead on regulated models.

Malfunctions in the charging system generally cause the battery to be undercharged and the tachometer to read erratically or totally fail. The following conditions will result in rectifier, rectifier/regulator or external alternator failure.

1. Reversing the battery leads.

2. Disconnecting the battery leads while the engine is running.

3. Loose connections in the charging system circuits, including battery connections and ground circuits. Wing nuts are not acceptable fasteners for battery connections. Use corrosion resistant hex nuts and lockwashers.

> ### CAUTION
> *If an outboard equipped with an unregulated charging system must be operated with the battery removed or disconnected, the positive battery cable end must be insulated (taped or sleeved) from the negative battery cable and/or ground. Do not operate an outboard equipped with a regulated charging system with the battery disconnected.*

System Inspection (All Models)

Before troubleshooting the charging system, check the following:

1. Make sure the battery is properly connected. If the battery polarity is reversed, the rectifier or rectifier/regulator will be damaged.

2. Check for loose or corroded connections. A terminal strip or bullet connectors are used on all charging system connections. Clean, tighten, repair or replace as necessary. Replace battery wing nuts with corrosion resistant hex nuts and lockwashers. Place the lockwasher under the battery cable as shown in **Figure 41**. Loose battery cable connections will cause a charging system failure.

3. Check the rectifier or rectifier/regulator (**Figure 39** or **Figure 40**, typical) mounting hardware for corrosion, evidence of electrical arcing and loose fasteners. These components are grounded through their mounting hardware. The mounting screws and bosses must be free of paint and corrosion and the screws must be securely tightened. Loose mounting screws will cause erratic operation and premature failure.

4. Check the battery condition. Charge or replace the battery as necessary.

5. Check the wiring harness between the stator and battery for cut, chafed or deteriorated insulation and corroded,

loose or disconnected connections. Repair or replace the wiring harness as necessary.

6. Visually inspect the stator windings for discoloration and burned windings. Replace any stator that shows evidence of overheating.

CAUTION
Unless otherwise noted, perform all voltage tests with the leads connected and the terminals exposed to accommodate test lead connection. All electrical components must be securely grounded to the power head any time the engine is cranked or started or the components will be damaged.

Current Draw Test

Use this test to determine if the total load of the engine electrical system and boat accessories exceeds the capacity of the charging system.

NOTE
If a clamp-on or inductive ammeter is used, install the probe on the positive battery cable (near the battery) and go directly to Step 3. If a conventional ammeter is used, make sure the ammeter is rated for at least 20 amps.

1. Disconnect the negative battery cable from the battery.
2. Disconnect the positive battery cable from the battery. Securely connect a suitable ammeter between the positive battery post and the positive battery cable. Reconnect the negative battery cable.
3. Turn the ignition switch ON (RUN) and turn on all accessories. Note the ammeter reading. Turn the ignition switch OFF (STOP) and turn off all accessories. If the ammeter reading exceeds the rated capacity of the charging system, reduce the accessory load connected to the charging system.

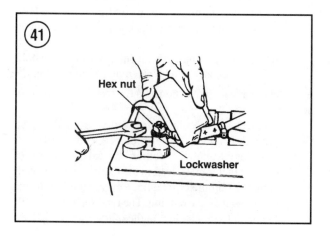

Hex nut

Lockwasher

Troubleshooting 4 and 5 Amp Unregulated Models

Refer to **Table 10** and **Table 11** for specifications and the back of the manual for wiring diagrams. The 9.9 and 15 hp (5 amp) models use bullet connectors on the stator-to-rectifier connections. All other models use a terminal strip and ring terminals (**Figure 39**). The rectifier red lead is always a ring terminal connection.

NOTE
If a clamp-on or inductive ammeter is used, install the probe on the rectifier red lead and go directly to Step 4.

1. Disconnect the negative battery cable from the battery.

2A. *9.9 and 15 hp (5 amp) models*—Install a conventional ammeter (10 amp, recommended) as follows:
  a. Remove the rectifier red lead from the terminal stud on the electrical component bracket. Then reinstall the nut to secure the positive battery cable and engine harness red lead.
  b. Connect an ammeter of sufficient size to measure the maximum rated output of the charging system in series between the rectifier red lead and its corresponding engine harness red lead. Connect the red lead of the ammeter to the rectifier red lead and the black lead of the ammeter to the engine harness red lead at the terminal stud on the electrical component bracket.
  c. Make sure the connections are secure and insulated from any other leads or grounds.

2B. *All other (4 amp) models*—Install a conventional ammeter (10 amp, recommended) as follows:
  a. Remove the rectifier red lead from the terminal strip. Then reinstall the screw to secure the engine harness red lead to the terminal strip.
  b. Connect an ammeter of sufficient size to measure the maximum rated output of the charging system in series between the rectifier red lead and its corresponding engine harness red lead. Connect the red lead of the ammeter to the rectifier red lead and the black lead of the ammeter to the engine harness red lead at the terminal strip.
  c. Make sure the connections are secure and insulated from any other leads or grounds.

3. Reconnect the negative battery cable.

4. Install a shop tachometer according to its manufacturer's instructions.

CAUTION
Do not run the engine without an adequate water supply and do not exceed 3000 rpm

3

without an adequate load. Refer to **Safety Precautions** *at the beginning of this chapter.*

5. Start the engine and run it as specified in **Table 11** while observing the ammeter readings. If amperage output is less than specified, continue with Step 6. If amperage output is within specification, the charging system is functioning correctly.

NOTE
The stator on 9.9 and 15 hp models has an extra yellow/gray bullet connector to allow easy connection of an accessory tachometer. If a tachometer is not being used, this extra bullet connector must be capped (or sleeved) to prevent it from touching ground or any other lead.

6A. *9.9-15 hp (5 amp) models*—To check the resistance of the stator, proceed as follows:
   a. Disconnect the negative battery cable. Then disconnect the yellow, yellow/blue and yellow/gray stator leads from the rectifier bullet connectors. If an accessory tachometer is installed, disconnect its gray lead from the second yellow/gray stator lead.
   b. Calibrate an ohmmeter on the lowest scale possible. Connect the ohmmeter to the stator's two yellow/gray bullet connectors. The meter must indicate continuity. Repair or replace the lead between the two yellow/gray bullet connectors if any other reading is noted.
   c. Move the red ohmmeter lead to the stator's yellow lead bullet connector. The meter must now indicate 0.80-0.90 ohm.
   d. Move the ohmmeter black lead to the stator's yellow/blue connector. The meter must again indicate 0.80-0.90 ohm.
   e. Move the red ohmmeter lead back to either stator yellow/gray bullet connector. The meter must now indicate 1.5-1.7 ohms.
   f. Replace the stator assembly if it does not perform as specified.

6B. *All other (4 amp) models*—To check the resistance of the stator, proceed as follows:
   a. Disconnect the negative battery cable. Then disconnect the yellow, yellow/blue and yellow gray stator leads from the terminal strip.
   b. Calibrate an ohmmeter on the lowest scale possible. Then connect the red ohmmeter lead to the stator's yellow lead and the ohmmeter black lead to the stator's yellow/blue lead. The meter must indicate 0.50-0.60 ohm.

   c. Move the red ohmmeter lead to the stator yellow/gray lead. The meter must again indicate 0.50-0.60 ohm.
   d. Replace the stator coil if it does not perform as specified.

7. To perform the stator short-to-ground tests, proceed as follows:
   a. Calibrate an ohmmeter on the highest scale available. Connect the ohmmeter black lead to a clean engine ground. If the stator is removed, connect the ohmmeter to the stator's metal laminations (mounting screw bore).
   b. Connect the red ohmmeter lead to the stator yellow lead. The meter must read no continuity. If any other reading is noted, inspect the yellow lead for damaged insulation and repair if possible. If the lead is not damaged, replace the stator coil (or stator assembly). Repeat this step for the stator yellow/gray and yellow/blue leads. All stator leads must indicate no continuity to ground.

8. To check the positive diodes in the rectifier, proceed as follows:
   a. Disconnect all rectifier leads (red, yellow, yellow/gray and yellow/blue). Calibrate the ohmmeter on the appropriate scale to test diodes.
   b. Connect the red ohmmeter lead to the rectifier red lead and the ohmmeter black lead to the rectifier yellow lead. Note the ohmmeter reading. Reverse the ohmmeter leads and note the reading. The reading must be high in one polarity and low in the other.
   c. Reconnect the red ohmmeter lead to the rectifier red lead and move the ohmmeter black lead to the rectifier yellow/gray lead. Note the ohmmeter reading. Reverse the ohmmeter leads and note the reading. The reading must be high in one polarity and low in the other.
   d. Reconnect the red ohmmeter lead to the rectifier red lead and move the ohmmeter black lead to the rectifier yellow/blue lead. Note the ohmmeter reading. Reverse the ohmmeter leads and note the reading. The reading must be high in one polarity and low in the other.
   e. If the reading is high in both polarities or low in both polarities on any or all tests, replace the rectifier.

9. To check the negative diodes in the rectifier, proceed as follows:
   a. Connect the red ohmmeter lead to a good engine ground. If the rectifier is removed, connect the red ohmmeter lead to the rectifier's metal case. Connect the ohmmeter black lead to the rectifier yellow lead. Note the ohmmeter reading. Reverse the ohmmeter leads and note the reading. The reading must be high in one polarity and low in the other.

b. Reconnect the red ohmmeter lead to ground. Move the ohmmeter black lead to the rectifier yellow/gray lead. Note the ohmmeter reading. Reverse the ohmmeter leads and note the reading. The reading must be high in one polarity and low in the other.

c. Reconnect the red ohmmeter lead to ground. Move the ohmmeter black lead to the rectifier yellow/blue lead. Note the ohmmeter reading. Reverse the ohmmeter leads and note the reading. The reading must be high in one polarity and low in the other.

d. If the reading was high in both polarities or low in both polarities on any or all tests, the rectifier must be replaced.

10. To check the continuity of the rectifier red lead back to the battery, make sure the negative lead of the battery is disconnected. Disconnect the rectifier red lead from its engine harness bullet connector or terminal strip. Calibrate the ohmmeter on a high ohms scale. Connect one ohmmeter lead to the battery positive terminal and the other ohmmeter lead to the engine harness red lead that connected to the rectifier red lead. Note the ohmmeter reading. A good circuit will read continuity (very low resistance). If not, repair or replace the red lead and/or connections between the rectifier and the battery.

11. Reconnect all leads when finished.

Troubleshooting 12 Amp Regulated Models

Refer to **Table 10** and **Table 11** for specifications and Chapter Fourteen for wiring diagrams.

NOTE
A regulated charging system only develops the current necessary to maintain 14.5 volts at the battery. If the battery is fully charged, the alternator will not produce its rated output unless enough accessory demand is present. If a clamp-on or inductive ammeter is used, install the probe on the rectifier/regulator red lead and go directly to Step 4.

1. Disconnect the negative battery cable from the battery.
2A. *25 and 35 hp (three-cylinder) models*—Install a conventional ammeter (20 amp, recommended) as follows:
   a. Remove the air silencer from the front of the engine.
   b. Disconnect the rectifier/regulator red lead bullet connector from the engine harness.
   c. Connect an ammeter of sufficient size to measure the maximum rated output of the charging system in *series* between the rectifier red lead and its corresponding engine harness red lead. Connect the red lead of the ammeter to the red rectifier lead bullet connector and the black lead of the ammeter to the engine red harness bullet connector.

d. Make sure the connections are secure and insulated from any other leads or grounds.

2B. *40-70 hp and 35 jet models*—Install a conventional ammeter (20 amp, recommended) as follows:
   a. Remove the rectifier/regulator red lead from the terminal strip. Then reinstall the screw to secure engine harness red lead to the terminal strip.
   b. Connect an ammeter of sufficient size to measure the maximum rated output of the charging system in *series* between the rectifier red lead and its corresponding engine harness red lead. Connect the red lead of the ammeter to the rectifier red lead and the black lead of the ammeter to the engine harness red lead at the terminal strip.
   c. Make sure the connections are secure and insulated from any other leads or grounds.

3. Reconnect the negative battery cable.

4. Install a shop tachometer according to its manufacturer's instructions.

5. Connect a voltmeter to the battery terminals.

CAUTION
*Do not run the engine without an adequate water supply and do not exceed 3000 rpm without an adequate load. Refer to **Safety Precautions** at the beginning of this chapter.*

6. Start the engine and run it as specified in **Table 11** while noting both the ammeter and voltmeter readings. If the voltage exceeds 12.5 volts, turn on accessories or attach accessories to the battery to maintain battery voltage at 12.5 volts or less. If amperage output is less than specified, continue to Step 7. If amperage output is within specification, turn off or disconnect the accessories and run the engine at approximately 3000 rpm while observing the voltmeter. As the battery approaches full charge, the voltage must rise to approximately 14.5 volts and stabilize. If the voltage stabilizes at approximately 14.5 volts, the voltage regulator is functioning correctly. If the voltage exceeds 15 volts, go to Step 9 and test the stator for a short-to-ground. If the stator tests satisfactorily, replace the rectifier/regulator.

NOTE
Loose or corroded battery connections and/or damaged battery cables can cause inaccurate results in the next test. Make sure the cables are in good condition and that all connections are clean and tight.

7. To test the rectifier/regulator excite and sense circuits, proceed as follows:
   a. Connect the black lead of the voltmeter to the negative battery terminal.

3

b. Connect the voltmeter red lead to the red lead at the terminal strip or rectifier/regulator bullet connector. The voltmeter must read battery voltage. If the voltmeter indicates a difference of more than 0.5 volt below battery voltage, clean and tighten the connections, or repair or replace the red lead between the terminal strip (or bullet connector) and the starter solenoid.

c. Move the voltmeter red lead to the purple lead at the terminal strip or rectifier/regulator bullet connector. Turn the ignition (key) switch to the ON or RUN position and note the meter reading. The voltmeter must read battery voltage. If the voltmeter indicates a difference of more than 1.0 volt below battery voltage, clean and tighten the connections or repair or replace the purple lead between the terminal strip (or bullet connector) and the ignition switch.

d. If the voltage on both the red and purple leads is as specified, continue at Step 8.

8. To check the resistance of the stator, proceed as follows:

a. Disconnect the negative battery cable. Then disconnect the yellow and yellow/gray stator leads from the terminal strip or the large, locking two-pin connector.

b. Calibrate an ohmmeter on the appropriate scale to read 0.4-0.6 ohm. Connect one lead of the ohmmeter to each of the stator leads. Note the reading.

c. The meter must read 0.4-0.6 ohms. If not, replace the stator assembly.

9. To check the stator for a short-to-ground, proceed as follows:

a. Calibrate the ohmmeter on the highest scale possible. Connect the ohmmeter black lead to a clean engine ground. If the stator is removed, connect the ohmmeter to the stator's metal laminations (mounting screw bore).

b. Connect the red ohmmeter lead to the stator yellow lead. The meter must read no continuity. If any other reading is noted, inspect the yellow lead for damaged insulation and repair if possible. If the lead is not damaged, replace the stator assembly.

c. Repeat this step for the stator yellow/gray leads. Both stator leads must indicate no continuity to ground.

10. If all ohmmeter and voltage tests are satisfactory to this point, yet the system does not perform as described in Step 6, replace the rectifier/regulator.

11. Reconnect all leads when finished.

Rectifier/Regulator Tachometer Circuit Tests

If the tachometer fails to operate correctly, the rectifier/regulator may not be sending a good tachometer signal out its gray lead. The following procedure is intended to determine if a good signal is being sent to the tachometer. If any charging system related symptom is present, troubleshoot that symptom *before* attempting to diagnose the tachometer symptom.

A voltmeter capable of measuring peak volts is required to check the tachometer circuit voltages. A conventional voltmeter will not work. OMC specifically recommends one of the following peak voltage meters: the Stevens Instruments CD-77 or the Merc-O-Tronic 781. If any other meter is used, it must provide equivalent readings to these meters. Refer to the back of the manual for wiring diagrams.

1. Verify that the tachometer is receiving battery voltage (or within 1.0 volt of battery voltage) at its purple lead terminal when the ignition switch is in the ON or RUN position. Repair the purple lead (including the ignition switch, 20 amp fuse and applicable connectors) as necessary.

2. Verify that the tachometer black lead has continuity to the negative battery terminal with an ohmmeter or test light. Repair the black lead and applicable connectors as necessary.

3. Set the peak reading voltmeter to positive (POS) polarity and the 50-volt range. Connect the red meter lead to the tachometer's gray lead terminal and the black meter lead to the tachometer's black lead terminal.

4. Turn the ignition switch to the ON or RUN position, but do not start the engine. Note the meter reading. The meter must indicate zero volts. If the meter indicates any voltage, perform the following until the defect is located. Once the meter reads zero volts, proceed to Step 5.

a. Disconnect the rectifier/regulator gray lead from the engine's terminal strip or rectifier/regulator bullet connector. If the meter now indicates zero volts, replace the rectifier/regulator.

b. Disconnect the four-pin Amphenol connector at the oil injection pump. If the meter now indicates 0 volts, repair the four-pin connector, replace the pump's circuit board, or replace the pump as an assembly.

c. If voltage is still indicated, the engine and/or boat wiring harness has a short-to-power between the gray lead and the red, red/purple or purple leads. Isolate and repair or replace the defective harness.

CAUTION
*Do not run the engine without an adequate water supply and do not exceed 3000 rpm without an adequate load. Refer to **Safety Precautions** at the beginning of this chapter.*

5. With the engine running at 1000 rpm in NEUTRAL, measure the voltage at the tachometer's gray lead terminal as described in Step 3. The meter must indicate no more than 8 volts.

   a. If the meter indicates 0 volts, check the continuity of the gray lead from the rectifier/regulator to the tachometer. Repair or replace the gray lead as necessary. If the gray lead has continuity, replace the rectifier/regulator.

   b. If the voltmeter shows more than 8 volts, replace the tachometer.

6. If the voltage in Step 5 was more than zero, but less than 8 volts, proceed as follows:

   a. Disconnect the gray lead from the tachometer and retest the gray lead voltage at 1000 rpm. Voltage must increase by approximately 1 volt over the amount noted in Step 5. If the voltage increases by more than approximately 1 volt, replace the tachometer.

   b. Disconnect the four-pin Amphenol connector at the oil injection pump and retest the gray lead voltage at 1000 rpm. Voltage must increase by approximately 2 volts over the amount noted in Step 5. If the voltage increases by more than approximately 2 volts, replace the pump's circuit board or replace the pump as an assembly.

   c. Disconnect the tachometer gray lead and the oil injection pump at the same time and retest the gray lead voltage at 1000 rpm. Voltage must increase by approximately 3 volts over the amount noted in Step 5. If the voltage increases by more than approximately 3 volts, replace the rectifier/regulator.

7. Reconnect all leads when finished. Connect the negative battery cable last.

Stator Resistance
(9.9 and 15 hp [5 Amp] Models)

> *NOTE*
> *The stator on 9.9 and 15 hp models has an extra yellow/gray bullet connector to allow easy connection of an accessory tachometer. If a tachometer is not used, this extra bullet connector must be capped (or sleeved) to prevent it from touching ground or any other lead.*

To check the resistance of the stator, proceed as follows:

1. Disconnect the negative battery cable. Then disconnect the yellow, yellow/blue and yellow/gray stator leads from the rectifier bullet connectors. If an accessory tachometer is installed, disconnect its gray lead from the second yellow/gray stator lead.

2. Calibrate an ohmmeter on the lowest scale possible. Connect the ohmmeter to the stator's two yellow/gray bullet connectors. The meter must indicate continuity. Repair or replace the lead between the two yellow/gray bullet connectors if any other reading is noted.

3. Move the red ohmmeter lead to the stator's yellow lead bullet connector. The meter must now indicate 0.80-0.90 ohm.

4. Move the ohmmeter black lead to the stator's yellow/blue connector. The meter must again indicate 0.80-0.90 ohm.

5. Move the red ohmmeter lead back to either stator yellow/gray bullet connector. The meter must now indicate 1.5-1.7 ohms.

6. Replace the stator assembly if it does not perform as specified.

7. Leave the stator leads disconnected and perform the stator short-to-ground test as described later in this section.

Stator Resistance (All 4 Amp Models)

To check the resistance of the stator, proceed as follows:

1. Disconnect the negative battery cable. Then disconnect the yellow, yellow/blue and yellow gray stator leads from the terminal strip.

2. Calibrate an ohmmeter on the lowest scale possible. Then connect the red ohmmeter lead to the stator's yellow lead and the ohmmeter black lead to the stator's yellow/blue lead. The meter must indicate 0.50-0.60 ohm.

3. Move the red ohmmeter lead to the stator yellow/gray lead. The meter must again indicate 0.50-0.60 ohm.

4. Replace the stator coil if it does not perform as specified.

5. Leave the stator leads disconnected and perform the stator short-to-ground tests as described later in this section.

Stator Resistance (All 12 Amp Models)

To check the resistance of the stator, proceed as follows:

1. Disconnect the negative battery cable. Then disconnect the yellow and yellow/gray stator lead at the terminal strip or the large, locking two-pin connector.

2. Calibrate an ohmmeter on the appropriate scale to read 0.4-0.6 ohm. Connect one lead of the ohmmeter to each of the stator leads. Note the reading. The meter must read 0.4-0.6 ohm.

3. Replace the stator coil if it does not perform as specified.

4. Leave the stator leads disconnected and perform the stator short-to-ground tests as described later in this section.

Stator Short-To-Ground Tests

Perform this test only after performing the preceding Stator resistance tests. To perform the stator short-to-ground tests, proceed as follows:

1. Calibrate an ohmmeter on the highest scale available. Connect the ohmmeter black lead to a clean engine ground. If the stator is removed, connect the ohmmeter to the stator's metal laminations (mounting screw bore).

2. Connect the red ohmmeter lead to the stator yellow lead. The meter must read no continuity. If any other reading is noted, inspect the yellow lead for damaged insulation and repair if possible. If the lead is not damaged, replace the stator coil (or stator assembly). Repeat this step for the stator yellow/gray (and yellow/blue) leads. All stator leads must indicate no continuity to ground.

3. Reconnect all leads when finished. Connect the negative battery cable last.

Rectifier Ohmmeter Tests
(Unregulated 4 and 5 Amp Models)

1. To check the positive and negative diodes in the rectifier, disconnect the negative battery cable. Then disconnect all of the rectifier leads (red, yellow, yellow/gray and yellow/blue) from the terminal strip or bullet connectors.

2. Calibrate the ohmmeter on the appropriate scale to test diodes.

3. To check the positive diodes in the rectifier, proceed as follows:

    a. Connect the red ohmmeter lead to the rectifier red lead and the ohmmeter black lead to the rectifier yellow lead. Note the ohmmeter reading. Reverse the ohmmeter leads and note the reading. The reading must be high in one polarity and low in the other.

    b. Reconnect the red ohmmeter lead to the rectifier red lead and move the ohmmeter black lead to the rectifier yellow/gray lead. Note the ohmmeter reading. Reverse the ohmmeter leads and note the reading. The reading must be high in one polarity and low in the other.

    c. Reconnect the red ohmmeter lead to the rectifier red lead and move the ohmmeter black lead to the rectifier yellow/blue lead. Note the ohmmeter reading. Reverse the ohmmeter leads and note the reading. The reading must be high in one polarity and low in the other.

    d. If the reading was high in both polarities or low in both polarities on any or all tests, the rectifier must be replaced.

4. To check the negative diodes in the rectifier, proceed as follows:

    a. Connect the red ohmmeter lead to a good engine ground. If the rectifier is removed, connect the red ohmmeter lead to the rectifier's metal case. Connect the ohmmeter black lead to the rectifier yellow lead. Note the ohmmeter reading. Reverse the ohmmeter leads and note the reading. The reading must be high in one polarity and low in the other.

    b. Reconnect the red ohmmeter lead to ground. Move the ohmmeter black lead to the rectifier yellow/gray lead. Note the ohmmeter reading. Reverse the ohmmeter leads and note the reading. The reading must be high in one polarity and low in the other.

    c. Reconnect the red ohmmeter lead to ground. Move the ohmmeter black lead to the rectifier yellow/blue lead. Note the ohmmeter reading. Reverse the ohmmeter leads and note the reading. The reading must be high in one polarity and low in the other.

    d. If the reading was high in both polarities or low in both polarities on any or all tests, the rectifier must be replaced.

5. Reconnect all leads when finished. Connect the negative battery cable last.

ELECTRICAL ACCESSORIES

The wiring harness used between the ignition switch and outboard motor is adequate to handle the electrical requirements of the outboard motor. It will not handle the electrical requirements of accessories. Whenever an accessory is added, run new wiring between the battery and the accessory, installing a separate fuse panel on the instrument panel.

If the ignition switch requires replacement, never install an automotive-type switch. Use only a switch approved for marine use.

WARNING SYSTEMS

Two types of warning systems are used on the models covered in this manual. The 1995 (EO) model year engines are intended to be used with *traditional wiring harnesses*, which use only a warning horn. The 1996-2003 (ED-ST) models are intended to be used with the modular wiring harness (MWS) and the system check engine monitoring gauge which uses warning lights and a warning horn.

Adaptor kits are available from OMC Genuine Parts to allow the use of the MWS and system check gauge on

1995 (EO) models and to allow the use of the traditional wiring harness on 1996-2003 (ED-ST) models. For additional information, refer to *Wiring Harnesses* located previously in this chapter.

Traditional Wiring Harness (1995 [EO] Models)

The warning system used on 1995 (EO) models equipped with traditional wiring harnesses provides the operator with audible warning signals only. The system can warn the operator of engine overheat, oil pump failure (no oil) and low oil level in the remote oil tank. Each warning signal is unique, and must be correctly identified by the operator. The 4 signals produced by the warning horn are as follows:

NOTE
*The **no oil** and **low oil** warning signals only apply to engines equipped with an oil injection system.*

1. *Engine overheat*—An overheating engine will produce a constant horn signal. If the overheat signal occurs during operation, reduce the engine speed to idle and check the water discharge (tell-tale) indicator for a steady stream of water, indicating that the water pump is operating correctly. If adequate water discharge is not noted at the tell-tale indicator, make sure that the boat has come off plane, then shift the gearcase into reverse and briefly apply throttle to clear any debris that may be covering the water intake screens. If the overheat signal is still sounding, and/or water discharge is not noted at the tell-tale indicator, the engine must be turned off, allowed to cool and the cause of the overheat determined and corrected.

2A. *No oil/empty oil tank (25 and 35 hp [three-cylinder models])*—If the engine-mounted oil reservoir is empty (or very low), the warning horn will sound continuously and engine speed will be limited to approximately 2500 rpm by the S.L.O.W. (speed limiting operational warning) system. The engine must be immediately stopped and the oil reservoir refilled. The system only detects oil level, not oil flow.

2B. *No oil (oil pump failure [all other models])*—If the motion sensor in the oil injection pump detects that the oil pump is not pumping oil, the warning system will produce an urgent, pulsing horn. The engine must be immediately stopped and the remote oil tank's oil level checked. If the oil level in the remote oil tank is satisfactory, the engine must be operated on a premixed 50:1 ratio fuel/oil mix until the cause of the warning can be determined. Refer to Chapter Eleven for oil injection system troubleshooting procedures.

3A. *Low oil level (25 and 35 hp [three-cylinder] models)*—This warning is indicated by a constant warning horn signal and the illumination of the low oil warning light, mounted on the engine. A float switch in the engine mounted oil reservoir activates the horn when the oil level reaches a predetermined level. The horn will continue to sound and the light will stay illuminated until the oil tank is refilled.

3B. *Low oil level (all other models)*—This warning is indicated by a single beep of the horn, approximately once every 40 seconds. A float switch in the remote oil tank activates the warning program in the oil tank whenever the oil level drops to approximately 1/3 to 1/4 of the tank's full capacity. The horn will continue to sound once every 40 seconds, until the oil tank is refilled.

4. *Self-test*—The warning horn performs a brief self-test each time the key is turned to the ON or RUN position. The self-test will sound a single beep of the warning horn. If the self-test does not occur, the warning horn's purple lead must be checked for battery voltage (whenever the ignition switch is in the RUN or ON position) and the black lead for continuity to the negative battery terminal (at all times).

The warning horn must sound whenever the horn's tan lead is grounded and the ignition switch is in the ON or RUN position. The tan lead does not affect the self-test unless it is shorted to ground. If the tan lead is shorted to ground the horn will sound continuously if the ignition switch is in the ON or RUN position.

On 20-30 hp (two-cylinder) remote control models, 40-70 hp electric start (remote control and tiller handle) models and 35 jet models a blocking diode is used in the engine harness tan lead to prevent the horn's self-test and other warning signals from activating the S.L.O.W. (speed limiting overheat warning) program in the power pack (ignition module). The S.L.O.W. system must only activate if the engine is actually overheating and the temperature switch is closed, shorting the tan lead to ground. The diode is positioned in the tan lead, near the large, red, ten-pin main harness connector. Testing the blocking diode is covered in the appropriate *Ignition* section of this chapter. Refer to the end of the manual for wiring diagrams.

Manually Testing The Warning Horn

The warning horn must sound whenever the horn's tan lead is grounded and the ignition switch is in the ON or RUN position. To prevent possible power head damage, the warning horn must be tested at the beginning of each boating season and periodically during the season. The horn is most quickly tested at the engine temperature switch, located near the top of the cylinder head on all models. The switch has a tan lead and is connected to the engine harness with a bullet connector or a two-pin Amphenol connector. The engine harness lead is a plain tan lead.

The warning horn's black lead is only needed for the self-test function and only indicates that the switch is receiving power and ground. The following test will make sure that the boat and engine harness's tan lead has continuity and that the warning horn will sound if the tan lead is grounded. To manually test the warning horn, refer to the back of the manual for wiring diagrams and proceed as follows:

1A. *25-70 hp (three-cylinder) models*—Disconnect the temperature switch two-pin Amphenol connector from the engine harness. On electric start models, the connector is located under the electrical component access cover on the starboard side of the power head.

1B. *All other models*—Disconnect the temperature switch lead (A, **Figure 42**, typical) from the one-pin Amphenol connector (40-50 hp [two-cylinder] and 35 jet) or engine harness tan lead bullet connector (all other models). See B, **Figure 42**, typical.

2. Turn the ignition (key) switch to the ON or RUN position.

3. Using a suitable jumper wire, hold the engine harness end of the tan lead to a good engine ground. The warning horn must sound continuously as long as the tan lead is held to ground.

NOTE
If the key-on self-test begins functioning during Step 4B, discontinue Step 4B and continue troubleshooting at Step 4A.

4A. If the horn does not sound, but the key-on self-test sounds normally, one of the following has occurred:
   a. The blocking diode has failed in an open circuit.
   b. The tan lead has an open circuit between the engine temperature switch and the warning horn. This includes the large, red, ten-pin main harness connector, the blocking diode (if equipped) and the boat wiring harness.
   c. The warning horn has failed (not likely, if the self-test functions).

4B. If the horn does not sound *and* the key-on self test did not sound, one of the following has occurred:
   a. The warning horn has failed.
   b. The warning horn is not receiving battery voltage through its purple lead with the ignition switch in the ON or run position. Test the purple lead and repair or replace it as necessary.
   c. The warning horn black lead is not properly grounded. Test the black lead for continuity back to the negative battery terminal. Clean and tighten the

connections, or repair or replace the ground circuit (boat harness black lead) as necessary.

5. Turn the ignition switch OFF and reconnect all leads when finished.

System Check Engine Monitor

The warning system used on 1996-1998 models equipped with the modular wiring system (MWS) and the system check engine monitor provides the operator with visual and audible warning signals. The system can warn the operator of engine overheat, oil pump failure (no oil) and low oil level in the oil tank. If a warning occurs, one of four light emitting diodes (LEDs) will illuminate on the system check gauge (**Figure 43**) and the warning horn will sound continuously for ten seconds. This warning system allows positive identification of the engine system that caused the warning, with no interpretation of warning signals required by the operator. The warning LED will stay illuminated for 30 seconds after the problem has been corrected, allowing easy identification of intermittent problems.

NOTE
*The **check engine** LED, while present in all gauges, is not functional on 70 hp and*

*smaller engines. These engines do not incorporate a sensor for the check engine LED. Additionally, the **low oil** and **no oil** LEDs will only function on engines equipped with an oil injection system.*

There are no longer any electronic modules in the remote oil tank or warning horn. All control of the warning horn, the gauge's LEDs and the system's self-test function, is contained in the system check engine monitor gauge.

Separate leads are used to carry the signal from the engine-mounted and remote oil tank sensors to the system check gauge through an eight-pin Deutsch connector (4, **Figure 44**). The engine temperature switch's engine overheat signal is carried by the tan lead, the oil injection pump's no oil signal is carried by the tan/yellow lead and the oil tank's *low oil* signal is carried by the tan/black lead. Each sending unit connects its lead to ground if a problem is noted. While the MWS boat harness contains a tan/orange lead that controls the check engine LED, the engine harness does not contain a tan/orange lead (or an appropriate sensor) to control the check engine LED.

The remaining leads in the eight-pin connector are: ground (black lead), key-switched battery voltage (purple lead), tachometer signal from the engine (gray lead) and warning horn control (tan/blue lead).

The warning horn uses only two leads. The purple lead supplies key-switched battery voltage to the horn and the

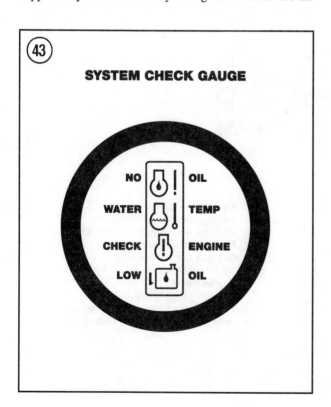

tan/blue lead is grounded by the system check gauge to sound the horn.

CAUTION
*A warning horn must be connected to the purple and tan/blue two-pin Deutsch connector (3, **Figure 44**), regardless of whether a system check gauge or the audible driver module (part No. 176458) is used.*

On 20-30 hp (two-cylinder) remote control models, 40-70 hp electric start (remote control and tiller handle) models and 35 jet models, a blocking diode is used in the *engine* harness tan lead to prevent the system's self-test and other electrical signals from activating the S.L.O.W. (speed limiting overheat warning) program in the power pack (ignition module). The S.L.O.W. program must only activate when the engine is actually overheating and the temperature switch is closed, shorting the tan lead to ground. The diode is positioned near the six-pin Deutsch System Check harness connector. Testing of the blocking diode is covered in the appropriate *Ignition* section of this chapter.

Self-test mode

The self-test function activates each time the key is turned to the ON or RUN position. The electronics in the gauge will sound the warning horn for a 1/2 second and illuminate all four gauge LEDs, then turn off each LED in sequence *each* time the ignition switch is turned to the ON or RUN position. Each self-test will make sure the warning horn and all LEDs are functioning, and that the electronic control circuits in the gauge are operating correctly.

NOTE
If the battery voltage at the gauge drops below 7 volts, the gauge may re-enter self-test mode.

If the gauge does not self-test correctly, refer to **Figure 44** and proceed as follows:

1. *LED(s) does not illuminate*—If one-three of the LEDs do not illuminate, the gauge is defective and must be replaced. If all four LEDs do not illuminate, proceed as follows:

   a. Test the purple lead at the gauge's eight-pin Deutsch connector (4, **Figure 44**) for battery voltage whenever the ignition switch is in the ON or RUN position. Repair or replace the purple lead, 20 amp fuse and/or ignition switch as necessary.

   b. Test the black lead at the gauge's eight-pin Deutsch connector for continuity back to the negative battery terminal. Repair or replace the black lead as necessary.

c. If the purple lead indicates battery voltage and the black lead indicates continuity, replace the system check gauge.

2. *Warning horn does not sound for a 1/2 second*—If the LEDs also do not illuminate, go back and complete Step 1 before proceeding. If the LEDs illuminate, but the horn does not sound, proceed as follows:

 a. Disconnect the eight-pin Deutsch connector (4, **Figure 44**) at the system check gauge. Turn the ignition switch to the ON or RUN position. Using a suitable jumper lead, ground the connector's tan/blue lead (pin No. 8) to the black lead (pin No. 2). If the warning horn sounds, replace the system check gauge. If the warning horn does not sound, leave the gauge disconnected and proceed.

 b. Disconnect the warning horn from its two-pin Deutsch connector (3, **Figure 44**). Test the tan/blue lead for continuity between the warning horn (two-pin) and gauge (eight-pin) Deutsch connectors (3 and 4, **Figure 44**). If continuity is not noted, repair

or replace the tan/blue lead (and/or connectors) as necessary. When finished, reconnect the eight-pin Deutsch connector to the gauge.

 c. Test the two-pin Deutsch connector's (3, **Figure 44**) purple lead (on the wiring harness side) for battery voltage whenever the ignition switch is in the ON or RUN position. Repair or replace the purple lead, 20 amp fuse and/or ignition switch as necessary. Reconnect the two-pin Deutsch connector when finished.

 d. If at this point, the warning horn will not sound for a 1/2 second during the self-test, replace the warning horn.

Operational mode

The operational mode is entered each time the self-test mode is complete *and* the gauge receives a tachometer signal (gray lead) from the engine. The warning horn control circuits are not enabled until the gauge receives at least a 1000 rpm tachometer signal. In this mode, if a

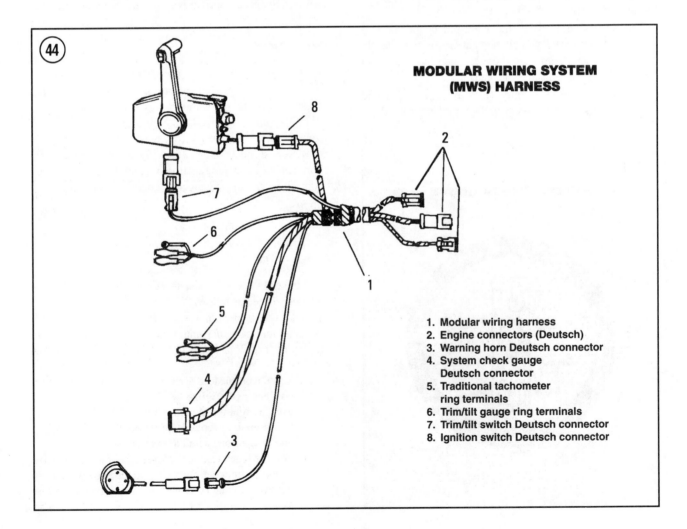

44

MODULAR WIRING SYSTEM (MWS) HARNESS

1. Modular wiring harness
2. Engine connectors (Deutsch)
3. Warning horn Deutsch connector
4. System check gauge Deutsch connector
5. Traditional tachometer ring terminals
6. Trim/tilt gauge ring terminals
7. Trim/tilt switch Deutsch connector
8. Ignition switch Deutsch connector

sensor activates (is shorted to ground), the appropriate LED will illuminate and the warning horn will sound for ten seconds. The LED will illuminate for a minimum of 30 seconds, even if the problem only occurrs momentarily. This allows easy identification of intermittent warning signals. However, the LED will remain illuminated as long as the sensor remains activated. When the sensor deactivates (opens from ground), the LED will remain illuminated for an additional 30 seconds.

If an additional sensor activates, the warning horn will again sound for ten seconds and the appropriate LED will illuminate as described in the previous paragraph. On the engines covered in this manual, it is possible to have three LEDs illuminated at the same time.

If the warning system activates under operation, identify which LED is illuminated and refer to the following:

1. *Water Temp*—If the overheat signal occurs during operation, reduce the engine speed to idle and check the water discharge (tell-tale) indicator for a steady stream of water, indicating that the water pump is operating correctly. If adequate water discharge is not noted at the tell-tale indicator, stop the boat, then shift the gearcase into reverse and briefly apply the throttle to clear any debris that may be covering the water intake screens. If the water temp LED is still illuminated, and/or water discharge is not noted at the tell-tale indicator, the engine must be turned off, allowed to cool and the cause of the overheat determined and corrected.

2A. *No oil (25 and 35 hp [three-cylinder] models)*—If the engine-mounted oil reservoir is empty (or very low), a float

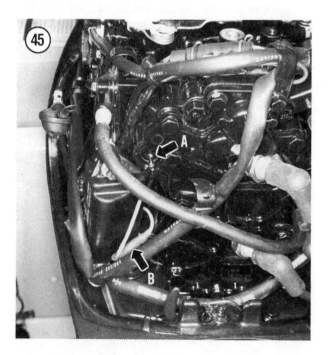

switch will close, activating the no oil LED (and the warning horn will sound). The engine must be immediately stopped and the oil reservoir refilled. The system does not detect oil flow, only oil level.

2B. *No oil (all other models)*—If the motion sensor in the oil injection pump detects that the oil pump is not pumping oil, the no oil LED will illuminate (and the warning horn will sound). The engine must be immediately stopped and the remote oil tank's oil level checked. If the oil level in the remote oil tank is satisfactory, the engine must be operated on a 50:1 fuel/oil mixture until the cause of the warning can be determined. Refer to Chapter Eleven for oil injection system troubleshooting procedures.

3A. *Low oil (25 and 35 hp [three-cylinder] models)*—A float switch in the engine-mounted oil reservoir activates this LED (and the gauge will sound the horn) whenever the oil tank's oil level drops below a predetermined level. The LED will remain illuminated until the oil tank is refilled.

3B. *Low oil (all other models)*—A float switch in the remote oil tank activates this LED (and the gauge will sound the horn) whenever the oil level drops to approximately 1/3 to 1/4 of the tank's full capacity. The LED will remain illuminated until the oil tank is refilled.

Diagnostic Mode

The system also features a diagnostic mode. The diagnostic mode is entered by turning the ignition switch to the ON or RUN position, but without actually starting the engine. The gauge will go through its self-test mode, then automatically enter the diagnostic mode. In this mode, the warning horn circuits are disabled. If a sensor is activated, the appropriate LED will illuminate only as long as the sensor is activated.

NOTE
Do not attempt to use the diagnostic mode unless the self-test mode has satisfactorily activated. Refer to the end of the book for wiring diagrams.

This mode allows a technician to manually ground the sensors (or sensor leads) to quickly verify that the wiring harness and gauge are functioning correctly. To test the wiring harness warning circuits, turn the ignition switch to the ON or RUN position, verify that the self-test successfully activated and completed, then proceed as follows:

1. *Water Temp*—Proceed as follows:
   a. Disconnect the engine temperature switch (A, **Figure 45**, typical) from the engine harness two-pin Amphenol connector (25-70 hp [three-cylinder] models), one-pin Amphenol connector (40-50 hp

[two-cylinder] and 35 jet) or bullet connector (all other models [B, **Figure 45**]).

b. Using a suitable jumper wire, hold the engine harness end of the tan lead to a good engine ground.

c. The *Water Temp* LED must illuminate as long as the tan lead is held to ground. If not, repair or replace the tan lead between the engine harness two-pin Amphenol (or bullet) connector and the system check gauge eight-pin Deutsch connector (4, **Figure 44**). This includes the blocking diode on models so equipped.

2A. *No oil (25 and 35 hp [three-cylinder] models)*—Proceed as follows:

a. Remove the nut securing the oil level sending unit into the oil tank. See **Figure 46**. Lift the oil sending unit from the tank while observing the gauge.

b. The *no oil* LED must illuminate when the float reaches the bottom of its travel. If not, disconnect the sending unit three-pin Amphenol connector.

c. Connect a suitable jumper wire between the tan/yellow lead (pin A) and the black lead (pin B) on the engine harness side of the three-pin Amphenol connector. If the LED now illuminates, replace the oil level sending unit.

d. The *no oil* LED must illuminate as long as the tan/yellow lead is connected to the black lead. If not, test the black lead for continuity to the negative battery terminal. Repair or replace the black lead as necessary.

e. If the black lead tests satisfactorily, repair or replace the tan/yellow lead between the three-pin Amphenol connector and the system check gauge eight-pin Deutsch connector.

2B. *No oil (all other models)*—Proceed as follows:

a. Disconnect the oil injection pump (**Figure 47**) from the engine harness four-pin Amphenol connector. The harness leaves the pump at the very back of the pump.

b. Using a suitable jumper wire, connect the tan/yellow lead (pin A) to the black lead (pin B) on the engine harness side of the connector.

c. The *no oil* LED must illuminate as long as the tan/yellow lead is connected to the black lead. If not, test the black lead for continuity to the negative battery terminal. Repair or replace the black lead as necessary.

d. If the black lead tests satisfactorily, repair or replace the tan/yellow lead between the four-pin Amphenol connector and the system check gauge eight-pin Deutsch connector (4, **Figure 44**).

3A. *Low oil (25 and 35 hp [three-cylinder] models)*—Proceed as follows:

a. Remove the nut securing the oil level sending unit to the oil tank. See **Figure 46**. Lift the oil sending unit from the tank while observing the gauge.

b. The *low oil* LED must illuminate when the oil pickup is lifted *before* the *no oil* light illuminates. If not, disconnect the oil level sending unit three-pin Amphenol connector from the engine harness.

c. Connect a suitable jumper lead between the tan/black lead (pin C) and the black lead (pin B) on the engine harness side of the connector. If the LED now illuminates, replace the oil level sending unit.

d. If the LED does not illuminate after connecting the jumper lead in the previous step, test the black lead for continuity from the engine harness side of the oil level sending unit's three-pin Amphenol connector to the negative battery terminal. Repair or replace the black lead as necessary.

e. If the black lead tests satisfactorily, repair or replace the tan/black lead between the engine harness side of the oil level sending unit's three-pin Amphenol connector and the system check gauge eight-pin Deutsch connector (4, **Figure 44**).

3B. *Low oil (all other models)*—Gain access to the remote oil tank, then proceed as follows:

a. Remove four Torx head screws securing the oil pickup assembly to the remote oil tank.

b. Lift the oil pickup assembly from the tank while observing the gauge.

c. The *low oil* LED must illuminate when the oil pickup is lifted high enough to cause the float switch to drop. If not, disconnect the oil tank two-pin Deutsch connector from the engine harness. Connect a suitable jumper lead between the tan/black and black leads on the engine harness side of the connector. If the LED now illuminates, repair or replace the oil pickup leads or replace the pickup as an assembly.

d. If the LED does not illuminate after connecting the jumper lead in the previous step, test the black lead for continuity from the engine harness side of the oil

tank's two-pin Deutsch connector to the negative battery terminal. Repair or replace the black lead as necessary.

e. If the black lead tests satisfactorily, repair or replace the tan/black lead between the engine harness side of the oil tank's two-pin Deutsch connector and the System Check gauge eight-pin Deutsch connector.

4. Turn the ignition switch to the OFF position and reconnect all leads when finished.

Audible driver module

If a system check gauge was not installed when the boat was rigged, an audible driver module *must* have been installed in its place. The audible driver module will provide only audible signals—there will be no LEDs. Because the LEDs are not present, some interpretation of the warning horn signals will be required on the operator's part. The module plugs into the eight-pin Deutsch connector, replacing the gauge. The warning signals are as follows:

NOTE
A constant warning horn and the activation of S.L.O.W. (speed limiting operational warning) means an overheat situation on all models (except the 25-35 hp [three-cylinder]). On these engines an empty oil tank will also engage S.L.O.W.

1A. *Engine overheat and Low Oil level (25 and 35 hp [three-cylinder] models)*—An overheating engine and/or low oil level in the oil tank will produce a constant horn signal. If the constant horn signal occurs during operation, reduce the engine speed to idle and check the water discharge (tell-tale) indicator for a steady stream of water, indicating that the water pump is operating correctly. If adequate water discharge is not noted at the tell-tale indicator, stop the boat, then shift the gearcase into reverse and briefly apply the throttle to clear any debris that may be

covering the water intake screens. If water discharge is still not noted at the tell-tale indicator, the engine must be turned off, allowed to cool and the cause of the overheat determined and corrected. A float switch in the engine-mounted oil reservoir also activates the warning horn continuously whenever the oil level drops to a predetermined value. The float switch holds the tank's tan/black (or tan) lead to the tank's black lead, sounding the horn until the tank is refilled.

1B. *Engine overheat and low oil level (all other models)*—An overheating engine and/or low oil level in the oil tank will produce a constant horn signal. If the constant horn signal occurs during operation, reduce the engine speed to idle and check the water discharge (tell-tale) indicator for a steady stream of water, indicating that the water pump is operating correctly. If adequate water discharge is not noted at the tell-tale indicator, stop the boat, then shift the gearcase into reverse and briefly apply the throttle to clear any debris that may be covering the water intake screens. If water discharge is still not noted at the tell-tale indicator, the engine must be turned off, allowed to cool and the cause of the overheat determined and corrected. A float switch in the remote oil tank also activates the warning horn continuously whenever the remote oil tank's oil level drops to approximately 1/3 to 1/4 of the tank's full capacity. The float switch holds the tank's tan lead to the tank's black lead, sounding the horn until the tank is refilled.

NOTE
*If the boat is operated in rough water, the oil sloshing in the oil tank may cause the float switch to open and close, resulting in an intermittent warning horn signal. Do not confuse this signal with the consistently pulsing **no oil** signal.*

2A. *No oil (25 and 35 hp [three-cylinder] models)*—If the oil level sending unit in the engine-mounted oil reservoir detects that the oil tank is empty (or very low), the warning horn will sound continuously and the engine will go into S.L.O.W. mode. The engine must be immediately stopped and the oil reservoir refilled. The system only detects oil level, not oil flow.

2B. *Oil pump failure (all other models)*—If the motion sensor in the oil injection pump detects that the oil pump is not pumping oil, the warning system will produce an urgent, pulsing horn. The engine must be immediately stopped and the oil level checked. If the oil level in the remote oil tank is satisfactory, the engine must be operated on a pre-mixed 50:1 fuel/oil mixture until the cause of the warning can be determined. Refer to Chapter Eleven for oil injection system troubleshooting procedures.

3

3. *Self-test*—The audible driver module sounds the warning horn as part of a brief self-test each time the key is turned to the ON or RUN position. The self-test sounds a single beep of the warning horn. If the self-test does not occur, refer to *Troubleshooting the audible driver module* in the next section.

Troubleshooting the audible driver module

If the audible driver module does not self-test correctly, proceed as follows:

1. Test the purple lead at the module's eight-pin Deutsch connector for battery voltage while the ignition switch is in the ON or RUN position. Repair or replace the purple lead, 20 amp fuse and/or ignition switch as necessary.

2. Test the black lead at the module's eight-pin Deutsch connector for continuity back to the negative battery terminal. Repair or replace the black lead as necessary.

3. Turn the ignition switch to the ON or RUN position. Using a suitable jumper lead, ground the connector's tan/blue lead (pin No. 8) to the black lead (pin No. 2). If the warning horn sounds, replace the audible driver module. If the warning horn does not sound, leave the module disconnected and proceed to Step 4.

4. Disconnect the warning horn from its two-pin Deutsch connector. Test the tan/blue lead for continuity between the warning horn (two-pin) and module (eight-pin) Deutsch connectors. If continuity is not noted, repair or replace the tan/blue lead (and/or connectors) as necessary. When finished, reconnect the eight-pin Deutsch connector to the audible driver module.

5. Test the two-pin Deutsch connector's purple lead (on the wiring harness side) for battery voltage while the ignition switch is in the ON or RUN position. Repair or replace the purple lead, 20 amp fuse and/or ignition switch as necessary. Reconnect the two-pin Deutsch connector when finished.

6. If at this point, the warning horn will not sound a single beep during the self-test, replace the warning horn.

IGNITION SYSTEM

This section deals with troubleshooting the various ignition systems used on Evinrude and Johnson outboard motors. Review the introduction to this chapter and the *Safety Precautions, Operating Requirements* and *Test and Repair Equipment* sections (all located at the front of this chapter) before continuing. Once the defective component is identified, refer to Chapter Seven for component removal and replacement procedures. Refer to **Table 12** for ignition system identification and features.

General Description

All of the engines in this manual use a magneto-powered, capacitor discharge ignition system. **Figure 48** shows an operational block diagram of a common two-cylinder ignition system (CD2). Ignition systems are self-powered and do not require battery voltage to operate. The rotation of the flywheel magnets induces voltage (approximately 300 volts AC) into the charge coil windings. This voltage is sent to the power pack where it is rectified (changed to DC) and stored in a capacitor. The voltage remains in the capacitor until a small voltage signal (approximately 3 volts AC) from the sensor coil(s) tells the SCRs (silicon-controlled rectifiers) in the power pack to send the stored voltage to the ignition coil(s). A SCR is simply an electronic switch. The ignition coil(s) transform the relatively low (300 volts) voltage into very high voltage (up to 40,000 volts). This high voltage is sufficient to jump the spark plug gap under all operating conditions.

> *NOTE*
> *On the 25 and 35 hp (three-cylinder) models, the sensor coil windings are replaced with an optical sensor assembly . The sensor assembly contains two optical sensors. A flywheel-mounted encoder (trigger wheel) passes windows and vanes through the optical sensors. The signals from the sensors are used in the same manner as conventional sensor coil windings.*

The system will continue to induce voltage and create spark until the stop circuit is engaged. The stop circuit is always a black/yellow lead that is connected to one side of the capacitor in the power pack. Grounding the stop circuit (black/yellow) lead will short the capacitor to ground, preventing it from storing electricity, causing the ignition system to cease operation.

There is always one charge coil and one power pack per engine, one ignition coil and spark plug for each cylinder and one stop circuit black/yellow lead. The number of sensor coils varies from model to model, depending on the charging system used and the features the ignition system is equipped with, such as QuikStart. Charge coil leads are always brown and brown/yellow. Power pack primary output leads are always orange (or orange with a tracer).

The QuikStart system is used on the 25-70 hp (three-cylinder) models. The system advances the ignition timing (below 1100-1500 rpm) whenever the engine temperature is below 105° F (41° C). This is done to reduce the amount of throttle movement required by the operator, making the starting procedure simpler. QuikStart is enabled and the timing is advanced for 7-10 seconds on each start-up,

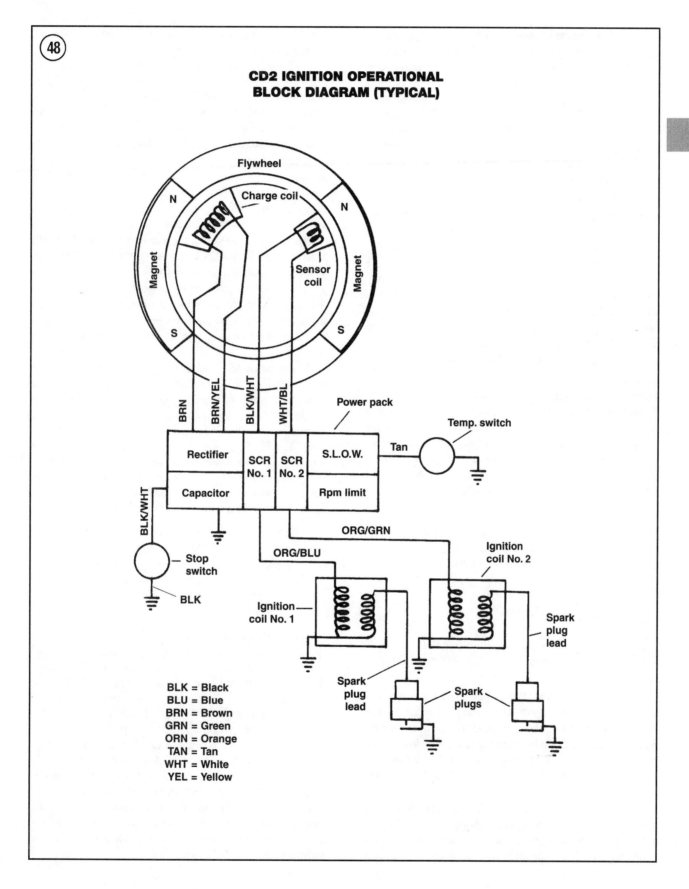

**CD2 IGNITION OPERATIONAL
BLOCK DIAGRAM (TYPICAL)**

BLK = Black
BLU = Blue
BRN = Brown
GRN = Green
ORN = Orange
TAN = Tan
WHT = White
YEL = Yellow

regardless of engine temperature. If the engine speed exceeds 1100-1500 rpm, timing advance returns to normal. The QuikStart system is a function of both the power pack and timer base (sensor coils) on the 50-70 hp (three-cylinder) models and a function of only the power pack (ignition module) on 25 and 35 hp (three-cylinder) models. A special engine temperature switch with a white/black lead (in addition to the standard tan lead) is used to indicate whether the engine's temperature is above or below the 105° F (41° C) threshold.

All 20-70 hp and 18-35 jet models also incorporate a rpm limit program and the S.L.O.W. (speed limiting operational warning) system into their power packs. The rpm limit program interrupts the ignition system any time engine speed exceeds the pack's preprogrammed value. If the engine is incorrectly propped, a high-speed misfire may simply be the rpm limit trying to prevent the engine from over-speeding. Always compare the wide-open throttle speed of the engine against specifications (Chapter Five) when troubleshooting a high speed misfire.

The S.L.O.W. program is designed to limit engine speed to approximately 2000-3000 rpm anytime the engine temperature switch (A, **Figure 45**, typical) is closed to ground. Engine operation when in S.L.O.W. is distinct. Once S.L.O.W. is engaged, the engine must be slowed to idle (or stopped and restarted) to reset the program. If the engine is still overheating, S.L.O.W. will re-engage once the engine's speed exceeds 2000-3000 rpm. S.L.O.W. does not affect engine operation below 2000-3000 rpm.

NOTE
On 25 and 35 hp (three-cylinder) models, the no-oil switch in the engine-mounted oil reservoir will also engage S.L.O.W.

Required Special Equipment

In addition to a conventional ohmmeter and the normal hand tools, the following test equipment is required to correctly test OMC ignition systems.

1. *Air gap spark tester*—The air gap spark tester replaces the spark plug with a known electrical load and is used as the first step in troubleshooting all OMC ignition systems. The tester is connected between the spark plug lead(s) and a good engine ground. The tester checks the total output of the ignition system. Recommended air gap testers are listed in **Table 1**.

2. *Four Amphenol jumper wires*—These can be fabricated using 8 in. (203 mm) lengths of 16-gauge wire. Crimp a pin (part No. 511469) to one end of a wire and a socket (part No. 581656) to the other end, using crimp tool (part

No. 322696). Insulate the socket and the crimped area of the pin with heat shrink tubing (part No. 510628).

3. *Peak reading voltmeter*—The peak reading voltmeter (PRV) is an essential tool for troubleshooting OMC ignition systems. A conventional voltmeter cannot be used as it will give inaccurate readings, leading to needless replacement of good components. OMC specifically recommends one of the meters listed in **Table 1**.

In the marine industry, the term peak volts is used interchangeably with DVA (direct volts adapter). The Mercury Marine (part No. 91-99750)/Electronic Specialties (Model 530) multimeter can be used for troubleshooting an OMC ignition system, as long as the DVA scale is used whenever the specification is given in peak volts. Mercury Marine also offers a DVA adapter (part No. 91-98045) to adapt most analog voltmeters (with a 400 DC volt scale) to read peak volts. If using this meter (or adaptor), it is normally necessary to reverse the meter test leads (reverse polarity) to obtain the specified results. If your initial test results are unsatisfactory, reverse your meter test leads and retest.

4. *Power pack load adaptor*—The Stevens Instrument Company part No. PL-88 power pack load adaptor is required to test power pack output at cranking speed. If a PL-88 is not available, it can be fabricated using a 10 ohm, 10 watt resistor (Radio Shack part No. 271-132, or equivalent). The PL-88 applies a known, calibrated load to the power pack and ensures that the pack will deliver its maximum output. The PL-88 also prevents a failed ignition coil from causing a no-output condition. Failure to use the PL-88 as specified, will result in no output during testing.

CAUTION
The PL-88 must be connected to the power pack primary (orange or orange/xxx) lead(s). Do not connect the PL-88 to the ignition coil secondary (spark plug) leads. See Figure 49.

5. *Terminal extenders (ignition coil)*—Terminal extenders (part No. TS-77) are small brass terminals with a coil spring soldered to one end. They are available from Stevens Instrument Company. The terminal extenders are installed on each ignition coil's primary terminal, then the power pack primary lead is installed over the extender. This allows the power pack output test to be performed with the engine running. The terminal extenders are used to diagnose running problems, not cranking problems.

6. *Test wheel*—Refer to *Test wheels (propellers)* in this chapter. OMC recommends the use of test wheels for all test procedures that require the engine to be run under load, such as the power pack running output test. Test wheel part numbers are listed in the *Quick Reference Data* section, located at the front of this manual.

Optional Test Equipment

To completely test the ignition coils used on OMC ignition systems, an ignition analyzer is required. The ST-75, available from Stevens Instrument Company or the Merc-O-Tronic Model 98 series are both recommended by OMC and can fully test the ignition coil(s) under actual operating conditions. These analyzers are expensive, but can usually be found at marine dealerships where the cost can be justified. The ignition coil can be quickly bench tested by any marine dealership that possesses an appropriate analyzer.

Troubleshooting Notes And Precautions (All Models)

Several troubleshooting precautions must be strictly observed to avoid damaging the ignition system or injuring yourself.

1. Do not reverse the battery connections. Reverse battery polarity will damage electronic components.

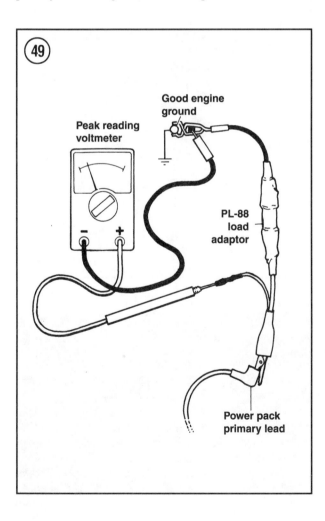

49

Peak reading voltmeter

Good engine ground

PL-88 load adaptor

Power pack primary lead

2. Do not spark the battery terminals with the battery cable connections to determine polarity.

3. Do not disconnect the battery cables with the engine running.

4. Do not crank or run the outboard if any electrical components are not grounded to the power head.

5. Do not touch or disconnect any ignition components when the outboard is running, while the ignition switch is ON or while the battery cables are connected.

6. Do not rotate the flywheel when performing ohmmeter tests. The meter will be damaged by the voltage induced.

7. If a sudden unexplained timing change is noted:
   a. Check the trigger magnets in the hub of the flywheel (if so equipped) for damage or a possible shift in magnet position. If the magnets are cracked, damaged or have shifted position, the flywheel must be replaced. See Chapter Seven.
   b. Check the flywheel key for a sheared condition. See Chapter Seven.
   c. 12 amp charging system models—Check the sensor coil common white lead for continuity, loose connections or other damage. If the common (white) lead is open, the ignition timing (and spark) will generally be erratic. Make repairs or replace components as necessary.

8. The ignition system on electric start models requires that the electric starter crank the engine at normal speed in order for the ignition system to produce adequate spark. If the starter motor cranks the engine slowly or not at all, go back to the *Starting System* section and correct the starting system problem before continuing.

9. The spark plug(s) must be installed during the troubleshooting process. The ignition system must produce adequate spark at normal cranking speed. Removing the spark plug(s) artificially raises the cranking speed and may prevent diagnosing a problem in the ignition system.

10. Check the battery cable connections (on models so equipped) for secure attachment to both battery terminals and the engine. Clean any corrosion from all connections. Discard any wing nuts and install corrosion resistant hexnuts at all battery cable connections. Place a corrosion resistant locking washer between the battery terminal stud and battery cable terminal end to ensure a positive connection. Loose battery connections can cause every symptom imaginable.

11. Check all ignition component mounting hardware and/or ground leads for secure attachment to the power head. Clean and tighten all ground leads, connections and fasteners as necessary.

CAUTION
If an outboard equipped with an unregulated charging system must be operated with the battery removed or disconnected, the posi-

3

tive battery cable end must be insulated (taped or sleeved) from the negative battery cable and/or ground. Do not operate an outboard equipped a regulated charging system with the battery disconnected.

Resistance Tests

The resistance values specified in the following test procedures are based on tests performed at room temperature. Actual resistance readings obtained during testing will generally be slightly higher if checked on hot components. In addition, resistance readings may vary depending on the manufacturer of the ohmmeter. Therefore, use discretion when failing any component that is only slightly out of specification. Many ohmmeters have difficulty reading less than 1 ohm accurately. If this is the case, specifications of less than 1 ohm generally appear as a very low (continuity) reading.

Peak Voltage Tests

Peak voltage tests are designed to check the voltage output of the charge coil, sensor coil(s) and the power pack (ignition module) at normal cranking speed. If an ignition misfire or failure occurs only when the engine is running and cranking speed tests do not show any defects, perform the power pack running output test(s) at the engine speed at which the ignition symptom or failure occurs. **Table 15** lists the cranking and high speed running voltages for all applicable tests.

> *NOTE*
> *All peak voltage specifications in the text and **Table 15** are **minimum** voltages. As long as the measured voltage meets or exceeds the specification, consider the test results satisfactory. On some components, the voltage may **greatly** exceed the minimum specification.*

When checking the peak voltage during the power pack running output test, observe the meter needle for fluctuations, which indicates erratic voltage output. The voltage output of the power pack will change with engine speed, but must not be erratic.

> *WARNING*
> *High voltage is present during ignition system operation. Do not touch ignition components, leads or test leads while cranking or running the engine.*

Push Button Stop Switch/Safety Lanyard Switch Tests (Tiller Handle Models [If So Equipped])

Refer to the back of the manual for wiring diagrams.

> *NOTE*
> *The safety lanyard must be installed (when specified) for the following tests.*

1A. *2.0, 3.3 and 3.5 hp*—To test the push button stop switch, disconnect the stop switch black lead from the engine harness black/yellow lead bullet connector.

1B. *3.0 and 4 hp (except 4 Deluxe)*—To test the push button stop switch, disconnect the six-pin Packard connector from the ignition module (combined charge coil and power pack). See **Figure 50**. If an OMC test harness (part No.

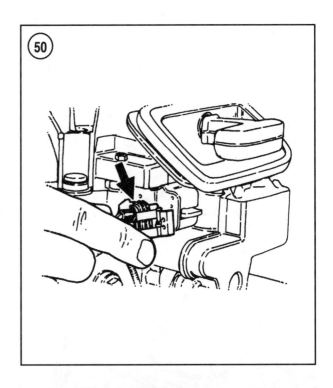

434127) is available, connect the test harness to the six-pin Packard connector.

1C. *4 Deluxe-50 hp (two-cylinder)*—To test the push button stop switch, disconnect the five-pin Amphenol connector from the power pack. See **Figure 51**, typical.

1D. *25 and 35 hp (three-cylinder)*—To test the push button stop switch, disconnect the stop switch black lead from the engine harness black/yellow lead at the one-pin Amphenol connector.

2A. *2.0, 3.3 and 3.5 hp*—Connect one lead of an ohmmeter, calibrated on the R × 1 scale, to the disconnected stop switch lead bullet connector. Connect the other ohmmeter lead to the ring terminal (or its retaining screw) of the stop switch lead that is still connected to engine ground.

2B. *3.0 and 4 hp (except 4 Deluxe)*—Connect one lead of an ohmmeter, calibrated on the R × 1 scale, to the

black/yellow terminal of the six-pin Packard connector. Be careful not to damage the connector pin. Connect the other ohmmeter lead to the ring terminal (or its retaining screw) of the stop switch black lead that is still connected to ground.

2C. *4 Deluxe-50 hp (two-cylinder)*—Using an amphenol jumper lead, connect one lead of an ohmmeter, calibrated on the R × 1 scale, to the black lead (pin E) of the ignition plate side of the five-pin Amphenol connector (male body, female pins). Connect the other ohmmeter lead to the ring terminal (or its retaining screw) of the stop switch black lead that is still connected to engine ground at an ignition coil mounting screw.

2D. *25 and 35 hp (three-cylinder)*—Using an Amphenol jumper lead, connect one lead of an ohmmeter, calibrated on the R × 1 scale, to the stop switch black lead at the 1-pin Amphenol connector. Connect the other ohmmeter lead to the ring terminal (or its retaining screw) of the stop switch black lead that is still connected to engine ground near the ignition module.

3. With the safety lanyard installed and the stop switch released, the meter must indicate no continuity.

4. With the stop switch depressed, the meter must indicate continuity (1 ohm or less).

5. With the safety lanyard removed and the stop switch released, the meter must indicate continuity (1 ohm or less)

6. Replace the stop switch if it does not perform as specified.

Lanyard Safety Switch Test (Traditional Harness Remote Control Models)

Remote control models using the traditional wiring harness will a dedicated safety lanyard switch mounted in the remote control box or on the dash. If correctly installed, the switch will be connected between the boat harness black/yellow and black leads. This switch is not used on models equipped with the modular wiring system (MWS).

The switch must have no continuity in the RUN position and must have continuity in the STOP position. Refer to the end of the book for an OMC remote control box wiring diagram (traditional harness).

The switch may be quickly tested at the engine's main harness connector or tested directly at the switch.

Testing at the main harness connector

1. Disconnect the negative battery cable, then disconnect the large, red 10-pin main engine harness connector.

2. Connect an ohmmeter, calibrated on the R × 1 scale, between the black (10, **Figure 52**) and black/yellow (4,

TRADITIONAL HARNESS TEN-PIN CONNECTOR (BOAT SIDE)

1. Red/purple lead
2. Not used
3. Gray lead
4. Black/yellow lead
5. Not used
6. Yellow/red lead
7. Tan lead
8. Purple/white lead
9. Purple lead
10. Black lead

52

Figure 52) pins of the boat side of the main harness connector.

3. Make sure the ignition switch is in the ON or RUN position and the lanyard is installed on the lanyard safety switch.

4. The meter must indicate no continuity. If not, either the ignition switch, lanyard safety switch or main harness is defective. Test the lanyard safety switch as described in the next section and test the ignition switch as described previously in this chapter. If the switches test satisfactorily, repair or replace the boat's main wiring harness.

5. Pull the lanyard from the safety switch while noting the meter reading. The meter must now indicate continuity. If not, test the lanyard safety switch directly as described in the next section. If the lanyard safety switch tests satisfactorily, repair or replace the boat's main wiring harness.

6. If the ohmmeter indicates continuity when the lanyard is removed and indicates no continuity when the lanyard is installed, the lanyard safety switch and boat wiring harness are operating correctly.

7. Reconnect all leads when finished. Connect the negative battery cable last.

Testing at the safety lanyard switch

1. Disconnect the negative battery cable.

2. Gain access to the safety lanyard switch and disconnect the black and black/yellow leads from the electrical harness.

3. Connect an ohmmeter, calibrated on the R × 1 scale, between the disconnected lanyard switch leads.

4. With the lanyard switch in the RUN position (lanyard installed), the meter must indicate no continuity.

5. With the lanyard switch in the OFF position (lanyard removed), the meter must indicate continuity (1 ohm or less).

6. Replace the lanyard safety switch if it does not perform as specified.

7. Reconnect all leads when finished. Connect the negative battery cable last.

Ignition Coil Tests

A total of 5 separate tests are required to fully test each ignition coil. The first 3 tests may be performed with a conventional ohmmeter. The power and leakage tests require the use of an ignition analyzer such as the ST-75, available from Stevens Instrument Company or the Merc-O-Tronic Model 98 series (no longer available). Both of these analyzers are recommended by OMC and can fully test the ignition coil(s) under actual operating conditions. These analyzers are expensive, and can usually be found at marine dealerships where the cost can be justified. The ignition coil can be quickly bench tested by any marine dealership that possesses an appropriate analyzer.

To test any ignition coil, perform the following tests, in the order listed:

1. Primary resistance.
2. Secondary resistance.
3. Spark plug lead continuity.
4. Ignition coil power test.
5. Ignition coil surface leakage test.

Primary and secondary resistance tests

The ignition coil on 6-15 hp, 40-50 hp (two-cylinder), 28 jet and 35 jet models contain two separate windings encased in a single housing (secondary windings [A, **Figure 53**] and primary windings [B, **Figure 53**]). Straps secured by the coil mounting screws provide the coil ground circuit.

The ignition coil may be left installed, or removed for these tests.

TROUBLESHOOTING   **85**

1. To measure the ignition coil's primary resistance, disconnect all primary and secondary leads from each ignition coil with a gentle twisting and pulling motion.

2. Calibrate an ohmmeter on the lowest scale possible. Connect the black meter lead to the ignition coil ground tab. Connect the red meter lead to the primary (small) terminal. If testing a dual-potted coil, you must connect the black lead to the ground tab closest to the primary terminal being tested.

3A. *25 and 35 hp (three-cylinder) models*—The meter must read 0.23-0.32 ohm.

3B. *All other models*—The meter must read 0.05-0.15 ohm.

4A. *25 and 35 hp (three-cylinder) models*—To test the ignition coil's secondary resistance, calibrate an ohmmeter on the appropriate scale to read 2000-2600 ohms.

4B. *All other models*—To test the ignition coil's secondary resistance, calibrate an ohmmeter on the appropriate scale to read 225-325 ohms.

5. Connect the black meter lead to the ignition coil's primary (small) terminal and the red meter lead to the coil's secondary (large) terminal. If testing a dual-potted coil, you must connect the black lead to primary terminal closest to the secondary terminal being tested.

6A. *25 and 35 hp (three-cylinder) models*—The meter must read 2000-2600 ohms.

6B. *All other models*—The meter must read 225-325 ohms.

7. Replace the ignition coil if it does not perform as specified.

8. Repeat this procedure for the remaining set of windings in a dual-potted coil or the remaining ignition coils.

Spark plug lead continuity test

Some models may use spark plug leads that are RFI (radio frequency interference) suppression leads. RFI suppression leads can be identified by color (any color except black, usually gray). Black spark plug leads are solid core leads. Never replace an RFI suppression lead with a solid core lead as erratic ignition operation may result.

No resistance specifications are available for RFI suppression leads. However, RFI suppression leads must basically have the same resistance and the reading must remain steady as the lead is gently flexed.

To test the continuity of the spark plug lead(s), proceed as follows:

1. Remove the spark plug lead from each ignition coil and spark plug with a gentle twisting and pulling motion.

2. Visually inspect the spark plug lead and boots for cracked insulation or damaged spring terminals. Replace the boots (and spring terminals) or the spark plug lead as an assembly as necessary.

3. Calibrate an ohmmeter on the R × 1 scale. Connect one ohmmeter lead to each end of the spark plug lead.

4A. *Solid core leads*—The meter must indicate continuity. Carefully flex the lead while noting the meter. The meter must continue to indicate continuity as it is flexed. If not, replace the suspect boot (and spring terminal) or replace the spark plug lead.

4B. *RFI Suppression leads*—Note the meter reading for comparison with the other leads. All leads must indicate approximately the same reading. Carefully flex the lead while noting the meter. The meter must continue to indicate a steady reading as it is flexed. If not, replace the suspect boot (and spring terminal) or replace the spark plug lead.

5. Reinstall the spark plug lead(s) to the ignition coil(s) when finished. Make sure the end with the shorter boot is installed on the ignition coil. The long boot must attach to the spark plug.

Ignition coil power and leakage tests

The ignition coil must be removed from the power head for the following tests. The following tests also require the use of an ignition analyzer. To perform the ignition coil power and leakage tests, proceed as follows:

> *WARNING*
> *The following tests produces high voltage sparks. Do not touch the ignition coil or the analyzer's primary or secondary leads during these tests. Make sure the test is performed on an insulated workbench or a suitable piece of dry wood or thick plastic sheet.*

1. Remove the ignition coil(s) from the engine as described in Chapter Seven. Make sure the spark plug lead(s) are attached to the ignition coil(s) with the shorter boot end installed on the ignition coil.

2. Position the ignition analyzer's high tension (large) lead into the spark plug boot cavity and securely attach it to the terminal spring.

3. Connect the analyzer's red primary (small) lead to the ignition coil's primary (small) terminal. If testing a dual-potted coil, you must connect the red lead to the primary terminal closest to the secondary lead being tested.

4. Connect the analyzer's black primary (small) lead to the ignition coil's ground tab terminal. If testing a dual-potted coil, you must connect the black lead to the ground tab closest to the primary (small) terminal being tested.

5. To perform the coil power test, follow the analyzer manufacturer's instructions. Use the normal polarity setting, then turn the analyzer on. Adjust the current flow knob to achieve 1.1 amps on the Stevens unit or 1.5

amps on the Merc-O-Tronic unit. Do not exceed these values.

NOTE
Do not continue the coil power test any longer than necessary. The coil will overheat and be damaged by prolonged testing at the maximum amperage setting.

6. Note the spark in the analyzer's window. The ignition coil must produce a steady blue spark at the specified amperage setting. It is acceptable for the coil to produce good spark at a lower amperage setting, but it must maintain good spark at the maximum amperage rating.

7. When the power test is completed, turn the tester off, but do not change the amperage setting.

8. To test the ignition coil and spark plug lead for surface leakage, disconnect the analyzer's high tension (large) lead from the spark plug lead. No spark will be visible if this test is successfully completed.

WARNING
The leakage test creates the maximum voltage the coil can produce, while leaving it nowhere to go. This puts maximum stress on the coil's insulation and spark plug lead. Be very careful not to allow your body to get near (or touch) the ignition coil and spark plug lead.

NOTE
Do not continue the coil surface leakage test any longer than necessary. The coil will overheat and be damaged by prolonged testing at the maximum amperage setting.

9. Turn on the analyzer and verify that the amperage setting is still 1.1 amps on the Stevens unit, or 1.5 amps on the Merc-O-Tronic unit. Adjust the amperage settings as necessary, but do not exceed these values.

10. Using the analyzer's leakage probe, trace the complete outer surface of the ignition coil's case and spark plug lead. Do not touch the coil's primary terminal, ground strap or probe inside of the spark plug boot.

11. Leakage will be apparent as it jumps to the leakage probe. Do not be confused by a slight or hazy glow (corona effect). Real leakage will snap and pop as it jumps to the probe. Turn the analyzer off as soon as you are finished. Replace the ignition coil and/or spark plug lead if any leakage is noted.

12. Repeat this procedure for the remaining set of windings in a dual-potted coil or the remaining ignition coils.

13. Reinstall the ignition coil(s) and reconnect all leads when finished. See Chapter Seven.

INDEXING FLYWHEEL (ERRATIC SPARK [TWO- AND THREE-CYLINDER MODELS])

If the outboard motor runs erratically, or if a high-speed misfire is noted, the power pack (ignition module) may be defective. Internal malfunctions can cause the pack to fire the ignition coil(s) twice per crankshaft revolution, erratically or continuously. The following procedure will determine if the pack is firing each cylinder at the correct time.

NOTE
For this procedure, it is not critical to determine each cylinder's exact TDC (top dead center). However, it is important to locate the general location of each cylinder's TDC.

1. Disconnect the negative battery cable (if equipped). Then disconnect and ground the spark plug leads to the power head to prevent accidental starting.

2. Remove all of the spark plugs.

3. Position the No. 1 piston at TDC. Insert a pencil or similar tool into the No. 1 spark plug hole and slowly rotate the flywheel clockwise to extend the pencil as far as possible, ensuring the piston is at TDC. The flywheel may be turned slightly counterclockwise to ensure TDC has been located.

4. With the No. 1 piston at TDC, place a mark on the flywheel directly across from the timing pointer or starter pivot screw. Label the mark No. 1.

5. Repeat Steps 3-4 for the remaining cylinder(s). Label each mark with its corresponding cylinder number.

6. Reinstall the spark plugs and connect the plug leads. Then reconnect the negative battery cable (if equipped).

CAUTION
*Do not run the engine without an adequate water supply and do not exceed 3000 rpm without an adequate load. Refer to **Safety Precautions** at the beginning of this chapter.*

7. Start the engine and run it at the speed at which the ignition symptom is present.

NOTE
All 20-70 hp and 18-35 jet models are equipped with an rpm limit program in the power pack. Make sure that the engine is correctly propped and is not exceeding its recommended wide-open throttle speed (Chapter Five), causing the rpm limit program to activate.

8. Alternately, connect a timing light to each spark plug lead. The timing light must indicate the cylinder number that is connected to the timing light. For example, if the

timing light is connected to the No. 1 cylinder (top) spark plug lead, only the No. 1 mark must be visible at or near the timing pointer.

NOTE
On 40-70 hp and 35 jet models equipped with a 12 amp charging system, an open circuit in the sensor coil (timer base) white lead will cause erratic spark and unstable timing. Refer to the back of the manual for wiring diagrams and check all sensor coil leads and connectors for proper pin location, dislodged pins (in the Amphenol connector bodies) or other damage that would affect continuity.

9A. *Two-cylinder models*—If a different cylinder number appears, or if the number jumps around, appears erratically or appears at a position other than near the timing pointer, first check the power pack's primary ignition coil leads for correct routing. The orange/blue primary lead must be connected to the No. 1 (top) ignition coil and the pack's orange/green primary lead must be connected to the No. 2 cylinder (lower) ignition coil. If the primary leads are correctly routed, replace the power pack (ignition module) and repeat this test.

9B. *Three-cylinder models*—If a different cylinder number appears, or if the number jumps around or appears at a position other than near the timing pointer, first check the power pack's primary ignition coil leads for correct routing. The orange/blue lead must be connected to the No. 1 cylinder (top) ignition coil, the orange/purple lead must be connected to the No. 2 cylinder (middle) ignition coil and the orange/green lead must be connected to the cylinder No. 3 (bottom) ignition coil. If the primary leads are correctly routed, replace the power pack (ignition module) and repeat this test procedure.

CD1 (CAPACITOR DISCHARGE ONE CYLINDER) IGNITION (2, 3.3 AND 3.5 HP MODELS)

Description

The CD1 ignition system used on 2, 3.3 and 3.5 hp models consists of the flywheel, charge coil, sensor coil, power pack, ignition coil, spark plug and a combination push button stop/safety lanyard switch. The charge coil and sensor coil are mounted under the flywheel, and the power pack and ignition coil are mounted on the side of the power head. The power pack is stamped CD1.

This system incorporates a nonadjustable, single-step electronic spark advance built into the power pack.

Troubleshooting

Refer to Tables 13-15 for specifications. The recommended troubleshooting procedure is:
1. Preliminary checks.
   a. Total output (spark) test.
   b. Stop circuit isolation.
2. Charge coil tests.
3. Sensor coil tests.
4. Power pack cranking output test.
5. Ignition coil tests.
6. Power pack running output test.

WARNING
High voltage is present in the ignition system. Do not touch or disconnect ignition components while the engine is being cranked or running.

Preliminary checks

NOTE
Before proceeding, inspect the power pack ground lead and ignition coil ground straps for corrosion, damage, loose connections or loose mounting screws. These components must be securely grounded to operate properly.

1. Disconnect the spark plug lead from the spark plug and install an air gap spark tester (**Table 1**) to the spark plug lead. Adjust the air gap to 3/8 in. (9.5 mm). Then, connect the body of the spark tester to a clean engine ground.
2. Make sure the safety lanyard is installed on the push button stop switch.

NOTE
Spark advance is controlled by the power pack. If spark output is good, but timing does not advance, replace the power pack.

3. Crank the engine while observing the tester. If a crisp, blue spark is noted, the ignition system is functioning correctly.
   a. If good spark is noted, yet the engine will not start or does not run correctly, make sure the correct spark plug is installed and that it is in satisfactory condition. Replace the spark plug if its condition is questionable. If the engine still does not run correctly, proceed to the Ignition module running output test.
   b. If the engine backfires or pops when attempting to start, remove the flywheel and check for a sheared flywheel key.
   c. If no spark, weak spark or erratic spark is noted, continue with Step 4.

4. Disconnect the push button stop switch black lead from the power pack black/yellow bullet connector. Crank the engine while observing the spark tester. If good spark is now noted, replace the push button stop switch.

5. Reconnect the stop switch lead when finished.

Charge coil output

A peak-reading voltmeter (PRV) is required for this procedure.

1. Disconnect the charge coil's brown and brown/yellow leads from the power pack bullet connectors.

2. Adjust a PRV to the positive and 500 settings (or equivalent).

3. To check the charge coil for a short to ground, connect the black meter lead to a clean engine ground.

4. Connect the red meter lead to the charge coil's brown lead. Crank the engine while noting the meter reading.

5. The meter must read 0 volts. If not, the charge coil is shorted to ground and must be replaced.

6. Repeat Steps 4-5 for the charge coil's brown/yellow lead.

7. To check the output of the charge coil, attach the red meter lead to the coil's brown lead and the black meter lead to the coil's brown/yellow lead.

8. Crank the engine while noting the meter reading. The meter must indicate180 peak volts or higher. If not, inspect the wiring and connectors for damage. Repair any damage and retest the coil's output. If the output is still below 180 volts, replace the charge coil and retest spark output.

9. Reconnect the charge coil leads when finished.

Charge coil resistance

The charge coil resistance tests can be used to confirm the results of the output tests performed in the previous section, or to determine the charge coil's condition if a PRV is not available.

1. Disconnect the brown and brown/yellow charge coil leads from the power pack bullet connectors.

2. Calibrate an ohmmeter on the appropriate scale to read 550-760 ohms.

3. Connect one ohmmeter lead to the charge coil brown lead and the other ohmmeter lead to the charge coil brown/yellow lead.

4. If the reading is not within specification (550-760 ohms), replace the charge coil and retest spark output.

5. To check the charge coil for a short to ground, calibrate the ohmmeter on the highest scale available. Connect the black ohmmeter lead to a good engine ground. If the coil is removed, connect the lead to a mounting screw bore.

6. Connect the red ohmmeter lead to the coil's brown lead. The meter must indicate no continuity. If, not the charge coil is shorted to ground and must be replaced.

7. Repeat Step 6 for the charge coil brown/yellow lead.

Sensor coil output

A peak-reading voltmeter (PRV) is required for this procedure.

1. Disconnect the sensor coil's blue lead from the power pack bullet connector.

2. Adjust a PRV to the positive (or sensor [SEN]) and 5 settings (or equivalent).

3. Connect the black meter lead to a good engine ground. Connect the red meter lead to the sensor coil's blue lead.

4. Crank the engine while noting the meter reading. The meter must indicate 1.0 peak volt or higher. If not, inspect the wiring and connector for damage. Repair any damage and retest the coil's output. If the output is still below 1.0 volt, replace the sensor coil and retest spark output.

Sensor coil resistance

The sensor coil resistance test can be used to confirm the results of the output test performed in the previous section, or to troubleshoot the sensor coil's condition if a PRV is not available.

1. Disconnect the blue sensor coil lead from the power pack bullet connector.

2. Calibrate an ohmmeter on the appropriate scale to read 50-70 ohms.

3. Connect the black ohmmeter lead to a good engine ground. If the coil is removed, connect the meter lead to the black ground lead at one of the coil's mounting screws.

4. Connect the red ohmmeter lead to the sensor coil blue lead. The meter must indicate 50-70 ohms. If not, replace the sensor coil and retest spark output.

Power pack cranking output

A peak-reading voltmeter (PRV) and a PL-88 pack load resistor (**Table 1**) are required for this procedure.

1. Disconnect the power pack's orange/blue primary lead from the ignition coil with a gentle twisting and pulling motion.

2. Connect the small, insulated alligator clip of the PL-88 to the power pack orange/blue lead. Then connect the large uninsulated alligator clip to a good engine ground. See **Figure 49**.

3. Adjust a PRV to the positive and 500 settings (or equivalent). Connect the black meter lead to a good engine

ground. Connect the red meter lead to the PL-88 pigtail lead (with the Amphenol socket). See **Figure 49**.

4. Crank the engine while noting the meter reading. The meter must indicate 180 peak volts or higher. If not, inspect the wiring and connector for damage. Repair any damage and retest the output. If the output is still below 180 volts, replace the power pack and retest spark output.

5. Remove the PL-88 and reconnect the power pack's orange/blue lead to the ignition coil primary terminal when finished.

Ignition coil

If all tests to this point are satisfactory, yet spark output at the air gap tester is not satisfactory, refer to *Ignition Coil Tests* at the beginning of the ignition section and test the ignition coil.

Power pack running output test

This test is intended to diagnose a misfire or ignition failure that occurs at a particular engine speed. Make sure that you operate the engine at the speed that the misfire or failure occurs during this test.

A peak-reading voltmeter (PRV) and a TS-77 terminal extender (**Table 1**) are required for this procedure.

It is possible for a defective ignition coil to cause the power pack output to be below specification. If there is any doubt as to the ignition coil's condition, refer to Ignition Coil Tests at the beginning of the ignition section and test the ignition coil.

1. Disconnect the power pack's orange/blue primary lead from the ignition coil with a gentle twisting and pulling motion.

2. Install the TS-77 terminal extender onto the ignition coil's primary terminal. Then, install the power pack's orange/blue lead onto the extender.

3. Adjust a PRV to the positive and 500 settings (or equivalent).

4. Connect the black meter lead to a good engine ground. Connect the red meter lead to the exposed metal of the terminal extender.

CAUTION
*Do not run the engine without an adequate water supply and do not exceed 3000 rpm without an adequate load. Refer to **Safety Precautions** at the beginning of this chapter.*

5. Run the engine to the speed that the misfire or ignition failure occurs while noting the meter reading. The meter must indicate a steady 220 peak volts or higher. If not, check for loose or damaged bullet connectors, damaged

leads, loose ground leads and/or component mounting hardware. If all checks are satisfactory, yet the voltage is below 220 volts or erratic, replace the power pack.

6. Remove the terminal extender and reconnect the orange/blue power pack lead to the ignition coil primary terminal when finished.

CD2 (CAPACITOR DISCHARGE TWO-CYLINDER) IGNITION (3 AND 4 HP [EXCEPT 4 DELUXE] MODELS)

Description

The CDI (capacitor discharge ignition) system used on 3 and 4 hp models (except 4 Deluxe) consists of the flywheel, sensor coil, ignition module (power pack and charge coil combined), dual-potted ignition coil, spark plugs and a combination push button stop/safety lanyard switch.

The ignition module is externally mounted to the front of the power head. The sensor coil is also externally mounted, but is mounted to an ignition plate that rotates the sensor coil along the outer diameter of the flywheel. The ignition plate is rotated by a mechanical linkage to advance and retard ignition timing.

The ignition coil assembly is mounted on the starboard side of the cylinder head.

Troubleshooting

Refer to **Tables 13-15** for specifications and the back of the manual for wiring diagrams. The recommended troubleshooting procedure is:

1. Preliminary checks.
   a. Total output (spark) test.
   b. Stop circuit isolation.
   c. Indexing the flywheel.
2. Sensor coil tests.
3. Ignition module cranking output test.
4. Ignition coil tests.
5. Ignition module running output test.

WARNING
*High voltage is present in the ignition system. **Do not** touch or disconnect ignition components while the engine is being cranked or running.*

Preliminary checks

NOTE
Before proceeding, inspect the ignition module ground lead (black lead to the stop

switch) and ignition coil ground straps for corrosion, damage, loose connections or loose mounting screws. These components must be securely grounded to operate properly.

1. Disconnect the spark plug leads from the spark plugs and install an air gap spark tester (**Table 1**) to the spark plug leads. Adjust the air gap to 3/8 in. (9.5 mm). Then, connect the body of the spark tester to a clean engine ground.

2. Make sure the safety lanyard is installed on the push button stop switch.

3. Crank the engine while observing the tester. If an alternating crisp, blue spark is noted at each air gap, the ignition system is functioning correctly.

    a. If good spark is noted, yet the engine will not start or does not run correctly, make sure the correct spark plugs are installed and that they are in satisfactory condition. Replace the spark plugs if their condition is questionable. If the engine still does not run correctly, proceed to Ignition module running output test.

    b. If good spark is noted, yet the engine backfires or pops when attempting to start, ensure that the power pack primary leads and secondary leads are correctly routed on the ignition coil. The orange/blue primary lead must be connected to the ignition coil's upper primary terminal and the coil's upper spark plug lead must be connected to the top (No. 1 cylinder) spark plug. If the leads are routed correctly, remove the flywheel and check for a sheared flywheel key.

    c. If the engine runs erratically or misfires at certain engine speeds (usually high rpm), refer to Indexing flywheel (erratic spark [two- and three-cylinder models]).

    d. If no spark, weak spark or erratic spark is noted on one or both cylinders, continue with Step 4.

4. Disconnect the six-pin Packard connector from the ignition module. See **Figure 54**.

5. Carefully insert a paper clip (or terminal tool) into pin E (black/yellow lead) from the front of the Packard connector. See **Figure 55**. Depress the terminal locking tab, then pull the black/yellow lead and terminal from the connector body. Tape or sleeve the lead's terminal to prevent contact with the power head.

6. Reconnect the six-pin Packard connector to the ignition module. Crank the engine while observing the spark tester. If good spark is now noted, replace the push button stop switch.

7. Reinstall the black/yellow lead and terminal into the Packard connector body. If necessary, carefully bend the terminal locking tab upward to ensure it will securely lock

in the connector body. Then reconnect the six-pin Packard connector to the ignition module when finished.

Sensor coil output

A peak-reading voltmeter (PRV) is required for this procedure. In addition, jumper leads, such as the six-pin Packard test adapter (part No. 434127), or equivalent test leads are highly recommended to prevent damage to the Packard connector terminals during testing. If no test leads are available, great care must be taken not to damage the terminals during the test procedure.

1. Disconnect the six-pin Packard connector from the ignition module. See **Figure 54**. Install the test adaptor or suitable jumper leads to the white (pin D) and white/blue (pin C) sensor coil leads at the Packard connector.

2. Adjust a PRV to the positive (or sensor [SEN]) and 5 settings (or equivalent).

3. To check the sensor coil for a short-to-ground, connect the black meter lead to a good engine ground. Connect the red meter lead to the Packard connector's white (pin D) lead.

4. Crank the engine while noting the meter reading. The meter must indicate 0 volts. If not, inspect the wiring and connector for damage. Repair any damage and retest. If the meter still indicates any reading other than 0, replace the sensor coil.

5. Repeat Steps 3-4 for the sensor coil white/blue (pin C) lead.

6. To check the sensor coil's peak voltage output, connect the black meter lead to the Packard connector's white (pin D) lead and the red meter lead to the connector's white/blue (pin C) lead.

7. Crank the engine while noting the meter reading. The meter must indicate 4.0 peak volts or higher. If not, inspect the wiring and connector for damage. Repair any damage and retest the coil's output. If the output is still below 4.0 volts, replace the sensor coil and retest the spark output.

8. Reconnect the six-pin Packard connector when finished.

Sensor coil resistance

The sensor coil resistance test can be used to confirm the results of the output test performed in the previous section, or to troubleshoot the sensor coil's condition if a PRV is not available.

1. Disconnect the six-pin Packard connector from the ignition module. See **Figure 54**. Install the test adaptor or suitable jumper leads to the white (pin D) and white/blue (pin C) sensor coil leads at the Packard connector.

2. To check the sensor coil for shorts-to-ground, calibrate an ohmmeter on the highest scale available.

NOTE
The sensor coil can be tested for a short-to-ground only when installed.

3. Connect the black ohmmeter lead to a good engine ground. Then connect the red ohmmeter lead to the Packard connector's white (pin D) lead. The meter must

indicate no continuity. If not, replace the sensor coil and retest spark output.

4. Repeat Step 3 for the Packard connector's white/blue (pin C) lead.

5. To check the sensor coil's resistance, calibrate an ohmmeter on the appropriate scale to read 85-115 ohms.

6. Connect the black ohmmeter lead to the Packard connector's white (pin D) lead and the red ohmmeter lead to the connector's white/blue (pin C) lead.

7. The meter must indicate 85-115 ohms. If not, replace the sensor coil and retest spark output.

8. Reconnect the six-pin Packard connector to the ignition module when finished.

Ignition module cranking output test

A peak-reading voltmeter (PRV) is required for this procedure. A PL-88 pack load resistor is not *required*.

1. Disconnect the ignition module's orange/blue primary lead from the ignition coil with a gentle twisting and pulling motion.

2. Adjust a PRV to the negative and 500 settings (or equivalent). Connect the black meter lead to a good engine ground. Connect the red meter lead to the spring clip inside the boot of the orange/blue primary lead.

3. Crank the engine while noting the meter reading. The meter must indicate 125 peak volts or higher. If not, inspect the wiring and connector for damage. Repair any damage and retest the output. If the output is still below 125 volts, replace the ignition module and retest spark output.

4. Reconnect the ignition module's orange/blue lead to the ignition coil primary terminal when finished.

5. Repeat this procedure for the ignition module's orange/green lead.

Ignition coil

If all tests to this point are satisfactory, yet spark output at the air gap tester is not satisfactory, refer to *Ignition Coil Tests* at the beginning of the ignition section and test the dual-potted ignition coil.

Ignition module running output test

This test is intended to diagnose a misfire or ignition failure that occurs at a particular engine speed. Make sure that you operate the engine at the speed that the misfire or failure occurs during this test.

A peak-reading voltmeter (PRV) and two TS-77 terminal extenders (**Table 1**) are required for this procedure.

It is possible for a defective ignition coil to cause the ignition module's output to be below specification. If there

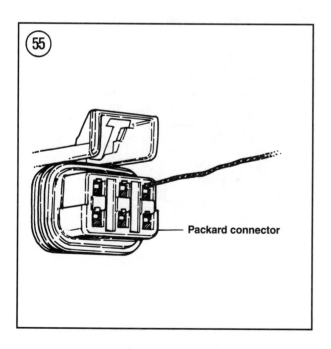

(55)

Packard connector

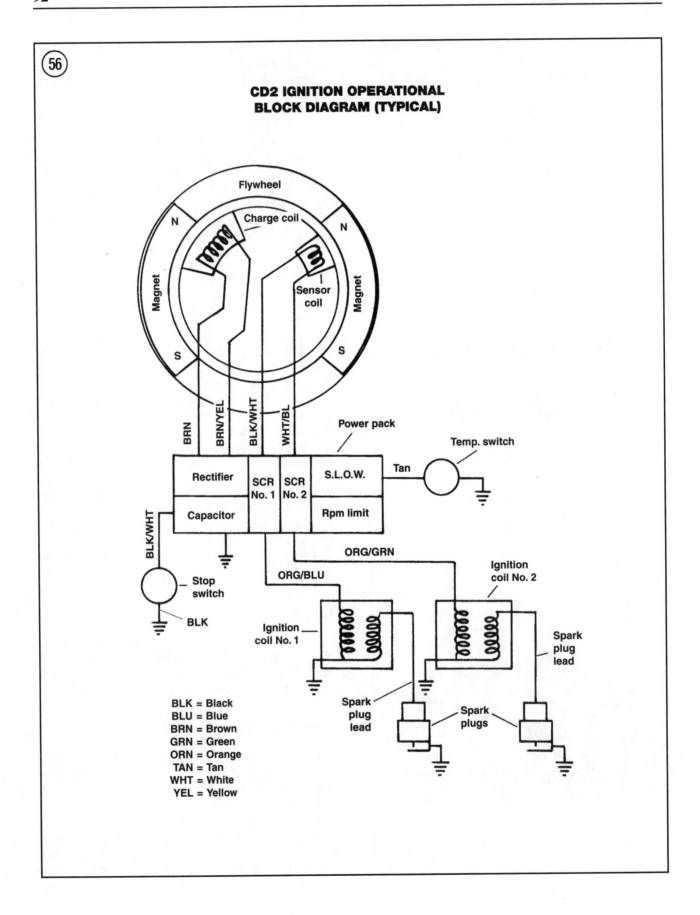

(56)

**CD2 IGNITION OPERATIONAL
BLOCK DIAGRAM (TYPICAL)**

BLK = Black
BLU = Blue
BRN = Brown
GRN = Green
ORN = Orange
TAN = Tan
WHT = White
YEL = Yellow

is any doubt as to the ignition coil's condition, refer to *Ignition Coil Tests* at the beginning of the ignition section and test the dual-potted ignition coil.

1. Disconnect the ignition module's orange/blue and orange/green primary leads from the ignition coil with a gentle twisting and pulling motion.

2. Install a TS-77 terminal extender onto each primary terminal. Then, install the module's orange/blue and orange/green leads onto the appropriate extender.

3. Adjust a PRV to the negative and 500 settings (or equivalent).

4. Connect the black meter lead to a good engine ground. Connect the red meter lead to the exposed metal of the upper (No. 1 cylinder) terminal extender.

CAUTION
Do not run the engine without an adequate water supply and do not exceed 3000 rpm without an adequate load. Refer to Safety Precautions at the beginning of this chapter.

5. Run the engine at the speed that the misfire or ignition failure occurs, while noting the meter reading. The meter must indicate a steady 150 peak volts or higher. If not, check for loose or damaged bullet connectors, damaged leads, loose ground leads and/or component mounting hardware. If all checks are satisfactory, yet the voltage is below 150 volts or erratic, replace the ignition module.

6. Repeat Steps 4-5 for the lower (No. 2 cylinder) terminal extender.

7. Remove the terminal extenders and reconnect the ignition module's primary leads to the appropriate ignition coil primary terminals, making sure the orange/blue lead is connected to the upper (No. 1 cylinder) primary terminal.

CD2 (CAPACITOR DISCHARGE TWO CYLINDER) IGNITION (4 DELUXE, 6-48 HP, 18 JET AND 28 JET EQUIPPED WITH ROPE START AND/OR 4 OR 5 AMP CHARGING SYSTEM)

Description

This ignition system is used on the 4 Deluxe, 6-48 hp, 18 jet and 28 jet models that are rope start or equipped with a 4 or 5 amp unregulated charging system. This ignition system is not used on 40 and 50 hp models equipped with the 12 amp regulated charging system. Refer to **Figure 56** for an operational block diagram of this ignition system and the end of the manual for wiring diagrams.

The major components are the:

1. *Flywheel*—The flywheel contains two magnets along the inner surface of its outer diameter. The magnets leading edge polarities are opposite. Do not attempt to use an older, breaker-point ignition flywheel on these engines. Even though it may fit, it will not operate due to the incorrect polarity of the magnets. The magnets provide power to the charge and sensor coils and the AC lighting coil or 4 amp battery charging system stator coil (if so equipped).

2. *Charge coil*—The charge coil windings provide the power pack with the voltage it needs to operate the ignition system. Charge coil voltage is AC voltage and must be measured with a PRV (peak reading voltmeter). Charge coil failure will always affect both cylinders.

3. *Power pack*—The power pack stores the electricity from the charge coil until the sensor coil tells it to send the electricity to the ignition coils. The power pack uses an internal rectifier to change the charge coil AC voltage to DC (direct current) voltage. The DC voltage is stored in a capacitor (an electrical storage tank) until it is released by an SCR (silicon controlled rectifier), which is simply an electronic switch. There is one SCR for each cylinder. Each SCR is controlled by a sensor coil lead.

The power pack on 20-48 hp, 18 jet and 28 jet models is also equipped with the S.L.O.W. and rpm limit programs described at the beginning of ignition section. Refer to **Table 12** for rpm limit specifications.

For easy identification, the programmed rpm limit and other information is stamped into the power pack. For example, the power pack shown in **Figure 57** is a part No. 484767 CD2 power pack equipped with S.L.O.W. (stamped S) and the rpm limit feature (stamped L/6100).

Use this information to determine if the correct power pack is installed.

On models equipped with a warning horn (all remote control and larger tiller handle models), a blocking diode is used in the engine harness tan lead to prevent the warning system self-test (and oil injection warning signals [40 hp and 28 jet]) from causing the power pack to falsely engage S.L.O.W.

4. *Sensor coil*—The sensor coil tells the power pack when to release the stored electricity in the capacitor to the appropriate ignition coil. The sensor coil on these models uses a single winding and two leads (black/white and white/black). The leads are connected to the SCRs in the power pack.

An SCR is triggered by the first positive pulse of voltage it receives. Because of the polarity of the magnets in the flywheel, one magnet will always cause a positive pulse to first appear in the black/white lead, while the other magnet will always cause a positive pulse to first appear in the white/black lead. Sensor coil failure will always affect both cylinders.

Ignition timing is advanced and retarded by rotating the sensor coil (armature plate assembly) with a mechanical linkage.

5. *Ignition coils*—There is one set of ignition coil windings for each cylinder. The ignition coil transforms the relatively low voltage from the charge coil into voltage high enough (40,000 volts) to jump the spark plug gap and ignite the air/fuel mixture. All models except the 4 Deluxe, 20-30 hp and 18 jet use a dual-potted ignition coil (**Figure 53**). Two sets of ignition coil windings are potted inside one case, but are electrically separate. The 4 Deluxe, 20-30 hp and 18 jet use two separate ignition coils.

6. *Spark plugs*—There is one spark plug for each cylinder. Use only the recommended spark plugs or engine damage may result. Suppressor plugs are designed to reduce RFI (radio frequency interference) emissions that can cause interference with electrical accessories and the ignition system. Failure to use the recommended suppressor spark plug will cause the ignition system to operate erratically.

7. *Stop circuit*—The stop circuit is connected to one end of the capacitor in the power pack. Whenever the stop circuit is connected to ground, the capacitor is shorted and cannot store electricity. At this point, there is no voltage available to send to the ignition coil and the ignition system ceases producing spark. The stop circuit must have an open circuit (to ground) in order for the engine to run.

8. *Engine temperature switch (9.9 and 15 hp [remote control models] and all 20-48 hp, 18 jet, and 28 jet models)*—The engine temperature switch triggers the warning horn (if so equipped) and the S.L.O.W. system (20-48 hp, 18 jet and 28 jet models). The engine temperature switch is normally open and closes when it reaches its specified temperature. Refer to *Engine Temperature Switches*, located later in this chapter.

Troubleshooting

Refer to **Tables 13-15** for specifications and the back of the manual for wiring diagrams. The recommended troubleshooting procedure is:
1. Preliminary checks.
    a. Total output (spark) test.
    b. Stop circuit isolation.
    c. Indexing the flywheel.
2. Sensor coil tests.
3. Power pack cranking output test.
4. Ignition coil tests.
5. Power pack running output test.
6. S.L.O.W. system.
    a. Functional test.
    b. Blocking diode test.

> *WARNING*
> *High voltage is present in the ignition system. **Do not** touch or disconnect ignition components while the engine is being cranked or running.*

Preliminary checks

> *NOTE*
> *Before proceeding, inspect the power pack ground lead and ignition coil ground straps for corrosion, damage, loose connections or loose mounting screws. These components must be securely grounded to operate properly.*

1. Disconnect the spark plug leads from the spark plugs and install an air gap spark tester (**Table 1**) to the spark plug leads. Adjust the air gap to 1/2 in. (12.7 mm). Then, connect the body of the spark tester to a clean engine ground.

2A. *Tiller handle models*—Make sure the safety lanyard is installed on the push-button stop switch. If equipped with an ignition (key) switch, turn the switch to the ON or RUN position.

2B. *Remote control models*—Turn the ignition switch to the ON or RUN position. If equipped with a lanyard safety switch, make sure the lanyard is correctly installed on the switch.

3. Crank the engine while observing the tester. If a crisp, blue spark is noted at each air gap, the ignition system is functioning correctly.
    a. If good spark is noted, yet the engine will not start or does not run correctly, ensure that the correct

spark plugs are installed and that they are in satisfactory condition. Replace the spark plugs if their condition is questionable. If the engine still does not run correctly, proceed to Power pack running output test.

b. If good spark is noted, yet the engine backfires or pops when attempting to start, ensure that the power pack primary leads and secondary leads are correctly routed.

The orange/blue primary lead must be connected to the top ignition coil (or upper primary terminal on dual-potted coils), and the top coil's (or upper secondary terminal on dual-potted coils) spark plug lead must be connected to the top (No. 1 cylinder) spark plug. If the leads are routed correctly, remove the flywheel and check for a sheared flywheel key.

c. If the engine runs erratically or misfires at certain speeds (usually mid-range or above), refer to Indexing flywheel (erratic spark [two- and three-cylinder models]).

d. 20-48 hp, 18 jet and 28 jet models—If the engine only misfires at or very near wide-open throttle, refer to Chapter Five and verify that the engine's W.O.T. (wide-open throttle) speed is within the recommended range. If the speed is exceeding the recommended range, the rpm limit program in the power pack may be the cause of the high speed misfire. Change propellers as necessary to reduce the W.O.T. speed to the recommended range.

e. 20-48 hp, 18 jet and 28 jet models—If the engine speed is limited to approximately 2000-3000 rpm, go to *Engine Temperature and Overheating* and make sure the engine is not overheating. If engine temperature is within specification, go to *S.L.O.W. System Operation (20-48 hp, 18 jet and 28 jet models)*.

f. If no spark, weak spark or erratic spark is noted on one or both cylinders, continue with Step 4.

4. Isolate the stop circuit (black/yellow) lead by disconnecting the power pack's five-pin Amphenol connector.

See **Figure 58**, typical. Connect four jumper leads between the connector bodies so that pins A-D (brown, black/white, white/black and brown/yellow) are connected, but pin E (black/yellow lead) is not connected.

5. Crank the engine while observing the spark tester. If good spark is now noted, the stop circuit (black/yellow lead) is shorted to ground.

a. Tiller handle models—If equipped with an ignition (key) switch, refer to substeb b. If not, replace the push-button stop switch and retest spark output.

b. Remote control models—A short to ground is present in the ignition (key) switch, safety lanyard switch (if equipped), or the main engine harness (and/or boat harness) black/yellow lead. Test, repair or replace the circuit or component as necessary.

6. Remove the jumper leads. Reconnect the five-pin Amphenol connector after completing ignition system troubleshooting.

Charge coil output

A peak-reading voltmeter (PRV), is required for this procedure.

1. Disconnect the power pack's five-pin Amphenol connector. See **Figure 58**, typical. Install suitable Amphenol jumper leads to pins A and D (brown and brown/yellow leads) in the armature plate side of the connector (male body, female pins).

2A. *4 Deluxe-15 hp models*—Adjust a PRV to the negative and 500 settings (or equivalent).

2B. *20-48 hp, 18 jet and 28 jet models*—Adjust a PRV to the positive and 500 settings (or equivalent).

3. To check the charge coil for a short-to-ground, connect the black meter lead to a clean engine ground.

4. Connect the red meter lead to the charge coil's brown lead (Pin A). Crank the engine while noting the meter reading.

5. The meter must read 0 volts. If not, the charge coil (or lead) is shorted to ground. Inspect the lead for damage and repair any found. If the lead is in satisfactory condition, the charge coil must be replaced.

6. Repeat Steps 4-5 for the charge coil's brown/yellow (pin D) lead.

7. To check the output of the charge coil, connect the red meter lead to the coil's brown lead (pin A) and the black meter lead to the coil's brown/yellow lead (pin D).

8. Crank the engine while noting the meter reading. The meter must indicate 230 peak volts or higher. If not, inspect the wiring and connectors for damage. Repair any damage and retest the coil's output. If the output is still below 230 volts, replace the charge coil and retest spark output.

9. Remove the jumper leads and reconnect the five-pin Amphenol connector if ignition troubleshooting is completed.

Charge coil resistance

The charge coil resistance test can be used to confirm the results of the output test performed in the previous section or to determine the charge coil's condition if a PRV is not available.

1. Disconnect the power pack's five-pin Amphenol connector. See **Figure 58**, typical. Install suitable Amphenol jumper leads to pins A and D (brown and brown/yellow leads) in the armature plate side of the connector (male body, female pins).

2A. *4 Deluxe-15 hp (rope start) models*—Calibrate an ohmmeter on the appropriate scale to read 680-840 ohms.

2B. *9.9 and 15 hp (electric start), 20-48 hp, 18 jet and 28 jet models*—Calibrate an ohmmeter on the appropriate scale to read 800-1000 ohms.

3. Connect one ohmmeter lead to the brown charge coil lead (pin A) and the other ohmmeter lead to the brown/yellow charge coil lead (pin D).

4A. *4 Deluxe-15 hp (rope start) models*—If the reading is not within 680-840 ohms, inspect the leads for damage and repair any found. If the leads are in satisfactory condition, the charge coil must be replaced.

4B. *9.9 and 15 hp (electric start), 20-48 hp, 18 jet and 28 jet models*—If the reading is not within 800-1000 ohms, inspect the leads for damage and repair any found. If the leads are in satisfactory condition, the charge coil must be replaced.

5. To check the charge coil for a short-to-ground, calibrate the ohmmeter on the highest scale available. Connect the black ohmmeter lead to a good engine ground. If the coil is removed, connect the lead to a mounting screw bore.

6. Connect the red ohmmeter lead to the coil's brown lead (pin A). Note the meter reading. The meter must indicate no continuity. If not, the charge coil (or lead) is shorted to ground. Inspect the lead for damage and repair any found. If the lead is in satisfactory condition, the charge coil must be replaced.

7. Repeat Step 6 for the charge coil brown/yellow lead (pin D).

8. Remove the jumper leads and reconnect the five-pin Amphenol connector when troubleshooting is completed.

Sensor coil output

A peak-reading voltmeter (PRV) is required for this procedure.

1. Disconnect the power pack's five-pin Amphenol connector. See **Figure 58**, typical. Install suitable Amphenol jumper leads to pins B and C (black/white and white/black leads) in the armature plate side of the connector (male body, female pins).

2A. *4 Deluxe-15 hp models*—Adjust a PRV to the negative (or sensor [SEN]) and 5 settings (or equivalent).

2B. *20-48 hp, 18 jet and 28 jet models*—Adjust a PRV to the positive (or sensor [SEN]) and 5 settings (or equivalent).

3. To check the sensor coil for a short-to-ground, connect the black meter lead to a good engine ground. Connect the red meter lead to the sensor coil's black/white (pin B) lead.

4. Crank the engine while noting the meter reading. The meter must indicate 0 volts. If not, inspect the wiring and connector for damage. Repair any damage and retest. If the meter still indicates any reading other than 0, the sensor coil is shorted to ground and must be replaced.

5. Repeat Steps 3-4 for the sensor coil white/black (pin C) lead.

6. To check the sensor coil's peak voltage output, connect the black meter lead to the sensor coil's black/white (pin B) lead and the red meter lead to the coil's white/black (pin C) lead.

7. Crank the engine while noting the meter reading. The meter must indicate 1.5 peak volts or higher. If not, inspect the wiring and connector for damage. Repair any damage and retest the coil's output. If the output is still below 1.5 volts, replace the sensor coil and retest spark output.

8. Remove the jumper leads and reconnect the five-pin Amphenol connector if ignition troubleshooting is completed.

Sensor coil resistance

The sensor coil resistance test can be used to confirm the results of the output test performed in the previous section, or to troubleshoot the sensor coil's condition if a PRV is not available.

1. Disconnect the power pack's five-pin Amphenol connector. See **Figure 58**, typical. Install suitable Amphenol jumper leads to pins B and C (black/white and white/black leads) of the armature plate side of the connector (male body, female pins).

2. To check the sensor coil for a short-to-ground, calibrate an ohmmeter on the highest scale available.

NOTE
The sensor coil must be installed (on the armature plate) to be tested for a short-to-ground.

3. Connect the black ohmmeter lead to a good engine ground, such as the armature plate. Then connect the red ohmmeter lead to the sensor coil's black/white (pin B) lead. Note the meter reading. The meter must indicate no continuity. If not, inspect the lead for damage and repair any found. If the lead is in satisfactory condition, replace the sensor coil and retest the spark output.

4. Repeat Step 3 for the sensor coil's white/black (pin C) lead.

5. To check the sensor coil's resistance, calibrate an ohmmeter on the appropriate scale to read 30-50 ohms.

6. Connect the black ohmmeter lead to the sensor coil's black/white (pin B) lead and the red ohmmeter lead to the coil's white/black (pin C) lead.

7. Note the meter reading, the meter must indicate 30-50 ohms. If not, replace the sensor coil and retest spark output.

8. Remove the jumper leads and reconnect the five-pin Amphenol connector when finished.

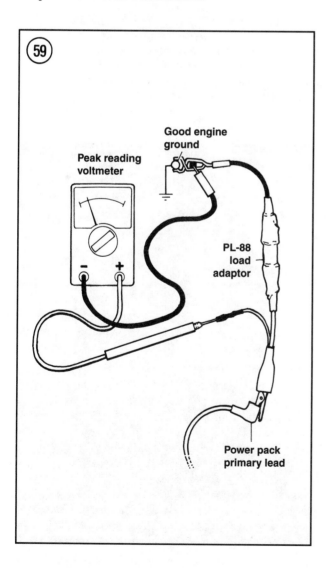

(59)

Peak reading voltmeter

Good engine ground

PL-88 load adaptor

Power pack primary lead

Power pack cranking output

A peak-reading voltmeter (PRV) and a PL-88 pack load resistor (**Table 1**) are required for this procedure.

1. Disconnect the power pack's orange/blue primary lead from the top ignition coil (or upper primary terminal on dual-potted coils) with a gentle twisting and pulling motion.

2. Connect the small, insulated alligator clip of the PL-88 to the power pack orange/blue lead. Then connect the large uninsulated alligator clip to a good engine ground. See **Figure 59**.

3A. *4 Deluxe-15 hp models*—Adjust a PRV to the negative and 500 settings (or equivalent).

3B. *20-48 hp, 18 jet and 28 jet models*—Adjust a PRV to the positive and 500 settings (or equivalent).

4. Connect the black meter lead to a good engine ground. Connect the red meter lead to the PL-88's pigtail lead (with the Amphenol socket). See **Figure 59**.

5. Crank the engine while noting the meter reading.

    a. 4 Deluxe-30 hp and 18 jet models—The meter must indicate 175 peak volts or higher. If not, inspect the wiring and connector for damage. Repair any damage and retest the output. If the output is still below 175 volts, replace the power pack and retest spark output.

    b. 40-48 hp and 28 jet models—The meter must indicate 150 peak volts or higher. If not, inspect the wiring and connector for damage. Repair any damage and retest the output. If the output is still below 150 volts, replace the power pack and retest spark output.

6. Remove the power pack's orange/blue lead from the PL-88 and reconnect it to the top ignition coil (or upper primary terminal).

7. Repeat Steps 1-6 for the power pack's orange/green primary lead (bottom ignition coil [or lower primary terminal on dual-potted coils]).

8. Remove the PL-88 and reconnect the power pack's orange/green lead to the ignition coil primary terminal when finished.

Ignition coil

If all tests to this point are satisfactory, yet spark output at the air gap tester is not satisfactory, refer to *Ignition Coil Tests* at the beginning of the ignition section and test the ignition coil(s).

Power pack running output test

This test is intended to diagnose a misfire or ignition failure that occurs at a particular engine speed. Make sure that you operate the engine at the speed that the misfire or failure occurs during this test.

A peak-reading voltmeter (PRV) and two TS-77 terminal extenders (**Table 1**) are required for this procedure.

It is possible for a defective ignition coil to cause the power pack output to be below specification. If there is any doubt as to the ignition coil's condition, refer to *Ignition Coil Tests* at the beginning of the ignition section and test the ignition coil(s).

1. Disconnect the power pack's orange/blue and orange/green primary leads from the ignition coil(s) with a gentle twisting and pulling motion.

2. Install a TS-77 terminal extender onto each primary terminal. Then, install the pack's orange/blue and orange/green leads onto the appropriate extender.

3A. *4 Deluxe-15 hp models*—Adjust a PRV to the negative and 500 settings (or equivalent).

3B. *20-48 hp, 18 Jet and 28 Jet models*—Adjust a PRV to the positive and 500 settings (or equivalent).

4. Connect the black meter lead to a good engine ground. Connect the red meter lead to the exposed metal of the upper (No. 1 cylinder) terminal extender.

CAUTION
*Do not run the engine without an adequate water supply and do not exceed 3000 rpm without an adequate load. Refer to **Safety Precautions** at the beginning of this chapter.*

5. Run the engine at the speed that the misfire or ignition failure occurs, while noting the meter reading

   a. *4 Deluxe-30 hp and 18 jet models*—The meter must indicate a steady 200 peak volts or higher. If not, check for loose or damaged connectors, damaged leads, loose ground leads and/or component mounting hardware. If all checks are satisfactory, yet the voltage is below 200 volts or erratic, replace the power pack and retest spark output.

   b. *40-48 hp and 28 jet models*—The meter must indicate a steady 175 peak volts or higher. If not, check for loose or damaged connectors, damaged leads, loose ground leads and/or component mounting hardware. If all checks are satisfactory, yet the voltage is below 175 volts or erratic, replace the power pack and retest spark output.

6. Repeat Steps 4-5 for the lower (No. 2 cylinder) terminal extender.

7. Remove the terminal extenders and reconnect the power pack's primary leads to the appropriate ignition coil terminals, making sure the orange/blue lead is connected to the top ignition coil or upper primary terminal (No. 1 cylinder).

S.L.O.W. System Operation
(20-48 hp, 18 Jet and 28 Jet Models)

These models are equipped with the speed limiting overheat warning (S.L.O.W.) system. The system is designed to activate the warning system and limit engine speed to approximately 2000-3000 rpm anytime the engine temperature exceeds the temperature switch's closing value. To deactivate S.L.O.W., the engine must be throttled back to idle (or stopped), and allowed to cool to a point below the temperature switch's opening value. Temperature switch values are as follows:

1. *20-30 hp (two-cylinder) and 18 jet models*—These models use a 180° F (82° C) temperature switch. The switch is identified by its tan/red lead. The switch must close at 174-186° F (79-86° C) and open at 140-170° F (60-77° C).

NOTE
Early 1995 (EO) 40 hp, 48 hp and 28 jet models were factory-equipped with a 203° F (95° C) temperature switch, identified by its solid tan lead. This switch can cause false overheat signals in some circumstances. If false overheat signals are an ongoing problem, these engines can be upgraded to the

237° F (114° C) switch described below. Also replace the thermostat spring with part No. 342421 (color-coded red).

2. *40 hp, 48 hp and 28 jet models*—These models use a 237° F (114° C) temperature switch. The switch is identified by its tan/blue lead. The switch must close at 231-243° F (111-117° C) and open at 192-222° F (89-106° C).

S.L.O.W. system troubleshooting

If the S.L.O.W. system engages during normal operation, proceed as follows:

1. Refer to *Engine Temperature and Overheating* and verify that the engine is not overheating. If the engine is overheating, repair the cooling system as necessary and recheck the engine's operating temperature.

2. If the engine temperature is within specification, disconnect the temperature switch lead at its bullet (or 1-pin Amphenol) connector. See **Figure 60** and **Figure 61**, typical. Tape or sleeve the engine harness end of the lead if necessary, to make sure it cannot contact engine ground.

3. Start the engine and check for S.L.O.W. engagement.

NOTE
If the temperature switch's tan lead is routed too close to the spark plug leads or ignition coil(s), RFI (radio frequency interference) can cause the power pack to falsely engage S.L.O.W. Route the tan lead as far away from the ignition coils and spark plug leads as possible.

4A. If the S.L.O.W. system still engages, refer to *Blocking diode tests* located later in this section. If the blocking diode tests satisfactorily, test the engine (and boat) harness tan lead for a short-to-ground. Repair or replace the lead as necessary. If the tan lead tests satisfactorily, replace the power pack.

4B. If the S.L.O.W. system no longer engages, the temperature switch is shorted to ground and must be replaced.

S.L.O.W. system functional tests

The S.L.O.W. system is activated by input from the engine temperature switch. The temperature switch is located near the top of the cylinder head. To perform a functional test of S.L.O.W. operation and troubleshoot all system functions, proceed as follows:

CAUTION
*Do not run the engine without an adequate water supply and do not exceed 3000 rpm without an adequate load. Refer to **Safety Precautions** at the beginning of this chapter.*

1. Connect an accurate shop tachometer to the spark plug lead following its manufacturer's instructions.

2. Disconnect the engine temperature switch at its bullet (or 1-pin Amphenol) connector. See **Figure 60** and **Figure 61**, typical.

3. Start the engine and allow it to warm to normal operating temperature. Then increase engine speed to approximately 3500 rpm.

4. Using a suitable jumper lead, connect the engine harness end of the tan lead to a clean engine ground while noting the engine speed.

5. If S.L.O.W. engages, engine speed will quickly be reduced to approximately 2000-3000 rpm and stabilize. It is not necessary to continue to hold the tan lead to ground once S.L.O.W. engaged (latched).

  a. If S.L.O.W. did not engage, test the blocking diode for an open condition as described in *Blocking diode test*. If the blocking diode tests satisfactorily, test the tan lead for an open circuit between the power pack tan lead bullet (or one-pin Amphenol) connector and the temperature switch connector. Repair or replace the tan lead as necessary. If the diode and the tan lead test satisfactorily, replace the power pack and retest the S.L.O.W. function.

b. If S.L.O.W. correctly engages, proceed to Step 6.

6. If S.L.O.W. engages in Step 5, disconnect the tan lead from ground and reduce engine speed to idle (or briefly turn the engine off). Then attempt to accelerate the engine to 3500 rpm.

a. If the engine will now freely accelerate above the S.L.O.W. limit (2000-3000 rpm), the power pack programming and engine wiring harness is functioning correctly.

b. If the engine still remains in S.L.O.W., disconnect the power pack tan lead at its bullet (or one-pin Amphenol) connector and retest. If the engine will now freely accelerate above the S.L.O.W. limit, the tan lead is shorted to ground. Repair or replace the tan lead as necessary. If the tan lead is not shorted to ground and the engine still will not rev above the S.L.O.W. limit, replace the power pack.

Blocking diode tests

On 20-30 hp (two-cylinder) remote control models and all 40-48 hp electric start models a blocking diode is used to prevent the warning system from activating the S.L.O.W. function during the warning system's self-test. The S.L.O.W. program must only activate if the engine is actually overheating. The blocking diode is located in the engine wiring harness tan lead.

The diode is positioned near the large, red ten-pin main harness connector on 1995 (EO) models and near the six-pin Deutsch system check harness connector on 1996-2003 (ED-ST) models.

If the diode fails in an open circuit, the S.L.O.W. program will still engage, but the operator will not get a warning horn signal (or LED on system check models).

If the diode fails in a closed circuit, the S.L.O.W. program may engage when the warning system self-tests and/or when the oil injection system's low oil or no oil warning signals are activated.

To test the blocking diode, refer to the back of the manual for wiring diagrams and proceed as follows:

1. Disconnect the negative battery cable. Then disconnect and ground the spark plug leads to the power head to prevent accidental starting.

2A. *Traditional wiring harnesses (1995 [EO] models)*—Disconnect the large, red ten-pin main harness connector. Then disconnect the engine temperature switch at its bullet (or one-pin Amphenol) connector.

2B. *Modular wiring harnesses (1996-2003 [ED-ST] models)*—Disconnect the engine harness from the boat wiring harness at the engine's six-pin Deutsch connector. Then disconnect the engine temperature switch at its bullet (or one-pin Amphenol) connector.

3. Calibrate an ohmmeter on the appropriate scale to test diodes.

4A. *Traditional wiring harnesses*—Using suitable jumper leads, connect one ohmmeter lead to the engine harness side of the tan temperature switch lead connector and the other ohmmeter lead to the tan pin (7, **Figure 62**) of the engine harness side of the large, red ten-pin connector.

4B. *Modular wiring harnesses*—Using suitable jumper leads, connect one ohmmeter lead to the engine harness side of the temperature switch's tan lead connector and the other ohmmeter lead to the tan lead (pin 6) of the engine harness side of the six-pin Deutsch connector.

5. Note the ohmmeter reading, then reverse the meter leads (or meter polarity).

a. The meter must indicate no continuity (very high reading) in one polarity and continuity (low reading) in the opposite polarity.

b. If the meter reads no continuity (very high reading) in both polarities, the diode has failed in an open circuit and must be replaced.

c. If the meter reads continuity (low reading) in both polarities, the diode has failed in a closed circuit (shorted) and must be replaced.

6. Reconnect all leads when finished. Connect the spark plug leads and negative battery cable last.

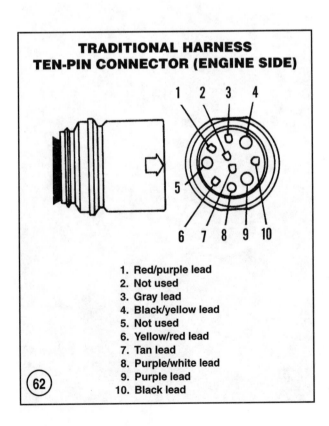

TRADITIONAL HARNESS TEN-PIN CONNECTOR (ENGINE SIDE)

1. Red/purple lead
2. Not used
3. Gray lead
4. Black/yellow lead
5. Not used
6. Yellow/red lead
7. Tan lead
8. Purple/white lead
9. Purple lead
10. Black lead

62

CD2 (CAPACITOR DISCHARGE TWO CYLINDER) IGNITION (40 HP, 50 HP AND 35 JET MODELS EQUIPPED WITH 12 AMP REGULATED CHARGING SYSTEM)

Description

This ignition system is used on 40 hp and 50 hp (two-cylinder) and 35 jet models equipped with the 12 amp regulated charging system. It is not used on 40 hp and 50 hp models equipped with the 4 amp unregulated charging system (or any three-cylinder models). The 12 amp charging system can be easily identified by the presence of the large, finned (air-cooled) rectifier/regulator. See **Figure 63**. Refer to the end of the manual for wiring diagrams.

The major components are the:

1. *Flywheel*—The flywheel contains magnets along the inner surface of its outer diameter and around the center hub. The outer magnets provide power to the charge and power coils, as well as the 12 amp stator coil windings. The inner magnets provide power to the sensor coils. The flywheel is unique to this charging system and cannot be substituted with a 4 amp flywheel.

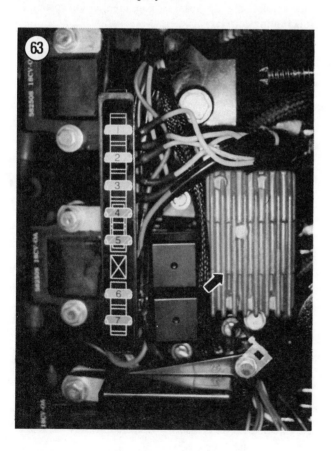

2. *Charge coil*—The charge coil windings provide the power pack with the voltage it needs to operate the ignition system. Charge coil output is AC voltage and must be measured with a PRV (peak reading voltmeter). Charge coil failure will always affect both cylinders. The charge coil is potted into the stator assembly along with the alternator stator coils and the power coil.

3. *Power pack*—The power pack stores the electricity from the charge coil until the sensor coil tells it to send the electricity to the ignition coils. The power pack uses an internal rectifier to change the charge coil AC voltage to DC (direct current) voltage. The DC voltage is stored in a capacitor (an electrical storage tank), until it is released by an SCR (silicon controlled rectifier), which is simply an electronic switch. There is one SCR for each cylinder. Each SCR is controlled by a sensor coil lead.

The power pack on these models is also equipped with the S.L.O.W. and rpm limit programs described at the beginning of ignition section. Refer to **Table 12** for rpm limit specifications.

The power pack is marked with information that can be used to determine if the correct power pack is installed. For example, a power pack stamped CD2SL/6700 indicates that it is for a CD2 ignition system equipped with S.L.O.W. (stamped S) and a 6700 rpm limit (stamped L/6700).

All models are equipped with a blocking diode in the engine harness tan lead. The blocking diode prevents the warning system self-test and oil injection warning signals from causing the power pack to falsely engage the S.L.O.W. function.

4. *Sensor coil*—The sensor coil tells the power pack when to release the stored electricity in the capacitor to the appropriate ignition coil. The sensor coil on these models uses two separate windings connected by a common white (return) lead. The blue lead triggers cylinder No. 1 and the green lead triggers cylinder No. 2. The blue and green leads are connected to the SCRs in the power pack.

An SCR is triggered by the first positive pulse of voltage it receives. Since there are two windings, each SCR is triggered by its dedicated sensor coil winding. Failure of a single coil or single lead (blue or green) will cause only one cylinder to fail. Failure of the common (white) lead will generally cause erratic spark and erratic ignition timing.

Ignition timing is advanced and retarded by rotating the sensor coils (timer base) with a mechanical linkage.

5. *Ignition coils*—There is one set of ignition coil windings for each cylinder. The ignition coil transforms the relatively low voltage from the charge coil into voltage high enough (40,000 volts) to jump the spark plug gap and ignite the air/fuel mixture. All models use a dual-potted

ignition coil. Two sets of ignition coil windings are potted inside one case, but are electrically separate.

6. *Spark plugs*—There is one spark plug for each cylinder. Use only the recommended spark plugs or engine damage may result. Suppressor plugs are designed to reduce RFI (radio frequency interference) emissions that can cause interference with electrical accessories and the ignition system. Failure to use the recommended suppressor spark plug will cause the ignition system to operate erratically.

7. *Stop circuit*—The stop circuit is connected to one end of the capacitor in the power pack. Whenever the stop circuit is connected to ground the capacitor is shorted and cannot store electricity. At this point there is no voltage available to send to the ignition coil and the ignition system ceases producing spark. The stop circuit must have an open circuit (to ground) for the engine to run. Tiller handle (electric start models) and all remote control models use an ignition (key) switch.

8. *Engine temperature switch*—The engine temperature switch triggers the warning system and the S.L.O.W. system. The engine temperature switch is normally open and closes when it reaches its specified temperature. Refer to *Engine Temperature Switches*, located in this chapter.

9. *Power coil*—The power coil provides the electricity the power pack needs to operate the S.L.O.W. system. The power coil is potted in the stator assembly along with the charge coil and alternator stator coils. The power coil windings are connected to the power pack with two leads (orange and orange/black). Failure of the power coil will result in the S.L.O.W. system not functioning.

Troubleshooting

Refer to **Tables 13-15** for specifications and the back of the manual for wiring diagrams. The recommended troubleshooting procedure is:

1. Preliminary checks.
   a. Total output (spark) test.
   b. Stop circuit isolation.
   c. Indexing the flywheel.
2. Sensor coil tests.
3. Ignition module cranking output test.
4. Ignition coil tests.
5. Ignition module running output test.
6. S.L.O.W. system.
   a. Functional test.
   b. Power coil test.
   c. Blocking diode test.

> *WARNING*
> *High voltage is present in the ignition system.* ***Do not*** *touch or disconnect ignition components while the engine is being cranked or running.*

Preliminary checks

> *NOTE*
> *Before proceeding, inspect the power pack ground lead and ignition coil ground straps for corrosion, damage, loose connections or loose mounting screws. These components must be securely grounded in order to operate properly.*

1. Disconnect the spark plug leads from the spark plugs and install an air gap spark tester (**Table 1**) to the spark plug leads. Adjust the air gap to 1/2 in. (12.7 mm). Then, connect the body of the spark tester to a clean engine ground.

2A. *Tiller handle models*—Make sure the safety lanyard is installed on the push-button stop switch. Then turn the ignition (key) switch to the ON or RUN position.

2B. *Remote control models*—Turn the ignition switch to the ON or RUN position. If equipped with a lanyard safety switch, make sure the lanyard is correctly installed on the switch.

3. Crank the engine while observing the tester. If a crisp, blue spark is noted at each air gap, the ignition system is functioning correctly.
   a. If good spark is noted, yet the engine will not start or does not run correctly, ensure that the correct spark plugs are installed and that they are in satisfactory condition. Replace the spark plugs if their condition is questionable. If the engine still does not run correctly, proceed to Power pack running output test.
   b. If good spark is noted, yet the engine backfires or pops when attempting to start, ensure that the power pack primary leads and secondary leads are correctly routed on the ignition coil. The orange/blue primary lead must be connected to the upper primary terminal and the upper secondary terminal's spark plug lead must be connected to the top (No. 1 cylinder) spark plug. If the leads are routed correctly, remove the flywheel and check for a sheared flywheel key.
   c. If the engine runs erratically or misfires at certain speeds (usually mid-range or above), refer to Indexing flywheel (erratic spark [two- and three-cylinder models]). Make sure you check the sensor coil common (white) lead for an open circuit or loose connection.
   d. If the engine only misfires at or very near wide-open throttle, refer to Chapter Five and verify that the engine's W.O.T. (wide-open throttle) speed is within the recommended range. If the W.O.T. speed is exceeding the recommended range, the rpm limit pro-

gram in the power pack may be the cause of the high speed misfire. Change propellers as necessary to reduce the W.O.T. speed into the recommended range.

   e. If the engine speed is limited to approximately 2000-3000 rpm, go to *Engine Temperature and Overheating* and make sure the engine is not overheating. If engine temperature is within specification, go to *S.L.O.W. System Operation (40-50 hp [two-cylinder] and 35 jet models)*.

   f. If no spark, weak spark or erratic spark is noted on one or both cylinders, continue with Step 4.

4. Isolate the stop circuit (black/yellow) lead by disconnecting the power pack's five-pin Amphenol connector. Connect few jumper leads between the connector bodies so pins A-D (brown, brown/yellow, orange and orange/black) are connected, but pin E (black/yellow lead) is not connected.

5. Crank the engine while observing the spark tester. If good spark is now noted, the stop circuit (black/yellow lead) is shorted to ground.

   a. Tiller handle models—A short to ground is present in the combination push-button stop switch/safety lanyard switch, the ignition (key) switch or the main engine harness black/yellow lead. Test, repair or replace the circuit or component as necessary.

   b. Remote control models—A short to ground is present in the ignition (key) switch, safety lanyard switch (if equipped) or the main engine harness (and/or boat harness) black/yellow lead. Test, repair or replace the circuit or component as necessary.

6. Remove the jumper leads. Reconnect the five-pin Amphenol connector if finished with ignition system troubleshooting.

Charge coil output

   A peak-reading voltmeter (PRV) is required for this procedure.

1. Disconnect the power pack's five-pin Amphenol connector. Install suitable Amphenol jumper leads to pins A and B (brown and brown/yellow leads) of the stator side of the connector (male body, female pins).

2. Adjust a PRV to the *positive* and *500* settings (or equivalent).

3. To check the charge coil for a short to ground, connect the black meter lead to a clean engine ground.

4. Connect the red meter lead to the charge coil's brown lead (pin A). Crank the engine while noting the meter reading.

5. The meter must read 0 volts. If not, the charge coil (or lead) is shorted to ground. Inspect the lead for damage and

repair any found. If the lead is in satisfactory condition, the charge coil (stator assembly) must be replaced.

6. Repeat Steps 4-5 for the charge coil's brown/yellow (pin B) lead.

7. To check the output of the charge coil, connect the red meter lead to the coil's brown lead (pin A) and the black meter lead to the coil's brown/yellow lead (pin B).

8. Crank the engine while noting the meter reading. The meter must indicate 230 peak volts or higher. If not, inspect the wiring and connectors for damage. Repair any damage and retest the coil's output. If the output is still below 230 volts, replace the charge coil (stator assembly) and retest spark output.

9. Remove the jumper leads and reconnect the five-pin Amphenol connector if ignition troubleshooting is completed.

Charge coil resistance

   The charge coil resistance tests can be used to confirm the results of the output test performed in the previous section, or to determine the charge coil's condition if a PRV is not available.

1. Disconnect the power pack's five-pin Amphenol connector. Install suitable Amphenol jumper leads to pins A and B (brown and brown/yellow leads) of the stator side of the connector (male body, female pins).

2. Calibrate an ohmmeter on the appropriate scale to read 750-950 ohms.

3. Connect one ohmmeter lead to the charge coil brown lead (pin A) and the other ohmmeter lead to the charge coil brown/yellow lead (pin B).

4. If the reading is not within 750-950 ohms, inspect the leads for damage and repair any found. If the leads are in satisfactory condition, the charge coil (stator assembly) must be replaced.

5. To check the charge coil for a short to ground, calibrate the ohmmeter on the highest scale available. Connect the black ohmmeter lead to a good engine ground. If the coil is removed, connect the lead to a mounting screw bore.

6. Connect the red ohmmeter lead to the coil's brown lead (pin A). Note the meter reading. The meter must indicate no continuity. If not, the charge coil (or lead) is shorted to ground. Inspect the lead for damage and repair any found. If the lead is in satisfactory condition, the charge coil (stator assembly) must be replaced.

7. Repeat Step 6 for the charge coil brown/yellow lead (pin B).

8. Remove the jumper leads and reconnect the five-pin Amphenol connector if ignition troubleshooting is completed.

3

Sensor coil output

A peak-reading voltmeter (PRV) is required for this procedure. There are two sensor windings in this sensor coil assembly. One winding consists of the blue (pin A) and white (pin B) leads. The second winding consists of the green (pin C) and white (pin B) leads. The white lead is the common (return) lead for both windings.

1. Disconnect the power pack's three-pin Amphenol connector. Install suitable Amphenol jumper leads to pins A, B and C (blue, white and green) of the timer base side of the connector (male body, female pins).

2. Adjust a PRV to the *positive (or sensor [SEN])* and *5* settings (or equivalent).

3. To check the sensor coil for a short-to-ground, connect the black meter lead to a good engine ground. Connect the red meter lead to the sensor coil's blue (pin A) lead.

4. Crank the engine while noting the meter reading. The meter must indicate 0 volts. If not, inspect the wiring and connector for damage. Repair any damage and retest. If the meter still indicates any reading other than 0, the sensor coil is shorted to ground and must be replaced.

5. Repeat Steps 3-4 for the sensor coil white and green (pins B and C) leads.

6. To check the sensor coil's peak voltage output, connect the black meter lead to the sensor coil's white (pin B) lead and the red meter lead to the coil's blue (pin A) lead.

7. Crank the engine while noting the meter reading. The meter must indicate 0.5 peak volt or higher. If not, inspect the wiring and connector for damage. Repair any damage and retest the coil's output. If the output is still below 0.5 volt, replace the sensor coil (timer base) and retest the spark output.

8. Repeat Steps 6-7 with the red meter lead connected to the sensor coil green (pin C) lead.

9. Remove the jumper leads and reconnect the three-pin Amphenol connector if ignition troubleshooting is completed.

Sensor coil resistance

The sensor coil resistance test can be used to confirm the results of the output test performed in the previous section, or to troubleshoot the sensor coil's condition if a PRV is not available.

1. Disconnect the power pack's three-pin Amphenol connector. Install suitable Amphenol jumper leads to pins A, B and C (blue, white and green leads) of the armature plate side of the connector (male body, female pins).

2. To check the sensor coil for a short to ground, calibrate an ohmmeter on the highest scale available.

3. Connect the black ohmmeter lead to a good engine ground, such as a metal portion of the timer base. Then connect the red ohmmeter lead to the sensor coil's blue (pin A) lead. Note the meter reading. The meter must indicate no continuity. If not, inspect the lead for damage and repair any found. If the lead is in satisfactory condition, replace the sensor coil (timer base) and retest spark output.

4. Repeat Step 3 for the sensor coil's white and green (pins B and C) leads. Each lead must indicate no continuity to ground.

5. To check the sensor coil's resistance, calibrate an ohmmeter on the appropriate scale to read 22-32 ohms.

6. Connect the black ohmmeter lead to the sensor coil's white (pin B) lead and the red ohmmeter lead to the coil's blue (pin A) lead.

7. The meter must indicate 22-32 ohms. If not, replace the sensor coil (timer base) and retest spark output.

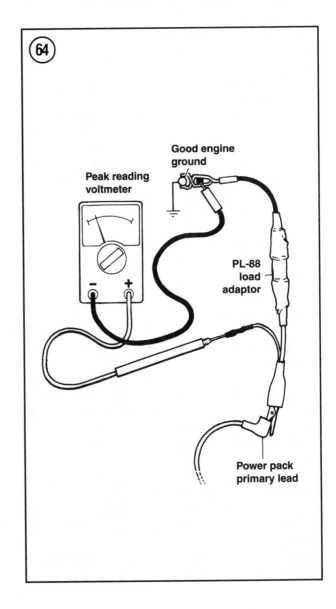

8. Move the meter's red lead to the sensor coil's green (pin C) lead. The meter must indicate 22-32 ohms. If not, replace the sensor coil (timer base) and retest spark output.

9. Remove the jumper leads and reconnect the three-pin Amphenol connector when finished.

Power pack cranking output

A peak-reading voltmeter (PRV) and a PL-88 pack load resistor (**Table 1**) are required for this procedure.

1. Disconnect the power pack's orange/blue primary lead from the ignition coil's upper primary terminal with a gentle twisting and pulling motion.

2. Connect the small, insulated alligator clip of the PL-88 to the power pack orange/blue lead. Then connect the large uninsulated alligator clip to a good engine ground. See **Figure 64**.

3. Adjust a PRV to the *positive* and *500* settings (or equivalent).

4. Connect the black meter lead to a good engine ground. Connect the red meter lead to the PL-88's pigtail lead (with the Amphenol socket). See **Figure 64**.

5. Crank the engine while noting the meter reading. The meter must indicate 150 peak volts or higher. If not, inspect the wiring and connector for damage. Repair any damage and retest the output. If the output is still below 150 volts, replace the power pack and retest spark output.

6. Remove the power pack's orange/blue lead from the PL-88 and reconnect it to the ignition coil's upper primary terminal.

7. Repeat Steps 1-6 for the power pack's orange/green primary lead (ignition coil's lower primary terminal).

8. Remove the PL-88 and reconnect the power pack's orange/green lead to the ignition coil's lower primary terminal when finished.

Ignition coil

If all tests to this point are satisfactory, yet spark output at the air gap tester is not satisfactory, refer to *Ignition Coil Tests* at the beginning of the ignition section and test the ignition coil(s).

Power pack running output test

This test is intended to diagnose a misfire or ignition failure that occurs at a particular engine speed. Make sure that you operate the engine at the speed that the misfire or failure occurs during this test.

A peak-reading voltmeter (PRV) and two TS-77 terminal extenders (**Table 1**) are required for this procedure.

It is possible for a defective ignition coil to cause the power pack output to be below specification. If there is any doubt as to the ignition coil's condition, refer to *Ignition Coil Tests* at the beginning of the ignition section and test the ignition coil(s).

1. Disconnect the power pack's orange/blue and orange/green primary leads from the ignition coil primary terminals with a gentle twisting and pulling motion.

2. Install a TS-77 terminal extender onto each primary terminal. Then install the pack's orange/blue and orange/green leads onto the appropriate extender.

3. Adjust a PRV to the *positive* and *500* settings (or equivalent).

4. Connect the black meter lead to a good engine ground. Connect the red meter lead to the exposed metal of the upper (No. 1 cylinder) terminal extender.

CAUTION
Do not run the engine without an adequate water supply and do not exceed 3000 rpm without an adequate load. Refer to Safety Precautions at the beginning of this chapter.

5. Run the engine at the speed that the misfire or ignition failure occurs, while noting the meter reading. The meter must indicate a steady 175 peak volts or higher. If not, check for loose or damaged connectors, damaged leads, loose ground leads and/or component mounting hardware. If all checks are satisfactory, yet the voltage is below 175 volts or erratic, replace the power pack and retest spark output.

6. Repeat Steps 4-5 for the lower (No. 2 cylinder) terminal extender.

7. Remove the terminal extenders and reconnect the power pack's primary leads to the appropriate ignition coil terminals, making sure the orange/blue lead is connected to the top ignition coil or upper primary terminal (No. 1 cylinder).

S.L.O.W. System Operation (40 hp and 50 hp [Two-cylinder] and 35 Jet Models With 12 Amp Charging System)

These models are equipped with the speed limiting overheat warning (S.L.O.W.) system. The system is designed to activate the warning system and limit engine speed to approximately 2000-3000 rpm anytime the engine temperature exceeds the temperature switch's closing value.

To deactivate (reset) the S.L.O.W. system, the engine must be stopped and allowed to cool to a point below the temperature switch's opening value. These engines must be equipped with a 237° F (114° C) temperature switch.

3

The switch is identified by its tan/blue lead. The switch must close at 231-243° F (111-117° C) and open at 192-222° F (89-106° C).

> *NOTE*
> *Early 1995 (EO) models were factory-equipped with a 203° F (95° C) temperature switch, identified by its solid tan lead. This switch can cause false overheat signals in some circumstances. If false overheat signals are an ongoing problem, these engines can be upgraded to the 237° F (114° C) switch described previously. The thermostat spring must also be replaced with part No. 342421 (color-coded red).*

The S.L.O.W. system receives its operating voltage from the power coil. The power coil is potted in the stator assembly along with the charge coil and alternator stator coil. If the power coil fails, the S.L.O.W. system will not operate.

S.L.O.W. system troubleshooting

If the S.L.O.W. system engages during normal operation, proceed as follows:

1. Refer to *Engine Temperature and Overheating* and verify that the engine is not overheating. If the engine is overheating, repair the cooling system as necessary and recheck the engine's operating temperature.

2. If engine temperature is within specification, disconnect the temperature switch lead at its bullet (or one-pin Amphenol) connector. See **Figure 65**, typical. To make sure it cannot contact engine ground, tape or sleeve the engine harness end of the lead if necessary.

> *NOTE*
> *If the temperature switch's tan or tan/blue lead is routed too close to the spark plug leads or ignition coil(s), RFI (radio frequency interference) can cause the power pack to falsely engage S.L.O.W. Route the tan lead as far away from the ignition coils and spark plug leads as possible.*

3. Start the engine and check for S.L.O.W. engagement.

4A. If the S.L.O.W. system still engages, refer to *Blocking diode tests* located later in this section. If the blocking diode tests satisfactorily, test the engine (and boat) harness tan lead for a short-to-ground. Repair or replace the lead as necessary. If the tan lead tests satisfactorily, replace the power pack.

4B. If the S.L.O.W. system no longer engages, the temperature switch is shorted to ground and must be replaced.

S.L.O.W. system functional tests

The S.L.O.W. system is activated by input from the engine temperature switch. The temperature switch is located near the top of the cylinder head. To perform a functional test of S.L.O.W. operation and troubleshoot all system functions, proceed as follows:

> *CAUTION*
> *Do not run the engine without an adequate water supply and do not exceed 3000 rpm without an adequate load. Refer to **Safety Precautions** at the beginning of this chapter.*

1. Connect an accurate shop tachometer to the spark plug lead following its manufacturer's instructions.

2. Disconnect the engine temperature switch at its bullet (or one-pin Amphenol) connector. See **Figure 65**, typical.

3. Start the engine and allow it to warm to normal operating temperature. Then increase engine speed to approximately 3500 rpm.

4. Using a suitable jumper lead, connect the engine harness tan lead to a clean engine ground while noting the engine speed.

5. If S.L.O.W. engages, engine speed will quickly be reduced to approximately 2000-3000 rpm and stabilize. It

is not necessary to continue to hold the tan lead to ground once S.L.O.W. has been engaged (latched). If S.L.O.W. correctly engages, proceed to Step 6. If not, proceed as follows:

a. Test the blocking diode for an open condition as described in *Blocking diode tests*.

b. If the blocking diode tests satisfactorily, test the tan lead for an open circuit between the power pack tan lead bullet (or one-pin Amphenol) connector and the temperature switch connector. Repair or replace the tan lead as necessary.

c. If the diode and the tan lead test satisfactorily, test the power coil as described in *Power coil tests*. If the power coil tests satisfactorily, replace the power pack and retest the S.L.O.W. function.

6. If S.L.O.W. engages in Step 5, disconnect the tan lead from ground and stop the engine. Restart the engine and attempt to accelerate the engine to 3500 rpm.

a. If the engine will now freely accelerate above the S.L.O.W. limit (2000-3000 rpm), the power pack programming and engine wiring harness are functioning correctly.

b. If the engine still remains in S.L.O.W., disconnect the power pack tan lead at its bullet (or one-pin Amphenol) connector and retest. If the engine will now freely accelerate above the S.L.O.W. limit, the tan lead is shorted to ground. Repair or replace the tan lead as necessary. If the tan lead is not shorted to

ground and the engine still will not accelerate above the S.L.O.W. limit, replace the power pack.

Blocking diode tests

A blocking diode located in the engine wiring harness tan lead is used to prevent the warning system's self-test and oil injection warning signals from activating the S.L.O.W. (speed limiting overheat warning) program in the power pack. The S.L.O.W. program must only activate if the engine is actually overheating and the temperature switch has closed, shorting the tan lead to ground.

The diode is positioned near the large, red ten-pin main harness connector on 1995 (EO) models and near the six-pin Deutsch system check harness connector on 1996-1998 (ED-EC) models.

If the diode fails in an open circuit, the S.L.O.W. program will still engage, but the operator will not get a warning horn signal (or LED on System Check models).

If the diode fails in a closed circuit, the S.L.O.W. program may engage when the warning system self-tests, and/or when the oil injection system's low oil or no oil warning signals are activated.

To test the blocking diode, refer to the back of the book for wiring diagrams and proceed as follows:

1. Disconnect the negative battery cable. Then disconnect and ground the spark plug leads to the power head to prevent accidental starting.

2A. *Traditional wiring harnesses (1995 [EO] models)*—Disconnect the large, red ten-pin main harness connector. Then disconnect the engine temperature switch at its bullet (or one-pin Amphenol) connector.

2B. *Modular wiring harnesses (1996-1998 [ED-EC] models)*—Disconnect the engine harness from the boat wiring harness at the engine's six-pin Deutsch connector. Then disconnect the engine temperature switch at its bullet (or one-pin Amphenol) connector.

3. Calibrate an ohmmeter on the appropriate scale to test diodes.

4A. *Traditional wiring harnesses*—Using suitable jumper leads, connect one ohmmeter lead to the engine harness side of the temperature switch tan lead connector and the other ohmmeter lead to the tan pin (7, **Figure 66**) of the engine harness side of the large, red ten-pin connector.

4B. *Modular wiring harnesses*—Using suitable jumper leads, connect one ohmmeter lead to the engine harness side of the temperature switch's tan lead connector and the other ohmmeter lead to the tan lead (pin 6) of the engine harness side of the six-pin Deutsch connector.

5. Note the ohmmeter reading, then reverse the meter leads (or meter polarity).

TRADITIONAL HARNESS TEN-PIN CONNECTOR (ENGINE SIDE)

1. Red/purple lead
2. Not used
3. Gray lead
4. Black/yellow lead
5. Not used
6. Yellow/red lead
7. Tan lead
8. Purple/white lead
9. Purple lead
10. Black lead

66

a. The meter must indicate no continuity (very high reading) in one polarity and continuity (low reading) in the opposite polarity.

b. If the meter reads no continuity (very high reading) in both polarities, the diode has failed in an open circuit and must be replaced.

c. If the meter reads continuity (low reading) in both polarities, the diode has failed in a closed circuit (shorted) and must be replaced.

6. Reconnect all leads when finished. Connect the spark plug leads and negative battery cable last.

Power coil tests

Test the power coil using an ohmmeter. There are no specifications for a peak-reading voltmeter (PRV).

1. Disconnect the power pack's five-pin Amphenol connector. Install suitable Amphenol jumper leads to pins C and D (orange and orange/black leads) of the stator side of the connector (male body, female pins).

2. Calibrate an ohmmeter on the appropriate scale to read 360-440 ohms.

3. Connect one ohmmeter lead to the power coil orange lead (pin C) and the other ohmmeter lead to the power coil orange/black lead (pin D).

4. If the reading is not within 360-440 ohms, inspect the leads for damage and repair any found. If the leads are in satisfactory condition, replace the power coil (stator assembly).

5. To check the power coil for a short to ground, calibrate the ohmmeter on the highest scale available. Connect the black ohmmeter lead to a good engine ground. If the stator is removed, connect the lead to a mounting screw bore.

6. Connect the red ohmmeter lead to the coil's orange lead (pin C). Note the meter reading. The meter must indicate no continuity. If not, the power coil (or lead) is shorted to ground. Inspect the lead for damage and repair any found. If the lead is in satisfactory condition, the power coil (stator assembly) must be replaced.

7. Repeat Step 6 for the power coil orange/black lead (pin D).

8. Remove the jumper leads and reconnect the five-pin Amphenol connector when finished.

OIS2000 IGNITION SYSTEM (25 AND 35 HP [THREE-CYLINDER] MODELS)

Description

This ignition system is used on 25 and 35 hp (three-cylinder) models. Refer to the back of the manual for wiring diagrams.

The major components are the:

1. *Flywheel*—The flywheel contains magnets along the inner surface of its outer diameter. The magnets provide power to the charge and power coils, as well as the 12 amp stator coil windings. An encoder ring is secured to the center hub of the flywheel. The encoder ring works in conjunction with the optical sensor to replace the sensor coil (timer base) used on other OMC ignition systems. The encoder ring is constructed to pass windows and vanes through the optical sensor, providing the ignition module with crankshaft position (timing) and engine speed information.

2. *Charge coil*—The charge coil windings provide the ignition module with the voltage it ultimately sends to the ignition coils. Charge coil output is AC voltage and must be measured with a PRV (peak reading voltmeter). Charge coil failure will always affect all cylinders. The charge coil is potted into the stator assembly along with the alternator stator coils and the power coil. On these models, both charge coil leads are solid brown.

3. *Power coil*—The power coil provides the electricity the ignition module needs to operate its electronic circuits, including the S.L.O.W. and QuikStart systems, and the optical sensor. The power coil is potted in the stator along with the charge coil and alternator stator coils. The power coil windings are connected to the ignition module with two solid orange leads. The engine will not run if the power coil fails.

4. *Ignition module (power pack)*—The ignition module (**Figure 67**) stores the electricity from the charge coil until

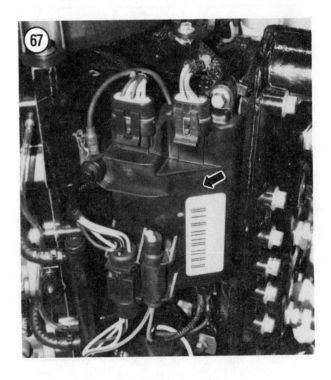

the optical sensor tells it to send the electricity to the ignition coils. The ignition module uses an internal rectifier to change the charge coil AC voltage to DC (direct current) voltage. The DC voltage is stored in a capacitor (an electrical storage tank), until it is released by a SCR (silicon controlled rectifier), which is simply an electronic switch. There is one SCR for each cylinder. Each SCR is controlled by internal electronic circuits, based on optical sensor input.

The ignition module is also equipped with the QuikStart, S.L.O.W. and rpm limit programs described at the beginning of the ignition section. The rpm limit specification is 6200 rpm.

5. *Optical sensor*—The optical sensor works in conjunction with the flywheel mounted encoder ring to tell the ignition module when to release the stored electricity in the capacitor to the appropriate ignition coil. The optical sensor assembly actually contains two optical sensors. Two sensors are required to provide the ignition module with the No. 1 cylinder location and anti-reverse protection. Dirt or grease on the optical sensor lenses will cause erratic spark. Ignition timing is advanced and retarded by rotating the optical sensor assembly (timer base) with a mechanical linkage.

6. *Ignition coils*—There is one ignition coil for each cylinder (**Figure 68**). The ignition coil transforms the relatively low voltage from the charge coil into voltage high enough (40,000 volts) to jump the spark plug gap and ignite the air/fuel mixture.

7. *Spark plugs*—There is one spark plug for each cylinder. Use only the recommended spark plugs or engine damage may result. Suppressor plugs are designed to reduce RFI (radio frequency interference) emissions that can cause interference with electrical accessories and the ignition system. Failure to use the recommended suppressor spark plug will cause the ignition system to operate erratically.

8. *Stop circuit*—The stop circuit is connected to one end of the capacitor in the power pack. Whenever the stop circuit is connected to ground, the capacitor is shorted and cannot store electricity. At this point there is no voltage available to send to the ignition coil and the ignition system ceases producing spark. The stop circuit must have an open circuit (to ground) in order for the engine to run. Both tiller handle and remote control models use an ignition (key) switch.

9. *Engine temperature switch*—The engine temperature switch (**Figure 69**) on these models has a dual function:

    a. The tan/blue lead of the switch triggers the warning system and the S.L.O.W. system.

    b. The white/black lead in the switch triggers the Quik-Start program.

Both engine temperature switch leads are normally open to ground and are closed when each reaches its specified temperature. Refer to *Engine Temperature Switches* located later in this chapter.

Troubleshooting

Refer to **Tables 13-15** for specifications and the end of the book for wiring diagrams. The recommended troubleshooting procedure is:
1. Preliminary checks.
   a. Total output (spark) test.
   b. Stop circuit isolation.
2. Power coil test.
3. Charge coil test.
4. Ignition module cranking output test.
5. Ignition coil tests.
6. Ignition module running output test.
7. S.L.O.W. system tests
   a. Temperature switch.
   b. Oil level switch.
8. QuikStart system tests.

> *WARNING*
> *High voltage is present in the ignition system. **Do not** touch or disconnect ignition components while the engine is being cranked or running.*

Preliminary checks

> *NOTE*
> *Before proceeding, inspect the ignition module ground leads and ignition coil ground straps for corrosion, damage, loose connections or loose mounting screws. These components must be securely grounded in order to operate properly.*

1. Disconnect the spark plug leads from the spark plugs and install an air gap spark tester (**Table 1**) to the spark plug leads. Adjust the air gap to 3/8 in. (9.5 mm). Then, connect the body of the spark tester to a clean engine ground.

2A. *Tiller handle models*—Make sure the safety lanyard is installed on the push-button stop switch. Then turn the ignition (key) switch to the ON or RUN position.

2B. *Remote control models*—Turn the ignition switch to the ON or RUN position. If equipped with a lanyard safety switch, make sure the lanyard is correctly installed on the switch.

3. Crank the engine while observing the tester. If a crisp, blue spark is noted at each air gap, the ignition system is functioning correctly.
   a. If good spark is noted, yet the engine will not start or does not run correctly, make sure the correct spark

plugs are installed and that they are in satisfactory condition. Replace the spark plugs if their condition is questionable. If the engine still does not run correctly, proceed to *Ignition module running output tests*.

   b. If good spark is noted, yet the engine backfires or pops when attempting to start, make sure the power pack primary and secondary leads are correctly routed on the ignition coils (**Figure 68**). The orange/blue primary lead must be connected to the top ignition coil. The orange/purple lead must be connected to the middle ignition coil. The orange/green lead must be connected to the bottom ignition coil. Each ignition coil secondary lead must be connected to the spark plug immediately adjacent to it. If the leads are routed correctly, remove the flywheel and check for a sheared flywheel key or damaged encoder wheel.

   c. If the engine runs erratically or misfires at certain speeds (usually mid-range or above), remove the flywheel and inspect the encoder wheel for damage or loose mounting screws. Check the optical sensors for dirt or oil on the lenses. Clean the four lenses with rubbing alcohol and a cotton swab.

   d. If the engine only misfires at or very near wide-open throttle, refer to Chapter Five and verify that the

W.O.T. (wide-open throttle) speed is within the recommended range. If the W.O.T. speed is exceeding the recommended range, the rpm limit program in the power pack may be the cause of the high speed misfire. Change propellers as necessary to reduce the W.O.T. speed to the recommended range.

e. If the engine speed is limited to approximately 2000-3000 rpm, check the oil reservoir's oil level. Fill the oil reservoir as necessary. If the speed is still limited, go to *Engine Temperature and Overheating* and make sure the engine is not overheating. If engine temperature is within specification, refer to *S.L.O.W. System Operation (25-35 hp [three-cylinder] models)*.

f. If no spark, weak spark or erratic spark is noted on one or more cylinders, continue with Step 4.

4. Isolate the stop circuit (black/yellow) lead by disconnecting the ignition module's four-pin Amphenol connector (**Figure 70**). Connect three jumper leads between the connector bodies so that pins A, C and D (tan, tan/yellow and white/black) are connected, but pin B (black/yellow lead) is not connected.

5. Crank the engine while observing the spark tester. If good spark is now noted, the stop circuit (black/yellow lead) is shorted to ground.

a. Tiller handle models—A short to ground is present in the combination push-button stop switch/safety lanyard switch, the ignition (key) switch, or the main engine harness black/yellow lead. Test, repair or replace the circuit or component as necessary.

b. Remote control models—A short to ground is present in the ignition (key) switch, safety lanyard switch (if equipped), or the main engine harness (and/or boat harness) black/yellow lead. Test, repair or replace the circuit or component as necessary.

6. Remove the jumper leads. Reconnect the four-pin Amphenol connector if ignition system troubleshooting is complete.

Power coil output tests

A peak-reading voltmeter (PRV) is required for this procedure. Test lead set part No. 342228 (or equivalent) is highly recommended to prevent damage to the Packard connectors during this procedure.

1. Disconnect the ignition module's four-pin Packard connector (A, **Figure 71**). Install suitable test leads to pins B and C (both orange leads) of the stator side of the connector (not the ignition module).

2. Adjust a PRV to the *positive* and *500* settings (or equivalent).

3. To check the power coil for a short to ground, connect the black meter lead to a clean engine ground.

4. Connect the red meter lead to power coil's first orange lead (Pin B). Crank the engine while noting the meter reading.

5. The meter must read 0 volts. If not, the power coil (or lead) is shorted to ground. Inspect the lead for damage and repair any found. If the lead is in satisfactory condition, the power coil (stator assembly) must be replaced.

6. Repeat Steps 4-5 for the power coil's second orange (pin C) lead.

7. To check the output of the power coil, connect the red meter lead to the coil's first orange lead (pin B) and the black meter lead to the coil's second orange lead (pin C).

8. Crank the engine while noting the meter reading. The meter must indicate 100 peak volts or higher. If not, inspect the wiring and connectors for damage. Repair any damage and retest the coil's output. If the output is still below 100 volts, replace the power coil (stator assembly) and retest spark output.

9. Remove the test leads and reconnect the four-pin Packard connector (A, **Figure 71**) to the ignition module when ignition troubleshooting is complete.

Power coil ohmmeter test

The power coil resistance tests can be used to confirm the results of the output tests performed in the previous section or to determine the power coil's condition if a PRV is not available. Test lead set part No. 342228 (or equivalent) is highly recommended to prevent damage to the Packard connectors during this procedure.

1. Disconnect the ignition module's four-pin Packard connector (A, **Figure 71**). Install suitable test leads to pins B and C (both orange leads) of the stator side of the connector (not the ignition module).

2A. *Rope start models*—Calibrate an ohmmeter on the appropriate scale to read 76-92 ohms.

2B. *Electric start models*—Calibrate an ohmmeter on the appropriate scale to read 52-62 ohms.

3. Connect one ohmmeter lead to the first power coil orange lead (pin B) and the other ohmmeter lead to the second power coil orange lead (pin C).

4. If the reading is not within 76-92 ohms (rope start) or 52-62 ohms (electric start), inspect the leads for damage and repair any found. If the leads are in satisfactory condition, the power coil (stator assembly) must be replaced.

5. To check the power coil for a short to ground, calibrate the ohmmeter on the highest scale available. Connect the black ohmmeter lead to a good engine ground. If the stator is removed, connect the lead to a mounting screw bore.

6. Connect the red ohmmeter lead to the coil's first orange lead (pin B). Note the meter reading. The meter must indicate no continuity. If not, the power coil (or lead) is shorted to ground. Inspect the lead for damage and repair any found. If the lead is in satisfactory condition, the power coil (stator assembly) must be replaced.

7. Repeat Step 6 for the coil's other orange lead (pin C).

8. Remove the test leads and reconnect the four-pin Packard connector (A, **Figure 71**) to the ignition module if ignition troubleshooting is complete.

Charge coil output

A peak-reading voltmeter (PRV) is required for this procedure. Test lead set part No. 342228 (or equivalent) is highly recommended to prevent damage to the Packard connectors during this procedure.

1. Disconnect the ignition module's four-pin Packard connector (A, **Figure 71**). Install suitable test leads to pins A and D (both brown leads) of the stator side of the connector (not the ignition module).

2. Adjust a PRV to the *positive* and *500* settings (or equivalent).

3. To check the charge coil for a short to ground, connect the black meter lead to a clean engine ground.

4. Connect the red meter lead to the charge coil's first brown lead (Pin A). Crank the engine while noting the meter reading.

5. The meter must read 0 volts. If not, the charge coil (or lead) is shorted to ground. Inspect the lead for damage and repair any found. If the lead is in satisfactory condition, the charge coil (stator assembly) must be replaced.

6. Repeat Steps 4-5 for the charge coil's second brown lead (Pin D).

7. To check the output of the charge coil, connect the red meter lead to the coil's first brown lead (pin A) and the black meter lead to the coil's second brown lead (pin D).

8. Crank the engine while noting the meter reading. The meter must indicate 300 peak volts or higher. If not, inspect the wiring and connectors for damage. Repair any damage and retest the coil's output. If the output is still below 300 volts, replace the charge coil (stator assembly) and retest spark output.

9. Remove the test leads and reconnect the four-pin Packard connector (A, **Figure 71**) to the ignition module if ignition troubleshooting is complete.

Charge coil resistance

The charge coil resistance tests can be used to confirm the results of the output tests performed in the previous section, or to determine the charge coil's condition if a PRV is not available. Test lead set part No. 342228 (or equivalent) is highly recommended to prevent damage to the Packard connectors during this procedure.

1. Disconnect the ignition module's four-pin Packard connector (A, **Figure 71**). Install suitable test leads to pins A and D (both brown leads) of the stator side of the connector (not the ignition module).

2A. *Rope start models*—Calibrate an ohmmeter on the appropriate scale to read 1010-1230 ohms.

2B. *Electric start models*—Calibrate an ohmmeter on the appropriate scale to read 720-880 ohms.

3. Connect one ohmmeter lead to the charge coil's first brown lead (pin A) and the other ohmmeter lead to the charge coil's second brown lead (pin D).

4. If the reading is not within 1010-1230 ohms (rope start) or 720-880 ohms (electric start), inspect the leads for damage and repair any found. If the leads are in satisfactory condition, replace the charge coil (stator assembly).

5. To check the charge coil for a short to ground, calibrate the ohmmeter on the highest scale available. Connect the black ohmmeter lead to a good engine ground. If the coil is removed, connect the lead to a mounting screw bore.

6. Connect the red ohmeter lead to the coil's first brown lead (pin A). Note the meter reading. The meter must indicate no continuity. If not, the charge coil (or lead) is shorted to ground. Inspect the lead for damage and repair

any found. If the lead is in satisfactory condition, the charge coil (stator assembly) must be replaced.

7. Repeat Step 6 for the coil's second brown lead (pin D).

8. Remove the test leads and reconnect the four-pin Packard connector (A, **Figure 71**) to the ignition module.

Ignition module cranking output

A peak-reading voltmeter (PRV) and a PL-88 pack load resistor (**Table 1**) are required for this procedure.

1. Disconnect the ignition module's orange/blue primary lead from the top ignition coil with a gentle twisting and pulling motion.

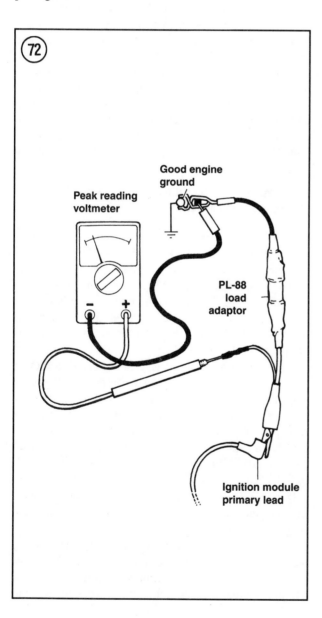

any found. Connect the small, insulated alligator clip of the PL-88 to the ignition module orange/blue lead. Then connect the large uninsulated alligator clip to a good engine ground. See **Figure 72**.

2. Connect the small, insulated alligator clip of the PL-88 to the ignition module orange/blue lead. Then connect the large uninsulated alligator clip to a good engine ground. See **Figure 72**.

3. Adjust a PRV to the *positive* and *500* settings (or equivalent).

4. Connect the black meter lead to a good engine ground. Connect the red meter lead to the PL-88's pigtail lead (with the Amphenol socket). See **Figure 72**.

5. Crank the engine while noting the meter reading. The meter must indicate 100 peak volts or higher. If not, inspect the orange lead and its spring terminal end for damage. Repair any damage and retest the output. If the output is still below 100 volts, the optical sensor or the ignition module is defective and must be replaced.

   a. If the optical sensor has not yet been cleaned and visually inspected, remove the flywheel and inspect the encoder wheel for damage or loose mounting screws. Check the optical sensors for dirt or oil on the lenses. Clean the four lenses with rubbing alcohol and a cotton swab.

   b. Inspect the optical sensor assembly's five leads and its five-pin Packard connector (B, **Figure 71**) for damage, loose connections or corrosion. Repair any damage found.

NOTE
There is no specific test for the optical sensor. If the ignition module output is below specification, either the optical sensor or the ignition module may be defective. The manufacturer recommends substituting a known good sensor or module to determine which is faulty.

   c. If all tests to this point are satisfactory, yet the ignition module output is below specification on one or more cylinders, replace either the ignition module or optical sensor assembly and retest ignition module output. If necessary, replace the remaining component.

6. Remove the ignition module's orange/blue lead from the PL-88 and reconnect it to the top ignition coil.

7. Repeat Steps 1-6 for the module's orange/purple (middle cylinder) and orange/green (bottom cylinder) primary leads.

8. Remove the PL-88 and reconnect the ignition module's orange/green lead to the bottom ignition coil when finished.

Ignition coil

If all tests to this point have been satisfactory, yet spark output at the air gap tester is not satisfactory, refer to

Ignition Coil Tests at the beginning of the ignition section and test the ignition coils.

Ignition module running output test

This test is intended to diagnose a misfire or ignition failure that occurs at a particular engine speed. Make sure you operate the engine at the same speed that the misfire or failure occurs during this test.

A peak-reading voltmeter (PRV) and three TS-77 terminal extenders (**Table 1**) are required for this procedure.

It is possible for a defective ignition coil to cause the ignition module output to be below specification. If there is any doubt as to the ignition coil's condition, refer to *Ignition Coil Tests* at the beginning of the ignition section and test the ignition coil(s).

1. Disconnect the ignition module's orange/blue, orange/purple and orange/green primary leads from the ignition coils with a gentle twisting and pulling motion.

2. Install a TS-77 terminal extender onto each primary terminal. Then install the module's orange/blue, orange/purple and orange/green leads onto the appropriate extender.

3. Adjust a PRV to the *positive* and *500* settings (or equivalent).

4. Connect the black meter lead to a good engine ground. Connect the red meter lead to the exposed metal of the upper (No. 1 cylinder) terminal extender.

CAUTION
*Do not run the engine without an adequate water supply and do not exceed 3000 rpm without an adequate load. Refer to **Safety Precautions** at the beginning of this chapter.*

5. Run the engine at the speed that the misfire or ignition failure occurs, while noting the meter reading. The meter must indicate a steady 240 peak volts or higher. If not, check for loose or damaged connectors, damaged leads, loose ground leads and/or component mounting hardware.

   a. If all checks are satisfactory, yet the voltage is below 240 volts or erratic, make sure that all charge coil tests were performed and that the charge coil performed satisfactorily.

   b. If the optical sensor has not yet been cleaned and visually inspected, remove the flywheel and inspect the encoder wheel for damage or loose mounting screws. Check the optical sensors for dirt or oil on the lenses. Clean the four lenses with rubbing alcohol and a cotton swab.

   c. Inspect the optical sensor assembly's five leads and its five-pin Packard connector (B, **Figure 71**) for

damage, loose connections or corrosion. Repair any damage found.

NOTE
There is no specific test for the optical sensor. If the ignition module output is below specification, either the optical sensor or the ignition module may be defective. The manufacturer recommends substituting a good sensor or module to determine which is faulty.

   d. If all tests to this point are satisfactory, yet the ignition module running output is below 240 peak volts (or erratic) on one or more cylinders, replace either the ignition module or optical sensor assembly and retest ignition module output. If necessary, replace the remaining component.

6. Repeat Steps 4-5 for the middle (No. 2 cylinder) and lower (No. 3 cylinder) terminal extender.

7. Remove the terminal extenders and reconnect the power pack's primary leads to the ignition coils, making sure the orange/blue lead is connected to the top ignition coil, orange/purple lead is connected to the middle ignition coil and the orange/green lead is connected to the bottom ignition coil.

S.L.O.W. System Operation (25 and 35 hp [Three-cylinder] Models)

These models are equipped with the speed limiting overheat warning (S.L.O.W.) system. The system is designed to activate the warning system and limit engine speed to approximately 2500 rpm if the engine temperature exceeds the engine temperature switch's closing value *and/or* if the oil level in the engine mounted oil reservoir falls below a predetermined level (reservoir almost empty).

If the engine overheats, deactivate (reset) the S.L.O.W. system by slowing engine speed to less than 1500 rpm (or stop engine) and allow the engine to cool below the temperature switch opening value. These engines must be equipped with a 237° F (114° C) temperature switch. The switch is identified by its tan/blue lead. The switch must close at 231-243° F (111-117° C) and open at 192-222° F (89-106° C).

If the S.L.O.W. system is activated by a low-oil condition, stop the engine and refill the oil reservoir to deactivate (reset) the S.L.O.W. system.

The S.L.O.W. system circuits (in the ignition module) receive operating voltage from the power coil. The power coil is potted in the stator assembly along with the charge coil and alternator stator coil. If the power coil fails, the ignition module will not operate and the engine will not run.

S.L.O.W. system troubleshooting

If the S.L.O.W. system engages during normal operation, proceed as follows:

1. Check the engine-mounted oil reservoir's oil level. Fill the reservoir as necessary.

2. Refer to *Engine Temperature and Overheating* and verify that the engine is not overheating. If the engine is overheating, repair the cooling system as necessary and recheck the engine's operating temperature.

3. If engine temperature is within specification, disconnect the temperature switch tan/blue lead at its bullet (or two-pin Amphenol) connector.

4. Rerun the engine and check for S.L.O.W. engagement. If the S.L.O.W. system no longer engages, the temperature switch is shorted to ground and must be replaced.

5. If the S.L.O.W. system still engages, disconnect the oil level sending unit at its three-pin Amphenol connector. Rerun the engine and check for S.L.O.W. engagement.

6. If the S.L.O.W. system no longer engages, the oil level sending unit is stuck or defective. Repair or replace the sending unit as necessary.

7. If the S.L.O.W. system still engages, one of the following conditions is present:

   a. The tan lead is shorted to ground between the temperature switch bullet connector (or two-pin Amphenol connector) and the ignition module's four-pin Amphenol connector (**Figure 70**).

   b. The tan/yellow lead is shorted to ground between the oil level sending unit's three-pin Amphenol connector and the ignition module's four-pin Amphenol connector (**Figure 70**).

   c. The ignition module is defective.

8. Test the tan and tan/yellow leads for shorts to ground and repair or replace the leads as necessary. If the tan and tan/yellow leads are not shorted to ground, replace the ignition module.

S.L.O.W. system functional test

The S.L.O.W. system is activated by input from the engine temperature switch's tan/blue lead and/or the oil level sending unit's tan/yellow lead. The temperature switch is located near the top of the cylinder head (**Figure 69**) and the oil level sending unit is located in the top of the engine-mounted oil reservoir (**Figure 73**). To perform a functional test of S.L.O.W. operation and troubleshoot all system functions, proceed as follows:

> *CAUTION*
> *Do not run the engine without an adequate water supply and do not exceed 3000 rpm without an adequate load. Refer to **Safety Precautions** at the beginning of this chapter.*

1. Connect an accurate shop tachometer to the spark plug lead following its manufacturer's instructions.

2. Disconnect the engine temperature switch tan/blue lead at its bullet (or two-pin Amphenol) connector and the oil level sending unit at its three-pin Amphenol connector.

3. Start the engine and allow it to warm to normal operating temperature. Then increase engine speed to approximately 3500 rpm.

4. Using a suitable jumper lead, connect the engine harness tan lead to a clean engine ground, while noting the engine speed.

5. If S.L.O.W. engages, engine speed will quickly be reduced to approximately 2500 rpm and stabilize. It is not necessary to continue to hold the tan lead to ground once S.L.O.W. has been engaged (latched). If S.L.O.W. correctly engages, proceed to Step 6. If not, proceed as follows:

   a. Test the tan lead for an open circuit between the ignition module's four-pin Amphenol connector's tan lead (pin A) and the temperature switch bullet (or two-pin Amphenol) connector (pin B). Repair or replace the tan lead as necessary.

   b. If the tan lead has continuity, replace the ignition module and retest S.L.O.W. function.

6. If S.L.O.W. engages in Step 5, disconnect the tan lead from ground and reduce engine speed to below 1500 rpm (or stop the engine). Then restart the engine and attempt to accelerate the engine to 3500 rpm.

   a. If the engine will now freely accelerate above the S.L.O.W. limit (2500 rpm), the ignition module programming and engine wiring harness are functioning correctly.

b. If the engine still remains in S.L.O.W., disconnect the ignition module's four-pin Amphenol connector (**Figure 74**). Connect jumper leads between pins B and D (black/yellow and white/black), but not between pins A and C (tan and tan/yellow).

c. If the engine will now freely accelerate above the S.L.O.W. limit, the tan or tan/yellow lead is shorted to ground. Test, repair or replace the tan and tan/yellow leads as necessary. If the tan and tan/yellow leads are not shorted to ground and the engine still will not accelerate above the S.L.O.W. limit, replace the ignition module.

7. Reconnect all leads except the oil level sending unit's three-pin Amphenol connector.

8. Start the engine and increase engine speed to 3500 rpm.

9. Using a suitable jumper lead, connect pin A (tan/yellow) to pin B (black) on the engine harness side (male plug/female pins) of the oil level sending unit's connector while noting the engine speed.

10. After a four-second delay, S.L.O.W. must engage and engine speed will quickly be reduced to approximately 2500 rpm and stabilize. It is not necessary to continue to hold the tan/yellow lead to the black lead once S.L.O.W. has been engaged (latched). If S.L.O.W. correctly engages, proceed to Step 11. If not, proceed as follows:

a. Test the tan/yellow lead for an open circuit between the ignition module's four-pin Amphenol connector's tan/yellow lead (pin C) and the oil level sending unit's three-pin Amphenol connector (pin A). Repair or replace the tan/yellow lead as necessary.

b. Test the black lead for continuity from pin B of the engine harness side (male plug/female pins) of the oil level sending unit's connector to engine ground at the lower starter motor mounting screw. Repair or replace the black lead as necessary.

c. If the tan/yellow and black leads have continuity, replace the ignition module and retest the S.L.O.W. function.

11. If S.L.O.W. engages in Step 10, remove the jumper lead from the three-pin Amphenol connector and reduce engine speed to below 1500 rpm (or stop the engine). Then restart the engine and attempt to accelerate the engine to 3500 rpm.

a. If the engine will now freely accelerate above the S.L.O.W. limit (2500 rpm), the ignition module programming and engine wiring harness are functioning correctly.

b. If the engine still remains in S.L.O.W., replace the ignition module.

12. Reconnect all leads when finished.

QuikStart System Operation (25 and 35 hp [Three-cylinder] Models)

The QuikStart circuit automatically advances the ignition timing approximately 5° when the engine temperature is below 105° F (41° C) to improve engine running quality during warm-up. The ignition timing will remain advanced until the engine temperature exceeds 105° F (41° C). To prevent power head damage from over-advanced timing (such as preignition or detonation), the ignition module disables the QuikStart program as soon as engine speed exceeds 1500 rpm, regardless of engine temperature.

NOTE
If the ignition timing stays advanced (above the normal engine timing specification) as the engine is accelerated above 1500 rpm, the ignition module is defective and must be replaced.

The QuikStart program also advances the ignition timing each time the engine is started (for approximately 7 seconds), regardless of engine temperature.

QuikStart system functional test

The QuikStart system is activated by input from the engine temperature switch's white/black lead. The temperature switch is located near the top of the cylinder head (**Figure 69**). If the white/black lead is open to ground, the

QuikStart program will be activated. If the white/black lead is grounded, the QuickStart program will be deactivated. To perform a functional test of QuikStart operation and troubleshoot all system functions, proceed as follows:

CAUTION
Do not run the engine without an adequate water supply and do not exceed 3000 rpm without an adequate load. Refer to Safety Precautions at the beginning of this chapter.

1. Refer to Chapter Five and perform all synchronization and linkage adjustments.

2. Connect an accurate shop tachometer and timing light to the No. 1 spark plug lead following its manufacturer's instructions.

3. Start the engine and allow it to warm to normal operating temperature. Refer to *Engine temperature check* located later in this chapter. Engine operating temperature must be well above 105° F (41° C) before proceeding.

4. Disconnect the engine temperature switch's white/black lead at its bullet (or two-pin Amphenol) connector.

5. Shift the engine into FORWARD gear and make sure that it is idling at no more than 900 rpm.

6. Check the ignition timing. Timing must be approximately 1° BTDC (before top dead center). Normal timing is 4° ATDC after top dead center. If timing is 1° BTDC, continue at Step 7. If not, proceed as follows:

a. If timing is not advanced (approximately 1° BTDC), test the white/black lead for a short to ground between its bullet (or two-pin Amphenol [pin B]) connector and the ignition module four-pin connector (pin D). Repair or replace the lead or connectors as necessary.

b. If the white/black lead is not shorted to ground, replace the ignition module.

7. Reconnect the engine temperature switch's white/black lead to the engine harness. Check the ignition timing again (at no more than 900 rpm). After approximately 7 seconds, the ignition timing must indicate approximately 4° ATDC. If the timing is retarded to 4° ATDC, the system is functioning correctly. If not, proceed as follows:

a. Test the engine temperature switch as described in *Engine Temperature Switches* located later in this Chapter. The white/black lead's function must be verified.

b. If the engine temperature switch tests satisfactorily, test the white/black lead for continuity between its bullet (or two-pin Amphenol [pin B]) connector and the ignition module four-pin connector (pin D). Repair or replace the lead or connectors, as necessary.

c. If the engine temperature switch tests satisfactorily, the white/black lead has continuity and timing does not retard to 4° ATDC when the switch is reconnected, replace the ignition module.

CD3 (CAPACITOR DISCHARGE THREE-CYLINDER) IGNITION (50-70 HP MODELS)

Description

This ignition system is used on 50-70 hp (three-cylinder) models equipped with the 12 amp regulated charging system. Refer to the back of the manual for wiring diagrams.

The major components are the:

1. *Flywheel*—The flywheel contains magnets along the inner surface of its outer diameter and around the center hub. The outer magnets provide power to the charge and power coils, as well as the 12 amp stator coil windings. The inner magnets provide power to the sensor coils.

2. *Charge coil*—The charge coil windings provide the power pack with the voltage it needs to operate the ignition system. Charge coil output is AC voltage and must be measured with a PRV (peak reading voltmeter). Charge coil failure will always affect all cylinders. The charge coil is potted into the stator assembly along with the alternator stator coils and the power coil.

3. *Power pack*—The power pack (A, **Figure 75**) stores the electricity from the charge coil until the sensor coil tells it

to send the electricity to the ignition coils. The power pack uses an internal rectifier to change the charge coil AC voltage to DC (direct current) voltage. The DC voltage is stored in a capacitor (an electrical storage tank) until it is released by a SCR (silicon controlled rectifier), which is simply an electronic switch. There is one SCR for each cylinder. Each SCR is controlled by a sensor coil lead.

The power pack on these models is equipped with the QuikStart, S.L.O.W. and rpm limit programs described at the beginning of the ignition section. The rpm limit specification is 6700 rpm.

All models are equipped with a blocking diode in the engine harness tan lead. The blocking diode prevents the warning system self-test and oil injection warning signals from causing the power pack to falsely engage S.L.O.W.

4. *Sensor coils*—The sensor coil tells the power pack when to release the stored electricity in the capacitor to the appropriate ignition coil. The sensor coil assembly (timer base) on these models uses three windings for normal operation (and three for QuikStart operation) connected by a common white (return) lead. The blue lead triggers cylinder No.1, the purple lead triggers cylinder No. 2 and the green lead triggers cylinder No. 3. The blue, purple and green leads are connected to the SCRs in the power pack.

The fifth timer base lead (black/white) is used by the power pack to internally switch the timer base over to the QuikStart set of sensor coil windings. These windings are located approximately 12° advanced from the normal sensor coil windings. When the power pack sends the correct signal through the black/white lead, electronic circuits in the timer base switch operation to the advanced sensor coil windings.

A SCR is triggered by the first positive pulse of voltage it receives. Since there is a normal and QuikStart winding for each cylinder (connected to the power pack by one lead), each SCR is triggered by its dedicated sensor coil windings through the appropriate blue, purple or green lead. Failure of a single coil or single lead (blue, purple or green) will cause only one cylinder to fail. Failure of the common (white) lead will generally cause erratic spark and erratic ignition timing. Failure of the black/white lead (or the QuikStart set of windings) will only cause a loss of QuikStart.

During normal operation, the ignition timing is advanced and retarded by rotating the sensor coils (timer base) with a mechanical linkage.

5. *Ignition coils*—There is one ignition coil (B, **Figure 75**) for each cylinder. The ignition coil transforms the relatively low voltage from the charge coil into voltage high enough (40,000 volts) to jump the spark plug gap and ignite the air/fuel mixture.

6. *Spark plugs*—There is one spark plug for each cylinder. Use only the recommended spark plugs or engine damage may result. Suppressor plugs are designed to reduce RFI (radio frequency interference) emissions that can cause interference with electrical accessories and the ignition system. Failure to use the recommended suppressor spark plug will cause the ignition system to operate erratically.

7. *Stop circuit*—The stop circuit is connected to one end of the capacitor in the power pack. Whenever the stop circuit is connected to ground, the capacitor is shorted out and cannot store electricity. At this point, there is no voltage available to send to the ignition coil, and the ignition system ceases producing spark. The stop circuit must have an open circuit (to ground) in order for the engine to run. Tiller handle (electric start) and all remote control models use an ignition (key) switch.

8. *Engine temperature switch*—The engine temperature switch (**Figure 76**) has a dual function:
   a. The tan/blue lead of the switch triggers the warning system and the S.L.O.W. system.
   b. The white/black lead in the switch triggers the Quik-Start program.

Both engine temperature switch leads are normally open to ground and are closed when each reaches its specified temperature. Refer to *Engine Temperature Switches*, located later in this chapter.

9. *Power coil*—The power coil provides the electricity the power pack needs to operate the QuikStart and S.L.O.W. systems. The power coil is potted in the stator assembly along with the charge coil and alternator stator coils. The power coil windings are connected to the power pack with two leads (orange and orange/black). Failure of the power coil will result in the QuikStart and S.L.O.W. systems not functioning.

Troubleshooting

Refer to **Tables 13-15** for specifications and the end of the book for wiring diagrams. The recommended troubleshooting procedure is:

1. Preliminary checks.
   a. Total output (spark) test.
   b. Stop circuit isolation.
   c. Indexing the flywheel.
2. Charge coil tests.
3. Sensor coil tests.
4. Power pack cranking output test.
5. Ignition coil tests.
6. Power pack running output test.
7. S.L.O.W. system.
   a. Functional test.
   b. Power coil tests.
   c. Blocking diode test.
8. QuikStart system.
   a. Functional test.
   b. Power coil tests.

WARNING
*High voltage is present in the ignition system. **Do not** touch or disconnect ignition components while the engine is being cranked or running.*

Preliminary checks

NOTE
Before proceeding, inspect the power pack ground lead and ignition coil ground straps for corrosion, damage, loose connections or loose mounting screws. These components must be securely grounded to operate properly.

1. Disconnect the spark plug leads from the spark plugs and install an air gap spark tester (**Table 1**) to the spark plug leads. Adjust the air gap to 1/2 in. (12.7 mm). Then, connect the body of the spark tester to a clean engine ground.

2A. *Tiller handle models*—Make sure the safety lanyard is installed on the push-button stop switch. Then turn the ignition (key) switch to the ON or RUN position.

2B. *Remote control models*—Turn the ignition switch to the ON or RUN position. If equipped with a lanyard safety switch, make sure the lanyard is correctly installed on the switch.

3. Crank the engine while observing the tester. If a crisp, blue spark is noted at each air gap, the ignition system is functioning correctly.

a. If good spark is noted, yet the engine will not start or does not run correctly, make sure the correct spark plugs are installed and that they are in satisfactory condition. Replace the spark plugs if their condition is questionable. If the engine still does not run correctly, proceed to *Power pack running output tests*.

b. If good spark is noted, yet the engine backfires or pops when attempting to start, make sure that the power pack primary leads and secondary leads are correctly routed on the ignition coil. The orange/blue primary lead must be connected to the top ignition coil, the orange/purple lead must be connected to the middle ignition coil and the orange/green lead must be connected to the bottom coil. Each ignition coil secondary lead must be connected to the spark plug immediately adjacent to it. If the leads are routed correctly, remove the flywheel and check for a sheared flywheel key.

c. If the engine runs erratically or misfires at certain engine speeds (usually mid-range or above), refer to *Indexing flywheel (erratic spark [two- and three-cylinder models])*. Make sure you check the sensor coil common (white) lead for an open circuit or loose connection.

d. If the engine only misfires at or very near wide-open throttle, refer to Chapter Five and verify that the engine's W.O.T. (wide-open throttle) speed is within the recommended range. If the engine speed is exceeding the recommended range, the rpm limit program in the power pack may be the cause of the high-speed misfire. Change propellers as necessary to lower W.O.T. speed to the recommended range.

e. If the engine speed is limited to approximately 2000-3000 rpm, go to *Engine Temperature and Overheating* and make sure the engine is not overheating. If engine temperature is within specification, go to *S.L.O.W. System Operation (50-70 hp [three-cylinder] models)*.

f. If no spark, weak spark or erratic spark is noted on one or two cylinders, continue with Step 4.

NOTE
*It is necessary to loosen the power pack mounting screws to gain access to the connector in the following step. Make sure the power pack mounting screws and its ground lead (A, **Figure 77**) are securely tightened before cranking or running the engine.*

4. Isolate the stop circuit (black/yellow) lead by disconnecting the power pack-to-stator five-pin Amphenol connector containing the black/yellow lead (B, **Figure 77**). Do not disconnect the power pack-to-timer base five-pin Amphenol connector. Connect four jumper leads between the

connector bodies so that pins A-D (brown, brown/yellow and both orange leads) are connected, but pin E (black/yellow lead) is not connected.

5. Crank the engine while observing the spark tester. If good spark is now noted, the stop circuit (black/yellow lead) is shorted to ground.

    a. Tiller handle models—A short to ground is present in the combination push-button stop switch/safety lanyard switch, the ignition (key) switch, or the main engine harness black/yellow lead. Test, repair or replace the circuit or component as necessary.

    b. Remote control models—A short to ground is present in the ignition (key) switch, safety lanyard switch (if equipped) or the main engine harness (and/or boat harness) black/yellow lead. Test, repair or replace the circuit or component as necessary.

6. Remove the jumper leads. Reconnect the five-pin Amphenol connector if finished with ignition system troubleshooting. Make sure the power pack mounting screws and ground lead are securely tightened.

Charge coil output

A peak-reading voltmeter (PRV) is required for this procedure.

> *NOTE*
> *It is necessary to loosen the power pack mounting screws to gain access to the connector in the following step. Make sure the power pack mounting screws and its ground lead (A, **Figure 77**) are securely tightened before cranking or running the engine.*

1. Disconnect the power pack-to-stator five-pin Amphenol connector (B, **Figure 77**). Install suitable Amphenol jumper leads to pins A and B (brown and brown/yellow leads) of the stator side of the connector (male body, female pins).

2. Adjust a PRV to the *positive* and *500* settings (or equivalent).

3. To check the charge coil for a short to ground, connect the black meter lead to a clean engine ground.

4. Connect the red meter lead to the charge coil's brown lead (Pin A). Crank the engine while noting the meter reading.

5. The meter must read 0 volts. If not, the charge coil (or lead) is shorted to ground. Inspect the lead for damage and repair any found. If the lead is in satisfactory condition, replace the charge coil (stator assembly).

6. Repeat Steps 4-5 for the charge coil's brown/yellow (pin B) lead.

7. To check the output of the charge coil, connect the black meter lead to the coil's brown lead (pin A) and the red meter

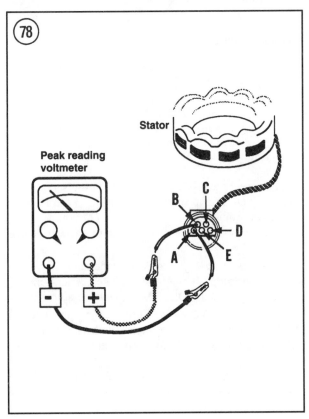

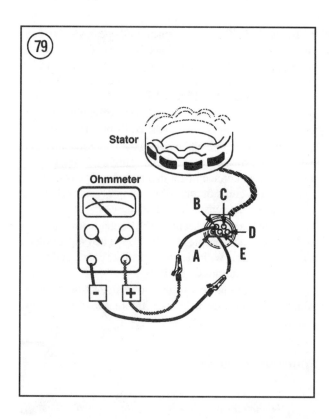

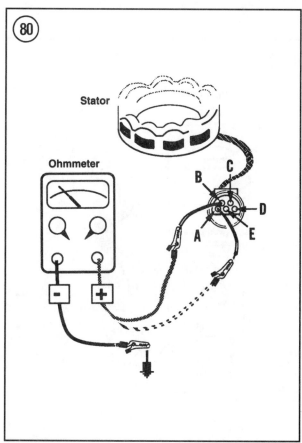

lead to the coil's brown/yellow lead (pin B). See **Figure 78**.

8. Crank the engine while noting the meter reading. The meter must indicate 250 peak volts or higher. If not, inspect the wiring and connectors for damage. Repair any damage and retest the coil's output. If the output is still below 250 volts, replace the charge coil (stator assembly) and retest spark output.

9. Remove the jumper leads and reconnect the five-pin Amphenol connector if ignition troubleshooting is completed. Make sure the power pack mounting screws and ground lead are securely tightened.

Charge coil resistance

The charge coil resistance tests can be used to confirm the results of the output test performed in the previous section or to determine the charge coil's condition if a PRV is not available.

NOTE
*It will be necessary to loosen the power pack mounting screws to gain access to the connector in the following step. Make sure the power pack mounting screws and its ground lead (A, **Figure 77**) are securely tightened before cranking or running the engine.*

1. Disconnect the power pack-to-stator five-pin Amphenol connector (B, **Figure 77**). Install suitable Amphenol jumper leads to pins A and B (brown and brown/yellow leads) of the stator side of the connector (male body, female pins).

2. Calibrate an ohmmeter on the appropriate scale to read 750-950 ohms.

3. Connect one ohmmeter lead to the charge coil brown lead (pin A) and the other ohmmeter lead to the charge coil brown/yellow lead (pin B). See **Figure 79**.

4. If the reading is not within 750-950 ohms, inspect the leads for damage and repair any found. If the leads are in satisfactory condition, the charge coil (stator assembly) must be replaced.

5. To check the charge coil for a short to ground, calibrate the ohmmeter on the highest scale available. Connect the black ohmmeter lead to a good engine ground. If the coil is removed, connect the lead to a mounting screw bore.

6. Alternately connect the red ohmeter lead to the coil's brown and brown/yellow leads (pins A and B). See **Figure 80**. Note the meter reading at each connection. The meter must indicate no continuity. If not, the charge coil (or leads) is shorted to ground. Inspect the leads for damage and repair any found. If the leads are in satisfactory condition, replace the charge coil (stator assembly).

7. Remove the jumper leads and reconnect the five-pin Amphenol connector if ignition troubleshooting is completed. Make sure the power pack mounting screws and ground lead are securely tightened.

Sensor coil output

A peak-reading voltmeter (PRV) is required for this procedure. Three normal operation windings and three QuickStart windings will be tested in this procedure. All six windings use the white lead for a common (return) lead.

1. Disconnect the power pack-to-timer base five-pin Amphenol connector (C, **Figure 77**). Install suitable Amphenol jumper leads to all five pins (A-E [blue, purple, green, black/white and white]) of the timer base side of the connector (male body, female pins).

2. Adjust a PRV to the *positive (or sensor [SEN])* and *5* settings (or equivalent).

3. To check the sensor coil for a short to ground, connect the black meter lead to a good engine ground. Connect the red meter lead to the sensor coil's blue (pin A) lead.

4. Crank the engine while noting the meter reading. The meter must indicate 0 volts. If not, inspect the wiring and connector for damage. Repair any damage and retest. If the meter still indicates any reading other than 0, the sensor coil is shorted to ground and must be replaced.

5. Repeat Steps 3-4 for the sensor coil purple, green, black/white and white (pins B, C, D and E) leads.

6. To check the normal operation sensor coil's peak voltage output, connect the black meter lead to the sensor coil's white (pin E) lead and the red meter lead to the coil's blue (pin A) lead.

7. Crank the engine while noting the meter reading. The meter must indicate 1.5 peak volts or higher. If not, inspect the wiring and connector for damage. Repair any damage and retest the coil's output. If the output is still below 1.5 volts, replace the sensor coil (timer base) and retest spark output.

8. Repeat Steps 6-7 with the red meter lead connected to the sensor coil purple (pin B) lead. Then repeat Steps 6-7 a final time with the red meter lead connected to the sensor coil green (pin C) lead.

NOTE
The QuickStart sensor coils are activated by the power pack through the power pack-to-timer base black/white lead. If the power pack is not receiving voltage through its yellow/red lead (from the starter solenoid/ignition switch) during cranking, or the power pack's QuikStart circuits are defective, the QuickStart sensor coils will not be activated.

9. To check the QuikStart sensor coil's peak voltage output, connect two jumper leads between the connector bodies so that pins D and E (black/white and white leads) are connected, but pins A-C (blue, purple and green leads) are not connected. See **Figure 81**.

10. Connect the black meter lead to a good engine ground. Connect the red meter lead to the coil's blue (pin A) lead.

11. Crank the engine while noting the meter reading. The meter must indicate 1.5 peak volts or higher. If not, inspect the wiring and connector for damage. Repair any damage and retest the coil's output. If the output is still below 1.5 volts, replace the sensor coil (timer base).

12. Repeat Steps 10-11 with the red meter lead connected to the sensor coil purple (pin B) lead. Then repeat Steps 10-11 a final time with the red meter lead connected to the sensor coil green (pin C) lead.

13. Remove the jumper leads and reconnect the five-pin Amphenol connector if ignition troubleshooting is complete.

Sensor coil resistance

NOTE
Ohmmeter polarity must be determined before testing the sensor coil resistance. A di-

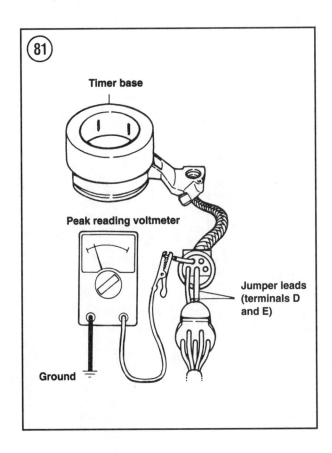

(81)

Timer base

Peak reading voltmeter

Ground

Jumper leads (terminals D and E)

ode, known to be in good condition, is required. A diode may be obtained from OMC Genuine Parts (part No. 583898) or Radio Shack (part No's. 276-1101, 276-1102, 276-1103 or 276-1104).

To determine ohmmeter polarity, calibrate the meter on appropriate scale to test a diode. Connect the leads to a known-good diode as shown in **Figure 82** and note the meter reading. The meter must indicate a very low reading (continuity). Reverse the leads at the diode and note the meter reading. The meter must indicate a very high reading (no continuity).

If the meter readings are as specified, the red meter lead is positive (+) and the black meter lead is negative (−).

If the opposite results were noted, reverse the meter leads at the meter, so the red lead will be true positive (+).

To test the resistance of the sensor coil windings, proceed as follows:

1. Disconnect the power pack-to-timer base five-pin Amphenol connector (C, **Figure 77**). Install suitable Amphenol jumper leads to all five pins (A-E [blue, purple, green, black/white and white]) of the timer base side of the connector (male body, female pins).

NOTE
The sensor coil resistance specifications vary based on the brand and model of ohmmeter used due to the timer base's internal electronic circuits. While specifications are given for three common meters, resistance

measured with any other meter may be different (higher or lower). The key concern is that all readings in Steps 3-4 are approximately the same.

2. Calibrate an ohmmeter on the appropriate scale to read approximately 270-950 ohms. If you are using the Fluke 29, the meter must be calibrated on the 40 ohm scale as specified in the manufacturer's instructions.

3. Connect the red (true positive) ohmmeter lead to the timer base white lead (pin E). Then alternately connect the black (negative) meter lead to the blue, purple and green leads (pins A, B and C), while noting the meter reading at each connection.

4. The meter must read as follows:
   a. Stevens Model AT-101 meter—270-330 ohms.
   b. Merc-O-Tronic Model M-700 meter—630-770 ohms.
   c. Fluke Model 29 meter—850-950 ohms.

5. If the sensor coil resistance is not as specified, replace the timer base and recheck spark output. If using an ohmmeter other than that recommended and the three resistance readings are not approximately the same, replace the timer base and recheck spark output.

6. To check the QuikStart lead, calibrate an ohmmeter on the appropriate scale to read 400-500 ohms.

7. Connect the red (true positive) meter lead to the timer base white lead (pin E). Connect the meter black (negative) lead to the timer base black/white lead (pin D).

8. The meter must read 400-500 ohms. If not, replace the timer base.

9. To test the timer base for a short to ground, calibrate the ohmmeter on the highest scale available.

10. Connect the black meter lead to a good engine ground. If the timer base is removed, connect the red meter lead to a metal portion of the timer base body.

11. Alternately connect the red meter lead to each of the five timer base leads (blue, purple, green, black/white and white [pins A-E]) while noting the meter reading at each connection.

12. The meter must indicate no continuity at each connection. If not, inspect the suspect lead for damage and repair any found. If the lead(s) is in satisfactory condition, replace the timer base and retest spark output.

13. Remove the jumper leads and reconnect the five-pin Amphenol connector when finished.

Power pack cranking output

A peak-reading voltmeter (PRV) and a PL-88 pack load resistor (**Table 1**) are required for this procedure.

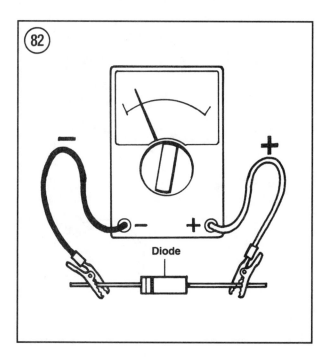

82

Diode

1. Disconnect the power pack's orange/blue primary lead from the top (No. 1 cylinder) ignition coil with a gentle twisting and pulling motion.

2. Connect the small, insulated alligator clip of the PL-88 to the power pack orange/blue lead. Then connect the large uninsulated alligator clip to a good engine ground. See **Figure 83**.

3. Adjust a PRV to the *positive* and *500* settings (or equivalent).

4. Connect the black meter lead to a good engine ground. Connect the red meter lead to the PL-88's pigtail lead (with the Amphenol socket). See **Figure 83**.

5. Crank the engine while noting the meter reading. The meter must indicate 190 peak volts or higher. If not, inspect the wiring and connector for damage. Repair any damage and retest the output. If the output is still below 190 volts, replace the power pack and retest the spark output.

6. Remove the power pack's orange/blue lead from the PL-88 and reconnect it to the top (No. 1 cylinder) ignition coil.

7. Repeat Steps 1-6 for the power pack's orange/purple (middle ignition coil) and orange/green (bottom ignition coil) primary leads.

8. Remove the PL-88 and reconnect the power pack's orange/green lead to the bottom (No. 3 cylinder) ignition coil when finished.

Ignition coil

If all tests to this point are satisfactory, yet spark output at the air gap tester is not satisfactory, refer to *Ignition Coil Tests* at the beginning of the ignition section and test the ignition coil(s).

Power pack running output test

This test is intended to diagnose a misfire or ignition failure that occurs at a particular engine speed. Make sure that you operate the engine at the speed that the misfire or failure occurs during this test.

A peak-reading voltmeter (PRV) and three TS-77 terminal extenders (**Table 1**) are required for this procedure.

It is possible for a defective ignition coil to cause the power pack output to be below specification. If there is any doubt as to the ignition coil's condition, refer to *Ignition Coil Tests* at the beginning of the ignition section and test the ignition coil(s).

1. Disconnect the power pack's orange/blue (No. 1 cylinder), orange/purple (No. 2 cylinder) and orange/green (No. 3 cylinder) primary leads from the ignition coils with a gentle twisting and pulling motion.

2. Install a TS-77 terminal extender onto each primary terminal. Then install the pack's orange/blue, orange/purple and orange/green leads onto the appropriate extender.

3. Adjust a PRV to the *positive* and *500* settings (or equivalent).

4. Connect the black meter lead to a good engine ground. Connect the red meter lead to the exposed metal of the upper (No. 1 cylinder) terminal extender.

> *CAUTION*
> *Do not run the engine without an adequate water supply and do not exceed 3000 rpm without an adequate load. Refer to* **Safety Precautions** *at the beginning of this chapter.*

5. Run the engine at the speed that the misfire or ignition failure occurs, while noting the meter reading. The meter must indicate a steady 220 peak volts or higher. If not, check for loose or damaged connectors, damaged leads, loose ground leads and/or component mounting hardware. If all checks are satisfactory, yet the voltage is below 220

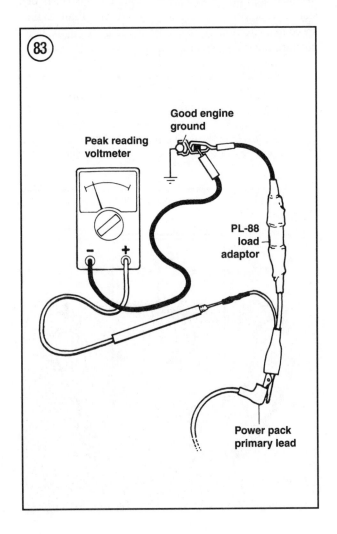

(83)

Peak reading voltmeter

Good engine ground

PL-88 load adaptor

Power pack primary lead

volts or erratic, replace the power pack and retest spark output.

6. Repeat Steps 4-5 for the middle (No. 2 cylinder) and bottom (No. 3 cylinder) terminal extenders.

7. Remove the terminal extenders and reconnect the power pack's primary leads to the appropriate ignition coil terminals, making sure the orange/blue lead is connected to the top (No. 1 cylinder) ignition coil, the orange/purple lead is connected to the middle (No. 2 cylinder) ignition coil and the orange/green lead is connected to the bottom (No. 3 cylinder) ignition coil.

S.L.O.W. System Operation (50-70 hp [Three-cylinder] Models)

These models are equipped with the speed limiting overheat warning (S.L.O.W.) system. The system is designed to activate the warning system and limit engine speed to approximately 2000-3000 rpm if the engine temperature exceeds the temperature switch's closing value.

To deactivate (reset) the S.L.O.W. system, the engine must be stopped and allowed to cool to a point below the temperature switch's opening value. These engines are equipped with a 237° F (114° C) temperature switch. The switch is identified by its tan/blue lead. The switch must close at 231-243° F (111-117° C) and open at 192-222° F (89-106° C).

The S.L.O.W. system receives its operating voltage from the power coil. The power coil is potted in the stator assembly along with the charge coil and alternator stator coil. If the power coil fails, the S.L.O.W. system will not operate.

S.L.O.W. system troubleshooting

If the S.L.O.W. system engages during normal operation, proceed as follows:

1. Refer to *Engine Temperature and Overheating* and verify that the engine is not overheating. If the engine is overheating, repair the cooling system as necessary and recheck the engine's operating temperature.

2. If engine temperature is within specification, disconnect the temperature switch lead at its bullet (or two-pin Amphenol [A, **Figure 84**]) connector. Tape or sleeve the engine harness end of the lead if necessary, to make sure it cannot contact engine ground.

NOTE
If the temperature switch's tan/blue lead is routed too close to the spark plug leads or ignition coil(s), RFI (radio frequency interference) can cause the power pack to falsely engage the S.L.O.W. function. Route the tan/blue lead as far from the ignition coils and spark plug leads as possible.

3. Start the engine and check for S.L.O.W. engagement.
4A. If the S.L.O.W. system still engages, refer to *Blocking diode tests* located later in this section. If the blocking diode tests satisfactorily, test the engine (and boat) harness tan lead for a short to ground. Repair or replace the lead as necessary. If the tan lead tests satisfactorily, replace the power pack.
4B. If the S.L.O.W. system no longer engages, the temperature switch is shorted to ground and must be replaced.

S.L.O.W. system functional tests

The S.L.O.W. system is activated by input from the engine temperature switch. The temperature switch is located near the top of the cylinder head. On 1995 (EO) models, the temperature switch tan lead is connected to the switch and power pack with bullet connectors. On 1996-1998 (ED-EC) models, the temperature switch tan lead is connected to the switch and power pack with Amphenol connectors.

To perform a functional test of S.L.O.W. operation and troubleshoot all system functions, proceed as follows:

CAUTION
*Do not run the engine without an adequate water supply and do not exceed 3000 rpm without an adequate load. Refer to **Safety Precautions** at the beginning of this chapter.*

1. Connect an accurate shop tachometer to the spark plug lead following its manufacturer's instructions.

2. Disconnect the engine temperature switch at its bullet (or two-pin Amphenol [A, **Figure 84**]) connector.

3. Start the engine and allow it to warm to normal operating temperature. Then increase engine speed to approximately 3500 rpm.

4. Using a suitable jumper lead, connect the engine harness tan lead to a clean engine ground, while noting the engine speed.

5. If S.L.O.W. engages, engine speed will quickly be reduced to approximately 2000-3000 rpm and stabilize. It is not necessary to continue to hold the tan lead to ground once S.L.O.W. has been engaged (latched). If S.L.O.W. correctly engages, proceed to Step 6. If not, proceed as follows:

   a. Test the blocking diode for an open condition as described in *Blocking diode tests*.

   b. If the blocking diode tests satisfactorily, test the tan lead for an open circuit between the power pack tan lead bullet (or three-pin Amphenol [B, **Figure 84**]) connector and the temperature switch connector. Repair or replace the tan lead as necessary.

   c. If the diode and the tan lead test satisfactorily, test the power coil as described in *Power coil tests*. If the power coil tests satisfactorily, replace the power pack and retest the S.L.O.W. function.

6. If S.L.O.W. engages in Step 5, disconnect the tan lead from ground and stop the engine. Restart the engine and attempt to accelerate the engine to 3500 rpm.

   a. If the engine will now freely accelerate above the S.L.O.W. limit (2000-3000 rpm), the power pack programming and engine wiring harness are functioning correctly.

   b. If the engine still remains in S.L.O.W., disconnect the power pack tan lead at its bullet (or three-pin Amphenol [B, **Figure 84**]) connector and retest. If the engine will now freely accelerate above the S.L.O.W. limit, the tan lead is shorted to ground. Repair or replace the tan lead as necessary. If the tan lead is not shorted to ground and the engine still will not accelerate above the S.L.O.W. limit, replace the power pack.

Blocking diode tests

A blocking diode located in the *engine* wiring harness tan lead is used to prevent the warning system's self-test and oil injection warning signals from activating the S.L.O.W. (speed limiting overheat warning) program. The S.L.O.W. program must only activate if the engine is actually overheating.

The diode is positioned near the large, red ten-pin main harness connector on 1995 (EO) models and near the six-pin Deutsch system check harness connector on 1996-1998 (ED-EC) models.

If the diode fails in an open circuit, the S.L.O.W. program will still engage, but the operator will not get a warning horn signal (or LED on system check models).

If the diode fails in a closed circuit, the S.L.O.W. program may engage when the warning system self-tests, and/or when the oil injection system's low oil or no oil warning signals are activated.

To test the blocking diode, refer to the back of the manual for wiring diagrams and proceed as follows:

1. Disconnect the negative battery cable. Then disconnect and ground the spark plug leads to the power head to prevent accidental starting.

2A. *Traditional wiring harnesses (1995 [EO] models)*—Disconnect the large, red ten-pin main harness connector. Then disconnect the engine temperature switch at its bullet connector.

2B. *Modular wiring harnesses (1996-1998 [ED-EC] models)*—Disconnect the engine harness from the boat wiring harness at the engine's six-pin Deutsch connector. Then disconnect the engine temperature switch at its two-pin Amphenol connector (A, **Figure 84**).

3. Calibrate an ohmmeter on the appropriate scale to test diodes.

4A. *Traditional wiring harnesses*—Using suitable jumper leads, connect one ohmmeter lead to the engine harness side of the temperature switch tan lead connector and the other ohmmeter lead to the tan pin (7, **Figure 66**) of the engine harness side of the large, red ten-pin connector.

4B. *Modular wiring harnesses*—Using suitable jumper leads, connect one ohmmeter lead to the engine harness side of the temperature switch's tan lead connector and the other ohmmeter lead to the tan lead (pin 6) of the engine harness side of the six-pin Deutsch connector.

5. Note the ohmmeter reading, then reverse the meter leads (or meter polarity).

   a. The meter must indicate no continuity (very high reading) in one polarity and continuity (low reading) in the opposite polarity.

   b. If the meter reads no continuity (very high reading) in both polarities, the diode has failed in an open circuit and must be replaced.

   c. If the meter reads continuity (low reading) in both polarities, the diode has failed in a closed circuit (shorted) and must be replaced.

6. Reconnect all leads when finished. Connect the spark plug leads and negative battery cable last.

Power coil test

Test the power coil using an ohmmeter. There are no output specifications for test using peak-reading voltmeter (PRV).

> *NOTE*
> *It is necessary to loosen the power pack mounting screws to gain access to the connector in the following step. Make sure the power pack mounting screws (and its ground lead [A, Figure 85]) are securely tightened before cranking or running the engine.*

1. Disconnect the power pack-to-stator five-pin Amphenol connector (B, **Figure 85**). Install suitable Amphenol jumper leads to pins C and D (orange/black and orange leads) of the stator side of the connector (male body, female pins).

2. Calibrate an ohmmeter on the appropriate scale to read 360-440 ohms.

3. Connect one ohmmeter lead to the power coil orange/black lead (pin C) and the other ohmmeter lead to the power coil orange lead (pin D).

4. If the reading is not within 360-440 ohms, inspect the leads for damage and repair any found. If the leads are in satisfactory condition, replace the power coil (stator assembly).

5. To check the power coil for a short-to-ground, calibrate the ohmmeter on the highest scale available. Connect the

black ohmmeter lead to a good engine ground. If the stator is removed, connect the lead to a mounting screw bore.

6. Connect the red ohmmeter lead to the coil's orange/black lead (pin C). Note the meter reading. The meter must indicate no continuity. If not, the power coil (or lead) is shorted to ground. Inspect the lead for damage and repair any found. If the lead is in satisfactory condition, replace the power coil (stator assembly).

7. Repeat Step 6 for the power coil orange lead (pin D).

8. Remove the jumper leads and reconnect the five-pin Amphenol connector when finished. Make sure the power pack mounting screws and ground lead are securely tightened.

QuikStart System Operation (50-70 hp [Three-cylinder] Models)

The QuikStart circuit automatically advances the ignition timing approximately 12° when the engine temperature is below 105° F (41° C) to improve engine running quality during warm-up and reduce the amount of fast idle lever movement required by the operator. The ignition timing will remain advanced until either the engine temperature exceeds 105° F (41° C) or an internal timer (in the power pack) reaches 1-2 minutes. To prevent power head damage from over-advanced timing (such as preignition or detonation), the power pack disables the QuikStart program as soon as engine rpm exceeds 1100 rpm, regardless of engine temperature or time elapsed.

> *NOTE*
> *If the ignition timing stays 12° advanced (above the normal engine timing specifications) as the engine is accelerated above 1100 rpm, the power pack is defective and must be replaced.*

The power pack contains an internal timer that limits the maximum duration of the QuikStart program to approximately 1-2 minutes, even if the temperature switch remains open from an overcooling engine or defective switch. Also, a second temperature switch (located inside the power pack) monitors the temperature under the motor cover. Warmer temperatures will cause the maximum duration of the QuikStart program to be shorter, while colder temperatures will allow the program to operate up to the maximum (1-2 minute) limit. Finally, the QuikStart program advances the ignition timing each time the engine is started (for approximately 5-10 seconds), regardless of engine temperature.

QuikStart system functional tests

The QuikStart system is activated by input from the engine temperature switch's white/black lead. The temperature switch is located near the top of the cylinder head (**Figure 76**). On 1995 (EO) models, the temperature switch white/black lead is connected to the switch and power pack with bullet connectors. On 1996-2003 (ED-ST) models, the temperature switch white/black lead is connected to the switch and power pack with Amphenol connectors.

If the white/black lead is open to ground, the QuikStart program will be activated. If the white/black lead is grounded, the QuickStart program will be deactivated.

A yellow/red lead (from the ignition switch and/or starter solenoid) powers the QuikStart circuits during engine startup (cranking), when the power coil has not yet begun to produce electricity.

The power pack signals the timer base to switch to the advanced set of sensor coils by applying voltage to the timer base black/white lead.

To perform a functional test of QuikStart operation and troubleshoot all system functions, proceed as follows:

CAUTION
*Do not run the engine without an adequate water supply and do not exceed 3000 rpm without an adequate load. Refer to **Safety Precautions** at the beginning of this chapter.*

1. Refer to Chapter Five and perform all synchronization and linkage adjustments.

2. Connect an accurate shop tachometer and timing light to the No. 1 spark plug lead following their manufacturer's instructions.

3. Refer to *Indexing flywheel (erratic spark [two- and three-cylinder models])* and mark the flywheel with the TDC (top dead center) location for cylinders No. 2 and No. 3.

4. Start the engine and allow it to warm to normal operating temperature. Refer to *Engine temperature check* located later in this chapter. Engine operating temperature must be well above 105° F (41° C) before proceeding.

5. Disconnect the engine temperature switch's white/black lead at its bullet (or two-pin Amphenol [A, **Figure 84**]) connector.

6. Shift the engine into FORWARD gear and make sure that it is idling at no more than 900 rpm.

7A. *50 hp models*—Check the ignition timing. Timing must be approximately 4° BTDC (before top dead center), which is 12° more than the normal timing figure of 8° ATDC (after top dead center). If the timing advances (to 4° BTDC), proceed to Step 9. If not, proceed to Step 8.

7B. *60-70 hp models*—Check the ignition timing. Timing must be approximately 8° BTDC (before top dead center),

which is 12° more than the normal timing figure of 4° ATDC (after top dead center). If the timing advanced (to 8° BTDC), proceed to Step 9. If not, proceed to Step 8.

8. If timing does not advance as specified in Step 7A (or Step 7B), proceed as follows:
   a. If timing is not advanced, test the white/black lead for a short to ground between its bullet connector (or two-pin Amphenol connector [A, **Figure 84**] pin B) and the power pack bullet connector (or three-pin connector's [B, **Figure 84**] pin A). Repair or replace the lead or connectors as necessary.
   b. If the white/black lead tests satisfactorily (is not shorted to ground), replace the power pack.

NOTE
The engine must be stopped to reset the QuickStart program before testing each remaining cylinder.

9. If the timing advances as specified in Step 7A (or Step 7B), stop the engine and repeat Steps 4-7 for the No. 2 and 3 (middle and bottom) cylinders. Make sure the engine is shut off before testing another cylinder and the timing light pickup assembly is moved to the spark plug lead of the cylinder being tested.
   a. If timing does not advance as specified on one or two cylinders (Steps 4-7), replace the timer base assembly.
   b. If timing does not advance as specified on all cylinders (Steps 4-7), refer to *QuikStart inoperative* in this chapter.

10. Reconnect the engine temperature switch's white/black lead to the engine harness. Start the engine and recheck the ignition timing (at no more than 900 rpm). The ignition timing must indicate approximately 8° ATDC (50 hp models) or 4° ATDC (60-70 hp models). If the timing retarded (approximately 12° from the QuikStart advanced figure), the system is functioning correctly. If not, proceed as follows:
   a. Test the engine temperature switch as described in *Engine Temperature Switches* located later in this Chapter. The white/black lead's function must be verified.
   b. If the engine temperature switch tests satisfactorily, test the white/black lead for continuity between its bullet connector (or two-pin Amphenol connector's [A, **Figure 84**] pin B) and the power pack bullet connector (or three-pin connector's [B, **Figure 84**] pin A). Repair or replace the lead or connectors, as necessary.
   c. If the engine temperature switch tests satisfactorily, the white/black lead has continuity and timing does not retard to 4° ATDC when the switch is recon-

nected, refer to *QuikStart always activated* located in the next section.

QuikStart always on

If QuikStart remains on constantly when the engine is operated *above* 1100 rpm, the power pack is defective and must be replaced. If QuikStart remains on constantly (regardless of time and/or engine temperature) when the engine is operated *below* 1100 rpm, proceed as follows:

1A. *1995 (EO) models*—Check for a defective starter solenoid or key switch bleeding voltage into the yellow/red lead connected to the power pack. This small voltage can activate the QuikStart circuit.
   a. Disconnect the power pack yellow/red lead bullet connector. Connect a voltmeter to the engine harness side of the bullet connector.
   b. Check for voltage with the ignition switch in the ON or RUN position. There must be zero volts. Any reading above zero can cause false activation of the QuickStart program.
   c. Repair or replace the lead or components (starter solenoid or ignition switch) as necessary.

1B. *1996-1998 (ED-EC) models*—Check for a defective starter solenoid or key switch bleeding voltage into the yellow/red lead connected to the power pack. This small voltage can activate the QuikStart circuit.
   a. Disconnect the power pack three-pin Amphenol connector (B, **Figure 84**). Connect an Amphenol jumper lead to the yellow/red lead (pin C) of the engine harness side of the connector (female body, male pins).
   b. Check for voltage at the yellow/red lead (pin C) with the ignition switch in the ON or RUN position. There must be zero volts. Any reading above zero can cause false activation of the QuickStart program.
   c. Repair or replace the lead or components (starter solenoid or ignition switch) as necessary.

NOTE
*In the preceding tests, the yellow/red lead must not indicate **any** voltage when the ignition switch is in the OFF (or STOP) and ON (or RUN) positions. However the yellow/red lead must indicate battery voltage when the ignition switch is in the START position (motor being cranked).*

2. Check for an open circuit or loose or corroded connections in the power pack white/black lead. Begin checking at the power pack bullet connector (or three-pin Amphenol connector [B, **Figure 84**]) and continue to the point the lead enters the power pack potting. Repair any damage noted or replace the power pack as necessary.

3. Test the engine temperature switch's white/black lead function as described in *Engine temperature switches*.

4. Check the engine operating temperature as described in *Engine temperature check* and verify that the engine is not overcooling.

5. If no problems are noted in Steps 1-4, replace the power pack.

3

QuikStart inoperative

A peak reading voltmeter (PRV) and a suitable Amphenol connector breakout box (or jumper leads) are necessary to complete this test. Two commonly used breakout boxes are the Stevens Model SA-6 or the Merc-O-Tronic Model 55-861. The breakout box is connected inline with the timer base circuit and allows voltage measurements while the circuit remains intact.

NOTE
*Use this procedure only if directed by Step 9 of **QuickStart functional tests**.*

To troubleshoot an inoperative QuikStart circuit, proceed as follows:

1A. *Using break out box*—Disconnect the power pack-to-timer base five-pin Amphenol connector (C, **Figure 85**). Attach each connector body to the appropriate lead or connector on the breakout box (Table 1). Verify that all breakout box switches are in the ON position.

1B. *Using jumper leads*—Disconnect the power pack-to-timer base five-pin Amphenol connector (C, **Figure 85**). Connect five jumper leads between the connector bodies so that all pins are connected. The jumper lead being used for pin D (black/white) must allow a voltage reading to be taken while the engine is running. Either strip a small amount of insulation from the jumper lead or install a suitable terminal in the middle of the jumper lead.

2. Adjust a PRV to the *positive* and *50* settings (or equivalent). Connect the black meter lead to a good engine ground. Connect the red meter lead to the black/white lead (pin D) at the breakout box or jumper lead.

CAUTION
*Do not run the engine without an adequate water supply and do not exceed 3000 rpm without an adequate load. Refer to **Safety Precautions** at the beginning of this chapter. Also, do not run the engine with any of the timer base leads disconnected or the power pack will be destroyed. Be certain the breakout box or jumper leads are installed as directed in Step 1.*

3. Start the engine and run at 900 rpm in FORWARD gear while observing the meter.

    a. If the meter indicates 8-12 volts, the timer base is defective and must be replaced and QuikStart function rechecked.

    b. If the meter does not indicate 8-12 peak volts, test the power coil as described in the following steps.

NOTE
*It is necessary to loosen the power pack mounting screws to gain access to the connector in the following step. Make sure the power pack mounting screws (and its ground lead [A, **Figure 85**]) are securely tightened before cranking or running the engine.*

4. Disconnect the power pack-to-stator five-pin Amphenol connector (B, **Figure 85**). Install suitable Amphenol jumper leads to pins C and D (orange/black and orange leads) of the stator side of the connector (male body, female pins).

5. Calibrate an ohmmeter on the appropriate scale to read 360-440 ohms.

6. Connect one ohmmeter lead to the power coil orange/black lead (pin C) and the other ohmmeter lead to the power coil orange lead (pin D).

7. If the reading is not within 360-440 ohms, inspect the leads for damage and repair any found. If the leads are in satisfactory condition, the power coil (stator assembly) must be replaced.

8. To check the power coil for a short to ground, calibrate the ohmmeter on the highest scale available. Connect the black ohmmeter lead to a good engine ground. If the stator is removed, connect the lead to a mounting screw bore.

9. Connect the red ohmmeter lead to the coil's orange/black lead (pin C). Note the meter reading. The meter must indicate no continuity. If not, the power coil (or lead) is shorted to ground. Inspect the lead for damage and repair any found. If the lead is in satisfactory condition, the power coil (stator assembly) must be replaced.

10. Repeat Step 6 for the power coil orange lead (pin D).

11. If the power coil tests satisfactory, yet the power pack does not supply the 8-12 peak volts to the black/white lead as specified in Step 3, replace the power pack and retest QuickStart function.

12. Remove the jumper leads and reconnect the five-pin Amphenol connector when finished. Make sure power pack mounting screws and ground lead are securely tightened.

FUEL SYSTEM

Outboard owners often assume the carburetor(s) is at fault if the engine does not run properly. While fuel system problems are not uncommon, carburetor adjustment is seldom the solution. In many cases, adjusting the carburetor only compounds the problem by making the engine run worse.

Never attempt to adjust the carburetor(s) idle speed and/or idle mixture until the following conditions have been met:

1. The ignition timing is correctly adjusted (Chapter Five).

2. The engine throttle and ignition linkage are correctly synchronized and adjusted (Chapter Five).

3. The engine is running at normal operating temperature. See *Engine Temperature Checks* located in this chapter.

4. The outboard is in the water, running in FORWARD gear with the correct propeller installed.

If the engine appears to be running lean or starving for fuel, first determine whether the boat fuel system or the engine fuel system is causing the problem. Engines that appear to be running rich or receiving excessive fuel, will usually have a problem located in the engine fuel system, not the boat fuel system.

The boat fuel system consists of the fuel tank, fuel vent line and vent fitting, the fuel pickup tube and antisiphon valve, the fuel distribution lines, boat-mounted water-separating fuel filter (recommended) and the primer bulb.

The typical engine fuel system consists of an engine fuel filter, crankcase pulse driven fuel pump (or combination fuel pump/oil injection pump), carburetor(s), fuel primer valve (mechanical or electric) and the necessary lines and fittings.

Conventional Fuel Pump Operation

All conventional fuel pumps are operated by pressure pulses created by the movement of the pistons in their bores. The pressure pulses reach the fuel pump(s) through a drilled passage in the crankcase or by a pulse fitting and hose.

The upward motion of the piston creates a low pressure in the crankcase and against the pump diaphragm. This low pressure opens the inlet check valve in the pump, drawing fuel

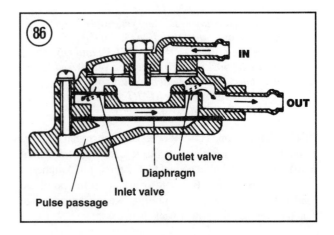

(86)

IN

OUT

Outlet valve

Diaphragm

Inlet valve

Pulse passage

from the supply line into the pump. The downward motion of the piston creates a high pressure in the crankcase and against the pump diaphragm. This pressure closes the inlet check valve and opens the outlet check valve, forcing the fuel into the fuel line to the carburetor(s). See **Figure 86**.

If the cylinder(s) that drives the fuel pump(s) fails, the fuel pump(s) cannot operate. Therefore, if a fuel delivery problem is encountered, first check the cranking compression before continuing with troubleshooting. Make sure the fuel tank vent line is not kinked, plugged or restricted. After a thorough visual inspection of the fuel system, continue with the fuel pump pressure and vacuum tests.

Troubleshooting

The first Step is to make sure that fresh fuel is present in the fuel tank. If the fuel is stale or sour, drain the fuel tank and dispose of the fuel in an approved manner. Clean the fuel filters and flush the fuel lines to remove all traces of the stale or sour fuel. Inspect all fuel lines for evidence of leakage or deterioration. Replace any questionable components. Make sure the fuel tank vent is open and not restricted. Refer to Chapter Four for fuel filter service procedures and Chapter Six for component removal, rebuild and replacement procedures.

NOTE
When troubleshooting an engine equipped with remote fuel tank or fuel tank permanently mounted in the boat, connect a substitute fuel tank (and fuel line) filled with fresh fuel to the engine. If the symptom is eliminated, the problem is in the original fuel tank and lines. If the symptom is still present, the problem is located on the engine. On models without oil injection, make sure the substitute tank contains the correct fuel/oil mix.

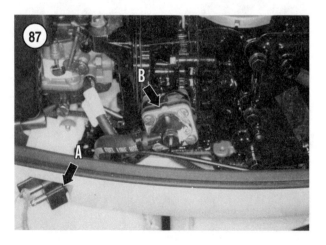

2, 3.3 and 3.5 hp (Gravity Feed System)

The 2.0, 3.3 and 3.5 hp models use a gravity feed fuel system and are not equipped with oil injection. Make sure fuel is present in the fuel tank and the fuel tank vent is not obstructed. Disconnect the fuel line from the fuel tank to the carburetor and place the line in a suitable container. Turn the fuel valve on and check for free fuel flow into the container. If the fuel flow is restricted, clean or replace the fuel valve and filter. See Chapters Four and Six.

If the fuel flows freely and the problem is still believed to be fuel related, service the carburetor as described in Chapter Six.

3 hp Models

These models are equipped with an integral fuel tank and a carburetor that has an internal fuel pump and fuel shutoff valve. An inline fuel filter is used between the fuel tank and the carburetor. These models are not equipped with oil injection.

Make sure fuel is present in the fuel tank and the fuel tank vent is not obstructed. Disconnect the fuel line from the carburetor and place the line in a suitable container and check for free fuel flow into the container.

If the fuel flow is restricted, clean or replace the inline fuel filter and check the fuel lines for obstructions. See Chapters Four and Six.

If the fuel flows freely and the problem is still believed to be fuel related, service the carburetor as described in Chapter Six.

4 hp Models (Except 4 Deluxe)

On 4 hp (4BR) models, an integral fuel tank and a quick-disconnect fitting for a remote fuel tank is used. A conventional fuel pump pulls fuel from the remote fuel tank when the fuel shut-off valve is in the OFF position and the engine is running. When the fuel shutoff valve is in the ON position, the carburetor's internal fuel pump pulls fuel from the integral fuel tank and inline fuel filter.

If the motor will run satisfactorily on the remote fuel tank, but not on the integral tank, the problem lies in the integral fuel tank, inline fuel filter or carburetor.

If the motor runs satisfactorily on the integral fuel tank, but not the remote fuel tank, begin troubleshooting by referring to *Conventional Fuel Pump Operation* located previously in this chapter.

The 4 hp (4R) models are equipped with a quick-disconnect fitting (A, **Figure 87**, typical) for a remote fuel tank. There is no integral fuel tank. A conventional fuel pump (B, **Figure 87**, typical) pulls fuel from the remote fuel tank whenever the engine is running. There is no fuel shutoff valve. A primer bulb in the remote tank's fuel supply line must be squeezed (by the operator) to fill the carburetor with fuel, prior to starting. To begin troubleshooting, refer to *Conventional Fuel Pump Operation* located previously in this chapter.

4 Deluxe, 6-30 hp (Two-cylinder), 18 and 28 Jet, 40 hp (rope start) and 48 Special models

These engines are not equipped with oil injection. A conventional fuel pump is used to supply fuel to the single carburetor (6-30 hp and 18 jet) or dual carburetors (40 hp, 48 Special and 28 jet) when the engine is running. A small, conventional fuel pump (B, **Figure 87**) is used on the 4 Deluxe-8 hp models and a large, conventional fuel pump (**Figure 88**) is used on 9.9-48 hp models. A primer bulb in the fuel supply line must be squeezed by the operator to fill the carburetor(s) with fuel, prior to starting. To begin troubleshooting, refer to *Conventional Fuel Pump Operation* located previously in this chapter.

25 and 35 hp (Three-cylinder) Models

These models use two conventional fuel pumps (connected in series) to supply fuel to the three carburetors when the engine is running. Prior to starting, a primer bulb in the fuel supply line must be squeezed by the operator to fill the carburetors with fuel.

The first (port) pump (A, **Figure 89**) is primarily a vacuum pump that lifts the fuel from the fuel tank. The second (starboard) pump (B, **Figure 89**) is primarily a pressure pump that pushes the fuel from the first pump to the carburetor.

These engines are also equipped with a separate oil injection pump and engine-mounted oil reservoir. The oil injection pump is mounted on the pressure side of the second fuel pump and is operated by fuel pressure. Refer to Chapter Eleven for an operational description of the oil injection system and service procedures.

To begin troubleshooting, refer to *Conventional Fuel Pump Operation* located previously in this chapter.

VRO^2 Systems

The 40 hp (electric start), 35 jet and all 50-70 hp models are equipped with a combination fuel pump/oil injection pump, referred to as the VRO^2 pump unit (**Figure 90**). The VRO^2 pump unit supplies the engine with fuel and oil when the engine is running. The correct amount of oil is mixed with the fuel inside of the pump unit. A primer bulb

in the fuel supply line must be squeezed to fill the carburetors with fuel, prior to starting.

The pump unit is driven by crankcase pressure and vacuum pulses. The pulse line is equipped with a pulse limiter that prevents damage to the pump unit's diaphragm during engine backfire.

Refer to Chapter Eleven for complete operational description, testing and repair procedures. It is important to note that any fuel restriction causing a vacuum above 4 in. Hg (13.5 kPa) in the fuel supply line will cause the unit to mix excessive oil in the fuel, resulting in excessive smoke, fouled spark plugs, carbon buildup and excessive oil consumption.

If the cylinder that drives the VRO^2 pump unit fails, the pump cannot operate. If a fuel delivery problem is evident, check the cranking compression before troubleshooting the fuel system. If the boat is equipped with a permanent fuel system make sure the fuel tank vent line is not kinked or obstructed. If all visual checks are satisfactory continue with the fuel pump pressure and vacuum tests.

Fuel Supply (Vacuum) Test

Make sure that all fuel filters have been cleaned (or replaced) as described in Chapter Four before continuing. This test is intended to determine if there is a restriction in the fuel supply system that would affect engine operation.

The fuel pump(s) cannot be tested for pressure until an unrestricted fuel supply has been verified.

The test is best performed with the vacuum gauge connected as close to the fuel pump inlet fitting as possible. The further the gauge is from the pump, the more likely that the source of a problem will be missed. Since the fuel pressure test is performed following the vacuum test, also install the pressure gauge at this time. Refer to **Figure 91** for a block diagram of a typical vacuum and pressure gauge installation.

CAUTION
*Do not run the engine without an adequate water supply and do not exceed 3000 rpm without an adequate load. Refer to **Safety Precautions** at the beginning of this chapter.*

NOTE
*The 25 and 35 hp (three-cylinder) models use two mechanical fuel pumps in series. Check the vacuum into the port pump and the pressure out of the starboard pump. See **Figure 89**.*

1A. *Permanent fuel tank*—Ensure that the fuel vent fitting and vent line are not obstructed.

1B. *Portable fuel tank*—Open the fuel tank cap to relieve any pressure that may be present, verify the fuel tank vent

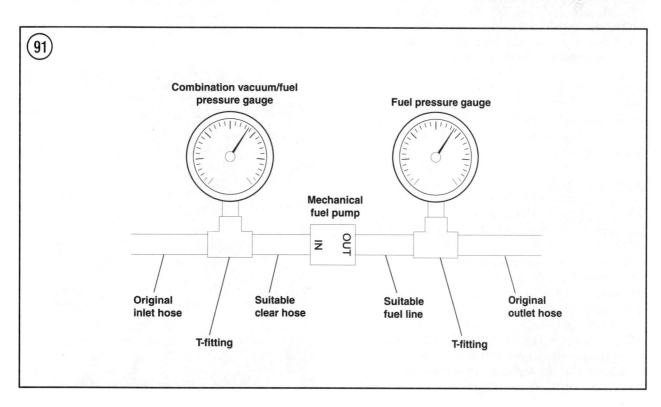

(91)

Combination vacuum/fuel
pressure gauge

Fuel pressure gauge

Mechanical
fuel pump

IN   OUT

Original
inlet hose

Suitable
clear hose

Suitable
fuel line

Original
outlet hose

T-fitting

T-fitting

is fully open and make sure that the tank is no more than 30 in. (762 mm) below the level of the fuel pump.

2A. *Conventional pump*—Disconnect the fuel inlet hose from the fuel pump. This is always the hose connected to the filter cover. See **Figure 92**, typical. On 25 and 35 hp (three-cylinder) models, the vacuum gauge must be connected to the port fuel pump.

2B. *VRO^2 pump*—Disconnect the fuel inlet hose (A, **Figure 93**) from the pump. Do not disconnect the oil inlet hose (B, **Figure 93**) or the pulse line hose (C, **Figure 93**) from the pump.

3. Connect a combination vacuum and fuel pressure gauge between the fuel pump and the inlet line using a T-fitting, a short piece of clear vinyl hose and the appropriate fittings and clamps. See **Figure 91**, typical.

4A. *Conventional pump*—Disconnect the fuel pump output hose that leads to the carburetor(s). On 25 and 35 hp (three-cylinder) models, the pressure gauge must be connected to the starboard pump's outlet fitting.

4B. *VRO^2 pump*—Disconnect the pump outlet hose (D, **Figure 93**) that leads to the carburetors.

5. Connect a fuel pressure gauge between the fuel pump and the output line using a T-fitting and appropriate piece of fuel line and clamps. See **Figure 94** for a typical conventional pump installation. Gently squeeze the primer bulb and check for leaks.

> *CAUTION*
> *Do not run the engine without an adequate water supply and do not exceed 3000 rpm without an adequate load. Refer to Safety Precautions at the beginning of this chapter.*

6. Start the motor and allow it to reach operating temperature. Then run the engine in FORWARD gear at wide-open throttle for a minimum of two minutes, while observing the clear hose on the inlet side of the fuel pump.

7. If air bubbles are visible in the clear hose on the inlet side of the pump, check the fuel supply line back to the pickup tube in the fuel tank for loose fittings, loose clamps, a defective primer bulb, damaged filter or any problems that would allow air to leak into the fuel line. There can be no air leaks into the fuel supply line. Correct any problems and retest.

8. If the vacuum gauge reading exceeds 4 in. Hg (13.5 kPa) during the wide-open throttle test, a restriction is present in the fuel delivery system. Check for flow restrictions caused by:

   a. Kinked or collapsed fuel lines.

   b. Fuel lines or fuel fittings that are too small. On a permanently installed fuel system, the fuel pickup tube (in the fuel tank) and all fuel distribution lines must be a minimum of 5/16 in. (7.94 mm) inside

diameter and all fuel fittings must be a minimum of 1/4 in. (6.35 mm) inside diameter.

   c. Defective antisiphon valve, primer bulb and fuel selector valves. Temporarily bypass any component in question with a suitable piece of fuel line. If the vacuum reading drops, the bypassed component is causing a restriction and must be replaced. Antisiphon valves may be tested as described in *Antisiphon Valve Tests*, in this chapter.

9. If no air bubbles are visible in the clear hose and the vacuum gauge reading does not exceed 4 in. Hg (13.5 kPa), the fuel supply system is in satisfactory condition. Do not disconnect any test gauges or lines. Continue to *Fuel pump output (pressure) test*.

Fuel Pump Output (Pressure) Test

Do not attempt this test unless the *Fuel restriction (vacuum) test* has been completed. The pressure gauge was installed along with the vacuum gauge in the preceding procedure.

> *CAUTION*
> *Do not run the engine without an adequate water supply and do not exceed 3000 rpm without an adequate load. Refer to Safety Precautions at the beginning of this chapter.*

1A. *Convention fuel pump (except 25 and 35 hp [three-cylinder] models)*—Start the motor and allow it to reach operating temperature. Run the engine in FORWARD gear

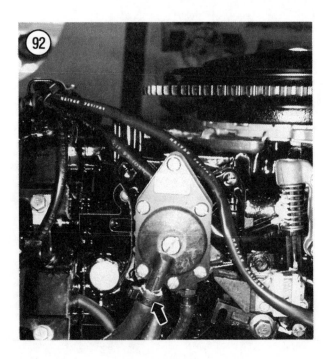

at idle speed, 2500-3000 rpm and wide-open throttle while observing the fuel pressure gauge at each speed. The pressure must be at least 1 psi (6.9 kPa) at idle speed, 1.5 psi (10.3 kPa) at 2500-3000 rpm and 2.5 psi (17.2 kPa) at wide-open throttle (above 4500 rpm).

1B. *25 and 35 hp (three-cylinder) models*—Start the motor and allow it to reach operating temperature. Run the engine in FORWARD gear at wide-open throttle while observing the fuel pressure gauge. The fuel pressure must be at least 3.0 psi (20.7 kPa) at wide-open throttle.

NOTE
Each time a VRO^2 pump cycles, the fuel pressure will momentarily drop. This is normal. A cycle occurs each time the oil piston injects oil into the mixing chamber. The frequency at which this occurs depends on engine load

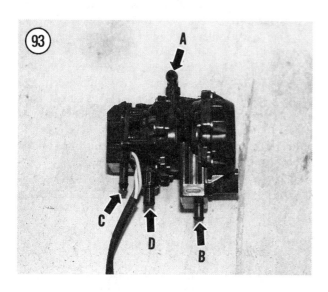

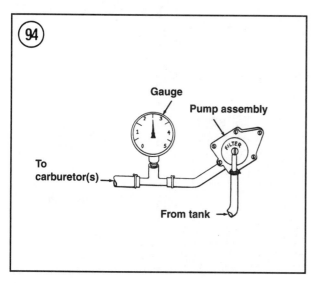

and speed, but will be consistent for any given load and speed. See Chapter Eleven.

1C. *VRO^2 equipped models*—Start the motor and allow it to reach operating temperature. Run the engine in FORWARD gear at 800 rpm while observing the fuel pressure gauge. The fuel pressure must stabilize at a minimum of 3.0 psi (20.7 kPa) between pump cycles.

2A. *Conventional fuel pump (except 25 and 35 hp [three-cylinder] models)*—If fuel pump pressure is not as specified, the fuel pump must be repaired or replaced.

2B. *25 and 35 hp (three-cylinder) models*—If fuel pump pressure is not as specified, both fuel pumps (port and starboard) must be repaired or replaced.

2C. *VRO^2 equipped models*—If the fuel pressure is not as specified, refer to Chapter Eleven and repair or replace the VRO^2 pump unit as directed.

3. If the fuel pump(s) is in acceptable condition, but the outboard motor still has a fuel-related problem, service the carburetors as described in Chapter Six.

NOTE
Make sure the fuel distribution line(s), fuel fitting(s) and any fuel manifold(s) between the fuel pump outlet fitting and at each carburetor (as equipped) are not restricted, kinked or blocked in any manner. Fuel must be able to flow unrestricted from the fuel pump(s) to the carburetor(s).

ANTISIPHON VALVE TESTS

Antisiphon valves are installed in boats to prevent fuel from being siphoned into the bilge area should a fuel line break at a point below the fuel level in the tank. OMC outboard engines are designed to operate with an antisiphon valve installed, as long as the valve meets OMC's specifications. The part No. 173273 (for 5/16 in. inside diameter fuel line) or part No. 173274 (for 3/8 in. inside diameter fuel line) antisiphon valves meet OMC's specifications and are highly recommended replacement parts if the antisiphon valve is suspected of causing a fuel restriction.

While antisiphon protection can also be provided by securing the fuel distribution lines above the top of the fuel tank (with the boat floating in an unloaded, static position), an antisiphon valve must never be removed from a boat so equipped.

If an antisiphon valve is suspected of causing a fuel starvation problem, the valve must be tested as described in the following procedure. This procedure uses the weight of a column of water pressing against the spring and check valve to test the valve's ability to stay closed (resist siphoning) and its ability to open and allow fuel flow without causing an excessive restriction on the engine's fuel pump. To test the valve, refer to **Figure 95** and proceed as follows:

1. Remove the valve from the fuel tank. Clean the valve in a suitable mild solvent.

2. Inspect the valve for correct size. The valve must have a hose barb designed to fit 5/16 in. inside diameter fuel line. Replace the valve (and/or fuel distribution line) if it (or the distribution line) is too small.

3. Inspect the valve for corrosion. Replace the valve if the check valve and/or spring are corroded.

4. Obtain a 30 in. (762 mm) piece of clear vinyl hose of the appropriate diameter that will allow the antisiphon valve to be threaded into the hose. If desired, an appropriate hose barb fitting may be installed to the threaded end of the valve to allow a more secure fit. The clear hose must be installed on the fuel tank end of the valve so that the water column will push against the check ball and spring.

5. Make a mark on the clear hose at a point 20 in. (508 mm) from the end of the valve. Then make a mark on the hose at a point 25 in. (635 mm) from the end of the valve. See **Figure 95**.

6. Fill the hose with water to the 20 in. (508 mm) mark with the hose held vertical (valve end down). The valve must hold the water. An occasional drip is acceptable, but a continuous drip is not acceptable.

7. Continue filling the hose with water while watching the valve. The valve must begin to leak water (drip or dribble continuously) by the time the water level reaches the 25 in. (635 mm) mark.

8. Replace the valve if it does not test as specified.

FUEL PRIMER SYSTEMS

A conventional choke system is used on all 2-8 hp models, 9.9-15 hp rope start models and the 25 and 35 hp (three-cylinder) tiller handle models. When the choke is closed, airflow to the engine is restricted, causing the overall air/fuel mixture to be enriched, allowing the engine to be started when cold. On 25 and 35 hp (three-cylinder) models, each carburetor is equipped with a choke plate, and the choke linkage will open and close all three valves simultaneously.

All remote control electric start models (and 40-70 hp tiller handle electric start models) use an electrically operated fuel primer solenoid. The 20-40 hp (two-cylinder) rope start, 20-30 hp (two-cylinder) tiller handle electric start models and the 18-28 jet use a manual fuel primer valve.

Fuel primer valves inject fuel (under pressure) behind the carburetor's throttle plate, directly into the reed valves.

This provides more positive enrichment of the air/fuel mixture, allowing faster starts than a conventional choke.

Manual Fuel Primer Valve

A plunger-type fuel primer valve is used on 20-40 hp (two-cylinder) rope start models, the 18 and 28 jet and the 20-30 hp (two-cylinder) tiller handle electric start models. See **Figure 96**, typical. When operated, the primer valve delivers fuel from the carburetor float chamber (A, **Figure 96**), into the carburetor's primer fitting, generally located near the mounting flange. The primer is basically a simple, plunger-type mechanical fuel pump.

The primer has three distinct operating modes (and positions).

1. *Off*—When the plunger (B, **Figure 96**) is pressed fully inward (past the detent) all fuel passages are blocked and fuel cannot flow. The plunger must be pushed fully inward (past the detent) after the engine is warmed up, or the engine will run rich, smoke excessively and stall at idle.

2. *Warm-up*—When the plunger is pulled out (past the detent) and released, an internal spring will return it to a position just outside of the detent. This position opens internal valving and allows a metered amount of fuel to be pulled through the valve by the engine's intake manifold vacuum. This position is a temporary position and is used only to enrich the mixture during warm-up.

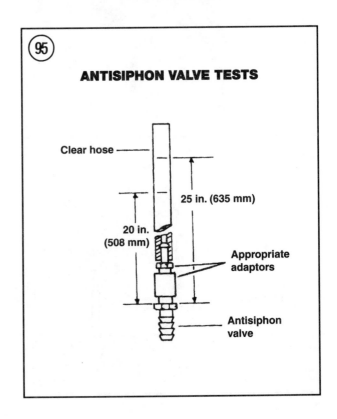

95

ANTISIPHON VALVE TESTS

Clear hose

25 in. (635 mm)

20 in. (508 mm)

Appropriate adaptors

Antisiphon valve

3. *Prime*—When the plunger is pulled to its full extension, fuel is pumped under pressure into the carburetor's primer fitting. Releasing the plunger causes the valve to refill with fuel from the carburetor's float chamber. The primer will only pump fuel as it is pulled outward. A discharge check valve in the discharge nipple (C, **Figure 96**) prevents the fuel (or air) in the discharge line from being drawn back into the valve. An inlet check valve in the valve's plunger prevents the fuel from being pushed back into the carburetor's float chamber during operation.

Manual Primer Operational Test

On some models, the fuel primer valve may be connected to the fuel recirculation system. See Chapter Six. To test the operation of the manual fuel primer valve, proceed as follows:

1. Disconnect the primer outlet hose from the carburetor fitting. Inspect the carburetor's primer fitting to make sure it is not blocked or obstructed. Clean the fitting as necessary.

2. Place the disconnect end of the primer hose into a graduated container.

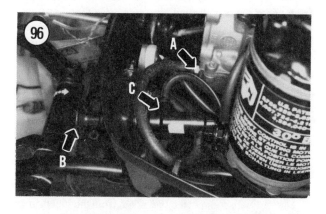

3. Fill the carburetor(s) with fuel by squeezing the primer bulb (in the fuel supply line) until it is firm.

4. Operate the primer while observing the quantity of fuel discharged into the container. Approximately 1 cc of fuel must be discharged from the primer with each full extension of the plunger. If fuel is forcefully discharged from the hose, the primer is functioning properly.

5. If no fuel is discharged, remove the primer hose from the primer valve outlet fitting (C, **Figure 96**). Operate the primer while observing the fitting. If fuel is now discharged, inspect the primer hose for kinks, blockage or a restriction. If fuel is not discharged, proceed to Step 6.

6. Disconnect the primer valve's fuel supply hose from the carburetor float chamber fitting (A, **Figure 96**). If fuel runs from the fitting, check the hose for kinks, blockage, or a restriction. If the hose is in acceptable condition, repair or replace the primer valve assembly.

Electric Fuel Primer Solenoid

The electric fuel primer solenoid (**Figure 97**) has replaced choke valves on all larger engines as the primary means of enriching the air/fuel mixture for cold starting. Fuel primer solenoid equipped models enrich the air/fuel mixture by injecting fuel (under pressure) directly into the carburetor(s). The fuel is injected on the intake manifold side of the throttle plate(s). The fuel primer solenoid is an electric solenoid valve which simply opens and closes. The fuel primer valve does not pump fuel. Fuel must be supplied by the primer bulb or engine's fuel pump. When electricity is applied to the purple/white lead, the solenoid is energized and the fuel valve opens. An internal spring forces the valve closed when the solenoid is not energized. The fuel primer valve is equipped with a manual valve (A, **Figure 97**) to allow manual operation of the valve if the electric circuit fails. Rotating the valve so that it extends away from the solenoid body will open the valve and allow fuel to flow continuously (as long as fuel pressure is present in the solenoid's fuel supply line). Make sure the valve is only opened momentarily to prime the engine, just as if you were using the valve electrically. The valve shown in **Figure 97** is in the OFF position.

A Schrader-type valve located under the removable cap on the manual valve (A, **Figure 97**) allows quick and simple injection of OMC Storage Fogging Oil and/or OMC Engine Tuner as described in Chapter Four. Both of these products are available in an injection-style can designed to attach directly to the primer's manual valve fitting.

Functional test

Proceed as follows to determine if the primer is functioning properly.

> *CAUTION*
> *Do not run the engine without an adequate water supply and do not exceed 3000 rpm without an adequate load. Refer to **Safety Precautions** at the beginning of this chapter.*

1. Start the motor and allow it to warm to normal operating temperature.

2. Adjust the engine speed to approximately 2000 rpm, then engage the primer by pressing the key inward.

3. The engine must quickly lose a noticeable amount of speed (approximately 1000 rpm) and begin to run roughly, indicating that fuel is being injected into the engine and the mixture has been enriched.

4. If not, check the primer solenoid's fuel supply hose and all discharge hoses and fittings for kinks, blockage or restriction. If the hoses and fittings are in acceptable condition, proceed to Step 5.

> *CAUTION*
> *Be careful not to break the primer solenoid fittings when removing the hoses. Push the hoses off of the fittings; do not pull. If necessary, slit the hose (and replace it) to prevent damaging the solenoid.*

5. Carefully disconnect the fuel hoses from the fuel primer valve and connect a short length of hose to the large (inlet) fitting.

6. Using a syringe filled with isopropyl alcohol, attempt to force fluid into the hose while rotating the manual valve to the open position. Fluid must flow through the valve with the valve opened, but not when the valve is closed.

7. Repair or replace the valve if it does not perform as specified.

8. Reconnect all lines when finished.

Troubleshooting

Refer to the back of the manual for wiring diagrams.

> *NOTE*
> *The ignition switch must be held in the CHOKE or PRIME position for all of the following tests.*

1. Check the fuel lines going to and from the fuel primer valve for deterioration and obstructions. Correct any problems found.

2. Check that the black lead (B, **Figure 97**) coming out of the fuel primer valve is connected to a clean ground. Clean and tighten the connection as necessary.

3. Connect a test lamp lead to a good engine ground.

4. Gain access to the ignition switch purple/white lead (terminal C). Connect the test lamp probe to this lead. With the ignition switch in the CHOKE or PRIME position, the test lamp must light. If the test lamp lights, go to Step 6. If the test lamp does not light, go to Step 5.

5. Connect the test lamp probe to the ignition switch red/purple lead (terminal B or BAT). The test lamp must light regardless of the ignition switch position. If the test lamp lights, replace the ignition switch and retest Step 4. If the test lamp does not light, repair or replace the red/purple lead from terminal B of the ignition switch back through the main 20 amp fuse to the starter solenoid.

6. Disconnect the purple/white lead from the fuel primer valve bullet connector (C, **Figure 97**). Connect the test lamp probe to the purple/white lead on the engine harness side. With the ignition switch in the CHOKE or PRIME position, the test lamp must light. If the test lamp does not light, repair or replace the purple/white lead from the fuel primer valve to the ignition switch.

7. Disconnect the purple/white lead from its bullet connector (C, **Figure 97**) and the black lead (B, **Figure 97**) from under the primer mounting screw. Calibrate an ohmmeter on the appropriate scale to read 4-7 ohms. Connect one meter lead to the fuel primer valve's purple/white lead and the other meter lead to the valve's black lead. Replace the solenoid if the resistance is not within 4-7 ohms.

> *CAUTION*
> *Be careful not to break the primer solenoid fittings when removing the hoses. Push the hoses off of the fittings; do not pull. If necessary, slit the hose (and replace it) to prevent damaging the solenoid.*

8. Carefully disconnect the fuel hoses from the fuel primer valve and connect a short length of hose to the inlet (large)

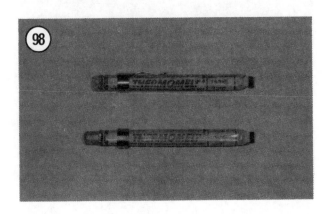

fitting. Using a syringe filled with isopropyl alcohol, attempt to force fluid into the hose while rotating the manual valve to the open position. Fluid must flow through the valve with the valve opened, but not when the valve is closed. Repair or replace the valve if it does not perform as specified.

9. Reconnect all leads and lines when finished.

ENGINE TEMPERATURE
AND OVERHEATING

Proper engine temperature is critical to good engine operation. Internal engine damage will occur if the engine is operated in an overheat condition. Engines that are overcooling will experience fouled spark plugs, poor idle quality and acceleration, excessive carbon buildup in the combustion chamber and reduced fuel economy. All recreational outboard models 6 hp and larger are equipped with a thermostat and a pressure relief valve, both mounted in the thermostat pocket of the cylinder head.

The thermostat controls the flow of water leaving the cylinder block. The pressure relief valve controls the water pressure in the cooling system. When water pressure exceeds the spring pressure of the valve, cooling water flows out the water discharge, bypassing the thermostat. Therefore, the thermostat controls the engine temperature during idle and low-speed operation and the pressure relief valve controls engine temperature at higher speeds.

It is important to note that on all thermostat-equipped engines, the thermostat always controls the maximum temperature that the engine can reach. The number stamped on the thermostat is the initial opening or *cracking* temperature. The thermostat will not reach full opening (full water flow) until it is 15°-20° F above the rated temperature. If the engine temperature drops at high engine speeds, but returns to thermostat controlled temperature at idle and low speeds, the system is working correctly. In no case must engine temperature exceed the thermostat rated temperature by more than 20° F.

Troubleshooting

Engine temperature can be checked with the use of Markal Thermomelt Stiks (**Figure 98**) available from Stevens Instrument Company, P.O. Box 193, Waukegan, Illinois 60079-0193. Thermomelt Stiks come in 100, 125, 131, 163, and 175° F ratings. The Thermomelt Stik looks similar to a piece of chalk. When the engine is marked with the thermomelt compound (**Figure 99**), the mark will stay dull and chalky until the temperature of the engine exceeds the rating of the compound, at which point the mark will become liquid and glossy. The 100° and 163° Thermomelt Stiks are required to test 2-8 hp models and the 125° and 163° Thermomelt Stiks are required to test 9.9-70 hp and 18-35 jet models.

The preferred and most accurate way of checking engine temperature is to use a pyrometer or an infrared temperature gun, such as the OMC temperature gun (part No. 772018). A pyrometer is an electronic thermometer. Pyrometers can be stand alone instruments or an adapter module designed to fit a standard digital multimeter. When using a pyrometer, a dab of silicone grease on the end of the probe will help to create a good thermal bond between the probe and the power head. If using the temperature gun, be sure to point the gun at the specified location when taking temperature measurements.

The temperature check must be taken as follows:

1. *2, 3.3 and 3.5 hp models*—Take the temperature reading on the head of the lower starboard cylinder head screw.

2. *4-8 hp models (including 4 Deluxe)*—Take the temperature reading on the top surface of the cylinder's water jacket, as close to the cylinder head as possible.

3. *9.9-30 hp (two-cylinder) and 18 jet models*—Take the temperature reading on top of the cylinder head, on the flat area between the thermostat housing and the head gasket. See **Figure 99**, typical.

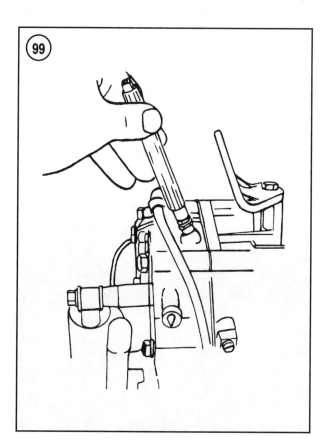

99

4. *25 and 35 hp (three-cylinder) models*—Take the temperature reading on the top of the thermostat housing, midway between the thermostat cover and the cylinder block mating surface.

5. *40-70 hp, 28 jet and 35 jet models*—Take the temperature reading on the top surface of the cylinder head's thermostat cavity, midway between the thermostat cover and the head gasket. See **Figure 100**, typical.

Engine temperature check using Thermomelt Stiks

To be accurate, the cooling water inlet temperature must be within 60°-80° F (18-24° C). Extreme variations in water inlet temperature can affect engine operating temperature. All engines equipped with a thermostat use a 140° F (60° C) thermostat. An acccurate engine temperature check cannot be performed with the outboard running on a flushing device.

> *CAUTION*
> *Do not run the engine without an adequate water supply and do not exceed 3000 rpm without an adequate load. Refer to **Safety Precautions** at the beginning of this chapter.*

1. Start the engine and run it at 2000-3000 rpm in FORWARD gear for 5-10 minutes to allow it to reach operating temperature. Then reduce speed to 900 rpm for 5 minutes.

2A. *2-8 hp models*—Mark the engine at the location previously specified with the 100° and 163° compound.

2B. *9.9-70 hp and 18-35 jet models*—Mark the engine at the location previously specified with the 125° and 163° compound.

3. Observe the 100° (or 125°) Thermomelt mark:
   a. If the 100° (or 125°) Thermomelt mark does not melt (remains dull and chalky), the engine is overcooling. Make sure the inlet water temperature is above 60° F (18° C). Check the thermostat and relief valve (if so equipped) for corrosion or debris preventing the thermostat and valve from closing. If the thermostat and valve are in acceptable condition, test the thermostat as described in the following section.
   b. If the 100° (or 125°) Thermomelt mark melts (turns liquid and glossy), the engine is at least reaching operating temperature and is not overcooling.

4. Next, observe the 163° Thermomelt mark:
   a. If the 163° Thermomelt mark does not melt (stays dull and chalky), the engine is not overheating at this speed. Proceed to Step 6.
   b. If the 163° mark melts (turns liquid and glossy), the engine is overheating. Proceed to Step 5.

5. If the engine is overheating:

   a. Check the water inlet screens (or cast inlet holes) in the lower gearcase for blockage from debris or corrosion and clean as necessary.
   b. Test the thermostat (if so equipped) as described in this chapter.
   c. Remove the lower gearcase and inspect the water pump assembly. Inspect the water tube from the water pump to the power head for damage, debris, blockage or corrosion.
   d. If necessary, remove the cylinder head and inspect for debris and corrosion in the water jackets surrounding the cylinder(s). On models so equipped, check for missing, mislocated, or damaged water passage restrictors.

> *CAUTION*
> *If running the engine in a test tank, it may not be possible to accurately perform the following 5000 rpm test due to the aeration of the test tank water and subsequent overheating.*

6A. *40-50 hp, 28 jet and 35 jet models*—Repeat the temperature test at 5000 rpm.
   a. If the 125° Thermomelt mark does not melt (stays dull and chalky) at 5000 rpm, the engine's cooling system is operating correctly and testing is finished.
   b. If the 125° mark melts (turns liquid and glossy), the engine is overheating at this speed. Proceed to Step 7.

6B. *All other models*—Repeat the temperature test at 5000 rpm.
   a. If the 163° Thermomelt mark does not melt (stays dull and chalky) at 5000 rpm, the engine's cooling system is operating correctly and testing is finished.
   b. If the 163° mark melts (turns liquid and glossy), the engine is overheating at this speed. Proceed to Step 7.

7. If the engine overheats in Step 6:

a. Check the water inlet screens (or cast inlet holes) in the lower gearcase for blockage from debris or corrosion, clean as necessary.

b. Inspect the thermostat and relief valve (if so equipped) for corrosion or debris preventing the valve from opening.

c. Test the thermostat (if so equipped) as described in this chapter.

d. Remove the lower gearcase and inspect the water pump assembly. Inspect the water tube from the water pump to the power head for damage, debris, blockage or corrosion.

e. If necessary, remove the cylinder head and inspect for debris and corrosion in the water jackets surrounding the cylinder(s). On model so equipped, check for missing, mislocated or damaged water passage restrictors.

Engine temperature check
(using a pyrometer or heat gun)

To be accurate, the cooling water inlet temperature must be within 60°-80° F (18-24° C). Extreme variations in water inlet temperature can affect engine operating temperature. All engines equipped with a thermostat use a 140° F (60° C) thermostat. Engine temperature checks cannot be performed on a flushing device.

CAUTION
*Do not run the engine without an adequate water supply and do not exceed 3000 rpm without an adequate load. Refer to **Safety Precautions** at the beginning of this chapter.*

1. Start the engine and run it at 2000-3000 rpm in FORWARD gear for 5-10 minutes to allow it to reach operating temperature. Then reduce the speed to 900 rpm for 5 minutes.

2A. *2-8 hp models*—Using a pyrometer or temperature gun, note the temperature of the engine at the previously specified location.

a. If the temperature is less than 100° F (37.8° C), the engine is overcooling. Make sure the inlet water temperature is above 60° F (18° C).

b. If the temperature reads at least 100° F (37.8° C), the engine is at least reaching operating temperature and is not overcooling.

2B. *9.9-70 hp and 18-35 jet models*—Note the temperature of the engine at the previously specified location.

a. If the temperature is less than 125° F (51.7° C), the engine is overcooling. Check the thermostat and poppet valve for debris preventing the thermostat and poppet valve from closing. If the thermostat and poppet valve are in acceptable condition, test the thermostat as described in the following section.

b. If the temperature reads at least 125° F (51.7° C), the engine is at least reaching operating temperature and is not overcooling.

3. *All models*—If the temperature reads less than 160° F (71.2° C), the engine is not overheating at this speed. Proceed to Step 4. If the temperature reads more than 160° F (71.2° C), the engine is overheating at this speed. Proceed as follows:

a. Test the thermostat as described in the following section.

b. Check the water inlet screens (or cast inlet holes) in the lower gearcase for blockage from debris or corrosion and clean as necessary.

c. Remove the lower gearcase and inspect the water pump assembly. Inspect the water tube from the water pump to the power head for damage, debris, blockage or corrosion.

d. If necessary remove the cylinder head and inspect for debris and corrosion in the water jackets surrounding the cylinder(s). On models so equipped, check for missing, mislocated, or damaged water passage restrictors.

CAUTION
If you are running the engine in a test tank, it may not be possible to accurately perform the following 5000 rpm tests due to the aeration of the test tank water and subsequent overheating.

4A. *40-50 hp, 28 jet and 35 jet models*—Repeat the temperature test at 5000 rpm.

a. If the temperature reads below 120° F (48.9° C) at 5000 rpm, the engine's cooling system is operating correctly and testing is finished.

b. If the temperature reads more than 120° F (48.9° C) at 5000 rpm, the engine is overheating at this speed. Proceed to Step 5.

4B. *All other models*—Repeat the temperature test at 5000 rpm.

a. If the temperature reads below 160° F (71.2° C) at 5000 rpm, the engine's cooling system is operating correctly and testing is finished.

b. If the temperature reads more than 160° F (71.2° C) at 5000 rpm, the engine is overheating at this speed. Proceed to Step 5.

5. If the engine overheats in Step 4:

a. Inspect the thermostat and relief valve (if so equipped) for corrosion or debris preventing the valve from opening.

b. Test the thermostat (if so equipped) as described in the following section.

3

c. Check the water inlet screens (or cast inlet holes) in the lower gearcase for blockage from debris or corrosion, clean as necessary.

d. Remove the lower gearcase and inspect the water pump assembly. Inspect the water tube from the water pump to the power head for damage or corrosion.

e. If necessary remove the cylinder head and inspect for debris and corrosion in the water jackets surrounding the cylinder(s). On models so equipped, check for missing, mislocated or damaged water passage restrictors.

Thermostat test

The thermostat on 20-30 hp (two-cylinder) and 18 jet models can be tested in the following procedure.

All other models use an assembly that is not compatible for testing when removed from the engine. The assembly consists of a vernatherm (thermostat), diaphragm, spring(s) and on some models, plastic housing(s). Replace the vernatherm (thermostat) if its condition is questionable. See Chapter Eight.

1. Remove the thermostat assembly as described in Chapter Eight.

2. Wash the thermostat (**Figure 101**) with clean water. Remove the thermostat grommet (if so equipped) and discard it. Read the thermostat-rated opening temperature stamped on the thermostat. All OMC thermostats are rated at 140° F (60° C).

3. Manually open the thermostat and insert a thread (or narrow feeler gauge) through the valve and seat. Let the thermostat shut, pinching the thread (or feeler gauge) in the valve.

4. Suspend the thermostat from the thread in a container of water that can be heated. Then suspend an accurate thermometer in the container of water. See **Figure 102**.

> *NOTE*
> *The thermostat and thermometer must not touch the sides or bottom of the container of water.*

5. Heat the water and note the temperature at which the thermostat falls free from the thread (or feeler gauge). The thermostat must begin to open between 135-145° F (57.3-62.8° C).

6. Continue to heat the water until the thermostat fully opens. The thermostat must fully open by 160° F (71.2° C).

7. Replace the thermostat(s) if it fails to open at the specified temperature or if it does not open completely. Install new gaskets, seals and/or grommets (as equipped).

> *NOTE*
> *Make sure the relief valve diaphragm, spring and seat are not damaged and correctly orientated before reinstalling the thermostat cover. Replace any damaged or worn parts (Chapter Eight).*

Engine temperature switches

All 20-70 hp (and 9.9-15 hp remote control models) are equipped with an engine temperature switch. Temperature

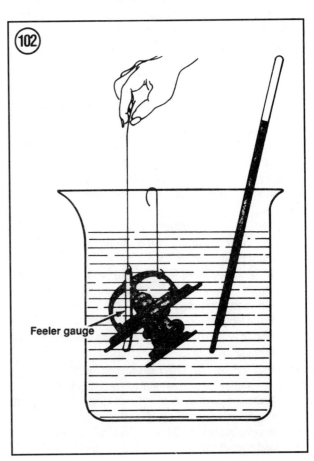

Feeler gauge

switches are normally open and close (short) to ground if the engine temperature exceeds the rated temperature of the switch. The temperature switch grounds through direct contact with the cylinder head. **Figure 103** shows a typical temperature switch installation.

On 20-70 hp models, the temperature switch activates the S.L.O.W. (speed limiting operational warning) system in the power pack (or ignition module). The S.L.O.W. program will limit engine speed to approximately 2000-3000 rpm if an overheat occurs.

Remote control and 40-70 hp tiller electric models are equipped with a warning horn (or system check warning gauge and horn). The warning horn provides an audible warning to the operator. On models equipped with S.L.O.W., this also allows the operator to be alerted of an overheat if the engine is being operated below the S.L.O.W. rpm limit (2000-3000 rpm).

On 25-70 hp (three-cylinder) models, the temperature switch (**Figure 104**) has an additional white/black lead that triggers the QuikStart program in the power pack (or ignition module). The QuikStart program advances the ignition timing during starting and warm-up. The white/black lead is normally open to ground when the engine is cold, and is shorted to ground when engine temperature exceeds 105° F (41° C).

Temperature switch functional test
(except QuikStart models)

1. Disconnect the engine wiring harness tan lead from the temperature switch tan/red (or tan/blue) lead at its bullet (or Amphenol) connector. See B, **Figure 105** or B, **Figure 103**.

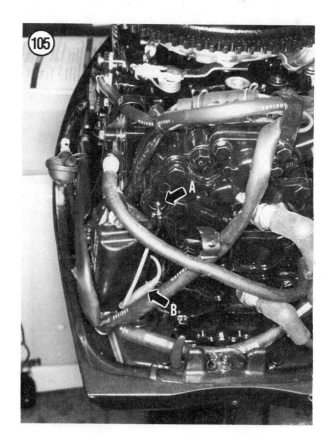

2. Calibrate an ohmmeter on the highest scale available. Connect one meter lead to a clean engine ground and the other ohmmeter lead to the temperature switch tan/red (or tan/blue) lead. The ohmmeter must read no continuity. Replace the temperature switch if any other reading is noted.

> *CAUTION*
> *Do not run the engine without an adequate water supply and do not exceed 3000 rpm without an adequate load. Refer to **Safety Precautions** at the beginning of this chapter.*

3. Run the engine up to operating temperature as described in *Engine temperature check* in this chapter. The ohmmeter must continue to indicate no continuity when the engine is at normal operating temperature. Replace the temperature switch if any other reading is noted. The only time the switch should indicate continuity is if the engine is actually overheating.

4. Reconnect all leads when finished.

Temperature switch functional test (QuikStart models)

The engine must be below 90° F (32° C) before beginning this procedure. Allow the engine to cool as necessary.

1. Disconnect the engine wiring harness tan and white/black leads from the temperature switch tan/blue and white/black leads at their bullet (or Amphenol) connector(s). See **Figure 106**, typical.

2. Calibrate an ohmmeter on the highest scale available. Connect the black meter lead to a clean engine ground and the red meter lead to the temperature switch tan/blue lead. The ohmmeter must read no continuity. Replace the temperature switch if any other reading is noted.

3. Move the red ohmmeter lead to the temperature switch white/black lead. The ohmmeter must read no continuity. Replace the temperature switch if any other reading is noted.

> *CAUTION*
> *Do not run the engine without an adequate water supply and do not exceed 3000 rpm without an adequate load. Refer to **Safety Precautions** at the beginning of this chapter.*

4. Run the engine up to operating temperature as described in *Engine temperature check* in this chapter. The ohmmeter must indicate continuity as the engine warms up and engine temperature exceeds 105° F (41° C). The meter must continue to indicate continuity when the engine is at normal operating temperature. Replace the temperature switch if any other reading is noted.

5. Move the red ohmmeter lead to the temperature switch tan/blue lead. With the engine at operating temperature, the ohmmeter must read no continuity. Replace the temperature switch if any other reading is noted. The only time the switch's tan/blue lead should indicate continuity is if the engine is actually overheating.

6. Reconnect all leads when finished.

Temperature switch bench test

The following procedure requires that the temperature switch be removed from the cylinder head. Refer to Chapter Eight for additional information on the removal and installation procedure. If a continuity tester is used in place of an ohmmeter, the light must illuminate when the specification is continuity and the light must not illuminate when the specification is no continuity. To remove and test the switch, proceed as follows:

1A. *9.9-15 hp (remote control) models*—Remove the 3 screws securing the thermostat cover to the cylinder head. Remove the cover and pull the temperature switch from its bore. Discard the cover seal.

1B. *20-30 hp (two-cylinder) and 18 jet models*—Remove the cylinder head cover from the cylinder head. Discard the cover gasket. See Chapter Eight.

1C. *All other models*—Remove the plastic nut securing the switch to the cylinder head. Then remove (pull) the switch from its bore.

> *WARNING*
> *To prevent fire or explosion when testing the temperature switch, be sure to use a suitable container to heat the oil. Use oil with a flash point above 300° F (150° C), such as OMC Cobra 4-Cycle Motor Oil. **Never** use an open flame to heat the oil.*

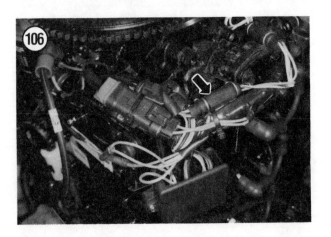

2. Calibrate an ohmmeter on the highest scale available. Connect the black meter lead to the metal body of the switch. Then connect the red meter lead to the switch's tan/red (or tan/blue) lead. The meter must indicate no continuity at room temperature. Replace the switch if any other reading is noted.

3. Place the switch and an accurate thermometer in a container of engine oil. Slowly increase the temperature of the oil using a suitable heat source (such as an electric hot plate). *Do not* use an open flame to heat the oil. Observe the ohmmeter and thermometer as the oil is heated and note the temperature at which the ohmmeter indicates continuity.

4A. *Tan/red lead*—The ohmmeter must indicate continuity as the temperature reaches 174-186° F (79-86° C). If not, replace the switch. If the switch indicates continuity at the specified temperature, continue with Step 5A.

4B. *Tan/blue lead*—The ohmmeter must indicate continuity as the temperature reaches 231-243° F (111-117° C). If not, replace the switch. If the switch indicates continuity at the specified temperature, continue with Step 5B.

5A. *Tan/red lead*—Allow the oil to cool while observing the temperature and ohmmeter. The ohmmeter must indicate no continuity as the temperature falls to 140-170° F (60-77° C). If not, replace the temperature switch.

5B. *Tan/blue lead*—Allow the oil to cool while observing the temperature and ohmmeter. The ohmmeter must indicate no continuity as the temperature falls to 192-222° F (89-106° C). If not, replace the temperature switch.

6. *QuikStart models*—Repeat this procedure for the white/black lead. When the oil is warmed, the lead must indicate continuity (close) at 102-108° F (39-42° C). As the oil cools, the lead must indicate no continuity (open) at 87-93° F (31-34° C). Replace the switch if it does not perform as specified.

7. Clean all corrosion and/or sealant from the switch's bore before reinstalling the switch. Lightly coat the outer diameter of the switch's metal body with OMC Gasket Sealing Compound, but do not allow any sealer onto the body's face.

8. Install the switch into its bore, making sure it is seated.

9A. *9.9 and 15 hp (remote control) models*—Install the thermostat cover (using a new seal) as described in Chapter Eight.

9B. *20-30 hp (two-cylinder) and 18 jet models*—Install the cylinder head cover (using a new gasket) as described in Chapter Eight.

9C. *All other models*—Coat the threads of the plastic retaining nut with OMC Gasket Sealing Compound. Install the nut and tighten it snugly.

ENGINE

Engine (power head) problems are generally the result of a failure in another system, such as the ignition, fuel (and lubrication) or cooling systems. If a power head is properly cooled, lubricated, timed correctly and given the correct air/fuel ratio, the engine should experience no mechanical problems other than normal wear. If a power head fails, the emphasis must be to determine why the power head failed. Just replacing failed mechanical components will do no good if the cause of the failure is not corrected.

Overheating and Lack of Lubrication

Overheating and lack of lubrication cause the majority of engine mechanical problems. Anytime an outboard motor is to be run, adequate cooling water must be supplied by immersing the gearcase water inlets in the water (test tank or lake) or using an approved flushing device. The motor must only be run at low speeds when operating on a flushing device. The motor must *never* be started without a water supply; water pump damage will occur in seconds.

Carbon buildup in a two-stroke outboard motor *will* cause premature power head failure. Carbon buildup comes from two possible sources: the lubricating oil and the fuel. The use of a premium quality outboard motor lubricant cannot be overemphasized. The current TCW-3 specification for power head lubricants ensures that maximum lubrication is delivered with minimal carbon deposit buildup. Using gasoline from a major brand manufacturer ensures that the fuel contains the detergents necessary to minimize carbon buildup from the fuel. Fuels that contain alcohol tend to accumulate carbon at an accelerated rate. The manufacturer recommends avoiding alcohol blended fuels whenever possible. Refer to Chapter Four for additional fuel and oil recommendations.

Use OMC Engine Tuner periodically (as described in Chapter Four) to remove carbon deposits from the combustion chamber and piston rings before they can contribute to high combustion chamber temperatures.

Preignition

Preignition is the premature ignition of the air/fuel charge in the combustion chamber. Preignition is caused by hot spots in the combustion chamber. See **Figure 107**. Basically, anything in the combustion chamber that gets hot enough to ignite the air/fuel charge will cause preignition. Glowing carbon deposits, inadequate cooling, improperly installed thread inserts, incorrect head gaskets, sloppy machine work, previous combustion chamber damage (nicks and scratches) or overheated (incorrect) spark plugs can all cause preignition. Preignition is usually first noticed in the form of power loss, but will eventually result in extensive damage to the internal engine components (especially pistons) because of excessive combustion chamber pressure and temperature. Preignition damage typically looks like an acetylene torch was used to melt away the top of the piston. Sometimes the piston will actually have a hole melted through the piston crown. It is important to remember that preignition can lead to detonation and detonation can lead to preignition. Both types of damage may be evident when the engine is disassembled.

Detonation

Commonly referred to as *spark knock* or *fuel knock*, detonation is the violent, spontaneous explosion of fuel in the combustion chamber, as opposed to the smooth, progressive, even burning of the air/fuel mixture that occurs during normal combustion. See **Figure 108**. When detonation occurs, combustion chamber pressure and temperature rise dramatically, creating severe shock waves in the engine. This will cause severe engine damage.

It is not unusual for detonation to break a connecting rod or crankshaft.

Detonation occurs when the octane requirements of the engine exceed the octane of the fuel being used. It does not necessarily mean that the wrong fuel was being used. It does mean that at the time of detonation, the engine needed higher octane fuel than was being used. All fuel will spontaneously explode if it is subjected to enough pressure and high enough temperature.

The fuel octane requirements of an engine are generally determined by the:

a. Compression ratio—Higher compression ratios require higher octane fuel. It is important to note that carbon buildup raises compression ratios.
b. Combustion chamber temperature—Higher temperatures require higher octane fuel. Water pump and thermostat malfunctions typically raise the combustion chamber temperature.
c. Air/fuel mixture—Leaner mixtures require higher octane fuels; richer mixtures require lower octane fuels.
d. Spark advance—Spark occurring too early causes excessive combustion chamber pressure, spark occurring extremely late causes the combustion flame front to quench along a larger surface area of the cylinder walls, exceeding the cooling system capacity to remove the heat. Both of these situations raise the octane requirements.
e. Operating speed—Propping an engine so it cannot reach the recommended operating speed range is considered *lugging* or *over-propping* the engine. This is like trying to drive a manual shift car or truck up a hill in high gear. If an engine is over-propped to the point that it cannot reach its recommended speed, combustion chamber temperatures will skyrocket, increasing the octane requirement.

Fuel degrades over time causing the actual octane rating of the fuel to drop. Even though the fuel may have exceeded the manufacturer's recommendations when the fuel was fresh, it may have dropped well below recommendations over time. Use a fuel conditioner, such as OMC 2+4 fuel conditioner to prevent octane deterioration. The fuel conditioner must be added to fresh fuel; it will not raise the octane of stale or sour fuel.

It is better to properly and safely dispose of questionable fuel and start with a fresh tank, rather than risk a power

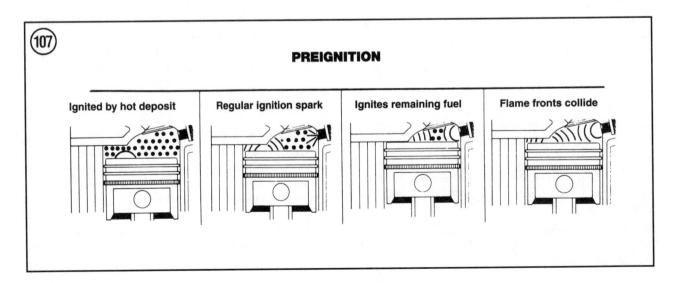

(107)

PREIGNITION

| Ignited by hot deposit | Regular ignition spark | Ignites remaining fuel | Flame fronts collide |

head failure. Power head failure typically occurs in a few seconds or less when an engine is detonating, so rarely can an operator detect detonation and reduce engine speed in time to save the power head. It is important to remember that detonation can lead to preignition and preignition can lead to detonation. Both types of damage may be evident when the engine is disassembled.

Poor Idle Quality

Poor idle quality can usually be attributed to one of the following conditions:

1. *Overcooling*—If the power head does not reach normal operating temperature, fuel tends to puddle in the crankcase, resulting in a lean air/fuel ratio in the combustion chamber. This tends to produce a lean spit or backfire through the carburetor at idle. Overheating is usually caused by debris caught in the thermostat(s) or poppet valve (if so equipped). A few selected models will not be equipped with thermostats. Refer to *Engine Temperature and Overheating* section in this chapter for engine temperature checks.

2. *Crankcase seal failure*—A two-stroke engine cannot function unless the crankcase is adequately sealed. As the piston travels downward, the crankcase must pressurize and push the air/fuel mixture into the combustion chamber as the intake ports are uncovered. Conversely, as the piston travels upward, the crankcase must create a vacuum to pull the air/fuel mixture into the crankcase from the carburetor in preparation for the next cycle.

Leaks in the crankcase cause the air/fuel charge to leak into the atmosphere under crankcase compression. During the intake cycle, crankcase leakage will cause air from the atmosphere to be drawn into the crankcase, diluting the air/fuel charge. The net result is inadequate fuel in the combustion chamber. On multiple cylinder engines, each crankcase must be sealed from all other crankcases. Internal leakage will allow the air/fuel charge to leak to another cylinder's crankcase, rather than travel to the correct combustion chamber. Refer to *Starting Difficulties* at the beginning of this chapter for additional information.

3. *Fuel recirculation system failure*—Multiple cylinder motors are equipped with a fuel recirculation system designed to collect unburned fuel and oil from the low spots of the individual crankcase areas. Since the intake system used by two-stroke engines does not completely transfer all of the fuel sent through the crankcase to the combustion chamber (especially during low speed operation), the recirculation system provides a method of collecting the fuel and oil pooled in the low spots of the crankcase and transferring it to the intake ports or intake manifold where it can be burned.

Correct recirculation system operation is vitally important to efficient engine operation. If the system fails, excessive amounts of fuel and oil will puddle in the crankcase and not reach the combustion chamber during low speed operation, causing a lean mixture. When the engine is accelerated, the puddles of fuel and oil are quickly drawn into the engine causing a temporary excessively rich mixture. This will result in poor low-speed performance, poor acceleration, spark plug fouling, stalling or spitting at idle and excessive smoke on acceleration. Refer to Chapter Six for fuel recirculation system service.

4. *Incorrect carburetor adjustments or carburetor malfunction*—The carburetor idle mixture screw must be correctly adjusted for the engine to idle and accelerate properly. An engine that is too lean at idle will spit or backfire through the carburetor at idle and hesitate on

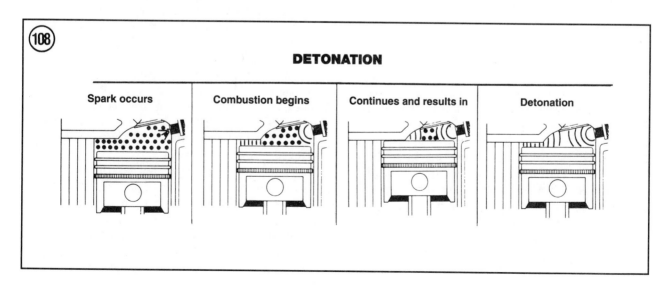

(108)

DETONATION

Spark occurs	Combustion begins	Continues and results in	Detonation

acceleration. Refer to Chapter Six for carburetor adjustments.

Misfiring

True misfiring is an ignition system malfunction, generally caused by weak (or erratic) spark or defective spark plugs. The ignition system is simply not able to deliver enough spark energy to fire the spark plug at the time of the misfire.

Four-stroking is a form of misfire caused by an air/fuel ratio so rich that it cannot consistently ignite. The term four-stroking comes from the fact that the engine is typically firing every other revolution (like a four-stroke engine), instead of every revolution. Four-stroking is caused by a fuel system malfunction. Check for excessive fuel pump pressure, carburetor(s) with a leaking inlet needle and seat or a fuel primer system stuck in the on position.

Mechanical failure (insufficient compression) can cause a misfire at all speeds, but will often cause a cylinder to not fire at idle and low speeds, while firing at mid-range and high speed. Always perform a compression test to verify the mechanical integrity of the combustion chamber.

Flat Spots and Hesitation On Acceleration

If the engine seems to hesitate or bog when the throttle is opened, but then recovers, check for a restricted main jet in the carburetor(s), water in the fuel or an excessively lean fuel mixture. Incorrect synchronization of the spark advance to the throttle opening (on models with adjustments) can cause flat spots and hesitation on acceleration.

Water Leakage into Cylinder(s)

A simple method to check for water leakage into a cylinder is to check the spark plugs. Water in the combustion chamber tends to clean the spark plug. If one spark plug in a multicylinder engine is clean and the others have normal deposits, a water leak is likely in the cylinder with the clean spark plug. Perform a compression test to check the mechanical integrity of the combustion chamber. Inspect the piston crown for the absence of carbon deposits. A cylinder crown that looks steam cleaned, is a typical indication of water leakage into that combustion chamber. If the exhaust port area can be accessed, look for evidence of hard mineral deposits and the absence of soft, wet carbon deposits.

Water Damage in Power Head Lower Cylinder(s)

While water leakage into the combustion chamber is generally caused by a defective or failed head gasket, water can also enter the lower cylinder(s) of a power head through the exhaust ports and carburetor(s). When a steep unloading ramp or tilted trailer bed is used to launch the boat from a trailer and the boat enters the water too quickly, water can be forced into the drive shaft housing and up through the exhaust chamber into the cylinders if the pistons are not covering the exhaust ports.

Sudden deceleration, with the engine shut off, can cause a wave to swamp the engine and enter the exhaust ports or enter through the lower carburetor(s). This is most prevalent with stern-heavy boats. Operating a boat with twin engines, with one engine shut off, is considered hazardous because there is no exhaust back pressure to keep water out of the engine that is not running. This is most likely when backing the boat with one engine stopped. It is recommended that the engine that is not being used (for docking or low speed maneuvering) be left running at idle speed to reduce the risk of water entry.

Water entering a cylinder can result in a bent connecting rod, a broken piston and/or piston pin, a cracked cylinder and/or cylinder head or any combination of these conditions. Even if no immediate physical damage is done to the power head, the entry of water will result in rust and corrosion of all internal surfaces (bearings, crankshaft, cylinder walls, connecting rods and piston rings).

Power Loss

Several factors can cause a loss of power. Remember that an engine needs three things to run properly: compression, fuel and ignition. Check the mechanical integrity of the combustion chamber by performing a cranking compression test. Test the ignition system with an air gap tester and verify ignition timing at wide-open throttle. Check the fuel system for air leaks into the fuel lines and fittings and test the fuel pump for adequate output pressure at wide-open throttle. Clean or replace all fuel filters. Remove the carburetor(s) and inspect the float chamber for water in the fuel and gum or varnish buildup in the metering passages and jets. Clean all of the carburetors if any debris or buildup is found in any one carburetor.

If the compression test reveals a mechanical defect in a combustion chamber, treat the engine with OMC Engine Tuner. Many times the piston rings are stuck to the piston and cannot adequately seal to the cylinder walls. Engine Tuner can free stuck piston rings and prevent unnecessary disassembly if no mechanical damage has yet occurred. Follow the instructions on the can and retest cranking compression after the treatment. If the compression is now within specification, consider changing lubricant and fuel to a higher-quality brand. See Chapter Four.

If the compression is still not within specifications after the Engine Tuner treatment, the motor must be disassembled, and the defect must be located and repaired. After rebuilding the power head, make sure the carburetors and fuel pump are rebuilt, a new water pump and thermostat(s) are installed and all synchronization and linkage adjustments are made (Chapter Five).

Marine growth on the bottom of the hull and lower gearcase will drastically reduce the top speed and fuel economy of any boat. If the motor is in a good state of tune and has no apparent malfunction, yet fuel economy and top speed are inadequate, inspect the bottom of the hull and lower gearcase for marine growth and clean as necessary.

Power output verification

This procedure requires the installation of a test wheel (**Figure 109**, typical). Test wheel part numbers and minimum test speed are listed in the Quick Reference Data section at the front of this manual. A test wheel is designed to apply a calibrated load to the engine, while producing minimum thrust.

> *CAUTION*
> *Do not run the engine without an adequate water supply and do not exceed 3000 rpm without an adequate load. Refer to **Safety Precautions** at the beginning of this chapter.*

To determine if the engine is producing its rated output, proceed as follows:

1. Remove the propeller and install the correct test wheel. Install the test wheel as you would a normal propeller. See Chapter Nine.

2. Connect an accurate tachometer to the power head according to its manufacturer's instructions.

3. Place the outboard in a test tank or back the boat and trailer into the water until the gearcase is submerged to at least its normal operating depth.

4. Start the engine and allow it to warm to normal operating temperature. Then shift into FORWARD gear and run the engine at wide-open throttle while noting the tachometer.

5. If the engine's speed meets or exceeds the minimum speed listed in the test wheel table, the engine is producing its rated horsepower.

6. If the engine's speed is less than the specified speed, the engine is not producing its rated horsepower. The problem will be located in one of the following areas:

   a. *Stuck piston rings or excessive carbon deposits in the combustion chambers*—Remove any carbon deposits from the combustion chambers by using OMC Engine Tuner as described in Chapter Four.

   b. *Insufficient cranking compression on one or more cylinders*—Check the cranking compression as described in Chapter Four.

   c. *Incorrect synchronization and linkage adjustments*—Refer to Chapter Five and perform all synchronization and linkage adjustments.

   d. *Ignition system malfunction*—Check the ignition system spark output as specified in *Preliminary checks* in the appropriate ignition section (Chapter Seven).

   e. *Fuel system malfunction*—Test the fuel system for restrictions and the fuel pump output as described in this chapter.

   f. *Carburetor malfunction*—If the fuel delivery system is in acceptable condition (single-cylinder engine), remove and rebuild the carburetor. On a multicarburetted engine, connect a timing light to the engine and shine its beam down each carburetor throat as the engine is run at various speeds. The fuel plume from each carburetor must be of the same volume and shape as the other carburetor(s). Remove and rebuild any questionable carburetors. See Chapter Six.

   g. If all tests to this point are satisfactory, inspect the reed valves for damage (Chapter Six). If the reed valves are in good condition, the engine may simply be worn out (cranking compression even, but low). The engine will have to be rebuilt to achieve its rated output. See Chapter Eight.

Piston Seizure

Piston seizure can be caused by insufficient piston-to-cylinder bore clearance, improper piston ring end gap, inadequate or inferior lubrication, cooling system failure (overheating), preignition or detonation.

Excessive Vibration

Excessive vibration can be caused by an engine misfiring on one or more cylinders, loose or broken motor mounts and worn or failed bearings. Gearcase problems that can cause excessive vibration are a bent propeller shaft, damaged propeller or a propeller with marine growth on the blades. A propeller that is ventilating from damage or defects on the leading edge of the gearcase, improperly mounted speedometer or a depth finder sending unit or any hull deformity that disturbs the water flow to the propeller can cause excessive vibration.

Engine Noise

Experience is needed to diagnose engine noises accurately. Noises are difficult to differentiate and harder yet to describe. Even a properly assembled two-stroke power head produces much more mechanical noise than its four-stroke counterpart and a two-stroke power head produces substantial intake (induction) noise. Deep knocking noises usually mean crankshaft main or rod bearing failure. A light slapping noise generally comes from a loose piston; however, some piston noise is normal, especially during warm-up. Any knocking noise on acceleration or at high speed could be preignition or detonation and must be investigated immediately.

Table 1 TEST EQUIPMENT AND TOOLS

Description	Part No.	Manufacturer
Air gap spark tester		
Two-cylinder	S-21	Stevens Instruments
Four-cylinder	S-48 H	Stevens Instruments
Four-cylinder	55-4S	Merc-O-Tronic
Amphenol type terminal tools		
Crimping pliers	322696	OMC
Pin insertion tool	322697	OMC
Pin removal tool (male)	322698	OMC
Pin removal tool (female)	322699	OMC
Amphenol connector break out boxes		
SA-6	SA-6	Stevens Instruments
Model 55-861	55-861	Merc-O-Tronic
Deutsch type terminal tools		
Crimping pliers	322696	OMC
Terminal service tool	342667	OMC
Terminal service kit	507197	OMC
Ignition analyzer		
ST-75	ST-75	Stevens Instruments
Model 98	NLA*	Merc-O-Tronic
Packard test lead sets		
3.0 and 4 hp	434127	OMC
25-35 hp (3-cylinder)	342228	OMC
Peak reading voltmeter (PRV)		
CD-77	CD-77	Stevens Instruments
Model 781	781	Merc-O-Tronic
Power pack load adaptor	PL-88	Stevens Instruments
Standard crimping pliers	500906	OMC
Temperature gun (infrared)	772018	OMC
Terminal extenders (ignition coil)	TS-77	Stevens Instruments
Thermomelt Stiks	T-100, 125, 163	Stevens Instruments

*No longer available from Merc-O-Tronic.

Table 2 WIRING HARNESS COLOR CODES (TRADITIONAL HARNESS)

Main harness circuits	Color code	Trim/tilt circuits	Color code
Starter engagement	Yellow/red	Trim motor up	Blue
Tachometer	Gray	Trim motor down	Green
Stop 1 (ignition side)	Black/yellow	Switching up	Blue/white
Stop 2 (ground side)	Black	Switching down	Green/white
Choke or primer	Purple/white	Switching circuit B+	Red/white
Warning horn	Tan	Trim sender circuit	White/tan
Switched B+	Purple	Grounds	Black or black/tan
Protected B+	Red/purple	Grounds	Black

Table 3 WIRING HARNESS COLOR CODES (MODULAR WIRING HARNESS)

Main harness circuits	Color code	Trim/tilt circuits	Color code
Starter engagement	Yellow/red	Trim motor up	Blue
Tachometer	Gray	Trim motor down	Green
Stop 1 (ignition side)	Black/yellow	Switching up	Blue/white
Stop 2 (ground side)	Black/white	Switching down	Green/white
Choke or primer	Purple/white	Switching circuit B+	Red/white
Overheat warning	Tan	Trim sender circuit	White/tan
No oil warning	Tan/yellow	–	–
Low oil warning	Tan/black	–	–
Warning horn control	Tan/blue	–	–
Protected B+	Red/purple	–	–
Grounds	Black	–	–

Table 4 MINIMUM BATTERY CABLE SIZES (AWG)

Cable length	9.9-15 hp	20-50 hp (two-cylinder)	50-70 hp (three-cylinder)
1-10 ft. (0.3-3.0 m)	10 gauge	6 gauge	4 gauge
11-15 ft. (3.4-4.6 m)	8 gauge	4 gauge	2 gauge
16-20 ft. (4.9-6.1 m)	6 gauge	3 gauge	1 gauge

Table 5 STARTER SYSTEM TROUBLESHOOTING

Symptom	Probable cause	Remedy
Low no-load speed with high current draw	Tight or dirty bushings	Clean and lubricate bushings.
	Shorted armature	Test armature on growler.
Low no-load speed with low current draw	High resistance in the armature circuit	Check brushes and springs. Test armature on growler. Clean and inspect commutator.
High current draw with no rotation	Stuck armature	Clean and lubricate bushings, remove internal corrosion.
	Internal short to ground	Check brush leads for shorts.
No current draw with no rotation	Open armature circuit	Check brushes and springs. Test armature on growler. Clean and inspect commutator.

(continued)

Table 5 STARTER SYSTEM TROUBLESHOOTING (continued)

Symptom	Probable cause	Remedy
Starter continues running after key is released	Solenoid stuck on Key switch failure Yellow or yellow/red wire circuit malfunction	Replace solenoid. Test key switch. Remove yellow or yellow/red wire from solenoid. If starter now stops, repair or replace the yellow/red wire from the key switch to the starter solenoid.
Starter turns motor over too slowly	Solenoid has high internal resistance	Measure voltage drop across the solenoid while starter is engaged. Connect red voltmeter lead to battery side of solenoid and black voltmeter lead to the starter side. Measure voltage with starter engaged.
	Mechanical failure of power head or gearcase	Turn flywheel by hand. If resistance is excessive, remove gearcase and recheck. Repair gearcase or power head.
	Battery cables too small or excessively long	Do not use cables smaller than the manufacturer installed. If extending cable length, use larger diameter cables.
Starter spins but starter drive does not engage	Starter drive is corroded or needs lubrication	Clean thoroughly and lubricate the splines under the starter drive.

	Starter is not producing necessary speed and torque to engage the drive	Check the battery charge, battery cables and connections. Test the solenoid voltage drop (see Starter turns motor slowly).
		Disassemble the starter and:
		  Clean and lubricate bushings.
		  Clean and inspect commutator.
		  Check brushes and springs.
		  Test armature on growler.

Table 6 CHARGING SYSTEM TROUBLESHOOTING

Symptom	Probable cause	Remedy
Battery overcharges Unregulated system	Extended high-speed running	Turn on accessories during high-speed runs.
Regulated system	Regulator failure	Test sense circuit. If good, replace regulator.
	Stator shorted to ground	Perform stator resistance tests.

(continued)

Table 6 CHARGING SYSTEM TROUBLESHOOTING

Symptom	Probable cause	Remedy

Battery gasses excessively	Overcharging
	Defective battery
	  (internally shorted)
		See battery overcharges
		
		Substitute another
		  battery and retest

Battery loses charge with engine running	Alternator failure Excessive accessory load	Test system per text. Perform current draw test

Battery loses charge
  during storage
	Current drain from
	  engine components
	  ohmmeter tests.
	
	Current drain from
	  accessories left on
	
	Defective battery
		Perform rectifier or
		  rectifier/regulator.
		
		Turn accessories off,
		  consider installing battery switch.
		Disconnect battery cables.
		  If battery still loses charge,
		  battery is defective.

Table 7 IGNITION SYSTEM TROUBLESHOOTING

Symptom	Probable cause	Remedy
Engine does not start (spark tests good)	Fouled spark plugs Incorrect timing from sheared flywheel key	Clean or replace spark plugs Check flywheel key.
Engine backfire	Improper timing Incorrect firing order Cracked spark plug insulator	Check timing. Check primary and secondary lead routing and connections. Replace spark plugs.

High-speed misfire	Insufficient spark
	Incorrect spark plug gap
	Loose electrical connections
	
	Secondary spark leakage
		Perform air gap spark test.
		Gap spark plugs (if applicable).
		Check battery connections,
		  engine harness connections
		  and terminals.
		Inspect ignition coils and spark
		  plug leads for cracks, arcing
		  and evidence of leakage.

Engine pre-ignition	Excessively high combustion chamber temperature.	Check for correct spark plugs Check for excessive spark advance. Inspect cooling system. Check fuel system for restricted supply (lean mixture).
Spark plug failure	Incorrect spark plug Spark plugs not torqued Air/fuel mixture incorrect Excessive carbon buildup Engine overheat	Use correct spark plug(s). Torque spark plug(s). Check fuel supply and carburetor(s). Use recommended fuel and oil. Inspect cooling system.
Ignition component failure	Loose electrical connections Loose mounting (vibration) Overheating Corrosion (water damage)	Clean and tighten all connections. Tighten mounting hardware. Inspect cooling system. Locate source of moisture.

3

Table 8 FUEL SYSTEM TROUBLESHOOTING

Symptom	Probable cause	Remedy
Engine does not start	No fuel to carburetor	Verify fuel in tank. Check fuel tank air vents. Check fuel tank pickup filter. Clean all fuel filters. Verify primer bulb operation.
	Carburetor failure	Rebuild and adjust carburetor.
Flooding at carburetor	Carburetor float malfunction	Disassemble carburetor and replace inlet needle and seat. Adjust the float level.
	Excessive fuel pump pressure overcoming float system.	Check fuel pump pressure. Check for stuck piston rings.
Loss of power, hesitation on acceleration	Restricted fuel supply (lean air/fuel mixture)	Clean fuel filters, check fuel lines for kinks and restrictions. Check carburetor jets for obstructions.
	Air leaks into fuel supply	Check all connections and hoses between fuel pickup and fuel pump.
Engine backfire Rough operation	Lean air/fuel ratio Water or dirt in fuel Broken or damaged reed valve(s)	Adjust idle mixture and speed. Clean fuel system. Inspect reed valves.
Engine preignition	Restricted fuel supply (lean air/fuel mixture)	Clean fuel filters, check fuel lines for kinks and restrictions. Check carburetor jets for obstructions.
	Low fuel pump pressure Air leaks into fuel supply	Check fuel pump pressure Check all connections and hoses between fuel pickup and fuel pump.
Engine detonation	Fuel octane does not meet engine octane requirements	Use higher octane fuel. Check for excessive carbon buildup in combustion chamber. See preignition.
Excessive fuel consumption	Carburetor float malfunction Blocked air bleeds Gasket failure Cracked carburetor casting(s) Incorrect metering jets High fuel pump pressure	Rebuild and adjust carburetor. Clean air bleeds. Replace all gaskets. Replace castings as needed. Install correct jets. Test fuel pump pressure and check for stuck piston rings.
Spark plug fouling	Fuel mixture too rich Excessive oil in fuel	See excessive fuel consumption Mix fuel and oil at recommended ratio. Test oil injection pump.

Table 9 STARTER NO-LOAD CURRENT DRAW SPECIFICATIONS

Model	Maximum current	Rpm range
9.9 and 15 hp	7 amps	7000-9200
20-35 hp	30 amps	6500-7500
40-50 hp (two-cylinder) and 35 jet	32 amps	5700-8000
50-70 hp (three-cylinder)	32 amps	5750-8000

Table 10 STATOR (ALTERNATOR COIL) IDENTIFICATION AND RESISTANCE SPECIFICATIONS

Model	Resistance[1]	Resistance[2]	Resistance[3]
4 Deluxe, 6 and 8 hp			
60 watt AC lighting[4]	0.81-0.91	Not applicable	1.19-1.23
4 amp unregulated DC[4]	Not applicable	0.50-0.60	0.50-0.60
9.9 and 15 hp			
5 amp AC lighting[4]	0.80-0.90	0.80-0.90	1.5-1.7
5 amp unregulated DC	0.80-0.90	0.80-0.90	1.5-1.7
18 jet			
60 watt AC lighting[4]	0.81-0.91	Not applicable	1.19-1.23
20-30 hp (two-cylinder)			
60 watt AC lighting[4]	0.81-0.91	Not applicable	1.19-1.23
4 amp unregulated DC[4]	Not applicable	0.50-0.60	0.50-0.60
25 and 35 hp (three-cylinder)			
71 watt AC lighting[4]	1.38-1.68	Not applicable	Not applicable
12 amp regulated DC	0.45-0.54	Not applicable	Not applicable
40 hp rope start and 28 jet			
60 watt AC[4]	0.81-0.91	Not applicable	1.19-1.23
4 amp unregulated DC[4]	Not applicable	0.50-0.60	0.50-0.60
40 hp electric start			
12 amp regulated DC	0.4-0.6	Not applicable	Not applicable
48 Special (SPL) models			
4 amp unregulated DC	Not applicable	0.50-0.60	0.50-0.60
50-70 hp and 35 jet			
12 amp regulated DC	0.4-0.6	Not applicable	Not applicable

1. Measured between the yellow and yellow/gray leads.
2. Measured between the yellow and yellow/blue leads.
3. Measured between the yellow/gray and yellow/blue leads.
4. Optional accessory on rope start models.

Table 11 BATTERY CHARGING SYSTEM OUTPUT SPECIFICATIONS

RPM	4 amp unregulated	5 amp unregulated	12 amp regulated
1000	0.4 amps	1.0 amps	5.0 amps
2000	1.2 amps	2.8 amps	9.0 amps
3000	2.2 amps	4.1 amps	11.0 amps
4000	3.2 amps	5.0 amps	11.8 amps
5000	4.0 amps	5.2 amps	12.0 amps

Table 12 IGNITION SYSTEM IDENTIFICATION

Model	System	Advance	Features	Rpm limit
2, 3.3 and 3.5 hp	CD1	Electronic	Not applicable	Not applicable
3 and 4 hp	CD	Mechanical	Not applicable	Not applicable
4 Deluxe, 6 and 8 hp	CD2	Mechanical	Not applicable	Not applicable
9.9 and 15 hp	CD2	Mechanical	Not applicable	Not applicable
20-30 hp (two-cylinder) and 18 jet	CD2	Mechanical	S.L.O.W.	6100
25 and 35 hp (three-cylinder)	OIS2000	Mechanical	QuickStart, S.L.O.W.	6200
28 jet and 40 hp (rope)	CD2	Mechanical	S.L.O.W.	6100
40 hp (electric)	CD2	Mechanical	S.L.O.W.	6700
48 Special	CD2	Mechanical	S.L.O.W.	6100
35 jet and 50 hp (two-cylinder)	CD2	Mechanical	S.L.O.W.	6700
50-70 hp (three-cylinder)	CD3	Mechanical	QuickStart, S.L.O.W.	6700

Table 13 IGNITION COIL RESISTANCE SPECIFICATIONS

Model	Primary windings	Secondary windings
25 and 35 hp (three-cylinder)	0.23-0.32	2000-2600
All other models	0.05-0.15	225-325

Table 14 IGNITION SYSTEM RESISTANCE SPECIFICATIONS

Model	Charge coil	Sensor coil	Power coil
2, 3.3 and 3.5 hp	550-670	40-60	NA
3 and 4 hp	NA	85-115	NA
4 Deluxe, 6-8 hp	800-1000	30-50	NA
9.9 and 15 hp (rope)	800-1000	30-50	NA
9.9 and 15 (electric)	680-840	30-50	NA
20-30 hp (two-cylinder) and 18 jet	800-1000	30-50	NA
25 and 35 hp (three-cylinder) (rope)	1010-1230	NA	76-92
25 and 35 hp (three-cylinder) (electric)	720-880	NA	52-62
28 jet and 40 hp (rope)	800-1000	30-50	NA
35 jet and 50 hp (two-cylinder)	750-950	22-32	360-440
40 and 48 hp (4 amp stator)	800-1000	30-50	NA
40 hp (12 amp stator)	750-950	22-32	360-440
50-70 hp (three-cylinder)	750-950	See text	360-440

Table 15 IGNITION SYSTEM MINIMUM PEAK VOLTAGE SPECIFICATIONS

Model	Charge coil cranking	Sensor coil cranking	Power coil cranking	Power pack output cranking (running)
2, 3.3 and 3.5 hp	180	1.0	NA	180 (220)
3 and 4 hp	NA	4.0	NA	125 (150)
4 Deluxe, 6-15 hp	230	1.5	NA	175 (200)
20-30 hp (two-cylinder) and 18 jet	230	1.5	NA	175 (200)
25 and 35 hp (three-cylinder)	300	NA	100	100 (240)
28 jet and 40 hp (rope)	230	1.5	NA	150 (175)
35 jet and 50 hp (two-cylinder)	230	0.5	NA	150 (175)
40 hp (4 amp stator)	230	1.5	NA	150 (175)
40 hp (12 amp stator)	230	0.5	NA	150 (175)
48 Special	230	1.5	NA	150 (175)
50-70 hp (three-cylinder)	250	1.5	NA	190 (220)

Chapter Four

Lubrication, Maintenance and Tune-up

The modern outboard motor delivers more power and performance than ever before, with improved designs, manufacturing methods, electrical and fuel systems and other advances. Proper lubrication, maintenance and tune-up are increasingly important as ways to maintain a high level of performance, extend engine life and extract the maximum economy of operation.

The owner's operation and maintenance manual is a valuable resource that must be read by anyone operating or maintaining the engine. The owner's manual is also a helpful supplement to this service manual. If it is missing, purchase an owner's manual through an Evinrude or Johnson dealership. The complete model number of the outboard motor is required to obtain the correct owner's manual.

You can do your own lubrication, maintenance and tune-up if you follow the correct procedures and use common sense. The following information is based on recommendations from Outboard Marine Corporation that will help you maintain your Evinrude or Johnson outboard motor and keep it operating at its peak performance level. **Tables 1-5**, covering the recommended preventive maintenance schedule, recommended spark plugs, cylinder head bolt torque values, gearcase lubricant capacities and test wheel recommendations are located at the end of this chapter

HOUR METER

Since a boat is not equipped with an odometer, service schedules for an outboard motor are based on hours of engine operation. An engine hour meter is highly recommended to help the owner keep track of the actual hours of engine operation. Many types of hour meters are available. The most accurate type (for maintenance purposes) is triggered by a spark plug lead. This makes sure that only actual running time is recorded. If an hour meter is operated by the key-switch, any time the operator forgets to turn off the key artificial running hours are recorded.

OMC Genuine Parts offer many models of ignition switch operated hour meters. Mercury Marine offers the Quicksilver Service Monitor (part No. 79-828010A-1), which is a spark plug wire-driven hour meter. The monitor can be set to flash an alarm at any time interval set by the operator.

FUELS AND LUBRICATION

Proper Fuel Selection

Two-stroke engines are lubricated by mixing oil with the fuel. The oil is either mixed with the fuel in the fuel tank (by the operator) or automatically mixed by an oil injection system. The various components of the engine are thus lubricated as the fuel/oil mixture passes through the crankcase and cylinders. Since two-stroke fuel serves the dual function of producing combustion and distributing the lubrication, never use marine white gasolines or any other fuel that is not intended to be used in modern gasoline powered engines. Any substandard fuel (and lubricating oil) will aggravate combustion chamber deposits, which leads to piston ring sticking, exhaust port blockage and abnormal combustion (preignition and detonation).

NOTE
The simplest way to reduce combustion chamber deposits and the resulting problems, is to use the highest quality fuel (without alcohol) and lubricating oil available.

The *recommended* fuel for all models is regular, midgrade or premium unleaded gasoline from a major supplier with a minimum pump posted octane rating of 87 AKI (anti-knock index) *and* no alcohol.

The AKI figure is determined (by the fuel supplier) by taking the RON (research octane number) and adding it to the MON (motor octane number), then dividing the result by 2 (RON+MON/2). The RON and MON are the fuel manufacturer's ratings of the fuel's ability to resist detonation in a test engine when operated at low and high power settings, respectively. The AKI figure is simply the average of these 2 ratings.

The minimum fuel requirements for the 2-30 hp (1- and two-cylinder) and 18 jet models is regular unleaded with a pump posted octane rating of 67 AKI and no more than 10% ethanol *or* 5 percent methanol with 5 percent cosolvents.

The *minimum* fuel requirements for the 25-35 hp (three-cylinder), 40-70 hp and 28-35 jet models is regular unleaded with a pump posted octane rating of 87 AKI and no more than 10 percent ethanol *or* 5 percent methanol with 5 percent cosolvents.

Methanol generally requires the use of special cosolvents to keep the methanol from phasing out of the fuel mix. The amount of cosolvents cannot exceed 5 percent of the total fuel mix. Methanol generally causes more side effects than ethanol, and its use is therefore discouraged.

Any fuel containing more than 10 percent ethanol *or* 5 percent methanol with 5% cosolvents is considered unacceptable fuel.

Recently *reformulated* fuels have been introduced in parts of the United States that have not achieved federally mandated reductions in emissions. Reformulated fuels are specifically blended to reduce emissions. Reformulated fuels normally contain oxygenates, such as ethanol, methanol or MTBE (methyl tertiary butyl ether). Reformulated

fuels may be used as long as they do not contain more than 10 percent ethanol *or* 5 percent methanol with 5 percent cosolvents and the normal precautions for alcohol (ethanol) extended fuels are taken. See *Alcohol Extended Gasoline.*

If the engine is used for severe service, hard working conditions or if detonation is suspected to be caused by poor grade gasoline, use mid-grade or premium grades of gasoline from a major supplier (as long as they contain no alcohol).

The installation of a water separating fuel filter is recommended as a preventative measure on all permanently installed fuel systems. The manufacturer specifically recommends the installation of the OMC Water Separating Fuel Filter if any alcohol blended or alcohol extended gasoline is used.

Sour Fuel

Fuel must not be stored for more than 60 days (under ideal conditions). As gasoline ages, it forms gum and varnish deposits that restrict carburetor and fuel system passages, causing the engine to starve for fuel. The octane rating of the fuel also deteriorates over time, increasing the likelihood of preignition or detonation. A fuel additive such as OMC 2+4 Fuel Conditioner must be used on a regular basis to stabilize the octane rating and prevent gum and varnish formation. Fuel conditioner must be added to fresh fuel. It cannot rejuvenate sour fuel. If the fuel is known to be sour or stale, it must be drained and replaced with fresh gasoline. Dispose of the sour fuel in an approved manner. Always use fresh gasoline when mixing fuel for your outboard motor.

Alcohol Extended Gasoline

Although the manufacturer does not encourage the use of gasoline that contains alcohol, the minimum gasoline specifications allow for a maximum of 10 percent ethanol *or* 5 percent methanol with 5 percent cosolvents to be used. Methanol is not recommended since the detrimental effects of methanol are more extreme than ethanol. If alcohol extended gasoline is used, the following must be considered.

1. Alcohol extended gasoline promotes leaner air/fuel ratios, which can:
   a. Raise combustion chamber temperature, leading to preignition and/or detonation.
   b. Cause hesitation or stumbling on acceleration.
   c. Cause hard starting, hot and cold.

d. Cause the engine to produce slightly less horse-power.

2. Alcohol extended gasoline attracts moisture, which can:
   a. Cause a water buildup in the fuel system.
   b. Block fuel filters.
   c. Block fuel metering components.
   d. Cause corrosion of metallic components in the fuel system and power head.

3. Alcohol extended gasoline deteriorates nonmetallic components, such as:
   a. Rubber fuel lines.
   b. Primer bulb.
   c. Fuel pump internal components.
   d. Carburetor internal components.
   e. Fuel recirculation components.

4. Alcohol extended gasoline promotes vapor lock and hot soak problems.

5. Alcohol extended fuels tend to build up combustion chamber deposits more quickly, which leads to:
   a. Higher compression ratios, increasing the likelihood of preignition or detonation.
   b. Piston ring sticking, which causes elevated piston temperature, loss of power and ultimately preignition or detonation.
   c. Exhaust port blockage or obstruction on engines with small or multiple exhaust ports.

NOTE
When the moisture content of the fuel reaches 0.5 percent, the water separates from the fuel and settles to the low points of the fuel system. This includes the fuel tank, fuel filters and carburetor float chambers. Alcohol extended fuels aggravate this situation.

If any or all of these symptoms are regularly occurring, consider testing the fuel for alcohol or simply changing to a different gasoline supplier. If the symptoms are no longer present after the change, continue using the gasoline from the new supplier.

If usage of alcohol extended fuels is unavoidable, perform regular maintenance and inspections more often than normally recommended. Pay special attention to: changing or cleaning the fuel filters, inspecting rubber fuel system components for deterioration, inspecting metallic fuel system components for corrosion and monitoring the power head for warning signs of pre-ignition and/or detonation on a regular basis. It is sometimes necessary to enrichen the carburetor's metering circuits to compensate for the leaning effect of these gasolines.

Reformulated gasolines that contain MTBE (methyl tertiary butyl ether) in normal concentrations have no side effects other than those previously listed. This does not apply to reformulated gasoline that contains ethanol or methanol.

Testing For Alcohol

The following procedure is an accepted and widely used field procedure for detecting alcohol in gasoline. Note that the gasoline must be checked prior to mixing with oil. Use any small transparent bottle or tube that can be capped and provided with graduations or a mark at approximately 1/3 full. A pencil mark on a piece of adhesive tape is sufficient.

1. Fill the container with water to the 1/3 full mark.
2. Add gasoline until the container is almost full. Leave a small air space at the top.
3. Shake the container vigorously, then allow it to sit for 3-5 minutes. If the volume of water appears to have increased, alcohol is present. If the dividing line between the water and gasoline becomes cloudy, reference from the center of the cloudy band.

This procedure can not differentiate between types of alcohol (ethanol or methanol). Also, it is not considered to be absolutely accurate from a scientific standpoint, but it is accurate enough to determine if sufficient alcohol is present to cause the user to take precautions.

Gasoline Additives

The only recommended fuel additives and the associated benefits from their use are:

1. *OMC 2+4 Fuel Conditioner*—This additive, when added to fresh fuel, provides the following benefits:
   a. Prevents fuel octane degradation and oxidation.
   b. Deactivates the fuel to prevent reactions with brass or copper fuel system components.
   c. Prevents the formation of gum and varnish in the fuel system components.
   d. Prevents moisture buildup in the fuel tank, fuel system and carburetors.

2. *OMC Carbon Guard*—Carbon Guard is designed to help prevent combustion chamber deposits from forming. Use Carbon Guard if substandard or questionable fuels (or oils) are being used, or if combustion chamber deposits are an ongoing problem.

Unless the boat is consistently operated with fresh fuel, the use of a fuel conditioner on an ongoing basis is recommended.

CAUTION
Some marinas are blending valve recession additives into their fuel to accommodate owners of older four-stroke marine engines. Valve recession additives are designed to help prevent premature valve seat wear on

older four-stroke engines. The valve recession additives may react with some outboard motor oils causing certain two-stroke oil additives to precipitate (gel). This precipitation can plug fuel system filters and smaller passages; therefore, the use of any fuel containing valve recession additives must be avoided.

Recommended Fuel/Oil Mixtures

The recommended oil for all models is Evinrude or Johnson TCW-3, 2-Cycle Outboard Oil. This oil meets or exceeds TCW-3 standards set by the NMMA (National Marine Manufacturers Association). If Evinrude or Johnson brand oil is not available, use a NMMA certified TCW-3 outboard oil from another engine manufacturer.

TCW-3 oils are designed to improve lubrication over previous standards (TCW and TCW-II), as well as reduce combustion chamber deposits caused by the lubricating oil. Do not use any oil other than a NMMA approved TCW-3 outboard motor oil.

CAUTION
Do not, under any circumstances, use automotive engine oil or gear lubricant. These types of lubricants will cause power head failure. Use only a NMMA approved TCW-3 outboard oil.

The recommended fuel/oil mixture for normal operation in all models without oil injection is 50 parts of fuel to 1 part of oil. This is the standard 6 gallons of fuel to one pint (16 fl. oz. [473 mL]) of oil.

All 2.0-3.3 hp models are not equipped with an oil injection system and no such system is available as an accessory. These engines require premixing of the fuel and oil in a separate tank, before filling the engine's integral fuel tank.

All 4-30 hp (two-cylinder), 18 and 28 jet, 40 hp rope start and 48 Special models are not factory-equipped with an oil injection system and require premixing of the fuel and oil in the remote fuel tank, unless they are equipped with the optional AccuMix R system. The AccuMix R system is mounted in the fuel line between the fuel tank and the outboard motor. The AccuMix R system automatically mixes the oil with the fuel at the recommended 50:1 ratio. Refer to Chapter Eleven for an operational description and service procedures on the AccuMix R system.

All 25 and 35 hp (three-cylinder) models are equipped with an engine mounted oil injection pump and reservoir and do not require premixing of the fuel and oil, except during power head break-in.

All 40 hp electric start, 35 jet and 50-70 hp engines are equipped with an oil injection system which can be readily identified by the presence of the engine-mounted VRO^2 pump (**Figure 1**) and a boat-mounted oil reservoir (**Figure 2**). These engines do not require premixing of the fuel and oil, except during power head break-in, or if the oil injection system has been disabled. See Chapter Eleven.

Power Head Break-in Procedures

A new outboard motor or rebuilt power head must be operated in accordance with the manufacturer's recommended break-in procedure. Additionally, Outboard Marine Corporation requires that a new motor or rebuilt power head be operated on a 25:1 fuel/oil mixture (often called double oiling) for the entire 10 hour break-in period.

CAUTION
*Do not run the engine without an adequate water supply and do not exceed 3000 rpm without an adequate load. Refer to **Safety Precautions** at the beginning of Chapter Three. Monitor water pump function by checking for a steady stream of water being discharged from the tell-tale (water pump indicator) fitting at the rear of the lower cowl.*

1. During the first 10 minutes of engine operation, operate the engine only at a fast idle (1500-2000 rpm) in NEUTRAL.
2. During the remaining 50 minutes (of the first hour of engine operation), change the engine speed frequently and avoid full-throttle operation (except to quickly plane the boat). Do not exceed 3500 rpm.

NOTE
During the remainder of the break-in period, the engine must not be allowed to exceed its

*recommended wide-open throttle (W.O.T.) range. Refer to **Wide-Open-Throttle Speed Verification** in Chapter Five.*

3. During the second hour of engine operation, use full throttle to plane the boat, then reduce the throttle setting to a maximum of 3/4 throttle. Occasionally, apply full throttle for one-two minutes, then reduce the throttle setting to a maximum of 3/4 throttle to allow the combustion chambers to cool. Do not operate the engine at any one throttle setting for more than 15 minutes. Frequently vary the throttle setting.

4. During the remaining 8 hours of the 10 hour break-in period, avoid continuous full-throttle operation. Do not operate the engine at any one throttle setting for more than 15 minutes. Frequently vary the throttle setting.

After the 10 hour break-in period, the engine can be operated as desired within normal operating guidelines.

2-30 hp (One and Two-cylinder), 18 and 28 Jet, 40 hp Rope Start and 48 Special Models (Without Accumix R Oil Injection)

To provide the required 25:1 fuel/oil mixture during the engine break-in period, mix 16 fl. oz. of the recommended outboard oil for every 3 gallons of the recommended fuel.

To provide the required 50:1 fuel/oil mixture after break-in and for all normal operation, mix eight fl. oz. of the recommended outboard oil for every three gallons of the recommended fuel. On models with an integral fuel tank, mix the fuel and oil in a separate container. On models equipped with a remote (portable) fuel tank, mix the fuel and oil directly in the remote fuel tank.

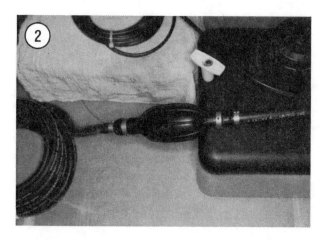

4-30 hp (Two-cylinder), 18 and 28 Jet, 40 hp Rope Start and 48 Special Models (Equipped with Accumix R Oil Injection)

To provide the required 25:1 fuel/oil mixture during the engine break-in period, mix eight fl. oz. of the recommended outboard oil for every three gallons of the recommended fuel. This will provide a 50:1 fuel/oil mix in the gas tank that will be supplemented by the AccuMix R's 50:1 fuel/oil mixture. The final result will be a 25:1 fuel/oil mixture to the engine.

To provide the required 50:1 fuel/oil mixture after break-in and for all normal operation, do not mix any oil in the gas tank. The AccuMix R system will provide the engine with the required 50:1 fuel/oil mixture. Monitor the Accu-Mix R's oil tank and keep it filled with the recommended outboard oil.

> *CAUTION*
> *If the oil injection system is disabled on 35 jet and 40-70 hp models, use a 25:1 fuel/oil mixture during engine break-in and a 50:1 mixture during normal operation.*

25 and 35 hp (Three-cylinder), 35 Jet and 40-70 hp Models Equipped with Oil Injection

To provide the required 25:1 fuel/oil mixture during the engine break-in period, mix eight fl. oz. of the recommended outboard oil for every three gallons of the recommended fuel. This will provide a 50:1 fuel/oil mix in the gas tank that will be supplemented by the engine-mounted oil injection system. The final result will be a 25:1 fuel/oil mixture to the engine.

To provide the required fuel/oil mixture for normal operation, do not add any oil to the fuel tank. The engine-mounted oil injection system will provide the engine with the required fuel/oil mixture. Monitor the engine-mounted oil tank (25-35 hp [three-cylinder] models) or the boat-mounted oil tank (35 jet and 40-70 hp models) and keep the tank filled with the recommended outboard oil.

Fuel Mixing Procedures

> *WARNING*
> *Gasoline is an extreme fire hazard. Never use gasoline near heat, spark or flame. Do not smoke while mixing fuel.*

Mix the fuel and oil outside or in a well-ventilated area. Mix the fuel and oil to the recommended fuel/oil ratio. Using less than the specified amount of oil can result in insufficient lubrication and serious engine damage. Using more oil than specified causes spark plug fouling, erratic fuel metering, excessive smoke and accelerated carbon accumulation.

Cleanliness is of prime importance when mixing fuel. Even a very small particle of dirt can restrict fuel metering passages.

Use fresh fuel only. If the fuel is sour, dispose of the fuel in an approved manner and start over with fresh fuel. If the fuel mix is not going to be used immediately, add OMC 2+4 Fuel Conditioner (or equivalent) to the fuel mix, following the instructions on the container.

Above 32° F (0° C)

Measure the required amount of gasoline and recommended outboard oil accurately. Pour the oil into the remote tank and add the fuel. Install the tank fill cap and mix the fuel by tipping the tank from side to side several times. See **Figure 3**.

If a built-in tank is used, insert a large filter-type funnel into the tank fill neck. Carefully pour the specified oil and gasoline into the funnel at the same time. See **Figure 4**.

Below 32° F (0° C)

Measure the required amount of gasoline and the recommended outboard oil accurately. Pour approximately one gallon of gasoline into the tank and then add the required amount of oil. Install the tank fill cap and shake the tank vigorously to mix thoroughly the fuel and oil. Remove the cap, add the balance of the gasoline and shake the tank again.

If a built-in tank is used, insert a large filter-type funnel into the tank fill neck. Mix the required amount of oil with one gallon of gasoline in a separate container. Carefully pour the mixture into the funnel at the same time the tank is being filled with gasoline.

Consistent Fuel Mixtures

The carburetor idle mixture adjustment is sensitive to fuel mixture variations which result from the use of different oils and gasolines or from inaccurate measuring and mixing. This may require constant readjustment of the idle mixture screw(s). To prevent carburetor readjustment or erratic running qualities from one fuel batch to another, always be consistent when mixing fuel. Prepare each batch of fuel exactly the same as previous ones.

Caution must be used if considering the use of premixed fuel sold at some on-water locations, since the quality and consistency of premixed fuel can vary greatly. The possi-

bility of engine damage resulting from use of an incorrect or substandard fuel/oil mixture often outweighs the convenience of premixed fuel. Premixed fuel must not be used if there is any concern that the fuel and oil mixture does not meet or exceed the engine fuel and oil requirements as previously stated in this manual.

AccuMix R Oil Injection System

The AccuMix R oil and gasoline mixing system is an optional accessory on 4-30 hp (two-cylinder), 18 and 28 jet, 40 hp rope start and 48 Special models. The AccuMix R system (**Figure 5**) is designed to deliver a constant 50:1 fuel/oil mixture to the engine's fuel system at all engine speeds and load conditions.

A bracket-mounted tank with a 2 qt. (1.89 L) oil reservoir is connected between the fuel tank and the engine, providing enough oil capacity for approximately 22 gal. (83 L) of fuel. The diaphragm operated fuel and oil mixing

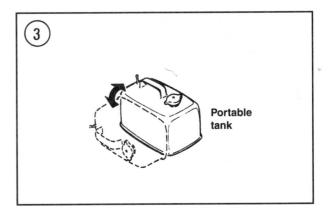

(3) Portable tank

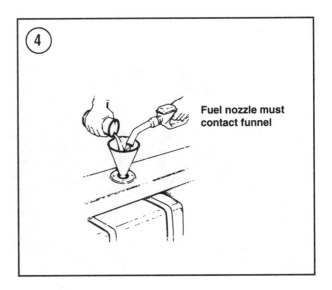

(4) Fuel nozzle must contact funnel

4

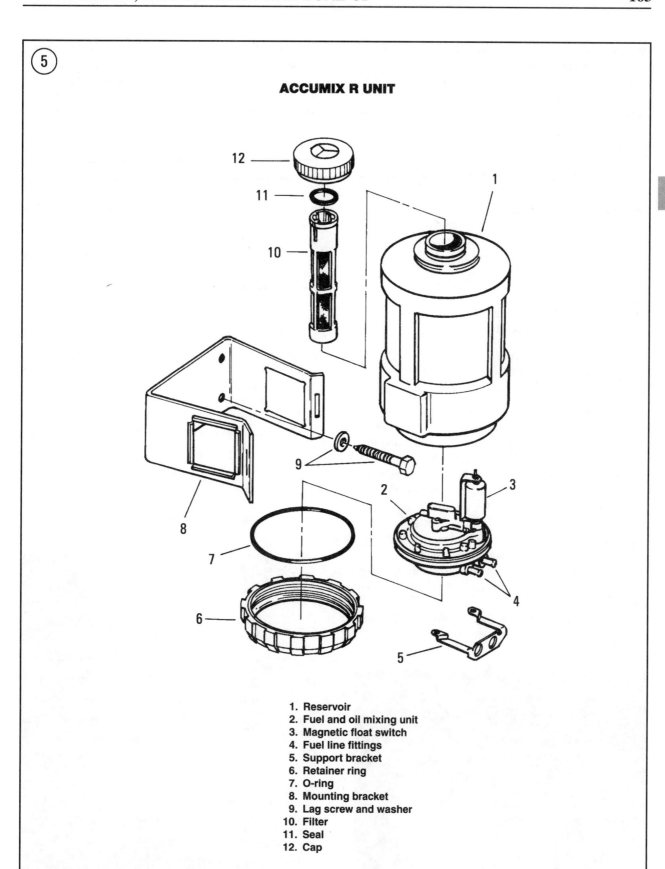

ACCUMIX R UNIT

1. Reservoir
2. Fuel and oil mixing unit
3. Magnetic float switch
4. Fuel line fittings
5. Support bracket
6. Retainer ring
7. O-ring
8. Mounting bracket
9. Lag screw and washer
10. Filter
11. Seal
12. Cap

chamber is actuated by the vacuum of the engine's fuel pump drawing fuel to the engine. The AccuMix R system is not equipped with a warning system. If the oil level falls below the predetermined level, a magnetic float switch (3, **Figure 5**) will pull a fuel piston valve closed, preventing fuel flow to the engine. Refill the oil to resume fuel flow to the engine.

A serviceable filter (10, **Figure 5**) filters all oil added to the reservoir. The filter must be removed and cleaned (or replaced) anytime debris is evident, or if it is difficult to fill the reservoir.

The fuel and oil mixing unit is not serviceable and is replaced as an assembly. Currently, the complete unit is less expensive to purchase than the fuel and oil mixing unit (2, **Figure 5**) alone.

Constant Ratio Oil Injection (25 and 35 hp [Three-cylinder])

NOTE
Electric fuel supply pumps are not recommended by OMC.

This oil injection system is used on all 25 and 35 hp (three-cylinder) models and provides the engine with a constant 50:1 fuel/oil ratio at all engine speeds and load conditions. The fuel and oil mixing unit is externally mounted near the bottom of the engine-mounted oil reservoir and is driven by the starboard fuel pump's pressure.

The engine-mounted oil tank's (**Figure 6**) capacity is 1.9 qt. (1.8 L). An internal float switch (A, **Figure 6**), provides a *low oil* signal if the oil tank's level is low and a separate *no oil* signal if the oil tank is almost empty. The oil tank must be filled as soon as possible after the *low oil* signal is noted and must be filled immediately upon noting the *no oil* signal.

On tiller handle models. an engine-mounted LED (light emitting diode) located near the starter rope handle, will il-luminate if the oil tank reaches the *low oil* level. If engine operation is continued, the ignition module will engage the S.L.O.W. (speed limiting operational warning) system when the oil tank reaches the *no oil* level. The *low oil* LED will remain illuminated at both the *low oil* and *no oil* levels.

On 1995 remote control models, an engine-mounted LED (light emitting diode) will illuminate when the oil tank reaches the *low oil* level. If engine operation is continued, the warning horn will sound *and* the ignition module will engage the S.L.O.W. (speed limiting operational warning) system when the oil tank reaches the *no oil* level. The *low oil* LED will remain illuminated at both the *low oil* and *no oil* levels. The warning system incorporates a self-test function, refer to *Warning Systems* in Chapter Three.

On 1996-2003 remote control models, the system check gauge's *low oil* LED will illuminate and the warning horn will sound for 10 seconds if the oil tank reaches the *low oil* level. If engine operation is continued and the oil tank reaches the *no oil* level, the system check gauge's *no oil* LED will illuminate, the ignition module will engage the S.L.O.W. (speed limiting operational warning) system and the warning horn will sound for 10 seconds. The *low oil* LED will remain illuminated at both the *low oil* and *no oil* levels. The warning system incorporates a self-test function, refer to *Warning Systems* in Chapter Three.

WARNING
Continued operation of the engine with the ***no oil*** *warning engaged will cause power head failure.*

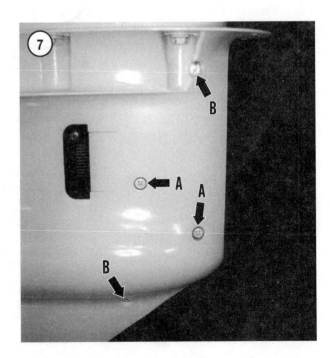

Filling the oil tank requires removing the engine cowl. Remove the fill cap (B, **Figure 6**) and fill with the recommended outboard oil. Reinstall the fill cap securely. Refer to Chapter Eleven for additional system information and service procedures.

VRO^2 System (35 Jet, 40 hp [Electric start] and 50-70 hp Models)

NOTE
Electric fuel supply pumps are not recommended by OMC.

The VRO^2 unit is a combination fuel and oil pump (**Figure 1**) driven by crankcase pressure and vacuum pulses. The oil is mixed with the fuel in an internal mixing chamber. The output from the pump is approximately 50:1 (fuel to oil).

A *no oil* motion sensor located in the pump engages the warning system if a no oil flow condition is noted. See *Warning Systems* in Chapter Three for warning signals and system operation. If the *no oil* signal is noted, the engine must be immediately stopped and the remote oil tank's oil level checked. If the oil tank's level is satisfactory, the engine must be operated on a 50:1 fuel/oil mix until the cause of the warning can be determined and corrected.

A 1.8 or 3 gallon (6.8 or 11.4 L) remote oil tank (**Figure 2**) supplies oil directly to the pump. A primer bulb in the oil line is used to purge air and prime the system during rigging, when the oil line has been disconnected (or serviced) or the oil tank has run dry. Never squeeze the oil tank's primer bulb during normal operation.

NOTE
Do not squeeze the oil tank's primer bulb before starting the engine. The engine's carburetors will become flooded with oil and starting will be difficult, if not impossible.

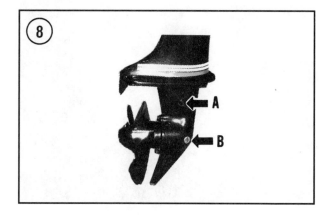

A low-oil switch attached to the oil tank's pickup assembly activates the *low oil* warning signal if the oil level in the reservoir becomes low. If this occurs, the engine must be stopped as soon as possible and the reservoir refilled. Power head damage will occur if the oil tank runs dry.

A filter attached to the pickup assembly keeps debris out of the oil lines and VRO^2 pump. The filter must be changed whenever the oil pickup assembly is removed from the oil tank or when any major service work is being performed on the oil injection system. See Chapter Eleven.

The warning system incorporates a self-test function as described in *Warning Systems*, located in Chapter Three.

WARNING
*Continued operation of the engine with the **no oil** warning engaged will cause power head failure.*

Remove the fill cap and fill the tank with the recommended outboard oil. When finished, reinstall the fill cap securely. Refer to Chapter Eleven for additional system information and service procedures.

Checking Lower Gearcase Lubricant

NOTE
*Some gearcases have one or two Pozidriv (similar to Phillips) screws (A, **Figure 7**, typical) located near (or between) the drain/fill and/or vent plugs. These screws retain shift system components and/or the pinion bearing and must not be removed by mistake. The drain/fill and vent plugs (B, **Figure 7**, typical) always have slotted heads.*

After being refilled, the lower gearcase lubricant level must be rechecked after 20 hours of operation or 10 days, then every 50 hours of operation or once a month thereafter. The recommended lubricant for all models is OMC Ultra HPF Gear Lubricant.

CAUTION
Do not use regular automotive gear lubricant in the gear housing. The expansion and foam characteristics and water tolerance of automotive gear lube are not suitable for marine use.

1. Place the outboard motor in an upright (vertical) position. Place a suitable container under the gear housing. Loosen the gearcase drain/fill plug (B, **Figures 8-12**). Allow a small amount of lubricant to drain. If water is present inside the gear housing, it will drain before the lubricant, or the lubricant will have a white or cream tint

to the normal lubricant color. If the lubricant looks satisfactory, retighten the drain/fill plug securely. If water was present in the lubricant, or if the lubricant is dirty, fouled or contains substantial metal shavings, allow the remaining lubricant to completely drain from the gearcase.

> *NOTE*
> *The presence of a small amount of metal filings and fine metal particles in the lubricant is normal, while an excessive amount of metal filings and larger chips indicates a problem. Remove and disassemble the gearcase to determine the source and cause of the metal filings and chips. Replace any damaged or worn parts. See Chapter Nine.*

> *CAUTION*
> *If water is present in the gearcase, but it is not possible to perform the repair at this time, completely drain the contaminated lubricant and refill the gearcase with fresh lubricant. Crank the engine through several revolutions and spin the propeller shaft several turns to spread the fresh lubricant throughout the gearcase.*

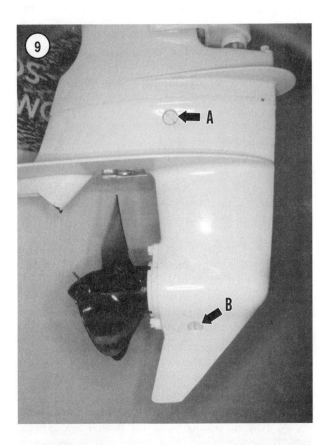

2. Remove the gearcase vent plug. See A, **Figures 8-12**. Replace the accompanying sealing washer (or O-ring) on the plug. The lubricant level must be level with the vent plug hole on all models.

> *CAUTION*
> *The vent plug is provided to vent displaced air while lubricant is added to the gearcase. Never attempt to fill or add lubricant to the gearcase without first removing the vent plug.*

3. If the lubricant level is low, temporarily reinstall the vent plug and remove the drain/fill plug. Insert the gearcase filling tube into the drain/fill plug hole (B, **Figures 8-12**), then remove the vent plug again.

4. Replace the sealing washer on the drain plug.

5. Inject the recommended lubricant into the drain/fill plug hole until excess lubricant flows from the vent plug hole (A, **Figures 8-12**). Then install and snug the vent plug.

6. Remove the gearcase filling tube and quickly install the drain/fill plug to minimize fluid loss. Then tighten both plugs to the following specifications:
   a. *2 and 3.3 hp*—31-40 in.-lb. (3.5-4.5 N•m).
   b. *3, 3.5 and 4 hp (except 4 Deluxe)*—40-50 in.-lb. (4.5-5.6 N•m).
   c. *4 Deluxe-70 hp*—84-86 in.-lb. (9.5-9.7 N•m).

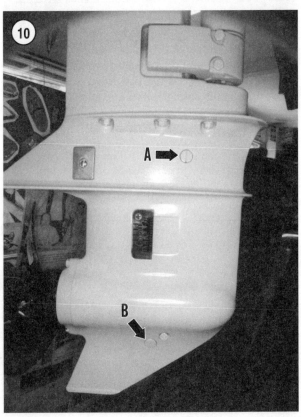

Changing Lower Gearcase Lubricant

NOTE
*Some gearcases have one or two Pozidriv (similar to Phillips) screws (A, **Figure 7**, typical) located near (or between) the drain/fill and/or vent plugs. These screws retain shift system components and/or the pinion bearing and must not be removed by mistake. The drain/fill and vent plugs (B, **Figure 7**, typical) always have slotted heads.*

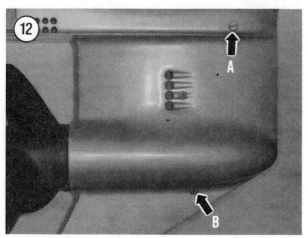

The lower gearcase lubricant must be changed after the first 20 hours of operation and every 100 hours (or seasonally) thereafter. Refer to **Table 4** for lower gearcase lubricant capacities.

1. Remove the engine cover. Disconnect and ground the spark plug leads to the power head to prevent accidental starting.

2. Place the outboard motor in an upright (vertical) position. Place a suitable container under the lower gearcase.

3. Remove the drain/fill plug (B, **Figures 8-12**), then the vent plug (A, **Figures 8-12**). Allow the lubricant to fully drain into the container.

4. Inspect the drained lubricant. Lubricant that is contaminated with water will have a white or cream tint to the normal lubricant color. The presence of a small amount of metal filings and fine metal particles in the lubricant is normal, while an excessive amount of metal filings and larger chips indicates a problem.

NOTE
If excessive metal filings and larger chips are present, remove and disassemble the gearcase to determine the source and cause of the metal filings and chips. Replace any damaged or worn parts. See Chapter Nine.

CAUTION
If water is present in the gearcase, but it is not possible to perform the repair at this time, completely drain the contaminated lubricant and refill the gearcase with fresh lubricant. Crank the engine through several revolutions and spin the propeller shaft several turns to spread the fresh lubricant throughout the gearcase.

5. Refill the gearcase with the recommended lubricant as described under *Checking Lower Gearcase Lubricant* in the previous section. Refer to **Table 4** for lower gearcase lubricant capacities.

Jet Pump Maintenance

The jet pump unit used on 18-35 jet models requires that the drive shaft bearings be lubricated daily or every 10 hours of operation, whichever comes first. After every 30 hours of operation, extra lubricant must be pumped in to purge the old grease and any moisture that may have accumulated.

The clearance between the jet pump impeller and the impeller liner must be 0.020-0.030 in. (0.51-0.76 mm). If the jet pump is operated consistently in silt laden or sandy waters, the clearance must be checked frequently. There are shims located above and below the impeller that are repositioned to set the required clearance. Refer to Chapter Nine for jet pump service procedures.

1. To lubricate the drive shaft bearings, disconnect the vent hose (1, **Figure 13**) from the grease fitting.

2. Connect a grease gun filled with OMC EP/Wheel Bearing Grease to the grease fitting (2, **Figure 13**).

3. Pump in grease until grease exits the vent hose (3, **Figure 13**).

4. Reconnect the vent hose to the grease fitting.

NOTE
Every 30 days, pump in extra grease until fresh grease exits the vent hose. If more than slight traces of water are present in the exiting grease, the drive shaft seals must be replaced. See Chapter Nine.

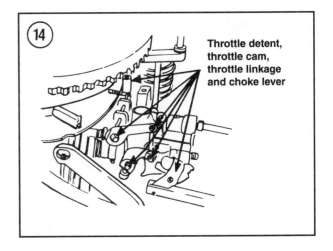

Throttle detent, throttle cam, throttle linkage and choke lever

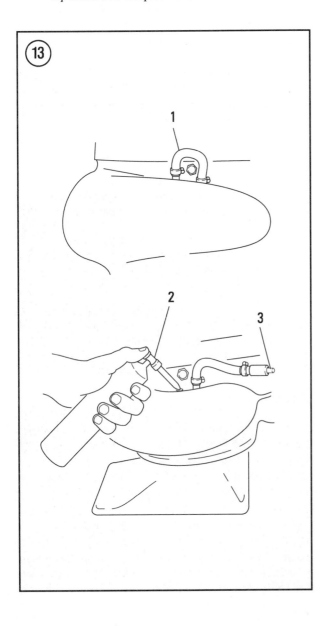

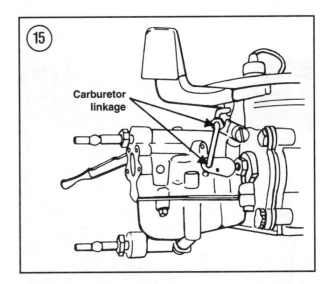

Carburetor linkage

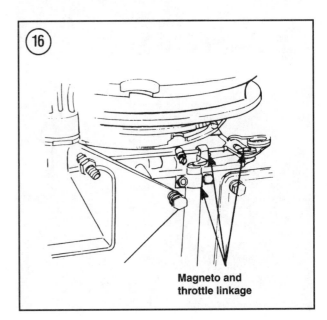

Magneto and throttle linkage

Propeller Shaft

To prevent corrosion and to ease the future removal of the propeller, remove and lubricate the propeller shaft at least once each season during freshwater operation or every 60 days of saltwater operation. Remove the propeller (Chapter Nine) and thoroughly clean any corrosion or dried grease, then coat the propeller shaft splines with OMC Triple Guard Grease or another suitable waterproof anti-corrosion grease.

Recommended Preventive Maintenance and Lubrication

Refer to **Table 1** for recommended preventive maintenance procedures. Common engines and typical lubrication points are shown in **Figures 14-25**.

Figure 17 shows the carburetor linkage on a typical multi-carbureted engine, **Figure 18** shows the throttle and spark linkage lubrication points for the 25-35 hp (three-cylinder) models and **Figure 19** shows typical spark control linkage lubrication points. **Figure 20** shows typical shift linkage lubrication points.

The factory supplied operation and maintenance manual is an excellent source for detailed pictures of the lubrica-

tion points for your specific engine. If you do not have an operation and maintenance manual for your engine, one can be ordered from any Evinrude/Johnson dealership. Make sure you have the complete engine model number before attempting to order the manual.

Basically, lubricate every grease fitting on the mid-section with OMC Triple Guard grease (or equivalent). Also lubricate all pivoting or sliding throttle, shift and ignition linkages, and the steering cable ram's sliding surfaces with Triple Guard grease. Lubricate the steering arm pivot points (remote control models) with SAE 30 engine oil.

Use a small, stiff bristle brush to apply the recommended lubricant to linkages and pivot points. Always wipe off all old lubricant and any dirt or debris before applying new grease.

CAUTION
When lubricating a steering cable equipped with a grease fitting, make sure the ram (core) is fully retracted into the engine's tilt tube. Lubricating these cables (via the grease fitting) with the ram extended can cause grease to be trapped behind the ram, resulting in a hydraulic lock situation. This will cause difficult steering, and in some situations, a complete loss of steering control.

On electric start models, manually rotate the starter pinion to expose the armature shaft's spiral splines (A, **Figure 25**). Clean any debris or dried lubricant from the splines, then lightly coat them with OMC Starter Pinion Lubricant. Allow the pinion to return to its resting position,

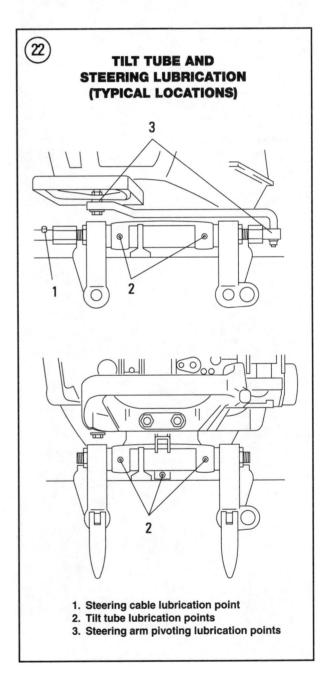

CLAMP SCREW LUBRICATION (PORTABLE MODELS)

㉑

TILT TUBE AND STEERING LUBRICATION (TYPICAL LOCATIONS)

㉒

1. Steering cable lubrication point
2. Tilt tube lubrication points
3. Steering arm pivoting lubrication points

then lift the protective cap and lightly coat the armature shaft (B, **Figure 25**) with the same lubricant.

Corrosion of the Propeller Shaft Bearing Carrier

Saltwater corrosion that is allowed to accumulate between the propeller shaft bearing carrier and gearcase

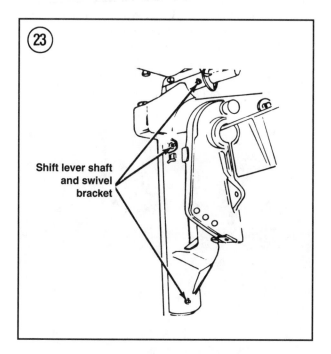

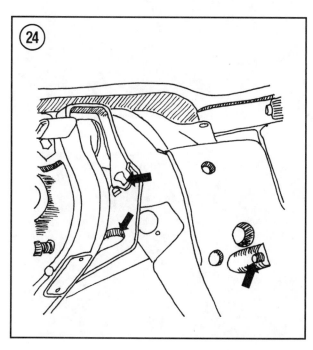

housing can eventually split the housing and destroy the lower gearcase assembly. If the outboard motor is operated in saltwater, remove the propeller shaft bearing carrier at least once a season. Refer to Chapter Nine for bearing carrier removal procedures for all models.

Thoroughly clean all corrosion and dried lubricant from each end of the propshaft bearing carrier's flanges (**Figure 26**, typical).

Always replace the bearing carrier O-ring(s) and propeller shaft seals if the carrier is removed. Apply OMC Gasket Sealing Compound (or equivalent) to the outer diameter of both carrier flanges and the carrier O-rings. Do not allow any sealing compound to flow into the gears or bearings.

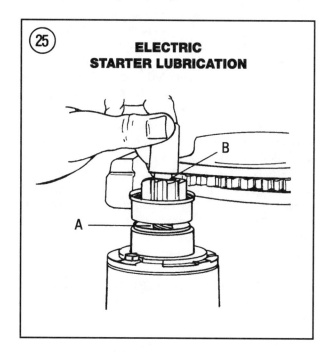

Then reinstall the bearing carrier as described in Chapter Nine.

Make sure all available anodes are installed and securely grounded to the gearcase or mid-section. Replace any anode that is deteriorated to two-thirds of its original size (one-third gone). Refer to Chapter One for anode theory. Refer to *Anti-corrosion maintenance* in this chapter for additional corrosion prevention procedures.

OFF-SEASON STORAGE

The two major considerations for preparing an outboard motor for storage are to protect it from rust, corrosion, dirt or other contamination and to protect it from physical damage. Two methods of *fogging* the engine can be used.

The fogging oil may be sprayed directly into the carburetor throat or injected through the service port located on the fuel primer solenoid (or pressed into the intake manifold on 25-35 hp [three-cylinder] models). This method is referred to as the *spray can method* and is usually the simplest if only one engine is to be stored. The service port is easily identified by its resemblance to a tire's air valve.

The fogging oil may be mixed into the fuel in what is referred to as a *storage mix*. Normally this is done in a six gallon remote fuel tank. This method is the easiest if several engines are to be stored. However, the quantity of storage mix can be reduced as long the same proportions (ratios) of the fuel, fogging oil, conditioner and outboard lubricant are maintained.

To prepare the motor for storage, proceed as follows:

1. Remove the engine cowling.

2. Treat all fuel tanks with OMC 2+4 Fuel Conditioner (or equivalent). Mix according to the manufacturer's recommendations for storage

> *CAUTION*
> *Do not run the engine without an adequate water supply and do not exceed 3000 rpm without an adequate load. Refer to Safety Precautions at the beginning of Chapter Three.*

3. Start the engine and run at fast idle until warmed up to operating temperature (at least 15 minutes). This ensures that the gasoline stabilizer has time to circulate through the entire fuel system. Then stop the engine.

> *CAUTION*
> *On engines equipped with oil injection, **do not** attempt to run the fuel system dry. The oil injection system will continue to pump oil even when no fuel is present. The result will be excessive oil in the carburetor(s). Restarting the engine will be extremely difficult. If*

the fuel in the fuel tank is fresh and properly stabilized, it is not necessary to attempt to run the engine fuel system dry. However, it may be desirable on small, portable engines (without oil injection) to allow transport or storage in a position that could cause spillage.

4A. *Storage mix method*—Using a 6 gallon remote fuel tank, prepare the following storage mixture:
  a. Add 5 gallons of fresh fuel. Avoid alcohol-extended fuels for storage whenever possible.
  b. Add 2 quarts of OMC Storage Fogging Oil. Fogging oil is available in 1 gallon cans (part No. 772030).
  c. Add 1 pint of the recommended outboard lubricant.
  d. Add 2.5 oz. of OMC 2+4 Fuel Conditioner.

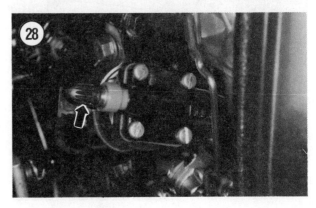

e. Thoroughly blend the mixture in the remote fuel tank by rocking it side-to-side.

f. Connect the storage mix tank to the engine. Start the engine and allow to run at approximately 1500 rpm for 5-10 minutes.

g. When finished, stop the engine, remove the motor from the water supply and disconnect the portable fuel tank containing the storage mix.

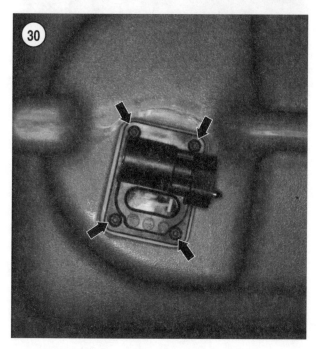

4B. *Spray can method (without service port)*—This method applies to 2-8 hp, 9.9-30 hp (two-cylinder) rope start and/or tiller electric models, 18-28 jet models and 40 hp rope start models.

a. Remove the carburetor air box cover (if so equipped) to gain access to the carburetor's throat (**Figure 27**, typical).

b. Start the engine and run it at fast idle (1500-2000 rpm) in NEUTRAL.

NOTE
On 28 jet and 40 hp rope start models, it is necessary to obtain two cans of fogging oil and spray into both carburetors at the same time.

c. Following the instructions printed on the fogging oil can(s), spray the recommended amount of fogging oil into the carburetor throat(s).

d. When finished, stop the engine, remove the motor from the water supply and reinstall the carburetor air box cover (if so equipped).

4C. *Spray can method (with service port)*—This method applies to remote control models, all 25 and 35 hp (three-cylinder) models and 40-70 hp tiller electric models.

a. Attach a can of fogging oil to the service port (**Figure 28**) located on the fuel primer solenoid or the port side of the intake manifold (just behind the middle carburetor) on 25 and 35 hp (three-cylinder) models. See **Figure 29**.

b. Start the engine and run it at fast idle (1500-2000 rpm) in NEUTRAL.

c. Following the instructions printed on the fogging oil can, inject the recommended amount of fogging oil into the service port.

d. When finished, stop the engine and remove the motor from the water supply. Then, remove the oil injection can from the service port and reinstall the service port's protective cover.

5. Remove the spark plugs as described in this chapter. Spray about one ounce of fogging oil into each spark plug hole. Crank the engine (clockwise) by hand several revolutions to distribute the fogging oil throughout the cylinders. Reinstall the spark plugs.

6. *Portable fuel tanks*—Service the portable fuel tank filter by removing the four T25 Torx screws (**Figure 30**) from the fuel pickup assembly. Remove the pickup assembly and clean the mesh filter at the end of pickup tube. If the filter cannot be satisfactorily cleaned, replace the pickup tube. When finished, reinstall the pickup assembly and tighten the 4 Torx screws securely.

NOTE
These engines use one of three types of engine-mounted fuel filters: 2, 3.3 and 3.5 hp

models use a filter in the integral fuel tank outlet valve and 4-48 hp (including 4 Deluxe), 18 jet and 28 jet models with conventional fuel pumps use a wire screen located under the fuel pump cover(s). All 3 hp, 4 hp (BR models), 25 and 35 hp (three-cylinder), 35 jet, 40 hp electric start and 50-70 hp models use an inline filter.

7. To service the fuel filter on 2, 3.3 and 3.5 hp models, proceed as follows:

   a. Remove the fuel tank as described in Chapter Five. Drain the fuel into a suitable container. If the fuel is contaminated or sour, dispose of the fuel in an approved manner.

   b. Loosen the clamp screw securing the fuel valve and filter assembly to the fuel tank. Remove the fuel valve and filter assembly from the fuel tank (**Figure 31**, typical).

   c. Clean any dirt or debris from the fuel tank.

   d. Clean the filter screen in the fuel outlet valve with solvent and low pressure compressed air. If the screen cannot be cleaned, replace the outlet valve assembly.

   e. Reinstall the valve assembly to the fuel tank and tighten the clamp screw securely.

   f. Reinstall the fuel tank to the motor and check for fuel leaks.

8. To service models equipped with conventional fuel pumps (4-35 hp, 18 and 28 jet, 40 hp rope start and 48 Special models), proceed as follows:

NOTE
*The 25 and 35 hp (three-cylinder) models are equipped with two conventional fuel pumps. See **Figure 32**. The filter on each pump must be cleaned as described in the following procedure. An in-line filter is also incorporated between the fuel/oil mixing unit and the carburetors. Service this filter as described in Step 9.*

   a. Remove the screw from the center of each fuel pump's inlet cover. See 1, **Figure 33** (small pumps) or 1, **Figure 34** (large pumps).

   b. Pull the inlet cover away from the fuel pump. Locate and secure the gasket on small (square) pumps or the small and large O-rings on large pumps. Inspect the gasket (or O-rings) and replace them if they are damaged or worn.

   c. Carefully remove the filter screen from the cover. Do not damage the screen in the process.

   d. Clean the screen in clean solvent and dry with compressed air. Replace the screen if it cannot be satisfactorily cleaned.

   e. Install the screen into the inlet cover. On small (square) pumps, position the gasket onto the pump body. On large pumps, position the small O-ring on to the pump body and the large O-ring into the groove in the inlet cover.

   f. Align the inlet cover to the pump body while being careful not to disturb the screen, gasket or O-ring positions.

   g. Tighten the center screw securely. Then test the installation by squeezing the primer bulb and checking for leaks.

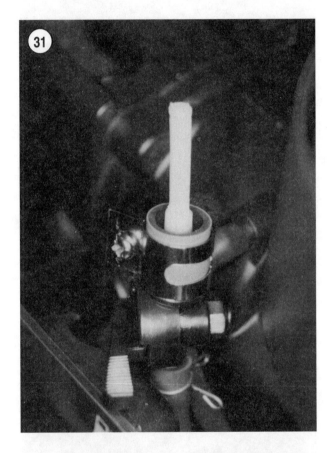

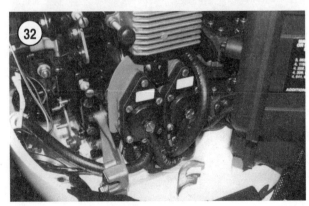

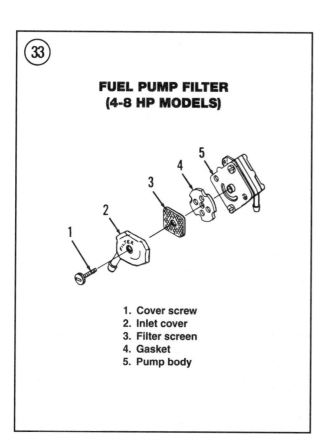

**FUEL PUMP FILTER
(4-8 HP MODELS)**

1. Cover screw
2. Inlet cover
3. Filter screen
4. Gasket
5. Pump body

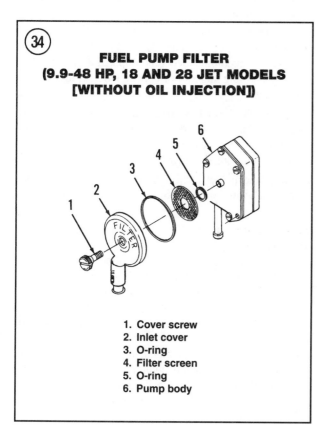

**FUEL PUMP FILTER
(9.9-48 HP, 18 AND 28 JET MODELS
[WITHOUT OIL INJECTION])**

1. Cover screw
2. Inlet cover
3. O-ring
4. Filter screen
5. O-ring
6. Pump body

NOTE
It may be necessary to remove the starboard split lower cowl to gain access to the inline fuel filter on 25 and 35 hp (three-cylinder) models.

9. On 3 hp, 4 hp (BR models), 25 and 35 hp (three-cylinder) models, 35 jet, 40 hp electric start and 50-70 hp models equipped with an inline fuel filter (**Figure 35**, typical), service the inline filter as follows:

  a. Carefully compress the spring clamps or cut the tie-strap clamps from each end of the filter.
  b. Disconnect the fuel lines from the filter. Discard the filter and replace any fuel lines damaged in the filter removal process.
  c. Connect the fuel lines to the new filter. Make sure the arrow is pointing in the direction of correct fuel flow (toward the carburetor). Securely fasten the hoses to the filter with the original spring clamps or new tie-straps.
  d. Test the installation by squeezing the primer bulb and checking for leaks.

10. Drain and refill the lower gearcase with the recommended lubricant as described previously in this chapter. Install new sealing washers (or O-rings) on the drain and vent plugs.

11. *Jet pump models*—Refer to *Jet pump maintenance* (in this chapter) for drive shaft bearing lubrication.

12. Refer to **Figures 14-25** and **Table 1** (as appropriate) for preventive maintenance and general lubrication recommendations.

13. Clean all exterior areas of the outboard motor, including all accessible power head parts. In saltwater or high-corrosion environments, spray the entire power head, including all electrical connections with OMC Anti-Corrosion Spray, or equivalent.

14. Install the engine cowling and apply a quality marine wax to all remaining metal surfaces (engine cowl, midsection and lower gearcase). In saltwater or high-corrosion environments, spray a thin film of Anti-Corrosion Spray

on all remaining metal painted surfaces (midsection and lower gearcase).

15. Remove the propeller and inspect the propshaft seals and propeller as described in Chapter Nine. Clean and lubricate the propeller shaft with OMC Triple Guard Grease, then reinstall the propeller as described in Chapter Nine.

> *CAUTION*
> *Make certain all water drain holes in the gear housing are clear to allow water to drain. Water expands as it freezes and can crack the gear housing or water pump. If the boat is equipped with a speedometer, disconnect the pickup tube and allow it to drain completely, then reconnect the tube.*

16. Drain the cooling system completely (to prevent freeze damage) by positioning the motor in a vertical position. Check all water drain holes for blockage.

17. Store the motor in a vertical position. In no case can an outboard motor be stored with the power head below the lower gearcase. The power head must be higher than the lower gearcase to prevent water from entering the engine through the exhaust ports.

18. Prepare the battery for storage as follows:
    a. Disconnect the negative, then the positive battery cables.
    b. Clean all grease, sulfate or other contamination from the battery case and terminals.
    c. Remove the vent caps (if possible) and check the electrolyte level of each cell. Add distilled water to the level recommended by the battery manufacturer. Do not overfill.
    d. Lubricate the terminals and terminal fasteners with OMC Electrical Grease or equivalent.

> *CAUTION*
> *A discharged battery can be damaged by freezing. Consider a battery **float** style charger to maintain the battery charge indefinitely. A float charger is an inexpensive way to keep the battery at peak charge without causing excessive venting or gassing (and subsequent water loss). The Guest Battery Pal No. 2602 is available from Evinrude/Johnson dealerships as part No. 508344.*

    e. With the battery in a fully-charged condition (specific gravity at 1.260-1.280), store the battery in a cool, dry location where the temperature will not drop below freezing.
    f. Recharge the battery every 45 days or whenever the specific gravity drops below 1.230. Maintain the

recommended electrolyte level at all times. Add distilled water as necessary to maintain the level recommended by the battery manufacturer. For maximum battery life, avoid charge rates in excess of 6 amps. Discontinue charging when the specific gravity reaches 1.260 at 80° F (27° C).

    g. Remove the grease from the battery terminals prior to returning the battery to service. Make sure the battery is installed in a fully-charged state.

19. If the storage fuel mixture is not to be used on any other outboard motors, *safely* drain and dispose of the mixture in an approved manner. It is not necessary to flush the fuel tank.

ANTI-CORROSION MAINTENANCE

> *NOTE*
> *Some manufacturers market magnesium sacrificial anodes. These anodes are designed to provide extra corrosion protection in freshwater. Do not use magnesium anodes in saltwater. The unit will be overprotected, causing the paint to blister and peel off.*

1. Flush the cooling system with freshwater as described in this chapter after each outing in saltwater. Wash and flush the exterior of the motor with freshwater.

2. Dry the exterior of the outboard and apply primer over any paint nicks and scratches. Use only Outboard Marine Corporation recommended touch-up paint. Do not use paints containing mercury or copper. Do not paint sacrificial anodes.

3. Apply OMC Black Neoprene Dip to all exposed electrical connections (such as ring terminals and terminal studs), except the positive battery terminal. Remove all corrosion and moisture before application.

4. Spray the power head and all electrical connections with OMC Anti-Corrosion Spray (or equivalent).

5. Inspect all of the sacrificial anodes. Replace any that have deteriorated to less than two-thirds their original size (one-third gone).
    a. To check for proper anode grounding, calibrate an ohmmeter on the highest scale available.
    b. Connect one meter lead to a power head ground. Connect the other meter lead to the anode. The ohmmeter must indicate continuity (very low reading).
    c. If no continuity is noted, remove the anode and thoroughly clean the mounting surfaces of the anode and the motor. Wire brush the threads of the mounting hardware and run a thread chaser into the mounting holes.

d. Reinstall the anode and retest as previously described. If the meter reading is still unsatisfactory, replace the anode and check the gearcase-to-midsection and midsection-to-power head mounting hardware for corrosion and high resistance.

6. If the outboard motor is operated consistently in saltwater, polluted or brackish water, reduce lubrication intervals (**Table 1**) by one-half.

ENGINE SUBMERSION

An outboard motor which has been lost overboard must be recovered and attended to as quickly as possible. Any delay will result in irreparable rust and corrosion damage to internal components. The following emergency steps must be attempted immediately if the motor is submerged in freshwater.

NOTE
If the outboard motor should fall overboard in saltwater, completely disassemble and clean the motor before any attempt to start the engine. If it is not possible to disassemble and clean the motor immediately, flush and resubmerge the outboard in freshwater to minimize rust and corrosion until it can be properly attended to.

1. Wash the outside of the motor with clean water to remove mud and other debris.

2. Remove the engine cowling.

3. Rinse the power head clean of all mud, silt, sand and other debris with freshwater.

4. Remove, clean and dry the spark plug(s).

5. Drain the carburetor float bowl(s). Do not reinstall the float chamber plugs. See Chapter Six.

6A. *25 and 35 hp (three-cylinder) models*—Drain and clean the engine-mounted oil tank. Flush all lines. Refill the system with the recommended oil.

6B. *35 jet, 40 hp (electric start) and 50-70 hp models*—Disconnect the remote oil tank's oil line from the engine connector. Drain, clean and flush the remote tank and its line. Install a new oil filter. Then purge all air from the system and reconnect the oil line to the engine as described in Chapter Eleven.

7. Disconnect, drain and clean all fuel lines. Then replace all fuel filters.

8. Connect a clean fuel tank to the engine fuel line connector. Squeeze the primer bulb repeatedly to flush fresh fuel through the entire fuel system and purge the system of water.

NOTE
If a boat with a permanent fuel system and remote controls was involved in the submersion, the boat's fuel system and electrical system must be serviced in the same manner as the engine's fuel and electrical systems.

9. Reinstall the carburetor drain plugs.

CAUTION
If there is a possibility that sand may have entered the power head, do not attempt to start the engine or severe internal damage could occur. If the outboard is lost overboard while running, internal engine damage is likely. Do not force the motor if it fails to turn easily with the spark plug(s) removed. This is an indication of internal damage such as a bent connecting rod or broken piston.

10. Drain as much water as possible from the power head by placing the motor in a horizontal position. Position the spark plugs facing downward and manually rotate the flywheel to expel water from the cylinder(s).

11. Pour liberal amounts of isopropyl (rubbing) alcohol into each carburetor throat while rotating the flywheel to help absorb any remaining moisture.

12. Disconnect all electrical connectors and dry with electrical contact cleaner or isopropyl alcohol. Lubricate all electrical connectors with OMC Electrical (dielectric) Grease (or equivalent).

13. Remove the electric starter motor. Disassemble the starter motor and dry all components with electrical contact cleaner or isopropyl alcohol. Reassemble and install the starter. See Chapter Seven.

14. Pour approximately one teaspoon of engine oil into each cylinder through the spark plug hole(s). Rotate the flywheel by hand to distribute the oil.

15. Position the outboard with the induction system facing upward. Pour engine oil into each carburetor throat while rotating the flywheel by hand to distribute the oil.

16. Reinstall the spark plug(s).

CAUTION
*Do not run the engine without an adequate water supply and do not exceed 3000 rpm without an adequate load. Refer to **Safety Precautions** at the beginning of Chapter Three.*

17. Attempt to start the engine using a fresh tank of 50:1 fuel/oil mixture (all models). If the outboard motor will start, allow it to run at least one hour to evaporate any remaining water inside the engine. Purge any remaining air from the oil injection system on models so equipped.

18. If the motor will not start, attempt to diagnose the cause as fuel, electrical or mechanical and repair as necessary. If the engine cannot be started the same day it was submerged, completely disassemble, clean and oil all internal components as soon as possible.

COOLING SYSTEM FLUSHING

Periodic flushing with clean freshwater will prevent salt or silt deposits from accumulating in the cooling system passageways. Perform the flushing procedure after each outing in saltwater, polluted or brackish water.

> *WARNING*
> *For safety's sake, remove the propeller if the motor must be run during the flushing procedure.*

Keep the motor in an upright (vertical) position during and after flushing. This prevents water from passing into the power head through the drive shaft housing and exhaust ports during the flushing procedure. It also eliminates the possibility of residual water being trapped in the drive shaft housing or other passages.

2-8 hp (Including 4 Deluxe) Models

> *WARNING*
> *The 2 and 3.3 hp engines are equipped with a direct drive gearcase. The propeller will be spinning any time the engine is running. The propeller must be removed before beginning flushing procedure.*

The 2-8 hp models do not have a flushing kit (adaptor) available from OMC Genuine Parts. The 2 and 3.3 hp water pickup is located on the starboard side of the gearcase, just in front of the propeller (**Figure 36**). The 3, 3.5 and 4 hp (except 4 Deluxe) water pickups are near the leading edge of the gearcase, just under the antiventilation plate. The 4 Deluxe, 6 and 8 hp water pickup is located at the rear of the gearcase and is part of the exhaust snout (**Figure 37**). In either case, the gearcase must be immersed in a test tank or suitable container of freshwater (such as a 55 gallon drum) and the engine run at idle speed for approximately 5-10 minutes to flush all cooling passageways satisfactorily.

1. Remove the propeller as described in Chapter Nine.

2. Place the outboard motor in a test tank or immerse the gearcase in a suitable container of freshwater (such as a 55 gallon drum). Position the outboard in the normal operating position.

3. Start the engine and operate at low speed (idle to 1500 rpm).

4. Verify that cooling water is being discharged from the water pump indicator fitting (tattle-tale). If it is not, stop the motor immediately and determine the cause of the problem.

5. Flush the motor for 5-10 minutes. If the outboard was last used in saltwater, flush for 10 minutes minimum.

6. Remove the outboard motor from the water supply.

7. Keep the outboard in the normal operating position to allow all water to drain from the drive shaft housing. If this

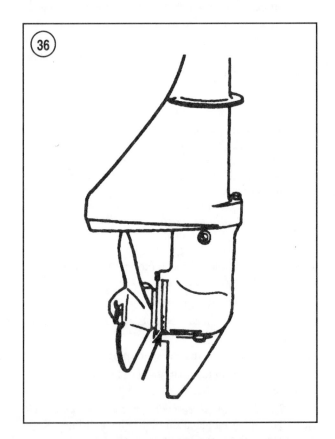

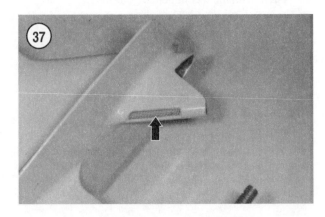

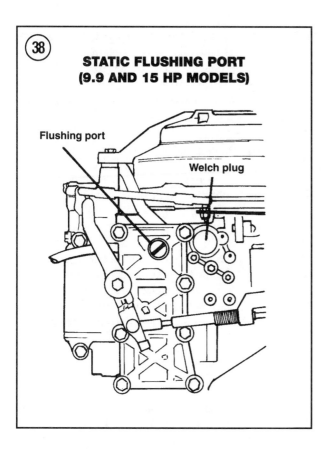

**STATIC FLUSHING PORT
(9.9 AND 15 HP MODELS)**

Flushing port

Welch plug

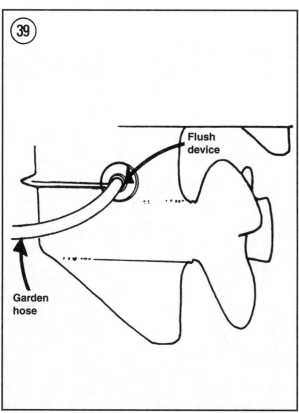

Flush device

Garden hose

is not done, water can enter the power head through the exhaust ports.

8. Reinstall the propeller as described in Chapter Nine.

9.9 and 15 hp Models

These models can be statically flushed using flushing adaptor (part No. 435299) or flushed with the engine running using a standard lower gearcase flushing adaptor, such as part No. 500542, 500543, 500544 or 500572.

Static flushing (9.9 and 15 hp models)

1. Remove the plug (marked Flush) and sealing washer from the starboard side of the power head. The fitting is located just behind the power head serial number plug as shown in **Figure 38**.
2. Install the part No. 435299 flushing adaptor into the power head flushing port.
3. Connect a garden hose between a water tap and the flushing adaptor.
4. Open the water tap to provide approximately 20-45 psi (138-310 kPa) water pressure.
5. Flush the motor for 5-10 minutes or until the discharged water is clear. If the outboard was last used in saltwater, flush for at least 10 minutes.
6. Stop the engine and shut off the water supply. Remove the flushing adaptor from the power head.
7. Replace the flushing port plug's sealing washer if it is worn or damaged. Lightly coat the plug's threads with OMC Gasket Sealing Compound or equivalent. Then install and tighten the plug securely.
8. Keep the outboard in the normal operating position to allow all water to drain from the power head and drive shaft housing. If this is not done, water can enter the power head through the exhaust ports if the motor is laid down.

Running flushing (9.9 and 15 hp models)

1. Remove the propeller as described in Chapter Nine.
2. Position the flushing adaptor over the lower gearcase water intake screens. See **Figure 39**, typical.
3. Make sure the outboard is positioned in the normal operating position.
4. Connect a garden hose between a water tap and the flushing device.
5. Open the water tap and adjust the flow to provide approximately 20-45 psi (138-310 kPa) water pressure. A significant amount of water must escape from around the flushing cups, but do not apply full pressure.
6. Shift the outboard into NEUTRAL and start the engine. Adjust the engine speed to approximately 1000-1500 rpm.

7. Adjust the water flow as necessary to maintain a slight loss of water around the rubber cups of the flushing device.

8. Check the motor to make sure that water is being discharged from the water pump indicator hose or fitting (tattle-tale). If not, stop the motor immediately and determine the cause of the problem.

9. Flush the motor for 5-10 minutes or until the discharged water is clear. If the outboard was last used in saltwater, flush for at least 10 minutes.

10. Stop the engine, then shut off the water supply. Remove the flushing device from the lower gearcase.

11. Keep the outboard in the normal operating position to allow all water to drain from the power head and drive shaft housing. If this is not done, water can enter the power head through the exhaust ports if the motor is laid down.

12. Reinstall the propeller as described in Chapter Nine.

25 and 35 hp (Three-cylinder) Outboard Models

These models can be flushed using the built-in flushing port (**Figure 40**) or by using a standard lower gearcase flushing adaptor, such as part No. 500542, 500543, 500544 or 500572.

If so desired, the motor can be statically flushed when vertical or tilted, using the built-in adaptor. Do not attempt to run the engine with the motor tilted. To statically flush the engine, follow the procedure outlined below, but do not start the engine.

1. Remove the propeller as described in Chapter Nine.

2A. *Built-in flushing port*—Remove the water discharge fitting (tattle-tale) from the rear of the engine. See **Figure 40**.

2B. *Gearcase flushing adaptor*—Position the flushing adaptor over the lower gearcase water intake screens. See **Figure 39**, typical.

3. Make sure the outboard is positioned in the normal operating position.

4. Connect a garden hose between a water tap and the flushing device or built in adaptor.

5. Open the water tap and adjust the flow to provide approximately 20-45 psi (138-310 kPa) water pressure. A significant amount of water must escape from around the flushing cups, but do not apply full pressure.

6. Shift the outboard into NEUTRAL and start the engine. Adjust the engine speed to approximately 1000-1500 rpm.

7A. *Built-in flushing port*—The flushing adaptor takes the place of the water pump indicator fitting (tattle-tale). Make sure that water is being discharged from the lower gearcase exhaust passages. If not, stop the motor immediately and determine the cause of the problem.

7B. *Gearcase flushing adaptor*—Adjust the water flow as necessary to maintain a slight loss of water around the rubber cups of the flushing device. Check the motor to

make sure that water is being discharged from the water pump indicator (tattle-tale). If not, stop the motor immediately and determine the cause of the problem.

8. Flush the motor for 5-10 minutes or until the discharged water is clear. If the outboard was last used in saltwater, flush for at least 10 minutes minimum.

9A. *Built-in flushing port*—Stop the engine, then shut off the water supply. Remove the garden hose from the built-in flushing port. Reinstall the water indicator fitting. Make sure the discharge port is pointing to one side of the motor where it can be observed while under way.

9B. *Gearcase flushing adaptor*—Stop the engine, then shut off the water supply. Remove the flushing device from the lower gearcase.

10. Keep the outboard in the normal operating position to allow all water to drain from the power head and drive shaft housing. If this is not done, water can enter the power head through the exhaust ports if the motor is laid down.

11. Reinstall the propeller as described in Chapter Nine.

20-30 hp (Two-cylinder) and 40-70 hp Outboard Models

A lower gearcase flushing adaptor, such as part No. 500542, 500543, 500544 or 500572 is the only recommended method of flushing these engines.

1. Remove the propeller as described in Chapter Nine.

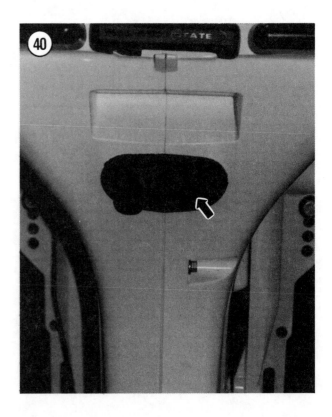

2. Position the outboard in the normal operating position.

3. Attach the flushing device to the lower gearcase as shown in **Figure 39**, typical.

4. Connect a garden hose (1/2 in. or larger) between a water tap and the flushing device.

5. Open the water tap and adjust the flow to provide approximately 20-45 psi (138-310 kPa) water pressure. A significant amount of water must escape from around the flushing cups, but do not apply full pressure.

6. Shift the outboard into NEUTRAL and start the engine. Adjust the engine speed to approximately 1000-1500 rpm.

7. Adjust the water flow as necessary to maintain a slight loss of water around the rubber cups of the flushing device.

8. Check the motor to be certain that water is being discharged from the water pump indicator fitting (tattle-tale). If not, stop the motor immediately and determine the cause of the problem.

9. Flush the motor for 5-10 minutes or until the discharged water is clear. If the outboard was last used in saltwater, flush at least for 10 minutes.

10. Stop the engine, then shut off the water supply. Remove the flushing device from the lower gearcase.

11. Keep the outboard in the normal operating position to allow all water to drain from the power head and drive shaft housing. If this is not done, water can enter the power head through the exhaust ports if the engine is laid down.

12. Reinstall the propeller as described in Chapter Nine.

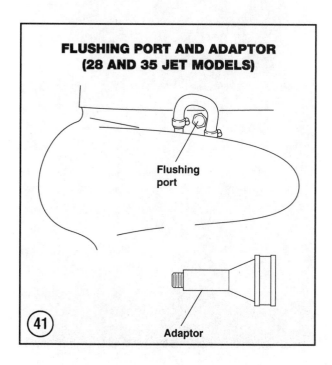

FLUSHING PORT AND ADAPTOR (28 AND 35 JET MODELS)

Flushing port

Adaptor

(41)

18-35 Jet Models

The 18 jet models do not have a flushing port or adaptor. The jet pump unit must be submerged in a suitable tank (or body) of freshwater and the engine run for at least 10 minutes at approximately 1000 rpm.

The 28 and 35 jet models have a flushing port built into the jet pump unit. A flushing adaptor is available from OMC Genuine Parts as part No. 435299. See **Figure 41**.

The water intake grate area, impeller and the entire outside surface of all jet pump units must be flushed with freshwater. Direct a garden hose into the grate area and over the outer surfaces of the pump unit after the recommended flushing procedure has been completed.

1. Position the outboard in the normal operating position.

2. Remove the flushing port plug and washer (**Figure 41**). Then install the flushing adapter into the jet pump unit.

3. Connect a garden hose (1/2 in. or larger) between a water tap and the flushing adaptor.

4. Open the water tap and adjust the flow to provide approximately 20-45 psi (138-310 kPa) water pressure. Do not apply full water pressure.

5. Shift the outboard into NEUTRAL and start the engine. Adjust the engine speed to approximately 1000 rpm.

6. Make sure the motor to be certain that water is being discharged from the water pump indicator fitting (tattle-tale). Adjust the water tap's flow as necessary. If no water is being discharged, stop the motor immediately and determine the cause of the problem.

7. Flush the motor for 5-10 minutes or until the discharged water is clear. If the outboard was last used in saltwater, flush for at least 10 minutes.

8. Stop the engine, then shut off the water supply. Remove the flushing device from the jet pump unit.

9. Replace the flushing port plug's sealing washer if it is worn or damaged. Lightly coat the plug's threads with OMC Gasket Sealing Compound. Then install and tighten the plug securely.

10. Thoroughly rinse the intake grate area and all outer surfaces of the pump unit with the garden hose.

11. Keep the outboard in the normal operating position to allow all water to drain from the power head and drive shaft housing. If this is not done, water can enter the power head through the exhaust ports if the engine is laid down.

TUNE-UP

A tune-up consists of a series of inspections, adjustments and parts replacement to compensate for normal wear and deterioration of the outboard motor components. Regular tune-ups are important to maintain the proper power, performance and economy. Recommended tune-up intervals are once a season or every 100 hours of operation. Individual operating conditions may dictate that a tune-up be performed more often. A tune-up must also be performed any time the outboard exhibits a substantial performance loss.

Since proper outboard motor operation depends upon a number of interrelated system functions, a tune-up consisting of only one or two of the recommended procedures will seldom provide satisfactory results. For best results, a thorough and systematic procedure of analysis and correction is necessary.

Prior to performing a tune-up, flush the outboard cooling system as described in this chapter to check for proper water pump operation.

The recommended tune-up procedure is listed below. Any procedure not covered in this chapter or section is so identified.

1. OMC Engine Tuner treatment—*Removing Combustion Chamber Deposits.*
2. Compression test.
3. Cylinder head bolt torque (**Table 3**).
4. Electrical wiring harness inspection.
5. Spark plug service.
6. Gearcase lubricant change and propshaft spline lubrication.
7. General engine lubrication (all applicable lubrication points). See **Table 1**.
8. Fuel filter service.
9. Lower gearcase water pump service.
10. Fuel system and oil injection system (if so equipped) service.
11. Ignition system service.
12. Charging system service (if so equipped).
13. Battery and starter system service (if so equipped).
14. All synchronization and linkage adjustments (Chapter Five).
15. On-water performance test.

Anytime the fuel or ignition system is adjusted or defective parts replaced, all engine synchronization and linkage adjustments *must* be verified. These procedures are described in Chapter Five. Perform all synchronization and linkage adjustments *before* running the on-water performance test.

Removing Combustion Chamber Deposits

During operation, carbon deposits will accumulate on the piston(s), rings, cylinder head(s) and exhaust ports. If the carbon is allowed to build up unchecked, the effective compression ratio will increase, raising the fuel octane requirements of the power head.

If the carbon builds up in the piston ring area, the piston rings will stick in the piston ring grooves causing a loss of

compression and the loss of heat transfer to the cylinder walls (and water passages). When the piston rings stick, performance suffers and combustion chamber temperatures skyrocket leading to preignition and detonation. All of these situations will eventually lead to power head failure.

OMC Engine Tuner is designed to remove combustion chamber deposits and free stuck piston rings, restoring engine performance and lowering the risk of engine failure.

> *NOTE*
> *Using quality gasolines and NMMA approved TCW-3 outboard oils will minimize combustion chamber deposits and piston ring sticking. If the use of poor quality gasoline and outboard oil is unavoidable, or combustion chamber deposits are an ongoing problem, use OMC Carbon Guard fuel additive regularly.*

For effective preventive maintenance, all engines must have OMC Engine Tuner applications performed every 50-100 hours of operation or as required. The manufacturer's instructions printed on the container will supersede the following instructions.

CAUTION
Do not run the engine without an adequate water supply and do not exceed 3000 rpm without an adequate load. Refer to Safety Precautions at the beginning of Chapter Three.

1A. *Models without service port*—This method applies to 2-8 hp (including 4 Deluxe), 9.9-30 hp (two-cylinder) rope start and/or tiller electric models, 18 and 28 jet models and 40 hp rope start models.

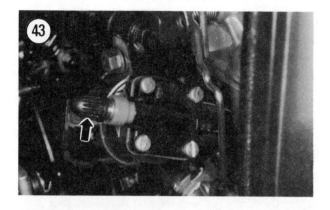

a. Remove the carburetor air box cover (if so equipped) to gain access to the carburetor's throat (**Figure 42**, typical).
b. Start the engine and allow it to reach operating temperature. Adjust the engine speed to 1000-1500 rpm in NEUTRAL.

NOTE
On 28 jet and 40 hp rope start models, it is necessary to obtain two cans of engine tuner and spray into both carburetors at the same time.

c. Following the instructions printed on the OMC Engine Tuner can(s), spray the recommended amount of tuner into the carburetor throat(s).
d. When finished, stop the engine, remove the motor from the water supply and reinstall the carburetor air box cover (if so equipped).

1B. *Models with service port*—This method applies to remote control models, all 25 and 35 hp (three-cylinder) models and 40-70 hp tiller electric models.

a. Attach an injection can of OMC Engine Tuner to the service port (**Figure 43**) located on the fuel primer solenoid or the port side of the intake manifold (just behind the middle carburetor) on 25 and 35 hp (three-cylinder) models. See **Figure 44**.
b. Start the engine and allow it to reach operating temperature. Adjust the engine speed to 1000-1500 rpm in NEUTRAL.
c. Following the instructions printed on the OMC Engine Tuner can, inject the recommended amount of tuner into the service port.
d. When finished, stop the engine and remove the motor from the water supply. Then remove the injection can from the service port and reinstall the service port's protective cover.

2. Allow the engine tuner to soak in the engine for 3-16 hours. Then restart the engine and run at 1500-2000 rpm for a *minimum* of 15 minutes to flush the deposits and tuner residue from the engine.

Compression Test

An accurate cylinder cranking compression check provides an indication as to the mechanical condition of the combustion chamber. It is an important preliminary step in any tune-up as a motor with low or unequal compression between cylinders *cannot* be satisfactorily tuned. Any compression problem discovered during this test must be corrected before continuing with the tune-up procedure. A thread-in compression tester is recommended for best results.

While specifications for the minimum amount of compression are not available, a variation of more than 15 psi (103.4 kPa) between any two cylinders indicates a problem. If the compression is unacceptable, remove the cylinder head and inspect the cylinder wall(s), piston(s) and head gasket condition. If the cylinder wall(s), piston(s) and head gasket show no evidence of damage or failure, the piston rings are worn or damaged and the power head will have to be rebuilt.

CAUTION
Do not run the engine without an adequate water supply and do not exceed 3000 rpm without an adequate load. Refer to Safety Precautions at the beginning of Chapter Three.

1. Warm the engine to operating temperature.
2. Remove the spark plug(s) as described in this chapter.
3. Securely ground the spark plug lead(s) to the engine to disable the ignition system and prevent possible ignition system damage.
4. Following the compression gauge manufacturer's instructions, connect the gauge to the No. 1 cylinder (top) spark plug hole (**Figure 45**, typical).
5. Manually hold the throttle plate(s) in the wide-open throttle position. Crank the engine through at least four compression strokes and record the gauge reading.
6. Repeat Step 4 and Step 5 for all remaining cylinders. A variation of more than 15 psi (103.4 kPa) between two cylinders indicates a problem with the lower reading cylinder, such as worn or sticking piston rings and/or scored pistons or cylinder walls. In such cases, pour a tablespoon of engine oil into the suspect cylinder and repeat Step 4 and Step 5. If the compression increases significantly (by 10 psi [69 kPa] or more), the rings are worn or damaged and the power head must be disassembled and rebuilt.

If the compression is acceptable, but the outboard motor is difficult to start or has poor idle quality, refer to *Starting Difficulties* in Chapter Three.

Cylinder Head Bolt Torque

CAUTION
Excessive torque will distort the cylinder bores or cylinder head(s). Insufficient torque will allow the cylinder head gaskets or seals to leak. The motor must be cool to the touch for this operation.

Retorque the cylinder head bolts during a tune-up. Loosen each bolt slightly and retorque to the specification listed in **Table 3**. Refer to Chapter Eight for cylinder head service procedures and tightening sequences if the cylinder

head has been removed from the power head. Install the cylinder head screws clean and dry on all models. Do not lubricate or seal the threads or the underside of the screw head.

Electrical Wiring Harness Inspection

Inspect all harnesses, leads, connectors and terminals for loose connection, corrosion, mechanical damage, damaged insulation and improper routing. Harnesses that are close to moving components must be checked for chafing or rubbing damage. Reroute, retape and secure harnesses as necessary. Inspect all harnesses, leads and components on or near the cylinder head and exhaust passages for heat damage. Repair any damage found. Refer to Chapter Three for recommended tools and repair kits.

Spark Plug Service

Improper installation and incorrect application are common causes of poor spark plug performance in outboard motors. The gasket on the plug must be fully compressed against a clean plug seat for heat transfer to take place effectively. If heat transfer cannot take place, the spark plug will overheat and fail. This may also lead to preignition and detonation. Make sure the spark plugs are correctly torqued.

Incorrect application can not only cause spark plug problems, but it can also lead to ignition system symptoms or failure from RFI (radio frequency interference). Most engines require inductive suppression spark plugs that reduce the RFI caused by the spark jumping the air gap of the spark plug. Always use the recommended spark plugs.

If the engine does not require inductive suppression spark plugs, yet ignition interference with onboard acces-

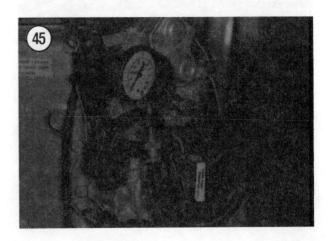

sories is noted, install the recommended inductive suppression spark plug as specified in **Table 2**.

> *CAUTION*
> *When the spark plug(s) is removed, dirt or other foreign material surrounding the spark plug hole(s) can fall into the cylinder(s). Foreign material inside the cylinders can cause engine damage when the engine is started.*

1. Clean the area around the spark plug(s) using compressed air or an appropriate brush.

2. Disconnect the spark plug lead(s) by twisting the boot back and forth on the spark plug insulator while pulling outward. Pulling on the lead instead of the boot can cause internal damage to the lead.

3. Remove the spark plugs using an appropriate size spark plug socket. Arrange the spark plugs in order of the cylinder from which they were removed.

4. Examine each spark plug. Conventional gap spark plugs (**Figure 46**) are recommended for the engines covered in this manual; however, in some extreme conditions, the use of surface gap spark plugs (**Figure 47**) may be warranted. Consult an Evinrude or Johnson dealer as needed. Compare the spark plug condition to **Figure 48**

(conventional gap) or **Figure 49** (surface gap). Spark plug condition is a good indicator of piston, rings and cylinder condition, and can provide a warning of developing trouble.

5. Check each plug for the make and heat range. All spark plugs must be identical. The spark plug *reach* must be correct or the spark plug may contact the piston, causing mechanical damage. See **Figure 50**. Refer to **Table 3** and check that the spark plugs are correct for your application.

6. If the spark plugs are in good condition, they may be cleaned and regapped (if applicable). Install new spark plugs if there is any question as to the condition of the spark plugs.

7. Inspect the spark plug threads in the engine and clean them with a thread chaser (**Figure 51**) if necessary. Wipe the spark plug seats clean before installing new spark plugs.

8. Install the spark plugs with new gaskets and tighten to 18-21 ft.-lb. (24.4-28.5 N•m) on all models. If a torque wrench is not available, seat the plugs finger-tight, then tighten an additional 1/4 turn with a wrench.

9. Inspect each spark plug lead before reconnecting it to its spark plug. If the insulation is damaged or deteriorated, install a new plug lead. Push the boot onto the plug terminal making sure it is fully seated.

Spark Plug Gap Adjustment
(Conventional Gap Only)

New spark plugs must be carefully gapped to ensure a reliable, consistent spark. Use a special spark plug gapping tool with wire gauges. **Figure 52** shows a common type of gapping tool.

1. Make sure the gaskets are installed on the spark plugs.

> *NOTE*
> *Some spark plug brands require that the terminal end be screwed on the plug before installation. See* **Figure 53**.

2. Insert a 0.030 in. (0.76 mm) wire feeler gauge (**Figure 54**, typical) between the electrodes. If the gap is correct, there will be a slight drag as the wire is pulled through. To adjust the gap, carefully bend the side electrode with a gapping tool (**Figure 52**), then remeasure the gap.

> *CAUTION*
> *Never attempt to close the gap by tapping the spark plug on a solid surface. This can damage the spark plug. Always use the proper adjusting tool to open or close the gap.*

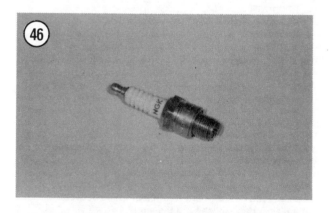

SPARK PLUG ANALYSIS
(CONVENTIONAL SPARK PLUG GAPS)

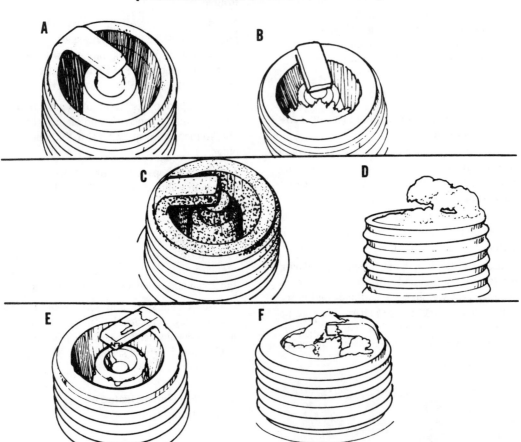

A. **Normal**—Light tan to gray color of insulator indicates correct heat range. Few deposits are present and the electrodes are not burned.

B. **Core bridging**—These defects are caused by excessive combustion chamber deposits striking and adhering to the firing end of the plug. In this case, they wedge or fuse between the electrode and core nose. They originate from the piston and cylinder head surfaces. Deposits are formed by one or more of the following:
  a. Excessive carbon in cylinder.
  b. Use of non-recommended oils.
  c. Immediate high-speed operation after prolonged trolling.
  d. Improper fuel-oil ratio.

C. **Wet fouling**—Damp or wet, black carbon coating over entire firing end of plug. Forms sludge in some engines. Caused by one or more of the following:
  a. Spark plug heat range too cold.
  b. Prolonged trolling.
  c. Low-speed carburetor adjustment too rich.

  d. Improper fuel-oil ratio.
  e. Induction manifold bleed-off passage obstructed.
  f. Worn or defective breaker points.

D. **Gap bridging**—Similar to core bridging, except the combustion particles are wedged or fused between the electrodes. Causes are the same.

E. **Overheating**—Badly worn electrodes and premature gap wear are indicative of this problem, along with a gray or white "blistered" appearance on the insulator. Caused by one or more of the following:
  a. Spark plug heat range too hot.
  b. Incorrect propeller usage, causing engine to lug.
  c. Worn or defective water pump.
  d. Restricted water intake or restriction somewhere in the cooling system.

F. **Ash deposits or lead fouling**—Ash deposits are light brown to white in color and result from use of fuel or oil additives. Lead fouling produces a yellowish brown discoloration and can be avoided by using unleaded fuels.

SURFACE GAP
SPARK PLUG ANALYSIS

A

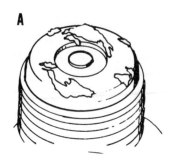

B

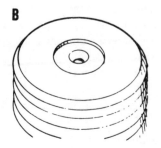

C

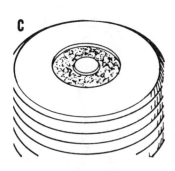

D

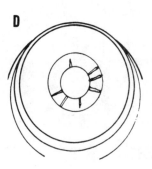

E

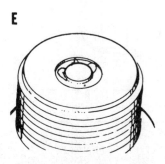

F

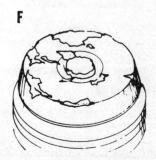

4

A. **Normal**—Light tan or gray colored deposits indicate that the engine/ignition system condition is good. Electrode wear indicates normal spark rotation.

B. **Worn out**—Excessive electrode wear can cause hard starting or a misfire during acceleration.

C. **Cold fouled**—Wet oil-fuel deposits are caused by "drowning" the plug with raw fuel mix during cranking, overrich carburetion or an improper fuel-oil ratio. Weak ignition will also contribute to this condition.

D. **Carbon tracking**—Electrically conductive deposits on the firing end provide a low-resistance path for the voltage. Carbon tracks form and can cause misfires.

E. **Concentrated arc**—Multi-colored appearance is normal. It is caused by electricity consistently following the same firing path. Arc path changes with deposit conductivity and gap erosion.

F. **Aluminum throw-off**—Caused by preignition. This is not a plug problem but the result of engine damage. Check engine to determine cause and extent of damage.

Lower Gearcase (and Jet Pump Unit) Water Pump

Overheating and extensive power head damage can result from a faulty water pump. Therefore, as a preventive maintenance measure, it is recommended that you replace the water pump impeller, seals and gaskets once a year or every 100 hours of operation. Individual operating conditions may dictate that the pump requires service less (or more) often. It is also recommended that the water pump be serviced anytime the lower gearcase (or jet pump unit) is removed for service. See Chapter Nine for water pump service procedures.

NOTE
Anytime the lower gearcase is removed, the
drive shaft splines must be cleaned and lu-

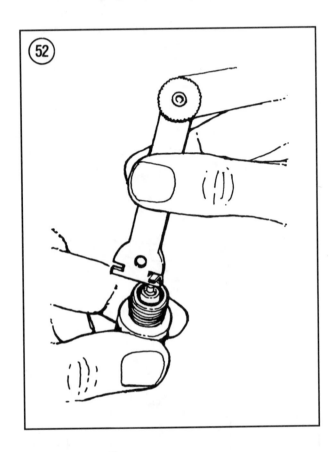

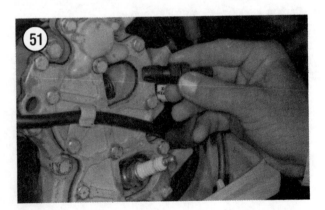

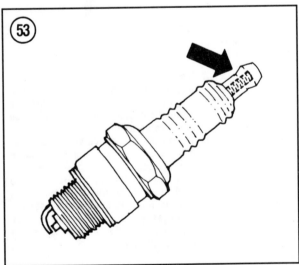

bricated with OMC Moly Lube. Do not apply any lubricant to the top drive shaft surface as this may prevent the drive shaft from fully seating into the crankshaft.

Many outboard owners depend upon the visual indication provided by the water pump indicator hose or *tattle-tale* as the sole indicator of water pump performance. While it is important to monitor the water pump indicator hose, the installation of a water pressure gauge kit (available from any Evinrude/Johnson dealership) is a more effective method to ensure that the pump is actually operating correctly. The kit contains a fitting and hose that attaches to the power head and a water pressure gauge that is mounted in the boat.

After installing the pressure gauge kit and every time the water pump is serviced, it is important to note the normal water pressure reading (at various speeds) for your motor. If the pressure reading shows a gradual drop from the normal reading, impeller wear is indicated and impeller replacement must be planned in the near future. If the pressure reading shows a sudden drop, water pump damage has occurred and the pump must be serviced immediately (Chapter Nine).

Fuel and Oil Injection Systems

During a tune-up, perform all synchronization and linkage adjustments as described in Chapter Five. Clean and replace all fuel filters. Inspect all fuel lines, fuel system components and all spring clamps, worm clamps or tie-straps for leaks, deterioration, mechanical damage and secure mounting. All replacement fuel lines must be alcohol resistant. See Chapter Six. If the fuel system is suspected of not functioning correctly, refer to Chapter Three for troubleshooting procedures.

Refer to *Fuel and Lubrication* in this chapter for basic oil injection system description and component function. Inspect the oil injection system (if so equipped) for leaks, loose lines and fittings and deterioration. Inspect warning system wiring (if so equipped) as described under *Electrical Wiring Harness Inspection* in this chapter. If the oil injection system is suspected of not functioning correctly, refer to Chapter Eleven for oil injection system troubleshooting and service procedures.

Fuel filters

1. *Portable fuel tanks*—Service the portable fuel tank filter by removing the four T25 Torx screws (**Figure 55**) from the fuel pickup assembly. Remove the pickup assembly and clean the fine mesh filter at the end of pickup tube. If the filter cannot be satisfactorily cleaned, the pickup tube must be replaced. When finished, reinstall the pickup assembly and tighten the four Torx screws securely.

> *NOTE*
> *These engines will use one of three types of engine-mounted fuel filters: 2, 3.3 and 3.5 hp models use a filter in the integral fuel tank outlet valve and 4-48 hp (including 4 Deluxe) with conventional fuel pumps will use a wire screen located under the fuel pump cover(s). All 3 hp, 4 hp (BR models), 25 and*

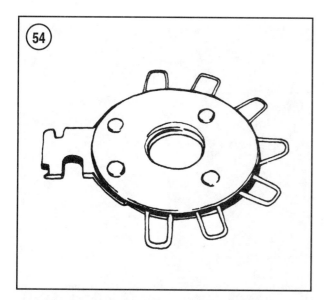

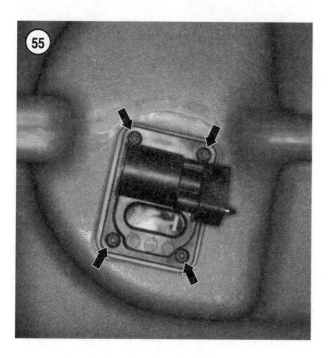

35 hp (three-cylinder), 40 hp electric start (and 50-70 hp models [with VRO[2] oil injection]) use an inline filter.

2. To service the fuel filter on 2 and 3.3 hp models, proceed as follows:

   a. Remove the fuel tank as described in Chapter Five. Drain the fuel into a suitable container. If the fuel is contaminated or sour, dispose of the fuel in an approved manner.

   b. Loosen the clamp screw securing the fuel valve and filter assembly to the fuel tank. Remove the fuel valve and filter assembly from the fuel tank (**Figure 56**, typical).

   c. Clean any dirt or debris from the fuel tank.

   d. Clean the filter screen in the fuel outlet valve assembly with solvent and low pressure compressed air. If the screen cannot be cleaned, replace the outlet valve assembly.

   e. Reinstall the valve assembly to the fuel tank and tighten the clamp screw securely.

   f. Reinstall the fuel tank to the motor and check for fuel leaks.

3. To service models equipped with conventional fuel pumps (4-35 hp [including 4 Deluxe], 18 and 28 jet, 40 hp rope start and 48 Special models), proceed as follows:

NOTE
*The 25 and 35 hp (three-cylinder) models are equipped with two conventional fuel pumps. See **Figure 57**. The filter on each pump must be cleaned as described in the following procedure. An inline filter is also incorporated between the fuel/oil mixing unit and the carburetors. This filter is serviced in Step 9.*

   a. Remove the screw from the center of each fuel pump's inlet cover. See 1, **Figure 58** (small pumps) or 1, **Figure 59** (large pumps).

   b. Pull the inlet cover(s) away from the fuel pump(s). Locate and secure the gasket on small (square) pumps or the small and large O-rings on large pumps. Inspect the gasket (or O-rings) and replace them if they are damaged or worn.

   c. Carefully remove the filter screen from the cover. Do not damage the screen in the process.

   d. Clean the screen in clean solvent and dry with compressed air. Replace the screen if it cannot be satisfactorily cleaned.

   e. Install the screen into the inlet cover. On small (square) pumps, position the gasket onto the pump body. On large pumps, position the small O-ring onto the pump body and the large O-ring into the groove in the inlet cover.

   f. Carefully align the inlet cover(s) to the pump body being careful not to disturb the screen, gasket or O-ring positions.

   g. Tighten the center screw(s) securely. Then test the installation by squeezing the primer bulb and checking for leaks.

NOTE
It may be necessary to remove the starboard split lower cowl to gain access to the inline fuel filter on 25 and 35 hp (three-cylinder) models.

FUEL PUMP FILTER (4-8 HP MODELS)

1. Cover screw
2. Inlet cover
3. Filter screen
4. Gasket
5. Pump body

FUEL PUMP FILTER (9.9-48 HP, 18 AND 28 JET MODELS [WITHOUT OIL INJECTION])

1. Cover screw
2. Inlet cover
3. O-ring
4. Filter screen
5. O-ring
6. Pump body

4

4. On 3 hp, 4 hp (BR models), 25 and 35 hp (three-cylinder) models, 40 hp electric start and 50-70 hp models equipped with an inline fuel filter (**Figure 60**, typical), service the inline filter as follows:

    a. Carefully compress the spring clamps or cut the tie-strap clamps from each end of the filter.

    b. Disconnect the fuel lines from the filter. Discard the filter and replace any fuel lines damaged in the filter removal process.

    c. Connect the fuel lines to the new filter. Make sure the arrow is pointing in the direction of correct fuel flow (toward the carburetor). Fasten the hoses to the filter securely with the original spring clamps or new tie-straps.

    d. Test the installation by squeezing the primer bulb and checking for leaks.

Fuel pump

The fuel pump does not generally require any specific service during a tune-up. However, conduct a visual inspection of the fuel (and/or oil injection) pump, pump mounting hardware, all fuel and crankcase pulse lines and all spring clamps, worm clamps or tie-straps. Replace any damaged or deteriorated components. If the fuel (or combination fuel and oil [VRO^2]) pump or fuel system is suspected of not functioning correctly, refer to Chapter Three for fuel system troubleshooting procedures. If the combination fuel and oil (VRO^2) pump is suspected of not injecting oil correctly, refer to Chapter Eleven.

Ignition System Service

Other than inspecting or replacing the spark plugs, the ignition system is relatively maintenance free. During a tune-up, verify all synchronization and linkage adjustments as described in Chapter Five. If the ignition system

is suspected of not functioning correctly, refer to Chapter Three for troubleshooting procedures.

Charging System Service

No maintenance is required on the charging system. If the charging system is suspected of not functioning correctly, refer to Chapter Three for troubleshooting procedures.

Battery and Electric Starter System

During a tune-up, the electric starting system requires minimal maintenance. Manually rotate the starter pinion to expose the armature shaft's spiral splines (A, **Figure 61**). Clean any debris or dried lubricant from the splines, then lightly coat them with OMC Starter Pinion Lubricant. Allow the pinion to return to its resting position, then lift the protective cap and lightly coat the armature shaft (B, **Figure 61**) with the same lubricant.

Inspect the battery cable connections for evidence of corrosion, loose connections or mechanical damage. If wing nuts are present, discard them and replace them with corrosion resistant hex nuts and lockwashers. Place a lockwasher under each battery cable to ensure positive contact with the battery terminal. Tighten the battery connections securely. Loose battery connections can cause every imag-

inable symptom. To verify correct operation of the electric starter system, proceed as follows:

1. Check the battery state of charge. See Chapter Seven.

2. Disable the ignition system by removing the spark plug lead from each spark plug and securing the spark plug leads to the power head.

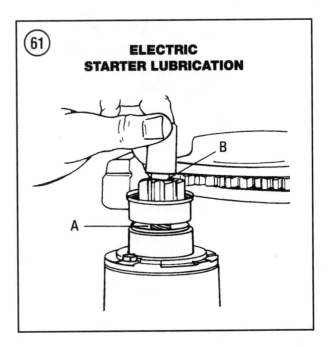

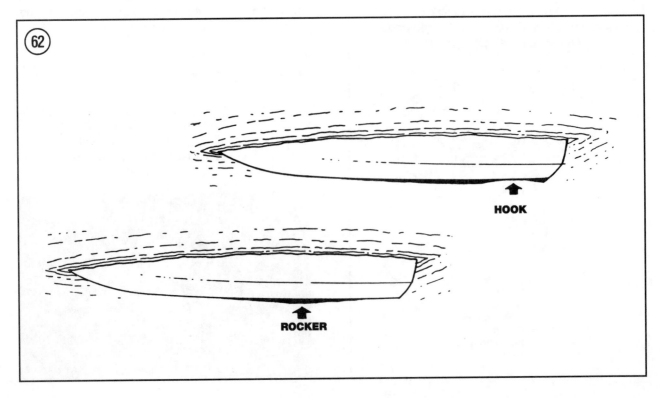

3. Connect a multimeter, set to the 20 volt DC scale, to the battery positive and negative terminals.

4. Turn the ignition switch to the START position and note the meter reading while the engine is cranking for several seconds.

    a. If the voltage is 9.5 volts or higher and the cranking speed is normal, the starting system is functioning normally and the battery is of sufficient capacity for the engine.

    b. If the voltage is below 9.5 volts and/or the cranking speed is below normal, the starting system is malfunctioning. Refer to Chapter Three for troubleshooting procedures.

5. Reconnect the spark plug leads when finished.

On Water Performance Testing

Before performance testing the outboard motor, make sure that the boat bottom is cleaned of all marine growth and that no *hook* or *rocker* is present in the boat bottom (**Figure 62**). Any of these conditions will reduce the boat performance considerably.

The boat must be performance tested with an average load on board. The outboard motor must be tilted or trimmed at an angle that will produce optimum performance and balanced steering control. If equipped with an adjustable trim tab, it must be properly adjusted to allow the boat to steer in either direction with equal ease at the boat's normal cruising speed.

CAUTION
Evinrude/Johnson outboard motors tend to perform best when propped toward the middle of the recommended wide-open throttle speed range. In no case should the engine be allowed to operate above or below the recommended speed range at wide-open throttle or engine damage will occur.

Check the engine speed at wide-open throttle. If engine speed is not within the specified range (Chapter Five) and the engine is in a proper state of tune, change the propeller. Use a higher pitch propeller to reduce engine speed or a lower pitch propeller to increase engine speed.

Table 1 RECOMMENDED PREVENTIVE MAINTENANCE SCHEDULE

Component or system	Recommended procedure	OMC lubricant or service manual reference
Lower gearcase		
Lubricant level	Check lubricant level	Ultra HPF Gear Lube
Gear lubricant	Change lubricant	Ultra HPF Gear Lube
Drive shaft splines	Remove gearcase and lubricate	Moly Lube
Propeller shaft splines	Remove propeller and lubricate	Triple Guard grease
Water pump	Replace impeller	Chapter Nine
Jet pump unit		
Bearing housing	Lubricate after each use	EP/Wheel Bearing grease
Mid-section		
Swivel housing fittings	Lubricate	Triple Guard grease
Tilt tube fittings	Lubricate	Triple Guard grease
Clamp screws	Clean and lubricate	Triple Guard grease
Engine cowl latches	Clean and lubricate	Triple Guard grease
Tilt lock linkage	Clean and lubricate	Triple Guard grease
Tilt lever shaft/strap	Clean and lubricate	Triple Guard grease
Reverse lock linkage	Clean and lubricate	Triple Guard grease
Shift linkages	Clean and lubricate	Triple Guard grease
Steering arm link	Clean and lubricate pivot points	SAE 30 engine oil
Steering cable/ram	Clean and lubricate	Triple Guard grease
Tiller handle	Clean and lubricate	Triple Guard grease
Power trim and tilt		
Lubricant	Check fluid level	Chapter Ten
Trim ram ends	Clean and lubricate	Triple Guard grease
(continued)		

Table 1 RECOMMENDED PREVENTIVE MAINTENANCE SCHEDULE (continued)

Component or system	Recommended procedure	OMC lubricant or service manual reference
Power head		
Electric starter motor	Clean/lightly lubricate drive splines	Starter Pinion lube
Fuel Filters	Clean or replace all fuel filters	Chapter Four
Ignition system	Synchronization/linkage adjustments	Chapter Five
Fuel system	Synchronization/linkage adjustments	Chapter Five
Throttle/shift linkage	Clean and lubricate all pivot points	Triple Guard grease
Combustion chambers	Remove carbon deposits	Engine tuner

Table 2 RECOMMENDED CHAMPION SPARK PLUGS*

Model	Standard (alternate)	Extended idle operation
2, 3.3 and 3.5 hp	QL87YC (L87YC)	Not applicable
3 hp, 4 hp and 4 Deluxe	QL86C (L86C)	L90C
6 and 8 hp	QL86C (L86)	QL82YC
9.9 and 15 hp	QL82C (no alternate)	QL86C
18 Jet	QL82C (no alternate)	Not applicable
20-30 hp (two-cylinder)	QL82C (QL77JC4)	Not applicable
25 and 30 hp (three-cylinder)	QL86C (L86)	QL82YC
40 hp and 28 jet	QL78YC (no alternate)	Not applicable
48, 50 hp (two-cylinder) and 35 jet	QL78YC (no alternate)	QL82C
50 hp (three-cylinder)	QL78YC (no alternate)	QL82C
60 and 70 hp	QL78YC (no alternate)	Not applicable
65 hp (commercial)	QL78YC (no alternate)	QL82C

*On 1998-2003 models, use the spark plug type printed on the emission control decal (affixed onto the engine).

Table 3 CYLINDER HEAD BOLT TORQUE SPECIFICATIONS

Model	in.-lb.	ft.-lb.	N•m
2-4 hp (except 4 Deluxe)	60-84	–	6.8-9.5
4 Deluxe, 6 and 8 hp	144-168	12-14	16.3-19.0
9.9-30 hp (two-cylinder) and 18 jet	216-240	18-20	24.4-27.1
25 and 35 hp (three-cylinder)	180-204	15-17	20.3-23.1
40-70 hp, 28 and 35 jet models	216-240	18-20	24.4-27.1

Table 4 GEARCASE GEAR RATIO AND APPROXIMATE LUBRICANT CAPACITY

Outboard model	Gear ratio	Tooth count	Lubricant capacity
2 and 3.3 hp	1.85:1	13.24	3 oz. (89 ml)
3.5 hp	1.85:1	13:24	2.7 oz. (80 ml)
3 and 4 hp	2.08:1	12:25	2.7 oz (80 ml)
4 Deluxe and 6-8 hp	2:23:1	13:29	11 oz. (325 ml)
9.9 and 15 hp	2.42:1	12:29	9 oz. (266 ml)
20, 25, 30 and 35 hp	2.15:1	13:28	11 oz. (325 ml)
28 Special	1.75:1	12:21	8 oz. (237 ml)
40-50 hp (two-cylinder)	2.42:1	12:29	16.4 oz. (485 ml)
50-70 hp (three-cylinder)	2.42:1	12:29	22 oz. (651 ml)
18-35 jet models	Not applicable	–	–

Table 5 TEST WHEEL (PROPELLER) RECOMMENDATIONS

Model	OMC part No.	Minimum test rpm
2 hp	115208 (standard propeller)	4500
3.3 and 3.5 hp	115306	5000
3 and 4 hp	317738	4400
4 Deluxe	390123	5100
6 hp	390239	4800
8 hp	390239	5300
9.9 hp	340177	4900
15 hp	340177	5700
20-30 hp (two-cylinder)		
20 hp	386891	4550
25 hp	434505	4800
28 Special	398948	4800
30 hp	434505	5400
25 hp (three-cylinder)		
1995	434505	4400
1996-2003	434505	4200
35 hp (three-cylinder)	434505	5000
40-50 hp (two-cylinder)		
40 hp	432968	4900
48 and 50 hp	432968	5200
50-70 hp (three-cylinder)		
50 hp	386665	4600
60 hp	386665	5000
70 hp	386665	5700
18-35 jet models	Not applicable	Not applicable

4

Chapter Five

Synchronization and Linkage Adjustments

For an outboard motor to deliver maximum efficiency, performance and reliability, the ignition and fuel systems must be correctly adjusted. This adjustment procedure is referred to as *synch and link*.

Failure to properly synch and link an engine will not only result in a loss of engine performance and efficiency, but can lead to power head damage. All synch and link adjustments must be performed during a tune-up or whenever any ignition or fuel system components are replaced, serviced or adjusted.

On a typical mid-sized engine, a synch and link procedure generally involves the following:

1. Synchronizing and adjusting the ignition and fuel systems linkages.
2. Verifying that the carburetor throttle plate(s) fully open and close, and that all throttle plates are synchronized to open and close at exactly the same time.
3. Synchronizing the ignition system spark advance with throttle plate(s) operation to provide optimum off-idle acceleration and smooth part-throttle operation.
4. Adjusting the ignition timing at wide-open throttle engine speeds.
5. Setting the idle speed correctly and the wide-open throttle speed.

Synch and link procedures for Evinrude/Johnson outboard motors differ according to engine model and the specific ignition and fuel systems used. This chapter is divided into self-contained sections for fast and easy reference. Each section specifies the appropriate procedure and sequence to be followed. **Table 1** lists recommended tools and test equipment required to perform these procedures

and **Tables 2-9** provide general specifications. All tables are located at the end of the chapter.

Read the safety precaution and general information in the next two sections, then proceed directly to the section pertaining to your particular outboard motor.

SERVICE PRECAUTIONS— 1998-2004 MODEL YEAR ENGINES

The EPA (Environmental Protection Agency) certifies emission output for all 1998-2004 models. Certified models have an EPA certification plate mounted near the model identification plate on the engine midsection. Refer to *Model Identification* in Chapter Eight for illustrations and information regarding the certification plate.

All repairs or service procedures must be performed exactly as specified to ensure the engine will continue to comply with EPA requirements. For the same reason, all replacement parts must meet or exceed the manufacturer's specifications.

If in doubt as to whether a repair or service procedure will adversely affect the engine's ability to maintain EPA compliance, contact an Evinrude or Johnson dealer before beginning the repair or procedure.

SAFETY PRECAUTIONS

Wear approved eye protection at all times, especially when machinery is in operation or when using a hammer. Wear approved ear protection during all running tests and in the presence of noisy machinery. Keep loose clothing tucked in and long hair tied back and secured. Refer to *Safety First* in Chapter Two for additional safety guidelines.

When making or breaking any electrical connection, always disconnect the negative battery cable first. When performing tests that require cranking the engine without starting, disconnect and ground the spark plug leads to prevent accidental starts and sparks.

Securely cap or plug all disconnected fuel lines to prevent fuel discharge when the motor is cranked or the primer bulb is squeezed.

Thoroughly read any manufacturer's instructions and safety sheets for test equipment and special tools being used.

Do not substitute parts unless you know they meet or exceed the original manufacturer's specifications.

Never run an outboard motor without an adequate water supply. Never run an outboard motor at wide-open throttle without an adequate load. Do not exceed 3000 rpm in neutral (no load).

Safely performing on-water tests requires two people: one person to operate the boat, the other to monitor the gauges or test instruments. All personnel must remain seated inside the boat at all times. It is not acceptable to lean over the transom while the boat is under way. Use extensions to allow all gauges and meters to be located in the normal seating area.

Test wheels (propellers)

OMC recommends using the specified test wheel (propeller) for procedures that require running the engine under load. The correct test wheel will suitably load the engine while producing a minimal amount of thrust. A test wheel can be used in an adequately sized test tank with the

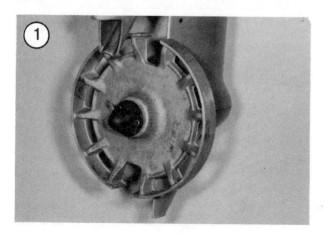

boat on a trailer (backed into the water) or with the boat launched and tied to a dock.

Test wheels are available from OMC Genuine Parts and are listed in **Tables 2-9**. The test wheel is also used to determine if the engine is producing its rated power. See **Figure 1**, typical. The minimum test speed for each engine is listed in **Tables 2-9**. If the engine can reach or exceed the specified minimum test speed with the specified test wheel installed, the engine is producing its rated power. The gearcase must be submerged in water to at least its normal operating depth and the gearcase must be shifted into FORWARD gear for this test.

A suitable test propeller can also be made by modifying (turning down) the diameter of a standard low pitch aluminum propeller until the recommended wide-open throttle speed can be obtained. Be careful of tying the boat to a dock as considerable thrust is produced by this type of test propeller. Some docks may not be able to withstand the load.

Propeller repair stations can provide the modification service. Normally, approximately 1/3 to 1/2 of the blade length is removed. However, it is far better to remove too little at first, than too much. It may take several tries to achieve the correct full-throttle speed, but once achieved, no further modifications are required. Many propeller repair stations have experience with this type of modification and may be able to recommend a starting point.

Test wheels and/or propellers allow simple tracking of engine performance. The full-throttle test speed of an engine fitted with the correct test wheel can be tracked (recorded) from season to season. It is not unusual for a new or rebuilt engine to show a slight increase in test propeller speed as complete break-in is achieved. The engine will generally hold this speed over the normal service life of the engine. As the engine begins to wear out, the test wheel (propeller) speed will show a gradual decrease that deteriorates to a marked or drastic decrease, as the point of engine failure is reached.

GENERAL INFORMATION

Synch and link adjustments that require the engine to be running, must be made with the engine running under actual operating conditions for adjustments to be as accurate as possible. Carburetor idle mixture and idle speed adjustments are very sensitive to engine load and exhaust system back pressure. If the adjustments are made with the engine running on a flushing device, the adjustments will not be correct when the motor is operated in the water under load.

The manufacturer recommends that idle speed and idle mixture adjustments be made only under normal operating conditions. Normal operating conditions are defined as follows:

1. The correct propeller must be installed.
2. The boat must be floating in the water with its movement unrestrained.
3. The motor must be warmed to operating temperature.
4. The motor must be in forward gear.

CAUTION
Do not run the engine without an adequate water supply and do not exceed 3000 rpm without an adequate load. Refer to Safety Precautions at the beginning of this chapter.

Ignition Timing

All 20-70 hp and 18-35 jet models use some form of timing marks to allow the ignition timing to be checked using a suitable stroboscopic timing light. If the timing is not within specification (**Tables 2-9**), a linkage adjustment must be made to bring the timing into specification.

The maximum timing specification must be checked at wide-open throttle. While this method is not always practical, attempts to set the timing at lower engine speeds will result in incorrect timing at wide-open throttle. This may lead to preignition or detonation (Chapter Three) and ultimately, power head damage.

The outboard can only be operated at full throttle when in forward gear and with a suitable load. This requires the use of a test wheel, test propeller or a dynamometer, since timing an engine while speeding across open water is not safe and is not recommended. Refer to *Safety Precautions* in the previous section.

High Speed Air/Fuel Mixture

CAUTION
Running an engine with high-speed jets that are too small (too lean) can cause catastrophic power head failure. It is better to have the high-speed air/fuel mixture slightly rich, rather than slightly lean. A lean air/fuel mixture causes high combustion chamber temperature that leads to preignition and detonation (Chapter Three).

The high speed air/fuel ratio is controlled by a fixed high speed jet (main jet). **Tables 2-9** list standard main jet sizes. The standard main jet must only be changed to compensate for changes in elevation, fuel blends or unique operating conditions. Changing the high speed jet can affect the air/fuel ratio across the entire engine speed range. If the engine runs satisfactorily, do not attempt to change the high-speed jet size. If changes to the high-speed jet sizes are warranted, see Chapter Six for additional information.

Wide-Open Throttle Speed Verification

All outboard motors have a specified wide-open throttle (W.O.T.) speed range (**Tables 2-9**). This means that when the engine is mounted on a boat and run at wide-open throttle, the engine speed must be within the specified range. If the speed is above or below the specified range, engine damage will result.

NOTE
Use an accurate shop tachometer (Table 1) for checking W.O.T. speed. Do not use the boat's tachometer for W.O.T. speed verification.

Operating an engine with a propeller that will not allow the engine to reach its specified range is called over-propping. This causes the combustion chamber temperature to rise dramatically, leading to preignition and detonation (Chapter Three).

Operating an engine with a propeller that allows an engine to exceed its specified range is called over-speeding. Over-speeding an engine will lead to mechanical failure of the reciprocating engine components. The 9.9-70 hp and 18-35 jet models are equipped with rpm-limiting power packs (or ignition modules) that interrupt the ignition system to limit engine speed. Over-speeding these engines can cause ignition misfire symptoms that can cause troubleshooting difficulties.

Changing propellers (pitch, diameter or style) changes the load on the engine and the resulting W.O.T. speed. If the W.O.T. speed exceeds the specified range, a propeller with more pitch or larger diameter must be installed and the speed rechecked. If the W.O.T. speed is below the specified range, a propeller with less pitch or smaller diameter must be installed.

Required Equipment

Verification of the timing pointer position requires the use of a suitable piston stop tool (such as part No. 384887).

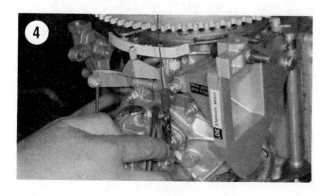

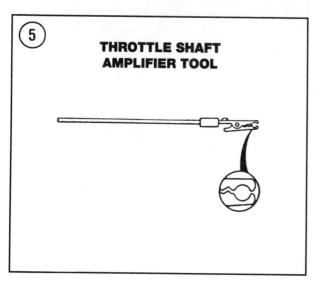

THROTTLE SHAFT
AMPLIFIER TOOL

Verify timing pointer position by removing the No. 1 spark plug and installing the piston stop tool into the spark plug hole and following the procedure as specified in the appropriate *synch and link* procedure.

The timing pointer position may also be verified using a suitable dial indicator and spark plug hole adaptor (**Table 1**). See **Figure 2**, typical. However, this method does not work on engines that the spark plugs come into the cylinder head at an angle.

Regardless of the method used, the timing pointer must be aligned with the flywheel's cast or stamped TDC (top dead center) mark when the No. 1 cylinder piston is at its TDC position.

All ignition timing checks and adjustments require the use of a stroboscopic timing light connected to the No. 1 spark plug lead. As the engine is cranked or operated, the light flashes each time the spark plug fires. When the light is pointed at the moving flywheel (**Figure 3**, typical), the mark on the flywheel appears to stand still. The appropriate timing marks will be aligned if the timing is correctly adjusted.

NOTE
*Timing lights with built-in features (such as a timing advance function) are not recommended for use on outboard motors. A basic high-speed timing light with an inductive pick up is all that is recommended. Both Stevens and Merc-O-Tronic Instruments (**Table 1**) offer timing lights that meet OMC's requirements.*

An accurate shop tachometer must be connected to the engine to determine engine speed during timing adjustments. Do not rely on the tachometer installed in a boat to provide accurate engine speed readings.

A simple tool, called a throttle shaft amplifier, can be made with an alligator clip and a length of stiff wire (a paper clip or piece of coat hanger will do). This tool is attached to the throttle shaft and exaggerates throttle shaft movement. This makes it easier to determine the exact instant the throttle shaft begins to move. **Figure 4** shows the tool installed in a typical application. The tool is especially useful if the throttle cam and cam follower are partially hidden by the flywheel. When making the tool, it may be necessary to enlarge the alligator clip's gripping surface (to fit the throttle shaft) by grinding out the front teeth as necessary. Then secure the wire to the end of the clip by crimping or soldering. See **Figure 5**.

2, 3.3 AND 3.5 HP

While ignition timing is not adjustable and no specifications are given, the system incorporates a single-step electronic advance. Timing is determined by the mechanical mounting of the ignition components and the flywheel. If timing is suspected of being incorrect, remove the flywheel and inspect the ignition component mounting hardware, the flywheel key and the flywheel magnets.

Refer to **Table 2** for specifications. The synch and link procedure must be performed in the following order:
1. Setting the throttle lever friction.
2. Adjusting the idle speed.
3. Adjusting the carburetor mixture needle E-clip position.
4. Wide-open throttle speed verification.

Setting Throttle Lever Friction

1. Remove the engine cowl.
2. Adjust the throttle lever friction screw (A, **Figure 6**) as necessary to provide the desired throttle lever friction.

Idle Speed Adjustment

For this adjustment to be accurate, the engine must be operated in a body of water with the correct propeller installed.

> *CAUTION*
> *Do not run the engine without an adequate water supply and do not exceed 3000 rpm without an adequate load. Refer to **Safety Precautions** at the beginning of this chapter.*

1. Start the engine and allow to warm to normal operating temperature.
2. Connect an accurate shop tachometer (**Table 1**) to the spark plug lead.
3. Place the throttle lever in the slowest speed position. On 3.5 hp models, shift the engine into *forward* gear.
4. Adjust the idle speed screw (B, **Figure 6**) to obtain 1100-1300 rpm for 2 and 3.3 hp models and 1000-1200 rpm for 3.5 hp models.

Carburetor Mixture Needle E-clip Adjustment

The carburetor mixture needle E-clip position must only be adjusted to compensate for changes in elevation, fuel blends or unique operating conditions. Moving the E-clip position affects the air/fuel ratio across most of the engine speed range. If the engine runs satisfactorily, do not at-

tempt to adjust the E-clip position. If adjustment is warranted, move the E-clip position as shown in Chapter Six to change the air/fuel ratio as desired. Further mixture adjustments will require changing the main jet. It is preferable to have the mixture slightly rich, rather than slightly lean.

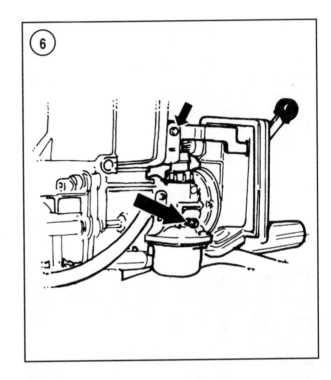

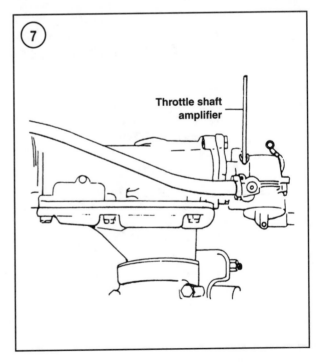

Throttle shaft amplifier

**Wide-Open Throttle
Speed Verification**

1. Connect an accurate shop tachometer (**Table 1**) to the spark plug lead.

2. With the engine mounted on a boat, the boat unrestrained in the water and the engine running at wide-open throttle in forward gear, record the maximum speed noted on the tachometer.

3. If the maximum speed exceeds the recommended range listed in **Table 2**, check the propeller for damage or incorrect application. Repair or replace the propeller as necessary.

4. If the maximum speed does not reach the recommended speed range listed in **Table 2**, check the propeller for incorrect application. If the correct propeller is installed, the engine is not producing its rated horsepower. Start troubleshooting by checking the cranking compression as described in Chapter Four.

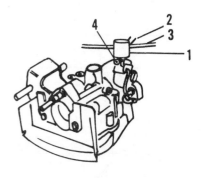

**CAM FOLLOWER PICKUP POINT
(3 AND 4 HP [EXCEPT 4 DELUXE])**

1. Cam follower (roller)
2. Mark
3. Throttle cam
4. Adjustment screw

3 AND 4 HP (EXCEPT 4 DELUXE)

Ignition timing is mechanically advanced and retarded during operation by rotating the sensor coil (ignition plate) via the throttle cable. Ignition timing is not adjustable and no specifications are given for verification.

If timing is suspected of being incorrect or not advancing, remove the flywheel and inspect the sensor coil (ignition plate), the flywheel key and the flywheel magnets. Make sure the ignition plate rotates freely as the throttle linkage is operated.

Refer to **Table 3** for specifications. The synch and link procedure must be performed in the following order:

1. Cam follower pickup point.
2. Idle mixture and idle speed adjustments.
3. Throttle cable adjustment.
4. Wide-open throttle speed verification.

5

Cam Follower Pickup Point

A 7/64 in. ball hex screwdriver is required for this procedure.

1. Position the throttle linkage in the low-speed (full idle) position.

2. Attach a throttle shaft amplifier to the starboard end of the carburetor's throttle shaft (opposite the cam follower linkage). See **Figure 7**, typical. Bend the tool as necessary to allow easy viewing.

3. Advance the throttle until the tip of the amplifier begins to move, indicating the throttle valve is starting to open.

4. With the throttle in this position, the single mark on the throttle cam must be aligned with the center of the cam follower roller. See **Figure 8**.

5. If adjustment is necessary, turn the cam follower adjustment screw (4, **Figure 8**) as necessary and repeat Steps 3-4. The throttle plate must just begin to open as the throttle cam mark aligns with the center of the cam roller.

6. Remove the throttle shaft amplifier when finished.

Idle Mixture and Idle Speed Adjustments

For these adjustments to be accurate, the engine must be operated in a body of water with the correct propeller installed.

*CAUTION
Do not run the engine without an adequate water supply and do not exceed 3000 rpm without an adequate load. Refer to **Safety Precautions** at the beginning of this chapter.*

1. Turn the idle mixture screw (**Figure 9**) one full turn. Do not force the screw tightly into the carburetor or the tip and the carburetor will be damaged.

2. Back out the mixture screw.

3. Loosen the throttle cable jam nuts (**Figure 10**) and back out the idle speed screw (**Figure 11**) as necessary to allow the ignition plate to contact its stop on the power head. The idle speed screw and/or throttle cable must not be holding the plate from its stop.

4. Connect an accurate shop tachometer (**Table 1**) to the No. 1 spark plug lead.

5. Start the engine and run it at approximately 2000 rpm until warmed to normal operating temperature.

6. Set the throttle control to the idle position and shift the gearcase into FORWARD gear. If necessary, adjust the idle speed screw (**Figure 11**) temporarily to obtain 700-800 rpm in FORWARD gear.

> *NOTE*
> *Idle mixture cannot be properly set unless the carburetor is operating on the idle circuit. Setting the idle mixture at higher speeds will give inaccurate results. It may be necessary to switch back and forth between idle mixture adjustment and idle speed adjustment several times to achieve proper adjustment. Always adjust the idle speed last.*

7. Slowly turn the idle mixture screw (**Figure 9**) counterclockwise in 1/8 turn increments, pausing at least 15 seconds between turns. Continue this step until the idle speed decreases and idle becomes rough due to an overly rich mixture. Note the position of the mixture screw slot.

8. Slowly turn the idle mixture screw clockwise in 1/8 turn increments, pausing at least 15 seconds between turns. The idle speed will gradually become smooth and speed will increase. Continue this step until the engine speed begins to slow again and/or misfires due to an excessively lean mixture. Note the position of the mixture screw slot.

9. Position the mixture screw at a midpoint between the settings of Step 6 and Step 7. See **Figure 12**.

> *NOTE*
> *It is a natural tendency to adjust the idle mixture too lean. Although the engine appears to run smoothly at idle, it will not accelerate without hesitation or continue to idle smoothly after wide-open throttle operation. If the engine does not perform satisfactorily in the following 2 steps, the idle mixture is most likely too lean.*

10. Run the engine at wide-open throttle for one minute to clear any fuel puddles from the crankcase. Then quickly reduce engine speed to idle. The engine will idle smoothly without stalling or spitting if the mixture is adjusted correctly. Readjust the mixture as necessary.

11. Quickly accelerate the engine to wide-open throttle and back to idle. The engine will accelerate cleanly without hesitation if the mixture is adjusted correctly. Readjust the mixture as necessary.

12. Adjust the idle speed screw (**Figure 11**) to obtain 700-800 rpm in FORWARD gear.

13. Stop the engine and proceed to *Throttle Cable Adjustment* in the next section.

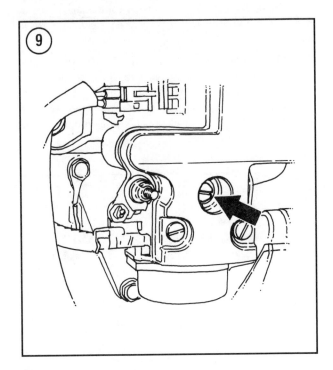

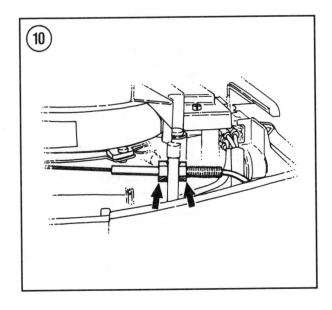

Throttle Cable Adjustment

1. Position the tiller handle throttle control in the full idle position and rotate the ignition plate so it is contacting the idle speed screw (**Figure 11**).

2. With the ignition plate contacting the idle speed screw and the throttle control in the full idle position, adjust the throttle cable nuts (**Figure 10**) as necessary to remove any slack in the cable.

3. Tighten the throttle cable nuts securely.

4. Operate the twist grip throttle and verify that the ignition plate rotates freely, yet contacts the idle speed screw when returned to idle. Readjust the throttle cable nuts as necessary.

Wide-Open Throttle Speed Verification

1. Connect an accurate shop tachometer (**Table 1**) to a spark plug lead.

2. With the engine mounted on a boat, the boat unrestrained in the water and the engine running at wide-open throttle in FORWARD gear, record the maximum speed noted on the tachometer.

3. If the maximum speed exceeds 5500 rpm, check the propeller for damage or incorrect application. Repair or replace the propeller as necessary.

4. If the maximum speed does not reach 4500 rpm, check the propeller for incorrect application. If the correct pro-

peller is installed, check the engine's power output using a test wheel as described in *Power output verification* at the end of Chapter Three. If the engine is not producing its rated power, start troubleshooting by checking the cranking compression as described in Chapter Four.

4 DELUXE MODELS

Ignition timing is mechanically advanced and retarded during operation by rotating the sensor coil (armature plate) via the throttle cable and associated linkage. Ignition timing is not adjustable and no specifications are given for verification.

If timing is suspected of being incorrect or not advancing, remove the flywheel and inspect the sensor coil (ignition plate), the flywheel key and the flywheel magnets. Make sure the armature plate rotates freely as the throttle linkage is operated.

Refer to **Table 4** for specifications. The synch and link procedure must be performed in the following order:

1. Cam follower pickup point.

2. Idle mixture and idle speed adjustments.

3. Wide-open throttle speed verification.

Cam Follower Pickup Point

A 7/64 in. ball hex screwdriver is required for this procedure.

1. Position the throttle linkage in the low-speed (full idle) position.

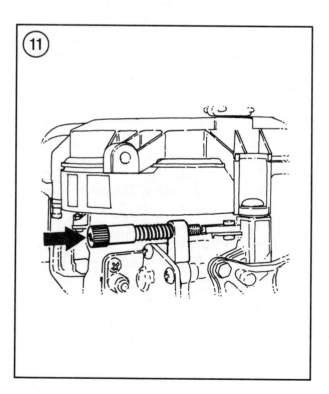

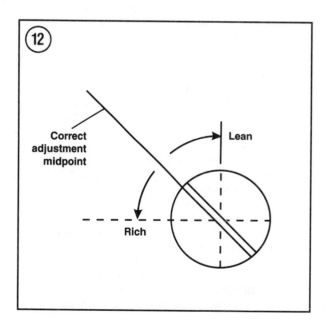

2. Attach a throttle shaft amplifier to either end of the carburetor's throttle shaft. See **Figure 13**, typical. Bend the tool as necessary to allow easy viewing.

3. Advance the throttle until the tip of the amplifier begins to move, indicating the throttle valve is starting to open.

4. With the throttle in this position, the single mark on the throttle cam must be aligned with the center of the cam follower roller. See **Figure 13**, typical.

5. If adjustment is necessary, turn the cam follower adjustment screw (**Figure 13**, typical) as necessary and recheck Steps 3-4. The throttle plate must just begin to open as the throttle cam mark aligns with the center of the cam roller.

6. Remove the throttle shaft amplifier when finished.

Idle Mixture and Idle Speed Adjustments

For these adjustments to be accurate, the engine must be operated in a body of water with the correct propeller installed.

CAUTION
*Do not run the engine without an adequate water supply and do not exceed 3000 rpm without an adequate load. Refer to **Safety Precautions** at the beginning of this chapter.*

1. Remove the idle mixture (low speed) control knob and turn the idle mixture screw clockwise until it is lightly seated. Do not force the screw tightly into the carburetor or the tip and the carburetor will be damaged.

2. Back out the mixture screw one turn.

3. Connect an accurate shop tachometer (**Table 1**) to the No. 1 spark plug lead.

4. Start the engine and run it at approximately 2000 rpm until warmed to normal operating temperature.

5. Set the throttle control to the idle position and shift the gearcase into FORWARD gear. If necessary, adjust the idle speed temporarily to obtain 600-650 rpm. To adjust the idle speed, remove the screw securing the throttle cable anchor to the engine and rotate the anchor around the throttle cable threaded area as necessary. Reinstall the screw, recheck idle speed and fully tighten the screw when finished.

NOTE
Idle mixture cannot be properly set unless the carburetor is operating on the idle circuit. Setting the idle mixture at higher speeds will give inaccurate results. It may be necessary to switch back and forth between idle mixture adjustment and idle speed adjustment several times to achieve proper adjustment. Always adjust the idle speed last.

6. Slowly turn the idle mixture screw counterclockwise in 1/8 turn increments, pausing at least 15 seconds between

turns. Continue this step until the idle speed decreases and idle becomes rough due to an overly rich mixture. Note the position of the mixture screw slot.

7. Slowly turn the idle mixture screw clockwise in 1/8 turn increments, pausing at least 15 seconds between turns. The idle speed will gradually become smooth and speed will increase. Continue this step until the engine speed begins to slow again and/or misfires due to the excessively lean mixture. Note the position of the mixture screw slot.

8. Position the mixture screw at a midpoint between the settings of Step 6 and Step 7. See **Figure 12**.

NOTE
It is a natural tendency to adjust the idle mixture too lean. Although the engine appears to run smoothly at idle, it will not accelerate without hesitation or continue to idle smoothly after wide-open throttle operation. If the engine does not perform satisfactorily in the following 2 steps, the idle mixture is most likely too lean.

9. Run the engine at wide-open throttle for one minute to clear any fuel puddles from the crankcase. Then quickly reduce engine speed to idle. The engine will idle smoothly without stalling or spitting if the mixture is adjusted correctly. Readjust the mixture as necessary.

10. Quickly accelerate the engine to wide-open throttle and back to idle. The engine will accelerate cleanly and without hesitation if the mixture is adjusted correctly. Readjust the mixture as necessary.

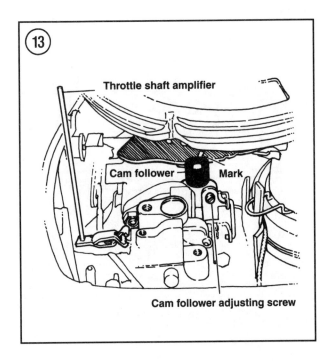

11. Make a final adjustment to the throttle cable anchor to obtain an idle speed of 600-650 rpm in FORWARD gear. If necessary, remove the screw securing the throttle cable anchor to the engine and rotate the anchor around the throttle cable threaded area as necessary. Reinstall the screw, recheck the idle speed, then fully tighten the screw when finished.

12. Reinstall the idle mixture (slow speed) control knob. Position the knob so that it is in the middle of its available travel. Do not disturb the idle mixture screw position when installing the knob.

Wide-Open Throttle Speed Verification

1. Connect an accurate shop tachometer (**Table 1**) to a spark plug lead.

2. With the engine mounted on a boat, the boat unrestrained in the water and the engine running at wide-open throttle in FORWARD gear, record the maximum speed noted on the tachometer.

3. If the maximum rpm 5500 rpm, check the propeller for damage or incorrect application. Repair or replace the propeller as necessary.

4. If the maximum speed does not reach 4500 rpm, check the propeller for incorrect application. If the correct propeller is installed, check the engine's power output using a test wheel as described in *Power output verification* at the end of Chapter Three. If the engine is not producing its rated power, start troubleshooting by checking the cranking compression as described in Chapter Four.

6 AND 8 HP MODELS

Ignition timing is mechanically advanced and retarded during operation by rotating the sensor coil (armature plate) via the throttle cable and associated linkage. Ignition timing is not adjustable and no specifications are given for timing verification.

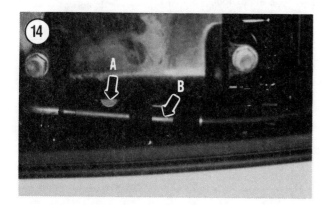

If timing is suspected of being incorrect or not advancing, remove the flywheel and inspect the sensor coil (armature plate), the flywheel key and the flywheel magnets. Make sure the armature plate rotates freely as the throttle linkage is operated.

Refer to **Table 4** for specifications. The synch and link procedure must be performed in the following order:
1. Throttle cable adjustment.
2. Idle mixture and idle speed adjustments.
3. Wide-open throttle stop adjustment.
4. Wide-open throttle speed verification.

Throttle Cable Adjustment

1. Grasp the twist grip throttle control and turn its idle speed adjustment knob fully counterclockwise to the minimum idle speed position. Then rotate the twist grip throttle control to the full idle position.

2. Position the throttle cam (rotate the armature plate) so that it is contacting its stop on the power head.

NOTE
It may be necessary to remove the power pack to gain access to the throttle cable anchor screw. Make sure the power pack is reinstalled and its ground lead securely fastened to the power head before cranking or starting the engine.

3. Remove the screw (A, **Figure 14**) securing the throttle cable anchor bracket to the power head. The screw and bracket are located on the starboard side of the power head, below the power pack.

4. With the (throttle cam) armature plate contacting its power head stop and the throttle control in the full idle position, adjust the throttle cable anchor bracket (B, **Figure 14**) as necessary to align the anchor with its mounting screw hole.

5. Preload the throttle cable to the closed (idle) position by rotating the throttle cable anchor one turn toward the rear of the engine (clockwise as viewed from the front of the engine). Then secure the anchor to the power head with the single screw. Tighten the screw securely.

6. Operate the twist grip throttle and verify that the armature plate rotates freely, yet contacts the idle stop when returned to idle. Readjust the throttle cable anchor as necessary.

Idle Mixture and Idle Speed Adjustments

For these adjustments to be accurate, the engine must be operated in a body of water with the correct propeller installed. For best results, the boat must be floating in the water and its movement unrestrained. A 7/64 in. ball hex screwdriver is required for this procedure.

CAUTION
*Do not run the engine without an adequate water supply and do not exceed 3000 rpm without an adequate load. Refer to **Safety Precautions** at the beginning of this chapter.*

1. Turn the idle mixture screw (**Figure 15**) clockwise until it is lightly seated. Do not force the screw tightly into the carburetor or the tip and the carburetor will be damaged.
2. Back out the mixture screw three full turns.

NOTE
If it is necessary to advance the throttle to access the throttle cam follower adjusting screw in the next step, be sure to return the throttle to the full idle position and confirm that the follower is not touching the throttle cam when finished.

3. Turn the throttle cam follower screw counterclockwise until the follower is not contacting the throttle cam. Access the cam follower screw by inserting the tool through the hole in the air silencer as shown in **Figure 16**.
4. Turn the idle speed screw (A, **Figure 17**) clockwise until its spring is fully compressed. Do not continue to tighten the screw after the spring is compressed.
5. Connect an accurate shop tachometer (**Table 1**) to the No. 1 spark plug lead.
6. Start the engine and run it at approximately 2000 rpm until warmed to normal operating temperature.
7. Set the throttle control to the idle position, verify that the armature plate is against its power head stop and shift the gearcase into FORWARD gear. Adjust the idle speed screw (A, **Figure 17**) temporarily to obtain 675-725 rpm in FORWARD gear.

NOTE
Idle mixture cannot be properly set unless the carburetor is operating on the idle circuit. Setting the idle mixture at higher speeds will give inaccurate results. It may be necessary to switch back and forth between idle mixture adjustment and idle speed adjustment several times to achieve proper adjustment. Always adjust the idle speed last.

8. Slowly turn the idle mixture screw (**Figure 15**) counterclockwise in 1/8 turn increments, pausing at least 15 seconds between turns. Continue this step until the idle speed decreases and idle becomes rough due to an overly rich mixture. Note the position of the mixture screw slot.

9. Slowly turn the idle mixture screw clockwise in 1/8 turn increments, pausing at least 15 seconds between turns. The idle speed will gradually become smooth and speed will increase. Continue this step until the engine speed begins to slow again and/or misfires due to an excessively lean mixture. Note the position of the mixture screw slot.

10. Position the mixture screw at a midpoint between the settings of Step 6 and Step 7. See **Figure 18**. Then turn the

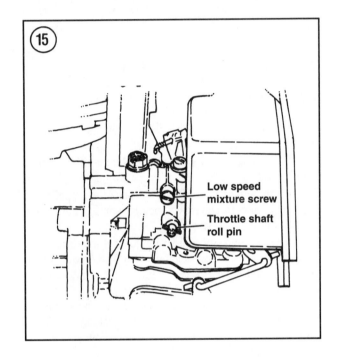

Low speed mixture screw

Throttle shaft roll pin

Air silencer

Cam follower screw

Ball-hex tool

screw counterclockwise (outward) 1/8 turn to slightly enrich the mixture.

NOTE
It is a natural tendency to adjust the idle mixture too lean. Although the engine appears to run smoothly at idle, it will not accelerate without hesitation or continue to idle smoothly after wide-open throttle operation. If the engine does not perform satisfactorily in Step 11 and Step 16, the idle mixture is most likely too lean.

11. Run the engine at wide-open throttle (in FORWARD gear) for one minute to clear any fuel puddles from the crankcase. Then quickly reduce engine speed to idle. The engine will idle smoothly without stalling or spitting if the mixture is adjusted correctly. Readjust the mixture as necessary.

12. Make a final adjustment to the idle speed screw (A, **Figure 17**) to obtain 675-725 rpm in FORWARD gear.

13. Stop the engine and remove the carburetor's air intake cover. Then install a throttle amplifier to either end of the throttle shaft.

NOTE
The cam follower roller and any mark that may be present on the throttle cam need not be aligned in the next step. It is only necessary that the twist grip and throttle cam are held in the specified position when adjusting the throttle cam follower.

14. With the twist grip handle held in the full idle position and the throttle cam (armature plate) against its stop, turn the throttle cam follower screw (B, **Figure 17**) clockwise until the throttle amplifier just indicates movement. Then turn the screw counterclockwise 1/8 turn.

15. Remove the throttle amplifier and reinstall the air intake cover.

16. Restart the engine and shift it into FORWARD gear. Quickly accelerate the engine to wide-open throttle and back to idle. The engine will accelerate cleanly without hesitation if the mixture is adjusted correctly. Readjust the mixture as necessary. If the mixture is readjusted, the idle speed (Step 12) and the cam follower (Steps 13-14) must also be readjusted.

Wide-Open Throttle Stop

1. Disconnect and ground the spark plug leads to the power head to prevent accidental starting.

2. While rotating the propeller, shift the gearcase into FORWARD gear.

3. Turn the twist grip handle to the full-throttle (wide open) position.

4. Check the position of the throttle shaft's roll pin (**Figure 15**). The roll pin must be perfectly vertical (indicating that the throttle plate is horizontal) when the throttle is wide open.

5

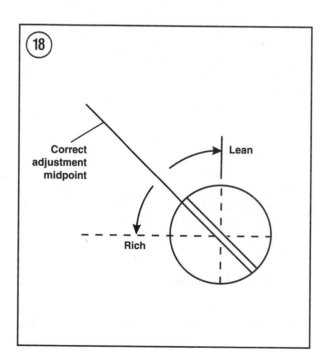

5. If adjustment is necessary, adjust the screw on the starboard end of the throttle cam (**Figure 19**) until the throttle shaft roll pin is exactly vertical when the throttle is wide open.

Wide-Open Throttle Speed Verification

1. Connect an accurate shop tachometer (**Table 1**) to a spark plug lead.

2. With the engine mounted on a boat, the boat unrestrained in the water and the engine running at wide-open throttle in FORWARD gear, record the maximum speed noted on the tachometer.

3. If the maximum speed exceeds 5500 rpm (6 hp) or 6000 rpm (8 hp), check the propeller for damage or incorrect application. Repair or replace the propeller as necessary.

4. If the maximum speed does not reach 4500 rpm (6 hp) or 5000 rpm (8 hp), check the propeller for incorrect application. If the correct propeller is installed, check the engine's power output using a test wheel as described in *Power output verification* at the end of Chapter Three. If the engine is not producing its rated power, start troubleshooting by checking the cranking compression as described in Chapter Four.

9.9 AND 15 HP MODELS

Ignition timing is mechanically advanced and retarded during operation by rotating the sensor coil (armature plate) via the throttle cable and associated linkage. Ignition timing is not adjustable and no specifications are given for verification.

If timing is suspected of being incorrect or not advancing, remove the flywheel and inspect the sensor coil or stator assembly (armature plate), the flywheel key and the flywheel magnets. Make sure the armature plate rotates freely as the throttle linkage is operated.

Refer to **Table 5** for specifications. The synch and link procedure must be performed in the following order:
1. Preliminary adjustments.
2. Cam follower pickup point adjustment.
3. Wide-open throttle stop adjustment.
4. Idle speed and idle mixture adjustments.
5. Shift lever detent position adjustment.
6. Wide-open throttle speed verification.

Preliminary Adjustments

1A. *Remote control models*—Disconnect the throttle and shift cables from the power head as described in Chapter Twelve.

1B. *Tiller handle models*—Grasp the twist grip throttle control and turn its idle speed adjustment knob fully counterclockwise to the minimum idle-speed position. Then rotate the twist grip throttle control to the full idle position.
   a. Remove the pin (A, **Figure 20**) connecting the throttle cable to the spark control arm.
   b. Turn the connector (B, **Figure 20**) on the end of the throttle cable until it is seated on the throttle cable. Then rotate the connector just enough to allow the throttle cable to be reinstalled to the spark control arm. Do not turn the connector more than 1/2 turn.

c. Secure the throttle cable to the spark control arm with the retaining pin.

2. *Tiller handle models*—Verify that the throttle cable anchor bracket is threaded as far forward on the cable's threads as possible. The bulk of the cable's threads must be visible as shown in **Figure 20**. If not, remove the screw (C, **Figure 20**) and rotate the anchor bracket on the cable's

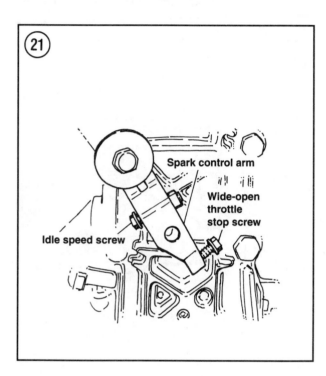

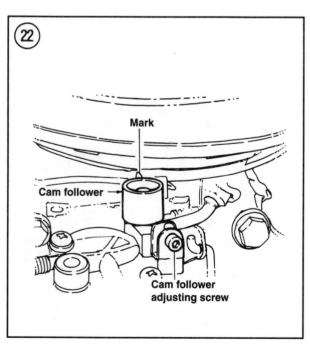

threads until it is as far forward as possible, without running off of the barrel's threads.

3. *All models*—Hold the spark control arm so that the idle speed screw (**Figure 21**) is against its power head stop. The idle speed screw is the screw just above the throttle cable attachment point on the spark control arm and its screw head faces the rear of the engine.

   a. When the arm is held against the idle stop, the centerline of the cam follower's roller must be exactly halfway between the cast mark on the throttle cam and the port end of the throttle cam. These components are at the front of the engine, just above the carburetor and just below the flywheel.

   b. If the roller is closer to the port end of the cam, turn the idle speed screw inward to move the cam's mark closer to the roller.

   c. If the roller is closer to the throttle cam's cast mark, turn the idle speed screw outward to move the cam's mark further from the cam follower's roller.

5

Cam Follower Pickup Point

A 7/64 in. ball hex screwdriver is required for this procedure. If the air intake cover is installed, remove its plastic plug to allow access to the adjustment screw. Make sure the plug is reinstalled when finished.

1. Position the throttle linkage in the low-speed (full idle) position. The idle speed screw must be held against its power head stop.

2. Attach a throttle shaft amplifier to the either end of the carburetor's throttle shaft.

3. Advance the spark control arm until the tip of the amplifier just begins to move, indicating the throttle valve is starting to open.

4. With the throttle in this position, the single mark on the throttle cam must be aligned with the center of the cam follower roller. See **Figure 22**.

5. If adjustment is necessary, turn the cam follower adjustment screw (**Figure 22**) as necessary and repeat Steps 3-4. The throttle plate must just begin to open as the throttle cam's mark aligns with the center of the cam roller.

6. Remove the throttle shaft amplifier when finished.

Wide-Open Throttle Stop

1. Disconnect and ground the spark plug leads to the power head to prevent accidental starting.

2. While rotating the propeller, shift the gearcase into FORWARD gear.

3. Adjust the wide-open throttle stop screw (**Figure 21**) so the tip of the screws extends through the spark control

arm 1/4 in. (6.4 mm). The wide-open throttle stop screw is the lowest screw on the spark control arm and its screw head faces the front of the engine. The screw has not yet correctly positioned in **Figure 21**.

4A. *Remote control models*—Manually hold the spark control arm against its wide-open stop.

4B. *Tiller handle models*—Turn the twist grip handle to the full-throttle (wide open) position.

5. Check the position of the throttle shaft's roll pin (**Figure 23**, typical). The roll pin must be perfectly vertical (indicating that the throttle plate is horizontal) when the throttle is wide open.

6. If adjustment is necessary, adjust the screw on the starboard end of the throttle cam (**Figure 24**) until the throttle shaft roll pin is exactly vertical when the throttle is wide open.

7. Reconnect the spark plug leads when finished.

Idle Speed and Idle Mixture Adjustments

For these adjustments to be accurate, the engine must be operated in a body of water with the correct propeller installed. For best results, the boat must be floating in the water with its movement unrestrained.

CAUTION
Do not run the engine without an adequate water supply and do not exceed 3000 rpm without an adequate load. Refer to **Safety Precautions** *at the beginning of this chapter.*

1. Turn the idle mixture screw (**Figure 25**) clockwise until it is lightly seated. Do not force the screw tightly into the carburetor or the tip and the carburetor will be damaged.

2. Back out the mixture screw three full turns.

3. Connect an accurate shop tachometer to the No. 1 spark plug lead.

4. Start the engine and run it at approximately 2000 rpm until warmed to normal operating temperature.

5A. *Remote control models*—Hold the spark control arm against its idle stop and manually shift the gearcase into FORWARD gear. Adjust the idle speed screw (**Figure 21**) to obtain 675-725 rpm in FORWARD gear.

5B. *Tiller handle models*—Rotate the twist grip throttle to its full idle position. Make sure the spark control arm is against its idle stop and shift the gearcase into FORWARD gear. Adjust the idle speed screw (**Figure 21**) to obtain 675-725 rpm in FORWARD gear.

NOTE
Idle mixture cannot be properly set unless the carburetor is operating on the idle circuit. Setting the idle mixture at higher speeds will give inaccurate results. It may be necessary

to switch back and forth between idle mixture adjustment and idle speed adjustment several times to achieve proper adjustment. Always adjust the idle speed last.

6. Slowly turn the idle mixture screw (**Figure 25**) counterclockwise in 1/8 turn increments, pausing at least 15 seconds between turns. Continue this step until the idle

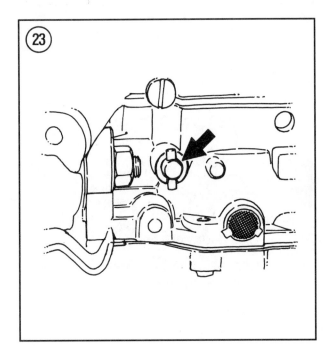

speed decreases and idle becomes rough due to an overly rich mixture. Note the position of the mixture screw slot.

7. Slowly turn the idle mixture screw clockwise in 1/8 turn increments, pausing at least 15 seconds between turns. The idle speed will gradually become smooth and speed will increase. Continue this step until the engine speed begins to slow again and/or misfires due to an excessively lean mixture. Note the position of the mixture screw slot.

8. Position the mixture screw at a midpoint between the settings of Step 6 and Step 7. See **Figure 26**. Then turn the screw counterclockwise (outward) 1/8 turn to slightly enrichen the mixture.

NOTE
It is a natural tendency to adjust the idle mixture too lean. Although the engine appears to run smoothly at idle, it will not

accelerate without hesitation or continue to idle smoothly after wide-open throttle operation. If the engine does not perform satisfactorily in the following 2 steps, the idle mixture is most likely too lean.

CAUTION
On remote control models, the engine must be manually shifted into FORWARD gear before attempting to operate it at wide-open throttle in the following steps.

9. Run the engine at wide-open throttle (in FORWARD gear) for one minute to clear any fuel puddles from the crankcase. Then quickly reduce engine speed to idle. The engine will idle smoothly without stalling or spitting if the mixture is adjusted correctly. Readjust the mixture as necessary.

10. Quickly accelerate the engine to wide-open throttle and back to idle. The engine will accelerate cleanly without hesitation if the mixture is adjusted correctly. Readjust the mixture as necessary.

11. Make a final adjustment to the idle speed screw to obtain 675-725 rpm in FORWARD gear.

12. *Tiller handle models*—With the twist grip handle held in the full idle position, adjust the throttle cable anchor to provide a slight amount of preload on the spark control arm. The spark control arm must firmly hold the idle speed screw in contact with the power head when the cable is correctly adjusted. If adjustment is necessary, proceed as follows:

    a. Remove the screw and rotate the anchor bracket (**Figure 27**) to provide a small amount of preload.

5

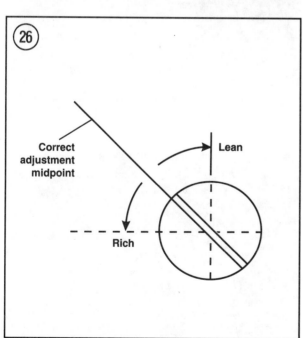

Correct adjustment midpoint

Lean

Rich

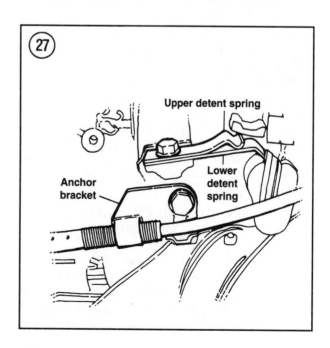

Upper detent spring

Anchor bracket

Lower detent spring

b. Position the bracket on the power head. Install the screw and tighten it securely.

c. Verify the adjustment by opening the throttle to the wide-open throttle position and back to the idle position. The idle speed screw must firmly contact the power head stop.

d. Readjust as necessary.

Shift Lever Detent Adjustment

1. Disconnect and ground the spark plug leads to the power head to prevent accidental starting.

2. While rotating the propeller, shift the gearcase into the NEUTRAL position.

3. With the outboard in NEUTRAL, the lower detent spring (**Figure 27**) must be centered in the notch in the shift lever.

4. If not, loosen the screw securing the detent springs and move the *lower* spring as necessary. Retighten the screw and recheck the adjustment.

5. *Remote control models*—Reinstall and adjust the throttle and shift cables as described in Chapter Twelve.

6. Reconnect the spark plugs leads when finished.

Wide-Open Throttle Speed Verification

1. Connect an accurate shop tachometer to a spark plug lead.

2. With the engine mounted on a boat, the boat unrestrained in the water and the engine running at wide-open throttle in FORWARD gear, record the maximum speed noted on the tachometer.

3. If the maximum speed exceeds 6000 rpm, check the propeller for damage or incorrect application. Repair or replace the propeller as necessary.

4. If the maximum speed does not reach 5000 rpm, check the propeller for incorrect application. If the correct propeller is installed, check the engine's power output using a test wheel as described in *Power output verification* at the end of Chapter Three. If the engine is not producing its rated power, start troubleshooting by checking the cranking compression as described in Chapter Four.

20-30 HP (TWO-CYLINDER) AND 18 JET MODELS

Ignition timing is mechanically advanced and retarded during operation by rotating the sensor coil (armature plate) via the throttle cable and associated linkage. Ignition timing is adjustable and must be verified and/or correctly adjusted as part of the synch and link procedure. Incorrect

ignition timing can lead to power head failure from preignition and/or detonation (Chapter Three).

On remote control models, the throttle and shift cables must be disconnected from the power head (as described in Chapter Twelve), before beginning the synch and link procedure. When the throttle or gearshift operation is necessary, manually operate the appropriate linkage from the point that the control cable normally attaches.

Refer to **Table 6** for specifications. The synch and link procedure must be performed in the following order:

1. Cam follower pickup point adjustment.

2. Throttle control rod adjustment (25 hp, 30 hp and 18 jet only).

3. Maximum spark advance verification/adjustment.

4. Idle speed and idle mixture adjustments.

5. Wide-open throttle speed verification.

Cam Follower Pickup Point

1. *Remote control models*—Disconnect the throttle and shift cables from the power head as described in Chapter Twelve.

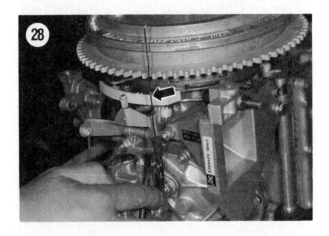

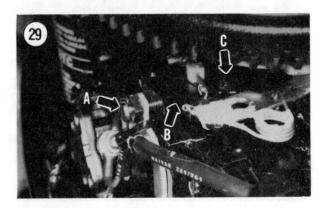

2. Connect a throttle shaft amplifier to either end of the carburetor's throttle shaft. Bend the tool as necessary to provide easy viewing. See **Figure 28**, typical.

3. *Tiller handle models*—Grasp the twist grip throttle control and turn its idle speed adjustment knob fully counterclockwise to the minimum idle speed position. Then rotate the twist grip throttle control to the full idle position.

4. Loosen the jam nut and back out the idle speed screw (A, **Figure 29**) until the end of the screw is flush with the bracket. Then retighten the jam nut to prevent the screw from vibrating out during later adjustments. The spark and

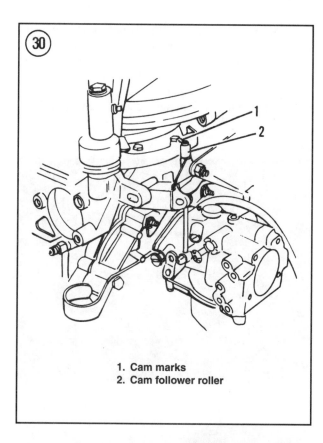

1. **Cam marks**
2. **Cam follower roller**

throttle control arm (B, **Figure 29**) must be able to contact the idle speed screw's mounting bracket.

5. Starting with the throttle in the full idle position (throttle arm against the idle speed screw mounting bracket), slowly advance the throttle until the tip of the amplifier begins to move, indicating that the throttle valve is starting to open. The cam follower (roller) must be centered between the two marks on the throttle cam as the throttle valve just begins to open as shown in **Figure 30**.

6. If adjustment is necessary, loosen the adjustment screw on the starboard end of the throttle shaft (A, **Figure 31**) and move the linkage as necessary. Hold the linkage in the desired position and retighten the adjustment screw. Repeat Step 5 to verify the adjustment. The throttle plate must just begin to open as the cam follower roller is centered between the two marks on the throttle cam.

7. Remove the throttle shaft amplifier when finished.

Throttle Control Rod Adjustment
(25 hp, 30 hp and 18 Jet)

This procedure does not apply to 20 hp models. This procedure ensures that the throttle plate is fully opened when the throttle linkage is in the wide-open throttle position. The engine cannot produce its rated power if the throttle plate is not opening fully or is rotated past full open.

WARNING
To prevent accidental starting, disconnect and ground the spark plug leads to the power head.

1. While rotating the propeller shaft, shift the outboard into FORWARD gear.

2A. *Tiller handle models*—Rotate the twist grip throttle to the wide-open position. The upper arm of the spark control shaft (B, **Figure 29**) must contact the power head stop (C, **Figure 29**) under the flywheel.

2B. *Remote control models*—Manually move the spark control shaft to the wide-open throttle position. The upper arm of the spark control shaft (B, **Figure 29**) must contact the power head stop (C, **Figure 29**) under the flywheel.

3. Look into the carburetor's intake throat and note the position of the throttle plate. The throttle plate must be exactly horizontal, allowing maximum air flow into the engine. If not, proceed to Step 4.

NOTE
If the throttle control rod (A, Figure 32) is removed from the pivot block (B, Figure 32), the pivot block's offset must face forward (toward the adjustment collar) when reas-

5

sembled. It is not necessary to remove the rod from the block to perform this adjustment.

4. If adjustment is necessary, loosen the screw on the adjustment collar (C, **Figure 32**). Move the collar toward the rear of the engine to open the throttle plate further. Move the collar toward the front of the engine to open the throttle plate less. Retighten the set screw, making sure the collar is positioned horizontally as shown in **Figure 32**.

5. Repeat Steps 2-3 to verify the adjustment. Readjust as necessary until the throttle plate is exactly horizontal when the spark control arm is held against its power head stop.

Maximum Spark Advance

1. Connect a suitable timing light (**Table 1**) to the top (cylinder No.1) spark plug lead.

> *CAUTION*
> *Do not run the engine without an adequate water supply and do not exceed 3000 rpm without an adequate load. Refer to **Safety Precautions** at the beginning of this chapter.*

2. Start the engine and allow it to warm to normal operating temperature.

> *CAUTION*
> *On remote control models, the gearcase linkage must be manually moved to the FORWARD gear position in the next step. Do not run the engine at wide-open throttle in NEUTRAL.*

3. Reduce the engine speed to idle and shift the gearcase into FORWARD gear.

> *NOTE*
> *Two timing scales may be present on the flywheel. If so, use the grid marked **ELEC CD** on electric start models or the grid marked **CD** on rope start models.*

4A. *Rope start models*—Point the timing light at the flywheel and timing pointer. The timing pointer is cast into the rope start housing and is located just above the spark control arm on the port side of the engine.

4B. *Electric start models*—Point the timing light at the flywheel and timing pointer. The timing pointer is part of the electric starter motor mounting bracket. Align the timing light to point to the center of the flywheel as shown in **Figure 33**.

5. Advance the throttle to the wide-open position and make sure the armature plate is rotated up against the rubber bumper on the maximum spark advance screw (A, **Figure 34**). Note the timing reading.

6A. *1995-1997 (EO-EU) 20 hp models*—The timing must be 33-35° BTDC at wide-open throttle (4500 rpm minimum).

6B. *1998 (EC) 20 hp models*—The timing must be 32-34° BTDC at wide-open throttle (4500 rpm minimum).

6C. *25 hp, 30 hp and 18 jet models*—The timing must be 29-31° BTDC at wide-open throttle (4500 rpm minimum on 25 hp, 28 hp and 18 jet or 5200 rpm on 30 hp).

> *WARNING*
> *To prevent accidental contact with the rotating flywheel, stop the motor prior to adjusting maximum spark advance.*

7. If adjustment is required, stop the engine and loosen the jam nut on the maximum advance screw (B, **Figure 34**). Turn the adjustment screw clockwise to retard timing; turn the screw counterclockwise to advance timing. Note that one turn of the screw equals approximately 1° timing change. Retighten the jam nut securely, then repeat Steps 2-6 as necessary.

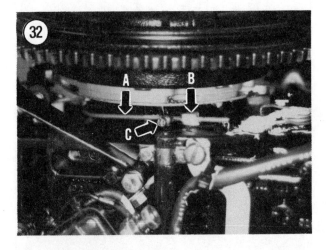

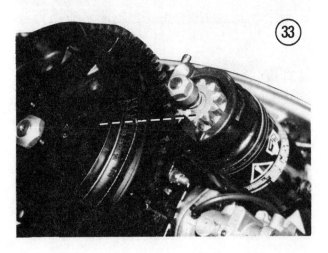

Idle Speed and
Idle Mixture Adjustments

For these adjustments to be accurate, the engine must be operated in a body of water with the correct propeller installed. For best results, the boat must be floating in the water with its movement unrestrained.

The idle mixture screw location depends on whether a TR or SV series carburetor is used. SV carburetors are easily identified by their black plastic top covers. TR carburetors (**Figure 35**, typical) are all metal.

CAUTION
*Do not run the engine without an adequate water supply and do not exceed 3000 rpm without an adequate load. Refer to **Safety Precautions** at the beginning of this chapter.*

1A. *TR carburetors*—Turn the idle mixture screw (**Figure 35**) clockwise until it is lightly seated. Do not force the

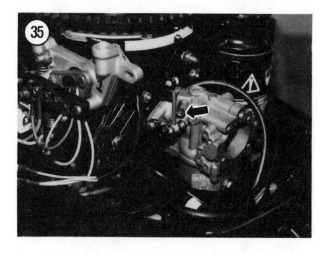

screw tightly into the carburetor, or the tip and the brass adaptor base will be damaged.

1B. *SV carburetors*—Turn the idle mixture screw (B, **Figure 31**) clockwise until it is lightly seated. Do not force the screw tightly into the carburetor, or the tip and the carburetor will be damaged.

2. Back out the mixture screw as follows:
   a. *20 hp models*—3 turns from a lightly seated position.
   b. *25 hp (TR carburetor)*—1-3/4 turns from a lightly seated position.
   c. *25 hp, 30 hp and 18 jet (SV carburetor)*—2-1/2 turns from a lightly seated position.

3. Connect an accurate shop tachometer to the No. 1 spark plug lead.

4. Start the engine and run it at approximately 2000 rpm until warmed to normal operating temperature.

5A. *Remote control models*—Hold the spark control arm against the idle speed screw and manually shift the gearcase into FORWARD gear. Adjust the idle speed screw (A, **Figure 29**) to obtain 675-725 rpm in FORWARD gear. Make sure the jam nut is tightened before proceeding.

5B. *Tiller handle models*—Rotate the twist grip throttle to its full idle position. Make sure the spark control arm is against the idle speed screw and shift the gearcase into FORWARD gear. Adjust the idle speed screw (A, **Figure 29**) to obtain 675-725 rpm in FORWARD gear. Make sure the jam nut is tightened before proceeding.

NOTE
Idle mixture cannot be properly set unless the carburetor is operating on the idle circuit. Setting the idle mixture at higher speeds will give inaccurate results. It may be necessary to switch back and forth between idle mixture adjustment and idle speed adjustment several times to achieve proper adjustment. Always adjust the idle speed last.

6. Slowly turn the idle mixture screw counterclockwise in 1/8 turn increments, pausing at least 15 seconds between turns. Continue this step until the idle speed decreases and the idle becomes rough due to an overly rich mixture. Note the position of the mixture screw slot.

7. Slowly turn the idle mixture screw clockwise in 1/8 turn increments, pausing at least 15 seconds between turns. The idle speed will gradually become smooth and speed will increase. Continue this step until the engine speed begins to slow again and/or misfires due to an excessively lean mixture. Note the position of the mixture screw slot.

5

8. Position the mixture screw at a midpoint between the settings of Step 6 and Step 7. See **Figure 36**. Then turn the screw counterclockwise (outward) 1/8 turn to slightly enrichen the mixture.

NOTE
It is a natural tendency to adjust the idle mixture too lean. Although the engine appears to run smoothly at idle, it will not accelerate without hesitation or continue to idle smoothly after wide-open throttle operation. If the engine does not perform satisfactorily in the following two steps, the idle mixture is most likely too lean.

CAUTION
On remote control models, the engine must be manually shifted into FORWARD gear before attempting to operate it at wide-open throttle in the following steps.

9. Run the engine at wide-open throttle (in FORWARD gear) for one minute to clear any fuel puddles from the crankcase. Then quickly reduce engine speed to idle. The engine will idle smoothly without stalling or spitting if the mixture is adjusted correctly. Readjust the mixture as necessary.

10. Quickly accelerate the engine to wide-open throttle and back to idle. The engine will accelerate cleanly without hesitation if the mixture is adjusted correctly. Readjust the mixture as necessary.

11. Make a final adjustment to the idle speed screw to obtain 675-725 rpm in FORWARD gear. Make sure the spark control arm is held against the idle speed screw during this procedure and that the jam nut is securely tightened when finished.

12. *Tiller handle models*—With the twist grip handle held in the full idle position, adjust the throttle cable anchor (**Figure 37**) to provide a slight amount of preload on the spark control arm. The spark control arm must be firmly held against the idle speed screw when the cable is correctly adjusted. If adjustment is necessary, proceed as follows:

  a. Remove the cotter pin and upper and lower washers securing the throttle cable to the bottom of the spark control arm. This is not an easy task. A pair of bent-tip needlenose pliers will make the job easier.

  b. Loosen the jam nut and rotate the throttle cable anchor bracket (**Figure 37**) as necessary to provide a slight amount of preload.

  c. Install the throttle cable to the spark control arm and secure it in place with the upper and lower washers and a new cotter pin. Bend both prongs of the cotter pin for a secure attachment.

  d. Verify the adjustment by moving the throttle to the wide-open throttle position and back to the full idle position. The spark control arm must firmly contact the idle speed screw.

  e. Readjust as necessary.

Wide-Open Throttle Speed Verification

1. Connect an accurate shop tachometer to a spark plug lead.

2. With the engine mounted on a boat, the boat unrestrained in the water and the engine running at wide-open throttle in FORWARD gear, record the maximum speed noted on the tachometer.

3A. *Except jet models*—If the maximum speed exceeds 5500 rpm on 20-28 hp or 5800 rpm on 30 hp, check the propeller for damage or incorrect application. Repair or replace the propeller as necessary.

3B. *18 jet models*—If the maximum speed exceeds 5500 rpm, check the jet pump impeller for damage, excessive impeller-to-liner clearance. Also, make sure the motor is not mounted too high on the transom, causing ventilation. See Chapter Nine.

4A. *Except jet models*—If the maximum speed does not reach 4500 rpm on 20-28 hp and 18 jet or 5200 rpm on 30 hp, check the propeller for incorrect application. If the correct propeller is installed, check the engine's power output using a test wheel as described in *Power output verification* at the end of Chapter Three. If the engine is not producing its rated power, start troubleshooting by

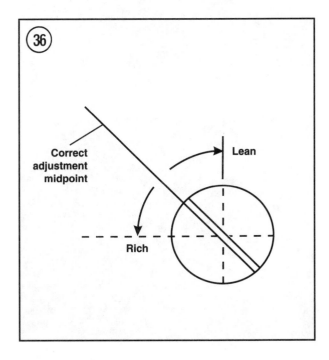

36

Correct
adjustment
midpoint

Lean

Rich

checking the cranking compression as described in Chapter Four.

4B. *18 jet models*—If the maximum speed does not reach 4500 rpm, the engine is not producing its rated power. Start troubleshooting by checking the cranking compression as described in Chapter Four.

25 AND 35 HP (THREE-CYLINDER) MODELS

Ignition timing is mechanically advanced and retarded during operation by rotating the optical sensor (timer base) via the throttle cable and associated linkage. Ignition timing is adjustable and must be verified and/or correctly adjusted as part of the synch and link procedure. Incorrect ignition timing can lead to power head failure from preignition and/or detonation (Chapter Three).

On remote control models, the throttle and shift cables must be disconnected from the power head (as described in Chapter Twelve) before beginning the synch and link procedure. When throttle or shift linkage operation is necessary, manually operate the appropriate control arm from the point that the control cable normally attaches.

Refer to **Table 7** for specifications. The synch and link procedure must be performed in the following order:

1. Preliminary adjustments.
2. Timing pointer verification.
3. Throttle plate synchronization.
4. Idle timing adjustment (idle speed and idle mixture adjustments).
5. Cam follower pickup point adjustment.

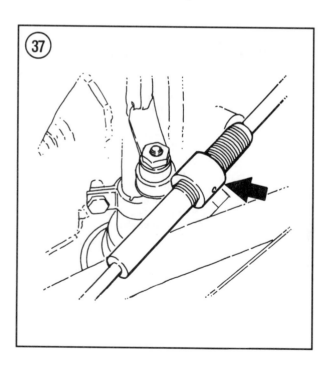

6. Maximum spark advance adjustment.
7. Wide-open throttle carburetor opening verification.
8. Neutral detent adjustment.
9. Wide-open throttle speed verification.

Preliminary Adjustments

The following adjustments must be made to correctly position the linkages. Failure to correctly position the linkages will give inaccurate and undesirable results. Some of these settings may be readjusted at a point later in the synch and link procedure.

The split lower cowls may be removed to gain direct access to the control cables.

1. Disconnect and ground the spark plug leads to the power head to prevent accidental starting.

2. *Remote control models*—Disconnect the throttle and shift cables from the power head as described in Chapter Twelve.

3. Adjust the idle stop screw (5, **Figure 38**) to set a dimension of 3/4 in. (19 mm) from the end of the screw (protective cap) to the face of its mounting boss as shown in **Figure 38**. Tighten the jam nut securely when finished.

4. *1995 and 1996 (EO and ED) models*—Adjust the timer base link (1, **Figure 38**) to a dimension of 2-1/2 in. (63.5 mm) as measured from the center of each ball socket as shown in **Figure 38**. Starting in 1997 (EU models), the timer base link is not adjustable.

5. *Tiller handle models*—Grasp the twist grip throttle control and turn its idle speed adjustment knob fully counterclockwise to the minimum idle speed position. Then rotate the twist grip throttle control to the full idle position.

6. *Tiller handle models*—Verify that the spark control arm (2, **Figure 38**) is securely held against the idle stop screw.

   a. If not, remove the throttle cable anchor bracket screw (8, **Figure 38**) and rotate the throttle cable anchor (7, **Figure 38**) around the threaded portion of the throttle cable until the anchor bracket is aligned with its mounting screw hole.

   b. Rotate the anchor bracket an additional turn (toward the rear of the engine) to slightly preload the cable.

   c. Secure the anchor bracket to the engine with its mounting screw. Make sure the flat washer is positioned between the anchor bracket and the engine. Tighten the mounting screw securely.

Timing Pointer Verification

The timing pointer's position may also be verified using a suitable dial indicator and spark plug hole adaptor. The timing pointer must point directly at the cast-in *TDC* mark on the flywheel when the No. 1 cylinder (top) piston is at the top of its travel (TDC).

1. Remove all of the spark plugs as described in Chapter Four.

2. Loosen the timing pointer mounting screw, then position the pointer at the center of its adjustment slot and retighten the screw. See **Figure 39**.

NOTE
*Never **turn** the flywheel counterclockwise.*

3. Turn the flywheel in a *clockwise* direction until the cast-in *TDC* mark on the flywheel is approximately 1 in. (25.4 mm) past the timing pointer.

4. Install OMC piston stop tool (part No. 384887) into the No. 1 spark plug hole. Screw the body of the tool in until it is bottomed, then turn the tool plunger inward until it contacts the piston. Secure the plunger in place by tightening the knurled locking ring. See **Figure 40**, typical.

5. Hold the piston firmly against the tool by applying counterclockwise turning pressure against the flywheel. While holding the flywheel in this position, place a mark on the flywheel directly adjacent to the timing pointer. Label this mark *A*.

6. Rotate the flywheel in a clockwise direction until the No. 1 piston contacts the piston stop tool again (almost a full turn). Hold the piston firmly against the tool by applying clockwise turning pressure against the flywheel, then place another mark on the flywheel directly in line and adjacent to the timing pointer. Label this mark *B*.

7. Remove the piston stop tool.

8. Measure the distance around the outer diameter of the flywheel between marks *A* and *B* using a flexible scale. A piece of paper or index card may also be cut or folded to match the distance between the *A* and *B* marks.

9. Place a third mark on the flywheel at the exact midpoint between the *A* and *B* marks. If using a piece of paper, simply fold the paper in half to achieve the midpoint. Label the third mark *C*. See **Figure 41**, typical.

10. If mark *C* is in direct alignment with the flywheel's cast-in TDC mark, the timing pointer is properly adjusted. If not, turn the flywheel in a clockwise direction to align mark *C* with the timing pointer.

NOTE
During Step 11, the flywheel's position cannot be disturbed from where it was set in Step 10.

11. While holding the flywheel in this position, loosen the timing pointer screw and move the pointer into alignment

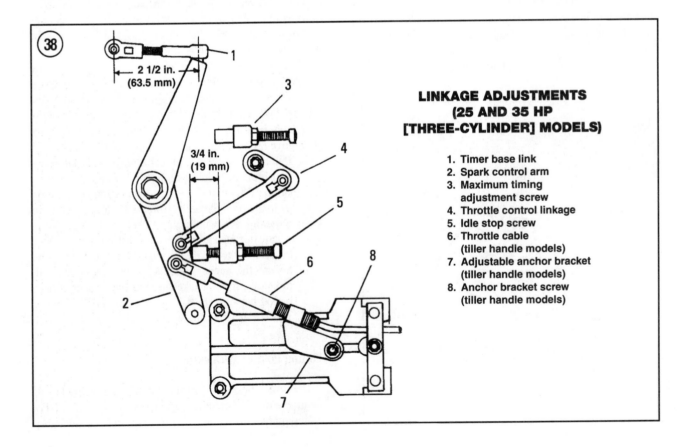

(38)

2 1/2 in.
(63.5 mm)

3/4 in.
(19 mm)

1
2
3
4
5
6
7
8

**LINKAGE ADJUSTMENTS
(25 AND 35 HP
[THREE-CYLINDER] MODELS)**

1. Timer base link
2. Spark control arm
3. Maximum timing
   adjustment screw
4. Throttle control linkage
5. Idle stop screw
6. Throttle cable
   (tiller handle models)
7. Adjustable anchor bracket
   (tiller handle models)
8. Anchor bracket screw
   (tiller handle models)

with the flywheel's cast-in TDC mark. Once the pointer is aligned, tighten the pointer screw securely.

Throttle Plate Synchronization

Since this engine uses three separate carburetors, they must be synchronized to open and close at exactly the same time.

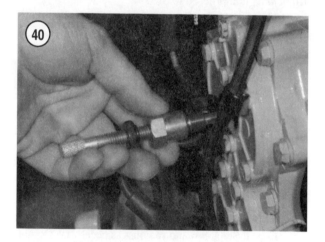

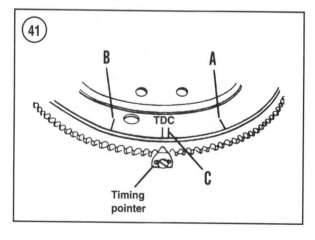

1. Remove the carburetor's air intake cover.

2. Using a 5/64 in. ball hex screwdriver, loosen the cam follower adjustment screw in a counterclockwise direction until an air gap is present between the cam and cam follower. The adjustment screw is located between the port fuel pump and the middle carburetor, below the throttle cam (**Figure 42**).

3A. *1995 and 1996 (EO and ED) models*—Loosen the adjustment screw on each of the center-to-upper and center-to-lower carburetor linkages using a No. 20 Torx screwdriver.

3B. *1997-2003 (EU-ST) models*—Loosen the linkage adjustment screw on the port side of each of the upper and lower carburetor's throttle shafts using a standard slotted screwdriver. See A, **Figure 43**.

5

4. Open the throttle plates and allow them to snap closed. Visually verify that each throttle plate is completely closed.

5A. *1995 and 1996 (EO and ED) models*—Apply a *slight* amount of downward pressure to the lower carburetor's linkage, then tighten its adjustment screw securely. Do not apply pressure to the large, plastic, main body of the linkage connector attached to the center carburetor.

5B. *1997-2003 (EU-ST) models*—Apply a *slight* amount of upward pressure to the lower carburetor's linkage arm, then tighten its adjustment screw securely. Do not apply pressure to the carburetor's throttle shaft. Repeat this procedure for the upper carburetor's link arm.

6. Open and close the throttle plates using the cam follower on the starboard side of the middle carburetor. Visually verify that all throttle plates are opening and closing at the same time and that all completely close. Readjust as necessary.

7. When finished, install the spark plugs as described in Chapter Four.

Idle Timing Adjustment

Adjusting the idle timing is in effect, setting the idle speed. If the engine is being used in a normal application, setting the idle timing to 4° ATDC (after top dead center) will normally provide an idle speed of 700-800 rpm when in forward gear.

For these specifications to provide the desired results, the boat must be floating in the water with its movement unrestrained and the correct propeller must be installed.

In unusual conditions, the idle timing can be adjusted (within reason) to provide a satisfactory idle speed. Advancing the idle timing will increase the idle speed. Before doing so, make sure that the carburetor idle mixture screws are correctly adjusted (as described in the following section) and that the engine is reaching operating temperature (Chapter Three).

It should not be necessary to retard the timing to decrease the idle speed. If the engine idles too fast, check for an intake system air leak. Also, make sure the carburetor throttle plate(s) are fully closing.

On 1995 and 1996 (EO and ED) models, adjust the idle timing by changing the length of the timer base link (1, **Figure 38**).

On 1997-2003 (EU-ST) models, adjust the idle timing by turning the idle stop screw (5, **Figure 38**) in or out. The idle stop screw was adjusted to 3/4 in. (19 mm) during the preliminary adjustments. Turn the screw inward to advance the idle timing and turn the screw outward to retard the idle timing. Step 6 of the *Preliminary Adjustments*

must again be verified if the idle stop screw's position is changed in this procedure.

To set the idle timing (and the idle speed) proceed as follows:

1. Start the engine and allow it to warm to operating temperature.

2. Stop the engine and disconnect the temperature switch's white/black lead at its bullet (or two-pin Amphenol) connector. See Chapter Three.

3. Connect a suitable jumper lead between the ignition module side of the white/black lead and a good engine ground. This will disable the ignition system's QuikStart program.

4. Attach a suitable timing light and shop tachometer to the No. 1 spark plug lead.

5. Start the engine, make sure the spark control arm (2, **Figure 38**) is held against the idle stop screw and shift the gearcase into FORWARD gear.

6. Aim the timing light at the timing pointer and flywheel (**Figure 39**). Note the timing and tachometer reading. The timing must read 4° ATDC and the engine speed must be 700-800 rpm. If so, proceed to *Cam Follower Pickup Adjustment*. If not, proceed to Step 7.

7A. *1995 and 1996 (EO and ED) models*—If the timing reading is incorrect, stop the engine.

   a. Remove the timer base link (1, **Figure 38**) from the spark control lever using a ball socket remover, such as OMC part No. 342226 (or equivalent).

   b. Turn the ball socket clockwise (lengthen the link) to advance the timing. Each complete turn advances timing approximately 1/2°.

   c. Turn the ball socket counterclockwise (shorten the link) to retard the timing. Each complete turn retards timing approximately 1/2°.

   d. Reconnect the timer base link to the spark control lever using a ball socket installer, such as OMC part No. 342225 (or equivalent).

   e. Repeat Steps 5-6 and readjust as necessary. Do not proceed until the timing is 4° ATDC.

7B. *1997-2003 (EU-ST) models*—If the timing reading is incorrect, stop the engine.

   a. Loosen the jam nut and adjust the idle stop screw (5, **Figure 38**) to correct the ignition timing.

   b. Turn the screw clockwise (inward) to advance the timing.

   c. Turn the screw counterclockwise (outward) to retard the timing.

   d. Tighten the jam nut and repeat Steps 5-6. Readjust as necessary. Do not proceed until the timing is 4° ATDC.

   e. *Tiller handle models*—Repeat Step 6 of the *Preliminary Adjustments* to make sure the throttle cable returns the spark lever to the idle stop screw.

8. Once correct timing is verified, observe the tachometer while the engine is idling in FORWARD gear with the spark control lever held against the idle stop screw.

a. If the engine speed is between 700-800 rpm and idle quality is acceptable, proceed to *Cam Follower Pickup Adjustment.*

b. If the idle quality is not acceptable, adjust the idle mixture screws as described in the next section.

c. If the idle quality is acceptable, but the idle speed is too high, make sure the correct propeller is installed, all of the carburetor throttle plates are closed and that the boat is being operated under normal conditions. If the engine still idles too fast, check the intake system for air leaks. Items to check include the intake manifold gaskets, carburetor base gaskets or crankcase seals. Also, check for loose or damaged primer and recirculation lines.

d. If the idle quality is acceptable, but the idle speed is too low and the engine does not suffer from any apparent defects, the idle timing may be advanced to increase the engine idle speed. Do not advance the timing more than necessary to bring the idle speed within specification. To advance the timing, follow the instructions in Step 7. The new timing figure must be recorded for later reference.

Idle mixture adjustments

For these adjustments to be accurate, the engine must be operated in a body of water with the correct propeller installed. For best results, the boat must be floating in the water with its movement unrestrained.

If the engine idle speed is acceptable, do not attempt to adjust the idle mixture. Perform this procedure only if the carburetors have been rebuilt, the mixture screws have been tampered with or if the idle quality is unsatisfactory.

The idle mixture on each carburetor must be individually set. When adjusting the idle mixture, attempt to keep all of the mixture screw settings as close to each other as possible. Some variation is normal, however. Try to turn each screw (in sequence) equal amounts in the same direction, noting that clockwise rotation leans the air/fuel mixture and counterclockwise rotation enrichens the air/fuel mixture. If it seems impossible to correctly adjust the idle mixture, try resetting all of the carburetors' mixture screws to their initial setting (Step 1) and start over.

> *CAUTION*
> *Do not run the engine without an adequate water supply and do not exceed 3000 rpm without an adequate load. Refer to **Safety Precautions** at the beginning of this chapter.*

1A. *All 1995 (EO) models and 1996 (ED) models with model numbers ending in C*—Adjust each idle mixture screw (B, **Figure 43**) to provide a dimension of 0.350 in. (8.9 mm) between the top cover and the underside of the screw head (simply measure the length of the idle mixture screw's spring).

1B. *1996 (ED) models with model numbers ending in G and all 1997-2003 (EU-ST) models*—Adjust each idle mixture screw (B, **Figure 43**) to provide a dimension of 0.390 in. (9.9 mm) between the top cover and the underside of the screw head (simply measure the length of the idle mixture screw's spring).

2. Connect an accurate shop tachometer to the No. 1 spark plug lead.

3. Start the engine and run it at approximately 2000 rpm until warmed to normal operating temperature.

4A. *Remote control models*—Hold the spark control arm (2, **Figure 38**) against the idle stop screw (5, **Figure 38**) and manually shift the gearcase into FORWARD gear. Adjust the idle timing/idle speed as described in the previous section. The engine must be idling at approximately 700-800 rpm in FORWARD gear before continuing.

4B. *Tiller handle models*—Rotate the twist grip throttle to its full idle position. Make sure the spark control arm is against the idle speed screw and shift the gearcase into FORWARD gear. Adjust the idle timing/idle speed as described in the previous section. The engine must be idling at approximately 700-800 rpm in FORWARD gear before continuing.

> *NOTE*
> *Idle mixture cannot be properly set unless the carburetor is operating on the idle circuit. Setting the idle mixture at higher speeds will give inaccurate results. It may be necessary to switch back and forth between idle mixture adjustment and idle timing/speed adjustment several times to achieve proper adjustment. Always adjust the idle timing/speed last.*

5. Slowly turn each idle mixture screw (B, **Figure 43**) counterclockwise in 1/8 turn increments, pausing at least 15 seconds between turns. Continue this step until the idle speed decreases and idle becomes rough due to an overly rich mixture. Note the position of each mixture screw's slot.

6. Slowly turn each idle mixture screw clockwise in 1/8 turn increments, pausing at least 15 seconds between turns. The idle speed will gradually become smooth and speed will increase. Continue this step until the engine speed begins to slow again and/or misfires due to an excessively lean mixture. Note the position of each mixture screw's slot.

5

7. Position each mixture screw at the midpoint of the settings achieved in Step 5 and Step 6. See **Figure 44**. Then turn each screw counterclockwise (outward) 1/8 turn to slightly enrichen the mixture.

> *NOTE*
> *It is a natural tendency to adjust the idle mixture too lean. Although the engine appears to run smoothly at idle, it will not accelerate without hesitation or continue to idle smoothly after wide-open throttle operation. If the engine does not perform satisfactorily in the following two steps, the idle mixture is most likely too lean.*

> *CAUTION*
> *On remote control models, the engine must be manually shifted into FORWARD gear before attempting to operate it at wide-open throttle in the following steps.*

8. Run the engine at wide-open throttle (in FORWARD gear) for one minute to clear any fuel puddles from the crankcase. Then quickly reduce engine speed to idle. The engine will idle smoothly without stalling or spitting if the mixture is adjusted correctly. Readjust the mixture on each carburetor as necessary.

9. Quickly accelerate the engine to wide-open throttle and back to idle. The engine will accelerate cleanly without hesitation if the mixture is adjusted correctly. Readjust the mixture on each carburetor as necessary.

10. Make a final adjustment to the idle timing/idle speed as described in the previous section.

Cam Follower Pickup Point

The engine does not need to be running for this procedure. This adjustment synchronizes the throttle opening to the spark advance.

1. Locate the timing grid on the timer base (optical sensor) at the front of the engine, under the flywheel. It is necessary to remove the carburetor's air intake cover (if not already removed) to see the grid.

2. Hold the spark control arm (2, **Figure 38**) securely against the idle stop screw (5).

3. Using a fine-point marker or scribe, make a precise, narrow mark on the raised boss of the crankcase, directly aligned with the timer base mark that indicates the current idle timing setting.

4. Advance the spark control arm until the 0° mark is aligned with the scribed mark on the crankcase. Hold the linkage in this position and do not allow it to move.

5. Using a 5/64 in. ball hex screwdriver, adjust the throttle cam follower's adjustment screw until it just touches the

throttle cam. The throttle cam and follower are located between the port fuel pump and the middle carburetor (**Figure 42**).

6. Hold the spark control arm securely against the idle stop screw, then advance the arm until the 0° mark is again aligned with the scribed mark on the crankcase. Verify that the cam follower is just barely touching the throttle cam. Readjust as necessary.

Maximum Spark Advance

Since this engine uses an optical ignition system, the engine does not need to be running to set (or verify) the maximum spark advance. However, all previous adjustments must be correct or this procedure will not be accurate.

1. Move the spark control arm to the wide-open throttle position.

2. Observe the timer base timing grid and note which timing grid mark aligns with the mark scribed on the crankcase during *Cam Follower Pickup Point Adjustment*.

3A. *25 hp models*—The scribed mark on the crankcase must align with the 19-21° timing marks on the timer base grid.

3B. *35 hp models*—The scribed mark on the crankcase must align with the 21-23° timing marks on the timer base grid.

4. If the specified timing marks do not align with the scribed crankcase mark (when the spark control arm is held

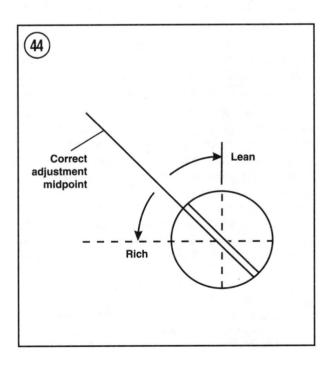

in the wide-open throttle position), loosen the jam nut on the maximum timing screw (3, **Figure 38**).

   a. To advance the timing, turn the screw clockwise (inward). Each complete turn advances the timing approximately 2°.

   b. To retard the timing, turn the screw counterclockwise (outward). Each complete turn advances the timing approximately 2°.

   c. Cycle the spark control arm through its full range of travel several times. Make sure the specified timing marks align each time the throttle is advanced to the wide-open throttle position.

   d. Tighten the jam nut securely when finished.

Wide-Open Throttle Carburetor Opening Verification

Although the wide-open throttle opening is not adjustable, it must be checked to be sure that all throttle linkage is in good condition and operating correctly.

1. Remove the air intake cover.

2. Hold the spark control arm in the wide-open throttle position. Look into the carburetors and note the throttle plate positions.

3. If the plates are not fully open (exactly horizontal), check all throttle linkage for mechanical binding, corrosion, obstructions or incorrect assembly. Correct any defects noted.

Neutral Detent Adjustment

It may prove easiest to remove the starboard side of the split lower engine cowl to gain access to the shift lever (A, **Figure 45**) for this procedure.

1. Disconnect and ground the spark plug leads to the engine to prevent accidental starting.

2. *Tiller handle models*—Disconnect the shift linkage from the engine shift lever.

3. Manually move the shift lever to the true NEUTRAL position. This will be the exact center of total shift linkage travel from full FORWARD to full REVERSE gear engagements. Always rotate the propeller when shifting the gearcase. Once in NEUTRAL, the propshaft must rotate freely in both directions.

4. Loosen the two neutral detent screws (B, **Figure 45**) on the shift lever arm.

5. Carefully locate the center of play in the shift lever arm without disturbing the neutral detent cam. Make a mark at each of the forward and rearward limits of shift lever free play on the detent cam.

6. Position the shift lever arm at the midpoint of the free play marks. Hold the shift lever in this position and tighten the two neutral detent screws. Tighten the screws to 60-84 in.-lb. (6.8-9.5 N•m).

7A. *Tiller handle models*—Reconnect the shift linkage to the shift lever (A, **Figure 45**).

7B. *Remote control models*—Reconnect and adjust the throttle and shift cables as described in Chapter Twelve.

Wide-Open Throttle Speed Verification

1. Connect an accurate shop tachometer to a spark plug lead.

2. With the engine mounted on a boat, the boat unrestrained in the water and the engine running at wide-open throttle in FORWARD gear, record the maximum speed noted on the tachometer.

3. If the maximum speed exceeds 5800 rpm, check the propeller for damage or incorrect application. Repair or replace the propeller as necessary.

4. If the maximum speed does not reach 5200 rpm, check the propeller for incorrect application. If the correct propeller is installed, check the engine's power output using a test wheel as described in *Power output verification* at the end of Chapter Three. If the engine is not producing its rated power, start troubleshooting by checking the cranking compression as described in Chapter Four.

5

40-50 HP (TWO-CYLINDER), 28 JET AND 35 JET MODELS

Ignition timing is mechanically advanced and retarded during operation by rotating the sensor coils (timer base assembly) via the throttle cable and associated linkage. Ignition timing is adjustable and must be verified and/or correctly adjusted as part of the synch and link procedure. Incorrect ignition timing can lead to power head failure from preignition and/or detonation (Chapter Three).

On remote control models, the throttle and shift cables must be disconnected from the power head (as described in Chapter Twelve), before beginning the synch and link procedure. When throttle or gearshift operation is necessary, manually operate the appropriate linkage from the point that the control cable normally attaches.

Refer to **Table 8** for specifications. The synch and link procedure must be performed in the following order:
1. Preliminary adjustments.
2. Throttle plate synchronization.
3. Cam follower pickup point adjustment.
4. Idle speed and idle mixture adjustments.
5. Throttle control rod adjustment.
6. Wide-open throttle stop adjustment.
7. Neutral detent adjustment and control cable installation.
8. Maximum spark advance verification/adjustment.
9. Wide-open throttle speed verification.

Preliminary Adjustments

The following adjustments must be made to correctly position the linkages. Failure to correctly position the linkages will give inaccurate and undesirable results. Some of these settings may be readjusted at a point later in the synch and link procedure. Disregard the two arrows cast into the throttle lever's roller slot (**Figure 46**) as they serve no function on these engines.

The split lower cowls may be removed to gain more direct access to the control cables.

1. Disconnect and ground the spark plug leads to the power head to prevent accidental starting.

2A. *Remote control models*—Disconnect the throttle and shift cables from the power head as described in Chapter Twelve.

2B. *Tiller handle models*—Disconnect the throttle cable from the throttle lever. To remove the locking clip, grasp the bent end of the locking clip with needlenose pliers and pull it outward toward the looped end of the clip.

3. Adjust the idle speed screw (1, **Figure 46**) to set a dimension of 1/2 in. (12.7 mm) as shown in A, **Figure 46**. Tighten the jam nut securely when finished.

NOTE
To prevent damage to the control linkage and components when disconnecting and connecting ball sockets, use suitable tools such as ball socket remover (part No. 342226) and ball socket installer (part No. 342225).

4. Carefully disconnect the throttle control rod (2, **Figure 46**) ball link from the throttle cam (3, **Figure 46**).

NOTE
Refer to Chapter Three for charging system identification.

5A. *40 hp rope start, 28 jet and 48 Special models*—Adjust the timer base link (4, **Figure 46**) to a dimension of 2 in. (50.8 mm) as measured from the center of each ball socket

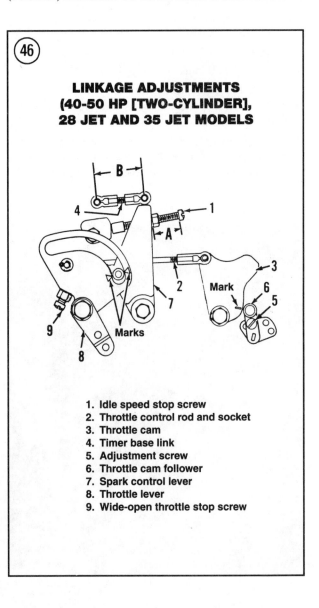

LINKAGE ADJUSTMENTS (40-50 HP [TWO-CYLINDER], 28 JET AND 35 JET MODELS

1. Idle speed stop screw
2. Throttle control rod and socket
3. Throttle cam
4. Timer base link
5. Adjustment screw
6. Throttle cam follower
7. Spark control lever
8. Throttle lever
9. Wide-open throttle stop screw

as shown in B, **Figure 46**. Disconnect and adjust only the *forward* link.

5B. *40 hp electric start, 50 hp and 35 jet*—Adjust the timer base link (4, **Figure 46**) to a dimension of 2-1/2 in. (63.5 mm) as measured from the center of each ball socket as shown in B, **Figure 46**. Disconnect and adjust only the *forward* link.

Throttle Plate Synchronization

Since these engines use two separate carburetors, they must be synchronized to open and close at exactly the same time.

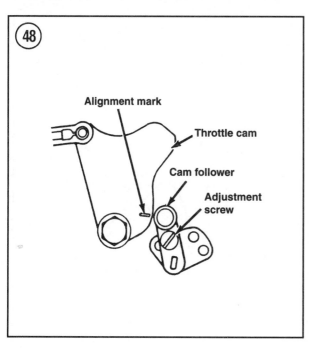

Alignment mark

Throttle cam

Cam follower

Adjustment screw

1. Loosen the throttle cam follower adjustment screw (5, **Figure 46**) and move the cam follower away from the throttle cam.

2. Loosen the linkage arm adjustment screw (A, **Figure 47**) on the upper carburetor.

3. Open the throttle plates and allow them to snap closed. If necessary, visually verify that each throttle plate is completely closed by removing the air intake cover and looking into each carburetor's bore.

4. Apply a *slight* amount of upward pressure to the upper carburetor's linkage arm (B, **Figure 47**), then tighten its adjustment screw securely. Do not apply pressure to the carburetor's throttle shaft.

5. Open and close the throttle plates using the cam follower on the starboard side of the lower carburetor. Verify that both throttle plates open and close at exactly the same time. Readjust as necessary.

Cam Follower Pickup Point Adjustment

1. Loosen the throttle cam follower adjustment screw (**Figure 48**) on the lower carburetor.

2. Rotate the throttle cam and cam follower roller toward each other until they contact. With the cam and roller touching each other and the carburetor throttle valves fully closed, continue to rotate the cam and roller (together) to align the mark on the throttle cam with the center of the cam follower roller, then tighten the adjustment screw securely.

3. When finished, install the spark plugs as described in Chapter Four.

Idle Speed Adjustments

Adjust the idle timing to correctly set idle speed. If the engine is used in a normal application, setting the idle speed to 775-825 rpm in FORWARD gear will normally result in an idle timing reading of 0-2° ATDC.

For these specifications to provide the desired results, the boat must be floating in the water with its movement unrestrained and the correct propeller installed.

To set the idle speed (and the idle timing), proceed as follows:

1. Start the engine and allow it to warm to operating temperature.

2. Attach a suitable timing light and shop tachometer to the No. 1 spark plug lead.

3. Start the engine, make sure the idle speed screw (1, **Figure 46**) is held against the power head stop, then shift the gearcase into FORWARD GEAR.

4. Loosen the idle speed screw's jam nut and adjust the screw to provide an idle speed of 775-825 rpm in FOR-

WARD GEAR. Make sure the idle speed screw is held against the power head stop at all times. Tighten the jam nut when finished.

5. Aim the timing light at the timing pointer and flywheel. The timing pointer is located at the top, center of the intake manifold, just behind the base of the top carburetor. Note the timing reading. The timing must read 0-2° ATDC with the engine idling at 775-825 rpm in FORWARD gear (with the idle speed screw against its stop). If so, proceed to *Throttle Control Rod Adjustment*. If not, proceed to Step 6.

6. If the idle timing is not within specification, verify that the engine is reaching operating temperature (Chapter Three), the boat is unrestrained in a body of water and the gearcase is in FORWARD gear with the correct propeller installed. If these conditions are satisfactory, then proceed as follows:

    a. If the idle quality is not acceptable (engine does not idle smoothly), adjust the idle mixture screws as described in the next section.

    b. If the idle quality is acceptable, but the idle timing is not within specification, check the mechanical condition of the power head by performing a cranking compression test as described in Chapter Four.

    c. If the compression test is satisfactory, but the idle timing is still not within specification, check the intake system for air leaks. Check the intake manifold gaskets, carburetor base gaskets and crankcase seals. Also, check for loose or damaged primer, balance and recirculation lines.

    d. If the idle quality is acceptable and the engine does not suffer from any apparent defects, the idle timing may be adjusted as necessary to achieve the specified idle speed. Do not adjust the timing any more than necessary to obtain 775-825 rpm in FORWARD gear.

Idle mixture adjustments

For these adjustments to be accurate, the engine must be operated in a body of water with the correct propeller installed. For best results, the boat must be floating in the water with its movement unrestrained.

If the engine idles satisfactory, do not attempt to adjust the idle mixture. Perform this procedure only if the carburetors have been rebuilt, the mixture screws have been tampered with, or if the idle quality is unsatisfactory.

The idle mixture on each carburetor must be individually set. When adjusting the idle mixture, attempt to keep both mixture screws settings as close to each other as possible. Some variation is normal, however. Try to turn each screw (in sequence) equal amounts in the same direction; noting

that clockwise rotation leans the air/fuel mixture and counterclockwise rotation enrichens the air/fuel mixture. If it seems impossible to correctly adjust the idle mixture, try resetting all of the carburetors mixture needles to their initial setting (Step 1) and starting over.

> *CAUTION*
> *Do not run the engine without an adequate water supply and do not exceed 3000 rpm without an adequate load. Refer to **Safety Precautions** at the beginning of this chapter.*

1. Turn each carburetor's idle mixture screw (**Figure 49**, typical) clockwise until it is lightly seated. Do not force the screw tightly into the carburetor or the tip and the carburetor will be damaged.

2. Back out each mixture screw to specification.

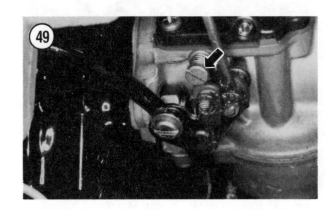

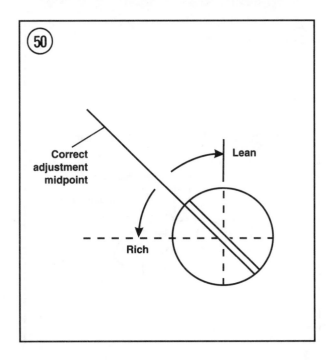

a. *40 hp and 28 jet*—2-1/2 turns from a lightly seated position.

b. *48 hp, 50 hp and 35 jet*—3-1/2 turns from a lightly seated position.

3. Connect an accurate shop tachometer to the No. 1 spark plug lead.

4. Start the engine and allow it to warm to normal operating temperature.

5. Hold the idle stop screw (1, **Figure 46**) against its power head stop and manually shift the gearcase into FORWARD gear. Temporarily adjust the idle speed as described in the previous section. The engine must be idling at 775-825 rpm in FORWARD gear before continuing.

> *NOTE*
> *Idle mixture cannot be properly set unless the carburetor is operating on the idle circuit. Setting the idle mixture at higher speeds will give inaccurate results. It may be necessary to switch back and forth between idle mixture adjustment and idle timing/speed adjustment several times to achieve proper adjustment. Always adjust the idle timing/speed last.*

6. Slowly turn each idle mixture screw (**Figure 49**, typical) counterclockwise in 1/8 turn increments, pausing at least 15 seconds between turns. Continue this step until the idle speed decreases and idle becomes rough due to an overly rich mixture. Note the position of each mixture screw's slot.

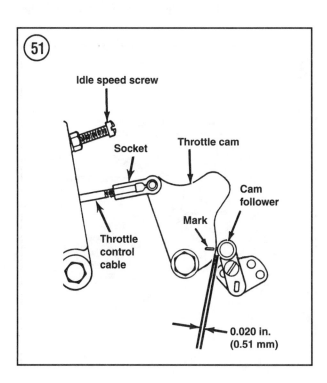

7. Slowly turn each idle mixture screw clockwise in 1/8 turn increments, pausing at least 15 seconds between turns. The idle speed will gradually become smooth and speed will increase. Continue this step until the engine speed begins to slow again and/or misfires due to an excessively lean mixture. Note the position of each mixture screw's slot.

8. Position each mixture screw at the midpoint of the settings achieved in Step 5 and Step 6. See **Figure 50**. Then turn each screw counterclockwise (outward) 1/8 turn to slightly enrichen the mixture.

> *NOTE*
> *It is a natural tendency to adjust the idle mixture too lean. Although the engine appears to run smoothly at idle, it will not accelerate without hesitation or continue to idle smoothly after wide-open throttle operation. If the engine does not perform satisfactorily in the following two steps, the idle mixture is most likely too lean.*

> *CAUTION*
> *The engine must be shifted into FORWARD gear before attempting to operate it at wide-open throttle in the following steps.*

9. Run the engine at wide-open throttle (in FORWARD gear) for one minute to clear any fuel puddles from the crankcase. Then quickly reduce engine speed to idle. The engine will idle smoothly without stalling or spitting if the mixture is adjusted correctly. Readjust the mixture on each carburetor as necessary.

10. Quickly accelerate the engine to wide-open throttle and back to idle. The engine will accelerate cleanly without hesitation if the mixture is adjusted correctly. Readjust the mixture on each carburetor as necessary.

11. Make a final adjustment to idle speed as described in the previous section.

Throttle Control Rod Adjustment

1. Disconnect and ground the spark plug leads to the power head to prevent accidental starting.

2. Hold the idle speed screw (1, **Figure 46**) against its power head stop.

3. Hold the throttle control rod (2, **Figure 46**) ball socket over the throttle cam's ball. Do not snap the socket onto the ball, just hold it against (over) the ball.

4. With the idle speed screw against its stop, adjust the rod's ball socket to obtain a clearance of 0.020 in. (0.51 mm) clearance between the throttle cam and cam follower as shown in **Figure 51**.

5

5. Snap the socket onto the throttle cam, then recheck the 0.020 in. (0.51 mm) clearance. Readjust as necessary.

Wide-Open Throttle Stop Adjustment

1. Disconnect the spark plug leads and ground them to the power head.

2. Hold the throttle lever arm in the wide-open throttle position. Make sure the wide-open throttle stop adjustment screw (9, **Figure 46**) is against its power head stop.

3. Note the position of each carburetor's shaft roll pins. The roll pins must be exactly vertical as shown in **Figure 52**. If one carburetor's roll pin is in a different position from the other, the throttle plates are incorrectly synchronized. Repeat *Throttle Plate Synchronization*.

4. If both roll pins are not vertical, loosen the jam nut on the wide-open throttle stop screw and adjust the screw as necessary to position the roll pins vertical (with the wide-open throttle stop screw against its power head stop).

5. Securely tighten the jam nut, then repeat steps 2-3. Readjust as necessary.

Neutral Detent Adjustment and Control Cable Installation

This procedure covers adjustments for propeller-driven models only. Refer to *Jet Drive Models* in Chapter Nine for adjustment procedures on jet drive models.

It may prove easiest to remove the starboard side of the split lower engine cowl to gain access to the shift lever for this procedure. The shift lever is located just below the mounting point for the throttle cable adjustable anchor and can be identified by the two hex head screws on its upper half and the metal link rod attached to its lower half. An illustration of the shift lever is located in Chapter Nine, in the appropriate *Gearcase Removal/Installation* section.

1. Disconnect the spark plug leads and ground them to the power head.

2. *Tiller handle models*—Disconnect the shift linkage from the engine shift lever.

3. Loosen the two neutral detent screws on the shift lever arm.

4. Manually move the shift lever to the true NEUTRAL position. This is the exact center of total shift linkage travel from full FORWARD to full REVERSE gear engagements. Always rotate the propeller when shifting the gearcase. Once in NEUTRAL, the propshaft must rotate freely in both directions.

5. Make sure the neutral detent cam (located behind the engine shift lever) is in its neutral detent. Then carefully locate the center of the play in the shift lever arm, being

careful not to shift the lower gearcase out of its neutral detent.

6. Position the shift lever arm at the midpoint of the free play. Hold the shift lever in this position and tighten the two neutral detent screws. Tighten the screws to 60-84 in.-lb. (6.8-9.5 N•m).

7A. *Tiller handle models*—Reconnect the shift linkage to the shift lever, then install and adjust the throttle cable as described in the next section.

7B. *Remote control models*—Reconnect and adjust the throttle and shift cables as described in Chapter Twelve.

Throttle cable installation (tiller handle models)

1. Verify that the spark plug leads are still disconnected and grounded to the power head.

2. Grasp the twist grip throttle control and turn its idle speed adjustment knob fully counterclockwise to the minimum idle speed position. Then rotate the twist grip throttle control to the full idle position.

> *NOTE*
> *The tiller handle throttle cable must be installed in the throttle lever's upper hole. The lower hole is for remote control models. Using the wrong hole will prevent the throttle from fully opening and closing.*

3. Connect the throttle cable to the *upper* hole in the throttle lever (8, **Figure 46**) using the clevis pin and

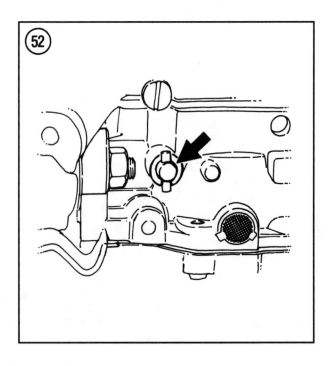

52

locking clip. Install the clip so it is parallel to the cast rib on the throttle lever (pointing fore and aft).

4. While holding the twist grip throttle control in the minimum idle position, pull on the throttle cable casing to remove any slack and position the idle speed screw against its stop. Then rotate the throttle cable anchor (7, **Figure 38**, similar) around the threaded portion of the throttle cable until the anchor bracket is aligned with its mounting screw hole.

5. Rotate the anchor bracket an additional two turns (toward the rear of the engine) to slightly preload the cable.

6. Secure the anchor bracket to the engine with its mounting screw. Make sure the flat washer is positioned between the anchor bracket and the engine. Tighten the mounting screw to 36 in.-lb. (4.1 N•m).

7. Open and close the throttle with the twist grip throttle several times, making sure the idle speed screw contacts its stop when the twist grip is in the minimum idle speed position. Readjust the cable anchor bracket's position as necessary.

8. Reconnect the spark plug leads when finished.

Maximum Spark Advance

1. Connect a suitable timing light to the top (No.1 cylinder) spark plug lead.

CAUTION
Do not run the engine without an adequate water supply and do not exceed 3000 rpm without an adequate load. Refer to Safety Precautions at the beginning of this chapter.

2. Start the engine and allow it to warm to normal operating temperature.

CAUTION
The gearcase linkage must be manually moved to the FORWARD gear position in the next step. Do not run the engine at wide-open throttle in NEUTRAL.

3. Reduce the engine speed to idle and shift the gearcase into FORWARD gear.

4. Point the timing light at the flywheel and timing pointer. The timing pointer is part of the intake manifold and is located at the front center of the engine. Align the timing light to point to the center of the flywheel through the timing pointer.

5. Advance the throttle to the wide-open position and make sure the wide-open throttle stop screw is against its power head stop. Note the timing reading.

6. The timing must be 18-20° BTDC at wide-open throttle (5000 rpm minimum).

WARNING
To prevent accidental contact with the rotating flywheel, stop the motor prior to adjusting maximum spark advance.

7. If adjustment is required, stop the engine and disconnect the timer base link's (4, **Figure 46**) forward socket from the spark control arm. Turn the socket clockwise (shortening the link) to retard timing; turn the socket counterclockwise (lengthening the link) to advance timing. Note that two turns of the socket equals approximately 1° timing change. Reconnect the timer base link to the spark control arm. Tighten the jam nut securely, then repeat Steps 2-6 as necessary.

8. If the timer base link's length is changed by more than two revolutions, it is necessary to readjust the *Idle speed* and *Throttle control rod* adjustments.

Wide-Open Throttle Speed Verification

1. Connect an accurate shop tachometer to a spark plug lead.

2. With the engine mounted on a boat, the boat unrestrained in the water and the engine running at wide-open throttle in FORWARD gear, record the maximum speed noted on the tachometer.

3A. *Except jet drive models*—If the maximum speed exceeds 5500 rpm, check the propeller for damage or incorrect application. Repair or replace the propeller as necessary.

3B. *Jet models*—If the maximum speed exceeds 5500 rpm, check the jet pump impeller for damage, excessive impeller-to-liner clearance, or that the motor is mounted too high on the transom, causing ventilation. See Chapter Nine.

4A. *Except jet drive models*—If the maximum speed does not reach 4500 rpm, check the propeller for incorrect application. If the correct propeller is installed, check the engine's power output using a test wheel as described in *Power output verification* at the end of Chapter Three. If the engine is not producing its rated power, start troubleshooting by checking the cranking compression as described in Chapter Four.

4B. *Jet models*—If the maximum speed does not reach 4500 rpm, the engine is not producing its rated power. Start troubleshooting by checking the cranking compression as described in Chapter Four.

50-70 HP (THREE-CYLINDER) MODELS

Ignition timing is mechanically advanced and retarded during operation by rotating the sensor coils (timer base assembly) via the throttle cable and associated linkage. Ignition timing is adjustable and must be correctly adjusted

5

as part of the synch and link procedure. Incorrect ignition timing can lead to power head failure from preignition and/or detonation (Chapter Three).

On remote control models, the throttle and shift cables must be disconnected from the power head (as described in Chapter Twelve), before beginning the synch and link procedure. When throttle or gearshift operation is necessary, manually operate the appropriate linkage from the point that the control cable normally attaches.

The order and content of the synch and link procedure varies depending on whether the engine is a tiller handle or remote control model. Refer to **Table 9** for specifications.

On tiller handle models, the synch and link procedure *must* be performed in the following order:
1. Timing pointer verification.
2. Throttle cable adjustment.
3. Throttle plate synchronization.
4. Cam follower pickup point adjustment.
5. Idle timing (speed) and idle mixture adjustments.
6. Throttle control rod adjustment.
7. Wide-open throttle stop adjustment.
8. Maximum spark advance verification/adjustment.
9. Neutral detent adjustment.
10. Wide-open throttle speed verification.

On remote control models, the synch and link procedure *must* be performed in the following order.
1. Timing pointer verification.
2. Throttle plate synchronization.
3. Cam follower pickup point adjustment.
4. Throttle control rod adjustment.
5. Wide-open throttle stop adjustment.
6. Idle timing (speed) and idle mixture adjustments.
7. Maximum spark advance verification/adjustment.
8. Wide-open throttle speed verification.

Timing Pointer Verification

The timing pointer's position may also be verified using a suitable dial indicator and spark plug hole adaptor (**Table 1**). The timing pointer must point directly at the cast-in *T (TDC)* mark on the flywheel when the No. 1 cylinder (top) piston is at the top of its travel (TDC).

The timing pointer is part of the engine's cowling brace and is located on the top of the intake manifold at the front and centerline of the engine as shown in **Figure 53**.

1. Remove all of the spark plugs as described in Chapter Four.
2. *Remote control models*—Disconnect the throttle and shift cables from the power head as described in Chapter Twelve.

3. Loosen the timing pointer mounting screw, then position the pointer at the center of its adjustment slot and retighten the screw.

> *NOTE*
> *Never **turn** the flywheel counterclockwise. Also, two timing grids are present on the flywheel. As the flywheel is rotated clockwise, the first grid that appears is not used. Use only the second timing grid that appears as the flywheel is rotated clockwise.*

4. Turn the flywheel in a *clockwise* direction until the cast-in *T* mark (representing top dead center) on the flywheel's second timing grid is approximately 1-1/2 in. (38 mm) past the timing pointer.

5. Install OMC Piston Stop Tool (part No. 384887) into the No. 1 spark plug hole. Screw the body of the tool in until it is bottomed, then turn the tool plunger inward until it contacts the piston. Secure the plunger in place by tightening the knurled locking ring. See **Figure 54**, typical.

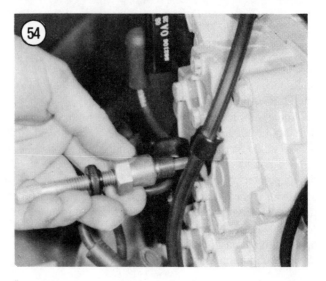

6. Hold the piston firmly against the tool by applying counterclockwise turning pressure against the flywheel. While holding the flywheel in this position, place a mark on the flywheel directly adjacent to the timing pointer. Label this mark *A*.

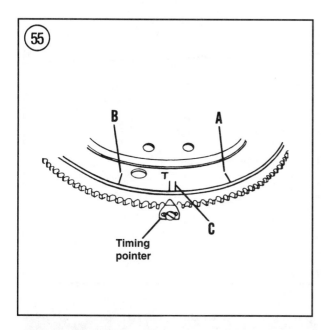

55

Timing
pointer

7. Rotate the flywheel in a clockwise direction until the No. 1 piston contacts the piston stop tool again (almost a full turn). Hold the piston firmly against the tool by applying clockwise turning pressure against the flywheel, then place another mark on the flywheel directly adjacent to the timing pointer. Label this mark *B*.

8. Remove the piston stop tool.

9. Measure the distance around the outer diameter of the flywheel between marks *A* and *B* using a flexible scale. A piece of paper or index card may also be cut or folded to match the distance between the *A* and *B* marks.

10. Place a third mark on the flywheel at the exact midpoint between the *A* and *B* marks. If using a piece of paper, simply fold the paper in half to achieve the midpoint. Label the third mark *C*. See **Figure 55**, typical.

11. If mark *C* is in direct alignment with the flywheel's cast-in T (TDC) mark, the timing pointer is properly adjusted. If not, turn the flywheel in a clockwise direction to align mark *C* with the timing pointer.

NOTE
Do not allow flywheel to move during Step 12.

12. While holding the flywheel in this position, loosen the timing pointer screw and move the pointer into alignment with the flywheel's cast-in T (TDC) mark. Once the pointer is aligned, tighten the pointer screw securely.

13. Reinstall the spark plugs as described in Chapter Four, but do not connect the spark plug leads at this time.

**Throttle Cable Adjustment
(Tiller Handle Models)**

This procedure ensures that the throttle cable can operate the throttle linkage through its full range of travel, ensuring that both idle and wide-open throttle can be reached.

1. Grasp the twist grip throttle control and turn its idle speed adjustment knob fully counterclockwise to the minimum idle speed position. Then rotate the twist grip throttle control to the full idle position.

2. Make sure the throttle cable mounting bracket is affixed to the power head using its most forward mounting hole. This will position the cable as far aft as possible.

3. Back out the idle speed and wide-open throttle stop screws until the ends of the screws are flush with the anchor block. See **Figure 56**.

4. Rotate the twist grip throttle to the wide-open throttle position.

5

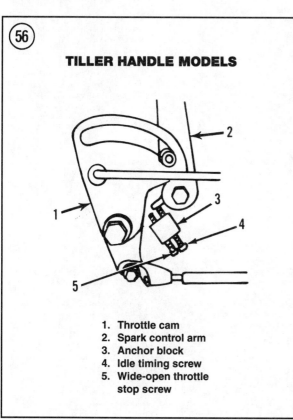

56

TILLER HANDLE MODELS

1. Throttle cam
2. Spark control arm
3. Anchor block
4. Idle timing screw
5. Wide-open throttle
stop screw

5. Measure the gap between the spark control cam follower (roller) and the end of the slot in the spark control cam (**Figure 57**).

6. Rotate the twist grip throttle to the minimum idle position and repeat Step 5, measuring the opposite end of the slot as shown in **Figure 58**.

7. The gap must be approximately 1/4 in. (6.3 mm) at each end of the slot, indicating the throttle cable's total travel is centered in the spark control arms slot. The actual dimension is not as important as the fact that the travel is centered.

8. If the travel is not centered, loosen the jam nut (**Figure 58**) and turn the knurled thumb wheel on the throttle cable as necessary to center the throttle cable's throw in the spark control arm's slot. Retighten the jam nut securely and repeat Steps 4-7.

Throttle Valve Synchronization

Since this engine uses three separate carburetors, they must be synchronized to open and close at exactly the same time.

1. Loosen the throttle cam follower adjustment screw (A, **Figure 59**) and move the cam follower roller away from the throttle cam.

2. Loosen the linkage arm adjustment screw (B, **Figure 59**) on the starboard side of each of the upper and lower carburetor's throttle shafts using a slotted screwdriver.

3. Open the throttle plates and allow them to snap closed. If necessary, visually verify that each throttle plate is

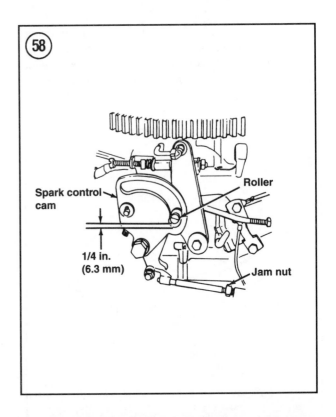

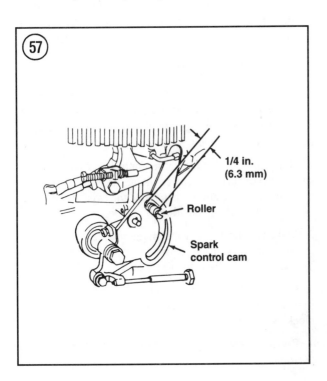

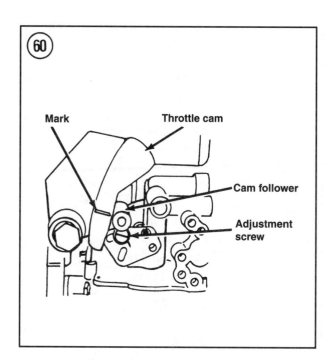

Mark   Throttle cam

Cam follower

Adjustment screw

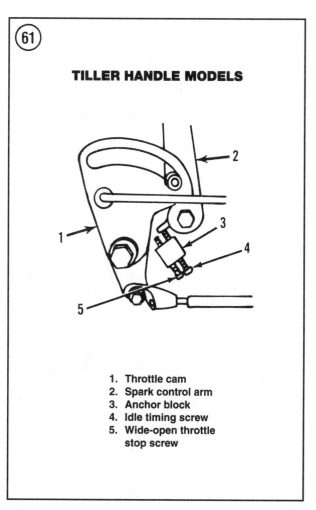

TILLER HANDLE MODELS

1. Throttle cam
2. Spark control arm
3. Anchor block
4. Idle timing screw
5. Wide-open throttle stop screw

completely closed by removing the air intake cover and looking into each carburetor's bore.

4. Apply a *slight* amount of upward pressure to the lower carburetor's linkage arm, then tighten its adjustment screw securely. Do not apply pressure to the carburetor's throttle shaft. Repeat this procedure for the upper carburetor's link arm.

5. Open and close the throttle plates using the cam follower on the starboard side of the middle carburetor. Verify that all throttle plates open and close at exactly the same time. Readjust as necessary.

Cam Follower Pickup
Point Adjustment

NOTE
To prevent damage to the control linkage and components when disconnecting and connecting ball sockets, use suitable tools such as ball socket remover (part No. 342226) and ball socket installer (part No. 342225).

1. Carefully disconnect the throttle control rod's ball socket link from the throttle cam.

2. Loosen the throttle cam follower adjustment screw (**Figure 60**) on the middle carburetor.

3. Rotate the throttle cam and cam follower roller toward each other until they contact. With the cam and roller touching each other and the carburetor throttle valves fully closed, continue to rotate the cam and roller (together) to align the mark on the throttle cam with the center of the cam follower roller, then tighten the adjustment screw securely. See **Figure 60**.

4. Attach a throttle shaft amplifier to the top carburetor's throttle shaft.

5. Slowly advance the throttle cam while observing the throttle amplifier. The mark on the throttle cam must align with the center of the cam follower roller just as the amplifier begins to move. If not, repeat Step 3.

Throttle Control
Rod Adjustment

1. *Tiller handle models* —Disconnect and ground the spark plug leads to the power head to prevent accidental starting.

2A. *Tiller handle models*—Rotate the twist grip throttle to the minimum idle speed position. Make sure the spark control arm (2, **Figure 61**) is against the idle timing screw (4, **Figure 61**).

2B. *Remote control models*—Hold the throttle arm (1, **Figure 62**) against its idle stop screw (2, **Figure 62**).

3. Hold the throttle control rod's ball socket over the throttle cam's ball as shown in **Figure 63**. Do not snap the socket onto the ball, just hold it against (over) the ball.

4. With the throttle arm against its stop, adjust the rod's ball socket to obtain a clearance of 0.010 in. (0.25 mm) clearance between the throttle cam and cam follower as shown in **Figure 63**.

5. Snap the socket onto the throttle cam, then recheck the 0.010 in. (0.25 mm) clearance. Readjust as necessary.

Wide-Open Throttle Stop Adjustment

1. Verify that the spark plug leads are disconnected and grounded to the power head to prevent accidental starting.

2A. *Tiller handle models*—Rotate the twist grip throttle to the wide-open throttle position. Make sure the throttle cam (1, **Figure 61**) is against the wide-open throttle stop adjustment screw (5, **Figure 61**).

2B. *Remote control models*—Hold the throttle control arm (1, **Figure 62**) in the wide-open throttle position. Make sure the lever is against the wide-open throttle stop adjustment screw (3, **Figure 62**).

3. Note the position of each carburetor's shaft roll pins. The roll pins must be exactly vertical as shown in **Figure 64**. If one carburetor's roll pin is in a different position from the other, the throttle plates are incorrectly synchronized. Repeat *Throttle Plate Synchronization.*

4. If both roll pins are not vertical, adjust the wide-open throttle stop screw as necessary to position the roll pins exactly vertical (with the spark control arm against the wide-open throttle stop screw).

5. Repeat Steps 2-3 to verify the adjustment.

6. *Remote control models*—Reinstall and adjust the throttle and shift cables as described in Chapter Twelve.

7. Reconnect the spark plug leads when finished.

Idle Timing (Idle Speed) Adjustment

Adjust the idle timing to set the correct idle speed. If the engine is used in a normal application, setting the idle timing to specification will normally provide an idle speed of 750-850 rpm when in forward gear.

For these specifications to provide the desired results, the boat must be floating in the water with its movement unrestrained and the correct propeller must be installed.

In unusual conditions, the idle timing can be adjusted (within reason) to provide a satisfactory idle speed. Advancing the idle timing will increase the idle speed. Before doing so, make sure that the carburetor idle mixture screws

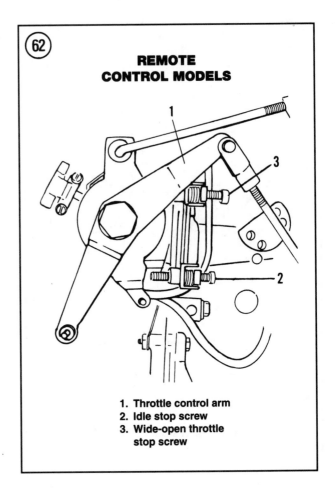

REMOTE CONTROL MODELS

1. Throttle control arm
2. Idle stop screw
3. Wide-open throttle stop screw

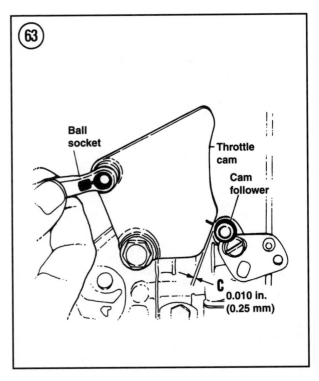

Ball socket

Throttle cam

Cam follower

C

0.010 in. (0.25 mm)

are correctly adjusted and that the engine is reaching operating temperature (Chapter Three).

It should not be necessary to retard the timing to decrease the idle speed. If the engine idles too fast, check for an intake system air leak and make sure the carburetor throttle plates are fully closing.

On tiller handle models, adjust the idle timing by changing the position of the idle timing screw (4, **Figure 61**).

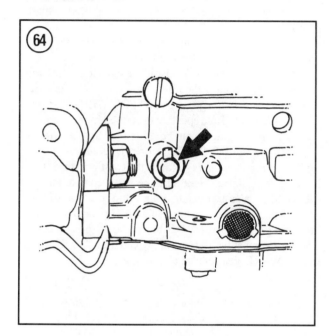

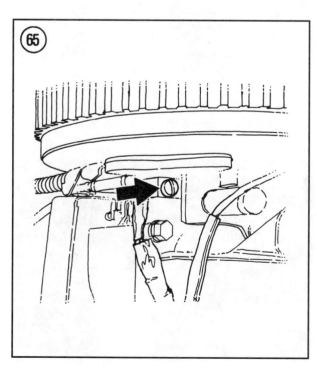

Turn the screw inward (clockwise) to advance the timing. Turn the screw outward (counterclockwise) to retard the timing.

On remote control models, adjust the idle timing by turning the timer base stop screw (**Figure 65**) in or out. Turn the screw inward (clockwise) to advance the idle timing and turn the screw outward (counterclockwise) to retard the idle timing.

To set the idle timing (and the idle speed) proceed as follows:

1. Reconnect the spark plug leads to the spark plugs.

2. Start the engine and allow it to warm to operating temperature. If the engine is not fully warmed, the Quik-Start program will advance the timing, causing the timing to be incorrectly adjusted.

3. Attach a suitable timing light and shop tachometer to the No. 1 spark plug lead.

4A. *Tiller handle models*—Rotate the twist grip throttle to the minimum idle speed position. Make sure the spark control arm (2, **Figure 61**) is against the idle timing screw (4, **Figure 61**).

4B. *Remote control models*—Hold the throttle arm (1, **Figure 62**) against its idle stop screw (2, **Figure 62**).

5. Aim the timing light at the timing pointer and flywheel. Note the timing and tachometer reading. The timing must read 7-9° ATDC on 50 hp models or 3-5° ATDC on 60-70 hp models, and the engine speed must be 750-850 rpm. If so, proceed to the next adjustment in the synch and link procedure. If not, proceed to Step 6.

6A. *Tiller handle models*—If the timing reading is incorrect, stop the engine.
    a. Adjust the idle timing screw (4, **Figure 61**) to correct the ignition timing.
    b. Turn the screw clockwise (inward) to advance the timing.
    c. Turn the screw counterclockwise (outward) to retard the timing.
    d. Repeat Steps 3-4. Readjust as necessary. Do not proceed until the timing is 7-9° ATDC on 50 hp models or 3-5° ATDC on 60-70 hp models.

6B. *Remote control models*—If the timing reading is incorrect, stop the engine.
    a. Adjust the timer base stop screw (**Figure 65**) to correct the ignition timing.
    b. Turn the screw clockwise (inward) to advance the timing.
    c. Turn the screw counterclockwise (outward) to retard the timing.
    d. Repeat Steps 3-4. Readjust as necessary. Do not proceed until the timing is 7-9° ATDC on 50 hp models or 3-5° ATDC on 60-70 hp models.

7. Once correct timing is verified, observe the tachometer as the engine is idling in FORWARD gear with the spark control lever held against the idle stop screw (or the twist grip throttle in the minimum idle position).

   a. If the engine speed is between 750-850 rpm and idle quality is acceptable, proceed to the next adjustment in the synch and link procedure.

   b. If the idle quality is not acceptable, adjust the idle mixture screws as described in the next section.

   c. If the idle quality is acceptable, but the idle speed is too high, make sure the correct propeller is installed, all of the carburetor throttle plates are closed and that the boat is being operated under normal conditions. If the engine still idles too fast, check the intake system for air leaks. Check the intake manifold gaskets, carburetor base gaskets or crankcase seals. Also, check for loose or damaged primer and recirculation lines.

   d. If the idle quality is acceptable, yet the idle speed is too low and the engine does not suffer from any apparent defects, the idle timing may be advanced to increase the engine idle speed. Do not advance the timing any more than necessary to bring the rpm within specifications. To advance the timing, follow the procedure as described in Step 6.

Idle Mixture Adjustments

For these adjustments to be accurate, the engine must be operated in a body of water with the correct propeller installed. For best results, the boat must be floating in the water with its movement unrestrained.

If the engine idle is acceptable, do not attempt to adjust the idle mixture. Perform this procedure only if the carburetors have been rebuilt, the mixture screws have been tampered with or if the idle quality is unsatisfactory.

The idle mixture on each carburetor must be individually set. When adjusting the idle mixture, attempt to keep all of the mixture screws settings as close to each other as possible. Some variation is normal, however. Try to turn each screw (in sequence) equal amounts in the same direction; noting that clockwise rotation leans the air/fuel mixture and counterclockwise rotation enriches the air/fuel mixture. If it seems impossible to correctly adjust the idle mixture, try resetting all of the carburetors' mixture needles to their initial setting (Step 1) and start over.

> *CAUTION*
> *Do not run the engine without an adequate water supply and do not exceed 3000 rpm without an adequate load. Refer to **Safety Precautions** at the beginning of this chapter.*

1. Turn each carburetor's idle mixture screw (**Figure 66**, typical) clockwise until it is lightly seated. Do not force the screw tightly into the carburetor or the tip and the carburetor will be damaged.

2. Back out each mixture screw to specification.

   a. *60-70 hp and 1995 (EO) 50 hp models*—2-1/2 turns from a lightly-seated position.

   b. *1996-2003 (ED-ST) models*—3-1/2 turns from a lightly-seated position.

3. Connect an accurate shop tachometer to the No. 1 spark plug lead.

4. Start the engine and run it at approximately 2000 rpm until warmed to normal operating temperature.

5A. *Remote control models*—Hold the throttle control arm (1, **Figure 62**) against the idle stop screw (2, **Figure 62**) and manually shift the gearcase into FORWARD gear. Adjust the idle timing/idle speed as described in the previous section. The engine must be idling at approximately 750-850 rpm in FORWARD gear before continuing.

5B. *Tiller handle models*—Rotate the twist grip throttle to its full idle position. Make sure the spark control arm (2, **Figure 61**) is against the idle timing stop screw (4, **Figure 61**) and shift the gearcase into FORWARD gear. Adjust the idle timing/idle speed as described in the previous section. The engine must be idling at approximately 750-850 rpm in FORWARD gear before continuing.

> *NOTE*
> *Idle mixture cannot be properly set unless the carburetor is operating on the idle circuit. Setting the idle mixture at higher speeds will give inaccurate results. It may be necessary to switch back and forth between idle mixture adjustment and idle timing/speed adjustment several times to achieve proper adjustment. Always adjust the idle timing/speed last.*

6. Slowly turn each idle mixture screw (**Figure 66**, typical) counterclockwise in 1/8 turn increments, pausing at

least 15 seconds between turns. Continue this step until the idle speed decreases and idle becomes rough due to an overly rich mixture. Note the position of each mixture screw's slot.

7. Slowly turn each idle mixture screw clockwise in 1/8 turn increments, pausing at least 15 seconds between turns. The idle speed will gradually become smooth and speed will increase. Continue this step until the engine speed begins to slow again and/or misfires due to an excessively lean mixture. Note the position of each mixture screw's slot.

8. Position each mixture screw at the midpoint of the settings achieved in Step 6 and Step 7. See **Figure 67**. Then turn each screw counterclockwise (outward) 1/8 turn to slightly enrichen the mixture.

> *NOTE*
> *It is a natural tendency to adjust the idle mixture too lean. Although the engine appears to run smoothly at idle, it will not accelerate without hesitation or continue to idle smoothly after wide-open throttle operation. If the engine does not perform satisfactorily in the following two steps, the idle mixture is most likely too lean.*

> *CAUTION*
> *On remote control models, the engine must be manually shifted into FORWARD gear before attempting to operate it at wide-open throttle in the following steps.*

9. Run the engine at wide-open throttle (in FORWARD gear) for one minute to clear any fuel puddles from the

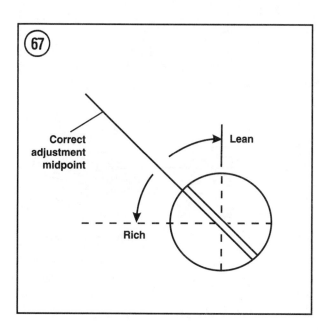

crankcase. Then quickly reduce engine speed to idle. The engine will idle smoothly without stalling or spitting if the mixture is adjusted correctly. Readjust the mixture on each carburetor as necessary.

10. Quickly accelerate the engine to wide-open throttle and back to idle. The engine will accelerate cleanly without hesitation if the mixture is adjusted correctly. Readjust the mixture on each carburetor as necessary.

11. Make a final adjustment to the idle timing/idle speed as described in the previous section.

Maximum Spark Advance

1. Connect a suitable timing light to the top (No. 1 cylinder) spark plug lead.

> *CAUTION*
> *Do not run the engine without an adequate water supply and do not exceed 3000 rpm without an adequate load. Refer to Safety Precautions at the beginning of this chapter.*

2. Start the engine and allow it to warm to normal operating temperature.

> *CAUTION*
> *The gearcase linkage must be manually moved to the FORWARD gear position in the next step. Do not run the engine at wide-open throttle in NEUTRAL.*

3. Reduce the engine speed to idle and shift the gearcase into FORWARD gear.

4. Point the timing light at the flywheel and timing pointer. The timing pointer is part of the engine's cowling brace and is located on the top of the intake manifold at the front and centerline of the engine as shown in **Figure 53**. Align the timing light to point to the center of the flywheel through the timing pointer.

5A. *Tiller handle models*—Rotate the twist grip throttle to the wide-open throttle position. Make sure the throttle cam (1, **Figure 61**) is against the wide-open throttle stop adjustment screw (5, **Figure 61**). Note the timing reading.

5B. *Remote control models*—Hold the throttle control arm (1, **Figure 62**) in the wide-open throttle position. Make sure the lever is against the wide-open throttle stop adjustment screw (3, **Figure 62**). Note the timing reading.

6. The timing must be 16-18° BTDC at wide-open throttle (5000 rpm minimum).

> *WARNING*
> *To prevent accidental contact with the rotating flywheel, stop the motor prior to adjusting maximum spark advance.*

7A. *Tiller handle models*—If adjustment is required, stop the engine and loosen the jam nut on the spark control arm's eccentric adjusting screw (**Figure 68**). Turn the screw and move the spark control arm forward to advance the timing and rearward to retard the timing. Turn the adjustment screw as necessary, then tighten the jam nut securely, making sure the screw does not turn with it. Repeat Steps 2-6 until the correct timing is verified.

7B. *Remote control models*—If adjustment is required, stop the engine and loosen the maximum spark advance adjustment screw's jam nut (**Figure 69**). Turning the screw clockwise retards timing and turning the screw counterclockwise advances timing. Note that one turn of the screw equals approximately 1° timing change. Turn the adjustment screw as necessary, then tighten the jam nut securely, making sure the screw does not turn with it. Repeat Steps 2-6 until the correct timing is verified.

Shift Lever Neutral Detent Adjustment

The shift lever detent spring is located just below the mounting point for the throttle cable adjustable anchor and is identified by the single hex head screw securing it in place. See **Figure 70**.

1. Disconnect and ground the spark plug leads to the power head to prevent accidental starting.

2. While rotating the propeller, shift the gearcase into the NEUTRAL position.

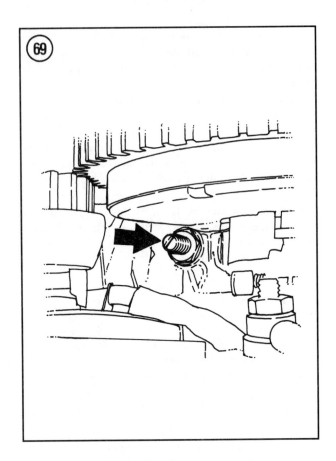

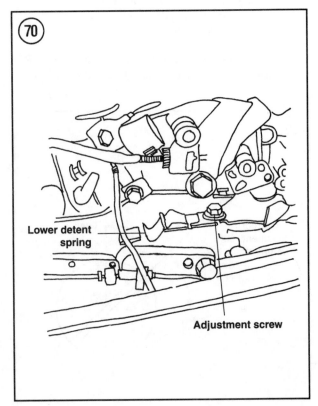

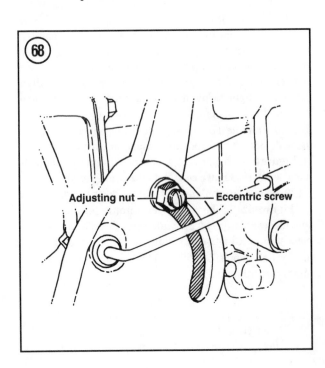

3. With the outboard in NEUTRAL, the lower detent spring (**Figure 70**) must be centered in the notch in the shift lever.

4. If not, loosen the screw (**Figure 70**) securing the detent springs and move the lower spring as necessary. Retighten the screw and recheck the adjustment.

5. Reconnect the spark plug leads when finished.

Wide-Open Throttle Speed Verification
(Final Step, All Models)

1. Connect an accurate shop tachometer (**Table 1**) to a spark plug lead.

2. With the engine mounted on a boat, the boat unrestrained in the water and the engine running at wide-open-throttle in FORWARD gear, record the maximum speed noted on the tachometer.

3. If the maximum speed exceeds 6000 rpm, check the propeller for damage or incorrect application. Repair or replace the propeller as necessary.

4. If the maximum speed does not reach 5000 rpm, check the propeller for incorrect application. If the correct propeller is installed, check the engine's power output using a test wheel as described in *Power output verification* at the end of Chapter Three. If the engine is not producing its rated power, start troubleshooting by checking the cranking compression as described in Chapter Four.

5

Table 1 RECOMMENDED TEST EQUIPMENT AND TOOLS

Description	Part No.	Manufacturer
Ball hex screwdriver	327622	OMC
Ball socket link remover	342226	OMC
Ball socket link installer	342225	OMC
Dial indicator set (for TDC verification)	91-58222A-1	Mercury Marine
Dial indicator set (for TDC verification)	350 EKA	Merc-O-Tronic
Piston stop tool	384884	OMC
Timing light	91-99379	Mercury Marine
Timing light	Model 712	Merc-O-Tronic
Timing light	ST-80	Stevens Instruments
Shop tachometer	TD-96	Stevens Instruments
Shop tachometer	67-100TA	Merc-O-Tronic
Shop tachometer	91-59339	Mercury Marine

Table 2 GENERAL SPECIFICATIONS: 2, 3.3 AND 3.5 HP

Rated output	
2 hp	2 hp (1.5 kw) at 4500 rpm
3.3 hp	3.3 hp (2.5 kw) at 5000 rpm
3.5 hp	3.5 hp (2.6 kw) at 5000 rpm
Weight	Approximately 29.7 lb. (13.5 kg)
Induction type	Loop-charged
No. of cylinders and configuration	1
Recommended full throttle operating range	
2 hp	4000-5000
3.3 and 3.5 hp	4500-5000
Recommended test wheel	
2 hp	115208 (standard propeller)
3.3 and 3.5 hp	115306
Minimum test rpm	
2 hp	4500 rpm
3.3 and 3.5 hp	5000 rpm
Idle speed in forward gear	
2 and 3.3 hp	1100-1300
3.5 hp	1000-1200
Carburetor specifications	
Initial idle mixture screw adjustment	Not applicable
Ignition timing	Not adjustable

Table 3 GENERAL SPECIFICATIONS: 3 AND 4 HP (EXCEPT 4 DELUXE)

Rated output	
3 hp	3 hp (2.2 kW) at 5000 rpm
4 hp	4 hp (3 kW) at 5000 rpm
Weight	approximately 35 lb. (15.9 kg)
Induction type	Cross-charged
Number of cylinders and configuration	2 inline
Recommended full throttle operating range	4500-5500 rpm
Idle speed in forward gear	700-800 rpm
Carburetor specifications	
Initial idle mixture screw adjustment	1 turn from lightly seated position
Ignition timing	Not adjustable
Firing order	1-2

Table 4 GENERAL SPECIFICATIONS: 4 DELUXE AND 6-8 HP

Rated output	
4 Deluxe	4 hp (3 kW) at 5000 rpm
6 hp	6 hp (4.5 kW) at 5000 rpm
8 hp	8 hp (6 kW) at 5500 rpm
Weight	
4 Deluxe	approximately 51.5 lb. (23.4 kg)
6 and 8 hp	approximately 57 lb. (25.9 kg)
Induction type	Cross-charged
Number of cylinders and configuration	2 in-line
Recommended full throttle operating range	
4 Deluxe and 6 hp	4500-5500 rpm
8 hp	5000-6000 rpm
Idle speed in forward gear	
4 Deluxe	600-650 rpm
6 and 8 hp	675-725 rpm
Initial idle mixture screw adjustment	
4 Deluxe	1 turn from lightly seated position
6 and 8 hp	3 turns from lightly seated position
Ignition timing	Not adjustable
Firing order	1-2

Table 5 GENERAL SPECIFICATIONS: 9.9 AND 15 HP

Rated output	
9.9 hp	9.9 hp (7.4 kW) at 5500 rpm
15 hp	15 hp (11.2 kW) at 5500 rpm
Weight	
Rope start	approximately 74.5 lb. (33.8 kg)
Electric start	approximately 77.5 lb. (35.2 kg)
Induction type	Cross-charged
Number of cylinders and configuration	2 inline
Recommended full throttle operating range	5000-6000 rpm
Idle speed in forward gear	675-725 rpm
Initial idle mixture screw adjustment	3 turns from lightly seated position
Ignition timing	Not adjustable, no specifications
Firing order	1-2

5

Table 6 GENERAL SPECIFICATIONS: 20-30 HP (TWO-CYLINDER) AND 18 JET

Rated output	
20 hp	20 hp (14.9 kW) at 5000 rpm
25 hp	25 hp (18.7 kW) at 5000 rpm
28 Special	28 hp (20.9 kW) at 5000 rpm
30 hp	30 hp (22.4 kW) at 5500 rpm
18 jet	25 hp (18.7 kW) at 5000 rpm
Weight	
Outboard models	approximately 114-122 lb. (52-55 kg)
18 jet	approximately 137 lb. (62.1 kg)
Induction type	Cross-flow
Number of cylinders and configuration	2 inline
Recommended full throttle operating range	
20, 25, 28 hp and 18 jet	4500-5500 rpm
30 hp	5200-5800 rpm
Idle speed in forward gear	650-700 rpm
Initial idle mixture screw adjustment	
20 hp	3 turns from lightly seated position
25 hp (TR carburetor)	1-3/4 turns from lightly seated position
25 hp, 30 hp and 18 jet (SV carburetor)	2-1/2 turns from lightly seated position
Ignition timing at W.O.T.	
20 hp (1995-1997 [EO-EU])	33-35° BTDC
20 hp (1998-2003 [EC-ST])	32-34° BTDC
25-30 hp and 18 jet	29-31° BTDC
Firing order	1-2

Table 7 GENERAL SPECIFICATIONS: 25 AND 35 HP (THREE-CYLINDER)

Rated output	
25 hp	25 hp (18.7 kW) at 5500 rpm
35 hp	35 hp (26.1 kW) at 5500 rpm
Weight	
Tiller handle models	approximately 151-159 lb. (68-82 kg)
Remote control models	approximately 170 lb. (77.1 kg)
Induction type	Loop-charged
Number of cylinders and configuration	3 inline
Recommended full throttle operating range	5200-5800 rpm
Idle speed in forward gear	See text
Initial idle mixture screw adjustment	See text
Idle timing	4° ATDC
Pickup timing	0° (TDC)
	(continued)

Table 7 GENERAL SPECIFICATIONS: 25 AND 35 HP (THREE-CYLINDER) (continued)

Maximum timing	
25 hp	19-21° BTDC
35 hp	21-23° BTDC
Firing order	1-2-3

Table 8 GENERAL SPECIFICATIONS: 40-50 HP (TWO-CYLINDER) AND 28-35 JET

Rated output	
40 hp	40 hp (29.8 kW) at 5000 rpm
48 Special	48 hp (35.8 kW) at 5000 rpm
50 hp/50 Special	50 hp (37.3 kW) at 5000 rpm
28 jet	40 hp (29.8 kW) at 5000 rpm
35 jet	50 hp (37.3 kW) at 5000 rpm
Weight	
Outboard models	approximately 182 lb. (82.6 kg)
Jet models	approximately 198 lb. (89.8 kg)
Induction type	Loop-charged
Number of cylinders and configuration	2 inline
Recommended full throttle operating range	4500-5500 rpm
Idle rpm in forward gear	775-825 rpm
Initial idle mixture screw adjustment	
40 hp and 28 jet	2-1/2 turns from lightly seated position
48 hp, 50 hp and 35 jet	3-1/2 turns from lightly seated position
Idle timing	0° (TDC)-2° ATDC
Timing at wide-open throttle	18-20° BTDC
Firing order	1-2

Table 9 GENERAL SPECIFICATIONS: 50-70 HP (THREE-CYLINDER)

Rated output	
50 hp	50 hp (37.3 kW) at 5500 rpm
60 hp	60 hp (44.8 kW) at 5500 rpm
70 hp	70 hp (52.2 kW) at 5500 rpm
Weight	
Tiller handle models	approximately 250 lb. (113.4 kg)
Remote control models	approximately 237 lb. (107.5 kg)
Induction type	Loop-charged
Number of cylinders and configuration	3 inline
Recommended full throttle operating range	5000-6000 rpm
Idle speed in forward gear	See text
Initial idle mixture screw adjustment	
1995 (EO) models	2-3/4 turns from lightly seated position
1996-2003 (ED-ST) models	
50 hp	1-3/4 turns from lightly seated position
60 and 70 hp	2-3/4 turns from lightly seated position
Idle timing	
50 hp	7-9° ATDC
60 and 70 hp	3-5° ATDC
Timing at wide-open throttle	16-18° BTDC
Firing order	1-2-3

Chapter Six

Fuel System

This chapter contains removal, overhaul, installation and adjustment procedures for fuel pumps, carburetors, reed valves, fuel primer solenoids and manual primer valves, fuel recirculation systems, portable fuel tanks and connecting lines used with the Evinrude/Johnson outboard motors covered in this manual. General fuel system troubleshooting is covered in Chapter Three.

Carburetor specifications are listed in **Tables 1-6**. Fuel pump, reed valve and intake manifold torque specifications are listed in **Table 7**. Carburetor torque values are listed in **Table 8**.

> *CAUTION*
> *Metric **and** American fasteners may be used on newer model outboards. Always match a replacement fastener to the original. Do not run a tap or thread chaser into a hole (or over a screw or bolt) without first determining the thread size and pitch.*

SERVICE PRECAUTIONS—1996-2003 MODEL YEAR ENGINES

The EPA (Environmental Protection Agency) certifies emission output for all 1996-2003 models. Certified models have an EPA certification plate mounted near the model identification plate on the engine midsection. Refer to *Model Identification* in Chapter Eight for illustrations and information regarding the certification plate.

All repairs or service procedures must be performed exactly as specified to ensure the engine will continue to comply with EPA requirements. For the same reason, all replacement parts must meet or exceed the manufacturer's specifications.

If in doubt as to whether a repair or service procedure will adversely affect the engine's ability to maintain EPA compliance, contact an Evinrude or Johnson dealer, before beginning the repair or procedure.

FUEL SYSTEM DESCRIPTIONS

2, 3.3 and 3.5 hp (Gravity Feed System)

The 2, 3.3 and 3.5 hp models use a gravity feed fuel system with an integral tank and are not equipped with oil injection. See **Figure 1**. A fuel shutoff valve at the base of the tank controls fuel flow from the fuel tank to the slide-valve carburetor. The fuel shutoff valve also contains an integral filter which can be cleaned or replaced with the valve assembly. The fuel tank cap contains an air vent that must be open to atmosphere. A choke plate and mechanical linkage are used to enrich the air/fuel mixture during starting and warm-up.

3 hp Models

These models are equipped with an integral fuel tank and a carburetor that has an internal fuel pump (bladder) and fuel shutoff valve. A replaceable inline fuel filter is used between the fuel tank and the carburetor. These models are not equipped with oil injection. The fuel tank cap contains an air vent that must be open to atmosphere. A choke plate and mechanical linkage are used to enrich the air/fuel mixture during starting and warm-up.

4 hp Models (Except 4 Deluxe)

A choke plate and mechanical linkage are used to enrich the air/fuel mixture during starting and warm-up on both of the following models.

The 4BR models are equipped with an integral fuel tank and a quick-disconnect fitting (A, **Figure 2**, typical) for a remote fuel tank. A conventional fuel pump (B, **Figure 2**, typical) pulls fuel from the remote fuel tank when the fuel shutoff valve is in the OFF position and the engine is running. When the shutoff valve is in the ON position, the carburetor's internal fuel pump (bladder) pulls fuel from the integral fuel tank and inline fuel filter.

The 4R models are equipped with a quick-disconnect fitting (A, **Figure 2**, typical) for a remote fuel tank. There is no integral fuel tank. A conventional fuel pump (B, **Figure 2**, typical) pulls fuel from the remote fuel tank whenever the engine is running. There is no fuel shutoff valve. A primer bulb in the remote tank's fuel supply line must be squeezed by the operator to fill the carburetor with fuel, prior to starting.

4 Deluxe, 6-30 hp (Two-Cylinder), 18-28 Jet, 40 hp (Rope Start) and 48 Special Models

These engines are not equipped with oil injection. A conventional fuel pump is used to supply fuel to the single carburetor (6-30 hp and 18 jet) or two carburetors (40 hp, 48 Special and 28 jet) when the engine is running. A small, conventional fuel pump (B, **Figure 2**) is used on the 4 Deluxe-8 hp models and a large, conventional fuel pump (**Figure 3**) is used on 9.9-48 hp models. A primer bulb in the fuel supply line must be squeezed by the operator to fill the carburetor(s) with fuel, prior to starting. A choke plate and mechanical linkage are used on the 4 Deluxe-15 hp rope start models, while a fuel primer system (either mechanical or electric) injects fuel directly behind the throttle

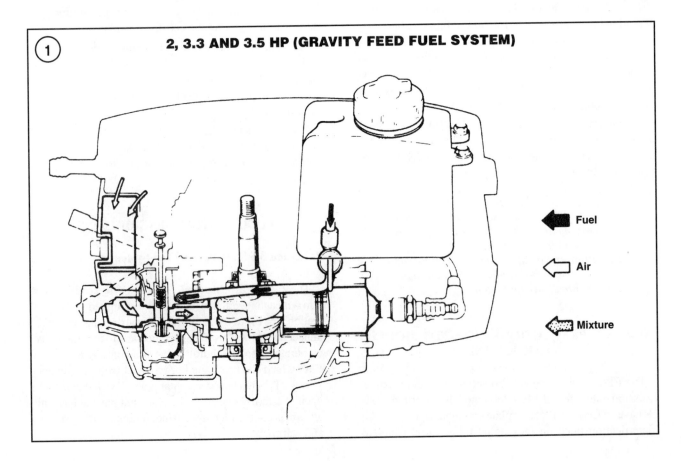

① 2, 3.3 AND 3.5 HP (GRAVITY FEED FUEL SYSTEM)

◄ Fuel

◁ Air

◁ Mixture

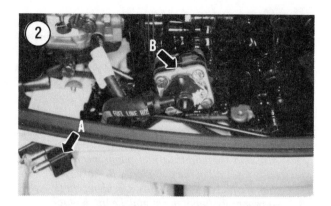

throttle plate on 9.9-15 hp (remote electric) and all larger models. Both systems enrich the air/fuel mixture during starting and warm-up.

25 and 35 hp (Three-cylinder) Models

These models use two conventional fuel pumps (connected in series) to supply fuel to the three carburetors when the engine is running. A primer bulb in the fuel supply line must be squeezed by the operator to fill the carburetors with fuel, prior to starting.

On rope start and tiller electric models, a choke plate (on each carburetor) and mechanical linkage are used to enrich the air/fuel mixture during starting and warm-up.

On remote control models, an electric fuel primer system injects fuel directly into the top of the intake manifold to enrich the air/fuel mixture during starting and warm-up.

The first (port) pump (A, **Figure 4**) is primarily a vacuum pump that lifts the fuel from the fuel tank. The second (starboard) pump (B, **Figure 4**) is primarily a pressure pump that pushes the fuel from the first pump to the carburetor.

These engines are also equipped with a separate oil injection pump and engine-mounted oil reservoir. The oil injection pump is mounted on the pressure side of the second fuel pump and is operated by fuel pressure. Refer to Chapter Eleven for an operational description, test and repair procedures on the oil injection system.

VRO^2 (Variable Ratio Oiling) Equipped Models

The 40 hp (electric start), 50-70 hp and 35 jet models are equipped with a combination fuel pump/oil injection pump, commonly referred to as the VRO^2 (variable-ratio oil) pump (**Figure 5**, typical). The VRO^2 pump supplies the engine with fuel and oil when the engine is running. The correct amount of oil is mixed with the fuel inside of the pump unit.

6

A primer bulb in the fuel supply line must be squeezed by the operator to fill the carburetors with fuel prior to starting. An electric fuel primer system injects fuel directly behind the throttle plates to enrich the air/fuel mixture during starting and warm-up.

The VRO^2 pump is driven by crankcase pressure and vacuum pulses. The pulse line is equipped with a pulse limiter that prevents damage to the pump's diaphragm should the engine backfire (typically from a lean air/fuel mixture).

Refer to Chapter Eleven for an operational description, test and repair procedures.

CONVENTIONAL FUEL PUMP SERVICE

The conventional fuel pump(s) used on Evinrude/Johnson outboard motors are extremely simple in design and reliable in operation. Diaphragm and check valve failures from aging and/or fatigue are generally the most common problem, although the use of contaminated fuel and/or fuel containing excessive amounts of alcohol or other additives can cause accelerated check valve and diaphragm failure. Refer to Chapter Four for fuel recommendations.

If the fuel pump is suspected of not functioning correctly, refer to Chapter Three for fuel system troubleshooting.

The manufacturer offers repair kits to overhaul any defective conventional fuel pump assembly. Always follow the instructions included with the fuel pump.

CAUTION
Fuel pump assemblies and internal fuel pump components may vary between models. Be certain that the correct fuel pump (or fuel pump repair kit) is used when replacing (or rebuilding) the fuel pump. Using the wrong fuel pump or internal components can cause reduced fuel flow to the engine, resulting in poor performance or power head failure. Never interchange fuel pump components from another model.

Conventional Fuel Pump Operation

All conventional fuel pumps are operated by pressure pulses created by the movement of the pistons in their cylinder bores. The pressure pulses reach the fuel pump(s) through a drilled passage in the crankcase, or by a pulse fitting (pressed or threaded into the crankcase) and hose.

The upward motion of the piston creates a low pressure in the crankcase (and against the pump diaphragm). This low pressure opens the inlet check valve in the pump,

drawing fuel from the supply line into the pump. The downward motion of the piston creates a high pressure in the crankcase (and against the pump diaphragm). This pressure closes the inlet check valve and opens the outlet check valve, forcing the fuel into the discharge line (to the carburetor[s]). See **Figure 6**.

NOTE
If the cylinder that supplies crankcase pressure and vacuum to a fuel pump mechanically fails, all of the cylinders will starve for fuel. If a fuel delivery failure is evident, check the compression of the engine before replacing the fuel pump. See Chapter Four.

Conventional Fuel Pump Removal/Installation

When removing fuel lines from fuel fittings, push the fuel line off of the fitting whenever possible. Pulling on the line only tightens its grip on the fitting. Plastic fittings can be easily damaged or broken, causing unnecessary component replacement.

If necessary, cut the fuel line with a razor knife (or similar tool) and peel the line from the fitting. Replacing the line is always more economical than replacing a fuel pump or any other fuel system component. See *Fuel Lines, Primer Bulbs, Fittings and Connectors* in this chapter.

25 and 35 hp (three-cylinder) models

These engines use two pumps, connected in series. The port pump is the suction pump and primarily draws fuel from the fuel tank via the quick-disconnect fitting on the engine's lower cowl. The starboard pump is the pressure pump and primarily pushes the fuel to the fuel/oil mixing unit and onto the carburetors. An inline filter is mounted

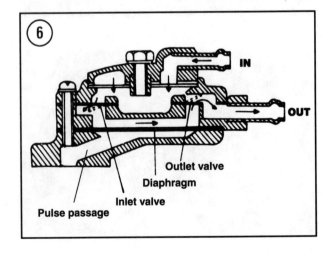

6

IN

OUT

Outlet valve
Diaphragm
Inlet valve
Pulse passage

between the starboard fuel pump and the fuel/oil mixing unit.

A heat shield is mounted behind both fuel pumps and is designed to keep the pumps thermally isolated from the power head, helping to prevent fuel system vapor lock. Make sure the shield is repositioned behind the pumps as shown in **Figure 4** during pump installation.

1. *Electric start models*—Disconnect the negative battery cable.

2. Disconnect and ground the spark plug leads to the power head to prevent accidental starting.

3. Remove the carburetor's air intake cover.

4. Disconnect the fuel supply line from the engine's quick-disconnect fitting located on the lower cowl.

5. Note the position of the lines on each pump (**Figure 4**). Each pump has a fuel inlet line connected to the filter cover, a fuel outlet line and a pulse line connected to a crankcase fitting. Note that the output line from the port pump is connected to the inlet cover of the starboard pump.

6. If the pumps are to be rebuilt and reinstalled, mark each pump body as to its location. The pump's positions cannot be switched.

7. Remove the screw at the center of each pump's inlet cover.

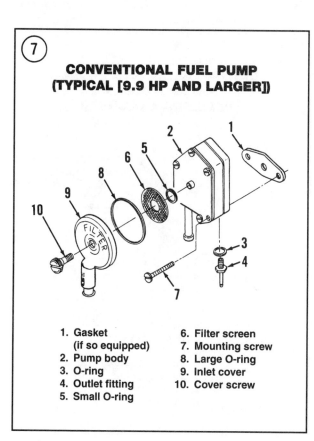

CONVENTIONAL FUEL PUMP (TYPICAL [9.9 HP AND LARGER])

1. Gasket (if so equipped)	6. Filter screen
2. Pump body	7. Mounting screw
3. O-ring	8. Large O-ring
4. Outlet fitting	9. Inlet cover
5. Small O-ring	10. Cover screw

8. Pull the inlet covers away from the pumps. Locate and secure the small and large O-rings on each pump. Inspect the O-rings and replace them if they are damaged or worn. See **Figure 7**, typical.

9. If the pumps are being replaced, remove the tie-straps or other clamps securing the fuel line to each inlet cover. Carefully push the fuel line from each inlet cover.

10. Remove the tie-straps or spring clamps securing the fuel outlet lines and crankcase pulse lines to the fuel pump bodies. Carefully push each fuel and pulse line from each pump.

11. Remove the 2 Torx-head screws securing each pump to the crankcase cover. These are screws are located at the lower outer corners of each pump. Support the heat shield as the last screw is removed. Then remove both pumps and the heat shield from the power head.

12. To install the pumps, begin by coating the threads of the pump mounting screws with OMC Nut Lock thread-locking adhesive or equivalent.

13. Position the heat shield and the port (suction) pump onto the crankcase cover. Secure the pump with two screws. Finger-tighten the screws at this time.

14. Position the starboard (pressure) pump onto the crankcase cover. Align the heat shield and pump, then secure the pump with two screws.

15. Evenly tighten each pump's two mounting screws to 24-36 in.-lb. (2.7-4.1 N•m).

16. Reconnect the crankcase pulse line and pump outlet line to each pump's body. Secure the connections with new tie-straps or the original spring clamps.

17. Carefully remove the filter screens (6, **Figure 7**) from the inlet covers. Do not damage the screens in the process. Clean the screens in clean solvent and dry with compressed air. Replace the screens if they cannot be satisfactorily cleaned.

18. Install the screens into the inlet covers. Position the small O-ring onto each pump body and the large O-ring into the groove in each inlet cover.

19. Carefully align the inlet cover(s) to the pump body being careful not to disturb the screen or O-ring positions.

20. Tighten the center screw(s) securely. Then reconnect each pump's inlet line to the inlet covers. Secure the connections with new tie-straps or the original spring clamps.

21. Reconnect the fuel supply line to the engine's quick-disconnect connector on the lower cowl and test the installation by squeezing the primer bulb and checking for leaks. Repair any leaks noted.

22. Reinstall the carburetor's air intake cover and reconnect the spark plug leads.

23. *Electric start models*—Reconnect the negative battery cable.

6

All other models

Refer to **Figure 7** (9.9 hp and larger) or **Figure 8** (4-8 hp) for this procedure.

1. *Electric start models*—Disconnect the negative battery cable.

2. Disconnect and ground the spark plug leads to the power head to prevent accidental starting.

3. Disconnect the fuel supply line from the engine's quick-disconnect fitting located on the lower cowl.

4. Note the position of the lines on the pump. The fuel inlet line is connected to the filter cover, the outlet line is connected to the carburetor(s). Some models are equipped with a pulse line connected to a crankcase fitting. If no pulse line is present, the pump uses a gasket to seal the back of the pump body to the crankcase pulse port.

5. Remove the screw at the center of the pump's inlet cover.

6. Pull the inlet cover away from the pump. On small (rectangular) pumps, locate and secure the gasket (3, **Figure 8**). On large (rectangular) pumps, locate and secure the small and large O-rings (5 and 8, **Figure 7**). Inspect the gasket or O-rings and replace if damaged or worn.

7. If the pump is being replaced, remove the tie-straps or other clamps securing the fuel line to the inlet cover. Carefully push the fuel line from the inlet cover.

8. Remove the tie-straps (or spring clamps) securing the fuel outlet line and crankcase pulse line (if so equipped) to the fuel pump body. Carefully push the line(s) from the pump.

9. Remove the two screws securing the pump to the crankcase. On small (square) pumps, the screws can easily be visually identified. On large (rectangular) pumps, the screws are located at the pump's lower outer corners as shown in **Figure 9**.

10. Remove the pump from the power head. On models not equipped with a pulse line, remove and discard the gasket.

11. To install the pumps, begin by coating the threads of the pump mounting screws with OMC Nut Lock thread-locking adhesive or equivalent.

NOTE
On models without a pulse line, make sure a new gasket is installed between the pump body and the crankcase.

12. Position the pump onto the crankcase (using a new gasket, if so equipped). The pump's fuel outlet fitting must face down. Secure the pump with two screws. Evenly tighten the screws to 24-36 in.-lb. (2.7-4.1 N•m).

13. Reconnect the crankcase pulse line (if so equipped) and pump outlet line to the pump's body. Secure the connections with new tie-straps or the original spring clamps.

14. Carefully remove the filter screen from the inlet cover. Do not damage the screen in the process. Clean the screen in clean solvent and dry with compressed air. Replace the screen if it cannot be satisfactorily cleaned.

15. Install the screen into the inlet cover. On small (square) pumps, position the gasket onto the pump body. On large pumps, position the small O-ring on to the pump body and the large O-ring into the groove in the inlet cover.

16. Carefully align the inlet cover(s) to the pump body being careful not to disturb the screen, gasket or O-ring positions.

17. Tighten the center screw securely. Then reconnect the pump's inlet line to the inlet cover. Secure the connection with a new tie-strap or the original spring clamp.

18. Reconnect the fuel supply line to the engine's quick-disconnect connector on the lower cowl and test the installation by squeezing the primer bulb and checking for leaks. Repair any leaks noted.

19. Reconnect the spark plug leads.

20. *Electric start models*—Reconnect the negative battery cable.

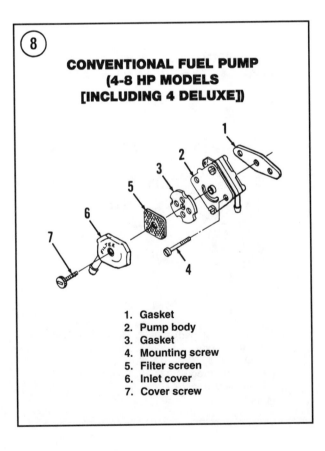

**CONVENTIONAL FUEL PUMP
(4-8 HP MODELS
[INCLUDING 4 DELUXE])**

1. Gasket
2. Pump body
3. Gasket
4. Mounting screw
5. Filter screen
6. Inlet cover
7. Cover screw

Disassembly/Assembly

Always replace the diaphragm, check valves and all O-rings and gaskets when assembling a fuel pump. Make sure the fuel pump repair kit is in hand before beginning disassembly. Follow all special instructions included with the repair kit, especially those covering check valve replacement.

1. Remove the remaining screws holding the pump body together.

2. Separate the pump body from the cover and back plate, being careful to note each component's location and orientation. Remove and discard the diaphragm, check valves and all gaskets and/or O-rings.

3. Assemble the pump following the instruction sheet provided in the repair kit. Install the new diaphragm, check valves and all gaskets and O-rings, along with any other components provided in the repair kit. Lightly coat the threads of the pump body screws with OMC Nut Lock threadlocking adhesive (or equivalent) before installing them.

4. Evenly tighten the pump body screws to 24-36 in.-lb. (2.7-4.1 N•m).

CARBURETORS

When removing fuel (or primer) lines from fuel fittings, push the fuel line off of the fitting whenever possible. Pulling on the line only tightens its grip on the fitting. Plastic fittings can be easily damaged or broken

from excessive force, causing unnecessary component replacement.

If necessary, cut the fuel (or primer) line with a razor knife (or similar tool) and peel the line from the fitting. Replacing the line is always more economical than replacing the component. See *Fuel Lines, Primer Bulbs, Fittings and Connectors*, in this chapter.

Carburetor Identification

Current (1995-1998) model Evinrude/Johnson outboard motors use the following carburetors:

1. *2, 3.3 and 3.5 hp*—One slide valve carburetor (imported).

2. *3 and 4 hp (including 4 Deluxe)*—One butterfly valve carburetor with an integral fuel pump (bladder) and fuel selector valve, with the exception of the 4 hp (R) and 4 Deluxe models. The fuel pump bladder and fuel selector valve are not installed on these models.

3. *6-20 hp*—One butterfly valve carburetor, referred to as a *modular* style carburetor.

4. *25 and 35 hp (three-cylinder)*—Three butterfly valve carburetors, referred to as *modular* style carburetors.

5. *25 and 30 hp (two-cylinder) and 18 jet*—One *TR* or *SV* series butterfly valve carburetor.

   a. The *TR* carburetor is easily identified by its all-metal construction.

   b. The *SV* carburetor is easily identified by its black plastic top cover.

6. *40-50 hp (two-cylinder), 28 jet and 35 jet*—Two *SV* series carburetors.

7. *50-70 hp (three-cylinder)*—Three *SV* series carburetors.

Carburetor Adjustments (Static)

Refer to **Tables 1-6** for carburetor specifications. OMC Carburetor gauge part No. 324891 is recommended for float level adjustments (except 2 and 3.3 hp) and a suitable T-gauge (such as Quicksilver part No. 91-36392 [or equivalent]) is recommended for the float level adjustment (except 2, 3.3 and 3.5 hp).

The 2, 3.3 and 3.5 hp models require only a float level setting that can be measured with a T-gauge (or equivalent).

Float level adjustments

Setting the float level correctly is crucial to proper carburetor calibration. Setting the float level too high or too low will affect the air/fuel mixture at all engine speeds, especially high speed. Setting the float level is adjusting the level of the fuel reservoir in the carburetor's float chamber.

If the float level is too low, insufficient fuel will be present in the float chamber and the air/fuel mixture will be leaned accordingly. A lean mixture can lead to hesitation on acceleration, surging at high speeds and ultimately preignition and/or detonation (Chapter Three).

If the float level is too high, excessive fuel will be present in the float chamber and the air/fuel mixture will be enriched accordingly. A rich mixture can cause flooding, excessive fuel consumption, rough engine operation, fouled spark plugs, excessive smoke and hard starting (when warm).

Float drop adjustments

Setting the float drop correctly is crucial to carburetor operation, especially at wide-open throttle. This adjustment ensures that the inlet valve needle opens fully, allowing adequate fuel flow into the float chamber at all times.

If the float drop is less than specified, the inlet valve will not open fully and fuel starvation at high speed will result, causing the engine to run lean (see float level adjustments).

If the float drop is excessive (more than specified), the inlet valve needle can be pulled far enough from its seat to fall out of the seat or become cocked. If this happens, the float chamber will overfill, causing severe carburetor flooding.

Carburetor Adjustments (Engine Running)

NOTE
*After service or repair is performed on the carburetor(s), perform the **Synchronization and Linkage Adjustments** as described in Chapter Five.*

All running adjustments are detailed in Chapter Five. The engine must be provided with an adequate supply of cooling water when performing any procedure that involves starting and running the engine. Refer to *Safety Precautions* at the beginning of Chapter Three or Chapter Four.

NOTE
Idle speed and idle mixture adjustments cannot be satisfactorily performed with the engine running on a cooling system flushing device.

When performing idle speed and idle mixture adjustments, the outboard must be running in FORWARD gear at normal operating temperature with the correct propeller installed. The best results will be obtained if the motor is operated in the normal operating environment (mounted on a boat, in the water, running in forward gear with the boat's movement unrestrained).

High Altitude Compensation

As an outboard motor is operated at higher altitudes, several things happen that affect how the engine must be adjusted and operated. As the altitude is increased, the air becomes less dense. Since an outboard motor is essentially an air pump, the less dense air will reduce the efficiency of the engine, reducing the horsepower output proportionally to the change in air density. The loss of horsepower will require propeller pitch and diameter changes to maintain the recommended full-throttle operating speed.

CAUTION
*Regardless of what altitude the engine is operated at, the engine must operate within the recommended full-throttle speed range as described in **Wide-Open-Throttle Speed Verification** in Chapter Five. Change the propeller pitch and diameter as necessary to maintain the specified full throttle speed.*

The less dense air also affects the engine's carburetor calibration, causing the engine's air/fuel mixture to become richer. Richer mixtures will cause the engine to produce less horsepower and lead to fouled spark plugs, reduced fuel economy and accelerated carbon buildup in the combustion chamber.

All Evinrude and Johnson motors come from the factory calibrated to operate efficiently between sea level and 3000 ft. (914 m). It may be necessary to change the high-speed jet at altitudes higher than 3000 ft. (914 m), while operation at altitudes of 6000 ft. (1829 m) or higher will require rejetting.

High altitude main jets are smaller than the standard main jets and will correct the air/fuel ratio for the specified altitude. The engine will still produce less power than at low altitude, but the running quality will be restored and the rich air/fuel mixture problems will be eliminated.

Refer to **Tables 1-6** for standard main jet size specifications. The general specifications for high-altitude operation are to reduce the size of the standard main jet by 0.002 (0.05 mm) for operation between 3000-6000 ft. (1829 m), reduce by 0.004 in. (0.10 mm) for operation between 6000-9000 ft. (1829-2743 m) and reduce by 0.006 in. (0.15 m) for operation above 9000 ft. (2743 m). The high-speed air/fuel mixture should be verified after any high-speed jet changes. Do *not* reduce the size of the high-speed jet(s) more than specified, unless the engine still exhibits symptoms of an overly rich high-speed air/fuel mixture. If the jet size is reduced more than the general specification, the high-speed air/fuel mixture *must* be verified as described in the next section.

CAUTION
If an engine has been rejetted for high altitude, it must again be rejetted to the specified standard main jet(s) before operating at low altitude, or serious power head damage will occur from the engine operating on an air/fuel mixture that is too lean. To prevent an overly lean mixture, always rejet the carburetor(s) for the lowest anticipated altitude that the engine will be operated at.

After the main jets are changed, the idle speed and idle mixture must also be reset (at the new altitude) as described in Chapter Five. Expect the new idle mixture screw position to be slightly leaner (clockwise) than the original setting.

NOTE
If the jet is visible from outside of the carburetor (without removing a plug), the jet is an air bleed and controls airflow into a metering circuit. If the jet is not visible from outside of the carburetor, or if a plug must be removed to see the jet, the jet controls fuel flow.

If it is necessary to change the intermediate fuel jet (or air bleed) to improve the running quality at 1/4-1/2 throttle, make changes in 0.001 in. (0.025 mm) increments for carburetors equipped with intermediate fuel jets or 0.004 in. (0.10 mm) increments for carburetors with intermediate air bleed jets. Avoid overly lean air/fuel mixtures. An engine with an overly lean intermediate circuit will tend to hesitate on acceleration and surge when operated at 1/4-1/2 throttle.

High-speed air/fuel mixture verification

An engine must not be allowed to operate with the air/fuel mixture too lean. A lean air/fuel mixture will cause the combustion chamber temperature to be excessive and lead to preignition and/or detonation (Chapter Three).

An engine that is running lean will tend to surge, hesitate and/or lose speed at wide-open throttle. If audible preignition and/or detonation (pinging sounds) can be heard over normal engine noise, *immediately* stop the engine, remove the spark plugs and examine them for signs of overheating (Chapter Four). Also, examine the combustion chambers for damage (melted pistons, aluminum deposits on the cylinder walls or cylinder wall scoring).

To verify the air/fuel mixture at wide-open throttle, proceed as follows:

1. Install a new set of spark plugs into the engine or clean the original spark plugs. Make sure the correct spark plugs are used as specified in Chapter Four.

2. With the boat in a body of water and the correct propeller installed, start the engine and allow it to reach operating temperature.

CAUTION
Regardless of what altitude the engine is operated at, the engine must operate within the recommended full-throttle speed range as described in Chapter Five. Change the propeller pitch and diameter as necessary to maintain the specified full-throttle speed.

3. Run the engine at wide-open throttle for approximately 1-2 minutes, then stop the engine as quickly (and safely) as possible. Do not allow the engine to idle.

4. Remove and examine the spark plugs. Refer to Chapter Four for a spark plug analysis chart.

5. Each spark plug's insulator must have a tan to light tan color and show no evidence of overheating or any other defects. If so, the mixture is correct and the engine can be operated normally at this altitude.

6. If the insulator is more white than tan, or appears to be blistered, the air/fuel mixture is too lean. Increase the main jet size on each carburetor by 0.002 in. (0.51 mm) and repeat the mixture verification procedure.

CAUTION
If in doubt, it is better to have the air/fuel mixture on the rich side (slightly darker tan, or brown color on the insulator), rather than too lean (very light tan, or almost white color on the insulator). Rich mixtures run cooler than lean mixtures.

7. If the insulator is more brown or dark brown than light tan, the air/fuel mixture is too rich. If so desired, decrease the main jet size on each carburetor by 0.001 in. (0.025 mm) and repeat the mixture verification procedure.

Carburetor Cleaning and Inspection (All Models)

Do not submerge the carburetor, or any carburetor parts in a hot tank or caustic carburetor cleaner. A sealing compound is used around the metering tubes and in other locations to improve sealing and eliminate porosity problems. A hot tank or caustic cleaner will remove this sealing compound, effectively destroying the carburetor.

6

A small syringe, such as the *Monoject No. 412 glue syringe* is an excellent tool for injecting isopropyl alcohol through the carburetor cast passages, and to check for leakage in the carburetor body. Craft stores and hobby shops are good places to locate a glue syringe.

CAUTION
Do not remove the throttle plate and throttle shaft on an Evinrude/Johnson carburetor. Replacement parts are not available.

1. Thoroughly and carefully remove any gasket material from all mating surfaces. Do not nick, scratch or damage the mating surfaces.

2. If equipped with core plug(s), remove the core plug(s) as described in *Core plug service*, located in the next section. The core plug(s) must be removed before cleaning the carburetor.

3. Clean the carburetor body and all metal parts using an aerosol carburetor and choke cleaning solvent (available from OMC Genuine Parts or any auto parts store) to remove gum, dirt and varnish. Use a small bristle brush to scrub stubborn gum and varnish deposits.

4. Wash all carburetor components in clean, mild solvent (such as mineral spirits), then thoroughly rinse the components with hot water. Finally, blow all components dry with compressed air. Be sure to blow out all orifices, nozzles and passages thoroughly.

5. Check all drillings and cast passages in the carburetor body for leakage and blockage using a small syringe filled with isopropyl alcohol.

   a. Inject the alcohol into each passage while watching the casting (and any lead-shot plugs) for leakage.

   b. Make sure that all passages are open. Check the float chamber vent, screen(s), drilled or cast passages or plastic fitting (shield) for debris or blockage. The carburetor will not function correctly if the float chamber vent(s) is blocked or restricted.

   c. If any lead-shot plugs are leaking, refer to *Lead shot service* in this chapter.

   d. On models equipped with an emulsion tube (brass tube passing completely through the carburetor venturi), check for leaks between the emulsion tube and the upper main body. If leakage is noted, clean and dry the area thoroughly, then invert the carburetor body. Apply one drop of OMC Ultra Lock thread-locking adhesive (or equivalent) to the point where the emulsion tube enters the carburetor body (in the venturi).

CAUTION
Do not use wire or drill bits to clean any carburetor passages. Doing so will alter calibration and ruin the carburetor.

6. Check the carburetor body for stripped threads, cracks or other damage.

7. Check for excessive throttle shaft play, throttle valve misalignment and/or throttle shaft binding. The throttle shaft and valve are not available separately from the carburetor body. If excessive wear or damage is noted, replace the carburetor.

8. On carburetors equipped with a choke, repeat Step 7 for the choke shaft and choke valve.

9. Check the fuel bowl and top cover (if so equipped) for distortion, deterioration, corrosion, cracks, blocked passages or other damage.

10. Check the idle mixture screw(s) tip for grooving, nicks or other damage. Replace the idle mixture screw(s) as necessary. **Figure 10** shows a good tip (left) and a tip damaged (right) from excessive pressure (tightening)

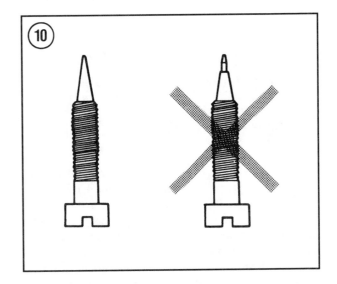

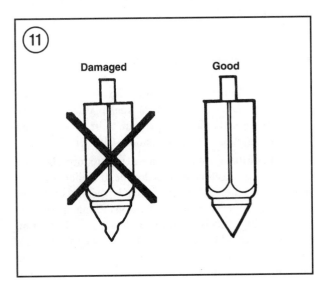

Damaged   Good

when seating. If wear is evident on one side of the needle tip only, the engine is vibrating excessively. Check for a damaged propeller or bent propshaft.

11. The inlet needle and seat and the float assembly are included in the repair kit and must always be replaced. If for some reason they must be reused, inspect as follows:

    a. Check the inlet needle and seat for excessive wear. Replace the needle and seat as an assembly if either are damaged or worn. See **Figure 11**.

    b. Check the float for fuel absorption, deterioration or other damage. Check the float arm for wear in the hinge pin and inlet needle contact areas. Replace the float as necessary.

LEAD SHOT REMOVAL

Core Plug Service

Core plugs must be removed during a carburetor rebuild. Debris and contaminants behind a core plug can only be removed by washing the carburetor after all core plugs are removed. New core plugs are included with the carburetor repair kit.

To remove the core plug(s), proceed as follows:

1. Secure the carburetor in a vise with protective jaws or set the carburetor on a shop towel and workbench. If removing a core plug on the top of the carburetor, make sure the emulsion tube and high-speed nozzle are protected by temporarily reinstalling the float chamber. Damage to the emulsion tube or high-speed nozzle cannot be repaired.

> *CAUTION*
> *Do not allow anything to penetrate more than 1/8 in. (3.2 mm) below any core plug or the carburetor casting will be irreparably damaged.*

2. Drive a 1/8 in. (3.2 mm) pin punch through the center of the core plug. Do not allow the punch to pass through the core plug by more than 1/8 in. (3.2 mm). Pry the core plug from the body by twisting the pin punch over to one side. Discard the core plug. See **Figure 12**.

3. Clean the carburetor as described in the previous section. Inspect the core plug hole. If the hole is out-of-round, damaged or distorted, replace the carburetor assembly.

4. Position a new core plug into the carburetor body with its convex (raised) side facing up.

5. Using a pin punch (or suitable steel rod) with a diameter as close to the core plug's diameter as possible and a perfectly flat end, drive the core plug until it is flattened. Do not drive the plug into a concave (depressed) position.

6. Coat the core plug-to-carburetor body mating surfaces with a light coat of Gasoila (varnish type) sealer or fingernail polish.

7. Check for leakage as described in *Carburetor Cleaning and Inspection*.

Lead Shot Service

1. If leakage is noted at a lead-shot plug, secure the carburetor in a vise with protective jaws or place the carburetor on a shop towel and work bench. Make sure the emulsion tube and high speed nozzle are protected by temporarily reinstalling the float chamber. Damage to the emulsion tube or high speed nozzle cannot be repaired.

2. Carefully pry the lead shot from its opening with a suitable knife, awl or other sharp instrument. See **Figure 13**.

3. Thoroughly clean the lead shot opening in the casting and all passages sealed by the shot.

6

4. Place a new lead shot in the opening. Using a suitable pin punch, flatten the shot only enough to seal the passage. Do not drive the shot down into the passage (blocking other passages).

5. Seal the lead shot with Gasoila (varnish-type) sealant or fingernail polish and allow it to fully dry.

6. Check for leakage as described in *Carburetor Cleaning and Inspection*.

Carburetor Removal/Installation (2, 3.3 and 3.5 hp)

Refer to **Figure 14** for an exploded view of the carburetor and **Table 1** for specifications. The 2 and 3.3 hp carburetors use gravity to supply fuel from the integral fuel tank to the carburetor fuel bowl.

1. Disconnect and ground the spark plug lead to the power head to prevent accidental starting.

2. Remove the knobs from the throttle and choke levers.

3. Remove the front 2 screws and loosen the rear screw securing the manual rewind starter assembly to the power head.

4. Remove the 2 screws from the front intake cover. Lift the front of the manual rewind starter and remove the front intake cover from the carburetor.

> *CAUTION*
> *Push the fuel line off of the fitting whenever possible. If necessary, cut the fuel line with a razor knife (or similar tool). Peel the line from the fitting.*

5. Close the fuel shutoff valve and disconnect the fuel supply hose (A, **Figure 15**) from the carburetor.

> *NOTE*
> *It may be necessary to remove the lower cowling to remove the carburetor.*

6. Loosen the carburetor mounting clamp (B, **Figure 15**) and remove the carburetor.

7. Remove the O-ring (26, **Figure 14**) from inside the carburetor's mounting flange. On 2 hp models, remove the air restrictor plate from behind the O-ring.

8. To install the carburetor, begin by installing a new O-ring (26, **Figure 14**) into the carburetor's mounting flange. On 2 hp models, the air restrictor plate must be installed first, then the O-ring. Position the restrictor plate's slot vertical.

9. Position the carburetor on the power head. Hold the carburetor toward the power head and tighten the mounting clamp (B, **Figure 15**).

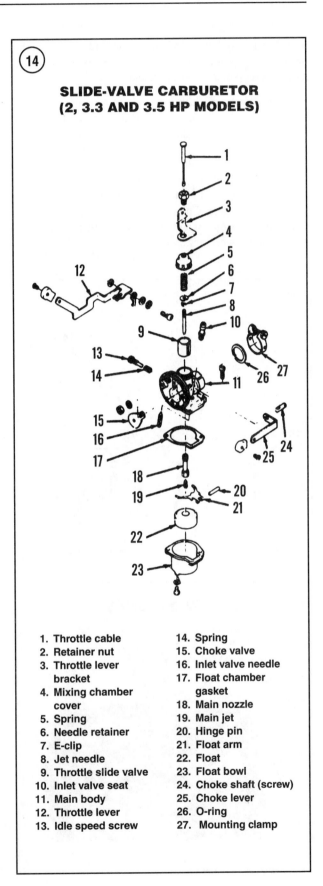

(14)

SLIDE-VALVE CARBURETOR (2, 3.3 AND 3.5 HP MODELS)

1. Throttle cable
2. Retainer nut
3. Throttle lever bracket
4. Mixing chamber cover
5. Spring
6. Needle retainer
7. E-clip
8. Jet needle
9. Throttle slide valve
10. Inlet valve seat
11. Main body
12. Throttle lever
13. Idle speed screw
14. Spring
15. Choke valve
16. Inlet valve needle
17. Float chamber gasket
18. Main nozzle
19. Main jet
20. Hinge pin
21. Float arm
22. Float
23. Float bowl
24. Choke shaft (screw)
25. Choke lever
26. O-ring
27. Mounting clamp

10. Reconnect the fuel delivery hose (A, **Figure 15**). Secure the connection with a new tie-strap or the original spring clamp.

11. Complete the installation by reinstalling the front intake cover, then reinstall the choke and throttle lever knobs.

12. Install the front two screws on the manual rewind starter. Tighten all three screws securely.

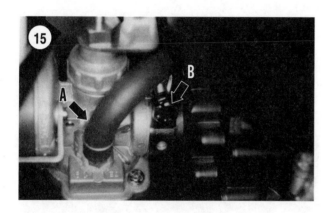

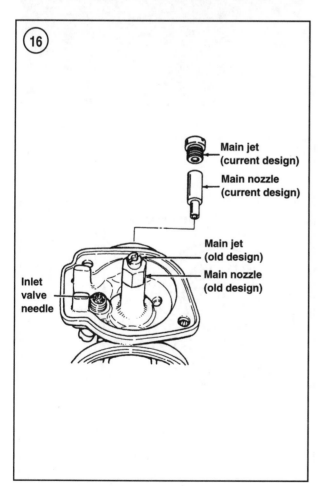

13. Reconnect the spark plug lead, then refer to Chapter Five for carburetor and linkage adjustment procedures.

Disassembly (2, 3.3 and 3.5 hp)

Make sure a carburetor repair kit is obtained prior to carburetor disassembly. The repair kit contains all of the O-rings, gaskets, inlet needle, float assembly and other necessary components. It is not recommended to reuse any of the components that are part of repair kit. Jet screwdriver (part No. 317002) is recommended for removing and installing the main jet.

Refer to **Figure 14** for the following procedure.

1. Remove the float chamber drain screw. Remove and discard the gasket.

2. Remove the two float chamber attaching screws. Separate the float chamber from the carburetor. Remove and discard the float chamber gasket.

3. Invert the carburetor and lift off the float. Then remove the float hinge pin and the float arm.

4. Remove the inlet valve needle. If the inlet valve seat (10, **Figure 14**) is removable, do not remove it unless a new one is included in the repair kit.

5. Remove the main jet using jet screwdriver (part No. 317002) or a suitable wide-blade screwdriver).

NOTE
The main nozzle on these models is held in place by the main jet. See **Figure 16**.

6. Invert the carburetor and catch the main nozzle as it falls out of the carburetor body.

7. Remove the throttle lever.

8. Loosen the retainer nut several turns, then unscrew the mixing chamber cover. Lift the throttle valve assembly out of the carburetor body. See **Figure 17**.

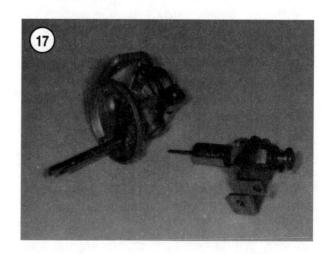

9. Compress the throttle valve spring and disconnect the throttle cable from the throttle valve. See **Figure 18**.

10. Remove the jet needle and jet retainer from the throttle valve. Do not lose the jet needle E-clip. Note the E-clip position for later reference.

11. Lightly seat the idle speed screw while noting the turns required for reference during reassembly. Remove the idle speed screw and spring to complete disassembly.

12. Refer to *Cleaning and Inspection* in this chapter. Also inspect the jet needle (8, **Figure 14**) for nicks, scratches, grooves or other damage. Replace the needle if any defects are noted.

Reassembly (2, 3.3 and 3.5 hp)

The position of the E-clip on the jet needle affects the air/fuel mixture across most of the engine's speed range. The factory setting should be acceptable for most operating conditions.

If an excessively rich or lean condition results from extreme changes in elevation or operating environments, the E-clip's position can be changed. The mixture becomes leaner as the E-clip is moved to the upper grooves and richer as it is moved to the lower grooves. See **Figure 19**.

> *CAUTION*
> *It is always better to run a slightly rich mixture as opposed to one that is too lean.*

Compare all components of the repair kit to be sure they match the original parts. To reassemble the carburetor, refer to **Figure 14** and proceed as follows:

1. Check the jet needle E-clip position. The factory setting is the third groove (1995-1997 [EO-EU] models) or fourth groove (1998-2003 [EC-ST] models) as shown in **Figure 19**. Your carburetor may not have the fifth (lowest) groove. Position the E-clip as specified (or desired).

2. Insert the jet needle into the throttle valve. Place the needle retainer into the throttle valve over the needle's E-ring. Align the retainer slot with the slot in the throttle valve. See **Figure 20**.

3. Reassemble the throttle valve components as follows:
   a. Place the throttle valve spring over the throttle cable.
   b. Compress the spring, then slide the throttle cable anchor through the slot and into position in the throttle valve. See **Figure 21**.

4. Slide the spring onto the idle speed screw. Install the screw into the carburetor body until lightly seated, then back out the number of turns noted during disassembly.

5. Align the slot in the throttle valve with the alignment pin in the carburetor body. Insert the throttle valve assembly into the body and tighten the mixing chamber cover. Tighten the cover retainer nut securely.

6. Reinstall the throttle lever.

7. Install the main nozzle and main jet (**Figure 16**).

8. If the inlet valve seat was removed, install a new valve seat at this time. Then install the inlet valve needle.

9. Install the float arm and hinge pin.

10. With the float chamber removed, invert the carburetor and measure from the mating surface of the carburetor body (with the fuel bowl gasket installed) to the float arm as shown in **Figure 22**. The distance must be 0.090 in. (2.3 mm).

11. If adjustment is necessary, bend the float arms evenly to obtain the specified measurement.

12. Install the float.

13. Install the float chamber with a new gasket. Tighten the bowl screws evenly and securely.

14. Reinstall the carburetor as described in this chapter.

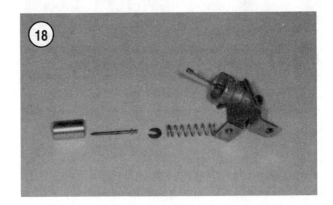
(18)

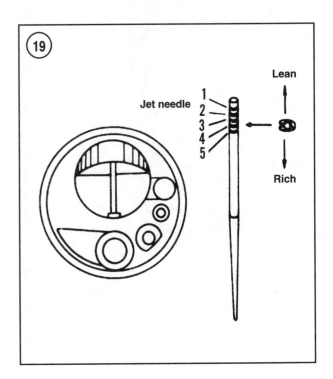
(19)

Jet needle

Lean

Rich

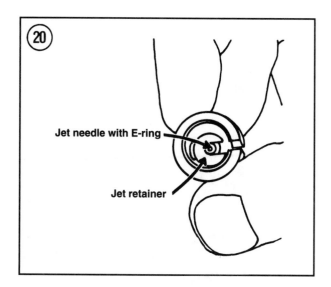

20

Jet needle with E-ring

Jet retainer

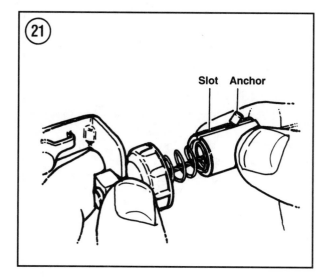

21

Slot   Anchor

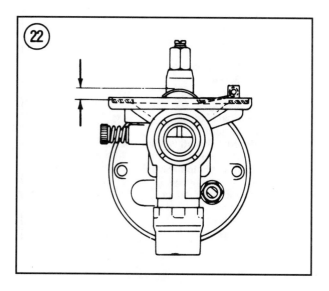

22

Carburetor Removal/Installation
(3 and 4 hp Models [Except 4 Deluxe])

Refer to **Figure 23** (3 and 4 hp models) or **Figure 24** (4 Deluxe models). Refer to **Table 2** for specifications.

1. Disconnect and ground the spark plug leads to the power head to prevent accidental starting.

2. Remove the choke knob by pulling it straight from the engine.

3. Remove the stop button's plastic mounting nut.

4. Remove the two screws from the bottom rear and two screws from the bottom front of the lower cowl assembly. Then slide the rear lower cowl from the engine.

5. *4 hp models*—Remove the tie-strap securing the fuel hose to the quick disconnect connector in the front lower cowl. Disconnect the fuel hose from the connector.

6. Remove the front lower cowl from the engine.

7. Remove the two screws securing the air intake cover to the carburetor. Then disconnect the choke linkage and remove the air intake cover.

8. *3 hp and 4 hp (BR) models*—Using a pair of side-cutter pliers, remove the roll pin that holds the fuel shutoff valve in the float chamber. See **Figure 25**. Then pull the shutoff valve from the float chamber.

> *CAUTION*
> *Push the fuel line(s) off of the fitting(s) whenever possible. If necessary, cut the fuel line with a razor knife (or similar tool), peel the line from the fitting. Do not apply excessive force or the carburetor will be damaged.*

9A. *3 hp and 4 hp (R) models*—Disconnect the single fuel supply hose from the carburetor.

9B. *4 hp (BR) models*—Disconnect the fuel supply lines (from the integral tank and conventional fuel pump) from the carburetor.

10. Remove the shoulder screw (8, **Figure 23**), throttle cam follower and cam follower link. Do not misplace the washer (5, **Figure 23**).

11. Remove the 2 nuts securing the carburetor to the intake manifold, then pull the carburetor from the engine. Remove and discard the carburetor gasket. Carefully clean any remaining gasket material from the carburetor and intake manifold.

> *NOTE*
> *Do not use gasket sealant on the carburetor-to-intake manifold gasket. Install the gasket dry.*

12. To reinstall the carburetor, begin by installing a new gasket (without sealant) onto the carburetor mounting studs.

6

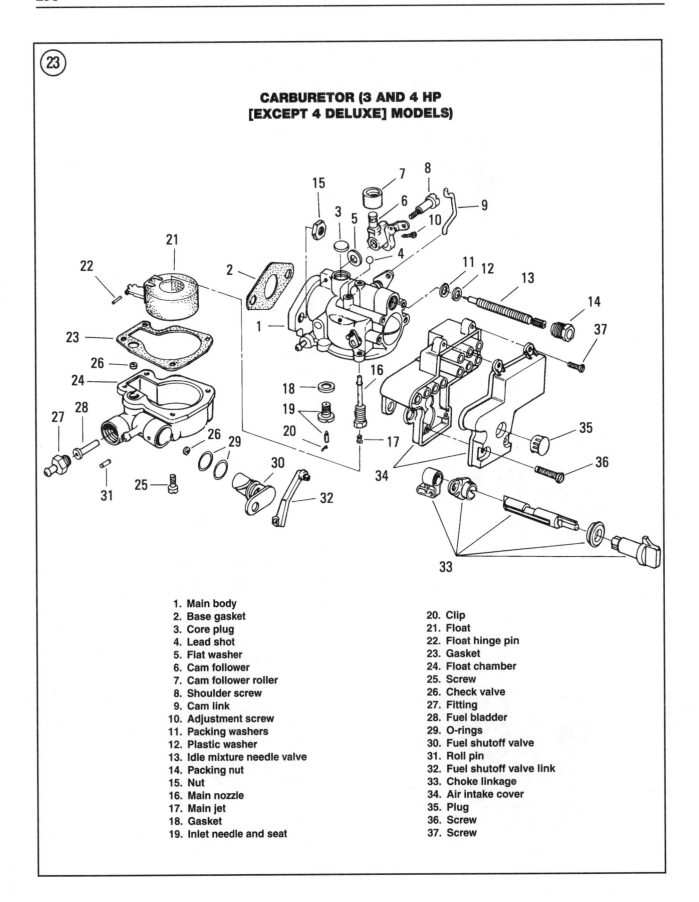

CARBURETOR (3 AND 4 HP [EXCEPT 4 DELUXE] MODELS)

1. Main body
2. Base gasket
3. Core plug
4. Lead shot
5. Flat washer
6. Cam follower
7. Cam follower roller
8. Shoulder screw
9. Cam link
10. Adjustment screw
11. Packing washers
12. Plastic washer
13. Idle mixture needle valve
14. Packing nut
15. Nut
16. Main nozzle
17. Main jet
18. Gasket
19. Inlet needle and seat
20. Clip
21. Float
22. Float hinge pin
23. Gasket
24. Float chamber
25. Screw
26. Check valve
27. Fitting
28. Fuel bladder
29. O-rings
30. Fuel shutoff valve
31. Roll pin
32. Fuel shutoff valve link
33. Choke linkage
34. Air intake cover
35. Plug
36. Screw
37. Screw

CARBURETOR (4 DELUXE MODELS)

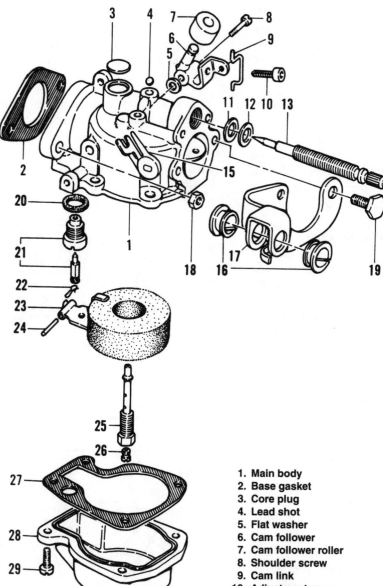

1. Main body
2. Base gasket
3. Core plug
4. Lead shot
5. Flat washer
6. Cam follower
7. Cam follower roller
8. Shoulder screw
9. Cam link
10. Adjustment screw
11. Packing washers
12. Plastic washer
13. Idle mixture
    needle valve
14. Packing nut
15. Choke shaft lever
16. Bushing
17. Choke linkage
    bracket
18. Nut
19. Screw
20. Gasket
21. Inlet needle valve
    and seat
22. Clip
23. Float
24. Float hinge pin
25. Main nozzle
26. Main jet
27. Gasket
28. Float chamber
29. Screw

6

13. Position the carburetor against the intake manifold. Secure the carburetor with two nuts. Evenly tighten the mounting nuts until they are secure.

14. Connect the fuel hose(s) to the carburetor. Secure the connection(s) with new tie-straps.

15. Install the throttle cam follower, cam follower link, shoulder screw and washer as shown in **Figure 23**. Tighten the shoulder screw securely, then make sure the linkage moves freely. Correct any problems found.

16. *3 hp and 4 hp (BR) models*—Make sure both O-rings are properly located on the fuel shutoff valve. Lightly lubricate the O-rings with outboard motor oil. To prevent damaging the O-rings, install the valve into the float chamber with a twisting motion. Secure the valve using a new roll pin. Do not damage the valve by driving the roll pin too far into the valve.

17. Install the air intake cover and choke linkage. Tighten the two air intake cover screws securely. Make sure the choke linkage moves freely. Correct any problems found.

18. *4 hp models*—Reconnect the fuel hose to the quick disconnect connector in the front lower cowl. Secure the connection with a new tie-strap.

19. Position the front lower cowl to the engine.

20. Position the rear lower cowl to the engine and the front lower cowl. Install the two screws at the bottom rear and two screws at the bottom front of the lower cowl assembly. Tighten all four screws securely.

21. Guide the stop button through the lower cowl and secure it in place with the plastic nut. Tighten the nut securely.

22. Install the choke knob onto the choke link shaft, then reconnect the spark plug leads.

23. Refer to Chapter Five for carburetor and linkage adjustment procedures.

Carburetor Removal/Installation (4 Deluxe)

1. Disconnect and ground the spark plug leads to the power head to prevent accidental starting.

2. Pull the idle mixture adjustment knob straight from the engine (and idle mixture adjustment screw).

3. Remove the retaining clip securing the choke knob to the choke shaft (**Figure 26**) using needlenose pliers. Then pull the choke knob from the lower cowl.

4. Remove the shoulder screw (8, **Figure 24**), throttle cam follower and cam follower link. Do not misplace the washer (5, **Figure 24**).

CAUTION
Push the fuel line off of the fitting whenever possible. If necessary, cut the fuel line with a razor knife (or similar tool), then peel the

line from the fitting. Do not apply excessive force or the carburetor will be damaged.

5. Disconnect the fuel hose from the carburetor.

6. Remove the two nuts securing the carburetor to the intake manifold, then pull the carburetor from the engine. Remove and discard the carburetor gasket. Carefully clean any remaining gasket material off of the carburetor and intake manifold.

NOTE
Do not use gasket sealant on the carburetor-to-intake manifold gasket. Install the gasket dry.

7. To reinstall the carburetor, begin by installing a new gasket (without sealant) onto the carburetor mounting studs.

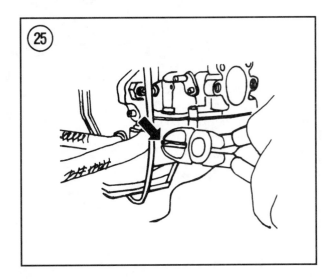

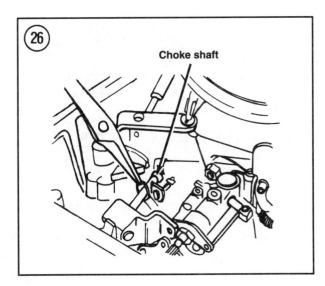

Choke shaft

8. Position the carburetor against the intake manifold. Install and tighten the two mounting nuts evenly and securely.

9. Connect the fuel hose to the carburetor. Secure the connection with a new tie-strap.

10. Install the throttle cam follower, cam follower link, shoulder screw and washer as shown in **Figure 24**. Tighten the shoulder screw securely, then make sure the linkage moves freely. Correct any problems found.

11. Install the choke knob and secure it with the retaining clip. Make sure the choke linkage moves freely. Correct any problems found.

12. Install the low-speed adjusting knob, then reconnect the spark plug leads.

13. Refer to Chapter Five for carburetor and linkage adjustment procedures.

Disassembly (3, 4 hp and 4 Deluxe)

Make sure a carburetor repair kit is obtained prior to carburetor disassembly. The repair kit will contain the O-rings, gaskets, inlet needle and seat, float assembly and other necessary components. It is not recommended to reuse any of the components that are part of repair kit. Jet screwdriver (part No. 317002) is recommended for removing and installing the main jet.

Refer to **Figure 23** (3 and 4 hp) or **Figure 24** (4 Deluxe) for this procedure.

1. Remove the four float chamber screws and separate the float chamber from the carburetor body. Remove and discard the float chamber gasket.

2. Unscrew the idle mixture needle valve's packing nut, then remove the needle valve.

3. Using a small seal pick or similar tool, carefully remove the washer (12, **Figure 23** or **Figure 24**) and needle valve

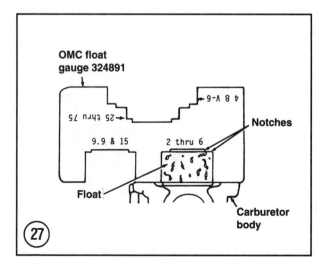

packing from the carburetor body. Be careful not to damage the packing nut threads.

4. *3 hp and 4 hp (BR) models*—Unscrew and remove the fuel pump fitting from the float chamber. Then remove the fuel pump bladder.

5. Using needlenose pliers, remove the float pivot pin. Then remove the float, retaining clip and inlet valve needle. Finally, unscrew the inlet valve seat using a wide-blade screwdriver or suitable tool.

6. Remove the main jet using jet screwdriver (part No. 317002) or a suitable wide-blade screwdriver). Then remove the main nozzle (16, **Figure 23** or 25, **Figure 24**).

7. Refer to *Cleaning and Inspection* in this chapter. On 3 hp and 4 hp (BR) models, also inspect the fuel pump bladder (28, **Figure 23**) and the two check valves (26, **Figure 23**) for damage, debris or deterioration. Replace the bladder and/or check valve(s) if any defects are noted.

Reassembly (3 hp, 4 hp and 4 Deluxe)

Refer to **Figure 23** (3 and 4 hp) or **Figure 24** (4 Deluxe) for this procedure. Compare all components of the repair kit (such as gaskets and the inlet valve assembly) to be sure they match the original parts.

1. Install the main nozzle into the carburetor body and tighten it securely. Then install and securely tighten the main jet into the nozzle.

2. Place a new gasket onto a new inlet valve seat, then thread the seat into the main body. Tighten the seat securely using a wide-blade screwdriver or suitable tool. The inlet seat must not be distorted or damaged during the tightening process.

3. Install the retaining clip onto a new inlet valve needle, then position the clip over the float arm. Install the float and inlet needle assembly to the carburetor and secure it in place with the hinge pin.

4. To set the float level, invert the carburetor so the float is facing upward. Allow the weight of the float to close the inlet valve assembly.

NOTE
*If the OMC carburetor gauge (part No. 324891) is not available, refer to **Table 2** for float level **direct measurement** specifications. Using a T gauge (or equivalent) tool, measure the float level at the same locations that the carburetor gauge checks as shown in **Figure 27**.*

5. Place the carburetor gauge (part No. 324891) with its notch marked 2 THRU 6 HP over the float. Make sure the gauge is resting directly on the float chamber gasket surface and that the gasket is not installed. See **Figure 27**.

6. The top of the float must be located at or between the notches as shown. Make sure the float gauge is not pushing downward on the float and that the float is not below the second notch.

7. If adjustment is necessary, carefully bend the float arm as required (between the float and the hinge pin bore) to position the float as specified. Do not force the inlet valve needle into the seat and do not bend the arm so that one side of the float is higher than the other. The float must be parallel with the carburetor body as viewed in **Figure 27**. Recheck the adjustment using the float gauge and readjust until the float level is correct.

8. To set the float drop, hold the carburetor in the upright position and allow the float to hang by its own weight. See **Figure 28**.

9. Measure the distance (D, **Figure 28**) from the float chamber gasket surface (without the gasket installed) to the bottom edge of the float as shown. The distance must be 1.125 to 1.5 in. (28.6-38.1 mm).

10. If adjustment is necessary, carefully bend the tab (T, **Figure 28**) as necessary. Do not bend the float arm or the float level setting will be altered.

11. *3 hp and 4 hp (BR) models*—Install the fuel pump bladder, then the fitting into the float chamber. Tighten the fitting securely.

12. Place a new gasket on the float chamber. Then install the bowl and secure it with four screws. Tighten the screws evenly in a crossing pattern to 15-22 in.-lb. (1.7-2.2 N•m).

13. Insert a new idle mixture needle valve packing assembly (three packing washers) into the carburetor body. Install the plastic washer, then install the packing nut into the carburetor body finger-tight.

14. Install the idle mixture needle valve. Turn the needle valve into the carburetor body until lightly seated. Then back out the valve one full turn.

15. Tighten the packing nut until the needle valve movement becomes stiff. The packing must be tight enough to prevent the valve from moving under engine vibration, but loose enough to allow adjustment when the mixture knob is installed. Readjust the packing nut as necessary.

16. Reinstall the carburetor as described in this chapter.

MODULAR CARBURETOR
(6-20 HP [TWO-CYLINDER], 25 AND
35 HP [THREE-CYLINDER] MODELS)

The term *modular* is used because the float chamber and top cover are constructed of a nonmetallic Minlon material (mineral reinforced nylon) while the carburetor body is made of aluminum. Different design top covers and float chambers are used to allow this carburetor to work on a wide range of engines.

On 6 and 8 hp models, the carburetors use a top cover with a pivot post for the throttle cam follower assembly, an idle mixture screw on the starboard rear corner and a filter screen inside the cover. There is no intermediate fuel (or air) jet in the top cover. An idle speed screw controls the throttle plate's position at idle. The main jet screws into the removable plastic main nozzle, which is connected to the carburetor body with a flexible tube. A wire screen, located on the starboard side of the main body protects the float chamber vent. All models use a choke assembly.

On 9.9 and 15 hp models, the carburetors use a top cover with a pivot post for the throttle cam follower assembly and an idle mixture screw on the starboard rear corner. There is no filter screen or intermediate fuel (or air) jet in the top cover. There is also no idle speed screw, and the throttle plate must be able to fully close in order for the engine to idle properly. Idle speed is controlled by adjusting the throttle cam (which controls throttle plate position). The main jet screws into the starboard side of the float chamber and is covered by the starboard float chamber drain screw. There is no removable main nozzle or flexible tube on these models. A plastic fitting, located near the top of the starboard side of the main body, shields the float chamber vent. Tiller handle models use a choke assembly and the primer fitting on the carburetor body or top cover must be capped, while remote control models use a primer system connected to the primer fitting on the carburetor body or top cover.

On 20 hp models, the carburetor uses a top cover without a pivot post (for a cam follower), but the idle mixture screw is still located on the starboard rear corner. There is no intermediate fuel (or air) jet in the top cover. There is also no idle speed screw and the throttle plate must be able to fully close in order for the engine to idle properly. Idle

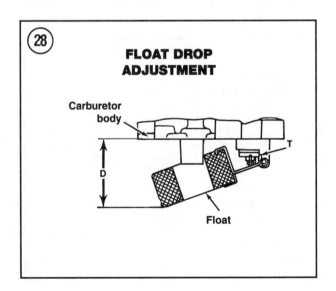

FLOAT DROP ADJUSTMENT

Carburetor body

Float

speed is primarily controlled by changing the idle timing. The main jet screws into the removable plastic main nozzle, which is connected to the carburetor body with a flexible tube. A wire screen, located on the starboard side of the main body, protects the float chamber vent. A primer system is used on all models and is connected to the port float chamber fitting (supply) and to the primer fitting on the starboard side of the carburetor mounting flange (delivery).

On 25 and 35 hp (three-cylinder) models, the carburetors use a top cover without a pivot post (for a cam follower). The idle mixture screw is located at the cover's port rear corner and an intermediate air bleed jet is mounted in a

special adaptor screw at the very front of the top cover. There is no idle speed screw and the throttle plate on each carburetor must be fully closed for the engine to idle properly. Idle speed is controlled by idle timing alone. The main jet screws into the port side of the float chamber and is covered by the port float chamber drain screw. A hole drilled on starboard side of the carburetor's body is the float chamber vent.

Refer to **Figure 29** (6, 8 and 20) or **Figure 30** (9.9, 15, 25 and 35 hp [three-cylinder]) for typical exploded views of these modular carburetors. Refer to **Tables 2-4** for specifications.

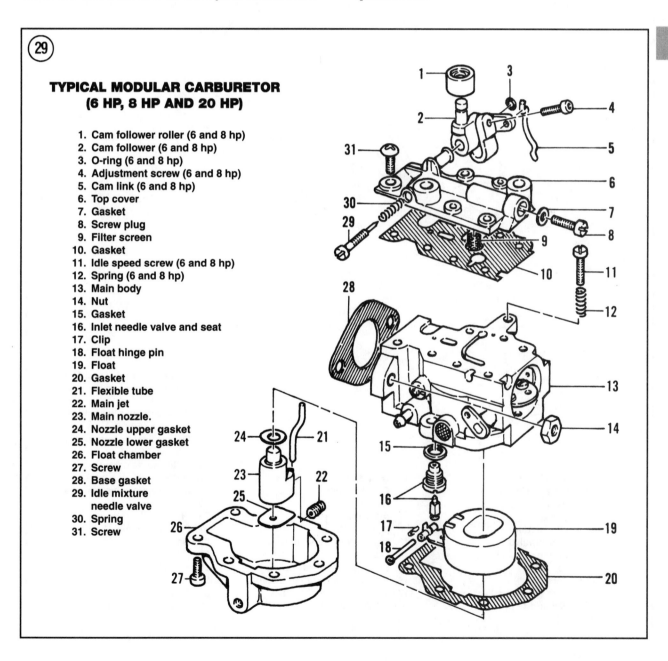

(29)

TYPICAL MODULAR CARBURETOR (6 HP, 8 HP AND 20 HP)

1. Cam follower roller (6 and 8 hp)
2. Cam follower (6 and 8 hp)
3. O-ring (6 and 8 hp)
4. Adjustment screw (6 and 8 hp)
5. Cam link (6 and 8 hp)
6. Top cover
7. Gasket
8. Screw plug
9. Filter screen
10. Gasket
11. Idle speed screw (6 and 8 hp)
12. Spring (6 and 8 hp)
13. Main body
14. Nut
15. Gasket
16. Inlet needle valve and seat
17. Clip
18. Float hinge pin
19. Float
20. Gasket
21. Flexible tube
22. Main jet
23. Main nozzle.
24. Nozzle upper gasket
25. Nozzle lower gasket
26. Float chamber
27. Screw
28. Base gasket
29. Idle mixture needle valve
30. Spring
31. Screw

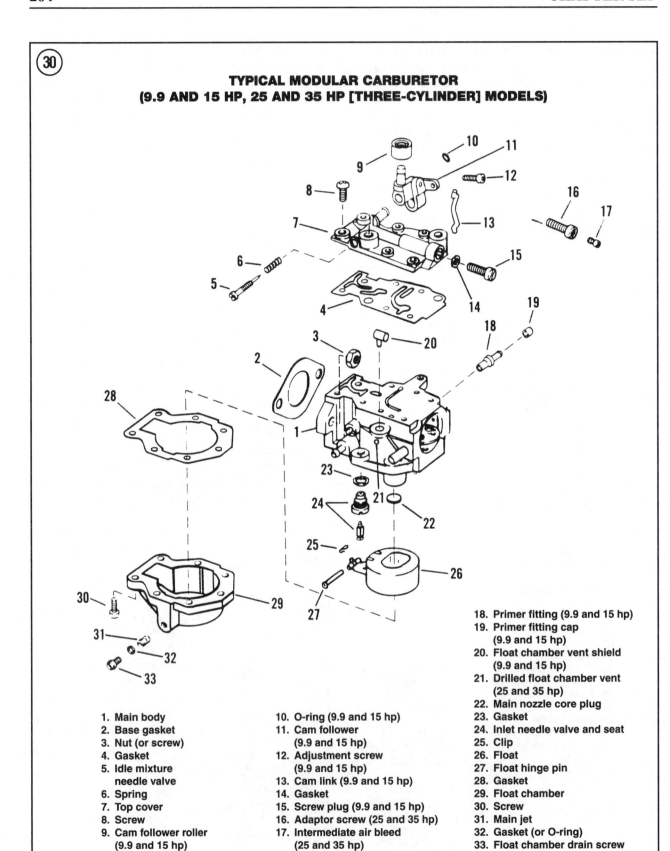

**TYPICAL MODULAR CARBURETOR
(9.9 AND 15 HP, 25 AND 35 HP [THREE-CYLINDER] MODELS)**

1. Main body
2. Base gasket
3. Nut (or screw)
4. Gasket
5. Idle mixture
   needle valve
6. Spring
7. Top cover
8. Screw
9. Cam follower roller
   (9.9 and 15 hp)
10. O-ring (9.9 and 15 hp)
11. Cam follower
    (9.9 and 15 hp)
12. Adjustment screw
    (9.9 and 15 hp)
13. Cam link (9.9 and 15 hp)
14. Gasket
15. Screw plug (9.9 and 15 hp)
16. Adaptor screw (25 and 35 hp)
17. Intermediate air bleed
    (25 and 35 hp)
18. Primer fitting (9.9 and 15 hp)
19. Primer fitting cap
    (9.9 and 15 hp)
20. Float chamber vent shield
    (9.9 and 15 hp)
21. Drilled float chamber vent
    (25 and 35 hp)
22. Main nozzle core plug
23. Gasket
24. Inlet needle valve and seat
25. Clip
26. Float
27. Float hinge pin
28. Gasket
29. Float chamber
30. Screw
31. Main jet
32. Gasket (or O-ring)
33. Float chamber drain screw

Removal/Installation (6-15 hp Models)

Refer to **Figure 29** or **Figure 30** for this procedure.

1. *Electric start models*—Disconnect the negative battery cable.

2. Disconnect and ground the spark plug leads to the power head to prevent accidental starting.

3. Remove the rope starter assembly as described in Chapter Twelve.

4. Remove the 2 screws (and washers) securing the air intake cover to the carburetor's top cover. Remove the air intake cover from the engine.

5A. *6 and 8 hp models*—Remove the shoulder screw (A, **Figure 31**) securing the choke linkage bellcrank to the starboard side of the carburetor's float chamber. Disconnect and remove the choke link from the carburetor's choke shaft arm (B, **Figure 31**).

5B. *9.9 and 15 hp tiller handle models*—Disconnect and remove the choke linkage from the carburetor.

> *CAUTION*
> *Push fuel (or primer) lines off of their fittings whenever possible. If necessary, cut the line with a razor knife (or similar tool) and peel the line from the fitting. Do not apply excessive force or the carburetor will be damaged.*

5C. *9.9 and 15 hp remote control models*—Disconnect the primer line from the fitting on the port side of the carburetor.

6. Remove the O-ring securing the cam follower to the port side of the carburetor's top cover. Then slide the cam follower off and disconnect the cam follower link from the throttle arm.

7. Remove the two nuts securing the carburetor to the intake manifold, then pull the carburetor from the engine.

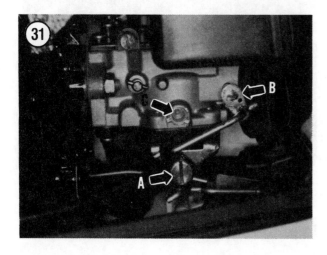

Once the carburetor is off of the studs, disconnect the fuel supply hose from the carburetor.

8. Remove and discard the carburetor gasket. Carefully clean any remaining gasket material from the carburetor and intake manifold.

> *NOTE*
> *Do not use gasket sealant on the carburetor-to-intake manifold gasket. Install the gasket dry.*

9. To reinstall the carburetor, begin by installing a new gasket (without sealant) onto the carburetor mounting studs.

10. Hold the carburetor near the intake manifold and attach the fuel line. Secure the connection with a new tie-strap.

11. Slide the carburetor over the studs and against the intake manifold. Install and tighten the nuts evenly and securely.

12. Install the throttle cam follower and cam follower link. Engage the link with the throttle arm, then slide the cam follower onto the carburetor's top cover. Secure the follower in place with a new O-ring. Then make sure the linkage moves freely.

13A. *6 and 8 hp models*—Connect the choke link to the choke shaft's arm. Position the choke linkage and bellcrank to side of the float chamber, then secure it in place with the shoulder screw. Tighten the screw securely. Verify that the choke linkage moves freely. See **Figure 31**.

13B. *9.9 and 15 hp tiller handle models*—Install the choke linkage to the carburetor. Make sure the choke linkage moves freely. Correct any problems found.

13C. *9.9 and 15 hp remote control models*—Reconnect the primer line to the fitting on the port side of the carburetor.

14. Position the air intake cover to the carburetor. Secure the cover in place with the two screws and washers. Tighten the screws to 8-10 in.-lb. (0.9-1.1 N•m).

15. Reinstall the rope starter as described in Chapter Twelve.

16. Reconnect the spark plug leads. On electric start models, reconnect the negative battery cable.

17. Refer to Chapter Five for carburetor and linkage adjustment procedures.

Removal/Installation (20 hp Models)

Refer to **Figure 29** for this procedure.

1. Disconnect and ground the spark plug leads to the power head to prevent accidental starting.

2. Disconnect the cam follower link from the snap connector on the starboard side of the carburetor's throttle arm. See **Figure 32**.

> *CAUTION*
> *Push fuel (or primer) lines off of their fittings whenever possible. If necessary, cut the line with a razor knife (or similar tool). Peel the line from the fitting and replace it. Do not apply excessive force or the carburetor will be damaged.*

3. Remove the two nuts securing the carburetor to the intake manifold, then pull the carburetor from the engine. Once the carburetor is off of the studs, disconnect the fuel hoses as follows:
   a. Disconnect the large primer line from the port side of the float chamber.
   b. Disconnect the small primer line from the starboard side of the carburetor's mounting flange.
   c. Disconnect the fuel line (from the fuel pump) from the 90° fitting on the starboard side of the carburetor body, just below the throttle shaft.

4. Remove and discard the carburetor gasket. Carefully clean any remaining gasket material off of the carburetor and intake manifold.

> *NOTE*
> *Do not use gasket sealant on the carburetor-to-intake manifold gasket. Install the gasket dry.*

5. To reinstall the carburetor, begin by installing a new gasket (without sealant) onto the carburetor mounting studs.

6. Hold the carburetor near the intake manifold and attach the fuel lines as follows:
   a. Connect the large primer line to the port side of the float chamber.
   b. Connect the small primer line to the starboard side of the carburetor's mounting flange.
   c. Connect the fuel line (from the fuel pump) to the 90° fitting on the starboard side of the carburetor body, just below the throttle shaft.
   d. Secure each connection with a new tie-strap.

7. Slide the carburetor over the studs and against the intake manifold. Install the two nuts and tighten them evenly and securely.

8. Reconnect the cam follower link to the snap connector on the starboard side of the carburetor's throttle arm. See **Figure 32**.

9. Reconnect the spark plug leads.

10. Refer to Chapter Five for carburetor and linkage adjustment procedures.

Removal/Installation
(25 and 35 hp [Three-cylinder] Models)

The following procedure describes the removal/installation of both carburetors. The carburetors can be removed/installed individually, if so desired.

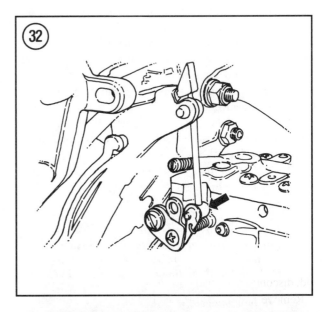

1. *Electric start models*—Disconnect the negative battery cable.

2. Disconnect and ground the spark plug leads to the power head to prevent accidental starting.

3. Remove the air intake cover from the engine. Make sure the drain hose at the bottom of the cover is disconnected.

4A. *Tiller handle models*—Disconnect the throttle (**Figure 33**) and choke linkage from the snap connectors on each carburetor's throttle and choke shaft arms. Also disconnect the choke cable from the middle carburetor's cable bracket.

4B. *Remote control models*—Disconnect the throttle linkage from the snap connectors on each carburetor's throttle shaft arm. See **Figure 33**.

CAUTION
Push fuel lines off of their fittings whenever possible. If necessary, cut the line with a razor knife (or similar tool). Peel the line from the fitting. Do not apply excessive force or the carburetor will be damaged.

5. Remove the two screws securing the top carburetor to the intake manifold, then pull the carburetor from the engine. Once the carburetor is free from the intake manifold, disconnect the fuel hose from the carburetor.

6. Remove and discard the carburetor gasket. Carefully clean any remaining gasket material off of the carburetor and intake manifold.

7. Repeat Steps 5-6 for each remaining carburetor.

NOTE
Do not use gasket sealant on the carburetor-to-intake manifold gasket. Install the gasket dry.

8. To reinstall the carburetors, hold the bottom carburetor near the intake manifold and attach the fuel line. Secure the connection with a new tie-strap.

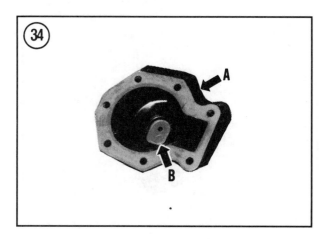

9. Position a new gasket (without sealant) between the carburetor and intake manifold. Align the screw holes and install the two screws. Evenly tighten the mounting screws to 60-84 in.-lb. (6.8-9.5 N•m).

10. Repeat Steps 8-9 for each remaining carburetor.

11A. *Tiller handle models*—Reconnect the throttle and choke linkage to the snap connectors on each carburetor's throttle and choke shaft arms. Then reconnect the choke cable to the middle carburetor's choke cable bracket.

11B. *Remote control models*—Reconnect the throttle linkage to the snap connectors on each carburetor's throttle shaft arm.

12. Reinstall the air intake cover. Make sure the cover's drain hose is reconnected.

13. Reconnect the spark plug leads and on electric start models, reconnect the negative battery cable.

14. Refer to Chapter Five for carburetor and linkage adjustment procedures.

Disassembly (All Modular Carburetors)

Make sure a carburetor repair kit is obtained prior to carburetor disassembly. The repair kit will contain the O-rings, gaskets, inlet needle and seat, float assembly and other necessary components. It is not recommended to reuse any of the components that are part of the repair kit. Jet screwdriver (part No. 317002) is recommended for removing and installing the main jet (and intermediate jet [if so equipped]).

Refer to **Figure 29** or **Figure 30** for this procedure.

1. *25 and 35 hp models*—Remove the two screws securing the air intake cover adaptor horn to the front face of the carburetor. Remove the adaptor, then remove and discard the gasket.

2. Remove the idle mixture screw and spring from the top cover.

3. Remove the top cover screws (or remaining top cover screws). Lift the cover and gasket off of the carburetor body. Discard the gasket. On 6 and 8 hp models, make sure the filter screen (9, **Figure 29**) is located and secured.

4A. *6-20 hp models*—Remove the screw plug from the top cover. See 8, **Figure 29** or 15, **Figure 30**. Then remove and discard the gasket (7, **Figure 29** or 14, **Figure 30**).

4B. *25 and 35 hp models*—Using jet screwdriver (part No. 317002) or equivalent, remove the intermediate air bleed jet (17, **Figure 30**) from the top cover. Then using a suitable screwdriver, remove the adaptor screw (16) and gasket (14). Discard the gasket.

5. Remove the seven float chamber screws. Separate the float chamber from the carburetor body. Remove and discard the float chamber gasket (A, **Figure 34**). On 6-8 hp and 20 hp models, remove the nozzle well lower gasket (B, **Figure 34**) from the float chamber.

6. Push the float pin (A, **Figure 35**, typical) from the carburetor body using a suitable tool, then remove the float (B) and the inlet valve needle and clip.

7. Using a wide-blade screwdriver (or suitable tool), unscrew and remove the inlet valve seat (A, **Figure 36**). Then remove and discard the seat gasket.

8. *6, 8 and 20 hp models*—Carefully slit the flexible tube (B, **Figure 36**) at each end's fitting. Then remove and discard the tube.

9. *6, 8 and 20 hp models*—Remove the high-speed orifice (**Figure 37**) using jet screwdriver (part No. 317002) or equivalent. Then lift the main nozzle (C, **Figure 36**) from the carburetor body. Remove and discard the nozzle's upper gasket (24, **Figure 29**).

10. Remove the float chamber drain plug(s) on 6-15, 25 and 35 hp models, or the primer fitting on 20 hp models. Then remove and discard the gasket(s) or O-ring(s).

11. *9.9, 15, 25 and 35 hp models*—Using jet screwdriver (part No. 317002) or equivalent, remove the high-speed jet from the float chamber's starboard drain hole on 9.9 and 15 hp models, or port hole on 25 and 35 hp models.

12. Refer to *Carburetor Cleaning and Inspection* in this chapter. On 6, 8 and 20 hp models, make sure the float chamber's vent screen (C, **Figure 31**) is not blocked or damaged. Replace the screen if it cannot be cleaned or is damaged.

Reassembly (All Modular Carburetors)

Refer to **Figure 29** (6, 8 and 20 hp) or **Figure 30** (9.9, 15, 25 and 35 hp) for this procedure. Compare all components of the repair kit (such as gaskets and the inlet valve assembly) to be sure they match the original parts.

1. *6, 8 and 20 hp models*—Install a new flexible tube onto the main body fitting. Then install a new main nozzle upper gasket over the main nozzle. Install the main nozzle to the main body, making sure the upper gasket is between the nozzle and body. Connect the flexible tube to the fitting on the main nozzle.

2A. *6, 8 and 20 hp models*—Using jet screwdriver (part No. 317002) or equivalent, install the main jet into the main nozzle. Tighten the jet securely. See **Figure 37**.

2B. *9.9, 15, 25 and 35 hp models*—Using jet screwdriver (part No. 317002) or equivalent, install the main jet into the starboard side of the float chamber on 9.9 and 15 hp models or the port side on 25 and 35 hp models. Tighten the jet securely.

3. Install the float chamber drain plug(s) on 6-15, 25 and 35 hp models or the primer fitting on 20 hp models, using a new gasket(s) or O-ring(s). Tighten the drain plug(s) or primer fitting securely.

4. Place a new gasket onto a new inlet valve seat, then thread the seat into the main body. Tighten the seat se-

curely using a wide-blade screwdriver or suitable tool. The inlet seat must not be distorted or damaged during the tightening process.

5. Install the retaining clip onto a new inlet valve needle, then position the clip over the float arm. Install the float and inlet needle assembly to the carburetor and secure it in place with the hinge pin.

NOTE
*If the OMC carburetor gauge (part No. 324891) is not available, refer to **Tables 2-4** for float level **direct measurement** specifications. Using a T gauge (or equivalent) tool, measure the float level at the same locations that the carburetor gauge checks as shown in **Figure 38**.*

6. To set the float level, invert the carburetor so the float is facing upward. Allow the weight of the float to close the inlet valve assembly.

7. Place the float gauge part No. 324891 with the notch marked *9.9 & 15 HP* over the float. Make sure the gauge

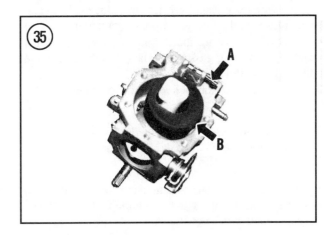

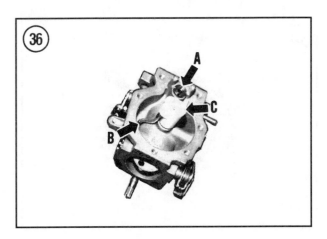

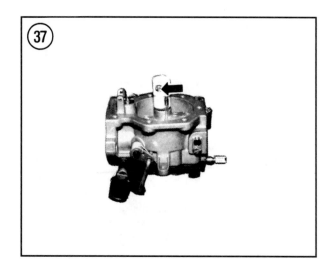

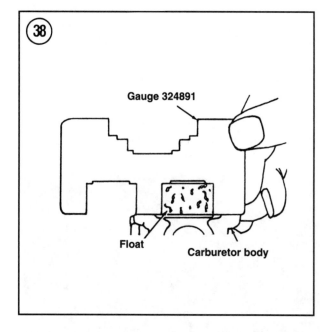

Gauge 324891

Float

Carburetor body

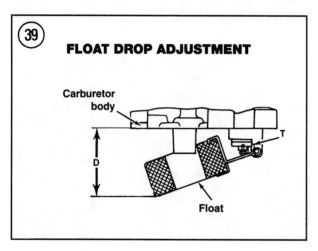

FLOAT DROP ADJUSTMENT

Carburetor body

D

T

Float

is resting directly on the float chamber gasket surface and that the gasket is not installed. See **Figure 38**, typical.

8. The top of the float must be located at or between the notches as shown. Make sure the float gauge is not pushing downward on the float and that the float is not below the second notch.

9. If adjustment is necessary, carefully bend the float arm as required (between the float and the hinge pin bore) to position the float as specified. Do not force the inlet valve needle into the seat and do not bend the arm so that one side of the float is higher than the other. The float must be parallel with the carburetor body as viewed in **Figure 38**. Recheck the adjustment using the float gauge and readjust until the float level is correct.

10. To set the float drop, hold the carburetor in the upright position and allow the float to hang by its own weight. See **Figure 39**.

11. Measure the distance (D, **Figure 39**) from the float chamber gasket surface (without the gasket installed) to the bottom edge of the float as shown. The distance must be 1.0 to 1.375 in. (25.4-34.9 mm).

12. If adjustment is necessary, carefully bend the tab (T, **Figure 39**) as necessary. Do not bend the float arm or the float level setting will be altered.

13. *6, 8 and 20 hp models*—Place a new main nozzle lower gasket into the float chamber relief. See B, **Figure 34**.

14. Place a new gasket on the float chamber, see A, **Figure 34**, typical. Then install the bowl and secure it with seven screws. Make sure the lower nozzle gasket is not displaced on 6, 8 and 20 hp models. Tighten the screws evenly in the pattern cast into the float chamber to 8-10 in.-lb. (0.8-1.2 N•m) on 6-20 hp models or 17-19 in.-lb. (1.9-2.2 N•m) on 25 and 35 hp models.

15. Using a new gasket, install the top cover to the main body. On 6 and 8 hp models, make sure the filter screen (9, **Figure 29**) is installed into the top cover before installing the cover to the body. Install and tighten the cover screws evenly in the pattern cast into the top cover to 8-10 in.-lb. (0.8-1.2 N•m) on 6-20 hp models or 17-19 in.-lb. (1.9-2.2 N•m) on 25 and 35 hp models.

16A. *6-20 hp models*—Install the screw plug (8, **Figure 29** or 15, **Figure 30**) into the top cover using a new gasket (7, **Figure 29** or 14, **Figure 30**). Tighten the screw plug securely.

16B. *25 and 35 hp models*—Install the adaptor screw (16, **Figure 30**) into the top cover using a new gasket (14). Tighten the adaptor screw securely. Then using jet screwdriver (part No. 317002) or equivalent, install the intermediate air bleed jet into the adaptor screw. Tighten the jet securely.

17A. *6-20 hp models*—Install the idle mixture needle valve and spring to the top cover. Turn the needle valve

6

carburetor body until *lightly* seated. Then back out the valve three full turns.

17B. *25 and 35 hp models*—Install the idle mixture needle valve and spring into the top cover. Adjust the screw as follows:

    a. *All 1995 (EO) models and 1996 (ED) models with model numbers ending in C*—Adjust each idle mixture screw to provide a dimension of 0.350 in. (8.9 mm) between the top cover and the underside of the screw head.

    b. *1996 (ED) models with model numbers ending in G and all 1997-2003 (EU-ST) models*—Adjust each idle mixture screw to provide a dimension of 0.390 in. (9.9 mm) between the top cover and the underside of the screw head.

18. *25 and 35 hp models*—Install the air intake cover adaptor using a new gasket. Secure the adaptor in place with two screws. Tighten both screws securely.

19. Reinstall the carburetor as described in this chapter.

TR AND SV CARBURETORS (25 AND 30 HP [TWO-CYLINDER], 40-70 HP AND 18-35 JET MODELS)

The manufacturer has assigned the identification terms of *TR* and *SV* to the carburetors covered in this section.

TR and SV Common Features

The TR (**Figure 40**, typical) and SV (**Figure 41**, typical) carburetors are very similar, with all differences located in the uppermost portion of the carburetor. Some common features are:

1. There is no idle speed screw and the throttle plate must be able to fully close for the engine to idle properly. Idle speed is primarily controlled by adjusting the idle timing.

2. A high-speed jet, mounted in the bottom of the float chamber (behind the drain screw), provides primary control of the air/fuel mixture at high speed.

3. An intermediate air bleed jet, mounted at the top of the carburetor (or in the top cover), provides primary control of the air/fuel mixture at part-throttle settings, typically off-idle to 1/4-1/3 throttle plate opening.

4. An adjustable idle mixture needle valve, located in the top portion of the carburetor, allows fine-tuning of idle low speed air/fuel mixture.

5. Float level and float drop adjustments are performed exactly the same on both styles.

6. All models use a primer fitting that is connected to the electric fuel primer solenoid or the manual primer. There is no choke assembly.

TR and SV Primary Differences

The primary differences between the TR and SV carburetors are as follows:

1. *TR carburetor*—This carburetor (**Figure 40**) is easily identified by its all metal construction and the absence of a removable top cover. **Figure 40** shows the location of the idle mixture screw (A), intermediate air bleed jet (B) and the float chamber vent (C). The primer fitting is located at the top of the carburetor on the port side of the main body. These carburetors are only used on some 25 hp models.

2. *SV carburetor*—These carburetors use a Minlon (black plastic) top cover that features an intermediate air bleed jet on the starboard side (A, **Figure 41**) and a fitting for the primer system on the port side (B, **Figure 41**). The idle mixture screw (C, **Figure 41**) is located just above the throttle shaft on the starboard side of the main body.

Refer to **Figure 42** (TR carburetor) or **Figure 43** (SV carburetor) for typical exploded views of each carburetor. Refer to **Table 3** or **Tables 5-6** for specifications.

Carburetor Removal/Installation (25 and 30 hp [Two-Cylinder] and 18 Jet Models)

1. Disconnect and ground the spark plug leads to the power head to prevent accidental starting.

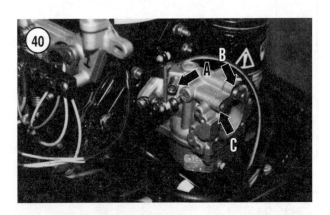

6

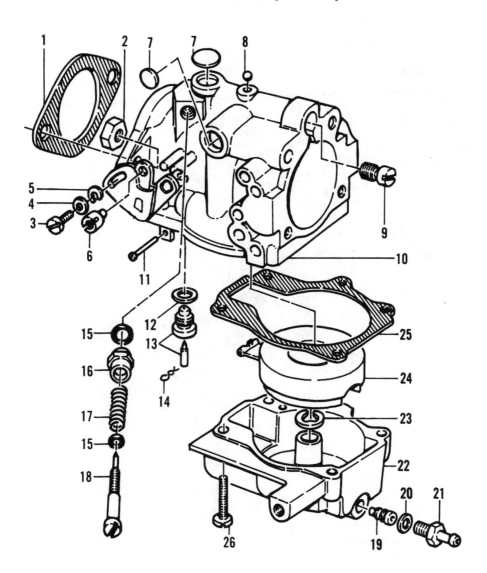

TR CARBURETOR (TYPICAL)

1. Base gasket
2. Mounting nut
3. Screw
4. Flat washer
5. Lockwasher
6. Linkage snap connector
7. Core plugs
8. Lead shot plug
9. Intermediate air bleed jet
10. Main body
11. Float hinge pin
12. Gasket
13. Inlet needle valve and seat
14. Clip
15. O-ring
16. Brass adaptor base
17. Spring
18. Idle mixture needle valve
19. High speed jet
20. Gasket
21. Fitting (or screw plug)
22. Float chamber
23. Nozzle gasket
24. Float
25. Gasket
26. Screw

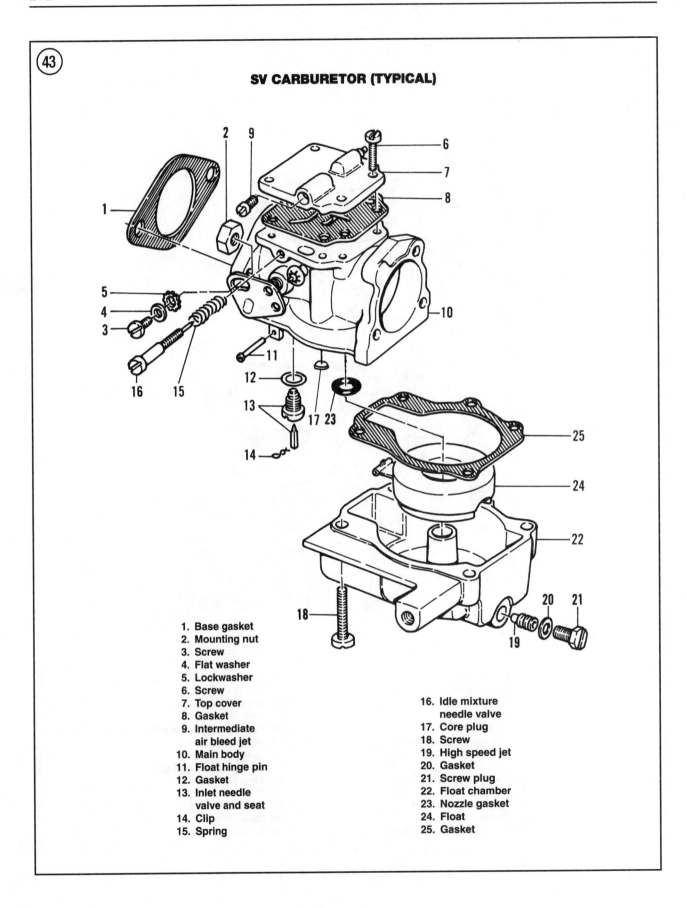

SV CARBURETOR (TYPICAL)

1. Base gasket
2. Mounting nut
3. Screw
4. Flat washer
5. Lockwasher
6. Screw
7. Top cover
8. Gasket
9. Intermediate
   air bleed jet
10. Main body
11. Float hinge pin
12. Gasket
13. Inlet needle
    valve and seat
14. Clip
15. Spring
16. Idle mixture
    needle valve
17. Core plug
18. Screw
19. High speed jet
20. Gasket
21. Screw plug
22. Float chamber
23. Nozzle gasket
24. Float
25. Gasket

2. *Electric start models*—Disconnect the negative battery cable. Then remove the starter motor and bracket assembly (Chapter Seven). It is not necessary to disconnect all of the electrical leads, just remove the mounting hardware and set the assembly to one side.

3. Disconnect the cam follower link from the snap connector on the starboard side of the carburetor's throttle arm. See **Figure 44**, typical.

4. *Remote control models*—If the fuel primer solenoid is mounted to the float chamber, remove the mounting screw, then lay the solenoid to one side.

> *CAUTION*
> *Push fuel (or primer) lines off of their fittings whenever possible. If necessary, cut the line with a razor knife (or similar tool), peel the line from the fitting. Do not apply excessive force or the carburetor will be damaged.*

5. Remove the two nuts securing the carburetor to the intake manifold, then pull the carburetor from the engine. Once the carburetor is off of the studs, disconnect the fuel and primer lines.

6. Remove and discard the carburetor gasket. Carefully clean any remaining gasket material off of the carburetor and intake manifold.

> *NOTE*
> *Do not use gasket sealant on the carburetor-to-intake manifold gasket. Install the gasket dry.*

7. To reinstall the carburetor, begin by installing a new gasket (without sealant) onto the carburetor mounting studs.

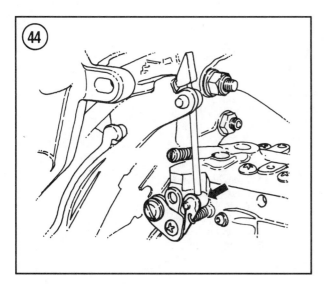

8. Hold the carburetor near the intake manifold and attach the fuel lines as follows:
   a. *Tiller handle models*—Connect the large primer line to the fitting at the front of the float chamber.
   b. Connect the fuel supply line (from the fuel pump) to the fitting at the lower, rear, port corner of the carburetor (or float chamber).
   c. Connect the primer line to the fitting at the top of the carburetor.
   d. Secure each connection with a new tie-strap.

9. Slide the carburetor over the studs and against the intake manifold. Install the two mounting nuts and tighten them securely.

10. Reconnect the cam follower link to the snap connector on the starboard side of the carburetor's throttle arm. See **Figure 44**, typical.

11. *Remote control models*—If so mounted, reattach the fuel primer solenoid to the starboard side of the float chamber. Tighten the mounting screw securely.

12. Reconnect the spark plug leads and on electric start models, reconnect the negative battery cable.

13. Refer to Chapter Five for carburetor and linkage adjustment procedures.

**Carburetor Removal/Installation
(40-50 hp [Two-Cylinder] and 28-35 Jet Models)**

The following procedure describes the removal/installation of both carburetors. The carburetors can be removed/installed individually, if so desired. **Figure 45** shows the carburetor and air intake cover installation for electric start models. Rope start models are similar.

1. Disconnect and ground the spark plug leads to the power head to prevent accidental starting.

2. *Electric start models*—Disconnect the negative battery cable.

3A. *Rope start models*—Remove the four screws securing the air intake cover to the air intake cover base. Remove the cover, then remove and discard the cover gasket.

3B. *Electric start models*—Remove the locknut and washer (2, **Figure 45**) from the bottom center of the air intake cover, then remove the seven screws around the perimeter of the cover. Remove the cover, then remove and discard the cover gasket.

> *NOTE*
> *The screws securing the air intake cover base to the carburetors are a special lock-patch screw that must only be used once. Discard the old screws and install new screws each time the base is removed.*

4. Remove the air intake cover base as follows:

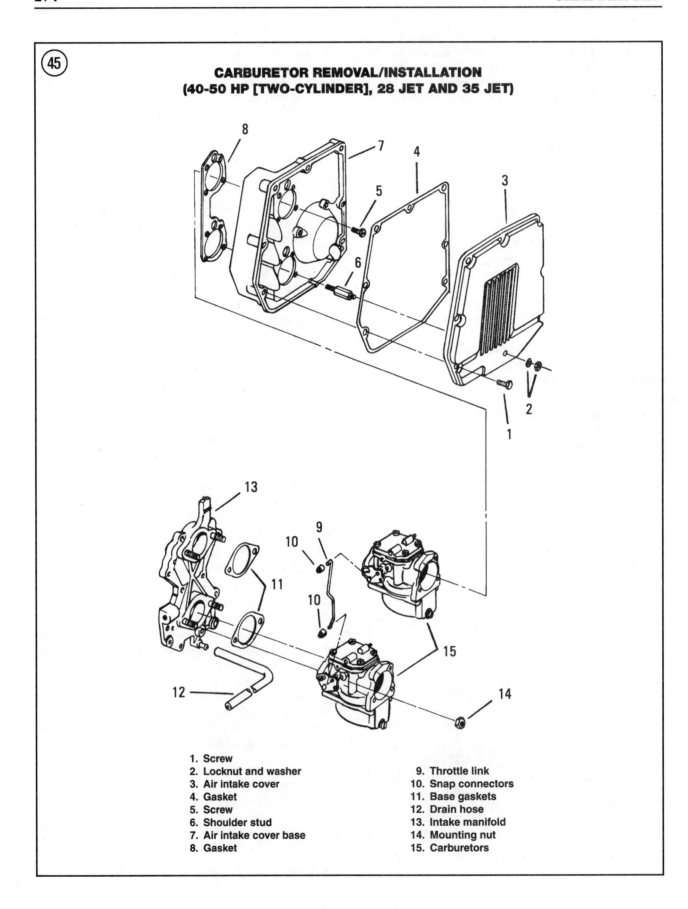

45

**CARBURETOR REMOVAL/INSTALLATION
(40-50 HP [TWO-CYLINDER], 28 JET AND 35 JET)**

1. Screw
2. Locknut and washer
3. Air intake cover
4. Gasket
5. Screw
6. Shoulder stud
7. Air intake cover base
8. Gasket
9. Throttle link
10. Snap connectors
11. Base gaskets
12. Drain hose
13. Intake manifold
14. Mounting nut
15. Carburetors

a. Remove and discard the base screws (5, **Figure 45**). Generally there are three screws holding the base to each carburetor. On electric start models, a special shoulder stud (6, **Figure 45**) is used in place of the lower port screw.

b. Disconnect the drain hose. On electric start models, detach the oil injection pump from the air intake cover base. The pump is held by rubber isolating mounts. Lubricate the mounts with isopropyl alcohol, then pull the mounts out the back side of the cover base.

c. Remove the air intake cover base from the engine. Then remove and discard the gasket.

5. Disconnect the upper-to-lower carburetor throttle link (9, **Figure 45**) from the snap connectors on the starboard side of each carburetor's throttle arm.

CAUTION
Push fuel (or primer) lines off of their fittings whenever possible. If necessary, cut the line with a razor knife (or similar tool). Peel the line from the fitting. Do not apply excessive force or the carburetor will be damaged.

6. Disconnect the primer line from the top of each carburetor.

7. Remove the two nuts securing each carburetor to the intake manifold, then pull each carburetor from the engine (one at a time). Once each carburetor is off of its studs, disconnect the fuel supply line from its fitting located at the lower, rear, port corner of the carburetor (or float chamber).

8. Remove and discard each carburetor's base gasket. Carefully clean any remaining gasket material off of each carburetor and the intake manifold.

NOTE
Do not use gasket sealant on the carburetor-to-intake manifold gasket. Install the gasket dry.

9. To reinstall the carburetor, begin by installing new gaskets (without sealant) onto each pair of carburetor mounting studs.

10. Hold the bottom carburetor near the intake manifold and attach the fuel supply line to the fitting on the lower, rear, port corner of the carburetor (or float chamber). Secure the connection with a new tie-strap.

11. Slide the carburetor over the studs and against the intake manifold. Install and tighten the two mounting nuts evenly and securely.

12. Repeat Steps 10-11 for the upper carburetor.

13. Connect the primer line to the primer fitting on the top of each carburetor.

14. Connect the upper-to-lower carburetor throttle link to each carburetor's throttle arm snap connector.

15. Install the air intake cover base as follows:

a. Position the air intake cover base to the engine. Connect the drain hose. On electric start models, lubricate the oil injection pump's rubber isolation mounts with isopropyl alcohol and pull each mount through the base until each is snapped in place.

b. Position a new gasket between the base and the carburetors. Using new screws, secure the base to the carburetors. On electric start models, install a new stud in the lower port screw hole.

c. Tighten the base mounting hardware evenly and securely.

16A. *Rope start models*—Install the air intake cover using a new gasket. Install and evenly tighten the four cover screws.

16B. *Electric start models*—Install the air intake cover using a new gasket. Install the perimeter screws and the single lock nut and washer at the bottom center of the air intake cover. Tighten the cover mounting hardware evenly and securely.

17. Reconnect the spark plug leads. On electric start models, reconnect the negative battery cable.

18. Refer to Chapter Five for carburetor and linkage adjustment procedures.

Carburetor Removal/Installation (50-70 hp [Three-Cylinder] Models)

The following procedure describes the removal/installation of all carburetors. The carburetors can be removed/installed individually, if so desired. Refer to **Figure 46** for this procedure.

1. Disconnect and ground the spark plug leads to the power head to prevent accidental starting.

2. Disconnect the negative battery cable.

3. Remove the ten screws (1, **Figure 46**) around the perimeter of the air intake cover. Remove the cover, then remove and discard the cover gasket.

NOTE
The screws securing the air intake cover base to the carburetors are a special lock-patch screw that must only be used once. Discard the old screws and install new screws each time the base is removed.

4. Remove the air intake cover base as follows:

a. Remove and discard the air silencer base screws (15, **Figure 46**). Generally there are two screws holding the base to each carburetor.

b. Disconnect the drain hose from the bottom of the air intake cover base.

6

46

**CARBURETOR REMOVAL/INSTALLATION
(50-70 HP [THREE-CYLINDER])**

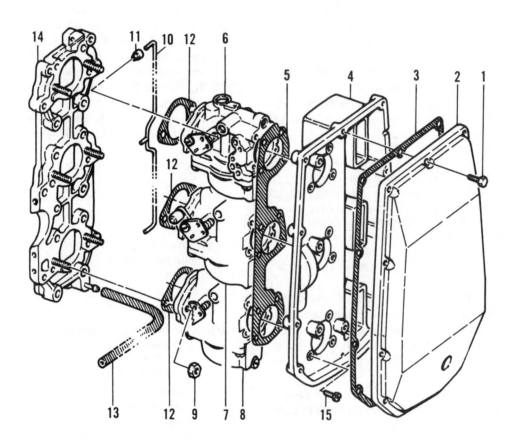

1. Screw
2. Air intake cover
3. Gasket
4. Air intake cover base
5. Gasket
6. Top carburetor
7. Middle carburetor
8. Bottom carburetor
9. Mounting nut
10. Throttle link
11. Snap connector
12. Base gaskets
13. Drain hose
14. Intake manifold
15. Screw

c. Remove the air intake cover base from the engine. Then remove and discard the gasket.

5. Disconnect the one-piece throttle link (10, **Figure 46**) from the snap connectors on the starboard side of each carburetor's throttle arm.

CAUTION
Push fuel (or primer) lines off of their fittings whenever possible. If necessary, cut the line with a razor knife (or similar tool). Peel the line from the fitting. Do not apply excessive force or the carburetor will be damaged.

6. Disconnect the primer line from the top of each carburetor.

7. Remove the two nuts securing each carburetor to the intake manifold, then pull each carburetor from the engine (one at a time). Once each carburetor is off of its studs, disconnect the fuel supply line from its fitting located at the lower, rear, port corner of the carburetor (or float chamber).

8. Remove and discard each carburetor's base gasket. Carefully clean any remaining gasket material from each carburetor and the intake manifold.

NOTE
Do not use gasket sealant on the carburetor-to-intake manifold gasket. Install the gasket dry.

9. To reinstall the carburetor, begin by installing new gaskets (without sealant) onto each pair of carburetor mounting studs.

10. Hold the bottom carburetor near the intake manifold and attach the fuel supply line to the fitting on the lower, rear, port corner of the carburetor (or float chamber). Secure the connection with a new tie-strap.

11. Slide the carburetor over the studs and against the intake manifold. Install and tighten the 2 mounting nuts evenly and securely.

12. Repeat Steps 10-11 for the middle and upper carburetors.

13. Connect the primer line to the primer fitting on the top of each carburetor.

14. Connect the throttle link to each carburetor's throttle arm snap connector.

15. Install the air intake cover base as follows:
   a. Position the air intake cover base to the engine and connect the drain hose.
   b. Position a new gasket between the base and the carburetors. Then using new screws, secure the base to the carburetors. The screws are installed in the starboard lower and port upper holes.
   c. Tighten all of the base mounting screws evenly to 24-36 in.-lb. (2.7-4.1 N•m).

16. Install the air intake cover using a new gasket. Install and evenly tighten the ten screws to 24-36 in.-lb. (2.7-4.1 N•m).

17. Reconnect the spark plug leads and the negative battery cable.

18. Refer to Chapter Five for carburetor and linkage adjustment procedures.

Disassembly (TR and SV Carburetors)

Make sure a carburetor repair kit is obtained prior to carburetor disassembly. The repair kit will contain the O-rings, gaskets, inlet needle and seat, float assembly and other necessary components. It is not recommended to reuse any of the components that are part of the repair kit. Jet screwdriver (part No. 317002) is recommended for removing and installing the main and intermediate jets.

Refer to **Figure 42** (TR) or **Figure 43** (SV) for this procedure.

1. Remove the float chamber drain plug (or fitting). Remove and discard the gasket.

2. Using jet screwdriver (part No. 317002) or equivalent, remove the high-speed jet from the float chamber's drain hole.

3. Using jet screwdriver (part No. 317002) or equivalent, remove the intermediate air bleed jet from the starboard side of the top cover on SV carburetors, or on TR carburetors, from its mounting bore at the top of the air intake cover mating surface.

4A. *TR carburetors*—Remove the idle mixture screw and spring from the adaptor base on the carburetor's top, rear, starboard corner. Then remove the brass adaptor base from the carburetor body. Remove and discard the O-rings from the mixture needle and adaptor base. See 15-18, **Figure 42**.

4B. *SV carburetors*—Remove the idle mixture screw (16, **Figure 43**) and spring (15) from the top cover.

5. *SV carburetors*—Remove the four top cover screws. Then lift the cover and gasket off the carburetor body. Discard the gasket.

6. Remove the float chamber screws. Separate the float chamber from the carburetor body (**Figure 47**). Remove

6

and discard the float chamber gasket and the nozzle well gasket (23, **Figure 42** or **Figure 43**).

7. Push the float pin from the carburetor body using a suitable tool, then remove the float and the inlet valve needle and clip. See **Figure 48**.

8. Using a wide-blade screwdriver (or suitable tool), unscrew and remove the inlet valve seat. Then remove and discard the seat gasket. See **Figure 49**.

9. Refer to *Carburetor Cleaning and Inspection* in this chapter. On TR models, make sure the top core plug is removed and the mixing pocket and all connecting passages thoroughly cleaned.

**Reassembly
(TR and SV Carburetors)**

Refer to **Figure 42** (TR carburetor) or **Figure 43** (SV carburetor) for this procedure. Compare all components of the repair kit (such as gaskets and the inlet valve assembly) to be sure they match the original parts.

1. Using jet screwdriver (part No. 317002) or equivalent, install the main jet into the float chamber. Tighten the jet securely.

2. Using jet screwdriver (part No. 317002) or equivalent, install the intermediate air bleed jet into the starboard side of the top cover on SV carburetors, or on TR carburetors, into its mounting bore at the top of the air intake cover mating surface. Tighten the jet securely.

3. Install the float chamber drain plug (or the primer fitting), using new gaskets. Tighten the drain plug (or primer fitting) securely.

4. Place a new gasket onto a new inlet valve seat, then thread the seat into the main body. Tighten the seat securely using a wide-blade screwdriver or suitable tool. The inlet seat must not be distorted or damaged during the tightening process.

5. Install the retaining clip onto a new inlet valve needle, then position the clip over the float arm. Install the float and inlet needle assembly to the carburetor and secure it in place with the hinge pin.

*NOTE
If the OMC carburetor gauge (part No. 324891) is not available, refer to **Table 3** or **Tables 5-6** for float level **direct measurement** specifications. Using a T gauge (or equivalent) tool, measure the float level at the same locations that the carburetor gauge checks as shown in **Figure 50**.*

6. To set the float level, invert the carburetor so the float is facing upward. Allow the weight of the float to close the inlet valve assembly.

7. Place the float gauge part No. 324891 with the notch marked *25 THRU 75 HP* over the float. Make sure the gauge is resting directly on the float chamber gasket surface and that the gasket is not installed. See **Figure 50**.

8. The top of the float must be located at or between the notches as shown. Make sure the float gauge is not pushing downward on the float and that the float is not below the second notch.

9. If adjustment is necessary, carefully bend the float arm as required (between the float and the hinge pin bore) to position the float as specified. Do not force the inlet valve needle into the seat and do not bend the arm so that one side of the float is higher than the other. The float must be parallel with the carburetor body as viewed in **Figure 50**. Recheck the adjustment using the float gauge and readjust until the float level is correct.

10. To set the float drop, hold the carburetor in the upright position and allow the float to hang by its own weight. See **Figure 51**.

11. Measure the distance (D, **Figure 51**) from the float chamber gasket surface (without the gasket installed) to the bottom edge of the float as shown. The distance must be 1.125 to 1.625 in. (28.6-41.3 mm).

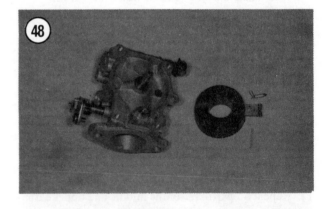

12. If adjustment is necessary, carefully bend the tab (T, **Figure 51**) as necessary. Do not bend the float arm or the float level setting will be altered.

13. Place a new gasket (23, **Figure 42** or **Figure 43**) around the main nozzle and a new gasket on the float chamber. Then install the bowl making sure the nozzle gasket is not displaced. Coat the float bowl's screw threads with OMC Screw Lock threadlocking adhesive. Install and evenly tighten the screws in a crossing pattern to 25-35 in.-lb. (2.8-4.0 N•m).

14. *SV carburetors*—Using a new gasket, install the top cover to the main body. Install and tighten the cover screws evenly in a crossing pattern to 15-22 in.-lb. (1.7-2.5 N•m).

15A. *TR carburetors*—Install the idle mixture needle valve as follows:
  a. Install the brass adaptor base into the carburetor body using a new O-ring. Tighten the adaptor snugly.

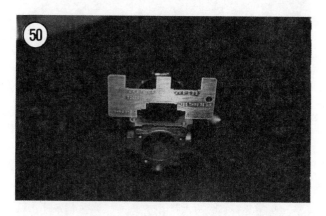

Be careful not to damage or distort the adaptor by over-tightening it.
  b. Install a new O-ring onto the inlet needle valve screw. Then install the spring over the valve and thread the assembly into the brass adaptor base until it is lightly seated in the adaptor base.
  c. Back the needle valve screw out 1-3/4 turns from a lightly seated position.

15B. *SV carburetors*—Install the idle mixture needle valve and spring into the carburetor body. Thread the needle valve into the body until it is *lightly* seated. Then back out the needle valve screw as follows:
  a. *25-40 hp and 18-28 jet*—2-1/2 turns from a lightly seated position.
  b. *48-50 hp (two-cylinder) and 35 jet*—3-1/2 turns from a lightly seated position.
  c. *50-70 hp (three-cylinder)*—2-3/4 turns from a lightly seated position on all 1995 (EO) models and 1996-1998 (ED-EC) 60-70 hp models. On 1996-1998 (ED-EC) 50 hp (three-cylinder) models, set the screws to 1-3/4 turns from a lightly seated position.

16. Reinstall the carburetor as described in this chapter.

FUEL PRIMER SYSTEMS

A conventional choke system is used on all 2-8 hp models, 9.9 and 15 hp (rope start models) and the 25 and 35 hp three-cylinder models equipped with a tiller handle. A metal plate at the front of the carburetor is actuated with a simple mechanical linkage. When the plate is closed, airflow to the engine is restricted, causing the overall air/fuel mixture to be enriched, allowing the engine to be started when cold. On 25 and 35 hp (three-cylinder) models, each carburetor is equipped with a choke plate and the choke linkage will open and close all three valves simultaneously.

All remote control electric start models (and 40-70 hp tiller handle electric start models) use an electrically operated fuel primer solenoid. The 20-40 hp (two-cylinder) rope start, 20-30 hp (two-cylinder) tiller handle electric start and the 18 and 28 jet models use a manual fuel primer valve.

Fuel primer valves inject fuel (under pressure) behind the carburetor's throttle plate, directly into the reed valves. This provides positive enrichment of the air/fuel mixture, allowing faster starts.

Manual Fuel Primer Valve

A plunger-type fuel primer valve is used on 20-40 hp (two-cylinder) rope start models, the 18 and 28 jet and the

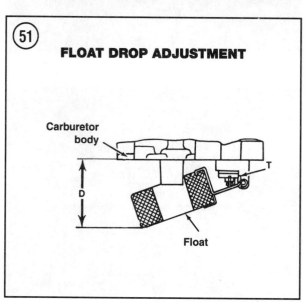

FLOAT DROP ADJUSTMENT

Carburetor body

D

Float

T

20-30 hp (two-cylinder) tiller handle electric start models. See **Figure 52**, typical. When operated, the primer valve delivers fuel from the carburetor float chamber (A, **Figure 52**), to the carburetor's primer fitting, generally located near the mounting flange. The pump is basically a simple plunger type mechanical fuel pump.

The primer has three distinct operating modes (and positions).

1. *Off*—When the plunger (B, **Figure 52**) is pressed fully inward (past the detent) all fuel passages are blocked and fuel cannot flow. The plunger must be pushed fully inward (past the detent) after the engine is warm, or the engine will run rich, smoke excessively and stall at idle.

2. *Warm-up*—When the plunger is pulled out (past the detent) and released, an internal spring will return it to a position just outside the detent (**Figure 53**). This position opens internal valving, allowing a metered amount of fuel to be pulled through the valve by the engine's intake manifold vacuum. This position is a temporary position, used only to enrich the mixture during warm-up.

3. *Prime*—When the plunger is pulled to its full extension (**Figure 54**), fuel is pumped under pressure into the carburetor's primer fitting. Releasing the plunger causes the valve to refill with fuel from the carburetor's float chamber. The primer will only pump fuel as it is pulled outward. A discharge check valve in the discharge fitting (small fitting [C, **Figure 52**]) prevents the fuel (or air) in the discharge line from being drawn back into the valve. An inlet check valve in the valve's plunger prevents the fuel from being pushed back into the carburetor's float chamber during operation.

> *NOTE*
> *It is a common mistake to forget to shut off the primer valve after the engine has warmed up. Remember to push the plunger fully inward (past its detent) after the engine has warmed up to the point where it has begun to sound excessively rich (runs rough and/or smokes excessively).*

On some models, the fuel primer valve may be teed into the fuel recirculation system. Refer to Chapter Three for operational checks and troubleshooting procedures.

Removal/installation

> *CAUTION*
> *Push fuel primer lines off of their fittings whenever possible. If necessary, cut the line with a razor knife (or similar tool) and peel the line from the fitting. Do not apply excessive force or the primer valve will be irreparably damaged.*

1. Disconnect and ground the spark plug leads to the power head to prevent accidental starting.

2. Disconnect the fuel supply hose from the carburetor float chamber (A, **Figure 52**) and discharge hose from the primer valve (C, **Figure 52**). Do not damage the primer valve during hose removal.

3. Remove the screw (13, **Figure 55**) securing the primer knob, then remove the knob. Remove the mounting nut (11, **Figure 55**) and remove the primer valve assembly from the inside of the lower cowl.

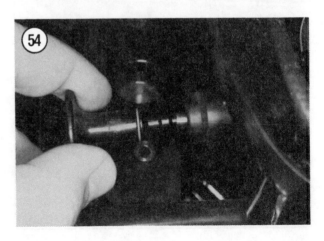

4. To install the primer valve, begin by positioning the valve into the lower cowl from the inside. Install and tighten the mounting nut securely.

5. Position the primer knob over the shaft and align the retaining screw hole. Install the screw (13, **Figure 55**) and tighten it securely.

6. Connect the fuel supply and primer discharge lines to the primer valve fittings. Secure the connections with new tie-straps.

7. Reconnect the spark plug leads.

Disassembly/assembly

Always replace all O-rings and the quad-ring each time the valve is disassembled.

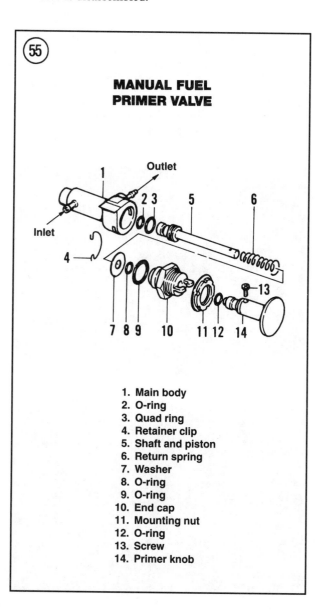

55

MANUAL FUEL PRIMER VALVE

Outlet

Inlet

1. Main body
2. O-ring
3. Quad ring
4. Retainer clip
5. Shaft and piston
6. Return spring
7. Washer
8. O-ring
9. O-ring
10. End cap
11. Mounting nut
12. O-ring
13. Screw
14. Primer knob

1. Remove the retainer clip (4, **Figure 55**) from the valve, using needlenose pliers.

2. Pull the shaft and piston assembly (5, **Figure 55**) from the main body (1). Then pull the end cap (10), spring (6) and washer (7) from the shaft and piston.

3. Remove and discard the piston O-ring (2, **Figure 55**) and quad-ring (3), then remove and discard the end cap external O-ring (9) and internal O-ring (8).

4. Clean and inspect all components as described in the next section.

NOTE
The primer O-rings (and quad-ring) are made of a special material to prevent deterioration and leakage. Be sure to install the correct O-rings (and quad-ring) during reassembly.

5. To reassemble the unit, begin by installing a new O-ring and quad-ring on the piston. Then install new internal and external O-rings to the end cap. Lubricate all O-rings (and quad-ring) with outboard motor oil.

6. Place the spring, then washer on the plunger shaft. Then slide the end cap over the shaft.

7. Insert the shaft and end cap assembly into the main body. Push the end cap into the housing until it is seated, then install the retainer clip (4, **Figure 55**).

Cleaning and inspection

A small glue syringe, such as the Monoject 412, is necessary to test the check valve function. The Monoject 412 syringe (or equivalent) is available at most craft stores and/or hobby shops.

1. Wash all components in a mild solvent, such as mineral spirits. Blow the components dry with compressed air.

2. Inspect the shaft and piston for nicks, scratches or other damage. Remove small scratches using crocus cloth. Replace the shaft and piston if deep scratches, nicks or burrs are noted.

3. Inspect the main body's piston bore for nicks, scratches or other damage. Replace the main body if it is damaged.

4. To check the main body's outlet fitting check valve, connect a small syringe filled with isopropyl alcohol to the outlet fitting (small nipple) using a suitable hose. Attempt to inject the alcohol into the small fitting.

   a. If alcohol freely enters the main body, the check valve is defective. Replace the main body.

   b. If alcohol cannot enter the main body, the check valve is functioning correctly.

5. Next connect the syringe to the main body's large fitting using a suitable hose. Cover the open end of the main body with your finger (where the end cap fits), but do not block

6

the main body's small fitting. Attempt to inject the alcohol into the large fitting.

   a. If alcohol freely enters the main body and is freely discharged from the small fitting, the main body is in satisfactory condition.

   b. If alcohol does not freely enter the main body *or* is not freely discharged from the small fitting, the main body is defective and must be replaced.

Electric Fuel Primer Solenoid

The electric fuel primer solenoid (**Figure 56**) has replaced choke valves on larger engines as the primary means of enriching the air/fuel mixture for cold starting. Fuel primer solenoid equipped models enrich the air/fuel mixture by injecting fuel (under pressure) directly into the carburetor(s) or intake manifold. If injected in the carburetor(s), the fuel is injected on the intake manifold (vacuum) side of the throttle plate.

The fuel primer solenoid is an electrical solenoid valve. The fuel primer valve does not pump fuel; fuel must be supplied by the primer bulb or engine's fuel pump. When electricity is applied to the purple/white lead, the solenoid is energized and the fuel valve opens. An internal spring forces the valve closed when the solenoid is not energized.

The fuel primer valve is equipped with a manual valve (A, **Figure 56**) to allow manual operation of the valve if the electrical circuit fails. Rotate the valve so it extends away from the solenoid body (**Figure 57**) to open the valve and allow fuel to flow continuously (as long as fuel pressure is present in the solenoid's fuel supply line). Make sure the valve is only opened momentarily to prime the engine, just as if you were using the valve electrically. The valve shown in **Figure 56** is in the OFF position, while the valve shown in **Figure 57** is in the ON position.

A schrader valve located under the removable cap on the manual valve (A, **Figure 56**) allows quick and simple injection of storage fogging oil and/or OMC Engine Tuner as described in Chapter Four. Both of these products are available in an injection style can, which is designed to attach directly to the primer's manual valve fitting.

Refer to Chapter Three for functional tests and troubleshooting procedures on the electric fuel primer solenoid.

Removal/installation

Refer to **Figure 56** for a typical primer solenoid installation. On some smaller engines, one of the two discharge (small) fittings is capped and secured with a tie-strap. If the cap is not installed or properly secured, fuel will leak out each time the valve is operated.

1. Disconnect the negative battery cable. Then disconnect and ground the spark plug leads to the power head to prevent accidental starting.

2. Disconnect the solenoid's purple/white lead at its bullet connector (B, **Figure 56**).

3. Remove the screw(s) securing the solenoid bracket and the black (ground) lead (C, **Figure 56**).

> *CAUTION*
> *Push fuel primer lines off of their fittings whenever possible. If necessary, cut the line with a razor knife (or similar tool) and peel the line from the fitting. Do not apply excessive force or the primer valve will be damaged.*

4. Carefully disconnect the fuel supply (large) hose and primer discharge (small) hose(s) from the solenoid, then remove the solenoid. See **Figure 58**.

5. To install the solenoid, begin by positioning the solenoid on the power head and connecting the fuel supply (large) hose to the solenoid's large fitting. Secure the connection with a new tie-strap.

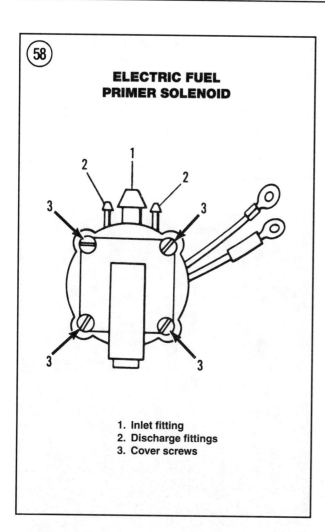

58

ELECTRIC FUEL PRIMER SOLENOID

1. Inlet fitting
2. Discharge fittings
3. Cover screws

6. Connect the primer discharge line(s) to the solenoid's small fitting(s). If only one discharge line is used, the second small fitting must be capped and the cap secured with a new tie-strap.

7. Secure the solenoid in place with its mounting bracket. Install the screw(s), making sure the black ground lead is secured by a screw. See B, **Figure 56**, typical. Tighten the screw(s) securely.

8. Connect the solenoid's purple/white lead to the matching engine harness bullet connector.

9. Squeeze the primer bulb and check for fuel leaks. Correct any problems found.

10. Reconnect the spark plug leads, then reconnect the negative battery cable.

Disassembly/assembly

Refer to **Figure 58** and **Figure 59** for this procedure. Replace any component that is damaged, deteriorated, corroded or worn.

1. Remove the four end cover screws (3, **Figure 58**). Then remove the cover (8, **Figure 59**) and gasket (7). Discard the gasket.

2. Remove the filter screen from the cover. Clean or replace the filter as necessary.

3. Pull the manual valve (11, **Figure 59**) from the cover with a twisting motion. Remove and discard the valve's O-ring (10).

4. Remove the needle valve, steel plunger and both springs. See **Figure 59**.

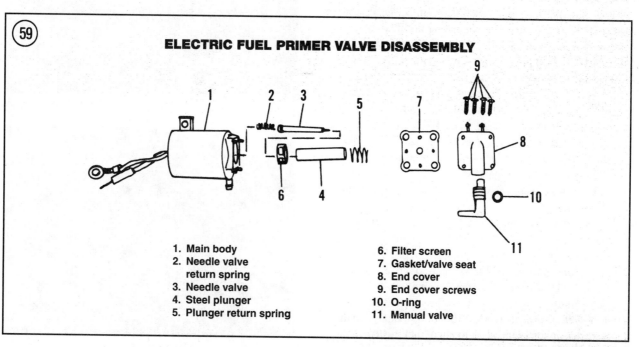

59

ELECTRIC FUEL PRIMER VALVE DISASSEMBLY

1. Main body
2. Needle valve return spring
3. Needle valve
4. Steel plunger
5. Plunger return spring
6. Filter screen
7. Gasket/valve seat
8. End cover
9. End cover screws
10. O-ring
11. Manual valve

5. Clean all components (except the main body) with a mild solvent, such as mineral spirits. Rinse the components using hot water, then blow dry with compressed air. Lightly oil the steel plunger and both springs with outboard oil to prevent rust.

6. To assemble the solenoid, begin by inserting the needle valve return spring, then the needle valve into the main body.

7. Install the plunger return spring into its groove on the plunger, then install the plunger into the main body and over the needle valve. The spring end of the plunger must face out.

8. Install a new O-ring in the manual valve's groove. Lubricate the O-ring with outboard motor oil, then install the valve into the end cover (with a twisting motion) until the valve is seated.

9. Position the filter screen onto the end cover, then install a new gasket (valve seat) so that the tapered side of the valve seat is facing the needle valve in the main body.

10. Position the end cover over the main body assembly. Make sure that all of the fittings (inlet and outlet) are pointing the same direction.

11. Install the end cover screws. Evenly and securely tighten the screws.

ANTISIPHON PROTECTION

In accordance with industry safety standards, boats equipped with a permanently mounted fuel tank must have some form of antisiphon device installed to prevent fuel from siphoning into the bilge if the fuel line should break or leak. The most common method of compliance is the antisiphon valve. Antisiphon valves are installed in boats to prevent fuel from being siphoned into the bilge area should the fuel supply line break at a point below the fuel level in the tank.

OMC outboard engines are designed to operate with an antisiphon valve installed, as long as the valve meets factory specifications. The part No. 173273 (for 5/16 in. inside diameter fuel line) or part No. 173274 (for 3/8 in. inside diameter fuel line) anti-siphon valves meet OMC's specifications and are highly recommended replacement parts if the anti-siphon valve is suspected of causing a fuel restriction.

For maximum antisiphon protection and maximum fuel system safety:

1. Use an appropriate antisiphon valve as discussed previously. If the antisiphon valve's condition is questionable, replace it with the appropriate OMC valve.

2. Make sure the primer bulb is located in the motor (splash) well. The primer bulb must not be mounted in the bilge area (on permanently mounted fuel systems), as

primer bulbs do not pass the Coast Guard fire test. Primers mounted in the splash well will not be able to leak fuel or vapor into the bilge (or passenger) compartment, should the bulb fail for any reason.

3. Use only fuel lines with a Coast Guard rating of A1 or A2 (as specified in the following sections) for all fuel lines that are located in the bilge area. This includes the fuel fill and vent lines and the fuel supply line between the fuel tank and the engine's fuel inlet fitting. Lines rated A1/A2

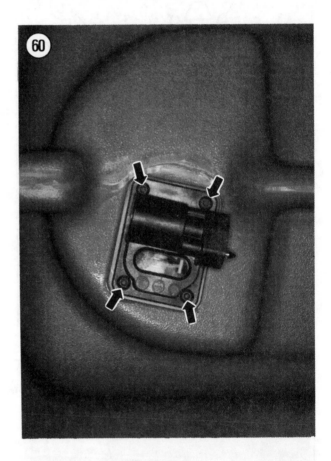

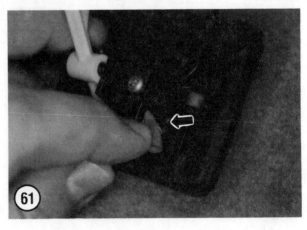

will provide superior protection from burn-through (and subsequent leakage) from an on-board fire, than lines rated B1/B2. Never use lines without a Coast Guard rating on permanently installed fuel systems.

4. Secure all fuel lines above the highest level of the fuel in the tank, as determined when the boat is floating in a static, unloaded position. Use appropriate stainless steel clamps and screws (spaced as necessary) for this purpose. Plastic clamps and tie-straps will quickly burn through in the event of a fire, allowing the fuel line to drop.

If an antisiphon valve is suspected of causing a fuel starvation problem, test the valve tested as described in Chapter Three. If it is defective, it must be replaced.

FUEL TANKS (INTEGRAL AND PORTABLE [REMOTE])

The 2, 3.3 and 3.5 hp models use an integral fuel tank with a tank mounted shutoff valve and fuel filter assembly. The 4 hp (BR) models are equipped with a dual fuel supply system. The engine can be run off the integral tank or a remote fuel tank.

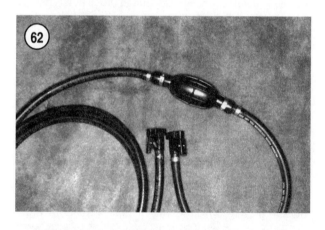

Inspect, clean and flush the integral tank (and fuel filter) at least once a season and during each tune-up or major repair procedure as described in Chapter Four.

Inspect the integral fuel tank, shutoff valve, lines, fittings, fuel filter and the fill cap and vent assembly for leaks, loose connections, deterioration, corrosion and contamination. Replace any suspect parts. Secure all fuel line connections with the original spring clamps or new tie-straps.

The fuel pickup in a factory remote tank is easily removed by removing the four screws (**Figure 60**) and lifting the pickup from the tank. A Viton valve (**Figure 61**) allows air into the tank, but prevents fuel vapor from escaping. The Viton valve is replaced with the pickup assembly.

The portable fuel tank (and pickup tube filter) must be inspected (and cleaned if necessary) at least once a season and during each tune-up or major repair procedure.

Inspect the portable fuel tank, pickup assembly, fuel lines, fittings, connectors and the fill cap and vent assembly for leaks, loose connections, deterioration, corrosion and contamination. Replace any suspect parts and secure all fuel line connections with new tie-straps.

NOTE
All integral and portable fuel tanks contain an air vent to allow air into the tank as the fuel is consumed. A plugged or blocked air vent will cause a vacuum to build up in the tank, and the engine will eventually starve for fuel. Always inspect the tank vent and make sure that it will allow air to enter the tank.

FUEL LINES, PRIMER BULBS, FITTINGS AND CONNECTORS

Figure 62 shows a typical fuel hose and primer bulb assembly. Current fuel lines, quick-disconnect connectors and primer bulbs are available in two different hose (inside diameter) sizes. The 5/16 in. (7.94 mm) sizes are acceptable for all engines covered in this manual, but the larger 3/8 in. (9.53 mm) sizes may be used as desired, and will reduce the likelihood of a restriction or blockage affecting the fuel system.

The engine connector (mounted on the lower cowl) is replaced as an assembly, while the fuel line connector's internal O-ring (**Figure 63**) may be individually replaced, or as an assembly with the connector. If replacing only the O-ring, great care must be taken not to damage the connector body and the new O-ring during the process.

Engine connectors used on smaller, portable engines (up to 30 hp [two-cylinder] models) are designed not to

6

A small internal valve is used to stop the fuel flow when the fuel line is disconnected. A protruding tip (**Figure 64**) opens the valve when the fuel line is reconnected. Do not use this design on larger engines as it will cause excessive fuel restriction. Debris in the valve or failure of its internal seals can also cause fuel restriction.

The primer bulb's check valves may be individually replaced, but keep in mind that the inlet and outlet check valves are different and that incorrect valve installation will prevent fuel flow and/or primer bulb function. It is usually more convenient to replace the primer bulb as an assembly.

When used with a permanently mounted fuel system, the engines in this manual require that the fuel pickup tube (in the fuel tank) and all fuel distribution lines be a *minimum* of 5/16 in. (7.94 mm) inside diameter and all fuel fittings must be a *minimum* of 1/4 in. (6.35 mm) inside diameter.

On engines permanently mounted to the transom and equipped with permanently mounted fuel tanks, consider eliminating the quick connector and connecting the fuel supply line directly to the fuel pump inlet (or fuel filter). This will minimize all possible fuel restrictions and help ensure adequate fuel supply to the engine.

Inspect the fuel hose and primer bulb periodically for leaks, deterioration, loose clamps, kinked or pinched lines and other damage. Make sure all fuel hose connections are tight and securely clamped. It is usually considered good practice to replace the fuel supply line and primer bulb as an assembly if there are any doubts as to its integrity.

Replacement Fuel Lines

The minimum size of the fuel supply line for engines covered in this manual is 5/16 in. (7.94 mm) inside diameter. All primer bulbs, anti-siphon valves, and other fittings must be compatible with this specification.

All replacement fuel line must be alcohol resistant. All replacement fuel line obtained from OMC Genuine Parts meets these requirements. Fuel line from other suppliers must be stamped *SAE J1527* indicating that it meets these requirements for alcohol resistance.

Fuel lines on permanently installed fuel systems, (including the vent and fill lines, and the supply line to the motor) must meet Coast Guard standards for permanently installed fuel systems in addition to the alcohol resistance specification. Portable fuel tanks are not required to meet these standards unless the tank and/or line is mounted to the boat (or line to the motor) in such a manner that tools are required to remove the tank and line assembly from the boat.

The Coast Guard fire test verifies that the fuel line can endure a fire for a specified amount of time without leaking more than a specified amount of fuel into an existing fire. Using line that passes this test is very desirable for obvious safety reasons. Using B1/B2 rated line simply means that the lines will burn through quicker than A1/A2 rated lines.

Four Coast Guard rating codes are used:

1. *A1 lines*—This code is used for fuel line that passes the Coast Guard fire test and is designed to have liquid fuel present in the line at all times. Typically, this type of fuel supply line is used between the fuel tank outlet and the engine's fuel inlet fitting. Antisiphon protection is highly recommended, but may not be required when using this line.

2. *A2 lines*—This code is used for fuel line that passes the Coast Guard fire test and is designed to have fuel vapor present in the fuel line at all times, but not liquid fuel. Typical applications are the fuel tank vent and fill lines where liquid fuel is present only temporarily. Fuel tank vent and fill lines must be self-draining.

3. *B1 lines*—This code is used for fuel line that does not pass the Coast Guard fire test, but is designed to have liquid fuel present in the line at all times. Typical applications are the fuel supply line between the fuel tank outlet and the engine's fuel inlet fitting. Antisiphon protection is mandatory when using this fuel line.

4. *B2 lines*—This code is used for fuel line that does not pass the Coast Guard fire test, but is designed to have fuel vapors present in the fuel line at all times, but not liquid fuel. Typical applications are the fuel tank vent and fill lines where liquid fuel is present only temporarily. Fuel tank vent and fill lines must be self-draining.

Fuel vent, fill and supply lines

Portable fuel tanks can use replacement fuel line assemblies as packaged from OMC Genuine Parts or fuel lines

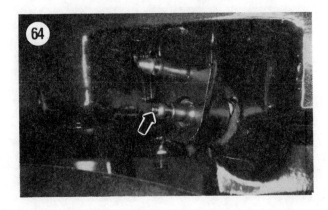

made from bulk line meeting the alcohol resistance specifications discussed previously.

The recommended fuel lines for permanent fuel systems are *A1* rated line for the fuel supply line and *A2* rated line for the fuel tank's vent and fill lines. It is very difficult to find *A1* rated line in the sizes necessary for the vent and fill lines. The primer bulb must not be mounted in the bilge area, as primer bulbs will not pass the Coast Guard fire test. Mount the primer bulb in the motor (splash) well, where if it fails, its leakage will exit the boat through the splash well drains and not enter the passenger or bilge compartments.

Fuel supply (distribution) lines must be secured above the highest level of the fuel in the tank to provide antisiphon protection. Use appropriate stainless steel clamps and screws, spaced as necessary, for this purpose. Plastic clamps and tie-straps will quickly burn through in a fire, allowing the fuel line to drop.

Always secure the connections with stainless steel worm clamps in the same manner they were originally secured. Fuel fill lines require two clamps at the fuel tank and two clamps at the hull's fill fitting. Make sure that any replacement worm clamps are *all* stainless steel. It is common to find clamps with non-stainless worm screws at automotive supply stores. These will quickly corrode and fail.

Fuel lines under the motor cowling

Fuel lines under the motor cowling do not have to meet the same requirements that fuel lines in the bilge area must meet. Straight lines can be replaced with bulk line cut to the same length. Make sure the same size replacement line is used as the original. A wide variety of line sizes are used to accommodate the primer, recirculation, air intake cover drain, oil injection system and fuel distribution systems. The manufacturer's parts catalog indicates the replacement line size and give the part number for the bulk roll.

Custom-molded (or preformed) lines can only be replaced with the correct preformed line as called out by part number in the manufacturer's parts catalogs.

Attempting to use straight (bulk) fuel line in an application calling out for a preformed line will inevitably result in a fuel restriction as the line collapses after several engine temperature cycles and the passing of time.

Always secure the connections with new tie-straps, snapper-type clamps, stainless steel spring clamps or stainless steel worm clamps in the same manner as they were originally secured.

The part No. 320107 tie-strap is specifically designed to clamp lines with a full 360° of clamping force. No other

tie-strap is recommended. Tie straps are commonly used on fuel and primer line connections under the motor cowl.

Snapper (ratchet) clamps are used on many oil injection and fuel system lines. Snapper clamps provide a more secure clamping action than a tie-strap. A snapper clamp service kit (part No. 500100) containing five of each size clamp in a tackle-box style container is available from OMC Genuine Parts. Replace any snapper clamp that is damaged, deteriorated or brittle.

Stainless steel spring clamps are now more commonly used on fuel line connections under the motor cowling because they can expand with the fuel line (during the heat of operation), yet will not cut or damage the line. When the motor cools (and the line contracts), the spring clamp will maintain the correct tension on the line. Spring clamps are reusable unless damaged or distorted.

Stainless steel worm clamps are used infrequently on fuel line connections on the actual motor. However, one is used to connect the oil supply line to the lower cowl fitting. Make sure that any replacement worm clamps are *all* stainless steel. It is common to find clamps with non-stainless worm screws at automotive supply stores. These will quickly corrode and fail. Do not tighten a worm clamp so tight that the clamp starts to cut into the fuel line.

FUEL FILTERS

Refer to Chapter Four for fuel filter service procedures on all models.

REED VALVE SERVICE

All Evinrude/Johnson two-stroke outboard motors are equipped with one set of reed valves per cylinder. The reed valves allow the air/fuel mixture from the carburetor to enter the crankcase, but not exit. They are in essence, one-way check valves.

Reed valves control the passage of air/fuel mixture into the crankcase by opening and closing as crankcase pressure changes. When the piston moves down, crankcase pressure is high, and the reed valves are pressed against their seats. When the piston moves up, crankcase pressure drops, and the reed valves are pulled away from their seats, allowing the air/fuel mixture to enter the crankcase. The maximum opening of a reed valve is controlled by its reed valve stop.

Reed valves are mounted to the intake manifold or to a reed plate, which is mounted between the intake manifold and crankcase cover.

Reed valves are essentially maintenance free and cause very few problems. However, if a reed valve does not seal,

6

the air/fuel mixture will escape the crankcase and not be transported to the combustion chamber. Some slight spitting of fuel back out of the carburetor throat at idle is considered normal, but any substantial discharge of fuel out of the carburetor throat indicates reed valve failure. Defective (leaking) reed valves will cause hard starting, poor idle quality and a loss of wide-open throttle speed.

> *CAUTION*
> *Do not run the engine without an adequate water supply and do not exceed 3000 rpm without an adequate load. Refer to **Safety Precautions** at the beginning of Chapter Three.*

If a defective reed valve is suspected, remove the air intake cover (if so equipped) and operate the motor at idle or fast idle, while holding a 3 × 5 index card approximately 1-2 in. (25-51 mm) from each carburetor's air inlet. If the card quickly becomes wet with fuel, the condition of the reed valve is questionable.

On most models, the reeds can be inspected with the carburetor removed. A small flashlight and mirror can be used to inspect for broken, cracked or chipped reeds. If reed damage is discovered, it is important to attempt to locate the missing pieces of the reed petal. The reed petals are made of stainless steel and will cause internal engine damage if allowed to pass through the crankcase and combustion chamber.

Inspect the reeds anytime the intake manifold is removed from the power head. On 2 and 3.3 hp models, the reed stop opening must be measured. Reed stops are not adjustable and will require replacement if not within specification.

Reed petals must never be turned over and reinstalled. This can lead to a pre-loaded condition. Preloaded reeds require higher crankcase vacuum levels to open. This causes acceleration and carburetor calibration problems. The reed petals must be flush to nearly flush along the entire length of the reed block mating surface with no preload.

2, 3.3 and 5 hp Models

The reed valves are mounted to the crankcase cover. Power head disassembly is required to service the reeds. Refer to Chapter 8 for power head removal and disassembly procedures. Once the crankcase cover is removed, inspect the reeds as follows:

Cleaning and inspection

1. Clean the crankcase cover and reed valve assembly (**Figure 65**) thoroughly with a mild solvent, such as mineral spirits.
2. Inspect the reed petals for cracks, chips or evidence of fatigue. The reeds must be flush (or nearly flush) to the seat along their entire length without being preloaded against the seat. Replace the reeds as necessary.
3. Check for indentation wear on the face of the seat area in the crankcase cover. If the reeds have worn indentations in the seat, the cylinder block and crankcase cover must be replaced.

> *NOTE*
> *Do not remove the reeds and reed stop unless replacement is necessary. Never turn reeds over for reuse.*

4. Measure the reed stop opening as shown in **Figure 66**. The reed stop opening must be between 0.236-0.244 in. (5.99-6.2 mm) and is not adjustable. Replace the reed stop if the measurement is not within specification.

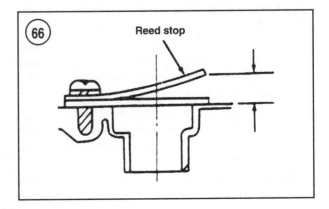

Reed stop

Reed valve replacement

1. Refer to Chapter Eight and remove the crankcase cover.

2. Remove the two screws securing the reed stop and reed petals to the crankcase cover. Remove the reed stop and reed petals. Discard the reed petals.

3. Clean and inspect the crankcase cover and reed stop. Check for indentation (wear) on the face of the seat area in the crankcase cover. If the reeds have worn indentations in the seat, the cylinder block and crankcase cover must be replaced.

4. Install a new reed petal assembly into the crankcase cover. Place the reed stop over the reed petals. Make sure the reed petals are centered over their openings.

5. Coat the threads of the two reed valve screws with OMC Nut Lock threadlocking adhesive or equivalent. Install and tighten the two screws to 27-35 in.-lb. (3-4.0 N•m).

6. Check the reed valves for preload and check the reed stop setting as described in *Cleaning and inspection* in the previous section.

7. Reinstall the crankcase cover as described in Chapter Eight.

3 and 4-8 hp (Including 4 Deluxe) Models

Two sets of reed petals are mounted to a single reed plate assembly. Each set of petals feeds one cylinder. The reed plate is mounted between the intake manifold and the crankcase cover.

On 3, 4 hp and 4 Deluxe models, the reed petals and reed stops are serviceable from the reed plate. A shim is located between each set of reed petals and their reed stop. See **Figure 67**.

On 6 and 8 hp models, the reed petals and reed stops are not serviceable and the reed plate is replaced as an assembly (**Figure 68**). A fuel recirculation system check valve and filter screen are mounted at the bottom of the reed plate. See *Fuel Recirculation Systems* in this chapter.

NOTE
On 3, 4 hp and 4 Deluxe models, do not remove the reed petals and reed stops from the reed plate assembly unless replacement is necessary. Never remove the reeds and turn over for reuse. Replace both sets of reed petals at the same time, regardless of condition.

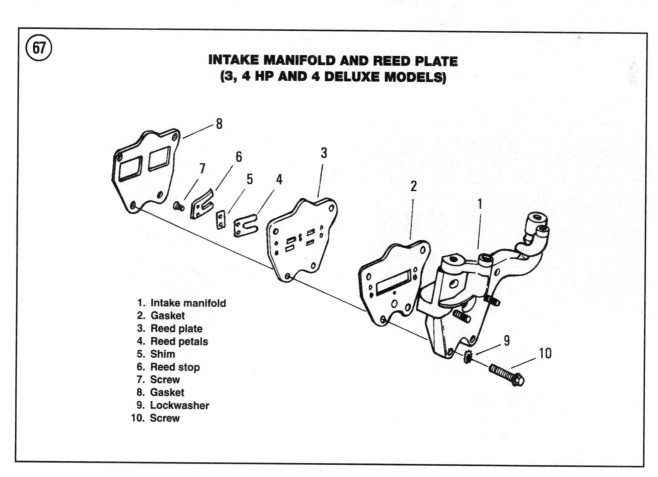

67

**INTAKE MANIFOLD AND REED PLATE
(3, 4 HP AND 4 DELUXE MODELS)**

1. Intake manifold
2. Gasket
3. Reed plate
4. Reed petals
5. Shim
6. Reed stop
7. Screw
8. Gasket
9. Lockwasher
10. Screw

Reed plate removal/installation

Refer to **Figure 67** or **Figure 68** for this procedure.

1. Disconnect and ground the spark plug leads to the power head to prevent accidental starting.

2. Remove the carburetor as described previously in this chapter.

3. *3 and 4 hp models (except 4 Deluxe)*—Remove the rope starter as described in Chapter Twelve and the ignition module as described in Chapter Seven.

4. Remove the four screws securing the intake manifold to the crankcase cover. The lower starboard screw secures the stop switch ground. Do not lose its star locking washer.

NOTE
Do not scratch, gouge, warp or damage the intake manifold, reed plate and crankcase cover during the disassembly procedure.

5A. *3, 4 hp and 4 Deluxe*—Carefully remove the intake manifold and reed plate assembly from the power head. Then separate the reed plate from the intake manifold.

5B. *6 and 8 hp*—Carefully remove the intake manifold, leaving the reed plate attached to the crankcase cover. Then remove the two screws securing the reed valve plate to the crankcase cover. Finally, remove the reed plate from the crankcase cover.

6. Carefully remove all gasket material from the intake manifold, reed plate and crankcase cover. Do not scratch, warp or gouge any of the components.

7. Clean and inspect the reed valve plate and intake manifold as described in the next section. Do not remove the reed petals from the reed plate on 3, 4 hp and 4 Deluxe models unless they are going to be replaced.

8A. *3, 4 hp and 4 Deluxe*—To install the reed plate and intake manifold, proceed as follows:

   a. Place a new gasket (without sealer) between the reed plate and intake manifold.

   b. Install the assembly to the crankcase cover using another new gasket (without sealer).

   c. Install the four intake manifold screws. Make sure the stop switch ground lead is secured with the star washer, under the lower starboard screw.

   d. Evenly tighten the four screws in a crossing pattern to 96-120 in.-lb. (10.9-13.6 N•m).

8B. *6 and 8 hp models*—To install the reed plate and intake manifold, proceed as follows:

   a. Position the reed plate to the crankcase cover using a new gasket (without sealer). Make sure the check

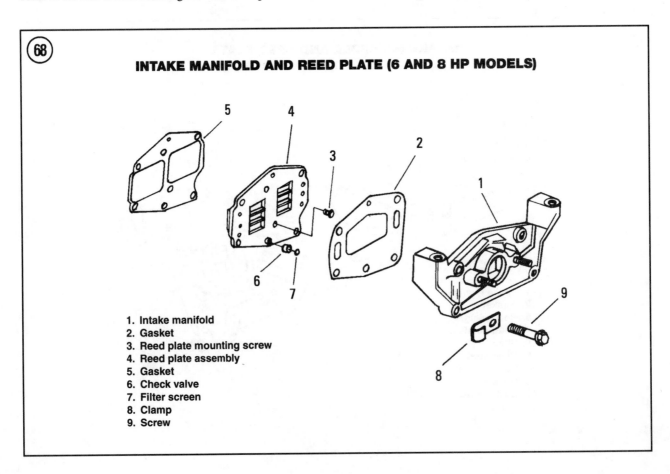

INTAKE MANIFOLD AND REED PLATE (6 AND 8 HP MODELS)

1. **Intake manifold**
2. **Gasket**
3. **Reed plate mounting screw**
4. **Reed plate assembly**
5. **Gasket**
6. **Check valve**
7. **Filter screen**
8. **Clamp**
9. **Screw**

valve and filter screen are not displaced during the installation process.

   b. Coat the threads of the two reed plate screws with OMC Gel Seal II sealant. Install and evenly tighten the screws to 60-84 in.-lb. (6.8-9.5 N•m).

   c. Position the intake manifold to the crankcase cover using another new gasket (without sealer).

   d. Install and evenly tighten the intake manifold screws in a crossing pattern to 60-84 in.-lb. (6.8-9.5 N•m).

9. Install the carburetor as described in this chapter.

10. *3 and 4 hp models (except 4 Deluxe)*—Install the rope starter as described in Chapter Twelve and the ignition module as described in Chapter Seven.

11. Reconnect the spark plug leads when finished.

Cleaning and inspection

1. Thoroughly clean the reed plate and intake manifold assemblies in a mild solvent, such as mineral spirits. On 6 and 8 hp models, inspect the check valve and screen (6 and 7, **Figure 68**) as described in *Fuel Recirculation Systems* in this chapter.

2. Check for excessive wear (indentations), cracks or grooves in the seat area of the reed plate. Replace the reed plate if any damage is noted.

3. Check the reed petals for cracks, chips or evidence of fatigue. Replace the reed petals (or reed plate assembly) if any damage is noted.

> *CAUTION*
> *Do not remove the reed petals and reed stops on 3, 4 hp and 4 Deluxe models, unless replacement is necessary. Never turn used reed petals over for reuse. Do not attempt to disassemble the reed plate on 6 and 8 hp models.*

4. Check the stand-open gap between the reed petals and the reed plate mating surface. It is acceptable (and normal) for a reed petal to stand open slightly if it can be closed with light pressure. If light pressure will not close the valve, inspect the seat area for burrs or high spots.

5. Check the reed petals for a preloaded condition. The reed petals must not be preloaded against their seats. Replace the reed petals (or reed plate assembly) if they are preloaded (stick tightly to the reed plate).

6. Check the reed stops for corrosion and mechanical damage. All stops must allow the reed petals to open the same amount. Replace the reed stops (or reed plate assembly) if the reed stops are damaged, corroded or deformed (not opening the same amount).

7. Using a machinist's straightedge (or equivalent) and a feeler gauge set, check the intake manifold and reed plate for warpage (flatness). The reed plate and intake manifold must be flat to within 0.003 in. (0.076 mm). If not, replace the reed plate and/or intake manifold.

8. *3, 4 hp and 4 Deluxe models*—To replace the reed petals (or reed stops), proceed as follows:

   a. Remove the screws attaching the reed petals and reed stops to the reed plate. Then remove the reed petals, shims and reed stops. Discard the reed petals.

   b. Determine which side of the new petals best seats to the reed plate without being preloaded. Position the reed petals to the reed plate and inspect their fit. Then, turn the petals over and inspect them again.

   c. Position the reed petals onto the reed plate with the best fitting side facing the reed plate. Then place a shim and reed stop over each reed petal.

   d. Apply OMC Nut Lock threadlocking adhesive (or equivalent) to the threads of the reed petal mounting screws. Install the screws finger-tight, then make sure the reed petals are centered over their seats (and openings).

   e. Tighten the screws evenly to 25-35 in.-lb. (2.8-4.0 N•m).

9.9 and 15 hp Models

Two sets of reed petals are mounted to a single reed plate assembly. Each set of petals feeds one cylinder. The reed plate is mounted between the intake manifold and the crankcase cover. See **Figure 69**.

The reed petals and reed stops are serviceable from the reed plate. A fuel recirculation system check valve and filter screen (9 and 10, **Figure 69**) are mounted at the top of the reed plate. See *Fuel Recirculation Systems* in this chapter.

> *NOTE*
> *Do not remove the reed petals and reed stops from the reed plate assembly unless replacement is necessary. Never remove the reeds and turn over for reuse. Replace both sets of reed petals at the same time, regardless of condition.*

Reed plate removal/installation

Refer to **Figure 69** for this procedure.

1. Disconnect and ground the spark plug leads to the power head to prevent accidental starting. On electric start models, disconnect the negative battery cable.

2. Remove the power head as described in Chapter Eight.

3. Remove the carburetor as described in this chapter.

6

4. Remove the six screws attaching the intake manifold to the crankcase cover.

> *NOTE*
> *Do not scratch, gouge, warp or damage the intake manifold, reed plate and crankcase cover during the disassembly procedure.*

5. Carefully remove the intake manifold and reed plate assembly from the power head. Then separate the reed plate from the intake manifold.

6. Carefully remove and discard all gasket material from the intake manifold, reed plate and crankcase cover. Do not scratch, warp or gouge any of the components.

7. Clean and inspect the reed valve plate and intake manifold as described in the next section. Do not remove the reed petals from the reed plate unless they are going to be replaced.

> *NOTE*
> *Make sure the check valve and filter screen are not displaced during the following installation procedure.*

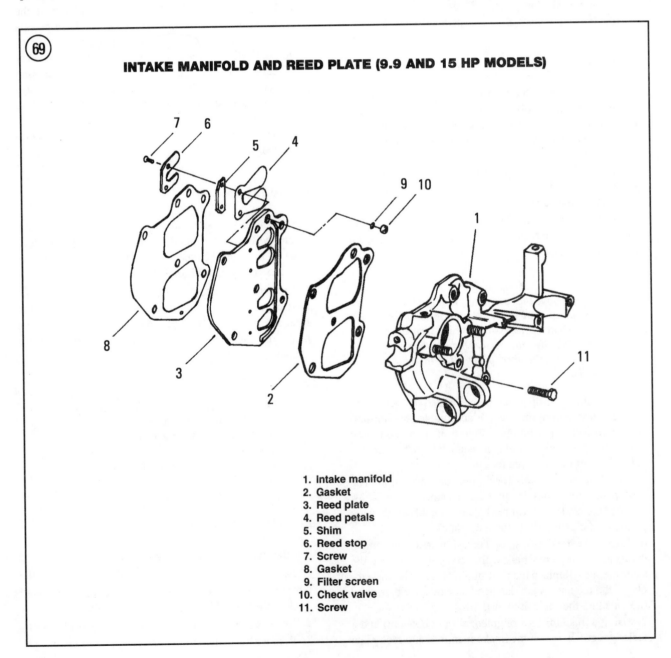

(69)

INTAKE MANIFOLD AND REED PLATE (9.9 AND 15 HP MODELS)

1. Intake manifold
2. Gasket
3. Reed plate
4. Reed petals
5. Shim
6. Reed stop
7. Screw
8. Gasket
9. Filter screen
10. Check valve
11. Screw

8. To install the reed plate and intake manifold, begin by placing a new gasket (without sealer) between the reed plate and intake manifold. Then install the assembly to the crankcase cover using another new gasket (without sealer). Install and evenly tighten the six intake manifold screws in a crossing pattern to 60-84 in.-lb. (6.8-9.5 N•m).

9. Install the carburetor as described in this chapter.

10. Install the power head as described in Chapter Eight.

11. When finished, reconnect the spark plug leads. On electric start models, correct the negative battery cable.

Cleaning and inspection

1. Thoroughly clean the reed plate and intake manifold assemblies in a mild solvent, such as mineral spirits. Inspect the check valve and screen (9 and 10, **Figure 69**) as described in *Fuel Recirculation Systems* in this chapter.

2. Check for excessive wear (indentations), cracks or grooves in the seat area of the reed plate. Replace the reed plate if any damage is noted.

3. Check the reed petals for cracks, chips or evidence of fatigue. Replace the reed petals (or reed plate assembly) if any damage is noted.

> *CAUTION*
> *Do not remove the reed petals and reed stops unless replacement is necessary. Never turn used reed petals over for reuse.*

4. Check the stand-open gap between the reed petals and the reed plate mating surface. It is acceptable (and normal) for a reed petal to stand open slightly if it can be closed with light pressure. If light pressure will not close the valve, inspect the seat area for burrs or high spots.

5. Check the reed petals for a pre-loaded condition. The reed petals must not be preloaded against their seats.

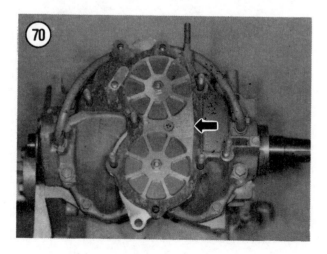

Replace the reed petals (or reed plate assembly) if they are preloaded (stick tightly to the reed plate).

6. Check the reed stops for corrosion and mechanical damage. All stops must allow the reed petals to open the same amount. Replace the reed stops (or reed plate assembly) if the reed stops are damaged, corroded or deformed (not opening the same amount).

7. Using a machinist's straightedge (or equivalent) and a feeler gauge set, check the intake manifold and reed plate for warpage (flatness). The reed plate and intake manifold must be flat to within 0.003 in. (0.076 mm). If not, replace the reed plate and/or intake manifold.

8. To replace the reed petals (or reed stops), proceed as follows:

   a. Remove the screws attaching the reed petals and reed stops to the reed plate. Then remove the reed petals, shims and reed stops. Discard the reed petals.

   b. Determine which side of the new petals best seats to the reed plate without being preloaded. Position the reed petals to the reed plate and inspect their fit. Then, turn the petals over and inspect them again.

   c. Position the reed petals onto the reed plate with the best fitting side facing the reed plate. Then place a shim and reed stop over each reed petal.

   d. Apply OMC Nut Lock threadlocking adhesive (or equivalent) to the threads of the reed petal mounting screws. Install the screws finger-tight, then make sure the reed petals are centered over their seats (and openings).

   e. Tighten the screws evenly to 25-35 in.-lb. (2.8-4.0 N•m).

20-30 hp (Two-cylinder) and 18 Jet

Two sets of reed petals are mounted to a single reed plate assembly. Each set of petals feeds one cylinder. The reed plate is mounted between the intake manifold and the crankcase cover. **Figure 70** shows the reed plate with the intake manifold removed.

The reed petals and reed stops are serviceable from the reed plate. A separate (single) reed petal (10, **Figure 71**) is used by the fuel recirculation system to pump fuel from the No. 1 cylinder crankcase out a fitting on the starboard side of the intake manifold. See *Fuel Recirculation Systems* in this chapter.

> *NOTE*
> *Do not remove the reed petals and reed stops from the reed plate assembly unless replacement is necessary. Never remove the reeds and turn over for reuse. Replace both sets of reed petals at the same time, regardless of condition.*

Reed plate removal/installation

Refer to **Figure 71** for this procedure.

1. Disconnect and ground the spark plug leads to the power head to prevent accidental starting. On electric start models, disconnect the negative battery cable.

2. Remove the carburetor as described previously in this chapter. Then disconnect the fuel recirculation hose from the fitting on the lower starboard corner of the intake manifold.

3. *25 hp, 30 hp and 18 jet models*—Disconnect the throttle control rod from the throttle cam follower (at the top of the intake manifold).

4. Remove a total of eight fasteners (screws and/or nuts and lockwashers), securing the intake manifold to the crankcase cover.

NOTE
Do not scratch, gouge, warp or damage the intake manifold, reed plate and crankcase cover during the disassembly procedure.

5. Carefully remove the intake manifold, leaving the reed plate attached to the crankcase cover. Then remove the screw (3, **Figure 71**) securing the reed valve plate to the crankcase cover. Carefully remove the reed plate from the crankcase cover.

6. Carefully remove all gasket material from the intake manifold, reed plate and crankcase cover. Do not scratch, warp or gouge any of the components.

7. Clean and inspect the reed valve plate and intake manifold as described in the next section. Do not remove the reed petals from the reed plate unless they are going to be replaced.

8. To install the reed plate and intake manifold, begin by placing a new gasket (without sealer) against the crankcase cover.

9. Coat the threads of the reed plate's flat head screw (3, **Figure 71**) with OMC Gel Seal II sealant. Position the reed plate against the crankcase cover and install the screw finger-tight. Align the reed plate to the crankcase cover, then tighten the screw securely.

10. Position another new gasket (without sealer) against the reed plate. Then position the intake manifold against the gasket.

11. Secure the assembly to the crankcase cover by installing the eight fasteners (screws and/or nuts and lockwashers). Tighten the fasteners (screws and/or nuts) evenly in a crossing pattern to 60-84 in.-lb. (6.8-9.5 N•m).

12. *25 hp, 30 hp and 18 jet models*—Connect the throttle control rod to the throttle cam follower (at the top of the intake manifold). Secure the connection with a new locking pin or small piece of stainless steel safety wire.

13. Install the carburetor as described in this chapter. Then reconnect the fuel recirculation line to the fitting on the starboard lower corner of the intake manifold. Secure the connection with a new tie-strap.

14. When finished, reconnect the spark plug leads. On electric start models, reconnect the negative battery cable.

Cleaning and inspection

1. Thoroughly clean the reed plate and intake manifold assemblies in a mild solvent, such as mineral spirits. Inspect the recirculation system reed petal as described in *Fuel Recirculation Systems*, located later in this chapter.

2. Check for excessive wear (indentations), cracks or grooves in the seat area of the reed plate. Replace the reed plate if any damage is noted.

3. Check the reed petals for cracks, chips or evidence of fatigue. Replace the reed petals (or reed plate assembly) if any damage is noted.

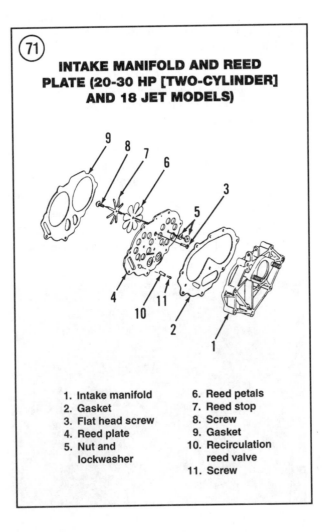

(71)

INTAKE MANIFOLD AND REED PLATE (20-30 HP [TWO-CYLINDER] AND 18 JET MODELS)

1. Intake manifold	6. Reed petals
2. Gasket	7. Reed stop
3. Flat head screw	8. Screw
4. Reed plate	9. Gasket
5. Nut and lockwasher	10. Recirculation reed valve
	11. Screw

CAUTION
Do not remove the reed petals and reed stops
unless replacement is necessary. Never turn
used reed petals over for reuse.

4. Check the stand-open gap between the reed petals and the reed plate mating surface. It is acceptable (and normal)

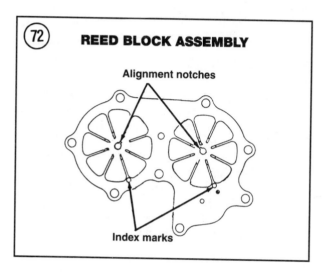

REED BLOCK ASSEMBLY

Alignment notches

Index marks

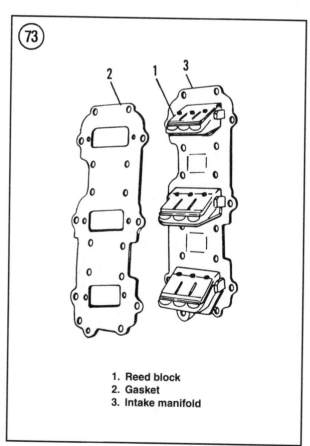

1. **Reed block**
2. **Gasket**
3. **Intake manifold**

for a reed petal to stand open slightly if it can be closed with light pressure. If light pressure will not close the valve, inspect the seat area for burrs or high spots.

5. Check the reed petals for a preloaded condition. The reed petals must not be preloaded against their seats. Replace the reed petals (or reed plate assembly) if they are preloaded (stick tightly to the reed plate).

6. Check the reed stops for corrosion and mechanical damage. All stops must allow the reed petals to open the same amount. Replace the reed stops (or reed plate assembly) if the reed stops are damaged, corroded or deformed (not opening the same amount).

7. Using a machinist's straightedge (or equivalent) and a feeler gauge set, check the intake manifold and reed plate for warpage (flatness). The reed plate and intake manifold must be flat to within 0.003 in. (0.076 mm). If not, replace the reed plate and/or intake manifold.

8. To replace the reed petals (or reed stops), proceed as follows:
   a. Remove the screw and nut attaching each set of reed petals and its reed stop to the reed plate. Then remove the reed petals and reed stops. Discard the reed petals.
   b. Determine which side of the new petals best seats to the reed plate without being preloaded. Position the reed petals to the reed plate and inspect their fit. Then, turn the petals over and inspect them again.
   c. Position the reed petals onto the reed plate with the best fitting side facing the reed plate. Position the alignment notches as shown in **Figure 72** or the reed petals will quickly fail. The port reed petal's notch must face the 1 o'clock position and the starboard petal's notch must face the 11 o'clock position.
   d. Apply OMC Nut Lock threadlocking adhesive (or equivalent) to the threads of the reed petal mounting screws. Install the screws (and nuts) finger-tight, then make sure the reed petals are centered over their seats (and openings) and the reed stops are centered over the reed petals.
   e. While holding the appropriate nut, tighten each screw to 25-35 in.-lb. (2.8-4.0 N•m).

25 and 35 hp (Three-cylinder),
40-70 hp, 28 Jet and 35 Jet Models

These models use a one-piece intake manifold with an individual reed valve block assembly for each cylinder. The reed blocks mount to the intake manifold as shown in **Figure 73**, typical. Each reed block contains two sets of reed petals, one on each side (**Figure 74**, typical). Each reed petal is secured to the reed block with screws.

The reed blocks on 25-35 hp (three-cylinder) models are not serviceable and are replaced as individual assemblies.

The reed blocks on 40-70 hp and the 28 and 35 jet models are serviceable. The reed petals and/or reed stops may be individually replaced. However, if any one reed petal has failed, it is recommended that all reed petals be replaced.

> *NOTE*
> *Do not remove the reed petals and reed stops from the reed plate assembly on 40-70 hp and the 28 and 35 jet models unless replacement is necessary. Never reuse the reeds. Also never attempt to reuse the reeds by removing them and turning them over. Replace all reed petals at the same time, regardless of condition.*

Reed block removal/installation

1. Disconnect and ground the spark plug leads to the power head to prevent accidental starting. On electric start models, disconnect the negative battery cable.

2. Remove the carburetors as described in this chapter.

3. Disconnect the air intake cover drain hose from the fitting at the bottom of the intake manifold.

4A. *25 and 35 hp (three-cylinder)*—Disconnect the fuel recirculation line from the elbow fitting near the bottom of the manifold. Then remove eight screws securing the manifold to the cylinder block. On remote control models, disconnect the primer line from the fitting near the top of the manifold.

4B. *40-50 hp (two-cylinder), 28 jet and 35 jet*—Remove the control cables from the anchor bracket on the bottom starboard corner of the intake manifold. Then remove the ten screws securing the manifold to the crankcase cover. The anchor bracket can be left attached to the intake manifold.

4C. *50-70 hp (three-cylinder)*—Remove the control cables from the anchor bracket on the bottom starboard corner of the intake manifold. Then remove the timing pointer (and cowl support) bracket at the top of the manifold. Finally, remove the 16 remaining screws securing the manifold to the crankcase cover. The anchor bracket can be left attached to the intake manifold.

> *NOTE*
> *Do not scratch, gouge, warp or damage the intake manifold, reed blocks and crankcase cover during the disassembly procedure.*

5. Carefully remove the intake manifold (and reed block) assembly. Then remove the two screws securing each reed block to the intake manifold. Carefully separate the reed blocks from the manifold.

6. Carefully remove all gasket material from the intake manifold, reed blocks and crankcase cover. Do not scratch, warp or gouge any of the components.

7. Clean and inspect the reed blocks and intake manifold as described in the next section. On 40-70 hp, 28 jet and 35 jet models, do not remove the reed petals from the reed blocks unless they are going to be replaced.

8A. *25 and 35 hp (three-cylinder)*—To install the reed blocks, proceed as follows:
   a. Peel the protective cover from a new self-adhesive gasket. Carefully position the gasket to the intake manifold, then press it in place. Do not use any sealer on the gasket.
   b. Coat the reed block screw threads with OMC Nut Lock threadlocking adhesive (or equivalent).
   c. Secure each reed block to the manifold with two screws. Make sure the gasket is correctly aligned with the manifold, then evenly tighten the reed block screws to 25-35 in.-lb. (2.8-4.0 N•m).

8B. *40-70 hp, 28 jet and 35 jet*—To install the reed blocks, proceed as follows:

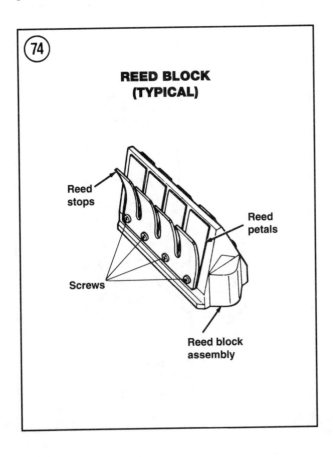

(74)

**REED BLOCK
(TYPICAL)**

Reed
stops

Reed
petals

Screws

Reed block
assembly

a. Position a new gasket (using no sealer) on the intake manifold. Then position each reed block to the gasket (and manifold).

b. Coat the reed block screw threads with OMC Nut Lock threadlocking adhesive (or equivalent).

c. Secure each reed block to the manifold with two screws. Make sure the gasket is correctly aligned with the manifold, then evenly tighten the reed block screws to 25-35 in.-lb. (2.8-4.0 N•m).

9A. *25 and 35 hp (three-cylinder)*—Position the intake manifold to the power head and secure it in place with eight screws. Evenly tighten the screws in a crossing pattern (starting at the center and working outward) to 60-84 in.-lb. (6.8-9.5 N•m). Then reconnect the fuel recirculation line to the fitting near the bottom of the manifold. On remote control models, reattach the primer line to the fitting near the top of the manifold.

9B. *40-50 hp (two-cylinder), 28 jet and 35 jet*—Position the intake manifold to the crankcase cover and secure it in place with ten screws. Evenly tighten the screws in a crossing pattern (starting at the center and working outward) to 60-84 in.-lb. (6.8-9.5 N•m). Then reinstall the control cables into the cable's anchor bracket.

9C. *50-70 hp (three-cylinder)*—Position the intake manifold to the crankcase cover and install the 16 lower screws. Then install the timing pointer bracket to the top of the manifold and secure it in place with two screws. Evenly tighten all 18 screws in a crossing pattern (starting at the center and working outward) to 60-84 in.-lb. (6.8-9.5 N•m). Then reinstall the control cables into the cable's anchor bracket.

10. Reconnect the air intake cover drain hose to the fitting at the bottom of the intake manifold.

11. Install the carburetors as described previously in this chapter.

12. Reconnect the spark plug leads. On electric start models, connect the negative battery cable.

Cleaning and inspection

1. Thoroughly clean each reed block and the intake manifold in a mild solvent, such as mineral spirits.

2. Inspect the intake manifold and reed blocks for distortion, cracks, blocked passages and fittings. Make sure that all machined (or cast) grooves in the intake manifold mating surface are clean and free from obstructions. On 25-35 hp (three-cylinder) models, inspect the recirculation system check valve as described in *Fuel Recirculation Systems* in this chapter.

3. Check the reed petal screws (**Figure 74**) for secure attachment. If any loose screws are located, remove the screw and lightly coat its threads with OMC Nut Lock

threadlocking adhesive (or equivalent). Install and tighten the screw to 25-35 in.-lb. (2.8-4.0 N•m).

4. Check for excessive wear (indentations), cracks or grooves in the seat areas of each reed block. Replace any damaged reed block(s).

5. Check the reed petals for cracks, chips or evidence of fatigue. Replace any damaged reed petals (or reed block assemblies) on which damage is noted.

CAUTION
On 40-70 hp, 28 jet and 35 jet models, do not remove the reed petals and reed stops unless replacement is necessary. Never turn used petals over and attempt to reuse them.

6. Check the stand-open gap between each reed petal and its reed box mating surface. It is acceptable (and normal) for a reed petal to stand open slightly, if it can be closed with light pressure. If light pressure will not close the valve, inspect the seat area for burrs or high spots.

7. Check the reed petals for a preloaded condition. The reed petals must not be preloaded against their seats. Replace the reed petals (or reed block assembly) if they are preloaded (stick tightly to the reed block).

8. Check the reed stops for corrosion and mechanical damage. All stops must allow the reed petals to open the same amount. Replace the reed stops (or the reed block assembly) if the reed stops are damaged, corroded or deformed (not opening the same amount).

9. Using a machinist's straight edge (or equivalent) and a feeler gauge set, check the intake manifold and reed blocks for warpage (flatness). The reed blocks must be flat to within 0.003 in. (0.076 mm) and the intake manifold must be flat to within 0.004 in. (0.102 mm). If not, replace the reed block(s) and/or intake manifold.

Reed petal replacement

To replace the reed petals (or reed stops) on 40-70 hp, 28 jet and 35 jet models, refer to **Figure 75** and proceed as follows:

NOTE
The reed petals are not replaceable on 25 and 35 hp (three-cylinder) models.

1. Remove the screws securing the reed stop and reed petals to each side of each reed block. See **Figure 74**. Then remove the reed stops, shim and reed petal from each side of the block. Discard the reed petals.

2. Determine which side of the new petals best seats to the reed plate without being preloaded. Position the reed petals to the reed plate and inspect their fit. Then, turn the petals over and inspect them again.

6

3. Position the reed petals onto each reed block with the best fitting side facing the block. Then position a shim and finally the reed stop over each reed petal. See **Figure 75**.

4. Apply OMC Nut Lock threadlocking adhesive (or equivalent) to the threads of the reed petal mounting screws. Install the screws finger-tight, then make sure the reed petals (and reed stop) are centered over their seats.

5. Evenly tighten the screws to 25-35 in.-lb. (2.8-4.0 N•m).

FUEL RECIRCULATION SYSTEMS

Multiple cylinder motors are equipped with a fuel bleed (recirculation) system designed to collect unburned fuel and oil from the low spots of the individual crankcase areas. Since the intake system used by two-stroke engines does not completely transfer all of the fuel sent through the crankcase to the combustion chamber (especially during low-speed operation), the recirculation system provides a method of collecting the fuel and oil pooled in the low spots of the crankcase and pumping it to the intake ports or intake manifold where it can be transferred into the combustion chamber and burned.

Many recirculation systems also collect the fuel and oil pooled in the lower crankshaft bearing area and pump it to the upper crankshaft bearing to ensure proper upper crankshaft bearing lubrication. These models can suffer an upper crankshaft bearing failure if the system malfunctions and does not pump fuel and oil to the upper bearing carrier.

Correct recirculation system operation is vitally important to efficient engine operation. If the system fails, excessive amounts of fuel and oil will puddle in the crankcase and not reach the combustion chamber during low-speed operation, causing a lean mixture. When the engine is accelerated, the puddles of fuel and oil are quickly drawn into the engine temporarily causing an excessively rich mixture. This will result in the following symptoms:

1. Poor low speed performance.
2. Poor acceleration.
3. Spark plug fouling.
4. Stalling or spitting at idle.
5. Excessive smoke on acceleration.

Fuel Recirculation System Service

A small glue syringe, such as the Monoject 412, is necessary to test check valve operation and test the fittings and lines for correct fluid flow. This syringe (or its equivalent) is available from most craft stores or hobby shops.

Some recirculation systems require one-way check valves for operation. External check valves are mounted directly in the cylinder block transfer port covers, crank-case cover or intake manifold. External check valves must flow fluid from the threaded end toward the nipple end, but not from the nipple toward the threaded end.

Internal check valves are mounted in the crankcase cover or in the intake manifold. Often the check valve will be protected by a wire mesh screen. The valve consists of a brass body with a fiber disc. Internal valves are always installed with the beveled (chamfered) end of the valve inserted into the crankcase cover (or intake manifold) first. Fluid must only flow from the non-beveled end to the beveled end. Refer to Chapter Eight for additional power head exploded views and check valve locations.

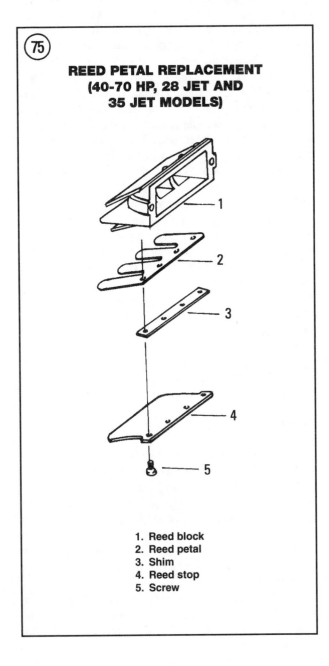

(75)

REED PETAL REPLACEMENT (40-70 HP, 28 JET AND 35 JET MODELS)

1. Reed block
2. Reed petal
3. Shim
4. Reed stop
5. Screw

Inspect internal check valves for gum, varnish and other debris. Make sure each valve's internal fiber disc is present and not damaged, distorted or stuck open or closed. The fiber disc must be free to move in the body.

NOTE
All check valves must flow fluid in one direction, but not the opposite. Any valve that allows fluid flow in both directions is defective and must be replaced.

Fittings and lines must always be open and allow fluid flow in either direction. A small syringe and a piece of recirculation line can quickly test the system. Replace or clean any fitting that will not flow in both directions. Replace any check valve that flows in both directions or will not flow in either direction. Push on the syringe plunger to check flow into a fitting or check valve. Pull on the syringe plunger to check flow out of a fitting or check valve. Also, inspect and replace any recirculation lines that are damaged or deteriorated.

When replacing threaded fittings, coat the threads with OMC Pipe Sealant with Teflon. Check valves (and fittings) that are press fit into the crankcase cover (or intake manifold) must be coated *lightly* with OMC Ultra Lock threadlocking adhesive. Do not allow sealant or adhesive into the valve or fitting.

2, 3.3 and 3.5 hp Models

These models do not incorporate a recirculation system.

3, 4 hp and 4 Deluxe Models

These models use a single, internal check valve mounted in the lower main bearing bore of the crankcase cover. See **Figure 76**, similar. A filter screen protects the valve. Drilled passages and a machined (or cast) slot in the crankcase cover connect the lower main bearing bore (and check valve) to the upper main bearing bore. Two small plastic metering rods are present in the drilled passages. The upper passage uses a 1.3 in. (33 mm) long plastic rod and the lower passage uses a 0.8 in. (20.32 mm) long plastic rod. There are no external lines. The plastic rods reduce the volume of the drilled passages, increasing the pumping efficiency of the system. See Chapter Eight for power head exploded views.

6

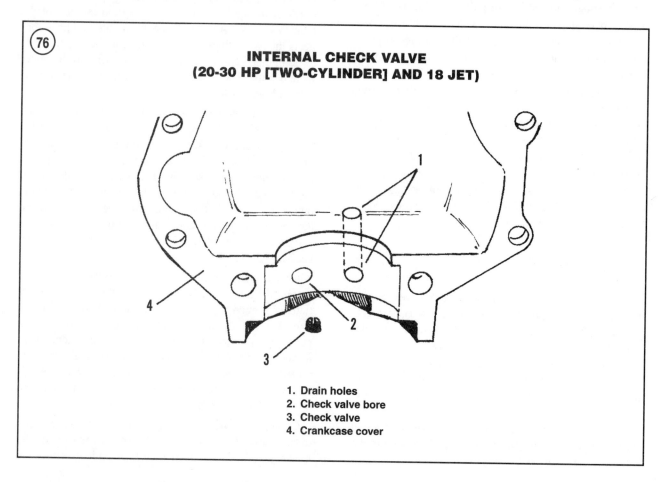

(76)

**INTERNAL CHECK VALVE
(20-30 HP [TWO-CYLINDER] AND 18 JET)**

1. Drain holes
2. Check valve bore
3. Check valve
4. Crankcase cover

This system keeps the upper main bearing properly lubricated and reduces the amount of puddled fuel in the bottom of the crankcase.

A severe engine overheat can melt the plastic metering rods block the passages. Any service on the system requires power head disassembly (Chapter Eight). Clean and inspect the internal check valve, filter screen, plastic metering rods and all passages. Replace any damaged parts.

6 and 8 hp Models

These models use a single, internal check valve mounted in the bottom of the reed plate assembly. A filter screen protects the valve. Refer to **Figure 68** for check valve location. Drilled passages connect the upper and lower main bearing bores to a machined (or cast) groove in the intake manifold. Two small plastic metering rods are present in the drilled passages. The upper passage uses a 1-5/8 in. (41.28 mm) long plastic rod and the lower passage uses a 1-1/4 in. (31.75 mm) long plastic rod. There are no external lines. The plastic rods reduce the volume of the drilled passages, increasing the pumping efficiency of the system. See Chapter Eight for power head exploded views.

This system keeps the upper main bearing properly lubricated and reduces the amount of puddled fuel in the bottom of the crankcase.

A severe engine overheat can melt the plastic metering rods and block the passages. Complete service on the system requires power head disassembly (Chapter Eight). However, removal of the intake manifold (and reed plate) will allow service on everything but the drilled main bearing passages and the plastic metering rods.

When servicing the system, clean and inspect the internal check valve, filter screen, plastic metering rods and all passages. Replace any damaged parts.

9.9 and 15 hp Models

These models use a single, internal check valve mounted in the top of the reed plate assembly. A filter screen protects the valve. Refer to **Figure 69** for check valve location. Drilled passages connect the upper and lower main bearing bores to a machined (or cast) groove in the reed plate and a short cast groove at the top of the intake manifold. There are no plastic metering rods in the drilled passages and there are no external lines.

This system keeps the upper main bearing properly lubricated and reduces the amount of puddled fuel in the bottom of the crankcase.

Complete service on the system requires power head disassembly (Chapter Eight). However, removal of the intake manifold (and reed plate) will allow service on everything but the drilled main bearing passages.

When servicing the system, clean and inspect the internal check valve, filter screen and all passages. Replace the valve and/or screen if damaged.

20-30 hp (Two-cylinder) and 18 Jet Models

These models incorporate two systems, each using a combination of internal and external components. The first system keeps the upper main bearing lubricated and removes puddled fuel from the bottom of the No. 2 cylinder crankcase. The second system removes puddled fuel from the No.1 cylinder crankcase and pumps it to either the carburetor's primer fitting or directly to the No. 1 cylinder transfer port cover.

The first system consists of an internal check valve mounted in the lower main bearing bore of the crankcase cover (**Figure 76**). A filter screen protects the valve. Drilled passages connect the lower and upper main bearing bores to fittings pressed into the bottom and top of the crankcase cover. A small diameter flexible fuel hose connects the two fittings together, allowing the puddled fuel to be pumped from the lower main bearing to the upper main bearing. The hose can be seen still attached to crankcase in **Figure 70**.

The second system consists of a small auxiliary reed valve (10, **Figure 71**) mounted to the reed plate. A drilled passage connects the reed valve to the lowest portion of the No. 1 cylinder crankcase. Each time the No. 1 piston moves down, crankcase pressure pushes any puddled fuel out the drilled passage, through the reed valve and out the intake manifold's fitting (starboard lower corner). When the piston moves up, crankcase vacuum pulls the reed valve closed, preventing the fuel (or air) from being drawn back into the crankcase.

A small diameter flexible fuel line connects the intake manifold fitting to either a fitting at the No. 1 cylinder transfer port cover, or a fitting in the carburetor's primer line. Any fuel discharged into the transfer port fitting is pulled into the No. 1 cylinder combustion chamber where it is consumed. Any fuel discharged into the primer line is pulled into the carburetor's primer fitting (by intake manifold vacuum), where it joins the normal air/fuel mixture on its way to both combustion chambers.

Complete service on the system requires power head disassembly (Chapter Eight). However, removal of the intake manifold (and reed plate) will allow service on everything but the drilled main bearing passages and the check valve in the lower main bearing bore.

When servicing the system, clean and inspect the reed valve (on the reed plate), the internal check valve and filter screen, all drilled passages and all flexible lines. Replace any damaged or deteriorated components.

25 and 35 hp (Three-cylinder) Models

These models use internal and external systems and components. The first system collects the puddled fuel from the lower main bearing and pumps the fuel to the upper main bearing. The second system (composed of two subsystems) collects the puddled fuel in each cylinder's transfer port passages and No. 3 cylinder reed box area and pumps this fuel to the appropriate boost passage, where it is pulled into the combustion chamber with the normal air/fuel mixture and consumed.

The first system consists of an internal check valve mounted in the lower main bearing bore of the crankcase cover, similar to that shown in **Figure 76**. Drilled passages connect the lower and upper main bearing bores to fittings pressed into the bottom and top of the crankcase cover. A small diameter clear hose connects the two fittings together, allowing the puddled fuel to be pumped from the lower main bearing to the upper main bearing. See Chapter Eight for an exploded view of the power head components.

The primary components of the second system consist of check valves threaded into the transfer port passages of each cylinder. A small diameter clear line connects each check valve to the appropriate boost passage fitting. All check valves and the boost port fittings are mounted in a vertical line on the port side of the block, near the intake manifold/crankcase cover mating line. The recirculation lines must be connected as follows:

1. No. 1 cylinder transfer port check valve to No. 3 cylinder boost port fitting. The line is 4.5 in. (114.3 mm) long.
2. No. 2 cylinder transfer port check valve to No. 1 cylinder boost port fitting. The line is 6.5 in. (165.1 mm) long.
3. No. 3 cylinder transfer port check valve to a T-fitting, then T-fitting to No. 2 cylinder boost port fitting. The first line is 3/4 in. (19.1 mm) long, the second is 5.5 in. (139.7 mm) long.

The secondary components of the second system consist of an internal check valve pressed into the No. 3 cylinder portion of the intake manifold and an external elbow fitting, near the bottom, port corner of the intake manifold. The internal check valve and external fitting are connected by a machined passage. A small diameter clear line (3 in. [76.2 mm] long) connects the external elbow fitting to the T-fitting described previously.

Complete service on the system requires power head disassembly (Chapter Eight). However, removal of the intake manifold (and reed plate) will allow service on everything but the drilled main bearing passages and the check valve in the lower main bearing bore.

When servicing the system, clean and inspect:
1. The intake manifold's internal check valve, external fitting and drilled passages.
2. The crankcase cover's internal check valve (lower main bearing bore) and the upper and lower main bearing fittings (and drilled passages).
3. The three transfer port external check valves, T-fitting and boost port fittings.
4. All other drilled or machined passages and all flexible lines.

Replace any damaged or deteriorated components.

40-50 hp (Two-cylinder), 28 Jet and 35 Jet Models

These models use an internal system only. The system consists simply of a machined passage in the intake manifold's crankcase cover mating surface and two drilled passages in the crankcase cover, one leading to the lower crankshaft main bearing area and one to the upper main bearing.

The pressure differential in the crankcase and intake manifold moves puddled fuel from the No. 2 cylinder crankcase (lower main bearing) to the upper main bearing and the No. 1 cylinder intake passage.

When servicing the system, clean and inspect the intake manifold's machined passage and the crankcase cover's drilled passages. Do not apply any sealer to the intake manifold gasket or the passages may become blocked.

50-70 hp (Three-cylinder) Models

These models use an internal system only. The system consists simply of machined passages in the intake manifold's crankcase cover mating surface and two drilled passages in the crankcase cover, one leading to the lower crankshaft main bearing area and one to the upper main bearing.

Pressure differentials in the crankcases and intake manifold passages move puddled fuel and fuel vapors from the No. 3 cylinder crankcase (lower main bearing) to each cylinder's intake passages and finally, the upper main bearing.

When servicing the system, clean and inspect the intake manifold's machined passages and the crankcase cover's drilled passages. Do not apply any sealer to the intake manifold gasket or the passages may become blocked.

6

Table 1 CARBURETOR SPECIFICATIONS: 2, 3.3 AND 3.5 HP

Float level (measured from gasket)	0.090 in. (2.3 mm)
Initial idle mixture screw adjustment	Not applicable
Mixture needle E-clip standard setting	
1995-1997 (EO-EU) models	3rd groove from flat (short) end
1998-2003 (EC-ST) models	4th groove from flat (short) end
Standard main jet	Part No. 115602
High altitude main jet compensation	Not applicable (adjust mixture needle)

Table 2 CARBURETOR SPECIFICATIONS: 3 AND 4-15 HP (INCLUDING 4 DELUXE)

Float level (direct measurement)	
3, 4 hp and 4 Deluxe	0.600-0.625 in. (15.24-15.88 mm)
6-15 hp	0.570-0.595 in. (14.48-15.11 mm)
Float drop	
3, 4 hp and 4 Deluxe	1.125 to 1.5 in. (28.6-38.1 mm)
6-15 hp	1.0-1.375 in. (25.4-34.9 mm)
Initial idle mixture screw adjustment	
3, 4 hp and 4 Deluxe	1 turn from lightly seated position
6-15 hp	3 turns from lightly seated position
Standard main jet	
3 hp	No. 33 (0.033 in. [0.84 mm])
4 hp (except 4 Deluxe)	No. 35 (0.035 in. [0.89 mm])
4 Deluxe, 6 hp (DR)	No. 33 (0.033 in. [0.84 mm])
6 hp (R)	No. 38 (0.038 in. [0.97 mm])
8 hp	No. 50 (0.050 in. [1.27 mm])
9.9 hp	No. 36 (0.036 in. [0.91 mm])
15 hp	No. 48 (0.048 in. [1.22 mm])
High altitude main jet compensation	
3000-6000 ft. (914-1829 m)	0.002 in. (0.05 mm) smaller than standard
6000-9000 ft. (1829-2743 m)	0.004 in. (0.10 mm) smaller than standard
9000 ft.-higher (2743 m -higher)	0.006 in. (0.15 mm) smaller than standard

Table 3 CARBURETOR SPECIFICATIONS: 20-30 HP (TWO-CYLINDER) AND 18 JET

Float level (direct measurement)	
20 hp	0.570-0.595 in. (14.48-15.11 mm)
25-30 hp and 18 jet	0.710-0.745 in. (18.03-18.92 mm)
Float drop	
20 hp	1.0-1.375 in. (25.4-34.9 mm)
25-30 hp and 18 jet	1.125-1.625 in. (28.6-41.3 mm)
Initial idle mixture screw adjustment	
20 hp	3 turns from lightly seated position
25 hp (TR carburetor)	1-3/4 turns from lightly seated position
25-30 hp and 18 jet (SV carburetor)	2-1/2 turns from lightly seated position
Standard intermediate jet	
20 hp	Not applicable
25 hp (TR series carburetor)	No. 30 (0.030 in. [0.76 mm])
25 hp (SV series carburetor)	No. 49D (0.049 in. [1.25 mm])
28 Special and 18 jet	No. 55D (0.055 in. [1.40 mm])
30 hp	No. 57D (0.057 in. [1.45 mm])
Standard main jet	
20 hp	No. 44 (0.044 in. [1.12 mm])
25 hp (TR series carburetor)	No. 51D (0.051 in. [1.30 mm])
25 hp (SV series carburetor)	No. 49D (0.049 in. [1.25 mm])
18 jet	
1995 (EO) models	No. 58D (0.058 in. [1.47 mm])
1996-2003 (ED-ST) models	No. 59D (0.059 in. [1.50 mm])
28 Special	No. 59D (0.059 in. [1.50 mm])
30 hp	No. 67D (0.067 in. [1.70 mm])

(continued)

Table 3 CARBURETOR SPECIFICATIONS: 20-30 HP (TWO-CYLINDER) AND 18 JET (continued)

High altitude main jet compensation	
3000-6000 ft. (914-1829 m)	0.002 in. (0.05 mm) smaller than standard
6000-9000 ft. (1829-2743 m)	0.004 in. (0.10 mm) smaller than standard
9000 ft.-higher (2743 m -higher)	0.006 in. (0.15 mm) smaller than standard

Table 4 CARBURETOR SPECIFICATIONS: 25 AND 35 HP (THREE-CYLINDER)

Float level (direct measurement)	0.570-0.595 in. (14.48-15.11 mm)
Float drop	1.0-1.375 in. (25.4-34.9 mm)
Initial idle mixture screw adjustment[1]	
1995 (EO) and 1996 (ED)[2] models	0.350 in. (8.9 mm)
1996 (ED)[3]-2003 (ST) models	0.390 in. (9.9 mm)
Standard intermediate jet	
25 hp	No. 31 (0.031 in. [0.79 mm])
35 hp	No. 32 (0.032 in. [0.81 mm])
Standard main jet	
1995 (EO) and 1996 (ED)[2] models	
25 hp	No. 38 (0.038 in. [0.97 mm])
35 hp	No. 42 (0.042 in. [1.07 mm])
1996 (ED)[3]-2003 (ST) models	
25 hp	No. 36 (0.036 in. [0.91 mm])
35 hp	No. 38 (0.038 in. [0.97 mm])
High altitude main jet compensation	
3000-6000 ft. (914-1829 m)	0.002 in. (0.05 mm) smaller than standard
6000-9000 ft. (1829-2743 m)	0.004 in. (0.10 mm) smaller than standard
9000 ft.-higher (2743 m -higher)	0.006 in. (0.15 mm) smaller than standard

1. Measure the idle mixture screw's spring length.
2. Model numbers ending with a C.
3. Model numbers ending with a G.

Table 5 CARBURETOR SPECIFICATIONS: 40-50 HP (TWO-CYLINDER) AND 28-35 JET

Float settings	
Float level (direct measurement)	0.710-0.745 in. (18.03-18.92 mm)
Float drop	1.125-1.625 in. (28.6-41.3 mm)
Initial idle mixture screw adjustment	
40 hp and 28 jet	2-1/2 turns from lightly seated position
48 hp, 50 hp and 35 jet	3-1/2 turns from lightly seated position
Standard intermediate jet	
40 hp and 28 jet	No. 71C (0.071 in. [1.80 mm])
48 hp, 50 hp and 35 jet	No. 56C (0.056 in. [1.42 mm])
Standard main jet	
40 hp and 28 jet	No. 49D (0.049 in. [1.25 mm])
48 hp, 50 hp and 35 jet	No. 55D (0.055 in. [1.40 mm])
High altitude main jet compensation	
3000-6000 ft. (914-1829 m)	0.002 in. (0.05 mm) smaller than standard
6000-9000 ft. (1829-2743 m)	0.004 in. (0.10 mm) smaller than standard
9000 ft.-higher (2743 m -higher)	0.006 in. (0.15 mm) smaller than standard

Table 6 CARBURETOR SPECIFICATIONS: 50-70 HP (THREE-CYLINDER)

Float settings	
Float level (direct measurement)	0.710-0.745 in. (18.03-18.92 mm)
Float drop	1.125-1.625 in. (28.6-41.3 mm)

(continued)

Table 6 CARBURETOR SPECIFICATIONS: 50-70 HP (THREE-CYLINDER) (continued)

Initial idle mixture screw adjustment	
1995 (EO) models	2-3/4 turns from lightly seated position
1996-2003 (ED-ST) models	
50 hp	1-3/4 turns from lightly seated position
60 hp and 70 hp	2-3/4 turns from lightly seated position
Standard intermediate jet	
50 hp	No. 40D (0.040 in. [1.02 mm])
60 hp	
1995 (EO) models	No. 40D (0.040 in. [1.02 mm])
1996-2003 (ED-ST) models	No. 35D (0.035 in. [0.89 mm])
70 hp	No. 60D (0.060 in. [1.52 mm])
Standard main jet	
50 hp	No. 41D (0.041 in. [1.04 mm])
60 hp	
1995 (EO) models	No. 46D (0.046 in. [1.17 mm])
1996-2003 (ED-ST)	No. 45D (0.045 in. [1.14 mm])
70 hp	No. 52D (0.052 in. [1.32 mm])
High altitude main jet compensation	
3000-6000 ft. (914-1829 m)	0.002 in. (0.05 mm) smaller than standard
6000-9000 ft. (1829-2743 m)	0.004 in. (0.10 mm) smaller than standard
9000 ft.-higher (2743 m -higher)	0.006 in. (0.15 mm) smaller than standard

Table 7 CARBURETOR TORQUE SPECIFICATIONS

Fastener	in.-lb.	ft.-lb.	N•m
Carburetor air intake cover			
50-70 hp (three-cylinder)	24-36	–	2.7-4.1
Carburetor air intake cover base			
50-70 hp (three-cylinder)	24-36	–	2.7-4.1
Carburetor float chamber screws			
3 hp, 4 hp and 4 Deluxe	15-22	–	1.7-2.5
6-20 hp	8-10	–	0.9-1.1
25 and 30 hp (two-cylinder) and 18 jet	25-35	–	2.8-4.0
25 and 35 hp (three-cylinder)	17-19	–	1.9-2.2
40-70 hp, 28 jet and 35 jet	25-35	–	2.8-4.0
Carburetor mounting			
25 and 35 hp (three-cylinder)	60-84	–	6.8-9.5
Carburetor top cover			
6-20 hp	8-10	–	0.9-1.1
25 and 30 hp (two-cylinder) and 18 jet	15-22	–	1.7-2.5
25 and 35 hp (three-cylinder)	17-19	–	1.9-2.2
40-70 hp, 28 jet and 35 jet	15-22	–	1.7-2.5

Table 8 FUEL PUMP, INTAKE MANIFOLD AND REED VALVE TORQUE SPECIFICATIONS

Fastener	in.-lb.	ft.-lb.	N•m
Intake manifold			
3 and 4 hp	96-120	–	10.9-13.6
4 Deluxe, 6-70 hp and 18-35 jet	60-84	–	6.8-9.5
Integral fuel tanks	60-84	–	6.8-9.5
Conventional fuel pumps			
Cover (filter) screw	securely	–	securely
Mounting screws	24-36	–	2.7-4.1
Reed valves			
Petal mounting screws	25-35	–	2.8-4.0
Reed box-to-intake manifold	25-35	–	2.8-4.0

Chapter Seven

Ignition and Electrical Systems

This chapter provides service procedures for the battery, starter motor and ignition systems used on the outboard motors covered in this manual. Wiring diagrams are located at the end of the book. Refer to Chapter Three for charging system identification.

Battery charge percentage, wire color codes, battery capacity and battery cable size recommendations are listed in **Tables 1-5**. Fastener torque values are listed in **Tables 6-7**. Ignition system identification is covered in **Table 8**. Refer to Chapter Three for charging system identification.

CAUTION
Metric and American fasteners may be used on newer model outboards. Always match a replacement fastener to the original. Do not run a tap or thread chaser into a hole (or over a screw or bolt) without first verifying the thread size and pitch.

SERVICE PRECAUTIONS—
1998-2003 MODEL YEAR ENGINES

The EPA (Environmental Protection Agency) certifies emission output for all 1998-2003 models. Certified models have an EPA certification plate mounted near the model identification plate on the engine midsection. Refer to *Model Identification* in Chapter Eight for illustrations and information regarding the certification plate.

All repairs or service procedures must be performed exactly as specified to ensure the engine will continue to comply with EPA requirements. For the same reason, all replacement parts must meet or exceed the manufacturer's specifications.

If in doubt as to whether a repair or service procedure will adversely affect the engine's ability to maintain EPA compliance, contact an Evinrude or Johnson dealer before beginning the repair or procedure.

BATTERY

Batteries used in marine applications endure far more rigorous treatment than those used in automotive electrical systems. Marine batteries have a thicker exterior case to cushion the plates during tight turns and rough water operation. Thicker plates are also used, with each one individually fastened within the case to prevent premature failure. Spill-proof caps on the battery cells prevent electrolyte from spilling into the bilge.

Use an automotive battery in a boat *only* during an emergency situation when a suitable marine battery is not available.

CAUTION
Sealed or maintenance-free batteries are not recommended for use with unregulated charging systems. Excessive charging during continued high-speed operation will cause the electrolyte to boil, resulting in its loss. Since water cannot be added to a

battery, prolonged overcharging will destroy the battery. Refer to Chapter Three for charging system identification.

Battery Rating Methods

The battery industry has developed specifications and performance standards to evaluate batteries and their energy potential. Several rating methods are available to provide meaningful information on battery selection.

Cold cranking amps (CCA)

This figure represents in amps the current flow the battery can deliver for 30 seconds at 0° F (-17.6° C) without dropping below 1.2 volts per cell (7.2 volts on a standard 12-volt battery).

Marine cranking amps (MCA)

This figure is similar to the CCA test figure except that the test is run at 32° F (0° C) instead of 0° F (-17.6° C). This is more aligned with actual boat operating environments. MCA times 0.77 equals CCA.

Reserve capacity

This figure represents the time (in minutes) that a fully charged battery at 80° F (26.7° C) can deliver 25 amps, without dropping below 1.75 volts per cell (10.5 volts on a standard 12-volt battery). The reserve capacity rating defines the length of time that a typical vehicle can be driven after the charging system fails. The 25 amp figure accounts for power required by the ignition, lighting and other accessories. The higher the reserve capacity rating, the longer the vehicle could be driven after a charging system failure.

Amp-hour rating

The ampere hour rating method is also called the 20 hour rating method. This rating represents the steady current flow that the battery will deliver for 20 hours at 80° F (26.7° C) without dropping below 1.75 volts per cell (10.5 volts on a standard 12-volt battery). The rating is actually the steady current flow times the 20 hours. Example: A 60 amp-hour battery will deliver 3 amps continuously for 20 hours. This method has been largely discontinued by the battery industry. Cold cranking amps (or MCA) and reserve capacity ratings are now the most common battery rating methods.

Battery Recommendations

The manufacturer recommends a battery with a minimum rating of 465 cold cranking amps (CCA) or 360 marine cranking amps (MCA) and 100 minutes reserve capacity for all models requiring a battery.

Battery Installation

Separate batteries may be used to provide power for accessories such as lighting, fish finders and depth finders. To determine the required capacity of such batteries, calculate the current (amperage) draw rate of the accessory and refer to **Table 4**.

Two batteries may be connected in parallel to double the ampere-hour capacity while maintaining the required 12 volts. See **Figure 1**. For accessories which require 24 volts,

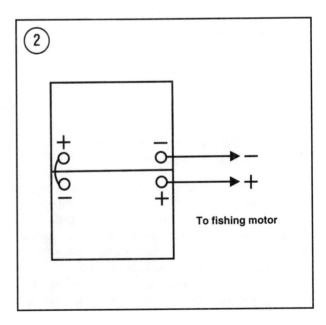

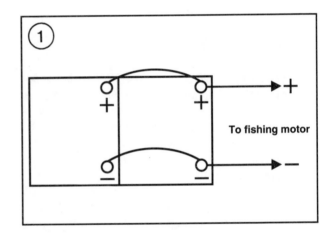

the batteries may be connected in series (**Figure 2**). If charging becomes necessary, batteries connected in a parallel or series circuit must be disconnected and charged individually.

Safety concerns

The battery must be securely fastened in the boat to prevent the battery from shifting or moving in the bilge area. The positive battery terminal (or the entire top of the battery) must also be covered with a nonconductive shield or boot.

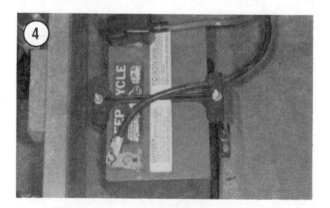

If the battery is not properly secured, it may contact the hull (or metal fuel tank) in rough water or while being transported. If the battery shorts against the metal hull or fuel tank, the resulting short circuit will cause sparks and an electrical fire. An explosion could follow if the fuel tank or battery case are compromised.

If the battery is not properly grounded and it contacts the metal hull, the battery will try to ground through the control cables or the boat's wiring harness. Again, the short circuit will cause sparks and an electrical fire and the control cables and boat wiring harness will be damaged.

The following preventive steps must be observed when installing a battery in any boat, especially a metal boat or a boat with a metal fuel tank.

1. Choose a location as far as practical from the fuel tank while still providing access for maintenance.

2. Secure the battery to the hull with a plastic battery box and tie-down strap (**Figure 3**) or a battery tray with a nonconductive shield or boot covering the positive battery terminal (**Figure 4**).

Make sure that all battery cable connections are clean and tight. Do *not* use wing nuts to secure battery cables. If wing nuts are present, discard them and replace them with corrosion resistant hex nuts and lockwashers to ensure positive electrical connections

4. Periodically inspect the installation to make sure the battery is physically secured to the hull and that the battery cable connections are clean and tight.

Care and Inspection

1. Remove the battery tray top or battery box cover. See **Figure 3** or **Figure 4**.

2. Disconnect the negative battery cable, then the positive battery cable.

> *NOTE*
> *Some batteries have a built-in carry strap (**Figure 5**) for use in Step 3.*

3. Attach a battery carry strap to the terminal posts. Remove the battery from the boat.

4. Inspect the entire battery case for cracks, holes or other damage.

5. Inspect the battery tray or battery box for corrosion or deterioration. Clean as necessary with a solution of baking soda and water.

> *CAUTION*
> *Do not allow the baking soda cleaning solution to enter the battery cells in Step 6 or the electrolyte will be severely weakened.*

7

6. Clean the top of the battery with a stiff bristle brush using the baking soda and water solution (**Figure 6**). Rinse the battery case with clear water and wipe dry with a clean cloth or paper towel.

7. Clean the battery terminal posts with a stiff wire brush or battery terminal cleaning tool (**Figure 7**).

NOTE
Do not overfill the battery cells in Step 8. The electrolyte expands due to heat from the charging system and will overflow if the level is more than 3/16 in. (4.8 mm) above the battery plates.

8. Remove the filler caps and check the electrolyte level. Add distilled water, if necessary, to bring the level to 3/16 in. (4.8 mm) above the plates in the battery case. See **Figure 8**.

9. Clean the battery cable clamps with a stiff wire brush (**Figure 9**).

10. Place the battery back into the boat and into the battery tray or battery box. If using a battery tray, install and secure the retaining bracket.

11. Reconnect the positive battery cable first, then the negative cable.

CAUTION
Be sure the battery cables are connected to their proper terminals. Reversing the battery polarity will result in charging and ignition system damage.

12. Securely tighten the battery connections. Coat the connections with petroleum jelly or a light grease to minimize corrosion. If you are using a battery box, install the cover and secure the assembly with a tie-down strap.

Battery Testing

Hydrometer testing

On batteries with removable vent caps, checking the specific gravity of the electrolyte using a hydrometer is the best method to check the battery state of charge. Use a hydrometer with numbered graduations from 1.100-1.300 points rather than one with color-coded bands. To use the hydrometer, squeeze the rubber bulb, insert the tip into a cell, then release the bulb to fill the hydrometer. See **Figure 10**.

NOTE
Do not test specific gravity immediately after adding water to the battery cells, as the water will dilute the electrolyte and lower the specific gravity. To obtain accurate hy-

drometer readings, the battery must be charged after adding water.

Draw sufficient electrolyte to raise the float inside the hydrometer. If using a temperature-compensated hydrometer, discharge the electrolyte back into the battery cell and repeat the process several times to adjust the temperature of the hydrometer to that of the electrolyte.

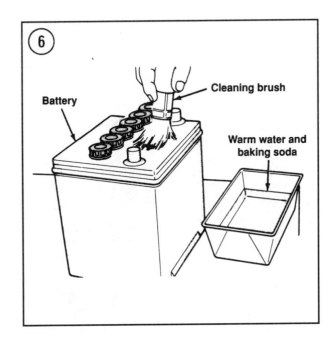

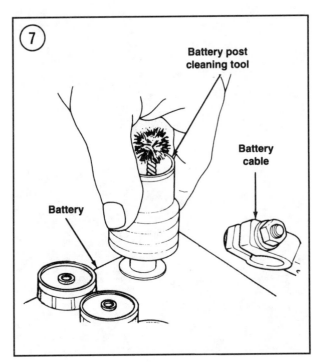

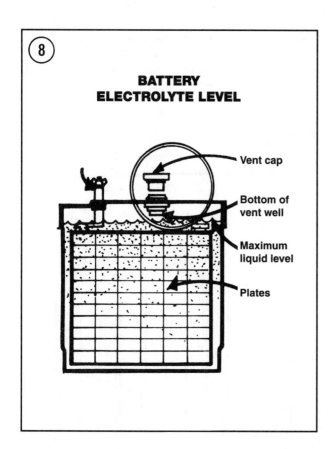

BATTERY ELECTROLYTE LEVEL

Vent cap

Bottom of vent well

Maximum liquid level

Plates

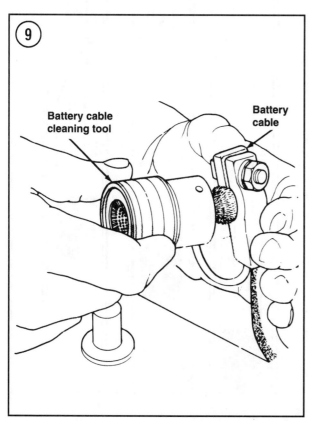

Battery cable cleaning tool

Battery cable

Hold the hydrometer upright and note the number on the float that is even with the surface of the electrolyte (**Figure 11**). This number is the specific gravity for the cell. Discharge the electrolyte into the cell from which it came.

The specific gravity of a cell is the indicator of the cell's state of charge. A fully charged cell will read 1.260 or more at 80° F (26.7° C). A cell that is 75% charged will read from 1.220-1.230 while a cell with a 50 percent charge will read from 1.170-1.180. Any cell reading 1.120 or less must be considered discharged. All cells must be within 30 points specific gravity of each other. If over 30 points variation is noted, the battery condition is questionable. Charge the battery and recheck the specific gravity. If 30 points or

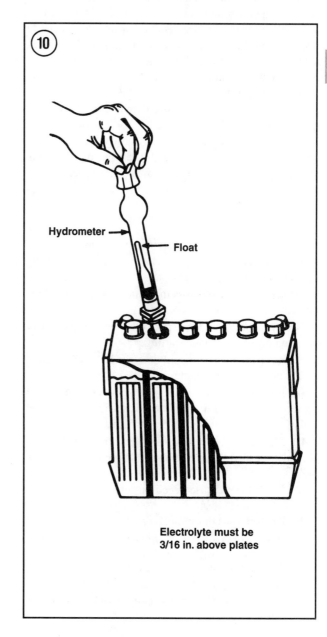

Hydrometer

Float

Electrolyte must be 3/16 in. above plates

7

more variation remains between cells after charging, the battery has failed and must be replaced.

NOTE
If a temperature-compensated hydrometer is not used, add 4 points specific gravity to the actual reading for every 10° above 80° F (26.7° C). Subtract 4 points specific gravity for every 10° below 80° F (26.7° C).

Open-circuit voltage test

On sealed or maintenance free batteries (vent caps not removable), the state of charge must be checked by measuring the open-circuit (no load) voltage of the battery. Use a digital voltmeter for best results. For the most accurate results, allow the battery to set at rest for at least 30 minutes to allow the battery to stabilize. Then, observing the correct polarity, connect the voltmeter to the battery and note the meter reading. If the open-circuit voltage is 12.7 volts or higher, the battery can be considered fully charged. A reading of 12.4 volts means the battery is approximately 75% charged, a reading of 12.2 means the battery is approximately 50% charged and a reading of 12.1 volts means that the battery is approximately 25% charged.

Load testing

To check the ability of the battery to maintain the starting system's minimum required voltage while cranking the engine, proceed as follows:
1. Attach a voltmeter across the battery as shown in **Figure 12**.
2. Remove and ground the spark plug leads to the power head to prevent accidental starting.
3. Crank the engine for approximately 15 seconds while noting the voltmeter reading.
4A. If the voltage is 9.5 volts or higher at the end of the 15 second time period, the battery is sufficiently charged and of sufficient capacity for the outboard motor.
4B. If the voltage is below 9.5 volts at the end of the 15 second time period, one of the following conditions is present:
   a. The battery is discharged or defective. Charge the battery and retest.
   b. The battery is of too small capacity for the outboard motor. Refer to *Battery Recommendations* in this chapter.
   c. The starting system is drawing excessive current causing the battery voltage to drop. Refer to Chapter Three for starting system troubleshooting procedures.

   d. A mechanical defect is present in the power head or gearcase creating excessive load (and current draw) on the starting system. Inspect the power head and gearcase for mechanical defects.

Battery Storage

Wet cell batteries slowly discharge when stored. They discharge faster when warm than when cold. Before stor-

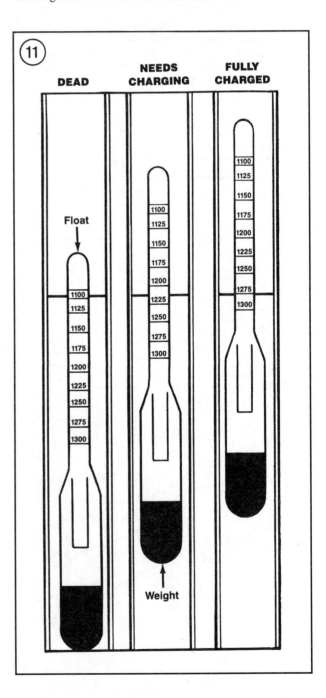

ing a battery, clean the case with a solution of baking soda and water. Rinse with clear water and wipe dry. The battery must be fully charged and then stored in a cool, dry location. Check electrolyte level and state of charge frequently during storage. If specific gravity falls to 40 points or more below full charge (1.260) or the open circuit voltage falls below 12.4 volts, recharge the battery.

Battery Charging

A good state of charge must be maintained in batteries used for starting. Check the state of charge with a hydrometer or digital voltmeter as described in the previous section.

The battery must be removed from the boat for charging, since a charging battery releases highly explosive hydrogen gas. In many boats, the area around the battery is not well ventilated, and the gas may remain in the area for hours after the charging process has been completed. Sparks or flames occurring near the battery can cause it to explode, spraying battery acid over a wide area.

If the battery cannot be removed for charging, make sure that the bilge access hatches, doors or vents are fully open to allow adequate ventilation. For this reason, it is important to observe the following precautions when charging batteries:

1. Never smoke in close proximity to any battery.

2. Make sure all accessories are off before disconnecting the battery cables. Disconnecting a circuit that is electrically active will create a spark that can ignite explosive gases that may be present.

3. Always disconnect the negative battery cable first, then the positive cable.

4. On batteries with removable vent caps, always check the electrolyte level before charging the battery. Maintain the correct electrolyte level throughout the charging process.

5. Never attempt to charge a battery that is frozen.

WARNING
Be extremely careful not to create any sparks around the battery when connecting the battery charger.

Connect the charger to the battery, negative charger lead to the negative battery terminal and positive charger lead to the positive battery terminal. If the charger output is variable, select a setting of approximately 4 amps. It is preferable to charge a battery slowly at low amp settings, rather than quickly at high amp settings.

If the charger has a dual voltage setting, set the voltage switch to 12 volts, then switch the charger on.

If the battery is severely discharged, allow it to charge for at least 8 hours. Check the charging process with a hydrometer. Consider the battery fully charged when the specific gravity of all cells does not increase when checked three times at one hour intervals, and all cells are gassing freely.

7

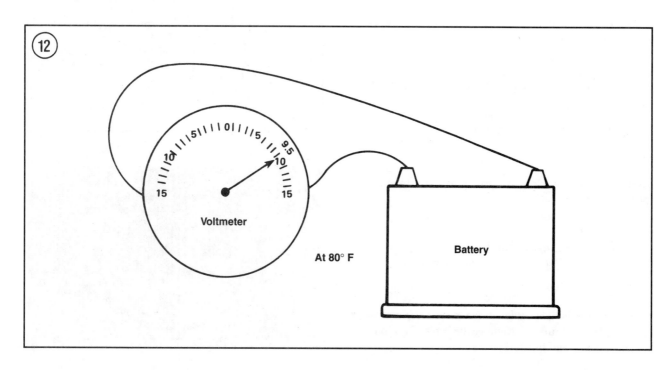

(12)   Voltmeter   At 80° F   Battery

Jump Starting

If the battery becomes severely discharged, it is possible to *jump start* the engine from another battery (in or out of a vehicle). However, jump starting can be dangerous if the proper procedure is not followed. Always use caution when jump starting.

Check the electrolyte level of the discharged battery before attempting the jump start. If the electrolyte is not visible or if it appears to be frozen, do not jump start the discharged battery.

> *WARNING*
> *Use extreme caution when connecting the booster battery to the discharged battery to avoid personal injury or damage to the system. **Be certain** the jumper cables are connected in the correct polarity.*

1. Connect the jumper cables in the order and sequence shown in **Figure 13**.

> *WARNING*
> *An electrical arc may occur when the final connection is made. This could cause an explosion if it occurs near the battery. For this reason, the final connection must be made to a good engine ground, away from the battery and not to the battery itself.*

2. Make sure all jumper cables are out of the way of moving engine parts.

> *CAUTION*
> *Do not run the engine without an adequate water supply and do not exceed 3000 rpm without an adequate load. Refer to **Safety Precautions** at the beginning of Chapter Three.*

3. Start the engine. Once it starts, run it at a moderate speed (fast idle).

> *CAUTION*
> *Running the engine at high speed with a fully discharged battery may damage the charging system.*

4. Remove the jumper cables in the exact reverse of the order shown in **Figure 13**. Remove the cables from point 4, then 3, then 2 and finally 1.

BATTERY CHARGING SYSTEM

Description

An alternator charging system is used on all electric start models. The job of the charging system is to keep the battery fully charged and supply current to run accessories. Charging systems can be divided into two basic designs: unregulated (4 or 5 amp) and regulated (12 amp).

The 9.9 and 15 hp models (if equipped with a battery charging system) use a 5 amp unregulated charging system. The 6, 8, 20-30 hp (two-cylinder), 40 hp (rope start), 48 Special, 18 jet and 28 jet models (if equipped with a battery charging system) use a 4 amp unregulated charging system.

The 25 and 35 hp (three-cylinder), 40 hp (electric start), 50-70 hp and 35 jet models are equipped with a 12 amp regulated charging system.

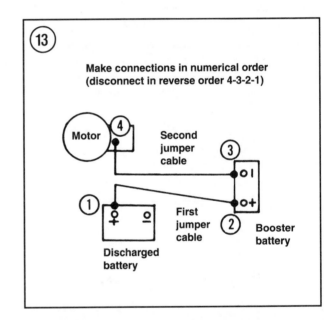

Make connections in numerical order (disconnect in reverse order 4-3-2-1)

All systems use permanent magnets mounted in the flywheel (**Figure 14**, typical) and a stator coil winding mounted to the power head (**Figure 15**, typical). As the flywheel rotates, the magnetic fields in the flywheel pass through the stator coil windings and induce AC (alternating current) into the stator coil. Unregulated systems use a rectifier (a series of six diodes) to change the AC current to DC (direct current). See **Figure 16**, typical. The output from an unregulated charging system is directly proportional to engine speed. Because an unregulated system has the potential to overcharge the battery during long periods of wide-open throttle operation, a maintenance-free battery is not recommended. Overcharging a battery causes the electrolyte level to drop, leading to premature battery failure. Vented batteries that allow removal of the vent caps and refilling of the electrolyte as needed will provide longer service life.

Regulated systems use the same type flywheel magnets and stator coil windings as the unregulated system, with the rectifier being replaced with a voltage regulator (rectifier/regulator). See **Figure 17**, typical. The rectifier portion of the voltage regulator changes the AC current to DC current, while the regulator portion monitors system voltage and controls the charging system output accordingly. Batteries that are maintained at 13-15 volts will stay fully charged without excessive venting. The regulator controls the output of the charging system to keep system voltage at approximately 14.5 volts. The red lead of the rectifier/regulator is DC output and also functions as the sense lead, allowing the regulator portion to monitor system voltage. A small purple lead turns the rectifier/regulator on whenever the ignition (key) switch is in the ON or RUN position.

Another function of the charging system is to provide the signal for the tachometer. All tachometers simply count the AC voltage pulses coming from the stator before the AC voltage is rectified to DC. Tachometer failure is always related to the charging system, not the ignition system. The tachometer connects to the stator's yellow/gray lead on unregulated systems or the voltage regulator's gray lead on regulated models.

Malfunctions in the charging system generally cause the battery to be undercharged and on integral systems, the tachometer to read erratically or totally fail. The following conditions will result in rectifier or voltage regulator (rectifier/regulator) failure.

a. Reversing the battery leads.
b. Disconnecting the battery leads while the engine is running.
c. Loose connections in the charging system circuits, including battery connections and ground circuits.

CAUTION
If an outboard motor equipped with an unregulated charging system must be operated

⑮ STATOR COIL (4 AMP)

Bullet or ring terminals

Stator coil

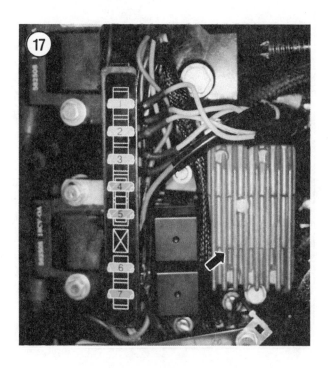

7

with the battery disconnected or removed, prevent the positive battery cable from contacting the negative battery cable and/or ground. Insulate the positive battery cable using tape. Never operate a regulated charging system with the battery disconnected.

Perform the following visual inspection to determine if the cause of the problem is of a simple origin. If the visual inspection does not locate the problem, refer to Chapter Three for complete charging system troubleshooting procedures.

1. Make sure that the battery cables are connected properly. The red cable (positive) must be connected to the positive battery terminal. If the polarity has been reversed, check for a damaged rectifier (or voltage regulator). See Chapter Three.

2. Inspect the battery terminals for loose or corroded connections. Tighten or clean as necessary. Replace any wing nuts with corrosion resistant hex nuts and lockwashers. See **Figure 18**.

3. Inspect the physical condition of the battery. Look for bulges or cracks in the case, leaking electrolyte and corrosion buildup. Clean, refill or replace the battery as necessary.

4. Carefully check the wiring between the stator coil and battery for damage or deterioration. Refer to the back of the manual for wiring diagrams. Repair or replace wires and connectors as necessary.

5. Check all accessory circuits and associated wiring for corroded, loose or disconnected connections. Clean, tighten or reconnect as necessary.

6. Determine if the accessory load on the battery is greater than the charging system's capacity by performing the *Current draw* test. See Chapter Three.

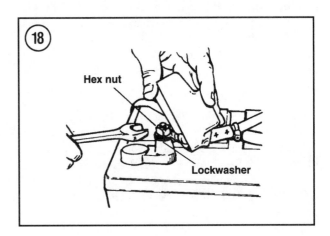

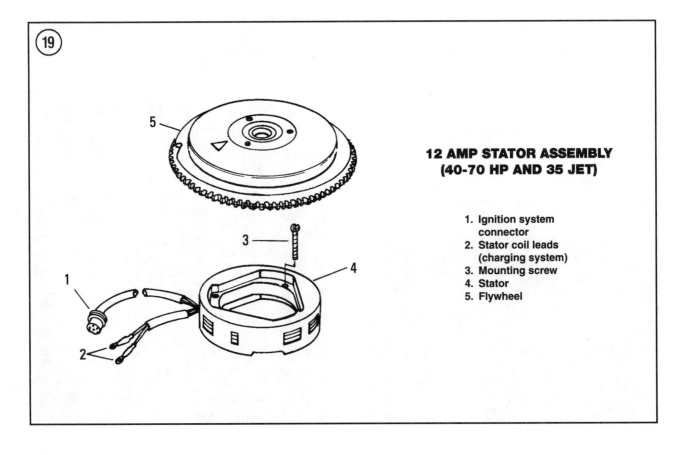

**12 AMP STATOR ASSEMBLY
(40-70 HP AND 35 JET)**

1. Ignition system connector
2. Stator coil leads (charging system)
3. Mounting screw
4. Stator
5. Flywheel

Stator Coil (or Stator Assembly) Replacement

On 4 amp charging systems, the stator coil is a separate component (**Figure 15**) mounted to the ignition (armature) plate and is easily identified by its yellow, yellow/gray and yellow/blue leads.

On 5 and 12 amp charging systems, the stator coil windings are integrated into a single stator assembly (**Figure 19**), which is mounted to the ignition (armature) plate on 5 amp models and directly to the power head on 12 amp models. The stator assembly includes the ignition system's charge coil windings and the battery charging system's stator coil windings. Other windings may be included in the stator assembly.

Removal and installation procedures for all stator windings (charging, ignition and integrated models) are covered under *Ignition Systems*, located later in this chapter.

Rectifier Removal/Installation (4 and 5 Amp Models)

If equipped with a charging system, the 9.9 and 15 hp models use a 5 amp unregulated charging system; while the 6, 8, 20-30 hp (two-cylinder), 40 hp (rope start), 48 Special, 18 jet and 28 jet models use a 4 amp unregulated charging system.

1. Disconnect and ground the spark plug leads to the power head to prevent accidental starting. Then disconnect the negative battery cable.

2A. *9.9 and 15 hp (5 amp) models*—Disconnect the rectifier's yellow, yellow/gray and yellow/blue leads at their bullet connectors. Then disconnect the rectifier red lead from the positive battery cable terminal stud.

2B. *All other (4 amp) models*—Remove the terminal strip protective cover. Then disconnect the rectifier's (A, **Figure 20**) red, yellow, yellow/gray and yellow/blue leads from the terminal strip.

3. If necessary, remove the two screws (B, **Figure 20**) securing the terminal strip to the power head and position the terminal strip out of the way.

4. Remove the large and small rectifier mounting screws. On 9.9-15 hp models, the negative battery cable (and stop switch ground lead) are under the large mounting screw. Remove the rectifier. See A, **Figure 20**, typical.

5. To install the rectifier, position it on the power head and secure it in place with large and small screws. On 9.9 and 15 hp (5 amp) models, make sure the negative battery cable (and stop switch ground lead) are secured under the large screw. Then tighten both screws to 48-96 in.-lb. (5.4-10.9 N•m).

6A. *9.9 and 15 hp (5 amp) models*—Connect the rectifier red lead to the positive battery cable terminal stud. Tighten the nut securely. Then connect the rectifier's yellow, yellow/gray and yellow/blue leads to their matching engine harness bullet connectors.

6B. *All other (4 amp) models*—If necessary, reposition the terminal strip and secure it in place with two screws. Then connect the rectifier's red, yellow, yellow/gray and yellow/blue leads to their matching leads on the terminal strip. Tighten each connection and the terminal strip mounting screws securely. Then reinstall the terminal strip's protective cap.

7A. *9.9 and 15 hp (5 amp) models*—Coat the larger rectifier mounting screw and the terminals of the leads connected to it with OMC Black Neoprene Dip. Then coat the rectifier red lead (and its terminal stud) with neoprene dip.

7B. *4 amp models*—Coat all connections with OMC Black Neoprene Dip.

8. Reconnect the spark plug leads and the negative battery cable when finished.

Voltage Regulator/Rectifier Removal/Installation (12 Amp Models)

On 40-50 hp (two-cylinder) and 35 jet models, it may be necessary to remove the starboard split lower cowl to gain access to the voltage regulator's lower mounting screw.

1. Disconnect and ground the spark plug leads to the power head to prevent accidental starting. Then disconnect the negative battery cable.

2. *25 and 35 hp (three-cylinder) models*—Remove the air intake cover. Make sure you disconnect the cover's drain hose during removal.

3A. *25 and 35 hp (three-cylinder) models*—Lift the lock tab on the regulator's large two-pin connector (yellow and yellow/gray leads) and separate the connector (A, **Figure 21**). Then disconnect the regulator's red, purple and gray leads at their bullet connectors.

3B. *40-70 hp and 35 jet models*—Remove the protective cap from the terminal strip (A, **Figure 22**). Then disconnect the regulator's red, gray, purple, yellow and yellow/gray leads from the terminal strip. Temporarily reinstall each screw after the regulator's lead is removed, to make sure each engine harness lead is held in its correct position.

4A. *25 and 35 hp (three-cylinder) models*—An extended starboard screw, nut and bumper cap (B, **Figure 21**) may be used on some models to provide support for the air intake cover. If so equipped, measure and record the installed height of the screw for reference during reinstallation. Then remove the two mounting screws and the regulator from the crankcase cover.

4B. *40-70 hp and 35 jet models*—Remove the two mounting screws (B, **Figure 22**), then remove the regulator (C, **Figure 22**) from the power head.

5A. *25 and 35 hp (three-cylinder) models*—To install the regulator, begin by positioning it on the crankcase cover and securing it in place with two screws. If equipped with an extended (starboard) screw (B, **Figure 21**), install the screw assembly in the starboard hole and readjust its installed height to that noted on disassembly. Then tighten both screws (or the port screw and starboard nut) to 60-84 in.-lb. (6.8-9.5 N•m).

5B. *40-70 hp and 35 jet models*—To install the regulator, begin by positioning the regulator (C, **Figure 22**) to the power head and secure it in place with two screws (B, **Figure 22**). Tighten both screws to 60-84 in.-lb. (6.8-9.5 N•m).

6A. *25 and 35 hp (three-cylinder) models*—Reconnect the regulator's large two-pin connector (yellow and yellow/gray leads) to its engine harness mate (A, **Figure 21**). Make sure the connector locks together. Then reconnect the regulator's red, purple and gray leads to their matching engine harness bullet connectors.

6B. *40-70 hp and 35 jet models*—Reconnect the regulator's red, gray, purple, yellow and yellow/gray leads to their mating engine harness leads at the terminal strip. Securely tighten each connection. Then reinstall the protective cap to the terminal strip (A, **Figure 22**).

7. *40-70 hp and 35 jet models*—Coat all connections with OMC Black Neoprene Dip.

8. Reconnect the spark plug leads and the negative battery cable when finished.

FUSES

Fuses are designed to protect wire and electrical components from damage due to excessive current (amperage)

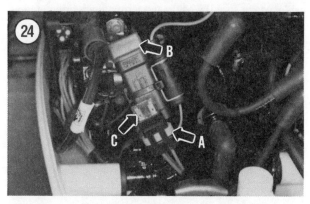

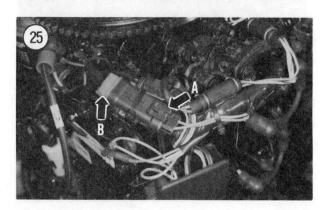

flow. A fuse that repeatedly blows indicates a problem with the circuit or component that the fuse is protecting.

Do not install a larger fuse in an attempt to remedy the problem. Refer to Chapter Three and locate the defect that is causing excessive current flow in the suspect circuit.

Do not trust a visual inspection alone when trying to determine if a fuse is good. Fuses can be quickly and accurately tested with an ohmmeter. A good fuse must indicate a full continuity reading (0 ohms). When testing fuses, be careful not to touch both ohmmeter probes at the same time with your hands. Ohmmeters set to higher scales will typically show a false continuity reading through your body.

Fuse Locations

Fuses are not used on rope start models or on 15 hp and smaller engines. On all other models, fuse location is as follows:

1. *20-30 hp (two-cylinder)*—A 20 amp blade-type fuse is located at the port rear corner of the engine, near the top of cylinder head. A spare fuse is contained in the plug located at the end of the fuse holder.

2. *25 and 35 hp (three-cylinder) models*—A 20 amp blade-type fuse is located on the starboard side of the engine, under the electrical/ignition component access cover at the point shown as A, **Figure 23**. A spare fuse is mounted in a pull-out plug (B, **Figure 23**) at the top of the access cover.

3. *40-50 hp (two-cylinder) and 35 jet*—A 20 amp blade-type fuse is located at the port rear corner of the engine, near the starter solenoid. A spare fuse is contained in the plug (B, **Figure 24**) located at the end of the fuse holder.

4. *50-70 hp (three-cylinder) models*—A 20 amp blade-type fuse is located at the port rear corner of the engine, on top of the cylinder head (A, **Figure 25**). A spare fuse is contained in the plug (B, **Figure 25**) located at the end of the fuse holder.

Fuse Replacement

1. *25 and 35 hp (three-cylinder) models*—Remove the electrical/ignition component access cover located on the starboard side of the engine. The cover is secured by two screws.

2. Carefully lift the lock clip and slide the fuse holder (A, **Figure 24**) out of the protective cover.

3. Pull the defective fuse (C, **Figure 24**) out of the fuse holder. Discard the fuse.

4. Push a new fuse into the fuse holder.

5. Push the fuse holder into the protective cover until the lock clip snaps into place.

6. *25 and 35 hp (three-cylinder) models*—Reinstall the electrical/ignition component access cover. Tighten the two screws securely.

ELECTRIC STARTING SYSTEM

Evinrude/Johnson outboard motors may be equipped with electric start only, manual (automatic rewinding rope) start only, or both electric and manual starters. Manual starters are covered in detail in Chapter Twelve.

A typical electric starter system consists of the battery, starter solenoid, neutral safety switch (or neutral safety linkage), starter motor, starter (or ignition) switch and the associated wiring.

Tiller handle models are equipped with a neutral safety switch (mounted on the shift linkage) or a mechanical linkage that prevents the starter button from being pushed unless the shift linkage is in NEUTRAL.

On remote control models, the neutral safety switch is mounted in the remote control box. Troubleshooting the electric starter system is covered in Chapter Three.

Starter Motor Description

Marine starter motors are very similar in design and operation to those found on automotive engines. The starter motors used on outboards covered in this manual have an inertia-type drive in which external spiral splines on the armature shaft mate with internal splines on the drive (or bendix) assembly.

The starter motor is an intermittent duty electric motor, capable of producing a very high torque, but only for a brief time. The high amperage flow through the starter motor causes the starter motor to overheat very quickly. To prevent overheating, never operate the starter motor continuously for more than 10-15 seconds. Allow the starter motor to cool for 2-3 minutes before cranking the engine again.

If the starter motor does not crank the engine, check the battery cables and terminals for loose or corroded connections. Correct any problems found. If this does not solve the starting problem, refer to Chapter Three for starting system troubleshooting procedures.

CAUTION
Evinrude/Johnson electric starter motors use permanent magnets glued inside main housing. Never strike a starter as this will damage the magnets, leading to total starter failure. Inspect the magnets anytime the starter is disassembled. Replace the housing

if the magnets are cracked, damaged or loose.

Starter Motor Removal/Installation (9.9 and 15 hp)

1. Disconnect and ground the spark plug leads to the power head.

2. Remove the rectifier as described previously in this chapter.

3. Remove the two screws holding the starter motor to the power head.

4. Lift the starter upward enough to gain access to the terminal stud on the bottom of the starter. Note the orientation of the cable and terminal, then disconnect the electrical cable from the starter motor.

CAUTION
When attaching the electrical cable to the starter motor, be certain the cable terminal does not turn and contact the starter motor or lower engine cover.

5. To install the starter, begin by positioning the starter close enough to the power head to install the electrical cable. Make sure the cable and terminal are orientated as noted on removal, then tighten the terminal nut securely.

6. Coat the connection with OMC Black Neoprene Dip.

7. Align the starter motor to the power head mounting bosses and secure it with two screws. Evenly tighten the screws to 10-12 ft.-lb. (13.6-16.3 N•m).

8. Reinstall the rectifier as described previously in this chapter.

9. Reconnect the spark plug leads and the negative battery cable when finished.

**Starter Motor Removal/Installation
(20-30 hp [Two-cylinder])**

1. Disconnect and ground the spark plug leads to the power head. Then disconnect the negative battery cable.

2. Note the location and orientation of the leads and cables connected to the starter solenoid, then disconnect all leads and cables from the solenoid except the cable to the starter motor.

3. Disconnect the negative battery cable from the starter motor bracket stud. Then remove the stud and lockwasher.

4. Remove the screws (A, **Figure 26**) securing the vertical throttle (and spark control) shaft clamp halves (B) to the power head. Remove the inner and outer clamp halves, then locate and secure the shaft's split nylon bushing.

5. Remove the locknut and flat washer from the stud at the front of the engine, located between the starter motor and the throttle cam follower assembly.

6. Remove the screw, lockwasher and ground strap at the bottom of the starter bracket, located between the starter motor and the starter solenoid. Use 1/4 in. drive tools and a flexible extension (or socket) to access the screw. The screw's head faces straight aft.

7. Remove the final screw (and lockwasher) securing the starter bracket to the power head. The screw is located just above the starter solenoid, close to the screws (A, **Figure 26**) removed previously.

8. Slide the starter bracket assembly forward and free from the stud on the front of the engine. Then lift the assembly from the power head.

9. To install the starter and bracket assembly, begin by making sure the solenoid and starter motor-to-solenoid cable are installed and their mounting hardware is securely tightened.

10. Slide the starter and bracket assembly over the stud on the front of the engine until it is seated to the engine.

11. Install the screw (and lockwasher) above the starter solenoid finger-tight, then install the lowest screw (and the lockwasher and ground strap) finger-tight. This is the screw that faces fore and aft.

12. Install the negative battery cable stud and lockwasher finger-tight, then install the locknut and flat washer over the stud at the front of the engine. Evenly tighten all four fasteners to 60-84 in.-lb. (6.8-9.5 N•m).

13. Make sure the split nylon bushing is installed on the vertical throttle (and spark control) shaft, then position the inner and outer clamp halves (B, **Figure 26**) around the bushing.

14. Secure the clamp halves with two screws (and washers). Tighten the screws (A, **Figure 26**) securely.

15. Reattach the leads and cables to the starter solenoid (as noted on disassembly). Tighten the nuts securely, then coat the connections with OMC Black Neoprene Dip. Make sure that none of the terminals are contacting (or close to contacting) the power head or starter bracket.

16. Reconnect the negative battery cable to the starter bracket stud, using a lockwasher and nut. Tighten the nut securely. Coat the connection with OMC Black Neoprene Dip.

17. Reconnect the spark plug leads and the negative battery cable when finished.

18. Verify all synch and link adjustments as described in Chapter Five.

**Starter Motor Removal/Installation
(25 and 35 hp [Three-cylinder])**

1. Disconnect and ground the spark plug leads to the power head. Then disconnect the negative battery cable.

2. Disconnect the negative battery cable and the two ground leads from the stud (A, **Figure 27**) on the starboard side of the engine. Then remove the stud and lockwasher from the power head.

3. Note the location and orientation of the leads and cables connected to the starter solenoid, then disconnect all leads and cables from the solenoid (except the metal strap connected directly to the starter motor's terminal stud).

7

4. Remove the screw (B, **Figure 27**) from the upper rear corner of the electrical component access cover, then pull the cover and bracket assembly away from the starter motor.

5. Remove the screw from the top rear corner of the oil reservoir and pull the reservoir far enough to the rear to gain access to the rear starter motor mounting screw.

6. Remove the two screws securing the starter motor assembly to the power head. Remove the starter motor assembly from the power head.

7. To install the starter motor assembly to the power head, first make sure the metal strap is connected between the solenoid's rear large stud and the starter motor's terminal stud. Make sure both nuts are securely tightened.

8. Coat the threads of the two starter motor mounting screws with OMC Nut Lock threadlocking adhesive. Then position the starter assembly to the power head and install the two screws. Evenly tighten both screws to 15-17 ft.-lb. (20.3-23 N•m).

9. Reposition the oil reservoir and install the top mounting screw. Tighten the screw to 72-108 in.-lb. (8.1-12.2 N•m).

10. Reposition the electrical component access cover and bracket and secure it in place with the screw (B, **Figure 27**) at the top rear corner and stud (and lockwasher) at the lower front corner (A, **Figure 27**). Tighten the screw and stud to 60-84 in.-lb. (6.8-9.5 N•m).

11. Reconnect all leads and cables to the starter solenoid as noted on disassembly. Tighten all connections securely, then coat all connections (except the positive battery cable connection) with OMC Black Neoprene Dip.

12. Reconnect the negative battery cable and the two engine harness ground leads to the stud at the lower front corner of the electrical component bracket. Secure the cable and leads with a nut and lockwasher. Tighten the nut securely. Then coat the connection with OMC Black Neoprene Dip.

13. Reconnect the spark plug leads and the negative battery cable when finished.

**Starter Motor Removal/Installation
(40-70 hp and 35 Jet)**

1. Disconnect and ground the spark plug leads to the power head. Then disconnect the negative battery cable.

2. *50-70 hp (three-cylinder) models*—Remove the air intake cover and cover base to allow easier access to the front starter motor mounting screw. See *Carburetor Removal/Installation (50-70 hp [Three-cylinder] Models)* in Chapter Six.

3. Disconnect the starter solenoid-to-starter motor cable from the starter motor's terminal stud. See A, **Figure 28**, typical.

NOTE
*The negative battery cable is not usually installed to the top starter motor mounting bolt as shown in **Figure 28**. The cable is normally attached to a dedicated ground stud on the power head. However, attaching the cable to a starter mounting screw is acceptable, if so desired.*

4. Remove the screw and lockwasher (B, **Figure 28**, typical) securing the starter motor to the front of the power head. Then remove the two screws and lockwashers (C, **Figure 28**, typical) securing the starter to the side of the power head.

5. Remove the starter motor from the power head.

6. To install the starter motor, begin by applying OMC Nut Lock threadlocking adhesive (or equivalent) to the threads of the three starter motor mounting screws.

7. Position the starter motor on the power head and install the mounting screws. Evenly tighten all of the screws snugly, then tighten the front screw to 14-16 ft.-lb. (19.0-21.7 N•m) and finally tighten the two side screws to 14-16 ft.-lb. (19.0-21.7 N•m).

8. Connect the starter cable to the starter motor's terminal stud. Install and tighten the nut securely, then apply OMC Black Neoprene Dip to the connection.

9. *50-70 hp (three-cylinder) models*—Install the air intake cover and base using new screws as directed under *Carburetor Removal/Installation (50-70 hp [Three-cylinder] Models)* in Chapter Six.

10. Reconnect the spark plug leads and the negative battery cable when finished.

Starter Motor Disassembly/Reassembly (9.9 and 15 hp Models)

Check the availability of parts for this starter before beginning disassembly. Replacement parts for all model years may not be available. If aftermarket replacement parts are used, they must meet or exceed the manufacturer's specifications. To disassemble and reassemble the starter, refer to **Figure 29** and proceed as follows:

1. Remove the starter motor as described previously in this chapter.

2. Scribe match marks across the starter housing and both the upper and lower end caps to ensure proper orientation on reassembly.

3. Remove the two through-bolts, then remove the drive end cap and armature assembly from the housing. Remove and discard the gasket (8, **Figure 29**).

4. Remove the end cap and brush plate from the housing. Remove and discard the gasket (10, **Figure 29**).

5. While carefully holding the bendix (pinion gear) with a pair of pliers, remove the locknut (1, **Figure 29**). Then slide the spacer (2), spring (3) and pinion gear (4) off of the armature shaft.

6. Slide the drive end cap off of the armature shaft, then locate and secure the thrust washer (6, **Figure 29**).

7. If necessary (and parts are available), remove the screw holding the negative brush and the nut holding the terminal stud (and the positive brush). See **Figure 30**. Remove both brushes from the plate. Discard the brushes.

8. Clean and inspect all components as described in *Starter motor cleaning and inspection (all models)*.

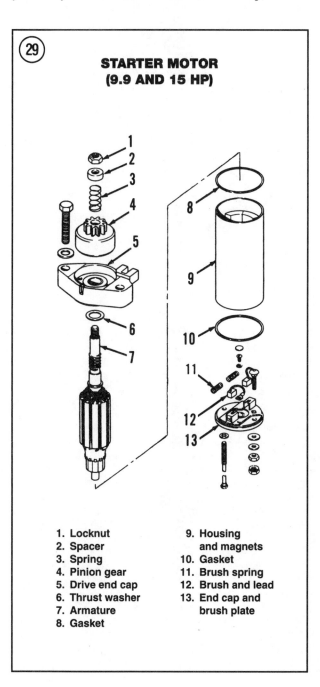

STARTER MOTOR (9.9 AND 15 HP)

1. Locknut
2. Spacer
3. Spring
4. Pinion gear
5. Drive end cap
6. Thrust washer
7. Armature
8. Gasket
9. Housing and magnets
10. Gasket
11. Brush spring
12. Brush and lead
13. End cap and brush plate

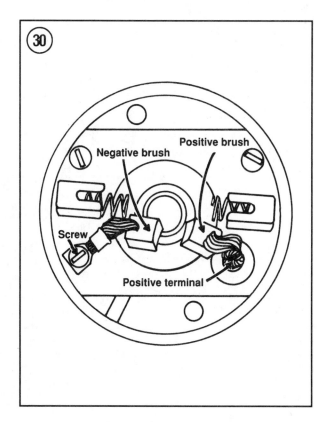

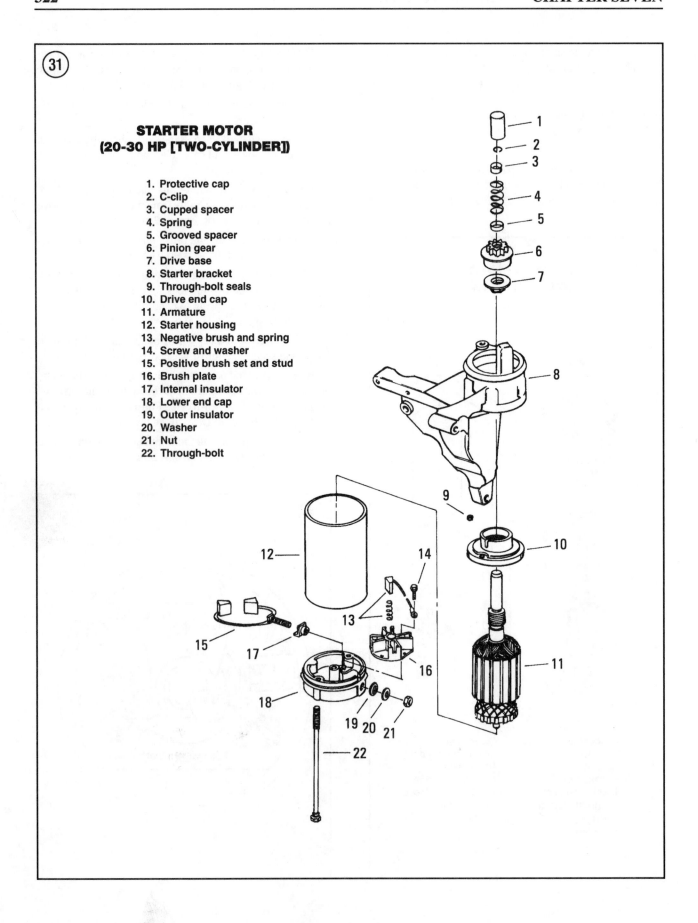

③1

**STARTER MOTOR
(20-30 HP [TWO-CYLINDER])**

1. Protective cap
2. C-clip
3. Cupped spacer
4. Spring
5. Grooved spacer
6. Pinion gear
7. Drive base
8. Starter bracket
9. Through-bolt seals
10. Drive end cap
11. Armature
12. Starter housing
13. Negative brush and spring
14. Screw and washer
15. Positive brush set and stud
16. Brush plate
17. Internal insulator
18. Lower end cap
19. Outer insulator
20. Washer
21. Nut
22. Through-bolt

9. To assemble the starter, begin by lubricating the bearing surfaces of the armature with one drop of SAE 10 engine oil. Then lightly lubricate the armature shaft's spiral splines and the bearing area above the splines with OMC Starter Pinion (Bendix) Lubricant.

10. If removed, install new brushes to the end cap (brush plate). See **Figure 30**. Place a spring behind each brush and compress the springs with the brushes. While holding the brushes compressed, insert the armature shaft into the brush plate's bushing, then release the brushes against the commutator.

11. Place a new gasket over the armature and against the end cap (brush plate).

12. Carefully slide the armature and end cap assembly into the starter housing, making sure the magnetic forces do not pull the armature from the end cap. Align the housing and end cap scribe marks.

13. Install the thrust washer (6, **Figure 29**) over the armature shaft. Then place a new gasket over the armature and against the starter housing.

14. Carefully slide the drive end cap over the armature shaft and seat it to the housing (and gasket). Align the housing and drive end cap scribe marks.

15. Lightly lubricate the through-bolt threads with clean engine oil. Install the through-bolts and evenly tighten them to 30-40 in.-lb. (3.4-4.5 N•m).

16. Apply OMC Black Neoprene Dip to both end cap-to-housing seams and to both through-bolt-to-end cap seams.

17. Install the pinion gear, spring, spacer and locknut onto the armature shaft. Carefully hold the pinion gear with a pair of pliers and tighten the locknut to 150-170 in.-lb. (17.0-19.2 N•m).

18. Test the starter's no-load current draw as described in Chapter Three.

19. Install the starter motor as described previously in this chapter.

Starter Motor Disassembly/Reassembly (20-30 hp [Two-cylinder] Models)

This starter uses a friction drive assembly. If any lubricant contacts the pinion gear-to-drive base mating surface, the starter drive will not operate. Keep these surfaces clean and dry.

Refer to **Figure 31** for this procedure. The starter solenoid does not have to be removed from the starter bracket, unless replacement is necessary.

1. Remove the protective cap (1, **Figure 31**) from the top of the armature shaft by pulling it upward while carefully prying between the pinion gear (6) and the protective cap.

2. Pull the cupped spacer (3, **Figure 31**) downward, exposing the C-clip (2). Then remove the C-clip with retaining ring pliers part No. 325937 (or equivalent). Discard the C-clip.

3. Remove the spring, grooved spacer, pinion gear and the drive base. See 4-7, **Figure 31**.

4. Scribe match marks across the starter bracket, starter housing and both the upper and lower end caps to ensure proper orientation on reassembly.

5. Remove the two through-bolts (22, **Figure 31**), then separate the motor from the starter bracket (8). Discard the through-bolt seals (9).

6. Remove the drive end cap and armature assembly from the housing, then slide the drive end cap from the armature. Remove the thrust washer from between the end cap and armature.

7. Separate the end cap and brush plate assembly from the housing.

8. If brush replacement is necessary, remove the screws (14, **Figure 31**) holding the negative brushes and the nut (21), washer (20), insulators (17 and 19) holding the terminal stud and the positive brushes (15) to the end cap.

9. Remove the brushes and springs from the brush plate. Then separate the brush plate from the end cap. Discard the brushes and springs.

10. Clean and inspect all components as described in *Starter motor cleaning and inspection (all models)*.

11. To assemble the starter, begin by lubricating the bearing surfaces of the armature with one drop of SAE 10 engine oil. Then lightly lubricate the armature shaft's spiral splines and the bearing area above the splines with OMC Starter Pinion (Bendix) Lubricant.

12. If removed, install a new terminal stud and positive brush set assembly into the end cap. The longest brush lead must be pressed into the slot as shown in **Figure 32**. Make sure the terminal stud passes through the inner insulator (17, **Figure 31**) first, then install the outer insulator (19), washer (20) and nut (21). Tighten the nut securely.

13. Position the brush plate into the end cap and install the negative brushes into it. Secure the brush plate and the negative brush leads with the screws and lockwashers. See **Figure 33**. Tighten both screws securely.

14. Install the armature into the starter housing. Allow the starter housing magnets to position the armature.

NOTE
A brush retaining tool can be fabricated from a putty knife. Cut or grind a 1/2 in. (12.7 mm) wide slot, approximately 1-1/2 in. (38 mm) deep, down the center of the putty knife. See **Figure 34**.

15. Fit all four springs and brushes into the brush plate and end cap assembly. Hold the brushes compressed with a suitable tool (**Figure 35**).

16. While holding the brushes compressed, carefully pilot the armature (and housing) into the end cap bushing, then remove the tool once the armature has firmly contacted the tool. Rotate the end cap to align the scribe marks.

17. Install the thrust washer over the armature. Then carefully slide the drive end cap over the armature shaft and seat it to the starter housing. Rotate the drive end cap to align the scribe marks, then install the through-bolts from the lower end cap and through the drive end cap.

18. Install a new seal (9, **Figure 31**) over each through-bolt and against the drive end cap.

19. Position the starter motor assembly to the starter bracket and align the scribe marks. Start the through-bolts

into the starter bracket threads, then evenly tighten the screws to 95-100 in.-lb. (10.7-11.3 N•m).

20. Apply OMC Black Neoprene Dip to both end cap-to-housing seams and to both through-bolt-to-end cap seams.

NOTE
Do not allow any lubricant to contact the bendix-to-drive base mating surfaces. Keep these surfaces clean and dry.

21. Install the drive base (7, **Figure 31**), pinion gear (6), grooved spacer (5), spring (4) and cupped spacer (3) over the armature shaft. Pull downward on the cupped spacer to expose the C-clip groove, then install a new C-clip (2) into

32

STARTER BRUSH REPLACEMENT (POSITIVE BRUSH SET)

1. Terminal stud
2. Long lead
3. Push lead into slot

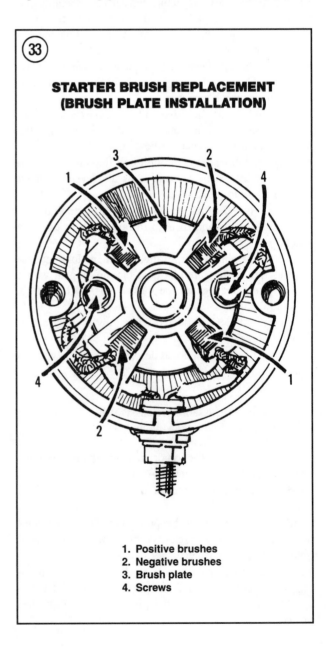

33

STARTER BRUSH REPLACEMENT (BRUSH PLATE INSTALLATION)

1. Positive brushes
2. Negative brushes
3. Brush plate
4. Screws

the groove. Release the cupped spacer and make sure it snaps up and over the C-clip, locking it in place.

22. Install the protective cap (1, **Figure 31**) over the armature shaft and make sure it snaps in place on the grooved spacer.

23. Test the starter's no-load current draw as described in Chapter Three.

24. Install the starter motor as described previously in this chapter.

Starter Motor Disassembly (25 and 35 hp [Three-cylinder], 40-70 hp and 35 Jet Models)

These starters use a friction drive assembly. If any lubricant contacts the pinion gear-to-drive base mating surface,

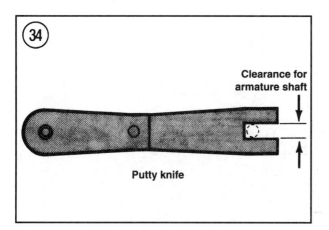

Clearance for armature shaft

Putty knife

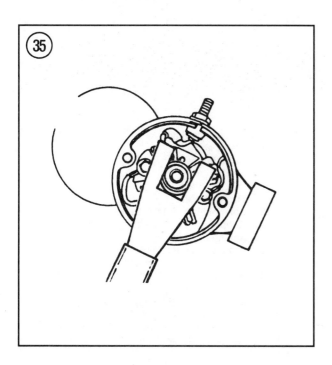

the starter drive will not operate. Keep these surfaces clean and dry.

The main differences between the 25 and 35 hp models and the 40-70 hp (and 35 jet) models are as follows:

   a. *25 and 35 hp models*—The starter solenoid mounts directly to the lower end cap and is connected to the starter motor with a metal strap. The through-bolts pass through the lower end cap and thread into the drive end cap. See **Figure 36**.

   b. *40-70 hp and 35 jet models*—The starter solenoid is remotely mounted and connects to the starter with a flexible cable. The through bolts pass through the drive end cap and thread into the lower end cap.

While outwardly different, service procedures for both starters are the same (once the solenoid is removed on 25 and 35 hp models). Refer to **Figure 36** for the following procedure.

1. Remove the protective cap (1, **Figure 36**) from the top of the armature shaft by pulling it upward while carefully prying between the pinion gear (6) and the protective cap.

2. Pull the cupped spacer (3, **Figure 36**) downward, exposing the C-clip (2). Then remove the C-clip with retaining ring pliers part No. 325937 (or equivalent). Discard the C-clip.

3. Remove the spring, grooved spacer, pinion gear and the drive base. See 4-7, **Figure 36**.

4. Scribe match marks across the starter housing and both the upper and lower end caps to ensure proper orientation on reassembly.

5. Remove the two through-bolts (20, **Figure 36**), then remove the drive end cap and armature assembly from the housing. Slide the drive end cap from the armature, then locate and remove the thrust washer from between the end cap and armature.

6. Separate the end cap and brush plate assembly from the housing.

7. *25 and 35 hp (three-cylinder) models*—Remove the nut and washer (26 and 25, **Figure 36**) securing the metal strap (24) to the terminal stud. Then remove the two screws and lockwashers (27 and 28, **Figure 36**) securing the solenoid bracket to the end cap. Remove the solenoid (and metal strap) from the lower end cap.

8. If brush replacement is necessary, remove the screws (11, **Figure 36**) holding the negative brushes and the nut (19), washer (18), insulators (15 and 17) holding the terminal stud and the positive brushes (14) to the end cap.

9. Remove the brushes and springs from the brush plate. Then separate the brush plate from the end cap. Discard the brushes and springs.

10. Clean and inspect all components as described in *Starter motor cleaning and inspection (all models)*.

11. To assemble the starter, begin by lubricating the bearing surfaces of the armature with one drop of SAE 10

7

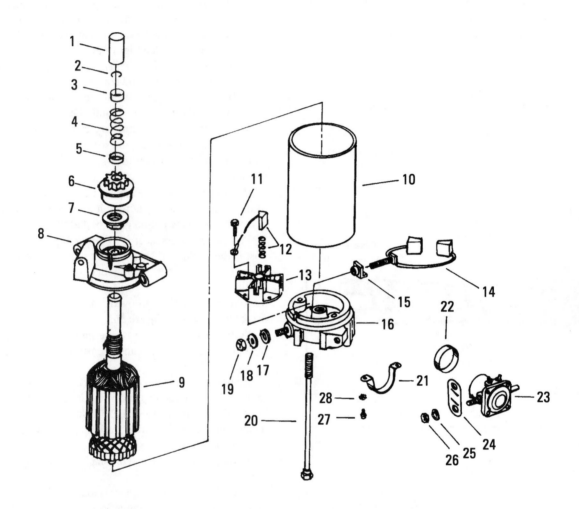

**STARTER MOTOR
(25 AND 35 HP [THREE-CYLINDER], 40-70 HP AND 35 JET MODELS)**

1. Protective cap
2. C-clip
3. Cupped spacer
4. Spring
5. Grooved spacer
6. Pinion gear
7. Drive base
8. Drive end cap
9. Armature
10. Starter housing
11. Screw and washer
12. Negative brush and spring
13. Brush plate
14. Positive brush set and stud

15. Internal insulator
16. Lower end cap
17. Outer insulator
18. Washer
19. Nut
20. Through-bolt
21. Solenoid bracket (25-35 hp)
22. Rubber grommet (25-35 hp)
23. Solenoid (25-35 hp)
24. Metal strap (25-35 hp)
25. Lockwasher (25-35 hp)
26. Nut (25-35 hp)
27. Screw (25-35 hp)
28. Lockwasher (25-35 hp)

engine oil. Then lightly lubricate the armature shaft's spiral splines and the bearing area above the splines with OMC Starter Pinion Lubricant.

12. If removed, install a new terminal stud and positive brush set assembly into the end cap. The longest brush lead must be pressed into the slot as shown in **Figure 32**. Make sure the terminal stud passes through the inner insulator (15, **Figure 36**) first, then install the outer insulator (17), washer (18) and nut (19). Tighten the nut securely.

13. Position the brush plate into the end cap and install the negative brushes into it. Secure the brush plate and the negative brush leads with the screws and lockwashers. See **Figure 33**. Tighten both screws securely.

14. Install the armature into the starter housing. Allow the starter housing magnets to position the armature.

NOTE
A brush retaining tool can be fabricated from a putty knife. Cut or grind a 1/2 in. (12.7 mm) wide slot, approximately 1-1/2 in. (38 mm) deep, down the center of the putty knife. See Figure 34.

15. Fit all four springs and brushes into the brush plate and end cap assembly. Hold the brushes compressed with a suitable tool (**Figure 35**).

16. While holding the brushes in a compressed position, carefully pilot the armature (and housing) into the end cap bushing, then remove the tool once the armature has firmly contacted the tool. Rotate the end cap to align the scribe marks.

17. Install the thrust washer over the armature. Then carefully slide the drive end cap over the armature shaft and seat it to the starter housing. Rotate the drive end cap to align the scribe marks, then install the through-bolts. Evenly tighten both through-bolts to 50-60 in.-lb. (5.7-6.8 N•m) on 25-35 hp models or 95-100 in.-lb. (10.7-11.3 N•m) on 40-70 hp and 35 jet models.

18. Apply OMC Black Neoprene Dip to both end cap-to-housing seams and to both through-bolt-to-end cap seams.

NOTE
Do not allow any lubricant to contact the bendix-to-drive base mating surfaces. Keep these surfaces clean and dry.

19. Install the drive base (7, **Figure 36**), pinion gear (6), grooved spacer (5), spring (4) and cupped spacer (3) over the armature shaft. Pull downward on the cupped spacer to expose the C-clip groove, then install a new C-clip (2) into the groove. Release the cupped spacer and make sure it snaps up and over the C-clip, locking it in place.

20. Install the protective cap (1, **Figure 36**) over the armature shaft and make sure it snaps in place on the grooved spacer.

21. Test the starter's no-load current draw as described in Chapter Three.

22. *25 and 35 hp (three-cylinder) models*—Install the starter solenoid to the lower end cap as follows:

   a. Make sure the rubber grommet is positioned around the solenoid and will isolate the solenoid from the end cap (and solenoid bracket).

   b. Position the solenoid to the end cap and place the bracket over the solenoid. Install and tighten the two screws (and lockwashers) finger-tight at this time.

   c. Install the metal strap (24, **Figure 36**) over the starter's terminal stud, then tighten the solenoid bracket screws (27) securely.

   d. Secure the metal strap with nuts and lockwashers. Tighten the nuts securely.

   e. Coat the strap and its connections with OMC Black Neoprene Dip.

23. Install the starter motor as described previously in this chapter.

Starter Motor Cleaning and Inspection (All Models)

1. Clean the armature and brush plate using an electrical parts cleaner (available at automotive parts stores). Then blow the parts dry with compressed air.

2. Wash all other parts in a mild solvent, such as mineral spirits, then thoroughly rinse with hot water. Blow the parts dry with compressed air.

3. Inspect the starter brushes in the end cap. Replace both brushes if either is pitted, chipped, oil soaked or excessively worn (1/2 of their original size).

4. Inspect the bendix (pinion gear) for cracked, chipped or excessively worn teeth and any other damage.

5. Inspect the armature shaft bushings in the drive end and lower end caps for excessive wear or other damage. Replace either end cap as necessary.

6. Using an ohmmeter, check for no continuity (an open circuit) between each commutator segment and the armature shaft (core). The armature must be replaced if any continuity is noted.

7. Clean the commutator using 300 grade emery cloth. Clean any copper particles or other contamination from between the commutator segments.

8. If the commutator is pitted, rough or worn unevenly, it can be resurfaced or replaced. If the armature shows water or overheat damage, have it checked for shorted windings using an armature growler. Most automotive electrical shops can perform commutator resurfacing and armature testing.

9. Inspect the starter housing for loose, cracked, chipped or damaged magnets. The magnets must strongly attract any steel or iron object held inside the starter housing.

7

Replace the housing if the magnets are weak, loose, cracked, chipped or damaged.

Starter Solenoid

Two types of starter solenoids are used on Evinrude/Johnson outboard motors. Both types of solenoids use the same type and quantity of electrical connections and are serviced in the same manner, but are not interchangeable.

The two large terminals always carry the electrical load from the battery to the starter motor. The large terminals have an open circuit across them when the solenoid is not energized. The large lead from the battery is usually black with red ends (sleeves). The large lead from the solenoid to the starter motor is usually yellow or black with yellow ends (sleeves).

The two small terminals are the control circuits of the solenoid. When battery voltage is applied to these terminals, the solenoid is energized and the large terminals will now have a closed circuit across them, allowing electricity to flow from the battery to the starter motor.

The polarity of the small terminals is not important as long as one is positive and one is negative. One small lead is always yellow/red, while the other small lead is black (or a second yellow/red).

The starter solenoid is always located near the starter motor. On 20-30 hp (two-cylinder models, it is mounted on the starter bracket (8, **Figure 31**). On 25-35 hp (three-cylinder) models, the solenoid is mounted on the starter's lower end cap (16, **Figure 36**). Refer to Chapter Three for troubleshooting procedures.

Starter Solenoid Removal/Installation

To replace the starter solenoid, refer to **Figure 37**, typical and proceed as follows:

1. Disconnect the negative battery cable.

2. Disconnect and ground the spark plug leads to the power head to prevent accidental starting.

3A. *20-30 hp (two-cylinder) models*—Remove the starter motor and bracket assembly as described previously in this chapter.

3B. *25 and 35 hp (three-cylinder) models*—Remove the starter motor and solenoid assembly as described previously in this chapter.

4. Note the location and position of all wires, cables and/or metal straps on the starter solenoid terminal studs and/or mounting screws.

5. Remove the nuts, lockwashers and all electrical cables (or metal straps) from the two large solenoid terminals.

6. Remove the nuts, lockwashers and electrical leads from the two small solenoid terminals.

7. Remove the two solenoid mounting screws, then remove the solenoid from the power head, starter bracket or starter motor

8. *20-70 hp and 35 jet models*—Remove the rubber grommet from around the solenoid and install the grommet onto the new solenoid.

9. To install the solenoid, position the solenoid on the power head, starter bracket or starter motor. Make sure any ground leads or ground straps are reconnected to the mounting screws as noted on removal. Tighten both mounting screws securely.

10A. *20-30 hp (two-cylinder) models*—Install the starter motor and bracket assembly as described previously in this chapter.

10B. *25 and 35 hp (three-cylinder) models*—Install the starter motor and solenoid assembly as described previously in this chapter.

11. Install the small leads, lockwashers and nuts. Tighten the nuts securely.

12. Install the large cables, lockwashers and nuts. Tighten the nuts securely. Make sure the positive battery cable is covered with a protective boot as shown in **Figure 37**.

13. Reconnect the spark plug leads and the negative battery cable when finished.

NEUTRAL SAFETY SWITCH

The neutral safety switch is designed to prevent electric starter operation unless the shift linkage is in the NEUTRAL position. If the electric starter motor can be engaged when the shift linkage is in NEUTRAL, but cannot be engaged when the shift linkage is in FORWARD or REVERSE gear, the switch is operating correctly.

The 9.9 and 15 hp and 40-70 hp tiller handle models are equipped with a neutral safety *mechanical linkage* that prevents the operator from fully depressing the starter button unless the shift linkage is in NEUTRAL. Refer to Chapter Nine for neutral safety linkage adjustment procedures.

Remote Control Models

All remote control models must be equipped with a neutral safety switch mounted in the control box. On standard OMC side mount control boxes, the switch is located inside the remote control assembly and is not adjustable. Refer to Chapter Three for troubleshooting procedures and Chapter Twelve for standard control box disassembly/reassembly procedures.

20-30 hp (Two-cylinder) Tiller Handle Models

The neutral safety switch is mounted on the starboard side of the engine, between the fuel pump and rectifier as shown in **Figure 38**. The switch is connected to the yellow/red lead coming from the ground side of the starter solenoid's control windings. The switch opens and closes this lead to ground, depending on shift linkage position. Refer to Chapter Three for troubleshooting procedures.

The neutral safety switch requires adjustment in order to operate correctly. If the switch has been replaced, or the electric starter can be engaged with the shift linkage in FORWARD or REVERSE gear, the switch needs adjustment or is defective. Prior to adjustment, make sure the engine's shift lever has been properly adjusted as described in Chapter Nine.

1. Disconnect and ground the spark plug leads to the power head to prevent accidental starting. Then disconnect the negative battery cable.

2. Disconnect the yellow/red wire from the neutral start switch.

3. Place the engine's shift lever in the NEUTRAL detent position. The propeller must spin freely in either direction.

4. Loosen the two neutral safety switch mounting screws. Insert a 1/16 in. drill bit between the top surface of the plunger's head and the bottom of the switch. Move the switch until the switch and plunger both are contacting the drill bit, then retighten the screws securely.

5. Remove the drill bit.

6. Calibrate an ohmmeter on the highest scale available. Connect one ohmmeter lead to the yellow/red lead's terminal on the switch. Connect the other ohmmeter lead to a good engine ground.

7. With the shift lever in the NEUTRAL position, the meter must indicate continuity.

8. Move the shift lever to the FORWARD and REVERSE gear positions while rotating the propeller and noting the meter reading at each position. The meter must indicate no continuity in both the FORWARD and REVERSE gear positions. If not, replace the switch and repeat this procedure.

9. To replace the switch, refer to **Figure 38** and proceed as follows:

   a. Disconnect the yellow/red lead from the switch's terminal.

   b. Remove the two screws (and washers), then remove the switch from its bracket.

   c. Position a new switch to the bracket and secure it in place with the two screws and washers.

   d. Connect the yellow/red lead to the switch's terminal.

   e. Adjust the switch and verify its operation as described in Steps 4-8.

10. Reconnect the spark plug leads and the negative battery cable when finished.

25 and 35 hp (Three-cylinder) Tiller Handle Models

The neutral safety switch is mounted on the starboard side of the engine, just in front of the fuel/oil mixing unit and above the shift lever. The switch requires no adjustments.

The switch is connected to the yellow/red lead between the ignition (key) switch and a starter solenoid primary terminal. The other starter solenoid primary terminal is directly wired to ground.

The switch must have continuity when the shift lever is in the NEUTRAL position and no continuity when the shift lever is in the FORWARD or REVERSE gear positions. Refer to Chapter Three for complete troubleshooting procedures.

To replace the switch, proceed as follows:

1. Disconnect and ground the spark plug leads to the power head to prevent accidental starting. Then disconnect the negative battery cable.

2. Remove the starboard split lower cowl. There are a total of six screws holding the lower cowls to each other.

3. Remove the two screws (and washers) securing the neutral safety switch to its bracket on the power head.

4A. *1995 (EO) models*—Disconnect the neutral safety switch's two yellow/red leads at the six-pin Amphenol connector (pins B and F). Refer to *Electrical Connector Service* in this chapter for Amphenol connector service procedures.

4B. *1996-1998 (ED-EC) models*—Disconnect the neutral safety switch's two yellow/red leads at the six-pin Deutsch connector, pins No. 2 and No. 6. Refer to *Electrical Connector Service* in this chapter for Deutsch connector service procedures.

5. Remove any tape, clamps or tie-straps securing the yellow/red leads. Then remove the switch.

6. To install the switch, begin by positioning the switch to its bracket and securing it in place with two screws (and washers). Tighten both screws securely but do not crush or distort the switch.

7. Reconnect the switch's two yellow/red leads to the six-pin connector, pins B (No. 2) and F (No. 6). Refer to *Electrical Connector Service* at the end of this chapter for connector service procedures.

8. Secure the two yellow/red leads with the original clamps, new tape or new tie-straps in the same manner as it was originally secured.

9. Install the starboard split lower cowl. Evenly tighten the six screws to 84-106 in.-lb. (9.5-12 N•m).

10. Reconnect the spark plug leads and the negative battery cable when finished.

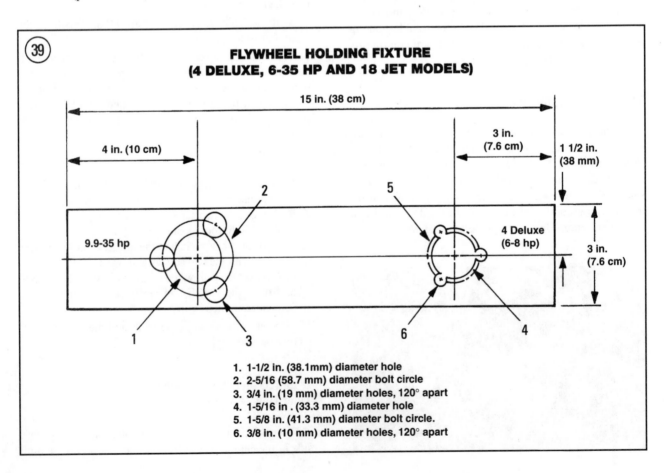

(39)

**FLYWHEEL HOLDING FIXTURE
(4 DELUXE, 6-35 HP AND 18 JET MODELS)**

1. 1-1/2 in. (38.1mm) diameter hole
2. 2-5/16 (58.7 mm) diameter bolt circle
3. 3/4 in. (19 mm) diameter holes, 120° apart
4. 1-5/16 in . (33.3 mm) diameter hole
5. 1-5/8 in. (41.3 mm) diameter bolt circle.
6. 3/8 in. (10 mm) diameter holes, 120° apart

FLYWHEEL SERVICE

The flywheel magnets must have an extremely strong charge order to produce sufficient voltage to correctly operate the ignition and charging systems. Weak magnets can cause misleading or erratic results during troubleshooting, which can lead to the unnecessary replacement of good parts.

On models using magnets glued into the outer rim of the flywheel, loose magnets can be glued back in place using epoxy repair kit part No. 431929 (or equivalent). The magnets must be positioned precisely in their original location and orientation (polarity), and must not be cracked, chipped or broken.

On 40-70 hp and 35 jet models equipped with the 12 amp charging system, the magnets around the flywheel's inner hub (sensor coil magnets) cannot be repaired. Should the magnets in the hub become loose, shift position or be cracked, the flywheel must be replaced.

On 25 and 35 hp (three-cylinder) models, there are no sensor coil magnets. Instead a plastic encoder ring (mounted around the flywheel's inner hub) is used to trigger the optical sensor.

If oil is present under the flywheel, the upper crankshaft seal may be leaking. On 3-15 hp (including 4 Deluxe) models, the upper seal can be replaced without disassembling the crankcase, if the proper special tools are used (as described in Chapter Eight). On all other models, the power head must be removed and the crankcase disassembled to replace the upper crankshaft seal (Chapter Eight).

Since the flywheel contains permanent magnets, the flywheel must never be struck with a hammer. Striking the flywheel (and/or magnets) can cause the magnets to lose their charge, leading to weak, erratic spark. Crankshafts are made of hardened steel, therefore striking the flywheel (and/or crankshaft) can also permanently damage the crankshaft. Use only the recommended flywheel puller tools (or their equivalents).

After removal, inspect the flywheel, key and crankshaft as directed in *Cleaning and inspection*. Replace all suspect components. Refer to **Table 7** for flywheel nut torque values.

Flywheel Holding Fixture
(4 Deluxe, 6-35 hp and 18 Jet Models)

To hold the flywheel when loosening or tightening the flywheel nut, the manufacturer recommends using a special holding fixture (**Figure 39**). The fixture is made from a piece of 1/4 in. (6.35 mm) thick by 3 in. (7.6 cm) wide, cold-rolled steel bar stock, 15 in. (38 cm) long.

If you do not have the equipment to fabricate the fixture, most welding or machine shops can manufacture the fixture for you. After all holes are drilled, remove all burrs and sharp edges with a file.

The tool is designed to fit over three puller bolts (from puller kit part No. 378103) threaded into the top of the flywheel. Make sure the puller bolts are securely tightened and that the tool is held as close to the flywheel as possible (to reduce the shearing load on the bolts). The puller bolts are specially hardened and are of a shoulder design; do not substitute.

Removal/Installation
(2-8 hp [including 4 Deluxe] Models)

The OMC universal puller kit (part No. 378103) is highly recommended for flywheel removal on these models. On 2 and 3.3 hp models, three puller screws (part No. 115308) are also required.

To hold the flywheel when loosening or tightening the flywheel nut, flywheel holder part No. 115315 (2 and 3.3 hp), part No. 333827 (3 and 4 hp) or the special holding fixture (4 Deluxe-8 hp [**Figure 39**]) is recommended.

The use of a piston stop (such as OMC part No. 384887 [**Figure 40**, typical]), is an acceptable alternative to prevent crankshaft rotation when removing or installing the flywheel nut. To use the piston stop to prevent crankshaft rotation, proceed as follows:

a. Remove the No. 1 cylinder spark plug. Using a pencil inserted into the spark plug hole, determine the approximate TDC position for No. 1 cylinder.

b. Continue to turn the flywheel clockwise until its outer diameter is approximately 2 to 3 in. (50-76

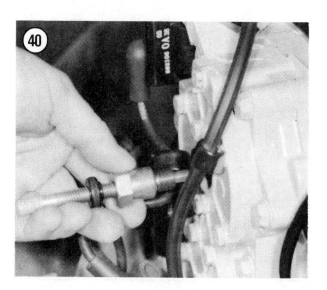

mm) past the TDC (top dead center) position of No. 1 cylinder.

c. Thread the piston stop's body fully into the spark hole. Then thread the stop rod in until it firmly contacts the piston. Tighten the knurled locking ring securely.

d. The crankshaft is now locked in position and the flywheel nut can be removed. When installing the nut, slowly rotate the crankshaft clockwise until the piston again seats against the piston stop.

e. Remove the piston stop when finished.

If the flywheel design so allows, a suitable strap wrench, such as Stevens Instruments part No. S-17 (or equivalent) may also be used as shown in **Figure 41**, typical.

To remove and install the flywheel, proceed as follows:

1. Disconnect and ground the spark plug lead(s) to the power head to prevent accidental starting.

2. Remove the rewind starter assembly as described in Chapter Twelve.

3. *2, 3.3 and 3.5 hp*—Remove the three screws (and washers) securing the starter cup to the flywheel. Then remove the starter cup. See **Figure 42**.

4A. *2, 3.3 and 3.5 hp*—Hold the flywheel using flywheel holder part No. 115315 (or equivalent) and remove the flywheel nut using a suitable socket and breaker bar.

4B. *3 and 4 hp (except 4 Deluxe)*—Hold the flywheel using flywheel holder part No. 333827 (or equivalent) and remove the flywheel nut using a suitable socket and breaker bar.

4C. *4 Deluxe, 6 and 8 hp*—Install three puller screws (part No. 307641) into the flywheel. Tighten the screws securely. Then place the smaller opening of the flywheel holding fixture (**Figure 39**) over the puller screws and against the flywheel (**Figure 43**). Remove the flywheel nut using a suitable socket and breaker bar. When finished, remove the holding fixture and puller screws.

5. Lubricate the puller pressing screw threads and the end of the crankshaft with OMC Moly Lube. Place the puller body (and screw) over the end of the crankshaft. Make sure the flat side of the puller plate is facing up.

6A. *2, 3.3 and 3.5 hp*—Secure the puller plate to the flywheel using three screws (part No. 115308) and three washers (part No. 307646). Tighten the puller screws securely.

6B. *3 hp and 4-8 hp*—Secure the puller plate to the flywheel using three screws (part No. 307641) and three washers (part No. 307639). Tighten the puller screws securely.

7. Hold the puller body with the puller handle and tighten the pressing screw (**Figure 44**, typical) until the flywheel breaks free from the crankshaft taper. Then lift the flywheel and puller assembly off the crankshaft. Remove the puller assembly from the flywheel.

8. Remove the flywheel key from the crankshaft.

9. Inspect and clean the flywheel, key and crankshaft as described in the following section.

10. To install the flywheel, begin by making certain the flywheel and crankshaft tapers are clean and dry.

11A. *2, 3.3 and 3.5 hp*—Install the flywheel key into the crankshaft groove. The key's outer edge must be parallel to the centerline of the crankshaft. See **Figure 45**.

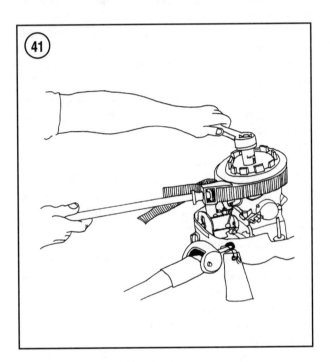

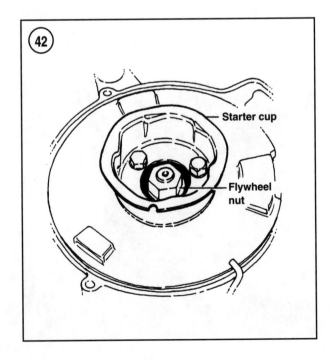

NOTE
*On 3 hp and 4-8 hp models (including 4 Deluxe), the single indented mark on the flywheel key **must** face down when installed.*

11B. *3 and 4-8 hp*—Install the flywheel key into the crankshaft groove with the single indent mark facing down. The key's outer edge must be parallel to the centerline of the crankshaft as shown in **Figure 45**.

12. Carefully lower the flywheel onto the crankshaft, making sure the key slot in the flywheel aligns with the key in the crankshaft.

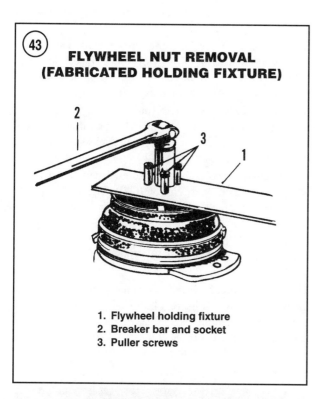

FLYWHEEL NUT REMOVAL (FABRICATED HOLDING FIXTURE)

1. Flywheel holding fixture
2. Breaker bar and socket
3. Puller screws

13. Coat the threads of the flywheel nut with OMC Gasket Sealing Compound. Then thread the nut onto the crankshaft.

14. Hold the flywheel with the appropriate holding tool and tighten the nut as follows:
   a. *2, 3.3 and 3.5 hp*—Tighten the nut to 29-33 ft.-lb. (39.3-44.7 N•m).
   b. *3 hp and 4 hp (including 4 Deluxe)*—Tighten the nut to 30-40 ft.-lb. (40.7-54.2 N•m).
   c. *6 and 8 hp*—Tighten the nut to 40-50 ft.-lb. (54.2-67.8 N•m).

15. *2, 3.3 and 3.5 hp*—Install the starter cup to the flywheel and secure it with three screws (and washers). Tighten the screws securely.

16. Install the rewind starter as described in Chapter Twelve.

17. Reconnect the spark plug lead(s).

Flywheel cleaning and inspection (2-8 hp)

WARNING
A damaged or defective flywheel must be replaced. A damaged or defective flywheel may fly apart at higher engine speeds, throwing fragments over a large area. Do not attempt to use or repair a damaged or defective flywheel.

1. Inspect the entire flywheel for cracks, chips, mechanical damage, wear and corrosion.

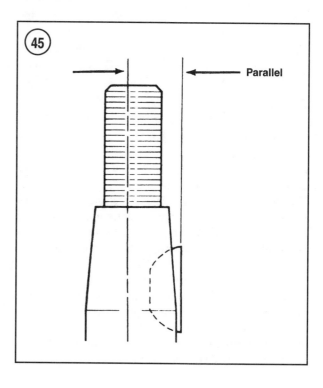

Parallel

2. Carefully inspect the flywheel and crankshaft tapers for cracks, wear, corrosion and metal transfer.

3. Inspect the flywheel and crankshaft key slots for wear, cracks or damage.

4. Carefully inspect the flywheel key. Replace the key if it is in questionable condition.

5. Inspect the flywheel for loose, cracked or damaged magnets. The flywheel must be replaced if the magnets are cracked or damaged. If a magnet glued to the outer diameter is loose (but is not damaged in any way), it can be reattached with flywheel magnet epoxy (part No. 431929). The magnet must be reinstalled in its original position and orientation (polarity).

6. Clean the flywheel and crankshaft tapers with a suitable solvent and blow dry with compressed air. The tapers must be clean, dry and free of oil or other contamination.

Removal/Installation
(9.9-35 hp and 18 Jet Models)

The OMC universal puller kit (part No. 378103) is highly recommended for flywheel removal on these models.

To hold the flywheel when loosening or tightening the flywheel nut, the special holding fixture (**Figure 39**) is recommended.

The use of a ring gear holding tool (such as OMC part No. 771311 [**Figure 46**, typical]) is an acceptable alternative to prevent crankshaft rotation when removing or installing the flywheel nut on models equipped with a ring gear.

If the flywheel design so allows, a suitable strap wrench, such as Stevens Instruments part No. S-17 (or equivalent) may also be used as shown in **Figure 41**, typical. Do not use a strap wrench on a flywheel with a ring gear.

To remove and install the flywheel, proceed as follows:

1. Disconnect and ground the spark plug leads to the power head to prevent accidental starting.

2A. *Rope start models*—Remove the rewind starter as described in Chapter Twelve.

2B. *Electric start models*—Disconnect the negative battery cable. On 25-35 hp (three-cylinder) models, remove the flywheel cover. Locate and secure the three spacer sleeves that prevent the three mounting screws from crushing the cover.

3A. *9.9 and 15 hp*—Install three puller screws (part No. 307641) into the flywheel. Tighten the screws securely. Then place the smaller opening of the flywheel holding fixture (**Figure 39**) over the puller screws and against the flywheel (**Figure 43**). Remove the flywheel nut using a suitable socket and breaker bar.

3B. *20-30 hp (two-cylinder) and 18 jet*—Install three puller screws (part No. 307642) into the flywheel. Tighten the screws securely. Then place the larger opening of the flywheel holding fixture (**Figure 39**) over the puller screws and against the flywheel (**Figure 43**, typical). Remove the flywheel nut using a suitable socket and breaker bar.

3C. *25 and 35 hp (three-cylinder)*—Install three puller screws (part No. 309492) into the flywheel. Tighten the screws securely. Then place the larger opening of the flywheel holding fixture (**Figure 39**) over the puller screws and against the flywheel (**Figure 43**, typical). Remove the flywheel nut using a suitable socket and breaker bar.

4. Remove the holding fixture and puller screws once the flywheel nut is removed.

5. Lubricate the puller pressing screw threads and the end of the crankshaft with OMC Moly Lube. Place the puller body (and screw) over the end of the crankshaft. Make sure the flat side of the puller plate is facing up.

6A. *9.9 and 15 hp*—Secure the puller plate to the flywheel using three screws (part No. 307641) and three washers (part No. 307639). Tighten the puller screws securely.

6B. *20-30 hp (two-cylinder) and 18 jet*—Secure the puller plate to the flywheel using three screws (part No. 307642) and three washers (part No. 307640). Tighten the puller screws securely.

6C. *25 and 35 hp (three-cylinder)*—Secure the puller plate to the flywheel using three screws (part No. 309492) and three washers (part No. 307639). Tighten the puller screws securely.

7. Hold the puller body with the puller handle and tighten the pressing screw (**Figure 44**, typical) until the flywheel breaks free from the crankshaft taper. Then lift the flywheel and puller assembly off the crankshaft. Remove the puller assembly from the flywheel.

8. Remove the flywheel key from the crankshaft.

9. Inspect and clean the flywheel, key and crankshaft as described in *Flywheel cleaning and inspection* in the following section.

10. To install the flywheel, begin by making certain the flywheel and crankshaft tapers are clean and dry.

> *NOTE*
> *The single, indented mark on the flywheel key **must** face down when installed.*

11A. *9.9 and 15 hp*—Install the flywheel key into the crankshaft groove with the single, indent mark facing down. The key's outer edge must be parallel to the taper of the crankshaft as shown in the left half of **Figure 47**.

11B. *20-35 hp and 18 jet*—Install the flywheel key into the crankshaft groove with the single, indent mark facing down. The key's outer edge must be parallel to the centerline of the crankshaft as shown in the right half of **Figure 47**.

12. Carefully lower the flywheel onto the crankshaft, making sure the key slot in the flywheel aligns with the key in the crankshaft.

13. Coat the threads of the flywheel nut with OMC Gasket Sealing Compound. Then thread the nut onto the crankshaft.

14. Hold the flywheel with the appropriate holding tool and tighten the nut as follows:

a. *9.9 and 15 hp*—Tighten the nut to 45-50 ft.-lb. (61-67.8 N•m).

b. *20-35 hp and 18 jet*—Tighten the nut to 100-105 ft.-lb. (136-142 N•m).

15A. *Rope start models*—Install the rewind starter as described in Chapter Twelve.

15B. *Electric start models*—Reconnect the negative battery cable. On 25-35 hp (three-cylinder) models, reinstall the flywheel cover. Make sure the spacer sleeves are installed with the screws, then tighten the three cover screws securely.

16. Reconnect the spark plug leads when finished.

Flywheel cleaning and inspection (9.9-35 hp and 18 jet)

> *WARNING*
> *A damaged or defective flywheel must be replaced. A damaged or defective flywheel may fly apart at higher engine speeds, throwing fragments over a large area. Do not attempt to use or repair a damaged or defective flywheel.*

1. Inspect the entire flywheel for cracks, chips, mechanical damage, wear and corrosion.

2. Carefully inspect the flywheel and crankshaft tapers for cracks, wear, corrosion and metal transfer.

7

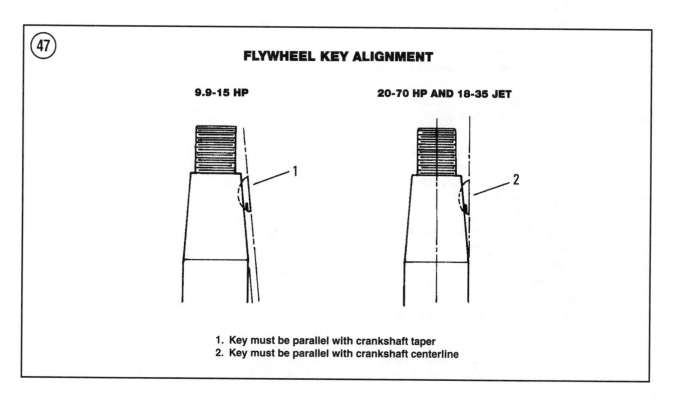

(47)

FLYWHEEL KEY ALIGNMENT

9.9-15 HP

20-70 HP AND 18-35 JET

1

2

1. Key must be parallel with crankshaft taper
2. Key must be parallel with crankshaft centerline

3. Inspect the flywheel and crankshaft key slots for wear, cracks or damage.

4. Carefully inspect the flywheel key. Replace the key if it is in questionable condition.

5. Inspect the flywheel for loose, cracked or damaged magnets. The flywheel must be replaced if the magnets are cracked or damaged. If a magnet glued to the outer diameter has become loose (but is not damaged in any way), it can be reattached with flywheel magnet epoxy (part No. 431929). The magnet must be reinstalled in its original position and orientation (polarity).

6. *25 and 35 hp (three-cylinder) models*—Inspect the plastic encoder ring for cracks, missing pieces, loose or missing mounting screws or any other damage. If replacement is necessary, proceed as follows:

    a. Remove the three screws securing the encoder to the flywheel, then remove the encoder.

    b. Position the new encoder to the flywheel. Rotate the encoder until the three mounting screw holes are aligned.

    c. Coat the encoder screw threads with OMC Nut Lock threadlocking adhesive.

    d. Install the screws and evenly tighten them to 24-36 in.-lb. (2.7-4.1 N•m).

7. Clean the flywheel and crankshaft tapers with a suitable solvent and blow dry with compressed air. The tapers must be clean, dry and free of oil or other contamination.

Removal/Installation (40-70 hp, 28 and 35 Jet Models)

The OMC universal puller kit (part No. 378103) is highly recommended for flywheel removal on these models.

To hold the flywheel when loosening or tightening the flywheel nut, a ring gear holding tool (such as OMC part No. 771311 [**Figure 46**, typical]) is recommended on models equipped with a ring gear. If the flywheel does not incorporate a ring gear, a suitable strap wrench, such as Stevens Instruments part No. S-17 (or equivalent) may also be used as shown in **Figure 48**, typical. Do not use a strap wrench on a flywheel with a ring gear.

To remove and install the flywheel, proceed as follows:

1. Disconnect and ground the spark plug leads to the power head to prevent accidental starting.

2A. *Rope start models*—Remove the rewind starter as described in Chapter Twelve.

2B. *Electric start models*—Disconnect the negative battery cable.

3. Hold the flywheel with a ring gear tool (**Figure 46**, typical) or a strap wrench (**Figure 48**, typical). Remove the flywheel nut using an appropriate socket and breaker bar.

4. Lubricate the puller pressing screw threads and the end of the crankshaft with OMC Moly Lube. Place the puller body (and screw) over the end of the crankshaft. Make sure the flat side of the puller plate is facing up.

5. Secure the puller plate to the flywheel using three screws (part No. 309492) and three washers (part No. 307639). Tighten the puller screws securely.

6. Hold the puller body with the puller handle and tighten the pressing screw (**Figure 44**, typical) until the flywheel breaks free from the crankshaft taper. Then lift the flywheel and puller assembly off the crankshaft. Remove the puller assembly from the flywheel.

7. Remove the flywheel key from the crankshaft.

8. Inspect and clean the flywheel, key and crankshaft as described in *Flywheel cleaning and inspection* in the following section.

9. To install the flywheel, begin by making certain the flywheel and crankshaft tapers are clean and dry.

NOTE
*The single, indented mark on the flywheel key **must** face down when installed.*

10. Install the flywheel key into the crankshaft groove with the single, indent mark facing down. The key's outer edge must be parallel to the centerline of the crankshaft as shown in the right half of **Figure 47**.

11. Carefully lower the flywheel onto the crankshaft, making sure the key slot in the flywheel aligns with the key in the crankshaft.

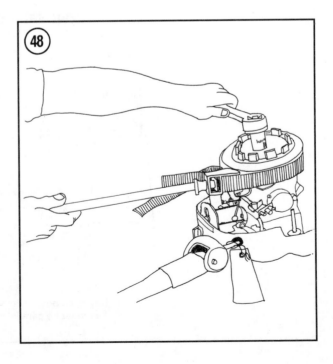

12. Coat the threads of the flywheel nut with OMC Gasket Sealing Compound. Then thread the nut onto the crankshaft.

13. Hold the flywheel with the appropriate holding tool and tighten the nut to 100-105 ft.-lb. (136-142 N•m).

14A. *Rope start models*—Install the rewind starter as described in Chapter Twelve.

14B. *Electric start models*—Reconnect the negative battery cable.

15. Reconnect the spark plug leads when finished.

Flywheel cleaning and inspection (40-70 hp, 28 and 35 jet)

> *WARNING*
> *A damaged or defective flywheel must be replaced. A damaged or defective flywheel may fly apart at higher engine speeds, throwing fragments over a large area. Do not attempt to use or repair a damaged or defective flywheel.*

1. Inspect the entire flywheel for cracks, chips, mechanical damage, wear and corrosion.

2. Carefully inspect the flywheel and crankshaft tapers for cracks, wear, corrosion and metal transfer.

3. Inspect the flywheel and crankshaft key slots for wear, cracks or damage.

4. Carefully inspect the flywheel key. Replace the key if it is in questionable condition.

5. Inspect the flywheel for loose, cracked or damaged magnets. The flywheel must be replaced if any of the magnets are cracked or damaged.

    a. If a magnet glued to the outer diameter has become loose (but is not damaged in any way), it can be reattached with flywheel magnet epoxy (part No. 431929). The magnet must be reinstalled in its original position and orientation (polarity).

    b. If the sensor magnets (around the inner hub) are loose, the flywheel must be replaced.

6. Clean the flywheel and crankshaft tapers with a suitable solvent and blow dry with compressed air. The tapers must be clean, dry and free of oil or other contamination.

IGNITION SYSTEMS

Refer to **Table 8** for ignition system identification. This section deals mainly with component removal and replacement. Refer to Chapter Three for additional illustrations, operational descriptions and ignition system troubleshooting procedures. Refer to the back of the manual for wiring diagrams.

CD1 (CAPACITOR DISCHARGE ONE-CYLINDER) IGNITION (2, 3.3 AND 3.5 HP MODELS)

Description

The CD1 (capacitor discharge, one cylinder) ignition system (**Figure 49**) used on 2 and 3.3 hp models consists of the flywheel, charge coil, sensor coil, power pack, ignition coil, spark plug and a combination push button stop/safety lanyard switch. The charge coil and sensor coil are mounted under the flywheel, and the power pack and ignition coil are mounted on the side of the power head. The power pack is stamped *CD1* for identification.

This system incorporates a nonadjustable, single-step electronic spark advance built into the power pack.

Operation

A series of permanent magnets is contained along the inner diameter of the outer rim of the flywheel. As the flywheel rotates, alternating current (AC) is induced into the charge coil windings. The AC current flows to the power pack, where it is converted (rectified) into direct current (DC) and stored in the capacitor contained within the power pack.

The magnets also pass by the sensor coil, inducing a low-voltage signal into the sensor coil windings. This voltage pulse causes an electronic switch in the power pack to close, allowing the stored voltage in the capacitor to discharge into the ignition coil. The ignition coil amplifies the voltage and discharges it into the spark plug lead. This sequence of events is repeated with each revolution of the flywheel unless the power pack's black/yellow lead is connected to ground. Connecting the black/yellow lead to ground shorts the capacitor, causing the ignition system to cease operation. Wiring diagrams are located at the end of the book.

Charge Coil and Sensor Coil Removal/Installation (2, 3.3 and 3.5 hp)

The ignition plate must be removed to service the charge coil and/or sensor coil. Coil locating tool (part No. 342674) is required to properly locate the coils on the armature plate. If the coils are too far from the flywheel magnets, the engine will be difficult to start and may run erratically. If the coils are too close to the magnets, they may be struck by the magnets, resulting in coil and magnet damage. Refer to **Figure 49** for this procedure.

1. Remove the flywheel as described previously in this chapter.

7

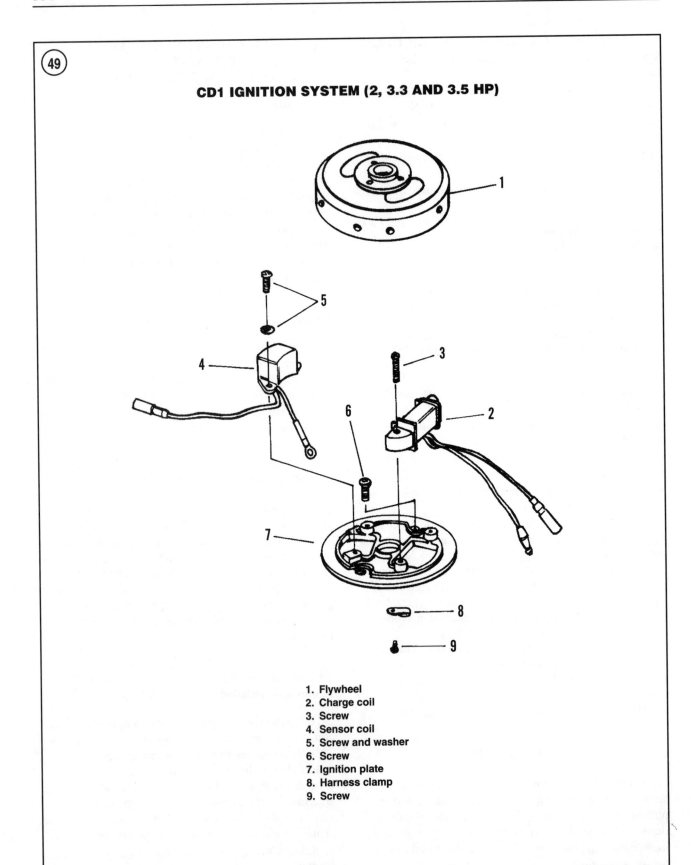

CD1 IGNITION SYSTEM (2, 3.3 AND 3.5 HP)

1. Flywheel
2. Charge coil
3. Screw
4. Sensor coil
5. Screw and washer
6. Screw
7. Ignition plate
8. Harness clamp
9. Screw

2. Disconnect the charge coil's brown and brown/yellow leads and the sensor coil's blue lead from the power pack bullet connectors.

3. Remove the two screws (6, **Figure 49**) holding the ignition plate to the power head. Loosen any clamps or remove any tie-straps securing the ignition plate leads, then lift the ignition plate from the power head.

4. Invert the ignition plate and remove the screw (and clamp) securing the leads to the plate. See 8 and 9, **Figure 49**. Then remove the braided mesh sleeve from the leads.

5. Position the ignition plate right side up, then remove the two screws and washers securing the sensor coil and the two screws securing the charge coil. Remove the sensor and charge coils from the ignition plate.

6. To assemble and install the ignition plate, begin by positioning the sensor and charge coils to their ignition plate mounting bosses. Route the coil leads out the bottom of the plate, then install the braided mesh sleeve over the leads.

7. Install the wire clamp over the leads. Coat the threads of the screw with OMC Screw Lock threadlocking adhesive (or equivalent), then install and tighten the clamp screw to 15-19 in.-lb. (1.7-2.2 N•m).

8. Install the coil locating tool through the ignition plate mounting screw holes. The S stamped on the tool must be next to the sensor coil (blue lead) and the C stamped on the tool must be next to the charge coil (brown and brown/yellow leads).

9. Coat the charge and sensor coil mounting screw threads with OMC Nut Lock threadlocking adhesive (or equivalent). Then install the screws finger-tight at this time. Note that the sensor coil requires a washer on each screw (5, **Figure 49**) and the sensor coil ground lead must be secured under the right hand screw (when looking from the center of the ignition plate outward).

10. Push the sensor coil outward against the coil locating tool. Make sure the alignment mark on the coil's left mounting ear is aligned with the second (right) mark on the ignition plate. Then evenly tighten both screws to 15-19 in.-lb. (1.7-2.2 N•m).

11. Push the charge coil outward against the coil locating tool. Evenly tighten both screws to 19-25 in.-lb. (2.2-2.8 N•m).

12. Remove the coil locating tool.

13. Position the ignition plate onto the power head and align the mounting screw holes. Coat the threads of the two mounting screws (6, **Figure 49**) with OMC Screw Lock threadlocking adhesive (or equivalent). Install and evenly tighten the screws to 27-44 in.-lb. (3.1-5.0 N•m).

14. Connect the charge coil's brown and brown/yellow leads and the sensor coil's blue lead to the power pack bullet connectors.

15. Secure the leads to the power head with new tie-straps or the original clamp(s).

16. Reinstall the flywheel as described previously in this chapter.

Ignition Coil Removal/Installation (2, 3.3 and 3.5 hp)

1. Disconnect the spark plug lead from the spark plug.

2. Disconnect the power pack's orange/blue primary lead from the ignition coil with a gentle twisting and pulling motion.

3. Remove the two ignition coil mounting screws (and four washers), then remove the coil from the power head.

4. To install the coil, begin by positioning the coil on the power head. On each screw, position a washer between the coil and the power head and between the screw head and coil. Once both screws (and all four washers) are installed, evenly tighten the mounting screws to 62-89 in.-lb. (7-10 N•m).

5. Coat the ignition coil's primary terminal with OMC Electrical (dielectric) Grease, then connect the power pack's orange/blue primary lead to the ignition coil's primary terminal. Make sure the connector is seated on the coil.

6. Coat the ribbed area of the spark plug with OMC Electrical (dielectric) Grease, then reconnect the spark plug lead to the spark plug. Make sure the connector is seated on the plug.

Power Pack Removal/Installation (2.2, 3.3 and 3.5 hp)

1. Disconnect the power pack's brown, brown/yellow, blue and black/yellow leads at their bullet connectors.

2. Disconnect the power pack's orange/blue primary lead from the ignition coil with a gentle twisting and pulling motion.

3. Remove the screw and washer securing the power pack's black ground lead to the cylinder head bracket.

4. Remove the two power pack mounting screws (and nuts, if present). Then remove the pack from the cylinder head.

5. To install the power pack, begin by positioning the pack on the cylinder head and securing it with the two mounting screws. Tighten both mounting screws securely.

6. Reconnect the power pack's black ground lead to the cylinder head bracket. Secure the ground lead with a screw and washer. Tighten the screw securely.

7. Coat the ignition coil's primary terminal with OMC Electrical (dielectric) Grease, then connect the power pack's orange/blue primary lead to the ignition coil's pri-

7

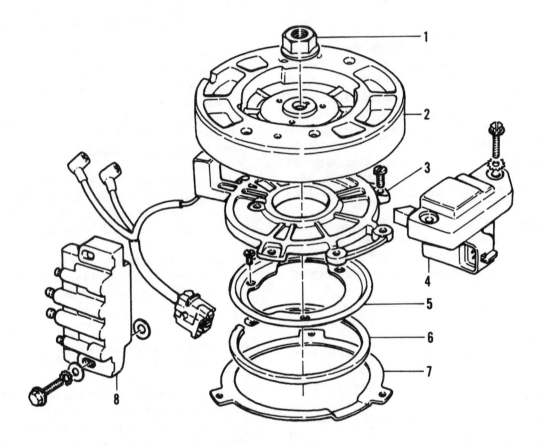

**IGNITION SYSTEM
(3 AND 4 HP [EXCEPT 4 DELUXE])**

1. Flywheel nut
2. Flywheel
3. Sensor coil
   (ignition plate assembly)
4. Ignition module
5. Support plate
6. Delrin bearing ring
7. Retainer plate
8. Dual-potted ignition coil

mary terminal. Make sure the connector is seated on the coil.

8. Connect the power pack's brown, brown/yellow, blue and black/yellow leads to the appropriate engine harness bullet connectors.

CAPACITOR DISCHARGE (TWO-CYLINDER) IGNITION (3 AND 4 HP MODELS EXCEPT 4 DELUXE])

Description

The CDI (capacitor discharge ignition) system (**Figure 50**) used on 3 and 4 hp models (except 4 Deluxe) consists of the flywheel, sensor coil, ignition module (power pack and charge coil combined), dual-potted ignition coil, spark plugs and a combination push button stop/safety lanyard switch.

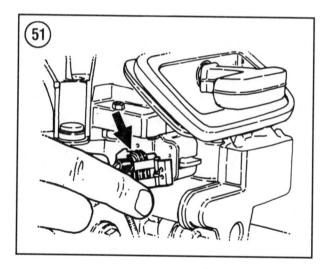

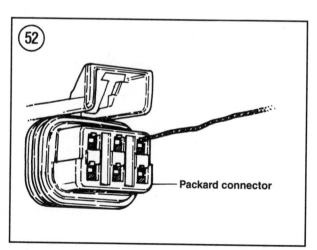

— **Packard connector**

The ignition module is externally mounted at the front of the power head and is fixed in position. An air gap between the module and flywheel must be set during installation. The sensor coil is also externally mounted, but is mounted to an ignition plate that rotates the sensor coil along the outer diameter of the flywheel. The ignition plate is rotated by a mechanical linkage to advance and retard ignition timing.

The ignition coil assembly is mounted on the starboard side of the cylinder head. The coil consists of two separate coils potted into one case. The coil windings are electrically separate. See Chapter Three.

Operation

A series of permanent magnets is contained along the outer rim of the flywheel. As the flywheel rotates, alternating current (AC) is induced into the charge coil windings and flows directly to the rectifier, where it is converted into direct current (DC) and stored in the capacitor (all contained within the ignition module).

The magnets also pass by an externally mounted sensor coil, inducing a series of low-voltage signals in the sensor coil windings. These voltage pulses cause electronic switches in the ignition module to close, allowing the stored voltage in the capacitor to discharge into the appropriate ignition coil winding. Each set of ignition coil windings amplifies the voltage and discharges it into the appropriate spark plug lead.

This sequence of events is repeated with each revolution of the flywheel, unless the ignition module's black/yellow lead is connected to ground. Connecting the black/yellow lead to ground shorts the capacitor, causing the ignition system to cease operation. Wiring diagrams are located at the back of the manual.

Sensor Coil (Ignition Plate) Removal/Installation (3 and 4 hp Models)

Refer to **Figure 50** for this procedure.

1. Disconnect and ground the spark plug leads to the power head to prevent accidental starting.

2. Remove the rope starter as described in Chapter Twelve.

3. Remove the flywheel as described previously in this chapter.

4. Disconnect the six-pin Packard connector from the ignition module. See **Figure 51**.

5. Carefully insert a paper clip (or terminal tool) into pin E (black/yellow lead) from the front of the Packard connector. See **Figure 52**. Depress the terminal locking tab,

then pull the black/yellow lead and terminal from the connector body.

6. Repeat Step 5 to remove the black lead from pin B of the Packard connector.

7. Disconnect the orange/blue and orange/green power pack primary leads from the ignition coil's primary terminals with a gentle twisting and pulling motion.

8. Remove the three screws securing the sensor coil (ignition plate) to the retainer plate (7, **Figure 50**). Lift the sensor assembly enough to disconnect the throttle cable from the assembly.

9. Remove any remaining clamps or tie-straps securing the sensor assembly's wiring harness to the power head. Then lift the sensor assembly and wiring harness from the power head.

10. If necessary, remove the three screws securing the support plate (5, **Figure 50**) to the power head. Lift the support plate from the power head, then disconnect the retainer plate spring and remove the retainer plate (7).

11. To reassemble, place the retainer plate on the power head and reconnect the spring. Position the support plate over the retainer plate.

12. Apply OMC Nut Lock threadlocking adhesive (or equivalent) to the threads of the screws, then install and evenly tighten the screws to 48-60 in.-lb. (5.4-6.8 N•m).

13. Lightly lubricate the groove of the Delrin bearing ring (6, **Figure 50**) with outboard motor oil. Then fit the ring to the support plate.

14. Lubricate the crankcase boss that the sensor coil assembly pivots around with OMC Moly Lube (or equivalent).

15. Connect the throttle cable to the retainer plate. Rotate the Delrin bearing ring until both open ends gap around the throttle cable connection.

NOTE
The gap in the timer base bearing (Delrin ring) must be centered around the throttle cable connection when installing the sensor coil.

16. Compress the Delrin bearing ring and fit the sensor coil assembly over the ring and into position. Rotate the sensor coil (ignition plate) as necessary to align the screw holes.

17. Apply OMC Screw Lock threadlocking adhesive (or equivalent) to the threads of the three sensor coil screws, then install and evenly tighten the screws to 25-35 in.-lb. (2.8-4.0 N•m).

18. Coat the ignition coil's primary terminals with OMC Electrical (dielectric) Grease, then connect the power pack's orange/blue primary lead to the ignition coil's upper primary terminal and the orange/green primary lead to the

coil's lower primary terminal. Make sure both connectors are seated on the coil.

19. Reconnect the stop switch leads to the six-pin Packard connector. Connect the black/yellow lead to pin E and the black lead to pin B. Push each lead into position until it locks securely in place. If necessary bend each terminal's locking tab slightly upward to ensure a positive lock.

20. Reconnect the six-pin Packard connector to the ignition module. Secure the wiring harness to the engine with new tie-straps or the original clamps.

21. Install the flywheel as described in this chapter and install the rope starter as described in Chapter Twelve.

22. Reconnect the spark plug leads, then refer to Chapter Five and verify all synch and link adjustments.

Ignition Module Removal/Installation (3 and 4 hp Models)

1. Disconnect and ground the spark plug leads to the power head to prevent accidental starting.

2. Disconnect the six-pin Packard connector from the ignition module. See **Figure 51**.

3. Remove the two module mounting screws (and lockwashers), then remove the module from the power head.

4. Clean the module mounting surfaces with a wire brush or emery cloth to ensure a good ground connection with the power head.

5. Apply a light coat of OMC Gasket Sealing Compound to the threads of the module mounting screws. Position the module to the power head, then install the mounting screws

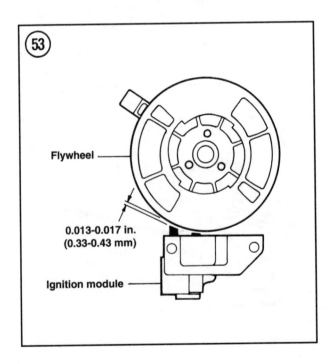

(53)

Flywheel

0.013-0.017 in.
(0.33-0.43 mm)

Ignition module

and lockwashers. Tighten the screws finger-tight at this time.

6. Using a suitable nonmetallic gauge, set the air gap between the ignition module and flywheel magnets to 0.013-0.017 in. (0.33-0.43 mm). See **Figure 53**.

7. When the correct air gap is established, tighten the module mounting screws to 60-84 in.-lb. (6.8-9.5 N•m). Recheck the air gap before proceeding. Readjust as necessary.

8. Reconnect the six-pin Packard connector to the ignition module.

9. Reconnect the spark plug leads when finished.

Ignition Coil Removal/Installation (3 and 4 hp Models)

1. Disconnect the spark plug leads from the spark plugs. Then disconnect the orange/blue and orange/green primary leads from the ignition coil (8, **Figure 50**) with a gentle twisting and pulling motion.

2. Loosen the two coil mounting screws, carefully noting the orientation of the flat washers, fiber washers and star-type lockwashers. Then remove the screws, washers and the ignition coil.

3. To install, position screws and washers through the ignition coil, then position the assembly on the power head. Normal washer stack-up is fiber washer, ignition coil, flat washer, star lockwasher and screw. See **Figure 50**. Once washer stack-up on both screws is verified, tighten both mounting screws to 48-96 in.-lb. (5.4-10.9 N•m).

4. Apply a light coat OMC Electrical (dielectric) Grease to the spark plug lead boots and both primary lead's boots. Connect the orange/blue primary lead to the ignition coil's upper primary terminal and the orange/green lead to the coil's lower primary terminal. The upper spark plug lead must connect to the No. 1 cylinder (upper) spark plug and the lower lead to the No. 2 cylinder (lower) spark plug. Make sure all connections are firmly seated.

CD2 (CAPACITOR DISCHARGE TWO CYLINDER) (4 DELUXE, 6-48 HP, 18 AND 28 JET MODELS WITH ROPE START AND/OR 4 [OR 5] AMP CHARGING SYSTEM)

Description

This ignition system is used on the 4 Deluxe, 6-48 hp, 18 jet and 28 jet models that are rope start or equipped with a 4 or 5 amp unregulated charging system. This ignition system is not used on 40 and 50 hp models equipped with the 12 amp regulated charging system. Refer to Chapter Three for an operational block diagram, additional illus-

trations and a complete description of this ignition system and its features. Refer to the back of the manual for wiring diagrams.

The major components of this ignition system are the:

1. *Flywheel*—The flywheel contains two magnets along the inner surface of its outer diameter. The magnets provide power to the charge and sensor coils, as well as the AC lighting coil or 4 amp battery charging stator coil (if so equipped).

2. *Charge coil*—The charge coil windings provide the power pack with the voltage it needs to operate the ignition system.

3. *Power pack*—The power pack uses an internal rectifier to change the charge coil AC voltage to DC (direct current) voltage. The DC voltage is stored in a capacitor, until it is released by a SCR (silicon controlled rectifier). There is one SCR for each cylinder. Each SCR is controlled by a sensor coil lead.

NOTE
The power pack on 20-48 hp, 18 jet and 28 jet models is equipped with the S.L.O.W. and RPM limit programs described in Chapter Three.

4. *Sensor coil*—The sensor coil tells the power pack when to release the stored electricity in the capacitor to the appropriate ignition coil. Ignition timing is advanced and retarded by rotating the sensor coil (armature plate assembly) with a mechanical linkage.

5. *Ignition coils*—There is one set of ignition coil windings for each cylinder. The ignition coil transforms the relatively low voltage from the charge coil into voltage high enough (40,000 volts) to jump the spark plug gap. All models except the 4 Deluxe, 20-30 hp (two-cylinder) and 18 jet use a dual-potted ignition coil. Two sets of ignition coil windings are potted into one case, but are electrically separate. The 4 Deluxe, 20-30 hp and 18 jet use two separate ignition coils.

6. *Spark plugs*—There is one spark plug for each cylinder. Suppressor plugs are designed to reduce RFI (radio frequency interference) emissions that can cause interference with electrical accessories and the ignition system. Failure to use the recommended suppressor spark plug will cause the ignition system to operate erratically. See Chapter Three.

7. *Stop circuit*—The stop circuit is connected to one end of the capacitor in the power pack. Whenever the stop circuit is connected to ground, the capacitor is shorted out and the ignition system ceases to operate. The stop circuit is always the black/yellow lead.

8. *Engine temperature switch (9.9-15 hp [remote control models] and all 20-48 hp and 18-28 jet models)*—The engine temperature switch triggers the warning horn (if so

7

equipped) and the S.L.O.W. system (20-48 hp and 18-28 jet models). See Chapter Three.

Armature Plate Removal/Installation (CD2 Ignition [Rope Start and/or 4 or 5 Amp Charging System])

This procedure removes the armature (ignition) plate from the power head as an assembly, with all of the coils (charge, sensor and stator [if equipped]) or stator assembly still attached. The armature plate must be removed before any of these components can be replaced.

1. Disconnect and ground the spark plug leads to the power head to prevent accidental starting.
2A. *Electric start models*—Disconnect the negative battery cable.
2B. *Rope start models*—Remove the rope starter as described in Chapter Twelve.
3. Remove the flywheel as described in this chapter.
4. Disconnect the armature plate-to-power pack five-pin Amphenol connector. This connector contains brown, brown/yellow, white/black, black/white and black/yellow leads.
5. *Electric start models*—Disconnect the stator coil yellow, yellow/gray and yellow/blue leads from the terminal strip (4 amp models) or bullet connectors (5 amp models).
6. Remove the screws (**Figure 54**, typical) securing the armature plate to the retainer plate. Then remove any clamps or tie-straps securing the armature plate electrical leads to the power head and lift the armature plate assembly from the power head.

> *NOTE*
> *To prevent damage to the spark control linkage (and armature plate) when disconnecting and connecting ball sockets, use suitable tools such as ball socket remover (part No. 342226) and ball socket installer (part No. 342225).*

7. If necessary, remove the four support plate mounting screws (**Figure 55**). Disconnect the spark control linkage from the retainer plate, then remove the support plate and retainer plate from the power head. Remove the Delrin bearing ring from the support plate.
8. To install the ignition plate assembly, begin by placing the retainer plate onto the power head and connecting the spark control linkage.
9. Lightly lubricate the groove of the Delrin bearing ring with OMC Moly Lube. Then fit the ring to the support plate.
10. Lubricate the crankcase boss (that the armature plate assembly pivots around) with OMC Moly Lube. Then

position the support plate over the retainer plate. Rotate the support ring to align the screw holes.

11. Apply OMC Nut Lock threadlocking adhesive (or equivalent) to the threads of the four support plate screws. Then install and evenly tighten the screws to 48-60 in.-lb. (5.4-6.8 N·m).

12. Compress the Delrin ring with a pair of needlenose pliers inserted into the notches near each end of the ring.

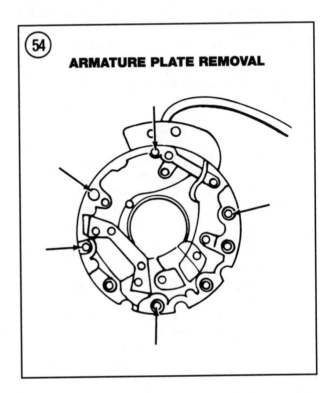

54

ARMATURE PLATE REMOVAL

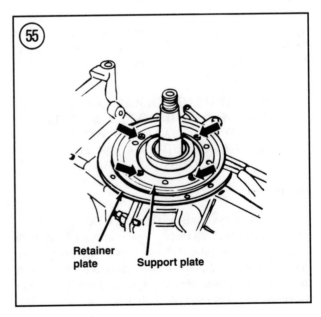

55

Retainer plate   **Support plate**

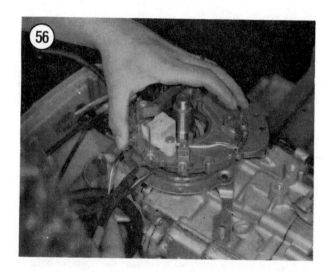

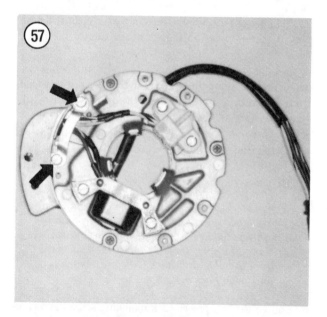

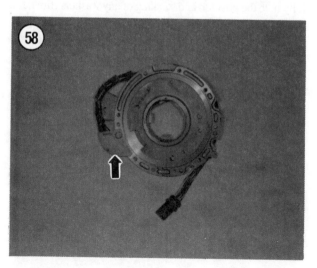

7

Carefully install the armature plate assembly over the crankshaft and seat it over the Delrin ring. See **Figure 56**.

13. Rotate the armature plate to align its screw holes with the retainer plate. Then apply OMC Nut Lock threadlocking adhesive (or equivalent) to the threads of the armature plate mounting screws.

14. Install the screws and evenly tighten hand tight. Inspect the armature plate and make sure the retainer plate is pulled up flush to the armature plate all the way around the plate. Also, make sure the throttle linkage rotates the armature plate freely. Correct any problems found.

15. Once the retainer plate is pulled flush to the armature plate, evenly tighten the screws to 25-35 in.-lb. (2.8-4.0 N•m).

16. Reconnect the five-pin Amphenol connector. On electric start models, reconnect the stator coil yellow, yellow/gray and yellow/blue leads to the terminal strip or bullet connectors.

17. Secure all electrical leads with new tie-straps or the original clamps. The armature plate must be free to rotate from its idle stop to its wide-open throttle stop. Adjust the harness as necessary.

18. Install the flywheel as described previously in this chapter.

19A. *Electric start models*—Reconnect the negative battery cable.

19B. *Rope start models*—Install the rope starter as described in Chapter Twelve.

20. Refer to Chapter Five and verify all synch and link adjustments.

Charge Coil, Sensor Coil and/or Stator Coil Removal/Installation (CD2 Ignition [Rope Start/4 or Amp])

On 9.9 and 15 hp electric start models (equipped with the 5 amp alternator), the sensor, charge and stator coils are all integrated into one assembly.

On 9.9 and 15 hp rope start (and all other rope start or 4 amp models), the coils (sensor, charge and stator [if equipped]) are each individually serviced.

1. Remove the armature (ignition) plate as described in the previous section.

2. Remove the two screws holding the upper wire clamp in place. See **Figure 57**.

3. Invert the armature plate and remove the lower wire clamp (cover plate). See **Figure 58**.

4A. *Rope start or 4 amp models*—Remove the two screws securing the sensor and/or charge coil (and/or three screws securing the stator coil).

4B. *5 amp models*—Remove the three screws securing the stator assembly to the armature plate.

5. The leads of the component(s) being replaced must be removed from the terminal body in order to pull the leads through the armature plate opening. Remove the appropriate leads and terminals from the five-pin Amphenol connector as described in *Electrical Connector Servicing* in this chapter.

6. Pull the leads of the defective coil(s) or the stator assembly from the spiral wrap insulation sleeve.

7. Remove the defective coil(s) or stator assembly from the armature plate.

8. Coat the threads of the coil (or stator assembly) mounting screws with OMC Ultra Lock threadlocking adhesive (or equivalent).

9. To install the coil(s) or stator assembly, position the coil(s) or stator assembly to the armature plate. Install the mounting screws finger-tight at this time. Carefully route the leads through the recess in the plate, making sure that none of the leads are twisted or wrapped around each other.

CAUTION
Make sure all wires routed through the upper clamp and lower clamp plate are not twisted or wrapped around each other. The wires must pass through the plate and clamp in one single layer.

10. Verify correct lead routing, then install the upper clamp (**Figure 57**) and lower clamp plate (**Figure 58**). Coat each clamp screw threads with OMC Nut Lock threadlocking adhesive (or equivalent). Tighten all screws securely. Then insert all armature plate leads into the spiral wrap insulation sleeve.

NOTE
The outer edges of each coil (charge, sensor or stator ([if equipped]) or the stator assembly, must be flush with the vertical machined surfaces on each armature plate mounting boss. This ensures the proper clearance between each component and the flywheel magnets. Coil Locating Ring (part No. 334994) will greatly simplify this process.

11. Place the coil locating ring (part No. 334994) over the machined bosses on the armature plate. See D, **Figure 59**. While holding the locating ring firmly in place, push each coil (A, B, and C) outward against the ring, then tighten each coil's mounting screws to 15-22 in.-lb. (1.7-2.5 N•m) while the coil is being held against the ring. If installing a stator assembly, make sure the stator assembly is centered in the coil locating ring (or centered on all of the mounting bosses).

12. Install the armature plate as described in this chapter.

13. Refer to Chapter Five and verify all synch and link adjustments.

**Power Pack Removal/Installation
(CD2 Ignition [Rope Start/4 Amp])**

The power pack is mounted on the starboard side of the power head on 4 Deluxe, 6 and 8 hp models. The power pack is mounted to the starboard side of the cylinder head on 9.9 and 15 hp models or the port side of the cylinder head on 20-30 hp (two-cylinder) and 18 jet models. On 40 hp models (rope start or 4 amp charging system), the power pack is mounted behind the electrical component access cover on the starboard side of the power head. On 48 Special models, the power pack is mounted to the electrical bracket on the starboard side of the power head.

1. Disconnect and ground the spark plug leads to the power head to prevent accidental starting.

2. *Electric start models*—Disconnect the negative battery cable.

3. *40 hp (rope start/4 amp)*—Remove the electrical component access cover on the starboard side of the power head.

4. Disconnect the power pack's five-pin Amphenol connector and the orange/blue and orange/green primary leads from the ignition coil(s). Remove the primary leads with a gentle twisting and pulling motion.

5. *20-48 hp, 18 jet and 28 jet*—Disconnect the power pack's tan lead at its bullet connector.

NOTE
The power pack on 4 Deluxe models is mounted on two spacers. The spacers are machined to allow the throttle cable and throttle linkage to be mounted over them. Carefully note the position of the spacers, throttle cable and linkage before removing the power pack mounting screws.

6. Loosen the two power pack mounting screws and carefully note the position and stacking of any washers (fiber, flat or star) between the power head and power pack, and power pack and screw heads. Also note the position of the power

pack ground (black) lead. On 4 Deluxe models, note the position of the spacers, throttle cable and throttle linkage.

7. Remove any clamps or tie-straps securing any of the power pack leads. If the power pack ground (black) lead is secured with a separate screw (and star washer), remove it at this time. Then remove the two screws, washers and the power pack.

8. To install the power pack, coat the threads of the mounting screws with OMC Nut Lock threadlocking adhesive (or equivalent). Then install the screws through the power pack with the washers stacked (or spacers positioned) as noted on disassembly. Make sure the ground lead is secured by a mounting screw or a separate screw (and star washer) as noted on disassembly. On 4 Deluxe models, make sure the throttle cable and throttle linkage is correctly positioned.

9. Position the assembly on the engine and thread the screws in finger-tight. Again verify the washer stack-up and that the ground lead is secured as noted during disassembly. Then tighten the mounting screws to 60-84 in.-lb. (6.8-9.5 N•m). If equipped with a separate ground screw, tighten it to 60-84 in.-lb. (6.8-9.5 N•m).

10. Reconnect the five-pin Amphenol connector and on 20-48 hp and 18-28 jet models, reconnect the power pack's tan lead to the tan/red or tan/blue temperature switch lead.

11. Coat the ignition coil(s) primary terminals with OMC Electrical (dielectric) Grease, then connect the orange/blue lead to the upper primary terminal and the orange/green lead to the lower primary terminal. Make sure the connectors are firmly seated to the coil(s).

12. *40 hp (rope start/4 amp)*—Reinstall the electrical component access cover.

13. *Electrical start models*—Reconnect the negative battery cable.

14. Reconnect the spark plug leads when finished.

15. Refer to Chapter Five and verify all synch and link adjustments.

Ignition Coil Removal/Installation (CD2 Ignition [Rope Start/4 Amp])

The ignition coil on 6-15, 40 and 48 hp and 28 jet models is two separate windings encased in a single housing. While potted together, the windings are electrically separate. Always treat this type of coil as two separate coils. The ground straps are secured by the coil mounting screws.

The 4 Deluxe, 20-30 hp (two-cylinder) and 18 jet models use two conventional separate coils. While the following procedure covers removal of both coils, they may be removed and installed separately.

1. *Electric start models*—Disconnect the negative battery cable.

2. Disconnect the spark plug leads from the spark plugs.

3. Disconnect the power pack's primary leads from the coil(s) with a gentle twisting and pulling motion.

4. Loosen the coil(s) mounting screws and note the stack-up of washers on each screw. A minimum of one flat washer and one star washer (on each screw) are used on all models, while fiber washers are used on 4 Deluxe, 6-30 hp and 18 jet models. On these models, the stop switch ground (black) is connected to a coil mounting screw (except remote control models).

5. Remove the screws, washers and coil(s).

6. To install the coils, begin by coating the screw threads with OMC Nut Lock threadlocking adhesive (or equivalent). Then install the screws and washers to the coil(s) as noted on disassembly, or as follows:

  a. *4 Deluxe*—The stack-up must be: fiber washer, coil, flat washer, star washer and screw. The stop switch ground lead is attached to the starboard coil's lower mounting screw, between the star and flat washers.

  b. *6 and 8 hp*—The fiber washers must be positioned between the ground straps and the coil body on the power head side. Then position the star washers between the screw heads and the outer ground straps. Finally, position the stop switch ground lead between the star washer and ground strap on the upper screw.

  c. *9.9 and 15 hp*—Note that fiber washers must be positioned between the coil body and the coil's metal (ground) straps as shown in **Figure 60** and that the

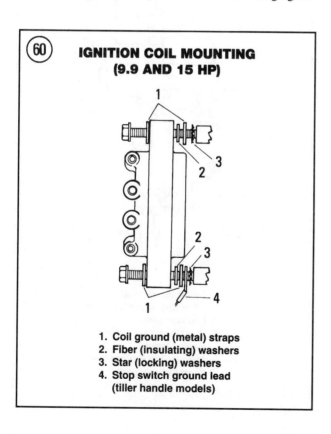

⑥⓪ IGNITION COIL MOUNTING (9.9 AND 15 HP)

1. Coil ground (metal) straps
2. Fiber (insulating) washers
3. Star (locking) washers
4. Stop switch ground lead (tiller handle models)

7

stop switch ground lead is attached to the lower mounting screw, between the coil ground strap and star washer.

d. *20-30 hp (two-cylinder) and 18 jet*—Position all washers, ground straps and the stop switch ground lead (tiller handle models) as shown in **Figure 61**. Note that each coil's ground strap must directly contact the power head and the fiber washers must be positioned between the ground strap and coil body on the power head side (as shown).

e. *40-48 hp and 28 jet*—The stack-up must be: coil, flat washer, star washer and screw.

7. Position the assembly on the power head and tighten the screws finger-tight. Recheck the washer stack-up, clamp position and stop switch ground lead position (as applicable). Then tighten the screws to 48-96 in.-lb. (5.4-10.9 N•m).

8. Coat the screw heads, ground straps, stop switch terminal (if equipped) and all other exposed washers with OMC Black Neoprene Dip.

9. Coat the ignition coil(s) primary terminals with OMC Electrical (dielectric) Grease, then connect the orange/blue lead to the upper primary terminal and the orange/green lead to the lower primary terminal. Make sure the connectors are firmly seated to the coil(s).

10. Coat the ribbed portion of each spark plug's insulator with OMC Electrical (dielectric) Grease. Then connect the spark plug leads to the spark plugs. The upper spark plug lead must connect to the No. 1 cylinder (upper) spark plug and the lower lead to the No. 2 cylinder (lower) spark plug. Make sure all connections are firmly seated.

CD2/CD3 (CAPACITOR DISCHARGE TWO/THREE CYLINDER) IGNITION (40-70 HP AND 35 JET MODELS WITH 12 AMP REGULATED CHARGING SYSTEM)

Description

This ignition system is used on 40-70 hp (two- and three-cylinder) and 35 jet models equipped with the 12 amp regulated charging system. It is not used on 40-50 hp (two-cylinder) models equipped with the 4 amp unregulated charging system. The 12 amp charging system can be easily identified by the presence of the large, finned (air-cooled) rectifier/regulator. Refer to Chapter Three for complete operational descriptions, additional illustrations and all troubleshooting procedures. Refer to the end of the book for wiring diagrams.

The major components are the:

1. *Flywheel*—The flywheel contains magnets along the inner surface of its outer diameter and around the center hub. The outer magnets provide power to the charge and power coils, as well as the 12 amp stator coil windings. The inner magnets provide power to the sensor coils.

2. *Charge coil*—The charge coil windings provide the power pack with the voltage it needs to operate the ignition system. Charge coil voltage output is AC voltage and must be measured with a PRV (peak reading voltmeter). Charge coil failure will always affect both cylinders. The charge coil is potted into the stator assembly along with the alternator stator coils and the power coil.

3. *Power pack*—The power pack stores the electricity from the charge coil until the sensor coil tells it to send the

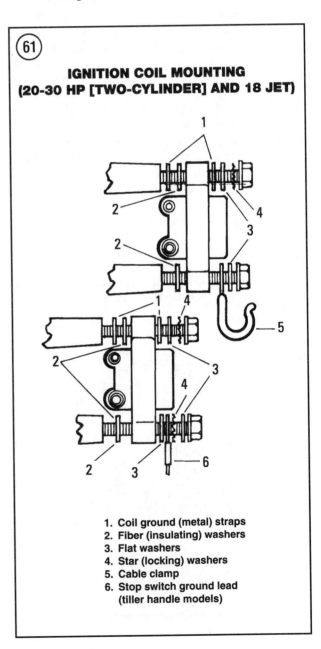

IGNITION COIL MOUNTING (20-30 HP [TWO-CYLINDER] AND 18 JET)

1. Coil ground (metal) straps
2. Fiber (insulating) washers
3. Flat washers
4. Star (locking) washers
5. Cable clamp
6. Stop switch ground lead (tiller handle models)

electricity to the ignition coils. The power pack uses an internal rectifier to change the charge coil AC voltage to DC (direct current) voltage. The DC voltage is stored in a capacitor (an electrical storage tank), until it is released by an SCR (silicon controlled rectifier). There is one SCR for each cylinder. Each SCR is controlled by a sensor coil lead.

The power pack is equipped with the S.L.O.W. and RPM limit programs described in Chapter Three. The three-cylinder models are also equipped with the QuikStart program (Chapter Three).

The power pack is stamped with the programmed RPM limit and other information. For example, if the power pack is stamped CD2SL/6700, it is a CD2 power pack with S.L.O.W. (stamped S) and RPM limit (stamped L/6700). Use this information to determine if the correct power pack is installed on your engine.

4. *Sensor coil*—The sensor coil tells the power pack when to release the stored electricity in the capacitor to the appropriate ignition coil.

   a. *Two-cylinder models*—The sensor coil assembly (timer base) uses two separate windings connected by a common white (return) lead. The blue lead triggers the No. 1 cylinder and the green lead triggers the No. 2 cylinder. The blue and green leads are connected to the SCRs in the power pack.

   b. *Three-cylinder models*—The sensor coil assembly (timer base) on these models uses three windings for normal operation (and three for QuikStart operation), connected by a common white (return) lead. The blue lead triggers the No. 1 cylinder, the purple lead triggers the No. 2 cylinder. The green lead triggers the No. 3 cylinder. The blue, purple and green leads are connected to the SCRs in the power pack.

A fifth timer base lead (black/white) is used by the power pack to internally switch the timer base over to the Quik-Start set of sensor coil windings. When the power pack sends the correct signal through the black/white lead, electronic circuits in the timer base switch operation to the advanced sensor coil windings.

5. *Ignition coils*—There is one set of ignition coil windings for each cylinder. The ignition coil transforms the relatively low voltage from the charge coil into voltage high enough (40,000 volts) to jump the spark plug gap and ignite the air/fuel mixture.

   a. Two-cylinder models use a dual-potted ignition coil. Two sets of ignition coil windings are potted into one case but are electrically separate and function independently from each other.

   b. Three-cylinder models use three separate conventional ignition coils.

6. *Spark plugs*—There is one spark plug for each cylinder. Failure to use the recommended suppressor spark plug will cause the ignition system to operate erratically.

7. *Stop circuit*—The stop circuit is connected to one end of the capacitor in the power pack. Whenever the stop circuit is connected to ground the ignition system will cease to operate. The stop circuit is always the black/yellow lead. Tiller handle (electric start models) and all remote control models use an ignition (key) switch.

8. *Engine temperature switch*—The engine temperature switch triggers the warning system and the S.L.O.W. system. On three-cylinder models, the switch also triggers the QuikStart program. See Chapter Three.

9. *Power coil*—The power coil provides the electricity the power pack needs to operate the S.L.O.W. system. On three-cylinder models, the power coil also powers the QuikStart system. The power coil is potted in the stator assembly along with the charge coil and alternator stator coils. The power coil windings are connected to the power pack with two leads (orange and orange/black).

Stator Assembly Removal/Installation (CD2/3 [12 Amp])

Refer to **Figure 62**, typical for this procedure.

1. Disconnect and ground the spark plug leads to the power head to prevent accidental starting.
2. Disconnect the negative battery cable.
3. Remove the flywheel as described in this chapter.
4. Disconnect the stator yellow and yellow/gray leads from the terminal strip. Reinstall the screws to retain the engine harness leads.

> *NOTE*
> *On three-cylinder models, it is necessary to loosen the power pack mounting screws to gain access to the connector in the following step. Make sure the power pack mounting screws (and its ground lead) are securely tightened after installation.*

5. Disconnect the stator's five-pin Amphenol connector. This connector contains brown, brown/yellow, orange, orange/black and black/yellow leads.
6. Remove the black/yellow lead and terminal from pin E of the stator side of the five-pin Amphenol connector. Refer to *Electrical Connector Servicing* near the end of this chapter.
7. Remove the three stator mounting screws. Then remove any tie-straps or clamps securing the stator harness to the power head or other leads.
8. Lift the stator assembly from the power head.
9. To install the stator, begin by removing any corrosion, varnish residue or other debris from the crankcase head's

7

mating surfaces. The stator must positively seat on the crankcase head to prevent it from vibrating loose under operation.

10. Clean the stator mounting screws using OMC Locquic Primer and allow to air dry. Then apply OMC Nut Lock threadlocking adhesive (or equivalent) to the threads of the screws.

11. Install the stator assembly, align the screw holes and make sure the stator has seated to the crankcase head. Install and evenly tighten the three mounting screws to 120-144 in.-lb. (13.6-16.3 N•m).

12. Connect the stator yellow and yellow/gray leads to the terminal strip. Tighten the connections securely, then coat the connections with OMC Black Neoprene Dip.

13. Install the black/yellow lead and terminal into the five-pin Amphenol connector, pin E. Refer to *Electrical Connector Service*, near the end of this chapter. Then connect the five-pin Amphenol connector to its power pack mate.

14. Verify the correct routing of all leads. Secure the leads with new tie-straps or the original clamps. On three-cylinder models, make sure the power pack mounting screws and ground lead have been re-tightened to 60-84 in.-lb. (6.8-9.5 N•m).

15. Install the flywheel as described in this chapter. Then reconnect the negative battery cable and the spark plug leads.

16. Refer to Chapter Five and verify all synch and link adjustments.

Sensor Coil (Timer Base) Removal/Installation (CD2/3 [12 Amp])

Refer to **Figure 62**, typical for this procedure.
1. Remove the stator assembly as described in this chapter.

NOTE
On three-cylinder models, it is necessary to loosen the power pack mounting screws to gain access to the connector in the following step. Make sure the power pack mounting screws (and its ground lead) are securely tightened after installation.

2A. *Two-cylinder models*—Disconnect the sensor coil (timer base) three-pin Amphenol connector. This connector has blue, green and white leads.

2B. *Three-cylinder models*—Disconnect the sensor coil (timer base) five-pin Amphenol connector. This connector has blue, purple, green, white and black/white leads.

NOTE
To prevent damage to the spark control linkage (and timer base) when disconnecting

and connecting ball sockets, use suitable tools such as ball socket remover (part No. 342226) and ball socket installer (part No. 342225).

3. Disconnect the spark control linkage from the timer base assembly.

4. Remove the three screws securing the three timer base retaining clips. Remove the three clips, then remove any clamps or tie-straps securing the timer base leads to the power head or other harnesses.

5A. *Two-cylinder models*—Lift the timer base from the power head. Then remove the retainer ring from the timer base groove. If so desired, remove the three screws secur-

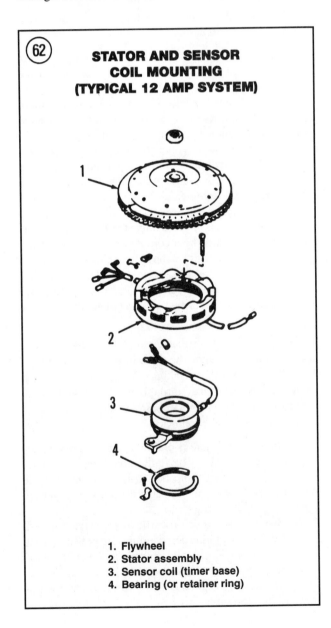

62 **STATOR AND SENSOR COIL MOUNTING (TYPICAL 12 AMP SYSTEM)**

1. Flywheel
2. Stator assembly
3. Sensor coil (timer base)
4. Bearing (or retainer ring)

ing the timer base adaptor to the power head. Then remove the adaptor.

5B. *Three-cylinder models*—Lift the timer base from the power head. Then remove the plastic bearing ring from the timer base.

6. Thoroughly clean the crankcase head and timer base bearing surfaces. Make sure the bearing surfaces are completely free of metal chips, corrosion or other contamination. On two-cylinder models, clean the adaptor base (if removed).

7. *Two-cylinder models*—If removed, install the adaptor base with the relieved side facing starboard. Coat the screw threads with OMC Nut Lock threadlocking adhesive (or equivalent), then install and evenly tighten the screws to 48-60 in.-lb. (5.4-6.8 N•m).

8. Lubricate the plastic bearing ring (or retainer ring) with outboard motor lubricant. Then coat the timer base groove, and the crankcase boss or timer base adaptor (that the timer base rotates around) with OMC Moly Lube. Finally, install the ring into the timer base's groove.

9A. *Two-cylinder models*—Rotate the open ends of the retainer ring until they are just in front of the timer base's linkage connector arm. Compress the open ends with needlenose pliers as you guide the base into position. The linkage arm must face starboard when installed. Make sure the base is seated into the adaptor and is not caught on the retainer ring.

9B. *Three-cylinder models*—Compress the plastic bearing ring while guiding the timer base into position on the power head. The ring must seat into the crankcase recess.

10. Apply OMC Nut Lock threadlocking adhesive to the three timer base retainer screws. Then position the clips and install the screws. Tighten the screws to 25-35 in.-lb. (2.8-4.0 N•m). Make sure the timer base rotates smoothly when finished. Correct any problems found.

11. Reconnect the spark control linkage to the timer base.

12A. *Two-cylinder models*—Connect the sensor coil (timer base) three-pin Amphenol connector to its power pack mate.

12B. *Three-cylinder models*—Connect the sensor coil (timer base) five-pin Amphenol connector to its power pack mate. Make sure the power pack mounting screws and ground lead have been re-tightened to 60-84 in.-lb. (6.8-9.5 N•m).

13. Install the stator assembly as described previously in this chapter.

Power Pack Removal/Installation (CD2/3 [12 Amp])

On two-cylinder models, the power pack is mounted low on the starboard side of the engine, beneath the ignition coil and voltage regulator. Removal of the starboard split lower cowl will allow easier access to the mounting screws and connectors.

On three-cylinder models, the power pack mounting screws (A and B, **Figure 63**) must be loosened to gain access to the Amphenol connector partially covered by the pack (C).

1. Disconnect and ground the spark plug leads to the power head to prevent accidental starting.

2. Disconnect the negative battery cable.

3. *Two-cylinder models*—Remove the starboard split lower cowl to gain better access to the power pack connectors and mounting screws. There are three internal screws (one front, two rear) and one external screw (just behind the steering arm).

4A. *Two-cylinder models*—Disconnect the power pack's five-pin and three-pin Amphenol connectors, and the orange/blue and orange/green primary leads from the ignition coil. Remove the primary leads with a gentle twisting and pulling motion.

4B. *Three-cylinder models*—Loosen the power pack mounting screws (A and B, **Figure 63**), then disconnect the power pack's two five-pin Amphenol connectors (C and D), and the orange/blue, orange/purple and orange/green primary leads from the ignition coils. Remove the primary leads with a gentle twisting and pulling motion.

5A. *Two-cylinder models*—Disconnect the power pack's tan lead at its bullet connector.

5B. *Three-cylinder (1995 [EO]) models*—Disconnect the power pack's tan and white/black leads at their bullet connectors (closest to the pack). Then remove the power pack's yellow/red lead from the like-colored small terminal of the starter solenoid.

5C. *Three-cylinder (1996-2003) models*—Disconnect the power pack's three-pin Amphenol connector. This connector has white/black, tan and yellow/red leads.

6. Loosen the two power pack mounting screws and carefully note the position and stacking of any washers (fiber, flat or star) between the power head and power pack, and power pack and screw heads. Also note the position of the power pack ground (black) lead. See **Figure 63** (three-cylinder models).

7. Remove any clamps or tie-straps securing any of the power pack leads. If the power pack ground (black) lead is secured with a separate screw (and star washer), remove it at this time. Then remove the two screws, washers and the power pack.

8A. *Two-cylinder models*—To install the power pack, position the pack to the power head and connect the power pack's five-pin and three-pin Amphenol connectors to their stator and timer base mates.

8B. *Three-cylinder models*—To install the power pack, position the pack to the power head and connect the power pack's five-pin Amphenol connectors to their stator and timer base mates. Then seat the connectors in their mounting brackets. See **Figure 63**.

9. Coat the threads of the mounting screws with OMC Nut Lock threadlocking adhesive (or equivalent). Then install the screws through the power pack with the washers stacked as noted on disassembly. Make sure the ground lead is secured by a mounting screw or a separate screw (and star washer) as noted on disassembly. See A, **Figure 63** (three-cylinder models). Thread the screws into the power head finger-tight.

10. Verify the washer stack-up and that the ground lead is secured as noted during disassembly. Then tighten the mounting screws to 60-84 in.-lb. (6.8-9.5 N•m). If equipped with a separate ground screw, tighten it to 60-84 in.-lb. (6.8-9.5 N•m).

11A. *Two-cylinder models*—Connect the power pack's tan lead to its engine harness mate.

11B. *Three-cylinder (1995 [EO]) models*—Connect the power pack's tan and white/black leads to their engine harness mates. Then install the power pack's yellow/red lead to the like-colored small terminal of the starter solenoid. Tighten the terminal nut securely, then coat the connection with OMC Black Neoprene Dip.

11C. *Three-cylinder (1996-2003) models*—Connect the power pack's three-pin Amphenol connector to its engine harness mate.

12A. *Two-cylinder models*—Coat the ignition coil primary terminals with OMC Electrical (dielectric) Grease, then connect the orange/blue lead to the upper primary terminal and the orange/green lead to the lower primary terminal. Make sure the connectors are firmly seated to the coil(s).

12B. *Three-cylinder models*—Coat the ignition coil primary terminals with OMC Electrical (dielectric) Grease, then connect the orange/blue lead to the top coil's primary terminal, the orange/purple lead to the middle coil's termi-

nal and the orange/green lead to the bottom coil's terminal. Make sure all connectors are firmly seated to the coil(s).

13. *Two-cylinder models*—Reinstall the starboard lower split cowl. Tighten the four screws securely.

14. Reconnect the negative battery cable and the spark plug leads when finished.

15. Refer to Chapter Five and verify all synch and link adjustments.

Ignition Coil Removal/Installation (CD2/3 [12 Amp])

1. Disconnect the negative battery cable, then disconnect the spark plug leads from the spark plugs.

2. Disconnect the power pack's primary leads from the coil(s) with a gentle twisting and pulling motion.

3. Remove the coil(s) mounting screws and washer(s), then remove the coil(s).

4. To install the coils, begin by coating the screw threads with OMC Nut Lock threadlocking adhesive (or equivalent). Then install the screws and washers to the coil(s) as follows:

    a. *Two-cylinder models*—The stack-up must be: coil, flat washer, star washer and screw.

    b. *Three-cylinder models*—Each coil's ground (metal) strap must face up. The top screw's stack-up must be coil, flat washer, star washer and screw. The bottom screws stack-up must be coil, flat washer and screw.

5. Position the assembly to the power head and tighten the screws finger-tight. Recheck the washer stack-up, then tighten the screws to 48-96 in.-lb. (5.4-10.9 N•m).

6. Coat the screw heads, washers and ground straps with OMC Black Neoprene Dip.

7A. *Two-cylinder models*—Coat the ignition coil primary terminals with OMC Electrical (dielectric) Grease, then connect the orange/blue lead to the upper primary terminal and the orange/green lead to the lower primary terminal. Make sure the connectors are firmly seated to the coil(s).

7B. *Three-cylinder models*—Coat the ignition coil primary terminals with OMC Electrical (dielectric) Grease, then connect the orange/blue lead to the top coil's primary terminal, the orange/purple lead to the middle coil's terminal and the orange/green lead to the bottom coil's terminal. Make sure all connectors are firmly seated to the coil(s).

8A. *Two-cylinder models*—Coat the ribbed portion of each spark plug's insulator with OMC Electrical (dielectric) Grease, then connect the spark plug leads to the spark plugs. The upper spark plug lead must connect to the No. 1 cylinder (upper) spark plug and the lower lead to the No. 2 cylinder (lower) spark plug. Make sure all connections are firmly seated.

8B. *Three-cylinder models*—Coat the ribbed portion of each spark plug's insulator with OMC Electrical (dielectric) Grease, then connect the spark plug leads to the spark plugs. The upper spark plug lead must connect to the No. 1 cylinder (upper) spark plug, the middle lead to the No. 2 cylinder (center) spark plug and the lower lead to the No. 3 cylinder (lower) spark plug. Make sure all connections are firmly seated.

OIS2000 IGNITION SYSTEM (25 AND 35 HP [THREE-CYLINDER] MODELS)

Description

This ignition system is used on 25 and 35 hp (three-cylinder) models. Refer to Chapter Three for a complete operational description, additional illustrations and all troubleshooting procedures. Refer to the back of the manual for wiring diagrams.

The major components are the:

1. *Flywheel*—The flywheel contains magnets along the inner surface of its outer diameter. The magnets provide power to the charge and power coils, as well as the 12 amp stator coil windings. An encoder ring is secured to the center hub of the flywheel. The encoder ring works in conjunction with the optical sensor to replace the sensor coil (timer base) used on other OMC ignition systems. The encoder ring is constructed to pass windows and vanes through the optical sensor, providing the ignition module with crankshaft position (timing) and engine speed information.

2. *Charge coil*—The charge coil windings provide the ignition module with the voltage it ultimately sends to the ignition coils. The charge coil is potted into the stator assembly along with the alternator stator coils and the power coil.

3. *Power coil*—The power coil provides the electricity the ignition module needs to operate its electronic circuits, including the S.L.O.W. and QuikStart systems, and the optical sensor. The power coil is potted in the stator along with the charge coil and alternator stator coils.

4. *Ignition module (power pack)*—The ignition module uses an internal rectifier to change the charge coil AC voltage to DC (direct current) voltage. The DC voltage is stored in a capacitor, until it is released by a SCR (silicon controlled rectifier). There is one SCR for each cylinder. Each SCR is controlled by internal electronic circuits, based on optical sensor input.

The ignition module is also equipped with the QuikStart, S.L.O.W. and RPM limit programs described in Chapter Three.

5. *Optical sensor*—The optical sensor works in conjunction with the flywheel mounted encoder ring to tell the ignition module when to release the stored electricity in the capacitor to the appropriate ignition coil. The optical

sensor assembly actually contains two optical sensors. Ignition timing is advanced and retarded by rotating the optical sensor assembly (timer base) with a mechanical linkage.

6. *Ignition coils*—There is one ignition coil for each cylinder. The ignition coil transforms the relatively low voltage from the charge coil into voltage high enough (40,000 volts) to jump the spark plug gap.

7. *Spark plugs*—There is one spark plug for each cylinder. Suppressor plugs are designed to reduce RFI (radio frequency interference) emissions that can cause interference with electrical accessories and the ignition system. Failure to use the recommended suppressor spark plug will cause the ignition system to operate erratically.

8. *Stop circuit*—The stop circuit is connected to one end of the capacitor in the power pack. Whenever the stop circuit is connected to ground, the capacitor is shorted out and the ignition system ceases to operate. The stop circuit is always the black/yellow lead. Both tiller handle and remote control models use an ignition (key) switch.

9. *Engine temperature switch*—The engine temperature switch on these models triggers the warning system, the S.L.O.W. system and the QuickStart program. See Chapter Three.

Stator Assembly Removal/Installation (25 and 35 hp [Three-cylinder])

Refer to **Figure 64** for this procedure.

1. Disconnect and ground the spark plug leads to the power head to prevent accidental starting.

2. *Electric start models*—Disconnect the negative battery cable.

3. Remove the flywheel as described in this chapter.

4. Remove the air intake cover from the carburetors. Make sure the cover's drain hose is disconnected before completely removing the cover from the engine.

5A. *Rope start models*—Check to see if any leads are connected to the stator coil's large two-pin locking connector (yellow and yellow gray leads). If so, disconnect the leads from the two-pin connector (7, **Figure 64**).

5B. *Electric start models*—Disconnect the stator coil yellow and yellow/gray leads from their large two-pin locking connector (7, **Figure 64**), just above the voltage regulator.

6. Disconnect the four-pin Packard connector (8, **Figure 64**) from the ignition module.

7. Remove the three screws (5, **Figure 64**) securing the stator assembly to the power head. Then remove any tie-straps or clamps securing the stator harness to the power head or other leads.

8. Lift the stator assembly from the power head.

9. To install the stator, begin by removing any corrosion, varnish residue or other debris from the crankcase head's

mating surfaces. The stator must positively seat on the crankcase head to prevent it from vibrating loose under operation. It is not necessary to remove any varnish from the new stator.

10. Clean the stator mounting screws using OMC Locquic Primer and allow to air dry. Then apply OMC Nut Lock threadlocking adhesive to the threads of the screws.

11. Install the stator assembly, align the screw holes and make sure the stator has seated to the crankcase head. Install and evenly tighten the three mounting screws to 84-106 in.-lb. (9.5-12 N•m).

12. Connect the stator's large two-pin connector (yellow and yellow/gray leads) to its mate from the voltage regulator (or other leads on rope start models). Make sure the connectors lock together.

13. Connect the stator's four-pin Packard connector to the ignition module. Make sure the connector locks to the ignition module.

14. Verify the correct routing of all leads. Secure the leads with new tie-straps or the original clamps.

15. Install the flywheel as described in this Chapter. Then install the air intake cover. Make sure drain hose is reconnected.

16. *Electric start models*—Reconnect the negative battery cable.

17. Reconnect the spark plug leads, then Refer to Chapter Five and verify all synch and link adjustments.

Optical Sensor Removal/Installation (25 and 35 hp [Three-cylinder])

Refer to **Figure 64** for this procedure.

1. Remove the stator assembly as described in the previous section.

> *NOTE*
> *To prevent damage to the spark control linkage (and timer base) when disconnecting and connecting ball sockets, use suitable tools such as ball socket remover (part No. 342226) and ball socket installer (part No. 342225).*

2. Disconnect the spark control linkage from the sensor assembly.

3. Disconnect the sensor's five-pin Packard connector (9, **Figure 64**) from the ignition module.

4. Remove the three screws securing the sensor retainer ring (11, **Figure 64**) to the power head.

5. Remove any tie-straps or clamps securing the sensor harness to the power head or other leads.

6. Lift the sensor assembly from the power head.

7. Clean the sensor and power head mating surfaces and the retainer ring.

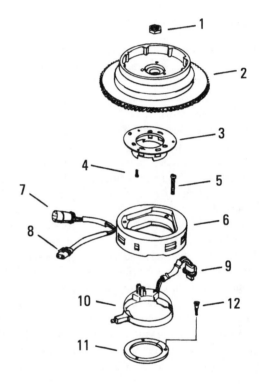

64

STATOR AND OPTICAL SENSOR MOUNTING (25 AND 35 HP [THREE-CYLINDER])

1. Flywheel nut
2. Flywheel
3. Encoder ring
4. Encoder screw
5. Stator screw
6. Stator assembly
7. Charging system connector
8. Ignition (4-pin Packard) connector
9. Ignition (5-pin Packard) connector
10. Optical sensor assembly
11. Sensor retainer ring
12. Screw

8. To install the sensor, begin by lightly lubricating the sensor-to-power head mating surfaces with outboard lubricant.

9. Position the retainer in the sensor assembly, then install the assembly to the power head.

10. Rotate the retainer ring to align the screw holes. Coat the screw threads with OMC Nut Lock threadlocking adhesive, then install and evenly tighten the retainer ring screws to 24-36 in.-lb. (2.7-4.1 N•m). Make sure the sensor can freely rotate. Correct any problems found.

11. Connect the sensor's five-pin Packard connector to the ignition module. Make sure the connector locks to the module.

12. Reconnect the spark control linkage to the sensor assembly.

13. Install the stator assembly as described previously in this chapter.

Ignition Module Removal/Installation (25 and 35 hp [Three-cylinder])

1. Disconnect and ground the spark plug leads to the power head to prevent accidental starting.

2. *Electric start models*—Disconnect the negative battery cable.

3. Disconnect the four- and five-pin Packard connectors from the top of the ignition module. See A and B, **Figure 65**.

4. Pull the Amphenol connectors from their holding clips on the side of the module. See **Figure 66**. Then separate the two and four-pin Amphenol connectors.

5. Remove the tan/black lead and terminal from pin B of the ignition module side of the two-pin Amphenol connector. Refer to *Electrical Connector Servicing* near the end of this chapter.

6. Remove the orange/blue, orange/purple and orange/green primary leads from the ignition coils. Remove the primary leads with a gentle twisting and pulling motion.

7. Note the orientation of the two module ground leads. The lower ground lead is secured by a separate screw (and star washer), and the upper ground lead is secured by the left center module mounting screw (and star washer). Remove the separate screw securing the module's lower ground (black) lead to the power head.

8. Remove the three screws (and any washers) securing the module to the power head and remove the module. Clean the mounting and ground screw bosses as necessary to ensure the ignition module will be properly grounded.

9. To install the module, coat the threads of the mounting (and separate ground) screws with OMC Nut Lock threadlocking adhesive. Position the upper ground lead to the module's center left mounting hole and place the screw (and star washer) through the hole as noted on disassembly.

10. Position the assembly to the engine and thread the screw in finger-tight. Then install the remaining two module screws. Evenly tighten all three screws to 84-106 in.-lb. (9.5-12 N•m).

11. Secure the module's lower ground lead to the power head using the separate screw and star washer as noted on disassembly. Tighten the screw to 84-106 in.-lb. (9.5-12 N•m).

12. Reconnect the four- and five-pin Packard connectors from the top of the ignition module. Make sure the connectors lock to the module. See A and B, **Figure 65**.

13. Install the tan/black lead and terminal into pin B of the ignition module side of the two-pin Amphenol connector. Refer to *Electrical Connector Servicing* near the end of this chapter.

14. Connect the module's two- and four-pin Amphenol connectors to their engine harness mates. Then push each

connector into their holding clips on the side of the module. See **Figure 66**.

15. Coat the ignition coil primary terminals with OMC Electrical (dielectric) Grease, then connect the orange/blue lead to the top coil's primary terminal, the orange/purple lead to the middle coil's terminal and the orange/green lead to the bottom coil's terminal. Make sure all connectors are firmly seated to the coil(s).

16. *Electric start models*—Reconnect the negative battery cable.

17. Connect the spark plug leads when finished, then refer to Chapter Five and verify all synch and link adjustments.

Ignition Coil Removal/Installation (25 and 35 hp [Three-cylinder])

These models use three separate coils unique to this engine. While the following procedure is written for removing all three coils, they may be removed and installed separately.

1. *Electric start models*—Disconnect the negative battery cable

2. Disconnect the spark plug leads from the spark plugs, then disconnect the ignition module's primary leads from the coil(s) with a gentle twisting and pulling motion.

3. Remove each coils mounting screw, flat washer and star (lock) washer, then remove each coil.

4. To install the coils, begin by coating the screw threads with OMC Nut Lock threadlocking adhesive. Then install a flat washer over each screw. Position each screw into each coil's mounting screw hole, then install the star washer over the screw and against the coil's ground (metal) strap. The stack-up must be: power head, star washer, coil, flat washer and screw.

5. Position each assembly to the power head and tighten the screw finger-tight. Recheck the washer stack-up, then tighten each coil's screw to 84-106 in.-lb. (9.5-12 N•m).

6. Coat the screw heads, washers and ground straps with OMC Black Neoprene Dip.

7. Coat the ignition coil primary terminals with OMC Electrical (dielectric) Grease, then connect the orange/blue lead to the top coil's primary terminal, the orange/purple lead to the middle coil's terminal and the orange/green lead to the bottom coil's terminal. Make sure all connectors are firmly seated to the coil(s).

8. Coat the ribbed portion of each spark plug's insulator with OMC Electrical (dielectric) Grease, then connect the spark plug leads to the spark plugs. The upper spark plug lead must connect to the No. 1 cylinder (upper) spark plug, the middle lead to the No. 2 cylinder (center) spark plug, and the lower lead to the No. 3 cylinder (lower) spark plug. Make sure all connections are firmly seated.

ELECTRICAL CONNECTOR SERVICE

Amphenol Connectors

Amphenol connectors have been widely used on Evinrude/Johnson engines since 1978. Amphenol connectors are identified by their round, dark rubber connector bodies. Often a wire locking clip (or wire bail) is used to keep the connector from vibrating apart. A disconnected Amphenol connector and its wire bail are shown in **Figure 67**. Connectors bodies are available in 1-6 pin configurations, with all configurations using the same male and

female connector pins; part No. 511469 (male) and part No. 581656 (female). Replacement connector body part numbers are listed in the manufacturer's parts catalog.

CAUTION
Always lubricate Amphenol connectors with isopropyl alcohol when connecting/disconnecting the bodies and/or replacing pins. The water resistant molded seals in the bodies will be irreparably damaged if no lubricant is used.

To separate the pin(s) from the body, a set of three special tools is required to prevent pin or body damage. The three tools are:

1. Insert tool part No. 322697, identified by its half-moon tip.
2. Male pin remover tool part No. 322698, identified by its round, hollow tip.
3. Female pin remover tool part No. 322699, identified by its round, solid tip.

Failure to use the recommended tools and lubricant will result in connector body damage and the connector will no longer be water resistant. Also, if the bodies are damaged, the pins will no longer be held in position and will tend to back out of the bodies as the connectors are joined. This will cause poor or erratic continuity, or no connection at all.

To replace the terminal pin(s) or connector body, refer to **Figure 68** and proceed as follows:

1. Remove the retaining clip (if so equipped).

2. Liberally lubricate the connector bodies mating line with isopropyl (rubbing) alcohol. Then carefully separate the halves. Apply additional lubricant if the connectors stick.

3. Lubricate the terminal pin to be removed with isopropyl alcohol at both ends of the connector cavity.

4. Hold the connector against the edge of a flat surface, allowing sufficient clearance for pin removal.

7

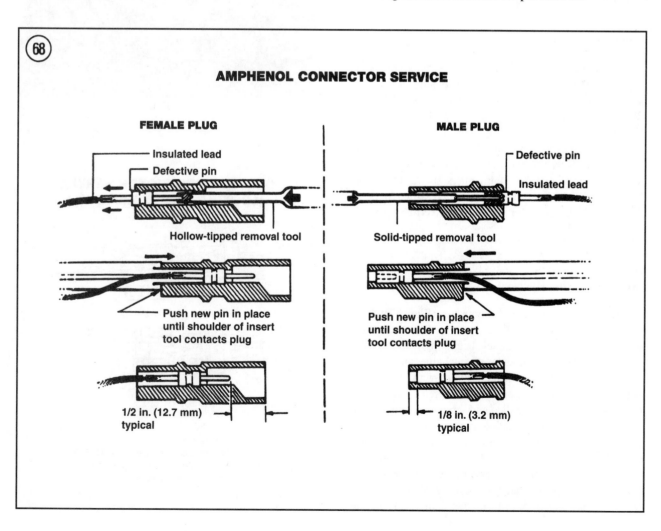

AMPHENOL CONNECTOR SERVICE

FEMALE PLUG — Insulated lead — Defective pin — Hollow-tipped removal tool — Push new pin in place until shoulder of insert tool contacts plug — 1/2 in. (12.7 mm) typical

MALE PLUG — Defective pin — Insulated lead — Solid-tipped removal tool — Push new pin in place until shoulder of insert tool contacts plug — 1/8 in. (3.2 mm) typical

5. Insert the proper removal tool into the connector end of the plug and carefully push the terminal pin from the plug. See **Figure 68**.

6. If the terminal pin (male or female) requires replacement, cut the lead as close to the pin as possible. Strip the lead back far enough to allow the new pin's crimping tabs to make complete contact with the wire strands. Do not nick or cut any of the wire strands.

7. Position the new pin to the lead and crimp it firmly with Amphenol crimping pliers (part No. 322696) or equivalent. A double roll crimp must be applied. Do not use a standard crimping pliers (such as Part No. 500906) for this operation.

8. Lubricate the connector cavity with rubbing alcohol.

9. Place the insert tool against the terminal pin's shoulder. Carefully guide the pin into the rear of the connector plug cavity and press it in place until the insert tool shoulder rests against the connector plug. Withdraw the insert tool.

10. Lubricate both connector bodies and connect the halves. Inspect the rear or each connector body to make sure the terminal pins did not back out. Then install the retaining clip (if so equipped).

Bullet Connectors

The bullet connector (**Figure 69**) is a common connector used widely in the marine industry. The bullet connectors used on Evinrude/Johnson engines will use vinyl sleeves with several internal sealing ribs to seal the sleeve to the lead as tightly as possible. Replacement male and female connectors, and their appropriate sleeves are listed in the manufacturer's parts catalog. The connectors are crimped in place with a standard crimping pliers, such as OMC part No. 500906. Make sure the correct vinyl sleeve (male or female) has been slid over the lead before crimping a new connector in place.

Deutsch Connectors
(Modular Wiring Harness)

OMC began using Deutsch connectors (**Figure 70**, typical) when the *Modular Wiring System (MWS)* was introduced on remote control models beginning with the 1996 (ED) model year. The modular wiring harness is designed to allow flexible, uncomplicated rigging with exceptional durability. These connectors are considered totally waterproof when correctly installed and serviced. Deutsch style connectors are easily identified by their hard plastic bodies, orange locking wedges and orange silicone elastomer seals. An external locking tab prevents the connectors from vibrating apart and must be manually released before the connectors can be separated. Each terminal pin is locked into the connector body with its own individual internal

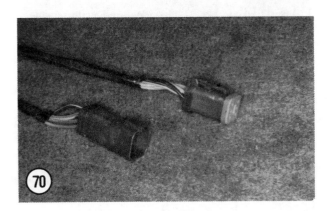

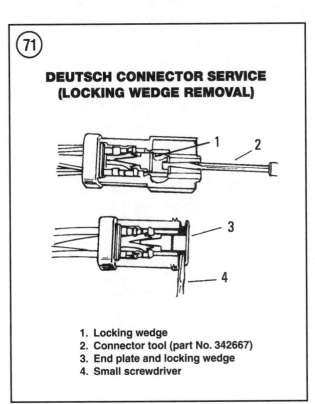

**DEUTSCH CONNECTOR SERVICE
(LOCKING WEDGE REMOVAL)**

1. Locking wedge
2. Connector tool (part No. 342667)
3. End plate and locking wedge
4. Small screwdriver

locking tab. Connectors bodies are available in 2-4, 6 and 8 pin configurations, with all configurations using the same male and female terminal pins, part No. 514679 (male) and part No. 514680 (female). Replacement connector body, locking wedge and seal part numbers are listed in the manufacturer's parts catalog.

CAUTION
Always lubricate the seals of Deutsch connectors with OMC Electrical Grease (QRD)

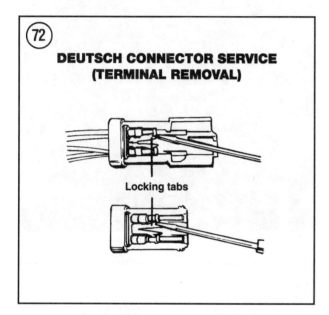

**DEUTSCH CONNECTOR SERVICE
(TERMINAL REMOVAL)**

Locking tabs

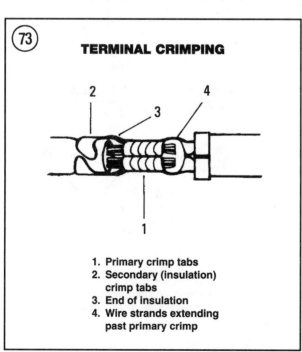

TERMINAL CRIMPING

1. Primary crimp tabs
2. Secondary (insulation) crimp tabs
3. End of insulation
4. Wire strands extending past primary crimp

when reconnecting the bodies and/or replacing the pins. If the locking wedge has been removed, the connector body cavity (for the wedge) must be filled with OMC Electrical Grease (QRD) to within 1/32 in. (0.8 mm) of the wedge to connector body mating surface.

To replace the terminal pins or connector body, proceed as follows:

1. Depress the locking latch and separate the connector.

2A. *Female body (male pins)*—Reach into the body with the hooked end of connector tool (part No. 342667) or equivalent, and pull the orange locking wedge from the body. See 1, **Figure 71**.

2B. *Male body (female pins)*—Carefully pry the orange end plate and locking wedge (3, **Figure 71**) from the end of the connector body with the flat end of connector tool (part No. 342667) or a small screwdriver (4, **Figure 71**).

3. Depress the internal locking tab (**Figure 72**) for the terminal pin (and lead) to be removed, then pull the lead (and terminal pin) from the rear of the connector body. Be careful not to damage the body's seal.

4. If the terminal pin (male or female) requires replacement, refer to **Figure 73** and proceed as follows:

   a. Cut the lead as close to the pin as possible, then strip the lead back 3/16 in. (4.8 mm). Do not nick or cut any of the wire strands.

   b. Using the OMC Amphenol crimping pliers (part No. 322696) or equivalent, position the terminal's primary tabs into the No. 18 notch of the pliers. Then position the wire strands into the terminal, making sure the wire strands extend past the primary tabs and the insulation is under secondary tabs.

   c. Crimp the terminal firmly, then inspect the crimp. All strands must be encapsulated in the crimp as shown in **Figure 73**. If not, remove the terminal and start over with a new terminal pin.

   d. If the primary crimp is satisfactory, position the secondary tabs in the No. 14-16 notch of the pliers and crimp the terminal firmly. Inspect the crimp. The secondary tabs must be folded over the insulation as shown in **Figure 73**. If not, remove the terminal and start over with a new terminal pin.

5. To install the terminal pin and lead, lubricate the pin with OMC Electrical (dielectric) Grease and insert the pin into the appropriate connector body socket. Push the pin and lead into the body until it locks in place. If the pin and lead do not lock in place, the connector body must be replaced.

6. Once all pins and leads have been installed, fill the locking wedge cavity with OMC Electrical Grease to a point approximately 1/32 in. (0.8 mm) below the internal ledge on female bodies or the end of the male body.

7

7. Inspect the male body's ribbed seal. Replace the seal if damaged. Then lubricate the seal ribs with OMC Electrical Grease. Align the connectors and push them together until the latch locks in place.

Packard Connectors

While the Packard connector is used extensively in the automotive industry, its use is somewhat limited on Evinrude/Johnson engines. This connector is only used to connect an engine harness directly to an electrical or ignition component and is not used to connect a harness to another.

> *CAUTION*
> *Always lubricate the seals of Packard connectors with OMC Electrical Grease (QRD) when reconnecting the bodies or replacing the pin(s), body or seal(s).*

There are two styles of Packard connector used on engines covered in this manual. The four- and five-pin Packard connectors are used on the 25 and 35 hp (three-cylinder) ignition module. The six-pin Packard connectors are used on the 3 and 4 hp (except 4 Deluxe) ignition module.

Four- and five-pin Packard connectors

This style is easily identified by a flat arrangement of the connector pins (in a straight row), the large U-shaped locking tab and the 3-ribbed replaceable seals; one sealing the leads to the body and the other sealing the body to the component. This connector is used in four- and five-pin configurations on the ignition module of the 25-35 hp (three-cylinder) engines as shown in **Figure 74**. This connector is of the *Pull-to-Lock* design.

To replace the body or the lead-to-body seal, all pins will have to be removed and cut from their leads. To do so, proceed as follows:

1. Carefully pry the lead-to-body seal out from the body at least 1 in. (25.4 mm). If the seal is nicked, cut or damaged, it will have to be replaced.

2. Unlock each terminal pin and lead by inserting a suitable terminal tool ([**Figure 75**] available from automotive tool suppliers) into the rear of the body until it releases the locking tab from the shoulder at the front of body. Then push the lead (and terminal pin) out the front of the connector body.

3. Cut the defective terminal pin from the lead as close to the pin as possible.

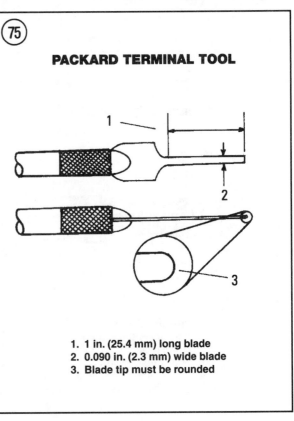

PACKARD TERMINAL TOOL

1. 1 in. (25.4 mm) long blade
2. 0.090 in. (2.3 mm) wide blade
3. Blade tip must be rounded

4. If changing the seal and/or connector body, note the position of each lead in the body, then pull the leads from the body and seal.

NOTE
Make sure all leads are routed through the new seal and/or connector body before crimping any new terminal pins to the leads.

5. If the leads were removed from the body and/or seal, lubricate the seal with OMC Electrical (dielectric) Grease

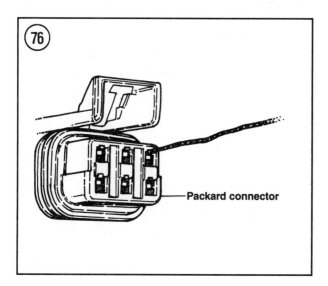

Packard connector

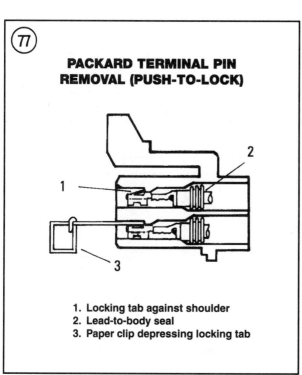

PACKARD TERMINAL PIN REMOVAL (PUSH-TO-LOCK)

1. **Locking tab against shoulder**
2. **Lead-to-body seal**
3. **Paper clip depressing locking tab**

and route the leads through the seal, then the connector body, in the positions noted during disassembly.

6. Strip the lead back far enough to allow the new pin's crimping tabs to make complete contact with the wire strands. Do not nick or cut any of the wire strands.

7. Using the OMC Amphenol crimping pliers (part No. 322696) or equivalent, position the terminal's primary tabs into the No. 18 notch of the pliers. Then position the wire strands into the terminal, making sure the wire strands extend past the primary tabs and the insulation is under secondary tabs.

8. Crimp the terminal firmly, then inspect the crimp. All strands must be encapsulated in the crimp as shown in **Figure 73**, typical. If not, remove the terminal and start over with a new terminal pin.

9. If the primary crimp is satisfactory, position the secondary tabs in the No. 14-16 notch of the pliers and crimp the terminal firmly. Inspect the crimp. The secondary tabs must be folded over the insulation as shown in **Figure 73**, typical. If not, remove the terminal and start over with a new terminal pin.

10. After crimping, inspect the locking tab on the terminal pin. If necessary, slightly bend the tab upwards to ensure a positive lock. Then pull each lead into the connector body until it locks in place. If any terminal pin will not lock in place (and the pin's locking tab is not damaged), the connector body's shoulder is rounded or damaged and the body must be replaced.

11. If the connector body-to-component seal is damaged, slide it from the body and discard it. Coat a new seal with OMC Electrical (dielectric) Grease and slide it over the connector body and against the body's shoulder.

Six-pin Packard connectors

This style of Packard connector is used on the ignition module of the 3 and 4 hp (except 4 Deluxe) models. The connector is easily identified by the two stacked rows of pins (3 each row). Each pin has its own individual rear seal, while a common 3-ribbed seal is used to seal the connector body to the component. This is a *Push-to-Lock* connector.

To service the connector, replacing the body, terminal pin(s) or the lead-to-body seal(s), proceed as follows:

1. Unlock the terminal pin and lead by inserting a suitable terminal tool (such as a paper clip) into the front of the body as shown in **Figure 76** and **Figure 77**. Then pull the lead, seal (and terminal pin) out the rear of the connector body.

2. If changing the body, note the position of each lead, then repeat Step 1 until all leads have been removed.

3. If necessary, cut the defective terminal pin from the lead as close to the pin as possible, then slide the seal (2, **Figure 77**) from the lead.

7

4. If removed, lubricate the seal with OMC Electrical (dielectric) Grease, then slide it over the lead.

5. Strip the lead back far enough to allow the new pin's crimping tabs to make complete contact with the wire strands. Do not nick or cut any of the wire strands.

6. Using the OMC Amphenol crimping pliers (part No. 322696) or equivalent, position the terminal's primary tabs into the No. 18 notch of the pliers. Then position the wire strands into the terminal, making sure the wire strands extend past the primary tabs and the insulation is under secondary tabs.

7. Crimp the terminal firmly, then inspect the crimp. All strands must be encapsulated in the crimp as shown in **Figure 73**, typical. If not, remove the terminal and start over with a new terminal pin.

8. If the primary crimp is satisfactory, position the secondary tabs in the No. 14-16 notch of the pliers and crimp the terminal firmly. Inspect the crimp. The secondary tabs must be folded over the insulation as shown in **Figure 73**, typical. If not, remove the terminal and start over with a new terminal pin.

9. After crimping, inspect the locking tab (1, **Figure 77**) on the terminal pin. If necessary, slightly bend the tab upwards to ensure a positive lock. Then push each lead into the connector body until it locks in place. If any terminal pin will not lock in place (and the pin's locking tab is not damaged), the connector body's shoulder is rounded or damaged and the body must be replaced.

10. Carefully push each lead's seal (2, **Figure 77**) into the rear of the connector body. Do not cut, nick or damage the seal during this operation.

11. If the connector body-to-component seal is damaged, slide it from the body and discard it. Coat a new seal with OMC Electrical (dielectric) Grease and slide it over the connector body and against the body's shoulder.

Table 1 BATTERY—STATE OF CHARGE PERCENTAGE

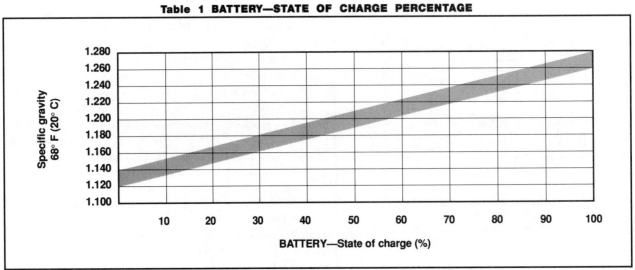

Table 2 WIRING HARNESS COLOR CODES (TRADITIONAL HARNESSES)

	Color code
Main harness circuits	
Starter engagement	Yellow/red
Tachometer	Gray
Stop 1 (ignition side)	Black/yellow
Stop 2 (ground side)	Black
Choke or primer	Purple/white
Warning horn	Tan
Switched B+	Purple
Protected B+	Red/purple
Grounds	Black
Trim/tilt circuits	
Trim motor up	Blue
Trim motor down	Green
Switching up	Blue/white
Switching down	Green/white
Switching circuit B+	Red/white
Trim sender circuit	White/tan
Grounds	Black or black/tan

7

Table 3 WIRING HARNESS COLOR CODES (MODULAR WIRING HARNESS)

	Color code
Main harness circuits	
Starter engagement	Yellow/red
Tachometer	Gray
Stop 1 (ignition side)	Black/yellow
Stop 2 (ground side)	Black/white
Choke or primer	Purple/white
Overheat warning	Tan
No oil warning	Tan/yellow
Low oil warning	Tan/black
Warning horn control	Tan/blue
Protected B+	Red/purple
Grounds	Black
Trim/tilt circuits	
Trim motor up	Blue
Trim motor down	Green
Switching up	Blue/white
Switching down	Green/white
Switching circuit B+	Red/white
Trim sender circuit	White/tan

Table 4 BATTERY CAPACITY (HOURS)

Accessory draw	Provides continuous power for:	Approximate recharge time
80 amp-hour battery		
5 amps	13.5 hours	16 hours
15 amps	3.5 hours	13 hours
25 amps	1.8 hours	12 hours
105 amp-hour battery		
5 amps	15.8 hours	16 hours
15 amps	4.2 hours	13 hours
25 amps	2.4 hours	12 hours

Table 5 MINIMUM BATTERY CABLE SIZES (AWG)

Cable length	9.9-15 hp	20-50[1] hp	50-70 hp[2]
1-10 ft. (0.3-3.0 m)	10 gauge	6 gauge	4 gauge
11-15 ft. (3.4-4.6 m)	8 gauge	4 gauge	2 gauge
16-20 ft. (4.9-6.1 m)	6 gauge	3 gauge	1 gauge

1. 50 hp (two-cylinder) models.
2. Three-cylinder models.

Table 6 ELECTRICAL AND IGNITION SPECIAL TORQUE VALUES

Fastener	in.-lb.	ft.-lb.	N•m
Charge coil			
2, 3.3 and 3.5 hp	19-25	–	2.2-2.8
All other models	15-22	–	1.7-2.5
Ignition coil(s)			
2, 3.3 and 3.5 hp	62-89	–	7-10
25 and 35 hp (three-cylinder)	84-106	–	9.5-12.0
All other models	48-96	–	5.4-10.9
Ignition (armature) plate			
Support plate-to-power head			
2, 3.3 and 3.5 hp	27-44	–	3.1-5.0
3-30 hp (two-cylinder)	48-60	–	5.4-6.8
40 hp[1], 48 Special, 18 and 28 jet	48-60	–	5.4-6.8
Armature-to-retainer plate	25-35	–	2.8-4.0
Power pack (ignition module)			
25 and 35 hp (three-cylinder)	84-106	–	9.5-12.0
All other models	60-84	–	6.8-9.5
Sensor coil (timer base)			
2, 3.3 and 3.5 hp	15-19	–	1.7-2.2
3 and 4 hp (except 4 Deluxe)	25-35	–	2.8-4.0
4 Deluxe, 6 and 8 hp	15-22	–	1.7-2.5
20-30 hp (two-cylinder) and 18 jet	15-22	–	1.7-2.5
25 and 35 hp (three-cylinder)	24-36	–	2.7-4.1
40 hp[1], 48 Special and 28 jet	15-22	–	1.7-2.5
40 hp[2], 50 hp and 35 jet			
Adaptor-to-power head	48-60	–	5.4-6.8
Timer base-to-adaptor	25-35	–	2.8-4.0
50-70 hp (three-cylinder)	25-35	–	2.8-4.0
Spark plugs	216-252	18-21	24.4-28.5
Stator assembly			
9.9 and 15 hp	25-35	–	2.8-4.0
25 and 35 hp (three-cylinder)	84-106	–	9.5-12.0
40 hp[2], 50-70 hp and 35 jet	120-144	10-12	13.6-16.3
Stator coil (4 amp systems)	15-22	–	1.7-2.5
Starter motor			
Mounting			
9.9 and 15 hp	120-144	10-12	13.6-16.3
20-30 hp (two-cylinder)	60-84	–	6.8-9.5
25 and 35 hp (three-cylinder)	–	15-17	20.3-23.0
40-70 hp and 35 jet	–	14-16	19.0-21.7
Bendix (pinion) nut (9.9 and 15 hp)	150-170	–	17.0-19.2
Through-bolts			
9.9 and 15 hp	30-40	–	3.4-4.5
20-30 hp (two-cylinder)	95-100	–	10.7-11.3
25 and 35 hp (three-cylinder)	50-60	–	5.7-6.8
40-70 hp and 35 jet	95-100	–	10.7-11.3
Rectifier	48-96	–	5.4-10.9
Voltage regulator (rectifier/regulator)	60-84	–	6.8-9.5

1. Rope start.
2. Electric start.

Table 7 FLYWHEEL NUT TORQUE VALUES

Model	in.-lb.	ft.-lb.	N•m
2, 3.3 and 3.5 hp	–	29-33	39.3-44.7
3, 4 hp and 4 Deluxe	–	30-40	40.7-54.2
6 and 8 hp	–	40-50	54.2-67.8
9.9 and 15 hp	–	45-50	61.0-67.8
20-70 hp and 18-35 jet	–	100-105	136-142

Table 8 IGNITION SYSTEM IDENTIFICATION

Model	System	Advance	Features	RPM limit
2, 3.3 and 3.5 hp	CD1	Electronic	Not applicable	Not applicable
3, 4 hp	CD	Mechanical	Not applicable	Not applicable
4 Deluxe, 6, 8 hp	CD2	Mechanical	Not applicable	Not applicable
9.9 and 15 hp	CD2	Mechanical	Not applicable	Not applicable
18 jet, 20-30 hp				
(two-cylinder)	CD2	Mechanical	S.L.O.W.	6100
25-35 hp (three-cylinder)	OIS2000	Mechanical	QuickStart, S.L.O.W.	6200
28 jet, 40 hp (rope)	CD2	Mechanical	S.L.O.W.	6100
40 hp (electric)	CD2	Mechanical	S.L.O.W.	6700
48 Special	CD2	Mechanical	S.L.O.W.	6100
35 jet, 50 hp				
(two-cylinder)	CD2	Mechanical	S.L.O.W.	6700
50-70 hp (three-cylinder)	CD3	Mechanical	QuickStart, S.L.O.W.	6700

7

Chapter Eight

Power Head

This chapter provides power head removal/installation, disassembly/reassembly and cleaning and inspection procedures for all power heads used on 2-70 hp and 18-35 jet models. The power head can be removed from the outboard motor, without removing the entire outboard from the boat, on all models.

Since this chapter covers a large range of models, spanning several model years, the power heads from different model groups differ in construction and require different service procedures. Whenever possible, engines with similar service procedures are grouped together.

The components shown in the accompanying illustrations are generally from the most common models. While it is possible that the components shown in the illustrations may not be identical with those being serviced, the step-by-step procedures cover every model in this manual. Exploded illustrations, typical of each power head model group, are located in the appropriate *Disassembly* section and are helpful references for many service procedures.

This chapter is arranged in a normal disassembly/assembly sequence. If only a partial repair is required, follow the procedure(s) to the point that the faulty parts can be replaced, then reassemble the unit. Many procedures require

the use of manufacturer recommended special tools, which can be purchased from an Evinrude or Johnson outboard dealership.

Power head work stands and holding fixtures are available from specialty shops, marine suppliers or marine and industrial product distributors.

Make sure that the work bench, work station, engine stand or holding fixture is of sufficient capacity to support the size and weight of the power head. This is especially important when working on larger engines, such as 50-70 hp models.

SERVICE CONSIDERATIONS

Performing internal service on the power head requires considerable mechanical ability. Carefully consider your capabilities before attempting any operation involving major disassembly of the engine.

If after studying the text and illustrations in this chapter, you decide not to attempt a major power head disassembly or repair, it may be financially beneficial to perform certain preliminary operations yourself. Consider separating the power head from the outboard motor and removing the fuel, ignition and electrical systems and all accessories yourself, taking only the basic power head to the dealership for the actual overhaul or major repair.

Since most marine dealers often have lengthy waiting lists for service (especially during the spring and summer seasons), this practice can reduce the time your unit is in the shop. If you have done much of the preliminary work, your repairs can be scheduled and performed much quicker. Always discuss your options with the dealer before appearing at the dealership with a disassembled engine. Dealers will often want to install, adjust and test run the engine to be comfortable providing warranty coverage for the overhaul or repair.

No matter who is doing the work, repairs will proceed much quicker and with less difficulty if the motor is cleaned before starting any service procedure. There are many special cleaners (degreasers) available from any automotive supply store. Most of these cleaners are simply sprayed on, then rinsed off with a garden hose after the recommended time period. Always follow all instructions provided by the manufacturer. Cleaning solvent must not be applied to electrical and ignition components and must never be sprayed into the induction system.

WARNING
Never use gasoline as a cleaning agent. Gasoline presents an extreme fire and explosion hazard. Be sure to work in a well-venti-

lated area when using cleaning solvents. Keep a large fire extinguisher rated for gasoline and oil fires nearby in case of an emergency.

Once you have decided to do the job yourself, read this chapter thoroughly until you have a good idea of what is involved in completing the repair satisfactorily. Make arrangements to buy or rent the necessary special tools and obtain a source for replacement parts *before* starting. It is frustrating and time-consuming to start a major repair and then be unable to finish because the necessary tools or parts are not available.

NOTE
A series of at least five photographs, taken from the front, rear, top and both sides of the power head (before removal), will be very helpful during reassembly and installation. The photographs are especially useful when trying to route electrical harnesses, fuel, primer and recirculation lines, and installing accessories, control linkages and brackets.

Before beginning the job, review Chapters One and Two of this manual. You will do a better job with this information fresh in your mind.

Tables 1-3 list torque values, **Tables 4-5** list all power head service specifications and **Table 6** lists the model number's design feature codes. All tables are located at the end of the chapter.

EVINRUDE/JOHNSON MODEL IDENTIFICATION

Johnson and Evinrude outboard motors are identified by a model identification plate (**Figure 1**, typical). The plate is actually a decal affixed to the port side of the swivel bracket, which is part of the engine's mid-section.

The identification plate contains at least the model and serial numbers and the name of the manufacturer. Newer model identification plates (**Figure 1**) contains all of the following information:

1. *Model number*—The model number is actually a series of letters and numbers. The model number is explained in the following section.

2. *Serial number*—The serial number is a letter followed by an eight-digit number. The serial number is unique to the engine and identifies it for title, insurance, warranty and theft recovery purposes. It is not normally required when ordering parts, but should be recorded and taken

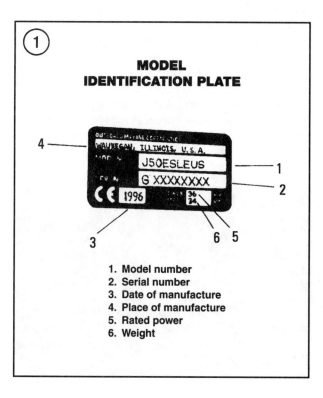

MODEL IDENTIFICATION PLATE

1. Model number
2. Serial number
3. Date of manufacture
4. Place of manufacture
5. Rated power
6. Weight

along. When the motor was built, the serial number was also stamped on a large core plug (**Figure 2**, typical) affixed to the cylinder block. If the power head has been replaced with an OMC Genuine Parts replacement power head assembly, the core plug will be stamped with the replacement power head's part number.

3. *Date of manufacture*—This is the date (year, or month and year) the motor was built. This does not always agree with the model year, as an OMC model year is not the same as a calendar year.

4. *Place of manufacture*—The engines in this manual may be assembled in the United States, Australia, Belgium, Hong Kong or South America.

5. *Rated power*—This figure is the motor's rated power output in kilowatts. Multiply kilowatts by 1.34 to get the horsepower equivalent.

6. *Weight*—This figure is the motor's weight in kilograms. Multiply kilograms by 2.2 to get the equivalent weight in pounds.

Model Number

The model number contains coded information in the following order:

1. *Model variation*—The model variation indicates if the engine is built in the United States, a foreign country or if the engine was specially styled for a boat manufacturer (custom paint and/or graphics). Typical model variations are: A (Australia), B (Belgium), H (Hong Kong) or S (South America). Other codes indicate models built for a particular boat manufacturer using special styling. If no code is present, the engine was built in the United States and contains no special styling.

2. *Style*—The style code will indicate if the engine is an Evinrude, Johnson or an OMC Commercial engine. Possible codes are E (Evinrude), J (Johnson) or none (OMC commercial engine). Commercial engines are not covered in this manual.

3. *Horsepower*—The horsepower is rounded to the nearest whole horsepower. For example, the 9.9 horsepower is listed as a 10 on the model identification plate. Horsepower ranges for the engines covered in this manual are 2-70 hp. Jet models are identified by their propshaft horsepower equivalent. The 18 jet is identified as a 25 hp, the 28 jet is identified as a 40 hp and the 35 jet is identified as a 50 hp.

4. *Design feature*—The design feature code will be one or two letters long. The design feature is always located immediately after the horsepower. See **Table 6** for common design feature codes. If your design feature code is not listed in **Table 6**, see your Evinrude/Johnson dealer.

5. *Transom height*—The transom height code is often called the shaft length. The transom height code is specifying the height of the motor as measured from the

antiventilation plate to the point where the stern brackets contact the top of the transom. This must match (or be very close) the boat's transom height. The height code is located between the design feature and the model year codes.

Only two codes are possible for the motors covered in this manual. If no code is given, the motor is a 15 in. (381 mm) model, often called a *standard* shaft. If the code is L, the motor is a 20 in. (508 mm) model, often called a *long* shaft. Sail models (and larger engines) may use codes X (extra-long) or Z (extra, extra-long), standing for 25 and 30 in. (635 and 762 mm) respectively. Sail models are not covered in this manual.

If the transom height does not match the motor, the gearcase is either too high or low in the water. If the gearcase is too high, the motor may not receive adequate cooling water and the propeller will ventilate excessively. If the gearcase is too low, the drag from the gearcase will reduce the boats speed and fuel economy. In either case, performance and handling will be adversely affected.

6. *Model year*—This is a two letter code, near the end of the model number, that can be used to determine the engine model year. These codes are based on the letters in the word INTRODUCES. A number is assigned to each letter of the word, in sequential order. I stands for 1, N for 2, T for 3 and so on. The last letter (S) represents 0. For example, the code EO stands for a 9 and a 5 or 1995. This coding system has been in effect since the 1981 (CI) model year.

7. *Model run*—This code (if present) is the last letter in the model number. A model run code is used to identify an engine change occurring within a model year. Any such change affects service procedures or replacement parts.

Possible model run codes for 1995 (EO) models are B, D, E, C, S, R, A, V. Possible model run codes for 1996 (ED) models are E, F, -2, D, S, C, G, A, R, M. Possible model run codes for 1997 (EU) models are D, K, C, S, R, A, M, B. Possible model run codes for 1998 (EC) models are S, R, A, C, M, B, E. Always note the model run code when ordering parts.

Model number (example)

The model number shown in **Figure 1** is J50ESLEUS. Separate the model number as follows: J, 50, ES, L, EU and S. The horsepower and model year codes are located first, if you are having difficulty. Remember that only certain letters are used as codes for each part of the model number and that there may be no model variation, transom height or model run codes. In this example, the engine is a Johnson 50 hp motor (style code J and horsepower code 50), built in the United States (because there is no model variation code). It has electric start and special styling (design feature code ES) and is a long shaft (transom height code L), designed for a 20 in. (508 mm) transom. It is a 1997 model year engine (model year code EU) and was built during the model run called S.

POWER HEAD BREAK-IN

Whenever a power head is rebuilt or replaced, or if *any* new internal parts are installed, it must be treated as a new engine. The engine must be run on the specified fuel/oil mix and operated in accordance with the recommended break-in procedure as described in Chapter Four.

CAUTION
Failure to follow the recommended break-in procedure will result in premature engine failure.

SERVICE PRECAUTIONS—
1998-2003 MODELS

The EPA (Environmental Protection Agency) certifies emission output for all 1998-2003 models. Certified models have an EPA certification plate (**Figure 3**) mounted near the model identification plate on the engine midsection.

The EPA certification plate contains the following information:

1. *The manufacturer*—In this case, the manufacturer is OMC (Outboard Marine Corporation).
2. *Statement of model year certification*—This lists the model year of emissions regulations that the engine is certified to meet. In this case, it is 1998.
3. *Certification data*—This section contains an engine family code, the family emissions level (FEL) indicating the hydrocarbon output in grams per kilowatt/hour, the engine displacement in cubic inches, the required engine oil and fuel and an exhaust emission control system code of EM (standing for engine modification [no catalytic converter]).
4. *Technical data*—This section lists the required spark plug(s) and gap, the W.O.T. (wide-open throttle) ignition timing and the idle timing and idle speed. The engine must be set to these specifications in order to comply with EPA certification.

All repairs and/or service procedures must be performed exactly as specified in this manual to ensure the engine will continue to comply with EPA requirements. For the same reason, all replacement parts must meet or exceed the manufacturer's specifications. Failure to properly maintain, repair or adjust the motor can result in substantial penalties.

Any modification that would affect the engine's emissions output is not allowed on an EPA certified engine. This includes:

a. Changing ignition timing and/or carburetors.
b. Carburetor re-jetting (other than standard high-altitude modifications).
c. Any performance modification such as changing cylinder and/or piston port timing (or shape) and/or any cylinder head alterations.

If in doubt as to whether a repair or service procedure will adversely affect the engine's ability to maintain EPA compliance, contact an Evinrude or Johnson dealer, before beginning the repair or procedure.

SERVICE RECOMMENDATIONS

If the engine has experienced a catastrophic failure, every attempt must be made to determine the cause of the failure. Refer to the *Engine* section at the end of Chapter Three for troubleshooting procedures.

Many failures are caused simply from using the incorrect (or stale) fuel and lubricating oil. Refer to Chapter Four for all fuel and oil recommendations.

When rebuilding or performing a major repair on the power head, consider performing the following steps to prevent the failure from reoccurring.

1. Service the water pump. Replace the impeller and all seals and gaskets. See Chapter Nine.

8

2. Replace the thermostat(s) and remove and inspect the poppet valve assembly (on models so equipped) as described in this chapter. Replace any suspect components.

3. Drain the fuel tank(s) and dispose of the old fuel in an approved manner.

4. Fill the fuel tank with fresh fuel and add the recommended oil to the fuel tank at the *break-in* ratio as described in Chapter Four.

5. Replace (or clean) all fuel filters. See Chapter Four.

6. Clean and adjust the carburetors. See Chapter Six.

7. *Oil-injected models*—Drain and clean the oil reservoir(s). Dispose of the old oil in an approved manner. Then refill the oil system with the specified oil (Chapter Four) and bleed the oil system as described in Chapter Eleven.

8. Install new spark plugs. Use only the recommended spark plugs listed in Chapter Four. Make sure the spark plugs are correctly torqued as described in Chapter Four.

9. Perform the synchronization and linkage adjustments as described in Chapter Five.

LUBRICANTS, SEALANTS AND ADHESIVES

The part numbers for the lubricants, sealants and adhesives called for in this chapter are all listed in the Quick Reference Data section at the front of this manual. Equivalent (after-market) products are acceptable for use, as long as they meet or exceed the original manufacturer's specifications.

During power head assembly, all internal engine components must be lubricated with Evinrude/Johnson 2-cycle (TCW-3) outboard motor oil. Do not assemble any components *dry*. Lubricate all seal lips and O-rings with OMC Triple Guard Grease. Lubricate and hold all needle and roller bearings in place with OMC Needle Bearing Assembly Grease.

To efficiently remove carbon deposits from the pistons and combustion chambers use OMC Engine Tuner. Allow ample time for the cleaner to soak into and soften carbon deposits.

If no other sealant or adhesive is specified, coat all gaskets with OMC Gasket Sealing Compound. However, do not apply any sealant to gaskets that are specified to be installed dry.

Coat the threads of all external fasteners (if no other sealant or adhesive is specified) with OMC Gasket Sealing Compound to help prevent corrosion and ease future removal.

When sealing the crankcase cover/cylinder block, both mating surfaces must be *completely* free of all sealant residue, dirt, oil or other contamination. The manufacturer specifically recommends using OMC Gel Seal and Gasket Remover (and a plastic scraper) to remove the original Gel Seal II sealant residue. The new Gel Seal II sealant will not properly seal and harden if the old sealant is not completely removed.

Locquic Primer, lacquer thinner, acetone or similar solvents may be used if OMC Gel Seal and Gasket Remover is not available. However, solvents with an oil, wax or petroleum base must not be used.

CAUTION
*Clean all mating surfaces carefully to avoid nicks and gouges. A plastic scraper can be improvised from a common household electrical outlet cover or a piece of Lucite with one edge ground to a 45° angle. Extreme caution must be used if a metal scraper, such as a putty knife is used. Nicks, scratches and gouges will prevent the sealant from curing. The crankcase cover-to-cylinder block surface must **not** be scratched or damaged and may **not** be lapped, surfaced or machined.*

OMC Gel Seal II Sealant is the only recommended sealant to seal the crankcase cover-to-cylinder block mating surfaces on all models. Prior to using Gel Seal II, the mating surfaces must be treated with OMC Locquic Primer, following the instructions on the container. If Locquic Primer is not used, the assembly must be allowed to set for 24 hours before returning the unit to service. The sealant bead must be applied to the inner (crankshaft) side of all crankcase cover screw holes, but must not be applied closer than 1/4 in. (6.35 mm) to crankshaft bearings or seal rings (if equipped).

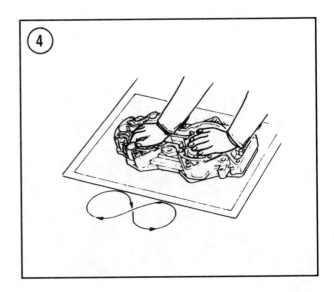

OMC Gel Seal II has a shelf life of approximately one year at room temperature. If the age of the Gel Seal II is in doubt, or it has been stored in a high-temperature area, use a new tube. Using Gel Seal that is too old will result in crankcase air leakage, requiring major disassembly to reseal the crankcase halves.

Apply OMC Ultra Lock threadlocking adhesive (or equivalent) to the threads of all internal fasteners (if no other adhesive is called for).

Whenever a threadlocking adhesive is called for, always clean the surface to be sealed (or threads to be secured) with OMC Locquic Primer. Locquic Primer cleans and primes the surface and ensures a quick secure bond by leaving a thin film of catalyst on the surface (or threads). The primer must be allowed to air dry, as blow drying will remove the catalyst.

Seal Installation

Apply OMC Gasket Sealing Compound to the outer diameter of all *metal-cased* seals before pressing the seal into place.

Apply OMC DPL (or WD-40) Lubricant to the outer diameter of all *rubber-cased* seals before pressing the seal into place. DPL will lubricate the seal and allow it to slide into position without cutting the rubber case. The DPL will then evaporate, preventing the seal from sliding out of its bore under operation. If gasket sealing compound or grease is used, the seal will be ejected from its bore under operation.

Lubricate the rubber lip(s) of *all* seals with OMC Triple Guard Grease, before the seal is slid over the shaft, or the shaft is inserted into the seal.

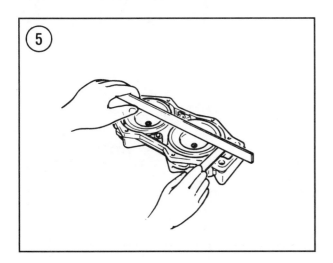

⑤

SEALING SURFACES

Clean all sealing surfaces carefully to prevent nicks and gouges. Often a shop towel soaked in solvent can be used to rub gasket material and/or sealant from a mating surface. If a scraper must be used, try using a plastic scraper (such as a household electrical outlet cover) or a piece of Lucite with one edge ground to a 45° angle to prevent damage to the sealing surfaces. If a metal scraper or putty knife is used, great skill and patience must be displayed to prevent destroying the component being cleaned.

NOTE
Plate glass (or a machinist's surface plate or straightedge) must be used for surface checking. Ordinary window glass does not have a uniform surface and will give a false reading. Plate glass has a very uniform surface flatness.

Once the surfaces are clean, check the component for warpage by placing the component onto a piece of plate glass or a machinist's surface plate. Apply uniform downward pressure and try to insert a selection of feeler gauges between the plate and the component. The maximum cylinder head warpage on all models is 0.004 in. (0.102 mm).

If a cylinder head is warped more than 0.004 (0.102 mm), it must be lapped, resurfaced or replaced. Do not remove more than 0.010 in. (0.254 mm) of material from a cylinder head.

On other components, no specifications are given, and it will be up to the technician to decide if the warpage is minor enough to be removed by lapping (or resurfacing), or if the component must be replaced.

CAUTION
The cylinder block-to-crankcase cover mating surfaces may not be lapped or resurfaced.

To remove minor warpage, minor nicks or scratches or traces of sealant or gasket material, place a large sheet of 320-400 grit wet sandpaper onto the plate glass or surface plate. Apply light downward pressure and move the component in a figure-8 pattern as shown in **Figure 4**. Use a light oil (such as WD-40) to keep the sandpaper from loading up. Remove the component from the sandpaper and recheck the sealing surface. Use a machinist's straightedge to check areas that cannot be accessed using the glass or surface plate. See **Figure 5**.

It may be necessary to repeat the lapping process several times to achieve the desired results. Never remove any more material than is absolutely necessary. Make sure the

8

component is thoroughly washed to remove all grit before reassembly.

FASTENERS AND TORQUE

Always replace a worn or damaged fastener with one of equal size, type and torque requirement. Power head torque values are listed in **Tables 1-3**. If a specification is not provided for a given fastener, use the standard torque values listed in the Quick Reference Data section at the front of this manual.

Determine the fastener size by measuring the shank of the screw (or bolt) as shown in **Figure 6**. Determine the thread pitch with the appropriate Metric or American thread pitch gauge as shown in **Figure 7**.

Damaged threads in components and castings may be repaired using a Heli-Coil (or equivalent) stainless steel threaded insert (**Figure 8**, typical). Thread insert kits are available from automotive, marine or industrial supply stores.

Never run a thread tap or thread chaser into a hole equipped with a Heli-Coil. Replace a damaged Heli-Coil by gripping the outermost coil with a needlenose pliers and unthreading the coil from the hole. Do not pull the coil straight out or the threads in the hole will be damaged.

CAUTION
*Metric **and** American fasteners may be used on these engines. Always match a replacement fastener to the original. Do not run a tap or thread chaser into a hole (or over a bolt) without first verifying the thread size and pitch.*

Unless otherwise specified, components secured by more than one fastener must be tightened in a *minimum* of three steps. Evenly tighten all fasteners hand-tight (snug) as a first step. Then evenly tighten all fasteners to 50 percent of the specified torque value as the second step. Finally, evenly tighten all fasteners to 100 percent of the specified torque value as the third step.

Be sure to follow torque patterns (sequences) as directed. If no pattern is specified, start at the center of the component and tighten in a circular pattern, working outward. All applicable torque sequences are listed in the appropriate *Assembly* section of this chapter.

The cylinder head screws must be retorqued after the engine has reached operating temperature and been allowed to cool to the touch. To retorque the cylinder head screws (and any other fasteners desired), loosen each fastener approximately one turn, then retighten to the specified torque value. Repeat the process until all of the fasteners are retorqued.

Spark plugs must be torqued to ensure proper heat transfer and to prevent preignition and detonation (Chapter Three). Spark plugs must be retorqued after the engine has reached operating temperature and cooled to the touch. Do not loosen the spark plug, simply retighten the plug to the specified torque value.

If no other sealant or adhesive is specified, coat the threads of all external fasteners with OMC Gasket Sealing Compound to help prevent corrosion and ease future removal.

FLYWHEEL

All flywheel service procedures are covered in Chapter Seven.

UPPER CRANKSHAFT SEAL REPLACEMENT (3, 4-30 HP [TWO-CYLINDER] AND 18 JET)

On the 3, 4-30 hp (two-cylinder) and 18 jet models, the upper crankshaft seal can be replaced without disassembling the crankcase assembly. On 3 and 4-15 hp models, seal remover/installer part No. 391060 (3-15 hp models)

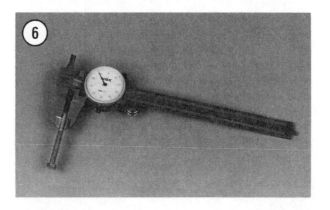

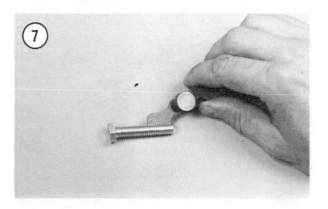

is required, while on 20-30 hp and 18 jet models, remover part No. 387780 *and* installer part No. 321539 are required.

To replace a defective upper crankshaft seal, proceed as follows:

1. Remove the flywheel as described in Chapter Seven.

2. *3 and 4-15 hp models*—Place the appropriate seal remover tip on the seal remover body. Use tip *A* on 3, 4 hp and 4 Deluxe models, tip *B* on 6 and 8 hp models, or tip *C* on 9.9 and 15 hp models. Tighten the tip securely.

3A. *3 and 4-15 hp models*—Place the seal remover/installer assembly over the crankshaft. Thread the remover tip firmly into the seal. Back out the pressing screw as necessary to ensure positive engagement to the seal.

3B. *20-30 hp and 18 jet models*—Place the seal remover (part No. 387780) over the crankshaft. Thread the tapered end firmly into the seal. Back out the pressing screw as necessary to ensure positive engagement to the seal.

4. Hold the remover/installer body and tighten the pressing screw to remove the seal.

5. Apply OMC Gasket Sealing Compound (metal-cased seal) or OMC DPL Lubricant (rubber-cased seal) to the outer diameter of a new upper crankshaft seal. Then lubricate the seal lip with OMC Triple Guard Grease. Carefully install the seal, with its lip facing down, over the crankshaft and into position over the crankcase bore.

6A. *3 and 4-15 hp models*—Remove the tip and pressing screw from the seal remover/installer body. Place the body over the crankshaft with the pressing screw hole facing up. Carefully drive the seal into the crankcase bore with a soft-faced mallet.

6B. *20-30 hp and 18 jet models*—Using seal installer part No. 321539, carefully drive the seal into the crankcase bore with a soft-faced mallet.

7. Install the flywheel as described in Chapter Seven.

POWER HEAD REMOVAL/INSTALLATION

The removal and installation procedures in this chapter represent the most efficient sequence for removing the power head while preparing for complete disassembly. If complete disassembly is not necessary, stop disassembly at the appropriate point, then begin reassembly where disassembly stopped. The power head should be removed as an assembly if major repairs are to be performed. On most models, power head removal is not required for certain service procedures such as cylinder head removal, intake and exhaust cover removal (if so equipped), ignition component replacement, fuel system component replacement and reed block/intake manifold removal.

Before removing the power head assembly, make a sketch or take a series of photographs showing the location, routing and positioning of wires, hoses and clamps for reference during reassembly. Note where wires, ground connections and washers are located so they can be reinstalled in their correct positions. Unless otherwise specified, install star washers on the engine side of ground connections.

8

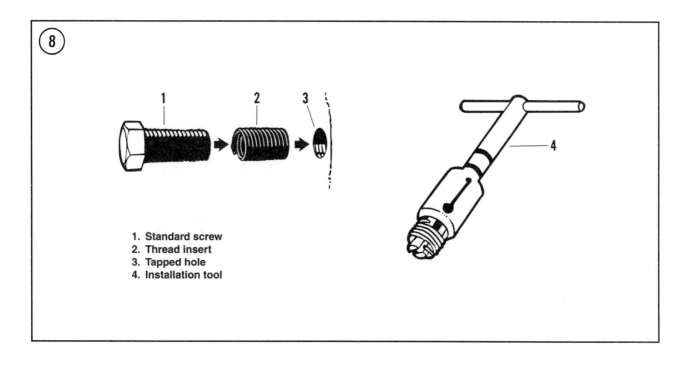

⑧

1. Standard screw
2. Thread insert
3. Tapped hole
4. Installation tool

Removal/Installation (2, 3.3 and 3.5 hp)

The power head may be removed from the drive shaft housing with all accessories and systems installed. If Steps 2-4 are to be skipped, make sure the safety lanyard switch leads are disconnected before continuing at Step 5.

1. Remove the split lower cowl. There are four screws securing the cowl to each side of the power head and six screws at the bottom of the engine, along the cowl parting line.

2. Disconnect the spark plug lead and remove the spark plug to prevent accidental starting.

3. Remove the rewind starter assembly as described in Chapter Twelve.

4. Remove the flywheel, charge coil, sensor coil, power pack and ignition coil as described in Chapter Seven.

5. Remove the fuel tank and carburetor as described in Chapter Six.

6. Remove the six screws and washers securing the power head to the drive shaft housing. See **Figure 9**.

7. Lift the power head off the drive shaft housing and place it on a clean bench. It may be necessary to tap the power head with a plastic or rubber mallet to help break the base gasket free.

8. Thoroughly clean all gasket material from the drive shaft housing and power head mating surfaces.

9. To install the power head, begin by installing a new gasket on the drive shaft housing. Lightly coat both sides of the gasket with OMC Gasket Sealing Compound.

10. Lubricate the drive shaft with OMC Moly Lube. Wipe any excess grease from the top surface of the drive shaft.

11. Install the power head onto the drive shaft housing. Rotate the crankshaft as necessary to align the drive shaft square splines.

12. Apply OMC Gasket Sealing Compound to the threads of the power head mounting screws. Install the six screws (and washers) and evenly tighten them to 60-84 in.-lbs (6.8-9.5 N•m).

13. Install the fuel tank and carburetor as described in Chapter Six.

14. Install the charge coil, sensor coil, power pack, ignition coil and flywheel as described in Chapter Seven.

15. Install the rewind starter as described in Chapter Twelve.

16. Install the spark plug and reconnect the spark plug lead. Tighten the spark plug to 18-21 ft.-lb. (24.4-28.5 N•m).

17. Refer to Chapter Four for fuel and oil recommendations and break-in procedures (as needed). Then refer to Chapter Five and perform all synchronization and linkage adjustments.

Removal/Installation
(3 and 4 hp [Except 4 Deluxe])

The power head may be removed from the drive shaft housing with most of the accessories and systems installed. If Steps 3-5 are to be skipped, make sure the safety lanyard switch leads, all applicable fuel supply lines, throttle control cable and choke valve linkage are disconnected before continuing at Step 6.

Make sure all cable clamps are reinstalled in their original positions and new tie-straps are installed to replace any that were removed.

1. Disconnect the spark plug leads and remove the spark plugs to prevent accidental starting.

2. Remove the split lower cowl. There are four bottom screws securing the lower cowl to the power head. Then remove the two internal screws securing the front and rear lower cowl halves to each other.

3. Remove the rewind starter as described in Chapter Twelve.

4. Remove the flywheel, ignition module, ignition coil and sensor coil (ignition plate) as described in Chapter Seven. Then remove the throttle cable from the power head.

5. Remove the fuel tank (if so equipped), fuel pump (if so equipped) and carburetor as described in Chapter Six.

6. Remove the six screws securing the power head to the drive shaft housing.

> *CAUTION*
> *At this point, there must be no hoses, leads or linkages connecting the power head to the drive shaft housing. Make sure that nothing will interfere with power head removal before continuing.*

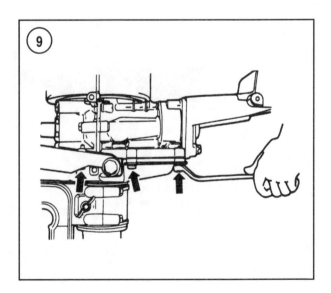

7. Lift the power head off the drive shaft housing and place it on a clean bench. It may be necessary to tap the power head with a plastic or rubber mallet to help break the base gasket free.

8. Thoroughly clean all gasket material from the power head and drive shaft housing mating surfaces.

9. To install the power head, begin by lubricating the drive shaft splines with OMC Moly Lube. Wipe any excess lubricant from the top of the drive shaft.

10. Place a new gasket onto the drive shaft housing.

11. Install the power head onto the drive shaft housing. Rotate the crankshaft as necessary to align the crankshaft and drive shaft splines.

12. Coat the threads of the six mounting screws with OMC Gasket Sealing Compound. Then install and evenly tighten the screws to 60-84 in.-lb. (6.8-9.5 N•m).

13. Install the fuel tank (if so equipped) and carburetor as described in Chapter Six.

14. Install the ignition coil, ignition module, sensor coil (ignition plate) and flywheel as described in Chapter Seven. Then reinstall the throttle cable to the power head.

15. Install the rewind starter as described in Chapter 12.

16. Reinstall the split lower cowl. Tighten the mounting screws securely.

17. Install the spark plugs and reconnect the spark plug leads. Tighten the spark plugs to 18-21 ft.-lb. (24.4-28.5 N•m).

18. Refer to Chapter Four for fuel and oil recommendations and break-in procedures (as needed). Then refer to Chapter Five and perform all synchronization and linkage adjustments.

Removal/Installation (4 Deluxe)

The power head may be removed from the drive shaft housing with most of the accessories and systems installed. If Steps 3-4 are to be skipped, make sure the safety lanyard switch leads, all applicable fuel supply lines, throttle/spark control and choke valve linkages are disconnected before continuing at Step 5.

Make sure all cable clamps are reinstalled in their original positions and new tie-straps are installed to replace any that were removed.

1. Disconnect the spark plug leads and remove the spark plugs to prevent accidental starting.

2. Remove the rewind starter as described in Chapter Twelve

3. Remove the flywheel, armature plate (containing the charge and sensor coils), power pack and ignition coils as described in Chapter Seven.

4. Remove the carburetor and fuel pump as described in Chapter Six.

5. Remove the six screws securing the power head to the exhaust housing.

> *CAUTION*
> *At this point, there must be no hoses, leads or linkages connecting the power head to the drive shaft housing. Make sure that nothing will interfere with power head removal before continuing.*

6. Lift the power head (and inner exhaust housing) off of the drive shaft housing and place it on a clean bench. It may be necessary to tap the power head with a plastic or rubber mallet to help break the base gasket free.

7. Remove the four screws securing the inner exhaust housing to the water tube, then separate the housing from the power head.

8. Remove the water tube retainer from the inner exhaust housing, then pull the water tube from the housing. Remove and discard the water tube grommet.

9. Thoroughly clean all gasket material from the power head, inner exhaust housing and drive shaft housing mating surfaces.

> *NOTE*
> *The gearcase must be removed from the drive shaft housing before the power head can be reinstalled.*

10. To install the power head, begin by removing the gearcase from the drive shaft housing as described in Chapter Nine.

11. Lubricate a new water tube grommet with soapy water. Then slide the grommet over the water tube and up against its flanged end.

12. Insert the water tube through the inner exhaust housing. Position the retainer over the water tube, then seat the water tube, grommet and retainer into the inner exhaust housing.

13. Position the power head so the base gasket surface is pointing upward. Then place a new power head gasket (without any sealer) onto the power head.

14. Position the inner exhaust housing and water tube assembly on the power head. Coat the four screws with OMC Nut Lock threadlocking adhesive (or equivalent). Install and evenly tighten the four screws to 60-84 in.-lb. (6.8-9.5 N•m).

15. Carefully lower the power head and exhaust housing assembly onto the drive shaft housing. Coat the threads of the six power head mounting screws with OMC Gasket Sealing Compound. Install and evenly tighten the screws to 60-84 in.-lb. (6.8-9.5 N•m).

16. Install the gearcase as described in Chapter Nine.

8

17. Install the armature plate (containing the charge and sensor coils), power pack, ignition coils and flywheel as described in Chapter Seven.

18. Install the carburetor and fuel pump as described in Chapter Six.

19. Install the rewind starter as described in Chapter Twelve.

20. Install the spark plugs and reconnect the spark plug leads. Tighten the spark plugs to 18-21 ft.-lb. (24.4-28.5 N•m).

21. Refer to Chapter Four for fuel and oil recommendations and break-in procedures (as needed). Then refer to Chapter Five and perform all synchronization and linkage adjustments.

Removal/Installation (6 and 8 hp)

The power head may be removed from the drive shaft housing with most of the accessories and systems installed. If Steps 2-4 are to be skipped, make sure the fuel supply line (at the fuel pump), choke linkage and the safety lanyard stop switch leads are disconnected before continuing at Step 5.

Make sure all cable clamps are reinstalled in their original positions and new tie-straps are installed to replace any that were removed.

1. Disconnect the spark plug leads and remove the spark plugs to prevent accidental starting.

2. Remove the rewind starter as described in Chapter Twelve.

3. Remove the flywheel, armature plate (containing the sensor and charge coils), the power pack and the ignition coil as described in Chapter Seven.

4. Remove the fuel pump and carburetor as described in Chapter Six.

5. Remove the screws (and washers) securing the throttle cable and the spark control lever to the starboard side of the power head. Then disengage the throttle cable from the spark control arm. Remove the spark control arm from the power head.

6. Disconnect the water discharge (tell-tale) hose from the starboard lower cowl.

7. Remove the three screws and nuts securing the split lower cowls to each other. All three screws are accessed from the starboard side of the engine.

8. Remove the two screws securing the front trim plate to the lower cowl halves. Then remove the split lower cowl halves.

9. Remove the six bottom screws securing the power head to the drive shaft housing.

10. Remove the three upper screws securing the rear of the adaptor plate to the drive shaft housing. See **Figure 10**.

CAUTION
At this point, there must be no hoses, leads or linkages connecting the power head to the drive shaft housing. Make sure that nothing will interfere with power head removal before continuing.

11. Rock the power head, or tap the power head with a plastic or rubber mallet to break the gasket seal between the drive shaft housing and power head. Then lift the power head, adaptor plate and inner exhaust housing assembly from the drive shaft housing and place it on a clean bench.

12. Remove the six screws securing the inner exhaust housing and the adaptor plate to the power head. Then carefully separate the housing and plate from each other and the power head. Do not scratch, gouge, distort or damage any of the components.

13. Remove the water tube from the inner exhaust housing. Remove and discard both the upper and lower grommets.

14. Thoroughly clean all gasket material from the power head, drive shaft housing, adapter plate, and inner exhaust housing mating surfaces.

NOTE
The gearcase must be removed from the drive shaft housing before the power head can be reinstalled.

15. To install the power head, begin by removing the gearcase from the drive shaft housing as described in Chapter Nine.

16. Lubricate two new water tube grommets with soapy water. Then slide one grommet over the water tube and up against its flanged end.

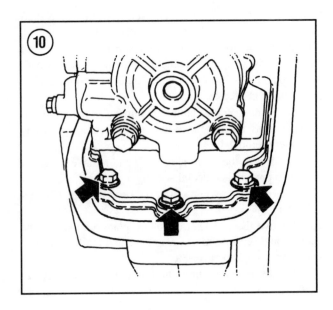

17. Insert the water tube through the inner exhaust housing, then seat the water tube and grommet into the inner exhaust housing. Position the second gasket on top of the water tube, in the adaptor plate's bore.

18. Position the power head so the base gasket surface is pointing upward. Then place a new power head gasket (without sealer) onto the power head.

19. Place the adaptor plate over the power head studs, then position a new gasket over the adaptor plate.

20. Position the inner exhaust housing and water tube assembly on the adaptor plate (and power head). Make sure the water tube's upper grommet is not displaced. Then coat the six mounting screws with OMC Nut Lock threadlocking adhesive (or equivalent). Align the exhaust housing, then install and evenly tighten the six screws to 60-84 in.-lb. (6.8-9.5 N•m).

21. Carefully lower the power head and exhaust housing assembly onto the drive shaft housing. Coat the threads of the nine power head mounting screws with OMC Gasket Sealing Compound. Install the six lower and three upper screws, then evenly tighten them to 60-84 in.-lb. (6.8-9.5 N•m).

22. Install the gearcase as described in Chapter Nine.

23. Reconnect the throttle cable to the spark control arm. Position the throttle cable and spark control arm on the power head with a washer on both sides of the control arm and a washer between the throttle cable anchor bracket and the power head, then secure each with a screw. Tighten each screw securely.

24. Install the armature plate (containing the sensor and charge coils), power pack, ignition coil and flywheel as described in Chapter Seven.

25. Install the fuel pump and carburetor as described in Chapter Six.

26. Install the rewind starter as described in Chapter Twelve.

27. Position the split lower cowl halves on the engine. Align the front plate to each cowl half and secure it to each half with one screw. Then install the three screws and nuts that secure the cowl halves to each other. Tighten all five screws securely.

28. Reconnect the water discharge (tell-tale) hose to the starboard lower cowl's fitting.

29. Install the spark plugs and tighten to 18-21 ft.-lb. (24.4-28.5 N•m). Reconnect the spark plug leads

30. Refer to Chapter Four for fuel and oil recommendations and break-in procedures (as needed). Then refer to Chapter Five and perform all synchronization and linkage adjustments.

Removal/Installation (9.9 and 15 hp)

The power head may be removed from the drive shaft housing with most of the accessories and systems installed.

If Steps 4-7 are to be skipped, make sure the fuel supply line (at the fuel pump), the safety lanyard switch leads, spark lever-to-armature plate link and the choke linkage are disconnected before continuing at Step 8.

Make sure all cable clamps are reinstalled in their original positions and new tie-straps are installed to replace any that were removed.

1. Disconnect the spark plug leads and remove the spark plugs to prevent accidental starting.

2. *Electric start models*—Disconnect both battery cables from the battery. Then remove the cables from the power head. Note each connection's location and the cable routing for reassembly.

3. Remove the split lower cowl as follows:
   a. Disconnect the water discharge (tell-tale) hose from the rear of the starboard lower cowl.
   b. Remove the three interior screws and nuts holding the rear of the cowl halves to each other.
   c. Remove the two interior screws and nuts holding the front of the cowl halves to the front panel (lower cowl support bracket).
   d. *1997-1998 (EU-EC) models*—Remove the rear exterior screw and nut holding the rear, lower edge of the cowls together.
   e. Remove the front exterior screw and nut holding the mid-point of the cowl halves together. The screw is located just above the swivel bracket (and steering arm) on the port side.

4. Remove the rewind starter as described in Chapter Twelve.

NOTE
Do not disconnect electrical and ignition components from each other unless absolutely necessary. Simply remove the mounting screws, cable clamps and tie-straps.

5. Remove the entire ignition system. This includes the flywheel, armature plate (containing the charge, sensor and stator coil [if equipped]), power pack and ignition coil. See Chapter Seven.

6. *Electric start models*—Remove the electric starter, starter solenoid (remote control models), rectifier and the remaining wiring harness. See Chapter Seven.

7. Remove the carburetor and fuel pump as described in Chapter Six.

NOTE
The shift shaft is located at the bottom of the intake manifold. The shaft does not need to be disassembled, unless so desired.

8

8A. *Tiller handle models*—Remove the screws (and washers) securing the throttle cable (A, **Figure 11**) and the spark control lever (B, **Figure 11**) to the starboard side of the power head. Then disengage the throttle cable from the spark control arm. Remove the spark control arm from the power head. If the ignition system is not removed, the spark control arm linkage must be disconnected from the armature plate.

8B. *Remote control models*—Disconnect the throttle and shift cables from the power head as described in Chapter Twelve. Then remove the screw (and washer) securing the spark and shift control arm assembly to the starboard rear corner of the power head. Disengage the shift link from the shift lever (at the front of the engine) and remove the control arm assembly and the shift link from the power head.

9. *Tiller handle models*—Disconnect the shift handle's link from the port end of the shift shaft by removing its special locking clip from the shift bellcrank.

10. Remove the rewind starter's neutral lock link from the shift bellcrank (port end of shift shaft). Then remove the cotter pin and clevis pin securing the lower gearcase shift shaft to the shift bellcrank.

11. Remove the six screws securing the power head to the drive shaft housing.

CAUTION
At this point, there must be no hoses, leads or linkages connecting the power head to the drive shaft housing. Make sure that nothing will interfere with power head removal before continuing.

12. Rock the power head, or tap the power head with a plastic or rubber mallet to break the gasket seal between the drive shaft housing and power head. Then lift the power head and inner exhaust housing assembly from the drive shaft housing and place it on a clean bench.

13. Remove the four screws securing inner exhaust housing to the power head. Then carefully separate the housing from the power head. Do not scratch, gouge, distort or damage any of the components.

14. Remove the two water tubes from the inner exhaust housing. Remove and discard both grommets.

15. Thoroughly clean all gasket material from the power head, drive shaft housing, and inner exhaust housing mating surfaces.

NOTE
The gearcase must be removed from the drive shaft housing before reinstalling the power head to ensure the water supply tube is correctly inserted into the water pump grommet after power head installation.

16. To install the power head, begin by removing the gearcase as described in Chapter Nine with the following exception. Since the shift shaft is already disconnected from the shift bellcrank, it is not necessary to disconnect the shift shaft at the gearcase as described in Chapter Nine.

17. Lubricate two new water tube grommets with soapy water. Install both water tubes into the inner exhaust housing using the new grommets. The short tube goes in the rear hole and the long tube goes in the front hole. Rotate both tubes to align the lower end of the tubes with the centerline of the engine (fore and aft). See **Figure 12**.

18. Position the power head so the base gasket surface is pointing upward. Then place a new power head gasket (without sealer) onto the power head.

19. Position the inner exhaust housing and water tube assembly on the power head. Make sure the water tube grommets are not displaced and that both tubes are aligned with the fore and aft centerline of the engine. Then coat the four mounting screws with OMC Nut Lock threadlocking adhesive (or equivalent). Align the exhaust housing, then install and evenly tighten the mounting screws to 60-84 in.-lb. (6.8-9.5 N•m).

20. Thoroughly coat the machined surface of the lower crankcase end cap (5, **Figure 12**) with Permatex No. 2 sealant.

21. Install a rubber band around the exhaust snout to hold the long water tube firmly against the cast rib on the snout as shown in **Figure 12**. Slowly lower the power head and exhaust housing assembly onto the drive shaft housing, while guiding the long water tube into its opening at the front and bottom of the drive shaft housing. Also guide the short water tube into its opening at the very rear of the housing. The short tube's opening is much higher in the housing than the long tube's opening.

NOTE
The two longest power head mounting screws go in the rearmost holes (1 on each side).

22. Once the power head is seated to the drive shaft housing, coat the threads of the six power head mounting

screws with OMC Gasket Sealing Compound. Install and evenly tighten the screws to 60-84 in.-lb. (6.8-9.5 N•m).

23. Install the gearcase as described in Chapter Nine with the following exception. Since the shift shaft is still connected to the gearcase, lubricate the top of the shift shaft with Triple Guard Grease and guide it through the drive shaft housing's lower grommet, then through the swivel bracket and finally through the cowl support plate when installing the gearcase. The bend in the top of the shift shaft must face forward.

24. Connect the rewind starter's neutral lock link to the shift bellcrank (port end of the shift shaft). Then align the shift rod with the shift bellcrank and secure it in place with the clevis pin and a new cotter pin. Bend both prongs of the cotter pin for a secure attachment.

25. *Tiller handle models*—Reconnect the shift handle's link to the shift bellcrank (port end of the shift shaft) and secure it in place with its special locking clip.

26A. *Tiller handle models*—Connect the throttle cable to the spark control arm, then position the spark control arm and the throttle cable anchor to the power head. Position a washer between the power head and the anchor, then secure the anchor and washer in place with a screw. Secure the spark control arm in place with a screw and washer. Tighten both screws securely. See **Figure 11**.

26B. *Remote control models*—Connect the shift link to the shift lever, then position the spark and shift control arm assembly to the starboard rear corner of the power head. Secure the assembly to the power head with a screw and washer. Tighten the screws securely. Then install the throttle and shift cables as described in Chapter Twelve.

27. Install the carburetor and fuel pump as described in Chapter Six.

28. *Electric start models*—Install the electric starter, starter solenoid (remote control models), rectifier and the remaining wiring harness. See Chapter Seven.

29. Install the entire ignition system. This includes the armature plate (containing the charge, sensor and stator coil [if equipped]), power pack, ignition coil and flywheel. Secure all harnesses and leads with the original clamps or new tie-straps. See Chapter Seven.

30. Install the rewind starter as described in Chapter Twelve.

31. Install the split lower cowl. Tighten all fasteners securely, then reconnect the water discharge (tell-tale) hose to the rear of the starboard lower cowl.

32. *Electric start models*—Connect both battery cables to the power head as noted on disassembly. Then connect both battery cables to the battery. Tighten all connections securely.

33. Install the spark plugs and tighten to 18-21 ft.-lb. (24.4-28.5 N•m). Reconnect the spark plug leads.

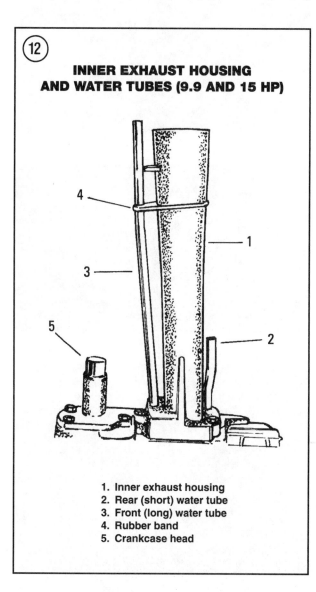

(12)

INNER EXHAUST HOUSING AND WATER TUBES (9.9 AND 15 HP)

1. Inner exhaust housing
2. Rear (short) water tube
3. Front (long) water tube
4. Rubber band
5. Crankcase head

8

34. Refer to Chapter Four for fuel and oil recommendations and break-in procedures (as needed). Then refer to Chapter Five and perform all synchronization and linkage adjustments.

Removal/Installation
(20-30 hp [Two-cylinder] and 18 Jet)

The power head may be removed from the drive shaft housing with most of the accessories and systems installed. If Steps 3-6 are to be skipped, make sure the fuel supply line (at the fuel pump), the primer lines (at the carburetor) and the applicable electrical leads are disconnected before continuing at Step 7.

Make sure all cable clamps are reinstalled in their original positions and new tie-straps are installed to replace any that were removed.

1. Disconnect the spark plug leads and remove the spark plugs to prevent accidental starting.

2. *Electric start models*—Disconnect both battery cables from the battery. Then remove the cables from the power head. Note each connection's location and the cable routing for reassembly.

3. *Rope start models*—Remove the rewind starter as described in Chapter Twelve.

4. Remove the fuel pump and carburetor as described in Chapter Six.

> *NOTE*
> *Do not disconnect electrical and ignition components from each other unless absolutely necessary. Simply remove the mounting screws, cable clamps and tie-straps.*

5. Remove the entire ignition system. This includes the flywheel, armature plate (containing the charge, sensor and stator coil [if equipped]), power pack and ignition coils. See Chapter Seven. Make sure the power head-to-drive shaft housing (or lower cowl) ground lead (or strap) is also disconnected.

6. *Electric start models*—Remove the electric starter and starter solenoid, rectifier, terminal block and the remaining wiring harness. Do not remove the neutral safety switch. See Chapter Seven.

7. If the ignition system is not going to be removed:
   a. Disengage the throttle arm spring (A, **Figure 13**) and washer from the throttle/spark control arm. Then remove the locking wire from the end of the throttle control rod (B, **Figure 13**). Separate the ignition plate link from the throttle control lever. Locate and secure the control arm's bushing.
   b. Remove one stop switch (black) lead and terminal from pin E of the armature side of the five-pin

Amphenol connector (male body, female pins). Refer to *Electrical Connector Service* in Chapter Seven.
   c. Remove the other stop switch (black) lead from the lower ignition coil mounting screw. Reinstall the screw temporarily to secure the washer(s).
   d. Disconnect the power head-to-drive shaft housing (or lower cowl) ground lead (or strap).

8. Disconnect the water discharge (tell-tale) hose from the exhaust cover fitting (**Figure 14**). Slide the hose through its clamp and remove it from the motor.

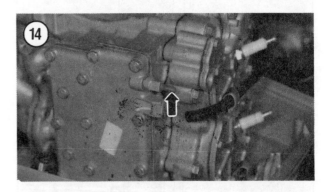

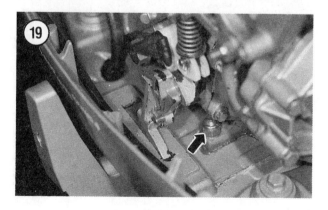

9. Remove the four screws and the upper and lower clamps holding the vertical throttle/spark control shaft. Then lift the shaft from the lower cowl's grommet. On tiller handle models, it is necessary to disconnect the throttle cable from the control shaft before it can be removed.

10. *Tiller handle models*—Proceed as follows:

    a. Disconnect the shift handle's linkage from the shift lever by removing the special locking clip and washer and sliding the link from its mounting stud.

    b. Install a small drill bit or paper clip through the hole in the top of the plunger shaft (A, **Figure 15**, typical) to secure the shaft to the bracket. If the hole is not visible, move the shift linkage until it is.

    c. Remove the cotter pin and washer holding the lower end of the cam link to the shift cam. Then disengage the link from the cam. Make sure you are disconnecting the lower end of the link (**Figure 16**), not the upper (B, **Figure 15**).

    d. Remove the screw and washer (A, **Figure 17**), then remove the mounting bracket. On electric start models, the neutral safety switch is removed with the bracket. On rope start models, the rewind starter lockout cable is removed with the bracket.

    e. Remove the screw (B, **Figure 17**) securing the cam link to the power head. Locate and secure the washer behind the cam link.

    f. Remove the screw and two locknuts (and washers) securing the plunger bracket to the engine. Then remove the cam link and plunger bracket assembly (**Figure 18**, typical).

11. Remove the four bottom mounting screws securing the power head to the drive shaft housing.

12. Locate and remove the two upper nuts and washers (one each side) securing the power head to the drive shaft housing (**Figure 19**). Use offset box-end wrench (part No. 322700) or an equivalent offset 1/2 in. box-end wrench to access the nuts.

CAUTION
At this point, there must be no hoses, leads or linkages connecting the power head to the drive shaft housing. Make sure that nothing will interfere with power head removal before continuing.

13. Rock the power head, or tap the power head with a plastic or rubber mallet to break the gasket seal between the drive shaft housing and power head. Then lift and remove the power head and inner exhaust housing assembly and place it on a clean bench.

14. Locate and secure the flat washer on the copper water tube in the drive shaft housing.

15. Remove the six screws securing the inner exhaust housing to the power head. Tap the lower end of the exhaust

8

snout with a soft-faced hammer to separate the housing from the power head. See **Figure 20**.

Remove and discard the water tube grommet located in the bore at the front of the inner exhaust housing.

17. Thoroughly clean all gasket material from the power head, drive shaft housing and inner exhaust housing mating surfaces. Then remove and discard the O-ring around the crankshaft's lower end cap.

18. To install the power head, begin by installing a new grommet in the inner exhaust housing. Lubricate the grommet with soapy water and push it into the housing with grommet installation tool (part No. 304148) or equivalent. Make sure the grommet's raised tab seats in the housing's hole.

19. Position the power head so the base gasket surface is pointing upward. Then place a new power head gasket (without sealer) onto the power head.

20. Position the inner exhaust housing against the power head and align the screw holes. Coat the six mounting screws with OMC Nut Lock threadlocking adhesive (or equivalent). Then install and evenly tighten the screws to 96-120 in.-lb. (10.9-13.6 N•m).

21. Lubricate a new O-ring with OMC Triple Guard Grease, then install it into the lower end cap's groove. Verify that the flat washer is in place (over the water tube) in the drive shaft housing, then coat the drive shaft splines with OMC Moly Lube. Wipe any excess lubricant from the top of the shaft.

22. Slowly lower the power head and exhaust housing assembly onto the drive shaft housing, while guiding the water tube into its opening at the front of the inner exhaust housing. Rotate the crankshaft clockwise as necessary to engage the drive shaft splines.

23. Once the power head is seated to the drive shaft housing, coat the threads of the four power head mounting screws and the two studs with OMC Gasket Sealing Compound. Install and hand-tighten the four screws. Then install the upper mounting nuts (and washers) hand tight. Finally tighten all six fasteners evenly to 192-216 in.-lb. (21.7-24.4 N•m).

24. *Tiller handle models*—Proceed as follows:

   a. Position the plunger bracket (**Figure 18**) to the power head and secure it in place with the screw and two locknuts (and washers). Tighten the fasteners securely.

   b. Position the cam link and plunger lever to the power head. Position the screw behind the plunger lever, then install the screw (B, **Figure 17**) through the cam link, plunger lever and washer. Tighten the screw securely.

   c. Position the mounting bracket (and neutral safety switch or rewind starter lockout cable) to the power

head and secure it with a screw (A, **Figure 17**). Tighten the screw securely.

   d. Connect the cam link to the shift cam. Secure the link with the flat washer and a new cotter pin (**Figure 16**). Bend both prongs of the cotter pin for a secure attachment.

   e. Remove the drill bit (or paper clip) securing the plunger shaft.

   f. Connect the shift handle linkage to the shift lever and secure it with the flat washer and special locking clip.

25. Connect the water discharge (tell-tale) hose to the exhaust cover fitting (**Figure 14**). Secure the hose in its clamp.

26. Position the vertical throttle/spark control shaft to the power head. Install the two upper and one lower half-clamps and secure them in place with a total of four screws. Tighten the screws securely. On tiller models, reconnect the throttle cable to the control shaft. Secure the cable with a flat washer and new cotter pin. Bend both prongs of the cotter pin for a secure attachment.

27A. If the ignition system was not removed:

   a. Reconnect one stop switch (black) lead to pin E of the armature side of the five-pin Amphenol connector. Refer to *Electrical Connector Service* in Chapter Seven.

   b. Connect the other stop switch (black) lead to the lower ignition coil mounting screw. The correct stack-up is coil ground tab, stop lead terminal, star washer, flat washer and screw. Tighten the mounting screw to 48-96 in.-lb. (5.4-10.9 N•m).

   c. Connect the throttle control rod to the control arm's link block. The offset of the block must face forward. Secure the control rod with a new lock wire and a suitable piece of stainless steel safety wire. See B, **Figure 13**.

   d. Position the armature plate link over the control arm's bushing and stud. Install the washer, then

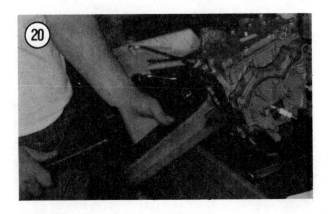

gage the link's spring to the groove in the control arm's stud. See A, **Figure 13**.

e. Reconnect the power head-to-drive shaft housing (or lower cowl) ground lead (or strap). Tighten the connections securely.

27B. If the ignition system was removed, reinstall the complete ignition system at this time. This includes the armature plate (and all coils), power pack, ignition coils and flywheel. See Chapter Seven. Make sure the power head-to-drive shaft housing (or lower cowl) ground lead (or strap) is reconnected and its connections are securely tightened.

28A. *Rope start models*—Install the rewind starter as described in Chapter Twelve.

28B. *Electric start models*—Install the electric starter and starter solenoid, rectifier, terminal block and wiring harness. See Chapter Seven.

29. Install the fuel pump and carburetor as described in Chapter Six.

30. *Electric start models*—Connect both battery cables to the power head as noted on disassembly. Then connect both battery cables to the battery. Tighten all connections securely.

31. Install the spark plugs and reconnect the spark plug leads. Tighten the spark plugs to 18-21 ft.-lb. (24.4-28.5 N•m).

32. Refer to Chapter Four for fuel and oil recommendations and break-in procedures (as needed). Then refer to Chapter Five and perform all synchronization and linkage adjustments.

Removal/Installation
(25 and 35 hp [Three-cylinder])

The power head is best removed with most of the accessories and systems left installed. These items can be removed after the power head is separated from the drive shaft housing. Refer to the back of the book for wiring diagrams. Make sure all cable clamps are reinstalled in their original positions and new tie-straps are installed to replace any that were removed.

Only Amphenol connectors are used on 1995 (EO) models, while Deutsch and Amphenol connectors are used on 1996-2003 (ED-ST) models.

1. Disconnect the spark plug leads and remove the spark plugs to prevent accidental starting.

2. *Electric start models*—Disconnect both battery cables from the battery. Then remove the cables from the power head. Note each connection's location and the cable routing for reassembly.

3. Remove the carburetor air intake cover by turning the knob in the middle of the cover. Then disconnect the drain hose and remove the cover from the power head.

4A. *Tiller handle models*—Disconnect the choke cable from the bracket mounted to the middle carburetor.

4B. *Trim/tilt models*—Disconnect the lower cowl mounted trim/tilt switch leads at their bullet connectors. The leads are green/white, blue/white and red/white.

5. Remove the split lower cowl as follows:

    a. Remove the six screws securing the cowl halves to each other. Access the screws from the starboard side.

    b. Pull the port cowl far enough from the engine to cut the tie-strap and remove the fuel line from the fuel tank connector. Then remove the port lower cowl.

    c. Remove the clamp securing the electrical leads to the starboard cowl. Then remove the starboard lower cowl.

6. *Electric start models*—Remove the two screws (**Figure 21**) securing the electrical component access cover to the starboard side of the engine. Then remove the cover. Note the location of each electrical connector and all leads, then disconnect all Amphenol (or Deutsch) connectors located under the access cover.

8

7. *Tiller handle electric start models*—Remove the two neutral safety switch (yellow/red) leads from the tiller handle side of the six-pin connector. These are pins B (or 2) and F (or 6) on the female body (male pins). Refer to *Electrical Connector Service* in Chapter Seven.

8. *Tiller handle models*—Disconnect the stop switch ground (black) lead from the starter motor ground stud (electric start models) or the ignition module ground screw (rope start models).

9. *Tiller handle models and 1995 (EO) remote control models*—Pull the oil warning light 2-pin Amphenol connector from the ignition module mounting clips. Then separate the connector.

10A. *Tiller handle models*—Proceed as follows:
   a. Disconnect the throttle cable's ball socket from the spark control arm. Use socket remover (part No. 342226) or equivalent to prevent damaging components.
   b. Disconnect the shift handle's linkage from the shift lever by removing the locking clip and sliding the shift linkage from the lever's stud.
   c. Remove the screw securing the throttle cable to its bracket assembly. Locate and secure the washer located between the throttle cable anchor and the bracket.
   d. Remove the two screws, locknuts and washers securing the tiller handle assembly to the steering arm (and tube).
   e. Remove the tiller handle assembly from the power head with the throttle cable, shift linkage, and all electrical leads and harnesses intact.

10B. *Remote control models*—Disconnect the throttle and shift cables as described in Chapter Twelve.

11. Remove the screw and washer securing the shift lever to the power head. This is the lowest screw on the shift lever. Do not loosen or remove the two upper screws (located side by side). Remove the shift lever from the power head.

12A. *Tiller handle models*—Remove the rewind starter as described in Chapter Twelve.

12B. *Electric start models*—Remove the three flywheel cover screws. Then remove the cover.

> ### CAUTION
> *At this point, there must be no hoses, wires or linkages connecting the power head to the drive shaft housing. Make sure that nothing will interfere with power head removal before continuing.*

13. Install a lifting eye, such as part No. 396748 (or equivalent) to the flywheel. Thread the three screws in only far enough to ensure adequate thread engagement. Threading the screws in too far will damage the encoder wheel or optical sensor mounted under the flywheel.

14. Attach a suitable hoist to the lifting eye, then remove the seven screws securing the power head to the drive shaft housing.

15. Apply upward pressure with a suitable hoist while rocking the power head to break the gasket seal between the power head and the drive shaft housing. Then lift the power head free from the drive shaft housing and set it on a clean bench or mount it to a suitable holding fixture.

16. Thoroughly clean all gasket material from the power head and drive shaft housing mating surfaces.

17. To install the power head, begin by coating both sides of a new power head base gasket with OMC Gasket Sealing Compound. Then position the gasket on the drive shaft housing.

18. Coat the drive shaft splines with OMC Moly Lube. Then wipe any excess lubricant from the top of the shaft.

19. Carefully lower the power head onto the drive shaft housing using the lifting eye and a suitable hoist. Rotate the crankshaft clockwise as necessary to engage the drive shaft splines.

20. Once the power head is seated to the drive shaft housing, coat the seven mounting screws with OMC Gasket Sealing Compound, then install and evenly tighten the screws to 180-204 in.-lb. (20.3-23.0 N•m). Remove the hoist and lifting eye.

21. Position the shift lever to the power head and secure it with a screw and washer. Tighten the screw to 84-106 in.-lb. (9.5-12.0 N•m).

22A. *Tiller handle models*—Install the rewind starter as described in Chapter Twelve.

22B. *Electric start models*—Install the flywheel cover. Coat the threads of the three mounting screws with OMC Nut Lock threadlocking adhesive (or equivalent). Then install and tighten the screws to 60-84 in.-lb. (6.8-9.5 N•m).

23A. *Tiller handle models*—Proceed as follows:
   a. Install the tiller handle assembly to the steering arm and secure it in place with two screws, washers and locknuts. Tighten the screws to 216-240 in.-lb. (24.4-27.1 N•m), then tighten the locknuts (while holding the screws) to 216-240 in.-lb. (24.4-27.1 N•m).
   b. Route the throttle cable, shift linkage and all electrical leads and harnesses to the power head.
   c. Position the throttle cable anchor to its bracket with a washer between the anchor and the bracket. Then install the screw and tighten it securely.
   d. Connect the shift handle's linkage to the shift lever and secure it with the locking clip.

e. Connect the throttle cable's ball socket to the spark control arm. Use socket installer (part No. 342225) or equivalent to prevent damaging components.

23B. *Remote control models*—Connect the remote control throttle and shift cables to the power head as described in Chapter Twelve.

24. *Tiller handle models and 1995 (EO) remote control models*—Connect the oil warning light Amphenol connector to its engine wiring harness mate. Then position the connector in the ignition module mounting clips.

25. *Tiller handle models*—Connect the stop switch ground (black) lead to the starter motor ground stud (electric start models) or the ignition module ground screw (rope start models). Tighten the connection securely.

26. *Tiller handle electric start models*—Reinstall the two neutral safety switch (yellow/red) leads to their six-pin connector body. These are pins B (or 2) and F (or 6) on the female body (male pins). Refer to *Electrical Connector Service* in Chapter Seven.

27. *Electric start models*—Reconnect all Amphenol or Deutsch connectors and secure them to their mounting clips on the electrical component bracket as noted on disassembly. Then install the access cover and secure it with two screws. Tighten the screws securely.

28. Install the split lower cowl as follows:

a. Position the port lower cowl close to the power head and reconnect the fuel supply line to its connector. Secure the connection with a new tie-strap, then seat the port lower cowl to the engine.

b. Position the starboard lower cowl close to the power head and secure the appropriate electrical leads to its clamp. Then seat the starboard lower cowl to the engine.

c. Install the six screws securing the cowl halves to each other. Install the screws from the starboard side. Tighten the screws to 84-106 in.-lb. (9.5-12.0 N•m).

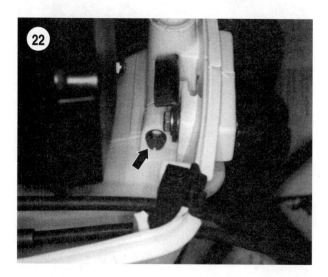

29A. *Tiller handle models*—Connect the choke cable to the bracket mounted on the middle carburetor.

29B. *Trim/tilt models*—Connect the lower cowl mounted trim/tilt switch leads to their engine harness bullet connector mates. The leads are green/white, blue/white and red/white.

30. Install the carburetor air intake cover. Make sure the drain hose is reconnected and the knob is turned to lock the cover to the engine.

31. *Electric start models*—Connect both battery cables to the power head as noted on disassembly. Then connect both battery cables to the battery. Tighten all connections securely.

32. Install the spark plugs and reconnect the spark plug leads. Tighten the spark plugs to 18-21 ft.-lb. (24.4-28.5 N•m).

33. Refer to Chapter Four for fuel and oil recommendations and break-in procedures (as needed). Then refer to Chapter Five and perform all synchronization and linkage adjustments.

Removal/Installation
(40-50 hp [Two-cylinder], 28 and 35 Jet)

The power head is best removed with most of the accessories and systems left installed. These items can be removed after the power head is separated from the drive shaft housing. Refer to the back of the book for wiring diagrams. Make sure all cable clamps are reinstalled in their original positions and new tie-straps are installed to replace any that were removed.

Only Amphenol connectors are used on 1995 (EO) models, while Deutsch and Amphenol connectors are used on 1996-2003 (ED-ST) models.

1. Disconnect the spark plug leads and remove the spark plugs to prevent accidental starting.

2. *Electric start models*—Disconnect both battery cables from the battery. Then remove the cables from the power head. Note each connection's location and the cable routing for reassembly.

3. Disconnect the fuel supply line from the quick-disconnect fuel connector on the port lower cowl. On oil injected models, also disconnect the oil line from the fitting next to the fuel connector. Plug the oil line and cap the fitting to prevent leakage and/or contamination.

4. Remove the split lower cowl as follows:

a. Remove the interior screw located at the very front of the cowl. See **Figure 22**.

b. Remove the two interior screws located at the very rear of the cowl. See **Figure 23**.

c. Remove the exterior screw located at the lower mid-point of the cowls, just behind the steering arm. See **Figure 24**.

d. Disconnect the water discharge (tell-tale) hose from the rear corner of the starboard cowl.

e. *Trim/tilt models*—Disconnect the lower cowl mounted trim/tilt switch leads at their bullet connectors. The leads are green/white, blue/white and red/white.

f. Remove the starboard and port lower cowl halves from the engine. Lift the control cable and fuel and electrical grommets from each cowl half as it is removed.

5A. *Tiller handle models*—Disconnect the shift linkage and throttle cable as follows:

a. Remove the special locking clip and clevis pin securing the shift handle's linkage to the rearmost shift lever.

b. Remove the screw securing the cable retaining plate to the trunnion anchor block. Remove the retaining plate.

c. Remove the special locking clip and clevis pin securing the throttle cable to the spark control arm.

d. Remove the screw securing the throttle cable anchor to the trunnion anchor block. Locate and secure the washer between the cable and the anchor block.

e. Position the throttle cable and shift handle's link to the side of the power head.

5B. *Remote control models*—Disconnect the throttle and shift cables as described in Chapter Twelve.

6. *Outboard models*—Remove the screw (**Figure 25**) securing the gearcase shift rod to the bellcrank at the port end of the shift shaft.

7A. *1995 (EO) Tiller handle electric start models*—Disconnect the electrical leads as follows:

a. Disconnect the stop switch black/yellow lead at its one-pin Amphenol connector. Then disconnect the stop switch black lead from the ignition coil (or power pack) mounting screw. Note the orientation of the washers before removing the lead, then reinstall the screw to secure the washers.

b. Disconnect the ignition (key) switch from its four-pin Amphenol connector. Then disconnect the warning horn from its three-pin Amphenol connector.

c. Disconnect the primer button purple lead from the terminal strip and the purple/white lead from the primer solenoid's bullet connector.

d. Disconnect the start button yellow/red lead from the starter solenoid and the purple lead from the terminal strip.

e. *Trim/tilt models*—Disconnect the trim/tilt motor from the engine harness at the large, locking 2-pin (blue and green leads) connector.

f. *Oil-injected models*—Disconnect the oil tank's tan and black leads at their bullet connectors.

7B. *1995 (EO) Remote control models*—Disconnect the electrical leads as follows:

a. Disconnect the main remote control harness at the large, red ten-pin connector.

b. Disconnect the remote oil tank's tan and black leads at their bullet connectors.

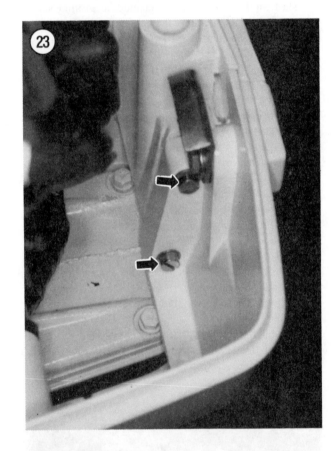

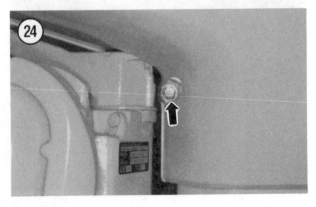

c. *Trim/tilt models*—Disconnect the trim/tilt motor from the engine harness from the large, locking two-pin (blue and green leads) connector.

d. *Trim/tilt models*—Disconnect the trim/tilt switch and sending unit harness from the engine at its five-pin Amphenol connector. The five leads are green/white, white/tan, tan/black, blue/white and red/purple.

7C. *1996-2003 (ED-ST) Tiller handle electric start models*—Disconnect the electrical leads as follows:

a. Disconnect one stop switch black/yellow lead from its one-pin Amphenol connector. Then disconnect the stator to power pack five-pin Amphenol connector. Remove the second stop switch black/yellow lead from pin E of the stator side of the Amphenol

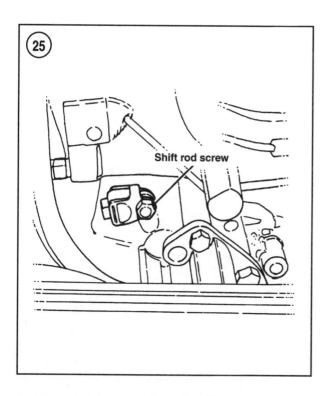

Shift rod screw

connector (male body, female pins). Refer to *Electrical Connector Service* in Chapter Seven.

b. Disconnect the stop switch black lead from its power head mounting screw. Note the orientation of the washers before removing the lead, then reinstall the screw to secure the washers.

c. Disconnect the ignition (key) switch from its six-pin Deutsch connector. Then disconnect the warning horn from its two-pin Deutsch connector. If equipped with a system check warning gauge (or an Audible Adaptor Module), disconnect it from the engine's eight-pin Deutsch connector.

d. Disconnect the primer button purple lead from the terminal strip and the purple/white lead from the primer solenoid's bullet connector.

e. Disconnect the start button yellow/red lead from the starter solenoid and the purple lead from the terminal strip.

f. *Trim/tilt models*—Disconnect the trim/tilt motor from the engine harness at the large, locking two-pin (blue and green leads) connector.

g. *Oil-injected models*—Disconnect the remote oil tank's tan and black leads from their two-pin Deutsch connector.

7D. *1996-2003 (ED-ST) remote control models*—Disconnect the electrical leads as follows:

a. Remove the access cover from the connector box on the port side of the power head. See **Figure 26**.

b. Disconnect the main harness six-pin Deutsch connector.

c. Disconnect the system check six-pin Deutsch connector.

d. Locate and disconnect the remote oil tank's two-pin Deutsch connector.

e. *Trim/tilt models*—Disconnect the switch and sending unit harness three-pin Deutsch connector. The connector should be in the connector box with the two 6-pin connectors.

f. *Trim/tilt models*—Disconnect the trim/tilt motor from the engine harness at the large, locking two-pin (blue and green leads) connector.

7E. *Rope start models*—Disconnect the electrical leads as follows:

a. Disconnect the armature plate five-pin Amphenol connector. Remove the black/yellow lead from pin E of the armature plate side of the connector (male body, female pin) as described in *Electrical Connector Service* in Chapter Seven.

b. Remove the screw securing the stop switch ground (black) lead to the power head.

c. If equipped with an AC lighting coil, disconnect the lighting system leads from the stator coil's yellow, yellow/gray and yellow/blue lead bullet connectors.

8

8. *Rope start models*—Remove the rewind starter as described in Chapter Twelve.

CAUTION
At this point, there must be no hoses, wires or linkages connecting the power head to the drive shaft housing. Make sure that nothing will interfere with power head removal before continuing.

9. Install a lifting eye, such as part No. 396748 (or equivalent) to the flywheel. Make sure the screws are threaded in far enough to ensure adequate thread engagement.

10. Attach a suitable hoist to the lifting eye, then remove the eight screws and washers securing the power head to the drive shaft housing.

11. Remove the nut and washer securing the rear of the power head to the adaptor plate. The nut is recessed into the pocket at the rear of the adaptor plate.

12. Apply upward pressure with a suitable hoist while rocking the power head to break the gasket seal between the power head and the drive shaft housing. Then lift the power head free from the drive shaft housing and set it on a clean bench or mount it to a suitable holding fixture.

13. Thoroughly clean all gasket material from the power head and drive shaft housing mating surfaces.

14. To install the power head, begin by positioning a new base gasket (without sealer) onto the drive shaft housing.

15. Coat the drive shaft splines with OMC Moly Lube. Then wipe any excess lubricant from the top of the shaft.

16. Carefully lower the power head onto the drive shaft housing using the lifting eye and a suitable hoist. Rotate the crankshaft clockwise as necessary to engage the drive shaft splines.

17. Once the power head is seated to the drive shaft housing, coat the eight mounting screws and the one stud with OMC Gasket Sealing Compound, then install and evenly tighten the screws and nut (and washers) to 18-20 ft.-lb. (24.4-27.1 N•m). Remove the hoist and lifting eye.

18. *Rope start models*—Install the rewind starter as described in Chapter Twelve.

19. Align the shift rod with the shift shaft bellcrank and install the retaining screw. Tighten the screw securely. See **Figure 25**.

20A. *Tiller handle models*—Connect the shift linkage and throttle cable as follows:

   a. Position the throttle cable in the upper relief of the trunnion anchor block, then position the cable end to the *upper* hole in the spark control arm. Secure the cable with the clevis pin and special locking clip.

   b. Align the throttle cable anchor with the hole behind the trunnion anchor block's upper pocket. Position a washer between the cable anchor and the block, then install the screw. Tighten the screw securely.

   c. Position the shift linkage's bushing in the lower relief of the trunnion anchor block. Then position the linkage end to the upper hole in the rearward shift lever. Secure the linkage with the clevis pin and special locking clip.

   d. Position the cable retaining plate over the trunnion anchor block and install the screw. Tighten the screw securely.

20B. *Remote control models*—Connect the throttle and shift cables as described in Chapter Twelve.

21. Reconnect all electrical leads and harnesses disconnected in Step 7. Refer to *Electrical Connector Service* in Chapter Seven as necessary. All ring terminal connections must be tightened securely and coated with OMC Black Neoprene Dip.

22. Install the split lower cowl as follows:

   a. Position the cowl halves to the power head. Lift the cables, leads and hoses (and their grommets) and seat them into each cowl half during installation.

   b. *Trim/tilt models*—Connect the lower cowl mounted trim/tilt switch leads to their engine harness mates.

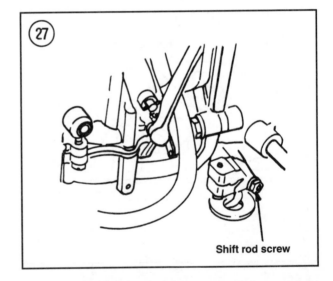

Shift rod screw

c. Connect the water discharge (tell-tale) hose to the rear corner of the starboard cowl.

d. Install and evenly tighten the one exterior (**Figure 24**) and three interior (**Figures 22-23**) screws.

23. Purge and connect the oil supply line as described in Chapter Eleven. Use a new snapper (ratchet) type clamp to secure the connection. Then reconnect the fuel supply line to the engine's quick-disconnect fitting.

24. *Electric start models*—Connect both battery cables to the power head as noted on disassembly. Then connect both battery cables to the battery. Tighten all connections securely.

25. Install the spark plugs and reconnect the spark plug leads. Tighten the spark plugs to 18-21 ft.-lb. (24.4-28.5 N•m).

26. Refer to Chapter Four for fuel and oil recommendations and break-in procedures (as needed). Then refer to Chapter Five and perform all synchronization and linkage adjustments.

Removal/Installation (50-70 hp [Three-cylinder])

The power head is best removed with most of the accessories and systems left installed. These items can be re-

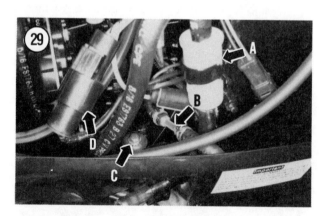

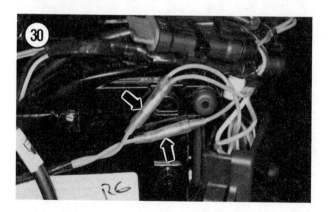

moved after the power head is separated from the drive shaft housing. Refer to the back of the book for wiring diagrams. Make sure all cable clamps are reinstalled in their original positions and new tie-straps are installed to replace any that were removed.

Only Amphenol connectors are used on 1995 (EO) models, while Deutsch and Amphenol connectors are used on 1996-1998 (ED-EC) models.

1. Disconnect the spark plug leads and remove the spark plugs to prevent accidental starting.

2. Disconnect both battery cables from the battery. Then remove the cables from the power head. Note each connection's location and the cable routing for reassembly.

3A. *Tiller handle models*—Disconnect the shift linkage and throttle cable as follows:

a. Remove the cotter pin, washer and clevis pin securing the shift handle's linkage to the shift lever.

b. Remove the screw securing the throttle cable to the spark control arm. Locate and secure the washer between the cable and control arm.

c. Remove the screw securing the throttle cable anchor to the intake manifold. Locate and secure the washer between the cable and the manifold.

d. Position the throttle cable and shift handle's link to the side of the power head.

3B. *Remote control models*—Disconnect the throttle and shift cables as described in Chapter Twelve.

4A. *Tiller handle models*—Remove the screw (**Figure 27**) securing the gearcase shift rod to the bellcrank at the port end of the shift shaft.

4B. *Remote control models*—Remove the clip (**Figure 28**) from the starboard end of the shift rod, then push the shaft toward the port side of the power head to disconnect the shift rod from the shift lever bellcrank.

NOTE
Do not disconnect any lines from the oil injection pump unless the pump is going to be replaced. It is very easy to damage the plastic fittings and body of the pump when removing the lines.

5. Disconnect the fuel supply line from either side of the inline fuel filter (A, **Figure 29**). Cap the filter and plug the line to prevent leakage and contamination.

6. Disconnect the oil supply line from the translucent site tube (B, **Figure 29**), located just below the oil injection pump. Cap the sight tube and plug the line to prevent leakage and contamination.

7. *Trim/tilt models*—Disconnect the lower cowl mounted trim/tilt switch leads at their bullet connectors. The leads are green/white, blue/white and red/purple. On remote control models, also disconnect the trim limit switch blue/white leads at their bullet connectors. See **Figure 30**.

8

8A. *1995 (EO) Tiller handle models*—Disconnect the electrical leads as follows:

a. Disconnect the stop switch black/yellow lead from its one-pin Amphenol connector. Then disconnect the stop switch black lead from the power pack mounting screw. Note the orientation of the washers before removing the lead, then reinstall the screw to secure the washers.

b. Disconnect the ignition (key) switch from its four-pin Amphenol connector. Then disconnect the warning horn from its three-pin Amphenol connector.

c. Disconnect the primer button red lead from the terminal strip and the purple/white lead from the primer solenoid's bullet connector.

d. Disconnect the start button yellow/red lead from the starter solenoid and the purple lead from its bullet connector.

e. Disconnect the trim/tilt motor from the engine harness at the large, locking two-pin (blue and green leads) connector (D, **Figure 29**).

f. Disconnect the oil tank's tan and black leads at their bullet connectors.

8B. *1995 (EO) Remote control models*—Disconnect the electrical leads as follows:

a. Disconnect the main remote control harness from the large, red ten-pin connector.

b. Disconnect the remote oil tank's tan and black leads at their bullet connectors.

c. *Trim/tilt models*—Disconnect the trim/tilt motor from the engine harness from the large, locking two-pin (blue and green leads) connector (D, **Figure 29**).

d. *Trim/tilt models*—Disconnect the trim/tilt switch and sending unit harness from the engine at its five-pin Amphenol connector. The five leads are green/white, white/tan, tan/black, blue/white and red/purple.

e. *Trim/tilt models*—Disconnect the trim sending unit's two-pin Amphenol connector and separate the ground lead at its bullet connector. This is a black lead connected to a green lead.

8C. *1996-2003 (ED-ST) Tiller handle models*—Disconnect the electrical leads as follows:

a. Disconnect two stop switch black/yellow leads from their two-pin Amphenol connector.

b. Disconnect the stop switch black lead from its power head mounting screw. Note the orientation of the washers before removing the lead, then reinstall the screw to secure the washers.

c. Disconnect the ignition (key) switch from its six-pin Deutsch connector. Then disconnect the warning horn from its two-pin Deutsch connector. If

equipped with a system check warning gauge (or an Audible Adaptor Module), disconnect it from the engine's eight-pin Deutsch connector.

d. Disconnect the primer button red lead at the terminal strip and the purple/white lead at the primer solenoid's bullet connector.

e. Disconnect the start button yellow/red lead from the starter solenoid and the purple lead from the terminal strip.

f. Disconnect the trim/tilt motor from the engine harness at the large, locking two-pin (blue and green leads) connector (D, **Figure 29**).

g. Disconnect the remote oil tank's tan and black leads from their two-pin Deutsch connector.

8D. *1996-2003 (ED-ST) Remote control models*—Disconnect the electrical leads as follows:

a. Remove the access cover from the connector box near the top of the cylinder head.

b. Disconnect the main harness six-pin Deutsch connector.

c. Disconnect the system check six-pin Deutsch connector.

d. Locate and disconnect the remote oil tank's two-pin Deutsch connector.

e. *Trim/tilt models*—Disconnect the switch and sending unit harness three-pin Deutsch connector. The connector should be in the connector box with the two 6-pin connectors.

f. *Trim/tilt models*—Disconnect the trim/tilt motor from the engine harness at the large, locking two-pin (blue and green leads) connector (D, **Figure 29**).

g. *Trim/tilt models*—Disconnect the trim sending unit's two-pin Amphenol connector and the separate ground lead at its bullet connector. This is a black lead connected to a green lead.

9. Disconnect the water discharge (tell-tale) hose from the fitting on the exhaust cover (early models) or top of the cylinder block (late models).

10. Remove the lower cowl's trim covers as follows:

a. Remove the four screws securing the front trim cover to the rear cover.

b. Remove the two screws securing the rear portion of the trim cover to the lower cowl. These screws are located just below and to the sides of the cylinder head. Then remove the rear trim cover.

c. Remove the two screws securing the front portion of the trim cover to the lower cowl. Then remove the front trim cover.

d. Remove the two screws (and eight washers) securing the lower cowl to the support brackets (near the intake manifold) on each side of the power head. See

C, **Figure 29**. Make sure you locate and secure the four washers from each screw.

e. Locate and disconnect the power head-to-lower cowl ground lead (or strap).

CAUTION
At this point, there must be no hoses, wires or linkages connecting the power head to the drive shaft housing. Make sure that nothing will interfere with power head removal before continuing.

11. Install a lifting eye, such as part No. 396748 (or equivalent) to the flywheel. Make sure the screws are threaded in far enough to ensure adequate thread engagement.

12. Attach a suitable hoist to the lifting eye, then remove the six screws and washers securing the power head to the drive shaft housing.

13. Remove the nut and washer securing the rear of the power head to the adaptor plate. The nut is recessed in the pocket at the rear of the adaptor plate.

14. Apply upward pressure with a suitable hoist while rocking the power head to break the gasket seal between the power head and the drive shaft housing. Then lift the power head free from the drive shaft housing and set it on a clean bench or mount it to a suitable holding fixture.

15. Thoroughly clean all gasket material from the power head and drive shaft housing mating surfaces.

16. To install the power head, begin by positioning a new base gasket (without sealer) onto the drive shaft housing.

17. Coat the drive shaft splines with OMC Moly Lube. Then wipe any excess lubricant from the top of the shaft.

18. Carefully lower the power head onto the drive shaft housing using the lifting eye and a suitable hoist. Rotate the crankshaft clockwise as necessary to align the drive shaft splines.

19. Once the power head is seated to the drive shaft housing, coat the six mounting screws with OMC Gel Seal II, then coat the one stud with OMC Gasket Sealing Compound. Install and evenly tighten the six screws and one nut (and their respective washers) to 18-20 ft.-lb. (24.4-27.1 N•m). Then remove the hoist and lifting eye.

20. Install the lower cowl's front and rear trim covers as follows:

a. Secure the lower cowl to the support brackets (near the intake manifold) on each side of the power head. Install the two screws, making sure the washer stack-up is large washer, small washer, rubber grommet (with inner support tube), small washer, large washer and screw. Tighten both screws securely. See C, **Figure 29**.

b. Position the front trim cover to the lower cowl and secure it with two screws. Tighten the screws securely.

c. Position the rear trim cover to the front trim cover. Install the four screws hand tight.

d. Secure the rear trim cover to the lower cowl with two screws. The screws are installed just below and to each side of the cylinder head. Tighten these screws securely, then tighten the four front-to-rear cover screws securely.

e. Reconnect the power head-to-lower cowl ground lead (or strap). Tighten the connection securely.

21. Connect the water discharge (tell-tale) hose to the fitting on the exhaust cover (early models) or top of the cylinder block (late models).

22. Reconnect all electrical leads and harnesses disconnected in Step 8. Refer to *Electrical Connector Service* in Chapter Seven as necessary. All ring terminal connections must be tightened securely, then coated with OMC Black Neoprene Dip.

23. *Trim/tilt models*—Connect the lower cowl mounted trim/tilt switch leads to their engine harness mates. On remote control models, reconnect the trim limit switch blue/white leads to their engine harness mates. See **Figure 30**.

24. Purge and connect the oil supply line to the translucent sight tube (B, **Figure 29**) as described in Chapter Eleven. Secure the oil line connection with the original spring clamp or a new snapper (ratchet) type clamp. Then reconnect the fuel supply line to the inline fuel filter (A, **Figure 29**). Secure the fuel line connection with the original spring clamp or a new tie-strap.

25A. *Tiller handle models*—Align the shift rod with the bellcrank at the port end of the shift shaft. Install and tighten the screw (**Figure 27**) to 60-84 in.-lb. (6.8-9.5 N•m) to secure the shift rod to the bellcrank.

25B. *Remote control models*—Align the shift rod with the bellcrank at the port end of the shift shaft. Then pull the shaft toward the starboard side of the power head to lock the shift rod to the bellcrank. Install the clip in the shift shaft hole at the starboard end of the shaft, making sure the flat and wave washers are behind the clip as shown in **Figure 28**.

26A. *Tiller handle models*—Connect the shift linkage and throttle cable as follows:

a. Position the shift linkage to the shift lever and secure it in place with the clevis pin, washer and a new cotter pin. Bend both prongs of the cotter pin for a secure attachment.

b. Position the throttle cable on the spark control arm. Install a washer between the arm and the cable, then secure the cable and washer to the arm with a screw. Tighten the screw securely.

8

c. Position the throttle cable anchor to the intake manifold. Position a washer between the anchor and the manifold, then secure the anchor and washer to the manifold with a screw. The screw must be installed in the cable anchor's most forward hole.

26B. *Remote control models*—Connect the throttle and shift cables to the power head as described in Chapter Twelve.

27. Connect both battery cables to the power head as noted on disassembly. Then connect both battery cables to the battery. Tighten all connections securely.

28. Install the spark plugs and reconnect the spark plug leads. Tighten the spark plugs to 18-21 ft.-lb. (24.4-28.5 N•m).

29. Refer to Chapter Four for fuel and oil recommendations and break-in procedures (as needed). Then refer to Chapter Five and perform all synchronization and linkage adjustments.

POWER HEAD DISASSEMBLY

Power head overhaul gasket sets are available for all models except 2, 3.3 and 3.5 hp models. It is often more economical and always simpler to order an overhaul gasket set instead of each component individually. Good mechanical practice requires every gasket, seal and O-ring be replaced during power head assembly. Replace the piston rings if the piston(s) are removed from the cylinders. It is strongly recommended that the connecting rod screws be replaced each time they are removed. If the piston is separated from the connecting rod, always install new piston pin locking clip(s) during assembly.

A large number of fasteners of different lengths and sizes are used in a power head. Plastic sandwich bags and/or cupcake tins are excellent methods of keeping small parts organized. Tag all larger internal parts for location and orientation. Use a felt-tipped permanent marker to mark components after they have been cleaned. Avoid scribing or stamping internal components as the marking process may damage or weaken the component.

> *NOTE*
> *Another series of at least six photographs, taken from the front, rear, top, bottom and both sides of the power head (before disassembly) will be very helpful during reassembly. The photographs are especially useful when trying to route electrical harnesses, fuel, primer and recirculation lines, and when installing accessories and control linkages.*

All power head components must be cleaned and inspected before any reassembly occurs. If the power head has had a major failure, it may be more economical (in time and money) to replace the basic power head as an assembly.

Remember that parts damaged by not using the correct tool can often be more expensive than the original cost of the tool. Recommended lubricant, sealants and adhesives are listed in the Quick Reference Data section at the front of this manual.

Taper Pin Service

Tapered pins are used to precisely align the crankcase halves to each other on all models except the 2, 3.3 and 3.5 hp and the 25 and 35 hp (three-cylinder) models. Taper pins must be removed before the crankcase cover can be separated from the cylinder block. The pins must be driven toward the intake manifold (front of the engine).

A special tool, fabricated as shown in **Figure 31**, is the only recommended method of removing the taper pins. The tool allows the pin to be driven straight from its bore, without damaging the pin or the crankcase halves. Fabricate the tool from a piece of cold-rolled steel, 1/2 in. (12.7 mm) thick, 2 in. (50.8 mm) wide and 11.5 in. (292.1 mm) long. A hole may be drilled in the tool's upper end for storage purposes.

If you do not have the equipment to fabricate the tool, most welding or machine shops can make it for you.

Under no circumstances should a punch (or any other tool) with a tip diameter smaller than the head of the taper pin be used to remove the pin. The pin's head will mushroom (expand), and/or the punch may enter the taper pin bore. In either case, the cylinder block may be damaged.

> *CAUTION*
> *Tapered pins must be driven out toward the intake manifold (front of the engine). Never drive tapered pins toward the cylinder block (cylinder head), or the block will be damaged.*

Guide Bushings and Dowel Pins

The 2, 3.3 and 3.5 hp and the 25 and 35 hp (three-cylinder) models use two hollow guide bushings (similar to very large roll pins) to locate the crankcase cover to the cylinder block. The bushings fit into machined reliefs in two of the crankcase cover-to-cylinder block screw bores. The bushings can be easily removed with an appropriate pair of needlenose pliers. When installing the bushings, use a soft-faced hammer to tap them into their bores.

Dowel pins are used to locate and secure the crankshaft main bearing races to the cylinder block (or crankcase cover) on some models. Dowel pins do not have to be removed if they are securely seated in their bores. However, they must be accounted for during disassembly and reassembly. If a dowel pin can be readily removed from its bore, it must be removed and stored with the other internal components until reassembly begins.

Wrist Pin
Locking Clips

The wrist pin is locked into each end of its bore with a wire-type locking clip. If removed, the clips must be discarded and new clips used during reassembly.

Wrist pin clip remover (part No. 325937) or equivalent, is highly recommended for easy removal of the locking clips. If the remover is not available, one can be fabricated from a pair of standard needlenose pliers. Modify the pliers by removing 3/16 in. (4.8 mm) from one tip, then grinding it as shown in **Figure 32**. Work slowly and with light pressure, stopping often and allowing the tip to cool. If not, the heat treatment will be lost and the modified tip will not be durable.

CAUTION
Always use new wrist pin locking clips on reassembly.

Connecting Rod Service

All connecting rods on 20-70 hp and 18-35 jet models are of the fractured cap design and require a special fixture (part No. 396749) to correctly align the cap. An accessory

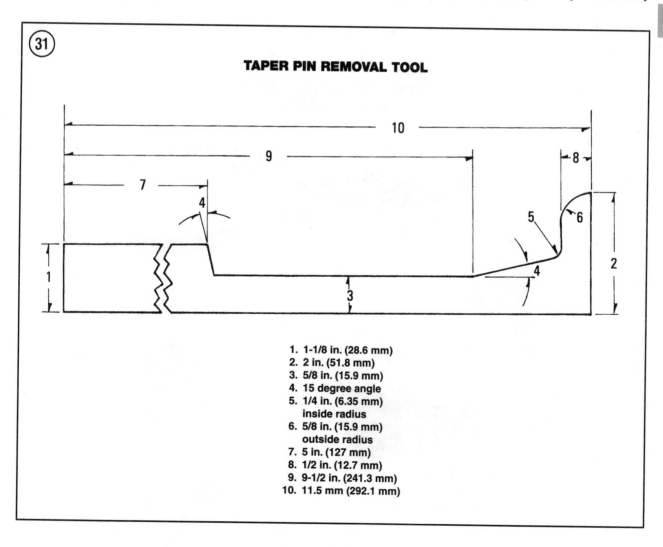

(31)

TAPER PIN REMOVAL TOOL

1. 1-1/8 in. (28.6 mm)
2. 2 in. (51.8 mm)
3. 5/8 in. (15.9 mm)
4. 15 degree angle
5. 1/4 in. (6.35 mm)
   inside radius
6. 5/8 in. (15.9 mm)
   outside radius
7. 5 in. (127 mm)
8. 1/2 in. (12.7 mm)
9. 9-1/2 in. (241.3 mm)
10. 11.5 mm (292.1 mm)

8

set of jaws (part No. 437273) is also required on 25 and 35 hp (three-cylinder) models.

NOTE
Smaller engines also use fractured cap connecting rods, but do not require a special fixture for reassembly. The cap is aligned by hand.

A fractured cap design means that the cap is broken from the rod during the manufacturing process, leaving a jagged (fractured) mating surface that will mate perfectly if installed in its original orientation. If the cap is installed reversed and the rod screws are tightened, the rod will be destroyed. Although alignment marks are provided, always mark the rod and cap with a permanent marker for redundancy. Correct orientation will be obvious if the time is taken to examine the mating surfaces of the rod and cap.

The special fixture contacts the rod cap and rod body on four beveled (machined) corners, applying a predetermined clamping force. The fixture is left in place during the torquing process, ensuring perfect rod cap alignment.

NOTE
Use new connecting rod bolts on reassembly.

If the rod cap is not perfectly aligned to the rod's body, the bearing surface will not be aligned, resulting in extremely noisy operation and premature bearing failure. This will destroy the connecting rod and the crankshaft.

Disassembly (2, 3.3 and 3.5 hp)

Refer to **Figure 33** for this procedure. Do not remove the large ball bearings from the crankshaft unless they must be replaced. Once the power head is disassembled, refer to *Power Head Cleaning and Inspection* in this chapter and clean and inspect all components before reassembling the power head.

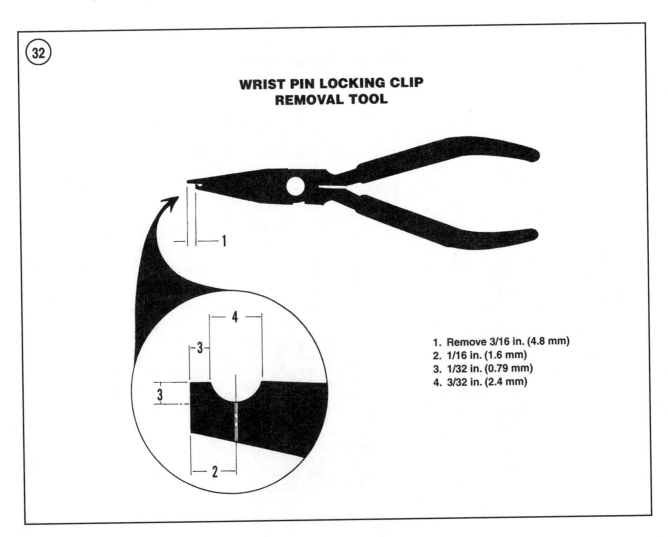

32

WRIST PIN LOCKING CLIP REMOVAL TOOL

1. Remove 3/16 in. (4.8 mm)
2. 1/16 in. (1.6 mm)
3. 1/32 in. (0.79 mm)
4. 3/32 in. (2.4 mm)

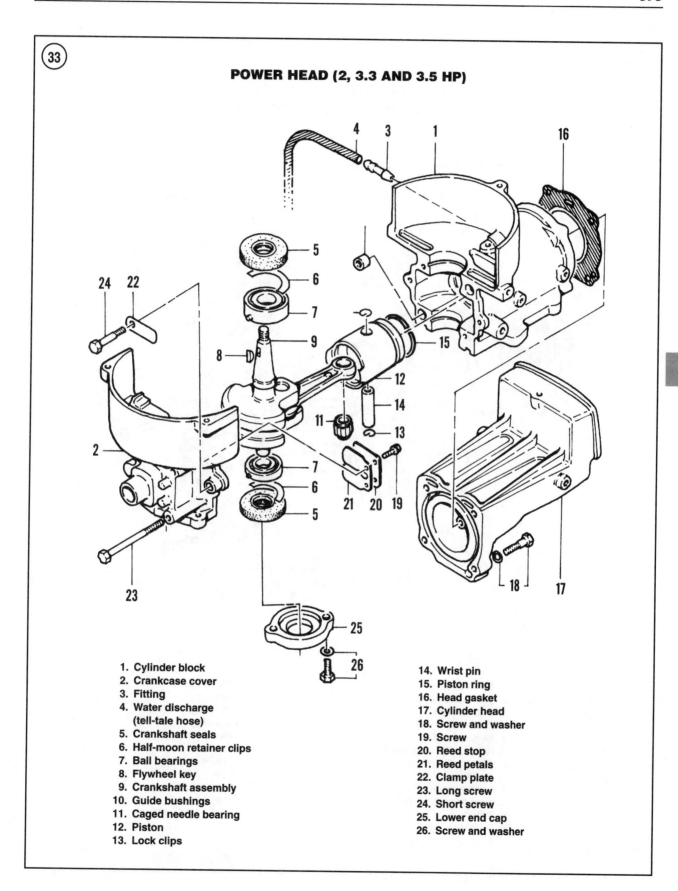

POWER HEAD (2, 3.3 AND 3.5 HP)

8

1. Cylinder block
2. Crankcase cover
3. Fitting
4. Water discharge
   (tell-tale hose)
5. Crankshaft seals
6. Half-moon retainer clips
7. Ball bearings
8. Flywheel key
9. Crankshaft assembly
10. Guide bushings
11. Caged needle bearing
12. Piston
13. Lock clips

14. Wrist pin
15. Piston ring
16. Head gasket
17. Cylinder head
18. Screw and washer
19. Screw
20. Reed stop
21. Reed petals
22. Clamp plate
23. Long screw
24. Short screw
25. Lower end cap
26. Screw and washer

CYLINDER BLOCK ASSEMBLY
(3, 4 HP AND 4 DELUXE)

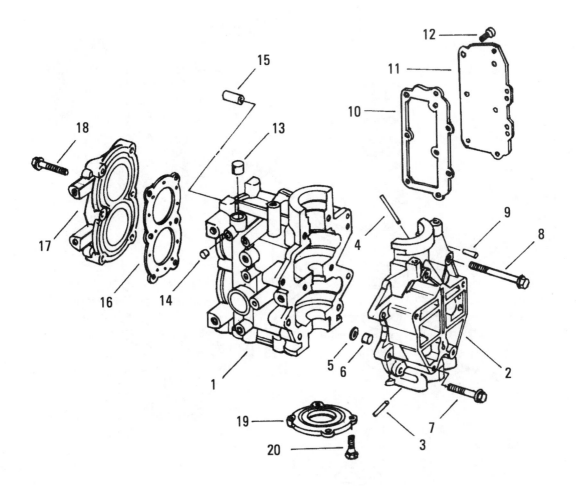

1. Cylinder block
2. Crankcase cover
3. Metering rod
   (1.3 in. [33 mm] long)
4. Metering rod
   (0.8 in. [20.3 mm] long)
5. Check valve screen
6. Check valve
7. Flange screws
8. Main bearing screws
9. Taper pin
10. Gasket
11. Exhaust cover
12. Screw
13. Large plug
14. Small plug
15. Water deflector
16. Gasket
17. Cylinder head
18. Screw
19. Lower end cap
   (3 and 4 hp)
20. Screw (3 and 4 hp)

1. Remove the two screws and washers securing the lower end cap to the power head. Remove the end cap from the power head.

2. Remove the four screws and washers securing the cylinder head to the power head. Tap the head with a soft-faced hammer to break it free from the power head. Remove and discard the gasket.

CAUTION
The crankcase cover and cylinder block are a matched, align-bored unit. Do not scratch, nick or damage the machined, mating surfaces.

3. Remove the six crankcase cover screws, then remove the crankcase cover from the cylinder block. Tap the cover with a soft-faced hammer to break it free from the cylinder block.

4. Lift the crankshaft, connecting rod and piston assembly from the cylinder block. Then locate and remove the two guide bushings (10, **Figure 33**) as necessary.

5. Slide the crankshaft seals and half-moon retainer rings from each end of the crankshaft. Discard the seals.

CAUTION
Wear suitable eye protection for piston ring and wrist pin locking clip removal.

6. Remove the piston ring from the piston using a standard piston ring expander. Retain the ring for cleaning the piston's ring groove.

7. Using locking clip remover (part No. 325937) or a modified pair of needlenose pliers (**Figure 32**), remove and discard the wrist pin locking clip from each end of the wrist pin bore.

8. Push the wrist pin out of the piston using a suitable mandrel. Remove the piston and the caged needle bearing from the connecting rod.

9. If either or both ball bearings must be replaced, remove the bearing(s) from the crankshaft using one of the following methods:

   a. Support the bearing in a knife-edged bearing plate. Press against the crankshaft until the bearing is free from the crankshaft. Then discard the bearing(s). When removing the upper bearing, install the flywheel nut to protect the crankshaft threads.

   b. Remove the bearing(s) using bearing puller (part No. 115316). Make sure each bearing's locating pin is positioned between the puller jaws, then tighten the through-bolts securely. Alternately tighten the puller bolts in 1/2 turn increments until the bearing is free from the crankshaft. Discard the bearing(s).

10. The connecting rod is not removable from the crankshaft. If the connecting rod or connecting rod big end bearing is excessively worn or damaged, replace the crankshaft as an assembly.

11. Clean and inspect the reed valves in the crankcase cover as described in Chapter Six.

12. Refer to *Power Head Cleaning and Inspection* in this chapter before beginning reassembly.

Disassembly
(3 and 4-8 hp [Including 4 Deluxe])

Two different styles of center main bearings are used on these models. All 3, 4 hp, 4 Deluxe and the 1995 (EO) 6 and 8 hp models use a center main bearing consisting of two stamped bearing liner halves and 30 loose bearing rollers.

On 1996-2003 (ED-ST) 6 and 8 hp models, the center main bearing consists of a machined outer race, 23 loose bearing rollers and a retaining ring. The outer race is fractured into two pieces (similar to a connecting rod) and a retaining ring holds the bearing together during assembly. A dowel pin aligns the race with the cylinder block.

On all models, a seal ring rides in the groove below the center main bearing.

All components (such as bearings, pistons and connecting rods) that are to be reused must be marked with their original location and orientation for reference during reassembly. Do not remove the large ball bearing from the crankshaft unless it must be replaced.

Refer to **Figure 34** (3, 4 hp and 4 Deluxe), **Figure 35** (6 and 8 hp) and **Figure 36** (all models, typical) for this procedure.

1. Remove the intake manifold and reed valves as described in Chapter Six.

2. If the rewind starter, ignition and fuel system components were not removed when the power head was removed:

   a. Refer to Chapter Six and remove the carburetor and fuel pump.

   b. Refer to Chapter Twelve and remove the rewind starter.

   c. Refer to Chapter Seven and remove the complete ignition system.

3. *6 and 8 hp*—Remove the three screws securing thermostat cover to the cylinder head, then remove the cover and thermostat components (17-25, **Figure 35**) from the cylinder head. Remove and discard the cover seal (24, **Figure 35**).

4. Remove the six screws securing the cylinder head to cylinder block. Carefully pull the head from the block, then remove and discard the gasket. If necessary, tap the head with a soft-faced (rubber or plastic) hammer to break the

8

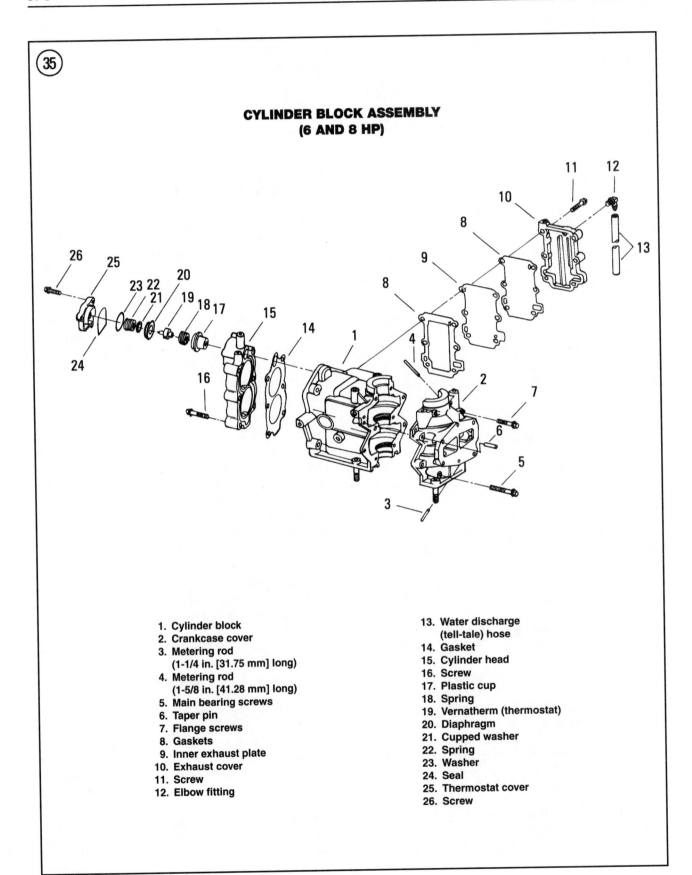

**CYLINDER BLOCK ASSEMBLY
(6 AND 8 HP)**

1. Cylinder block
2. Crankcase cover
3. Metering rod
   (1-1/4 in. [31.75 mm] long)
4. Metering rod
   (1-5/8 in. [41.28 mm] long)
5. Main bearing screws
6. Taper pin
7. Flange screws
8. Gaskets
9. Inner exhaust plate
10. Exhaust cover
11. Screw
12. Elbow fitting

13. Water discharge
    (tell-tale) hose
14. Gasket
15. Cylinder head
16. Screw
17. Plastic cup
18. Spring
19. Vernatherm (thermostat)
20. Diaphragm
21. Cupped washer
22. Spring
23. Washer
24. Seal
25. Thermostat cover
26. Screw

CRANKSHAFT ASSEMBLY
(3, 4-8 HP [TYPICAL])

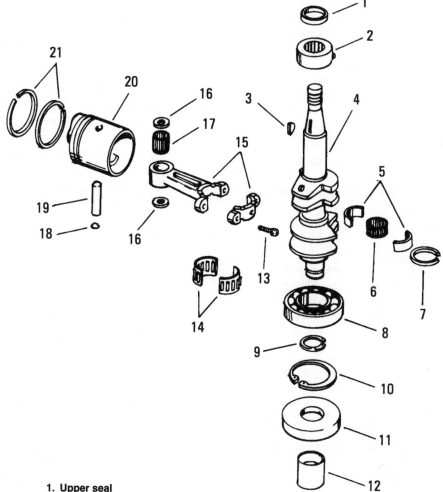

1. Upper seal
2. Upper main bearing
3. Flywheel key
4. Crankshaft
5. Center main bearing
   race (or liners)
6. Loose needles
7. Seal ring
8. Ball bearing
9. Retaining ring
10. Retaining ring
11. Lower seal
12. Sleeve/drive shaft seal
13. Rod cap screw
14. Caged roller bearing halves
15. Connecting rod
16. Thrust washers
    (3, 4 hp and 4 Deluxe)
17. Loose needles
    (or caged bearing)
18. Wrist pin lock clip
19. Wrist pin
20. Piston
21. Piston rings

8

gasket seal. Do not damage the sealing surfaces during the removal process.

5A. *3, 4 hp and 4 Deluxe*—Remove the eight screws securing the exhaust cover to the cylinder block. Carefully tap around the perimeter of the cover with a soft-faced mallet to break the gasket seal, then separate the cover from the block and remove and discard the gasket. Do not damage or distort the cover during the removal process.

5B. *6 and 8 hp*—Remove the six screws securing the exhaust cover and inner plate to the cylinder block. Carefully tap around the perimeter of the cover with a soft-faced mallet to break the gasket seal, then remove the assembly from the block and separate the inner plate from the cover. Remove and discard the gaskets. Do not damage or distort the cover or inner plate during the removal process.

6. *3 and 4 hp (except 4 Deluxe)*—Remove the four screws securing the lower end cap to the cylinder block. Then remove the lower end cap.

7. Remove the bottom crankshaft seal. If necessary, pierce the seal with a small punch and pry it from its bore. Then, using suitable snap ring pliers, remove the crankshaft retainer ring (10, **Figure 36**).

8. Mark the top piston *No.1* and the bottom piston *No. 2* with a permanent marker. Then temporarily install the cylinder head using only two screws. Tighten the screws finger-tight. This will prevent the pistons from falling out of their cylinders during disassembly.

CAUTION
Do not damage the taper pin or its bore during removal, or the cylinder block will be ruined.

9. Using a large punch, with a tip diameter larger than the taper pin's diameter, drive the taper pin toward the intake manifold side (front) of the power head. Then remove the pin from its bore.

10. Remove the ten crankcase cover-to-cylinder block screws. Note the length of each screw and its original location. There are six main bearing screws and four flange screws.

CAUTION
The crankcase cover and cylinder block are a matched, align-bored unit. Do not scratch, nick or damage the machined mating surfaces.

11. Position the power head with the crankcase cover facing upward. Using a soft-faced mallet, carefully tap the flywheel end of the crankshaft in an upward direction until the crankcase cover separates from the cylinder block. Then lift the cover off of the cylinder block. Use caution not to nick, scratch or damage the crankcase cover and cylinder block mating surfaces.

12. Mark the corresponding cylinder number on the connecting rods with a felt-tipped permanent marker. Mark the connecting rods and rod caps in such a manner that the rod caps can be reinstalled in their original orientation. Note any special alignment markings (such as cast dots).

NOTE
Always store all components from each connecting rod and piston assembly together. They must be reinstalled in their original locations.

13. *3, 4 hp, 4 Deluxe and 1995 (EO) 6 and 8 hp*—Remove the center main bearing liner from the crankcase cover and as many of the 30 loose needles as possible. Place the liner half and bearing rollers in a labeled container.

14. Remove each connecting rod cap and bearing assembly as follows:

   a. Remove the connecting rod screws from the upper (No. 1 cylinder) connecting rod. Alternately loosen each screw a small amount until all tension is off of both screws.

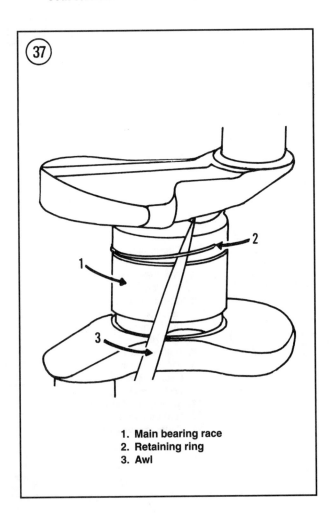

1. **Main bearing race**
2. **Retaining ring**
3. **Awl**

b. Tap the rod cap with a soft metal (brass) mallet to separate the cap from the rod.

c. Remove the cap and rod from the crankshaft, then remove the two caged roller bearing halves from the crankshaft. Carefully push the piston and rod assembly to the bottom of its bore.

d. Store the caged roller bearing assemblies in clean, numbered containers, corresponding to the cylinder number.

e. Repeat this procedure to remove the No. 2 cylinder connecting rod cap.

15. Lift the crankshaft out of the cylinder block, then slide the upper seal and bearing from the crankshaft. Note that the flywheel key must be removed before the bearing and seal can be removed. Discard the seal.

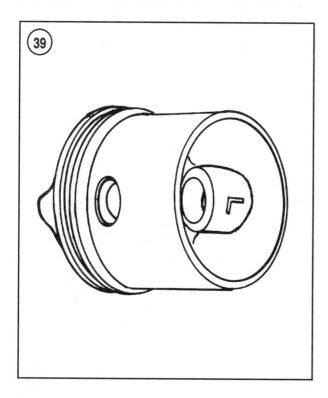

16. Reinstall each rod cap to its respective connecting rod in its original orientation. Tighten the rod cap screws finger-tight.

17A. *3, 4 hp, 4 Deluxe and 1995 (EO) 6 and 8 hp*—Remove the remaining loose needle bearings from the cylinder block, then remove the center main bearing liner from the cylinder block. Make sure all 30 loose needles are accounted for. Store these components with the components removed in Step 13.

17B. *1996-2003 (ED-ST) 6 and 8 hp*—Remove the retaining ring from the center main bearing as shown in **Figure 37**. Then remove the bearing race halves and the 23 loose needle bearings. Store the bearing components in a labeled container.

18. Remove the seal ring (7, **Figure 36**) from its groove at the center of the crankshaft. Discard the ring.

19. Remove the cylinder head and carefully push each piston from its cylinder. Store each piston with its bearing components removed in Step 14.

20. If the lower crankshaft sleeve/drive shaft seal (12, **Figure 36**) requires replacement, carefully grind or file a vertical groove through the sleeve, then slide the sleeve from the crankshaft. Do not damage the crankshaft surface when removing the sleeve. Discard the sleeve.

NOTE
Do not press directly against the end of the crankshaft in the next step as it and the sleeve/drive shaft seal (if installed) will be damaged.

21. If the ball bearing must be replaced, remove the retainer ring (9, **Figure 36**) using suitable snap ring pliers. Support the bearing in a knife-edged press plate. Press the bearing free from the crankshaft using a suitable mandrel that will pilot into and press against the bottom of the crankshaft splined bore. Then discard the bearing.

22. Remove the piston rings from both pistons using a standard piston ring expander. See **Figure 38**. Retain the rings for cleaning the piston ring grooves.

23. Using locking clip remover (part No. 325937) or a modified pair of needlenose pliers (**Figure 32**), remove and discard the two wrist pin locking clips from each piston.

NOTE
*On 3, 4 hp and 4 Deluxe models, the wrist pin is a press-fit on one side of the piston and a loose fit on the opposite side. The loose side is identified by an L cast on the underside of the wrist pin boss (**Figure 39**). To prevent piston damage, the pin must be pressed from the loose side, toward the press-fit side.*

8

24A. *3, 4 hp and 4 Deluxe*—Place the piston into the appropriate saddle of piston cradle part No. 326572 (or equivalent). See **Figure 40**. Make sure the *L* side of the piston is facing upward. Press the pin from the piston using pin remover part No. 326624 (or equivalent). Remove the tool and pin, then retrieve the two thrust washers and 21 loose needle bearings. Store the components in a labeled container.

> *NOTE*
> *On 6 and 8 hp models, the piston must be heated to 200-400° F (93-204° C) to relax the interference fit between the wrist pin and the wrist pin bore enough to allow wrist pin removal. Heat the entire piston using a suitable heat gun, heat lamp or by boiling in water. Do not use an open flame or heat a small area of the piston. Wear suitable insulated gloves when handling the hot piston.*

24B. *6 and 8 hp*—Evenly heat the piston to 200-400° F (93-204° C). Then place the piston into the appropriate saddle of piston cradle part No. 326573 (or equivalent). See **Figure 40**. Press the pin from the piston using pin remover part No. 333141 (or equivalent). Remove the tool and pin, then retrieve the two thrust washers. Store the components in a labeled container.

25. Repeat Step 20 to separate the No. 2 cylinder piston and connecting rod.

26. *6 and 8 hp*—If the caged needle bearing in the small end of the connecting rod requires replacement, support the small end of the rod and press the bearing from the rod using bearing remover part No. 327645 (or equivalent). Discard the bearing.

27. Refer to *Power Head Cleaning and Inspection* in this chapter before beginning reassembly.

Disassembly (9.9 and 15 hp)

All components (such as bearings, pistons and connecting rods) that are to be reused must be marked with their original location and orientation for reassembly purposes. Do not remove the large ball bearing from the crankshaft unless it must be replaced.

Refer to **Figure 41** and **Figure 42** for this procedure.

1. Remove the intake manifold and reed valves as described in Chapter Six.

2. If the rewind starter, ignition and fuel system components were not removed when the power head was removed, refer to Chapter Six and remove the carburetor and fuel pump, refer to Chapter Twelve and remove the rewind starter, and refer to Chapter Seven and remove the complete ignition (and electrical) system.

3. Remove the three screws securing the thermostat cover to the cylinder head, then remove the cover and thermostat components (18-26, **Figure 41**) from the cylinder head. Remove and discard the cover seal (25). If equipped with an engine temperature switch (17), remove it at this time.

4. Remove the six screws securing the cylinder head to the cylinder block. Carefully pull the head from the block, then remove and discard the gasket. If necessary, tap the head with a soft-faced (rubber or plastic) hammer to break the gasket seal. Do not damage the sealing surfaces during the removal process.

5. Remove the six screws securing the intake (bypass) cover to the cylinder block. Carefully tap around the perimeter of the cover with a soft-faced mallet to break the gasket seal, then separate the cover from the block and remove and discard the gasket. Do not damage or distort the cover during the removal process.

6. Remove the remaining seven screws securing the exhaust cover and inner manifold to the cylinder block. Carefully tap around the perimeter of the cover with a soft-faced mallet to break the gasket seal, then remove the assembly from the block and separate the manifold from the cover. Remove and discard the gaskets. Do not damage or distort the cover or manifold during the removal process.

7. Remove the three screws (and washers) securing the lower end cap to the cylinder block. Then remove the lower end cap. Remove and discard the O-ring and two seals. The seals may be driven from the end cap with a suitable punch. Do not damage the seal bores during the removal process.

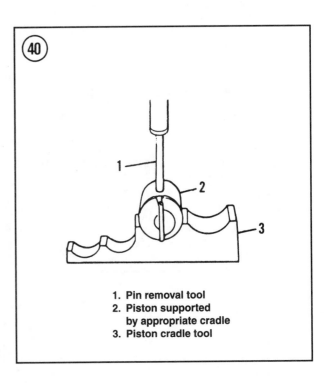

40

1. Pin removal tool
2. Piston supported by appropriate cradle
3. Piston cradle tool

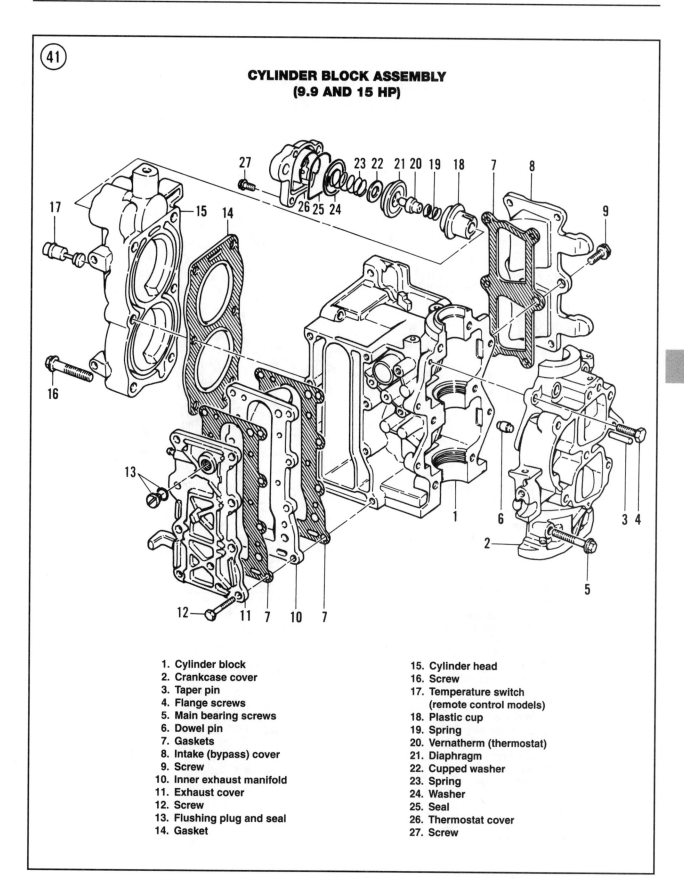

(41)

CYLINDER BLOCK ASSEMBLY
(9.9 AND 15 HP)

8

1. Cylinder block
2. Crankcase cover
3. Taper pin
4. Flange screws
5. Main bearing screws
6. Dowel pin
7. Gaskets
8. Intake (bypass) cover
9. Screw
10. Inner exhaust manifold
11. Exhaust cover
12. Screw
13. Flushing plug and seal
14. Gasket

15. Cylinder head
16. Screw
17. Temperature switch
    (remote control models)
18. Plastic cup
19. Spring
20. Vernatherm (thermostat)
21. Diaphragm
22. Cupped washer
23. Spring
24. Washer
25. Seal
26. Thermostat cover
27. Screw

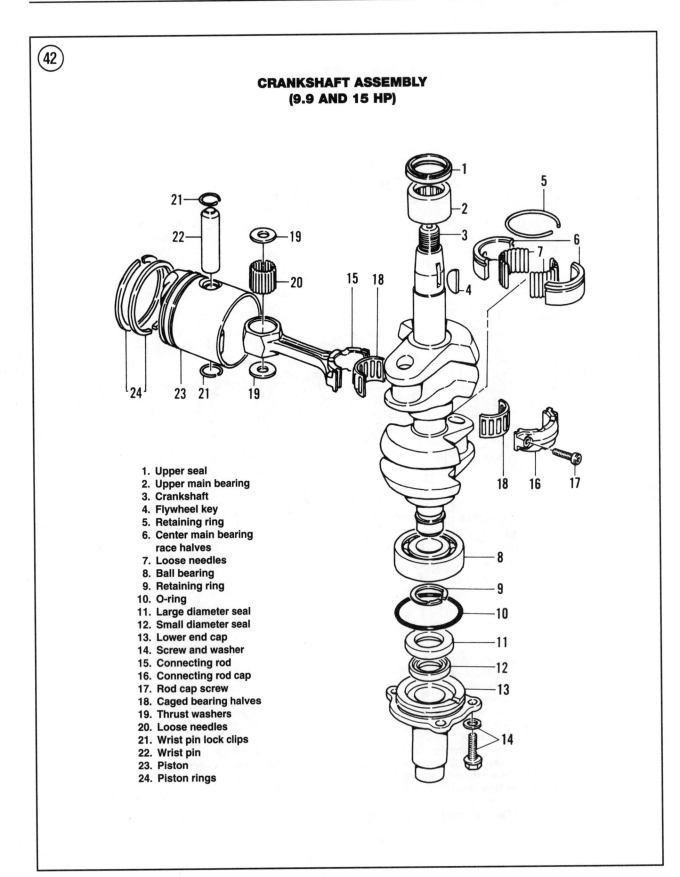

**CRANKSHAFT ASSEMBLY
(9.9 AND 15 HP)**

1. Upper seal
2. Upper main bearing
3. Crankshaft
4. Flywheel key
5. Retaining ring
6. Center main bearing
   race halves
7. Loose needles
8. Ball bearing
9. Retaining ring
10. O-ring
11. Large diameter seal
12. Small diameter seal
13. Lower end cap
14. Screw and washer
15. Connecting rod
16. Connecting rod cap
17. Rod cap screw
18. Caged bearing halves
19. Thrust washers
20. Loose needles
21. Wrist pin lock clips
22. Wrist pin
23. Piston
24. Piston rings

8. Mark the top piston *No.1* and the bottom piston *No. 2* with a permanent marker. Then temporarily install the cylinder head using only two screws. Tighten the screws finger-tight. This will prevent the pistons from falling out of their cylinders during disassembly.

CAUTION
Do not damage the taper pin or its bore during removal, or the cylinder block will be ruined.

9. Using the tool shown in **Figure 31** (or equivalent), drive the taper pin toward the intake manifold side (front) of the power head. Position the tool's extended toe over the taper pin and hold the main body of the tool parallel to the pin. Drive the pin from its bore.

10. Remove the ten crankcase cover-to-cylinder block screws. Note the length of each screw and its original location. There are six main bearing screws and four flange screws.

CAUTION
The crankcase cover and cylinder block are a matched, align-bored unit. Do not scratch, nick or damage the machined mating surfaces.

11. Position the power head with the crankcase cover facing upward. Using a soft-faced mallet, carefully tap the flywheel end of the crankshaft in an upward direction until the crankcase cover separates from the cylinder block. Then lift the cover off of the cylinder block. Use caution not to nick, scratch or damage the crankcase cover and cylinder block mating surfaces.

12. Mark the corresponding cylinder number on the connecting rods with a felt-tipped permanent marker. Mark the connecting rods and rod caps so that the rod caps can be reinstalled in their original orientation. Note any special alignment markings (such as cast dots).

NOTE
*Always store **all** components from each connecting rod and piston assembly together. They must be reinstalled in their original locations.*

13. Remove each connecting rod cap and bearing assembly as follows:
   a. Remove the connecting rod screws from the upper (No. 1 cylinder) connecting rod. Alternately loosen each screw a small amount until all tension is off of both screws.
   b. Tap the rod cap with a soft metal (brass) mallet to separate the cap from the rod.
   c. Remove the cap and rod from the crankshaft, then remove the two caged roller bearing halves from the

crankshaft. Carefully push the piston and rod assembly to the bottom of its bore.
   d. Store the caged roller bearing assemblies in clean, numbered containers, corresponding to the cylinder number.
   e. Repeat this procedure to remove the No. 2 cylinder connecting rod cap.

14. Lift the crankshaft out of the cylinder block, then slide the upper seal and bearing from the crankshaft. Note that the flywheel key must be removed before the seal and bearing can be removed. Discard the seal.

15. Reinstall each rod cap to its respective connecting rod in its original orientation. Tighten the rod cap screws finger-tight.

16. Remove the retaining ring from the center main bearing as shown in **Figure 37**. Then remove the bearing race halves and the 23 loose needle bearings. Store the bearing components in a labeled container.

17. If the ball bearing must be replaced, remove the retainer ring (9, **Figure 42**) using a suitable pair of retaining ring pliers. Support the bearing in a knife-edged pressing plate. Press the bearing free from the crankshaft using a suitable mandrel that will pilot into and press against the bottom of the crankshaft splined bore. Then discard the bearing.

18. Remove the cylinder head and carefully push each piston from its cylinder. Store each piston with its bearing components removed in Step 13.

19. Remove the piston rings from both pistons using a standard piston ring expander. See **Figure 38**. Retain the rings for cleaning the piston ring grooves.

20. Using locking clip remover (part No. 325937) or a modified pair of needlenose pliers (**Figure 32**), remove and discard the two wrist pin locking clips from each piston.

NOTE
The wrist pin is a slip fit to both sides of the piston. The pin can be pushed out in either direction.

21. Place the piston into the appropriate saddle of piston cradle part No. 326573 (or equivalent). See **Figure 40**. Press the pin from the piston using pin remover part No. 392511 (or equivalent). Remove the tool and pin, then retrieve the two thrust washers and 22 loose needle bearings. Store the components in a labeled container.

22. Repeat Step 20 to separate the No. 2 cylinder piston and connecting rod.

23. Refer to *Power Head Cleaning and Inspection* in this chapter before beginning reassembly.

8

Disassembly
(20-30 hp [Two-cylinder] and 18 Jet)

All components (such as bearings, pistons and connecting rods) that are to be reused must be marked as to their original location and orientation for reassembly purposes. Do not remove the large ball bearing from the crankshaft unless it is to be replaced.

Refer to **Figure 43** and **Figure 44** for this procedure.

1. Remove the carburetor, fuel pump, intake manifold, reed valves and all related fuel and recirculation lines. On remote control models, also remove the fuel primer solenoid and all related primer lines. See Chapter Six.

2. If the rewind starter is still installed, remove it as described in Chapter Twelve.

3. If the ignition and electrical components are still installed, remove the flywheel, armature plate assembly (with charge and sensor coils), power pack and ignition coils. If equipped with electric start, remove the starter motor and starter solenoid as an assembly, then remove the terminal strip, rectifier and remaining engine harness. Do not disconnect ignition and electrical components from each other unless absolutely necessary. Simply remove the mounting screws, cable clamps and tie-straps. See Chapter Seven.

4. Remove the 14 screws securing the cylinder head water cover to the cylinder head. Carefully tap around the pe-

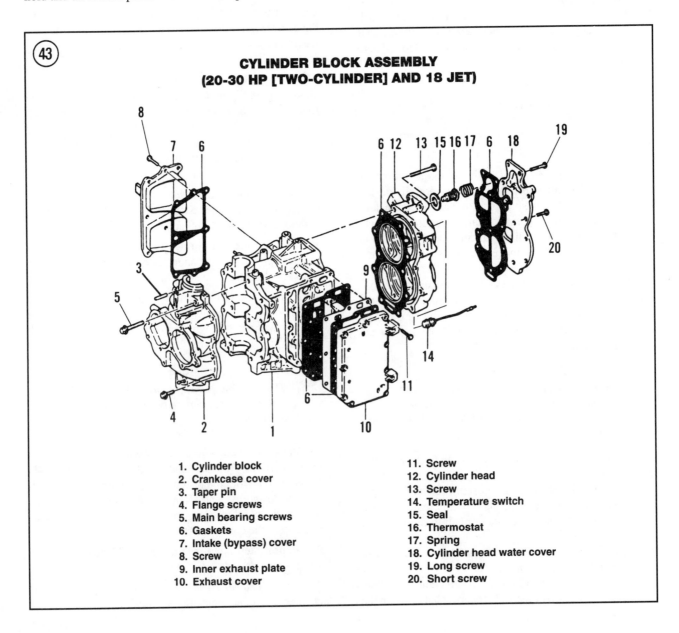

(43)

**CYLINDER BLOCK ASSEMBLY
(20-30 HP [TWO-CYLINDER] AND 18 JET)**

1. Cylinder block
2. Crankcase cover
3. Taper pin
4. Flange screws
5. Main bearing screws
6. Gaskets
7. Intake (bypass) cover
8. Screw
9. Inner exhaust plate
10. Exhaust cover
11. Screw
12. Cylinder head
13. Screw
14. Temperature switch
15. Seal
16. Thermostat
17. Spring
18. Cylinder head water cover
19. Long screw
20. Short screw

CRANKSHAFT ASSEMBLY
(20-30 HP [TWO-CYLINDER] AND 18 JET)

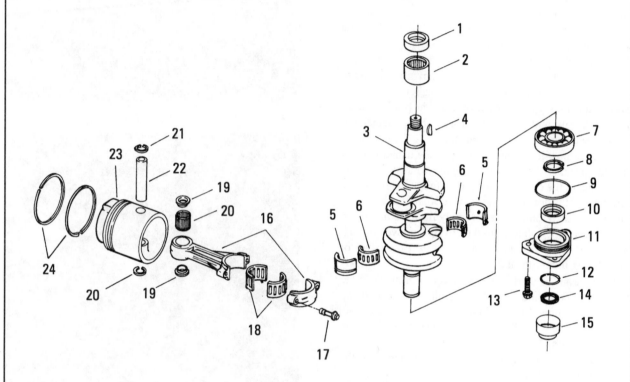

1. Upper seal
2. Upper main bearing
3. Crankshaft
4. Flywheel key
5. Bearing liner halves
6. Caged roller bearing halves
7. Ball bearing
8. Retaining ring
9. O-ring
10. Lower seal
11. Lower end cap
12. O-ring

13. Screw
14. O-ring (drive shaft seal)
15. Crankshaft sleeve/O-ring retainer
16. Connecting rod and cap
17. Rod cap screw
18. Caged bearing halves
19. Thrust washers
20. Loose needles
21. Wrist pin lock clips
22. Wrist pin
23. Piston
24. Piston rings

8

rimeter of the cover with a soft-faced mallet to break the gasket seal, then remove the cover from the cylinder head (**Figure 45**). Do not damage or distort the cover during the removal process.

5. Remove the engine temperature switch and the thermostat, spring and seal (**Figure 46**) from the cylinder head. Then remove and discard the cover gasket.

6. Remove the ten screws securing the cylinder head to the cylinder block. Carefully pull the head from the block (**Figure 47**), then remove and discard the gasket. If necessary, tap the head with a soft-faced (rubber or plastic) hammer to break the gasket seal. Do not damage the sealing surfaces during the removal process.

7. Remove the nine screws securing the intake (bypass) cover to the cylinder block. Carefully tap around the perimeter of the cover with a soft-faced mallet to break the gasket seal, then separate the cover from the block (**Figure 48**) and remove and discard the gasket. Do not damage or distort the cover during the removal process.

8. Note the position of all brackets on the exhaust cover, then remove the 15 screws securing the exhaust cover and inner plate to the cylinder block. Carefully tap around the perimeter of the cover with a soft-faced mallet to break the gasket seal, then remove the assembly from the block and separate the inner plate from the cover. Remove and discard the gaskets. Do not damage or distort the cover or plate during the removal process.

9. Remove and discard the three screws securing the lower end cap to the cylinder block. Carefully pry the end cap from the cylinder block (**Figure 49**). Do not damage, distort or gouge the end cap and sealing surfaces. Remove and discard the O-ring and seal. The seal may be driven from the end cap with a suitable punch. Do not damage the seal bore during the removal process.

10. Mark the top piston *No. 1* and the bottom piston *No. 2* with a felt-tipped permanent marker. Then temporarily install the cylinder head using only two screws. Tighten the screws finger-tight. This will prevent the pistons from falling out of their cylinders during disassembly.

> *CAUTION*
> ***Do not*** *damage the taper pin or its bore during removal, or the cylinder block will be ruined.*

11. Using the tool shown in **Figure 31** (or equivalent), drive the taper pin toward the intake manifold side (front) of the power head. Position the tool's extended toe over the taper pin and hold the main body of the tool parallel to the pin. Drive the pin from its bore.

12. Remove the 14 crankcase cover-to-cylinder block screws. See **Figure 50**. Note the length of each screw and its original location. There are six main bearing screws and eight flange screws.

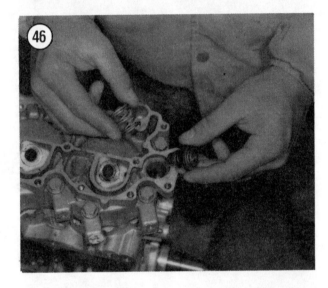

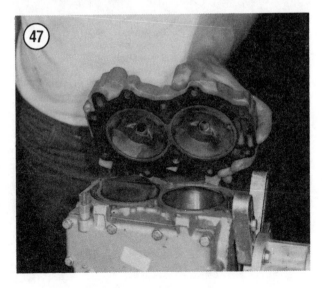

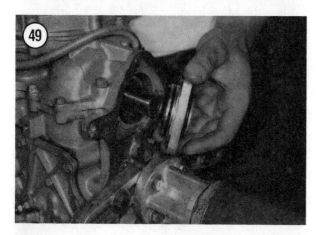

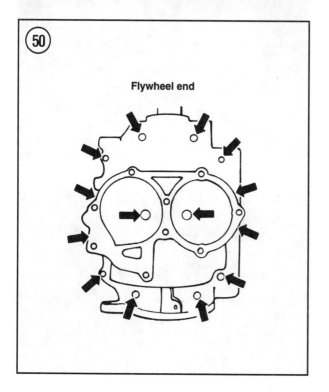

Flywheel end

CAUTION
The crankcase cover and cylinder block are a matched, align-bored unit. Do not scratch, nick or damage the machined mating surfaces.

13. Position the power head with the crankcase cover facing upward. Using a soft-faced mallet, carefully tap the flywheel end of the crankshaft in an upward direction until the crankcase cover separates from the cylinder block. Then lift the cover off of the cylinder block (**Figure 51**). Use caution not to nick, scratch or damage the crankcase cover and cylinder block mating surfaces.

14. Remove the center main bearing liner from the crankcase cover, then remove both caged needle bearing halves from around the crankshaft. Store these components in a labeled container.

15. Mark the corresponding cylinder number on the connecting rods with a felt-tipped permanent marker. Mark the connecting rods and rod caps so that the rod caps can be reinstalled in their original orientation. Note any special alignment marks (such as cast dots).

NOTE
Always store all components from each connecting rod and piston assembly together. They must be reinstalled in their original locations.

16. Remove each connecting rod cap and bearing assembly as follows:
   a. Remove the connecting rod screws from the upper (No. 1 cylinder) connecting rod using connecting rod screw socket (part No. 331638) or an equivalent heavy-duty 5/16 in., 12-point thin-wall socket. Alternately loosen each screw a small amount until all tension is off of both screws.

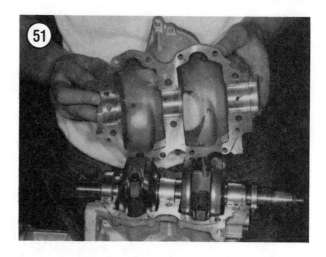

b. Tap the rod cap with a soft metal (brass) mallet to separate the cap from the rod.

c. Remove the cap and rod from the crankshaft, then remove the two caged roller bearing halves from the crankshaft. See **Figure 52**. Carefully push the piston and rod assembly to the bottom of its bore.

d. Store the caged roller bearing assemblies in clean, numbered containers, corresponding to the cylinder number.

e. Repeat this procedure to remove the No. 2 cylinder connecting rod cap.

17. Lift the crankshaft out of the cylinder block, then slide the upper seal and bearing from the crankshaft. Discard the seal.

18. Reinstall each rod cap to its respective connecting rod in its original orientation. Tighten the rod cap screws finger-tight.

19. Remove the center main bearing liner from the cylinder block. Store the liner with the components removed in Step 14.

20. Remove and discard the O-ring (drive shaft seal) from inside the sleeve located on the bottom of the crankshaft. If the sleeve requires replacement, pull it from the crankshaft with a suitable two-jaw puller, such as puller jaws (part No. 432129) and slide hammer (part No. 432128).

NOTE
Do not press directly against the end of the crankshaft in the next step as it and the sleeve (if installed) will be damaged.

21. If the ball bearing must be replaced, remove the retainer ring (8, **Figure 44**) using a suitable pair of retaining ring pliers. Support the bearing in a knife-edged pressing plate. Press the bearing free from the crankshaft using a suitable mandrel that will pilot into and press against the bottom of the crankshaft splined bore. Then discard the bearing.

22. Remove the cylinder head and carefully push each piston from its cylinder. Store each piston with its bearing components removed in Step 16.

23. Remove the piston rings from both pistons using a standard piston ring expander. See **Figure 53**. Retain the rings for cleaning the piston ring grooves.

24. Using locking clip remover (part No. 325937) or a modified pair of needlenose pliers (**Figure 32**), remove and discard the two wrist pin locking clips from each piston. See **Figure 54**.

NOTE
The wrist pin is a slip fit to both sides of the piston. The pin can be pushed out in either direction.

25. Place the piston into the appropriate saddle of piston cradle (part No. 326573) or equivalent. See **Figure 55**, typical. Press the pin from the piston using pin remover (part No. 326356) or equivalent. Remove the tool and pin, then retrieve the two thrust washers and 28 loose needle bearings. Store the components in a labeled container.

26. Repeat Step 24 to separate the No. 2 cylinder piston and connecting rod.

27. Refer to *Power Head Cleaning and Inspection* in this chapter before beginning reassembly.

Disassembly (25 and 35 hp [Three-cylinder])

Since the power head is removed with all accessories installed, it is necessary to first remove all accessories and systems from the power head.

All components (such as bearings, pistons and connecting rods) that are to be reused must be marked as to their original location and orientation for reassembly purposes. Do not remove the large ball bearing from the crankshaft unless it is to be replaced.

Refer to **Figure 56** and **Figure 57** for this procedure.

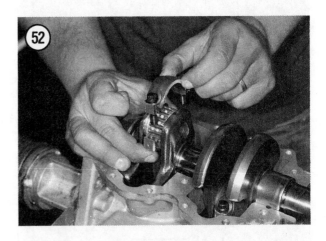

1. Remove the carburetors, fuel pumps, intake manifold, reed blocks and all external recirculation lines. On remote control models, also remove the fuel primer solenoid and all related primer lines. See Chapter Six.

2. Remove the oil reservoir, fuel/oil mixing unit and all related mounting brackets from the power head. See Chapter Eleven.

3. *Electric start models*—Remove the electric starter motor and starter solenoid as described in Chapter Seven.

4. Remove the flywheel and the entire ignition and electrical system as described in Chapter Seven. This includes the stator assembly, optical sensor, ignition module, ignition coils and the wiring harness. Remove the voltage regulator (on electric start models) and the trim/tilt relay bracket and harness on models with trim and tilt. Do not disconnect components from each other unless absolutely

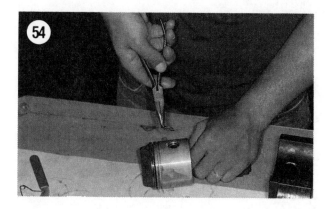

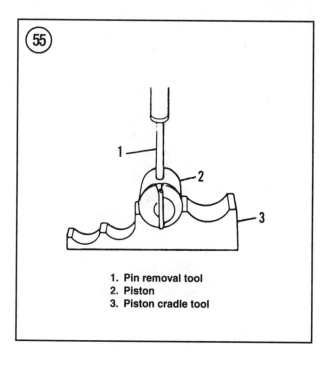

1. Pin removal tool
2. Piston
3. Piston cradle tool

necessary. Instead, simply remove the mounting screws, cable clamps and tie-straps.

5. *Remote control models*—Remove the two screws securing the trunnion anchor bracket (A, **Figure 58**) to the crankcase cover. Remove the bracket from the cover.

6. Remove the screw (and two washers) securing the spark control arm (B, **Figure 58**) to the starboard side of the cylinder block. See *Remove the spark control arm*.

7. If so desired, remove the nut and washer from the starboard end of the throttle control shaft (C, **Figure 58**). Remove the ball link arm and nylon spacer, then slide the shaft out (the port side) of the crankcase cover. Remove the two nylon bushings from the crankcase cover bosses.

8. If so desired, remove the retaining ring securing the shift lever's neutral detent assembly to the lower, starboard, front corner of the cylinder block, near the crankcase cover parting line. Then remove the retainer (guide), ball and spring.

9. Remove the thermostat cover from the cylinder head. Unscrew the cover using a spark plug socket. Remove and discard the cover O-ring. Then remove the thermostat components (20-26, **Figure 56**) from the cylinder head.

10. Remove the plastic nut securing the engine temperature switch to the cylinder head. The switch is located between the No. 1 and No. 2 spark plugs. Then pull the switch from the cylinder head.

11. Loosen the 12 cylinder head screws in small increments, until there is no tension on the screws. Then remove the screws. Carefully pull the head from the block, then remove the three O-rings (13, **Figure 56**) from their grooves in the cylinder block and discard them. If necessary, tap the head with a soft-faced (rubber or plastic) hammer to break the seal. Do not damage the sealing surfaces during the removal process.

12. Remove the 20 crankcase cover-to-cylinder block screws. Remove the 12 flange screws (4, **Figure 56**) first, then loosen the eight main bearing screws (5) in several stages until there is no tension on the screws. Remove the main bearing screws, noting the length of each screw and its original location.

CAUTION
The crankcase cover and cylinder block are a matched, align-bored unit. Do not scratch, nick or damage the machined mating surfaces.

13. Position the power head with the crankcase cover facing upward. Using a soft-faced mallet, carefully tap the flywheel end of the crankshaft in an upward direction until the crankcase cover separates from the cylinder block. Then lift the cover off of the cylinder block. Use caution

8

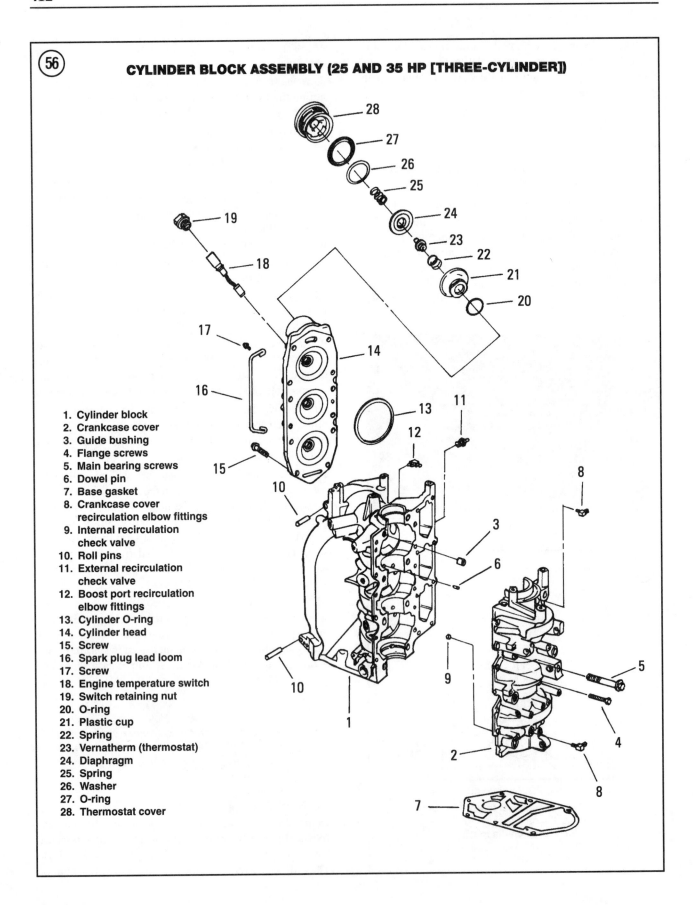

56

CYLINDER BLOCK ASSEMBLY (25 AND 35 HP [THREE-CYLINDER])

1. Cylinder block
2. Crankcase cover
3. Guide bushing
4. Flange screws
5. Main bearing screws
6. Dowel pin
7. Base gasket
8. Crankcase cover recirculation elbow fittings
9. Internal recirculation check valve
10. Roll pins
11. External recirculation check valve
12. Boost port recirculation elbow fittings
13. Cylinder O-ring
14. Cylinder head
15. Screw
16. Spark plug lead loom
17. Screw
18. Engine temperature switch
19. Switch retaining nut
20. O-ring
21. Plastic cup
22. Spring
23. Vernatherm (thermostat)
24. Diaphragm
25. Spring
26. Washer
27. O-ring
28. Thermostat cover

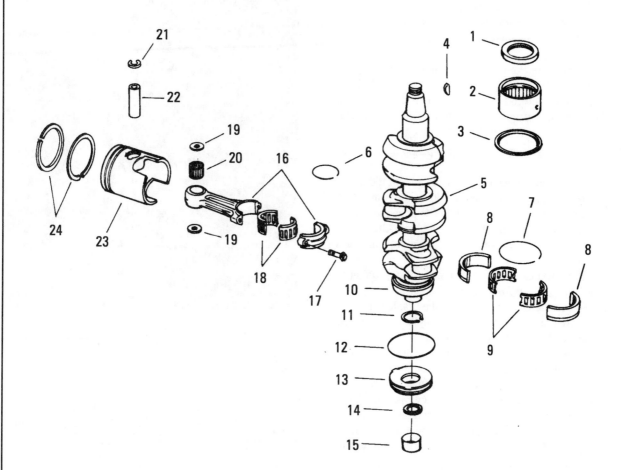

**CRANKSHAFT ASSEMBLY
(25 AND 35 HP [THREE-CYLINDER])**

8

1. Upper seal
2. Upper main bearing
3. O-ring
4. Flywheel key
5. Crankshaft
6. Seal ring
7. Retaining ring
8. Bearing race halves
9. Caged roller bearing halves
10. Ball bearing and
    locating ring
11. Retaining ring
12. O-ring
13. Crankcase head and seal
14. O-ring (drive shaft seal)
15. Crankshaft
    sleeve/O-ring retainer
16. Connecting rod and cap
17. Rod cap screw
18. Caged bearing halves
19. Thrust washers
20. Loose needles
21. Wrist pin lock clips
22. Wrist pin
23. Piston
24. Piston rings

not to nick, scratch or damage the crankcase cover and cylinder block mating surfaces.

NOTE
At this point, only the connecting rods secure the crankshaft in the crankcase. Make sure the crankcase is not positioned where the crankshaft can fall out as the pistons are removed.

14. Mark the corresponding cylinder number on the connecting rods with a felt-tipped permanent marker. Mark the connecting rods and rod caps so that the rod caps can be reinstalled in their original orientation. Note any special alignment marks (such as cast dots).

15. Remove each connecting rod and piston assembly as follows:
   a. Remove the connecting rod screws from the upper (No. 1 cylinder) connecting rod using connecting rod screw socket (part No. 342664) or an equivalent heavy-duty 1/4 in., 12-point socket. Alternately loosen each screw a small amount until all tension is off of both screws.
   b. Tap the rod cap with a soft metal (brass) mallet to separate the cap from the rod.
   c. Remove the cap and rod from the crankshaft, then remove the two caged roller bearing halves from the crankshaft. See **Figure 52**, typical.
   d. Be prepared to catch and support the piston with one hand, then push the piston and connecting rod assembly from the cylinder bore. Make sure the connecting rod does not damage the cylinder wall, nor contact the piston skirt during and after removal.
   e. Reinstall the rod cap to the connecting rod in its original orientation. Tighten the rod cap screws finger-tight.
   f. Store the piston and connecting rod, and the caged roller bearing halves in clean, numbered containers, corresponding to the cylinder number.
   g. Repeat this procedure to remove the No. 2 and 3 cylinders connecting rod and piston assemblies.

16. Lift the crankshaft out of the cylinder block, then slide the upper seal and bearing assembly from the crankshaft. Remove and discard the O-ring. Then drive the seal from the bearing using a suitable punch. Do not damage or distort the bearing's seal bore during removal. Discard the seal.

17. Slide the seal carrier from the lower end of the crankshaft. Discard the carrier and its O-ring.

18. Remove the retaining ring from the upper center main bearing as shown in **Figure 59**. Then remove the bearing race and caged roller bearing halves. Store the bearing components in a labeled container. Repeat this step for the

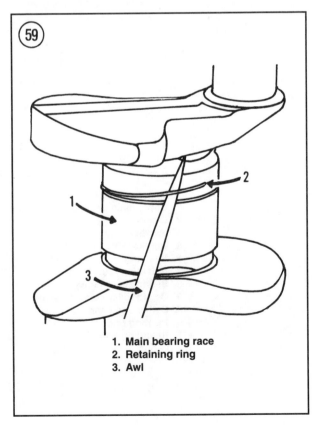

1. **Main bearing race**
2. **Retaining ring**
3. **Awl**

lower center main bearing. Store the lower bearing's components in a separate labeled container.

19. Remove the three seal rings. A seal ring is located just above each center main bearing and the ball bearing. Carefully expand the seal rings just far enough to slip them from their grooves and over the adjacent main bearing surface. If the ball bearing must be replaced, remove the lowest seal ring after the ball bearing is removed.

20. Remove and discard the O-ring (drive shaft seal) from inside the sleeve located on the bottom of the crankshaft. If the sleeve requires replacement, pull it from the crankshaft with a suitable two-jaw puller, such as puller jaws (part No. 432129) and slide hammer (part No. 432128).

NOTE
Do not press directly against the end of the crankshaft in the next step as it and the sleeve (if installed) will be damaged.

21. If the ball bearing must be replaced, remove the retainer ring (11, **Figure 57**) using a suitable pair of retaining ring pliers. Support the bearing in a knife-edged press plate. Press the bearing free from the crankshaft using a suitable mandrel (such as a scrap piece of drive shaft) that will pilot into and press against the bottom of the crankshaft splined bore. See **Figure 60**. Then discard the bearing.

22. Remove the piston rings from both pistons using a standard piston ring expander. See **Figure 61**, typical. Retain the rings for cleaning each piston's ring grooves.

23. Using locking clip remover (part No. 325937) or a modified pair of needlenose pliers (**Figure 32**), remove and discard the two wrist pin locking clips from each piston. See **Figure 54**, typical.

NOTE
The wrist pin is a slip fit to both sides of the piston. The pin can be pushed out in either direction.

24. Place the wrist pin remover (part No. 342657) or equivalent into one end of the No. 1 cylinder wrist pin bore. Support the bottom of the piston with one hand and drive the pin tool and pin from the piston.

25. Remove the piston from the connecting rod. Remove the two thrust washers and the 24 loose needle bearings (**Figure 62**, typical). Store the components in clean, numbered containers corresponding to the cylinder number.

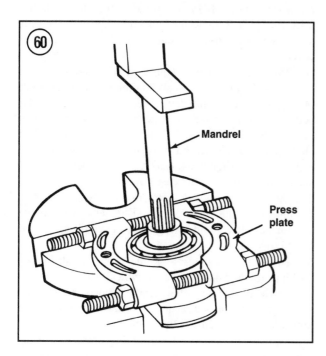

Mandrel

Press plate

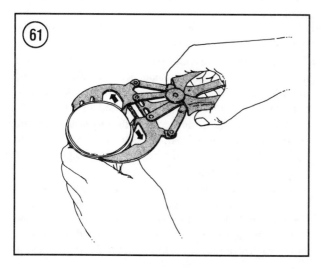

1. Loose needle bearings
2. Thrust washers

26. Repeat Step 24 and Step 25 to separate the remaining (No. 2 and No. 3 cylinders) pistons and connecting rods.

27. Refer to *Power Head Cleaning and Inspection* in this chapter before beginning reassembly.

Disassembly (40-70 hp, 28 and 35 Jet)

Since the power head is removed with all accessories installed, it is necessary to first remove all accessories and systems from the power head.

All components (such as bearings, pistons and connecting rods) that are to be reused must be marked as to their original location and orientation for reassembly purposes. Do not remove the large ball bearing from the crankshaft unless it is to be replaced.

Although the exploded illustrations show three-cylinder models, the two-cylinder models represented in this section are similar in construction. The primary difference between two- and three-cylinder models is the shift linkage. Shift linkage for three-cylinder models is shown in **Figure 63**. Illustrations of two-cylinder shift linkage is located in Chapter Five. All procedures specific to one model are so indicated in the text. Refer to **Figure 64** and **Figure 65** for this procedure.

1. Remove the entire ignition and electrical system (as equipped) and all related mounting brackets. This includes the stator (or armature plate) assembly, sensor coil (12 amp charging systems), power pack and ignition coil(s). On electric start models, this includes the starter motor, starter solenoid, terminal strip, rectifier (or voltage regulator) and the wiring harness. On models with trim/tilt, also remove the trim/tilt relay bracket and associated harness. Do not disconnect components from each other unless absolutely necessary. Simply remove the mounting screws, cable clamps and tie-straps. See Chapter Seven.

2. Remove the carburetors, intake manifold, reed blocks, fuel pump (or oil injection pump and pulse-limiter fitting), fuel primer solenoid (electric start models) and all related fuel, oil and primer lines. See Chapter Six.

3A. *Two-cylinder models*—Remove the shoulder screw (and washers) from both the throttle cam and spark control arms, located on the starboard side of the power head. Then remove the throttle cam and spark control arms. Refer to Chapter Five for an illustration of the throttle and spark linkages.

3B. *Three-cylinder (remote control) models*—Remove the cotter pin, washer and clevis pin (41, **Figure 64**) securing the shift link (40) to the shift shaft (42). Then remove the two shoulder screws (38, **Figure 64**) and washers securing the throttle cam (47) and the spark, throttle and shift control levers (29, 34 and 36) to the power head. Remove the control arms and throttle cam as an assembly.

3C. *Three-cylinder (tiller handle) models*—Remove the three shoulder screws (and washers) securing the spark control arm, throttle control arm and the throttle cam to the power head. Remove the control arms and throttle cam as an assembly.

4A. *Two-cylinder models*—Refer to **Figure 63** and remove the shoulder screw, wave washer and flat washers securing the rear shift lever to the starboard side of the power head. Then bend the lock tab away from the shift bellcrank screw (20, **Figure 63**) and remove the bellcrank screw. Slide the bellcrank (and the spacer behind it) from the shift shaft, then pull the shift shaft and rear shift lever (as an assembly) off from the starboard side of the power head.

4B. *Three-cylinder (remote control) models*—Remove the screw (46, **Figure 64**) holding the shift bellcrank to the shift lever (42). Remove the bellcrank, then slide the shift lever and washers from the starboard side of the crankcase cover.

4C. *Three-cylinder (tiller handle) models*—Remove the screw (46, **Figure 64**, typical) holding the shift bellcrank (45, typical) to the shift lever (42, typical). Remove the bellcrank, then remove the cotter pin, washer and clevis pin securing the shift handle's link to the shift lever. The clevis pin is located as shown in 41, **Figure 64**. Slide the shift shaft (42, **Figure 64**, typical) and washers from the starboard side of the crankcase cover.

5A. *Two-cylinder models*—Remove the two shift shaft bushings from the crankcase cover bosses. Then remove the retainer, detent and spring from the crankcase cover. See **Figure 63**.

5B. *Three-cylinder models*—Remove the two shift shaft bushings (30 and 44, **Figure 64**, typical) from the crankcase cover bosses. On tiller handle models, remove the screws securing the neutral detent spring and bracket to the power head. Then remove the detent bracket.

6. *Two-cylinder models*—Remove the two screws securing the lower cowl mount to the starboard side of the crankcase cover, just behind the shift shaft and lever (11, **Figure 63**) removed in the previous step. Remove the starboard lower cowl mount.

7. Remove the four screws securing the thermostat cover to the top of the cylinder head. Remove the cover and discard the gasket. Then remove the thermostat components (19-24, **Figure 64**) from the cylinder head.

8. Remove the plastic nut securing the engine temperature switch to the cylinder head. The switch is located just to the port side of the thermostat cover. Then pull the switch from the cylinder head.

9. Remove the 14 (three-cylinder) or ten (two-cylinder) screws securing the cylinder head to the cylinder block. Carefully pull the head from the block, then remove and discard the gasket. If necessary, tap the head with a soft-faced (rubber or plastic) hammer to break the gasket seal.

Do not damage the sealing surfaces during the removal process.

10. Mark the pistons (with their cylinder number) with a felt-tipped marker, starting with the top piston as *No.1* and working downward. Then temporarily install the cylinder head using only two screws. Tighten the screws finger-tight. This will prevent the pistons from falling out of their cylinders during disassembly.

11. Note the position of any clamps or brackets on the exhaust cover, then remove the 14 (three-cylinder) or 12

(two-cylinder) screws securing the exhaust cover to the cylinder block. Carefully tap around the perimeter of the cover with a soft-faced mallet to break the gasket seal, then remove the cover. Remove and discard the gasket. Do not damage or distort the cover during the removal process.

12. Remove and discard the four screws securing the lower end cap to the cylinder block. Carefully pry the end cap from the cylinder block. Do not damage, distort or gouge the end cap and sealing surfaces. Remove and discard the O-ring and two seals. Remove the seals with a

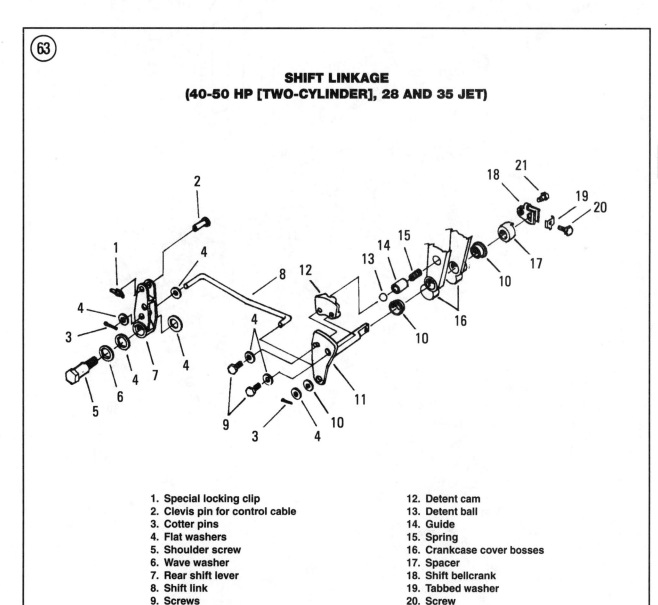

63

**SHIFT LINKAGE
(40-50 HP [TWO-CYLINDER], 28 AND 35 JET)**

1. Special locking clip
2. Clevis pin for control cable
3. Cotter pins
4. Flat washers
5. Shoulder screw
6. Wave washer
7. Rear shift lever
8. Shift link
9. Screws
10. Nylon bushings
11. Shift shaft and lever
12. Detent cam
13. Detent ball
14. Guide
15. Spring
16. Crankcase cover bosses
17. Spacer
18. Shift bellcrank
19. Tabbed washer
20. Screw
21. Gearcase shift shaft-to-bellcrank screw

8

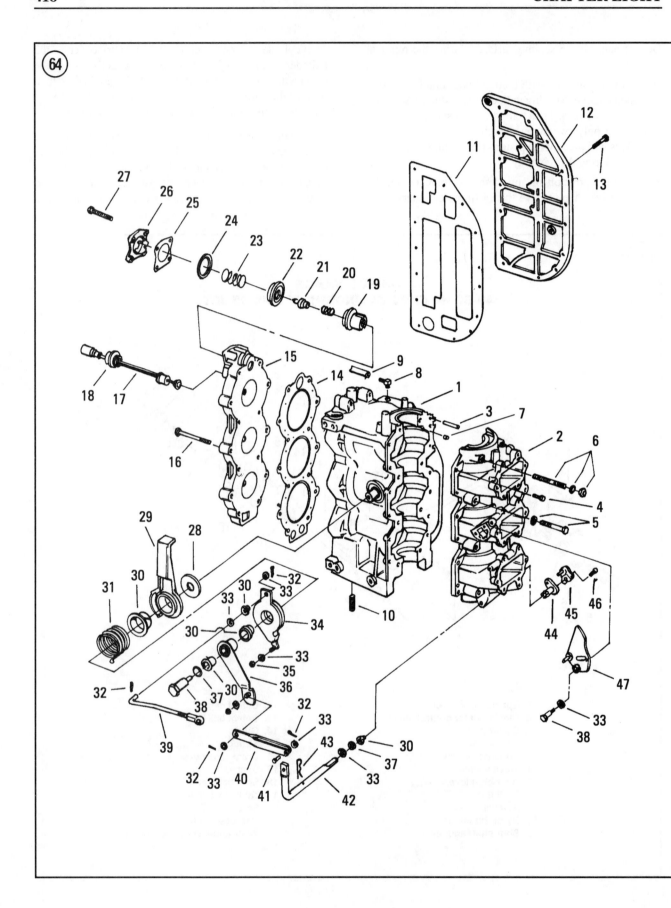

CYLINDER AND CRANKCASE ASSEMBLY
(40-70 HP, 28 AND 35 JET [THREE-CYLINDER SHOWN])

1. Cylinder block
2. Crankcase cover
3. Taper pin
4. Flange screws
5. Main bearing screws and washers
6. Stud, washer and nut (three-cylinder)
7. Dowel pin
8. Water discharge elbow fittings
9. Water discharge hose
10. Stud
11. Gasket
12. Exhaust cover
13. Screw
14. Gasket
15. Cylinder head
16. Screw
17. Engine temperature switch
18. Switch retaining nut
19. Plastic cup
20. Spring
21. Vernatherm (thermostat)
22. Diaphragm
23. Spring
24. Washer
25. Gasket
26. Thermostat cover
27. Screw
28. Washer
29. Spark control lever
30. Bushings
31. Spring
32. Cotter pins
33. Flat washers
34. Throttle lever
35. Locknuts
36. Shift lever
37. Wave washers
38. Shoulder screws
39. Throttle cam link
40. Shift link
41. Clevis pin
42. Shift shaft
43. Retaining clip
44. Bushing and keeper
45. Shift bellcrank
46. Screw
47. Throttle cam

CRANKSHAFT ASSEMBLY
(40-70 HP, 28 AND 35 JET [THREE-CYLINDER SHOWN])

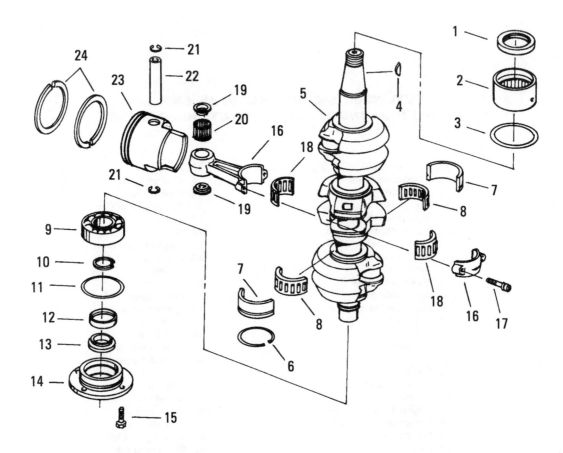

1. Upper seal
2. Upper main bearing
3. O-ring
4. Flywheel key
5. Crankshaft
6. Retaining ring
7. Bearing race halves
8. Caged roller bearing halves
9. Ball bearing and locating ring
10. Retaining ring
11. O-ring
12. Seal (double lip)

13. Seal (single lip)
14. Lower end cap
15. Screw
16. Connecting rod and cap
17. Rod cap screw
18. Caged bearing halves
19. Thrust washers
20. Loose needles
21. Wrist pin lock clips
22. Wrist pin
23. Piston
24. Piston rings

two-jaw seal puller, such as part No. 432127 puller and bridge and part No. 432131 jaws. Do not damage the seal bore during the removal process.

CAUTION
Do not *damage the taper pin or its bore during removal, or the cylinder block will be ruined.*

13. Using the tool shown in **Figure 31** (or equivalent), drive the taper pin (3, **Figure 64**) toward the intake manifold side (front) of the power head. Position the tool's extended toe over the taper pin and hold the main body of the tool parallel to the pin. Drive the pin from its bore.

14A. *Two-cylinder models*—Remove the eight crankcase cover-to-cylinder block flange screws (4, **Figure 64**, typical). Then evenly loosen and remove the six main bearing screws (5, **Figure 64**, typical). Note the length and original position of each screw and that there are no washers on the main bearing screws of two-cylinder models.

14B. *Three-cylinder models*—Note the position of the control linkage stop screw bracket, then remove the 12 crankcase cover-to-cylinder block flange screws (4, **Figure 64**). Next, evenly loosen and remove the ten main bearing fasteners. There are two nuts and washers (6, **Figure 64**) and eight screws and washers (5). Remove all fasteners, noting the length and original position of each screw.

CAUTION
The crankcase cover and cylinder block are a matched, align-bored unit. Do not scratch,

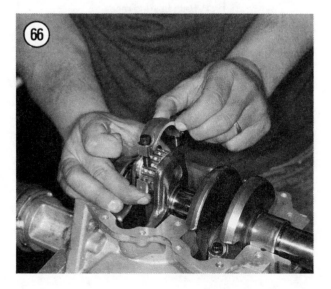

nick or damage the machined mating surfaces.

15. Position the power head with the crankcase cover facing upward. Using a soft-faced mallet, carefully tap the flywheel end of the crankshaft in an upward direction until the crankcase cover separates from the cylinder block. Then lift the cover off of the cylinder block. Use caution not to nick, scratch or damage the crankcase cover and cylinder block mating surfaces.

NOTE
*Always store **all** components from each connecting rod and piston assembly together. They must be reinstalled in their original locations.*

16. Mark the corresponding cylinder number on the connecting rods with a felt-tipped permanent marker. Mark the connecting rods and rod caps in such a manner that the rod caps can be reinstalled in their original orientation. Note any special alignment marks (such as cast dots).

17. Remove each connecting rod cap and bearing assembly as follows:
   a. Remove the connecting rod screws from the upper (No. 1 cylinder) connecting rod using connecting rod screw socket (part No. 331638) or an equivalent heavy-duty 5/16 in., 12-point thin-wall socket. Alternately loosen each screw a small amount until all tension is off of both screws.
   b. Tap the rod cap with a soft metal (brass) mallet to separate the cap from the rod.
   c. Remove the cap and rod from the crankshaft, then remove the two caged roller bearing halves from the crankshaft. See **Figure 66**, typical.
   d. Store the caged roller bearing assemblies in clean numbered containers, corresponding to the cylinder number.
   e. Repeat this procedure to remove the remaining (No. 2 cylinder [and No.3]) connecting rod caps.

18. Lift the crankshaft out of the cylinder block, then slide the upper seal and bearing assembly from the crankshaft. Remove and discard the O-ring.

19. Reinstall each rod cap to its respective connecting rod in its original orientation. Tighten the rod cap screws finger-tight.

20. Then drive the seal from the upper bearing using a suitable punch. Do not damage or distort the bearing's seal bore during removal. Discard the seal.

21. Remove the retaining ring from the center main bearing (upper center main bearing on three-cylinder models)

8

as shown in **Figure 67**. Then remove the bearing race and caged roller bearing halves. Store the bearing components in a labeled container. Repeat this procedure for the lower center main bearing on three-cylinder models. Store the second bearing's components in a separate labeled container.

22. If the ball bearing must be replaced, remove the retainer ring (10, **Figure 65**) using a suitable pair of retaining ring pliers. Support the bearing in a knife-edged press plate. Press the bearing free from the crankshaft using a suitable mandrel that will pilot into and press against the bottom of the crankshaft splined bore. Then discard the bearing.

23. Remove the cylinder head and carefully push each piston from its cylinder. Store each piston with its bearing components removed in Step 18.

24. Remove the piston rings from all pistons using a standard piston ring expander. See **Figure 61**, typical. Retain the rings for cleaning each piston's ring grooves.

25. Using locking clip remover (part No. 325937) or a modified pair of needlenose pliers (**Figure 32**), remove and discard the two wrist pin locking clips from each piston. See **Figure 68**, typical.

> *NOTE*
> *The wrist pin is a slip fit to both sides of the piston. The pin can be pushed out in either direction.*

26. Place the piston into the appropriate saddle of piston cradle (part No. 326573) or equivalent. See **Figure 69**, typical. Press the pin from the piston using pin remover (part No. 326356) or equivalent. Remove the tool and pin, then retrieve the two thrust washers and 28 loose needle bearings (**Figure 70**, typical). Store the components in clean, numbered containers corresponding to the cylinder number.

27. Repeat the previous step to separate the remaining piston(s) and connecting rod(s).

28. Refer to *Power Head Cleaning and Inspection* before beginning reassembly.

POWER HEAD CLEANING AND INSPECTION

Refer to Chapter Six and clean and inspect the reed valves and the fuel recirculation system components. Test all check valves in the recirculation system for correct function as described in Chapter Six.

Review the following sections: *Sealing Surfaces, Fasteners and Torque* and *Sealants, Lubricants and Adhesives*, located at the beginning of this chapter.

Replace all seals, O-rings, gaskets, wrist pin retainer clips and piston rings any time the power head is disassembled.

It is highly recommended that all connecting rod screws be replaced, if they have been removed.

Perform the cleaning and inspection procedure in each of the following sections that applies to your engine *before* beginning assembly.

Cylinder Block and Crankcase Cover (All Models)

The cylinder block and crankcase cover are a matched, align-bored assembly. For this reason, do not attempt to

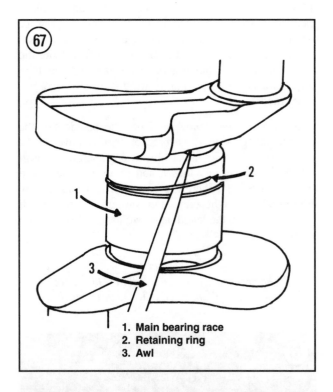

67

1. **Main bearing race**
2. **Retaining ring**
3. **Awl**

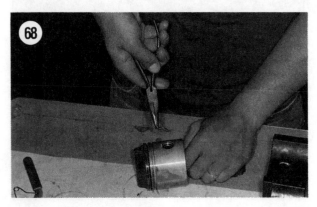

68

assemble an engine with parts salvaged from other blocks. If the following inspection procedure indicates that the block or cover requires replacement, replace the cylinder block and crankcase cover as an assembly.

NOTE
All fuel recirculation components (hoses, T-fittings, threaded fittings, check valves and metering rods) and the pulse limiter fitting (on VRO², oil-injected models) must be removed if it is necessary to submerge the block and/or cover in a strong cleaning solution. See Chapter Six or Chapter Eleven.

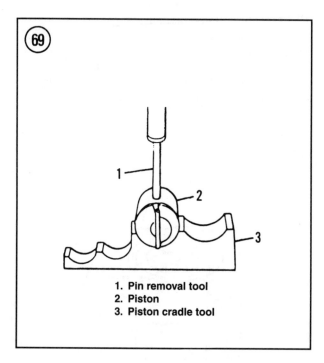

1. Pin removal tool
2. Piston
3. Piston cradle tool

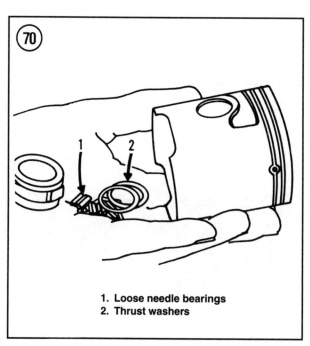

1. Loose needle bearings
2. Thrust washers

1. Clean the cylinder block and crankcase cover thoroughly with clean solvent and a parts washing brush. This is a preliminary cleaning to remove grease, grime and oil. On 3 and 4-8 hp (including 4 Deluxe) models, make sure the two plastic metering rods are removed from the recirculation passages in the crankcase cover.

2. Remove all carbon and varnish deposits from the combustion chambers, exhaust ports and exhaust cavities with a carbon removing solvent, such as OMC Engine Tuner. Allow ample time for the solvent to soften the deposits. Use a hardwood dowel or plastic scraper to remove stubborn deposits. Do not scratch, nick or gouge the combustion chambers or exhaust ports.

3. Completely remove the original Gel Seal sealant from the cylinder block-to-crankcase cover mating surface and all gasket residue from the cylinder head and all other sealing surfaces. OMC Gel Seal and Gasket Remover is the only solvent recommended for this purpose. Gel Seal and Gasket Remover is available either in an aerosol spray or in a liquid (gel).

WARNING
Wear hand and eye protection when working with OMC Gel Seal and Gasket Remover. Remove your wrist watch and all jewelry. The solvent is extremely potent.

a. Carefully spray (or brush) the OMC Gel Seal and Gasket Remover over the surface to be cleaned, then allow the solvent to stand for 5-10 minutes. Do not allow the solvent to contact any painted surfaces.

CAUTION
*The crankcase cover and cylinder block mating surfaces **must not** be scratched, nicked or damaged. Use a plastic scraper to clean the mating surfaces.*

b. Scrape the old sealant and/or gasket material from the mating surfaces with a plastic scraper (such as a household electrical outlet cover) or a piece of Lucite with one edge ground to a 45° angle.

4. After removing all traces of old Gel Seal and/or gasket material, wash the cylinder block and crankcase cover thoroughly with a mild solvent, such as mineral spirits. Then wash the cylinder block and crankcase cover thoroughly with hot, soapy water. Rinse the cylinder block and crankcase cover with clean hot water, then blow dry with

8

compressed air. Finally, lubricate the cylinder walls with outboard lubricant to prevent corrosion.

> *WARNING*
> *Use suitable hand and eye protection when using muriatic acid products. Avoid breathing the vapors. Use only in a well-ventilated area.*

5. If the cylinder bore(s) have aluminum transfer from the piston(s):
   a. Clean loose deposits from the bore with a stiff bristle brush.

> *CAUTION*
> *Do not allow muriatic acid to contact the aluminum surfaces of the cylinder block.*

   b. Apply a small quantity of diluted muriatic acid to the aluminum deposits. A bubbling action indicates the aluminum is being dissolved.
   c. Wait 1-2 minutes, then thoroughly wash the cylinder with hot water and detergent.
   d. Repeat this procedure until the aluminum deposits are completely removed.
   e. Lightly oil the cylinder walls with outboard lubricant to prevent rust.

6. Check the cylinder block and crankcase cover for cracks, fractures, stripped threads or other damage. Then carefully inspect the cylinder block-to-crankcase cover mating surface for nicks, grooves, cracks or distortion.

> *CAUTION*
> *The cylinder block-to-crankcase cover mating surfaces may **not** be lapped or resurfaced.*

7. Inspect all gasket mating surfaces for nicks, grooves, cracks or distortion. Any of these defects will cause leakage. Check the surfaces for distortion (warpage) as described under *Sealing Surfaces* located at the beginning of this chapter. **Figures 71-73** show typical directions in which to check for warpage on the cylinder head and exhaust cover mating surfaces.

Generally, a sealing surface with a distortion of more than 0.004 in. (0.1 mm) will require lapping, resurfacing or replacement. Small imperfections are best removed by lapping the component as described in *Sealing Surfaces*. Do not remove more than 0.010 in. (0.25 mm) of material when lapping or resurfacing.

8. Check all water, oil and fuel bleed passages in the block and cover for obstructions. Make sure all pipe plugs are installed tightly. Pipe plugs must be sealed with OMC Pipe Sealant with Teflon.

> *NOTE*
> *If metal particles (such as those that result from a bearing failure) are present in the cylinder block or crankcase cover, replace the recirculation system check valve(s) and make certain all recirculation hoses and fittings are free of debris and/or restrictions.*

9. *9.9-50 hp (two-cylinder), 50-70 hp (three-cylinder) and 18-35 jet*—Inspect the labyrinth seal grooves cast into the cylinder block and crankcase cover, near each center main bearing. The seal grooves must be free of debris and must not be excessively worn or damaged. The seals prevent internal leakage between each. Refer to *Starting Difficulties* in Chapter Three for additional information.

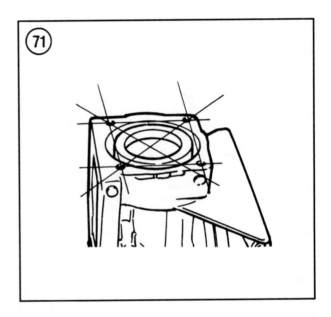

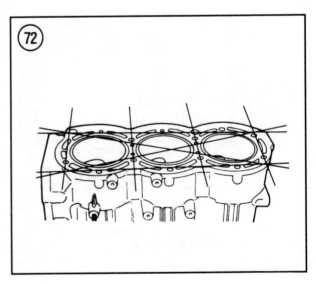

10. *3, 4 hp, 4 Deluxe, 20-30 hp (two-cylinder) and 18 jet*—Inspect the water passage deflectors. The deflector(s) ensure that the water flows correctly through the block. The deflector(s) must be pulled from the block and discarded if damaged, distorted or deteriorated.

The 3, 4 hp and 4 Deluxe models use one deflector mounted at the very top and center of the water jacket, while the 20-30 hp (two-cylinder) and 18 jet models use three deflectors placed as shown in **Figure 74**. The lower, port deflector is shorter than the upper and lower, starboard deflectors.

To function correctly, the deflector(s) must extend slightly past the cylinder head gasket surface of the block. If not, water will bypass the deflector, resulting in incorrect cooling water flow. Replacement deflectors are listed in the manufacturer parts catalog.

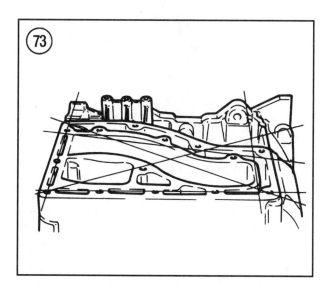

Cylinder Bore Inspection

Inspect the cylinder bores for scoring, scuffing, grooving, cracks or bulging and any other mechanical damage. Inspect the cylinder block (casting) and cast-iron liner for separation or delamination. There must be no gaps or voids between the aluminum casting and the liner. Remove any aluminum deposits (aluminum transfer from the pistons) as described previously in this section. If the cylinders are in a visually acceptable condition, hone the cylinders as described in *Cylinder wall honing*. If the cylinders are in unacceptable condition, bore the defective cylinder(s) or replace the cylinder block and crankcase cover as an assembly.

NOTE
It is not necessary to bore all cylinders in a cylinder block. Bore only the cylinders that are excessively worn or damaged. It is acceptable to have a mix of standard and oversize bores on a given power head as long as the correct piston (standard or oversize) is used to match each bore. Always check the manufacturer's parts catalog for oversize piston availability and bore sizes before beginning the boring process.

Cylinder Bore Honing

A rigid type cylinder hone is recommended for deglazing the bore to aid in the seating of new piston rings. If the cylinder is bored oversize, the rigid hone will be used in two steps: a rough (deburring) hone to remove the machining marks and a finish (final) hone to establish final bore diameter and the correct cross-hatch pattern in the cylinder bore.

Flex (ball type) hones and spring-loaded hones are not recommended as they will not produce a true (straight and perfectly round) bore.

NOTE
If you are not proficient with the correct use of a rigid cylinder hone, it is recommended that cylinder bore honing be performed by a qualified machine shop or a qualified dealer. Rigid hones are available from the Sunnen Products Company, 7910 Manchester Ace, St. Louis, Missouri 63143. Sunnen products are often available from tool and industrial suppliers.

If the cylinders are in a visually acceptable condition, prepare the cylinder bore for new piston rings and remove any glazing, light scoring and/or scuffing by lightly honing the cylinders as follows:

1. Follow the rigid hone manufacturer's instructions when using the hone. Make sure the correct stones for a cast-iron bore are installed on the hone.

2. A continuous flow of the recommended honing oil must be pumped into the bore during the honing operation. If an oil pumping system is not available, enlist the aid of an assistant (and an oil can) to keep the cylinder walls flushed with honing oil.

3. If the hone loads (slows down) at one location in the bore, this indicates the narrowest portion of the bore. Localize the stroking in this location to remove stock until the hone maintains the same speed (and load) throughout the entire bore.

4. Frequently remove the hone from the cylinder bore and inspect the bore. Do not remove any more material than necessary.

5. Attempt to achieve a stroke rate of approximately 30 cycles per minute, adjusting the speed of the hone to achieve a cross-hatch pattern with an intersecting angle of approximately 30°. Do not exceed a cross-hatch angle of more than 45°.

6. After honing, inspect each intake and exhaust port for sharp edges or burrs. Remove any burrs and chamfer all sharp edges with a suitable whetstone or emery cloth.

7. Thoroughly clean the cylinder block using hot water, detergent and a stiff bristle brush. Make certain all abrasive material from the honing process is removed. After washing and flushing, coat the cylinder walls with outboard motor oil to prevent rusting.

8. Proceed to *Cylinder bore measurements* in this chapter to determine if the cylinder bores are within the manufacturer's specifications for wear, taper and out-of-round.

Cylinder Bore Measurements

Measure each cylinder bore as follows. Oversize bore specifications are simply the standard bore specification *plus* the oversize dimension (check parts catalog for available oversize dimensions). All standard bore specifications, maximum taper and out-of-round specifications are listed in **Table 4** and **Table 5**. The maximum wear limit on a given cylinder is equal to the standard bore plus the maximum taper specification.

Use a cylinder bore gauge (**Figure 75**), inside micrometer or a telescoping gauge and an outside micrometer, to measure the entire area of ring travel in the cylinder bore. Take three sets of readings: at the top, middle and bottom of the ring travel area (**Figure 76**).

1. Take the first reading at the top of the ring travel area (approximately 1/2 in. [12.7 mm] from the top of the cylinder bore) with the gauge aligned with the crankshaft centerline. Record your reading. Then turn the gauge 90° to the crankshaft centerline and take (and record) another reading.

2. The difference between the two readings is the cylinder out-of-round. The reading must not exceed specifications (**Tables 4-5**).

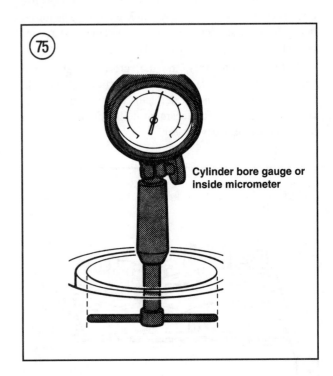

Cylinder bore gauge or inside micrometer

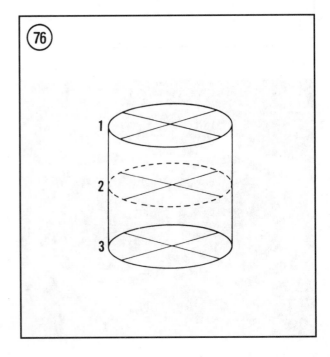

3. Take a second set of readings at the midpoint of the ring travel area (just above the ports) using the same alignments points described in Step 1. Record the readings. Calculate the cylinder out-of-round by determining the difference between the two readings. The reading must not exceed specifications (**Tables 4-5**).

4. Take a third set of readings at the bottom of the ring travel area (near the bottom of the cylinder bore) using the same alignment points described in Step 1. Record the readings. Calculate the cylinder out-of-round by determining the difference between the two readings. The reading must not exceed specifications (**Tables 4-5**).

5. To determine the cylinder taper, subtract the readings taken at the top of the cylinder bore from the readings taken at the bottom of the cylinder bore. The difference in these readings is the cylinder taper. The reading must not exceed specification (**Tables 4-5**).

NOTE
If the cylinder has already been bored over-size, add the oversize dimension to the stand-ard bore dimension and the maximum cylinder wear specification in the next step.

6. To determine if the cylinder is excessively worn, add the maximum cylinder wear specification (**Table 4** or **Table 5**) to the standard cylinder bore. If any of the readings taken in Steps 1-4 exceed this figure, the cylinder is excessively worn.

7. Repeat Steps 1-6 for each remaining cylinder.

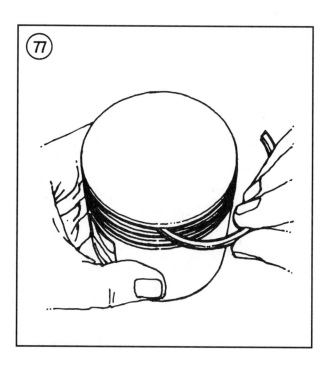

8. If any cylinder is excessively worn, bore the cylinder to the next oversize or replace the cylinder block/crankcase cover.

Piston

If the wrist pin and piston are to be reused, the pins must be reinstalled in the piston that they were removed from.

CAUTION
Do not use an automotive ring groove clean-ing tool as it will damage the ring grooves and loosen the ring locating pins.

1. Clean the piston(s), wrist pin(s), thrust (locating) wash-ers and the wrist pin needle bearing assemblies thoroughly with clean solvent and a parts washing brush. Do not wire brush the piston as metal from the wire wheel may become imbedded in the piston. This can lead to preignition and detonation.

2. Remove all carbon and varnish deposits from the top of the piston, piston ring groove(s) and the under the piston crown with a carbon removing solvent, such as OMC Engine Tuner. Use a piece of hardwood or a plastic scraper to remove stubborn deposits. Do not scratch, nick or gouge any part of the piston. Do not remove any stamped or cast identification marks.

3. Clean stubborn deposits from the ring groove(s) as follows:
   a. Fashion a ring cleaning tool from the original piston ring(s). Rings are different shaped for each ring groove. Make sure you are using the correct original ring for each ring groove.
   b. Break off approximately 1/3 of the original ring. Grind a beveled edge onto the broken end of the ring.

NOTE
On keystone and semi-keystone rings, it is necessary to grind off enough of the ring taper to allow the inside edge of the broken ring to reach the inside diameter of the ring groove.

   c. Use the ground end of the ring to gently scrape the ring groove clean (**Figure 77**). Be careful to only remove the carbon. Do not gouge the metal and do not damage or loosen the piston ring locating pin(s).

4. Polish any nicks, burrs or sharp edges on and about the piston skirt with emery cloth. Do not remove any cast or stamped identification markings. Wash the piston thor-oughly to remove all abrasive grit.

5. Inspect the piston(s) overall condition for scoring, cracks, worn or cracked wrist pin bosses and any other mechanical damage. Carefully inspect the crown and the

top outer diameter for burning, erosion, evidence of ring migration and mechanical damage (**Figure 78**). Replace the piston as necessary.

6. Check the piston ring grooves for wear, erosion, distortion and loose ring locating pins.

7. Inspect the wrist pin for water etching, pitting, scoring, heat discoloration, excessive wear, distortion and mechanical damage. Roll the pin across a machinist's surface plate to check the pin for distortion.

8. Inspect the thrust (locating) washers and needle bearings for water damage, pitting, scoring, overheating, wear and mechanical damage.

Piston Measurements

Measure each piston skirt with a micrometer as described in the following text and compare the readings to specifications. All piston specifications are listed in **Table 4** and **Table 5**.

To calculate the specified skirt diameter on oversize pistons, simply add the oversize dimension to the standard skirt diameter listed in **Table 4** and **Table 5**.

No specifications are given for cylinder-to-piston clearance. The correct clearance is obtained by verifying that the piston skirt and cylinder bore dimensions are correct.

1. *2-8 hp (including 4 Deluxe)*—Using a micrometer, measure each piston's skirt diameter as follows:

    a. Take a first reading at a point 1/8 in. (3.2 mm) up from the bottom of the skirt (**Figure 79**) at a 90° angle to the wrist pin bore as shown in **Figure 79**. Record your reading.

    b. Take a second reading (at the same distance from the bottom of the skirt) aligned with the wrist pin bore as shown in **Figure 80**, typical. Record the reading.

    c. The first reading must be within specification (**Table 4**), and both readings must be within 0.002 in. (.051 mm) of each other. If not, replace the piston(s).

2. *9.9 and 15 hp*—There are no piston skirt diameter specifications. Each piston can only be checked for out-of-round (with a micrometer) as follows:

    a. Take a first reading at a point 1/8 in. (3.2 mm) up from the bottom of the skirt (**Figure 79**) at a 90° angle to the wrist pin bore as shown in **Figure 79**. Record your reading.

    b. Take a second reading (at the same distance from the bottom of the skirt) aligned with the wrist pin bore as shown in **Figure 80**, typical. Record the reading.

    c. If the difference between the two measurements exceeds 0.002 in. (0.051 mm), the piston is out-of-round and must be replaced.

3. *20-30 hp (two-cylinder) and 18 jet*—The pistons used on these models are made by one of three possible vendors:

Art, Rightway or Zollner. The pistons manufactured by Art and Rightway have slightly different dimensions than those produced by Zollner. Refer to **Figure 81** for piston identification. Art and Rightway pistons have a clearly visible, raised semi-circle cast into the middle of the exhaust side of the deflector. This is not present on Zollner pistons.

The pistons used in these engines are cam-shaped. This means that the piston is intentionally built out-of-round. The piston is engineered to fit the bore perfectly when at

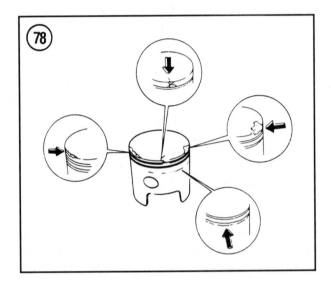

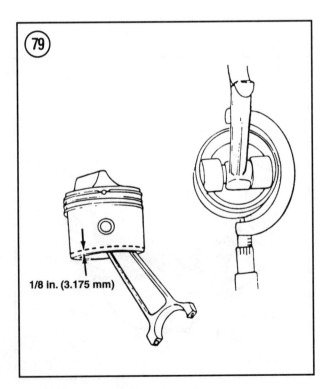

1/8 in. (3.175 mm)

operating temperature (and fully expanded), which makes the engine run more quietly and efficiently. The piston must be measured at the specified points or the readings will be inaccurate.

These pistons also have very fine, shallow grooves machined into the piston skirt. If the grooves are worn smooth in the triangular pattern shown in **Figure 82**, the piston(s) must be replaced.

Using a micrometer, measure each piston's skirt as follows:

    a. Measure the major diameter of each piston's skirt at a point 1/8 to 1/4 in. (3.2-6.35 mm) up from the

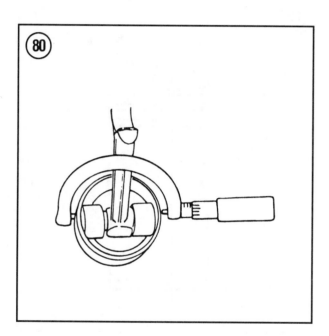

bottom of the skirt at a 90° angle to the wrist pin bore. See A, **Figure 81**. Record your readings. The piston major diameter must be within the major diameter specification listed in **Table 4**.

    b. Measure the minor diameter of each piston's skirt at a point 1/8 to 1/4 in. (3.2-6.35 mm) up from the bottom of the skirt, aligned with the wrist pin bore. See B, **Figure 81**. Record your readings. The piston minor diameter must be within the minor diameter specification listed in **Table 4**.

    c. Subtract the minor diameter from the major diameter. The resulting difference must be within the cam dimension specification listed in **Table 4**.

    d. Replace any piston that does not measure as specified.

4. *40-50 hp (two-cylinder), 28 jet and 35 jet*—The pistons used in these engines are cam-shaped. This means that the piston is intentionally built out-of-round. The piston is engineered to fit the bore perfectly when at operating temperature (and fully expanded), which makes the engine run more quietly and efficiently. The piston must be measured at the specified points or the readings will be inaccurate.

These pistons also have very fine, shallow grooves machined into the piston skirt. If the grooves are worn smooth in the pattern shown in **Figure 82**, the piston(s) must be replaced.

Using a micrometer, measure the piston skirt as follows:

    a. Measure the major diameter of each piston's skirt at a point 1/8 in. (3.2 mm) up from the bottom of the

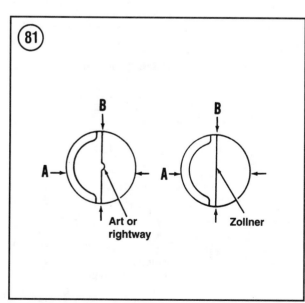

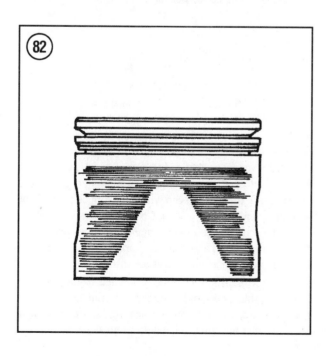

skirt directly aligned with the upper piston ring's dowel pin. See **Figure 83**. Record your reading.

b. The major diameter must be no less than 3.1831 in. (80.851 mm) on a standard piston. If not, replace the piston.

NOTE
No other point on the piston skirt can be larger than the major diameter specified in substep b.

c. Determine the minor diameter of each piston's skirt, by taking several readings (at a point 1/8 in. [3.2 mm] up from the bottom of the skirt) around the skirt, until the smallest diameter is located. Record the reading.

d. The minor diameter must be no more than 0.004 in. (0.102 mm) smaller than the major diameter. If not, replace the piston.

5. *25, 35 and 50-70 hp (three-cylinder)*—Using a micrometer, measure each piston skirt as follows:

a. Take a reading at a point 1/4 in. (6.35 mm) up from the bottom of the skirt at a 90° angle to the wrist pin bore as shown in A, **Figure 84**. Record your reading.

b. The piston diameter must be within the specification listed in **Table 5**. If not, replace the piston(s).

c. Take a second reading (at the same distance from the bottom of the skirt) as close to aligned with the wrist pin bore as possible (B, **Figure 84**). Record the reading.

d. The difference between the first and second readings must be within 0.003 in. (0.076 mm) of each other. If not, replace the piston(s).

Connecting Rods
(3, 4-70 hp and 18-35 Jet)

All connecting rods on 3, 4-70 hp and 18-35 jet models are of the fractured cap design. This means that the cap is broken from the rod during the manufacturing process, leaving a jagged (fractured) mating surface that will mate perfectly if installed in its original orientation. If the cap is installed reversed and the rod screws are tightened, the rod will be destroyed. While alignment marks are provided, always mark the rod and cap with a felt-tipped permanent marker for easy identification. Correct orientation is obvious if the time is taken to examine the mating surfaces of the rod and cap. The connecting rod cap must be held firmly in position as the screws are installed.

If the rod cap is not perfectly aligned to the rod, the bearing surface will not be aligned, resulting in extremely noisy operation and premature bearing failure. This will destroy the connecting rod and the crankshaft.

The use of new connecting rod screws on final assembly is highly recommended. However, the original screws must be used for cleaning and inspection. All connecting rod screw torque specifications are listed in **Table 1**.

All connecting rods on 20-70 hp and 18-35 jet models require a special fixture (part No. 396749) to correctly align the cap. An accessory set of jaws (part No. 437273) is also required on 25 and 35 hp (three-cylinder) models.

The special fixture contacts the rod cap and rod body on four beveled (machined) corners, applying a predeter-

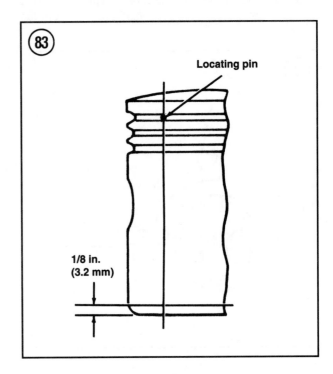

83

Locating pin

1/8 in.
(3.2 mm)

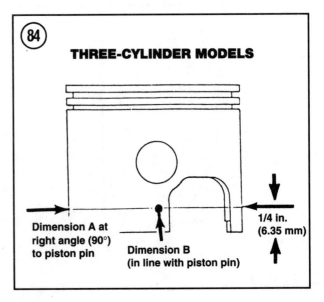

84

THREE-CYLINDER MODELS

Dimension A at right angle (90°) to piston pin

Dimension B (in line with piston pin)

1/4 in.
(6.35 mm)

mined clamping force. The fixture is left in place during the torquing process, ensuring perfect rod cap alignment. Use of the fixture is described in the following section, labeled *Connecting rod assembly (20-70 hp and 18-35 jet)*.

NOTE
Smaller engines also use fractured cap connecting rods, but do not require a special fixture for reassembly. The cap is aligned by hand.

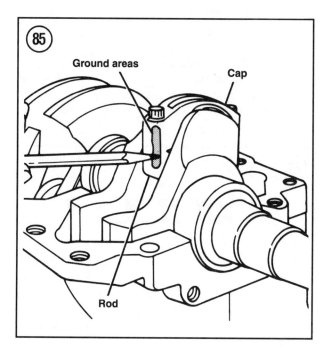

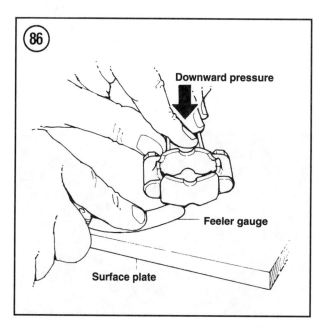

To clean and inspect the connecting rods, proceed as follows:

1. Clean the connecting rods thoroughly with clean solvent and a parts washing brush.

2. Check the connecting rod big and small end bearing surfaces for rust, water damage, pitting, spalling, chatter marks, heat discoloration and excessive or uneven wear. If the defect can be felt by dragging a pencil lead or a finger nail over it, the rod must be discarded. Stains or marks that cannot be felt can be removed by polishing the bearing surface.

3A. *3 and 4-15 hp*—Assemble the rod cap to the connecting rod as follows:

   a. Clamp the No. 1 cylinder connecting rod securely in a soft-jawed vise.

   b. Install the matching connecting rod cap to the connecting rod in its original orientation. Carefully observe the fracture and alignment marks to ensure correct installation.

   c. Lubricate the screw threads and underside of the screw head with outboard lubricant. Then, while holding the cap firmly in position, install the connecting rod screws and thread them fully into the rod.

   d. Tighten each screw finger-tight. Run a fingernail, pencil lead or dental pick over the four beveled edges of the rod-to-cap joint (**Figure 85**, typical). No ridge must be seen or felt. Realign and retorque the cap as necessary.

   e. Once the alignment is verified, finish torquing the rod screws to 60-70 in.-lb. (6.8-7.9 N•m) in three progressive steps. Make a final check of alignment after the final torque is applied. If correct alignment cannot be obtained, replace the connecting rod.

   f. Repeat this procedure for each remaining rod.

3B. *20-70 hp and 18-35 jet*—Assemble the rod cap to the connecting rod as described in *Connecting rod assembly (20-70 hp and 18-35 jet models)* in the following section.

4. Check the connecting rods for straightness. Place each rod/cap assembly on a machinist's surface plate and press downward on the rod beam. The rod must not wobble under pressure. While holding the rod against the plate, attempt to insert a 0.002 in. (0.051 mm) feeler gauge between the machined surfaces of the rod and the plate (**Figure 86**). If the feeler gauge can be inserted between any machined surface of the rod and the surface plate, the rod is bent and must be discarded.

5. Stains or slight defects in the connecting rod bearing bores can be cleaned using fine-grit abrasive cloth. First fabricate a holder for the abrasive cloth as follows:

   a. Using a hacksaw, cut a notch 1 in. (25 mm) long into the end of a rod or bolt. The rod or bolt should be approximately 4 in. (102 mm) long and 5/16 in. (8 mm) in diameter.

8

b. Insert a length of fine-grit abrasive cloth into the notch cut into the holder. Mount the holder in an electric drill.

c. Spin the cloth using the drill as shown in **Figure 87** to clean the bearing bores. Maintain a 90° angle as shown. Continue until the bearing bore is polished, but do not remove any more material from the rod than necessary.

d. Wash the connecting rod thoroughly in clean solvent to remove any abrasive grit, then inspect the bearing surfaces. Replace any connecting rod that does not clean up properly.

e. Remove and discard the rod cap screws. Wash the rod and cap again in clean solvent. Retag the rod and cap for identification. Lightly oil the bearing surfaces with outboard lubricant to prevent rust.

f. Repeat this process for each remaining connecting rod.

Connecting Rod Assembly
(20-70 hp and 18-35 Jet)

Rod cap alignment fixture (part No. 396749) is required for this procedure. On 25 and 35 hp (three-cylinder) models, jaw Kit (part No. 437273) is also required. Always refer to the instructions included with the tool for additional or updated information.

Rod cap screw socket (part No. 342664) or an equivalent heavy-duty 12-point, 1/4 in. socket is required to torque the rod cap screws on 25 and 35 hp (three-cylinder) models.

Rod cap screw socket (part No. 331638) or an equivalent heavy-duty 12-point, thin-wall, 5/16 in. socket is required to torque the rod cap screws on all other models.

> *CAUTION*
> *Failure to use the alignment fixture (and use it correctly) will result in premature connecting rod bearing failure, which will also result in the connecting rod and crankshaft being destroyed.*

1. If assembling the rod for cleaning and inspection, clamp the No. 1 cylinder connecting rod securely in a soft-jawed vise.

2. Install the matching connecting rod cap to the connecting rod in its original orientation. Carefully observe fracture and alignment marks to ensure correct installation.

3. Lubricate the screw threads and underside of the screw head with outboard lubricant. Then, while holding the cap firmly in position, install the connecting rod screws and thread them fully into the rod.

4. Tighten both screws to 25-30 in.-lb. (2.82-3.39 N•m).

5A. *20-50 hp (two-cylinder), 50-70 hp (three-cylinder) and 18-35 jet*—Assemble the rod cap alignment fixture as follows:

a. Move the flat on the knob marked *Set* to align with the arrow embossed on the tool's frame. Move the adjustment knob in or out until the outermost ring aligns with the surface of the tool frame. The instruction sheet refers to this as mark *A*. Then rotate the knob 180° to lock the adjustment.

b. Install the retaining jaw labeled *C* and the forcing jaw labeled *D* to the fixture frame as described by the tool's instruction sheet.

5B. *25 and 35 hp (three-cylinder)*—Assemble the rod cap alignment fixture as follows:

a. Move the flat on the knob marked *Set* to align with the arrow embossed on the tool's frame. Move the adjustment knob in or out until the outermost ring aligns with the surface of the tool's frame. The

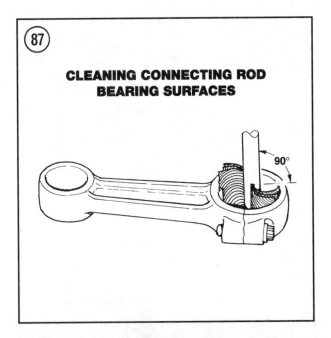

CLEANING CONNECTING ROD BEARING SURFACES

instruction sheet refers to this as mark *A*. Then rotate the knob 180° to lock the adjustment.

b. Install the retaining jaw labeled *G* and the forcing jaw labeled *H* from the jaw kit (part No. 437273) to the fixture frame as described by the tool and jaw kit's instruction sheets.

6. Lubricate the four precision ground corners of the connecting rod's big end, then position the fixture over the big end in the manner shown in **Figure 88**, typical.

7. Allow the stop plunger in the center of the frame to contact the rod cap. Then align the grooves machined into the jaws with the rod cap-to-connecting rod parting line.

8. Tighten the tool's forcing screw to 23 in.-lb. (2.6 N•m). Verify that the stop plunger is contacting the rod cap and

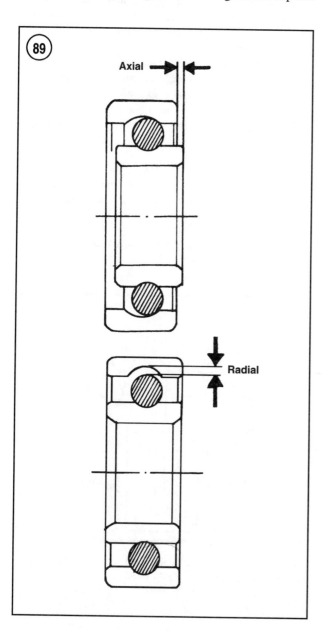

that the grooves in the jaws are aligned with the rod's parting line.

9. Loosen both rod cap screws 1/4 turn. Then retighten both screws to a preliminary torque of 40-60 in.-lb. (4.5-6.8 N•m).

10A. *20-50 hp (two-cylinder), 50-70 hp (three-cylinder) and 18-35 jet*—Tighten both rod cap screws to a final torque of 30-32 ft.-lb. (40.7-43.4 N•m) in a minimum of three progressive steps.

10B. *25 and 35 hp (three-cylinder)*—Tighten both rod caps' screws to a final torque of 170-190 in.-lb. (19.2-21.5 N•m) in a minimum of two progressive steps.

11. Loosen the forcing screw and remove the fixture. Run a fingernail or pencil lead over each of the four beveled (machined) edges of the rod-to-cap joint (**Figure 85**, typical). No ridge must be seen or felt. Replace the connecting rod if the correct alignment cannot be accomplished.

12. Repeat this procedure for each remaining connecting rod.

Crankshaft (2, 3.3 and 3.5 hp)

1. Thoroughly wash the crankshaft assembly and all bearings in clean solvent with a parts washing brush.

2. Inspect the square drive end of the crankshaft for corrosion, excessive wear or other damage.

3. Inspect the flywheel taper, flywheel key groove, and threads for corrosion, wear, cracks and mechanical damage.

4. Inspect the seal surfaces for excessive grooving, pitting, nicks or burrs. The seal surfaces may be polished with crocus cloth if necessary.

5. Inspect the connecting rod large end bearing by rotating the rod around its journal. The bearing must rotate smoothly with no binding, catches or noise.

6A. *Ball bearings removed*—Check the upper and lower ball bearing journals for overheating, corrosion and evidence of a bearing race spinning on the journal. The bearing's inner races must be an interference fit on the crankshaft. The journals may be polished with crocus cloth if necessary.

6B. *Ball bearings installed*—Rotate the ball bearings. The bearing must rotate smoothly with no rough spots, catches or noise. There must be no discernible radial or axial play between the inner and outer races of the bearings (**Figure 89**). If the bearing shows any visible wear, corrosion or deterioration, it must be replaced.

7. Clean the connecting rod small end bearing surfaces as necessary with crocus cloth. Use the same procedure as described in *Connecting Rods (3, 4-70 hp and 18-35 jet)*.

8. Inspect the connecting rod small end needle bearing assembly for water damage, wear, pitting, overheating and

mechanical damage. Replace the bearing if there is any question regarding its condition.

9. Support the crankshaft assembly as shown in **Figure 90**. Mount a dial indicator at the check points shown, then rotate the crankshaft assembly and check the runout. Replace the crankshaft if runout exceeds 0.001 in. (0.025 mm).

10. Determine connecting rod, crankpin and crankpin bearing wear by checking the connecting rod small end play (**Figure 91**). Replace the crankshaft assembly if play is not within 0.022-0.056 in. (0.56-1.42 mm).

11. Replace the crankshaft and connecting rod as an assembly if necessary.

Crankshaft (3, 4-70 hp and 18-35 Jet)

Crankshaft dimensions are listed in **Tables 4-5**. Replace the crankshaft if it is excessively worn. The lower main bearing journal cannot be measured unless the ball bearing is removed.

1. Thoroughly wash the crankshaft and the main and connecting rod bearing assemblies with clean solvent and a parts washing brush.

2. Measure the crankshaft journals and crankpins with a micrometer and compare to the specifications given in **Table 4** or **Table 5**.

3. Inspect the drive shaft splines, flywheel taper, flywheel key groove and flywheel nut threads for corrosion, cracks, excessive wear, and mechanical damage.

4. Inspect the upper and lower seal surfaces for excessive grooving, pitting, nicks or burrs. The seal surfaces may be polished with a fine grit abrasive cloth as necessary. If the crankshaft is equipped with a sleeve/drive shaft seal carrier on the drive shaft end, it can be replaced if damaged.

5A. *3 and 4-8 hp (including 4 Deluxe)*—Inspect the seal ring groove near the center main journal for wear and mechanical damage.

5B. *25 and 35 hp (three-cylinder)*—Inspect each of the three crankshaft seal rings for broken segments and excessive wear. Each ring must be at least 0.100 in (2.54 mm) thick. Replace any seal ring that is damaged or excessively worn.

5C. *All other models*—Inspect the journal surfaces that ride against the labyrinth seal grooves for scoring, overheating, grooving and excessive wear. These are the journals that ride against the grooves cast into the crankcase cover and cylinder block. The journals may be polished with fine grit abrasive cloth if necessary.

6. Check the crankshaft bearing surfaces for rust, water damage, pitting, spalling, chatter marks, heat discoloration and excessive or uneven wear. If the defect can be felt by dragging a pencil lead or a finger nail over it, the crankshaft must be discarded. Stains or marks that cannot be felt can

be removed by polishing the bearing surface with a strip of fine grit abrasive cloth. Work the cloth back and forth evenly over the entire journal until the surface is polished. Do not remove any more material than necessary.

7. Thoroughly clean the crankshaft again in clean solvent and recheck the crankshaft surfaces. Replace the crankshaft if it cannot be properly cleaned. If the crankshaft is in acceptable condition, lightly oil the crankshaft to prevent rust.

8. Inspect the bearings as follows:

a. *Ball bearing(s)*—Rotate the bearing(s). The bearing must rotate smoothly without noise or excessive play. There must be no discernible radial or axial play (**Figure 89**) between the inner and outer races of the bearing. If the bearing shows any visible signs of wear, corrosion or deterioration, it must be replaced.

b. *Roller/needle bearings*—Inspect the rollers and/or needles for water etching, pitting, chatter marks, heat discoloration and excessive or uneven wear. Inspect the cages for wear and mechanical damage. Replace bearings as an assembly; do not attempt to replace individual rollers or needles.

> *CAUTION*
> *The bearing cage on some needle bearings is designed to retain the bearing rollers (needles). The needles are loose on other bearings. Therefore, either all or none of the needle bearing rollers must be retained in the cage. If some of the rollers fall from the cage,*

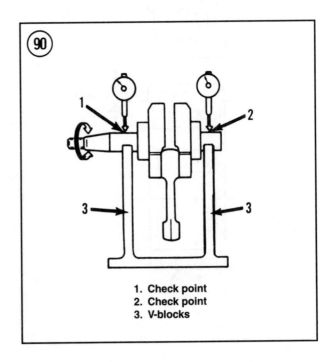

1. Check point
2. Check point
3. V-blocks

yet some are retained, the bearing has failed and must be replaced. Replace any bearing whose condition is questionable.

Lower End Cap, Cylinder Head, Exhaust, Intake and Cylinder Head Cover(s)

If your engine is equipped with any or all of these components, clean and inspect each as described in the following sections.

Cylinder head and cylinder head cover

The 20-30 hp (two-cylinder) and 18 jet models are equipped with a cylinder head cover, in addition to a cylinder head.

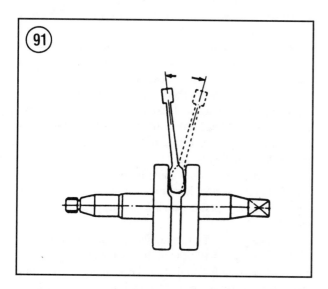

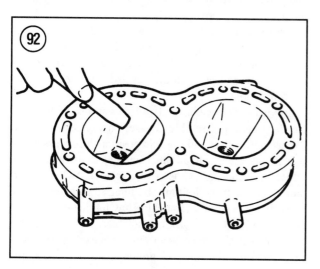

1. Clean the cylinder head and cylinder head cover thoroughly with clean solvent and a parts washing brush. Carefully remove all gasket and sealant material from the mating surfaces.

2. *Cylinder heads*—Remove all carbon and varnish deposits from the combustion chambers using a carbon removing solvent, such as OMC Engine Tuner. Use a sharpened hardwood dowel or plastic scraper to remove stubborn deposits (**Figure 92**, typical). Do not scratch, nick or gouge the combustion chambers.

> *NOTE*
> *The cylinder head can be lapped or resurfaced to remove warpage up to 0.010 in. (0.254 mm). Do not remove more than 0.010 in. (0.254 mm) of material from the cylinder head.*

3. Check the cylinder head and cylinder head cover for cracks, fractures, distortion or other damage. Check the cylinder head for stripped or damaged threads. Refer to *Sealing surfaces* in this chapter and check the cylinder head for warpage. Maximum warpage on all models is 0.004 in. (1.02 mm). Remove minor imperfections by lapping the cylinder head as described in *Sealing Surfaces*.

4. Inspect all gasket surfaces (or O-ring grooves) for nicks, grooves, cracks, corrosion or distortion. Replace the cylinder head or cylinder head cover if the defect is sufficient to cause leakage.

5. Check all water passages in the head(s) for obstructions. Make sure all pipe plugs are installed tightly. Pipe plugs must be sealed with OMC Pipe Sealant with Teflon.

Exhaust cover and inner plate

1. Clean the exhaust cover (and inner plate) thoroughly with clean solvent and a parts washing brush. Carefully remove all gasket and sealant material from the mating surfaces.

2. Remove all carbon and varnish deposits with a carbon removing solvent, such as OMC Engine Tuner. Use a hardwood dowel or plastic scraper to remove stubborn deposits. Do not scratch, nick or gouge the mating surfaces.

3. Inspect the component and all gasket surfaces for nicks, grooves, cracks, corrosion or distortion. Replace the cover/manifold/plate if the defect is sufficient to cause leakage.

Intake cover

1. Clean the intake cover(s) thoroughly with clean solvent and a parts washing brush. Carefully remove all gasket and sealant material from the mating surfaces.

2. Inspect the cover and all gasket surfaces for nicks, grooves, cracks, corrosion or distortion. Replace the cover if the defect could cause leakage.

Lower end caps

1. Clean the end cap thoroughly with clean solvent and a parts washing brush. Carefully remove all sealant material from mating surfaces.

2. Inspect the seal bore(s) for nicks, gouges or corrosion that could cause the seal to leak around its outer diameter. Replace the end cap if the seal bore is damaged.

3. Inspect the end cap mating surface and O-ring groove for nicks, grooves, cracks, corrosion or distortion. Replace the end cap(s) if the defect could cause leakage.

Thermostat Assembly
(6-70 hp and 18-35 Jet)

The thermostat (or Vernatherm) regulates the water leaving the power head. Correct thermostat operation is vital to engine break-in, spark plug life, smooth consistent idling, maximum performance and durability.

On all models, the thermostat assembly incorporates a relief (blow-off) function controlled by water pressure in the block. At higher engine speeds, the water pump pressure (against a diaphragm, housing or the thermostat) is sufficient to force the thermostat off of its seat. When this happens, an additional exit for heated cooling water is provided. This increased flow of heated water leaving the cylinder head (in addition to the thermostat flow), allows additional cold inlet water to enter the block, lowering the engine operating temperature.

The benefit of this system is that the block stays warm enough at low speeds (under thermostat control) to maintain smooth idle and keep the plugs from fouling, but cool enough at high speeds to prevent preignition and detonation. Consider installing a new thermostat assembly diaphragm (if equipped) and/or all grommets (or seals) during any major disassembly or repair.

Refer to the appropriate power head disassembly procedure for illustrations of the thermostat assembly specific to your model engine.

1. Carefully clean all gasket material and/or sealant from the thermostat housing and its mating surface on the cylinder head. Inspect the thermostat bore in the cylinder head for corrosion and debris. Check the thermostat housing for

corrosion and/or distortion. Clean or replace the cylinder head and/or thermostat housing as necessary.

2. Remove and discard all seals, grommets or other sealing devices in the thermostat assembly.

3. If the thermostat is to be reused, refer to *Engine Temperature* in Chapter Three for cleaning, inspection and testing procedures. A Vernatherm cannot be tested when removed from the engine.

4. Inspect the spring(s) for corrosion, distortion and mechanical or other damage. Replace the spring(s) as necessary.

5. Inspect the diaphragm (if equipped) for cracks, pin holes or deterioration. Replace the diaphragm if its condition is questionable.

POWER HEAD ASSEMBLY

Before beginning assembly, make sure you have completed all applicable sections of the *Power Head Cleaning and Inspection* in this chapter.

Review the following sections: *Sealing Surfaces, Fasteners and Torque* and *Sealants, Lubricants and Adhesives*, located at the beginning of this chapter.

The manufacturer recommends replacing all seals, O-rings, gaskets, wrist pin locking clips and piston rings anytime a power head is disassembled. It is highly recommended that new connecting rod cap screws be installed during the assembly procedure.

If the original bearings must be reused, each must be installed in its original location and orientation. The same applies for any pistons and/or connecting rods being reused.

Piston rings may be rectangular and/or semi-keystone. Rectangular rings will fit their grooves in either direction, but must be installed so that the beveled ends of the ring end gap correctly fit around (straddle) the locating pin in the piston ring groove.

Semi-keystone rings are beveled 7-1/2° on the upper surface only. These rings will not fit their groove correctly if installed upside down. Carefully examine each ring's construction and position the beveled side up (matching the ring groove).

Lubricate the needle and roller bearings with OMC Needle Bearing Assembly Grease. This grease will hold the needles, rollers and cages in position during assembly procedures. Lubricate all other internal components with OMC (Evinrude or Johnson) 2-Cycle TC-W3 outboard lubricant, which will simply be referred to as oil in the following procedures. Do not use any lubricant inside the power head that is not gasoline soluble.

Mating surfaces must be absolutely free of gasket material, sealant residue, dirt, oil, grease or any other contaminant. OMC Cleaning Solvent, lacquer thinner, acetone, isopropyl alcohol and similar solvents are excellent oil, petroleum and wax-free solvents to use for the final preparation of mating surfaces.

OMC Gel Seal II is the only recommended sealant for sealing the crankcase cover to the cylinder block. Prior to applying the Gel Seal II, the crankcase cover's mating surface must be treated with OMC Locquic Primer and allowed to air dry. If the surface is blown dry, the primer's catalyst will also be blown away. If Locquic Primer is not used, the crankcase assembly must be allowed to set for at least 24 hours (after assembly) before starting the engine.

CAUTION
OMC Gel Seal II has a shelf life of approximately one year. If the age of the Gel Seal II can not be determined, it must be replaced. Using old sealant will result in leakage.

A selection of torque wrenches is absolutely essential for correct assembly and to ensure maximum longevity of the power head assembly. Failing to torque items as specified will result in premature power head failure.

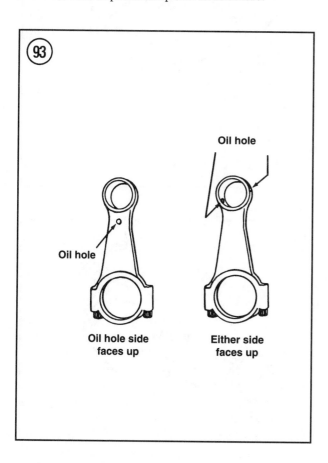

(93)

Oil hole

Oil hole

Oil hole

Oil hole side faces up

Either side faces up

Connecting Rod Orientation

The connecting rod must be correctly orientated when installed to the crankshaft to ensure adequate lubrication of the small end bearing. If the original rods are being reused, they must be installed in their original orientation as noted on disassembly. If installing one or more new connecting rods, position the rods in one of the following manners:

1. If the connecting rod's small end has a single hole through the I-beam of the rod and into the small end bore, the hole must face upward. See **Figure 93**.

2. If the connecting rod has two oil holes drilled in a straight line through the small end, the rod can be installed in either direction. See **Figure 93**.

3. If the small end of the connecting rod is scalloped (relieved) to expose some of the needle bearings to lubrication, the rod (when new) can be installed in either direction.

4. If the small end does not have any of the previous means of identification, position the part number (cast into the I-beam) and/or the rod cap alignment marks facing up.

**Piston Ring End Gap
(All Models)**

Before assembling the engine, the piston ring end gap must be checked (and adjusted if necessary) before installing the piston rings on the pistons.

Insufficient end gap will result in the piston sticking in the cylinder bore when the engine is hot. There must be adequate end gap to allow for heat expansion.

Excessive end gap will result in combustion gases leaking past the gap between the ring ends. This will cause a reduction in performance and can lead to excessive carbon buildup in the ring grooves and on the piston skirt.

Once the end gap is set, the rings must be tagged for correct installation into the bore in which they were checked (and fitted). Only the 2 and 3.3 hp have one piston ring. All other engines use two rings on each piston. Both rings must be checked (and fitted).

Excessive ring end gap can be caused by a worn or oversize bore. Recheck the cylinder bore as described in this chapter. Also make sure that the correct piston rings are used for the actual bore size.

Insufficient ring end gap can be corrected by carefully filing the ring ends until the correct end gap (**Tables 4-5**) is achieved. See **Figure 94**.

To check the piston ring end gap, refer to **Figure 94** and proceed as follows.

8

1. Select a piston ring and place it inside the No. 1 cylinder bore. Push the ring squarely into the bore using the piston. The ring must be square in the bore.

2. Measure the ring end gap with a feeler gauge as shown in **Figure 95**. If the ring gap is not within specification, repeat the measurement with the same ring in the No. 2 cylinder. Repeat the process as necessary until a bore is found that the ring fits correctly in or until there are no more cylinder bores to check.

3A. *Excessive end gap*—If the ring end gap is excessive in every bore, the ring is defective or the cylinder is oversize. Measure the cylinder bore and recheck the piston ring application (part number). If the bore is within specification and the correct ring is being used, the ring being checked is defective and must be replaced with another new ring.

3B. *Insufficient end gap*—If the ring end gap is insufficient in every bore, carefully file the ends of the ring as shown in **Figure 94**. Keep the file at a 90° angle to the ring. Do not remove any more material than necessary and do not create any burrs on the ring ends.

4. Once a ring correctly fits in a cylinder, tag the ring with the cylinder number so it can be installed on the correct piston during power head assembly.

5. If the ring is a rectangular ring, roll the ring around the piston's groove as shown in **Figure 96**, typical to check for binding. The piston ring must fit freely into its groove. If not, check for carbon deposits and remove any found. If the ring still binds, the piston must be replaced.

6. Repeat this process until all rings (top and bottom) are fitted to a specific cylinder bore and properly tagged for identification.

Assembly (2, 3.3 and 3.5 hp)

Refer to **Figure 97** for this procedure.

PISTON RING END GAP

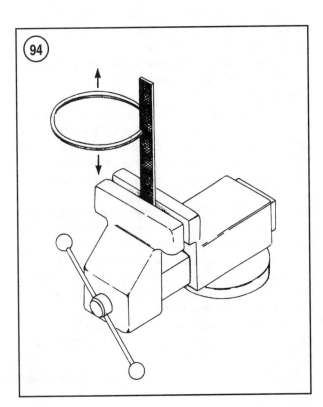

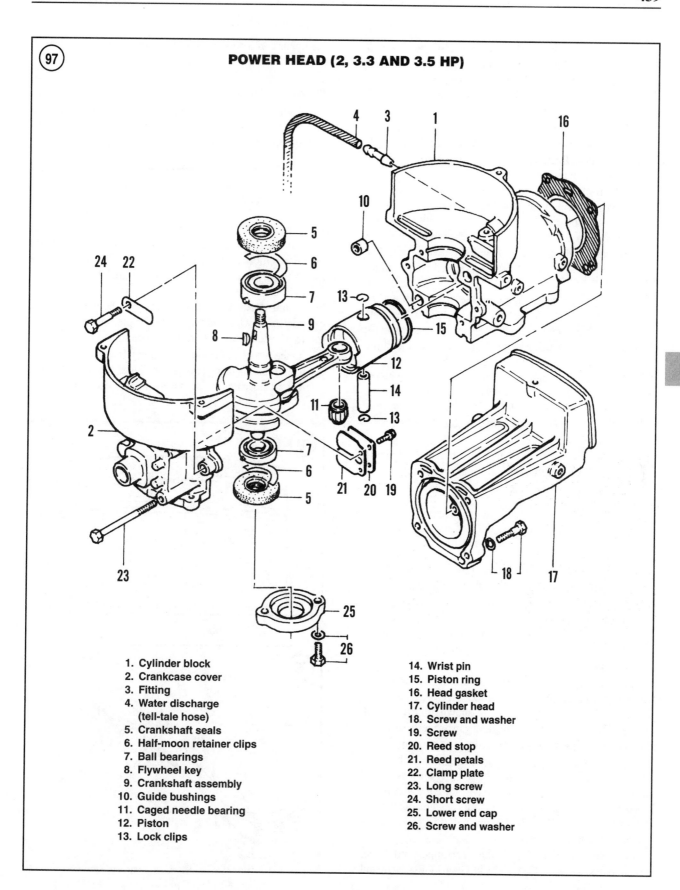

POWER HEAD (2, 3.3 AND 3.5 HP)

1. Cylinder block
2. Crankcase cover
3. Fitting
4. Water discharge (tell-tale hose)
5. Crankshaft seals
6. Half-moon retainer clips
7. Ball bearings
8. Flywheel key
9. Crankshaft assembly
10. Guide bushings
11. Caged needle bearing
12. Piston
13. Lock clips
14. Wrist pin
15. Piston ring
16. Head gasket
17. Cylinder head
18. Screw and washer
19. Screw
20. Reed stop
21. Reed petals
22. Clamp plate
23. Long screw
24. Short screw
25. Lower end cap
26. Screw and washer

1. Check the new piston ring's end gap as described in *Piston Ring End Gap* located in this chapter. The ring end gap must be 0.006-0.014 in. (0.15-0.36 mm).

2. If the crankshaft ball bearings were removed, install new bearings as follows:

    a. Oil the new bearings and the crankshaft journals.

    b. Slide the upper bearing over the flywheel end of the crankshaft. Position the locating pin in the bearing's outer race toward the bottom of the crankshaft, which should also result in the numbered side of the bearing facing away from the crankshaft.

    c. Support the crankshaft (under the upper counterweight) in a press. Press against the inner race of the bearing with a suitable mandrel, such as part No. 115309 (or equivalent) until it is seated on the crankshaft.

    d. Slide the lower bearing over the drive shaft end of the crankshaft. Position the locating pin in the bearing's outer race toward the bottom of the crankshaft, which should also result in the numbered side of the bearing facing away from the crankshaft.

    e. Support the crankshaft (under the lower counterweight) in a press. Press against the inner race of the bearing with a suitable mandrel, such as part No. 115309 (or equivalent) until it is seated on the crankshaft.

3. Lubricate the wrist pin bearing with needle bearing grease, then install the bearing into the connecting rod.

NOTE
The piston must be installed on the connecting rod so the arrow on the piston crown is facing down (toward the exhaust port).

4. Position the piston on the connecting rod with the arrow on the piston crown facing down. Oil the wrist pin and push the pin through the piston, bearing and connecting rod.

5. Secure the wrist pin with two new wrist pin retainers (13, **Figure 97**). Install the retainers with needlenose pliers. Make sure the retainers are completely seated in their grooves at each end of the wrist pin.

6. Using a standard ring expander, install the piston ring onto the piston. Install the ring with its grooved ends facing up (toward the piston crown) as shown in **Figure 98**, typical. Then make sure the ring end gap properly straddles the piston ring locating pin inside the ring groove.

7. Using a feeler gauge, measure the clearance between the piston ring and its ring groove. The ring must be seated in its groove. See **Figure 99**, typical. Take measurements at several locations around the piston. The clearance must not exceed 0.0026 in. (0.066 mm). If the clearance is excessive, replace the piston.

8. Lubricate the seal lips of the new upper and lower crankshaft seals with OMC Triple Guard Grease. Install

the upper and lower seals onto the crankshaft. The lips of both seals must face inward when installed.

9. Install the crankshaft bearing half moon retainers (6, **Figure 97**) into the cylinder block grooves.

10. Lubricate the piston ring, piston and cylinder bore with oil. Then position the end gap of the piston ring to straddle the ring locating pin in its groove.

NOTE
A ring compressor is not required as the cylinder bore has a tapered entrance.

11. Position the cylinder block so it is sitting on the cylinder head mating surface. Position the crankshaft and piston assembly over the cylinder block. Slowly lower the assembly toward the block while feeding the piston into the cylinder bore. The crankshaft must be kept perfectly horizontal. Rock the piston slightly to help it enter the cylinder bore while making sure the piston ring does not rotate or catch upon entering the bore.

12. Once the piston ring enters the cylinder bore, seat the crankshaft ball bearings into the cylinder block. Rotate the crankshaft bearings as necessary to position the bearing

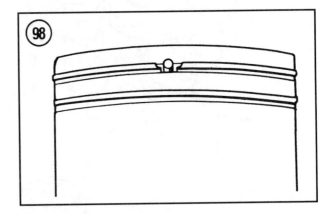

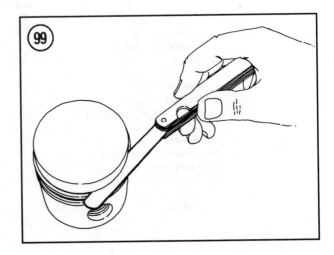

locating pins in the cylinder block notches in the port side of the mating surface.

13. Insert a thin screwdriver blade into the exhaust port and carefully depress the piston ring. If the ring fails to spring back when released, it was probably broken during installation. Replace the ring if it is damaged or broken.

14. Install new reed valves into the crankcase cover as described in Chapter Six.

15. Using an oil and wax free solvent, such as OMC Cleaning Solvent, acetone or lacquer thinner, clean the cylinder block and crankcase cover mating surfaces.

16. Install the two guide bushings (10, **Figure 97**) into the cylinder block or crankcase cover (if not already installed).

17. Spray the crankcase cover mating surface with OMC Locquic Primer and allow it to air dry.

18. Apply OMC Gel Seal II sealant to the mating surface of the cylinder block. Run a continuous sealant bead along the inside of all screw holes, then carefully spread the bead over the entire surface of the flange, making sure the sealant will not contaminate the bearings or ooze excessively into the crankcase.

19. Install the crankcase cover into position on the cylinder block. Seat the cover to the block with hand pressure. Coat the threads of the six crankcase cover screws with OMC Gel Seal II sealant, then install the cover screws. Tighten the cover screws evenly to 90-120 in.-lb. (10.2-

13.6 N•m) in a crossing pattern starting with the center screws and working outward.

20. Install the lower end cap with its recessed side facing the power head. Coat the threads of the two screws with OMC Gasket Sealing Compound, then install and tighten the screws to 60-84 in.-lb. (6.8-9.5 N•m).

21. Rotate the crankshaft several revolutions to check for binding or unusual noise. If binding or noise is noted, the power head must be disassembled and the cause of the defect located and corrected before proceeding.

NOTE
Do not use sealant on the cylinder head screws.

22. Apply a light coat of OMC Gasket Sealing Compound to both sides of a new cylinder head gasket. Position the cylinder head and new gasket on the cylinder block, then install the screws and washers (with no sealant). Evenly tighten the screws in a crossing pattern to 60-84 in.-lb. (6.8-9.5 N•m).

23. Install the power head as described previously in this chapter.

8

Assembly (3 and 4-8 hp [Including 4 Deluxe])

Refer to **Figure 100** or **Figure 101**, and **Figure 102** for the following procedure.

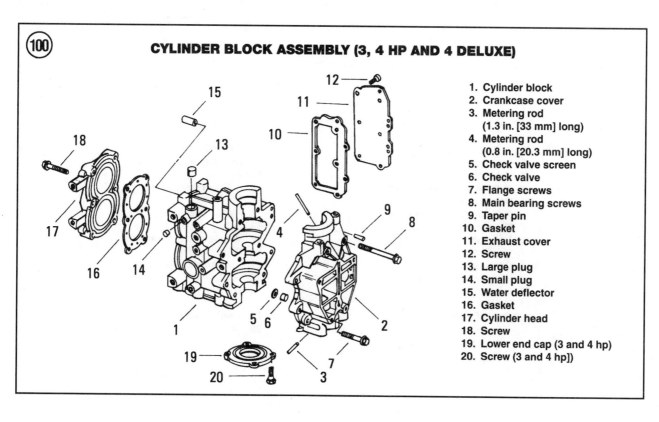

CYLINDER BLOCK ASSEMBLY (3, 4 HP AND 4 DELUXE)

1. Cylinder block
2. Crankcase cover
3. Metering rod (1.3 in. [33 mm] long)
4. Metering rod (0.8 in. [20.3 mm] long)
5. Check valve screen
6. Check valve
7. Flange screws
8. Main bearing screws
9. Taper pin
10. Gasket
11. Exhaust cover
12. Screw
13. Large plug
14. Small plug
15. Water deflector
16. Gasket
17. Cylinder head
18. Screw
19. Lower end cap (3 and 4 hp)
20. Screw (3 and 4 hp])

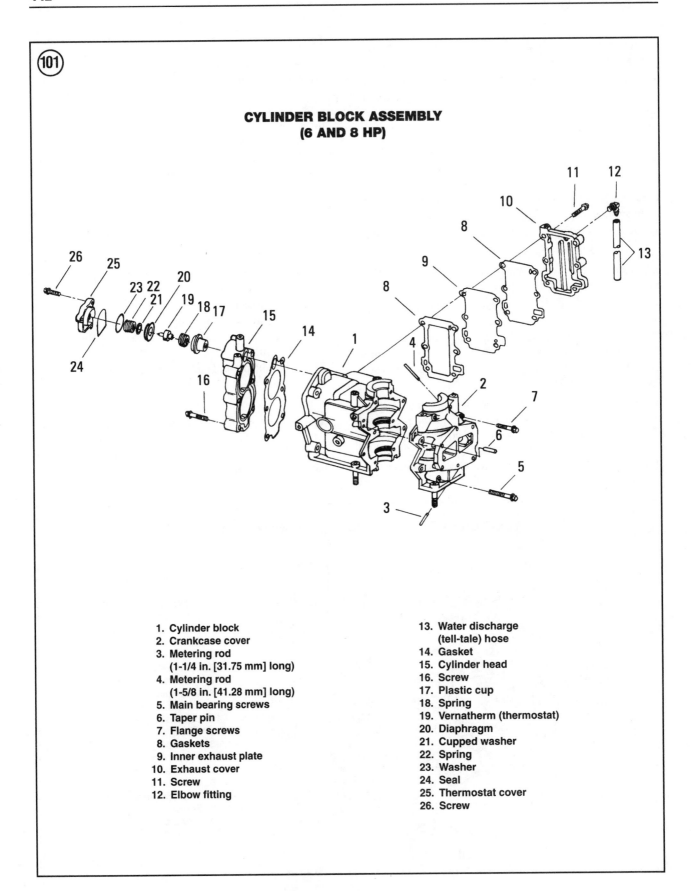

101

**CYLINDER BLOCK ASSEMBLY
(6 AND 8 HP)**

1. Cylinder block
2. Crankcase cover
3. Metering rod
   (1-1/4 in. [31.75 mm] long)
4. Metering rod
   (1-5/8 in. [41.28 mm] long)
5. Main bearing screws
6. Taper pin
7. Flange screws
8. Gaskets
9. Inner exhaust plate
10. Exhaust cover
11. Screw
12. Elbow fitting
13. Water discharge
    (tell-tale) hose
14. Gasket
15. Cylinder head
16. Screw
17. Plastic cup
18. Spring
19. Vernatherm (thermostat)
20. Diaphragm
21. Cupped washer
22. Spring
23. Washer
24. Seal
25. Thermostat cover
26. Screw

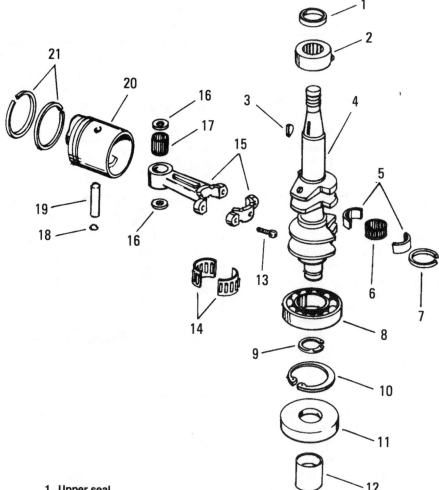

**CRANKSHAFT ASSEMBLY
(3, 4-8 HP [TYPICAL])**

1. **Upper seal**
2. **Upper main bearing**
3. **Flywheel key**
4. **Crankshaft**
5. **Center main bearing race (or liners)**
6. **Loose needles (see text)**
7. **Seal ring**
8. **Ball bearing**
9. **Retaining ring**
10. **Retaining ring**
11. **Lower seal**
12. **Sleeve/drive shaft seal**
13. **Rod cap screw**
14. **Caged roller bearing halves**
15. **Connecting rod**
16. **Thrust washers (3, 4 hp and 4 Deluxe)**
17. **Loose needles (or caged bearing)**
18. **Wrist pin lock clip**
19. **Wrist pin**
20. **Piston**
21. **Piston rings**

8

1. Check the end gap of the new piston rings for each cylinder as described in *Piston Ring End Gap* located previously in this chapter. The ring end gap must be 0.005-0.015 in. (0.13-0.38 mm).

2A. *3, 4 hp and 4 Deluxe*—If removed, install a new water deflector (15, **Figure 100**) into the water jacket at the top and center of the cylinder block.

2B. *6 and 8 hp*—Install the connecting rod small end bearings as follows:

    a. Lubricate the new bearing and No. 1 cylinder connecting rod with oil.

    b. Support the connecting rod in a press, then pilot a new bearing into the connecting rod small end bore, making sure the oil hole in the bearing case is aligned with the oil hole in the end of the connecting rod.

    c. Press the bearing into the rod using bearing installer part No. 327645 (or equivalent). Verify that the oil holes are aligned.

    d. Repeat this procedure for the remaining connecting rod.

> *CAUTION*
> *When installed, the narrow, steep and sharper side of the piston's deflector must face the intake ports (starboard side of the engine) and the longer, gently-sloped side must face the exhaust ports and cover (port side).*

Piston and connecting rod assembly (3, 4 hp and 4 Deluxe)

The wrist pin is a loose fit in one wrist pin boss, identified by the *L* cast into the boss (**Figure 103**), and a press-fit on the other side. To prevent damage during installation, the wrist pin must be inserted into the loose side first. Assemble the No. 1 cylinder components first, then repeat this procedure for the No. 2 cylinder components. Proceed as follows:

1. Install a new wrist pin lock clip into the side of the piston not marked *L*. Make sure the clip is fully seated in its groove.

2. Lubricate the wrist pin with oil and insert it into the loose side of the piston. Push the pin just far enough through the wrist pin boss to place a thrust washer over the pin, then do so.

3. Liberally apply OMC Needle Bearing Assembly Grease to the connecting rod's small end bore, then arrange the 21 loose needle bearings in the bore. A suitable dowel or socket can be used to help align the bearings.

4. Make sure the connecting rod is correctly orientated to the piston. Refer to *Connecting Rod Orientation* as necessary. Remember that the piston's deflector dome must be positioned so that the narrow, steep, sharper slope faces starboard when installed.

5. Align the rod to the piston. Push the wrist pin into the rod (and loose needles), then position the second thrust washer between the rod and the other wrist pin boss. Continue pushing the wrist pin through the second thrust washer until the pin is piloted in the wrist pin boss not marked *L*.

6. Place the piston/rod assembly into the appropriate saddle of Piston Cradle (part No. 326572) or equivalent. See **Figure 104**, typical. Press the pin using wrist pin installer (part No. 326624) or equivalent, until the remaining wrist pin lock clip groove is exposed. Do not press the pin any

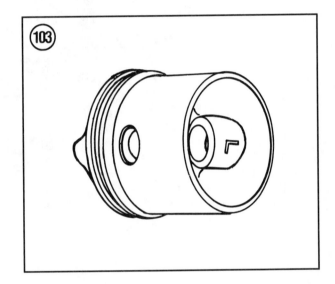

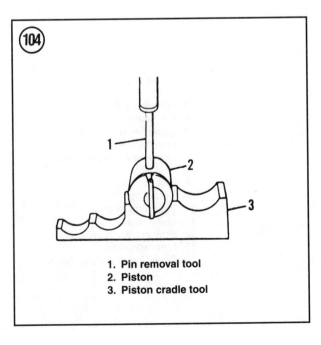

1. **Pin removal tool**
2. **Piston**
3. **Piston cradle tool**

further than necessary to expose the groove, or the piston and the lock clip (already installed) will be damaged.

7. Inspect the assembly and make sure that none of the 21 needle bearings or either of the thrust washers were displaced and that the rod pivots freely on the wrist pin. Correct any problems found.

8. Install a new wrist pin lock clip into the side of the piston marked *L*. Make sure the clip is fully seated in its groove.

Piston and connecting rod assembly (6 and 8 hp)

Because the wrist pin is a press-fit on these models, the piston must be heated to 200-400° F (93-204° C) to install the wrist pin without damaging or distorting the piston. Heat the piston using a suitable heat gun or heat lamp, but do not use an open flame. Assemble the No. 1 cylinder components first, then repeat this procedure for the No. 2 cylinder components. Proceed as follows:

1. Using cone (part No. 333142) and driver (part No. 333141) or equivalent, install a new wrist pin lock clip into one side of the wrist pin bore as follows:

   a. Insert a new lock clip into the internally tapered end of the cone.

   b. Insert the driver into the cone and push the lock clip until it is approximately 1/2 in. (12.7 mm) from the externally beveled end.

   c. Position the externally beveled end of the cone over the wrist pin bore and rotate the cone as necessary to ensure that the open ends of the clip are positioned 180° from the notch in the wrist pin bore.

   d. While holding the cone and piston aligned, briskly push downward on the driver to install the lock clip. See **Figure 105**, typical.

e. Remove the tools and inspect the clip. The open ends of the clip must be positioned 180° from the notch in the wrist pin bore and the clip must be fully seated in its groove.

2. Heat the piston to 200-400° F (93-204° C). Then place the piston into the appropriate saddle of piston cradle (part No. 326573) or equivalent, with the lock clip facing down. Use insulated gloves to handle the piston.

3. Make sure the connecting rod is correctly orientated to the piston. Refer to *Connecting Rod Orientation* as necessary. Remember that the piston's deflector dome must be positioned so that the narrow, steep, sharper slope faces starboard when installed.

4. Lubricate the wrist pin with oil, then align the connecting rod to the piston.

5. Press the pin into the piston using wrist pin installer (part No. 333141) or equivalent, until the remaining wrist pin retainer clip groove is exposed. See **Figure 104**, typical. Do not press the pin any further than necessary to expose the groove or the piston and the lock clip (already installed) will be damaged.

6. Inspect the assembly and make sure that the rod pivots freely on the wrist pin. Then measure the piston as described in *Piston measurements* to determine if the piston was distorted during the procedure. Correct any problems found.

7. Install the second wrist pin lock clip into its groove.

Piston installation (3 and 4-8 hp [including 4 Deluxe])

> **CAUTION**
> *Install the piston rings onto the pistons that match the cylinder bore for which the rings were fitted.*

1. Using a suitable ring expander, install the piston rings onto both pistons. Install the bottom ring first, then the top ring. Expand each ring only enough to fit over the piston crown and into its groove. Make sure the ring end gaps properly straddle the locating pin in each ring groove. See **Figure 98**, typical.

2. Using a feeler gauge, measure the clearance between each piston ring and its ring groove. Each ring must be seated in its groove during its measurement. See **Figure 99**, typical. Take measurements at several locations around the piston. The ring side clearance must not exceed 0.004 in. (0.102 mm). If the clearance is excessive, replace the piston(s).

3. Lubricate the No. 1 cylinder piston rings, piston and cylinder bore with oil.

4. Install the No. 1 cylinder piston and connecting rod assembly as follows:

8

a. Verify that the end gap of each piston ring is straddling the ring locating pin in each ring groove.

CAUTION
When installed, the narrow, steep and sharper side of the piston's deflector must face the intake ports (starboard side of the engine) and the longer, gently-sloped side must face the exhaust ports and cover (port side).

b. Using the appropriate tapered sleeve ring compressor (part No. 327017 [3, 4hp and 4 Deluxe] or (part No. 326589 [6-8 hp]), install the No.1 piston into the cylinder bore. Be careful to keep the rod's big end from damaging the cylinder bore.

c. Insert a small screwdriver through the exhaust port and depress each piston ring. If the ring does not spring back when the screwdriver is removed, it was probably broken during piston installation. Replace any broken or damaged rings.

5. Repeat Step 4 for the No. 2 cylinder, then temporarily install the cylinder head with two screws to prevent the pistons from falling from their bores. Tighten the two screws finger-tight.

Crankshaft installation
(3 and 4-8 hp [including 4 Deluxe])

Two different styles of center main bearings are used on these models. All 3, 4 hp, 4 Deluxe and the 1995 (EO) 6 and 8 hp models use a center main bearing consisting of two stamped bearing liner halves and 30 loose needles.

On 1996-2003 (ED-ST) 6 and 8 hp models, the center main bearing consists of a machined outer race, 23 loose needles and a retaining ring. The outer race is fractured into two pieces and a retaining ring holds the bearing together. A dowel pin locates the race to the cylinder block.

On all models, a seal ring rides in the groove below the center main bearing.

1. Install a new crankshaft ball bearing as follows:
   a. Lubricate the new bearing and the crankshaft journal with oil.
   b. Slide the bearing over the drive shaft end of the crankshaft with the numbered side of the bearing facing away from the crankshaft.
   c. Support the crankshaft (under the lower counterweight) in a press. Press against the inner race of the bearing with a suitable mandrel until it is seated on the crankshaft.
   d. Install the retaining ring (9, **Figure 102**) with its flat (or sharp-edged) side facing away from the bearing.

2. Install the crankshaft sleeve/drive shaft seal (12, **Figure 102**) as follows:
   a. Lubricate a new sleeve/seal with isopropyl alcohol.
   b. Pilot the sleeve over the lower end of the crankshaft.
   c. Support the crankshaft (under the lower counterweight) in a press. Press the sleeve onto the crankshaft until it is seated on the crankshaft.

3. Lubricate a new seal ring with oil, then install it into the groove at the middle of the crankshaft. Do not expand the ring any more than necessary for installation.

4. Oil the upper main bearing and slide it over the flywheel end of the crankshaft with the lettered side of the bearing facing toward the crankshaft (down).

5. Coat the outer diameter of a new upper seal with OMC Gasket Sealing Compound. Then lubricate the seal lip with OMC Triple Guard Grease. Slide the seal over the flywheel end of the crankshaft with the seal lip facing the crankshaft (down).

6A. *3, 4 hp, 4 Deluxe and 1995 (EO) 6 and 8 hp*—Assemble the center main bearing as follows:
   a. Install the main bearing liner (with the hole in it) into the cylinder block, making sure the liner's hole properly engages the cylinder block. Make sure the liner is seated in the block.
   b. Apply a thick coat of needle bearing assembly grease to the liner half.
   c. Install 14 loose needle bearings to the liner half. Apply additional grease as necessary.

6B. *1996-2003 (ED-ST) 6 and 8 hp*—Assemble the center main bearing as follows:
   a. Apply a thick coat of needle bearing assembly grease around the crankshaft's center main bearing journal.
   b. Install 23 loose needle bearings around the journal.
   c. Position the main bearing race halves around the journal with the retaining ring groove facing the flywheel (up).
   d. Carefully align the fractured parting lines, then install the retainer ring. Position the retainer ring to cover as much of both fracture lines as possible.

7. Position the cylinder block so that it is sitting on the cylinder head and the crankcase cover mating surface is facing up. Then push both pistons to the bottom of their bores and position both connecting rods to one side of the crankcase.

8. Position the crankshaft assembly over the cylinder block and slowly lower it into the block. Align the locating pin on the upper main bearing with its notch in the cylinder block. On 1996-2003 (ED-ST) 6 and 8 hp models, rotate the center main bearing as necessary to align the main bearing with the locating dowel in the cylinder block (**Figure 106**). Make sure the upper seal and the lower main (ball) bearing are seated in their bores.

9. *3, 4 hp, 4 Deluxe and 1995 (EO) 6 and 8 hp*—Finish assembling the center main bearing as follows:

    a. Verify that the 14 loose needle bearings are still in place, then apply a thick coat of needle bearing assembly grease to the exposed portion of the center main bearing journal.

    b. Install the remaining 16 loose needle bearings around the center main journal.

    c. Position the remaining center main bearing liner half over the needle bearings, making sure its dovetails are aligned with the liner already installed.

10. Install the No. 1 cylinder connecting rod to the crankshaft journal as follows:

    a. Grease the crankpin journal with a thick coat of needle bearing assembly grease. Install the caged bearing halves on the journal. If the original bearings are reused, they must be installed in their original position.

    b. Pull the No. 1 cylinder rod and piston assembly up to the crankpin journal and bearings. Rotate the crankshaft as necessary to allow mating of the rod and journal.

    c. Install the matching connecting rod cap in its original orientation. Carefully observe fracture and alignment marks to ensure correct installation.

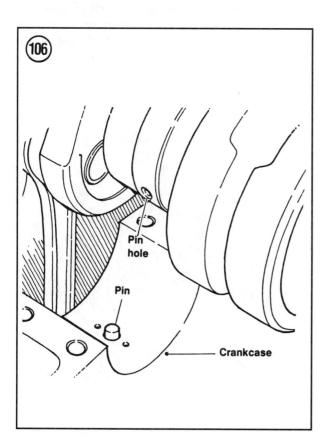

Pin hole

Pin

Crankcase

    d. Lubricate the screw threads and underside of the screw heads of new connecting rod screws with oil. Then, while holding the cap firmly in position, install the connecting rod screws and thread them fully into the rod.

    e. Tighten each screw to 15 in.-lb. (1.69 N•m). Run a fingernail or pencil lead over each edge of the rod-to-cap joint. The edges must be perfectly flush with no detectable misalignment. Realign and retorque the cap as necessary. Refer to *Cleaning and Inspection (Connecting Rod)* for additional information.

    f. Once correct alignment is verified, alternately tighten each screw to the final torque of 60-70 in.-lb. (6.8-7.9 N•m) in three progressive steps. Make a final check of alignment after the final torque is applied.

    g. Rotate the crankshaft several revolutions to check for binding or unusual noise. If noted, remove the piston and connecting rod just installed and correct the defect before proceeding.

11. Repeat Step 10 for the No. 2 cylinder piston and connecting rod assembly.

8

Final assembly (3 and 4-8 hp [including 4 Deluxe])

1. Using an oil and wax free solvent, such as OMC Cleaning Solvent, acetone or lacquer thinner, clean the cylinder block and crankcase cover mating surfaces.

2. Spray the crankcase cover mating surface with OMC Locquic Primer and allow it to air dry.

3. Apply OMC Gel Seal II sealant to the mating surface of the cylinder block. Run a continuous sealant bead along the inside of all screw holes, then carefully spread the bead over the entire surface of the flange, making sure the sealant will not contaminate the bearings or seals. Keep the sealant approximately 1/4 in. (6.35 mm) from the center seal ring and all crankshaft bearings.

4. *3, 4 hp, 4 Deluxe and 1995 (EO) 6 and 8 hp*—Verify that the center main bearing liner halves (and 30 loose needles) are still correctly installed and the dovetails on the liner halves are mated.

5. Install the plastic metering rods (3 and 4, **Figure 100** or **Figure 101**) into the crankcase cover recirculation passages. See Chapter Six.

6. Install the crankcase cover into position on the cylinder block. Seat the cover to the block with hand pressure.

NOTE
Before installing the taper pin, the crankcase cover must be seated to the cylinder block and held in place by the main bearing screws, but without substantial clamping load being applied by the screws. The cover

must be able to move (shift) slightly when the taper pin is installed, precisely aligning the cover to the cylinder block.

7. Lightly coat the threads of the ten crankcase cover screws with OMC Gel Seal II sealant, then install the screws. Tighten the six main bearing screws finger-tight until the cover is seated to the block. Then install the taper pin (9, **Figure 100** or 6, **Figure 101**) and seat it in its bore. Do not drive the taper pin too tightly into its bore or it will split the cylinder block and crankcase cover.

CAUTION
Do not strike the end of the crankshaft directly, or the crankshaft sleeve/drive shaft seal will be destroyed.

8. Insert a suitable mandrel into the crankshaft splined bore. The mandrel must fit into and contact the bottom of the splined bore. Carefully tap against the mandrel (with a soft-faced hammer) to seat the ball bearing in its bore. Then make sure the upper seal is seated in its bore.

9A. *3, 4 hp and 4 Deluxe*—Tighten the six main bearing screws evenly to 60-84 in.-lb. (6.8-9.5 N•m) in a crossing pattern starting with the center screws and working outward. Then tighten the four flange screws in the same manner to 60-84 in.-lb. (6.8-9.5 N•m).

9B. *6 and 8 hp*—Tighten the six main bearing screws evenly to 144-168 in.-lb. (16.3-19.0 N•m) in a crossing pattern starting with the center screws and working outward. Then tighten the four flange screws in the same manner to 60-84 in.-lb. (6.8-9.5 N•m).

10. Install the bearing retaining ring using a suitable pair of snap ring pliers. The beveled edge must face out and the open end of the ring must be centered over the lubrication hole as shown in **Figure 107**.

11. Rotate the crankshaft several revolutions to check for binding or unusual noise. If binding or noise is noted, the crankcase cover must be removed and the cause of the defect located and corrected before proceeding.

NOTE
Do not use sealant on the cylinder head screws. On 3, 4 hp and 4 Deluxe models, install the gasket with its tabbed end facing up and the numbered side facing the block.

12. Remove the cylinder head. Lightly coat both sides of a new head gasket with OMC Gasket Sealing Compound. Position the cylinder head and new gasket to the cylinder block, then install the screws (with no sealant). Tighten the screws finger-tight at this time.

13A. *3, 4 hp and 4 Deluxe*—Evenly tighten the cylinder head screws to 60-84 in.-lb. (6.8-9.5 N•m) in the pattern shown in **Figure 108**.

13B. *6 and 8 hp*—Evenly tighten the cylinder head screws to 144-168 in.-lb. (16.3-19.0 N•m.) in the pattern shown in **Figure 108**.

14. *6 and 8 hp*—Install the thermostat components as described in *Thermostat* in this chapter.

15. Apply OMC Gasket Sealing Compound to a new exhaust cover gasket(s). Install the exhaust cover (and inner plate on 6-8 hp models) and gasket(s). Evenly tighten the screws in a crossing pattern, starting at the center and working outward to 25-35 in.-lb. (2.8-4.0 N•m) on 3, 4 hp and 4 Deluxe models or 60-84 in.-lb. (6.8-9.5 N•m) on 6-8 hp models.

16A. *3, 4 hp and 4 Deluxe*—Apply OMC Gasket Sealing Compound to the outer diameter of a new crankshaft lower seal. Lubricate the seal lip with OMC Triple Guard Grease, then install the seal, with its lip facing away from the lower main bearing, until fully seated against the lower bearing retaining ring.

16B. *6 and 8 hp*—Apply OMC Gasket Sealing Compound to the outer diameter of a new crankshaft lower seal. Lubricate the seal lip with OMC Triple Guard Grease, then install the seal, with its lip facing toward the lower main bearing, until fully seated against the bearing retaining ring. The seal is retained by the inner exhaust housing.

17. *3 and 4 hp (excluding 4 Deluxe*—Install the lower end cap. Coat the threads of the four mounting screws with OMC Gasket Sealing Compound. Install and evenly

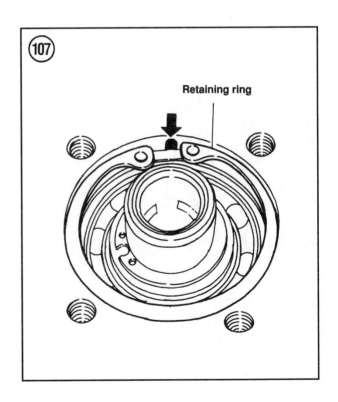

Retaining ring

tighten the fasteners in a crossing pattern to 25-35 in.-lb. (2.8-4.0 N•m).

18. Install the intake manifold and reed valves as described in Chapter Six.

19. Install the power head as described previously in this chapter.

Assembly (9.9 and 15 hp)

Refer to **Figure 109** and **Figure 110** for the following procedures.

Check the end gap of the new piston rings as described in *Piston Ring End Gap* in this chapter. The ring end gap must be 0.005-0.015 in. (0.13-0.38 mm).

> *CAUTION*
> *When installed, the narrow, steep and sharper side of the piston's deflector must*

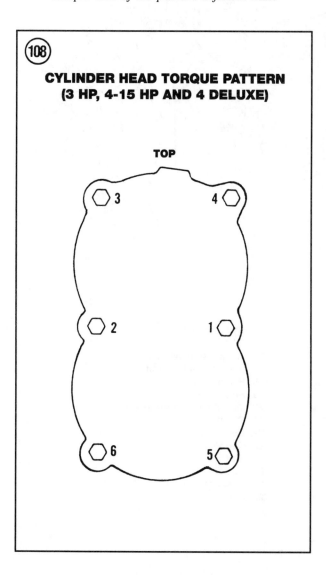

face the intake ports and cover (starboard side of the engine) and the longer, gently-sloped side must face the exhaust ports and cover (port side).

Piston and connecting rod assembly (9.9 and 15 hp)

Assemble the pistons and connecting rods. The wrist pin is a slip-fit to the piston and should not require more than moderate hand pressure to install. Assemble the No. 1 cylinder components first, then repeat this procedure for the No. 2 cylinder components. Proceed as follows:

1. Using Wrist Pin Lock Clip Installer (part No. 395112) or equivalent, install a new wrist pin lock clip into one end of the wrist pin bore as follows:

   a. Insert a new lock clip into the internally tapered end of the cone.

   b. Insert the driver into the cone and push the lock clip until it is approximately 1/2 in. (12.7 mm) from the externally beveled end.

   c. Position the externally beveled end of the cone over the wrist pin bore and rotate the cone as necessary to position the open ends of the clip 180° from the notch in the wrist pin bore.

   d. While holding the cone and piston aligned, briskly push downward on the driver to install the lock clip. See **Figure 105**, typical.

   e. Remove the tools and inspect the clip. The open ends of the clip must be positioned 180° from the notch in the wrist pin bore and the clip must be fully seated in its groove.

2. Lubricate the wrist pin with oil and insert it into the side of the piston without the lock clip installed. Push the pin just far enough through the wrist pin boss to place a thrust washer over the pin, then do so.

3. Liberally apply OMC Needle Bearing Assembly Grease to the connecting rod's small end bore, then arrange the 22 loose needle bearings in the bore. Use a suitable dowel or socket to help align the bearings. See **Figure 111**.

4. Make sure the connecting rod is correctly orientated to the piston. Refer to *Connecting Rod Orientation* as necessary.

5. Align the rod to the piston. Push the wrist pin into the rod (and loose needles), then position the second thrust washer between the rod and other wrist pin boss. Continue pushing the wrist pin through the second thrust washer until the pin just contacts the lock clip installed in Step 1. If the pin is difficult to install, continue to Step 6.

> *NOTE*
> *When using the pressing pin (from wrist pin lock clip installer [part No. 395112]) to push*

8

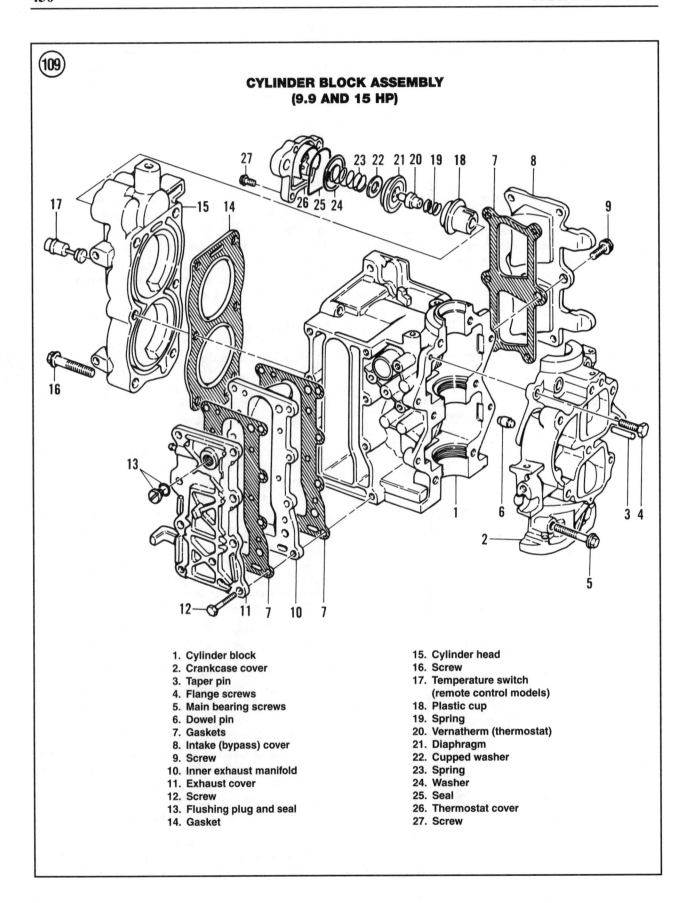

**CYLINDER BLOCK ASSEMBLY
(9.9 AND 15 HP)**

1. Cylinder block
2. Crankcase cover
3. Taper pin
4. Flange screws
5. Main bearing screws
6. Dowel pin
7. Gaskets
8. Intake (bypass) cover
9. Screw
10. Inner exhaust manifold
11. Exhaust cover
12. Screw
13. Flushing plug and seal
14. Gasket
15. Cylinder head
16. Screw
17. Temperature switch (remote control models)
18. Plastic cup
19. Spring
20. Vernatherm (thermostat)
21. Diaphragm
22. Cupped washer
23. Spring
24. Washer
25. Seal
26. Thermostat cover
27. Screw

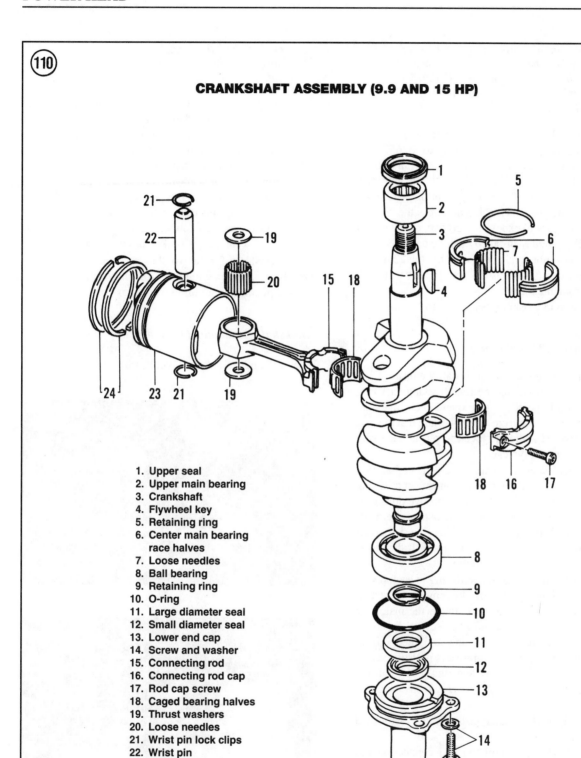

⑪⓪

CRANKSHAFT ASSEMBLY (9.9 AND 15 HP)

1. Upper seal
2. Upper main bearing
3. Crankshaft
4. Flywheel key
5. Retaining ring
6. Center main bearing
   race halves
7. Loose needles
8. Ball bearing
9. Retaining ring
10. O-ring
11. Large diameter seal
12. Small diameter seal
13. Lower end cap
14. Screw and washer
15. Connecting rod
16. Connecting rod cap
17. Rod cap screw
18. Caged bearing halves
19. Thrust washers
20. Loose needles
21. Wrist pin lock clips
22. Wrist pin
23. Piston
24. Piston rings

8

the wrist pin into position, it may be necessary to reduce the outer diameter of the guide portion of the pin approximately 0.015 in. (0.38 mm) to allow it to fit into the wrist pin's inner diameter.

6. If necessary, place the piston/rod assembly into the appropriate saddle of piston cradle part No. 326573 (or equivalent). See **Figure 104**, typical. Press the pin into the piston using the pressing pin from wrist pin lock clip installer part No. 395112 (or equivalent), until the remaining lock clip groove is exposed. Do not press the pin any further than necessary to expose the groove, or the piston and the lock clip (already installed) will be damaged.

7. Inspect the assembly and make sure that the 22 needle bearings and the two thrust washers are properly installed. Correct any problems found.

8. Install the second wrist pin lock clip into its groove.

Piston installation (9.9 and 15 hp)

1. Using a suitable ring expander, install the piston rings onto both pistons. Install the bottom (rectangular) ring first, then the top (tapered) ring. Expand each ring only enough to fit over the piston crown. Make sure that the ring end gaps properly straddle the locating pin in each ring groove. See **Figure 98**, typical.

2. Using a feeler gauge, measure the clearance between each piston's bottom (rectangular) piston ring and its ring groove. Each ring must be seated in its groove during its measurement. See **Figure 99**, typical. Take measurements at several locations around the piston. The ring side clearance must not exceed 0.004 in. (0.102 mm). If the clearance is excessive, replace the piston(s).

3. Check the fit of the upper (tapered) ring to each piston by placing a straightedge across the ring as shown in **Figure 112**. The straightedge must touch the piston on both sides of the ring. Check the fit at several locations around the piston. If the ring holds the straightedge from the piston at any point, the ring groove is not sufficiently cleaned or is damaged. Remove the ring and clean the groove as necessary. Refer to *Power Head Cleaning and Inspection.*

4. Lubricate the No.1 cylinder piston rings, piston and cylinder bore with oil.

5. Install the No.1 cylinder piston and connecting rod assembly as follows:

   a. Verify that the end gap of each piston ring is straddling the ring locating pin in each ring groove.

CAUTION
When installed, the narrow, steep and sharper side of the piston's deflector must face the intake ports (starboard side of the

engine) and the longer, gently-sloped side must face the exhaust ports and cover (port side).

   b. Using a tapered sleeve ring compressor, such as part No. 339754 (standard bore) or part No. 339755 (oversize bore), install the No.1 piston into the cylinder bore. Be careful to keep the rod's big end from damaging the cylinder bore.

   c. Insert a small screwdriver through the intake or exhaust port and depress each piston ring. If the ring does not spring back when the screwdriver is removed, it was probably broken during piston installation. Replace any broken or damaged rings.

6. Repeat Step 5 for the No. 2 cylinder piston, then temporarily install the cylinder head with two screws to prevent the pistons from falling from their bores.

Crankshaft installation (9.9 and 15 hp)

1. Install a new crankshaft ball bearing as follows:

a. Lubricate the new bearing and the crankshaft journal with oil.

b. Slide the bearing over the drive shaft end of the crankshaft with the numbered side of the bearing facing away from the crankshaft.

c. Support the crankshaft (under the lower counterweight) in a press. Press against the inner race of the bearing with a suitable mandrel until it is seated on the crankshaft.

d. Install the retaining ring (9, **Figure 110**) with the sharp-edged side of the ring facing away from the bearing.

2. Oil the upper main bearing and slide it over the flywheel end of the crankshaft with the lettered side of the bearing facing toward the crankshaft (down).

3. Assemble the center main bearing as follows:

a. Apply a thick coat of needle bearing assembly grease around the crankshaft's center main bearing journal.

b. Install 23 loose needle bearings around the journal.

c. Position the main bearing race halves around the journal with the retaining ring groove facing the flywheel (up).

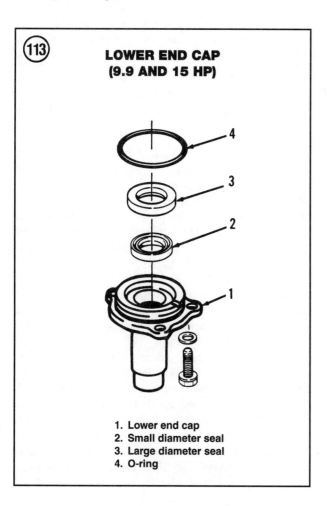

**LOWER END CAP
(9.9 AND 15 HP)**

1. Lower end cap
2. Small diameter seal
3. Large diameter seal
4. O-ring

d. Carefully align the fractured parting lines, then install the retainer ring. Position the retainer ring to cover as much of both fracture lines as possible.

4. Position the cylinder block so that it is sitting on the cylinder head and the crankcase cover mating surface is facing up. Then push both pistons to the bottom of their bores and position both connecting rods to one side of the crankcase.

5. Position the crankshaft assembly over the cylinder block and slowly lower it into the block. Align the locating pin on the upper main bearing with its notch in the cylinder block and rotate the center main bearing as necessary to align the main bearing with the locating dowel in the cylinder block (**Figure 106**). Make sure the lower main (ball) bearing is seated in its bore.

6. Install the No. 1 cylinder connecting rod to the crankshaft journal as follows:

a. Grease the crankpin journal with a thick coat of needle bearing assembly grease. Install the caged bearing halves to the journal. If the original bearings are being reused, they must be installed in their original position.

b. Pull the No. 1 cylinder rod and piston assembly up to the No. 1 crankpin journal and bearings. Rotate the crankshaft as necessary to allow mating of the rod and journal.

c. Install the matching connecting rod cap in its original orientation. Carefully observe fracture and alignment marks to ensure correct installation.

d. Lubricate the screw threads and underside of the screw heads of *new* connecting rod screws with oil. Then while holding the cap firmly in position, install the connecting rod screws and thread them fully into the rod.

e. Tighten each screw to 15 in.-lb. (1.69 N•m). Run a fingernail or pencil lead over each edge of the rod-to-cap joint. The edges must be perfectly flush with no detectable misalignment. Realign and retorque the cap as necessary. Refer to *Connecting Rod Cleaning and Inspection* for additional information.

f. Once the alignment is verified, alternately tighten each screw to 60-70 in.-lb. (6.8-7.9 N•m) in three progressive steps. Make a final check of alignment after the final torque is applied.

g. Rotate the crankshaft several revolutions to check for binding or unusual noise. If noted, remove the piston and connecting rod just installed and correct the defect before proceeding.

7. Repeat Step 6 for the No. 2 cylinder piston and connecting rod assembly.

8. Prepare the lower end cap for installation. Refer to **Figure 113** and proceed as follows:

8

a. Coat the outer diameter of two new seals with OMC Gasket Sealing Compound.

NOTE
The seal lips will face each other if correctly installed.

b. Using the longer-stepped side of seal installer (part No. 330251 or part No. 433391) or equivalent, press the smaller seal into the lower end cap bore with the lip (spring) facing up (toward the crankshaft) until the tool contacts the end cap.

c. Using the shorter-stepped side of the same tool, press the larger seal into the lower end cap bore with the lip (spring) facing down (away from the crankshaft) until the tool contacts the end cap.

d. Coat the seal lips and pack the area between the lips with a small amount (approximately 3 cc) of OMC Moly Lube.

e. Lightly coat a new O-ring with OMC Triple Guard Grease and install it in the lower end cap's groove.

Final assembly (9.9 and 15 hp)

1. Using an oil and wax free solvent, such as acetone or lacquer thinner, clean the cylinder block and crankcase cover mating surfaces.

2. Spray the crankcase cover mating surface with OMC Locquic Primer and allow it to air dry.

3. Apply OMC Gel Seal II sealant to the mating surface of the cylinder block. Run a continuous sealant bead along the inside of all screw holes, then carefully spread the bead over the entire surface of the flange, making sure the sealant will not contaminate the bearings or seals. Keep the sealant approximately 1/4 in. (6.35 mm) from the labyrinth seal grooves and all crankshaft bearings.

4. Place the crankcase cover into position on the cylinder block. Seat the cover to the block with hand pressure.

NOTE
Before installing the taper pin, the crankcase cover must be seated to the cylinder block and held in place by the main bearing screws. At this point, there should be no substantial clamping load applied by the screws. The cover must be able to move (shift) slightly when the taper pin is installed, precisely aligning the cover to the cylinder block.

5. Lightly coat the threads of the ten crankcase cover screws with OMC Gel Seal II sealant, then install the screws. Tighten the six main bearing screws finger-tight (until the cover is seated to the block). Then install the taper pin (3, **Figure 109**) and seat it in its bore. Do not drive the

taper pin too tightly into its bore or it will split the cylinder block and crankcase cover.

6. Carefully tap the lower end of the crankshaft using a soft hammer to seat the ball bearing in its bore and make sure the upper seal is seated in its bore.

7. Install the lower end cap. Coat the threads of the end cap screws with OMC Gasket Sealing Compound. Install the screws and washers. Tighten the screws finger-tight at this time.

8. Coat the outer diameter of a new upper seal with OMC Gasket Sealing Compound. Lubricate the lip of the seal with OMC Triple Guard Grease. Slide the seal over the flywheel end of the crankshaft with its lip facing the crankcase. Using seal installer (part No. 391060) or equivalent, drive the seal into position in the crankcase bore.

9. Tighten the six main bearing screws evenly to 144-168 in.-lb. (16.3-19.0 N•m) in a crossing pattern starting with the center screws and working outward. Then tighten the four flange screws in the same manner to 60-84 in.-lb. (6.8-9.5 N•m).

10. Evenly tighten the three lower end cap screws to 60-84 in.-lb. (6.8-9.5 N•m).

11. Rotate the crankshaft several revolutions to check for binding or unusual noise. If binding or noise is noted, the crankcase cover must be removed and the cause of the defect located and corrected before proceeding.

NOTE
Do not use sealant on the cylinder head screws.

12. Remove the cylinder head. Apply a dab of Permatex No. 2 to each of the two ribs bridging the water jacket at the top of the cylinder head.

13. Lightly coat both sides of a new head gasket with OMC Gasket Sealing Compound. Position the cylinder head and new gasket on the cylinder block, then install the screws (with no sealant). Evenly tighten the cylinder head screws to 216-240 in.-lb. (24.4-27.1 N•m) in the pattern shown in **Figure 108**.

14. Install the thermostat components as described in *Thermostat* in this chapter. On remote control models, install the engine temperature switch before installing the thermostat cover.

15. Apply OMC Gasket Sealing Compound to a new intake (bypass) cover gasket. Install the cover using the new gasket. Coat the threads of the nine screws with sealing compound, then install and evenly tighten the screws to 60-84 in.-lb. (6.8-9.5 N•m) in a crossing pattern, starting at the center and working outward.

16. Apply OMC Gasket Sealing Compound to two new exhaust cover gaskets. Install the exhaust cover and inner plate to the power head using the new gaskets. Install and

evenly tighten the screws in a crossing pattern, starting at the center and working outward to 95-130 in.-lb. (10.7-14.7 N•m).

17. Install the intake manifold and reed valves as described in Chapter Six.

18. Install the power head as described previously in this chapter.

Assembly (20-30 hp [Two-cylinder] and 18 Jet)

Refer to **Figure 114** and **Figure 115** for the following procedures.

1. If removed, install three new water deflectors. Coat each new deflector with STP Oil Treatment and push it into position in the water jacket. Install the short deflector in the lower, port position and the two long deflectors in the lower starboard and the upper positions. Do not shorten or modify the deflectors. It is normal for the deflectors to protrude slightly from the cylinder block. Refer back to **Figure 74** for exact deflector positioning in the water jacket.

2. Check the end gap of the new piston rings as described in *Piston Ring End Gap* in this chapter. The ring end gap must be 0.007-0.017 in. (0.18-0.43 mm).

> *CAUTION*
> *When installed, the narrow, steep and sharper side of the piston's deflector must*

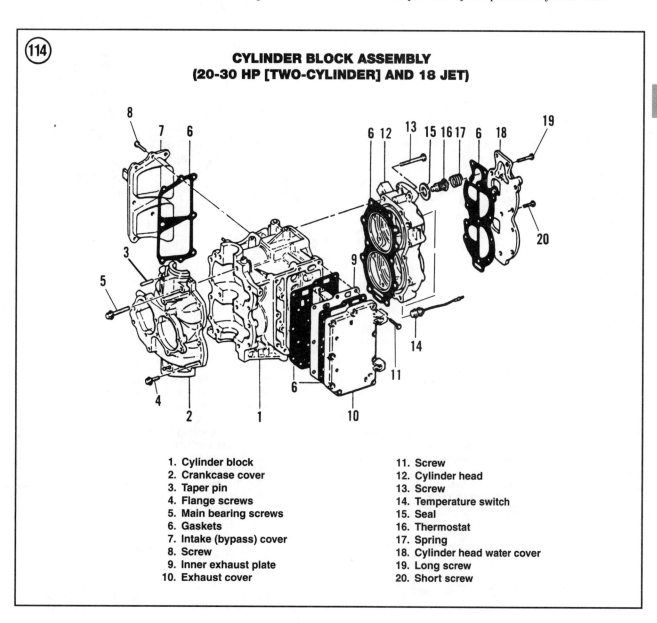

**CYLINDER BLOCK ASSEMBLY
(20-30 HP [TWO-CYLINDER] AND 18 JET)**

1. Cylinder block
2. Crankcase cover
3. Taper pin
4. Flange screws
5. Main bearing screws
6. Gaskets
7. Intake (bypass) cover
8. Screw
9. Inner exhaust plate
10. Exhaust cover
11. Screw
12. Cylinder head
13. Screw
14. Temperature switch
15. Seal
16. Thermostat
17. Spring
18. Cylinder head water cover
19. Long screw
20. Short screw

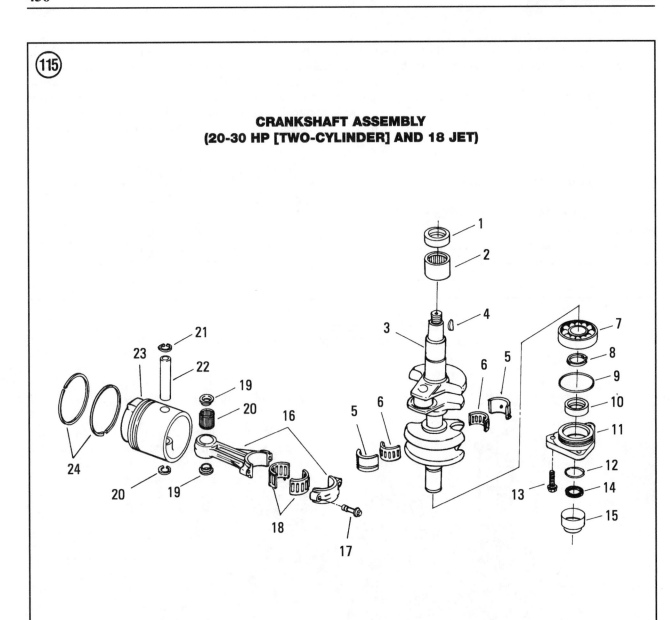

**CRANKSHAFT ASSEMBLY
(20-30 HP [TWO-CYLINDER] AND 18 JET)**

1. Upper seal
2. Upper main bearing
3. Crankshaft
4. Flywheel key
5. Bearing liner halves
6. Caged roller bearing halves
7. Ball bearing
8. Retaining ring
9. O-ring
10. Lower seal
11. Lower end cap
12. O-ring
13. Screw
14. O-ring (drive shaft seal)
15. Crankshaft sleeve/O-ring retainer
16. Connecting rod and cap
17. Rod cap screw
18. Caged bearing halves
19. Thrust washers
20. Loose needles
21. Wrist pin lock clips
22. Wrist pin
23. Piston
24. Piston rings

face the intake ports and cover (starboard side of the engine).

Piston and connecting rod assembly (20-30 hp [two-cylinder] and 18 jet)

Assemble the pistons and connecting rods. The wrist pin is a slip-fit in the piston and should not require more than moderate hand pressure to install. Assemble the No. 1 cylinder components first, then repeat this procedure for the No. 2 cylinder components. Proceed as follows:

1. Using Cone (part No. 318600) and Driver (part No. 318599) or equivalent, install a new wrist pin lock clip into one end of the wrist pin bore as follows:

   a. Insert a new lock clip into the internally tapered end of the cone.

   b. Insert the driver into the cone and push the lock clip until it is approximately 1/2 in. (12.7 mm) from the externally beveled end.

   c. Position the externally beveled end of the cone over the wrist pin bore and rotate the cone as necessary to position the open ends of the clip 180° from the notch in the wrist pin bore.

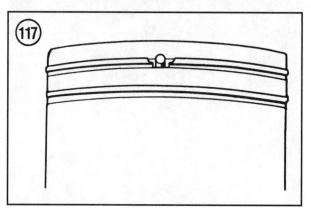

   d. While holding the cone and piston aligned, briskly push downward on the driver to install the lock clip. See **Figure 116**, typical.

   e. Remove the tools and inspect the clip. The open ends of the clip must be positioned 180° from the notch in the wrist pin bore and the clip must be fully seated in its groove.

2. Lubricate the wrist pin with oil and insert it into the side of the piston without the lock ring installed. Push the pin into the wrist pin boss until it is just flush with the connecting rod cavity.

3. Liberally apply OMC Needle Bearing Assembly Grease to the connecting rod's small end bore, then arrange the 28 loose needle bearings in the bore. Use bearing installation tool (part No. 336660) or a suitable dowel or socket to help align the bearings. See **Figure 111**, typical.

4. Position a thrust washer on each side of the connecting rod small end. Make sure the stepped side of each thrust washer is against the loose needle bearings (flat side facing out). Apply additional needle bearing grease as necessary to hold the washers in position.

5. Make sure the connecting rod is correctly orientated to the piston. Refer to *Connecting Rod Orientation* as necessary.

6. Align the rod to the piston. Push the wrist pin into the rod (and loose needles), then continue pushing the wrist pin until it just contacts the lock clip installed in Step 1. If the pin is difficult to install, continue to Step 7.

7. If necessary, place the piston/rod assembly into the appropriate saddle of piston cradle (part No. 326573) or equivalent. Refer back to **Figure 104**, typical. Press the pin into the piston using driver (part No. 318599) or equivalent, until the remaining lock clip groove is exposed. Do not press the pin any further than necessary to expose the groove, or the piston and the lock clip (already installed) will be damaged.

8. Inspect the assembly and make sure that none of the 28 needle bearings or either of the thrust washers were displaced and that the rod pivots freely on the wrist pin. Correct any problems found.

9. Install the second wrist pin lock clip into its groove in the same manner as Step 1.

Piston installation (20-30 hp [two-cylinder] and 18 jet)

1. Using a suitable ring expander, install the piston rings onto both pistons. Install the bottom (rectangular) ring first, then the top (tapered) ring. Expand each ring only enough to fit over the piston crown. Make sure that the ring end gaps properly straddle the locating pin in the ring grooves. See **Figure 117**, typical.

2. Using a feeler gauge, measure the clearance between each piston's bottom (rectangular) piston ring and its ring groove. Each ring must be seated in its groove during its measurement. See **Figure 118**, typical. Take measurements at several locations around the piston. The ring side clearance must not exceed 0.004 in. (0.102 mm). If the clearance is excessive, replace the piston(s).

3. Check the fit of the upper (tapered) ring to each piston by placing a straightedge across the ring as shown in **Figure 112**. The straightedge must touch the piston on both sides of the ring. Check the fit at several locations around the piston. If the ring holds the straightedge from the piston at any point, the ring groove is not sufficiently cleaned or is damaged. Remove the ring and clean the groove as necessary. Refer to *Power Head Cleaning and Inspection.*

4. Lubricate the No. 1 cylinder piston rings, piston and cylinder bore with oil.

5. Install the No. 1 cylinder piston and connecting rod assembly as follows:
   a. Verify that the end gap of each piston ring is straddling the ring locating pin in each ring groove.
   b. Using a tapered sleeve ring compressor, such as part No. 326591 (standard bore) or part No. 330223 (oversize bore), install the No. 1 piston into the cylinder bore with the narrow, steep and sharper side of the piston's deflector facing starboard as shown in **Figure 119**. Be careful to keep the rod's big end from damaging the cylinder bore.
   c. Insert a small screwdriver through the intake or exhaust port and depress each piston ring (**Figure 120**). If the ring does not spring back when the screwdriver is removed, it was probably broken during piston installation. Replace any broken or damaged rings.

6. Repeat Step 5 for the No. 2 cylinder piston, then temporarily install the cylinder head with two screws to prevent the pistons from falling from their bores. Tighten the two screws finger-tight.

Crankshaft installation
(20-30 hp [two-cylinder] and 18 jet)

The connecting rods on these models require a special fixture (part No. 396749) to correctly align the cap.

The special fixture contacts the rod cap and rod body on four beveled (machined) corners, applying a predetermined clamping force. The fixture is left in place during the torquing process, ensuring perfect rod cap alignment.

CAUTION
Failure to use the alignment fixture (and use it correctly) will result in premature connecting rod big end bearing failure.

Rod cap screw socket (part No. 331638) or an equivalent heavy-duty 12 point, thin-wall, 5/16 in. socket is required to torque the rod cap screws.

1. If the crankshaft ball bearing was removed, install a new bearing as follows:
   a. Lubricate the new bearing and the crankshaft journal with oil.
   b. Slide the bearing over the drive shaft end of the crankshaft with the numbered side of the bearing facing away from the crankshaft.
   c. Support the crankshaft (under the lower counterweight) in a press. Press against the inner race of the bearing with Bearing/Sleeve Installer (part No.

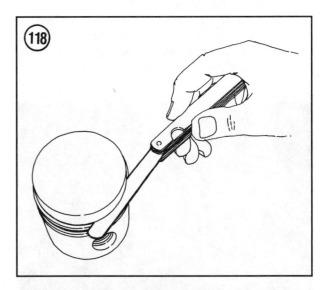

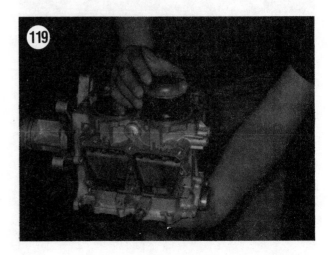

339749) or a suitable mandrel, until it is seated on the crankshaft.

NOTE
*If the crankshaft sleeve was removed, do not install the bearing retaining ring (8, **Figure 115**) until the sleeve is pressed into place.*

   d. If the crankshaft sleeve was not removed, install the retaining ring (8, **Figure 115**) with the flat (or sharp-edged) side of the ring facing away from the bearing.

2. If the crankshaft sleeve (15, **Figure 115**) was removed, install a new sleeve as follows:

   a. Lubricate a new sleeve and the crankshaft with oil.

   b. Place the sleeve into Bearing/Sleeve Installer (part No. 339749) or equivalent.

   c. Support the crankshaft (under the lower counterweight) in a press. Position the installer tool (and

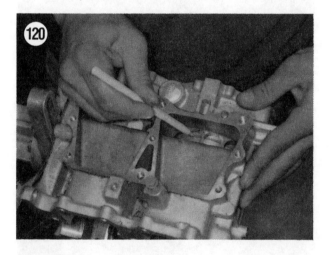

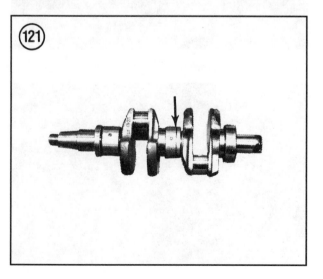

sleeve) over the crankshaft and press against the installer until the installer contacts the ball bearing.

   d. If the installer proves difficult to remove after pressing the sleeve in place, thread a suitable slide hammer, such as part No. 391008 into the installer and pull it from the crankshaft.

   e. Inspect the sleeve for distortion or deformation. The sleeve must be removed and replaced if it is damaged, distorted or deformed in any manner.

   f. Install the ball bearing retaining ring (8, **Figure 115**) with the flat (or sharp-edged) side of the ring facing away from the bearing.

3. Lubricate a new O-ring (14, **Figure 115**) with OMC Moly Lube, then install it into the crankshaft sleeve at the lower end of the crankshaft.

4. Oil the upper main bearing and slide it over the flywheel end of the crankshaft with the lettered side of the bearing facing toward the flywheel (up).

5. Assemble the center main bearing as follows:

   a. Apply a coat of needle bearing assembly grease around the crankshaft's center main bearing journal.

   b. Position the two caged needle bearing halves around the journal.

   c. Position the main bearing race halves around the journal with the retaining ring groove (**Figure 121**) facing the drive shaft housing (down).

   d. Carefully align the fractured parting lines, then install the retainer ring. Position the retainer ring to cover as much of both fracture lines as possible.

6. Position the cylinder block so it is sitting on the cylinder head and the crankcase cover mating surface is facing up. Then push the pistons to the bottom of their bores and position both connecting rods to one side of the crankcase.

7. Position the crankshaft assembly over the cylinder block and slowly lower it into the block. Align the locating pin on the upper main bearing with its notch in the cylinder block and rotate the center main bearing as necessary to align the main bearing with the locating dowel in the cylinder block (**Figure 106**, typical). Make sure the lower main (ball) bearing is seated in its bore.

8. Begin the installation of the No. 1 cylinder connecting rod onto the crankshaft journal as follows:

   a. Grease the crankpin journal with a thick coat of needle bearing assembly grease. Install the caged bearing halves to the journal. If the original bearings are reused, they must be installed in their original position.

   b. Pull the No. 1 cylinder rod and piston assembly up to the crankpin journal and bearings. Rotate the crankshaft as necessary to allow mating of the rod and journal.

   c. Install the matching connecting rod cap in its original orientation. Carefully observe fracture and align-

8

ment marks to ensure correct installation. See **Figure 122**.

  d. Lubricate the screw threads and underside of the screw heads of new connecting rod screws with oil. Then while holding the cap firmly in position, install the connecting rod screws and thread them fully into the rod.

  e. Tighten each screw initially to 25-30 in.-lb. (1.69 N•m).

9. Assemble the rod cap alignment fixture as follows:

  a. Move the flat on the knob marked *Set* to align with the arrow embossed on the tool's frame. Move the adjustment knob in or out until the outermost ring aligns with the surface of the tool frame. The instruction sheet will refer to this as mark *A*. Then rotate the knob 180° to lock the adjustment.

  b. Install the retaining jaw labeled *C* and the forcing jaw labeled *D* onto the fixture frame as described by the tool's instruction sheet.

  c. Lubricate the four precision ground corners of the connecting rod big end, then position the fixture over the big end in the manner shown in **Figure 123**, typical.

  d. Allow the stop plunger in the center of the frame to contact the rod cap. Then align the grooves machined into the jaws with the rod cap-to-connecting rod parting line.

  e. Tighten the tool's forcing screw to 23 in.-lb. (2.6 N•m). Verify that the stop plunger is contacting the rod cap and that the grooves in the jaws are aligned with the rod's parting line.

10. Loosen both rod cap screws 1/4 turn. Then retighten both screws to a preliminary torque of 40-60 in.-lb. (4.5-6.8 N•m). Apply a final torque of 30-32 ft.-lb. (40.7-43.4 N•m) in a minimum of three progressive steps.

11. Loosen the forcing screw and remove the fixture. Run a fingernail or pencil lead over each of the four beveled (machined) edges of the rod-to-cap joint (**Figure 124**, typical). The edges must be perfectly flush with no detectable misalignment. If any misalignment is detected, the connecting rod must be replaced.

12. Rotate the crankshaft several revolutions to check for binding or unusual noise. If binding or noise is noted, correct the defect before proceeding.

13. Repeat Steps 8-12 for the No. 2 cylinder piston and connecting rod assembly.

14. Prepare the lower end cap for installation.

  a. Coat the metal case of a new seal with OMC Gasket Sealing Compound.

  b. Using seal installer (part No. 333520) or equivalent, press the seal into the lower end cap bore with the extended lip facing down until the tool contacts the end cap.

  c. Coat the seal lips and the area between the lips with OMC Triple Guard Grease.

  d. Lightly coat two new O-rings with OMC Triple Guard Grease. Install each O-ring (small and large) into the appropriate end cap groove.

Final assembly (20-30 hp [two-cylinder] and 18 jet)

1. Using an oil and wax free solvent, such as acetone or lacquer thinner, clean the cylinder block and crankcase cover mating surfaces.

2. Spray the crankcase cover mating surface with OMC Locquic Primer and allow it to air dry.

3. Apply OMC Gel Seal II sealant to the mating surface of the cylinder block. Run a continuous sealant bead along the inside of all screw holes, then carefully spread the bead over the entire surface of the flange, making sure the sealant will not contaminate the bearings, labyrinth seals or ooze into the crankcase. Keep the sealant approximately 1/4 in. (6.35 mm) from the labyrinth seal grooves and all crankshaft bearings.

4. Install the crankcase cover into position on the cylinder block. Seat the cover to the block with hand pressure.

NOTE
Before installing the taper pin, the crankcase cover must be seated to the cylinder block and held in place by the main bearing screws, but without any substantial clamping load being applied by the screws. The cover must be able to move (shift) slightly when the taper pin is installed, to precisely align the cover to the cylinder block.

5. Lightly coat the threads of the 14 crankcase cover screws with OMC Gel Seal II sealant, then install the screws. Tighten the six main bearing screws finger-tight

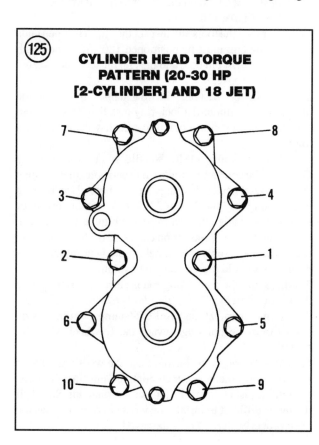

CYLINDER HEAD TORQUE PATTERN (20-30 HP [2-CYLINDER] AND 18 JET)

until the cover is seated to the block. Then install the taper pin (3, **Figure 114**) and seat it in its bore. Do not drive the taper pin too tightly into its bore or it will split the cylinder block and crankcase cover.

CAUTION
Do not strike the end of the crankshaft directly, or the crankshaft sleeve will be destroyed.

6. Insert a suitable mandrel into the crankshaft splined bore. The mandrel must fit into and contact the bottom of the splined bore. Carefully tap against the mandrel with a soft-faced hammer to seat the ball bearing in its bore.

7. Install the lower end cap. Coat the threads of three new end cap screws with OMC Gasket Sealing Compound. Install the screws and tighten them finger-tight at this time.

8. Tighten the six main bearing screws evenly to 168-192 in.-lb. (19.0-21.7 N•m) in a crossing pattern starting with the center screws and working outward. Then tighten the eight flange screws in the same manner to 60-84 in.-lb. (6.8-9.5 N•m).

9. Evenly tighten the three lower end cap screws to 60-84 in.-lb. (6.8-9.5 N•m).

10. Rotate the crankshaft several revolutions to check for binding or unusual noise. If binding or noise is noted, the crankcase cover must be removed and the cause of the defect located and corrected before proceeding.

11. Coat the metal case of a new upper crankshaft seal with OMC Gasket Sealing Compound. Lubricate the lip of the seal with OMC Triple Guard Grease. Slide the seal over the flywheel end of the crankshaft with its lip facing the crankcase. Using seal installer part No. 321539 (or equivalent), drive the seal into position in the crankcase bore.

NOTE
Do not sealant on the cylinder head screws.

12. Remove the cylinder head. Lightly coat both sides of a new head gasket with OMC Gasket Sealing Compound. Position the cylinder head and new gasket to the cylinder block, then install the screws (without sealant). Evenly tighten the cylinder head screws to 216-240 in.-lb. (24.4-27.1 N•m) in the pattern shown in **Figure 125**.

13. Install a new thermostat seal into the cylinder head cavity. Set the thermostat into the cavity and over the seal with the spring side of the thermostat facing the cylinder head. Then place the relief spring over the thermostat. Finally, install the engine temperature switch into its cylinder head bore.

14. Apply OMC Gasket Sealing Compound to a new cylinder head water cover gasket. Install the water cover using the new gasket. Coat the threads of the 14 screws with sealing compound, then install and evenly tighten the

screws to 60-84 in.-lb. (6.8-9.5 N•m) in a crossing pattern, starting at the center and working outward. Install the three longer screws around the thermostat.

15. Apply OMC Adhesive M to a new intake (bypass) cover gasket. The sealant dries quickly, so position the gasket to the power head as soon as possible. Install the cover using the new gasket. Coat the threads of the nine screws with OMC Gasket Sealing Compound, then install and evenly tighten the screws to 60-84 in.-lb. (6.8-9.5 N•m) in a crossing pattern, starting at the center and working outward.

NOTE
Be sure to install all brackets to the exhaust cover as noted on disassembly.

16. Apply OMC Gasket Sealing Compound to two new exhaust cover gaskets. Install the exhaust cover and inner plate to the power head using the new gaskets. Reposition all brackets, then install and evenly tighten the 15 screws in a crossing pattern, starting at the center and working outward to 60-84 in.-lb. (6.8-9.5 N•m).

17. Install the intake manifold, reed valves and fuel recirculation system lines as described in Chapter Six. If equipped with a fuel primer solenoid, install it at this time.

18. Install the power head as described previously in this chapter.

Assembly (25 and 35 hp [Three-cylinder])

Refer to **Figure 126** and **Figure 127** for the following procedures.

1. Check the end gap of the new piston rings as described in *Piston Ring End Gap* in this chapter. The ring end gap must be 0.005-0.020 in. (0.13-0.51 mm).

2. If removed, reinstall the shift lever's neutral detent assembly into the lower, starboard, front corner of the cylinder block, near the crankcase cover parting line, as follows:
   a. Lubricate the ball and retainer (guide) with OMC Moly Lube. Place the spring, then the detent ball into the crankcase cover cavity. Finally, place the retainer (guide) over the detent ball.
   b. Install the retaining ring with Installer part No. 342658 (or equivalent). Place the retaining ring into the larger tube, then position the larger tube over the retainer (detent ball guide).
   c. Push the retaining ring into position with the smaller (inner) tube, while holding the retainer (detent ball guide) and spring compressed with the larger tube.
   d. Remove the large tube, then the small tube, making sure the retaining ring is fully expanded in its groove.

Piston and connecting rod assembly
(25 and 35 hp [three-cylinder])

CAUTION
*When installed, the word **UP** on the piston dome must face **UP**.*

Assemble the pistons and connecting rods. The wrist pin is a slip-fit to the piston and should not require more than moderate hand pressure to install. Assemble the No. 1 cylinder components first, then repeat this procedure for the No. 2 cylinder and cylinder No. 3 components. Proceed as follows:

1. Using wrist pin lock clip installer part No. 342223 (or equivalent), install a new wrist pin lock clip into one end of the wrist pin bore as follows:
   a. Insert a new lock clip into the internally tapered end of the cone.
   b. Insert the driver into the cone and push the lock clip until it is approximately 1/2 in. (12.7 mm) from the externally beveled end.
   c. Position the externally beveled end of the cone over the wrist pin bore. Rotate the cone as necessary to position the open ends of the clip 180° from the notch in the wrist pin bore.
   d. While holding the cone and piston aligned, briskly push downward on the driver to install the lock clip. See **Figure 116**, typical.
   e. Remove the tools and inspect the clip. The open ends of the clip must be positioned 180° from the notch in the wrist pin bore and the clip must be fully seated in its groove.

2. Lubricate the wrist pin with oil and insert it into the side of the piston without the lock ring installed. Push the pin into the wrist pin boss until it is just flush with the connecting rod cavity.

3. Liberally apply OMC Needle Bearing Assembly Grease to the connecting rod's small end bore, then arrange the 24 loose needle bearings in the bore. Use bearing installation tool (part No. 342217) or a suitable dowel or socket to help align the bearings. See **Figure 128**, typical.

4. Position a thrust washer on each side of the connecting rod small end. Apply additional needle bearing grease as necessary to hold the washers in position.

5. Make sure the connecting rod is correctly orientated to the piston. Refer to *Connecting Rod Orientation* as necessary. Remember that the word UP (stamped on the piston dome) must be pointing toward the flywheel when installed.

6. Align the rod to the piston. Push the wrist pin into the rod (and loose needles), then continue pushing the wrist pin until it just contacts the lock clip installed in Step 1. If the pin is difficult to install, the wrist pin or piston has not been properly cleaned or is damaged.

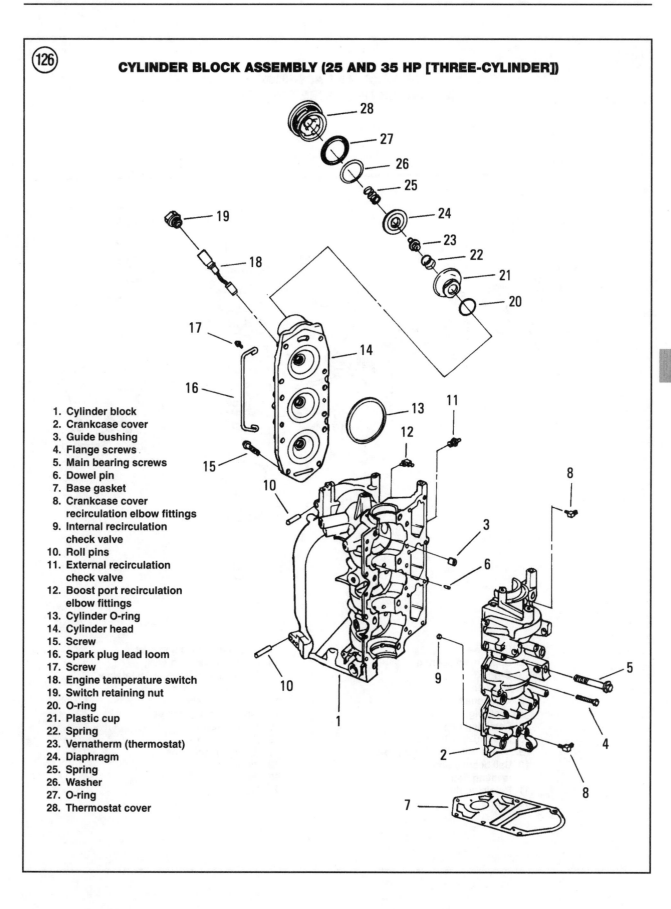

126

CYLINDER BLOCK ASSEMBLY (25 AND 35 HP [THREE-CYLINDER])

1. Cylinder block
2. Crankcase cover
3. Guide bushing
4. Flange screws
5. Main bearing screws
6. Dowel pin
7. Base gasket
8. Crankcase cover
   recirculation elbow fittings
9. Internal recirculation
   check valve
10. Roll pins
11. External recirculation
    check valve
12. Boost port recirculation
    elbow fittings
13. Cylinder O-ring
14. Cylinder head
15. Screw
16. Spark plug lead loom
17. Screw
18. Engine temperature switch
19. Switch retaining nut
20. O-ring
21. Plastic cup
22. Spring
23. Vernatherm (thermostat)
24. Diaphragm
25. Spring
26. Washer
27. O-ring
28. Thermostat cover

8

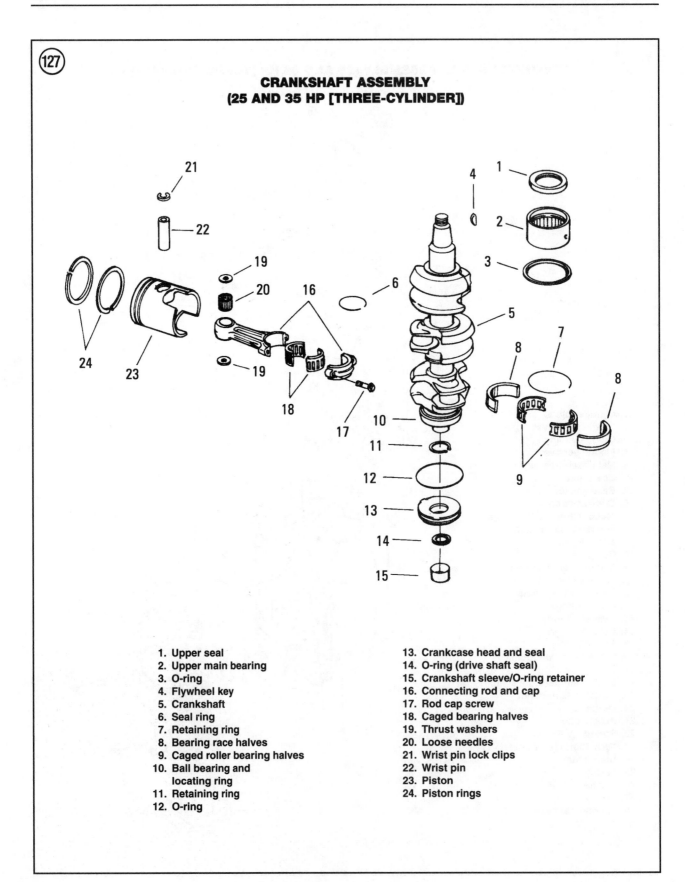

**CRANKSHAFT ASSEMBLY
(25 AND 35 HP [THREE-CYLINDER])**

1. Upper seal
2. Upper main bearing
3. O-ring
4. Flywheel key
5. Crankshaft
6. Seal ring
7. Retaining ring
8. Bearing race halves
9. Caged roller bearing halves
10. Ball bearing and
    locating ring
11. Retaining ring
12. O-ring
13. Crankcase head and seal
14. O-ring (drive shaft seal)
15. Crankshaft sleeve/O-ring retainer
16. Connecting rod and cap
17. Rod cap screw
18. Caged bearing halves
19. Thrust washers
20. Loose needles
21. Wrist pin lock clips
22. Wrist pin
23. Piston
24. Piston rings

7. Inspect the assembly and make sure that the 24 needle bearings and the two thrust washers are properly installed. Also, make sure the rod pivots freely on the wrist pin. Correct any problems found.

8. Install the second wrist pin lock clip into its groove in the same manner as Step 1.

Piston installation (25 and 35 hp [three-cylinder])

CAUTION
Install the piston rings onto the pistons that match the cylinder bore for which the rings were fitted.

1. Using a suitable ring expander, install the piston rings onto both pistons. Both rings are semi-keystone and either ring may be installed in either groove. Install the bottom ring first, then the top ring. Expand each ring only enough to fit over the piston crown. Make sure that the ring end gaps properly straddle the locating pin in each ring groove. See **Figure 129**, typical.

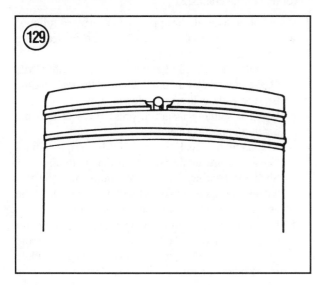

2. Check the fit of each ring to its piston by placing a straightedge across the ring as shown in **Figure 130**, typical. The straightedge must touch the piston on both sides of the ring. Check the fit at several locations around the piston. If the ring holds the straightedge from the piston at any point, the ring groove is sufficiently cleaned or is damaged. Remove the ring and clean the groove as necessary. Refer to *Power Head Cleaning and Inspection*.

3. Lubricate the No. 1 cylinder piston rings, piston and cylinder bore with oil.

4. Install the No. 1 cylinder piston and connecting rod assembly as follows:

   a. Verify that the end gap of each piston ring is straddling the ring locating pin in each ring groove.

CAUTION
*When installed, the word **UP** on the piston dome must face toward the flywheel.*

   b. Using a tapered sleeve ring compressor, such as part No. 342218 (25 hp standard bore), part No. 342219 (25 hp oversize bore), part No. 342220 (35 hp standard bore) or part No. 342221 (35 hp oversize bore), install the No. 1 piston into its cylinder bore with the word UP on the piston facing the flywheel end of the cylinder block. Be careful to keep the rod's big end from damaging the cylinder bore.

CAUTION
Due to the design of this block, the rings cannot be checked for damage after installation. Use extreme care (and the correct sleeve style compressor) to prevent piston ring damage or breakage. If in doubt, remove the piston and recheck the rings.

5. Repeat Steps 3-4 for the No. 2 and No. 3 pistons.

6. Install the cylinder head as follows:

8

a. Coat three new O-rings with OMC Triple Guard Grease and install them into the cylinder block grooves.

b. Apply a very fine bead (approximately 1/16 in. [1.6 mm]) of GE (General Electric) RTV sealant around each water passage on the cylinder head. Do not allow the sealer to ooze excessively into the cooling water passages and keep the adhesive away from the three cylinder block O-rings as much as possible.

NOTE
Do not use sealant on the cylinder head screws. If a torque pattern is cast into the cylinder head (near each screw hole), follow the pattern when tightening the screws.

c. Install the cylinder head making sure the three cylinder block O-rings are not displaced. Then install the screws (without sealant). Evenly tighten the cylinder head screws to 108-204 in.-lb. (20.3-23.0 N•m) in a crossing pattern, starting at the center and working outward.

Crankshaft installation
(25 and 35 hp [three-cylinder])

The connecting rods on these models require a special fixture (part No. 396749) and an accessory set of jaws (part No. 437373) to correctly align the cap.

The special fixture contacts the rod cap and rod body on four beveled (machined) corners, applying a predetermined clamping force. The fixture is left in place during the torquing process, ensuring perfect rod cap alignment.

CAUTION
Failure to use the alignment fixture (and use it correctly) will result in premature connecting rod big end bearing failure.

Rod cap screw socket (part No. 342664) or an equivalent heavy-duty 12 point, 1/4 in. socket is required to torque the rod cap screws.

1. Install a new crankshaft ball bearing as follows:
   a. Lubricate the new bearing and the crankshaft journal with oil.
   b. Slide the bearing over the drive shaft end of the crankshaft with the locating ring in the bearing's outer race positioned closest to the crankshaft seal ring groove. This should also result in the numbered side of the bearing facing away from the crankshaft.
   c. Support the crankshaft (under the lower counterweight) in a press. Press against the inner race of the bearing with bearing/sleeve installer (part No.

342222) or a suitable mandrel, until it is seated on the crankshaft.

NOTE
*If the crankshaft sleeve was removed, do not install the bearing retaining ring (11, **Figure 127**) until the sleeve has been pressed into place.*

   d. If the crankshaft sleeve was not removed, install the retaining ring (11, **Figure 127**) with the flat (or sharp-edged) side of the ring facing away from the bearing.

2. If the crankshaft sleeve (15, **Figure 127** was removed, install a new sleeve as follows:
   a. Lubricate a new sleeve and the crankshaft with oil.
   b. Place the sleeve into bearing/sleeve installer part No. 342222 (or equivalent).
   c. Support the crankshaft (under the lower counterweight) in a press. Position the installer tool (and sleeve) over the crankshaft and press against the installer until the installer contacts the ball bearing.
   d. If the installer proves difficult to remove after pressing the sleeve in place, thread a suitable slide hammer, such as part No. 391008 into the installer and pull it from the crankshaft.
   e. Inspect the sleeve for distortion or deformation. Replace the sleeve if it is damaged, distorted or deformed in any manner.
   f. Install the ball bearing retaining ring (11, **Figure 127**) with the flat (or sharp-edged) side of the ring facing away from the bearing, using a suitable pair of retaining ring pliers.

3. Lubricate a new O-ring (14, **Figure 127**) with OMC Moly Lube, then install it into the crankshaft sleeve at the lower end of the crankshaft.

4. Assemble and install the upper main bearing as follows:
   a. Set the main bearing in a press with its seal bore facing up.
   b. Coat the metal case of a new upper seal with OMC Gasket Sealing Compound, then set the seal into the bearing with its lip facing down.
   c. Using a suitable mandrel, press the seal into the bearing until it is seated.
   d. Lubricate the seal lip with OMC Triple Guard Grease. Lubricate the bearing rollers with oil.
   e. Slide the bearing and seal assembly over the flywheel end of the crankshaft with the seal side of the assembly facing toward the flywheel (up).
   f. Lubricate a new O-ring with OMC Triple Guard Grease, then slide the O-ring over the bearing and seal assembly. Position the O-ring near the middle of the bearing case.

4. Install the three crankshaft seal rings. Lubricate the rings with oil and expand them only as far as necessary to install them. Make sure the ends of each ring butt up flush against each other.

5. Assemble the center main bearings as follows:
    a. Apply a coat of needle bearing assembly grease around the crankshaft's upper center main bearing journal.
    b. Position the two caged needle bearing halves around the journal.
    c. Position the main bearing race halves around the journal with the retaining ring groove (**Figure 121**) facing the drive shaft housing (down).
    d. Carefully align the fractured parting lines, then install the retainer ring. Position the retainer ring to cover as much of both fracture lines as possible.
    e. Repeat this procedure for the lower center main bearing.

6. Install a new lower end cap as follows:
    a. Grease the seal lips in the lower end cap with OMC Triple Guard Grease.
    b. Coat a new O-ring with the same grease and position it in the end cap's groove.
    c. Carefully slide the end cap over the lower end of the crankshaft and seat it against the ball bearing.

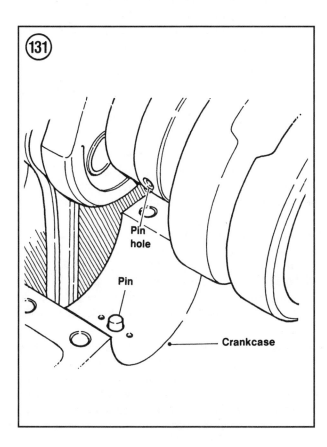

(131)

Pin hole

Pin

Crankcase

7. Position the cylinder block so the crankcase cover mating surface is facing up. Then position the pistons at the bottoms of their bores with the connecting rods to one side of the crankcase.

NOTE
There are many things to align when installing the crankshaft. Work slowly and patiently.

8. Position the crankshaft assembly over the cylinder block and slowly lower it into the block.
    a. Rotate the upper main bearing and both center main bearings as necessary to align each bearing with the locating dowel in the cylinder block (**Figure 131**, typical).
    b. Move the O-ring on the upper main bearing as necessary to fit it into its groove.
    c. Make sure the locating ring on the lower main (ball) bearing is seated in its bore.
    d. Rotate the lower end cap as necessary to position its tab into the cylinder block recess.

9. Begin the installation of the No. 1 cylinder connecting rod to the crankshaft journal as follows:
    a. Grease the crankpin journal with a thick coat of needle bearing assembly grease. Install the caged bearing halves to the journal. If the original bearings are reused, they must be installed in their original position.
    b. Pull the No. 1 cylinder rod and piston assembly up to the crankpin journal and bearings. Rotate the crankshaft as necessary to allow mating of the rod and journal.
    c. Install the matching connecting rod cap in its original orientation. Carefully observe fracture and alignment marks to ensure correct installation.
    d. Lubricate the screw threads and the underside of the screw heads of *new* connecting rod screws with oil. Then while holding the cap firmly in position, install the connecting rod screws and thread them fully into the rod.
    e. Tighten each screw initially to 25-30 in.-lb. (1.69 N•m).

10. Assemble the rod cap alignment fixture as follows:
    a. Move the flat on the knob marked *Set* to align with the arrow embossed on the tool's frame. Move the adjustment knob in or out until the outermost ring aligns with the surface of the tool frame. The instruction sheet refers to this as mark *A*. Then rotate the knob 180° to lock the adjustment.
    b. Install the retaining jaw labeled *G* and the forcing jaw labeled *H* from the jaw kit (part No. 437273) to the fixture frame as described by the tool and jaw kit's instruction sheets.

8

c. Lubricate the four precision ground corners of the connecting rod's big end, then position the fixture over the big end as shown in **Figure 123**, typical.

d. Allow the stop plunger in the center of the frame to contact the rod cap. Then align the grooves machined into the jaws with the rod cap-to-connecting rod parting line.

e. Tighten the tool's forcing screw to 23 in.-lb. (2.6 N•m). Verify that the stop plunger is contacting the rod cap and that the grooves in the jaws are aligned with the rod's parting line.

11. Loosen both rod cap screws 1/4 turn. Then retighten both screws to a preliminary torque of 40-60 in.-lb. (4.5-6.8 N•m). Apply a final torque of 170-190 in.-lb. (19.2-21.5 N•m) in a minimum of two progressive steps.

12. Loosen the forcing screw and remove the fixture. Run a fingernail or pencil lead over each of the four beveled (machined) edges of the rod-to-cap joint (**Figure 124**, typical). The edges must be perfectly flush with no detectable misalignment. If any misalignment is detected, replace the connecting rod.

13. Rotate the crankshaft several revolutions to check for binding or unusual noise. If binding or noise is noted, correct the defect before proceeding.

14. Repeat Steps 8-12 for the remaining piston and connecting rod assemblies.

Final assembly (25 and 35 hp [three-cylinder])

1. Using an oil and wax free solvent, such as acetone or lacquer thinner, clean the cylinder block and crankcase cover mating surfaces.

2. Spray the crankcase cover mating surface with OMC Locquic Primer and allow to air dry.

3. Apply OMC Gel Seal II sealant to the mating surface of the cylinder block. Run a continuous sealant bead along the inside of all screw holes, then carefully spread the bead over the entire surface of the flange, making sure the sealant will not contaminate the bearings, seal rings or ooze excessively into the crankcase's internal chambers. Keep the sealant approximately 1/4 in. (6.35 mm) from the crankshaft seal rings and bearings.

4. Make sure the two guide bushings (3, **Figure 126**) are in place in the crankcase cover or the cylinder block. Then install the crankcase cover into position on the cylinder block. Seat the cover to the block with hand pressure.

5. Lightly coat the threads of the eight main bearing screws with OMC Ultra Lock threadlocking adhesive. Install and tighten the eight main bearing screws finger-tight (until the cover is seated to the block). Install the two longer screws in the holes closest to the flywheel.

6. Lightly coat the threads of the 12 flange screws with OMC Ultra Lock threadlocking adhesive. Install and tighten the 12 flange screws finger-tight at this time.

7. Tighten the eight main bearing screws evenly to 216-240 in.-lb. (24.4-27.1 N•m) in a crossing pattern starting with the center screws and working outward. Then tighten the 12 flange screws in the same manner to 60-84 in.-lb. (6.8-9.5 N•m).

8. Rotate the crankshaft several revolutions to check for binding or unusual noise. If binding or noise is noted, the crankcase cover must be removed and the cause of the defect located and corrected before proceeding.

9. Install the thermostat components as described in *Thermostat* in this chapter.

10. Coat the outer diameter of the engine temperature switch's body with OMC Gasket Sealing Compound. Do not coat the metal face of the switch. Install the switch into its cylinder head bore and secure it in place by tightening the plastic retaining nut securely.

11. If removed, install the throttle control shaft to the crankcase cover. Lubricate the two bushings with OMC Triple Guard Grease, then install them into the cover's bosses. Slide the throttle shaft through the cover bushings from the port side. Install the nylon spacer and ball link arm to the shaft, then secure them with the nut and washer. Tighten the nut to 60-84 in.-lb. (6.8-9.5 N•m).

12. Install the spark control arm as follows:
    a. Position a washer over the shoulder screw, then insert the screw (and washer) through the spark control arm.
    b. Position another washer over the threads of the shoulder screw, then install the assembly to the starboard side of the cylinder block.
    c. Tighten the shoulder screw to 60-84 in.-lb. (6.8-9.5 N•m).

13. *Remote control models*—Position the trunnion anchor bracket to the crankcase cover. Coat the threads of the two mounting screws with OMC Nut Lock threadlocking adhesive, then install and tighten the screws to 84-106 in.-lb. (9.5-12.0 N•m).

14. Install the intake manifold (and reed blocks), carburetors, and all external fuel recirculation system lines as described in Chapter Six. On remote control models, install the fuel primer solenoid and all related lines.

15. Install the oil reservoir, fuel/oil mixing unit and all related mounting brackets to the power head. See Chapter Eleven.

16. *Electric start models*—Install the electric starter motor and starter solenoid as described in Chapter Seven.

17. Install the entire ignition and electrical system as described in Chapter Seven. This includes the stator assembly, optical sensor, ignition module, ignition coils, wiring harness and flywheel. Install the voltage regulator (on

electric start models) and the trim/tilt relay bracket and harness on models with trim and tilt. Secure all harnesses and leads with the original clamps or new tie-straps.

18. Install the power head as described previously in this chapter.

Assembly (40-70 hp, 28 and 35 Jet)

Although the exploded illustrations show three-cylinder models, the two-cylinder models represented in this section are similar in construction. The primary difference between two- and three-cylinder models is the shift linkage. Shift linkage for three-cylinder models is shown in **Figure 63**. An illustration of two-cylinder shift linkage is located in Chapter Five. All procedures specific to one model are so indicated in the text. Refer to **Figure 132** and **Figure 133** for this procedure.

Piston and connecting rod assembly (40-70 hp; 28 and 35 jet)

Assemble the pistons and connecting rods. The wrist pin is a slip-fit to the piston and should not require more than moderate hand pressure to install. Assemble the No. 1 cylinder components first, then repeat this procedure for the remaining cylinders. Proceed as follows:

CAUTION
*When installed, the word **UP** on the piston dome must face toward the flywheel.*

1. Using cone (part No. 318600) and driver (part No. 318599) or equivalent, install a new wrist pin lock clip into one end of the wrist pin bore as follows:
   a. Insert a new lock clip into the internally tapered end of the cone.
   b. Insert the driver into the cone and push the lock clip until it is approximately 1/2 in. (12.7 mm) from the externally beveled end.
   c. Position the externally beveled end of the cone over the wrist pin bore. Rotate the cone as necessary to position the open ends of the clip 180° from the notch in the wrist pin bore.
   d. While holding the cone and piston in position, quickly push downward on the driver to install the lock clip. See **Figure 116**, typical.
   e. Remove the tools and inspect the clip. The open ends of the clip must be positioned 180° from the notch in the wrist pin bore, and the clip must be fully seated in its groove.
2. Lubricate the wrist pin with oil and insert it into the side of the piston without the lock ring installed. Push the pin

into the wrist pin boss until it is just flush with the connecting rod cavity.

3. Liberally apply OMC Needle Bearing Assembly Grease to the connecting rod's small end bore, then arrange the 28 loose needle bearings in the bore. Use bearing installation tool (part No. 336660) or a suitable dowel or socket to help align the bearings. See **Figure 128**.

4. Position a thrust washer on each side of the connecting rod small end. Make sure the stepped side of each thrust washer is against the loose needle bearings (flat side facing out). Apply additional needle bearing grease as necessary to hold the washers in position.

5. Make sure the connecting rod is correctly orientated to the piston. Refer to *Connecting Rod Orientation* as necessary. Remember that the word UP, (stamped on the piston dome) must be positioned pointing UP (toward the flywheel) when installed.

6. Align the rod with the piston. Push the wrist pin into the rod (and loose needles), then continue pushing the wrist pin until it just contacts the lock clip installed in Step 1. If the pin is difficult to install, continue to Step 7.

7. If necessary, place the piston/rod assembly into the appropriate saddle of piston cradle (part No. 326573) or equivalent. Refer to **Figure 104**, typical. Press the pin into the piston using river part No. 318599 (or equivalent), until the remaining lock clip groove is exposed. Do not press the pin any further than necessary to expose the groove, or the piston and the lock clip (already installed) will be damaged.

8. Inspect the assembly and make sure that the 28 needle bearings and the thrust washers are in place. Also, make sure the rod pivots freely on the wrist pin. Correct any problems found.

9. Install the second wrist pin lock clip into its groove in the same manner as Step 1.

Piston installation (40-70 hp, 28 and 35 jet)

1. Check the piston ring end gap as described in *Piston Ring End Gap* in this chapter. The ring end gap must be 0.005-0.020 in. (0.13-0.51 mm).

CAUTION
Install the piston rings onto the pistons that match the cylinder bore for which the rings were fitted.

2. Using a suitable ring expander, install the piston rings onto both pistons. Both rings are semi-keystone and either ring may be installed in either groove. Install the bottom ring first, then the top ring. Expand each ring only enough to fit over the piston crown. Make sure the ring end gaps properly straddle the locating pin in each ring groove. See **Figure 129**, typical.

8

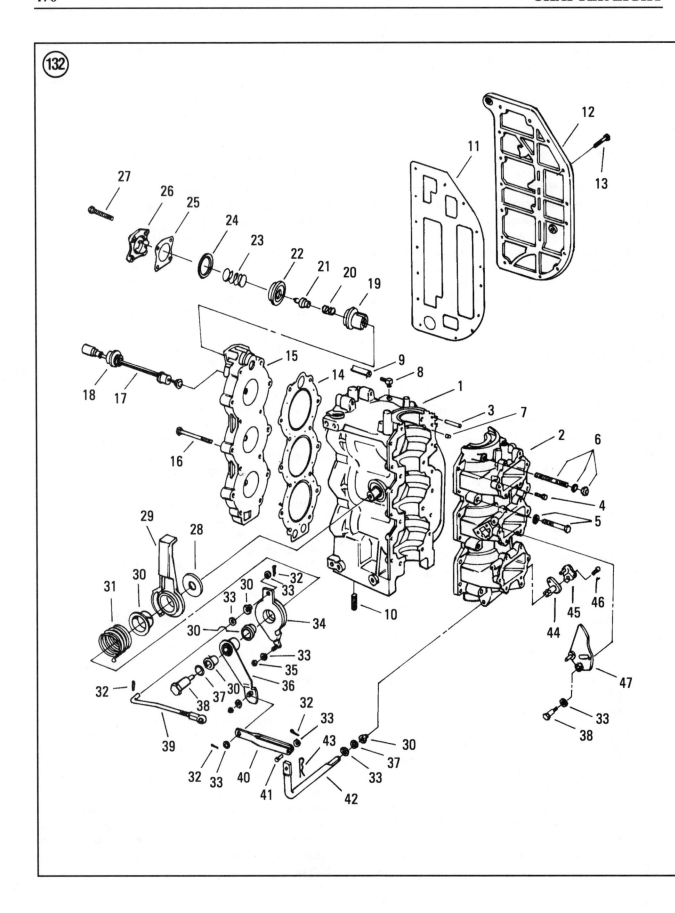

CYLINDER AND CRANKCASE ASSEMBLY
(40-70 HP, 28 AND 35 JET [THREE-CYLINDER SHOWN])

1. Cylinder block
2. Crankcase cover
3. Taper pin
4. Flange screws
5. Main bearing screws
   and washers
6. Stud, washer and nut
   (three-cylinder)
7. Dowel pin
8. Water discharge elbow fittings
9. Water discharge tell-tale hose
10. Stud
11. Gasket
12. Exhaust cover
13. Screw
14. Gasket
15. Cylinder head
16. Screw
17. Engine temperature switch
18. Switch retaining nut
19. Plastic cup
20. Spring
21. Vernatherm (thermostat)
22. Diaphragm
23. Spring
24. Washer
25. Gasket
26. Thermostat cover
27. Screw
28. Washer
29. Spark control
30. Bushings
31. Spring
32. Cotter pins
33. Flat washers
34. Throttle lever
35. Locknuts
36. Shift lever
37. Wave washers
38. Shoulder screws
39. Throttle cam link
40. Shift link
41. Clevis pin
42. Shift shaft
43. Cotter clip
44. Bushing and keeper
45. Shift bellcrank
46. Screw
47. Throttle cam

8

CRANKSHAFT ASSEMBLY
(40-70 HP, 28 AND 35 JET [THREE-CYLINDER SHOWN])

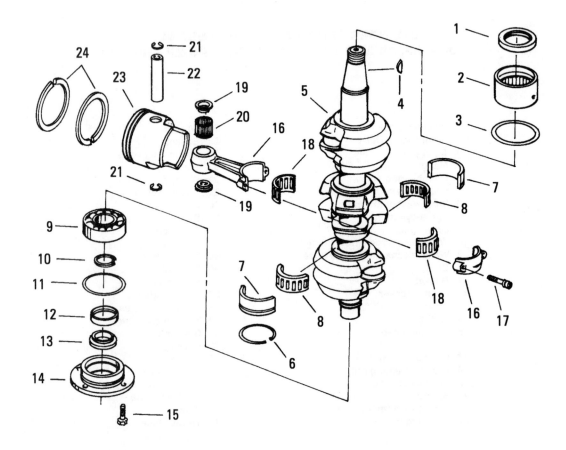

1. Upper seal
2. Upper main bearing
3. O-ring
4. Flywheel key
5. Crankshaft
6. Retaining ring
7. Bearing race halves
8. Caged roller bearing halves
9. Ball bearing and locating ring
10. Retaining ring
11. O-ring
12. Seal (double lip)
13. Seal (single lip)
14. Lower end cap
15. Screw
16. Connecting rod and cap
17. Rod cap screw
18. Caged bearing halves
19. Thrust washers
20. Loose needles
21. Wrist pin lock clips
22. Wrist pin
23. Piston
24. Piston rings

3. Check the fit of each ring to its piston by placing a straightedge across the ring as shown in **Figure 130**, typical. The straightedge must touch the piston on both sides of the ring. Check the fit at several locations around the piston. If the ring holds the straightedge from the piston at any point, the ring groove has not been sufficiently cleaned or is damaged. Remove the ring and clean the groove as necessary. Refer to *Power Head Cleaning and Inspection*.

4. Lubricate the No. 1 cylinder piston rings, piston and cylinder bore with oil.

5. Install the No. 1 cylinder piston and connecting rod assembly as follows:

   a. Verify that the end gap of each piston ring is straddling the ring locating pin in each ring groove.

   CAUTION
   *When installed, the word **UP** on the piston dome must face toward the flywheel.*

   b. Using a tapered sleeve ring compressor, such as part No. 326592 (standard bore) or part No. 330222 (oversize bore), install the No.1 piston into its cylinder bore with the word UP on the piston facing the

flywheel end of the cylinder block. Be careful to keep the rod's big end from damaging the cylinder bore.

CAUTION
Due to the design of this block, the rings cannot be checked for damage after installation. Use extreme care (and the correct sleeve style compressor) to prevent piston ring damage or breakage. If in doubt, remove the piston and recheck the rings.

6. Repeat Steps 4-5 for the remaining piston(s).

NOTE
Do not use sealant on the cylinder head screws.

7. Install the cylinder head. Lightly coat both sides of a new head gasket with OMC Gasket Sealing Compound. Position the cylinder head and new gasket on the cylinder block, then install the screws (without sealant). Evenly tighten the cylinder head screws to 216-240 in.-lb. (24.4-27.1 N•m) in the pattern shown in **Figure 134** (two-cylinder models) or **Figure 135** (three-cylinder models).

8

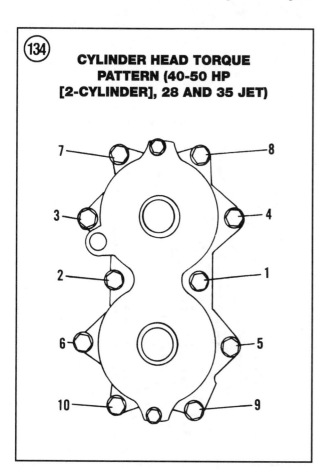

CYLINDER HEAD TORQUE PATTERN (40-50 HP [2-CYLINDER], 28 AND 35 JET)

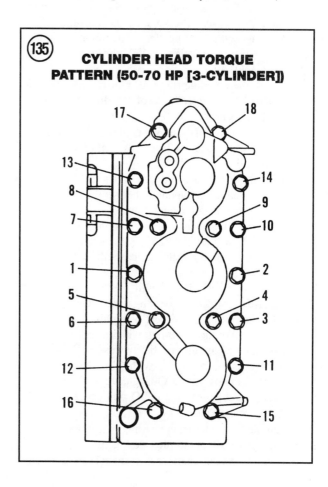

CYLINDER HEAD TORQUE PATTERN (50-70 HP [3-CYLINDER])

Crankshaft installation
(40-70 hp, 28 and 35 jet)

The connecting rods on these models require a special fixture (part No. 396749) to correctly align the cap.

The special fixture contacts the rod cap and rod body on four beveled (machined) corners, applying a predetermined clamping force. The fixture is left in place during the torquing process, ensuring perfect rod cap alignment.

> *CAUTION*
> *Failure to use the alignment fixture (and use it correctly) will result in premature connecting rod big end bearing failure.*

Rod cap screw socket (part No. 331638) or an equivalent heavy-duty 12-point, thin-wall, 5/16 in. socket is required to torque the rod cap screws.

1. Install a new crankshaft ball bearing as follows:
   a. Lubricate the new bearing and the crankshaft journal with oil.
   b. Slide the bearing over the drive shaft end of the crankshaft with the numbered side of the bearing facing away from the crankshaft.
   c. Support the crankshaft (under the lower counterweight) in a press. Press against the inner race of the bearing with bearing/sleeve installer (part No. 339749) or a suitable mandrel, until it is seated on the crankshaft.
   d. Install the retaining ring (10, **Figure 133**) with the flat (or sharp-edged) side of the ring facing away from the bearing.
2. Assemble and install the upper main bearing as follows:
   a. Set the main bearing in a press with its seal bore facing up.
   b. Coat the metal case of a new upper seal with OMC Gasket Sealing Compound, then set the seal into the bearing with its lip facing down.
   c. Using seal installer (part No. 334500 [two-cylinder models]) or (part No. 326567 [three-cylinder models]) or a suitable mandrel, press the seal into the bearing.
   d. Lubricate the seal lip with OMC Triple Guard Grease. Lubricate the bearing rollers with oil.
   e. Slide the bearing and seal assembly over the flywheel end of the crankshaft with the seal side of the assembly facing toward the flywheel.
   f. Lubricate a new O-ring with OMC Triple Guard Grease, then slide the O-ring over the bearing and seal assembly. Position the O-ring near the middle of the bearing case.
3. Assemble the center main bearing(s) as follows:
   a. Apply a coat of needle bearing assembly grease around the crankshaft's center main bearing journal

(two-cylinder models) or the crankshaft's upper center main bearing journal.
   b. Position the two caged needle bearing halves around the journal.
   c. Position the main bearing race halves around the journal with the retaining ring groove facing the drive shaft housing (down). See **Figure 136**.
   d. Carefully align the fractured parting lines, then install the retainer ring. Position the retainer ring to cover as much of both fracture lines as possible.
   e. Repeat this procedure for the lower center main bearing on three-cylinder models.
4. Position the cylinder block so it is sitting on the cylinder head and the crankcase cover mating surface is facing up. Push the pistons to the bottom of their bores, then position all connecting rods to one side of the crankcase.

> *NOTE*
> *There are many things to align when installing the crankshaft. Work slowly and patiently.*

5. Position the crankshaft assembly over the cylinder block and slowly lower it into the block.
   a. Rotate the upper main bearing and center main bearing(s) as necessary to align each bearing with the

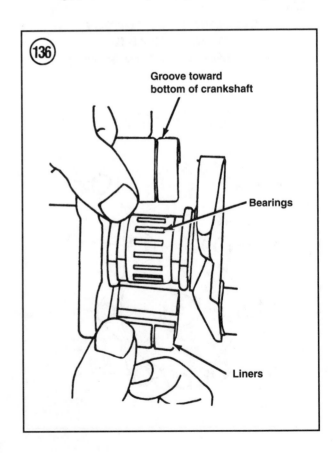

136

Groove toward
bottom of crankshaft

Bearings

Liners

locating dowel in the cylinder block (**Figure 131**, typical).

b. Move the O-ring on the upper main bearing as necessary to fit it into its groove.

c. Make sure the lower main bearing is seated in its bore.

6. Begin the installation of the No. 1 cylinder connecting rod to the crankshaft journal as follows:

a. Grease the crankpin journal with a thick coat of needle bearing assembly grease. Install the caged bearing halves to the journal. If the original bearings are reused, they must be installed in their original position.

b. Pull the No. 1 cylinder rod and piston assembly up to the crankpin journal and bearings. Rotate the

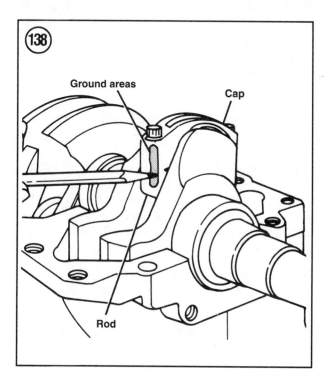

Ground areas

Cap

Rod

crankshaft as necessary to allow mating of the rod and journal.

c. Install the matching connecting rod cap in its original orientation. Carefully observe fracture and alignment marks to ensure correct installation.

d. Lubricate the screw threads and underside of the screw heads of new connecting rod screws with oil. Then while holding the cap firmly in position, install the connecting rod screws and thread them fully into the rod.

e. Tighten each screw initially to 25-30 in.-lb. (1.69 N•m).

7. Assemble the rod cap alignment fixture as follows:

a. Move the flat on the knob marked *Set* to align with the arrow embossed on the tool's frame. Move the adjustment knob in or out until the outermost ring aligns with the surface of the tool frame. The instruction sheet refers to this as mark *A*. Then rotate the knob 180° to lock the adjustment.

b. Install the retaining jaw labeled *C* and the forcing jaw labeled *D* to the fixture frame as described by the tool's instruction sheet.

c. Lubricate the four precision ground corners of the connecting rod's big end, then position the fixture over the big end in the manner shown in **Figure 137**, typical.

d. Allow the stop plunger in the center of the frame to contact the rod cap. Then align the grooves machined into the jaws with the rod cap-to-connecting rod parting line.

e. Tighten the tool's forcing screw to 23 in.-lb. (2.6 N•m). Verify that the stop plunger is contacting the rod cap and that the grooves in the jaws are aligned with the rod's parting line.

8. Loosen both rod cap screws 1/4 turn. Then retighten both screws to a preliminary torque of 40-60 in.-lb. (4.5-6.8 N•m). Apply a final torque of 30-32 ft.-lb. (40.7-43.4 N•m) in a minimum of three progressive steps.

9. Loosen the forcing screw and remove the fixture. Run a fingernail or pencil lead over each of the four beveled (machined) edges of the rod-to-cap joint (**Figure 138**, typical). The edges must be perfectly flush with no detectable misalignment. If any misalignment is detected, replace the connecting rod.

10. Rotate the crankshaft several revolutions to check for binding or unusual noise. If binding or noise is noted, correct the defect before proceeding.

11. Repeat Steps 6-10 for the remaining piston and connecting rod assemblies.

12. Prepare the lower end cap for installation as follows:

a. Coat the metal cases of two new seals with OMC Gasket Sealing Compound.

8

b. Using the extended side of seal installer part No. 339752 (or equivalent), press the smaller seal into the lower end cap bore with the lip (spring side) facing up (toward the flywheel).

c. Using the shorter side of seal installer part No. 339752 (or equivalent), press the larger diameter seal into the lower end cap bore with the extended lip facing down (toward the drive shaft housing).

c. Liberally coat the seal lips and fill the area between the seals with OMC Moly Lube.

d. Lightly coat a new O-ring with OMC Triple Guard Grease. Install the O-ring into the end cap groove.

Final assembly (40-70 hp, 28 and 35 jet)

1. Using an oil and wax free solvent, such as acetone or lacquer thinner, clean the cylinder block and crankcase cover mating surfaces.

2. Spray the crankcase cover mating surface with OMC Locquic Primer and allow it to air dry.

3. Apply OMC Gel Seal II sealant to the mating surface of the cylinder block. Run a continuous sealant bead along the inside of all screw holes, then carefully spread the bead over the entire surface of the flange, making sure the sealant will not contaminate the bearings, labyrinth seals or ooze excessively into the crankcase's internal chambers. Keep the sealant approximately 1/4 in. (6.35 mm) from the labyrinth seal grooves and the crankshaft bearings.

4. Install the crankcase cover into position on the cylinder block. Seat the cover to the block with hand pressure.

NOTE
Before installing the taper pin, the crankcase cover must be seated to the cylinder block and held in place by the main bearing screws, but without any substantial clamping load being applied by the screws. The cover must be able to move (shift) slightly when the taper pin is installed to precisely align the cover to the cylinder block.

5A. *Two-cylinder models*—Install and tighten the six main bearing screws finger-tight (until the cover is seated to the block). Then install the taper pin (3, **Figure 132**, typical) and seat it in its bore. Do not drive the taper pin too tightly into its bore, or it will split the cylinder block and crankcase cover.

5B. *Three-cylinder models*—Install and tighten the six main bearing screws (and washers) and two nuts (and washers) finger-tight (until the cover is seated to the block). Then install the taper pin (3, **Figure 132**) and seat it in its bore. Do not drive the taper pin too tightly into its bore or it will split the cylinder block and crankcase cover.

6. Install and finger-tighten the eight (two-cylinder) or 12 (three-cylinder) flange screws.

7. Tap the lower end of the crankshaft with a soft-faced mallet to seat the ball bearing in its bore. Then coat the flange of the lower end cap with OMC Gasket sealing compound and install it over the lower end of the crankshaft. Make sure the end cap is seated to the crankcase, then coat the threads of the four end cap screws with sealing compound. Install the screws and tighten them finger-tight at this time.

8A. *Two-cylinder models*—Tighten the six main bearing screws evenly to 216-240 in.-lb. (24.4-27.1 N•m) in a crossing pattern starting with the center screws and working outward. Then tighten the eight flange screws in the same manner to 60-84 in.-lb. (6.8-9.5 N•m).

8B. *Three-cylinder models*—Tighten the eight main bearing fasteners evenly to 216-240 in.-lb. (24.4-27.1 N•m) in a crossing pattern, starting with the center screws and working outward. Then tighten the 12 flange screws in the same manner to 60-84 in.-lb. (6.8-9.5 N•m).

9. Evenly tighten the four lower end cap screws to 60-84 in.-lb. (6.8-9.5 N•m) on two-cylinder models or 95-120 in.-lb. (10.7-13.6) on three-cylinder models.

10. Rotate the crankshaft several revolutions to check for binding or unusual noise. If binding or noise is noted, remove the crankcase cover, and correct the cause of the defect before proceeding.

11. Install the thermostat components as described in *Thermostat* in this chapter.

12. Coat the outer diameter of the engine temperature switch's body with OMC Gasket Sealing Compound. Do not coat the metal face of the switch. Install the switch into its cylinder head bore and secure it in place by tightening the plastic retaining nut securely.

13. Apply OMC Gasket Sealing Compound to a new exhaust cover gasket. Position the exhaust cover and gasket on the power head, then position any clamps or brackets to the exhaust cover as noted on disassembly. Install and evenly tighten the 12 (two-cylinder) or 14 (three-cylinder) screws in a crossing pattern to 60-84 in.-lb. (6.8-9.5 N•m).

14. *Two-cylinder models*—Install the lower cowl mount to the starboard side of the crankcase cover, just behind the shift shaft and lever. Secure the mount with two screws. Tighten the screws to 60-84 in.-lb. (6.8-9.5 N•m).

NOTE
Lubricate all shift and throttle linkage bushings and components with OMC Triple Guard Grease.

15A. *Two-cylinder models*—Refer to **Figure 139** and install the two shift shaft bushings into the crankcase cover bosses. Then install the detent spring, detent ball and detent ball guide (retainer) into the bore of the starboard side of the crankcase cover.

15B. *Three-cylinder models*—Install the two shift shaft bushings (30 and 44, **Figure 132**, typical) into the crankcase cover bosses. On tiller handle models, install the neutral detent spring and bracket to the power head. Tighten the mounting screws securely.

16A. *Two-cylinder models*—Refer to **Figure 139** and install the shift shaft and rear shift lever (as an assembly) to the starboard side of the power head. Secure the rear shift lever to the power head with the shoulder screw, wave washer and two flat washers. Tighten the shoulder screw securely. Install the spacer over the shift shaft, then install

the bellcrank. Secure the bellcrank with a screw and tabbed washer. Tighten the screw securely, then bend the tab firmly against the screw head.

16B. *Three-cylinder (remote control) models*—Refer to **Figure 132** and install the shift lever (and washers) on the starboard side of the power head. Position the bellcrank over the port end of the shift lever and secure it with a screw. Tighten the screw securely.

16C. *Three-cylinder (tiller handle) models*—Install the shift lever (and washers) on the starboard side of the power head. Position the bellcrank over the port end of the shift lever and secure it with a screw. Tighten the screw securely. Connect the shift handle's link to the shift lever with the

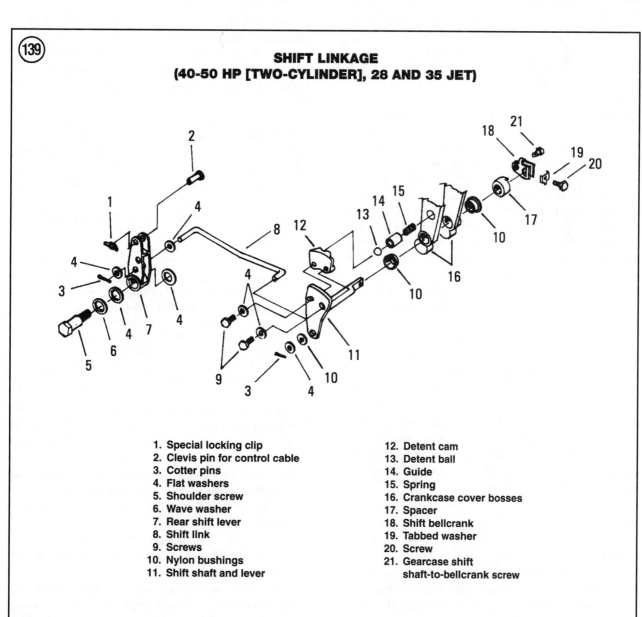

**SHIFT LINKAGE
(40-50 HP [TWO-CYLINDER], 28 AND 35 JET)**

1. Special locking clip
2. Clevis pin for control cable
3. Cotter pins
4. Flat washers
5. Shoulder screw
6. Wave washer
7. Rear shift lever
8. Shift link
9. Screws
10. Nylon bushings
11. Shift shaft and lever
12. Detent cam
13. Detent ball
14. Guide
15. Spring
16. Crankcase cover bosses
17. Spacer
18. Shift bellcrank
19. Tabbed washer
20. Screw
21. Gearcase shift shaft-to-bellcrank screw

8

clevis pin, washer and a new cotter pin. Bend both prongs of the cotter pin for a secure attachment.

17A. *Two-cylinder models*—Position the throttle cam and spark control arm on the starboard side of the power head. Secure each component in place with a shoulder screw (and two washers). Tighten each shoulder screw securely.

17B. *Three-cylinder (remote control) models*—Refer to **Figure 132** and position the spark, throttle and shift control arms and the throttle cam to the starboard side of the power head. Secure the arms and cam in place with two shoulder screws (and washers). Tighten the shoulder screws securely. Connect the shift link to the shift lever with the clevis pin, washer and a new cotter pin. Bend both prongs for a secure attachment.

17C. *Three-cylinder (tiller handle) models*—Position the spark control arm, throttle control arm and the throttle cam to the starboard side of the power head (as an assembly). Secure the arms and cam in place with three shoulder screws (and washers). Tighten the shoulder screws securely.

18. Install the intake manifold, reed blocks, carburetors, fuel pump (or oil injection pump and pulse-limiter fitting), fuel primer solenoid (electric start models) and all related fuel, oil and primer lines. See Chapter Six.

19. Install the entire ignition and electrical system (as equipped) and all related mounting brackets. This includes the stator (or armature plate) assembly, sensor coil (12 amp charging systems), power pack and ignition coil(s). On electric start models, this includes the starter motor, starter solenoid, terminal strip, rectifier (or voltage regulator) and the wiring harness. On models with trim/tilt, also install the trim/tilt relay bracket and associated harness. Secure all leads and harnesses with the original clamps or new tie-straps. See Chapter Seven.

20. Install the flywheel as described in Chapter Seven.

REED VALVES

Reed valves control the passage of air/fuel mixture into the crankcase by opening and closing as crankcase pressure changes. Reed valves are mounted to a reed plate (or block) and are positioned between the intake manifold and crankcase cover. Refer to Chapter Six for full system descriptions and all service procedures.

THERMOSTAT

On 6-70 hp and 18-35 jet models, a thermostat (or Vernatherm) regulates the water leaving the power head. Correct thermostat operation is vital to engine break-in, spark plug life, smooth consistent idling and maximum performance and durability.

On all models, the thermostat assembly incorporates a relief (blow-off) function controlled by water pressure in the cylinder block. At higher engine speeds, the water pump pressure (against a diaphragm, housing or the thermostat) will be sufficient to force the thermostat off of its seat.

Refer to the appropriate power head disassembly procedure for additional illustrations of the thermostat assembly specific to your model engine.

Removal/Installation
(6-15 and 40-70 hp, 28 and 35 Jet)

These models use a vernatherm. The vernatherm is a temperature sensitive device that moves a plunger in or out, based on the water temperature around its sensing pellet. The plunger controls whether the vernatherm is seated (closed) against the diaphragm or pushed away (open) from the diaphragm.

At higher engine speeds, the increased water pressure will push the diaphragm away from the vernatherm, allowing increased cooling water flow. At lower speeds, the relief (large) spring keeps the diaphragm seated to the vernatherm, allowing the vernatherm to control the water temperature.

To service the thermostat, refer to **Figure 140** and proceed as follows:

NOTE
On all models, the relief (large) spring pushes against the diaphragm via a cupped washer (5, Figure 140). On 6-15 hp models, the cupped washer is removable (loose) from the diaphragm. On 40-70 hp, 28 and 35 jet models, the cupped washer must be attached to the diaphragm. If it is loose or separated, replace the diaphragm.

1A. *6-15 hp*—Remove the three screws securing the thermostat cover to the cylinder head. Remove the cover, large spring and cupped washer. Then remove and discard the cover seal.

1B. *40-70 hp, 28 and 35 jet*—Remove the four screws securing the thermostat cover to the cylinder head. Remove the cover and large spring. Then remove and discard the cover gasket.

2. Remove the large washer, diaphragm, vernatherm, small spring and plastic cup (housing) from the cylinder head. Separate the components.

3. Refer to *Thermostat Assembly (6-70 hp and 18-35 jet)* in the *Power Head Cleaning and Inspection* section and clean and inspect the thermostat components. On 40-70 hp

(and 28-35 jet) models, the cupped washer must be attached to the diaphragm. If not, replace the diaphragm.

4. To install the thermostat components, begin by making sure the plunger is installed in the vernatherm. The rounded tip of the plunger must be exposed and facing away from the vernatherm.

5. Install the small spring over the pellet end of the vernatherm and seat it against the vernatherm's shoulder.

6. Insert the vernatherm and small spring assembly into the plastic cup. The spring must enter the cup first.

7. Place the diaphragm over the vernatherm and cup. The raised rib on the diaphragm must face out.

8. Place the large washer over the raised rib on the diaphragm. Then install the assembly into the cylinder head and seat it in its bore.

NOTE
If the relief spring is tapered (one end larger than the other), install the larger end into the thermostat cover.

9A. *6-15 hp*—Install a new seal to the thermostat cover. Position the relief (large) spring in the cover, then set the cupped washer over the spring. Carefully install the cover to the cylinder head, making sure the cupped washer fits

into the bore created by the diaphragm's raised rib and that the large washer is not displaced.

9B. *40-70 hp, 28 and 35 jet*—Lightly coat a new cover gasket with OMC Gasket Sealing Compound. Position the gasket on the cover. Install the relief (large) spring into the cover's bore and seat it in position. Carefully install the cover on the cylinder head, making sure the spring fits into the cupped washer attached to the diaphragm and that the large washer is not displaced.

10. Lightly coat the threads of the three or four cover screws with OMC Gasket Sealing Compound. Install and evenly tighten them to 60-84 in.-lb. (6.8-9.5 N•m).

11. Refer to *Engine Temperature and Overheating* in Chapter Three and verify that the engine operating temperature is correct.

Removal/Installation
(20-30 hp [Two-cylinder] and 18 Jet)

These models use a traditional thermostat (similar to an automotive design). The thermostat is held against the cylinder head (and a seal) by a water pressure relief spring. At higher speeds, the increased water pressure will force the entire thermostat off its seat, bypassing the thermostat and increasing water flow. At lower speeds, the spring holds the thermostat against the cylinder head, allowing the thermostat to control the water temperature.

To service the thermostat, proceed as follows:

1. Refer to the appropriate *Power Head Disassembly* section and remove the cylinder head cover, relief spring, thermostat and seal.

2. Refer to *Thermostat Assembly (6-70 hp and 18-35 jet)* in the *Power Head Cleaning and Inspection* section and clean and inspect the thermostat components.

3. Refer to the appropriate *Power Head Assembly* section and install the seal, thermostat, relief spring and cylinder head cover. Use a new thermostat seal and cylinder head cover gasket during assembly.

4. Refer to *Engine Temperature and Overheating* in Chapter Three and verify that the engine operating temperature is correct.

Removal/Installation
(25 and 35 hp [Three-cylinder])

These models use a thermostat cartridge assembly containing a vernatherm. The vernatherm is a temperature sensitive device that moves a plunger in or out, based on the water temperature around its sensing pellet. The plunger controls whether the vernatherm is seated (closed) against the diaphragm or pushed away (open) from the diaphragm.

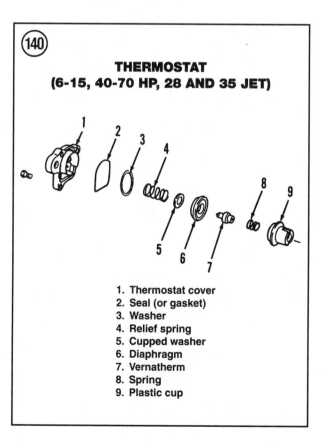

(140)

**THERMOSTAT
(6-15, 40-70 HP, 28 AND 35 JET)**

1. Thermostat cover
2. Seal (or gasket)
3. Washer
4. Relief spring
5. Cupped washer
6. Diaphragm
7. Vernatherm
8. Spring
9. Plastic cup

8

At higher engine speeds, the increased water pressure will push the diaphragm away from the vernatherm, allowing increased cooling water flow. At lower speeds, a spring keeps the diaphragm seated to the vernatherm, allowing the vernatherm to control the water temperature.

To service the thermostat, refer to **Figure 141** and proceed as follows:

1. Remove the thermostat cartridge assembly by unscrewing it from the cylinder head using a spark plug socket.

2. Remove the small O-ring from the protruding nose of the cover and the large O-ring from the housing flange. Discard both O-rings.

3. Unscrew the inner cover from the main housing. Separate the components, taking note of each component's location.

4. Refer to *Thermostat Assembly (6-70 Hp and 18-35 jet)* in the *Power Head Cleaning and Inspection* section and clean and inspect the thermostat components. The diaphragm's cupped washer must be attached to the diaphragm. If it is loose or separated, replace the diaphragm.

5. To assemble the thermostat cartridge, begin by making sure the plunger is installed in the vernatherm. The rounded tip of the plunger must be exposed and facing away from the vernatherm.

6. Install the small spring over the pellet end of the vernatherm and seat it against the vernatherm's shoulder.

7. Place the large washer over the raised rib on the diaphragm (same side as the cupped washer). Then position the plunger end of the vernatherm into the diaphragm's opening. The raised rib (and washers) on the diaphragm must face away from the vernatherm. Finally place the large spring over the diaphragm and against the cupped washer.

8. Carefully place the main housing over the assembled components, with the large spring entering the housing first. Then place the inner cover over the vernatherm and small spring. Tighten the cover securely to the housing, keeping in mind the components are plastic.

9. Install a new small O-ring in the inner cover's groove and a new large O-ring against the main housing's flange. Lubricate both O-rings with OMC Triple Guard Grease.

10. Thread the thermostat cartridge assembly into the cylinder head and tighten it securely.

Refer to *Engine Temperature and Overheating* in Chapter Three and verify that the engine operating temperature is correct.

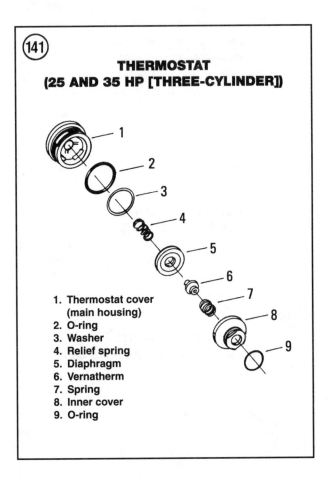

(141)

**THERMOSTAT
(25 AND 35 HP [THREE-CYLINDER])**

1. Thermostat cover
   (main housing)
2. O-ring
3. Washer
4. Relief spring
5. Diaphragm
6. Vernatherm
7. Spring
8. Inner cover
9. O-ring

Table 1 CONNECTING ROD SCREW TORQUE VALUES

Outboard model	Torque specification
2, 3.3 and 3.5 hp	Not applicable
3, 4-15 hp (including 4 Deluxe)	60-70 in.-lb. (6.8-7.9 N•m)
20-30 hp (two-cylinder) and 18 jet	30-32 ft.-lb. (40.7-43.4 N•m)
25 and 35 hp (three-cylinder)	170-190 in.-lb. (19.2-21.5 N•m)
40-70 hp, 28 and 35 jet	30-32 ft.-lb. (40.7-43.4 N•m)

Table 2 CYLINDER HEAD BOLT TORQUE VALUES

Outboard model	Torque specification
2-4 hp (including 4 Deluxe)	60-84 in.-lb. (6.8-9.5 N•m)
6 and 8 hp	144-168 in.-lb. (16.3-19.0 N•m)
9.9-50 hp (two-cylinder) and 18-35 jet	216-240 in.-lb. (24.4-27.1 N•m)
25 and 35 hp (three-cylinder)	180-204 in.-lb. (20.3-23 N•m)
50-70 hp (three-cylinder)	216-240 in.-lb. (24.4-27.1 N•m)

Table 3 POWER HEAD TORQUE VALUES

Fastener	in.-lb.	ft.-lb.	N•m
Crankcase cover			
2, 3.3 and 3.5 hp	90-120	–	10.2-13.6
3, 4 hp and 4 Deluxe	60-84	–	6.8-9.5
6-15 hp			
Large (main bearing) screws	144-168	12-14	16.3-19.0
Small (outer) screws	60-84	–	6.8-9.5
20-30 hp (two-cylinder) and 18 jet			
Large (main bearing) screws	168-192	14-16	19.0-21.7
Small (outer) screws	60-84	–	6.8-9.5
25 and 35 hp (three-cylinder)			
Large (main bearing) screws	216-240	18-20	24.4-27.1
Small (outer) screws	60-84	–	6.8-9.5
40-70 hp, 28 and 35 jet			
Large (main bearing) screws	216-240	18-20	24.4-27.1
Small (outer) screws	60-84	–	6.8-9.5
Crankshaft lower end cap			
2, 3.3 and 3.5 hp	60-84	–	6.8-9.5
3, 4 hp (except 4 Deluxe)	25-35	–	2.8-4.0
9.9-50 hp (two-cylinder) and 18-35 jet	60-84	–	6.8-9.5
50-70 hp (three-cylinder)	95-120	–	10.7-13.6
Cylinder head water cover	60-84	–	6.8-9.5
Exhaust cover			
3, 4 hp and 4 Deluxe	25-35	–	2.8-4.0
6 and 8 hp	60-84	–	6.8-9.5
9.9 and 15 hp	95-130	7.9-10.8	10.7-14.7
20-70 hp and 18-35 jet	60-84	–	6.8-9.5
Inner exhaust housing			
4 Deluxe, 6-15 hp	60-84	–	6.8-9.5
20-30 hp (two-cylinder) and 18 jet	96-120	8-10	10.9-13.6
Intake (transfer) port cover screws	60-84	–	6.8-9.5
Power head mounting hardware			
2-15 hp (including 4 Deluxe)	60-84	–	6.8-9.5
20-30 hp (two-cylinder) and 18 jet	192-216	16-18	21.7-24.4
25 and 35 hp (three-cylinder)	180-204	15-17	20.3-23.0
40-70 hp, 28 and 35 jet	216-240	18-20	24.4-27.1
Spark plug(s)	216-252	18-21	24.4-28.5
Thermostat cover	60-84	–	6.8-9.5

8

**Table 4 POWER HEAD DIMENSIONAL SPECIFICATIONS
(ONE- AND TWO-CYLINDER MODELS)**

Component	Specification–in. (mm)
Crankshaft	
Connecting rod deflection at small end	
2, 3.3 and 3.5 hp	0.022-0.056 (0.56-1.42)
Crankpin diameter	
2, 3.3 and 3.5 hp	0.6299-0.6301 (16.00-16.005)
3, 4-8 hp (including 4 Deluxe)	0.6695-0.6700 (17.01-17.02)
9.9 and 15 hp	0.8120-0.8125 (20.63-20.64)
20-50 hp and 18-35 jet	1.1823-1.1828 (30.03-30.04)
Center main journal diameter	
3, 4 hp and 4 Deluxe	0.6685-0.6690 (16.98-16.99)
6-15 hp	0.8120-0.8125 (20.63-20.64)
20-30 hp and 18 jet	1.1833-1.1838 (30.06-30.07)
40-50 hp and 28-35 jet	1.3745-1.3749 (34.91-34.92)
Top main journal diameter	
2, 3.3 and 3.5 hp	0.7875-0.7878 (20.003-20.010)
3, 4 hp and 4 Deluxe	0.7515-0.7520 (19.088-19.10)
6 and 8 hp	0.8762-0.8767 (22.26-22.27)
9.9 and 15 hp	0.8757-0.8762 (22.24-22.26)
20-30 hp and 18 jet	1.2510-1.2515 (31.78-31.79)
40-50 hp, 28 and 35 jet	1.4986-1.4991 (38.06-38.08)
Bottom main journal diameter	
2, 3.3 and 3.5 hp	0.5906-0.5910 (15.00-15.01)
3, 4-8 hp	
(including 4 Deluxe)	0.6691-0.6695 (17.00-17.01)
9.9 and 15 hp	0.7870-0.7874 (19.99-20.00)
20-30 hp and 18 jet	0.9842-0.9846 (25.00-25.01)
40-50 hp, 28 and 35 jet	1.1810-1.1815 (30.00-30.01)
Crankshaft runout	
2, 3.3 and 3.5 hp	0.001 (0.025)
Cylinder	
Bore diameter—standard	
2, 3.3 and 3.5 hp	1.8898-1.8906 (48.00-48.02)
3, 4 hp and 4 Deluxe	1.5643-1.5650 (39.73-39.75)
6 and 8 hp	1.9373-1.9380 (49.21-49.23)
9.9 and 15 hp	2.3745-2.3750 (60.31-60.33)
20-30 hp and 18 jet	2.9995-3.0005 (76.19-76.21)
40-50 hp, 28 and 35 jet	3.1870-3.1880 (80.95-80.98)
Maximum cylinder out-of-round	0.003 (0.076)
Maximum cylinder taper	0.002 (0.051)
Maximum cylinder wear	
2-15 hp (including (4 Deluxe)	0.002 (0.051)
20-50 hp and 18-35 jet	0.003 (0.076)
Maximum cylinder head warpage	0.004 (0.102)
Piston	
Piston-to-cylinder clearance	See text
Skirt diameter	
2, 3.3 and 3.5 hp	1.8868-1.8873 (47.925-47.937)
3, 4 hp and 4 Deluxe	1.5625-1.5631 (39.688-39.703)
6 and 8 hp	1.9345-1.9355 (49.136-49.162)
9.9 and 15 hp	See text
20-30 hp and 18 jet	
Zollner piston (see text)	
Major diameter	2.9956 (76.088)
Minor diameter	2.9886-2.9906 (75.910-75.961)
Cam dimension	0.005-0.007 (0.127-0.178)
Art (or Rightway) piston (see text)	
Major diameter	2.9969 (76.121)
Minor diameter	2.9944-2.9954 (76.058-76.083)
Cam dimension	0.0015-0.0025 (0.038-0.064)
	(continued)

Table 4 POWER HEAD DIMENSIONAL SPECIFICATIONS (ONE- AND TWO-CYLINDER MODELS) (continued)

Component	Specification–in. (mm)
Piston	
Skirt diameter (continued)	
40-50 hp, 28 and 35 jet	
Major diameter	3.1831 (80.851) minimum
Minor diameter	3.1791 (80.749) minimum
Cam dimension	0.004 in. (0.102) maximum
Maximum piston out-of-round	
2-15 hp (including 4 Deluxe)	0.002 (0.051)
Piston ring end gap	
2, 3.3 and 3.5 hp	0.006-0.014 (0.15-0.36)
3, 4-15 hp (including 4 Deluxe)	0.005-0.015 (0.13-0.38)
20-30 hp and 18 jet	0.007-0.017 (0.18-0.43)
40-50 hp, 28 and 35 jet	0.019-0.031 (0.48-0.79)
Piston ring side clearance	
2, 3.3 and 3.5 hp	0.0026 (0.066) maximum
3, 4-30 hp (including 4 Deluxe)	0.004 (0.102) maximum

Table 5 POWER HEAD DIMENSIONAL SPECIFICATIONS (THREE-CYLINDER MODELS)

Component	Specification–in. (mm)
Crankshaft	
Crankpin diameter	1.1823-1.1828 (30.03-30.04)
Center main journal diameters	1.3748-1.3752 (34.92-34.93)
Seal ring thickness (25 and 35 hp)	0.100 (2.54) minimum
Top main journal diameter	
25 and 35 hp	1.4979-1.4984 (38.05-38.06)
50-70 hp	1.4974-1.4979 (38.03-38.05)
Bottom main journal diameter	1.1810-1.1815 (30.00-30.01)
Cylinder	
Bore diameter - standard	
25 hp	2.3495-2.3505 (59.68-59.70)
35 hp	2.4995-2.5005 (63.49-63.51)
50-70 hp	3.1870-3.1880 (80.95-80.98)
Maximum cylinder out-of-round	
25 and 35 hp	0.004 (0.102)
50-70 hp	0.003 (0.762)
Maximum cylinder taper	0.002 (0.051)
Maximum cylinder wear	
25 and 35 hp	0.004 (0.102)
50-70 hp	0.003 (0.076)
Maximum cylinder head warpage	0.004 (0.102)
Piston	
Piston-to-cylinder clearance	See text
Skirt diameter	
25 hp	2.3440-2.3450 (59.54-59.56)
35 hp	2.4940-2.4950 (63.35-63.37)
50-70 hp	3.1806-3.1841 (80.79-80.88)
Maximum piston out-of-round	0.003 (0.0762)
Piston ring end gap	
25 and 35 hp	0.005-0.020 (0.13-0.51)
50-70 hp	0.019-0.031 (0.48-0.79)

Table 6 DESIGN FEATURE CODES

Code	Definition
AE	Alaska model, electric start
AR	Alaska model, rope start
	(continued)

8

Table 6 DESIGN FEATURE CODES (continued)

Code	Definition
BA	AC lighting coil, rope start
D	Remote control, electric start
DE	De-rated power head, electric start
DR	De-rated power head, rope start
DT	De-rated power head, electric start , trim and tilt
E	Electric start
ES	Electric start, special styling
F	Rope start or four stroke
G	Special styling
J	Jet drive
K	Tiller handle, electric start
M	Manual tilt, electric start
MS	Special styling, manual tilt, electric start
Q	Trim and tilt, electric start
R	Rope start
RD	Rope start, deluxe model
S	Special styling
SP	Special styling
ST	Special styling, trim and tilt
T	Trim and tilt, electric start
TE	Tiller handle, electric start
TK	Tiller handle, trim and tilt, electric start
TR	Tiller handle, special styling
TT	Tiller handle, trim and tilt, backtroller model
U	Manual tilt
V	Special gearcase

Chapter Nine

Lower Gearcase and Jet Drive Units

LOWER GEARCASE

This section provides lower gearcase removal/installation, rebuilding and resealing procedures for all gearcases used on 2-70 hp models. Jet drive units are covered in a separate section at the end of this chapter.

The lower gearcase can be removed from the outboard motor without removing the entire outboard from the boat. Exploded illustrations of each lower gearcase are located in the appropriate *Disassembly* section and are helpful references for many service procedures

This chapter is arranged in a normal disassembly/assembly sequence. If only a partial repair is required, follow the procedure(s) to the point that the faulty parts can be replaced, then reassemble the unit.

Table 1 lists the factory gear ratio and approximate lubricant capacity for each model, **Tables 2-4** list all torque values, **Table 5** lists all gearcase specifications and **Tables 6-8** list all manufacturer recommended tools. All Tables are located at the end of the chapter.

Make sure that the work bench, work station, gearcase stand or holding fixture is of sufficient capacity to support the size and weight of the gearcase. This is especially important when working on larger engines.

GEARCASE OPERATION

A drive shaft transfers engine torque from the engine crankshaft to the lower gearcase. A pinion (drive) gear on the drive shaft is in constant mesh with the forward and reverse (driven) gears in the lower gearcase housing. These gears are bevel cut to change the vertical power flow into the horizontal flow required by the propeller shaft. All models (except the 28 Special) use spiral bevel gears for smooth, quiet operation.

The 2 and 3.3 hp gearcase has only a pinion and forward gear. The propeller shaft and forward gear are permanently joined during the manufacturing process. This is a direct drive gearcase. Anytime the engine is cranked or running, the propeller shaft will be turning. Reverse thrust is achieved by rotating the outboard motor 360° using the tiller handle.

The 3, 3.5 and 4 hp (excluding 4 Deluxe) gearcase also has only a pinion and forward gear, but the propeller shaft is connected to the propshaft by a spiral (spring) clutch that allows NEUTRAL and FORWARD operation. There is no reverse. Reverse thrust is achieved by rotating the engine 360° using the tiller handle.

The 1995 and 1996 (EO and EU) 6 and 8 hp gearcase has full shifting capability but does not use a sliding clutch. A shift plunger, actuated by a shift cam (via a rotating shift shaft) forces detent balls into notches machined in the forward and reverse gear inner hubs. There are two detent balls for each gear.

All other models have full shifting capability. A sliding clutch (called a clutch dog), splined to the propeller shaft and actuated by a shift plunger and shift bellcrank (via a vertically traveling shift shaft), directly engages lugs on the face of forward and reverse gears. **Figure 1** shows the simplified arrangement of internal components in such a gearcase.

Since all shifting gearcases use direct mechanical means of shifting the gearcase, they must only be shifted at idle speed. Shifting at higher speeds will cause severe shock loads to the gears and shift system components, resulting in premature failure.

All lower gearcases incorporate a water pump to supply cooling water to the power head. The water pump on 2 and 3.3 hp models is driven by the propeller shaft and can be serviced without removing the gearcase from the engine. On all other models, the water pump is driven by the drive shaft, and the gearcase must be removed from the drive shaft housing to service the water pump. Water pump removal and installation procedures are covered in this chapter.

All 40-70 hp gearcases use a precisely located (shimmed) pinion gear. The pinion gear is precisely located (vertically positioned) in the gear housing by the use of very thin metal spacers, called shims. The forward and reverse gears are located during the manufacturing process and are properly positioned as long as the gearcase is correctly assembled and the internal parts are not excessively worn.

It is good practice to confirm the correct shim adjustment anytime the drive shaft and pinion gear are removed from the gearcase. If any drive shaft components (drive shaft, bearing housing, thrust washer(s), thrust bearing and/or pinion gear), are replaced, the shim adjustment procedure must be performed to prevent gearcase failure.

Shim fixture part No. 393185 and the appropriate gauge bar and adapter bushing are required to determine the correct shim thickness. No measurements or inspections are available to check shim adjustment after gearcase assembly.

For reference, gear lash is the measurement of the clearance between a tooth on the pinion and two teeth on the forward or reverse gear. This clearance is also referred to as gear backlash. If the pinion gear is positioned too high in the gearcase, gear lash will be excessive. Excessive lash will cause excessive gear noise and a reduction in gear

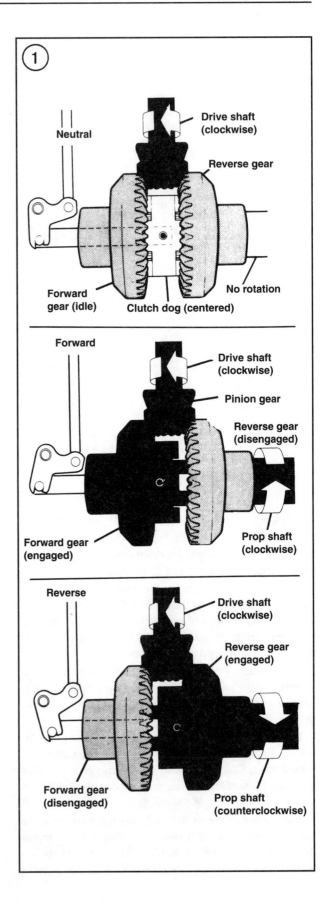

strength and durability. If the pinion gear is positioned too low in the gearcase, gear lash will be insufficient. If the gears are too close to maintain a film of lubricant between the gears, the gearcase is certain to fail. Insufficient gear lash will be compounded as the gearcase warms during operation.

GEAR RATIO

The gear ratio refers to the amount of gear reduction between the crankshaft and the propeller. Gear ratios range from as low as 2.42:1 to as high as 1.75:1. A gear ratio of 2.42:1 means that the crankshaft turns 2.42 times for every 1 turn of the propeller shaft. Higher number ratios are easier for the engine to turn. **Table 1** lists the factory gear ratio and tooth count for all models.

If the gear ratio is suspected of being incorrect, the gear ratio can be determined by two different methods. The first method does not require removing the gearcase. Mark the flywheel and a propeller blade for counting purposes. Manually shift the gearcase into FORWARD gear. While counting, turn the flywheel in the normal direction of rotation (clockwise as viewed from the top of the flywheel) until the propeller shaft makes exactly ten turns. Divide the number of flywheel rotations counted by ten and compare the result with the list of gear ratios in **Table 1**. Round the result to the nearest ratio listed.

The second method of determining gear ratio involves counting the actual number of teeth on the gears. This method requires at least partial disassembly of the gearcase. To determine the gear ratio, divide the driven gear tooth count (forward or reverse gear) by the drive gear tooth count (pinion or drive shaft gear).

For example, on a gearcase with a 13:28 (drive-to-driven) tooth count, divide 28 (driven) by 13 (drive) = 2.15 ratio.

It is very important that the engine be operated with the factory recommended gear ratio. Running the engine with an incorrect gear ratio can cause poor performance, poor fuel economy and make it difficult or impossible to obtain the correct wide-open speed.

Regardless of the gear ratio used, it is imperative that the engine operate within the recommended speed range at wide-open throttle. Change the propeller(s) pitch and diameter as necessary to adjust engine speed. Increasing the pitch or diameter increases the load on the engine and will reduce the wide-open throttle speed. Decreasing the pitch or diameter reduces the load on the engine and will increase the wide-open throttle speed. Use an accurate shop tachometer for wide-open throttle speed verification.

SERVICE PRECAUTIONS

When working on a gearcase, there are several good procedures to keep in mind that will make your work easier, faster and more accurate.

1. Never use elastic locknuts more than twice. It is a good practice to replace such nuts each time they are removed. Never use an elastic locknut that can be turned by hand (without the aid of a wrench).

2. Use special tools where noted. The use of makeshift tools can damage components and cause serious personal injury.

3. Use the appropriate fixtures to hold the gearcase housing whenever possible. A vise with protective jaws must be used to hold smaller housings or individual components. If protective jaws are not available, insert blocks of wood or similar padding on each side of the housing or component before clamping.

4. Remove and install pressed-on parts with an appropriate mandrel, support and press. Do not attempt to pry or hammer press-fit components on or off.

5. Refer to **Tables 3-6** for torque values and the Quick Reference Data section for standard torque values. Proper torque is essential to ensure long life and satisfactory service from gearcase components.

6. To help reduce corrosion, especially in saltwater areas, apply OMC Gasket Sealing Compound to all external surfaces of bearing carriers, housing mating surfaces and fasteners when no other sealant, adhesive or lubricant is recommended. Do not apply sealing compound where it can get into gears or bearings.

7. Replace all O-rings, seals and gaskets during assembly.

8. All 40-70 hp gearcases use a precision-shimmed pinion gear. Tag all shims with the thickness of each shim as it is removed from the gearcase. Shims are reusable as long as they are not physically damaged or corroded. Follow shimming instructions closely and carefully. The shims control the pinion gear's location. Incorrectly shimming a gearcase can cause failure of the gearcase assembly.

9. Work in an area of good lighting with sufficient space for component storage. Keep an ample number of clean containers available for parts storage. When not being worked on, cover parts and assemblies with clean shop towels or plastic bags.

CAUTION
*Metric **and/or** U.S. standard fasteners may be used on OMC gearcases. Always match a replacement fastener to the original. Do not run a tap or thread chaser into a hole (or over a bolt) without first verifying the thread size and pitch. Check all threaded holes for Heli-Coil stainless steel locking thread inserts. Never run a tap or thread chaser into*

9

a Heli-Coil equipped hole. Heli-Coil inserts are replaceable, if damaged.

10. Whenever a threadlocking adhesive is called for, always clean the surface to be sealed (or threads to be secured) with OMC Locquic Primer. Locquic Primer cleans and primes the surface and ensures a quick secure bond by leaving a thin film of catalyst on the surface (or threads). The primer must be allowed to air dry, as blow drying will remove the catalyst.

CORROSION CONTROL

Sacrificial zinc or aluminum anodes must have good electrical continuity to ground or they will not function. Anodes must not be painted or coated with any material. OMC Genuine Parts offers accessory anode kits for additional corrosion protection. See your Evinrude/Johnson dealership.

Refer to the exploded illustrations of each lower gearcase in the appropriate *Disassembly* section for exact anode location(s).

Sacrificial Anode Visual Inspection

Check for loose mounting hardware and make sure that the anodes are not painted. Also, check the amount of deterioration present. Replace anodes if they are 2/3 their original size (1/3 gone). Test the electrical continuity of each anode after installation as described in the next section.

Sacrificial Anode Electrical Testing

This test requires an ohmmeter.
1. Calibrate the ohmmeter on the lowest scale available.
2. Connect one ohmmeter lead to the anode. Connect the other ohmmeter lead to a good ground point on the gearcase. The meter must indicate a very low reading (zero or very near zero).
3. If the reading is not zero, remove the anode and clean the mounting surfaces of the anode, gearcase and mounting hardware. Reinstall the anode and retest continuity.
4. Test the continuity of the gearcase to the engine and negative battery post by connecting one ohmmeter lead to the negative battery cable and the other ohmmeter lead to a good ground point on the lower gearcase. The meter must indicate a very low reading (zero or very near zero).
5. If the reading is not zero, check the electrical continuity of the lower gearcase to the drive shaft housing, the drive shaft housing to the power head, and the power head to the negative battery terminal. Check for loose mounting hardware, broken or missing ground straps or excessive corro-

sion. Repair as necessary to establish a good electrical ground path.

GEARCASE LUBRICATION

To ensure maximum performance and durability, the gearcase requires periodic lubrication. The gearcase lubricant must be changed every 100 hours of operation or once each season.

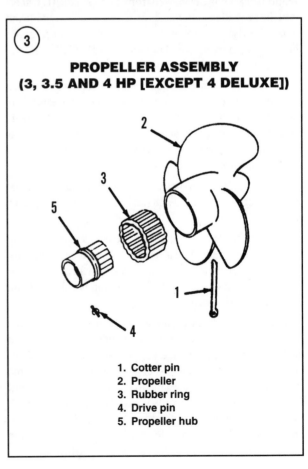

**PROPELLER ASSEMBLY
(3, 3.5 AND 4 HP [EXCEPT 4 DELUXE])**

1. Cotter pin
2. Propeller
3. Rubber ring
4. Drive pin
5. Propeller hub

The recommended lubricant for all models is OMC Ultra HPF Gear Lube (or equivalent). If the gearcase is subjected to severe duty, it may be necessary to change the lubricant more frequently.

Refer to Chapter Four for the correct procedure for changing the lower gearcase lubricant.

NEUTRAL START ADJUSTMENT (TILLER HANDLE MODELS)

The 9.9 and 15 hp and 40-70 hp tiller handle models are equipped with a neutral safety mechanical linkage that prevents the operator from depressing the starter button unless the shift linkage is in NEUTRAL. Adjustment procedures are covered in the appropriate *Gearcase Removal/Installation* section.

PROPELLER

The propellers used on 4 Deluxe and 6-70 hp models incorporates a shock-absorbing rubber hub. The hub is designed to absorb the shock loads produced from shifting

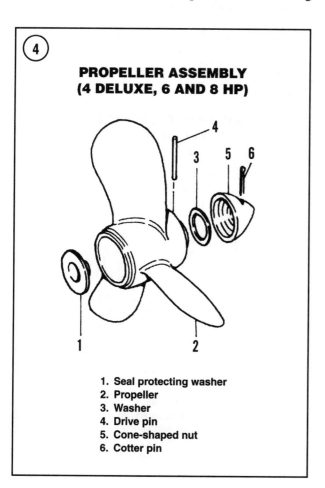

PROPELLER ASSEMBLY (4 DELUXE, 6 AND 8 HP)

1. Seal protecting washer
2. Propeller
3. Washer
4. Drive pin
5. Cone-shaped nut
6. Cotter pin

the unit into gear. If a hub fails, it will generally slip at higher throttle settings but will still allow the boater to return to port at reduced throttle. The defective rubber hub can be removed and a new hub pressed into the propeller (generally at a propeller repair station), or the propeller can be replaced.

The propellers used on 3 and 4 hp (except 4 Deluxe) models incorporate a separate inner hub, rubber shock absorbing sleeve and plastic propeller. Each part is individually replaceable without special tools or equipment.

The propellers on 2 and 3.3 models are solid plastic and do not feature a shock-absorbing hub.

The outboard motors covered in this manual use the following variations of propeller attachment:

1. *2 and 3.3 hp models*—These models use a propeller drive pin that engages notches in the propeller hub with a hole in the propeller shaft (**Figure 2**). The drive pin is secured in place by the propeller, which is secured by a cotter pin. The drive pin is designed to absorb the propeller thrust and shearing loads.

2. *3, 3.5 and 4 hp models (excluding 4 Deluxe)*—These models use a separate propeller hub that is engaged with the propeller shaft by a drive pin. A ribbed, rubber, shock-absorbing ring fits over the propeller hub, locking the drive pin in place. The propeller fits over the rubber ring (engaging the ribs) and is secured in place by a cotter pin. The hub, drive pin and rubber ring absorb all of the propeller's thrust and shearing loads. See **Figure 3**.

3. *4 Deluxe, 6 and 8 hp models*—These models use a propeller drive pin that engages holes in the rear of the propeller's hub with a hole in the propeller shaft. The drive pin is secured in place by a cone-shaped nut (not threaded), which is secured by a cotter pin. A washer is also located between the rear of the hub and the drive pin. The drive pin is designed to absorb the propeller thrust and shearing loads. A special washer, installed between the propeller and the gearcase, protects the seal from fish line and other debris. See **Figure 4**.

4. *28 Special models*—These models use propellers that push directly against a shoulder on the propeller shaft. There is no thrust washer or drive pin. The propeller is retained by a threaded, cone nut. The nut is secured by a cotter pin. The engine's power is transmitted through splines in the shaft and hub. The propeller's thrust is transmitted from the hub to a shoulder on the shaft.

5. *9.9-70 hp models (except 28 Special)*—These models use propellers that push against a thrust washer that rides against a tapered (or stepped) shoulder on the propeller shaft. The propellers are retained by a splined washer (plastic or brass) and a castellated nut. The castellated nut is secured by a cotter pin. Splines in the propeller shaft transmit the engine's power to the propeller, while the

9

thrust washer absorbs all thrust and transfers it to the shaft. See **Figure 5**, typical.

Removal/Installation

Inspect the propeller for wear, damage, cracks, missing pieces and cavitation damage (burning or erosion on the blade face). See A, **Figure 6**. If the propeller is driven by a drive pin, inspect the drive pin hole (or grooves) for wear or elongation. If the propeller is driven by splines (B, **Figure 6**), inspect the splines for wear or damage. If the splines are packed with dried grease or other debris, be sure to clean the splines before installing the propeller. If propeller damage is noted, replace the propeller or have it rebuilt at a competent propeller rebuild station. Do not operate an engine with a damaged propeller, as the resulting vibration will damage the gearcase and cause fasteners all over the engine to vibrate loose.

> *WARNING*
> *To prevent accidental engine starting during propeller service, disconnect and ground all spark plug leads to the power head. Remove the ignition key and safety lanyard from models so equipped.*

2 and 3.3 hp

1. Remove and discard the cotter pin securing the propeller to the propeller shaft. Slide the propeller off of the shaft.
2. Remove the drive pin (**Figure 2**) from the propeller shaft. Inspect the pin for damage and discard it if it is distorted, bent or worn.
3. Clean the propeller shaft and propeller hub thoroughly. Inspect the pin engagement hole for elongation, wear or cracks. Rotate the propeller shaft to check for a bent propeller shaft. Replace any damaged parts.
4. Liberally coat the propeller shaft and propeller hub bore with OMC Triple Guard Grease.
5. Install the drive pin into the propeller shaft hole, then slide the propeller over the propeller shaft and seat it against the drive pin.
6. Secure the propeller with a new stainless steel cotter pin. Bend both prongs of the cotter pin for a secure attachment.

3, 3.5 and 4 hp (except 4 Deluxe)

Refer to **Figure 3** for this procedure.
1. Remove and discard the cotter pin securing the propeller to the propeller shaft. Slide the propeller off of the shaft.

2. Remove the rubber ring (3, **Figure 3**) from the propeller drive hub. Then remove the drive pin from the propeller shaft. Inspect the pin for damage and discard it if it is distorted, bent or worn.
3. Slide the propeller hub from the propeller shaft.
4. Clean the propeller shaft and propeller hub thoroughly. Inspect the pin engagement hole for elongation, wear or cracks. Rotate the propeller shaft to check for a bent propeller shaft. Replace any damaged parts.
5. Liberally coat the propeller shaft and propeller hub bore with OMC Triple Guard Grease.
6. Slide the propeller hub over the propeller shaft and align the drive pin holes. Install the drive pin into the propeller shaft hole, then slide the rubber ring over the propeller hub.
7. Slide the propeller over the propeller shaft and seat it over the rubber ring and propeller hub.
8. Secure the propeller with a new stainless steel cotter pin. Bend both prongs of the cotter pin for a secure attachment.

4 Deluxe, 6 and 8 hp

Refer to **Figure 4** for this procedure.

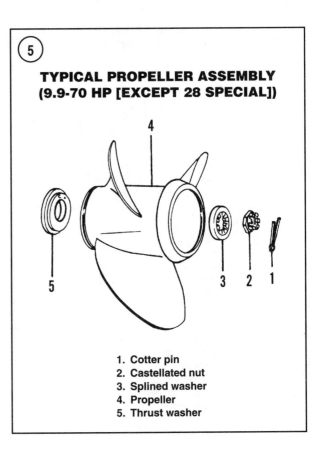

⑤

TYPICAL PROPELLER ASSEMBLY (9.9-70 HP [EXCEPT 28 SPECIAL])

1. Cotter pin
2. Castellated nut
3. Splined washer
4. Propeller
5. Thrust washer

1. Remove and discard the cotter pin securing the cone nut to the propeller shaft. Slide the cone nut off of the shaft.

2. Remove the drive pin from the propeller shaft. Inspect the pin for damage and discard it if it is distorted, bent or worn.

3. Remove the washer (3, **Figure 4**) from the rear of the propeller hub, then slide the propeller from the propeller shaft.

NOTE
*The seal protecting washer (1, **Figure 4**) is not normally removed during propeller re-*

moval unless it is loose or worn. If so, remove and discard the washer, then press a new washer (with the stepped side facing out) over the propshaft and into position with hand pressure.

4. Clean the propeller shaft and propeller hub thoroughly. Inspect the pin engagement hole for elongation, wear or cracks. Rotate the propeller shaft to check for a bent propeller shaft. Replace any damaged parts.

5. Liberally coat the propeller shaft and propeller hub bore with OMC Triple Guard Grease.

6. Slide the propeller hub over the propeller shaft and align the drive pin holes. Install the washer (3, **Figure 4**), then install the drive pin through the hub and propeller shaft.

7. Position the coned nut over the propshaft. Secure the nut with a new stainless steel cotter pin. Bend both prongs of the cotter pin for a secure attachment.

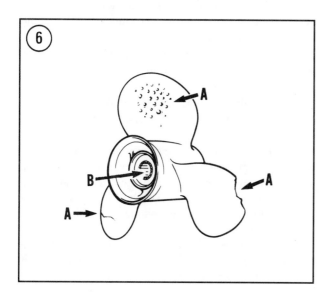

28 Special

1. Remove and discard the cotter pin from the cone-shaped propeller nut.

2. Place a block of wood between the propeller blades and antiventilation plate to prevent the propeller from turning. See **Figure 7**, typical.

3. Remove the cone-shaped propeller nut. Then slide the propeller from the propeller shaft.

4. Clean the propeller shaft thoroughly. Inspect the propeller shaft for cracks, wear or damage. Rotate the propeller shaft to check for a bent propeller shaft. Replace any damaged parts.

5. Lubricate the propeller shaft liberally with OMC Triple Guard Grease.

6. Slide the propeller onto the propeller shaft. Align the splines and seat the propeller against the shaft's shoulder.

7. Install the propeller nut. Place a block of wood between a propeller blade and the antiventilation plate (**Figure 7**) to prevent the propeller from turning.

8. Tighten the nut to 120 in.-lb. (13.6 N•m). Then continue tightening the nut until the cotter pin hole is aligned. Do not tighten the nut any more than necessary to align the holes.

9. Secure the nut with a new stainless steel cotter pin. Bend both prongs of the cotter pin for a secure attachment.

9.9-70 hp (except 28 Special)

Refer to **Figure 5** for this procedure.

1. Remove and discard the cotter pin from the propeller nut.

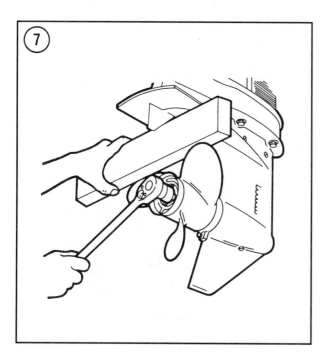

9

2. Place a block of wood between the propeller blades and antiventilation plate to prevent the propeller from turning. See **Figure 7**, typical.

3. Remove the propeller nut and splined washer. Then slide the propeller from the propeller shaft.

4. Remove the thrust washer.

5. Clean the propeller shaft thoroughly. Inspect the propeller shaft for cracks, wear or damage. Rotate the propeller shaft to check for a bent propeller shaft. Inspect the propeller thrust washer and splined washer for wear or damage. Replace any damaged parts.

6. Lubricate the propeller shaft liberally with OMC Triple Guard Grease.

7A. *9.9-35 hp*—Slide the propeller thrust washer onto the propeller shaft. The fish line trap's groove and the larger diameter of the thrust washer must face the gearcase. Align the splines and slide the propeller over the shaft and seat it against the thrust washer.

7B. *40-70 hp*—Position the thrust washer in the propeller hub. Make sure the washer fits into the hub. Slide the assembly over the propeller shaft, align the splines and seat the assembly against the shaft's shoulder.

8. Install the splined washer (3, **Figure 5**). Make sure the splines are aligned and engaged to the shaft.

9. Install the propeller nut. Place a block of wood between a propeller blade and the antiventilation plate (**Figure 7**) to prevent the propeller from turning.

10. Tighten the nut to 120 in.-lb. (13.6 N•m). Then continue tightening the nut until the cotter pin hole is aligned with the next slot in the nut. Do not tighten the nut any more than necessary to align the cotter pin hole.

11. Secure the nut with a new stainless steel cotter pin. Bend both prongs of the cotter pin for a secure attachment.

TRIM TAB ADJUSTMENT

Adjust the trim tab (on models so equipped) so the steering wheel will turn with equal ease in each direction at the normal cruising speed and trim angle. The trim tab can only provide neutral steering effort for the speed and trim angle for which it was set. Trimming the outboard out (up) or in (down) or changing engine speed will change the torque load on the propeller and the resultant steering effort.

If adjustment is desired, run the boat at the speed and trim angle desired. If the boat turns more easily to starboard than port, loosen the trim tab retaining screw and move the tab's trailing edge slightly to starboard. If the boat turns more easily to port, move the tab slightly to port. Tighten the trim tab retaining screw to specification (**Tables 3-5**).

GEARCASE REMOVAL/INSTALLATION

Exploded views of each gearcase are located in the appropriate *Disassembly* section of this chapter. Refer to these views as necessary during the removal and installation procedure.

2 and 3.3 hp Models

The water pump can be serviced without gear housing removal on these models. Refer to *Water Pump* in this chapter.

The square drive shaft runs inside of a removable support tube in the drive shaft housing. The tube must fit into the lower crankshaft seal.

1. Disconnect and ground the spark plug lead to the power head to prevent accidental starting.

2. Close the fuel shutoff valve.

3. Tilt the outboard to the fully UP position.

4. Remove the propeller as described previously in this chapter.

5. Remove the upper mounting screw, lockwasher and flat washer from the leading edge of the gearcase. Remove the lower mounting screw, lockwasher and flat washer from directly above the propeller. Then pull the gear housing from the drive shaft housing and place the gearcase on a clean workbench.

6. If the square drive shaft and support tube did not come out with the gearcase, remove the drive shaft and support tube from the drive shaft housing.

7. Remove and discard the water tube seal from the gearcase.

8. To install the gearcase, begin by tilting the outboard to the fully UP position.

9. Apply OMC Moly Lube to the outside diameter of the drive shaft support tube (**Figure 8**), then insert the tube into

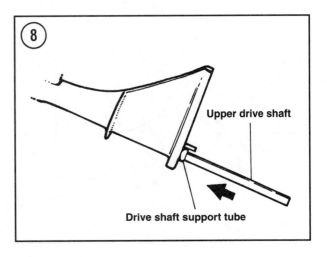

Upper drive shaft

Drive shaft support tube

the drive shaft housing until seated in the lower crankshaft seal.

10. Apply OMC Moly Lube to the inside diameter (both ends) of the square (upper) drive shaft. Insert the shaft into the tube (**Figure 8**), then engage the shaft to the crankshaft.

11. Glue a new water tube seal to the lower gearcase with OMC Adhesive M sealant. Then apply OMC Triple Guard Grease to the inside diameter of the water tube seal.

12. Apply OMC Nut Lock threadlocking adhesive to the threads of the two gear housing mounting screws.

13. Install the gear housing, making sure the water tube enters the water tube grommet and the lower drive shaft engages the square (upper) drive shaft. Rotate the propeller shaft clockwise as necessary to align the drive shafts.

14. Install the gear housing mounting screws, lockwashers and flat washers. Evenly tighten both screws to 89-115 in.-lb. (10.1-13.0 N•m).

15. Install the propeller as described in this chapter.

16. Check the lubricant level or refill the gearcase with the recommended lubricant as described in Chapter Four.

17. Reconnect the spark plug lead.

3, 3.5 and 4 hp (Except 4 Deluxe) Models

1. Disconnect and ground the spark plug leads to the power head to prevent accidental starting.

2. Remove the propeller (and hub) as described in this chapter.

3. Remove the two gearcase mounting screws. The screws are located under the antiventilation plate, at the front and rear of the gearcase strut.

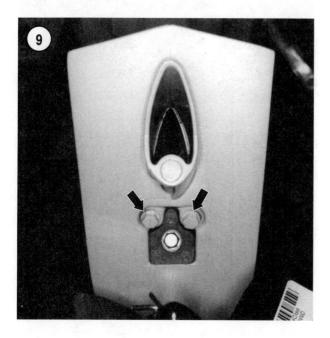

4. Carefully pull the gearcase straight down and away from the drive shaft housing. The shift shaft and water tube will stay in the drive shaft housing. Place the gearcase on a clean workbench or mount it in a suitable holding fixture.

5. Remove and discard the water tube grommet from the water pump housing.

6. To install the gearcase, begin by installing a new water tube grommet into the water pump housing. Make sure the raised tabs align with the holes in the water pump housing.

> *CAUTION*
> *Do not apply lubricant to the top of the drive shaft in the next step. Excess lubricant between the top of the drive shaft and the engine crankshaft can create a hydraulic lock, preventing the drive shaft from fully engaging the crankshaft.*

7. Clean the drive shaft splines as necessary, then coat the splines with OMC Moly Lube.

8. Apply OMC Triple Guard Grease to the inside diameter of the water tube seal. Then apply OMC Nut Lock threadlocking adhesive to the threads of the two gear housing mounting screws.

9. Install the gearcase to the drive shaft housing, guiding the water tube and shift shaft into place. Rotate the flywheel clockwise (as necessary) to align the crankshaft and drive shaft splines. When all components are correctly aligned, seat the gearcase to the drive shaft housing.

10. Install the two gearcase mounting screws and evenly tighten them to 60-84 in.-lb. (6.8-9.5 N•m).

11. Install the propeller as described in this chapter.

12. Check the lubricant level or refill the gearcase with the recommended lubricant as described in Chapter Four.

13. Reconnect the spark plug leads to the spark plugs.

4 Deluxe, 6 and 8 hp Models

If the engine is a long shaft (or equipped with an accessory 5 in. extension), it is not necessary to remove the extension housing from the drive shaft housing for the following procedure.

1. Disconnect and ground the spark plug leads to the power head to prevent accidental starting.

2. Remove the propeller (and hub) as described in this chapter.

3. While rotating the propeller shaft, move the shift lever into FORWARD gear.

4. Remove the three gearcase mounting screws. Two of the screws are located under the antiventilation plate, just in front of the exhaust snout (next to the anode) as shown in **Figure 9**. The final screw is located at the very front of

9

the gearcase, just below the lower motor mounts as shown in **Figure 10**.

> *NOTE*
> *The water tube will stay in the exhaust housing, unless an accessory extension kit has been installed. If so equipped, a water tube extension may remain in the extension housing or come out with the water pump. Models factory-equipped with an extension (long shaft models) use a one-piece, extended water tube.*

5. Carefully pull the gearcase straight down and away from the drive shaft housing. Place the gearcase on a clean workbench or mount it in a suitable holding fixture.

6. Remove and discard the water tube grommet from the water pump housing.

7. To install the gearcase, begin by installing a new water tube grommet into the water pump housing. Make sure the raised tabs align with the holes in the water pump housing. If equipped with a water tube extension, install the extension tube into the extension housing using a new seal.

> *CAUTION*
> *Do not apply lubricant to the top of the drive shaft in the next step. Excess lubricant between the top of the drive shaft and the engine crankshaft can create a hydraulic lock, preventing the drive shaft from fully engaging the crankshaft.*

8. Clean the drive shaft splines as necessary, then coat the splines with OMC Moly Lube.

9. Apply OMC Triple Guard Grease to the inside diameter of the water tube seal. Then apply OMC Nut Lock thread-locking adhesive to the threads of the three gearcase mounting screws.

10. Position the engine's shift lever in the FORWARD gear position. Then rotate the shift shaft (on the gearcase) fully clockwise to engage FORWARD gear, while rotating the propeller shaft to ensure gear engagement.

11. Position the gearcase under the drive shaft housing. Guide the shift shaft through the drive shaft housing grommet and into the steering tube. Be prepared to guide the water tube into the water pump's grommet.

> *CAUTION*
> *Do not rotate the flywheel counterclockwise in the next step or the water pump impeller will be damaged.*

12. Push the gearcase toward the drive shaft housing while rotating the flywheel clockwise (as required) to align the drive shaft and crankshaft splines.

> *NOTE*
> *If gearcase and drive shaft housing do not mate in the next step, the two shift shaft may not have engaged the shift linkage at the top of the drive shaft housing. Wiggle the shift lever to help align the shafts. If this does not help, remove the gearcase and make sure the engine shift linkage and the gearcase are in the full FORWARD gear position.*

13. Make sure the water tube is seated in the water pump seal and the shift shaft is aligned with the shaft linkage, then seat the gearcase against the drive shaft housing.

14. Install the gearcase mounting screws. Tighten the two rear (lower) screws to 60-84 in.-lb. (6.8-9.5 N•m) and the front (upper) screw to 120-144 in.-lb. (13.6-16.3 N•m).

15. Install the propeller as described in this chapter.

16. Check the lubricant level or refill the gearcase with the recommended lubricant as described in Chapter Four.

17. Reconnect the spark plug leads to the spark plugs.

9.9 and 15 hp Models

If the engine is a long shaft (or equipped with an accessory 5 in. extension), it is not necessary to remove the

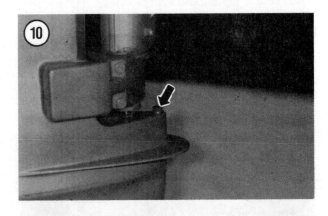

extension housing from the drive shaft housing for the following procedures.

1. Disconnect and ground the spark plug leads to the power head to prevent accidental starting.

2. Remove the propeller as described in this chapter.

3. While rotating the propeller shaft, move the shift lever to the REVERSE gear position.

4. Remove the gearcase mounting screws. There are three screws on each side of the gearcase as shown in **Figure 11**.

5. Pull the gearcase far enough from the drive shaft housing to expose the shift shaft connector (**Figure 12**). Remove the connector's *upper* screw (and washer).

NOTE
The water tube will stay in the drive shaft housing, unless an accessory extension kit has been installed. If so equipped, a water tube extension may remain in the extension housing or come out with the water pump. Models factory-equipped with an extension (long shaft models) use a one-piece, extended water tube.

6. Carefully pull the gearcase straight down and away from the drive shaft housing. Place the gearcase on a clean workbench or mount it in a suitable holding fixture.

7. Remove and discard the water tube grommet from the water pump housing.

8. To install the gearcase, begin by installing a new water tube grommet into the water pump housing. Make sure the raised tabs align with the holes in the water pump housing.

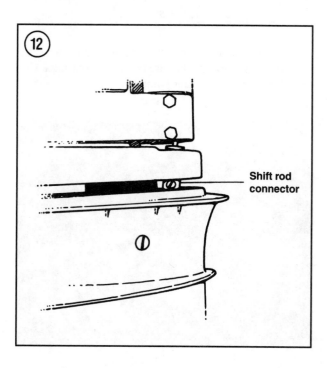

Shift rod connector

If equipped with a water tube extension, install the extension tube into the extension housing using a new seal.

CAUTION
Do not apply lubricant to the top of the drive shaft in the next step. Excess lubricant between the top of the drive shaft and the engine crankshaft can create a hydraulic lock, preventing the drive shaft from fully engaging the crankshaft.

9. Clean the drive shaft splines as necessary, then coat the splines with OMC Moly Lube.

10. Apply OMC Triple Guard Grease to the inside diameter of the water tube seal. Apply OMC Nut Lock thread-locking adhesive to the threads of the gearcase mounting screws. Apply OMC Gasket Sealing Compound to the threads of the shift shaft connector screw.

11. Move the engine's shift lever to the REVERSE gear position. Then pull the shift shaft on the gearcase upward while rotating the propeller shaft to ensure full gear engagement.

12. Position the gearcase under the drive shaft housing. Be prepared to guide the water tube into the water pump's grommet.

13. Push the gearcase toward the drive shaft housing until the shift shaft connector mates with the upper shift shaft. Align the groove in the upper shift shaft with the hole in the connector, then install the screw and washer. Tighten the screw to 60-84 in.-lb. (6.8-9.5 N•m).

CAUTION
Do not rotate the flywheel counterclockwise in the next step or the water pump impeller will be damaged.

14. Continue pushing the gearcase toward the drive shaft housing, while rotating the flywheel clockwise (as required) to align the drive shaft and crankshaft splines. Align the water tube with the water pump grommet, then seat the gearcase against the drive shaft housing.

15. Install the gearcase mounting screws. Evenly tighten the screws to 96-120 in.-lb. (10.9-13.6 N•m).

16. *Tiller handle models*—Adjust the neutral safety mechanical linkage as described in the following section.

17. Install the propeller as described in this chapter.

18. Check the lubricant level or refill the gearcase with the recommended lubricant as described in Chapter Four.

19. Reconnect the spark plug leads to the spark plugs.

Neutral safety mechanical linkage adjustment

This procedure applies only to 9.9 and 15 hp tiller handle electric start models. This procedure ensures that the electric starter motor can only be engaged when the shift linkage is in the NEUTRAL position.

1. Disconnect and ground the spark plug leads to the power head to prevent accidental starting.

2. Remove the propeller to prevent accidental contact with a rotating propeller.

3. Move the engine shift lever to the NEUTRAL position. Rotate the propeller shaft and verify that the gearcase is in NEUTRAL.

4. Loosen the slotted head screw (and locknut) securing the starter button and bracket to the shift lever (shift handle).

5. Move the starter button bracket as necessary to center the starter button over the starter switch's recess.

6. While holding the bracket in position, tighten the screw (and locknut) securely.

7. Make sure you are clear of the propeller shaft and flywheel. Then depress the starter button momentarily (with the shift linkage still in the NEUTRAL position). The electric starter must engage.

8. While rotating the propeller shaft, move the engine shift lever to the FORWARD position. Make sure you are clear of the propeller shaft and flywheel. Then depress the starter button momentarily. The electric starter must not engage.

9. While rotating the propeller shaft, move the engine shift lever to the REVERSE position. Make sure you are clear of the propeller shaft and flywheel. Then depress the starter button momentarily. The electric starter must not engage.

10. Readjust the starter button and bracket as necessary.

11. When finished, install the propeller and reconnect the spark plug leads.

20-35 hp Models
(Except 28 Special)

If the engine is equipped with an accessory 5 in. extension, it is not necessary to remove the extension housing from the drive shaft housing for the following procedures.

1. Disconnect and ground the spark plug leads to the power head to prevent accidental starting.

2. Remove the propeller as described previously in this chapter.

3. Mark the position of the trim tab with a grease pencil (or china marker). Remove the screw securing the trim tab. Then remove the trim tab.

4. Remove the two screws securing the water intake screen halves to each other and to the gearcase. Remove the screen halves.

5. Using the appropriate open-end wrenches, hold the lower shift shaft stationary and unscrew the upper shift shaft's retaining nut. See **Figure 13**. Remove the tapered plastic keeper from the upper shift shaft, then slide the retaining nut from the upper shift shaft.

6A. *Two-cylinder models*—Remove the four screws and one nut (and washer) securing the gearcase to the drive shaft housing. The nut (and washer) are located at the very front of the gearcase, just below the lower motor mounts, similar to **Figure 10**. The four screws (2 each side) are located toward the rear of the gearcase, above the anti-ventilation plate, similar to those shown in **Figure 11**.

6B. *Three-cylinder models*—Remove the screws (each side) securing the gearcase to the drive shaft housing. See **Figure 11**, typical.

> *NOTE*
> *On two-cylinder models, the water tube and drive shaft spacer tube may stay in the drive shaft housing or come out with the water pump. Three-cylinder models do not use these components.*

7. Carefully pull the gearcase straight down and away from the drive shaft housing. Place the gearcase on a clean workbench or mount it in a suitable holding fixture.

8. *Two-cylinder models*—Remove the water tube from the water pump or drive shaft housing. Locate and secure the washer that sits at the very top of the tube. Then pull the drive shaft spacer tube from the water pump or drive shaft housing.

9A. *Two-cylinder models*—Remove and discard the water tube grommet from the water pump housing and the two O-rings from the drive shaft spacer tube.

9B. *Three-cylinder models*—Remove and discard the grommet assembly from the top of the water pump housing.

10A. *Two-cylinder models*—To install the gearcase, proceed as follows:

   a. Install a new water tube grommet into the water pump housing. Make sure the raised tabs align with the holes in the water pump housing.

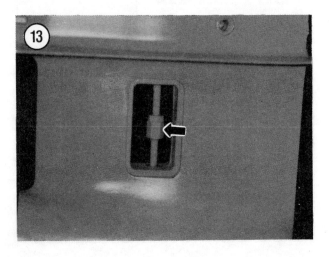

b. Grease the upper (straight) end of the water tube, then place the washer over the end of the tube. Install the water tube into the inner exhaust housing.

c. Grease two new O-rings with OMC Triple Guard Grease. Install an O-ring in each end of the drive shaft spacer tube.

d. Install the spacer tube into its drive shaft housing bore with the with tabs facing the rear of the housing. Make sure the tube is seated in the drive shaft bore.

10B. *Three-cylinder models*—Coat the groove of a new water pump grommet assembly with OMC Adhesive M sealant. Install the grommet over the drive shaft and seat it to the water pump housing.

CAUTION
Do not apply lubricant to the top of the drive shaft in the next step. Excess lubricant between the top of the drive shaft and the engine crankshaft can create a hydraulic lock, preventing the drive shaft from fully engaging the crankshaft.

11. Clean the drive shaft splines as necessary, then coat the splines with OMC Moly Lube. Coat the lower end of the upper shift shaft with OMC Triple Guard Grease.

12. Thread the upper shift shaft retaining nut temporarily into the lower shift shaft. This step is necessary as it is not possible to install the nut over the shift shaft after the gearcase is installed.

13. Position the gearcase under the drive shaft housing. Insert the drive shaft into the spacer tube (two-cylinder models) or the cast bore (three-cylinder) models. Push the gearcase toward the drive shaft housing until the upper shift shaft can be inserted through the hole at the rear of the water pump housing. Guide the shift shaft through the hole.

CAUTION
Do not rotate the flywheel counterclockwise in the next step or the water pump impeller will be damaged.

14A. *Two-cylinder models*—Continue pushing the gearcase toward the drive shaft housing, rotating the flywheel clockwise (as required) to align the drive shaft and crankshaft splines. Align the water tube with the water pump grommet, then seat the gearcase against the drive shaft housing.

14B. *Three-cylinder models*—Continue pushing the gearcase toward the drive shaft housing, rotating the flywheel clockwise (as required) to align the drive shaft and crankshaft splines. Then seat the gearcase against the drive shaft housing. It is not necessary to align any water passages.

15. Coat the threads of the gearcase mounting hardware with OMC Gasket Sealing Compound. Install the four screws and one nut (and washer) on two-cylinder models, or the six screws (three each side) on three-cylinder models. Evenly tighten the screws (and nut) to 192-216 in.-lb. (21.7-24.4 N•m).

16. Unthread the upper shift shaft retaining nut from the lower shift shaft. Slide the nut upward onto the upper shift shaft to expose the keeper groove. Install the plastic keeper with its widest edge facing down.

17. Connect the upper and lower shift shafts together by threading the retaining nut into the lower shift shaft. Using the appropriate open-end wrenches, hold the lower shift shaft stationary and tighten the upper shift shaft retaining nut. Tighten the nut securely. See **Figure 13**.

18. Install the water inlet screens and secure them in place with two screws. Tighten the screws securely. Make sure the openings in the screens are facing the rear of the gearcase.

19A. *Two-cylinder (tiller handle) models*—Adjust the shift lever's neutral detent position as described in *Shift lever detent adjustment (two-cylinder models)* located later in this chapter. On electric start models, also adjust the neutral safety switch as described in Chapter Seven.

19B. *Three-cylinder models*—Adjust the shift lever's neutral detent position as described in the appropriate *Synch and Link* procedure in Chapter Five.

20. Install the propeller as described previously in this chapter.

21. Install the trim tab. Coat the mounting screw's threads with OMC Gasket Sealing Compound. Align the trim tab with the mark made during removal, then install and tighten the screw to 60-84 in.-lb. (6.8-9.5 N•m).

22. Check the lubricant level or refill the gearcase with the recommended lubricant as described in Chapter Four.

23. Reconnect the spark plug leads to the spark plugs.

Shift lever detent adjustment
(two-cylinder [tiller handle] models)

1. Disconnect and ground the spark plug leads to the engine to prevent accidental starting.

2. Manually move the shift linkage to the true NEUTRAL position. This is the exact center of total shift linkage travel from full FORWARD to full REVERSE gear engagements. Always rotate the propeller shaft when shifting the gearcase. Once in NEUTRAL, the propshaft must rotate freely in both directions.

3. Loosen the two neutral detent screws on the shift lever arm. The arm is located on the starboard side of the drive shaft housing, just below the lower cowl and is easily identified by its grease fitting.

4. Carefully move the shift cam (inside the lower cowl) to locate the shift lockout lever in the detent notch of the shift

9

cam. Do not disturb the shift lever arm's position (the outer lever's position).

5. Tighten the two shift lever screws to 60-84 in.-lb. (6.8-9.5 N•m).

6. Reconnect the spark plug leads when finished.

28 Special Models

This engine is factory-equipped with a 5 in. extension housing. It is not necessary to remove the extension housing from the drive shaft housing for the following procedures.

1. Disconnect and ground the spark plug leads to the power head to prevent accidental starting.

2. Remove the propeller as described in this chapter.

3. Remove the two screws securing the shift linkage access plate (**Figure 14**) to the starboard side of the drive shaft housing. Remove the cover and gasket. Discard the gasket.

4. While rotating the propeller shaft, move the shift linkage to the FORWARD gear position.

5. Remove the lower screw (and washer) from the shift shaft linkage connector. See **Figure 14**.

6. Remove the nut (and washer) securing the gearcase extended stud to the drive shaft housing. The nut (A, **Figure 15**) is located at the very rear of the drive shaft housing, just above the extension housing. Do *not* remove the extension housing screws (B, **Figure 15**).

7. Remove the screws (two each side) securing the gearcase to the extension housing. The screws are located toward the front of the gearcase, above the antiventilation plate.

NOTE
*The water tube and drive shaft spacer tube (**Figure 16**) may stay in the drive shaft housing or come out with the water pump.*

8. Carefully pull the gearcase straight down and away from the drive shaft housing. Place the gearcase on a clean workbench or mount it in a suitable holding fixture.

9. Remove the water tube from the water pump or drive shaft housing. Locate and secure the washer that sits at the very top of the tube. Then pull the drive shaft spacer tube from the water pump or drive shaft housing.

10. Remove and discard the water tube grommet from the water pump housing and the two O-rings from the drive shaft spacer tube.

11. To install the gearcase, proceed as follows:
   a. Install a new water tube grommet into the water pump housing. Make sure the raised tabs align with the holes in the water pump housing.

b. Lubricate the upper (straight) end of the water tube, then place the washer over the end of the tube. Install the water tube into the inner exhaust housing.

c. Lubricate two new O-rings with OMC Triple Guard Grease. Install an O-ring in each end of the drive shaft spacer tube.

d. Install the spacer tube over the drive shaft and seat it into the impeller housing with the tabs facing the rear of the housing.

CAUTION
Do not apply lubricant to the top of the drive shaft in the next step. Excess lubricant be-

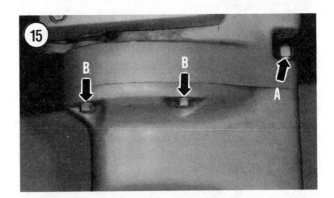

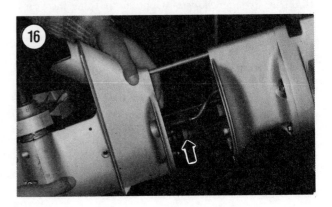

tween the top of the drive shaft and the engine crankshaft can create a hydraulic lock, preventing the drive shaft from fully engaging the crankshaft.

12. Clean the drive shaft splines as necessary, then coat the splines with OMC Moly Lube.

13. Move the engine's shift linkage to the FORWARD gear position. Then pull the shift shaft on the gearcase upward while rotating the propeller shaft to ensure full gear engagement.

14. Coat the threads of the gearcase mounting screws with OMC Gasket Sealing Compound. Coat the threads of the gearcase mounting stud with OMC Nut Lock threadlocking adhesive.

15. Position the gearcase under the drive shaft (extension) housing. Insert the drive shaft into its bore. Then push the gearcase toward the drive shaft housing until the upper

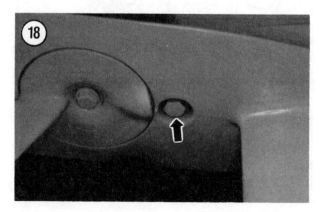

shift shaft and connector mates with the lower shift shaft. Align the connector and shift shaft as required.

> *CAUTION*
> *Do not rotate the flywheel counterclockwise in the next step or the water pump impeller will be damaged.*

16. Continue pushing the gearcase toward the drive shaft (extension) housing, rotating the flywheel clockwise (as required) to align the drive shaft and crankshaft splines. Align the water tube with the water pump grommet, then seat the gearcase against the drive shaft housing.

17. Install the four screws and one nut (and washer). Evenly tighten the screws to 192-216 in.-lb. (21.7-24.4 N•m). Tighten the nut to 45-50 ft.-lb. (61.0-67.8 N•m).

18. Align the groove in the lower shift shaft with the hole in the shift shaft connector, then install the screw (and washer). Tighten the screw to 120-144 in.-lb. (13.6-16.3 N•m). See **Figure 14**.

19. Coat a new gasket with OMC Adhesive M sealant, then install the shift connector cover using the new gasket. Coat the threads of the cover screws with OMC Gasket Sealing Compound. Install the screws and tighten them securely.

20. Install the propeller as described previously in this chapter.

21. Check the lubricant level or refill the gearcase with the recommended lubricant as described in Chapter Four.

22. Reconnect the spark plug leads to the spark plugs.

40-50 hp (Two-cylinder) Models

It is not necessary to remove the trim tab to remove and install the gearcase.

1. Disconnect and ground the spark plug leads to the power head to prevent accidental starting.

2. Remove the propeller as described in this chapter.

3. Remove the port side of the split lower cowl to gain easier access to the shift shaft screw. Split lower cowl removal is detailed in Chapter 8 under *Power Head Removal/Installation.*

4. Remove the screw securing the gearcase shift shaft to the bellcrank on the port side of the engine's shift lever shaft. The screw is located on the port side of the power head under the electric starter (and oil injection pump [if so equipped]) as shown in **Figure 17**.

5. Remove the five gearcase mounting screws as follows:

   a. Remove the recessed screw (and washer) from under the antiventilation plate, just behind the rear edge of the gearcase strut and in front of the trim tab as shown in **Figure 18**. A 5/8 in. thin wall socket is required to remove the screw.

9

b. Remove the four screws (and washers) above the antiventilation plate. Two screws are located on each side of the gearcase. See **Figure 19**.

6. Carefully pull the gearcase straight down and away from the drive shaft housing. Place the gearcase on a clean workbench or mount it in a suitable holding fixture.

7. Remove the water pump outlet and drive shaft grommets from the water pump housing. Discard the grommets.

8. To install the gearcase, begin by gluing new water pump outlet and drive shaft grommets to the water pump housing with OMC Adhesive M sealant. Use the adhesive sparingly.

CAUTION
Do not apply lubricant to the top of the drive shaft in the next step. Excess lubricant between the top of the drive shaft and the engine crankshaft can create a hydraulic lock, preventing the drive shaft from fully engaging the crankshaft.

9. Clean the drive shaft splines as necessary, then coat the splines with OMC Moly Lube. Coat the threads of the gearcase mounting screws with OMC Nut Lock thread-locking adhesive.

10. Verify the *Shift Shaft Height* as described in this chapter.

11. Position the gearcase under the drive shaft housing. Insert the drive shaft into its cast bore and the shift shaft through its grommet in the drive shaft housing and into the steering tube. Then push the gearcase toward the drive shaft housing until the drive shaft is ready to enter the crankshaft splines.

CAUTION
Do not rotate the flywheel counterclockwise in the next step or the water pump impeller will be damaged.

12. Continue pushing the gearcase toward the drive shaft housing, while rotating the flywheel clockwise (as required) to align the drive shaft and crankshaft splines. Then seat the gearcase against the drive shaft housing. It is not necessary to align any water passages.

13. Install the five gearcase mounting screws (and washers). Evenly tighten the four 3/8 in. screws (**Figure 19**) to 18-20 ft.-lb. (24.4-27.1 N•m). Then tighten the single 7/16 in. screw (**Figure 18**) to 28-30 ft.-lb. (28.0-30.7 N•m).

14. Align the shift shaft with the bellcrank, then install the retaining screw (**Figure 17**). Tighten the screw securely.

15. Adjust the shift lever's neutral detent as described in the next section.

16. *Tiller handle models*—Verify correct operation of the neutral start safety linkage as described in *Neutral Start*

Safety Linkage (40-70 hp [Tiller Handle] Models), located later in this chapter.

17. Install the propeller as described previously in this chapter.

18. Check the lubricant level or refill the gearcase with the recommended lubricant as described in Chapter Four.

19. Reconnect the spark plug leads to the spark plugs.

Shift lever detent adjustment (40-50 hp [two-cylinder] models)

1. Verify that the spark plug leads are disconnected and grounded to the power head.

2A. *Tiller handle models*—Disconnect the shift linkage from the engine shift lever.

2B. *Remote control models*—Disconnect the shift cable as described in Chapter Twelve.

3. Loosen the two neutral detent screws on the shift lever arm. See **Figure 20**.

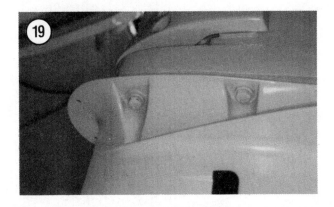

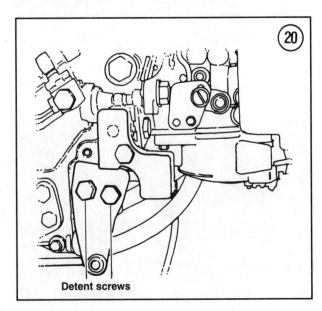

Detent screws

4. Manually move the shift lever to the true NEUTRAL position. This is the exact center of total shift linkage travel from full FORWARD to full REVERSE gear engagements. Always rotate the propeller when shifting the gearcase. Once in NEUTRAL, the propshaft must rotate freely in both directions.

5. Make sure the neutral detent cam (located behind the engine shift lever) is in its neutral detent. Then carefully locate the center of the play in the shift lever arm, being careful not to shift the lower gearcase out of its neutral detent.

6. Position the shift lever arm at the midpoint of the free play. Hold the shift lever in this position and tighten the

two neutral detent screws. Tighten the screws to 60-84 in.-lb. (6.8-9.5 N•m).

7A. *Tiller handle models*—Reconnect the shift linkage to the shift lever.

7B. *Remote control models*—Reconnect and adjust the shift cable as described in Chapter Twelve.

50-70 hp (Three-cylinder) Models

1. Disconnect and ground the spark plug leads to the power head to prevent accidental starting.

2. Remove the propeller as described previously in this chapter.

3A. *Tiller handle models*—Remove the screw securing the gearcase shift shaft to the bellcrank on the port end of the engine's shift shaft. See **Figure 21**.

3B. *Remote control models*—Remove the clip from the shift shaft. Push the shift lever toward the power head (to port) to disengage the shift shaft from the bellcrank on the port end of the engine's shift shaft. See **Figure 22**.

4. Mark the trim tab position relative to the gearcase housing with a grease pencil (or china marker). Remove the screw (A, **Figure 23**) securing the trim tab to the gearcase. Remove the trim tab.

5. Remove the six gearcase mounting screws as follows:

9

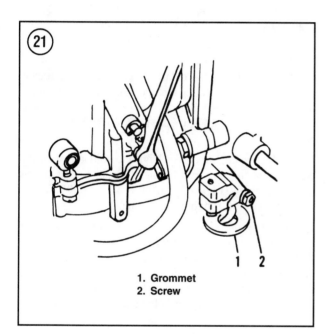

1. Grommet
2. Screw

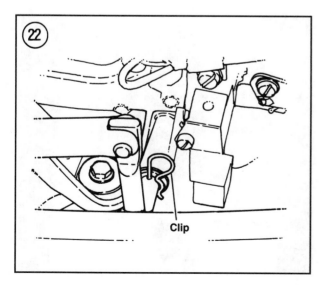

Clip

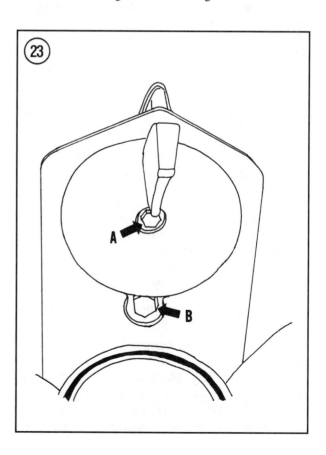

a. Remove the recessed screw and washer (B, **Figure 23**) from under the antiventilation plate, just behind the rear edge of the gearcase strut and in front of the trim tab pocket. A 5/8 in. thin wall socket is required to remove the screw.

b. Remove the screw (and washer) from inside the trim tab pocket. See **Figure 24**.

c. Remove the four screws (and washers) above the antiventilation plate. Two screws are located on each side of the gearcase. See **Figure 25**, typical.

6. Carefully pull the gearcase straight down and away from the drive shaft housing. Place the gearcase on a clean workbench or mount it in a suitable holding fixture.

7. To install the gearcase, begin by inspecting the exhaust seal on the inner exhaust housing located inside the drive shaft housing. If damaged, remove and discard the seal. Glue a new seal to the inner exhaust housing with OMC Adhesive M sealant.

8. Coat the outer surface of the exhaust seal (the portion that contacts the gearcase) with OMC Triple Guard Grease.

9. Remove and discard the drive shaft grommet at the top of the pump housing. Glue a new grommet to the pump housing with OMC Adhesive M sealant. Use the adhesive sparingly.

10. Replace the water tube seal as follows:

a. Remove the screw securing the water tube guide to the pump housing.

b. Remove the guide, then pull the water tube seal from the pump housing with a suitable tool and discard it.

c. Coat a new water tube seal with OMC Triple Guard Grease, then install the guide into the pump housing with its widest opening facing up.

d. Position the water tube guide over the seal and install its screw. Tighten the screw securely.

CAUTION
Do not apply lubricant to the top of the drive shaft in the next step. Excess lubricant between the top of the drive shaft and the engine crankshaft can create a hydraulic lock, preventing the drive shaft from fully engaging the crankshaft.

11. Clean the drive shaft splines as necessary, then coat the splines with OMC Moly Lube. Coat the threads of the gearcase mounting screws with OMC Gasket Sealing Compound.

12. Verify the *Shift Shaft Height* as described later in this chapter.

13. Position the gearcase under the drive shaft housing. Insert the drive shaft into its bore and the shift shaft through its grommet in the drive shaft housing and into the steering tube. Then push the gearcase toward the drive shaft hous-

ing and pilot the water tube into the water tube guide on top of the water pump housing.

CAUTION
Do not rotate the flywheel counterclockwise in the next step or the water pump impeller will be damaged.

14. Continue pushing the gearcase toward the drive shaft housing, while rotating the flywheel clockwise (as required) to align the drive shaft and crankshaft splines. Make sure the water tube fits into the water tube seal, then seat the gearcase against the drive shaft housing.

15. Install the six gearcase mounting screws (and washers). Evenly tighten the five 3/8 in. screws (**Figure 24** and **Figure 25**) to 18-20 ft.-lb. (24.4-27.1 N•m). Then tighten the single 7/16 in. screw (B, **Figure 23**) to 28-30 ft.-lb. (28.0-30.7 N•m).

16. Install the trim tab. Coat the mounting screw's threads with OMC Gasket Sealing Compound. Align the trim tab with the mark made during removal, then install and tighten the screw (A, **Figure 23**) to 35-40 ft.-lb. (47.5-54.2 N•m).

17A. *Tiller handle models*—Align the shift rod with the bellcrank at the port end of the shift shaft. Install and tighten the screw (**Figure 21**) to 60-84 in.-lb. (6.8-9.5 N•m) to secure the shift rod to the bellcrank.

17B. *Remote control models*—Align the shift rod with the bellcrank at the port end of the shift shaft. Then pull the shaft toward the starboard side of the power head to lock the shift rod to the bellcrank. Install the clip in the shift shaft hole at the starboard end of the shaft, making sure the flat and wave washers are behind the clip as shown in **Figure 22**.

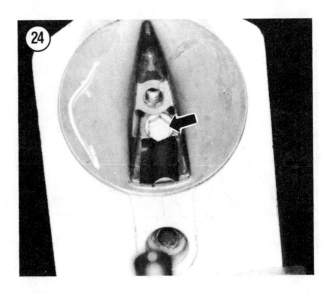

18. *Tiller handle models*—Adjust the shift lever's neutral detent as described in the appropriate *Synch and Link* section of Chapter Five. Then verify correct operation of the neutral start safety linkage as described in *Neutral Start Safety Linkage (40-70 hp Tiller Handle Models)*, located later in this chapter.

19. Install the propeller as described previously in this chapter.

20. Check the lubricant level or refill the gearcase with the recommended lubricant as described in Chapter Four.

21. Reconnect the spark plug leads to the spark plugs.

Neutral Start Safety Linkage (40-70 hp Tiller Handle Models)

The correct positioning of the shift lever's starter button over the electric starter switch is normally determined by the correct adjustment of the shift shaft height (on the lower gearcase) and the shift lever neutral detent adjustment (on the power head). When correctly positioned, the electric starter switch can only be engaged when the shift linkage is in the NEUTRAL position.

If necessary, a small amount of adjustment is provided on the shift control lever linkage to make sure the components are correctly aligned.

To adjust the neutral start safety linkage, proceed as follows:

1. If there is any reason to believe that the shift shaft height is incorrect, remove the lower gearcase and adjust the shift shaft height as described in this chapter.

2. Adjust the shift lever's neutral detent as described in this chapter (two-cylinder models) or in the appropriate section of Chapter Five (three-cylinder models) before continuing.

3. Position the engine-mounted shift control lever in the NEUTRAL detent position. The lever must positively click

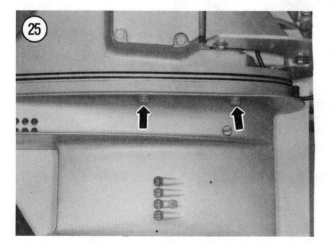

into the detent and the propeller must rotate freely in both directions.

4. Check the alignment of the starter button (on the shift control lever) to the electric starter switch (mounted in the tiller handle mounting base).

   a. If the button and switch are aligned, no adjustment is necessary. Proceed to Step 7 to verify correct operation.

   b. If the button and switch are not aligned, proceed to Step 5.

5. Remove the special locking clip (or cotter pin), washer (three-cylinder models) and clevis pin securing the shift control lever's link to the shift lever at the rear of the power head.

6. Rotate the link's connector to change the length of the link as necessary to align the button and switch. Make sure adequate thread engagement between the link and connector is maintained. When correctly aligned, connect the link to the shift lever by installing the clevis pin and securing the clevis pin with the washer (three-cylinder models) and special locking clip (or a new cotter pin). Bend both prongs of the cotter pin for a secure attachment.

NOTE
If the connector does not have enough adjustment to correct the button-to-switch alignment, the shift shaft height of the lower gearcase is incorrect, or the shift lever's neutral detent is not correctly adjusted.

7. Verify system operation as follows:

   a. Disconnect and ground the spark plug leads to the power head to prevent accidental starting.

   b. Remove the propeller to prevent accidental contact with a rotating propeller.

   c. Make sure you are clear of the propeller shaft and flywheel. Then depress the starter button momentarily (with the shift linkage still in the NEUTRAL position). The electric starter must engage.

   d. While rotating the propeller shaft, move the engine shift lever to the FORWARD position. Make sure you are clear of the propeller shaft and flywheel. Then depress the starter button momentarily. The electric starter must not engage.

   e. While rotating the propeller shaft, move the engine shift lever to the REVERSE position. Make sure you are clear of the propeller shaft and flywheel. Then depress the starter button momentarily. The electric starter must not engage.

   f. Readjust the linkage (or the shift shaft height or shift lever neutral detent) as necessary. When finished, install the propeller and reconnect the spark plug leads.

WATER PUMP

All models in this manual use an offset pump housing that causes the vanes of the impeller to flex during rotation. At low speeds the pump operates as a positive displacement pump. At high speeds, water resistance causes the impeller vanes to flex inward, causing the pump to operate as a centrifugal pump. See **Figure 26**.

The pump draws water into the intake port(s) as the vanes flex outward and pumps water out of the discharge port(s) as the vanes compress as shown in **Figure 27**.

On 2 and 3.3 hp models, the pump is located at the rear of the gearcase and is driven by a pin in the propeller shaft. On all other models, the pump is located on the gearcase upper deck and is driven by a key in the drive shaft.

The impeller only operates in a clockwise rotation with the drive shaft (or propeller shaft) and is held in a flexed (compressed) position at all times. Over time, this causes the impeller to take a set in one direction. Turning an impeller over and attempting to turn it against its natural set will cause premature impeller failure and power head damage from overheating. The manufacturer recommends replacing the impeller every time the water pump is disassembled. The impeller must only be reused if there is no

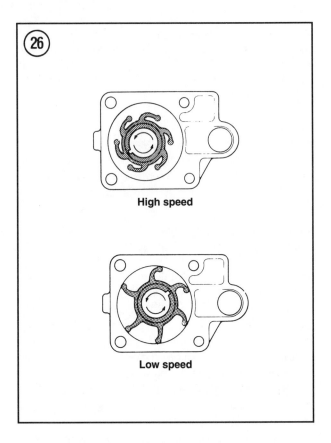

High speed

Low speed

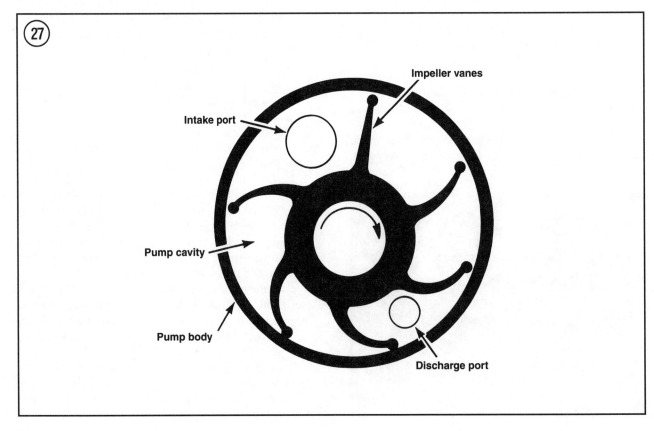

Impeller vanes

Intake port

Pump cavity

Pump body

Discharge port

other option. If the impeller must be reused, reinstall the impeller in its original position.

Overheating and extensive power head damage can result from a faulty water pump. Therefore, replace that the water pump impeller, seals and gaskets at least once a year as a preventative maintenance measure.

Individual operating conditions may dictate that the pump will require service more often. It is also recommended that the water pump be serviced anytime the lower gearcase (or jet pump unit) is removed for any type of service.

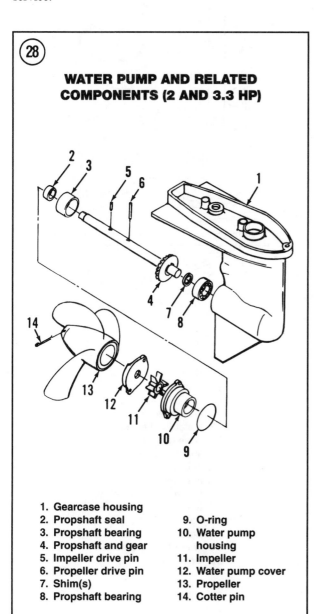

WATER PUMP AND RELATED COMPONENTS (2 AND 3.3 HP)

1. Gearcase housing
2. Propshaft seal
3. Propshaft bearing
4. Propshaft and gear
5. Impeller drive pin
6. Propeller drive pin
7. Shim(s)
8. Propshaft bearing
9. O-ring
10. Water pump housing
11. Impeller
12. Water pump cover
13. Propeller
14. Cotter pin

Water Pump Precautions

All impellers are made of some variation of rubber. The water pump liner (or housing) is either stainless steel or aluminum.

The water passing through the pump lubricates and cools the impeller and pump housing. Without the water, the pump will overheat and the impeller will begin to melt almost instantaneously. Continued operation without water can generate enough heat to melt the plastic pump housing (if so equipped). Of course, this can be secondary to the potential damage to the power head from overheating.

Once the impeller sustains *any* damage, its pumping ability is greatly diminished because the impeller can no longer seal adequately. The impeller must seal on its top and bottom surfaces, as well as the blade tips.

If you know that the engine was run without an adequate supply of water to the pump, the pump must be disassembled and the impeller (and any other damaged parts) replaced.

Extended cranking (such as during ignition system troubleshooting) can be detrimental to a water pump that is completely dry. Consider attaching a flushing device before initially cranking an engine with a dry water pump. This will make sure the pump is wet and will prevent it from being damaged. It is not necessary to keep the water supply flowing during all cranking periods—it is just important to keep the pump wet during extended cranking.

Removal and Disassembly

Replace the impeller, all seals and gaskets each time the water pump is disassembled.

On 2 and 3.3 hp models, the rubber water pump impeller is located inside the rear of the gearcase housing. The impeller is mounted on and driven by the propeller shaft. The water pump can be serviced without gearcase removal. Water is pumped to the power head through a copper water tube.

On all other models, the water pump impeller is secured to the drive shaft by a key or pin that fits between a flat area on the drive shaft and impeller hub. As the drive shaft rotates, the impeller rotates with it. Water is pumped up to the power head through a copper water tube or cast passage in the drive shaft housing.

2 and 3.3 hp

Refer to **Figure 28** for this procedure.

9

1. Remove the propeller and propeller drive pin as described previously in this chapter. Drain the gearcase lubricant as described in Chapter Four.

2. Remove the two screws and washers securing the pump cover to the rear of the gearcase. Separate the cover from the gearcase and slide it off of the propeller shaft.

3. Pry the impeller off of the propeller shaft using a screwdriver or needlenose pliers.

4. Remove the impeller drive pin from the propeller shaft.

5. Inspect the pump housing impeller wear surface. If damaged or excessively worn, drain the gearcase lubricant as described in Chapter Four, then remove and discard the pump housing (10, **Figure 28**) and O-ring (9).

6. Refer to *Water Pump Cleaning and Inspection* in this chapter before reassembling the water pump.

3, 3.5, 4-8 hp and 4 Deluxe

Refer to **Figure 29** or **Figure 30** for this procedure.

1. Remove the gearcase as described in this chapter.

2. Remove the three (3 and 4 hp) or four water pump housing mounting screws.

> *NOTE*
> *Hold down on the drive shaft during the next step to prevent it from being pulled up when removing the water pump components. On 3, 3.5 and 4 hp models (except 4 Deluxe), if the shaft moves upward enough to disengage the pinion gear, the gearcase must be completely disassembled to reinstall the drive shaft into the pinion gear.*

3. While holding DOWN on the drive shaft, carefully pry the pump housing loose using a putty knife or similar tool. Then slide the housing up and off the drive shaft. Remove and discard the body-to-impeller plate O-ring (3, 3.5 and 4 hp) or gasket (4 Deluxe, 6 and 8 hp).

> *NOTE*
> *If the impeller is corroded and frozen to the drive shaft, the impeller hub may have to be split with a chisel to remove it.*

4. If the impeller came off with the pump housing, proceed to Step 5. If the impeller remained on the gearcase, slide the impeller up and off the drive shaft while holding downward on the drive shaft. If the impeller sticks, hold the impeller in place and rotate the drive shaft counterclockwise to loosen the wedging action of the impeller drive key.

5. Locate and secure the impeller drive key. Carefully pry the impeller plate from the gearcase (or pump base) using a putty knife or similar tool. Remove the plate, then remove and discard the gasket.

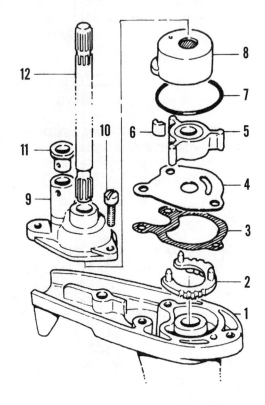

WATER PUMP AND RELATED COMPONENTS (3, 3.5 AND 4 HP)

1. Gearcase deck
2. Water inlet screen
3. Base gasket
4. Impeller plate
5. Impeller
6. Impeller key
7. Pump housing O-ring
8. Impeller liner
9. Pump housing
10. Screw
11. Water tube grommet
12. Drive shaft

**WATER PUMP AND RELATED COMPONENTS
(4 DELUXE, 6 AND 8 HP)**

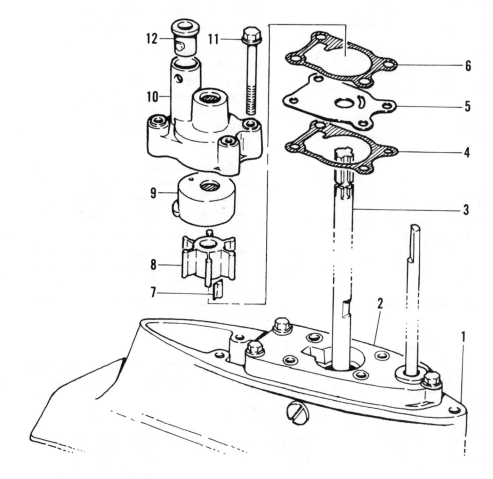

1. Gearcase housing
2. Pump base
3. Drive shaft
4. Gasket
5. Impeller plate
6. Gasket
7. Impeller key
8. Impeller
9. Impeller liner
10. Pump housing
11. Screw
12. Water tube grommet

9

6. *3, 3.5 and 4 hp (except 4 Deluxe)*—Remove the water intake screen from the gearcase. Discard the screen if it is damaged or cannot be satisfactorily cleaned.

NOTE
If the liner is to be removed, liberally apply OMC Cleaning Solvent or isopropyl alcohol to the liner-to-pump housing mating surfaces to soften the sealant. The liner will be much easier to remove.

7. If the impeller liner must be replaced, carefully pull the liner from the pump housing using needlenose pliers. Do not damage the pump housing during the removal process. Discard the liner.

8. Refer to *Water Pump Cleaning and Inspection* in this chapter before reassembling the water pump.

9.9 and 15 hp

Refer to **Figure 31** for this procedure.
1. Remove the gearcase as described in this chapter.
2. Remove the four water pump housing screws.
3. While holding DOWN on the drive shaft, carefully pry the pump housing loose using a putty knife or similar tool.

Then slide the housing up and off the drive shaft. There is no gasket or seal between the pump housing and impeller plate.

NOTE
If the impeller is corroded and frozen to the drive shaft, the impeller hub may have to be split with a chisel to remove it.

4. If the impeller came off with the pump housing, proceed to Step 5. If the impeller remained on the gearcase, slide the impeller up and off the drive shaft while holding downward on the drive shaft. If the impeller sticks, hold the impeller in place and rotate the drive shaft counterclockwise to loosen the wedging action of the impeller drive pin.

5. Locate and secure the impeller drive pin. Carefully pry the impeller plate from the gearcase (or pump base) using a putty knife or similar tool. There is no gasket or seal between the impeller plate and gearcase deck.

6. Remove and discard the large O-ring seal and the drive shaft seal from the top of the pump housing. Do not damage the pump housing during the removal process.

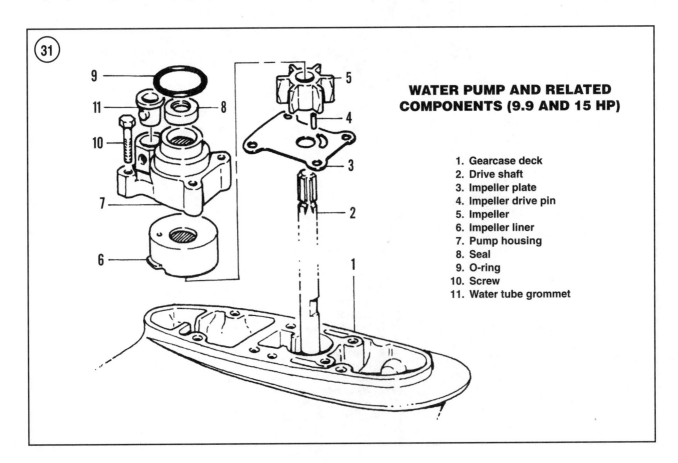

31

WATER PUMP AND RELATED COMPONENTS (9.9 AND 15 HP)

1. Gearcase deck
2. Drive shaft
3. Impeller plate
4. Impeller drive pin
5. Impeller
6. Impeller liner
7. Pump housing
8. Seal
9. O-ring
10. Screw
11. Water tube grommet

NOTE
If the liner is to be removed, liberally apply OMC Cleaning Solvent or isopropyl alcohol to the liner-to-pump housing mating surfaces to soften the sealant. The liner will be much easier to remove.

7. If the impeller liner must be replaced, carefully pull the liner from the pump housing using needlenose pliers. Do not damage the pump housing during the removal process. Discard the liner.

8. Refer to *Water Pump Cleaning and Inspection* (located later in this chapter) before reassembling the water pump.

20-35 hp and 18 jet

Refer to **Figure 32** for propeller-driven models (except 28 Special). Refer to **Figure 33** for 18 jet and 28 special.

1A. *Propeller-driven*—Remove the gearcase as described previously in this chapter.

1B. *18 jet models*—Remove the jet drive unit as described later in this chapter.

2A. *18 jet and 28 Special*—Remove the four water pump housing screws.

2B. *All other models*—Remove the six water pump housing screws.

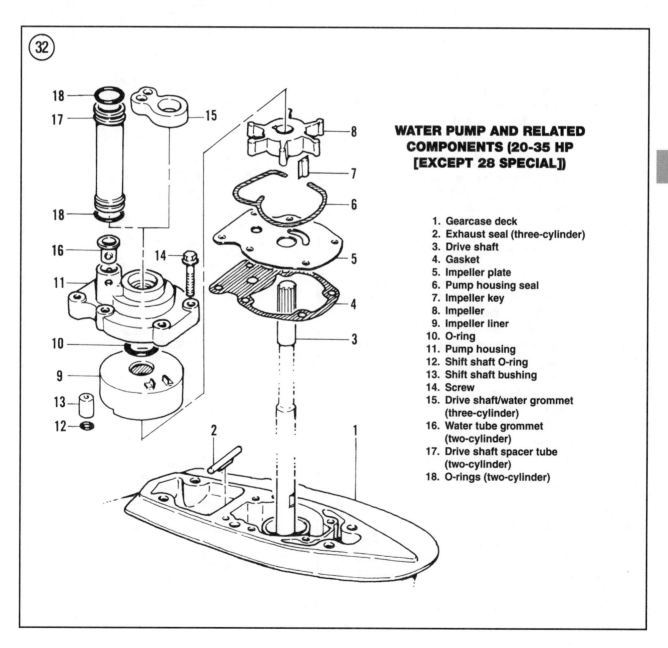

(32)

WATER PUMP AND RELATED COMPONENTS (20-35 HP [EXCEPT 28 SPECIAL])

9

1. Gearcase deck
2. Exhaust seal (three-cylinder)
3. Drive shaft
4. Gasket
5. Impeller plate
6. Pump housing seal
7. Impeller key
8. Impeller
9. Impeller liner
10. O-ring
11. Pump housing
12. Shift shaft O-ring
13. Shift shaft bushing
14. Screw
15. Drive shaft/water grommet (three-cylinder)
16. Water tube grommet (two-cylinder)
17. Drive shaft spacer tube (two-cylinder)
18. O-rings (two-cylinder)

3. While holding DOWN on the drive shaft, carefully pry the pump housing loose using a putty knife or similar tool. Then slide the housing up and off the drive shaft. Remove and discard the body-to-impeller plate gasket (18 jet and 28 Special) or O-ring (all other models).

NOTE
If the impeller is corroded and frozen to the drive shaft, the impeller hub may have to be split with a chisel to remove it.

4. If the impeller came off with the pump housing, proceed to Step 5. If the impeller remained on the gearcase, slide the impeller up and off the drive shaft while holding downward on the drive shaft. If the impeller sticks, hold the impeller in place and rotate the drive shaft counterclockwise to loosen the wedging action of the impeller drive key.

5. Locate and secure the impeller drive key (or pin). Carefully pry the impeller plate from the gearcase (or jet pump) using a putty knife or similar tool. Remove the plate, then remove and discard the gasket.

NOTE
Liberally apply OMC Cleaning Solvent or isopropyl alcohol to the liner-to-pump housing mating surfaces to soften the sealant. The liner will be much easier to remove.

6. Gently pry the liner from the pump housing with a suitable screwdriver. A pair of needlenose pliers may be used to help pull the liner from the body. The liner and pump housing must not be damaged if either must be reused. Remove and discard the O-ring or drive shaft seal (A, **Figure 34**) located under the liner.

7. *Except 28 Special and jet drive*—Remove the shift shaft O-ring and bushing from the water pump housing. Discard the O-ring. See **Figure 32**.

8. *Three-cylinder models*—Remove and discard the exhaust seal/water dam (2, **Figure 32**). The seal is recessed in the gearcase deck in a groove located just behind the pump housing mounting area.

9. Refer to *Water Pump Cleaning and Inspection* in this chapter before reassembling the water pump.

40-70 hp, 28 and 35 jet

Refer to **Figure 35** for this procedure. The water tube guide used on three-cylinder models is not shown in **Figure 35**, but is mounted directly over the seal (12, **Figure 35**) with a single screw. Jet drive models do not use the base gasket (1, **Figure 35**).

1. Remove the gearcase or jet pump unit as described in this chapter.

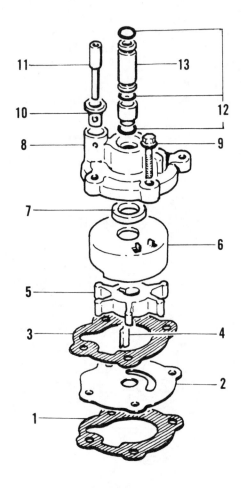

(33)

WATER PUMP AND RELATED COMPONENTS (28 SPECIAL AND 18 JET)

1. Base gasket
2. Impeller plate
3. Housing gasket
4. Impeller key (or pin)
5. Impeller
6. Impeller liner
7. Drive shaft seal
8. Pump housing
9. Screw
10. Water tube grommet
11. Water tube extension (18 jet)
12. O-rings
13. Drive shaft spacer tube adaptor (18 jet)

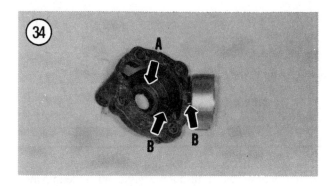

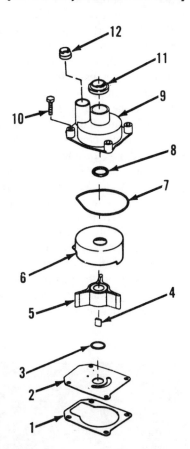

**WATER PUMP AND
RELATED COMPONENTS
(40-70 HP, 28 AND 35 JET)**

1. Base gasket
   (except jet)
2. Impeller plate
3. O-ring
4. Impeller key
5. Impeller
6. Impeller liner
7. Pump housing seal
8. O-ring
9. Pump housing
10. Screw
11. Drive shaft grommet
12. Water tube
    grommet/seal

2. Remove the four water pump housing screws.

3. Carefully pry the pump housing loose using a putty knife or similar tool. Then slide the housing up and off the drive shaft. Remove and discard the body-to-impeller plate O-ring.

> *NOTE*
> *If the impeller is corroded and frozen to the drive shaft, the impeller hub may have to be split with a chisel to remove it.*

4. If the impeller came off with the pump housing, proceed to Step 5. If the impeller remained on the gearcase, slide the impeller up and off the drive shaft. If the impeller sticks, hold the impeller in place and rotate the drive shaft counterclockwise to loosen the wedging action of the impeller drive key.

5. Locate and secure the impeller drive key. Then remove and discard the O-ring that seals the bottom of the impeller to the drive shaft.

6. Carefully pry the impeller plate from the gearcase (or jet pump) using a putty knife or similar tool. Remove the plate, then remove and discard the gasket on outboard models. Jet drive models do not use a gasket between the impeller plate and jet drive unit.

> *NOTE*
> *Liberally apply OMC Cleaning Solvent or isopropyl alcohol to the liner-to-pump housing mating surfaces to soften the sealant. The liner will be much easier to remove.*

7. Gently pry the liner from the pump housing with a suitable screwdriver. A pair of needlenose pliers may be used to help pull the liner from the body. The liner and pump housing must not be damaged if either must be reused. Remove and discard the O-ring (8, **Figure 35**) located under the liner.

8. Refer to *Water Pump Cleaning and Inspection* in this chapter before reassembling the water pump.

Water Pump Cleaning and Inspection (All Models)

1. Clean all metal parts in a mild solvent (such as mineral spirits) and dry with compressed air. Make sure all gasket material and sealant residue is removed.

2. Clean all plastic components with OMC Cleaning solvent or isopropyl alcohol. Make sure all gasket material and sealant residue is removed.

3. Clean all sealant and/or gasket material from the gearcase (or jet pump unit) deck and all other mating surfaces. Do not gouge or distort gasket sealing surfaces and do not

9

allow gasket material to fall into the gearcase housing or jet pump unit.

4. Check plastic pump housings and all other plastic parts for cracks, deformation or distortion from overheating or improper service procedures. Replace parts as needed.

5. Check metal pump housings for excessive wear, corrosion, distortion, mechanical or other damage. Replace parts as needed.

6. Check the impeller plate and impeller liner (or housing) for grooves, rough surfaces or excessive wear. While some grooving is normal, the grooves must not be deep or sharp. If a groove easily catches a fingernail, the part must be replaced. Replace the impeller liner (or housing) and impeller plate as necessary.

> *NOTE*
> *The water pump impeller must be able to float on the drive shaft. Clean the impeller area of the drive shaft thoroughly using emery cloth. Be certain the impeller slides onto the drive shaft easily.*

7. It is highly recommended that the impeller be replaced anytime it is removed. If the impeller must be reused, check the bonding of the rubber to the impeller hub for separation. Check the side seal surfaces and blade ends for cracks, tears, excessive wear or a glazed (or melted) appearance. If any of these defects are noted, do *not* reuse the original impeller under any circumstances.

Assembly and Installation

2 and 3.3 hp

Refer to **Figure 28** for this procedure.

1. If the pump housing is being replaced, coat a new O-ring with OMC Triple Guard Grease and install it over the new water pump housing assembly. Lubricate the housing, flange and propeller shaft seal lip with the same grease.

2. Install the pump housing into the gearcase.

3. Insert the impeller drive pin into the propeller shaft.

4. Lightly lubricate the impeller with gear lubricant. Slide the impeller onto the propeller shaft. Install the impeller into the pump housing while rotating the impeller in a clockwise direction. Make sure the impeller properly engages the drive pin.

5. Install the pump cover over the propeller shaft and seat it against the pump housing.

6. Apply OMC Gasket Sealing Compound to the threads of the pump housing retaining screws. Install the screws and tighten to 60-84 in.-lb. (6.8-9.5 N•m).

7. Install the propeller as described in this chapter.

8. Fill the gearcase with the recommended lubricant as described in Chapter Four.

3, 3.5 and 4 hp (except 4 Deluxe)

Refer to **Figure 29** for this procedure.

1. Install the water intake screen in the gearcase housing. Make sure the tabs on the screen are facing UP. See **Figure 36**.

2. Apply OMC Gasket Sealing Compound to both sides of a new base gasket. Install the gasket, then the impeller plate, over the drive shaft and into position on the gearcase housing.

3. Coat the drive shaft flat with a suitable grease, then position the impeller key on the flat. Rotate the drive shaft as necessary to position the impeller key as far from the water intake slot in the impeller plate as possible.

4. If removed, apply a *light* coat of OMC Gasket Sealing Compound to the exterior surfaces of the impeller liner. Install the liner into the housing, making sure its beveled lip is correctly aligned with the relief in the housing and that the liner is seated into the housing bore.

5. Lightly lubricate the impeller with gear lubricant. Insert the impeller into the liner with a counterclockwise twisting motion. Make sure all three blades enter the liner. Rotate the impeller (counterclockwise) until the impeller drive key slot is pointing at the liner's beveled lip.

6. Glue a new pump housing O-ring into the housing's groove using OMC Adhesive M sealant. Use the adhesive sparingly. Allow the adhesive to dry, then coat the O-ring with OMC Triple Guard Grease.

7. Place the pump assembly over the drive shaft. Carefully align the impeller drive key slot with the impeller key, then seat the assembly to the impeller plate. Rotate the drive shaft clockwise (and the pump housing counterclockwise) as necessary to align the components. Make sure the impeller key is not displaced during the installation process.

8. Apply OMC Gasket Sealing Compound to the threads of the three housing mounting screws. Verify that the housing is seated to the gearcase and that the screw holes are aligned, then install and evenly tighten the screws to 25-35 in.-lb. (2.8-4.0 N•m).

9. Install the gearcase to the outboard motor as described in this chapter.

4 Deluxe, 6 and 8 hp

The 4 Deluxe uses an impeller with three vanes, while the 6 and 8 hp models use an impeller with six vanes. Do not interchange the impellers, as overheating or overcooling problems will result.

Refer to **Figure 30** for this procedure.

1. Apply OMC Gasket Sealing Compound to both sides of a new base gasket. Install the gasket, then the impeller plate, over the drive shaft and into position on the water pump base.

2. Apply OMC Gasket Sealing Compound to both sides of a new pump housing gasket. Install the gasket over the drive shaft and into position on the impeller plate.

3. Coat the drive shaft flat with a suitable grease, then position the impeller key on the flat. Rotate the drive shaft as necessary to position the impeller key as far from the water intake slot in the impeller plate as possible.

4. If removed, apply a light coat of OMC Gasket Sealing Compound to the exterior surfaces of the impeller liner. Install the liner into the housing, making sure its beveled lip is correctly aligned with the relief in the housing and that the liner is seated in the housing bore.

NOTE
If the impeller drive key slot is not completely open through both sides of the impeller, install the impeller into the housing with the open end of the slot facing out. If the closed end of the slot is installed facing out, the impeller drive key will not be able to enter the slot when the housing is installed over the drive shaft.

5. Lightly lubricate the impeller with gear lubricant. Insert the impeller into the liner with a counterclockwise twisting motion. Make sure all blades completely enter the liner. Rotate the impeller counterclockwise until the impeller drive key slot is pointing at the liner's beveled lip.

6. Place the pump assembly over the drive shaft. Carefully align the impeller drive key slot with the impeller key, then seat the assembly to the impeller plate. Rotate the drive shaft clockwise (and the pump housing counterclockwise) as necessary to align the components. Make sure the impeller key is not displaced during the installation process.

7. Apply OMC Gasket Sealing Compound to the threads of the four housing mounting screws. Verify that the housing is seated on the gearcase, the gaskets are correctly positioned and that the screw holes are aligned, then install and evenly tighten the screws to 60-84 in.-lb. (6.8-9.5 N•m).

8. Install the gearcase to the outboard motor as described previously in this chapter.

9.9 and 15 hp

Refer to **Figure 31** for this procedure. These models do not use a base gasket or pump housing gasket (or seal).

1. Apply OMC Gasket Sealing Compound to the outer diameter of a new drive shaft seal (8, **Figure 31**). Using a suitable mandrel, press the seal into the bore at the top of the pump body with the seal lip facing down (toward the pump body).

2. Using OMC Adhesive M sealant, glue a new O-ring (9, **Figure 31**) to the shoulder at the top of the pump housing. Use the adhesive sparingly.

3. If removed, apply a *light* coat of OMC Gasket Sealing Compound to the exterior surfaces of the impeller liner. Install the liner into the housing, making sure its beveled lip is correctly aligned with the relief in the housing and that the liner is seated in the housing bore.

4. Lightly coat the impeller plate-to-gearcase deck mating surfaces with OMC Adhesive M sealant. Position the impeller plate over the drive shaft and into position on the gearcase deck.

5. Coat the drive shaft flat with a suitable grease, then vertically position the impeller pin on the center of the flat. Rotate the drive shaft to position the impeller drive pin straight aft.

NOTE
If the impeller drive pin slot is not completely open through both sides of the impeller, install the impeller into the housing with the open end of the slot facing out. If the closed end of the slot is installed facing out, the impeller drive pin will not be able to enter the slot when the housing is installed over the drive shaft.

6. Lightly lubricate the impeller with gear lubricant. Insert the impeller into the liner with a counterclockwise twisting motion. Make sure all blades completely enter the liner. Rotate the impeller (counterclockwise) until the impeller drive key slot is pointing straight aft.

7. Clean the pump housing-to-impeller plate mating surfaces of all oil and grease, then coat the pump housing mating surfaces with OMC Adhesive M sealant. Do not allow the adhesive to enter the impeller cavity.

9

8. Place the pump assembly over the drive shaft. Carefully align the impeller drive pin slot with the impeller drive pin, then seat the assembly to the impeller plate. Rotate the drive shaft clockwise (and the pump housing counterclockwise) as necessary to align the components. Make sure the impeller pin is not displaced during the installation process.

NOTE
Install the longer housing screws in the front holes.

9. Apply OMC Nut Lock threadlocking adhesive (or equivalent) to the threads of the four housing mounting screws. Verify that the housing is seated to the gearcase and that the screw holes are aligned, then install and evenly tighten the screws to 60-84 in.-lb. (6.8-9.5 N•m).

10. Install the gearcase to the outboard motor as described in this chapter.

20-35 hp and 18 jet

Refer to **Figure 32** for propeller-driven models (except 28 Special). Refer to **Figure 33** for 18 jet and 28 special.

1. *Three-cylinder models*—Apply a light coat of OMC Adhesive M sealant to the exhaust seal/water dam (2, **Figure 32**). Install the seal into its groove in the gearcase deck, just behind the pump mounting area. Seat the seal in its groove.

2. Apply OMC Gasket Sealing Compound to both sides of a new base gasket. Install the gasket, then the impeller plate, over the drive shaft and into position on the gearcase deck (prop-drive models) or bearing housing deck (jet drive models).

3A. *28 Special*—Coat the drive shaft flat with a suitable grease, then vertically position the impeller pin on the center of the flat. Rotate the drive shaft to position the impeller drive pin straight aft.

NOTE
On all models except the 28 Special, install the impeller drive key so its sharp edge is the leading edge as the drive shaft is rotated clockwise (as viewed from the top).

3B. *All other models*—Coat the drive shaft flat with a suitable grease, then position the impeller key on the flat. The sharp edge of the key must lead as the drive shaft is turned clockwise. Then rotate the drive shaft to position the thickest part of the impeller drive key straight aft.

4A. *28 Special and 18 jet models*—Coat the outer diameter of a new drive shaft seal (7, **Figure 33**) with OMC Gasket Sealing Compound. Press the seal into the pump housing (with the seal lip facing the power head) using seal installer

(part No. 330655) or a suitable mandrel. Press the seal until it is flush with the inside of the pump housing. See A, **Figure 34**.

4B. *All other models*—Glue a new O-ring (10, **Figure 32**) into the pump housing's groove (B, **Figure 37**) using OMC Adhesive M sealant. Use the adhesive sparingly.

5. Apply a *light* coat of OMC Gasket Sealing Compound to the exterior surfaces of the impeller liner. Install the liner into the housing, making sure the raised alignment tabs are correctly aligned with the pump housing's recesses. See B, **Figure 34**, typical. The liner must seat in the pump housing bore.

NOTE
If the impeller drive key (pin) slot is not completely open through both sides of the impeller, install the impeller into the housing with the open end of the slot facing out. If the closed end of the slot is installed facing out, the impeller drive key (pin) will not be able to enter the slot when the housing is installed over the drive shaft.

6. Lightly lubricate the impeller with gear lubricant. Insert the impeller into the liner with a counterclockwise twisting motion. Make sure all blades completely enter the liner. Rotate the impeller (counterclockwise) until the impeller drive key (or pin) slot is pointing straight aft.

7. *Prop-drive models (except 28 Special)*—Coat the shift shaft bushing with OMC Triple Guard Grease and install it into its bore (A, **Figure 37**) in the pump body. Then coat a new shift shaft O-ring with the same grease and install it over the shift shaft bushing (in the pump housing bore) (A, **Figure 37**).

8A. *18 jet and 28 Special*—Apply OMC Gasket Sealing Compound to both sides of a new pump housing gasket (3,

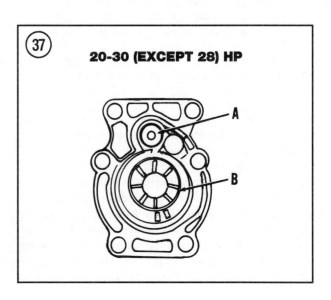
③⑦ **20-30 (EXCEPT 28) HP**

Figure 33). Install the gasket over the drive shaft and into position on the impeller plate.

8B. *All other models*—Glue a new pump housing seal (6, **Figure 32**) into the housing's groove using OMC Adhesive M sealant. Use the adhesive sparingly. Allow the adhesive to dry, then coat the O-ring with OMC Triple Guard Grease.

9. Place the pump assembly over the drive shaft. Carefully align the impeller drive key (or pin) slot with the impeller drive key (or pin), then seat the assembly to the impeller plate. Rotate the drive shaft clockwise (and the pump housing counterclockwise) as necessary to align the components. Make sure the impeller drive key (or pin) is not displaced during the installation process.

10. Apply OMC Gasket Sealing Compound to the threads of the housing mounting screws. Verify that the housing is seated to the gearcase, that the gasket(s) is correctly positioned and that the screw holes are aligned, then install and evenly tighten the screws to 60-84 in.-lb. (6.8-9.5 N•m).

11. Install the gearcase jet pump as described in this chapter.

40-70 hp, 28 and 35 jet

Jet drive models do not use the base gasket (1, **Figure 35**) even though the gasket is included in the manufacturer's water pump repair kit. The water tube guide used on three-cylinder models is not shown in **Figure 35**, but is mounted directly over the seal (12, **Figure 35**) with a single screw.

Refer to **Figure 35** for this procedure.

1A. *Prop-drive*—Apply OMC Gasket Sealing Compound to both sides of a new base gasket. Install the gasket, then the impeller plate, over the drive shaft and into position on the gearcase deck

1B. *Jet drive models*—Apply a light coat of OMC Gasket Sealing Compound to the impeller plate-to-bearing housing mating surfaces. Then install the impeller plate over the drive shaft and into position on the gearcase deck (without a gasket).

2. Lubricate a new impeller O-ring (3, **Figure 35**) with OMC Triple Guard Grease. Slide the O-ring over the drive shaft and into position against the impeller plate.

> *NOTE*
> *Install the impeller drive key so its sharp edge is the leading edge as the drive shaft is rotated clockwise (as viewed from top).*

3. Coat the drive shaft flat with a suitable grease, then position the impeller key on the flat. The sharp edge of the key must lead as the drive shaft is turned clockwise. Then rotate the drive shaft to position the thickest part of the impeller drive key straight aft.

4. Glue a new O-ring (8, **Figure 35**) into the pump housing's groove using OMC Adhesive M sealant. Apply four small drops of adhesive, using the four ribs shown in **Figure 38** as locating references for each drop. Do not apply any adhesive near the air bleed groove (**Figure 38**, typical) or the pump will not be able to prime under all conditions. Use the adhesive sparingly.

5. Apply a light coat of OMC Gasket Sealing Compound to the exterior surfaces of the impeller liner. Install the liner into the housing, making sure the raised alignment tab is correctly aligned with the pump housing's recess. See B, **Figure 34**, typical. The liner must seat in the pump housing bore.

> *NOTE*
> *The impeller drive key slot is not open through both sides of the impeller. The impeller must be installed into the housing with the open end of the slot facing out. If the closed end of the slot is installed facing out, the impeller drive key will not be able to enter the slot when the housing is installed over the drive shaft.*

6. Lightly lubricate the impeller with gear lubricant. Insert the impeller into the liner (with the impeller drive key slot facing out) using a counterclockwise twisting motion. Make sure all blades completely enter the liner. Rotate the impeller (counterclockwise) until the impeller drive key slot is pointing straight aft.

7. Glue a new pump housing seal (7, **Figure 35**) into the housing's groove using OMC Adhesive M sealant. Use the adhesive sparingly. Allow the adhesive to dry, then coat the seal with OMC Triple Guard Grease.

9

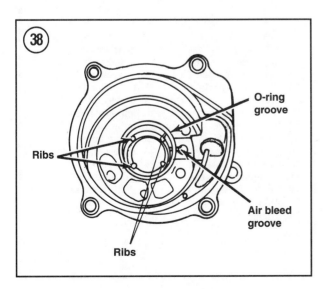

(38) O-ring groove

Ribs

Air bleed groove

Ribs

8. Place the pump assembly over the drive shaft. Carefully align the impeller drive key (or pin) slot with the impeller drive key, then seat the assembly to the impeller plate. Rotate the drive shaft clockwise (and the pump housing counterclockwise) as necessary to align the components. Make sure the impeller drive key is not displaced during the installation process.

9. Apply OMC Gasket Sealing Compound to the threads of the housing mounting screws. Verify that the housing is seated to the gearcase, that the base gasket and impeller plate are correctly positioned and that the screw holes are aligned, then install and evenly tighten the screws to 60-84 in.-lb. (6.8-9.5 N•m).

10. Install the gearcase or jet pump as described in this chapter.

GEARCASE DISASSEMBLY/ASSEMBLY

The section covers complete disassembly and assembly procedures for each lower gearcase covered in this manual. Once the gearcase is disassembled, refer to *GEARCASE CLEANING AND INSPECTION*, in this chapter before beginning assembly.

Larger (40-70 hp) models require that the pinion gear be shimmed (precisely located vertically) during assembly. The assembly procedure will refer you to *PINION GEAR SHIMMING* at the proper time.

Service Precautions (Bearing Installation)

If the specified special tools for removing and installing press-fit bearings are not available, make sure that you measure (and record) the installed position of each bearing before removal. Once a press-fit bearing is removed, it must be replaced. Install all new bearings in the exact same position as noted before removal.

Incorrect installation will damage a new bearing. A standard mechanic's rule is to press only against the numbered side of any bearing (unless otherwise specified). Refer to the following general guidelines when installing new bearings:

1. All caged needle bearings must be installed by pressing on the numbered side.

2. All one-piece ball bearing assemblies must be installed by pressing on the numbered side of the bearing.

   a. Press on the bearing's outer race if the bearing is pressed into a bore (such as a housing).

   b. Press on the bearing's inner race if the bearing is pressed over a shaft (such as a propshaft or gear hub).

3. A tapered roller bearing consists of a bearing race (also called the cup) and a roller bearing assembly (inner race, tapered rollers and a bearing cage). The race and roller

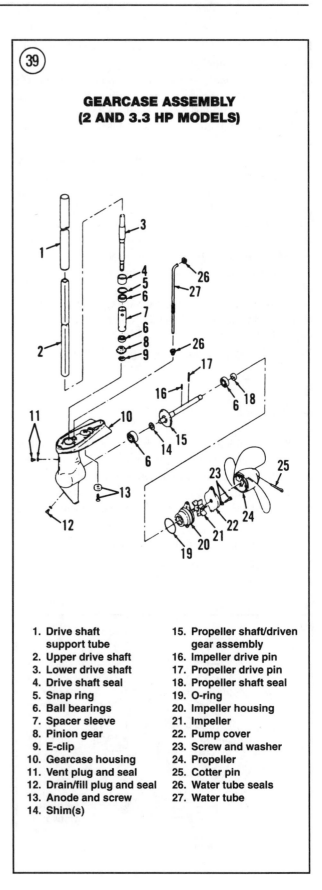

**GEARCASE ASSEMBLY
(2 AND 3.3 HP MODELS)**

1. Drive shaft support tube
2. Upper drive shaft
3. Lower drive shaft
4. Drive shaft seal
5. Snap ring
6. Ball bearings
7. Spacer sleeve
8. Pinion gear
9. E-clip
10. Gearcase housing
11. Vent plug and seal
12. Drain/fill plug and seal
13. Anode and screw
14. Shim(s)
15. Propeller shaft/driven gear assembly
16. Impeller drive pin
17. Propeller drive pin
18. Propeller shaft seal
19. O-ring
20. Impeller housing
21. Impeller
22. Pump cover
23. Screw and washer
24. Propeller
25. Cotter pin
26. Water tube seals
27. Water tube

bearing are a matched assembly and must be replaced as such. Do not attempt to replace only the race or only the roller bearing.

   a. The race is normally installed by pressing on the narrowest edge of its outer diameter, resulting in the tapered bearing surface facing the pressing tool (unless specified otherwise). The pressing tool must not be allowed to directly contact the precision ground bearing surface.

   b. The roller bearing must be installed by pressing on its inner race, with the rollers facing the pressing tool (unless specified otherwise). Do not allow the pressing tool to contact the rollers or the bearing cage.

Service Precautions (Seal Installation)

Apply OMC Gasket Sealing Compound to the outer diameter of all *metal-cased* seals before pressing the seal into place.

OMC DPL (or WD-40) Lubricant must be applied to the outer diameter of all *rubber-cased* seals before pressing the seal into place. DPL will lubricate the seal and allow it to slide into position without cutting the rubber case. The DPL will then evaporate, preventing the seal from sliding out of its bore under operation. If gasket sealing compound

or any grease is used, the seal will be ejected from its bore under operation.

Lubricate the rubber lip(s) of *all* seals with OMC Triple Guard Grease, before the seal is installed.

Disassembly (2 and 3.3 hp Models)

Refer to **Figure 39** for this procedure.

> *NOTE*
> *Do not remove the ball bearings (6, **Figure 39**) unless they must be replaced. However, the impeller housing ball bearing must be removed (and discarded) to access the propeller shaft seal.*

1. Remove the gearcase as described in this chapter.

2. Remove the water pump components as described in this chapter.

3. Remove the water pump impeller housing. If it is difficult to remove, tap the housing with a soft (plastic or lead) hammer to break it free. Remove and discard the housing O-ring.

4. Using a suitable tool, reach into the gearcase cavity and remove the E-clip securing the pinion gear to the lower drive shaft. Lift the drive shaft out of the top of the gearcase, then remove the pinion gear from the gear cavity.

5. Pull the propeller shaft and driven gear assembly from the gearcase. Be sure to retrieve the shim(s) located on the end of the shaft. See 14, **Figure 39**.

6. Pull the drive shaft and water tube seals from the gearcase deck using a suitable tool. Do not damage the seal bore during removal.

7. To replace the impeller housing's propshaft seal and ball bearing, proceed as follows:

   a. Remove the ball bearing using a suitable bearing puller, such as support plate (part No. 115312), 2-jaw puller head (part No. 432130) and puller bridge and threaded rod (part No. 432127) assembled in the manner shown in **Figure 40**. Discard the bearing.

   b. Remove the propeller shaft seal using the same tools. Pull the seal from the bearing side of the impeller housing. Discard the seal.

8. If the forward propeller shaft ball bearing must be replaced, pull the bearing from the gearcase with a suitable bearing puller, such as bearing puller kit (part No. 115307). Discard the bearing.

9. If the drive shaft ball bearings must be replaced, proceed as follows:

   a. Remove the snap ring securing the drive shaft upper bearing into the gearcase with a pair of No. 3 snap ring pliers (or equivalent).

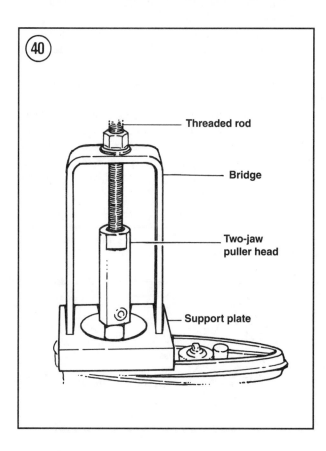

40

Threaded rod

Bridge

Two-jaw puller head

Support plate

9

b. Remove the drive shaft upper ball bearing using a suitable bearing puller, such as support plate (part No. 115312), 2-jaw puller head (part No. 432130) and puller bridge and threaded rod (part No. 432127), assembled as shown in **Figure 40**. Discard the bearing.

c. Reach into the drive shaft bore and remove the bearing spacer sleeve (7, **Figure 39**) from the gearcase.

d. Remove the drive shaft lower ball bearing using a suitable bearing puller, such as bearing puller kit (part No. 115307). Discard the bearing.

10. Refer to *Gearcase Cleaning and Inspection*. Clean and inspect all components as directed before beginning reassembly procedures.

Assembly (2 and 3.3 hp Models)

Lubricate all internal components with OMC Ultra HPF Gear Lube or equivalent. Do not assemble components *dry*. When installing ball bearings, press only against the bearing's outer race. Refer to **Table 3** for torque values and **Figure 39** for this procedure.

> *NOTE*
> *The drive shaft bearings must be precisely located to control the pinion gear position. OMC bearing and seal installer (part No. 115310) and collar (part No. 115314) are the only tools recommended for this procedure.*

1. If the drive shaft ball bearings were removed, install new bearings as follows:
   a. Position the collar (part No. 115314) over the narrow end of bearing installer (part No. 115310).
   b. Lubricate a new ball bearing and the drive shaft bore. Position the bearing over the narrow end of the bearing installer and up against the collar. The numbered side of the bearing must face the collar.
   c. Fit the assembly into the drive shaft bore. Drive the bearing into the drive shaft bore until the tool seats against the gearcase. Remove the tools. Separate the collar (part No. 115314) from the bearing installer (part No. 115310).
   d. Insert the spacer sleeve into the drive shaft bore.
   e. Lubricate another new ball bearing and the upper part of the drive shaft bore. Position the bearing over the narrow end of the bearing installer and against the large end's shoulder. The lettered side of the bearing must face the tool's shoulder. Do not use a collar when installing this bearing.

f. Fit the assembly into the drive shaft bore. Drive the bearing into the drive shaft bore until the tool seats against the gearcase. Remove the tool.

g. Install the bearing snap ring. The sharp edge of the ring must face up. See **Figure 41**, typical. Make sure the snap-ring is fully expanded into its groove.

2A. If the propeller shaft's front ball bearing was removed and bearing installer (part No. 115310) and collar (part No. 115313) are available, install a new bearing as follows:
   a. Position collar (part No. 115313) over the narrow end of bearing installer (part No. 115310).
   b. Lubricate a new ball bearing and the bearing bore. Position the bearing over the narrow end of the bearing installer and up against the collar. The numbered side of the bearing must face the collar.
   c. Fig the assembly into the propshaft bore. Drive the bearing into the propshaft bore until the bearing is seated in the gearcase. Remove the tools. Separate the collar (part No. 115313) from the bearing installer (part No. 115310).

2B. If the propeller shaft's front ball bearing was removed, but the special tools called for in Step 2A are not available, install a new bearing as follows:
   a. Lubricate a new ball bearing and the bearing bore. Position the bearing into the propeller shaft bore with the numbered side of the bearing facing up (out).
   b. Using a suitable mandrel that only contacts the bearing's outer race, drive the bearing into the propshaft bore until the bearing is seated in the gearcase.

3. Install a new seal and ball bearing into the impeller housing as follows:
   a. Coat the outer diameter of a new seal with OMC Ultra Lock threadlocking adhesive (or equivalent).
   b. Position the seal in the impeller housing with the spring side facing up. The spring side of the seal must face toward the gearcase when the impeller housing is installed.

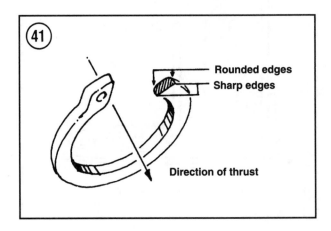
Rounded edges
Sharp edges
Direction of thrust

c. Using the longer stepped side of bearing and seal installer (part No. 115311) or a suitable mandrel, press the seal into the housing until it is seated.

d. Coat the seal lips with OMC Triple Guard Grease.

e. Lubricate a new ball bearing and the impeller housing's bearing bore.

f. Position the bearing into the housing with the numbered side facing up.

g. Using the short stepped side of bearing installer (part No. 115311) or a suitable mandrel, press the bearing into the housing until it is seated. Press only on the bearing's outer race.

4. Apply Scotch Grip Rubber Adhesive 1300 to the outer diameter of a new water tube seal. Install the water tube seal into the gearcase. Then lubricate the inner diameter of the seal with OMC Triple Guard Grease.

5. Apply OMC Gasket Sealing Compound to the outer diameter of a new drive shaft seal. Position the seal into the drive shaft bore with the spring side facing down (into the gearcase). Press the seal into the drive shaft bore until it is seated, using bearing and seal installer (part No. 115310) or a suitable mandrel.

6. Install the original shim(s) onto the front of the driven gear and propeller shaft assembly.

7. Install the drive gear and propeller shaft assembly into the gearcase. Make sure the shaft is fully engaged into the front ball bearing.

8. Position the pinion gear into the propeller shaft bore, then insert the lower drive shaft into its bore and engage the pinion gear. Rotate the pinion gear and drive shaft as necessary to align the splines.

9. Secure the pinion gear to the drive shaft by installing the E-clip into the drive shaft groove. The sharp edge of the E-clip must face away from the pinion gear. The sharp edge is identified in the same manner as the snap ring shown in **Figure 41**. Replace the E-clip if it does not lock securely in place.

10. Coat a new impeller housing O-ring with OMC Triple Guard Grease. Install the O-ring onto the impeller housing. Then coat the impeller housing and gearcase mating surfaces with the same grease.

11. Install the impeller housing on the gearcase. Align the screw holes and the water passage, then seat the housing to the gearcase.

12. Install the impeller drive pin into the propeller shaft.

13. Lubricate the impeller with gear lubricant. Install the water pump impeller onto the shaft. Rotate the impeller and propeller shaft clockwise while pushing the impeller into the housing. Make sure the impeller has fully engaged the drive pin.

14. Install the water pump cover over the propeller shaft and against the pump housing.

15. Apply OMC Gasket Sealing Compound to the threads of the pump housing retaining screws. Install the screws and tighten to 60-84 in.-lb. (6.8-9.5 N•m).

NOTE
*The drive shaft bore must be plugged before the pressure and vacuum tests can be performed. The best way to do this is to install the drive shaft support tube (1, **Figure 39**) into the drive shaft seal, then plug the upper end of the support tube with a suitable rubber plug. Be sure to hold the tube into the seal during the pressure tests, or air pressure will push the tube out of the seal.*

16. Test the integrity of the gearcase seals, O-rings and gaskets as described in *Gearcase Pressure and Vacuum Testing*. The drive shaft tube must be held in position during the pressure tests or it will push out of the drive shaft seal.

17. Fill the gearcase with the recommended lubricant as described in Chapter Four.

18. Install the gearcase as described previously in this chapter.

Disassembly
(3, 3.5 and 4 hp [Except 4 Deluxe] Models)

Refer to **Figure 42** for an exploded view of this gearcase (with the water pump and propeller removed). The propeller shaft bearing carrier can be removed without removing the gearcase from the drive shaft housing, if so desired. If the thrust washers and thrust bearings must be reused, reinstall them in their original location and orientation.

NOTE
*Do not remove the pressed-in needle bearings (3, 4, 14 and 21, **Figure 42**) unless they must be replaced.*

1. Drain the gearcase lubricant as described in Chapter Four.

2. Remove the gearcase as described in this chapter.

3. Remove the water pump as described in this chapter.

4. Pull the drive shaft up and out of the gearcase.

5. Remove the two screws securing the propshaft bearing carrier to the gearcase housing. Rotate the bearing carrier to break the O-ring seal, then pull the carrier from the gearcase. If necessary, gently tap the carrier's mounting screw ears with a soft-faced mallet to assist in rotating the carrier. Remove the O-ring (20, **Figure 42**) from the carrier groove. Discard the O-ring.

6. Pull the propeller shaft and driven gear assembly from the gearcase. Reach into the gearcase and remove the driven gear's thrust bearing and thrust washer (15-16,

Figure 42). Tag these components with their location and orientation. Do not intermix the driven gear components with the pinion gear components.

7. Remove the pinion gear, thrust bearing and thrust washer (11-13, **Figure 42**). Tag these components with their location and orientation.

8. Disassemble the propeller shaft and driven gear assembly as follows:

   a. Insert an appropriate size punch into the propeller shaft drive pin hole.

b. Hold the driven gear firmly while gently twisting the propeller shaft counterclockwise (as viewed from the propeller). Gently pull it away from the driven gear. The shaft and gear will separate (**Figure 43**).

c. Remove the spring from the gear (or shaft) by holding the gear (or shaft) firmly while gently twisting the spring in a counterclockwise direction (as viewed from the open end of the spring) and gently pulling it away from the gear (or shaft). Do not use any tools to grasp the spring as it will be damaged.

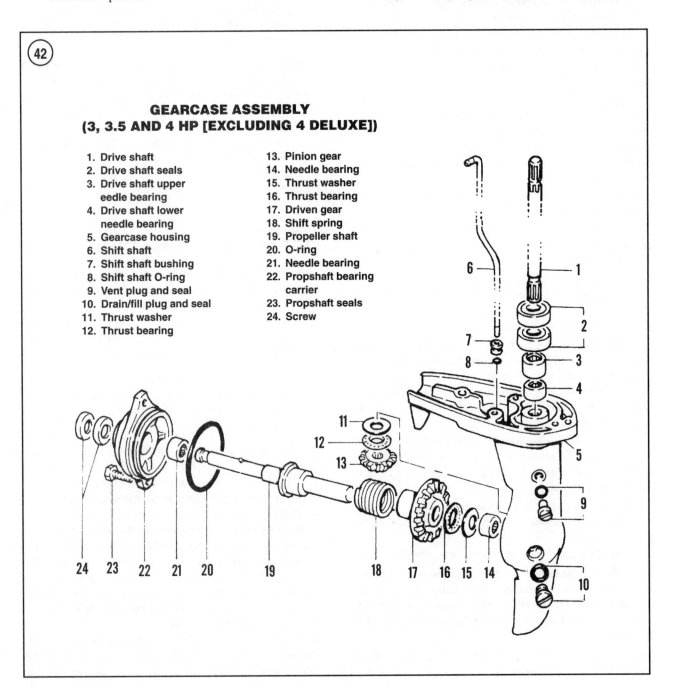

(42)

**GEARCASE ASSEMBLY
(3, 3.5 AND 4 HP [EXCLUDING 4 DELUXE])**

1. Drive shaft
2. Drive shaft seals
3. Drive shaft upper eedle bearing
4. Drive shaft lower needle bearing
5. Gearcase housing
6. Shift shaft
7. Shift shaft bushing
8. Shift shaft O-ring
9. Vent plug and seal
10. Drain/fill plug and seal
11. Thrust washer
12. Thrust bearing
13. Pinion gear
14. Needle bearing
15. Thrust washer
16. Thrust bearing
17. Driven gear
18. Shift spring
19. Propeller shaft
20. O-ring
21. Needle bearing
22. Propshaft bearing carrier
23. Propshaft seals
24. Screw

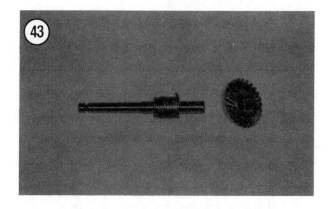

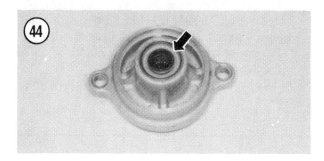

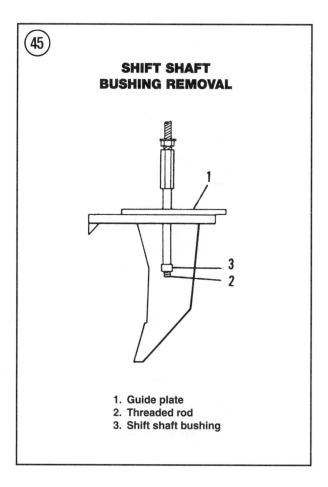

**SHIFT SHAFT
BUSHING REMOVAL**

1. Guide plate
2. Threaded rod
3. Shift shaft bushing

If necessary, place a shop towel over the spring to protect your hand.

9. Remove the two propeller shaft seals (**Figure 44**) from the propeller shaft bearing carrier by pulling them from the carrier with a suitable two-jaw puller. See **Figure 40**. Do not damage the seal bore during the removal process. Discard the seals.

10. Remove the two drive shaft seals (2, **Figure 42**) from the gearcase. Pull them out with a suitable two-jaw puller. Assemble the tools in the manner shown in **Figure 40**. Do not damage the seal bore during the removal process. Discard the seals.

11. The shift shaft bushing must be removed to access the shift shaft O-ring beneath it. To remove the bushing and O-ring, refer to **Figure 45** and proceed as follows:

   a. Place the guide plate from bearing remover/installer kit (part No. 392092) onto the gearcase deck. Make sure the alignment dowels are inserted in the gearcase mounting screw bores.

   b. Insert the threaded end of the rod (from the bearing kit) through the guide plate and into the shift shaft bushing. Thread the rod fully into the bushing.

   c. Attach a suitable slide hammer to the rod. Then pull the bushing from the gearcase.

   d. If the O-ring did not come out with the bushing, pull the O-ring from the gearcase with a suitable hooked tool.

   e. Discard the bushing and O-ring.

12. Remove the needle bearing from the propshaft bearing carrier as follows:

   a. Support the carrier in a press with the seal side of the carrier facing up.

   b. Press the bearing from the carrier using a suitable mandrel.

   c. Discard the bearing.

13. To remove the needle bearing from the very front of the propeller shaft bore, pull the bearing from the gearcase using a suitable bearing puller. Position the puller bridge to push against the two screw hole bosses at the top and bottom of the gearcase bore. Discard the bearing.

14. Refer to **Figure 46** and pull both drive shaft needle bearings from the drive shaft bore (at the same time) as follows:

   a. Place the guide plate from bearing remover/installer kit (part No. 392092) onto the gearcase deck. Make sure the alignment dowels are inserted in the gearcase mounting screw bores.

   b. Insert the rod (from the bearing kit) through the guide plate and into the drive shaft bore. Position the small disc (from the bearing kit) under the lower drive shaft needle bearing with the flat side of the disc facing the bearing. Thread the disc fully onto the rod.

9

c. Attach a suitable slide hammer to the upper end of the rod. Then pull both bearings from the drive shaft bore.

d. Discard both bearings.

15. Refer to *Gearcase Cleaning and Inspection*. Clean and inspect all components as directed before beginning reassembly procedures.

Assembly
(3, 3.5 and 4 hp [Except 4 Deluxe] Models)

Lubricate all internal components with OMC Ultra HPF Gear Lube. Do not assemble components *dry*. When installing new needle bearings (3, 4, 14 and 21, **Figure 42**), press only against the numbered side of the bearing. Refer to **Table 3** for torque values and **Figure 42** for this procedure.

1. Refer to **Figure 47** and install a new drive shaft lower bearing using the bearing remover/installer kit part No. 392092.

a. Install the cotter clip into the hole in the rod.

b. Pilot the rod through the guide plate. Then place the small disc onto the rod, making sure the concave side of the disc is facing away from the rod.

c. Lubricate a new needle bearing and the drive shaft bore. Position the bearing over the rod and against the concave side of the small disc. The numbered side of the bearing must face the disc.

d. Pilot the assembly into the drive shaft bore. Make sure the guide plate's alignment dowels are piloted into the gearcase mounting screw bores.

e. Drive the bearing into the gearcase until the cotter clip just contacts the guide plate. Then remove and disassemble the tool.

2. If the upper and lower drive shaft needle bearings were removed, refer to **Figure 48** and install a new upper bearing using bearing remover/installer kit part No. 392092.

a. Pilot the rod through the guide plate. Then place the large disc onto the rod, making sure the concave side of the disc is facing away from the rod.

b. Lubricate a new needle bearing and the drive shaft bore. Position the bearing over the rod and against the concave side of the large disc. The numbered side of the bearing must face the disc.

c. Pilot the assembly into the drive shaft bore. Make sure the guide plate's alignment dowels are piloted into the gearcase mounting screw bores.

d. Drive the bearing into the gearcase until the large disc contacts the shoulder in the drive shaft bore. Then remove and disassemble the tool.

3. If the needle bearing (14, **Figure 42**) at the front of the propshaft bore was removed, install a new bearing as follows:

a. Lubricate a new needle bearing and its bore.

b. Place the bearing onto bearing installer (part No. 392091) or a suitable mandrel. Make sure the numbered side of the bearing is facing the installer.

c. Press the bearing into its bore until the bearing is seated or the tool contacts the gearcase (whichever happens first).

4. If the needle bearing (A, **Figure 49**) in the propshaft bearing carrier was removed, install a new bearing as follows:

a. Position the carrier so that the O-ring groove (B, **Figure 49**) is facing up.

b. Lubricate a new needle bearing and its bore.

c. Place the bearing onto bearing installer (part No. 392091) or a suitable mandrel. Make sure the numbered side of the bearing is facing the installer.

d. Press the bearing into the carrier until it is seated in the carrier bore.

5. Install a new shift shaft bushing and O-ring using bearing remover/installer kit part No. 392092.

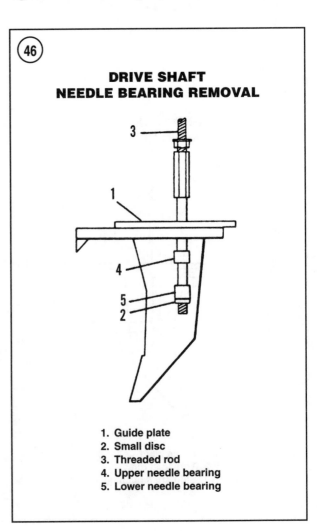

(46)

DRIVE SHAFT
NEEDLE BEARING REMOVAL

1. **Guide plate**
2. **Small disc**
3. **Threaded rod**
4. **Upper needle bearing**
5. **Lower needle bearing**

a. Lubricate a new O-ring with OMC Triple Guard Grease. Position the O-ring into the open end of a new shift shaft bushing.

b. Pilot the rod through the guide plate. Then place the bushing installer onto the rod.

c. Position the bushing assembly onto the Installer, making sure the O-ring end of the bushing is facing away from the Installer.

d. Coat the outer diameter of the shift shaft bushing with OMC Adhesive M sealant.

e. Pilot the assembly into the shift shaft bore. Make sure the guide plate's alignment dowels are piloted into the gearcase mounting screw bores.

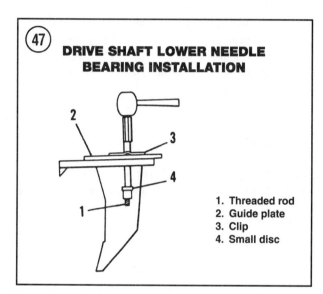

47

DRIVE SHAFT LOWER NEEDLE BEARING INSTALLATION

1. Threaded rod
2. Guide plate
3. Clip
4. Small disc

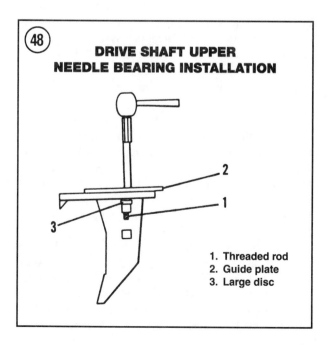

48

DRIVE SHAFT UPPER NEEDLE BEARING INSTALLATION

1. Threaded rod
2. Guide plate
3. Large disc

f. Drive the bushing into its bore until it is seated or the tool contacts the gearcase (whichever happens first).

6. Install two new seals into the drive shaft bore as follows:

a. Coat the outer diameter of each seal with OMC Gasket Sealing Compound.

b. Install the inner seal using the longer, stepped shoulder of seal installer (part No. 327431) or equivalent. The seal lip (spring side) must face into the gearcase. Press the seal until the installer contacts the gearcase.

c. Install the outer seal using the shorter shoulder of seal installer (part No. 327431) or equivalent. The seal lip (spring side) must face out of (away from) the gearcase. Press the seal until the installer contacts the gearcase. The seal must be flush with the gearcase when correctly installed.

d. Lubricate the seal lips and pack the area between the seal lips with OMC Triple Guard Grease.

7. Install two new seals into the propshaft bearing carrier as follows:

a. Position the carrier so that its seal bore is facing up.

b. If the seals are metal-cased, coat the outer diameter of each seal with OMC Gasket Sealing Compound. If the seals are rubber cased, lubricate the outer diameter of each seal with OMC DPL (WD-40) Lubricant.

c. Install the inner seal using the longer, stepped shoulder of seal installer (part No. 327572) or equivalent. The seal lip (spring side) must face into the carrier. Press the seal until the installer contacts the carrier.

d. Install the outer seal using the shorter shoulder of seal installer (part No. 327572) or equivalent. The seal lip (spring side) must face out of (away from) the carrier. Press the seal until the installer contacts the carrier. The seal must be flush with the carrier.

e. Lubricate the seal lips and pack the area between the seal lips with OMC Triple Guard Grease.

8. Lubricate a new O-ring (B, **Figure 49**) with OMC Triple Guard Grease. Install the O-ring into the propshaft bearing carrier's groove.

9. Set the gearcase on its deck so the skeg is pointing up and the propshaft bore is horizontal.

9

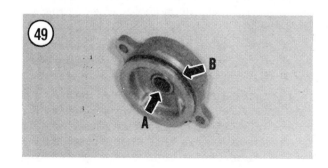

49

10. Position the pinion gear's thrust washer in the gearcase. The chamfered side of the thrust washer must be positioned against the gearcase (away from the pinion gear). Lubricate the thrust bearing and position it over the thrust washer. Finally install the pinion gear over the thrust bearing.

11. Lubricate the lower end of the drive shaft. Carefully pick up the gearcase and insert the drive shaft into its bore, being careful not to displace the pinion gear, bearing or thrust washer. Rotate the drive shaft as necessary to engage the splines, then seat the shaft into the gear.

NOTE
From this point on, do not allow the drive shaft to back out of its drive shaft bore. The pinion gear will disengage, and it may be necessary to disassemble the gearcase to re-install the gear.

12. Clamp the drive shaft in a soft-jawed vise so that the gearcase skeg is pointing up and the propshaft bore is horizontal. Do not allow the drive shaft to disengage the pinion gear.

13. Assemble the propshaft and driven gear as follows:
   a. Lubricate the driven gear hub, shift spring and propeller shaft.
   b. Position the spring over the gear hub with the protruding tang facing the gear.
   c. Position the propeller shaft into the open end of the spring.
   d. Rotate the gear and shaft counterclockwise (when viewing the ends of the assembly) while gently pushing the components toward each other. Make sure the spring is seated on both the gear and shaft.

14. Lubricate the driven gear's thrust bearing with OMC Needle Bearing Assembly Grease. Position the bearing over the front end of the propeller shaft.

15. Lubricate the driven gear's thrust washer with OMC Needle Bearing Assembly Grease. Position the washer over the front end of the propeller shaft with its chamfered side facing away from the gear.

16. Install the propeller shaft and driven gear assembly into the gearcase. Make sure the propshaft pilots into the needle bearing and that the thrust washer and bearing are not displaced.

17. Cover the groove at the rear of the propeller shaft with a single wrap of cellophane tape to prevent the sharp edges from damaging the propshaft seals.

18. Lubricate the prop shaft bearing carrier flange with OMC Triple Guard Grease. Install the propshaft bearing carrier over the propshaft. Align the screw holes, then seat the carrier in the gearcase bore. Remove the cellophane tape from the propshaft.

19. Coat the threads of the two carrier mounting screws with OMC Gasket Sealing Compound. Install and evenly tighten the screws to 60-84 in.-lb. (6.8-9.5 N•m).

NOTE
Do not allow the drive shaft to back out of its bore and disengage the pinion gear. Hold the drive shaft into the gearcase during the pressure tests in the next step.

20. Test the integrity gearcase seals, gaskets and O-rings as described in *Gearcase Pressure and Vacuum Testing*. The drive shaft must be held in position during the pressure tests, or it may be forced out of its bore by the internal pressure.

21. Install the water pump as described in this chapter.

22. Fill the gearcase with the recommended lubricant as described in Chapter Four.

23. Install the gearcase as described previously in this chapter.

Disassembly
(4 Deluxe, 6 and 8 hp Models)

Refer to **Figure 50** and **Figure 51** for this procedure. The 1995 and 1996 (EO and ED) models use detent balls (21, **Figure 50**), activated by the shift cam follower (20) to engage the forward and reverse gears. The 1997-2003 (EU-ST) models use a sliding clutch dog (6, **Figure 51**) to engage the forward and reverse gears. Any differences in service procedures are called out in the text.

The propshaft bearing carrier and propeller shaft on 1997-2003 (EU-ST) models can be removed without removing the gearcase from the outboard motor, if so desired. Because of its shift detent ball system, this type of partial disassembly is not recommended on 1995 and 1996 (EO and ED) models.

1. Drain the gearcase lubricant as described in Chapter Four.

2. Remove the gearcase as described in this chapter.

3. Remove the water pump as described in this chapter.

4. Remove the three screws securing the water pump base to the gearcase deck. See **Figure 52**. Then separate the base from the gearcase and slide it up and off of the drive and shift shafts. Remove and discard the gasket.

5. Pull the drive and shift shafts straight up and out of the gearcase.

6. Remove the two screws securing the propshaft bearing carrier to the gearcase housing. Rotate the bearing carrier to break the O-ring seal, then pull the carrier and propeller shaft from the gearcase as an assembly. If necessary, gently tap the carrier's mounting screw ears with a soft-faced mallet to assist in rotating the carrier.

**GEARCASE ASSEMBLY
(4 DELUXE, 6 AND 8 HP [1995 AND 1996 SHOWN])**

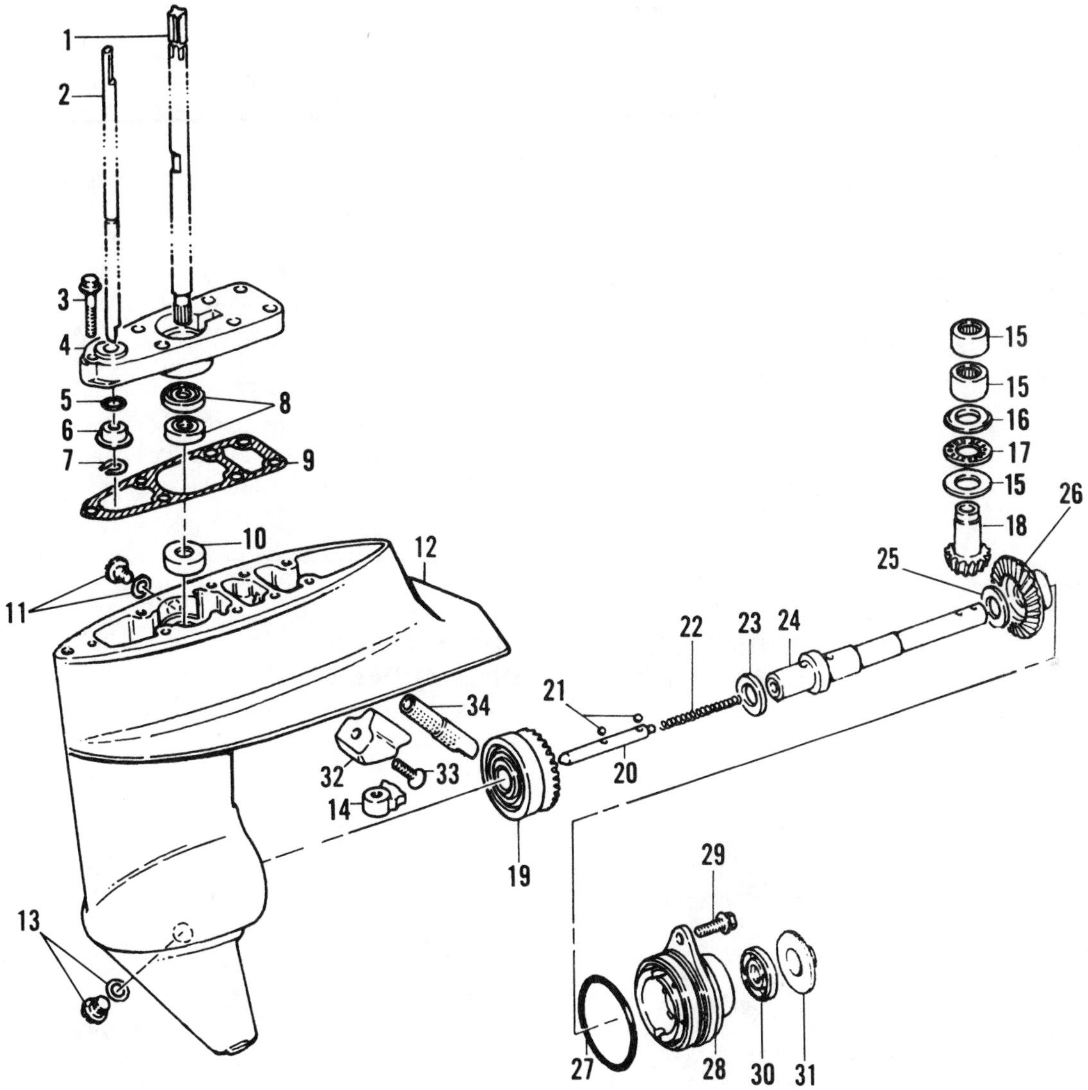

1. Drive shaft
2. Shift shaft
3. Screw
4. Water pump base
5. O-ring
6. Shift shaft bushing
7. Retaining ring
8. Drive shaft seals
9. Gasket
10. Sleeve and bearing assembly
11. Vent plug and seal
12. Gearcase housing
13. Drain/fill plug and seal
14. Shift cam
15. Pinion gear bearings
16. Thrust washers
17. Thrust bearing
18. Pinion gear
19. Forward gear and bearing assembly
20. Shift cam follower
21. Detent balls
22. Shift spring
23. Forward gear thrust washer
24. Propeller shaft
25. Reverse gear thrust washer
26. Reverse gear
27. O-ring
28. Propshaft bearing carrier
29. Screw
30. Propshaft seal
31. Seal protecting washer
32. Anode
33. Screw
34. Water inlet screen

9

7A. *1995 and 1996 models*—Make sure the shift cam follower, both thrust washers and all four detent balls came out with the propeller shaft. If not, reach into the gearcase and remove any components left behind.

7B. *1997-2003 models*—Make sure the shift cam follower (4, **Figure 51**) comes out with the propshaft. If not, reach into the gearcase bore and remove it.

8. Slide the propshaft bearing carrier from the propeller shaft. Remove and discard the carrier O-ring (27, **Figure 50**).

9A. *1995 and 1996 models*—Disassemble the propshaft by sliding the reverse gear and both thrust washers (forward and reverse) from the shaft. Then collect the four detent shift balls and pull the shift cam follower from the propshaft bore. Finally slide the cam follower spring from the propshaft bore. **Figure 53** shows all propshaft components except for the thrust washers.

NOTE
Spring compressor part No. 390766 (or equivalent) is required to disassemble and

assemble the propshaft on 1997 and 1998 models. The tool is designed to straddle the clutch dog pin and compress its spring. Once the spring is compressed, the clutch dog pin can be removed or installed.

9B. *1997-2003 models*—Refer to **Figure 51** and disassemble the propshaft as follows:

   a. Begin by sliding the reverse gear (and its thrust washer) from the shaft.
   b. Pull the shift cam follower from the propshaft bore.
   c. Remove and discard the clutch dog pin's retaining spring with a small screwdriver or awl. Insert the tool under one end of the spring and rotate the propeller shaft to unwind the spring. See **Figure 54**.
   d. Insert spring compressor (part No. 390766) into the open end of the propshaft and depress the clutch dog spring. See **Figure 55**.
   e. While holding the spring compressed, push the clutch dog pin out of the clutch dog with a suitable punch. Slowly release the pressure on the spring,

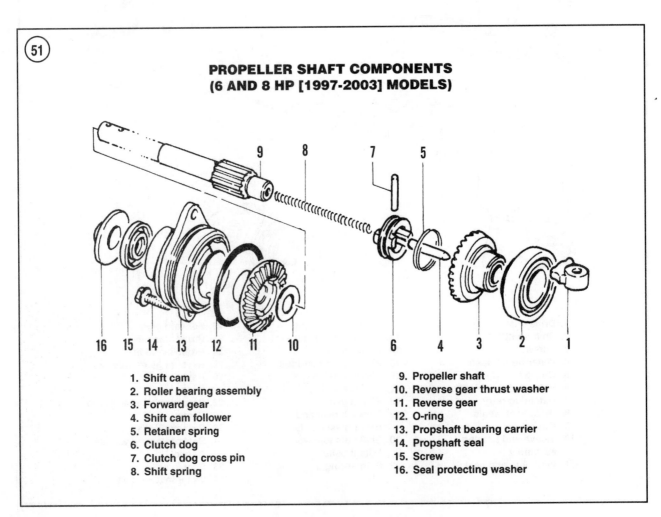

**PROPELLER SHAFT COMPONENTS
(6 AND 8 HP [1997-2003] MODELS)**

1. Shift cam
2. Roller bearing assembly
3. Forward gear
4. Shift cam follower
5. Retainer spring
6. Clutch dog
7. Clutch dog cross pin
8. Shift spring
9. Propeller shaft
10. Reverse gear thrust washer
11. Reverse gear
12. O-ring
13. Propshaft bearing carrier
14. Propshaft seal
15. Screw
16. Seal protecting washer

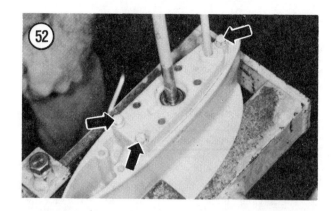

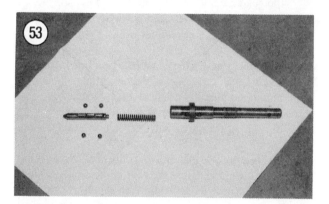

then remove the spring and clutch dog from the propshaft. See **Figure 56**.

10. Reach into the gearcase bore and tilt the forward gear out from under the pinion gear. Remove the forward gear.

11. Remove the pinion gear, thrust bearing and upper and lower thrust washers. See **Figure 57**.

12. Remove the shift cam from the front of the gearcase bore by tilting the gearcase until the cam falls from the gearcase bore.

13. Remove the seal protecting washer from the propshaft bearing carrier. Discard the washer if it is damaged or worn.

14. Remove the propeller shaft seal from the propeller shaft bearing carrier. Pull it from the carrier with a suitable two-jaw puller, and puller bridge, threaded rod and support plate (part No. 432127). Do not damage the seal bore during the removal process. Discard the seal.

15. Remove the two drive shaft seals from the bottom of the water pump base in the same manner as the propeller shaft seal. Discard the seals.

16. Remove and discard the shift shaft bushing from the bottom of the water pump base. Pry the bushing from the

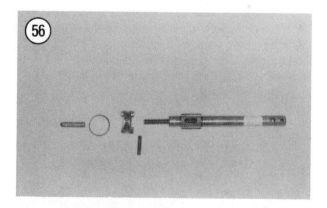

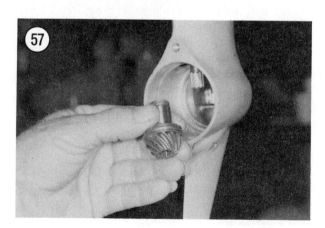

e shift shaft or a similar sized punch. Then discard the O-ring under the bushing.

> *NOTE*
> *On 1995 and 1996 models, the forward gear and its bearing are serviced as an assembly. On 1997-2003 models, the forward gear and its bearing are available separately. In either case, make sure the puller jaws are positioned in the relief slots behind the bearing race.*

17A. *1995 and 1996 models*—If the forward gear or its tapered roller bearing requires replacement, remove the bearing race by pulling it from the gearcase bore with a suitable bearing puller and slide hammer. Discard the race and the forward gear and bearing assembly.

17B. *1997-2003 models*—If the forward gear's tapered roller bearing requires replacement, proceed as follows:
   a. Remove the bearing race by pulling it from the gearcase bore with a suitable bearing and slide hammer.
   b. Discard the bearing race.
   c. Separate the roller bearing from the forward gear by supporting the bearing in a knife-edged bearing plate. Press on the gear hub (with a suitable mandrel) until the gear is separated from the bearing.
   d. Discard the roller bearing.

18. If the drive shaft upper bearing and sleeve assembly (10, **Figure 50**) requires replacement, pull the bearing and sleeve from the drive shaft bore using a suitable external two-jaw bearing puller. The puller must pull on the outside diameter of the sleeve.

> *NOTE*
> *The drive shaft upper bearing and sleeve assembly must be removed (and discarded) in order to remove the two lower drive shaft (pinion) bearings.*

19. If the two lower drive shaft (pinion) bearings require replacement, position a shop towel in the gearcase bore, directly under the bearings. Drive both bearings into the gearcase bore using bearing remover (part No. 319880) or an equivalent mandrel. Discard both bearings.

20. Refer to *Gearcase Cleaning and Inspection*. Clean and inspect all components as directed before beginning reassembly procedures.

Assembly (4 Deluxe, 6 and 8 hp Models)

Lubricate all internal components with OMC Ultra HPF Gear Lube. Do not assemble components *dry*. Refer to **Table 3** for torque values. Refer to **Figure 50** and **Figure 51** for this procedure.

> *NOTE*
> *The forward gear bearing and race are a matched assembly and must be replaced as such.*

1. If the forward gear bearing race was removed, install the race from the new bearing (or forward gear and bearing assembly) as follows:
   a. Lubricate the bearing race and its bore. Set the race into the bore with the tapered side of the race facing up (out).
   b. Position bearing installer (part No. 326025) or an equivalent mandrel over the race. Drive the race into the gearcase until it is seated in its bore.

2. If the forward gear roller bearing was removed from the forward gear, install a new roller bearing (from the new bearing assembly) onto the forward gear as follows:
   a. Place the gear in a press with the gear hub facing up. Use a suitable piece of wood or soft metal (such as aluminum plate) to protect the gear teeth.
   b. Lubricate the roller bearing and gear hub. Then position the bearing over the gear hub with the rollers facing up (away from the gear).
   c. Using a suitable mandrel that only contacts the bearing's inner race, press the bearing onto the gear hub until it is seated against the hub shoulder.

3. If the drive shaft upper bearing (and sleeve) assembly was removed, install a new bearing as follows:
   a. Lubricate the new bearing assembly and the drive shaft bore.
   b. Position the bearing assembly into the drive shaft bore. If one side of the bearing is numbered, position that side up.
   c. Drive the bearing assembly into the drive shaft bore using bearing installer part No. 326575, or an equivalent mandrel that contacts only the sleeve and not the bearing. Drive the sleeve (and bearing) until the sleeve is seated in its bore.

4. If the two lower drive shaft (pinion) bearings were removed, the new bearings must be pulled into position from the gearcase (propshaft) bore, one at a time. To install the new bearings, proceed as follows:
   a. Lubricate the new bearings and the drive shaft bore.
   b. Place a new bearing onto bearing installer (part No. 319878). The numbered side of the bearing must face the installer.
   c. Position the bearing (and installer) in the propshaft bore. Install a 6-1/2 in. long, 3/8 in., coarse-thread bolt (or match the threads of the installer) and a heavy-duty flat washer (wide enough to cover the upper drive shaft bearing's sleeve) into the drive shaft bore.
   d. Thread the bolt into the installer. Tighten the bolt to pull the bearing into the drive shaft bore. Tighten the

bolt until the installer seats against the gearcase. Then remove the tools.

e. Place a second new bearing onto the bearing installer. The numbered side of the bearing must face the installer.

f. Position the bearing (and installer) in the propshaft bore. Install the bolt and flat washer into the drive shaft bore.

g. Thread the bolt into the installer. Tighten the bolt to pull the bearing into the drive shaft bore (and push the first bearing deeper into the bore). Tighten the bolt until the installer seats against the gearcase. Remove the tools.

5. Install a new seal into the propshaft bearing carrier as follows:

a. Position the carrier so that its seal bore is facing up.

b. If the seal is metal cased, coat the outer diameter of the seal with OMC Gasket Sealing Compound. If the seal is rubber cased, lubricate the outer diameter of the seal with OMC DPL (WD-40) Lubricant.

c. Position the seal into the carrier bore with its numbered side facing up (out). Press the seal into the carrier (using a suitable mandrel or socket) until it is seated in the bore.

d. Lubricate the seal lips with OMC Triple Guard Grease.

6. Lubricate a new O-ring (27, **Figure 50**) with OMC Triple Guard Grease. Install the O-ring into the propshaft bearing carrier's groove.

7. Install two new drive shaft seals into the water pump base as follows:

a. Coat the outer diameter of each seal with OMC Gasket Sealing Compound.

b. Install the inner seal using the longer, stepped shoulder of seal installer (part No. 326547) or an equivalent mandrel. The seal lip (spring side) must face into the pump base (away from the gearcase). Press the seal until the installer contacts the pump base.

c. Install the outer seal using the shorter shoulder of seal installer (part No. 326547) or an equivalent mandrel. The seal lip (spring side) must face out of the pump base (into the gearcase). Press the seal until the installer contacts the pump base. The seal must be flush with the pump base when installed.

d. Lubricate the seal lips and pack the area between the seal lips with OMC Triple Guard Grease.

8. Lubricate a new shift shaft O-ring with OMC Triple-Guard grease and install it in the water pump base.

9. Lightly apply OMC Adhesive M sealant to the outer diameter of a new shift shaft bushing. Push the bushing into the water pump cover, over the shift shaft O-ring. Make sure the bushing is seated, then allow the adhesive to dry.

10. If the shift shaft retaining ring (7, **Figure 50**) was removed, reinstall it to the shift shaft at this time.

11. Using a pair of mechanical fingers or needlenose pliers, position the shift cam into the gearcase bore. The side marked *UP* must face the gearcase deck (toward the power head) and the cam's ramp must face the port side.

12. While holding the shift cam in position, insert the shift shaft into the gearcase bore (retaining ring end first) and engage the shift cam. Rotate the shaft as necessary to align the components, then seat the shaft into the cam. Then rotate the shift shaft as far clockwise as possible.

13. Lightly coat both sides of a new water pump base gasket with OMC Adhesive M sealant. Position the gasket to the gearcase deck, then carefully slide the water pump base over the shift shaft and into position against the gasket. Align the base and gasket with the gearcase deck screw holes.

14. Coat the threads of the three water pump base screws with OMC Nut Lock threadlocking adhesive. Install and evenly tighten the screws to 60-84 in.-lb. (6.8-9.5 N•m). See **Figure 52**.

15. Assemble the thrust washers and thrust bearing on the pinion gear. Use OMC Needle Bearing Assembly Grease to hold the components in position. The thrust bearing must be positioned between the thrust washers as shown in **Figure 57**.

16. Invert the gearcase and install the pinion gear and bearing assembly into the drive shaft bore.

17. Insert the forward gear and bearing assembly into the gearcase bore. Tilt the gear to get it past the pinion gear, then rotate it into position (meshed with the pinion gear). If it sticks, insert the propeller shaft into the gear to gain additional leverage. Remove the propeller shaft when finished.

18A. *1995 and 1996 models*—Assemble and install the propshaft as follows:

a. Coat the thrust washers with OMC Needle Bearing Assembly grease. Install the washers onto the propshaft. One washer must be positioned on each side of the propshaft flange.

b. Insert the shift spring into the open end of the propshaft. Then insert the shift cam follower over the spring. The stepped end of the follower must be against the spring.

c. Depress the cam follower (and rotate as necessary) until the rear set of detent notches are visible. Coat two detent balls with OMC Needle Bearing Assembly Grease, then install a ball on each side of the rear set of holes.

d. While continuing to hold the cam follower in position, slide the reverse gear over the propshaft and over the detent balls just installed. Seat the reverse

9

gear against its thrust washer (and propshaft flange). Then release the cam follower.

e. Coat the remaining two detent balls with OMC Needle Bearing Assembly Grease, then install a ball on each side of the forward set of holes.

NOTE
The forward detent balls must be positioned 90° from their engagement lugs (in the forward gear hub) for the balls to fit into the forward gear hub during propshaft installation.

f. While holding the propshaft, push against the reverse gear to lock it in place. Make sure the front thrust washer and detent balls are retained by the assembly grease, then install the propshaft into the gearcase with the forward detent balls positioned 90° from their engagement lugs in the forward gear hub. Seat the propshaft into the forward gear hub.

NOTE
Spring compressor part No. 390766 (or equivalent) is required to assemble the propshaft on 1997-2003 models. The tool is designed to straddle the clutch dog pin and compress its spring. Once the spring has been compressed, the clutch dog pin can be installed.

18B. *1997-2003 models*—Assemble the propshaft as follows:

a. Align the cross pin holes of the clutch dog with the slot in the propeller shaft. Position the end marked *PROP END* toward the propeller and slide the clutch dog onto the propeller shaft.

b. Install the spring into the propeller shaft. Insert spring compressor (part No. 390766) into the open end of the propshaft and depress the spring. See **Figure 55**.

c. With the spring held dompressed, insert the clutch dog pin into the clutch. The pin must pass in front of the clutch dog spring.

NOTE
When installed correctly, the clutch dog pin's retaining spring must lay flat, with no overlapping coils.

d. Secure the pin to the clutch dog with a new retainer spring. Do not open the spring any more than necessary to install it.

e. Coat the shift cam follower with OMC Needle Bearing Assembly Grease. Then insert the cam follower into the open end of the propshaft. The flat end must contact the clutch dog pin.

f. Insert the propshaft assembly into the gearcase and seat it into the forward gear hub.

g. Coat the reverse gear thrust washer with OMC Needle Bearing Assembly Grease, then position the washer into its recess in the reverse gear hub. Finally, install the reverse gear assembly over the propshaft and engage it to the pinion gear teeth.

19. Apply a light coat of OMC Gasket Sealing Compound to the propshaft bearing carrier-to-gearcase mating surfaces. Then install the propshaft bearing carrier. Rotate the carrier to align the screw holes, then seat the carrier on the gearcase.

20. Coat the threads of the two propshaft bearing carrier mounting screws with OMC Gasket Sealing Compound. Install and evenly tighten the screws to 60-84 in.-lb. (6.8-9.5 N•m).

21. Install the seal protecting washer over the propshaft and up against the propshaft seals. The stepped side of the washer must face away from the gearcase.

22. Lubricate the lower end of the drive shaft. Install the drive shaft into its bore and rotate the shaft as necessary to engage the pinion gear.

23. Test the integrity of the gearcase seals, gaskets and O-rings as described in *Gearcase Pressure and Vacuum Testing*. The drive shaft must be held in position during the pressure tests, or it may be forced out of its bore by the internal pressure.

24. Install the water pump as described in this chapter.

25. Fill the gearcase with the recommended lubricant as described in Chapter Four.

26. Install the gearcase as described in this chapter.

Disassembly (9.9 and 15 hp Models)

Early 1995 models may have two propshaft seals (installed back-to-back), while all later models use a single (double-lipped) seal.

The propshaft bearing carrier and propeller shaft can be removed without removing the gearcase from the outboard motor, if so desired. Refer to **Figure 58** for this procedure.

1. Drain the gearcase lubricant as described in Chapter Four.

2. Remove the gearcase as described in this chapter.

3. Remove the water pump as described in this chapter.

4. Remove the two screws securing the propshaft bearing carrier to the gearcase.

5. Pull the propshaft bearing carrier from the gearcase. If the carrier sticks, use puller kit part No. 368631 (or an equivalent puller) as follows:

a. Thread two screws (part No. 319873 [from the puller kit]) into the holes of the screws removed in Step 4.

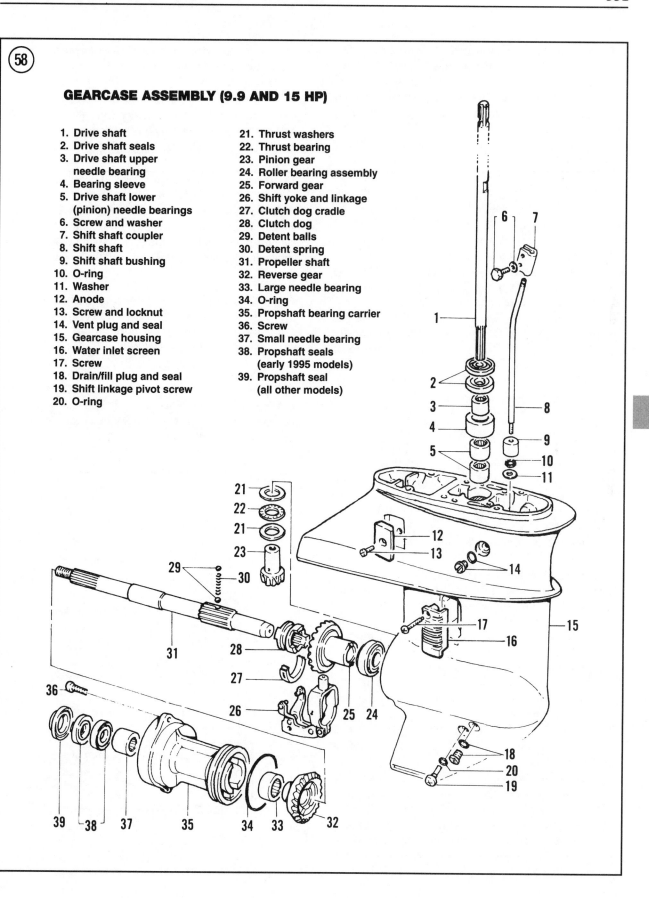

(58)

GEARCASE ASSEMBLY (9.9 AND 15 HP)

1. Drive shaft
2. Drive shaft seals
3. Drive shaft upper
   needle bearing
4. Bearing sleeve
5. Drive shaft lower
   (pinion) needle bearings
6. Screw and washer
7. Shift shaft coupler
8. Shift shaft
9. Shift shaft bushing
10. O-ring
11. Washer
12. Anode
13. Screw and locknut
14. Vent plug and seal
15. Gearcase housing
16. Water inlet screen
17. Screw
18. Drain/fill plug and seal
19. Shift linkage pivot screw
20. O-ring

21. Thrust washers
22. Thrust bearing
23. Pinion gear
24. Roller bearing assembly
25. Forward gear
26. Shift yoke and linkage
27. Clutch dog cradle
28. Clutch dog
29. Detent balls
30. Detent spring
31. Propeller shaft
32. Reverse gear
33. Large needle bearing
34. O-ring
35. Propshaft bearing carrier
36. Screw
37. Small needle bearing
38. Propshaft seals
    (early 1995 models)
39. Propshaft seal
    (all other models)

9

b. Place the bridge (part No. 319874 [from the puller kit]) over the propshaft and pilot it on the two puller screws.

c. Install the propeller nut onto the propshaft. Tighten the nut to pull the carrier (and the propshaft) from the gearcase bore. If necessary, add washers under the nut to allow the tool to pull the carrier further from its bore.

d. Once the carrier is loose, remove the nut, bridge and two screws. Pull the propshaft (and carrier) from the gearcase bore as an assembly.

6. Slide the bearing carrier from the propshaft. Remove and discard the carrier O-ring.

7. Slide the reverse gear and its thrust washer from the propeller shaft. Then locate and secure the two clutch dog detent balls and detent spring. The detent balls will most likely be in the gearcase bore.

8. Remove the shift linkage pivot screw (19, **Figure 58**) from the starboard side of the gearcase. The screw is easily identified by its *Posidriv* (similar to Phillips) screw head. Remove and discard the O-ring from under the screw head.

9. Pull the drive shaft straight up and out of the gearcase.

10. Fully unthread the shift shaft (counterclockwise), then pull the shaft from the gearcase.

11. Reach into the gearcase bore and remove the clutch dog.

12. Grasp the shift yoke with a pair of needlenose pliers and remove it and the forward gear as an assembly. Wiggle the components as necessary to allow removal. Then remove the forward gear's roller bearing from the front of the gearcase bore.

13. Remove the pinion gear, both thrust washers and the thrust bearing.

14. The shift shaft bushing must be pulled up and out of its bore to access the shift shaft O-ring. Remove the shift shaft bushing, O-ring and washer as follows:

a. Position the head of bushing remover (part No. 327693) into the gearcase bore and under the shift shaft bushing.

b. Insert a suitable slide hammer, such as part No. 391008 (and its adapter) through the shift shaft bushing (from the top of the gearcase) and engage the bushing remover.

c. Unthread the handle from the bushing remover, then pull the bushing up and out the gearcase using the slide hammer.

d. Locate and secure the washer, then remove and discard the bushing's O-ring.

15. Remove the two drive shaft seals from the gearcase by pulling them from their bore with a suitable two-jaw puller, puller bridge, threaded rod and support plate (part No. 432127). See **Figure 59**, typical. Do not damage the seal bore during the removal process. Discard the seals.

16. Remove the propshaft seal(s) from the propshaft bearing carrier in the same manner as the drive shaft seals. Discard the seal(s).

17. If the forward gear tapered roller bearing requires replacement, remove the bearing race. Pull it from the gearcase bore with a suitable bearing puller and slide hammer. Discard the race and the forward gear roller bearing.

18. If the drive shaft upper sleeve and bearing assembly (3 and 4, **Figure 58**) requires replacement, pull the bearing first, then the sleeve, from the drive shaft bore. Use a suitable bearing puller and puller bridge, threaded rod and support plate (part No. 432127). Assemble the tools as shown in **Figure 59**, typical. Discard the bearing.

NOTE
The drive shaft upper bearing and sleeve must be removed (and the bearing discarded) in order to remove the two lower drive shaft (pinion) bearings.

19. If the two pinion bearings require replacement, position a shop towel in the gearcase bore directly under the bearings. Drive both bearings into the gearcase bore using bearing remover (part No. 319880) or an equivalent mandrel. Discard both bearings.

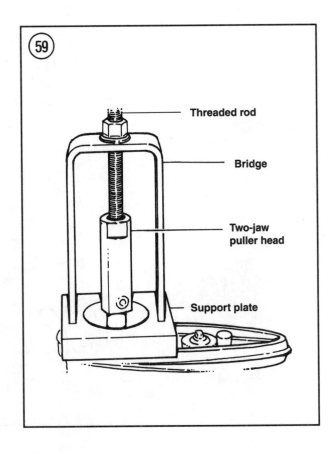

(59)

Threaded rod

Bridge

Two-jaw puller head

Support plate

20. If the propshaft bearing carrier's small bearing (37, **Figure 58**) requires replacement, insert bearing remover (part No. 319880) or an equivalent mandrel into the carrier (from the O-ring groove end) and press the bearing from the carrier. Discard the bearing.

21. If the propshaft bearing carrier's large bearing requires replacement, pull bearing from the carrier with a suitable bearing puller and puller bridge, threaded rod and support plate (part No. 432127). Discard the bearing.

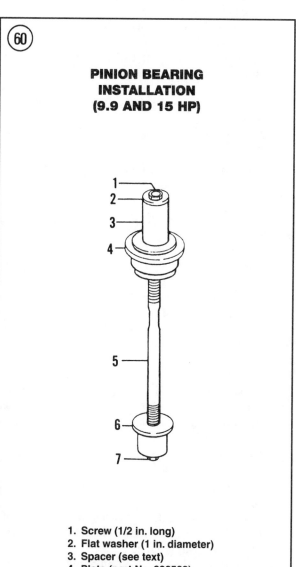

60

PINION BEARING INSTALLATION (9.9 AND 15 HP)

1. Screw (1/2 in. long)
2. Flat washer (1 in. diameter)
3. Spacer (see text)
4. Plate (part No. 326583)
5. Threaded rod (part No. 326582)
6. Installer (part No. 326578)
7. Screw (1-1/4 in. long)

22. Refer to *Gearcase Cleaning and Inspection*. Clean and inspect all components as directed before beginning reassembly procedures.

Assembly (9.9 and 15 hp Models)

Lubricate all internal components with OMC Ultra HPF Gear Lube. Do not assemble components *dry*. Refer to **Table 4** for torque values and **Figure 58** for this procedure.

> *NOTE*
> *The forward gear bearing and race are a matched assembly and must be replaced as such.*

1. If the forward gear bearing race was removed, install the new race as follows:
   a. Lubricate the bearing race and its bore. Set the race into the bore with the tapered side of the race facing up (out).
   b. Attach bearing installer (part No. 319929) to drive handle (part No. 311880).
   c. Position the Bearing Installer (or an equivalent mandrel) over the bearing race.
   d. Cushion the leading edge of the gearcase on a suitable block of wood, then drive the race into the gearcase until it is seated in its bore.

> *NOTE*
> *The pinion bearings (5, **Figure 58**) must be installed before the upper drive shaft sleeve and bearing assembly (3 and 4) can be installed.*

> *CAUTION*
> *The screws (1 and 7, **Figure 60**) must be securely tightened and the flat washer (2) must be perfectly flat or the bearings will not be correctly positioned in the next step.*

2. If the two pinion bearings were removed, the new bearings must be pressed into position from the top of the drive shaft bore, one at a time. Several components from the universal pinion bearing remover/installer kit (part No. 391257) and a second spacer (part No. 339753) are required to properly locate the bearings. To install the new bearings, refer to **Figure 60** and proceed as follows:
   a. Lubricate two new bearings and the drive shaft bore.
   b. To install the lower bearing, assemble the tool as shown in **Figure 60**, using the shorter spacer (part No. 326585). Make sure the screws (1 and 7, **Figure 60**) are securely tightened.
   c. Position the bearing over the installer (6, **Figure 60**) with the numbered side of the bearing against the tool's shoulder.

9

d. Insert the assembly into the drive shaft bore. Drive against the screw (1, **Figure 60**) with a soft-faced mallet until the flat washer (2) contacts the spacer (3).

e. Replace the short spacer (part No. 326585 [3, **Figure 60**]) with long spacer (part No. 339753). After changing the spacer, make sure the screws (1 and 7) are securely tightened.

f. Position the second bearing over the installer (6, **Figure 60**) with the numbered side of the bearing against the tool's shoulder.

g. Pilot the assembly into the drive shaft bore. Drive against the screw (1, **Figure 60**) with a soft-faced mallet until the flat washer (2) contacts the spacer (3).

3. If the drive shaft upper bearing (and sleeve) were removed, assemble a new bearing and sleeve and install the assembly as follows:

a. Lubricate the new bearing, the sleeve and the drive shaft bore.

b. Using bearing installer (part No. 319931) or a suitable mandrel, press the bearing into the sleeve. Press against the numbered side of the bearing only.

c. Position the sleeve and bearing assembly into the drive shaft bore. Make sure the numbered side of the bearing is facing up.

d. Drive the assembly into the drive shaft bore using a suitable mandrel. The mandrel must only push against the sleeve. Press the assembly into the drive shaft bore until it is seated.

4. If the propshaft bearing carrier bearings were removed, install new bearings as follows:

a. Position the carrier in a press with its propeller end facing down (O-ring groove facing up).

b. Lubricate a new small bearing (37, **Figure 58**) and position it into the carrier's bore with its numbered side facing up. Press the bearing into position using a suitable mandrel.

d. Lubricate a new large bearing (33, **Figure 58**) and position it into the carrier's bore with its numbered side facing up.

e. Press the bearing into position with the short-stepped side of bearing installer (part No. 339751) or an equivalent mandrel.

5A. *Double propshaft seal models*—Install two new propshaft seals as follows:

a. Coat the outer diameter of each seal with OMC Gasket Sealing Compound.

b. Install the inner seal using the longer, stepped shoulder of seal installer (part No. 335822) or an equivalent mandrel. The seal lip (spring side) must face into the carrier bore. Press the seal until the installer contacts the carrier.

c. Install the outer seal using the shorter shoulder of seal installer (part No. 335822) or an equivalent mandrel. The seal lip (spring side) must face out from the carrier. Press the seal until the installer contacts the carrier.

d. Lubricate the seal lips and pack the area between the seal lips with OMC Triple Guard Grease.

5B. *Single propshaft seal models*—Install a new propshaft seal as follows:

a. Lubricate the outer diameter of the seal with OMC DPL (WD-40) Lubricant.

b. Position the seal onto seal installer (part No. 342663) or an equivalent mandrel. The extended lip of the seal must pilot into the tool's relief (extended lip must face away from the carrier).

c. Position the installer (and seal) over the carrier's bore. Press the seal into the carrier until the tool contacts the carrier.

d. Lubricate the seal lips with OMC Triple Guard Grease.

6. Coat a new O-ring (34, **Figure 58**) with OMC Triple Guard Grease. Install the O-ring into the propshaft bearing carrier's O-ring groove.

7. Install two new drive shaft seals into the drive shaft bore as follows:

a. Coat the outer diameter of each seal with OMC Gasket Sealing Compound.

b. Install the inner seal using the longer, stepped shoulder of seal installer (part No. 326554) or an equivalent mandrel. The seal lip (spring side) must face into the gearcase. Press the seal until the installer contacts the gearcase deck.

c. Install the outer seal using the shorter shoulder of seal installer (part No. 326554) or an equivalent mandrel. The seal lip (spring side) must face out from the gearcase. Press the seal until the installer contacts the gearcase deck. The seal must be flush with the deck when installed.

d. Lubricate the seal lips and pack the area between the seal lips with OMC Triple Guard Grease.

8. Install the shift shaft bushing, O-ring and washer as follows:

a. Lubricate a new shift shaft O-ring with OMC Triple Guard Grease. Install the O-ring into the open end of the shift shaft bushing.

b. Position the shift shaft bushing and O-ring onto bushing installer (part No. 304515) or an equivalent mandrel. The O-ring end of the bushing must face away from the installer.

c. Position the washer (11, **Figure 58**) over the installer's tip and against the O-ring (and bushing).

d. Coat the bushing's outer diameter with OMC Gasket Sealing Compound. Place the bushing assembly into its bore, then drive the bushing into the gearcase until it is seated.

9. Lubricate the forward gear's roller bearing and position it in its cup at the bottom of the gearcase bore.

NOTE
Yoke locating tool (part No. 319991) is re-quired to install the shift yoke and forward gear assembly.

10. Push the threaded end of the yoke locating tool (part No. 319991) through the shift rod bushing and into the gearcase bore.

11. Position the forward gear's hub in the closed end of the yoke. Hold the assembly near the gearcase bore and thread the yoke locating tool into the closed end of the yoke.

12. Slowly pull on the yoke locating tool to pull the gear and yoke assembly into the gearcase bore. Guide the assembly into the bore until the gear is seated against its roller bearing and the shift yoke drops into its relief at the bottom of the gearcase bore. Do not remove the locating tool at this time.

13. Assemble the thrust washers and thrust bearing to the pinion gear. Use OMC Needle Bearing Assembly Grease to hold the components in position. The thrust bearing must be positioned between the thrust washers as shown in **Figure 57**, typical.

14. Install the pinion gear assembly into its bore. It may be necessary to momentarily push the top of the forward gear away from the pinion gear (using a screwdriver), to allow the pinion gear to enter its bore. Make sure the pinion gear is seated in its bore and properly meshed with the forward gear.

15. Install a new O-ring on the shift linkage pivot screw. Coat the threads of the screw and the O-ring with OMC Nut Lock threadlocking adhesive.

16. Using the yoke locating tool (installed previously), move the shift linkage until it is aligned with the hole for the shift linkage pivot screw. Then install and tighten the shift linkage pivot screw to 48-84 in.-lb. (5.4-9.5 N•m).

17. Remove the yoke locating tool. Lubricate the lower end of the shift shaft with OMC Triple Guard Grease, then carefully thread the rod through the shift shaft bushing to prevent damaging the O-ring. Then align the yoke with the shaft and thread the shaft into the yoke until it is seated.

18. Unthread the shift shaft to position the bend at the top of the shaft straight forward. Do not unthread the shaft any more than necessary to position the shaft as specified. The shaft must not be unthreaded more than one full turn.

19. Using a pair of needlenose pliers, install the saddle over the open arms of the shift yoke.

20. Coat the forward gear thrust washer with OMC Needle Bearing Grease. Position the washer into the recess of the forward gear's hub.

21. Install the clutch dog over the shift saddle and engage it with the forward gear. The grooved end of the clutch dog must face the forward gear. Move the shift shaft up or down as necessary to align the components. Make sure the saddle is not displaced from the shift yoke arms.

22. Coat the reverse gear thrust washer with OMC Needle Bearing Grease. Slide the washer over the propeller end of the propshaft and up against the shaft's shoulder.

23. Coat the detent spring, the two detent balls and their hole in the propshaft with OMC Needle Bearing Assembly Grease. Install the spring into the propshaft hole, then position a ball over each end of the spring.

24. Carefully insert the propshaft assembly into the clutch dog and forward gear. The detent balls must be aligned with the recesses in the clutch dog's internal splines. Use a long screwdriver to compress the detent balls and help guide them into the clutch dog. Push the shaft into the gearcase until it passes through the clutch dog, forward gear and forward gear bearing and seats in the gearcase.

25. Slide the reverse gear over the propshaft and engage it with the pinion gear.

26. Apply OMC Gasket Sealing Compound to the propshaft bearing carrier's rear flange-to-gearcase mating surfaces. Then coat the forward flange (and O-ring) with the same sealant. Install the propshaft bearing carrier over the propshaft. Rotate the carrier to align the screw holes, then seat the carrier to the gearcase.

27. Coat the threads of the propshaft bearing carrier mounting screws with OMC Gasket Sealing Compound. Install and evenly tighten the screws to 60-84 in.-lb. (6.8-9.5 N•m).

28. Lubricate the lower end of the drive shaft. Install the drive shaft into its bore and rotate the shaft as necessary to engage the pinion gear.

29. Test the integrity of the gearcase seals, gaskets and O-rings as described in *Gearcase Pressure and Vacuum Testing*. The drive shaft must be held in position during the pressure tests or it may be forced out of its bore by the internal pressure.

30. Install the water pump as described in this chapter.

31. Fill the gearcase with the recommended lubricant as described in Chapter Four.

32. Install the gearcase as described in this chapter.

Disassembly
(20-35 hp Models [Except 28 Special])

The propshaft bearing carrier can be removed without removing the gearcase from the outboard motor, if so

⑥①

GEARCASE ASSEMBLY (20-35 HP [EXCEPT 28 SPECIAL])

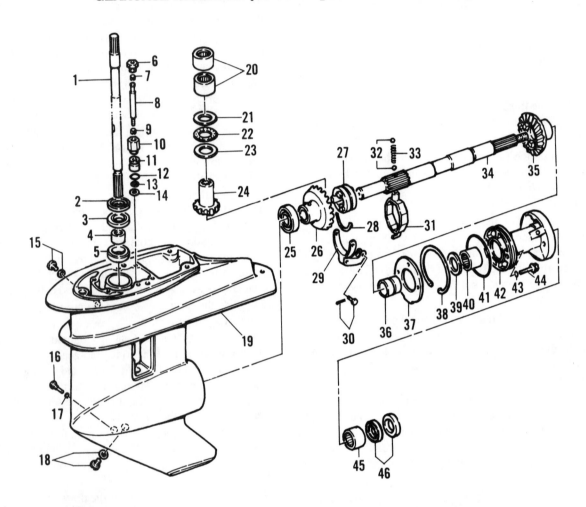

1. Drive shaft
2. Extended lip drive
   shaft seal
3. Flush lip drive shaft seal
4. Drive shaft upper
   needle bearing
5. Bearing sleeve
6. Upper shift shaft
   coupling nut
7. Upper shift shaft
   tapered plastic bushing
8. Lower shift shaft
9. Lower shift shaft
   tapered plastic bushing
10. Lower shift shaft coupling nut
11. Shift shaft bushing
12. External O-ring
13. Internal O-ring

14. Washer
15. Vent plug and seal
16. Shift linkage pivot screw
17. O-ring
18. Drain/fill plug and seal
19. Gearcase housing
20. Pinion gear
    needle bearings
21. Externally chamfered
    thrust washer
22. Thrust bearing
23. Internally chamfered
    thrust washer
24. Pinion gear
25. Roller bearing assembly
26. Forward gear
27. Clutch dog
28. Shift cradle

29. Shift lever
30. Clevis and cotter pin
31. Shift yoke
32. Detent balls
33. Detent spring
34. Propeller shaft
35. Reverse gear
36. Reverse gear bushing
37. Retainer plate
38. Retaining ring
39. Thrust washer
40. Large needle bearing
41. O-ring
42. Propshaft bearing carrier
43. O-ring
44. Screw
45. Small needle bearing
46. Propshaft seals

desired. Do not attempt to remove the propshaft without removing the gearcase from the outboard motor.

Refer to **Figure 61** for this procedure.

1. Drain the gearcase lubricant as described in Chapter Four.

2. Remove the gearcase as described in this chapter.

3. Remove the water pump as described in this chapter.

4. Pull the drive shaft straight up and out of the gearcase.

5. Remove the two screws (44, **Figure 61**) securing the propshaft bearing carrier in the gearcase bore. The screws are located inside the carrier's exhaust passages (**Figure 62**). Remove and discard the O-ring from each screw.

6. Using components of the universal puller kit part No. 378103 (or an equivalent puller) and two 1/4-20 by 6 in. screws , remove the propshaft bearing carrier.

    a. Position the puller head (part No. 307636) and pressing screw (part No. 307637) over the propshaft.

    b. Install the two 1/4-20 by 6 in. screws (with two flat washers) through the puller head slots and into the screw holes on the rear flange of the carrier.

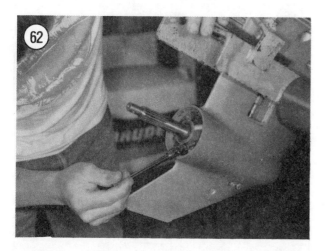

c. Insert the handle (part No. 307638) into the puller head to stabilize the assembly, then tighten the pressing screw to pull the carrier from the gearcase. See **Figure 63**.

d. Once free, pull the carrier from the gearcase bore. Remove and discard the O-ring (41, **Figure 61**). Locate and secure the thrust washer (39).

WARNING
*The retaining (snap) ring (38, **Figure 61**) is under extreme pressure. Wear suitable eye and hand protection when removing and installing the retaining ring.*

7. Remove the retaining ring from the gearcase bore using retaining ring pliers (part No. 331045), or equivalent snap ring pliers. Once clear of the gearcase bore, release all tension from the ring before removing the ring completely from the propshaft.

8. Remove the retainer plate (37, **Figure 61**) from the gearcase bore.

9. Slide the lower shift shaft coupling nut down toward the gearcase bore to expose the tapered plastic keeper. Remove and discard the keeper. Unthread the lower shift shaft from the shift yoke (in the gearcase bore), then remove the shaft and coupler nut from the gearcase.

10. Reach into the gearcase with needlenose pliers and remove the shift yoke (**Figure 64**).

11. Remove the shift linkage pivot screw (16, **Figure 61**) from the starboard side of the gearcase. The screw is easily identified by its *Posidriv* (similar to Phillips) screw head. Remove and discard the O-ring from under the screw head.

12. Pull the propshaft and reverse gear assembly from the gearcase bore. Then locate and secure the two clutch dog detent balls and detent spring. The detent balls will most likely be in the gearcase bore.

9

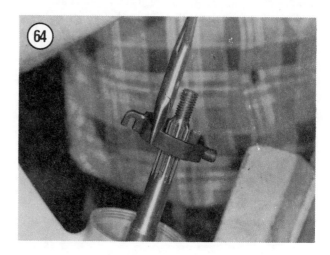

13. Slide the reverse gear off of the propeller shaft. Push the bushing from the gear's bore.

14. Reach into the gearcase bore with needlenose pliers and remove the clutch dog, shift lever and cradle as an assembly. Tilt the lever as necessary to allow easy removal. Do not force the removal. Do not separate the cradle from the shift lever unless one or both components are to be replaced.

15. Remove the forward gear and its roller bearing. Then remove the pinion gear, two thrust washers and thrust bearing. Note the location and orientation of the thrust washers before removing them from the pinion gear.

16. The shift shaft bushing must be pulled up and out of its bore to access the shift shaft O-ring. Remove the shift shaft bushing, O-rings and washer as follows:
   a. Position the head of bushing remover (part No. 327693) into the gearcase bore under the shift shaft bushing.
   b. Insert a suitable slide hammer through the shift shaft bushing (from the top of the gearcase) and engage the bushing remover.
   c. Unthread the handle from the bushing remover, then pull the bushing up and out the gearcase using the slide hammer.
   d. Locate and secure the washer, then remove and discard the bushing's internal and external O-rings.

17. Remove the two drive shaft seals from the gearcase by pulling them from their bore using a suitable two-jaw puller and puller bridge, threaded rod and support plate. See **Figure 59**, typical. Do not damage the seal bore during the removal process. Discard the seals.

18. Remove the propshaft seal(s) from the propshaft bearing carrier in the same manner as the drive shaft seals. Discard the seal(s).

19. If the forward gear tapered roller bearing requires replacement, remove the bearing race by pulling it from the gearcase bore using a suitable bearing puller and slide hammer (part No. 432128). Use angle wrench part No. 334359 (or an equivalent angled wrench) to hold the puller head while expanding its jaws. Discard the race and the forward gear roller bearing.

20. If the drive shaft upper needle bearing and sleeve (4 and 5, **Figure 61**) requires replacement, pull the bearing first, then the sleeve, from the drive shaft bore with a suitable bearing puller and puller bridge, threaded rod and support plate, assembled as shown in **Figure 59**, typical. Discard the bearing.

NOTE
The drive shaft upper bearing and sleeve must be removed in order to remove the two lower drive shaft (pinion) bearings.

21. If the two lower drive shaft (pinion) bearings require replacement, refer to **Figure 65** and proceed as follows:
   a. Position a shop towel in the gearcase bore, directly under the bearings.
   b. Assemble the components from pinion bearing kit part No. 391257 as shown in **Figure 65**.
   c. Insert the tool into the drive shaft bore. Drive against the screw (1, **Figure 65**) with a soft-faced mallet until both bearings are removed.
   d. Discard both bearings.

22. If either (or both) of the propshaft bearing carrier's bearings (40 and 45, **Figure 61**) require replacement, pull the defective bearing(s) from the carrier with a suitable bearing puller and puller bridge, threaded rod and support plate (part No. 432127). Discard the bearing(s).

23. Refer to *Gearcase Cleaning and Inspection*. Clean and inspect all components as directed before beginning reassembly procedures.

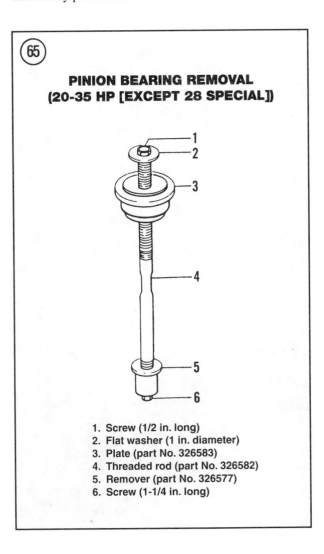

(65)

**PINION BEARING REMOVAL
(20-35 HP [EXCEPT 28 SPECIAL])**

1. Screw (1/2 in. long)
2. Flat washer (1 in. diameter)
3. Plate (part No. 326583)
4. Threaded rod (part No. 326582)
5. Remover (part No. 326577)
6. Screw (1-1/4 in. long)

Assembly
(20-35 hp Models [Except 28 Special])

Lubricate all internal components with OMC Ultra HPF Gear Lube. Do not assemble components dry. Refer to **Table 4** for torque values and **Figure 61** for this procedure.

NOTE
*The forward gear bearing and race (25, **Figure 61**) are a matched assembly and must be replaced as such.*

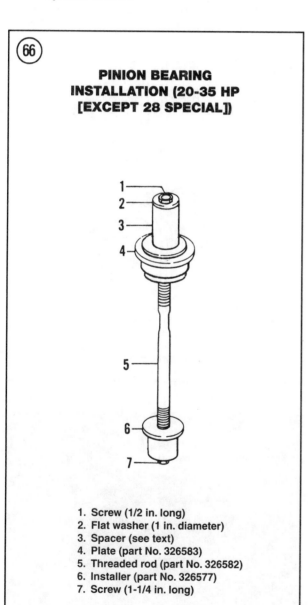

(66)

PINION BEARING INSTALLATION (20-35 HP [EXCEPT 28 SPECIAL])

1. Screw (1/2 in. long)
2. Flat washer (1 in. diameter)
3. Spacer (see text)
4. Plate (part No. 326583)
5. Threaded rod (part No. 326582)
6. Installer (part No. 326577)
7. Screw (1-1/4 in. long)

1. If the forward gear bearing race was removed, install the new race as follows:
   a. Lubricate the bearing race and its bore. Set the race into the bore with the tapered side of the race facing up (out).
   b. Attach bearing installer (part No. 319929) to drive handle (part No. 311880).
   c. Position the Bearing Installer (or an equivalent mandrel) over the bearing race.
   d. Cushion the leading edge of the gearcase on a block of wood, then drive the race into the gearcase until it is seated in its bore.

NOTE
*The pinion bearings (20, **Figure 61**) must be installed before the upper drive shaft sleeve and bearing assembly (4 and 5) can be installed.*

CAUTION
*The screws (1 and 7, **Figure 66**) must be securely tightened and the flat washer (2) must be perfectly flat or the bearings will not be correctly positioned in the next step.*

9

2. If the two lower drive shaft (pinion) bearings were removed, the new bearings must be pressed into position from the top of the drive shaft bore, one at a time. Several components from universal pinion bearing remover/installer kit (part No. 391257) and two spacers (part No. 330067 and part No. 330068) are required to properly locate the bearings. To install the new bearings, refer to **Figure 66** and proceed as follows:
   a. Lubricate two new bearings and the drive shaft bore.
   b. To install the lower bearing, assemble the tool as shown in **Figure 66**, using the shorter spacer (part No. 330067). Make sure the Screws (1 and 7, **Figure 66**) are securely tightened.
   c. Position the bearing over the installer (6, **Figure 66**) with numbered side of the bearing against the tool's shoulder.
   d. Insert the assembly into the drive shaft bore. Drive against the screw (1, **Figure 66**) with a soft-faced mallet until the flat washer (2) contacts the spacer (3).
   e. Replace the short spacer (part No. 330067 [3, **Figure 66**]) with long spacer (part No. 330068). After changing the spacer, make sure the screws (1 and 7) are securely tightened.
   f. Position the second bearing over the installer (6, **Figure 66**) with the numbered side of the bearing against the tool's shoulder.
   g. Insert the assembly into the drive shaft bore. Drive against the screw (1, **Figure 66**) with a soft-faced

mallet until the flat washer (2) contacts the spacer (3).

3. If the drive shaft upper bearing (and sleeve) were removed, assemble a new bearing and sleeve, and install the assembly as follows:

    a. Lubricate the new bearing, the sleeve and the drive shaft bore.

    b. Using bearing installer (part No. 322923) or a suitable mandrel, press the bearing into the sleeve. Press against the numbered side of the bearing only.

    c. Position the sleeve and bearing assembly into the drive shaft bore. Make sure the numbered side of the bearing is facing up.

    d. Drive the assembly into the drive shaft bore using bearing installer (part No. 322923) attached to plate (part No. 318122) with a suitable bolt. If these tools are not available, use a suitable mandrel that only contacts the sleeve. Press the assembly into the drive shaft bore until the plate contacts the gearcase deck (or the sleeve is positioned as noted on disassembly).

4. If the propshaft bearing carrier bearings were removed, install new bearings as follows:

    a. Position the carrier in a press with its propeller end facing down (O-ring groove facing up).

    b. Lubricate a new large bearing (40, **Figure 61**) and position it into the carrier's bore with its numbered side facing up.

    c. Press the bearing into position using bearing installer (part No. 335820) or an equivalent mandrel. Press until the tool contacts the bearing carrier.

    d. Position the carrier in a press with the propeller end facing up (O-ring groove facing down).

    e. Lubricate a new small bearing (45, **Figure 61**) and position it into the carrier's bore with its numbered side facing up.

    f. Press the bearing into position with bearing installer (part No. 321428) or an equivalent mandrel. Press until the tool contacts the bearing carrier.

5. Install two new propshaft seals as follows:

    a. Coat the outer diameter of each seal with OMC Gasket Sealing Compound.

    b. Install the inner seal using the longer, stepped shoulder of seal installer (part No. 335821) or an equivalent mandrel. The seal lip (spring side) must face into the carrier bore. Press the seal until the installer contacts the carrier.

    c. Install the outer seal using the shorter shoulder of seal installer (part No. 335821) or an equivalent mandrel. The seal lip (spring side) must face out from the carrier. Press the seal until the installer contacts the carrier.

    d. Lubricate the seal lips and pack the area between the seal lips with OMC Triple Guard Grease.

6. Coat a new O-ring (41, **Figure 61**) with OMC Triple Guard Grease. Install the O-ring into the propshaft bearing carrier's O-ring groove.

7. Install two new drive shaft seals into the drive shaft bore as follows:

    a. Coat the outer diameter of each seal with OMC Gasket Sealing Compound.

    b. Install the inner seal (with the flush lip) using the longer, stepped shoulder of seal installer (part No. 326552) or an equivalent mandrel. The seal lip (spring side) must face into the gearcase. Press the seal until the installer contacts the gearcase deck.

    c. Install the outer seal (with the extended lip) using the shorter shoulder of seal installer (part No. 326552)

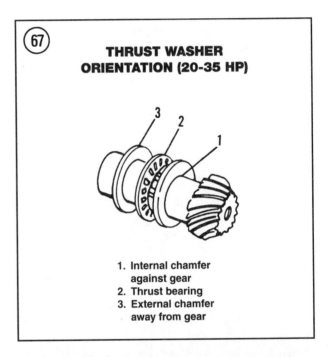

67

THRUST WASHER ORIENTATION (20-35 HP)

1. Internal chamfer against gear
2. Thrust bearing
3. External chamfer away from gear

68

or an equivalent mandrel. The extended lip must face away (out) from the gearcase. Press the seal until the installer contacts the gearcase deck.

    d. Lubricate the seal lips and pack the area between the seal lips with OMC Triple Guard Grease.

8. Install the shift shaft bushing, O-ring and washer as follows:

    a. Lubricate a new shift shaft O-ring with OMC Triple Guard Grease. Install the O-ring into the open end of the shift shaft bushing.

    b. Position the shift shaft bushing and O-ring onto bushing installer (part No. 304515) or an equivalent mandrel. The O-ring end of the bushing must face away from the installer.

    c. Position the washer (14, **Figure 61**) over the installer's tip and against the O-ring (and bushing).

    d. Install a new external O-ring into the groove in the bushing's outer diameter.

    e. Coat the bushing's outer diameter (and the external O-ring) with OMC Gasket Sealing Compound. Place the bushing assembly into its bore, then drive the bushing into the gearcase until it is seated.

9. Lubricate the forward gear's roller bearing and position it in its cup at the bottom of the gearcase bore.

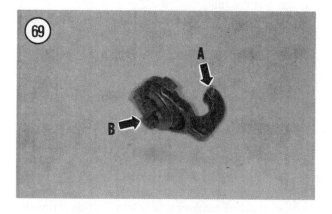

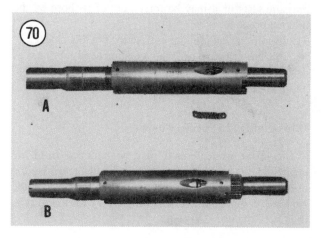

10. Refer to **Figure 67** and assemble the thrust washers and thrust bearing to the pinion gear as follows:

    a. Use OMC Needle Bearing Assembly Grease to hold the components in position.

    b. Position the washer with the chamfer on the internal diameter (1, **Figure 67**) onto the pinion gear with the chamfered edge facing the gear.

    c. Position the thrust bearing (2, **Figure 67**) over the washer.

    d. Position the washer with its chamfer on the outer diameter (3, **Figure 67**) onto the pinion gear with the chamfered edge facing away from the gear.

11. Install the pinion gear into its bore. It is helpful to use a right-angled rod, such as that shown in **Figure 68**, to install the gear.

12. Install the forward gear. Tilt the gear to get it behind the pinion gear, then rotate it into position over its roller bearing. Make sure the gear is sitting flush against its bearing and is engaged with the pinion gear.

13. Assemble and install the shift lever, cradle and clutch dog as follows:

    a. If the cradle and shift lever were separated, install the cradle into the shift lever arms.

    b. If the clevis pin (A, **Figure 69**) was removed, install the clevis pin into the shift lever and secure it with a new cotter pin. Bend both prongs of the cotter pin for a secure attachment.

    c. Set the clutch dog (B, **Figure 69**) into the cradle. The grooved end of the clutch dog must face the forward gear.

    d. Grasp the assembly with a pair of needlenose pliers and set it into position in the gearcase bore.

14. Install a new O-ring on the shift linkage pivot screw. Coat the threads of the screw and the O-ring with OMC Nut Lock threadlocking adhesive. Move the shift lever and cradle until it is aligned with the hole for the shift linkage pivot screw. Then install and tighten the shift linkage pivot screw to 48-84 in.-lb. (5.4-9.5 N•m).

NOTE
Shift detent sleeve (part No. 328081) is required to install the propshaft into the gearcase without displacing the detent spring and detent balls.

15. Refer to **Figure 70** and assemble and install the propshaft as follows:

    a. Install shift detent sleeve (part No. 328081) over the propshaft. Align the slot in the tool with one side of the hole in the propeller shaft. See A, **Figure 70**.

    b. Install one detent ball, then the detent spring through the slot in the tool and into the propshaft hole.

    c. Install the second detent ball over the spring, push it down with your thumb, then carefully pull the tool

9

back over the ball, locking it in place. Continue pulling the tool toward the rear of the propshaft until you feel the detent balls snap into the hole near end of the tool. See B, **Figure 70**.

NOTE
Work slowly and carefully in the following steps. The detent balls and spring will not engage the clutch dog if all components are not correctly aligned.

d. Carefully insert the propshaft into the gearcase bore and into the clutch dog, forward gear and forward bearing. Rotate the tool to engage the tool's lugs with the clutch dog and engage the clutch dog with the forward gear.

e. When all components are aligned, hold the tool firmly engaged with the clutch dog, then tap gently on the end of the propshaft to drive the shaft into position.

f. Remove the tool and visually verify that the detent balls and spring are not displaced.

16. Slide the reverse gear over the propshaft and engage it with the pinion gear. Lubricate the reverse gear bushing, then slide it over the propshaft and push it into the reverse gear.

17. Using needlenose pliers, install the shift yoke into the gearcase bore with the open end of the hook (at its bottom) facing in. Engage the hook with the clevis pin at the bottom of the shift lever and cradle.

18. Lubricate the lower end of the shift shaft with OMC Triple Guard Grease, then carefully thread the rod through the shift shaft bushing to prevent damaging the O-ring. Then align the yoke with the shaft and thread the shaft into the yoke until it is seated.

19. Slide the lower coupling nut over the shift shaft, then install a new tapered plastic keeper into the shaft's groove. The keeper's larger end must face up.

20. Install the retaining plate over the propshaft and into the gearcase bore. The plate's tab must face straight down (toward the skeg).

WARNING
*The retaining (snap) ring (38, **Figure 61**) is under extreme pressure. Wear suitable eye and hand protection when removing and installing the retaining ring.*

NOTE
Do not drag the open ends of the retaining ring in the gearcase bore during installation. This will scratch the bore, resulting in the carrier's O-ring being damaged when the carrier is installed.

21. Install the retaining ring. Position the ring over the propshaft and against the end of the gearcase bore. The sharp edge of the ring must face the propeller (outward). Compress the ring using suitable snap ring pliers, then push it into its bore. Continue to compress the ring as necessary to install the ring into its groove, then carefully release the ring, making sure it completely expands and seats in its groove.

22. Install a $\frac{1}{4}$-28 × 6 threaded rod into one of the threaded holes in the retainer plate. Do not thread the rod more than 2-3 turns into the plate.

23. Coat the reverse gear thrust washer with OMC Needle Bearing Grease. Position the washer into the recess in the propshaft bearing carrier.

24. Apply OMC Gasket Sealing Compound to the propshaft bearing carrier's rear flange. Then coat the forward flange (and O-ring) with the same sealant. Install the propshaft bearing carrier over the propshaft, making sure the word *UP* (cast into the rear flange), is pointing straight up and the guide pin fits into the appropriate hole in the carrier.

25. Push the carrier into the gearcase bore until it is seated. If necessary, tap the carrier with a wooden dowel (and suitable mallet).

26. Install new O-rings on the two carrier screws. Then coat the screw threads and O-rings with OMC Gasket Sealing Compound. Install one screw into the open carrier hole and engage the retaining ring threads. Do not tighten the screw at this time.

27. Remove the guide pin from the other carrier screw hole. Then install the second screw into the hole and engage the retaining ring threads. Once both screws engage the retaining ring threads, tighten both screws finger-tight.

28. Evenly tighten the carrier mounting screws to 60-84 in.-lb. (6.8-9.5 N•m) in a minimum of three progressive stages.

29. Lubricate the lower end of the drive shaft. Install the drive shaft into its bore and rotate the shaft as necessary to engage the pinion gear.

30. Test the integrity of the gearcase seals, gaskets and O-rings as described in *Gearcase Pressure and Vacuum Testing*. The drive shaft must be held in position during the pressure tests or it may be forced out of its bore by the internal pressure.

31. Install the water pump as described in this chapter.

32. Fill the gearcase with the recommended lubricant as described in Chapter Four.

33. Install the gearcase as described in this chapter.

Disassembly (28 Special Models)

The lower gearcase half may be removed from the gearcase housing while the gearcase is still attached to the outboard motor. This will allow access to most of the gearcase components. Refer to **Figure 71** for this procedure.

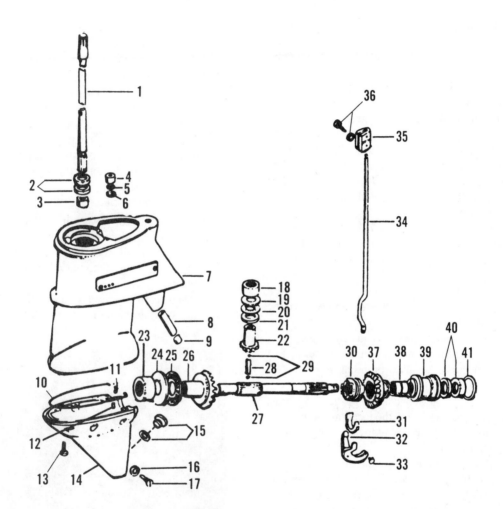

GEARCASE ASSEMBLY (28 SPECIAL)

1. Drive shaft
2. Drive shaft seals
3. Drive shaft upper needle bearing
4. Shift shaft bushing
5. Shift shaft O-ring
6. Washer
7. Upper gearcase housing
8. Water inlet screen
9. Plug
10. Seal
11. Magnet
12. Dowel pin
13. Screw
14. Lower gearcase housing
15. Plug and seal
16. O-ring
17. Shift linkage pivot screw
18. Pinion gear needle bearing
19. Externally chamfered thrust washer
20. Thrust bearing
21. Internally chamfered thrust washer
22. Pinion gear
23. Needle bearing
24. Thrust washer
25. Thrust bearing
26. Forward gear
27. Propeller shaft
28. Detent spring
29. Detent balls
30. Clutch dog
31. Clutch dog cradle
32. Shift lever
33. Clevis and cotter pins
34. Shift shaft
35. Shift shaft coupler
36. Screw and washer
37. Reverse gear
38. Reverse gear bushing
39. Gearcase head
40. Propshaft seals
41. O-ring

9

1. Drain the gearcase lubricant as described in Chapter Four.

2. Remove the gearcase as described in this chapter.

3. Remove the water pump as described in this chapter.

4. Pull the drive shaft straight up and out of the gearcase.

5. Verify that the shift shaft coupler (35, **Figure 71**) is not attached to the shift shaft. If still attached, remove it at this time.

6. Inspect the exposed end of the shift shaft for nicks and burrs. Remove any such damage with 400 grit wet/dry sandpaper. The shift shaft must slide through the shift shaft bushing without catching.

7. Position the gearcase so the lower gearcase housing is pointing up.

8. Remove the shift linkage pivot screw (17, **Figure 71**) from the starboard side of the lower gearcase housing. The screw is easily identified by its *Posidriv* (similar to Phillips) screw head. Remove and discard the O-ring from under the screw head.

9. Remove the 6 screws (13, **Figure 71**) holding the lower gearcase housing to the upper gearcase housing. Tap the skeg sideways with a soft-faced mallet to break the seal, then remove the lower gearcase housing. Remove and discard the rubber seal (10, **Figure 71**).

10. Lift the shift lever up and to the rear and remove the clutch dog cradle (**Figure 72**).

11. Lift the propeller shaft, forward and reverse gears and the gearcase head (as an assembly) from the gearcase. Lift the shift rod as necessary to allow propshaft removal. See **Figure 73**.

12. Remove the pinion gear, two thrust washers and thrust bearing from the gearcase. Note the location and orientation of the thrust washers before removing them from the pinion gear. See **Figure 74**.

13. Pull the shift shaft from the bottom of the gearcase.

14. The shift shaft bushing must be removed to access the shift shaft O-ring. Drive the bushing from the gearcase (toward the power head) with bushing remover part No. 304514 (or a suitable punch). Do not damage the bushing's bore during the removal process. Locate and secure the washer (6, **Figure 71**) and discard the O-ring (5).

15. Remove the two drive shaft seals from the gearcase by pulling them from their bore with a suitable 2-jaw puller and puller bridge, threaded rod and support plate (part No. 432127). Do not damage the seal bore during the removal process. Discard the seals.

CAUTION
Use extreme care when removing the clutch dog. The detent balls and spring may fly from the propshaft with considerable force.

16. Slide all components (except the clutch dog) from the propeller shaft. Then cover the clutch dog with a shop towel (to catch the detent balls and spring) and slowly slide the clutch dog off the front of the propeller shaft. Locate and secure the two detent balls and detent spring.

17. Remove and discard the O-ring from the gearcase head's groove.

18. Remove the two propshaft seals from the gearcase head by pulling them from their bore with a suitable 2-jaw puller and puller bridge and threaded rod (part No. 432127) and a suitable support plate. Do not damage the seal bore during the removal process. Discard the seals.

19. If the drive shaft upper needle bearing (3, **Figure 71**) requires replacement, remove the bearing as follows:

   a. Insert bearing remover part No. 326570 (or a suitable mandrel) through the pinion gear's bearing and against the upper drive shaft bearing.

   b. Drive the bearing out of the top of the gearcase with a suitable mallet.

   c. Discard the bearing.

20. If the pinion gear (lower drive shaft) needle bearing requires replacement, remove the bearing as follows:

   a. Insert the small, hooked end of bearing remover part No. 326571 into the pinion bearing until it locks in place.

   b. Insert bearing remover part No. 326570 (or a suitable mandrel) through the drive shaft bore (from the top

of the gearcase) and position it over the bearing remover (part No. 326571) installed in substep a.

c. Drive the bearing out the bottom of the gearcase with a suitable mallet.

d. Discard the bearing.

21. Refer to *Gearcase Cleaning and Inspection*. Clean and inspect all components as directed before beginning reassembly. Make sure the magnet (11, **Figure 71**) is thoroughly cleaned and all metal shavings and particles are removed.

Assembly (28 Special Models)

Lubricate all internal components with OMC Ultra HPF Gear Lube. Do not assemble components *dry*. Refer to **Table 4** for torque values and **Figure 71** for this procedure.

1. If the drive shaft upper bearing was removed, install a new bearing as follows:

a. Position the gearcase housing with the drive shaft housing mating surface facing up.

b. Lubricate the bearing and the drive shaft bore.

c. Set the bearing into the drive shaft bore with its numbered side facing up.

d. Press the bearing into position using the longer stepped side of bearing installer (part No. 326564) or an equivalent mandrel. Press the bearing until the tool seats against the gearcase housing.

2. If the pinion gear (lower drive shaft) bearing was removed, install a new bearing as follows:

a. Position the gearcase housing with the lower gearcase housing's mating surface facing up.

b. Lubricate the bearing and the drive shaft bore.

c. Set the bearing into the bottom of the drive shaft bore with its numbered side facing up.

d. Press the bearing into position using bearing installer (part No. 326565) or an equivalent mandrel. Press the bearing until the tool seats against the gearcase housing.

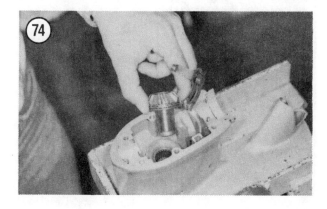

3. Install the shift shaft bushing, O-ring and washer as follows:

a. Lubricate a new shift shaft O-ring with OMC Triple Guard Grease. Install the O-ring into the open end of the shift shaft bushing.

b. Position the shift shaft bushing and O-ring onto bushing installer (part No. 304515) or an equivalent mandrel. The O-ring end of the bushing must face away from the installer.

c. Position the washer (6, **Figure 71**) over the installer's tip and against the O-ring (and bushing).

d. Coat the bushing's outer diameter with OMC Gasket Sealing Compound. Insert the bushing assembly into its bore, then drive the bushing into the gearcase until it is seated.

4. Install two new drive shaft seals into the drive shaft bore (at the same time) as follows:

a. Coat the outer diameter of each seal with OMC Gasket Sealing Compound.

b. Attach seal installer (part No. 330655) to drive handle (part No. 378737).

c. Position the outer (upper) seal onto the installer with the seal lip (spring side) facing the installer.

d. Position the inner (lower) seal onto the installer with the seal lip (spring side) facing away from the installer (and the upper seal).

e. Press both seals into the drive shaft bore until the installer contacts the gearcase deck.

f. Lubricate the seal lips and pack the area between the seal lips with OMC Triple Guard Grease.

NOTE
The outer propshaft seal is identified by the extended metal case that covers (protects) the seal lip from debris (such as fishing line).

5. Install two new propeller shaft seals into the gearcase head as follows:

a. Coat the outer diameter of each seal with OMC Gasket Sealing Compound.

b. Install the inner seal using the longer shoulder of seal installer (part No. 326691) or an equivalent mandrel. The seal lip (spring side) must face into the gearcase. Press the seal until the installer contacts the gearcase head.

c. Install the outer seal using the shorter shoulder of seal installer (part No. 326691) or an equivalent mandrel. The seal lip (covered by the extended metal case) must face out from the gearcase. Press the seal until the installer contacts the gearcase deck.

d. Lubricate the seal lips and pack the area between the seal lips with OMC Triple Guard Grease.

6. Coat a new O-ring with OMC Triple Guard Grease and install it into the gearcase head's groove.

9

7. Lubricate the shift shaft with OMC Triple-Guard grease. Insert the shaft into the shift shaft bushing and push it into place. Tilt the shift lever toward the rear of the gearcase and set the cradle onto the shift lever arms as shown in B, **Figure 75**.

8. Refer to **Figure 76** and assemble and install the pinion gear, thrust washers and thrust bearing as follows:

   a. Use OMC Needle Bearing Assembly Grease to hold the components in position.

   b. Position the washer with the chamfer on its internal diameter (1, **Figure 76**) onto the pinion gear with the chamfered edge facing the gear.

   c. Position the thrust bearing (2, **Figure 76**) over the washer.

   d. Position the washer with the chamfer on its outer diameter (3, **Figure 76**) onto the pinion gear with the chamfered edge facing away from the gear.

   e. Install the pinion gear and bearing assembly into its bore.

8. Coat the detent spring, the two detent balls and their hole in the propshaft with OMC Needle Bearing Assembly Grease. Install the spring into the propshaft hole, then position a ball over each end of the spring.

9. Carefully insert the propshaft assembly into the clutch dog. The clutch dog's grooved lugs must face forward and the detent balls must be aligned with the recesses in the clutch dog's internal splines. Compress the detent balls with your fingers and help guide them into the clutch dog. Push the shaft into the clutch dog until the detent balls engage the recesses in the clutch dog's inner bore.

10. Lubricate all of the following components and install them onto the propshaft as follows:

   a. Slide the forward gear over the front of the propshaft, then install the thrust bearing and thrust washer over the forward gear hub in that order.

   b. Install the needle bearing over the forward gear hub and seat it against the thrust washer. The numbered side of the bearing must face away from the gear.

   c. Install the reverse gear over the rear of the propshaft, then slide the reverse gear bushing over the shaft and into the gear.

   d. Install the gearcase head over the rear of the propshaft and seat it against the reverse gear hub.

11. Make sure the dowel pin (12, **Figure 71**) is securely installed in the upper gearcase. Then apply a thin bead of OMC Adhesive M sealant across the gearcase head's bore (just ahead of where the gearcase head's O-ring will ride) as shown in A, **Figure 75**.

12. Set the propshaft assembly into the upper gearcase (**Figure 77**). Rotate the gearcase head to align its hole with the dowel pin in the upper gearcase. Make sure all components are seated into the upper gearcase, then rotate the shift lever and cradle forward and engage the cradle with

the clutch dog groove. If necessary, move the shift lever up or down, and the clutch back and forth to align the cradle.

13. Hook the alignment tool (part No. 390880) on the upper gearcase housing. Tighten the alignment tool's screw to push the propeller shaft forward, seating and aligning the forward gear, thrust bearing and thrust washer against the front of the gearcase.

NOTE
The lower gearcase-to-upper gearcase sealing strip is sold only in bulk rolls. Obtain at least 13 in. (33 cm) from an Evinrude/Johnson dealership before proceeding.

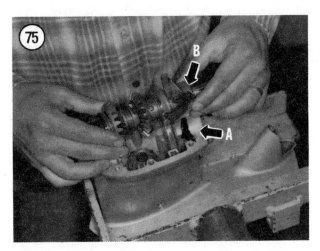

THRUST WASHER ORIENTATION (20-35 HP)

1. Internal chamfer against gear
2. Thrust bearing
3. External chamfer away from gear

14. Glue a new seal strip into the lower gearcase housing's groove using OMC Adhesive M sealant. Use the sealant sparingly. Allow the sealant to dry, then trim the ends of the sealing strip flush with the ends of the housing's groove.

15. Apply OMC Black Silicone RTV sealant to the last 1/2 in. (12.7 mm) of each end of the sealing strip. Spread the sealant over the adjoining lower-to-upper gearcase mating surfaces. Do not allow the sealer to ooze excessively into the gearcase cavity and contaminate the bearings and gears. Remove excess sealer.

16. Make sure the magnet (11, **Figure 71**) is securely installed in its pocket at the rear of the lower gearcase housing.

17. Coat the upper-to-lower gearcase mating surface of the upper gearcase with OMC Adhesive M sealant. Also apply the sealant to the exposed portion of the gearcase head's O-ring. Do not allow the sealer to ooze excessively into the gearcase cavity and contaminate the bearings and gears. Remove excess sealer.

18. Install the lower gearcase housing to the upper gearcase housing and seat it in place with hand pressure. Apply OMC Gasket Sealing Compound to the threads of the 6 gearcase screws. Install the screws and evenly tighten them finger-tight at this time.

NOTE
*The lower gearcase housing must be pushed backward **while** the screws are being tightened to align the housing with the forward gear thrust washer and bearing.*

19. While applying rearward pressure to the lower gearcase housing, tighten all six screws evenly to 60-84 in.-lb. (6.8-9.5 N•m) in a minimum of three progressive steps. Remove the alignment tool when finished.

20. Install a new O-ring on the shift linkage pivot screw. Coat the threads of the screw and the O-ring with OMC Nut Lock threadlocking adhesive. Move the shift shaft until the shift lever is aligned with the hole for the shift

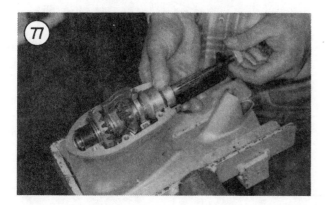

linkage pivot screw. Then install and tighten the shift linkage pivot screw to 48-84 in.-lb. (5.4-9.5 N•m).

21. Lubricate the lower end of the drive shaft. Install the drive shaft into its bore and rotate the shaft as necessary to engage the pinion gear.

22. Test the integrity of the gearcase seals, gaskets and O-rings as described in *Gearcase Pressure and Vacuum Testing*. The drive shaft must be held in position during the pressure tests or it may be forced out of its bore by the internal pressure.

23. Install the water pump as described in this chapter.

24. Fill the gearcase with the recommended lubricant as described in Chapter Four.

25. Install the gearcase as described in this chapter.

Disassembly (40-50 hp [Two-cylinder] Models)

Refer to **Figure 78** for this procedure. Record the location, orientation and thickness of all shims and thrust washers removed during disassembly, so that they may be correctly reinstalled.

The propshaft bearing carrier can be removed without removing the gearcase from the outboard motor, if so desired. Do not attempt to remove the propshaft without removing the gearcase from the outboard motor.

1. Drain the gearcase lubricant as described in Chapter Four.

2. Remove the gearcase as described in this chapter.

3. Remove the water pump as described in this chapter.

4. Remove the two screws securing the anode to the rear of the propshaft bearing carrier. Remove the anode.

5. Remove the two screws securing the retaining tabs (50, **Figure 78**) to the propshaft bearing carrier. Remove the screws and the tabs.

6. Using components of the universal puller kit part No. 378103 (or an equivalent puller) and two 1/4-20 × 8 in. screws , remove the propshaft bearing carrier.

   a. Position the puller head (part No. 307636) and pressing screw (part No. 307637) over the propshaft.

   b. Install the two 1/4-20 × 8 in. screws (with two flat washers) through the puller head slots and into the screws holes on the rear flange of the carrier.

   c. Insert the handle (part No. 307638) into the puller head to stabilize the assembly, then tighten the pressing screw to pull the carrier from the gearcase. See **Figure 63**, typical.

   d. Once free, pull the carrier from the gearcase bore. Remove and discard the O-ring (47, **Figure 78**). Locate and secure the reverse gear thrust washer (46).

7. Rotate the gearcase until the reverse gear and thrust bearing slide out. Be prepared to catch the components.

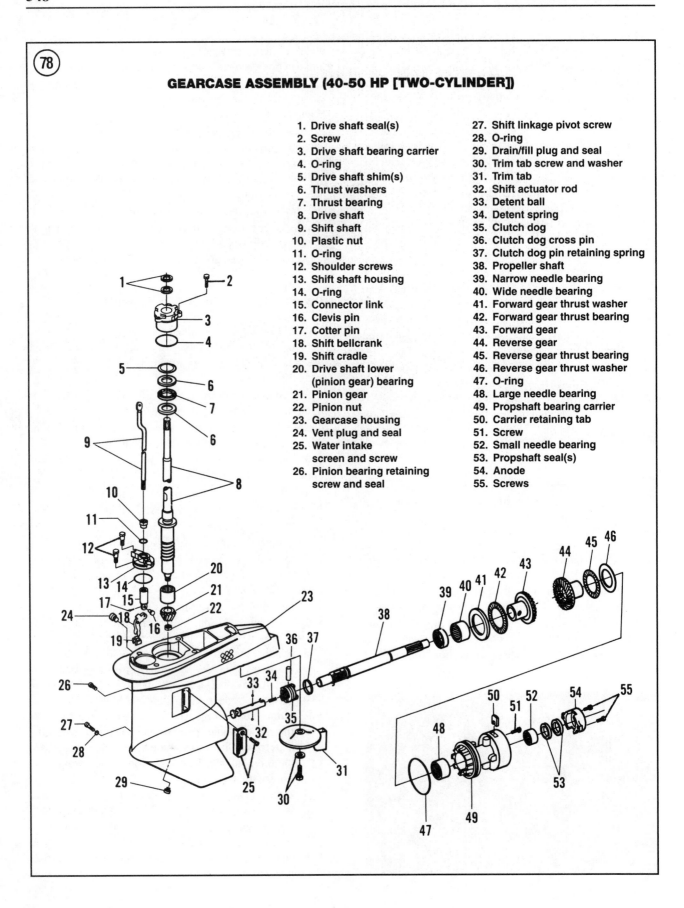

GEARCASE ASSEMBLY (40-50 HP [TWO-CYLINDER])

1. Drive shaft seal(s)
2. Screw
3. Drive shaft bearing carrier
4. O-ring
5. Drive shaft shim(s)
6. Thrust washers
7. Thrust bearing
8. Drive shaft
9. Shift shaft
10. Plastic nut
11. O-ring
12. Shoulder screws
13. Shift shaft housing
14. O-ring
15. Connector link
16. Clevis pin
17. Cotter pin
18. Shift bellcrank
19. Shift cradle
20. Drive shaft lower (pinion gear) bearing
21. Pinion gear
22. Pinion nut
23. Gearcase housing
24. Vent plug and seal
25. Water intake screen and screw
26. Pinion bearing retaining screw and seal
27. Shift linkage pivot screw
28. O-ring
29. Drain/fill plug and seal
30. Trim tab screw and washer
31. Trim tab
32. Shift actuator rod
33. Detent ball
34. Detent spring
35. Clutch dog
36. Clutch dog cross pin
37. Clutch dog pin retaining spring
38. Propeller shaft
39. Narrow needle bearing
40. Wide needle bearing
41. Forward gear thrust washer
42. Forward gear thrust bearing
43. Forward gear
44. Reverse gear
45. Reverse gear thrust bearing
46. Reverse gear thrust washer
47. O-ring
48. Large needle bearing
49. Propshaft bearing carrier
50. Carrier retaining tab
51. Screw
52. Small needle bearing
53. Propshaft seal(s)
54. Anode
55. Screws

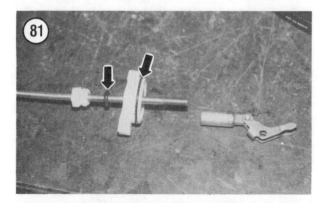

Once the gear and bearing are removed, reposition the gearcase so the drive shaft is pointing straight up.

8. Remove the shift linkage pivot screw (27, **Figure 78**) from the starboard side of the lower gearcase housing. The screw is easily identified by its *Posidriv* (similar to Phillips) screw head and is located at the very front of the gearcase bullet as shown in **Figure 79**. Remove and discard the O-ring from under the screw head.

9. Remove the two shoulder screws (**Figure 80**) securing the shift shaft housing to the gearcase deck. Then pull the shift shaft (and cover) from the gearcase. Disassemble the shift shaft as follows:

    a. Unthread the connector link from the lower end of the shift shaft.

    b. Unscrew the plastic nut, then pull the shaft from the housing. Remove and discard the two O-rings (**Figure 81**).

    c. If necessary, remove the cotter pin and clevis pin to separate the connector link from the shift bellcrank.

10. Pull the propeller shaft assembly from the gearcase. Locate and secure the shift cradle from the front of the shift actuator rod or the gearcase bore. See **Figure 82**.

11. Remove and discard the clutch dog cross pin's retaining spring with a small screwdriver or awl. Insert the tool under one end of the spring and rotate the propeller shaft to unwind the spring.

12. Using a small punch, push the cross pin out of the clutch dog. When the punch is removed, the tension on the detent spring will be relieved.

13. Slide the clutch dog off the front of the propshaft. Then pull the shift actuator rod from the propshaft. Locate and secure the three detent balls and one detent spring.

14. Remove the three screws securing the drive shaft bearing carrier to the gearcase housing. Do not remove the carrier at this time.

15. Install drive shaft spline socket part No. 334995 (or an equivalent splined socket) and a breaker bar onto the drive shaft splines. See **Figure 83**

16. Hold the pinion nut using an 11/16 in. wrench or socket. Pad the area around the tool's handle with shop towels to prevent housing damage. See **Figure 83**.

17. Loosen and remove the pinion nut by turning the drive shaft counterclockwise until the nut is free from the shaft. Remove the nut from the gearcase bore.

18. Pull the drive shaft assembly from its bore, then remove the pinion gear from the gearcase. If the pinion gear sticks to the drive shaft, proceed as follows:

    a. Position plate (part No. 325867) over the drive shaft and against the gearcase deck.

    b. Position puller (part No. 387206) over the drive shaft and position its set screw over the water pump drive key's flat.

9

c. Tighten the puller's two horizontal screws securely, then tighten the set screw against the drive shaft's flat.

d. Alternately tighten the puller's two vertical screws until the drive shaft is free from the pinion gear.

e. Remove the tools when finished.

19. Slide the drive shaft bearing carrier, shim(s), both thrust washers and the thrust bearing from the drive shaft. See **Figure 84**. Measure and record the thickness of the shim(s) for later reference. Tag the shim(s) for identification during reassembly.

20. Remove and discard the drive shaft bearing carrier's O-ring.

21. Rotate the gearcase until the forward gear, thrust bearing and thrust washer slide out. Be prepared to catch the components. Once the components are removed, reposition the gearcase so the drive shaft bore is pointing straight up.

NOTE
The needle bearing in the drive shaft bearing carrier is not serviceable. If the bearing is damaged, replace the carrier as an assembly.

22. Remove the drive shaft seal(s) from the drive shaft bearing carrier by driving the seal(s) from the carrier bore using a suitable punch and hammer. Do not damage the seal bore during the removal process. Discard the seal(s).

23. Remove the propshaft seal(s) from the propshaft bearing carrier by pulling the seal(s) from the carrier bore with a suitable two-jaw puller and puller bridge, threaded rod

and support plate (part No. 432127). Do not damage the seal bore during the removal process. Discard the seal(s).

24. If the forward gear needle bearings at the front of the gearcase bore require replacement, use the components from bearing service kit part No. 433034 (or an equivalent bearing puller), as specified in the following procedure, to remove both bearings at the same time.

a. Insert the hinged end of the rod assembly through the needle bearings and engage the hinged head with the front (narrow) bearing.

b. Slide the guide plate over the rod and insert it into the gearcase bore.

c. Slide the larger flat washer, then the smaller flat washer (from the bearing kit) over the rod and against the guide plate.

d. Lubricate the threads and washers, then install the nut (from the bearing kit) over the rod. Tighten the nut with a 15/16 in. socket (or wrench) to pull both bearings from the gearcase bore.

e. Discard both bearings.

25. If the lower drive shaft (pinion gear) bearing requires replacement, components from pinion bearing kits (part No. 391257 and part No. 433033) or equivalent tools are required to remove the bearing. To remove the bearing, proceed as follows:

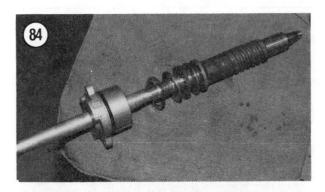

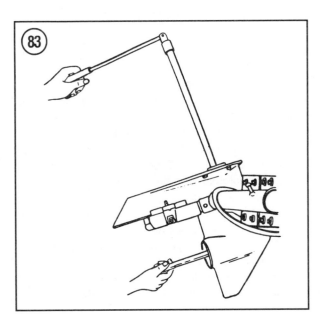

a. Remove the bearing retaining screw from the starboard side of the gearcase. The screw is easily identified by its *Posidriv* (similar to Phillips) screw head. The screw is located just in front of the starboard water inlet screen as shown in **Figure 85**. Remove and discard the O-ring from the screw.

b. Position a shop towel in the gearcase bore, directly under the bearing.

c. Assemble the components from pinion bearing kits part No. 391257 and part No. 433033, as shown in **Figure 86**. The guide plate is from kit part No. 433033. All other components are from kit part No. 391257.

d. Insert the tool into the drive shaft bore. Drive against the screw (1, **Figure 86**) with a soft-faced mallet until the bearing is removed.

e. Discard the bearing.

26. If either (or both) of the propshaft bearing carrier's bearings (48 and 52, **Figure 78**) require replacement, pull the defective bearing(s) from the carrier with a suitable bearing puller and puller bridge, threaded rod and support plate (part No. 432127). Discard the bearing(s).

27. Refer to *Gearcase Cleaning and Inspection*. Clean and inspect all components as directed before beginning reassembly.

Assembly
(40-50 hp [Two-cylinder] Models)

Lubricate all internal components with OMC Ultra HPF Gear Lube. Do not assemble components dry. Refer to **Table 5** for torque values, **Table 2** for specifications and **Figure 78** for this procedure.

The pinion gear is precisely located by a shimming process. Confirm the correct shim adjustment during any major disassembly. The text will refer you to *Pinion Gear Shimming* (located later in this chapter) at the correct time in the assembly sequence.

The shift shaft must be adjusted to a specific height in NEUTRAL gear. Failure to properly adjust the shift shaft will cause the shift system to be biased toward one gear. The other gear will not properly engage and will be quickly destroyed under operation. The text will refer you to *Shift Shaft Height Adjustment* at the correct time in the assembly sequence.

1. If the forward gear needle bearings were removed from the gearcase bore, install two new bearings as follows:

a. Lubricate the bearings and the gearcase bore.

b. Attach the bearing installer (from bearing service kit part No. 433034) to drive handle (part No. 311880) so that the installer's longer shoulder is facing away from the drive handle.

c. Install a new narrow bearing over the installer with the numbered side of the bearing facing the installer.

d. Insert the assembly into the gearcase bore. Slide the guide plate (from the bearing kit) over the drive handle and pilot it in the gearcase bore.

e. Drive the bearing into the gearcase until the installer contacts the gearcase.

f. Remove the tool and reverse the bearing installer on the drive handle so that the installer's shorter shoulder is facing away from the drive handle.

g. Install a new wide bearing over the installer with the numbered side of the bearing facing the installer.

h. Insert the assembly into the gearcase bore. Slide the guide plate (from the bearing kit) over the drive handle and pilot it in the gearcase bore.

i. Drive the bearing into the gearcase until the installer contacts the gearcase.

> *CAUTION*
> *The screws (1 and 7, **Figure 87**) must be securely tightened and the flat washer (2) must be perfectly flat or the pinion bearing will not be correctly positioned in the next step.*

9

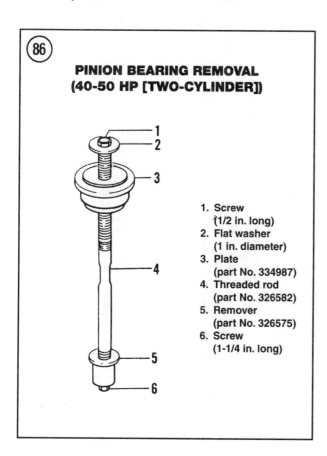

86

PINION BEARING REMOVAL (40-50 HP [TWO-CYLINDER])

1. Screw
   (1/2 in. long)
2. Flat washer
   (1 in. diameter)
3. Plate
   (part No. 334987)
4. Threaded rod
   (part No. 326582)
5. Remover
   (part No. 326575)
6. Screw
   (1-1/4 in. long)

2. If the lower drive shaft (pinion gear) bearing was removed, the new bearing must be pressed into position from the top of the drive shaft bore. Several components from universal pinion bearing remover/installer kit (part No. 391257), spacer (part No. 334986) and guide plate (part No. 334987) from bearing service kit (part No. 433033) are required to properly locate the bearing. To install the new bearing, refer to **Figure 87** and proceed as follows:

   a. Lubricate the new bearing and the drive shaft bore.

   b. Assemble the tool as shown in **Figure 87**, using the specified spacer and guide plate from bearing kit (part No. 433033). Make sure the screws (1 and 7, **Figure 87**) are securely tightened.

   c. Position the bearing over the installer (6, **Figure 87**) with the numbered side of the bearing against the tool's shoulder.

   d. Insert the assembly into the drive shaft bore. Drive against the screw (1, **Figure 87**) with a soft-faced mallet until the flat washer (2) contacts the spacer (3). Remove the installation tools.

   e. Install a new O-ring on the pinion bearing retaining screw. Apply OMC Nut Lock to the threads of the screw and the O-ring. Then install and tighten the screw to 48-84 in.-lb. (5.4-9.5 N•m). See **Figure 85**.

3. If the propshaft bearing carrier bearings were removed, install new bearings as follows:

   a. Position the carrier in a press with its propeller end facing down (O-ring groove facing up).

   b. Lubricate a new large bearing (48, **Figure 78**) and position it into the carrier's bore with the numbered side facing up.

   c. Press the bearing into position using the short shoulder of bearing installer (part No. 334997) or an equivalent mandrel. Press until the tool contacts the bearing carrier.

   d. Position the carrier in a press with the propeller end facing up (O-ring groove facing down).

   e. Lubricate a new small bearing (52, **Figure 78**) and position it into the carrier's bore with its numbered side facing up.

   f. Press the bearing into position with the longer shoulder of bearing installer (part No. 334997) or an equivalent mandrel. Press until the tool contacts the bearing carrier.

4A. *Double seal models*—Install two new propshaft seals as follows:

   a. Coat the outer diameter of each seal with OMC Gasket Sealing Compound.

   b. Install the inner seal using the longer, stepped shoulder of seal installer (part No. 326556 [or part No. 910585]) or an equivalent mandrel. The seal lip (spring side) must face into the carrier bore. Press the seal until the installer contacts the carrier.

   c. Install the outer seal using the shorter shoulder of seal installer (part No. 326556 [or part No. 910585]) or an equivalent mandrel. The seal lip (spring side) must face out from the carrier. Press the seal until the installer contacts the carrier.

   d. Lubricate the seal lips and pack the area between the seal lips with OMC Triple Guard Grease.

4B. *Single seal models*—Install a new propshaft seal as follows:

   a. Lubricate the outer diameter of a new seal with OMC DPL (WD-40) Lubricant.

   b. Position the propshaft bearing carrier in a press with the O-ring end facing down.

   c. Position the seal onto the appropriate end of seal installer (part No. 342666) or an equivalent mandrel. The seal's extended lip must face the Installer (away from the carrier). A recess is provided in the seal installer to protect the seal's lip.

   d. Press the seal into the carrier until the installer contacts the carrier.

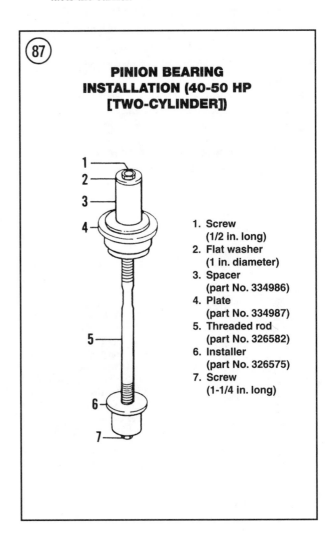

PINION BEARING INSTALLATION (40-50 HP [TWO-CYLINDER])

1. Screw (1/2 in. long)
2. Flat washer (1 in. diameter)
3. Spacer (part No. 334986)
4. Plate (part No. 334987)
5. Threaded rod (part No. 326582)
6. Installer (part No. 326575)
7. Screw (1-1/4 in. long)

e. Lubricate the seal lips with OMC Triple Guard Grease.

5. Coat a new O-ring (47, **Figure 78**) with OMC Triple Guard Grease. Install the O-ring into the propshaft bearing carrier's O-ring groove.

6A. *Double seal models*—Install two new drive shaft seals into the drive shaft bearing carrier as follows:

    a. Coat the outer diameter of each seal with OMC Gasket Sealing Compound.

    b. Install the inner seal (with the flush lip) using the longer, stepped shoulder of seal installer (part No. 335823) or an equivalent mandrel. The seal lip (spring side) must face into the carrier. Press the seal until the installer contacts the carrier.

    c. Install the outer seal (with the extended lip) using the shorter shoulder of seal installer (part No. 335823) or an equivalent mandrel. The extended lip must face away (out) from the carrier. Press the seal until the installer contacts the carrier.

    d. Lubricate the seal lips and pack the area between the seal lips with OMC Triple Guard Grease.

6B. *Single seal models*—Install a new drive shaft seal into the drive shaft bearing carrier as follows:

    a. Lubricate the outer diameter of a new seal with OMC DPL (WD-40) Lubricant.

    b. Position the drive shaft bearing carrier in a press with the needle bearing end facing down.

    c. Position the seal onto the appropriate end of seal installer (part No. 342666) or an equivalent mandrel. The seal's extended lip must face the installer (away from the carrier). A recess is provided in the seal installer to protect the seal's lip.

    d. Press the seal into the carrier until the installer contacts the carrier.

    e. Lubricate the seal lips with OMC Triple Guard Grease.

7. Coat a new O-ring (4, **Figure 78**) with OMC Triple Guard Grease. Install the O-ring into the drive shaft bearing carrier's O-ring groove.

CAUTION
The pinion gear must be precisely located in the drive shaft bore. If the shimming tool is not available, take the drive shaft assembly to an Evinrude/Johnson dealership and have a qualified technician perform the procedure.

8. Refer to *Pinion Gear Shimming* in this chapter and determine the quantity of shims required to properly locate the pinion gear. Once the shims are determined, tag the shim pack and store extra shims to avoid confusion during assembly.

9. Assemble the propeller shaft as follows:

    a. Align the cross pin holes of the clutch dog with the slot in the propeller shaft. Position the end of the clutch dog stamped *PROP END* toward the propeller and slide it onto the propeller shaft.

WARNING
Wear eye protection during assembly of the shift detent balls and spring.

    b. Coat the detent ball bore in the shift actuator rod with OMC Needle Bearing Assembly Grease. Position two balls into the bore.

    c. Install the third detent ball into the hole in the end of the actuator rod. Then insert the detent spring into the hole and push the ball and spring up until they contact the two balls installed previously.

    d. Carefully position the shift actuator rod into the open end of the propshaft. Align the detent balls with the holes in the propshaft and the cross pin hole in the rod with the hole in the clutch dog. Be careful not to displace the detent balls or spring.

NOTE
The wedge-shaped tool used in the next step must have a diameter of 9/32 in. (7.1 mm) and be 2-5/8 in. (67 mm) long. Grind an approximately 20° ramp on one end.

    e. While holding the components aligned, insert a suitable wedge-shaped tool into the clutch dog hole (with the angled ramp facing the front), through the propshaft slot and into the actuator rod hole. The tool must enter behind the detent spring and compress it toward the front of the shaft. Do not damage the detent spring by spearing it.

    f. Position the clutch dog cross pin over the tool and push the tool out of the clutch dog as the cross pin enters the clutch dog. See **Figure 88**.

NOTE
When installed correctly, the cross pin retaining spring must lay flat, with no overlap-

9

ping coils. There must be three wraps of wire over each end of the cross pin.

g. Secure the pin to the clutch dog with a new retainer spring. Do not open the spring any more than necessary to install it. Install one end of the spring over the clutch and into its groove. Then using a small screwdriver to guide the spring, rotate the propeller shaft to wind the spring into place. Make sure no coils overlap and that three wraps of wire are over each end of the pin.

h. Apply OMC Needle Bearing Grease to the groove at the front of the shift actuator rod. Then position the shift cradle into the groove. See **Figure 82**.

10. Position the forward gear thrust washer into the gearcase bore with the chamfered side of the washer facing the front of the gearcase (away from the gears).

11. Apply OMC Needle Bearing Assembly Grease to the forward gear's thrust bearing face. Then position the thrust bearing onto the forward gear. Carefully install the forward gear and bearing assembly into the gearcase bore. Make sure the thrust bearing is not displaced during installation.

12. Refer to **Figure 84** and assemble the drive shaft as follows:

a. Position a thrust washer over the drive shaft and against the shaft's shoulder with the chamfered side of the washer facing the shoulder.

b. Position the thrust bearing over the drive shaft and against the thrust washer. Then install the second thrust washer over the shaft and against the thrust bearing with the chamfered side of the washer facing away from the thrust bearing.

c. Position the predetermined amount of shims over the drive shaft and against the second thrust washer.

d. Carefully slide the drive shaft bearing carrier over the shaft, being careful not to damage the seals on the splines. Then seat the carrier against the shims.

e. Coat the gearcase side of the drive shaft bearing carrier-to-gearcase housing mating surface (not the bore) with a light coat of OMC Gasket Sealing Compound.

13. Install the drive shaft and pinion gear as follows:

a. Clean the pinion gear and drive shaft tapered mating surfaces thoroughly with OMC Cleaning Solvent, acetone, or a similar oil and wax-free solvent.

b. Position the pinion gear under the drive shaft bore, then insert the drive shaft assembly into its bore and engage the pinion gear. Rotate the shaft as necessary to engage the splines.

c. Lubricate the threads of a *new* pinion nut with outboard lubricant, then install the new pinion nut using a suitable nut holder, such as pinion nut starter (part

No. 342216). Tighten the nut finger-tight, then remove the pinion nut starter.

d. Apply OMC Gasket Sealing Compound to the three drive shaft bearing carrier screws, then install and evenly tighten the screws to 12-14 ft.-lb. (16.3-19.0 N•m).

e. Hold the pinion nut with an 11/16 in. wrench or socket. Pad the handle to prevent gearcase damage. Attach spline socket (part No. 334995) or an equivalent spline socket to a torque wrench. Then hold the pinion nut and turn the drive shaft until the torque wrench reads 40-45 ft.-lb. (54.2-61.0 N•m).

14. Refer to **Figure 81** and assemble the shift shaft as follows:

a. Apply OMC Triple Guard Grease to two new O-rings (11 and 14, **Figure 78**). Install the larger (thinner) O-ring into the shift shaft housing's groove.

b. Slide the plastic nut, then the small (thicker) O-ring and finally the shift shaft housing over the shift shaft.

c. Apply a small amount of OMC Adhesive M sealant to the plastic nut's threads. Then thread the nut into the shift shaft housing, locking the O-ring into the housing. Tighten the nut to 48-60 in.-lb. (5.4-6.8 N•m).

d. If the bellcrank was removed from the connector link, install the clevis pin to secure the bellcrank to the link. Secure the clevis pin with a new cotter pin. Bend both prongs of the cotter pin for a secure attachment.

e. Thread the connector link (and bellcrank) onto the shift shaft a total of *nine* turns.

15. Position the gearcase so that its leading edge is facing down. Carefully slide the propshaft assembly into the gearcase bore, making sure that the shift cradle is facing straight up so that the bellcrank will be able to engage it.

16. Carefully install the shift shaft assembly into its bore, making sure the bellcrank tangs engage the recesses in the top of the shift cradle. See **Figure 89**. This must be visually verified.

17. Install a new O-ring on the shift linkage pivot screw. Coat the threads of the screw and the O-ring with OMC Nut Lock threadlocking adhesive. Move the shift shaft (and bellcrank) until the shift bellcrank is aligned with the hole for the shift linkage pivot screw. Then install and tighten the shift linkage pivot screw to 48-84 in.-lb. (5.4-9.5 N•m).

18. Seat the shift shaft housing into its bore. Then coat the threads of the two shoulder screws with OMC Gasket Sealing Compound. Install and evenly tighten the shoulder screws to 60-84 in.-lb. (6.8-9.5 N•m). See **Figure 80**.

19. Apply OMC Needle Bearing Assembly Grease to the reverse gear's thrust bearing face, then position the thrust bearing onto the reverse gear. Carefully install the reverse

gear and bearing assembly over the propshaft and into the gearcase bore. Make sure the thrust bearing is not displaced during installation and that the gear's teeth engage the pinion gear.

20. Coat the reverse gear thrust washer with OMC Needle Bearing Grease and position it into its recess in the propshaft bearing carrier.

21. Apply OMC Gasket Sealing Compound to the propshaft bearing carrier's rear flange. Then coat the forward flange (and O-ring) with the same sealant. Install the propshaft bearing carrier over the propshaft, making sure

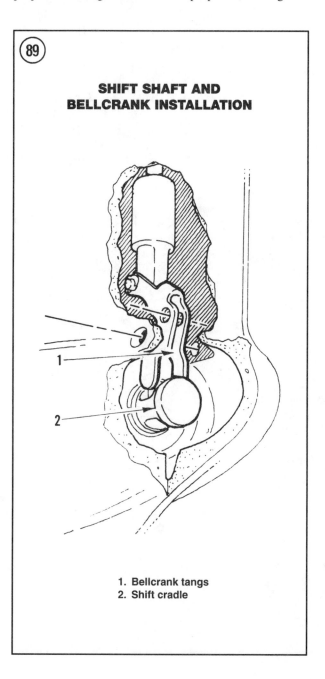

(89)

SHIFT SHAFT AND BELLCRANK INSTALLATION

1. Bellcrank tangs
2. Shift cradle

the screw holes are vertical and the drain slot is pointing down.

22. Push the carrier into the gearcase bore until it is seated. If necessary, tap the carrier with a wooden dowel (and suitable mallet). Do not attempt to pull the carrier into position with the retaining tabs and screws.

23. Coat the threads of the two carrier retaining screws with OMC Nut Lock threadlocking adhesive. Position the carrier retaining tabs over the screw holes and engage them into the notches in the gearcase bore. Secure each retainer with a screw. Tighten the screws to 120-144 in.-lb. (13.6-16.3 N•m).

24. Position the anode over the propshaft and against the bearing carrier. Secure the anode with two screws. Tighten the screws to 108-132 in.-lb. (12.2-14.9 N•m).

25. Test the integrity of the gearcase seals, gaskets and O-rings as described in *Gearcase Pressure and Vacuum Testing*.

26. Adjust the shift shaft height as described in *Shift Shaft Height Adjustment*, located later in this chapter. Failure to properly set the shift shaft height will result in premature gear failure.

27. Install the water pump as described previously in this chapter.

28. Fill the gearcase with the recommended lubricant as described in Chapter Four.

29. Install the gearcase as described previously in this chapter.

Disassembly
(50-70 hp [Three-cylinder] Models)

Refer to **Figure 90** for this procedure. Record the location, orientation and thickness of all shims and thrust washers removed during disassembly, so they can be correctly reinstalled.

The propshaft bearing carrier can be removed without removing the gearcase from the outboard motor, if so desired. Do not attempt to remove the propshaft without removing the gearcase from the outboard motor.

1. Drain the gearcase lubricant as described in Chapter Four.

2. Remove the gearcase as described in this chapter.

3. Remove the water pump as described in this chapter.

4. Remove the four screws (56, **Figure 90**) securing the propshaft bearing carrier into the gearcase bore. The screws are located inside the carrier's exhaust passages. Remove and discard the O-ring from each screw.

5. Using components of the universal puller kit part No. 378103 (or an equivalent puller) and two 5/16-18 × 8 in. screws or two heavy duty puller arms (part No. 330278), remove the propshaft bearing carrier.

9

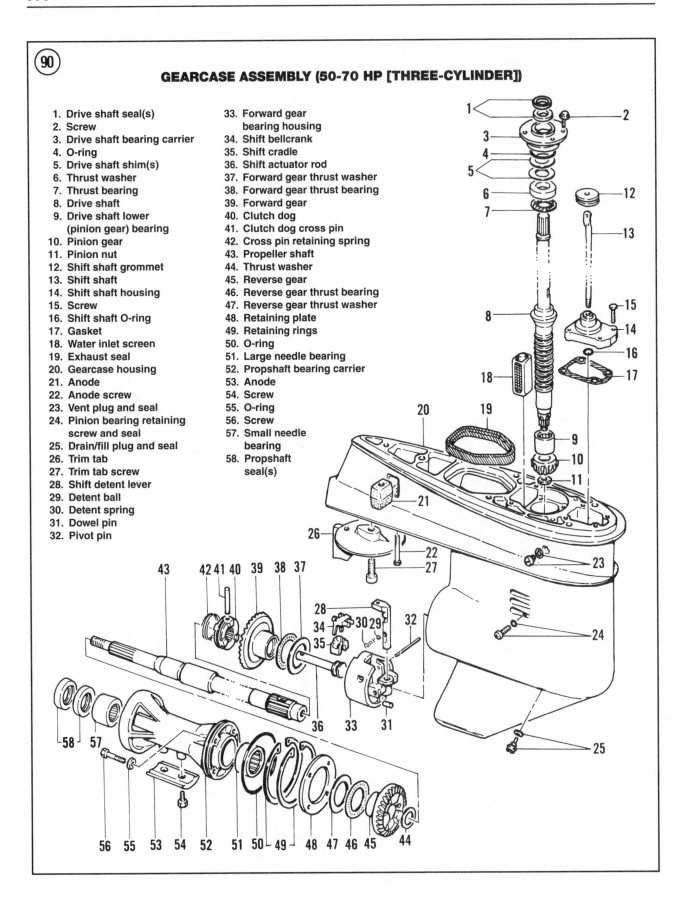

90

GEARCASE ASSEMBLY (50-70 HP [THREE-CYLINDER])

1. Drive shaft seal(s)
2. Screw
3. Drive shaft bearing carrier
4. O-ring
5. Drive shaft shim(s)
6. Thrust washer
7. Thrust bearing
8. Drive shaft
9. Drive shaft lower (pinion gear) bearing
10. Pinion gear
11. Pinion nut
12. Shift shaft grommet
13. Shift shaft
14. Shift shaft housing
15. Screw
16. Shift shaft O-ring
17. Gasket
18. Water inlet screen
19. Exhaust seal
20. Gearcase housing
21. Anode
22. Anode screw
23. Vent plug and seal
24. Pinion bearing retaining screw and seal
25. Drain/fill plug and seal
26. Trim tab
27. Trim tab screw
28. Shift detent lever
29. Detent ball
30. Detent spring
31. Dowel pin
32. Pivot pin
33. Forward gear bearing housing
34. Shift bellcrank
35. Shift cradle
36. Shift actuator rod
37. Forward gear thrust washer
38. Forward gear thrust bearing
39. Forward gear
40. Clutch dog
41. Clutch dog cross pin
42. Cross pin retaining spring
43. Propeller shaft
44. Thrust washer
45. Reverse gear
46. Reverse gear thrust bearing
47. Reverse gear thrust washer
48. Retaining plate
49. Retaining rings
50. O-ring
51. Large needle bearing
52. Propshaft bearing carrier
53. Anode
54. Screw
55. O-ring
56. Screw
57. Small needle bearing
58. Propshaft seal(s)

a. Position the puller head (part No. 307636) and pressing screw (part No. 307637) over the propshaft.

b. Install the two screws (with two flat washers) through the puller head slots and into the screw holes on the rear flange of the carrier. If using the heavy duty puller arms, hook each arm under a support leg on the carrier's rear flange and lock each arm into the puller head's slots with the pin attached to each arm.

c. Insert the handle (part No. 307638) into the puller head to stabilize the assembly, then tighten the pressing screw to pull the carrier from the gearcase. See **Figure 91**, typical.

d. Once free, pull the carrier from the gearcase bore. Remove and discard the O-ring (50, **Figure 90**).

WARNING
*The retaining (snap) rings (49, **Figure 90**) are under extreme pressure. Wear suitable eye and hand protection when removing and installing the retaining rings.*

7. Remove both retaining rings from the gearcase bore using retaining ring pliers (part No. 331045) or an equivalent pair of snap ring pliers. Once clear of the gearcase bore, release all tension from each ring *before* removing the ring completely from the propshaft.

8. Remove the retainer plate (48, **Figure 90**) from the gearcase bore.

9. Rotate the gearcase until the reverse gear and its thrust bearing and thrust washers slide out. Be prepared to catch the components. Make sure you locate and secure the thrust washer (44, **Figure 90**) located between the front of the reverse gear and the propshaft flange. Once the gear,

bearing and washers are removed, reposition the gearcase so that the drive shaft is pointing straight up.

10. Remove the four screws (2, **Figure 90**) securing the drive shaft bearing carrier to the gearcase. Do not remove the carrier at this time.

11. Pull up on the shift shaft (while rotating the propeller shaft) to engage FORWARD gear.

12. Hold the pinion nut using an 11/16 in. wrench. Pad the area around the wrench handle with shop towels to prevent housing damage.

13. Install drive shaft spline socket part No. 334995 (or an equivalent splined socket) and a breaker bar onto the drive shaft splines.

14. Loosen and remove the pinion nut by turning the drive shaft counterclockwise until the nut is free from the shaft. Remove the nut from the gearcase bore.

15. Pull the drive shaft assembly from its bore, then remove the pinion gear from the gearcase. If the pinion gear sticks to the drive shaft, proceed as follows:

a. Position plate (part No. 325867) over the drive shaft and against the gearcase deck.

b. Position puller (part No. 387206) over the drive shaft and position its set screw over the water pump drive key's flat.

c. Tighten the puller's two horizontal screws securely, then tighten the set screw against the flat on the drive shaft.

d. Alternately tighten the puller's two vertical screws until the drive shaft is free from the pinion gear.

e. Remove the tools when finished.

16. Slide the drive shaft bearing carrier, shim(s), thrust washer and thrust bearing from the drive shaft. Measure and record the thickness of the shim(s) for later reference. Tag the shim(s) for identification during assembly.

17. Remove and discard the drive shaft bearing carrier's O-ring (4, **Figure 90**).

18. Rotate the gearcase until the pinion gear slides out. Be prepared to catch the gear. Once the gear is removed, reposition the gearcase so that the drive shaft is pointing straight up.

19. Push the shift shaft downward as far as possible. Then unthread the shift shaft until it is free from the shift detent lever (28, **Figure 90**). The detent lever must remain in the fully down position to remove the propshaft assembly.

20. Remove the four screws securing the shift shaft housing to the gearcase deck. If necessary, tap the housing with a soft-faced hammer to break it free. Then remove the housing and shift shaft as an assembly. Remove and discard the cover gasket.

21. Pull the shift shaft from the shift shaft housing. Remove the housing's O-ring from the shift shaft bore with a hooked tool. Discard the O-ring.

9

22. Grasp the propeller shaft and pull the propshaft assembly from the gearcase (**Figure 92**). If it catches, make sure the drain/fill plug is removed and that the shift detent lever is pushed downward as far as possible. Set the assembly on a clean workbench.

23. Refer to **Figure 93** and disassemble the propshaft as follows:

a. Remove and discard the clutch dog cross pin's retaining spring with a small screwdriver or awl. Insert the tool under one end of the spring and rotate the propeller shaft to unwind the spring.

b. Using a small punch, push the cross pin out of the clutch dog. Then slide the forward gear and bearing housing assembly and the clutch dog off the front of the propshaft.

c. Separate the forward gear, thrust bearing and thrust washer from the bearing housing.

d. Using a small punch, push the pivot pin from the bearing housing, then pull the actuator rod and cradle from the bearing housing. Lift the cradle from the rod.

e. Remove the shift bellcrank (8, **Figure 93**) from the opening at the top and front of the bearing housing. If necessary, rotate the shift detent lever to provide clearance.

CAUTION
*Use extreme care when removing the shift detent lever. The detent ball and spring may fly from the access hole (2, **Figure 94**) with considerable force.*

f. Cover the detent ball and spring access hole (2, **Figure 94**) with a shop towel, then rotate the shift detent lever 90° to either side and pull the lever (1) from the bearing housing. Locate and secure the detent ball and spring.

NOTE
The needle bearings in the forward gear bearing housing and the drive shaft bearing carrier are not serviceable. If the bearing and/or the housing are worn or damaged, replace the bearing housing (or bearing carrier) as an assembly.

24. Remove the drive shaft seal(s) from the drive shaft bearing carrier by pulling the seal(s) from the carrier bore with a suitable two-jaw puller and puller bridge, threaded rod and support plate (part No. 432127). Do not damage the seal bore during the removal process. Discard the seal(s).

25. Remove the propshaft seal(s) from the propshaft bearing carrier by pulling the seal(s) from the carrier bore with a suitable two-jaw puller and puller bridge, threaded rod

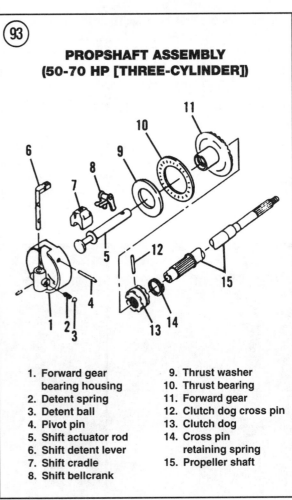

**PROPSHAFT ASSEMBLY
(50-70 HP [THREE-CYLINDER])**

1. Forward gear bearing housing
2. Detent spring
3. Detent ball
4. Pivot pin
5. Shift actuator rod
6. Shift detent lever
7. Shift cradle
8. Shift bellcrank
9. Thrust washer
10. Thrust bearing
11. Forward gear
12. Clutch dog cross pin
13. Clutch dog
14. Cross pin retaining spring
15. Propeller shaft

and support plate (part No. 432127). Do not damage the seal bore during the removal process. Discard the seal(s).

26. If the lower drive shaft (pinion gear) bearing requires replacement, several components from pinion bearing kit (part No. 391257) or equivalent tools are required to remove the bearing. To remove the bearing, proceed as follows:

a. Remove the bearing retaining screw from the starboard side of the gearcase. The screw is easily identified by its *Posidriv* (similar to Phillips) screw head. The screw is located just in front of the starboard water inlet screen as shown in **Figure 95**. Remove and discard the O-ring from the screw.

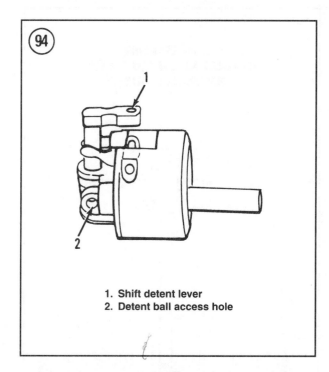

1. Shift detent lever
2. Detent ball access hole

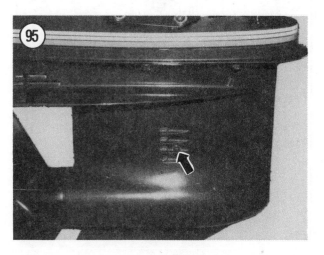

b. Assemble the components from pinion bearing kit part No. 391257 (except for the remover) as shown in **Figure 96**.

c. Inser the tool into the drive shaft bore. Hold the remover (4, **Figure 96**) under the pinion bearing and thread it fully onto the rod (3).

d. Tighten the flanged nut (1, **Figure 96**) to pull the bearing up and out of the drive shaft bore. If the remover rotates (slips), hold it stationary with a wrench.

e. Discard the bearing.

27. If either (or both) of the propshaft bearing carrier's bearings (51 and 57, **Figure 90**) require replacement, pull the defective bearing(s) from the carrier with a suitable bearing puller and puller bridge, threaded rod and support plate (part No. 432127). Discard the bearing(s).

28. Refer to *Gearcase Cleaning and Inspection*. Clean and inspect all components as directed before beginning assembly.

Assembly
(50-70 hp [Three-cylinder] Models)

Lubricate all internal components with OMC Ultra HPF Gear Lube. Do not assemble components dry. Refer to

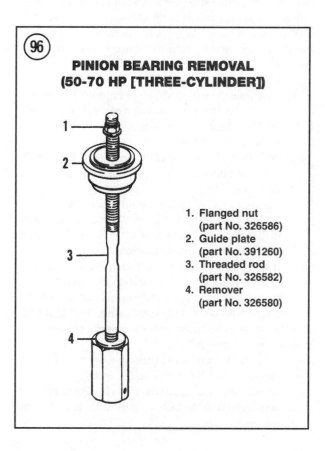

PINION BEARING REMOVAL
(50-70 HP [THREE-CYLINDER])

1. Flanged nut
   (part No. 326586)
2. Guide plate
   (part No. 391260)
3. Threaded rod
   (part No. 326582)
4. Remover
   (part No. 326580)

Table 5 for torque values, **Table 2** for specifications and **Figure 90** for this procedure.

The pinion gear is precisely located by a shimming process. The shimming should be verified during any major disassembly. However, if the pinion gear, drive shaft, drive shaft bearing carrier or the drive shaft thrust washer or thrust bearing is replaced, the pinion gear must be shimmed. The text will refer you to *Pinion Gear Shimming* at the correct time in the assembly sequence.

The shift shaft must be adjusted to a specific height in NEUTRAL gear. Failure to properly adjust the shift shaft will cause the shift system to be biased toward one gear. The other gear will not properly engage and will be quickly destroyed under operation. The text will refer you to *Shift Shaft Height Adjustment* (located later in this chapter) at the correct time in the assembly sequence.

CAUTION
*The screws (1 and 7, **Figure 97**) must be securely tightened and the flat washer (2) must be perfectly flat or the pinion bearing will not be correctly positioned in the next step.*

1. If the lower drive shaft (pinion gear) bearing was removed, the new bearing must be pressed into position from the top of the drive shaft bore. Several components from universal pinion bearing remover/installer kit (part No. 391257) are required to properly locate the bearing. To install the new bearing, refer to **Figure 97** and proceed as follows:

   a. Lubricate the new bearing and the drive shaft bore.

   b. Assemble the tool as shown in **Figure 97**, using the specified components of pinion bearing kit (part No. 391257). Make sure the screws (1 and 7, **Figure 97**) are securely tightened.

   c. Position the bearing over the installer (6, **Figure 97**) with the numbered side of the bearing against the tool's shoulder.

   d. Insert the assembly into the drive shaft bore. Drive against the screw (1, **Figure 97**) with a soft-faced mallet until the flat washer (2) contacts the spacer (3). Remove the installation tools.

   e. Install a new O-ring on the pinion bearing retaining screw. Apply OMC Nut Lock to the threads of the screw and the O-ring. Then install and tighten the screw to 48-84 in.-lb. (5.4-9.5 N•m). See **Figure 95**.

2. If the propshaft bearing carrier bearings were removed, install new bearings as follows:

   a. Position the carrier in a press with its propeller end facing down (O-ring groove facing up).

   b. Lubricate a new large bearing (51, **Figure 90**) and position it into the carrier's bore with its numbered side facing up.

   c. Press the bearing into position using the short shoulder of bearing installer (part No. 326562) or an equivalent mandrel. Press until the tool contacts the bearing carrier.

   d. Position the carrier in a press with the propeller end facing up (O-ring groove facing down).

   e. Lubricate a new small bearing (57, **Figure 90**) and position it into the carrier's bore with its numbered side facing up.

   f. Press the bearing into position with the longer shoulder of bearing installer (part No. 326562) or an equivalent mandrel. Press until the tool contacts the bearing carrier.

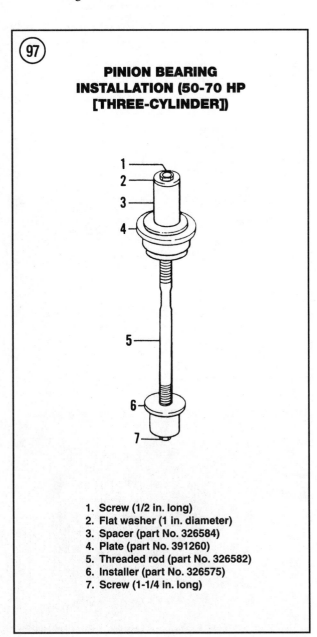

(97)

PINION BEARING INSTALLATION (50-70 HP [THREE-CYLINDER])

1. Screw (1/2 in. long)
2. Flat washer (1 in. diameter)
3. Spacer (part No. 326584)
4. Plate (part No. 391260)
5. Threaded rod (part No. 326582)
6. Installer (part No. 326575)
7. Screw (1-1/4 in. long)

3. If the propshaft bearing carrier's anode was removed, install the anode at this time. Secure the anode to the carrier with two screws. Tighten both screws securely.

4A. *Double seal models*—Install two new propshaft seals as follows:

   a. Coat the outer diameter of each seal with OMC Gasket Sealing Compound.

   b. Install the inner seal using the longer, stepped shoulder of seal installer (part No. 326551) or an equivalent mandrel. The seal lip (spring side) must face into the carrier bore. Press the seal until the installer contacts the carrier.

   c. Install the outer seal using the shorter shoulder of seal installer (part No. 326551) or an equivalent mandrel. The seal lip (spring side) must face out from the carrier. Press the seal until the installer contacts the carrier.

   d. Lubricate the seal lips and pack the area between the seal lips with OMC Triple Guard Grease.

4B. *Single seal models*—Install a new propshaft seal as follows:

   a. Lubricate the outer diameter of a new seal with OMC DPL (WD-40) Lubricant.

   b. Position the seal onto the appropriate end of seal installer (part No. 342665) or an equivalent mandrel. The seal's extended lip must face the Installer (away from the carrier). A recess is provided in the seal installer to protect the seal's lip.

   c. Press the seal into the carrier until the Installer contacts the carrier.

   d. Lubricate the seal lips with OMC Triple Guard Grease.

5. Coat a new O-ring (50, **Figure 90**) with OMC Triple Guard Grease. Install the O-ring into the propshaft bearing carrier's O-ring groove.

6A. *Double seal models*—Install two new drive shaft seals into the drive shaft bearing carrier as follows:

   a. Coat the outer diameter of each seal with OMC Gasket Sealing Compound.

   b. Install the inner seal (with the flush lip) using the longer, stepped shoulder of seal installer (part No. 326545) or an equivalent mandrel. The seal lip (spring side) must face into the carrier. Press the seal until the installer contacts the carrier.

   c. Install the outer seal (with the extended lip) using the shorter shoulder of seal installer (part No. 326545) or an equivalent mandrel. The extended lip must face away (out) from the carrier. Press the seal until the installer contacts the carrier.

   d. Lubricate the seal lips and pack the area between the seal lips with OMC Triple Guard Grease.

6B. *Single seal models*—Install a new drive shaft seal into the drive shaft bearing carrier as follows:

   a. Lubricate the outer diameter of a new seal with OMC DPL (WD-40) Lubricant.

   b. Position the drive shaft bearing carrier in a press with the needle bearing end facing down.

   c. Position the seal onto the appropriate end of seal installer (part No. 342665) or an equivalent mandrel. The seal's extended lip must face the installer (away from the carrier). A recess is provided in the seal installer to protect the seal's lip.

   d. Press the seal into the carrier until the installer contacts the carrier.

   e. Lubricate the seal lips with OMC Triple Guard Grease.

7. Coat a new O-ring (4, **Figure 90**) with OMC Triple Guard Grease. Install the O-ring into the drive shaft bearing carrier's O-ring groove.

CAUTION
The pinion gear must be precisely located in the drive shaft bore. If the shimming tool is not available, take the drive shaft assembly to an Evinrude/Johnson dealership and have a qualified technician perform the procedure.

8. Refer to *Pinion Gear Shimming* (in this chapter) and determine the quantity of shims required to properly locate the pinion gear. Once the shims are determined, tag the shim pack and put away any extra shims to avoid confusion during assembly.

9. Refer to **Figure 93** and assemble the forward gear bearing housing as follows:

   a. Support the bearing carrier so that the detent ball access hole (2, **Figure 94**) is pointing straight up.

   b. Grease the detent spring and ball with OMC Needle Bearing Grease. Install the spring, then the ball into their bore.

   c. Insert the shift detent lever into its bore until it is almost touching the detent ball and spring. Position the head of the shift lever pointing to either side of the bearing housing.

   d. Insert a screwdriver into the bottom of the shift detent lever bore and compress the detent ball and spring. While holding the ball and spring compressed, push the shift detent lever into its bore until it is flush with the bottom of the bore and pushes out the screwdriver.

   e. Insert the shift bellcrank lever through the hole at the top of the bearing carrier. Rotate the shift lever (1, **Figure 94**) until it points to the rear of the housing and engage the bellcrank tangs into the detent lever slots. Then push the shift detent lever down as far as possible.

9

f. Grease the shift cradle with OMC Needle Bearing Grease and set it into its groove in the shift actuator rod. Insert the rod and cradle into the bearing carrier and engage the cradle with the bellcrank tangs.

g. Align the hole in the shift bellcrank with the hole in the bearing carrier, then install the pivot pin.

10. Refer to **Figure 93** and assemble the propeller shaft as follows:

a. Install the forward gear thrust washer over the bearing carrier and seat it on the housing's shoulder.

b. Apply OMC Needle Bearing Assembly Grease to the forward gear's thrust bearing face, then position the thrust bearing onto the forward gear. Carefully install the forward gear and bearing assembly into the forward gear bearing carrier. Make sure the thrust bearing and shift actuator rod (and shift cradle) are not displaced during installation.

c. Align the cross pin holes of the clutch dog with the slot in the propeller shaft. Position the grooved end of the clutch dog toward the front of the propshaft and slide it onto the propeller shaft.

d. Carefully install the propshaft assembly to the forward gear bearing carrier assembly. Insert the shift actuator rod into the open end of the propshaft and the propshaft into the forward gear.

e. Align the hole in the shift actuator rod with the hole in the clutch dog, then install the clutch dog cross pin.

NOTE
When installed correctly, the cross pin retaining spring must lay flat, with no overlapping coils. There must be three wraps of wire over each end of the cross pin.

f. Secure the pin to the clutch dog with a new retainer spring. Do not open the spring any more than necessary to install it. Install one end of the spring over the clutch and into its groove. Then using a small screwdriver to guide the spring, rotate the propeller shaft to wind the spring into place. Make sure no coils overlap and that three wraps of wire are over each end of the pin.

11. Make sure the shift detent lever is pushed down as far as possible, then install the propshaft and forward gear assembly into the gearcase bore (**Figure 92**). The detent lever must be facing straight up and the locating pin on the bearing housing must engage the corresponding hole in the gearcase housing. Make sure the assembly is seated in the bore and that the thrust washer and bearing are displaced during installation.

12. Lubricate a new shift shaft housing O-ring with OMC Triple-Guard grease and install the O-ring into the hous-

ing's O-ring groove. Use a blunt tool to seat the O-ring into its groove.

13. Lubricate the threaded end of the shift shaft with OMC Triple Guard Grease and insert it into the housing's brass bushing. To prevent damaging the O-ring, rotate the shift shaft (clockwise) until all of the threads have pass through the O-ring. Continue pushing the shift shaft through the housing until it is centered on the shaft.

14. Coat a new shift housing gasket with OMC Gasket Sealing Compound. Then position the gasket on the gearcase deck.

15. Position the shift shaft and housing assembly to the gearcase. Thread the shift shaft into the shift detent lever approximately four turns.

NOTE
If the propshaft assembly is seated in the gearcase bore, the shift shaft housing will be closely aligned to the gearcase deck. If the screw holes are grossly misaligned, the forward bearing housing is not seated in its bore or the alignment pin is not aligned with its hole. Tap on the end of the propshaft with a soft-faced hammer and use the shift shaft to rotate the forward gear's bearing housing as necessary to ensure alignment and correct seating.

16. Coat the four shift shaft housing screws with OMC Gasket Sealing Compound. Align the screw holes, then install and evenly tighten the screws to 60-84 in.-lb. (6.8-9.5 N•m).

17. Assemble the drive shaft components (3-8, **Figure 90**) as follows:

a. Position the thrust bearing over the drive shaft and against the thrust washer. Then install the thrust washer over the shaft and against the thrust bearing.

b. Position the predetermined amount of shims over the drive shaft and against the thrust washer.

c. Install seal protector (part No. 312403) over the splined end of the drive shaft or wrap the splines with a single layer of cellophane tape to protect the drive shaft seal(s).

d. Carefully slide the drive shaft bearing carrier over the shaft, being careful not to damage the seals, then seat the carrier against the shims. Remove the seal protector or cellophane tape.

e. Coat the gearcase side of the drive shaft bearing carrier-to-gearcase housing mating surface (not the bore) with a light coat of OMC Gasket Sealing Compound.

18. Install the drive shaft and pinion gear as follows:

a. Clean the pinion gear and drive shaft tapered mating surfaces thoroughly with OMC Cleaning Solvent, acetone or a similar oil-free solvent.

b. Pull up on the shift rod while rotating the propshaft to fully engage the FORWARD gear.

c. Position the pinion gear under the drive shaft bore, then insert the drive shaft assembly into its bore and engage the pinion gear. Rotate the shaft as necessary to engage the splines and position the bearing carrier with the word *FRONT* facing the front of the gearcase.

d. Lubricate the threads of a new pinion nut with outboard lubricant, then install the new pinion nut using a suitable nut holder. Tighten the nut finger-tight, then remove the pinion nut starter.

e. Apply OMC Gasket Sealing Compound to the four drive shaft bearing carrier screws. Make sure the bearing carrier is positioned with the word *FRONT* facing the front of the gearcase, then seat the carrier into its bore with hand pressure.

f. Install and evenly tighten the four bearing carrier screws to 12-14 ft.-lb. (16.3-19.0 N•m).

g. Hold the pinion nut with an 11/16 in. wrench. Pad the handle to prevent gearcase damage. Attach spline socket (part No. 334995) or an equivalent spline socket to a torque wrench. Then hold the pinion nut and turn the drive shaft until the torque wrench reads 40-45 ft.-lb. (54.2-61.0 N•m).

19. Coat the reverse gear's inner thrust washer with OMC Needle Bearing Grease, then position the thrust washer into the recess in the face of the gear.

20. Lubricate the reverse gear thrust bearing and thrust washer. Install the bearing, then the washer over the reverse gear's hub.

21. Slide the reverse gear assembly over the propshaft and into position in the gearcase bore. Make sure that the washers and bearing are not displaced during installation.

22. Slide the retaining plate over the propshaft and into the gearcase bore. There is no specific orientation for the plate.

WARNING
*The retaining (snap) rings (49, **Figure 90**) are under extreme pressure. Wear suitable eye and hand protection when removing and installing the retaining rings.*

NOTE
Do not drag the open ends of the retaining rings in the gearcase bore during installation. This will scratch the bore, resulting in the carrier's O-ring being damaged when the carrier is installed.

23. Install the two retaining rings as follows:

a. Position the first ring over the propshaft and against the end of the gearcase bore. Engage retaining ring pliers (part No. 331045) or an equivalent pair of snap ring pliers to the ring.

b. Compress the ring, pushing it into its bore as soon as it will fit. Continue to compress the ring as necessary to install the ring into the lower groove, then carefully release the ring, making sure it completely expands and seats in its groove.

c. Repeat this procedure for the second ring. Install the second ring in the upper groove.

24. Install two ¼-28 × 10 in. rods into two opposing holes in the retainer plate. Do not thread the guide rods more than 2-3 turns into the plate.

25. Apply a light coat of OMC Gasket Sealing Compound to the propshaft bearing carrier's rear flange. Then coat the forward flange (and O-ring) with the same sealant. Install the propshaft bearing carrier over the propshaft, making sure the word *UP* (cast into the rear flange) is pointing straight up, the anode is pointing straight down and the guide pins are installed in the appropriate holes in the carrier.

26. Push the carrier into the gearcase bore until it is seated. If necessary, tap the carrier with a wooden dowel (and suitable mallet).

27. Install new O-rings on the four carrier screws. Then coat the screw threads and O-rings with OMC Gasket Sealing Compound. Install screws into the two open carrier holes and engage the retaining ring threads. Do NOT tighten the screws at this time.

28. Remove the guide pins from the other carrier screw holes. Then install the remaining two screws into the holes and engage the retaining ring threads. Once all screws are engaged with the retaining ring threads, tighten all four screws finger-tight.

29. Evenly tighten the four carrier mounting screws to 120-144 in.-lb. (13.6-16.3 N•m) in a minimum of three progressive stages.

30. Test the integrity of the gearcase seals, gaskets and O-rings as described in *Gearcase Pressure and Vacuum Testing*.

31. Adjust the shift shaft height as described in *Shift Shaft Height Adjustment* in this chapter. Failure to properly set the shift shaft height will result in premature gear failure.

32. Install the water pump as described in this chapter.

33. Fill the gearcase with the recommended lubricant as described in Chapter Four.

34. Install the gearcase as described in this chapter.

9

GEARCASE CLEANING AND INSPECTION

NOTE
Do not remove any pressed-on roller or ball bearing, pressed-in needle bearing, ball bearing or bushing unless they must be replaced. A tapered roller bearing consists of the roller assembly and a bearing race. The roller and race are a matched assembly and must be replaced as such.

1. Discard all seals, gaskets and O-rings removed during disassembly.

2. Clean all parts in a mild solvent (such as mineral spirits) and dry with compressed air. Lightly lubricate all internal components to prevent rusting.

CAUTION
*Metric **and** U.S. standard fasteners may be used on Evinrude/Johnson gearcases. Always match a replacement fastener to the original. Do not run a tap or thread chaser into a hole (or over a bolt) without first verifying the thread size and pitch. Check all threaded holes for Heli-Coil stainless steel locking thread inserts. Never run a tap or thread chaser into a Heli-Coil equipped hole. Heli-Coil inserts are replaceable, if damaged.*

3. Inspect all screws, bolts, nuts and other fasteners for damaged, galled or distorted threads. Replace any elastic locknuts that can be installed without the aid of a wrench. Clean all sealing compound, RTV sealant and threadlocking compound from the threaded areas. Minor thread imperfections can be corrected with an appropriate thread chaser.

4. Clean all gasket and sealant material from the gearcase housing. Make certain that all water and lubricant passages are clean and unobstructed. Make sure all threaded holes are free of corrosion, gasket sealant or threadlocking adhesive. Damaged or distorted threads may be repaired with stainless steel threaded inserts.

5. On models with hydrostatic seal rings cast into the very rear of the gearcase bore, inspect the rings for wear, damage, debris or excessive corrosion. The rings trap water between the propeller hub and gearcase, sealing the gearcase to the propeller hub. This prevents exhaust gases from leaking into the propeller blade area, resulting in ventilation. If the seal rings can no longer retain water, the propeller will ventilate excessively. If so, the gearcase housing must be replaced.

6. Inspect all castings for cracks, porosity, wear, distortion and mechanical damage. Replace any housing that shows evidence of having a bearing spun in its bore.

7. Inspect all anodes as described at the beginning of this chapter. Replace any anode that is deteriorated to 2/3 of its original size.

8. Inspect the water inlet screen(s) for damage or obstructions. Clean or replace the screen(s) as necessary.

9. Inspect the drive shaft and propeller shaft for worn, damaged or twisted splines. See A, **Figure 98**, typical. Excessively worn drive shaft splines are usually the result of shaft misalignment caused by a distorted drive shaft housing or lower gearcase housing, due to impact with an underwater object. Distorted housings must be replaced.

10. Inspect the drive shaft and propeller shaft threaded areas for damage. See A, **Figure 98**, typical. If equipped, check the impeller drive pin and propeller drive pin holes for wear, elongation and cracks.

11. Inspect each shaft's bearing and seal surfaces for excessive wear, grooving, metal transfer and discoloration from overheating. See B, **Figure 98**, typical.

12. Check for a bent propeller shaft by supporting the shaft with V-blocks at its bearing surfaces. Mount a dial indicator on a smooth machined area just forward of the shear pin hole or the propeller splines (as equipped). Rotate

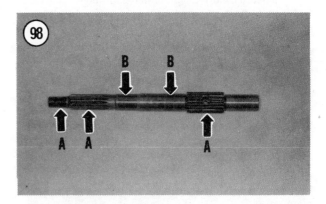

the propeller shaft while observing the dial indicator. Any noticeable wobble or a reading of more than 0.006 in. (0.15 mm) indicates excessive shaft runout and the propeller shaft must be replaced.

13. Check each gear for excessive wear, corrosion or rust and mechanical damage. Check the teeth for galling, chips, cracks, missing pieces, distortion or discoloration from overheating. Check the clutch dog and each gear's engagement lugs (**Figure 99**, typical) for chips, cracks and excessive wear. Check the pinion gear and clutch dog splines for wear, distortion or mechanical damage.

14. Inspect all shift components and shift linkage for excessive wear, grooving, metal transfer and discoloration from overheating. Inspect shift shafts for corrosion, wear, distortion or other damage. Inspect all pivot points and pivot pins for wear and elongated holes.

   a. *3, 3.5 and 4 hp (except 4 Deluxe)*—Inspect the shift spring. The coils must be positioned tightly against each other. If the coils gap at any point, replace the spring.

   b. *4 Deluxe, 6 and 8 hp models*—These models use a rotary shift shaft and a shift cam. Inspect the shaft for wear, distortion or twisting. Replace the shift shaft if it is twisted, damaged or worn. Inspect the shift cam for wear, grooving or other damage.

   c. *All other models*—Inspect the shift bellcrank and pivot pin or shift linkage pivot screw for excessive wear, distortion and elongated holes. Inspect the shift cradle or shift actuator rod (as equipped) for excessive wear, grooving, metal transfer and discoloration from overheating.

15. Inspect all bearings for water damage, pitting, discoloration from overheating and metal transfer. Be sure to locate and inspect all internal needle bearings. On models with bushings, inspect each bushing for excessive wear. Any bushing that is noticeably out of round or elongated, must be replaced.

16. Check the propeller for nicks, cracks or damaged blades. Minor nicks can be removed with a file, taking care to retain the original shape and contour of the blade. Replace the propeller or have it repaired if any of the blades are bent, cracked or badly chipped. If the propeller is excessively corroded, it must be replaced.

GEARCASE PRESSURE AND VACUUM TESTS

Anytime a gearcase is disassembled and reassembled, it must be pressure and vacuum tested before refilled it with lubricant. Failure to pressure and vacuum test a gearcase can lead to needless gearcase failure caused by the lubricant leaking out or water leaking in.

A total of four separate tests (two pressure and two vacuum) are required to verify the integrity of the gearcase seals, gaskets and O-rings. Do not fill the gearcase with lubricant until all four tests are satisfactorily performed (in the specified order) as described in the following procedure.

NOTE
*The tester can be attached to the vent plug/lubricant level hole or the drain/fill plug hole, as long as the gearcase is positioned to prevent lubricant from draining to the hole being used. If this is not done, the tester will draw lubricant into itself during the vacuum tests. See **Figure 100**.*

On 2 and 3.3 hp models, the drive shaft bore must be plugged during these tests. The easiest way to accomplish this is to install the drive shaft support tube into the drive shaft seal, then plug the top of the support tube with a suitable rubber plug. This will ensure the drive shaft seal is tested during the procedure. Hold the drive shaft support tube into the gearcase during the pressure tests, or it may be forced from its bore by the internal pressure.

On 3, 3.5 and 4-35 hp models, the drive shaft must be held into the gearcase during the pressure tests, or it may be forced from its bore by the internal pressure.

There are no special concerns when testing 40-70 hp models.

1. Perform a low pressure test as follows:

   a. Connect a pressure tester (such as Stevens S-34) to the lubricant level or drain plug hole. Make sure the opposite plug (drain plug or lubricant level) and seal is installed and securely tightened.

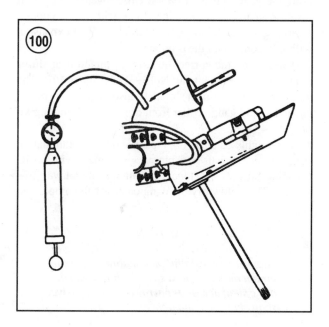

(100)

b. Position the gearcase to elevate the hole that the tester is attached to. See **Figure 100**.

c. Pressurize the gearcase to 3-5 psi (20.7-34.5 kPa) for a minimum of 3 minutes.

d. Rotate the drive shaft, propeller shaft and shift the gearcase into and out of gear (if applicable) during the test.

e. If any pressure drop is noted, spray soapy water on all seals and mating surfaces until the leak is found. Correct the leak and retest.

f. Do not proceed until the gearcase holds pressure for at least 3 minutes without any measurable leakage.

2. Perform a high pressure test as follows:

a. Increase the pressure to 16-18 psi (110-124 kPa) for a minimum of 3 minutes.

b. Rotate the drive shaft, propeller shaft and shift the gearcase into and out of gear (if applicable) during the test.

c. If any pressure drop is noted, spray soapy water on all seals and mating surfaces until the leak is found. Correct the leak and retest.

d. Do not proceed until the gearcase holds pressure, or loses no more than 1 psi (6.9 kPa) after a minimum of 3 minutes.

e. Remove the pressure tester when finished.

3. If both pressure tests are completed satisfactorily, perform a low vacuum test as follows:

a. Connect a vacuum tester (such as Stevens V-34) to the same hole and in the same manner as the pressure tester was connected.

b. Pull a vacuum of 3-5 in.-Hg. (10-16.8 kPa) for a minimum of three minutes.

c. Rotate the drive shaft, propeller shaft and shift the gearcase into and out of gear (if applicable) during the test.

d. If any vacuum loss is noted, apply gear lubricant to all seals and mating surfaces. The lubricant will be drawn into the gearcase at the point of the leak. Correct the leak and retest.

e. Do not proceed until the gearcase holds vacuum for at least three minutes without any measurable leakage.

4. Perform a high vacuum test as follows:

a. Increase the vacuum to 14-16 in.-Hg. (47-54 kPa).

b. Rotate the drive shaft, propeller shaft and shift the gearcase into and out of gear (if applicable) during the test.

c. If any vacuum loss is noted, apply gear lubricant to all seals and mating surfaces. The lubricant will be drawn into the drive unit at the point of the leak. Correct the leak and retest.

d. Do not proceed until the gearcase holds vacuum, or loses no more than 1 in.-Hg. (3.4 kPa) after a minimum of three minutes.

e. Remove the vacuum tester when finished.

5. Fill the gearcase with lubricant as described in Chapter Four.

PINION GEAR SHIMMING
(40-70 HP MODELS)

Proper pinion gear-to-forward/reverse gear engagement (and the corresponding gear lash) are crucial for smooth, quiet operation and long service life. Only one shimming procedure must be performed to set up the lower gearcase properly. The pinion gear must be shimmed to the correct height (depth). The forward and reverse gear are positioned by the manufacturing process and will be correctly positioned as long as the gearcase is correctly assembled and no parts are excessively worn. Refer to **Table 2** for all gearcase specifications.

The pinion gear's position is controlled by adding or subtracting very thin metal spacers, called shims. The shims must be positioned between the drive shaft bearing carrier and the adjoining thrust washer. Placing the shims anywhere else in the drive shaft assembly will cause immediate destruction of the shims.

If the pinion gear is positioned too high in the gearcase bore, the gear teeth will be too far apart. This will cause excessive gear noise (whine) and a reduction in gear strength and durability, since the gear teeth are not sufficiently overlapping.

If the pinion gear is positioned too low in the gearcase bore, the gear teeth will be too close together. This will result in gearcase failure since there will not be enough clearance to maintain a film of lubricant. Heat expansion will only compound the problem.

Determining the correct quantity of pinion gear shims requires shim gauge kit part No. 393185 (**Figure 101**). The 40-50 hp (two-cylinder) models also require a special gauge bar and gauge collar from drive shaft shimming kit part No. 433032.

1. Thoroughly clean all oil, grease or other contamination from the drive shaft and pinion gear tapers with OMC Cleaning Solvent, Acetone, or a similar oil and wax-free solvent. Then blow dry the components with compressed air.

CAUTION
Clamp the drive shaft in a soft-jawed vise to allow easier installation and torquing of the pinion nut in the next step. Do not clamp the drive shaft across its narrower surface (drive shaft seal area and above).

2. Install the pinion gear on the drive shaft and align the splines. Lubricate the threads of the original pinion nut with outboard lubricant, then install the pinion nut and tighten it to 40-45 ft.-lb. (54.2-61.0 N•m). Use spline socket (part No. 334995) or an equivalent spline socket to hold the splined end of the drive shaft and an 11/16 in. socket to hold the nut.

NOTE
No shims are installed at the beginning of the shimming process.

3A. *40-50 hp (two-cylinder)*—Refer back to **Figure 84** and assemble the drive shaft as follows:
   a. Position a thrust washer over the drive shaft against the shaft's shoulder with the chamfered side of the washer facing the shoulder.
   b. Position the thrust bearing over the drive shaft and against the thrust washer. Then install the second thrust washer over the shaft and against the thrust bearing with the chamfered side of the washer facing away from the thrust bearing. Do not install any shims at this time.
   c. Carefully slide the drive shaft bearing carrier over the shaft, being careful not to damage the seals on the splines, then seat the carrier against the thrust washer.

3B. *50-70 hp (three-cylinder)*—Refer back to **Figure 90** and assemble the drive shaft as follows:
   a. Position the thrust bearing over the drive shaft and against the thrust washer. Then install the thrust washer over the shaft and against the thrust bearing. Do not install any shims at this time.
   b. Install seal protector (part No. 312403) over the splined end of the drive shaft, or wrap the splines

with a single layer of cellophane tape to protect the drive shaft seal(s).
   c. Carefully slide the drive shaft bearing carrier over the shaft, being careful not to damage the seals, then seat the carrier against the thrust washer. Remove the seal protector or cellophane tape.

4. Slide the appropriate Collar (A, **Figure 101**) over the splined end of the drive shaft against the drive shaft bearing carrier. The large (flanged) end of the collar must face the bearing carrier.
   a. *40-50 hp (two-cylinder)*—Use collar part No. 334985 (from kit part No. 433032).
   b. *50-70 hp (three-cylinder)*—Use collar part No. 328363 (from kit part No. 393185).

5. Set the drive shaft assembly into the shim fixture.
   a. Make sure the flanged end of the gauge collar is piloted on the inner edge of the fixture's frame (C, **Figure 101**).
   b. Position the preload screw tip (E, **Figure 101**) into the recess in the pinion nut end of the shaft.
   c. Tighten the preload screw until the groove in the spring-loaded plunger (E, **Figure 101**) is flush with the end of the screw (D). The assembly must be properly preloaded for the results to be accurate.
   d. Tighten the preload screw's jam nut securely against the fixture's frame. Failure to tighten the jam nut will cause an inaccurate result.
   e. Rotate the drive shaft several turns to seat the thrust bearing.

6. Position the appropriate gauge bar (F, **Figure 101**) into the fixture frame and against the dowel pins in the tool base. Each gauge bar is machined a certain distance shorter than the distance required to properly locate the pinion gear. This distance is called the *gauge factor*.
   a. *40-50 hp (two-cylinder)*—Use gauge bar part No. 334984. The gauge bar is gold colored and has a gauge factor of 0.030 in. (0.762 mm).
   b. *50-70 hp (three-cylinder)*—Use gauge bar part No. 328366. The gauge bar is silver colored and has a gauge factor of 0.020 in. (0.508 mm).

7. Rotate the drive shaft bearing carrier to position the gauge bar exactly between two screw holes. Do not attempt to take any measurements when the gauge bar is positioned over a screw hole.

NOTE
When using a feeler gauge, a light drag must be felt as the gauge is pushed and pulled between the surfaces being measured. When the correct gauge is determined, verify your results by inserting the next larger and next smaller size gauges between the surfaces. The next larger gauge must result in a distinct increase in drag, while the next smaller

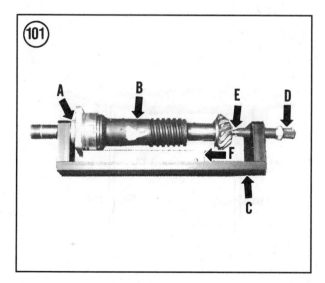
(101)

gauge must result in a distinct decrease in drag. Do not twist or cock the gauge, as this will give an inaccurate result.

8. Next, hold the gauge bar firmly against the pinion gear. Then measure the clearance (A, **Figure 102**) between the gauge bar and the drive shaft bearing carrier using a feeler gauge. Verify, then record your reading.

NOTE
The pinion gear cannot be rotated during Steps 8 and 9 or the results (Step 10) will be inaccurate.

9. Rotate the drive shaft bearing housing (while holding the pinion gear stationary) to position the gauge bar between the next pair of screw holes and repeat Step 8. Repeat this step until a measurement is taken between each pair of screw holes. This will be a total of three readings on two-cylinder models and four readings on three-cylinder models.

10. Subtract the smallest feeler gauge reading from the largest reading obtained in Steps 8 and 9. If the difference exceeds 0.004 in. (0.102 mm), the drive shaft bearing carrier is unacceptably warped and must be replaced. Replace the carrier and repeat this procedure.

NOTE
The bearing carrier cannot be rotated during Steps 11 and 12 or the results (Step 13) will be inaccurate.

11. Make sure the gauge bar is positioned between a pair of screw holes, then hold the gauge bar firmly against the drive shaft bearing carrier. Measure the clearance (B, **Figure 102**) between the gauge bar and the flat surface on the upper edge of the pinion gear using a feeler gauge. Verify, then record your reading.

12. Rotate the pinion gear (while holding the bearing carrier stationary) exactly 1/4 turn and repeat Step 11. Then repeat this step two more times until a total of four measurements are taken at 90° intervals around the pinion gear.

13. Subtract the smallest feeler gauge reading from the largest reading obtained in Steps 11 and 12. If the difference exceeds 0.002 in. (0.051 mm), the pinion gear is not running true to the drive shaft. Remove the pinion gear and clean the tapers again. Reinstall the pinion gear and repeat Steps 11-13. If the results are still unacceptable, either the drive shaft or the pinion gear are warped or distorted and must be replaced. Because the drive shaft is made of a softer steel, it is usually the cause of the problem. Replace either the drive shaft or the pinion gear and repeat this procedure.

14. If the bearing carrier and pinion gear are within specification to this point, determine the average of the meas-urements recorded in Steps 8 and 9 by adding the measurements together, then dividing by three (two-cylinder models) or four (three-cylinder models). Record this figure as the *Average feeler gauge measurement.*

NOTE
Shims can be reused if they are of the correct thickness and are not bent, kinked or grooved.

15A. *40-50 hp (two-cylinder)*—Determine the correct amount of shims required to locate the pinion gear as follows:
   a. Subtract the *average feeler gauge measurement* obtained in Step 14 from the *gauge factor* of 0.030 in. (0.762 mm). Record this figure as the *required shim thickness.*
   b. Shims are available in 0.003, 0.004, 0.005, 0.006 and 0.007 in. (0.076, 0.102, 0.127, 0.152 and 0.178 mm) sizes. Select the shim stack-up that will use the *least* number of shims to obtain the *required shim thickness.*

15B. *50-70 hp (three-cylinder)*—Determine the correct amount of shims required to locate the pinion gear as follows:
   a. Subtract the *average feeler gauge measurement* obtained in Step 14 from the *gauge factor* of 0.020 in. (0.508 mm). Record this figure as the *required shim thickness.*
   b. Shims are available in 0.003, 0.004 and 0.005 in. (0.076, 0.102 and 0.127 mm) sizes. Select the shim stack-up that will use the *least* number of shims to obtain the *required shim thickness.*

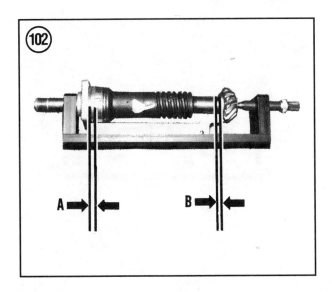

(102)

NOTE
The shims must be installed between the drive shaft bearing carrier and the thrust washer (upper thrust washer on two-cylinder models).

16. Remove the drive shaft assembly from the shim fixture. Remove the gauge collar and drive shaft bearing carrier and install the shim pack (determined in Step 15) over the drive shaft and against the thrust washer. Then reinstall the drive shaft bearing carrier and the gauge collar as described in this procedure.

17. Verify that the correct amount of shims are installed by repeating Steps 5-9.

    a. If the average of the feeler gauge readings now obtained in Steps 8 and 9 equals the *gauge factor* of the gauge bar, the pinion gear is properly shimmed.

    b. If the readings are very close to being correct (within 0.001-0.002 in. [0.025-0.051 mm]), add or subtract to the thickness of the shim pack to achieve an average feeler gauge clearance equal to the *gauge factor* of the gauge bar. Verify all corrections by repeating Steps 5-9.

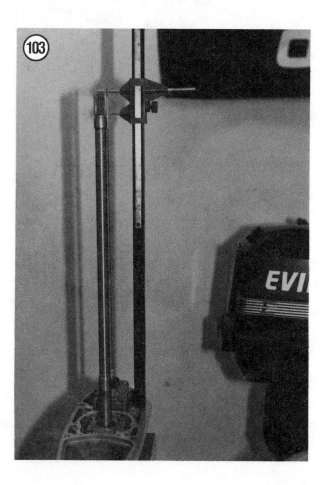

c. If the new readings are far from being correct, repeat the entire shimming procedure.

SHIFT SHAFT HEIGHT ADJUSTMENT (40-70 HP MODELS)

Shift shaft height adjustment is a critical adjustment. If the shift shaft height is incorrect, the geometry of the engine-mounted shift linkage will be incorrect and the shift linkage will have too much throw in one gear and too little throw in the other.

If the shift shaft height is too low, the shift system will be biased toward the forward gear, and the reverse gear will not receive adequate engagement. If the shift shaft height is too high, the shift system will be biased toward the reverse gear, and the forward gear will not receive adequate engagement.

If the clutch dog is not fully engaged into a gear, the clutch dog will tend to pop out of engagement with that gear's lugs under acceleration and high-power settings. This will quickly destroy (round) the engagement lugs as the clutch dog backs out of the gear (over the engagement lugs), then slams back into the next set of lugs. Eventually the lugs will become so rounded that the clutch dog will slip at low-power settings.

The shift shaft height adjustment must be performed with the gearcase removed and the shift mechanism in its NEUTRAL detent position. This can be quickly found by moving the shift shaft up and down, while feeling for the detent ball(s) to engage the detent notch in the shift detent lever (three-cylinder models) or the clutch dog (two-cylinder models). The propshaft will rotate freely when in NEUTRAL.

The shift shaft height gauge (part No. 389997) or another accurate measuring device is required for this procedure. The measurement is always taken from the top of the gearcase deck (not the shift shaft housing) and the center of the hole at the top of the shift shaft. Shift shaft height specifications are also listed in **Table 2**.

To adjust the shift shaft height, refer to **Figure 103** and proceed as follows:

1. Move the shift shaft up and down (while rotating the propeller) until you feel the shift mechanism click into its NEUTRAL detent position and the propeller rotates freely.

2A. *40-50 hp (two-cylinder)*—Make sure the shift shaft's offset is facing straight forward.

2B. *50-70 hp (three-cylinder)*—Make sure the shift shaft's offset is facing to port, but with the stamped flat on the head of the shaft pointing straight fore and aft (the hole pointing straight port and starboard).

3. Set the shift shaft height gauge (part No. 389997) to the following specification:

9

a. *40-50 hp (two-cylinder)*—The correct shift shaft height for standard shaft (15 in.) models is 16-29/32 to 16-31/32 in. (429.42-431.0 mm). The correct shift shaft height for long shaft (20 in.) models is 21-29/32 to 21-31/32 in. (556.42-558.0 mm).

b. *50-70 hp (three-cylinder)*—The correct shift shaft height for long shaft (20 in.) models is 21-11/16 to 21-3/4 in. (550.86-552.45 mm).

4. Set the gauge onto the gearcase deck (gearcase-to-drive shaft housing mating surface). Keep the gauge parallel to the shift shaft and attempt to insert the gauge's pin into the shift shaft's hole. Turn the shaft clockwise to shorten and counterclockwise to lengthen. The gauge's pin must fit cleanly into the shaft's hole without lifting the gauge from the deck or disturbing the shaft's position when the gauge and shaft are parallel (**Figure 103**). Readjust as necessary.

5. Once correctly adjusted, make sure the shift shaft's height is not disturbed before the gearcase is installed.

JET DRIVE MODELS

Jet drive models are based on the following propeller-driven models. The standard lower gearcase has been removed and a jet pump unit installed. An adaptor plate is used on all models. The adaptor plate does not normally require removal for service procedures.

1. *18 jet*—25 hp (two-cylinder) power head.
2. *28 jet*—40 hp (two-cylinder) power head.
3. *35 jet*—50 hp (two-cylinder) power head.

Service on the power head, ignition, electrical, fuel and power trim and tilt systems are the same as on propeller-driven outboard models. Refer to the appropriate chapter and service section for the engine models or component serviced. Only service on the jet drive assembly (and water pump) is covered in this chapter. Refer to **Table 9** for all torque values.

JET PUMP UNIT ADJUSTMENTS AND MAINTENANCE

Outboard Mounting Height

A jet drive outboard must be mounted higher on the transom plate than an equivalent propeller-driven outboard motor. However, if the jet drive is mounted too high, air will be allowed to enter the jet drive resulting in cavitation and power loss. If the jet drive is mounted too low, excessive drag, water spray and loss of speed will result.

NOTE
When operating in rough or extremely rough (white) water, it may be necessary to add a spray plate or a white water wedge between

*the bottom of the hull and the intake housing. See **Spray Plates**, in the next section.*

To set the initial height of the outboard motor, proceed as follows:

1. Place a straightedge against the boat bottom (not keel) and *abut* the end of the straightedge with the jet drive intake.

2. The fore edge of the water intake housing must align with the top edge of the straightedge (**Figure 104**).

3. Secure the outboard motor at this setting, then test run the boat.

4. If cavitation occurs (over-speeding and/or loss of thrust), the outboard motor must be lowered in 1/4 in. (6.35 mm) increments until uniform operation is noted.

NOTE
A slight amount of cavitation in rough water and sharp turns is normal. However exces-

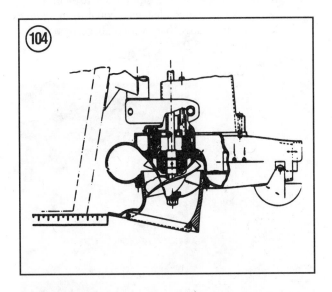

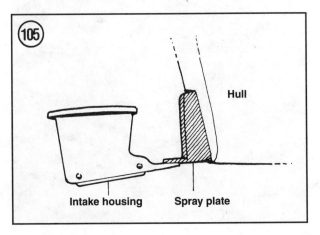

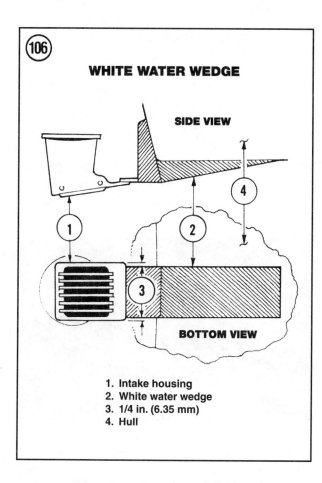

WHITE WATER WEDGE

SIDE VIEW

BOTTOM VIEW

1. Intake housing
2. White water wedge
3. 1/4 in. (6.35 mm)
4. Hull

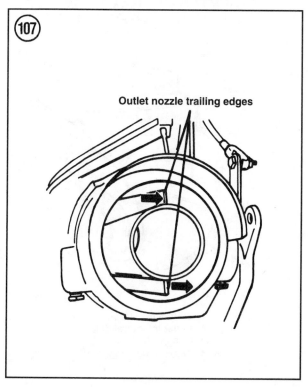

Outlet nozzle trailing edges

sive cavitation will damage the impeller and can cause power head overheating.

5. If uniform operation is noted with the initial setting, raise the outboard motor in 1/4 in. (6.35 mm) increments until cavitation is noted. Then lower the motor to the last uniform setting.

NOTE
The outboard motor must be in a vertical position when the boat is on plane. Adjust the motor trim setting as needed. If the outboard trim setting is altered, the outboard motor height must be checked and adjusted.

Spray Plates

If the boat is consistently operated in rough or very rough (white) water, it may not be possible to achieve optimum performance as described in the preceding procedure.

A spray plate (**Figure 105**) will typically enhance the performance of a boat operated in rough water. The plate simply enhances the water flow from the hull to the intake grate, minimizing the possibility of air being drawn into the jet drive unit intake. This generally allows the motor to be mounted as specified in the preceding section.

A white water wedge (**Figure 106**) will typically allow the boat to be operated in extremely rough water. The wedge allows the motor to be mounted lower (in undisturbed water), yet ensures smooth water flow into the intake grate.

The white water wedge must be 1/2 in. (12.7 mm) narrower than the intake grate as shown in **Figure 106**. Before modifying the bottom of the hull, consult a dealership with experience in jet drive propulsion and extremely rough water operation.

Steering Torque

A minor adjustment to the trailing edge of the drive outlet nozzle may be made if the boat tends to pull in one direction when the boat and outboard are pointed in a straight-ahead direction. Should the boat tend to pull to the starboard side, bend the top and bottom trailing edge of the jet drive outlet nozzle 1/16 in. (1.6 mm) toward the starboard side of the jet drive. See **Figure 107**.

Bearing Lubrication

The jet pump bearing(s) must be lubricated after each operating period, after every 10 hours of operation and prior to storage. In addition, after every 30 hours (15 hours in saltwater) of operation, additional grease must be pumped into the bearing(s) to purge any moisture.

Lubricate the bearing(s) by first removing the vent hose from the side of the jet pump housing to expose the grease fitting. See **Figure 108**. Use a grease gun and inject OMC EP/Wheel Bearing grease into the fitting until grease exits the end of the hose. After every 30 hours, pump fresh grease into the fitting until all dirty grease is expelled and fresh (clean) grease exits from the end of the hose. Reconnect the vent hose to the fitting when finished.

When lubricating the bearings, note the color of the grease expelled from the hose. During the break-in period (of new bearing and seals) some discoloration of the grease is normal. After the break-in period, the discoloration will be minimal.

If the grease contains moisture or excessive discoloration, the bearing housing must be removed, disassembled, the bearings inspected and all seals and O-rings replaced as described later in this chapter.

Directional Control

The boat's operational direction is controlled by a thrust gate. The thrust gate is controlled by an engine-mounted mechanical linkage on the 18 jet, an engine-mounted shift cable and mechanical linkage on the 28 jet and a remote control shift cable on 35 jet models.

When the directional control lever is placed in the full forward position, the thrust gate must completely uncover the jet drive housing's outlet nozzle opening and seat securely against the jet drive's pump housing (on a rubber stop). When the directional control lever is placed in full reverse position, the thrust gate must completely close off the pump housing's outlet nozzle opening. Neutral position is a separate detent on the shift cam plate, located midway between full forward and full reverse positions (detents).

Thrust Gate Adjustment (All Models)

The thrust gate adjustment sets the gate opening in the NEUTRAL position and verifies that the gate is secured when in the FORWARD position.

> *WARNING*
> *The thrust gate adjustment must be correct or water pressure from the boat's forward movement can engage the thrust gate, causing REVERSE to engage unexpectedly.*

1. Disconnect the shift link rod or shift cable from the shift cam.

2. Move the shift cam to the NEUTRAL position as shown in **Figure 109**.

3. With the shift cam in the NEUTRAL position, apply upward pressure on the reverse gate and measure the clearance between the gate and the water discharge passage as shown in **Figure 109**. The clearance must be 9/16 in. (14.3 mm). If so, proceed to Step 5. If not, proceed to Step 4.

4. To adjust the gate clearance, loosen the screw securing the eccentric nut (**Figure 110**), then rotate the eccentric nut to achieve the specified clearance. When achieved, hold

(108)

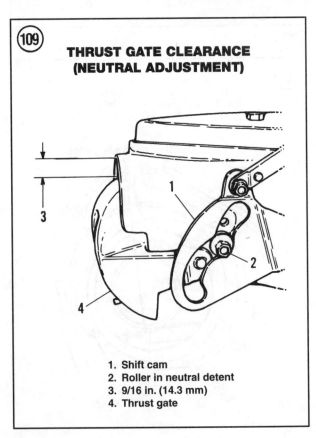

(109)

**THRUST GATE CLEARANCE
(NEUTRAL ADJUSTMENT)**

1. **Shift cam**
2. **Roller in neutral detent**
3. **9/16 in. (14.3 mm)**
4. **Thrust gate**

the eccentric nut in place and tighten the cam screw securely.

5. Move the shift cam to the full FORWARD position as shown in **Figure 111**. Attempt to move the thrust gate up toward the NEUTRAL position. The thrust gate must remain secured in the FORWARD position (shift cam roller in the FORWARD detent and gate secured against the rubber stop) and must not move toward NEUTRAL. If the gate is secure, adjustment is complete. If not, proceed to Step 6.

6. If the gate is not secure, loosen the screw securing the eccentric nut (**Figure 110**), then rotate the eccentric nut just enough to secure the thrust gate in the FORWARD position. Do not disturb the adjustment any more than necessary to secure the gate. When correct adjustment is achieved, hold the eccentric nut in place and tighten the cam screw securely.

Shift Link Rod Adjustment (18 Jet)

The shift link rod is properly adjusted if after placing the engine mounted directional control lever in the full FORWARD position, the thrust gate *cannot* be moved from the FORWARD position (shift cam roller in the FORWARD detent and gate secured against the rubber stop) and toward NEUTRAL.

> *WARNING*
> *Shift link rod adjustment must be correct or water pressure from the boat's forward movement can engage the thrust gate, causing REVERSE to engage unexpectedly.*

To adjust the shift link rod, refer to **Figure 112** and proceed as follows:

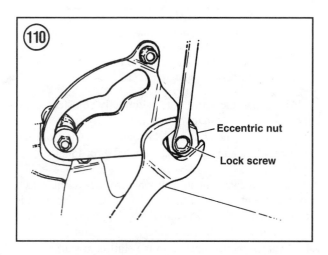

(110)

Eccentric nut

Lock screw

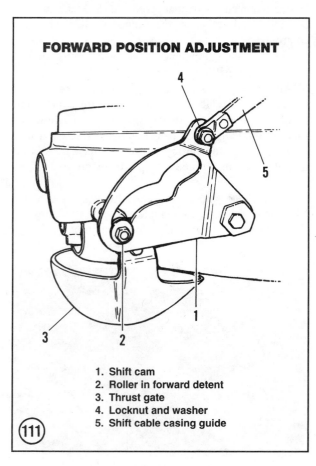

FORWARD POSITION ADJUSTMENT

(111)
1. Shift cam
2. Roller in forward detent
3. Thrust gate
4. Locknut and washer
5. Shift cable casing guide

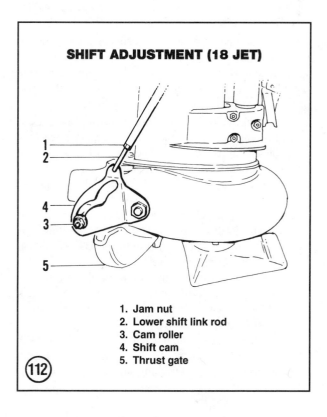

SHIFT ADJUSTMENT (18 JET)

(112)
1. Jam nut
2. Lower shift link rod
3. Cam roller
4. Shift cam
5. Thrust gate

9

1. Verify that the thrust gate is correctly adjusted as described previously in this chapter.

2. Place the engine-mounted directional control lever in the full FORWARD position.

3. Remove the special locking clip (or cotter pin), washer and tension spring securing the shift link rod to the shift cam.

4. Loosen the jam nut (1, **Figure 112**) and adjust the linkage by rotating the lower end of the shift link rod (2, **Figure 112**). Adjust the linkage to place the roller (3, **Figure 112**) in the forward detent (at the end of the shift cam slot) as shown in **Figure 112**.

5. Reattach the shift link rod to the shift cam. Install the tension spring, then the washer. Secure the connection with the special locking clip or a new stainless steel cotter pin. Bend both prongs of the cotter pin for a secure attachment.

6. Securely tighten the link rod jam nut.

7. Place the engine-mounted directional control lever in the full FORWARD position.

8. Attempt to move the thrust gate (5, **Figure 112**) up toward the NEUTRAL position. The thrust gate must remain secured in the FORWARD position (shift cam roller in the FORWARD detent and gate secured against the rubber stop) and must not move toward NEUTRAL. If the gate is secure, proceed to Step 10. If not, proceed to Step 9.

9. If the thrust gate can be moved upward toward the NEUTRAL position, shorten the shift link rod as necessary to prevent the gate from moving toward NEUTRAL.

10. Place the engine-mounted directional control lever in the NEUTRAL detent position. Push up on the thrust gate with moderate hand pressure. The shift cam must engage the NEUTRAL detent as shown in 2, **Figure 109**. If not, proceed to Step 11.

11. Adjust the engine-mounted neutral detent as follows:
  a. Loosen the two neutral detent screws (**Figure 113**) on the shift lever arm. The arm is located on the starboard side of the drive shaft housing, just below the lower cowl and is easily identified by its grease fitting.
  b. Manually move the directional control lever to position the jet drive unit in the NEUTRAL position. The shift cam must positioned in the NEUTRAL detent as shown in 2, **Figure 109**.
  c. Carefully move the shift cam (inside the lower cowl) to locate the shift lockout lever in the detent notch of the shift cam. Do not disturb the shift lever arm's position (the outer lever's position).
  d. Tighten the two neutral detent screws to 60-84 in.-lb. (6.8-9.5 N•m).
  e. Repeat Step 10 to verify the adjustment. Readjust as necessary.

Shift Cable and Linkage Adjustment (28 Jet)

The shift cable is properly adjusted if after placing the engine mounted directional control lever in the full FORWARD position, the thrust gate *cannot* be moved from the FORWARD position (shift cam roller in the FORWARD detent and gate secured against the rubber stop) and toward NEUTRAL.

> *WARNING*
> *Shift cable adjustment must be correct or water pressure from the boat's forward movement can engage the thrust gate, causing REVERSE to engage unexpectedly.*

1. Verify that the thrust gate is correctly adjusted as described previously in this chapter.

2. Disconnect the shift cable's connector ends from the shift cam stud and the engine mounted directional control lever.

3. Loosen the jam nut on each connector. Then adjust each connector until 1/8 in. (3.2 mm) of the cable core threads are exposed after passing through each connector. Tighten each connector's jam nut securely.

4. Reattach the connectors to the shift cam stud and the engine-mounted directional control lever. Make sure the bushing is reinstalled in the connector attached to the control lever.

5. Place the engine-mounted directional control lever in the full FORWARD position.

6. Attempt to move the thrust gate (3, **Figure 111**) up toward the NEUTRAL position. The thrust gate must remain secured in the FORWARD position (shift cam roller in the FORWARD detent and gate secured against the rubber stop) and must not move toward NEUTRAL. If the gate is secure, proceed to Step 8. If not, proceed to Step 7.

7. If the thrust gate can be moved upward toward the NEUTRAL position, loosen the two screws securing the shift cable's lower bracket to the jet pump unit housing.

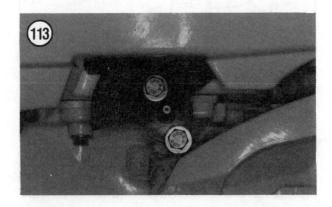

Move the bracket as necessary to prevent the gate from moving toward NEUTRAL, then tighten both screws securely.

8. Place the engine-mounted directional control lever in the NEUTRAL detent position. Push up on the thrust gate with moderate hand pressure. The shift cam must engage the NEUTRAL detent (2, **Figure 109**). If not, proceed to Step 9.

9. Adjust the engine-mounted neutral detent as follows:

   a. Loosen the two neutral detent screws on the engine-mounted shift lever arm. See **Figure 114**.

   b. Manually move the directional control lever to position the jet drive unit in the NEUTRAL position. The shift cam will be positioned as shown in **Figure 109**.

   c. Tighten the two neutral detent screws to 60-84 in.-lb. (6.8-9.5 N•m).

   d. Repeat Step 8 to verify the adjustment. Readjust as necessary.

Shift Cable Adjustment (35 Jet)

WARNING
Shift cable adjustment must be correct or water pressure from the boat's forward movement can engage the thrust gate, causing REVERSE to engage unexpectedly.

To adjust the remote control shift cable, proceed as follows:

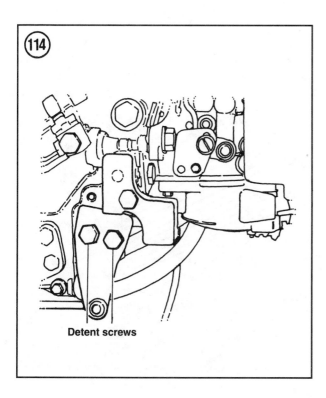

Detent screws

1. Verify the thrust gate adjustment as described in this chapter.

2. Remove the locknut and washer (4, **Figure 111**) securing the shift cable to the shift cam's stud. Pull the shift cable from the shift cam stud. Rotate the cable and remove it from the anchor block.

3. Reconnect the cable's casing guide (5, **Figure 111**) to the shift cam stud. Do not install the washer and locknut.

4. Place the remote control shift lever into the full FORWARD (full-throttle) position. Pull on the shift cable's adjustment barrel to remove all slack from the system and seat the shift cam in the full FORWARD position as shown in **Figure 111**.

5. Hold the shift cable barrel centered over the anchor bracket. Adjust the shift cable barrel to align with its anchor bracket.

6. Reinstall the cable's barrel into the anchor bracket and reconnect the cable guide to the shift cam stud.

7. Place the engine-mounted directional control lever in the NEUTRAL detent position. Push up on the thrust gate with moderate hand pressure. The shift cam must engage the NEUTRAL detent as shown in 2, **Figure 109**. If not, adjust the cable barrel slightly and recheck NEUTRAL detent engagement.

8. Place the remote control shift lever in the full FORWARD (full-throttle) position.

9. Attempt to move the thrust gate (3, **Figure 111**) up toward the NEUTRAL position. The thrust gate must remain secured in the FORWARD position (shift cam roller in the FORWARD detent and gate secured against the rubber stop) and must not move toward NEUTRAL. If the gate is secure, proceed to Step 11. If not, proceed to Step 10.

10. If the thrust gate can be moved upward, toward the NEUTRAL position, readjust the cable barrel as necessary to prevent the gate from moving toward NEUTRAL.

11. After the correct adjustment is obtained, securely tighten the cable casing guide retaining nut (4, **Figure 111**) until it bottoms, then back the nut off 1/8 to 1/4 turn.

CAUTION
The NEUTRAL position adjustment in Step 7 is secondary in importance to the FORWARD position adjustment in Steps 9-11.

Impeller Clearance Adjustment and Impeller Removal/Installation

If a loss of high-speed performance and/or a higher than normal full throttle engine speed (not boat speed) is evident, check the clearance between the edge of the impeller and the water intake casing liner. Also check the leading edge(s) of the impeller for wear or damage. If worn or damaged, refer to *Worn impeller* following this procedure.

> *NOTE*
> *Impeller wear can occur quickly when operated in water with excessive silt, sand or gravel.*

1. Disconnect the spark plug leads to prevent accidental starting.

2. Using a feeler gauge set, determine the clearance between the impeller blades and the intake liner. See **Figure 115**.

3. The impeller-to-liner clearance must be 0.020-0.030 in. (0.51-0.76 mm).

4. If the clearance is not as specified, remove the six water intake housing mounting screws. Remove the intake housing. See **Figure 116**, typical.

5. Bend the tabs on the tab washer retaining the impeller nut to allow a suitable tool to be installed on the impeller nut. Remove the nut, tab washer, lower shim impeller, drive key, plastic sleeve and upper shims. Note the number of lower and upper shims. See **Figure 117**.

> *NOTE*
> *If the impeller is stuck to the drive shaft, use a block of wood and hammer to rotate the impeller in the opposite direction of normal rotation. Rotate the impeller just enough to free the drive key and allow impeller removal.*

6. If the clearance is excessive, remove shims as needed from below the impeller (lower shims) and position them above the impeller (nut side). Moving one shim changes the clearance by approximately 0.004 in. (0.102 mm).

> *NOTE*
> *Lubricate the impeller shaft, impeller sleeve and drive key with OMC Triple Guard Grease, prior to reassembly.*

7. Install the impeller with the selected number of shims. Hold the upper shims on the drive shaft with grease. Then position the plastic sleeve in the impeller and install the impeller, drive key and lower shims.

8. Install a new tab washer and the impeller retaining nut on the drive shaft. Tighten the nut to 16-18 ft-lb. (21.7-24.4 N•m). Do not bend the tabs on the tab washer at this time.

9. Apply OMC Gasket Sealing Compound to the threads of the intake housing retaining screws. Install the housing and screws. Tighten the screws finger-tight.

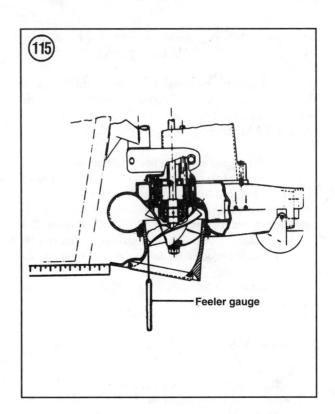

(115)

— Feeler gauge

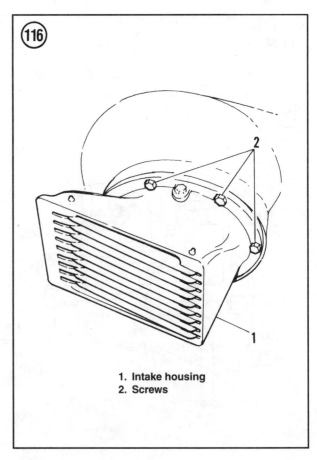

(116)

2

1

1. Intake housing
2. Screws

NOTE
The intake housing can be moved slightly on its mounting to center the liner over the impeller.

10. Rotate the impeller to check for rubbing or binding. Make sure the housing is centered over the impeller.

11. Repeat Step 2 and Step 3 to recheck impeller clearance. Readjust clearance as necessary.

12. After correct clearance is obtained, remove the intake housing screws and housing. Make sure the impeller nut is tightened to 16-18 ft.-lb. (21.7-24.4 N•m), then lock the nut in place with the tab washer. Make sure the tabs are bent securely against the nut.

13. Reinstall the intake housing, again making sure the housing is centered on the impeller. Tighten the housing screws in a crossing pattern to 60-84 in.-lb. (6.8-9.5 N•m).

Worn impeller

The leading edge(s) of the impeller can become worn due to the ingestion of gravel, silt and other debris. If a noticeable performance loss, increased wide-open throttle speed, or difficulty in getting the boat on plane is noted, check the leading edge(s) of the impeller for wear or damage.

1. If the leading edge(s) is damaged, remove the impeller as described in the previous section.

2. Sharpen the impeller by removing material (with a flat file) from the lower surface of the leading edge(s) as shown in **Figure 118**. Do not remove material from the upper surface or alter the top side lifting angle of the impeller.

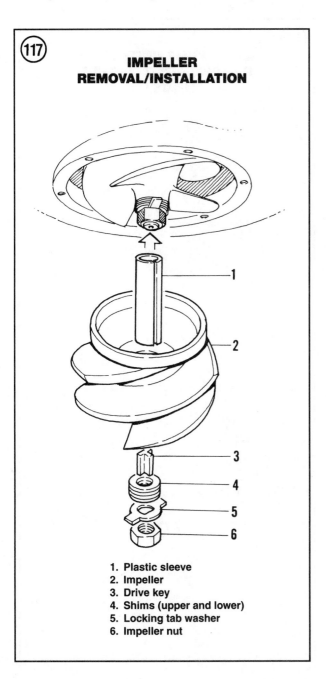

IMPELLER REMOVAL/INSTALLATION

1. Plastic sleeve
2. Impeller
3. Drive key
4. Shims (upper and lower)
5. Locking tab washer
6. Impeller nut

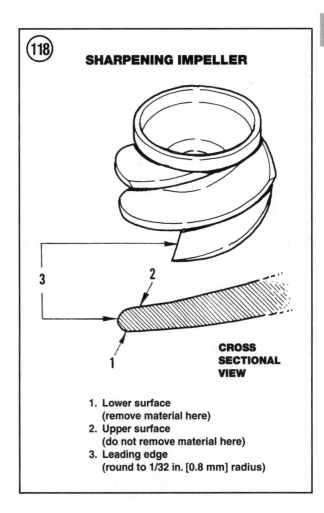

SHARPENING IMPELLER

CROSS SECTIONAL VIEW

1. Lower surface
   (remove material here)
2. Upper surface
   (do not remove material here)
3. Leading edge
   (round to 1/32 in. [0.8 mm] radius)

9

3. When finished, file or sand a 1/32 in. (0.8 mm) radius on the leading edge(s) as shown in **Figure 118**.

4. Reinstall the impeller and recheck the impeller clearance as described in the previous section.

Cooling System Flushing

The cooling system can become plugged by sand and salt deposits if it is not flushed occasionally. Clean the cooling system after each use in salt, brackish or silt-laden water. Refer to Chapter Four for cooling system flushing procedures.

Water Pump

The water pump is located at the top of the jet pump unit on all models as follows:

On 18 jet, the water pump is bolted directly to the bearing housing. Water pump service procedures for the 18 jet are covered along with the 28 Special models.

On 28 and 35 jet, a metal adaptor base is used to adapt the water pump to the jet pump unit housing. A gasket is not used between the water pump's impeller plate and the pump adaptor base, and no gasket is used between the pump adaptor base and the jet pump unit housing. However, these mating surfaces and adaptor base attachment screws must be coated with OMC Gasket Sealing Compound. Water pump service procedures are covered in the 40-50 hp (two-cylinder) section.

Since proper water pump operation is critical to outboard operation and durability, the water pump must be serviced anytime the jet pump unit is removed from the outboard. To service the water pump, remove the jet drive assembly as described in this chapter and refer to the appropriate water pump service section in this chapter for the related power head.

JET PUMP UNIT SERVICE

When removing the jet drive mounting fasteners, it is not uncommon to find that they are corroded. Such fasteners must be discarded and new ones installed. Apply OMC Gasket Sealing Compound to the threads of the mounting screws during installation.

Pump Unit Removal

1. Disconnect and ground the spark plug leads to the power head to prevent accidental starting.

2. Tilt the outboard to the fully UP position and engage the tilt lock lever, securely block the drive shaft housing or support the drive shaft housing with a suitable hoist.

3A. *18 jet*—Remove the special locking clip (or cotter pin), tension spring and washer securing the shift link rod (2, **Figure 112**) to the shift cam (4). Disconnect the shift link rod from the shift cam.

3B. *28 jet models*—Remove the nut and washer (4, **Figure 111**) securing the shift cable connector to the stud on the shift cam. Pull the connector from the stud, then locate and

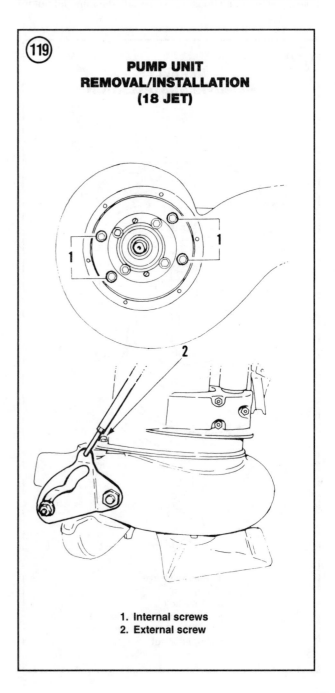

PUMP UNIT REMOVAL/INSTALLATION (18 JET)

1. Internal screws
2. External screw

secure the bushing. Remove the two screws and locknuts securing the shift cable retainer and backing plate to the anchor bracket. Remove the cable from the jet pump.

3C. *35 jet models*—Remove the nut and washer (4, **Figure 111**) securing the remote control shift cable's casing guide to the stud on the shift cam. Pull the casing guide from the stud, then rotate the shift cable as necessary to disengage the adjustment barrel from the anchor bracket.

4. Remove the six water intake housing mounting screws. Remove the intake housing. See **Figure 116**, typical.

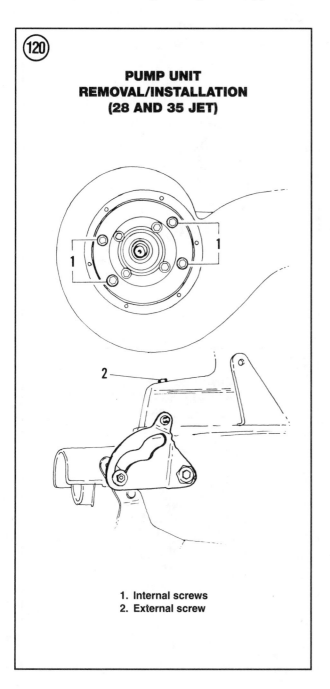

**PUMP UNIT
REMOVAL/INSTALLATION
(28 AND 35 JET)**

1. Internal screws
2. External screw

5. Bend the tabs on the impeller nut tab washer away from the impeller nut. Remove the impeller nut and tab washer. Discard the tab washer. See **Figure 117**.

NOTE
Note the number and location of impeller adjustment shims for reference during reassembly.

6. Remove the shims located below the impeller and note the number. Remove the impeller and the shims located above the impeller and note the number.

7. Slide the impeller sleeve and drive key off the drive shaft.

8A. *18 jet*—Remove the four hex head screws (1, **Figure 119**) from the bottom of the bearing carrier in the impeller cavity. Then remove the screw (2, **Figure 119**) from the rear of the adaptor plate. Support the pump unit as the last screw is removed.

8B. *28 and 35 jet*—Remove the four internal screws (1, **Figure 120**) located inside of the impeller cavity. Then remove the external screw (2, **Figure 120**, typical) from the rear of the adaptor plate. Support the pump unit as the last screw is removed.

9. Remove the jet pump unit by pulling it straight down and away from the drive shaft housing (adaptor plate) until the drive shaft is free from the housing. The adaptor plate will remain attached to the drive shaft housing. Place the pump unit on a clean workbench.

NOTE
On 18 jet models, the water tube, water tube extension, drive shaft spacer tube (and adaptor tube) may stay in the drive shaft housing or come out with the water pump. The 28-35 jet models do not use these components.

10A. *18 jet*—Remove the water tube and water tube extension from the water pump or drive shaft housing. Locate and secure the washer that sits at the very top of the tube. Then pull the drive shaft spacer tube (and adaptor tube) from the water pump or drive shaft housing. Remove and discard the water tube seal and all drive shaft support (and adaptor) tube O-rings.

10B. *28 and 35 jet*—Remove and discard the water tube and drive shaft grommets. Refer to *Water Pump* in this chapter for additional information.

Pump Unit Installation

1A. *18 jet*—Prepare the pump unit for installation as follows:

    a. Glue a new water tube grommet into the water pump housing using Scotch Grip 1300 Adhesive. Use the

9

adhesive sparingly and make sure the grommet's raised tabs align with the holes in the water pump housing.

b. Grease the upper (straight) end of the water tube, then place the washer over the end of the tube. Install the water tube into the inner exhaust housing.

c. Install the water tube extension over the water tube.

d. Grease two-new O-rings with OMC Triple Guard Grease. Install an O-ring in each end of the drive shaft spacer tube.

e. Install the spacer tube into its drive shaft housing bore with the tabs facing the rear of the housing. Make sure the tube is seated in the drive shaft bore.

f. Grease a new O-ring with OMC Triple Guard Grease. Install the O-ring into the drive shaft spacer tube adaptor. Install the adaptor tube over the drive shaft support tube (already in the drive shaft housing). Make sure the adaptor is seated to the support tube.

1B. *28 and 35 jet*—Glue a new water outlet grommet and drive shaft grommet to the top of the water pump housing using OMC Adhesive M sealant. Use the sealant sparingly.

> *CAUTION*
> *Do not apply lubricant to the top of the drive shaft in the next step. Excess lubricant between the top of the drive shaft and the engine crankshaft can create a hydraulic lock, preventing the drive shaft from fully engaging the crankshaft.*

2. Clean the drive shaft splines as necessary, then coat the splines with OMC Moly Lube.

3. Position the jet pump unit under the adaptor plate (drive shaft housing). Insert the drive shaft into the spacer tube (18 jet) or the cast bore (28 and 35 jet). Then push the pump unit toward the drive shaft housing.

> *CAUTION*
> *Do not rotate the flywheel counterclockwise in the next step or the water pump impeller will be damaged.*

4A. *18 jet*—Continue pushing the pump unit toward the drive shaft housing, rotating the flywheel clockwise (as required) to align the drive shaft and crankshaft splines. Align the water tube with the water pump grommet, then seat the pump unit against the adaptor plate (drive shaft housing).

4B. *28 and 35 jet*—Continue pushing the pump unit toward the drive shaft housing, rotating the flywheel clockwise (as required) to align the drive shaft and crankshaft spline. Then seat the pump unit against the adaptor plate (drive shaft housing). It is not necessary to align any water passages.

5A. *18 jet*—Coat the threads of the four interior screws with OMC Nut Lock threadlocking adhesive, then coat the threads of the one exterior screw with OMC Gasket Sealing Compound.

5B. *28 and 35 jet*—Coat the threads of the five mounting screws with OMC Gasket Sealing Compound.

6A. *18 jet*—Secure the pump unit to the drive shaft housing with the four internal screws (and washers) and one exter-

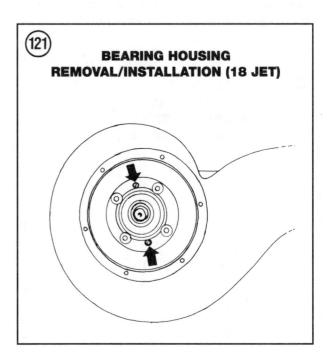

BEARING HOUSING REMOVAL/INSTALLATION (18 JET)

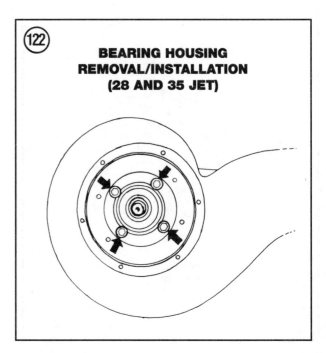

BEARING HOUSING REMOVAL/INSTALLATION (28 AND 35 JET)

nal screw (with no washer). See **Figure 119**. Evenly tighten the four internal screws to 60-84 in.-lb. (6.8-9.5 N•m), then tighten the external screw to 120-144 in.-lb. (13.6-16.3 N•m).

6B. *28 and 35 jet*—Secure the pump unit to the drive shaft housing with the four internal and 1 external screws (all with washers). See **Figure 120**. Evenly tighten the mounting screws to 10-12 ft.-lb. (13.6-16.3 N•m).

NOTE
Install the original upper and lower impeller shims if the original impeller and intake liner are used. If a new impeller or liner is installed, start with no upper shims, carefully adding shims until the correct clearance is obtained.

7. Install the impeller and water intake housing and check the impeller clearance as described in *Impeller Clearance Adjustment and Impeller Removal/Installation*.

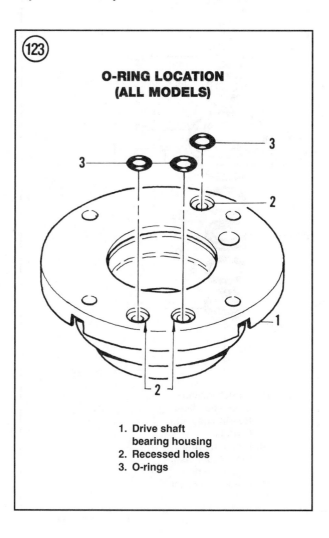

**O-RING LOCATION
(ALL MODELS)**

1. Drive shaft
   bearing housing
2. Recessed holes
3. O-rings

8. Connect and adjust the shift link rod (18 jet) or shift cable (28 and 35 jet) as described previously in this Chapter.
9. Reconnect the spark plug leads.

DRIVE SHAFT AND BEARING HOUSING

Removal

1. Remove the pump unit as described in this chapter.
2. Remove the water pump assembly. Refer to the appropriate water pump service section in this chapter.
3. *28 and 35 jet*—Remove the four screws securing the water pump base adaptor to the top of the pump unit housing. Then remove the adaptor.
4A. *18 jet*—Remove the two screws securing the bearing housing and drive shaft assembly to the pump unit housing. See **Figure 121**. Withdraw the bearing housing and drive shaft assembly from the pump unit housing and place on a clean work bench.
4B. *28 and 35 jet*—Remove the four screws securing the bearing housing and drive shaft assembly to the pump unit housing. See **Figure 122**. Withdraw the bearing housing and drive shaft assembly for the pump unit housing and place it on a clean work bench.
5. Remove and discard the three O-rings from bearing housing-to-drive shaft housing mating surface. See **Figure 123**.

Installation

1. Glue three new O-rings (using OMC Adhesive M sealant) into the recesses on the mating surface of the bearing housing as shown in **Figure 123**. Use the sealant sparingly. Allow the sealant to dry, then lubricate the O-rings with OMC Triple Guard Grease.
2. Install the bearing housing and drive shaft assembly into the pump unit housing. Make sure the retainer screw holes are aligned and that the O-rings are not displaced during installation.
3. Coat the threads of the two (18 jet) or four (28 and 35 jet) bearing housing screws with OMC Gasket Sealing Compound.
4A. *18 jet*—Install the two housing retaining screws (**Figure 121**) and tighten them securely.
4B. *28 and 35 jet*—Install the four housing retaining screws (**Figure 122**). Evenly tighten the screws to 60-84 in.-lb. (6.8-9.5 N•m).
5. *28 and 35 jet*—Install the water pump base adaptor to the top of the pump unit housing. Coat the mating surfaces with OMC Gasket Sealing Compound and the screws with OMC Nut Lock threadlocking adhesive. Tighten the four screws securely.

9

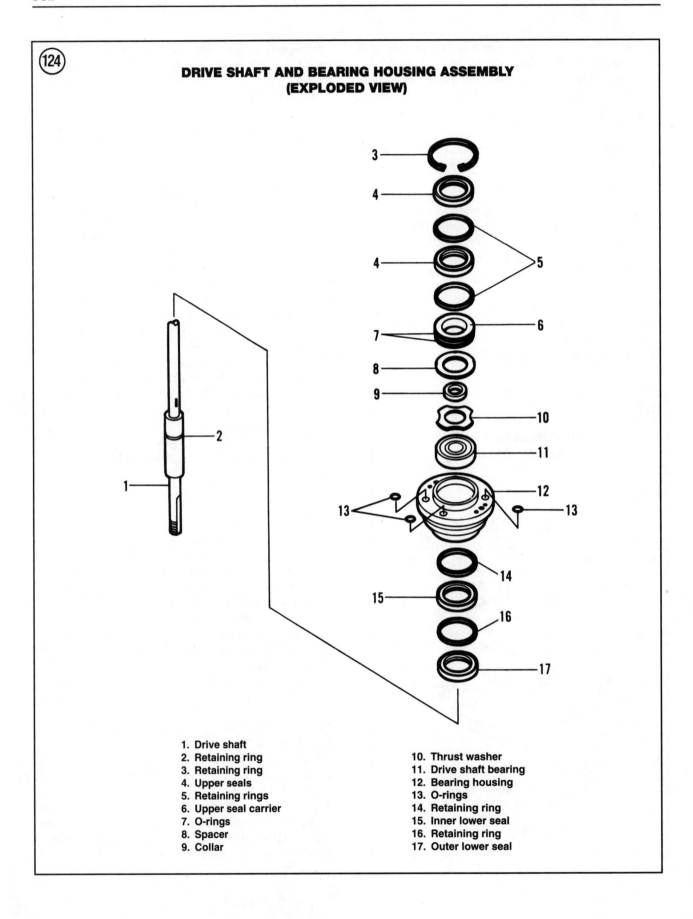

124

**DRIVE SHAFT AND BEARING HOUSING ASSEMBLY
(EXPLODED VIEW)**

1. Drive shaft
2. Retaining ring
3. Retaining ring
4. Upper seals
5. Retaining rings
6. Upper seal carrier
7. O-rings
8. Spacer
9. Collar
10. Thrust washer
11. Drive shaft bearing
12. Bearing housing
13. O-rings
14. Retaining ring
15. Inner lower seal
16. Retaining ring
17. Outer lower seal

6. Install the water pump assembly as described in the appropriate water pump servicing section near the front of this chapter.

7. Install the jet pump unit as described in this section. Lubricate the jet pump unit bearings before operation as described in this chapter.

Disassembly (All Models)

Refer to **Figure 124** and **Figure 125** for this procedure. The snap ring that secures the drive shaft bearing is not shown in either figure. The snap ring fits into a groove (in the drive shaft) located directly under the bearing (11, **Figure 124** or **Figure 125**).

1. Remove the bearing housing and drive shaft assembly from the jet pump housing as described in this chapter.

2. Remove the snap ring (3, **Figure 124**) from the bore in the top of the bearing housing with a suitable pair of internal snap ring pliers.

3. Support the bearing housing in a press with the impeller end of the drive shaft facing up. Heat the housing with a heat gun, heat lamp, or propane torch until it is thoroughly

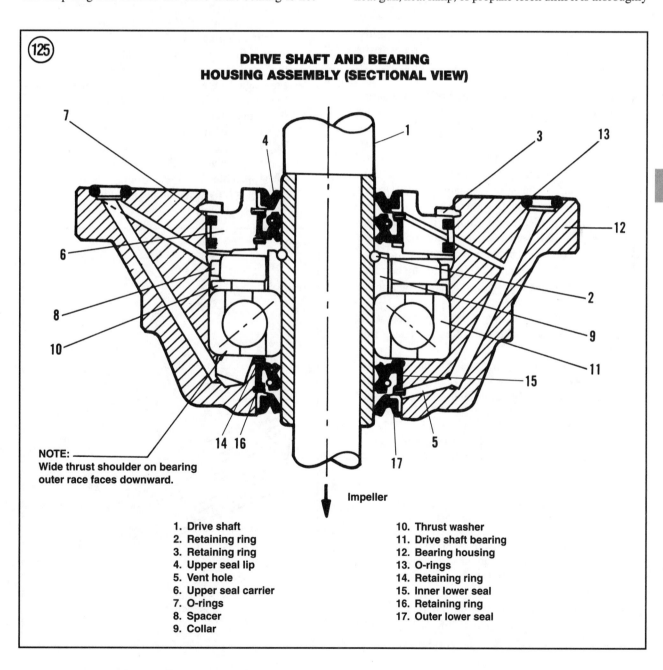

9

(125) **DRIVE SHAFT AND BEARING HOUSING ASSEMBLY (SECTIONAL VIEW)**

NOTE:
Wide thrust shoulder on bearing outer race faces downward.

Impeller

1. Drive shaft
2. Retaining ring
3. Retaining ring
4. Upper seal lip
5. Vent hole
6. Upper seal carrier
7. O-rings
8. Spacer
9. Collar
10. Thrust washer
11. Drive shaft bearing
12. Bearing housing
13. O-rings
14. Retaining ring
15. Inner lower seal
16. Retaining ring
17. Outer lower seal

warmed, yet not so hot that the grease (and seals) melts (or smoke). Do not apply heat to the drive shaft.

CAUTION
Wear insulated gloves when handling the heated housing.

4. Press on the impeller end of the drive shaft until it is free from the bearing housing. If the shaft sticks, repeat the application of heat and try again. When properly heated, the shaft should not require a great amount of effort to remove.

5. Allow the components to cool before proceeding.

6. Remove both seals from the bearing housing as follows:
   a. Remove the inner seal's retaining ring (14, **Figure 124**) by hooking its tang with a small screwdriver or awl. Lift the ring from its groove in a circular, unwinding motion.
   b. Drive the inner seal (15, **Figure 124**) into the interior of the bearing carrier with a suitable punch. Do not damage the seal bore. Discard the seal.
   c. Remove the outer seal's retaining ring (16, **Figure 124**) in the same manner as the inner seal's ring.
   d. Drive the outer seal (17, **Figure 124**) from the interior of the housing with a suitable punch. Do not damage the seal bore. Discard the seal.

7. Remove the upper seal carrier from the drive shaft. The carrier (6, **Figure 124**), seals (4) and retaining rings (5) are serviced as an assembly. Discard the carrier.

8. Slide the spacer (8, **Figure 124**) from the drive shaft.

9. If the drive shaft bearing requires replacement, remove the bearing as follows:
   a. Remove the retaining ring (located just below the bearing) with a suitable pair of external snap ring pliers.
   b. Support the thrust washer and bearing in a knife-edged bearing plate, then press against the impeller end of the drive shaft until the bearing and washer are free from the shaft.
   c. Discard the bearing.
   d. Slide the collar (9, **Figure 124**) from the drive shaft.
   e. If the retaining ring (2, **Figure 124**) requires replacement, remove and discard it.

Assembly (All Models)

Replace all seals and O-rings. If the drive shaft bearing was removed, it must be discarded and a new bearing installed. Lubricate all seals and O-rings with OMC Triple Guard Grease.

When installing the new bearing, press only on its inner race or the bearing will be destroyed. Refer to **Figure 124** and **Figure 125** for this procedure.

1. If the drive shaft bearing was removed, reassemble the drive shaft as follows:
   a. If the retaining ring (2, **Figure 124**) was removed, install a new ring into its groove on the drive shaft.
   b. Slide the collar over the impeller end of the drive shaft and seat it over the retaining ring. The larger stepped end of the collar must face the retaining ring.
   c. Slide the thrust washer over the impeller end of the drive shaft and up against the collar. The washer is bowed (curved). Install the washer so that its bow faces the top of the drive shaft. The washer must only contact the bearing's outer race.
   d. Lubricate a new drive shaft bearing and the drive shaft with OMC EP/Wheel Bearing grease. Then slide the bearing over the impeller end of the drive shaft with the numbered side of the bearing facing the impeller end of the shaft (downward).
   e. Press against the inner race of the bearing until it is seated against the collar. Do not press on the bearing's outer race.
   f. Secure the bearing in place by installing the retaining ring into the drive shaft groove with a suitable pair of external snap ring pliers. Make sure the sharp edge of the snap ring faces away from the bearing and that the ring is fully seated in the groove.

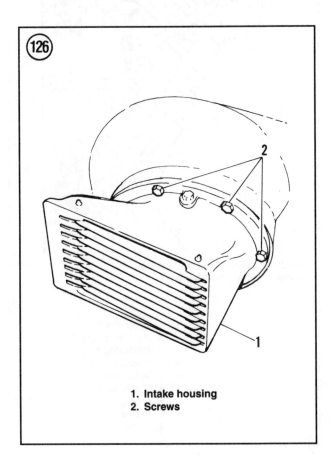

(126)

1. **Intake housing**
2. **Screws**

2. Grease the seal lips (4, **Figure 125**) of a new upper seal carrier (6, **Figure 125**) with OMC Triple Guard grease. If the O-rings (7, **Figure 124**) are not included with the carrier, install two new O-rings (lubricated with OMC Triple Guard Grease) into the grooves on the carrier's outer diameter.

3. Slide the spacer over the long end of the drive shaft and seat it against the thrust washer. Then carefully slide the upper seal carrier over the drive shaft and seat it against the spacer. Then set the drive shaft aside temporarily.

4. Install new seals into the bearing housing as follows:
   a. Position the housing so that the seal bore is facing up (bearing bore facing down).
   b. Install the retaining ring into the groove (16, **Figure 125**) closest to the outer edge (impeller side) of the carrier. Position the ring so that its notched ends are positioned over the small lubrication vent hole (5, **Figure 125**) in the seal bore.
   c. Coat the outer diameter of the outer seal (17, **Figure 125**) with OMC Gasket Sealing Compound, then

position the seal into the bore with the seal lip facing up (out). Press the seal into the bore (with a suitable mandrel) until it contacts the retaining ring.
   d. Invert the bearing housing so that the bearing bore is facing up (seal bore facing down).
   e. Coat the outer diameter of the inner seal (15, **Figure 125**) with OMC Gasket Sealing Compound, then position the seal into the seal bore (from the bearing side) with the spring side of the seal facing down (toward the outer seal). Press the seal into the bore (with a suitable mandrel) until it contacts the retaining ring.
   f. Install the second retaining ring (14, **Figure 125**) over the inner seal and into its groove. Make sure the ring has fully seated into its groove.
   g. Lubricate the seal lips and pack the area between the seals with OMC Triple Guard Grease.

5. Pack the cavity (in the bearing housing) between the seals and the bearing bore with OMC EP/Wheel Bearing grease.

6. Support the bearing housing in a press with the bearing bore facing up (seals facing down). Carefully insert the impeller end of the drive shaft assembly into the bearing housing and pilot the bearing into its bore. Be careful not to damage the seals with the drive shaft.

7. Heat the bearing carrier with a heat gun, heat lamp or a propane torch. Do not heat the carrier above the point where it can no longer be comfortably touched. Do not heat the carrier to the point that the grease begins to melt (or smoke).

8. Press against the impeller end of the drive shaft until the shaft (and bearing) are seated in the carrier. This should only require moderate pressure.

9. Push the upper seal carrier into its bore with hand pressure. The snap ring groove will be visible when the carrier is seated.

10. Install the retaining ring (3, **Figure 125**) into the bearing housing with the beveled side of the ring facing up (outward), using a suitable pair of internal snap ring pliers. Make sure the ring is fully expanded into its groove.

11. Install the drive shaft and bearing housing to the jet pump unit as described previously in this chapter.

WATER INTAKE HOUSING LINER

Replacement

1. Remove the six water intake housing mounting screws. See **Figure 126**. Then pull the water intake housing down and away from the pump unit housing.

2. Mark or tag the liner screws for reassembly in the same location, then remove the screws and washers. See **Figure 127**.

9

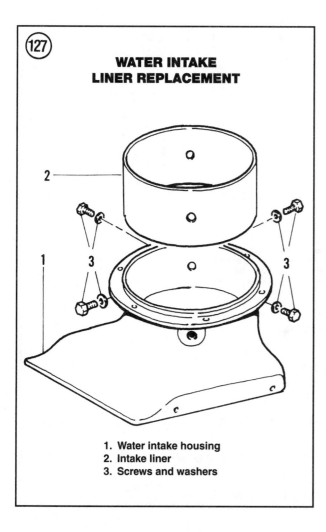

(127) **WATER INTAKE LINER REPLACEMENT**

2

1   3   3

1. **Water intake housing**
2. **Intake liner**
3. **Screws and washers**

3. Tap the liner loose by inserting a long drift punch through the intake housing grate. Place the punch on the edge of the liner and tap with a hammer.

4. Withdraw the liner from the liner housing.

5. Install the new liner into the intake housing. See **Figure 127**.

6. Align the liner screw holes with their respective intake housing holes. Gently tap the liner into place with a soft hammer if necessary.

7. Apply OMC Gasket Sealing Compound to the threads of the liner retaining screws.

8. Install the liner retaining screws (and washers). Evenly and securely tighten the screws.

9. Remove any burrs from the inner diameter of the liner and grind the end of the screws as necessary to ensure a flush inner surface.

10. Install the intake housing and set the impeller clearance as described previously in *Impeller Clearance Adjustment and Impeller Removal/Installation.*

Table 1 GEARCASE GEAR RATIO AND APPROXIMATE LUBRICANT CAPACITY

Outboard model	Gear ratio	Tooth count	Lubricant capacity
2.0 and 3.3 hp	1.85:1	13.24	3 oz. (89 ml)
3.5 hp	1.85:1	13:24	2.7 oz. (80 ml)
3.0 and 4 hp	2.08:1	12:25	2.7 oz (80 ml)
4 Deluxe, 6 and 8 hp	2:23:1	13:29	11 oz. (325 ml)
9.9 and 15 hp	2.42:1	12:29	9 oz. (266 ml)
20, 25, 30 and 35 hp	2.15:1	13:28	11 oz. (325 ml)
28 Special	1.75:1	12:21	8 oz. (237 ml)
40-50 hp (two-cylinder)	2.42:1	12:29	16.4 oz. (485 ml)
50-70 hp (three-cylinder)	2.42:1	12:29	22 oz. (651 ml)
18-35 jet models	Not applicable	–	–

Table 2 GEARCASE SPECIFICATIONS

Component	Specification (or part No.)
Pinion gear shimming	
40-50 hp (two-cylinder)	
Gauge bar	Part No. 334984
Clearance dimension	0.030 in. (0.762 mm)
Gauge collar	Part No. 334985
50-70 hp (three-cylinder)	
Gauge bar	Part No. 328366
Clearance dimension	0.020 in. (0.508 mm)
Gauge collar	Part No. 328363
Required remote control box shift stroke	
Neutral to Forward	1.125-1.330 in. (28.58-33.78 mm)
Shift shaft height (in NEUTRAL)	
40-50 hp (two-cylinder)	
Standard shaft (15 in.)	16-29/32 to 16-31/32 in. (429.42-431.0 mm)
Long shaft (20 in.)	21-29/32 to 21-31/32 in. (556.42-558.0 mm)
50-70 hp (three-cylinder)	
Long shaft (20 in.)	21-11/16 to 21-3/4 in. (550.86-552.45 mm)

Table 3 GEARCASE TORQUE VALUES (2-8 HP [INCLUDING 4 DELUXE])

Component	in.-lb.	ft.-lb.	N•m
2 and 3.3 hp			
Anode	60-84	–	6.8-9.5
Drain and vent plugs	30-40	–	3.4-4.5
Bearing carrier/pump cover	60-84	–	6.8-9.5
Gearcase mounting	89-115	–	10-13
3, 3.5 and 4 hp (except 4 Deluxe)			
Drain and vent plugs	40-50	–	4.5-5.7
Gearcase mounting	60-84	–	6.8-9.5
Propshaft bearing carrier	60-84	–	6.8-9.5
Water pump	25-35	–	2.8-4.0
4 Deluxe, 6 and 8 hp			
Drain and vent plugs	84-86	–	9.5-9.7
Gearcase mounting			
Front (upper) screw	120-144	10-12	13.6-16.3
Rear (lower) screws	60-84	–	6.8-9.5
Propshaft bearing carrier	48-60	–	5.4-6.8
Water pump and base	60-84	–	6.8-9.5

Table 4 GEARCASE TORQUE VALUES (9.9-35 HP)

Component	in.-lb.	ft.-lb.	N•m
9.9 and 15 hp			
Gearcase mounting	96-120	8-10	10.9-13.6
Drain and vent plugs	84-86	–	9.5-9.7
Propshaft bearing carrier	60-84	–	6.8-9.5
Propeller nut	120	10	13.6
Shift linkage pivot screw	48-84	–	5.4-9.5
Shift shaft coupler	60-84	–	6.8-9.5
Water pump	60-84	–	6.8-9.5
28 Special (two-piece gearcase)			
Drain and vent plugs	84-86	–	9.5-9.7
Gearcase halves	60-84	–	6.8-9.5
Gearcase mounting			
Screws (lower)	192-216	16-18	21.7-24.4
Nut (upper rear)	–	45-50	61.0-67.8
Propeller nut	120	10	13.6
Shift linkage pivot screw	48-84	–	5.4-9.5
Shift shaft coupler	120-144	10-12	13.6-16.3
Water pump	60-84	–	6.8-9.5
20-35 hp (one-piece gearcase)			
Anode			
25 and 35 hp (three-cylinder)	108-132	–	12.2-14.9
Drain and vent plugs	84-86	–	9.5-9.7
Gearcase mounting	192-216	16-18	21.7-24.4
Propshaft bearing carrier	60-84	–	6.8-9.5
Propeller nut	120*	10	13.6
Shift linkage pivot screw	48-84	–	5.4-9.5
Trim tab	60-84	–	6.8-9.5
Water pump	60-84	–	6.8-9.5

Table 5 GEARCASE TORQUE VALUES (40-70 HP)

Component	in.-lb.	ft.-lb.	N•m
Anode			
Two-cylinder	108-132	–	12.2-14.9
Three-cylinder	Securely		

(continued)

9

Table 5 GEARCASE TORQUE VALUES (40-70 HP)

Component	in.-lb.	ft.-lb.	N•m
Drain and vent plugs	84-86	–	9.5-9.7
Drive shaft bearing carrier	144-166	12-14	16.3-19.0
Gearcase mounting			
3/8 in. Screws	–	18-20	24.4-27.1
7/16 in. Screw	–	28-30	28.0-30.7
Pinion bearing retaining screw	48-84	–	5.4-9.5
Pinion nut	–	40-45	54.2-61.0
Propshaft bearing carrier	120-144	10-12	13.6-16.3
Propeller nut	120*	10	13.6
Shift linkage pivot screw	48-84	–	5.4-9.5
Shift shaft plastic nut (bushing)			
Two-cylinder	48-60	–	5.4-6.8
Shift shaft housing	60-84	–	6.8-9.5
Trim tab			
Two-cylinder	–	18-20	24.4-27.1
Three cylinder	–	35-40	47.5-54.2
Water pump	60-84	–	6.8-9.5

*See text on page 492

Table 6 PUMP TORQUE VALUES (JET DRIVES)

Component	in.-lb.	ft.-lb.	N•m
18 jet			
Adaptor-to-drive shaft housing	192-216	16-18	21.7-24.4
Impeller nut	192-216	16-18	21.7-24.4
Intake housing	60-84	–	6.8-9.5
Jet pump mounting			
Bearing housing screws	60-84	–	6.8-9.5
Rear (upper) screw	120-144	10-12	13.6-16.3
Water pump	60-84	–	6.8-9.5
28 and 35 jet			
Adaptor-to-drive shaft housing	192-216	16-18	21.7-24.4
Bearing housing	60-84	–	6.8-9.5
Impeller nut	192-216	16-18	21.7-24.4
Intake housing	60-84	–	6.8-9.5
Jet pump mounting	120-144	10-12	13.6-16.3
Thrust gate	60-84	–	6.8-9.5
Thrust gate cam roller	60-84	–	6.8-9.5
Water pump	60-84	–	6.8-9.5

Chapter Ten

Trim and Tilt Systems

Trimming refers to the process of changing the angle of the propeller shaft (and its thrust cone) relative to the bottom of the boat, or more simply, changing the trim angle. Trimming the outboard motor UP (out or away from the transom) raises the bow of the boat, while trimming the motor DOWN (in or toward the transom) lowers the bow.

On models without any form of power trim and tilt, the motor must be raised and lowered manually. The reverse lock must be released and the motor lifted by hand. To change the trim angle of the motor, the trim limit rod must be moved to another set of holes in the stern brackets. See **Figure 1**, typical. Depending on the model, there are 3-5 available trim rod positions. Different operating conditions and changes to the boat load require frequent changes to the trim limit rod position to maximize boat performance and efficiency.

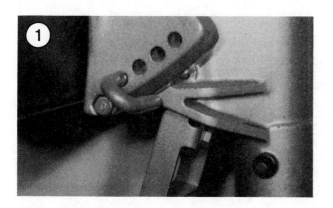

Power trim and tilt is designed to provide an easy and convenient way to infinitely change the trim angle while under way and allow hands-free tilting of the motor for trailer loading or beaching. OMC uses both manual (gas-charged) tilt systems and power (electro-hydraulic) trim and tilt systems.

The term *integral* refers to components being located between the stern brackets, while the term *external* refers to components being located outside of the stern brackets or inside of the boat. All OMC trim and tilt systems are integral.

This chapter includes maintenance, component replacement and troubleshooting procedures for manual and power trim and tilt systems. **Tables 1-3** list specifications, **Table 4** lists torque values and **Tables 5-9** list troubleshooting procedures. All tables are located at the end of the chapter.

Using Power Trim and Tilt

While a power trim and tilt system can be operated at any time, it is not recommended to change trim angle while operating in reverse gear. Correct adjustment of the trim angle assures maximum performance and efficiency under any given load and speed condition.

Trim the outboard motor out as necessary to achieve a bow-up position for cruising, running with choppy waves or to achieve maximum performance when running at wide-open throttle. Excessive trim UP will cause propeller ventilation (or cavitation), causing a reduction in performance (propeller slippage) and possible propeller damage from cavitation burns.

Trim the outboard motor in as necessary to hold the bow down when accelerating onto plane, operating at slow speeds or running against choppy waves. Excessive trim IN at high power settings and high speeds will cause the bow to plow or dive into the water, making handling difficult.

Trimming the outboard motor cannot correct operational problems resulting from overloading or incorrectly loading the hull. Trimming also will not overcome an incorrect engine installation, poor hull design or hull flaws, such as hook or rocker (**Figure 2**).

Trimming the outboard motor to the point that the swivel bracket is no longer supported by the stern brackets is considered *tilting*. The tilt function is normally used to reduce the draft of the boat for shallow water operation, beaching or launching, loading or transporting the boat.

Care should be taken to not operate the outboard motor above 1000 rpm when the unit is in the tilt range and in no case can the motor be operated if the cooling water intakes are above the water.

A malfunction of the trim and tilt system can result in the loss of the reverse lock function. This can cause the outboard motor to kick up when operating in reverse gear or trail out when decelerating. Both of these conditions will cause a loss of control. Any defect noted in the trim and tilt system must be repaired immediately, before returning the boat to service.

MANUAL TILT ASSIST CYLINDER

All 50-70 hp (three-cylinder) models (without power trim and tilt) use a gas-charged cylinder to assist the operator in manually tilting the engine. See **Figure 3**. The cylinder also acts as a shock absorber during impact. The cylinder is not serviceable and is simply replaced if it loses its charge (fails to assist in tilting) or develops any external leaks.

> *WARNING*
> *Do not attempt to disassemble the cylinder. The cylinder contains a high-pressure gas charge and could burst (causing personal injury) during any attempts at disassembly.*

Manual Tilt Assist Cylinder Service

The only maintenance required is periodic lubrication of the upper and lower pivot pins (3 and 8, **Figure 3**) with a heavy-duty penetrating lubricant, such as OMC 6-in-1 Lubricant or OMC Anti-corrosion Spray.

Manual Tilt Cylinder Removal

This procedure applies only to 50-70 hp (three-cylinder) models without power trim and tilt. Refer to **Figure 3** for this procedure.

1. Tilt the outboard motor to the full UP position and engage the tilt lock. Support the gearcase with a hoist or

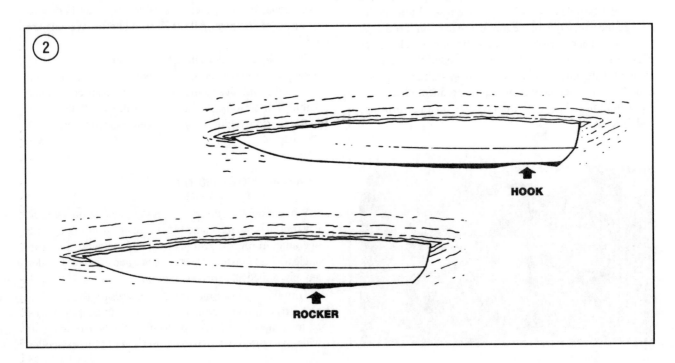

③

MANUAL TILT ASSIST (50-70 HP)

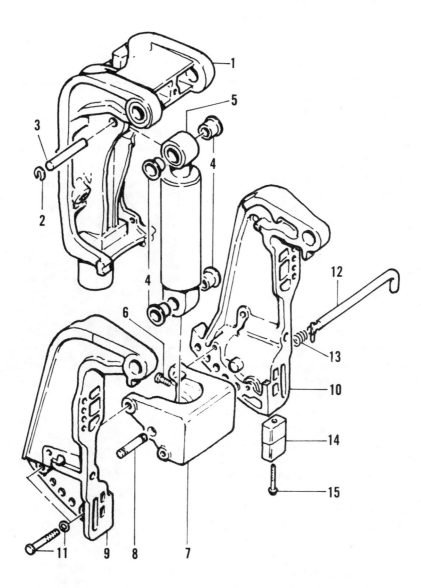

10

1. Swivel housing
2. Locking clip
3. Upper pivot pin
4. Bushings
5. Tilt cylinder
6. Set screw
7. Mounting bracket
8. Lower pivot pin

9. Starboard stern
   bracket
10. Port stern bracket
11. Screw and washer
12. Trim limit rod
13. Spring
14. Anode
15. Screw

block the gearcase to eliminate any possibility of it falling during this procedure.

2. Remove the locking clip from one end of the upper pivot pin. See **Figure 4**.

3. Drive the upper pivot pin from the swivel bracket using a suitable punch.

4. Remove the trim limit rod from the stern bracket assembly. Note the position of the pin for reassembly.

5. Remove the four screws and washers (two each side) securing the tilt cylinder mounting bracket to the stern bracket assembly. See 7 and 11, **Figure 3**.

6. Pull the tilt cylinder and mounting bracket assembly from the stern brackets.

7. Remove the set screw (6, **Figure 3**) securing the lower pivot pin into the bracket. Then drive the lower pivot pin from the bracket with a suitable punch.

8. Remove the four pivot pin bushings (4, **Figure 3**) from the tilt cylinder.

Manual Tilt Cylinder Installation

Use OMC Triple Guard Grease for all grease applications. Refer to **Figure 3** for this procedure.

1. Grease the pivot pin bushings and install them into the tilt cylinder's upper and lower pivot pin bores.

2. Grease the lower pivot pin. Position the tilt cylinder into the mounting bracket and align the pivot pin bores. Then install the lower pivot pin and center it in its bore.

3. Coat the threads of the lower pivot pin set screw (6, **Figure 3**) with OMC Gasket Sealing Compound. Install the set screw into the mounting bracket and tighten it to 24-26 in.-lb. (2.7-2.9 N•m).

4. Position the mounting bracket and cylinder assembly into the stern brackets.

5. Coat the threads of the four bracket screws with OMC Nut Lock threadlocking adhesive. Then align the screw holes and install the screws (and washers). Evenly tighten the screws to 18-20 ft.-lb. (24.4-27.1 N•m).

6. Grease the upper pivot pin. Align the tilt cylinder rod's eye with the swivel bracket bore, then install the pin. Secure the pin by installing the locking clip. See **Figure 4**.

7. Reinstall the trim limit rod (12, **Figure 3**) to the stern bracket assembly (in the position noted on disassembly).

8. Release the tilt lock, remove the hoist or remove the blocks and lower the outboard.

TOUCH-TRIM SYSTEM

This section applies to the 28-35 jet, 48 Special and all 40-50 hp (two-cylinder [and 50 Special]) models without power trim and tilt.

These models use a remote-control, gas-charged, tilt-assist cylinder to assist the operator in manually trimming and tilting the outboard (**Figure 5**). The system is referred to as the Touch Trim system.

WARNING
Do not attempt to disassemble the cylinder and manifold assembly. The system contains fluid under a high pressure gas charge and could burst (causing personal injury) during any attempts at disassembly.

The system consists of a sealed, pressurized cylinder, manifold assembly, control lever and cable (A, **Figure 5**). When

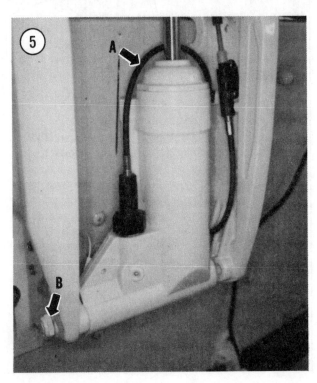

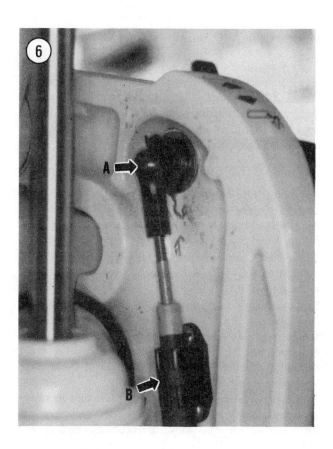

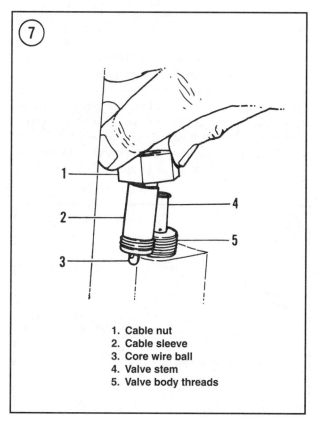

1. Cable nut
2. Cable sleeve
3. Core wire ball
4. Valve stem
5. Valve body threads

the control lever is moved to the TILT position, the cylinder's internal passages are opened, the internal pressure is directed to the tilt cylinder and the motor can be trimmed (and tilted) with minimal effort to any position desired. When the control lever is moved to the RUN position, the internal passages are closed, blocking all internal fluid flow, locking the motor in its present position.

The touch-trim system incorporates several special hydraulic functions:

1. *Impact*—This circuit is designed to absorb and dissipate the energy of an impact with an underwater object, while in forward motion. It does NOT protect the unit from impact damage when backing up. The circuit allows the sealed hydraulic system to act as a shock absorber. High-pressure springs and check balls in the tilt cylinder piston vent hydraulic fluid to the opposite side of the piston when the pressure reaches a predetermined value. When fluid is vented, the engine is allowed to tilt up as necessary, dissipating the energy of the impact.

2. *Reverse lock*—Reverse lock is a function of multiple circuits in the system. Its function is to hold the gearcase in the water during reverse thrust. Reverse thrust occurs during deceleration and when operating in reverse gear. If the gearcase is not held in the water during deceleration and reverse gear operation, the operator will not have control of the boat.

3. *Control valve*—The control valve allows the operator to raise or lower the engine as desired with little or no effort. Move the valve to the TILT position (opened) and position the engine as desired. After positioning the engine, the control lever must be moved to the RUN position (closed) in order for the engine to hold position and for the impact and reverse lock circuits to function.

WARNING
Do not operate a boat with the control lever left in the TILT (open) position.

Control Cable Replacement

If the control cable (A, **Figure 5**) is damaged, excessively worn or corroded, replace it as follows:

1. Tilt the outboard motor to the full UP position and engage the tilt lock. Support the gearcase with a hoist or block the gearcase to eliminate any possibility of it falling during this procedure.

2. Pull the cable from its anchor bracket (B, **Figure 6**), then carefully pry the cable's ball socket from the ball on the control lever arm (A).

WARNING
*If the valve body (5, **Figure 7**) unscrews as the cable nut (1) is loosened, discontinue nut*

10

removal. Carefully screw the nut (and valve body) back into the unit. If cable replacement is necessary, remove and replace the control cable and the cylinder as an assembly.

3. Unthread the cable nut (1, **Figure 7**) using a suitable open-end wrench.

4. Lift the cable upward to expose the core wire, then slide the ball at the end of the core wire (3, **Figure 7**) from the relief in the valve stem (4).

5. Remove the cable from the clamp on the starboard stern bracket. Note the routing of the cable (**Figure 5**), then remove the cable from the outboard motor.

NOTE
Do not discard the cable nut. The nut must be used with the new cable.

6. If installing a new cable, remove the cable nut for use with the new control cable. If reusing the original cable, remove the O-ring from the groove in the cable sleeve (2, **Figure 7**). Discard the O-ring.

7. To install the cable, begin by applying OMC Triple Guard Grease to the ball (3, **Figure 7**) at the end of the cable core wire, then fill the relief in the valve stem (4) with the same grease.

8A. If the cable is being reused, install a new O-ring (coated with OMC Triple Guard Grease) into the groove in the cable sleeve (2, **Figure 7**).

8B. If installing a new cable, coat the O-ring already installed in the groove with the same grease, then install the nut from the old cable onto the new cable.

9. Apply a light coat of Permatex No. 2 sealant to the exposed valve threads (5, **Figure 7**).

10. Hook the core wire's ball into the relief in the valve stem. Then seat the cable sleeve over the valve. Thread the nut onto the valve's threads and tighten it to 36-48 in.-lbs (4.1-5.4 N•m).

11. Route the cable as noted on removal. Secure the cable to the clamp on the starboard stern bracket.

12. Thread the ball socket onto the cable's core wire. With the control lever in the RUN position, adjust the ball socket (A, **Figure 6**) so that when the ball socket is held over the control lever's ball, the cable can just be aligned with its anchor bracket (B, **Figure 6**) as the slack is gently pulled from the cable.

13. Snap the ball socket onto the control lever and the cable casing into the anchor bracket.

14. Cycle the lever between the TILT and RUN positions a minimum of ten times, then adjust the cable as described in the next section.

Control Cable Adjustment

Correct adjustment of the ball socket (A, **Figure 6**) is necessary to ensure the trim valve can be fully opened and closed. The valve must open before the motor can be trimmed/tilted. In addition, the valve must fully close to hold a given trim position and to engage the reverse lock and impact protection circuits.

The valve must close the internal hydraulic circuits before the control lever reaches the end of its travel. The remaining travel is called *reserve motion*. The control lever must have approximately 1/8 in. (3.2 mm) reserve motion as shown in **Figure 8**. To adjust the control cable, refer to **Figure 8** and proceed as follows:

1. Move the control lever to the TILT position and tilt the motor to the fully UP position. Then move the control lever to the midpoint of its total travel (as shown as A, **Figure 8**).

2. While pushing the motor back down to its normal running position, slowly move the control lever toward the RUN position. Stop moving the control lever as soon as the motors ceases downward movement. Leave the control lever in this position.

3. Push down firmly on the gearcase to make sure the valve is closed and will not allow any downward movement. If the motor still moves downward, repeat step one and step two.

4. Hold a scale or tape measure behind the control lever. Anchor the scale to the stern bracket so that it cannot shift. Note the position of the control lever, then move the control lever to the end of its travel in the RUN position. Measure (and record) the additional lever movement.

5. The control lever must move approximately an additional 1/8 in. (3.2 mm). If insufficient or excessive reserve movement is noted, pry the ball socket from the control lever arm (A, **Figure 6**) and adjust as follows:

   a. To increase the reserve movement, turn the ball socket counterclockwise (lengthen the cable). Reat-

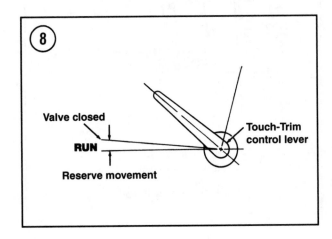

tach the ball socket and repeat this procedure until reserve movement is within specification.

b. To reduce the reserve movement, turn the ball socket clockwise (shorten the cable). Reattach the ball socket and repeat this procedure until reserve movement is within specification.

NOTE
If the reserve movement is excessive and cannot be adjusted because the ball socket bottoms on the cable threads, the cable is worn, stretched or damaged. If so, the cable must be replaced.

Cylinder and Manifold Assembly Removal

The position of the lower mounting through-bolt determines the maximum negative trim angle of the unit. Installing the bolt in the holes closest to the transom allows the maximum amount of negative trim angle, while installing the bolt in the holes furthest from the transom allows the minimum amount of negative trim. The unit comes from the factory with the bolt in the middle set of holes, which provides the proper amount of negative trim angle for an average application.

1. Tilt the outboard motor to the full UP position and engage the tilt lock. Support the gearcase with a hoist or block the gearcase to eliminate any possibility of it falling during this procedure.

2. Remove the locking clip from the upper pivot pin. See **Figure 4**, typical. Thread adaptor (part No. 340924) into the threaded end of tilt pin. Attach a suitable slide hammer, such as part No. 391008 into the thread adaptor and pull the pin from the swivel bracket.

3. Note the position of the lower mounting through-bolt in the stern bracket holes. Then remove the 3/4 in. locknut (B, **Figure 5**) from one end of the through-bolt. Push the bolt from the stern brackets and cylinder and manifold assembly. Do not damage the threaded ends of the through-bolt.

4. Remove the cylinder and manifold assembly from the stern brackets. Remove the two bushings from the cylinder rod eye and the two bushings from the bottom of the cylinder and manifold assembly.

Cylinder and Manifold Assembly Installation

Use OMC Triple Guard Grease for all grease applications.

1. Grease the four bushings. Install the two shorter bushings into the cylinder rod eye and the two longer bushings into the bottom of the cylinder and manifold assembly.

2. Grease the lower mounting bolt. Position the cylinder and manifold assembly into the mounting bracket and align the bolt holes (as noted on removal). Then install the lower mounting through-bolt.

3. Coat the threads of lower mounting bolt with OMC Gasket Sealing Compound. Install the lock nut and tighten it to 20-25 ft.-lb. (27.1-33.9 N•m). See B, **Figure 5**.

4. Grease the upper pivot pin. Align the cylinder rod eye with the swivel bracket bore, then install the pin. Secure the pin by installing the locking clip (**Figure 4**, typical).

5. Reinstall the control cable as described in this chapter.

6. Release the tilt lock, remove the hoist or remove the blocks and lower the outboard.

POWER TRIM AND TILT SYSTEMS

A power trim and tilt system is available as standard equipment on selected 25 and 35 hp (three-cylinder) and 40-70 hp models. Manual tilt (or Touch-Trim) models in these horsepower ranges can be converted to power trim and tilt with the appropriate conversion kit from OMC Genuine Parts. See your Evinrude/Johnson dealership.

Power trim and/or tilt is not available for 2.0-15 hp models.

System Description (General)

Power trim and tilt systems incorporate several special hydraulic circuits:

1. *Impact*—This circuit is designed to absorb and dissipate the energy of an impact with an underwater object, while in forward motion. It does not protect the unit from impact damage when backing up. The circuit allows the hydraulic system to act as a shock absorber. High-pressure springs and check balls in the tilt cylinder piston vent hydraulic fluid to the opposite side of the piston if the pressure caused by the impact reaches a predetermined value. When fluid is vented, the engine is allowed to tilt up as necessary, dissipating the energy of the impact.

2. *Reverse lock*—Reverse lock is a function of multiple circuits in the system. Its function is to hold the gearcase in the water during reverse thrust. Reverse thrust occurs during deceleration and when operating in reverse gear. If the gearcase is not held in the water during deceleration and reverse gear operation, the operator will not have control of the boat.

3. *Manual release*—The manual release valve allows the operator manually to raise or lower the engine should the electric motor or hydraulic system not function. The valve can be opened and the engine positioned as desired. After positioning the engine, the manual release valve must be closed for the engine to hold position and for the impact

and reverse lock circuits to function. Manual release valves must never be totally unscrewed (except during disassembly). Refer to *Manual Release Valve Operation* (in this chapter) for additional information.

WARNING
Do not operate a boat with the manual release valve opened.

4. *Hydraulic trim limit (three-ram models)*—All three-ram trim and tilt systems use hydraulic valving to limit the maximum amount of positive trim the unit can achieve while under way. The trim range is limited to approximately 15° (conventional systems) or 21° (FasTrak systems). The engine can be tilted higher than this when operating below planing speeds (shallow water drive) or when trailering the boat. If the unit is tilted above 15 (or 21) degree positive trim and the operator attempts to accelerate the boat, propeller thrust will overcome the tilt (or trim) relief valve and the unit will trim down to the maximum trim out (approximately 15 or 21°) position. If the operator tries to exceed the maximum trim out (up) limit while under way, the electric motor and pump will run, but the unit can trim no higher as the internal valving will bypass the pump's output to prevent additional trim.

5. *Thermal expansion*—The thermal expansion circuit protects the system from the destructive effects of the hydraulic fluid expansion. By nature, hydraulic fluid is incompressible, yet it will expand and contract as temperature fluctuates. If the system is subjected to a temperature increase, the fluid will expand. Since the system is sealed, there is no room for the fluid to expand. If unchecked, the internal hydraulic pressure will soar and hydraulically lock the system. Pressure may also increase enough to burst the cylinder and/or manifold, if unchecked. The thermal expansion valve is designed to open at a predetermined pressure, vent fluid to the reservoir and protect the system hydraulic from lock-up and damage.

System Identification

Three different power trim and tilt systems are used on outboard motors covered in this manual and are described in the following sections.

25 and 35 hp (three-cylinder), 40 and 50 hp (two-cylinder) models

These models use an OMC single-ram integral power trim and tilt system. See **Figure 9**. This system is referred to as the *single ram system* in this manual.

Total system travel is 65°. There is no separation between the trim and tilt ranges in this system. However, the

first 15° of movement is considered the trim range because the swivel bracket is still supported by the stern brackets. The remaining 50° of movement is considered the tilt range.

A two-wire electric motor, controlled by relays, powers the system. A trim gauge sending unit is standard on the 40-50 hp (remote control) models.

50-70 hp (three-cylinder) tiller handle models

These models use the *conventional* three-ram integral power trim and tilt system. See **Figure 10**. This system is referred to as the *conventional system* in this manual.

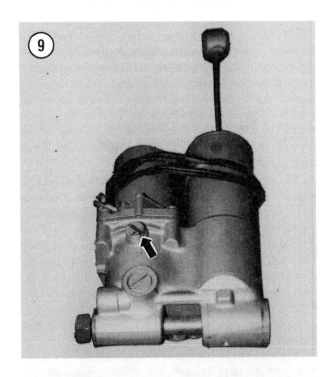

The system offers a 15° trim range, followed by a 50° tilt range for a total travel of 65°. A two-wire electric motor, controlled by relays, powers the system.

A trim gauge sending unit is standard equipment. The sending unit is mounted on the inner surface of the port stern bracket. The sending unit can only be accessed when the outboard is fully tilted UP.

A tilt lock is provided to relieve the pressure on the hydraulic system when trailering or during storage. The tilt lock is attached to the swivel bracket. To engage the tilt lock, tilt the outboard to the fully UP position, move the tilt lock arms into position over the stern brackets, then trim the outboard down until the trim rams are fully retracted and the motor is pulled firmly against the lock.

50-70 hp (three-cylinder) remote control models

These models use the *FasTrak* three-ram integral power trim and tilt system. See **Figure 11**. This system is referred to as the *FasTrak System* in this manual.

The system offers a 21° trim range, followed by a 54° tilt range for a total possible travel of 75°. A two-wire electric motor, controlled by relays, powers the system.

A trim gauge sending unit is standard equipment. The sending unit is mounted on the inner surface of the port stern bracket. The sending unit can only be accessed when the outboard is fully tilted UP.

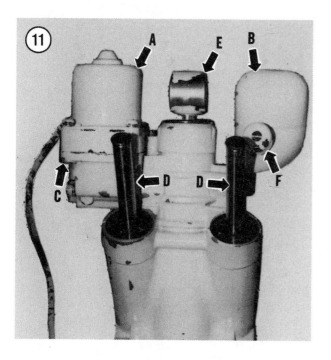

An adjustable tilt limit switch, mounted on the tilt tube, will shut off the trim and tilt system to prevent the outboard motor from tilting too far into the splash well.

A trailer lock is provided to relieve the pressure on the hydraulic system when trailering the boat and motor. The trailer lock is attached to the lower portion of the swivel bracket. To engage the trailer lock, tilt the unit to the fully UP position, then rotate the lock forward and down into the stern brackets. Trim the outboard down until the motor is pulled firmly against the lock. The trim rams will remain extended.

A tilt lock is provided to support the unit and relieve the hydraulic pressure when servicing or storing the boat and motor. It is not intended to be used for trailering. The tilt lock lever is attached to the top of the swivel bracket, near the tilt tube bore. The tilt lock can support the engine at a tilt angle of 50° or 73°. To engage the tilt lock, tilt the unit past the 50° or 73° tilt angle (as desired), then rotate the tilt lock lever to position the support cam (on the starboard side of the motor) over the stern bracket. Then bump the trim switch until the motor is resting on the tilt lock lever. Do not pull the motor down tightly against the lock.

Electric Motor Operation

All trim and tilt systems use permanent-magnet, two-wire electric motors. Strong permanent magnets glued to the main housing take the place of the field windings and electricity only flows through the rotating armature. Permanent magnet motors must never be struck with a hammer as this will crack the magnets and destroy the motor.

The two motor leads are blue and green and there is no dedicated ground (black) lead. Two relays (one for each motor lead) switch the polarity of the green and blue leads to change the motor direction.

When the blue lead is connected to positive and the green lead is grounded, the motor runs in the UP direction. When viewed from the drive end, the armature shaft must turn clockwise, which will turn the hydraulic pump counterclockwise (as viewed from the top of the pump).

When the green lead is connected to positive and the blue lead is grounded, the motor runs in the *DOWN* direction. When viewed from the drive end, the armature shaft must turn counterclockwise, which will turn the hydraulic pump clockwise (as viewed from the top of the pump).

If the boat is wired using a standard OMC harness, the trim and tilt system switching circuits are wired independently of the ignition switch. The unit will trim (and tilt) in and out, regardless of ignition switch position. However, the ignition switch must be in the ON or RUN position for the trim indicator gauge to operate. The trim

10

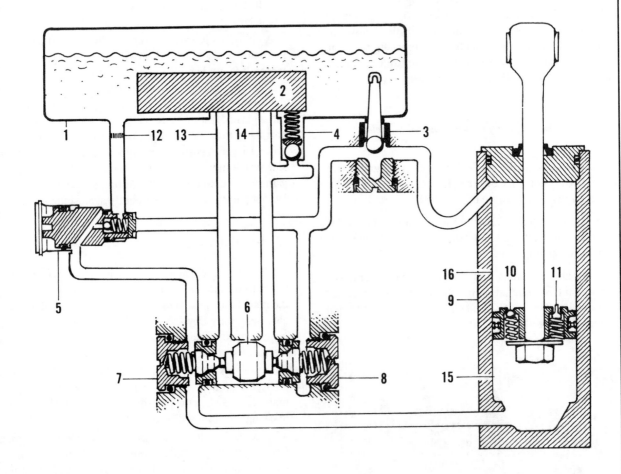

SINGLE RAM SYSTEM FLOW DIAGRAM

1. Reservoir
2. Pump assembly
3. Filter valve assembly
4. IN relief valve
5. Manual release (and thermal expansion) valve
6. Pump control piston
7. UP check valve assembly
8. DOWN check valve assembly
9. Cylinder
10. Impact relief valve
11. UP relief valve
12. Filter screen
13. Pump UP discharge
14. Pump DOWN discharge
15. High-volume chamber
16. Low-volume chamber

system receives power to operate the switching circuits through the 20 amp main fuse mounted on the power head. The fuse receives power directly from the starter solenoid's positive battery cable terminal.

Hydraulic Operation (Single Ram System)

Refer to **Figure 12** for the following operational description.

1. *UP mode*—When the motor is activated in the UP direction, the motor rotates the pump in a counterclockwise direction. The pump directs fluid under pressure (13, **Figure 12**) to the pump control piston (6), pushing it over and opening the DOWN check valve (8) to provide a path for fluid returning from the low-volume (top) side of the cylinder. The pump's pressure opens the UP check valve (7), allowing pressurized fluid to flow to the high-volume side (15) of the cylinder, forcing the piston upward. As the piston moves upward, the return fluid is directed back to the pump through the DOWN check valve (8) and passage (14). Additional fluid, required to make up the difference between the low-volume return and the high-volume requirements, is drawn directly into the pump from the reservoir. When the piston reaches the top of its bore, the UP relief valve (11) is mechanically opened, venting all hydraulic pressure through the piston (and back to the pump).

2. *DOWN mode*—When the motor is activated in the DOWN direction, the motor rotates the pump in a clockwise direction. The pump directs fluid under pressure (14, **Figure 12**) to the pump control piston (6), pushing it over and opening the UP check valve (7) to provide a path for fluid returning from the high-volume side (15) of the cylinder. The pump's pressure opens the DOWN check valve (8), allowing pressurized fluid to flow to the low-volume side (16) of the cylinder, forcing the piston downward. As the piston moves downward, the return fluid is directed back to the pump through the UP check valve (7) and passage (13). Since more fluid is returning (because the high-volume side is being emptied and the low-volume side is being filled), the excess fluid is vented to the reservoir through the DOWN relief valve (4). The DOWN relief valve opens at approximately 1600 psi (11032 kPa). When the piston reaches the bottom of its bore, all pressurized fluid is vented to the reservoir through the DOWN relief valve.

3. *Static mode*—When the electric motor is not running, the UP and DOWN check valves are closed (by internal springs) and all fluid flow is blocked.

4. *Manual release mode*—When the manual release valve (5, **Figure 12**) is opened, the reservoir and both sides of the cylinder (high and low volume) are opened to each other. This allows unrestricted fluid flow in either direction (UP or DOWN).

5. *Thermal expansion*—The manual release valve (5, **Figure 12**) incorporates the thermal expansion valve in its tip. If the trim and tilt unit is left in the fully tilted UP position and the system is exposed to an increase in temperature, the fluid in the high-volume side (15) of the cylinder will expand, causing a drastic pressure increase. When the pressure at the manual release valve's tip reaches approximately 8000 psi (55160 kPa), the thermal expansion valve will open and vent the excessive pressure (and fluid) into the reservoir (through the filter screen [12]), preventing hydraulic lock-up and system damage.

NOTE
*The UP relief valve (11, **Figure 12**) also functions as an impact relief valve.*

6. *Impact mode*—Impact mode activates whenever the motor is running in FORWARD gear and strikes an underwater object. The internal pressures instantaneously change from pressure in the high-volume side (15, **Figure 12**) of the cylinder, to pressure in the low-volume (16) side of the cylinder. The five impact valves (10) and the UP relief valve (11) are located in the cylinder's piston and are calibrated to open at a specific pressure, allowing fluid to vent across the piston, dissipating the energy of the impact over as long a time period as possible. Because the impact valves close as soon as the pressure dissipates (after impact), the engine will remain at or near the original trim angle.

Hydraulic Operation (Conventional System)

Refer to **Figure 13** for the following explanations.

1. *UP mode*—When the motor is activated in the UP direction, the motor rotates the pump in a counterclockwise direction. The pump directs fluid under pressure (19, **Figure 13**) to the pump control piston, pushing it over and opening the reverse lock check valve (10) to provide a path for fluid returning from the low-volume side (17) of the cylinder and trim rams. The pump's pressure opens the trim check valve (11), allowing pressurized fluid to flow to the high-volume side (16) of the trim rams, forcing them upward. The pump also directs fluid under pressure to the tilt check valve (6), opening it and allowing pressurized fluid to flow to the high-volume side (16) of the tilt cylinder, forcing it upward. The tilt cylinder and trim rams work together to lift the outboard motor for the first 15° of upward movement.

As the piston (and trim rams) moves upward, the return fluid from the low-volume chamber is directed back to the pump through the reverse lock check valve (10). Addi-

10

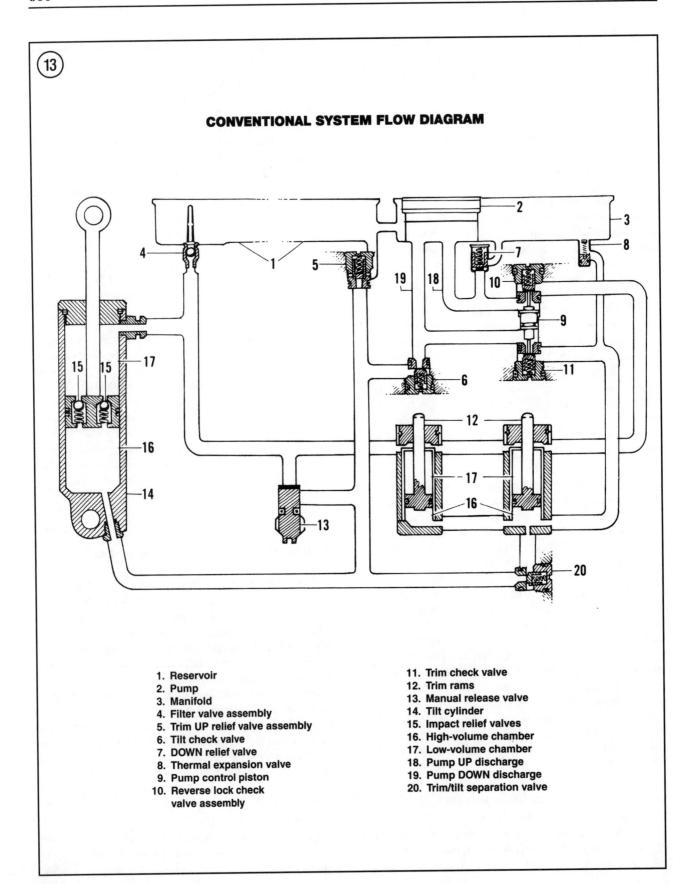

CONVENTIONAL SYSTEM FLOW DIAGRAM

1. Reservoir
2. Pump
3. Manifold
4. Filter valve assembly
5. Trim UP relief valve assembly
6. Tilt check valve
7. DOWN relief valve
8. Thermal expansion valve
9. Pump control piston
10. Reverse lock check valve assembly

11. Trim check valve
12. Trim rams
13. Manual release valve
14. Tilt cylinder
15. Impact relief valves
16. High-volume chamber
17. Low-volume chamber
18. Pump UP discharge
19. Pump DOWN discharge
20. Trim/tilt separation valve

tional fluid, required to make up the difference between the low-volume return and the high-volume requirements, is drawn directly into the pump from the reservoir.

When the trim rams reach the top of the bores, all fluid and pressure is directed against the high-volume side of the tilt cylinder. The tilt cylinder alone continues to lift the outboard motor until its piston contacts the cylinder's end cap. At this point, there is no place for the fluid to go, and pressure will increase until the trim UP relief valve (5) opens, venting all pressurized fluid to the reservoir. The trim UP relief valve opens at approximately 1500 psi (10,343 kPa).

2. *DOWN mode*—When the motor is activated in the DOWN direction, the motor rotates the pump in a clockwise direction. The pump directs fluid under pressure (19) to the pump control piston, pushing it over and opening the trim check valve (11, **Figure 13**) to provide a path for fluid returning from the high-volume side (16) of the cylinder and rams. The pump's pressure opens the reverse lock check valve (10), allowing pressurized fluid to flow to the low-volume side (17) of the tilt cylinder and trim rams, forcing them downward. As the piston and rams move downward, the return fluid is directed back to the pump through the trim check valve (11). Since more fluid is returning (because the high-volume side is being emptied and the low-volume side is being filled), the excess fluid is vented to the reservoir through the DOWN relief valve (7). The DOWN relief valve opens at approximately 800 psi (5516 kPa). When the piston and rams all reach the bottom of their bores, all pressurized fluid is vented to the reservoir through the DOWN relief valve.

3. *Static mode*—When the electric motor is not running, the UP and DOWN check valves are closed (by internal springs) and all fluid flow is blocked. If the outboard is in the tilt range, it may only be operated at idle speed. If higher power settings are attempted, the increased propeller thrust will cause the pressure in the tilt cylinder to rise to the point where the trim UP relief valve (5, **Figure 13**) will open (approximately 1500 psi [10343 kPa]), allowing the outboard to trim IN until it contacts the trim rams (15° trim angle). When this happens, the tilt cylinder's low-volume chamber is filled with fluid drawn from the reservoir through the filter valve (4).

4. *Manual release mode*—When the manual release valve (13, **Figure 13**) is opened, the reservoir and both sides of the tile cylinder are opened to each other. This allows unrestricted fluid flow in either direction with the tilt cylinder. However, only the low-volume side of the trim rams is opened, allowing them to extend, but not to extend. Electric motor operation is required to lower the system to the maximum trim IN position.

Once the manual release valve is open, the motor can be raised to any position desired, but if the trim rams are not extended, the motor will settle back down (after the valve is closed) until the rams are filled with fluid (and fully extended). If this happens, the valve must be reopened and the motor repositioned again.

5. *Thermal expansion*—If the trim and tilt unit is left in the fully tilted UP position and the system is exposed to an increase in temperature, the fluid in the high-volume side of the cylinder and trim rams will expand, causing a drastic pressure increase. If the pressure at the thermal expansion valve (8, **Figure 13**) reaches its predetermined value, it will open and vent the excessive pressure (and fluid) into the reservoir, preventing hydraulic lock-up and system damage.

6. *Impact mode*—Impact mode activates whenever the motor is running in FORWARD gear and strikes an underwater object. The internal pressures instantaneously change from pressure in the high-volume side (16, **Figure 13**) of the tilt cylinder (and trim rams) to pressure in the low-volume side (16) of the tilt cylinder. The trim rams are not affected and will remain in position because the trim/tilt separation valve (20) closes, locking the rams in position and isolating them from the cylinder.

The impact valves are located in the cylinder's piston and are calibrated to open at a specific pressure, allowing fluid to vent across the piston, dissipating the energy of the impact over as long a time period as possible. Because the impact valves close as soon as the pressure dissipates (after impact), the engine will remain at or near the original trim angle.

Hydraulic Operation (FasTrak Systems)

Refer to **Figure 14** for the following explanations.

1. *UP mode*—When the motor is activated in the UP direction, the motor rotates the pump in a counterclockwise direction. The pump directs fluid under pressure (17, **Figure 14**) past the check ball in the UP pump control piston (7) to the DOWN pump control piston (9). The DOWN pump control piston pushes down, opening the DOWN check valve (10) to provide a path for fluid returning from the low-volume (16) side of the cylinder and trim rams. The pump's pressure opens the UP check valve (8), allowing pressurized fluid to flow to the high-volume side (15) of the tilt cylinder and trim rams, forcing them upward. The tilt cylinder and trim rams work together to lift the outboard motor for the first 21° of upward movement.

As the tilt cylinder's piston moves upward, the return fluid from the tilt cylinder's low-volume chamber is directed back to the pump through the DOWN check valve (10). Additional fluid, required to make up the difference between the low-volume return and the high-volume requirements, is drawn directly into the pump from the

10

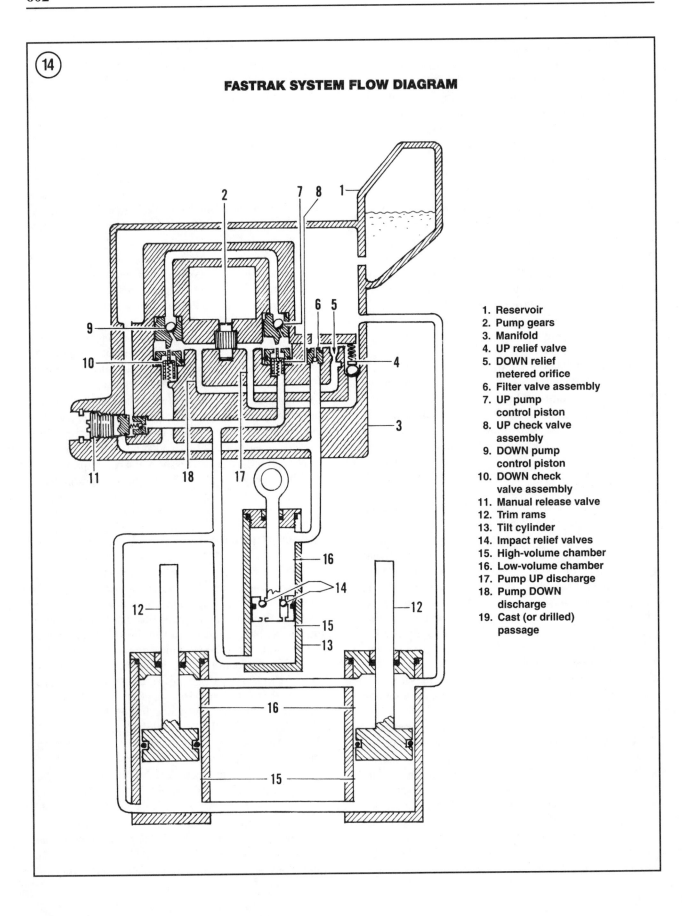

⑭

FASTRAK SYSTEM FLOW DIAGRAM

1. Reservoir
2. Pump gears
3. Manifold
4. UP relief valve
5. DOWN relief
   metered orifice
6. Filter valve assembly
7. UP pump
   control piston
8. UP check valve
   assembly
9. DOWN pump
   control piston
10. DOWN check
    valve assembly
11. Manual release valve
12. Trim rams
13. Tilt cylinder
14. Impact relief valves
15. High-volume chamber
16. Low-volume chamber
17. Pump UP discharge
18. Pump DOWN
    discharge
19. Cast (or drilled)
    passage

reservoir. As the trim rams move upward, the return fluid from each ram's low-volume chamber is pumped directly to the reservoir through a cast (or drilled) passage (19). The passage is always open.

When the trim rams reach the top of the bores, all fluid and pressure is directed against the high-volume side of the tilt cylinder. The tilt cylinder alone continues to lift the outboard motor until its piston contacts the cylinder's end cap. At this point there is no place for the fluid to go, and pressure will increase until the UP relief valve (4) opens, venting all pressurized fluid to the reservoir. The UP relief valve opens at approximately 1400-1600 psi (9653-11032 kPa).

2. *DOWN mode*—When the motor is activated in the DOWN direction, the motor rotates the pump in a clockwise direction. The pump directs fluid under pressure (18, **Figure 14**) past the check ball in the DOWN pump control piston (9) to the UP pump control piston (7). The UP pump control piston pushes down, opening the UP check valve (8) to provide a path for fluid returning from the high-volume side (15) of the cylinder and rams.

The pump's pressure opens the DOWN check valve (10), allowing pressurized fluid to flow to the low-volume side (16) of the tilt cylinder, forcing it downward. As the piston moves downward, the return fluid from the cylinder (and trim rams) is directed back to the pump through the UP check valve (8). Since more fluid is returning (because all of the high-volume chambers are being emptied and only the tilt cylinder's low-volume side is being filled), the excess fluid is vented to the reservoir through the DOWN relief metered orifice (5). This orifice is open at all times.

The trim rams are not retracted by hydraulic pressure. When the tilt cylinder lowers the motor far enough to contact the trim rams, the rams are retracted by the downward force of the tilt cylinder. The trim ram's low-volume chambers are filled with fluid pulled directly from the reservoir through a cast passage (19).

3. *Static mode*—When the electric motor is not running, the UP and DOWN check valves are closed (by internal springs) and all fluid flow is blocked. If the outboard is in the tilt range, it may only be operated at idle speed. If higher power settings are attempted, the increased propeller thrust will cause the pressure in the tilt cylinder to rise to the point where the tilt UP relief valve (located in the tip of the manual release valve [11, **Figure 14**]) will open, allowing the outboard to trim IN until it contacts the trim rams (21° trim angle). When this happens, the tilt cylinder's low-volume chamber is filled with fluid drawn from the reservoir through the filter valve (6).

4. *Manual release mode*—When the manual release valve (11, **Figure 14**) is opened, the reservoir and both the high- and low-volume sides of the tilt cylinder and high-volume

side of the trim rams are opened to each other. The low-volume side of the trim rams is always open to the reservoir. With all the chambers open, unrestricted fluid flow is allowed in either direction (UP or DOWN) within the tilt cylinder and trim rams.

Once the valve is open, the motor can be raised to any position desired, but if the trim rams are not extended, the motor will settle back down (after the valve is closed) until the rams are filled with fluid and fully extended. If this happens, the valve must be reopened and the motor repositioned again. If the motor is already tilted, the motor can be lowered to any position desired.

NOTE
*The tilt UP relief valve also functions as the thermal expansion valve. The valve is located in the tip of the manual release valve (11, **Figure 14**).*

5. *Thermal expansion*—If the trim and tilt unit is left in the fully tilted UP position and the system is exposed to an increase in temperature, the fluid in the high-volume side of the cylinder and trim rams will expand, causing a drastic pressure increase. When the pressure at the tilt UP relief (thermal expansion) valve reaches its predetermined value, it will open and vent the excessive pressure (and fluid) into the reservoir, preventing hydraulic lock-up and system damage.

6. *Impact mode*—Impact mode activates whenever the motor is running in FORWARD gear and strikes an underwater object. The internal pressures instantaneously change from pressure in the high-volume side (15, **Figure 14**) of the tilt cylinder, to pressure in the low-volume side (16) of the tilt cylinder. The four impact valves are located in the cylinder's piston (14) and are calibrated to open at a specific pressure, allowing fluid to vent across the piston, dissipating the energy of the impact over as long a time period as possible. Because the impact valves close as soon as the pressure dissipates (after impact), the engine will remain at or near the original trim angle.

Maintenance

Periodically check the wiring system for corrosion and loose or damaged connections. Tighten any loose connections, replace damaged components and clean corroded terminals as necessary. Coat the terminals and connections with anti-corrosion grease or OMC Black Neoprene Dip. Check the reservoir fluid level as outlined in the following procedure.

Inspect the anode(s) for loose mounting hardware, loose or damaged ground straps (if equipped) and excessive deterioration. The anode must be replaced if it is reduced

10

to two-thirds its original size (1/3 gone). Make sure the anode is not painted or coated with any substance. If paint or any other coating covers the anode, the anode must be removed and the coating stripped or the anode replaced.

Reservoir Fluid Check

The fill plug is located just below the electric motor on single ram systems (**Figure 9**). On conventional and Fas-Trak systems, the fill plug is located on the reservoir. See **Figure 10** (conventional system) or F, **Figure 11** (FasTrak system).

1. Trim the outboard to the fully *UP* position. Thoroughly clean the area around the fill plug.

2. Cover the fill plug with a shop towel and carefully and slowly remove the fill plug, allowing any internal pressure (and possibly fluid) to vent before fully removing the plug.

3. The fluid level must be even with the bottom of the fill plug hole. If necessary, add OMC Power Trim/Tilt and Power Steering Fluid (or Dexron II automatic transmission fluid) to bring the fluid level up to the bottom of the level hole.

> *CAUTION*
> *Do not overfill the unit. The oil level rises as the unit is trimmed down and there must be room for the thermal expansion of the fluid in the reservoir.*

4. Install the fill plug and tighten it securely. Then cycle the outboard fully down and up several times to purge any air that might be in the system.

5. Recheck the fluid level as described in Steps 1 and 2. Make sure the fill plug is tightened as follows:
   a. *Single ram system*—Tighten the fill plug to 45-55 in.-lb. (5.1-6.2 N•m).
   b. *Conventional system*—Tighten the fill plug to 45-50 in.-lb. (5.1-5.7 N•m).
   c. *FasTrak system*—Tighten the fill plug securely.

Bleeding Air From Hydraulic System

All of these trim and tilt systems are considered self-bleeding. Simply cycle the unit fully up and down a total of 3-5 times to bleed all the air from the system. Make sure the fluid level in the reservoir is maintained as described previously in this section. If the fluid appears foamy, allow the unit to sit for a minimum of 30 minutes to allow the air to separate from the fluid.

Manual Release Valve Operation

All models incorporate a manual release valve. The manual release valve allows the motor to be raised or lowered if the electric motor fails for any reason.

Single ram system—Once the valve is open, the motor can be positioned anywhere (as desired) in the trim or tilt range. The valve is located at the lower port corner of the trim and tilt unit as shown in **Figure 15**.

Conventional system—The valve is accessed through a hole in the starboard stern bracket as shown in **Figure 16**. Once the valve isopen, the motor can be raised to any position desired, but if the trim rams are not extended, the motor will settle back down (after the valve is closed) until

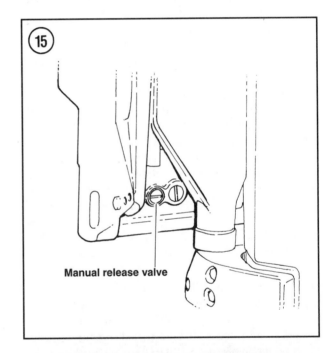
Manual release valve

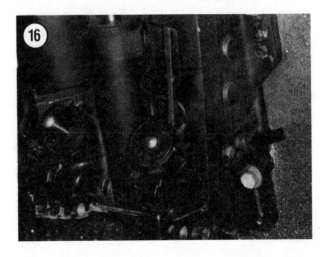

the rams are filled with fluid and fully extended. If this happens, the valve must be reopened and the motor repositioned again. If the motor is already tilted, the motor can only be lowered to the maximum *trim out* position (trim rams fully extended). Electric motor operation is required to lower the system to the maximum *trim in* position (trim rams retracted).

FasTrak system—The valve is accessed through a hole in the port stern bracket as shown in **Figure 17**. Once the valve is open, the motor can be raised to any position desired. However, if the trim rams are not extended, the motor will settle back down (after the valve is closed) until the rams have filled with fluid and fully extended. If this happens, the valve must be reopened and the motor repositioned again. If the motor is already tilted, the motor can be lowered to any position desired.

> *WARNING*
> *Do not operate the engine with the manual release valve in the open position. Reverse lock protection will be disabled. There would be nothing to prevent the engine from tilting out of the water when backing in reverse gear and when decelerating in forward gear. This will cause a loss of directional control. Retighten the manual release valve securely once the motor has been positioned as desired.*

1A. *Single ram system*—To raise or lower the motor manually, open the manual release valve a minimum of three full turns, but no further than the point where it just contacts its retaining ring.

1B. *Three-ram systems*—To raise or lower the motor manually, open the manual release valve approximately

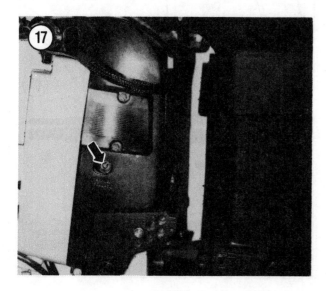

3-1/2 turns, or until it just contacts its retaining ring. Do not open the valve further than the point where it just contacts its retaining ring.

2A. *Single ram system*—Position the engine at the tilt or trim position desired.

2B. *Three-ram systems*—Position the engine as described previously in this section.

3. Retighten the manual release valve.

Maximum Trim-In Limit Adjustment

On some boats, excessive negative trim can cause instability at high operating speeds. To limit the total amount of negative (down) trim an engine can achieve, an adjustable trim limit rod (or an adjustable lower mounting through-bolt) is used.

On single ram systems, the lower mounting through-bolt can be positioned in any one of the three pairs of holes in the stern brackets. The unit comes from the factory with the bolt in the innermost holes, which provides the maximum amount of negative trim angle. Moving the bolt to the middle, or outer holes limits the negative trim angle accordingly.

On conventional systems, the trim limit rod can be positioned in any one of the five pairs of holes in the stern brackets. The unit comes from the factory with the rod in the innermost set of holes, which provides the maximum amount of negative trim angle. Moving the bolt to any of the other sets of holes limits the negative trim angle accordingly

On FasTrak systems, the trim limit rod can be positioned in any one of the six pairs of numbered holes in the stern brackets. The holes are staggered in two rows (three holes each) and are numbered according to their trim limiting potential. Installing the rod in the No. 1 holes provides the maximum amount of negative trim angle, while installing the rod in the No. 6 holes provides the least amount of negative trim angle. The unit comes from the factory with the rod in the No. 1 holes.

Trim Gauge Sending Unit Adjustment

40 and 50 hp (two-cylinder) models

The trim gauge sending unit must be adjusted so the gauge needle is aligned with the DOWN mark when the outboard is fully trimmed IN. The trim and tilt system's lower mounting bolt must be installed in its correct position before the sending unit can be adjusted.

1. Trim the outboard motor to the full down position. Turn the ignition (key) switch to the ON or RUN position and

10

note the position of the gauge. The gauge needle must be aligned with the DOWN mark on the face of the gauge.

2. If adjustment is needed, tilt the outboard motor to the full UP position. Engage the tilt lock, support the gearcase with a hoist or block the gearcase to eliminate any possibility of it falling during this procedure.

3. Loosen the screw securing the eccentric cam (**Figure 18**) to the port stern bracket.

   a. *Needle too low*—Rotate the eccentric cam to position a thicker portion against the sending unit's arm. Retighten the screw securely.

   b. *Needle too high*—Rotate the eccentric cam to position a thinner portion against the sending unit's arm. Retighten the screw.

4. Release the tilt lock, remove hoist or blocks and trim the outboard motor to the full down position. Note the position of the gauge. The gauge needle must be aligned with the DOWN mark on the face of the gauge. If not, repeat Steps 2-4 as necessary, until correct alignment is obtained.

5. Turn off the ignition switch when finished.

50 and 70 hp (three-cylinder) models

The trim gauge sending unit must be adjusted so the gauge needle is aligned with the DOWN mark when the outboard is fully trimmed IN. The trim limit rod must be installed in its correct position before the sending unit can be adjusted. The trim gauge sending unit is attached to the port stern bracket as shown in **Figure 19**, typical.

1. Trim the outboard motor to the full down position. Turn the ignition (key) switch to the ON or RUN position and note the position of the gauge. The gauge needle must be aligned with the DOWN mark on the face of the gauge.

2. If adjustment is needed, tilt the outboard motor to the full UP position. Engage the tilt lock, support the gearcase with a hoist or block the gearcase to eliminate any possibility of it falling during this procedure.

3. Loosen the two screws securing the trim sending unit (**Figure 19**) just enough to allow the sending unit to be rotated with moderate effort.

> *NOTE*
> *If the sending unit cannot be accessed between the swivel bracket and port stern bracket, tilt the motor up and rotate the sending unit as necessary. Then, lower the motor and check the adjustment. Repeat this sequence until the adjustment is correct.*

4. Release the tilt lock, remove the hoist or blocks and trim the outboard motor to the full DOWN position. Turn the ignition (key) switch to the ON or RUN position and note the position of the gauge.

   a. Reach into the gap between the swivel bracket and port stern bracket (with a suitable screwdriver) and rotate the sending unit as necessary to align the gauge needle with the DOWN mark.

   b. When the sending unit is correctly adjusted, tilt the outboard motor to the full UP position and engage the tilt lock. Support the gearcase with a hoist or block the gearcase to eliminate any possibility of it falling.

   c. Tighten the two sending unit screws securely. Then release the tilt lock or remove the hoist (or blocks) and trim the motor to the full DOWN position.

   d. Note the position of the gauge. The gauge needle must be aligned with the DOWN mark on the face of the gauge. If not, readjust as necessary, until correct alignment is obtained.

5. Turn off the ignition switch when finished.

Tilt Limit Switch Adjustment (FasTrak System)

If the lower cowl, upper cowl or steering arm contacts the splash well or any other part of the boat's hull when fully tilted, adjust the tilt limit switch to limit the upward tilt range and prevent motor-to-hull contact. The switch is located behind the tilt (steering) tube, directly between the

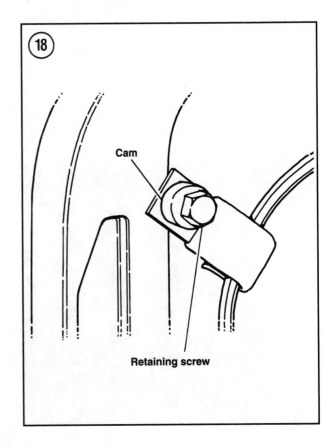

stern brackets. Rotate the cam mechanism around the tilt tube to adjust the switch setting. Refer to **Figure 20** for this procedure.

> *CAUTION*
> *If the tilt limit switch is being used to prevent contact between the motor and hull, remember that the motor can tilt past the tilt limit switch setting during a severe impact or when the motor is being tilted manually (via the manual release valve).*

1. Trim the outboard motor to the full down position.

2A. *To increase the tilt limit*—Push the cam's lower tab upward to rotate the cam slightly (as desired).

2B. *To decrease the tilt limit*—Push the cam's upper tab downward to rotate the cam slightly (as desired).

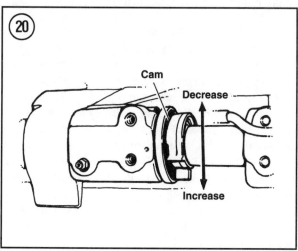

3. Tilt the outboard to the full UP position, while observing the clearance between the motor and the hull. Be prepared to stop tilting the motor if necessary. If the motor stops at the tilt angle desired, adjustment is complete. If not, repeat Steps 1-3.

POWER TRIM AND TILT HYDRAULIC TROUBLESHOOTING

If a problem develops in the trim and tilt system, the initial step is to determine whether the problem is located in the electrical system or in the hydraulic system. If the electric motor runs normally, the problem is hydraulic in nature. If the electric motor does not run or runs slowly, go to *Electric system testing* in this chapter. It is possible (but not likely) for an internal hydraulic problem to cause the pump to turn slowly or lock up completely.

If the electric motor seems to run abnormally fast in both directions, remove the electric motor and check for a sheared pump drive shaft (or coupler).

If the unit will only tilt or trim partially, or the system's movement is erratic, check the reservoir fluid level as described in this chapter.

Any external leakage, no matter how small, must be immediately corrected. The troubleshooting procedures in this section do not list any external seals and/or O-rings as probable causes of system malfunction. Correct any external leakage before proceeding with troubleshooting possible internal leakage.

> *NOTE*
> *The seating area of the manual release valve must be in perfect condition or leak-down or other operational problems may occur. Carefully check the valve seat using a magnifying glass. Replace the valve body/manifold if any defects are noted.*

If the unit will not trim out (up) under load, but otherwise functions normally, the problem is most likely in the pump assembly. On some units, the pump can be replaced without having to replace the valve body or manifold assembly. Consult a parts catalog or the appropriate illustrations in this chapter to determine your best course of action.

The recommended fluid for all systems is OMC Power Trim/Tilt and Power Steering Fluid (or Dexron II automatic transmission fluid). Lubricate all seals and O-rings with the recommended fluid during assembly.

> *NOTE*
> *Always replace all O-rings, seals and gaskets that are removed. O-ring and seal kits are available for all models. Clean the out-*

10

side of the component before disassembly. Always use a lint-free cloth when handling trim and tilt components. Dirt or lint can cause blocked passages, sticking valves and prevent O-rings from sealing.

CAUTION
Use caution when only partially disassembling the unit to replace a specific component. If the fluid is contaminated with metal shavings, water or other debris, the system must be completely disassembled, cleaned, inspected and all O-rings, seals and gaskets replaced. If not, the contamination will soon cause the newly installed component to fail.

Relieving System Pressure

WARNING
Eye protection must be worn during any procedure involving disassembly of the power trim and tilt system.

Relieve the system hydraulic pressure before beginning any form of disassembly.

NOTE
When opening the reservoir plug to check or add fluid, all units must be in the fully UP position (all rams extended). However, on conventional systems, unique hydraulic circuitry requires the unit be in the fully DOWN position (all rams retracted) during disassembly.

FasTrak and single ram systems

To relieve the internal pressure on the single ram and FasTrak systems proceed as follows:
1. Tilt the outboard motor to the fully UP position. Engage the tilt lock, support the gearcase with a hoist or block the gearcase to eliminate any possibility of it falling during this procedure.
2. Open the manual release valve until it just contacts its retaining ring. Allow the outboard motor to settle onto the tilt lock, hoist or blocks.
3. Cover the reservoir fill plug with a shop towel and carefully and slowly remove the fill plug, allowing any internal pressure (and fluid) to vent before fully removing the plug.
4. Reinstall the fill plug and close the manual release valve to prevent fluid loss and contamination.
5. Use caution during system disassembly, as there still may be residual pressure in the system. During disassembly, cover each component with a shop towel and slowly

loosen the component and/or its fasteners, allowing any internal pressure (and fluid) to vent before fully removing the component.

Conventional systems

To relieve the internal pressure on the conventional system proceed as follows:
1. Tilt the outboard motor to the fully UP position. Engage the tilt lock, support the gearcase with a hoist or block the gearcase to eliminate any possibility of it falling during this procedure.
2. Remove the locking clip securing the upper pivot pin to the swivel bracket, then remove the upper pivot pin to free the tilt cylinder from the swivel bracket.
3. Operate the trim and tilt system in the DOWN direction until the tilt cylinder and both trim rams are fully retracted.
4. Briefly *bump* the trim switch up, then down, then up again. The motor must run *briefly* in each direction, as specified. This will help relieve internal pressure.
5. Open the manual release valve until it just contacts its retaining ring.
6. If the unit must be disassembled, cover the reservoir fill plug with a shop towel and carefully and slowly remove the fill plug, allowing any internal pressure (and fluid) to vent before fully removing the plug.
7. Reinstall the fill plug and close the manual release valve to prevent fluid loss and contamination.
8. Use caution during system disassembly, as there still may be residual pressure in the system. During disassembly, cover each component with a shop towel and slowly loosen the component and/or its fasteners, allowing any internal pressure (and fluid) to vent before fully removing the component.

Single Ram System Troubleshooting

Remove and install these units as an assembly. There is no specific troubleshooting procedure to isolate the cylinder components from the pump and manifold components.

The cylinder and manifold are manufactured (cast) as a single unit and are not available separately. The electric motor and the hydraulic pump assembly are not serviceable and each is replaced as a separate assembly. All other components are available individually.

Refer to **Table 2** for normal system cycle times, **Table 4** for torque specifications and **Table 5** for troubleshooting procedures. The troubleshooting table lists common problems, their most likely cause and the course of action to remedy the problem. Refer to **Figure 21** for an exploded view of this system.

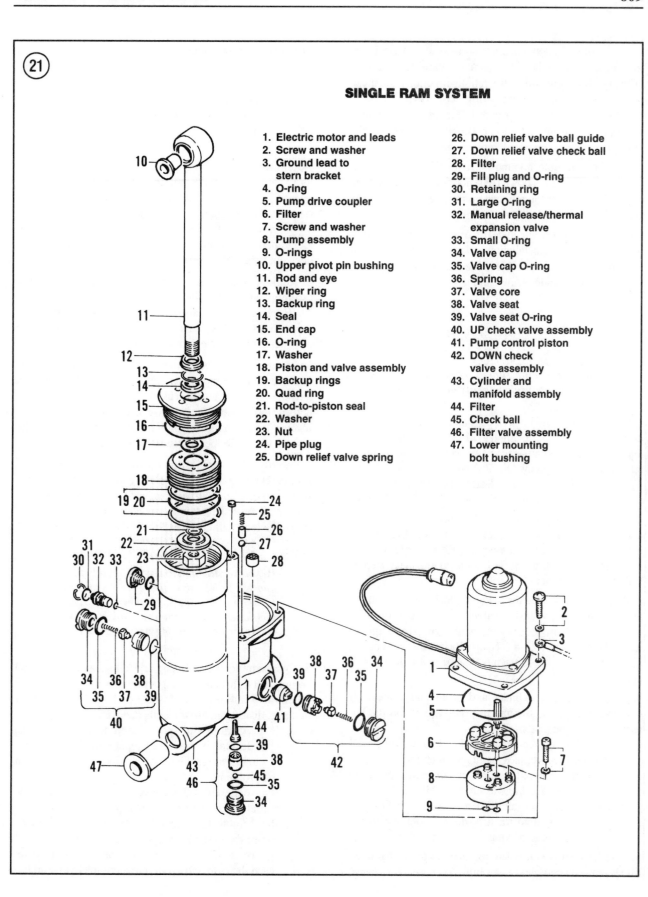

SINGLE RAM SYSTEM

1. Electric motor and leads
2. Screw and washer
3. Ground lead to stern bracket
4. O-ring
5. Pump drive coupler
6. Filter
7. Screw and washer
8. Pump assembly
9. O-rings
10. Upper pivot pin bushing
11. Rod and eye
12. Wiper ring
13. Backup ring
14. Seal
15. End cap
16. O-ring
17. Washer
18. Piston and valve assembly
19. Backup rings
20. Quad ring
21. Rod-to-piston seal
22. Washer
23. Nut
24. Pipe plug
25. Down relief valve spring
26. Down relief valve ball guide
27. Down relief valve check ball
28. Filter
29. Fill plug and O-ring
30. Retaining ring
31. Large O-ring
32. Manual release/thermal expansion valve
33. Small O-ring
34. Valve cap
35. Valve cap O-ring
36. Spring
37. Valve core
38. Valve seat
39. Valve seat O-ring
40. UP check valve assembly
41. Pump control piston
42. DOWN check valve assembly
43. Cylinder and manifold assembly
44. Filter
45. Check ball
46. Filter valve assembly
47. Lower mounting bolt bushing

If the unit leaks down *and* has no reverse lock (leaks in both directions), replace the manual release valve and its 2 O-rings. If the unit still leaks in both directions, the most likely cause is a failed piston O-ring, scored cylinder walls or failed piston valves (impact or UP relief). Disassemble the cylinder and inspect these components. If no visible damage or defects are noted, replace the piston assembly.

Additional troubleshooting is divided into two failure modes: The unit leaks down (will not hold a trim position in forward gear) or the unit has no reverse lock (kicks up in reverse or trails out on deceleration).

Refer to *Power Trim and Tilt System Service* in this chapter for removal/installation and disassembly/reassembly procedures. Refill and bleed the system after reassembly as described under *Maintenance*.

Unit leaks down

CAUTION
*Relieve system pressure as described in this chapter before beginning **any** disassembly.*

1. Remove, clean and inspect the manual release valve and its O-rings. See 30-33, **Figure 21**. Replace the manual release valve if it is damaged in any way. Install the manual release valve (using new O-rings) and tighten the valve to 45-55 in.-lb. (5.1-6.2 N•m). Retest the system for leak-down. Continue to the next step if leak-down is still noted.

2. Remove, clean and inspect the UP check valve assembly and pump control piston. See 41 and 42, **Figure 21**. Replace any damaged components. Reassemble the unit and retest for leak-down. Continue to the next step if leak-down is still noted.

3. Remove and replace the manual release valve to eliminate the thermal expansion valve as a problem. Install a new manual release valve (using new O-rings) and tighten it to 45-55 in.-lb. (5.1-6.2 N•m). Retest the system for leak-down. Continue to the next step if leak-down is still noted.

4. Disassemble the cylinder and clean and inspect all components. Inspect the impact relief valves and the UP relief valve in the piston.
   a. If the O-rings are undamaged and the cylinder wall is not scored, replace the piston assembly.
   b. If the cylinder wall is scored or damaged, replace the cylinder and manifold as an assembly.
   c. Reassemble the unit with new seals and O-rings. Retest the system for leak-down. Continue to the next step if leak-down is still noted.

5. If leak-down is still noted, replace the power trim and tilt system as a complete assembly.

Unit has no reverse lock

CAUTION
*Relieve system pressure as described previously in this chapter before beginning **any** disassembly.*

1. Remove, clean and inspect the manual release valve and its O-rings. See 30-33, **Figure 21**. Replace the manual release valve if it is damaged in any way. Install the manual release valve (using new O-rings) and tighten the valve to 45-55 in.-lb. (5.1-6.2 N•m). Retest the system for reverse lock function. Continue to the next step if reverse lock still does not function correctly.

2. Remove, clean and inspect the DOWN check valve assembly and pump control piston. See 41 and 42, **Figure 21**. Replace any damaged components. Reassemble the unit and retest the reverse lock function. Continue to the next step if the reverse lock still does not function correctly.

3. Remove and replace the manual release valve to eliminate the thermal expansion valve as a problem. Install a new manual release valve (using new O-rings) and tighten it to 45-55 in.-lb. (5.1-6.2 N•m). Retest the system for reverse lock function. Continue to the next step if the reverse lock still does not function correctly.

4. Remove, clean and inspect the filter valve assembly (46, **Figure 21**). Replace any damaged components. Install the filter valve assembly using new O-rings and retest the system for reverse lock function. Continue to the next step if reverse lock still does not function correctly.

NOTE
Pay close attention to the impact relief valve and UP relief valve springs in the next step. If the unit does not leak down, but reverse lock does not function, a broken or weak valve spring is a strong possibility.

5. Disassemble the cylinder and clean and inspect all components. Inspect the impact relief valves and the UP relief valve in the piston. Inspect each valve's spring for damage, distortion, broken coils and weakness.
   a. If the O-rings and springs are undamaged and the cylinder wall is not scored, replace the piston assembly to eliminate the piston's valves as the source of the problem.
   b. If the cylinder wall is scored or damaged, replace the cylinder and manifold as an assembly.
   c. Reassemble the unit with new seals and O-rings. Retest the system for reverse lock function.
   d. If reverse lock still does not function properly, replace the trim and tilt unit as a complete assembly.

Conventional System Troubleshooting

This is a complex trim and tilt system. Make sure the anticipated repairs are within your capabilities before beginning any disassembly. If you are unsure of yourself, it may be better to remove the unit and take it to an Evinrude/Johnson dealership that employs a competent technician.

Remove and install these units as an assembly. There is no specific troubleshooting procedure to isolate the tilt cylinder from the trim rams and the manifold assembly. Parts are available to service most of the tilt cylinder, trim rams and manifold assembly. A test gauge set is available to assist in the troubleshooting procedure and to verify that the system is functioning correctly after reassembly. Refer to *Pressure Testing* in this chapter.

Test specifications are listed in **Tables 1-3**. Torque specifications are listed in **Table 4** and troubleshooting procedures are listed in **Table 6**. The troubleshooting table lists common problems, their most likely cause and the course of action to remedy the problem. Refer to **Figure 22** for an exploded view of this system and **Figure 13** for a hydraulic flow diagram.

If the unit leaks down in the tilt range and has no reverse lock, clean and inspect the manual release valve. Replace the valve if its tip shows any damage. If the unit still leaks in both directions, the cause is most likely a failed tilt cylinder piston O-ring, scored cylinder walls or failed piston impact relief valves. Disassemble the cylinder and inspect these components. If no visible damage or defects are noted, replace the piston assembly.

Refer to *Power Trim and Tilt System Service* in this chapter for removal/installation and disassembly/reassembly procedures as necessary. Refill and bleed the system after reassembly as described under *Maintenance*.

CAUTION
*Relieve system pressure as described in this chapter before beginning **any** disassembly.*

Check valve pressure test

All of the cartridge style check valves (21, 24, 25 and 26, **Figure 22**) can be quickly tested using the check valve tester kit (part No. 390063).

1. Screw the suspect check valve into the tester body and tighten it to 50-60 in.-lb. (5.7-6.8 N·m).
2. Attach a suitable gearcase pressure tester (such as Stevens S-34) to the tester body.
3. Apply 30 psi (207 kPa) of pressure and check for leakage.

4. If the valve exhibits leakage from the external O-rings, replace the O-rings. If the valve exhibits leakage from the hole at the center of its tip, the valve is defective and must be replaced.

Complete system pressure test

Pressure tester kit (Part No. 391010) consists of a gauge and two adaptors (**Figure 23**). The adaptor stamped *A* (part No. 395618) must be used when testing the UP circuit and the adaptor stamped *B* (part No. 395619) must be used when testing the DOWN circuit.

CAUTION
The adaptors use an O-ring (part No. 332930) glued to the very tip of the adaptor. The O-ring will wear out during normal use. Replace worn O-rings immediately. Glue the new O-ring(s) to the adaptor(s) using a suitable instant glue, such as Dupont Krazy Glue or Loctite Black Max adhesive.

Pressure testing requires that the complete trim and tilt unit be removed from the outboard motor, and that the unit be supported in a suitable stand, such as part No. 390008. Refer to *Power Trim and Tilt System Service* in this chapter for system removal/installation procedures.

Operate the pump and note the pressure required to extend or retract the rams. Then, continue running the pump until the relief valve opens, noting the pressure as the pump forces fluid through the relief valve. The relief valve makes a distinct noise when it opens, caused by the rapid fluctuations of the valve bouncing on and off of its seat. This is also called measuring the stall pressure. The gauge needle will vibrate during the stall test and will be difficult to read. Simply note the average or midpoint of the needle oscillations.

Once the stall pressure is noted, stop the electric motor and begin the leak-down test. Leak-down is measured from the first point of needle stabilization as the electric motor is shut off and the relief valve closes. The needle may jump up slightly or drop slightly as this occurs. It is only important to note where the needle stabilizes, immediately after the trim motor is stopped.

The acceptable leak-down rate for all tests is a maximum pressure drop of 200 psi (1379 kPa) in a minimum time span of five minutes. For example, if the trim out stall pressure is 1450 psi (9998 kPa) and the needle stabilizes at 1400 psi (9653 kPa) when the electric motor stopped, the gauge cannot indicate lower than 1200 psi (8274 kPa) after a minimum of five minutes. Refer to **Table 3** for all pressure specifications.

10

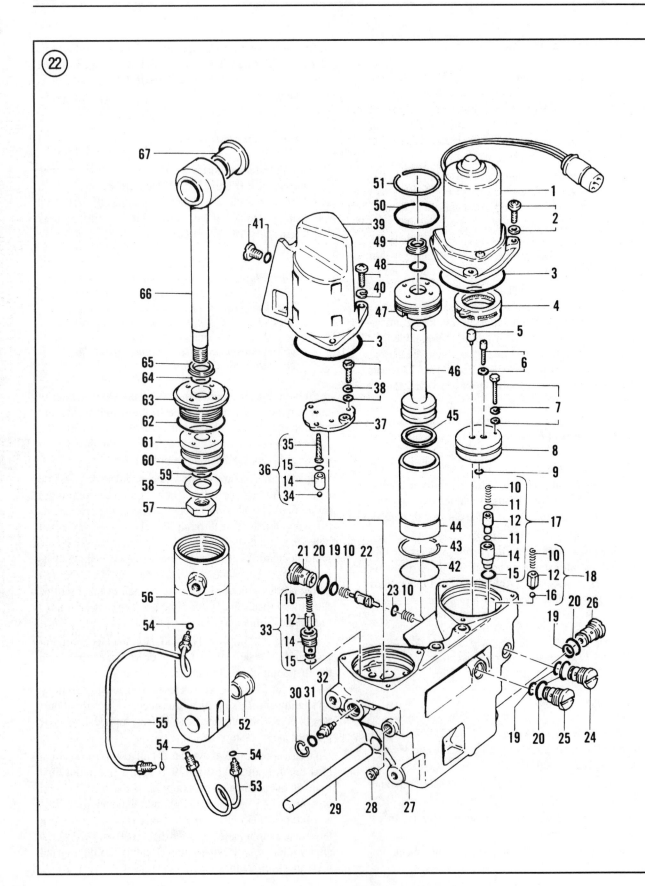

CONVENTIONAL SYSTEM

1. Electric motor and lead assembly
2. Screw and lockwasher
3. O-ring
4. Filter
5. Pump drive coupler
6. Socket screw and lockwasher
7. Hex screw, lockwasher and flat washer
8. Pump assembly
9. O-ring
10. Spring
11. O-ring
12. Valve core
13. Valve core O-rings
14. Valve seat
15. Valve seat O-ring
16. Valve core tip seal
17. Down relief valve assembly
18. Thermal expansion valve assembly
19. Check valve small O-rings
20. Check valve large O-rings
21. Reverse lock check valve cartridge
22. Pump control piston
23. Pump control piston O-ring
24. Trim check valve cartridge
25. Tilt check valve cartridge
26. Trim/tilt separation valve cartridge
27. Manifold assembly
28. Pipe plug
29. Tilt cylinder lower pivot pin
30. Retaining ring
31. O-ring
32. Manual release valve
33. Trim UP relief valve assembly
34. Check ball
35. Filter
36. Filter valve assembly
37. Plate
38. Screw, lockwasher and flat washer
39. Reservoir
40. Screw and lockwasher
41. Level plug and O-ring
42. Sleeve O-ring
43. Sleeve backup ring
44. Trim ram sleeve
45. Trim ram seal
46. Trim ram
47. Trim ram end cap
48. Quad ring
49. Wiper
50. End cap outer O-ring
51. End cap backup ring
52. Lower pivot pin bushing
53. Lower (high-volume chamber) line
54. Line fitting O-rings
55. Upper (low-volume chamber) line
56. Tilt cylinder
57. Nut
58. Washer
59. Rod-to-piston O-ring
60. O-ring
61. Piston assembly
62. End cap O-ring
63. Tilt cylinder end cap
64. O-ring
65. Wiper
66. Rod and eye
67. Upper pivot pin bushing

1. Remove the power trim and tilt unit as described in this chapter. Make sure the internal pressure is relieved as described in *Relieving System Pressure*.

2. Mount the unit in a suitable work stand, such as part No. 390008. The system must be mounted in its normal operating position. See **Figure 24**.

3. Make sure the tilt cylinder and trim rams are fully retracted. If necessary, connect the motor to the outboard motor's two-pin connector and operate it using the boat-mounted switch. If this is not feasible, connect the trim motor green lead to the battery's positive terminal and the motor blue lead to the negative terminal. Operate the electric motor in the DOWN direction until the rams are fully retracted.

4. To help relieve internal pressure, briefly operate the trim motor in the UP direction, then DOWN, then UP again. If the motor is being connected directly to the battery, simply switch the polarity of the blue and green leads to reverse the motor.

5. Remove the manual release valve's retaining ring (30, **Figure 22**) with a suitable pair of internal snap ring pliers.

6. Cover the manual release valve with a shop towel and carefully remove it from the manifold (by turning it coun-

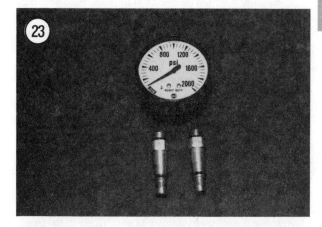

10

terclockwise). Work slowly and allow any pressure and fluid to vent before completely removing the valve.

7. To test the UP circuits, assemble the adaptor stamped *A* (part No. 395618) to the pressure gauge and body. Make sure all three adaptor O-rings (tip, middle and gauge end) are in satisfactory condition. Replace any worn or damaged O-rings.

8. Screw the gauge and adaptor assembly into the manual release valve port in the manifold. Tighten the assembly to 5-10 in.-lb. (0.6-1.1 N•m). Do not overtighten the assembly or the adapter O-ring will be damaged. See **Figure 24**.

9. Operate the unit fully UP and DOWN through several cycles. Check the fluid level each time the unit is in the full UP position (all rams extended). Add the recommended fluid as necessary to keep the fluid level flush with the bottom of the fill plug hole. Once the correct fluid level is verified, operate the system in the DOWN direction until all of the rams are fully retracted.

10. To finish testing the UP circuits, operate the system in the UP direction while observing the pressure gauge.
   a. Note the running pressure required to extend the rams (as the rams are being extended).
   b. Note the stall pressure (after the rams are fully extended and the motor is still running).
   c. Turn off the electric motor and immediately note the pressure at which the needle stabilizes. Then note the pressure drop after a *minimum* of 5 minutes.

11. A good system must indicate approximately 200 psi (1379 kPa) as the cylinder and rams are extending, approximately 1500 psi (10343 kPa) during the full UP stall and must not leak down more than 200 psi (1379 kPa) after the electric motor is stopped.

12. Operate the unit in the DOWN direction until all rams are fully retracted. Then repeat Step 4 to help relieve internal pressure. Cover the pressure gauge with a shop towel and carefully remove it from the manifold (by turning it counterclockwise). Work slowly and allow any pressure (and fluid) to vent before completely removing the valve.

13. Remove the adaptor stamped *A* (part No. 395618) from the gauge and body.

14. To test the DOWN circuits, assemble the adaptor stamped *B* (part No. 395619) to the pressure gauge and body. Make sure all three adaptor O-rings (tip, middle and gauge end) are in satisfactory condition. Replace any worn or damaged O-rings.

15. Screw the gauge and adaptor assembly into the manual release valve port in the manifold. Tighten the assembly to 5-10 in.-lb. (0.6-1.1 N•m). Do not overtighten the assembly or the adapter O-ring will be damaged. See **Figure 24**.

16. Operate the unit fully UP and DOWN through several cycles. Check the fluid level each time the unit is in the full UP position (all rams extended). Add the recommended

fluid as necessary to keep the fluid level flush with the bottom of the fill plug hole. Once the correct fluid level is verified, leave the system in the full UP position (all rams fully extended).

17. To finish testing the DOWN circuits, operate the system in the DOWN direction while observing the pressure gauge.
   a. Note the running pressure required to retract the rams (as the rams are being retracted).
   b. Note the stall pressure (after the rams are fully retracted and the motor is still running).
   c. Turn off the electric motor and immediately note the pressure at which the needle stabilizes. Then note the pressure drop after a minimum of five minutes.

18. A good system must indicate approximately 800 psi (5516 kPa) as the cylinder and rams are retracting, approximately 900 psi (6206 kPa) during the full DOWN stall and must not leak down more than 200 psi (1379 kPa) after the electric motor has been turned off.

19. If the UP or DOWN pressure tests are not as specified, refer to **Table 7** for pressure test results. The table lists failure modes, their probable causes and the corrective action necessary.

20. Operate the unit in the DOWN direction until all rams are fully retracted. Then repeat Step 4 to help relieve internal pressure. Cover the pressure gauge with a shop towel and carefully remove it from the manifold (by turning it counterclockwise). Work slowly and allow any pressure (and fluid) to vent before completely removing the valve.

21. If service is complete, install the manual release valve using a new O-ring. Tighten the valve to 45-55 in.-lb. (5.1-6.2 N•m). Then install the retaining ring using a suitable pair of internal snap ring pliers. Make sure the ring's sharp edge is facing out.

22. Operate the unit fully UP and DOWN through several cycles. Check the fluid level each time the unit is in the full UP position (all rams extended). Add the recommended fluid as necessary to keep the fluid level flush with the bottom of the fill plug hole. Once the correct fluid level is verified, leave the system in the full DOWN position (all rams fully retracted) to make installation easier.

FasTrak System Troubleshooting

While this is a complex trim and tilt system, it is serviced in a modular fashion. With the exception of the manual release valve, the pump (and valve body) assembly is available only as an assembly. The trim rams and tilt cylinder may be resealed or repaired, but if the tilt cylinder or either trim ram bore is scored, replace the system as an assembly. With the exception of the electric motor O-ring (4, **Figure 25**), the O-rings and seals are only available in

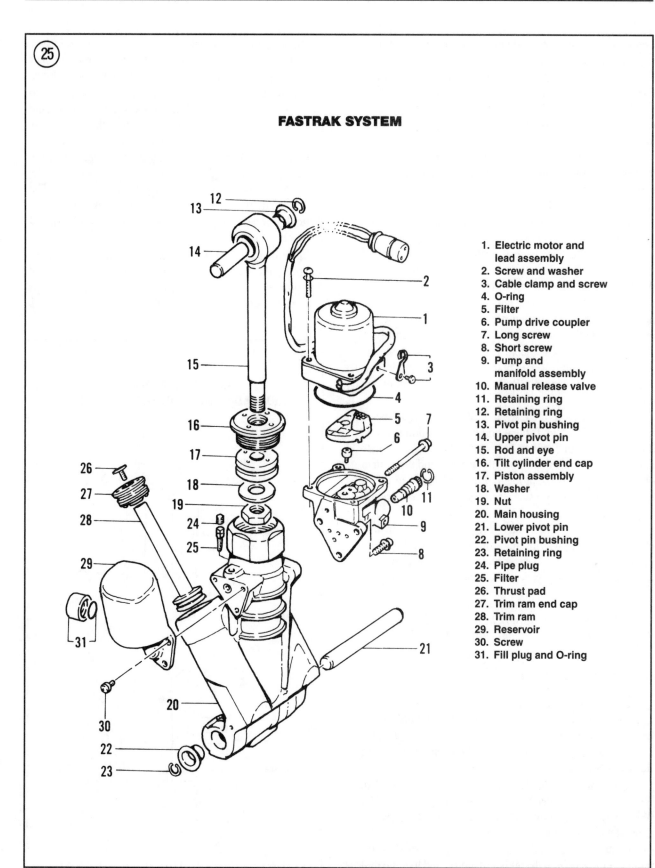

FASTRAK SYSTEM

1. Electric motor and lead assembly
2. Screw and washer
3. Cable clamp and screw
4. O-ring
5. Filter
6. Pump drive coupler
7. Long screw
8. Short screw
9. Pump and manifold assembly
10. Manual release valve
11. Retaining ring
12. Retaining ring
13. Pivot pin bushing
14. Upper pivot pin
15. Rod and eye
16. Tilt cylinder end cap
17. Piston assembly
18. Washer
19. Nut
20. Main housing
21. Lower pivot pin
22. Pivot pin bushing
23. Retaining ring
24. Pipe plug
25. Filter
26. Thrust pad
27. Trim ram end cap
28. Trim ram
29. Reservoir
30. Screw
31. Fill plug and O-ring

10

a repair kit and are not shown in the exploded view shown in **Figure 25**.

The FasTrak system is also used on larger engines. Different manual release valves (incorporating the tilt relief/thermal expansion valve) and tilt pistons (impact relief valves) are used to provide the correct operating pressures for the different weight and thrust of the larger engines.

The manual release valve for 50-70 hp (three-cylinder) models must have a groove in its outer face as shown in **Figure 26**. If not, remove the valve and replace it with the correct (grooved) valve.

The tilt cylinder piston's four impact relief holes all must measure 0.093 in. (2.36 mm) in diameter. The impact relief valve springs must be identical, with the exception that one spring is slightly shorter than the other three. If not, replace the piston (as an assembly) with the correct one.

Remove and install these units as an assembly. There is no specific troubleshooting procedure to isolate the tilt cylinder from the trim rams and the manifold assembly.

A test gauge set is available to assist in the troubleshooting procedure and to verify that the system is functioning correctly after reassembly. Refer to *Pressure Testing* in this chapter.

Test specifications are listed in **Tables 1-3**, torque specifications are listed in **Table 4** and troubleshooting procedures are listed in **Table 8**. The troubleshooting table lists common problems, their most likely cause and the course of action to remedy the problem. Refer to **Figure 25** for an exploded view of this system and **Figure 14** for a hydraulic flow diagram.

Refer to *Power Trim and Tilt System Service*, in this chapter, for removal/installation and disassembly/reassembly procedures as necessary. Refill and bleed the system after reassembly as described under *Maintenance*.

> *CAUTION*
> *Relieve system pressure as described in this chapter before beginning **any** disassembly.*

Complete system pressure test

Pressure tester kit (Part No. 434524) consists of two adaptors. The adaptor stamped *A* (part No. 336658) must be used when testing the UP circuit, and the adaptor stamped *B* (part No. 336659) must be used when testing the DOWN circuit.

A pressure gauge and body, either from the part No. 390010 pressure tester kit, or available alone as part No. 983975 is also required. **Figure 23** shows the pressure gauge and a typical set of adaptors.

Pressure testing requires that the complete trim and tilt unit be removed from the outboard motor, and that the unit be supported in a suitable stand (or in a soft-jawed vise). Refer to *Power Trim and Tilt System Service*, located later in this chapter, for system removal/installation procedures.

Operate the pump and note the pressure required to extend or retract the tilt cylinder, then continue running the pump until the relief valve opens, noting the pressure as the pump forces fluid through the relief valve. The relief valve makes a distinct noise when it opens, caused by the rapid fluctuations of the valve bouncing on and off of its seat. This is also called measuring the stall pressure. The gauge needle will vibrate during the stall test and will be difficult to read. Simply note the average or mid-point of the needle oscillations.

Once the stall pressure is noted, stop the electric motor and begin the leak-down test. Measure leak-down from the first point of needle stabilization as the electric motor stops and the relief valve closes. The needle may jump up

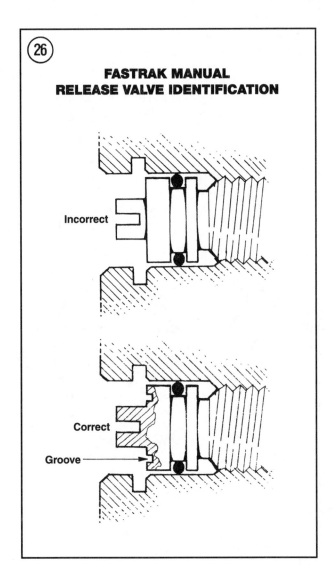

FASTRAK MANUAL RELEASE VALVE IDENTIFICATION

Incorrect

Correct

Groove

slightly or drop slightly as this occurs. It is only important to note where the needle stabilizes at, immediately after the trim motor is stopped.

The acceptable leak-down rate for all tests is a maximum pressure drop of 200 psi (1379 kPa) in a minimum time span of five minutes. For example, if the trim out stall pressure was 850 psi (5861 kPa) and the needle stabilized at 825 psi (5688 kPa) when the electric motor stopped, the gauge cannot indicate lower than 625 psi (4309 kPa) after a minimum of five minutes. Refer to **Table 3** for all pressure specifications.

NOTE
The pressure tester takes the place the of the manual release valve. If the unit passes all pressure tests, yet still malfunctions, replace the manual release valve.

1. Remove the power trim and tilt unit as described later in this chapter. Make sure the internal pressure is relieved as described in *Relieving System Pressure* in this chapter.
2. Mount the unit in a suitable work stand or in a soft-jawed vise. The system must be mounted in its normal operating position.
3. Make sure the tilt cylinder and trim rams are extended. If necessary, connect the motor to the outboard motor's two-pin connector and operate it using the boat-mounted switch. If this is not feasible, connect the trim motor blue lead to the battery's positive terminal and the motor green lead to the negative terminal. Operate the electric motor in the UP direction until the rams are fully extended.
4. To relieve internal pressure, briefly operate the motor in the DOWN direction. If the motor is being connected directly to the battery, simply switch the polarity of the blue and green leads to reverse the motor.
5. Open the manual release valve until it just contacts its retaining ring. Then cover the fill plug with a shop towel and carefully and slowly remove the fill plug, allowing any internal pressure (and fluid) to vent before fully removing the plug. It is normal for some fluid to be expelled at this time.
6. Remove the manual release valve's retaining ring (11, **Figure 25**) with a suitable pair of internal snap ring pliers.
7. Cover the manual release valve with a shop towel and carefully remove it from the manifold (by turning it counterclockwise). Work slowly and allow any pressure (and fluid) to vent before completely removing the valve.
8. To test the UP circuits, assemble the adaptor stamped *A* (part No. 336658) to the previously specified pressure gauge and body. Make sure all four adaptor O-rings are in satisfactory condition. Replace any worn or damaged O-rings.
9. Screw the gauge and adaptor assembly into the manual release valve port in the manifold. Tighten the assembly to

5-10 in.-lb. (0.6-1.1 N•m). Do not overtighten the assembly or the adapter O-ring will be damaged. See **Figure 24**, typical.

NOTE
Once the trim rams are extended, they will not retract when bench testing the unit. The trim rams are retracted by the swivel bracket pushing against them as the tilt cylinder lowers the motor.

10. Operate the unit fully UP and DOWN through several cycles. Check the fluid level each time the unit is in the full UP position (all rams extended). Add the recommended fluid as necessary to keep the fluid level flush with the bottom of the fill plug hole. Once the correct fluid level is verified, operate the system in the DOWN direction until the tilt cylinder is fully retracted.
11. To finish testing the UP circuits, operate the system in the UP direction while observing the pressure gauge.
   a. Note the running pressure required to extend the tilt cylinder (as the cylinder is being extended).
   b. Note the stall pressure (after the rams are fully extended and the motor is still running).
   c. Turn off the electric motor and immediately note the pressure at which the needle stabilizes. Then note the pressure drop after a *minimum* of 5 minutes.
12. A good system must indicate between 0-200 psi (0-1379 kPa) as the cylinder is extending; 1400-1600 psi (9653-11032 kPa) during the full UP stall; and must not leak down more than 200 psi (1379 kPa) after the electric motor is turned off.
13. To relieve internal pressure, briefly operate the motor in the DOWN direction. If the motor is being connected directly to the battery, simply switch the polarity of the blue and green leads to reverse the motor.
14. Unscrew the pressure gauge approximately 3-1/2 turns. Then cover the fill plug with a shop towel and carefully and slowly remove the fill plug, allowing any internal pressure (and fluid) to vent before fully removing the plug. It is normal for some fluid to be expelled at this time.
15. Cover the pressure gauge with a shop towel and carefully remove it from the manifold (by turning it counterclockwise). Work slowly and allow any pressure (and fluid) to vent before completely removing the valve.
16. Remove the adaptor stamped *A* (part No. 336658) from the gauge and body.
17. To test the DOWN circuits, assemble the adaptor stamped *B* (part No. 336659) to the pressure gauge and body. Make sure all three adaptor O-rings are in satisfactory condition. Replace any worn or damaged O-rings.
18. Screw the gauge and adaptor assembly into the manual release valve port in the manifold. Tighten the assembly to 5-10 in.-lb. (0.6-1.1 N•m). Do not overtighten the assembly

10

18. Screw the gauge and adaptor assembly into the manual release valve port in the manifold. Tighten the assembly to 5-10 in.-lb. (0.6-1.1 N•m). Do not overtighten the assembly or the adapter O-ring will be damaged. See **Figure 24**, typical.

19. Operate the unit fully UP and DOWN through several cycles. Check the fluid level each time the unit is in the full UP position (all rams extended). Add the recommended fluid as necessary to keep the fluid level flush with the bottom of the fill plug hole. Once the correct fluid level is verified, leave the system in the full UP position (all rams fully extended).

20. To finish testing the DOWN circuits, operate the system in the DOWN direction while observing the pressure gauge.

    a. Note the running pressure required to retract the tilt cylinder ram (as the ram is being retracted).

    b. Note the stall pressure (after the tilt cylinder is fully retracted and the motor is still running).

    c. Turn off the electric motor and immediately note the pressure at which the needle stabilizes. Then note the pressure drop after a *minimum* of five minutes.

21. A good system must indicate 0-200 psi (1379 kPa) as the tilt cylinder ram is retracting; approximately 800 psi (5516 kPa) during the full DOWN stall; and must not leak down more than 200 psi (1379 kPa) after the electric motor is turned off.

22. If the UP or DOWN pressure tests are not as specified, refer to **Table 9** for pressure test results. The table lists failure modes, their probable causes and the corrective action necessary.

23. To relieve internal pressure, briefly operate the motor in the DOWN direction.

24. Unscrew the pressure gauge approximately 3-1/2 turns. Then cover the fill plug with a shop towel and carefully and slowly remove the fill plug, allowing any internal pressure (and fluid) to vent before fully removing the plug. It is normal for some fluid to be expelled at this time.

25. Cover the pressure gauge with a shop towel and carefully remove it from the manifold (by turning it counterclockwise). Work slowly and allow any pressure (and fluid) to vent before completely removing the valve.

26. If service is complete, install the manual release valve using a new O-ring. The two nylon seal rings are not replaceable and if damaged, replace the valve as an assembly. Tighten the valve to 45-55 in.-lb. (5.1-6.2 N•m). Then install the retaining ring using a suitable pair of internal snap ring pliers. Make sure the ring's sharp edge is facing out.

27. Operate the unit fully UP and DOWN through several cycles. Check the fluid level each time the unit is in the full UP position (all rams extended). Add the recommended fluid as necessary to keep the fluid level flush with the bottom of the fill plug hole. Once the correct fluid level is verified, leave the system in the full DOWN position (tilt cylinder fully retracted) to make installation easier.

POWER TRIM AND TILT SYSTEM ELECTRICAL TROUBLESHOOTING

Troubleshooting procedures vary slightly between 1995 (EO) models equipped with the traditional wiring harness and Amphenol connectors and the 1996-2003 (ED-ST) models equipped with the modular wiring system (MWS) and Deutsch connectors. Refer to *Wiring Harnesses* in Chapter Three for harness information. Regardless of the connectors used, the wire color codes and their function remain constant.

Green-colored leads are primarily used for the down circuits. Blue-colored leads are primarily used for the up circuits. The switching circuits for the trim and tilt system are protected by the main 20 amp fuse (on the motor).

Tiller handle models have only one trim and tilt switch mounted to the starboard side of the lower motor cowl. Remote control models have the lower cowl-mounted switch and one or more boat mounted (or remote control) switches.

Electrical testing is performed most accurately with a multimeter (Chapter Three). However, a 12 volt test lamp and a self-powered continuity tester may be used if a multimeter is unavailable. Before beginning any troubleshooting with a test lamp, connect the test lamp directly to the battery and observe the brightness of the bulb. You must reference the rest of your tests against this test. Whenever the bulb does not glow as brightly as when it was hooked directly to the battery, a problem is indicated.

If a multimeter is used, take a battery voltage reading to reference all of your readings against. When the voltmeter reads one or more volts less than battery voltage, a definite problem is indicated. When checking continuity with an ohmmeter, a zero reading is good. The higher the ohmmeter reads above zero, the worse the condition of that circuit.

Relay Function

It is important to understand the function of each relay terminal before attempting to troubleshoot the system.

All relays (1, **Figure 27**) used in these systems use standard electrical connector positioning. Each relay has five terminals which are labeled 30, 85, 86, 87 and 87A.

Terminal No. 87 (4, **Figure 27**) is *Power IN* to the relay from the battery (terminal strip or starter solenoid). Terminal No. 87 is connected to a solid red lead and is part of the load circuits.

Terminals No. 85 and No. 86 (3, **Figure 27**) are the control circuits of the relay. Whenever one of these terminals is grounded and the other terminal is connected to battery voltage, the relay is energized. The polarity of terminals No. 85 and No. 86 is not important, as long as one is positive and one is negative. On the engines covered in this manual, terminal No. 85 is connected to a black (ground) lead and terminal No. 86 is connected to a trim and tilt switch (blue/white or green/white) lead.

Terminals No. 30 (2, **Figure 27**) and No. 87A (5) make up the remainder of the load circuits of the relay. Terminal No. 30 is normally open to terminal No. 87 (Power IN). When the relay is energized, terminal No. 87 has continuity to terminal No. 30. Terminal No. 87A is normally closed to terminal No. 30. When the relay is energized, terminal No. 87A has no continuity to terminal No. 30. On the engines covered in this manual, terminal No. 87A is always connected to a black (ground) lead and terminal No. 30 is connected to a trim motor (blue or green) lead.

Preliminary Checks

Before attempting to troubleshoot any electrical circuit:

1. Make sure that all connectors are properly engaged and that all terminals and leads are free of corrosion. Clean and tighten all connections as required. This includes the battery cable connections at the engine and at the battery terminals. Refer to *Connector Service* in Chapter Three for additional information.

> *NOTE*
> *If wing nuts are used to secure the battery cables to the battery terminals, remove and discard the wing nuts. Place a corrosion resistant lock washer over each battery terminal, then place the battery cable over the washer. Secure the connection with a corrosion resistant hex nut. Tighten the hex nut securely.*

2. Make sure the battery is fully charged. Charge or replace the battery as required. Refer to Chapter Seven for battery information.

Electrical Troubleshooting (Complete System)

Refer to **Figure 28** for a typical trim and tilt system wiring diagram. The tilt limit switch shown in **Figure 28** is only present on FasTrak systems. On other systems, the blue/white lead goes straight from the trim and tilt switch(es) to the relay bracket. Refer to the back of the

10

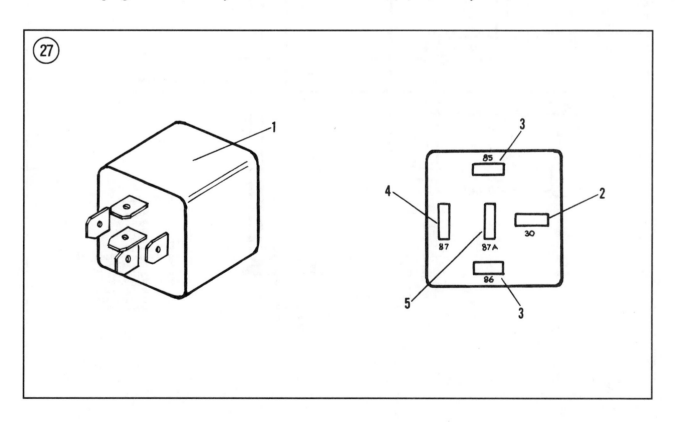

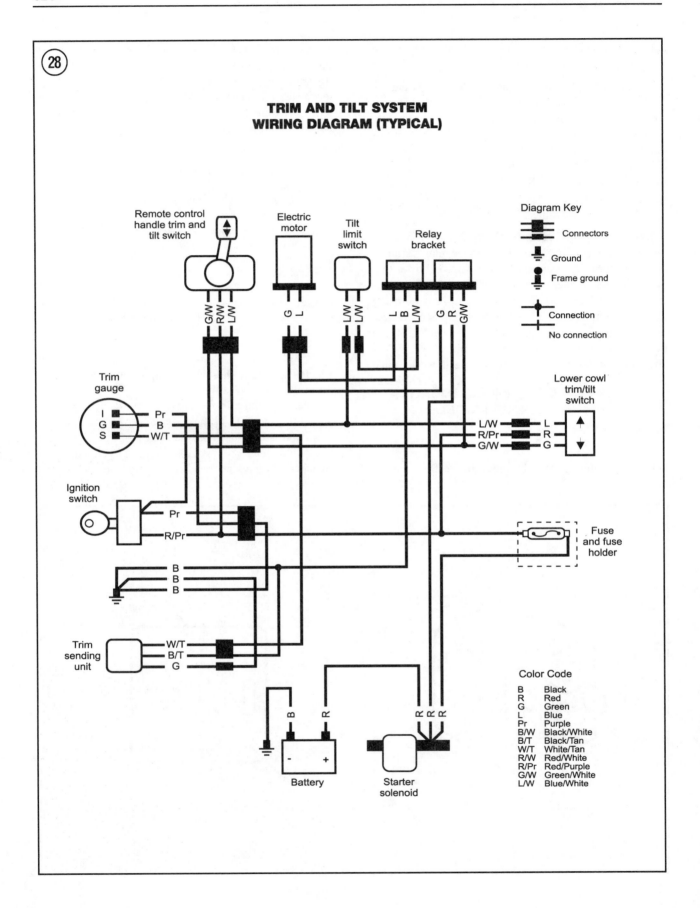

Refer to **Figure 29** for the terminal location at the relay bracket for all three-cylinder models. Note that the position of the blue and green leads (and the blue/white and green/white leads) are reversed on the 40-50 hp (two-cylinder) models.

The two-wire motor is reversed by switching the polarity of the motor's blue and green leads. There are two relays, one for each motor lead. The relays are bracket-mounted to the top of the power head on 25-35 hp (three-cylinder) models (**Figure 30**) or the starboard side of the power head near the voltage regulator and terminal strip on 40-70 hp models (**Figure 31**, typical).

Both relays hold their motor lead (blue or green) to ground when they are not activated. When the UP relay is activated, it takes the blue motor lead off of ground and connects it to positive. The DOWN relay is inactive and holds the green lead to ground. Current can then flow from the positive terminal to the UP relay to the trim motor and back to ground through the down relay causing the motor to run in the UP direction.

When the DOWN relay is activated, it takes the green trim motor lead off of ground and connects it to positive. The UP relay is inactive and holds the blue lead to ground. Current can then flow from the positive terminal to the DOWN relay to the trim motor and back to ground through the UP relay, causing the motor to run in the DOWN direction.

If the motor will run in one direction, but not the other, the problem *cannot* be the trim motor.

To troubleshoot the electric motor and switching circuits, proceed as follows:

1. Disconnect and ground the spark plug leads to the power head to prevent accidental starting.

2. Verify that the starter system will crank the engine normally. If not, refer to Chapter Three and troubleshoot the starting system. The starting system must be functioning correctly for this procedure to be accurate.

(29)

RELAY BRACKET TERMINAL LOCATION
(THREE-CYLINDER MODELS)

Green/white*

Red

Green*

Black

Blue/white*

Blue*

Red

Black

*See text for two-cylinder models

3. Mark each relay as to its original position in the relay bracket, then remove both trim and tilt relays from the relay mounting bracket.

NOTE
The connections in Steps 4 and 5 are made at the specified terminals in the relay mounting bracket.

4. Connect the test lamp probe to the battery voltage (B+) terminal of each relay. These are the solid red leads (**Figure 29**). The test lamp must light at each point. If not, repair or replace the red lead from the starter solenoid to the relay bracket. See **Figure 28**, typical. On 40-50 hp (2-cylinder) models, the red lead goes from the starter solenoid to the terminal strip, then to the relay bracket.

5. Connect the test lamp lead to the positive terminal of the battery and touch the test lamp probe to each of the two ground (black lead) terminals of each relay. The test lamp must light at each point. See **Figure 29**. If not, repair or replace the black lead (from the relay bracket to ground).

NOTE
Each trim and tilt switch present on the motor and/or boat must be tested as described in the appropriate following step.

6A. *Lower cowl mounted trim switch*—Disconnect the red/purple lead from the trim and tilt switch's bullet connector (**Figure 28**). Connect the test lamp probe to the engine harness side of the red/purple lead's bullet connector. The test lamp must light. If not, repair or replace the red/purple lead between the fuse holder and the bullet connector. Reconnect the leads when finished.

6B. *Remote control mounted trim switch*—Proceed as follows:
 a. Follow the trim and tilt switch leads from the control box until the three-pin connector (**Figure 28**) is located. The three leads are green/white, red/white and blue/white. Disconnect the three-pin connector.
 b. Connect the test lamp probe to the red/white lead on the engine harness side of the connector. The test lamp must light.
 c. If not, repair or replace the red/purple (changing to red/white) lead between the fuse holder and trim and tilt switch connector (**Figure 28**). This includes one or more connectors depending on the model.
 d. Reconnect all leads when finished.

6C. *Boat-mounted trim switch*—Connect the test lamp probe to the center terminal (red/white, red/purple or red lead) of each trim and tilt switch. The test lamp must light. If not, repair or replace the lead between the fuse holder output terminal and center terminal of the suspect trim/tilt switch. If it is necessary to disconnect any leads to test the switch, reconnect all leads when finished.

NOTE
The connections in Steps 7 and 8 are made at the specified terminals in the relay mounting bracket.

7A. *Conventional and single ram systems*—Connect the test lamp probe to the blue/white terminal in the relay bracket. See **Figure 29**.
 a. Hold each trim and tilt switch in the UP position and observe the test lamp. The test lamp must light as each switch is activated.
 b. If not, connect the test lamp probe to the blue/white lead (or terminal) at each trim and tilt switch. Hold each trim and tilt switch in the UP position and observe the test lamp. The test lamp must light when each switch is activated.
 c. If not, replace the defective trim and tilt switch. If the test lamp lights at the trim and tilt switch, but not at the UP relay blue/white terminal, repair or replace the blue/white lead between the suspect trim and tilt switch and relay bracket.

7B. *FasTrak systems*—Connect the test lamp probe to the blue/white terminal in the relay bracket. See **Figure 29**.
 a. Hold each trim and tilt switch in the UP position and observe the test lamp. The test lamp must light as each switch is activated.
 b. If not, connect the test lamp probe to the blue/white lead (or terminal) at each trim and tilt switch. Hold each trim and tilt switch in the UP position and observe the test lamp. The test lamp must light when each switch is activated.
 c. If not, replace the defective trim and tilt switch. If the test lamp lights at the trim and tilt switch, but not at the relay bracket blue/white terminal, proceed to substep d.
 d. Disconnect the tilt limit switch leads from the main engine harness at their bullet connectors (**Figure 32**, typical). Connect the engine side of the connectors to each other, bypassing the tilt limit switch.
 e. Repeat substep b. If the test lamp now lights, the tilt limit switch is defective or improperly adjusted. If

the test lamp still does not light, repair or replace the blue/white lead between the suspect trim and tilt switch and relay bracket.

8. Connect the test lamp probe to the green/white terminal in the relay bracket (**Figure 29**).

   a. Hold each trim and tilt switch in the DOWN position and observe the test lamp. The test lamp must light as each switch is activated.

   b. If not, connect the test lamp probe to the green/white lead (or terminal) at each trim and tilt switch. Hold each trim switch in the DOWN position and observe the test lamp. The test lamp must light when each trim switch is activated.

   c. If not, replace the defective trim and tilt switch. If the test lamp lights at the trim and tilt switch, but not at the relay bracket green/white terminal, repair or replace the green/white lead between the suspect trim and tilt switch and relay bracket.

9. Install both trim and tilt relays into the relay bracket. Then pull the relays out far enough to allow access to the relay terminals, but remain engaged to the relay bracket.

10. Connect the test lamp probe to the solid blue terminal in the relay bracket. See **Figure 29**. Hold a trim and tilt switch in the UP position and observe the test lamp. The test lamp must light. If not, replace the UP relay.

11. Connect the test lamp probe to the solid green terminal in the relay bracket. Hold a trim and tilt switch in the DOWN position and observe the test lamp. The test lamp must light. If not, replace the DOWN relay.

NOTE
Each relay grounds its respective blue or green trim motor lead when not activated. Step 12 confirms that the relays are providing the required ground path.

12. Connect the test lamp lead to the positive terminal of the battery. Alternately touch the test lamp probe to the solid blue terminal and the solid green terminal in the relay bracket (**Figure 29**). The test lamp must light at each test point. If not, replace the defective relay(s).

13. Push both relays into the relay bracket until they are seated.

14. Connect the test lamp lead to the negative terminal of the battery. Then separate the trim and tilt motor's large two-pin connector (**Figure 28**).

15. Connect the test lamp probe to the blue lead on the engine harness side of the two-pin connector. Hold a trim and tilt switch in the UP position and observe the test lamp. The test lamp must light. If not, the blue lead has an open circuit between the relay bracket and the two-pin connector. Repair or replace the blue lead as necessary.

16. Connect the test lamp probe to the green lead on the engine harness side of the two-pin connector. Hold a trim and tilt switch in the DOWN position and observe the test lamp. The test lamp must light. If not, the green lead has an open circuit between the relay bracket and the two-pin connector. Repair or replace the green lead as necessary.

17. Reconnect the large two-pin trim and tilt motor connector.

18. If all previous tests are satisfactory and the electric motor still does not operate correctly, repair or replace the electric motor.

10

Relay Ohmmeter Tests

The relays can be bench-tested using an ohmmeter. Refer to *Relay Function* in this chapter for a description of the function of each relay terminal. Refer to **Figure 33** for this procedure.

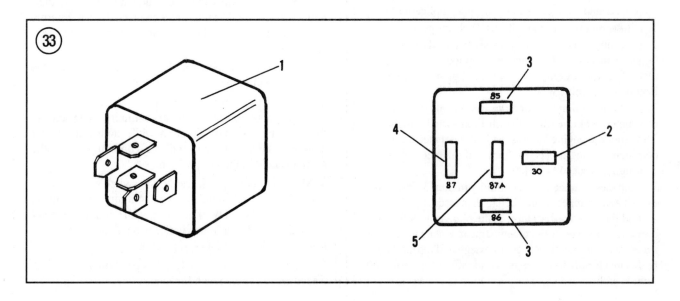

1. Remove the suspect relay from the relay bracket. See **Figure 30** or **Figure 31**.

2. Calibrate an ohmmeter on the R × 1 scale.

3. Connect the meter red lead to terminal No. 30 (2, **Figure 33**) and the meter black lead to terminal No. 87A (5). The meter must indicate continuity.

4. Move the meter black lead to terminal No. 87 (4, **Figure 33**). The meter must indicate no continuity.

5. Calibrate the ohmmeter on the appropriate scale to read 70-100 ohms. Connect one meter lead to terminal No. 85 and the other meter lead to terminal No. 86. See 3, **Figure 33**. The meter must read 70-100 ohms.

6. Using a suitable pair of jumper leads, connect a 12-volt battery to terminals No. 85 and No. 86 (3, **Figure 33**). Polarity is not important as long as one terminal is negative and the other terminal is positive.

7. Calibrate the ohmmeter on the R × 1 scale.

8. With the jumper leads and battery attached, connect the meter red lead to terminal No. 30 (2, **Figure 33**) and the meter black lead to terminal No. 87A (5). The meter must indicate no continuity.

9. Move the meter black lead to terminal No. 87 (4, **Figure 33**). The meter must indicate continuity.

10. Remove the jumper leads from the relay and battery.

11. Replace the relay if it does not perform as specified.

Tilt Limit Switch Test (FasTrak Models)

The 50-70 hp (three-cylinder) models equipped with the FasTrak trim and tilt system incorporate a tilt limit switch, which can be adjusted as needed to prevent the motor from tilting too high. If the switch fails in an open circuit, the motor will not trim UP. If the switch fails in a closed circuit, the tilt limiting feature will be lost, and the motor may trim UP too far and contact the hull (in some applications).

1. Tilt the outboard to the fully DOWN (in) position.

2. Disconnect the two tilt limit switch leads from their bullet connectors. The connectors are located at the port, rear, top corner of the power head as shown in **Figure 32**. Both leads are blue/white.

3. Calibrate an ohmmeter on the R × 1 scale. Connect an ohmmeter lead to each of the tilt limit switch blue/white leads (not the engine harness leads). The meter must read continuity. If not, proceed to Step 5. If the meter indicates continuity, proceed to Step 6.

4. If the meter indicates no continuity in Step 3, verify that the switch plunger is not being depressed by the cam around the tilt (steering) tube. If the plunger is depressed, the switch is severely out of adjustment. Rotate the cam as necessary to allow the plunger to extend and repeat Step 4. If the meter still indicates no continuity, replace the tilt limit switch.

5. Manually depress the tilt limit switch's plunger while noting the meter reading. The meter must indicate no continuity when the plunger is depressed. If not, the switch is defective and must be replaced.

6. If the meter indicates no continuity when the plunger is depressed in Step 5, the switch is functioning correctly. Reconnect both switch leads to the engine harness bullet connectors. If necessary, adjust the switch as described previously in this chapter.

Trim and Tilt Switch (and Boat Harness) Tests

All trim and tilt switches are simple three-position, three terminal switches. The switches are spring loaded to the OFF position. Trim and tilt switches are supplied battery voltage through a red, red/white or red/purple lead that is protected by the engine's 20 amp fuse. When activated, the switch takes the battery voltage and connects it to the blue/white (UP) lead *or* the green/white (DOWN) lead. The switch(es) can be quickly tested with an ohmmeter. On remote control models, the trim and tilt boat harness can be tested along with the switch, or the switch can be tested alone.

Refer to *Wiring Harnesses* in Chapter Three for description and identification of the *traditional wiring harness* and *modular wiring harness (MWS)* systems. Refer to the back of the manual for wiring diagrams.

Lower cowl mounted switch

1. Disconnect the lower cowl mounted trim and tilt switch's red, green/white and blue/white leads at their bullet connectors. The red lead is connected to a red/purple engine harness lead. All three connectors are located very close to the switch.

2. Calibrate an ohmmeter on the R × 1 scale. Connect the meter red lead to the switch's red lead.

3. Connect the meter black lead to the switch's blue/white lead. The meter must indicate no continuity. Then activate the switch in the UP direction while noting the meter reading. The meter must indicate continuity while the switch is held in the UP position.

4. Move the meter black lead to the switch's green white lead. The meter must indicate no continuity. Then activate the switch in the DOWN direction while noting the meter reading. The meter must indicate continuity while the switch is held in the DOWN position.

5. Replace the switch if it does not perform as specified. Reconnect all leads when finished.

Remote control mounted switch

Standard OMC boat wiring harness trim and tilt switching circuits use blue/white (UP), green/white (DOWN) and red/white or red/purple leads. Other harness manufacturers may use solid blue and green leads instead of the blue/white and green/white leads. The red/white (or red/purple) lead may also be replaced with a solid red lead.

1. Disconnect the negative battery cable from the battery.

2A. *Testing switch only*—Follow the trim and tilt switch leads from the control box until the three-pin connector is located. See **Figure 28**. The three leads are green/white, red/white and blue/white. Disconnect the three-pin connector.

2B. *Testing switch and boat harness*—Proceed as follows:

    a. *Traditional harness*—Locate the trim and tilt harness five-pin Amphenol connector on the outboard engine. The harness contains green/white, white/tan, black/tan, blue/white and purple/red leads. Separate the connector.

> *NOTE*
> *The electrical harness junction box is located on the starboard side of the engine on 25-35 hp (three-cylinder models), on the exhaust cover on 40-50 hp (two-cylinder) models and near the top of the cylinder head on 50-70 hp (three-cylinder models).*

    b. *MWS harness*—Remove the cover from the electrical harness junction box. Separate the three-pin Deutsch connector (green/white, blue/white and white/tan leads) and the 6-pin Deutsch connector (black/yellow, yellow/red, black/white, purple, red/purple and purple/white leads).

3. Calibrate an ohmmeter on the R × 1 scale.

4A. *Testing switch only*—Connect the meter red lead to the red/white lead at the switch harness's three-pin connector.

4B. *Testing switch and boat harness*—Connect the meter red lead to the red/white (or red/purple) lead of the boat wiring harness. This is pin E of the five-pin Amphenol connector on traditional harnesses or pin No. 5 of the six-pin Deutsch connector on MWS systems.

5A. *Testing switch only*—Connect the meter black lead to the blue/white lead at the switch harness's 3-pin connector.

5B. *Testing switch and boat harness*—Connect the meter black lead to the blue/white lead of the *boat* wiring harness. This is pin D of the five-pin Amphenol connector (traditional harnesses) or pin A of the three-pin Deutsch connector (MWS systems).

6. Note the meter reading. The meter must indicate no continuity.

    a. *Testing switch only*—If not, replace the switch.

    b. *Testing switch and harness*—If not, start this procedure over and follow the *Testing switch only* steps. If the switch now tests satisfactorily, the boat harness is defective. Locate and repair the short circuit between the blue/white and red/white (and/or red/purple) leads in the boat harness.

7. Activate the trim and tilt switch in the UP direction. Note the meter reading. The meter must indicate continuity while the switch is held activated in the UP position.

    a. *Testing switch only*—If not, replace the switch.

    b. *Testing switch and harness*—If not, start this procedure over and follow the *Testing switch only* steps. If the switch now tests satisfactorily, the boat harness is defective. Locate and repair the open circuit in the blue/white or red/white (and/or red/purple) leads in the boat harness.

8A. *Testing switch only*—Move the meter black lead to the green/white lead of the switch harness's three-pin connector.

8B. *Testing switch and boat harness*—Move the meter black lead to the green/white lead of the boat wiring harness. This will be pin D of the five-pin Amphenol connector (traditional harnesses) or pin B of the three-pin Deutsch connector (MWS systems).

9. Note the meter reading. The meter must indicate no continuity.

    a. *Testing switch only*—If not, replace the switch.

    b. *Testing switch and harness*—If not, start this procedure over and follow the *Testing switch only* steps. If the switch now tests satisfactorily, the boat harness is defective. Locate and repair the short circuit between the green/white and red/white (and/or red/purple) leads in the boat harness.

10. Activate the trim and tilt switch in the DOWN direction. Note the meter reading. The meter must indicate continuity while the switch is held activated in the DOWN position.

    a. *Testing switch only*—If not, replace the switch.

    b. *Testing switch and harness*—If not, start this procedure over and follow the *Testing switch only* steps. If the switch now tests satisfactorily, the boat harness is defective. Locate and repair the open circuit in the green/white or red/white (and/or red/purple) leads in the boat harness.

11. Reconnect all leads and connectors when finished. Reconnect the negative battery cable last.

Boat mounted switch

Standard OMC boat wiring harness trim and tilt switching circuits use blue/white (UP), green/white (DOWN) and red/white or red/purple leads. Other harness manufacturers may use solid blue and green leads instead of the

10

blue/white and green/white leads. The red/white (or red/purple) lead may also be replaced with a solid red lead.

1. Disconnect the negative battery cable from the battery.

2A. *Testing switch only*—Gain access to the trim and tilt switch. Note the position of the three leads, then disconnect all leads from the switch.

2B. *Testing switch and boat harness*—Proceed as follows:

  a. *Conventional harness*—Locate the trim and tilt harness five-pin Amphenol connector on the outboard engine. The harness will contain green/white, white/tan, black/tan, blue/white and purple/red leads. Separate the connector.

NOTE
The electrical harness junction box is located on the starboard side of the engine on 25-35 hp (three-cylinder models), on the exhaust cover on 40-50 hp (two-cylinder) models and near the top of the cylinder head on 50-70 hp (three-cylinder models).

  b. *MWS harness*—Remove the cover from the electrical harness junction box. Separate the three-pin Deutsch connector (green/white, blue/white and white/tan leads) and the six-pin Deutsch connector (black/yellow, yellow/red, black/white, purple, red/purple and purple/white leads).

3. Calibrate an ohmmeter on the R × 1 scale.

4A. *Testing switch only*—Connect the meter red lead to the switch's center terminal (terminal that was connected to red/white, red/purple or red lead).

4B. *Testing switch and boat harness*—Connect the meter red lead to the red/purple lead of the boat wiring harness. This will be pin E of the five-pin Amphenol connector on traditional harnesses or pin No. 5 of the six-pin Deutsch connector on MWS systems.

5A. *Testing switch only*—Connect the meter black lead to the switch terminal that originally contained the blue/white (or blue) lead.

5B. *Testing switch and boat harness*—Connect the meter black lead to the blue/white lead of the boat wiring harness. This will be pin D of the five-pin Amphenol connector (traditional harnesses) or pin A of the three-pin Deutsch connector (MWS systems).

6. Note the meter reading. The meter must indicate no continuity.

  a. *Testing switch only*—If not, replace the switch.

  b. *Testing switch and harness*—If not, start this procedure over and follow the *Testing switch only* steps. If the switch now tests satisfactorily, the boat harness is defective. Locate and repair the short circuit between the blue/white and red/white (or red/purple [or red]) leads in the boat harness.

7. Activate the trim and tilt switch in the UP direction. Note the meter reading. The meter must indicate continuity while the switch is held activated in the UP position.

  a. *Testing switch only*—If not, replace the switch.

  b. *Testing switch and harness*—If not, start this procedure over and follow the *Testing switch only* steps. If the switch now tests satisfactorily, the boat harness is defective. Locate and repair the open circuit in the blue/white or red/purple (or red/white [or red]) leads in the boat harness.

8A. *Testing switch only*—Move the meter black lead to the switch terminal that originally contained the green/white (or green) lead.

8B. *Testing switch and boat harness*—Move the meter black lead to the green/white lead of the *boat* wiring harness. This will be pin D of the five-pin Amphenol connector (traditional harnesses) or pin B of the three-pin Deutsch connector (MWS systems).

9. Note the meter reading. The meter must indicate no continuity.

  a. *Testing switch only*—If not, replace the switch.

  b. *Testing switch and harness*—If not, start this procedure over and follow the *Testing switch only* steps. If the switch now tests satisfactorily, the boat harness is defective. Locate and repair the short circuit between the green/white and red/purple (and/or red/white [and/or red]) leads in the boat harness.

10. Activate the trim and tilt switch in the DOWN direction. Note the meter reading. The meter must indicate continuity while the switch is held activated in the DOWN position.

  a. *Testing switch only*—If not, replace the switch.

  b. *Testing switch and harness*—If not, start this procedure over and follow the *Testing switch only* steps. If the switch now tests satisfactorily, the boat harness is defective. Locate and repair the open circuit in the green/white or red/purple (or red/white [or red]) leads in the boat harness.

11. Reconnect all leads and connectors when finished. Reconnect the negative battery cable last.

ELECTRIC MOTOR TESTING

Operating Amperage Draw Test (Single Ram Systems)

This procedure applies to the single ram trim and tilt system used on the 25-35 hp (three-cylinder) and 40-50 hp (two-cylinder) models. This test determines the time required for the system to cycle from full DOWN to full UP, then from full UP to full DOWN. The test also measures the amperage draw of the trim/tilt motor during full UP or full DOWN stall.

The outboard motor must not be running, and no external forces must be applied to it during this test. Refer to **Table 1** for all amperage specifications and **Table 2** for normal system cycle times.

A suitable stop watch and a DC ammeter capable of measuring up to 25 amps are necessary to perform the following procedure. The battery must be fully charged and in acceptable condition for the following test to be valid. Refer to Chapter Seven for battery information. Refer to the back of the manual for wiring diagrams.

NOTE
If a clamp-on or inductive ammeter is used, install the probe onto the relay bracket red lead and continue at Step 4.

1. Disconnect the negative battery cable from the battery.
2A. *25-35 hp (three-cylinder) models*—Install a conventional ammeter (25 amp recommended) as follows:
   a. Disconnect the red lead (that connects to the trim and tilt relay bracket) from the starter solenoid battery positive terminal. Then reinstall the nut to secure the battery cable and other engine harness red leads to the starter solenoid. See **Figure 28**.
   b. Connect an ammeter in series between the relay bracket red lead and the starter solenoid positive terminal. Hook the red lead of the ammeter to the starter solenoid positive terminal and the black lead of the ammeter to the relay bracket red lead.
   c. Make sure the connections are secure and insulated from any other leads or grounds.
2B. *40-50 hp (two-cylinder) models*—Install a conventional ammeter (25 amp, recommended) as follows:
   a. Disconnect the red lead (that connects to the trim and tilt relay bracket) from the terminal strip (on the starboard side of the engine). Then reinstall the screw to secure the other engine harness red leads to the terminal strip.
   b. Connect an ammeter in series between the relay bracket red lead and its corresponding engine harness red lead(s). Connect the red lead of the ammeter to the engine harness red lead(s) at the terminal strip and the black lead of the ammeter to the relay bracket red lead.
   c. Make sure the connections are secure and insulated from any other leads or grounds.
3. Reconnect the negative battery cable.
4. Operate the trim and tilt system through several full UP and DOWN cycles. Record the following:
   a. Note the time required to travel from the full UP to full DOWN positions and full DOWN to full UP positions. Compare your results to **Table 2**.
   b. Note the ammeter reading during a full UP stall (motor fully tilted UP and electric motor running) and during a full DOWN stall (motor fully trimmed DOWN and electric motor running). Compare your results to **Table 1**.
5. If the cycle times and amperage draw readings are within specification, and all hydraulic functions are normal, the system is operating correctly and testing is complete.

NOTE
If the tilt tube nut is over-tightened, the amperage draw readings and system cycle times will be excessive.

6. If the system cycle time (and/or the amperage draw) is excessive in one or both directions, loosen one tilt (steering) tube nut several turns. Retighten the nut to 40-45 ft.-lb. (54.2-61.0 N•m), then loosen the nut exactly 1/4 turn. Recheck the system cycle times.

7. If the amperage draw is excessive, remove the electric motor and perform the *No-Load Amperage Draw Test* as described in this chapter. If the no-load current draw is within specification, check the hydraulic pump for binding, blocked passages or plugged check valves.

8. If the current draw is below specification, remove the electric motor and perform the *No-Load Amperage Draw Test* as described in this chapter. If the no-load current draw is within specification, check the hydraulic system for a worn or damaged hydraulic pump, valves stuck open, broken valve springs or other internal leakage.

9. Disconnect the negative battery cable from the battery. Remove the ammeter and reconnect the relay bracket red lead to the starter solenoid battery positive terminal (25-35 hp) or to the terminal strip (40-50 hp). Tighten the fastener securely, then coat the connection with OMC Black Neoprene Dip.

10. Reconnect the negative battery cable when finished.

Operating Amperage Draw Test (Three-Ram Systems)

Specifications vary depending on the manufacturer and model of the electric motor. The motor is manufactured by either Prestolite, Bosch or Showa. Identify the motors by measuring the outer diameter of the motor' main housing and noting the exit location of the motor leads. Note that all motors are interchangeable as assemblies.
   a. *Prestolite*—The main housing is 3.0 in. (76.2 mm) in diameter. The motor leads exit from the top of the motor and pass through (and are secured by) a hollow retainer nut.
   b. *Bosch*—The main housing is 2.5 in. (63.5 mm) in diameter. The motor leads exit from the top of the motor through a molded rubber grommet.

10

c. *Showa*—The main housing is 3.0 in. (76.2 mm) in diameter. The motor leads exit from the top of the motor and are secured by a retainer plate, held by 2 screws.

d. *Showa*—The main housing is 2.4 in. (61 mm) in diameter. The motor leads exit from the side of the mounting flange end of the motor. The motor main housing is a single piece of stamped steel.

This procedure applies to conventional and FasTrak three-ram trim/tilt systems used on 50-70 hp (three-cylinder) models. This test determines the time required for the system to cycle from full DOWN to full UP, then from full UP to full DOWN. The test also measures the amperage draw of the trim/tilt motor during the following modes of operation:

1. Full UP and full DOWN stall (ram at end of travel, electric motor running).

2. Trimming UP and Tilting UP (conventional systems). The trim UP measurements are taken as the trim rams are extending and the tilt UP measurements are taken after the trim rams are fully extended and as the tilt cylinder is extending.

3. Trimming UP and Trimming IN (FasTrak systems). These measurements are only taken when the trim rams are extending (trimming UP) or retracting (trimming DOWN), but not in the Tilt UP or Tilt DOWN ranges (any point above full trim ram extension).

NOTE
*The trim range of both conventional and FasTrak systems is defined as the range that the trim rams remain in contact with the swivel bracket. Once the swivel bracket loses contact with the trim rams, the **tilt** range begins. The trim range on Conventional systems is approximately 15° and the trim range on FasTrak systems is approximately 21°.*

4. During the following test, the outboard motor must not be running and no external forces can be applied to it. Refer to **Table 1** for all amperage specifications and **Table 2** for normal system cycle times.

5. A suitable stop watch and a DC ammeter capable of measuring up to 50 amps (conventional systems) or 100 amps (FasTrak systems) are necessary to perform the following procedure. The battery must be fully charged and in acceptable condition for the following test to be valid. Refer to Chapter Seven for battery information. Refer to Chapter Fourteen for wiring diagrams.

NOTE
If a clamp-on or inductive ammeter is being used, install the probe onto the relay bracket red lead and continue at Step 4.

6. Disconnect the negative battery cable from the battery.

7. Install a conventional ammeter as follows:
   a. Disconnect the red lead that connects to the trim and tilt relay bracket from the starter solenoid battery positive terminal. Then reinstall the nut to secure the battery cable and other engine harness red leads to the starter solenoid. See **Figure 28**.
   b. Connect an ammeter in series between the relay bracket red lead and the starter solenoid positive terminal. Connect the red lead of the ammeter to the starter solenoid positive terminal and the black lead of the ammeter to the relay bracket red lead.
   c. Make sure the connections are secure and insulated from any other leads or grounds.

8. Reconnect the negative battery cable.

9A. *Conventional systems*—Operate the trim and tilt system through several full UP and DOWN cycles. Record the following:
   a. Note the time required to travel from the full UP to full DOWN positions and full DOWN to full UP positions. Compare your results to **Table 2**.
   b. Note the ammeter reading during a full UP stall (motor fully tilted UP and electric motor running) and during a full DOWN stall (motor fully trimmed DOWN and electric motor running). Compare your results to **Table 1**.
   c. Note the ammeter reading as the trim rams are extending (trimming out). Compare your results to **Table 1**.
   d. Note the ammeter reading as the unit is tilting out (after the swivel bracket breaks contact with the trim rams).

9B. *FasTrak systems*—Operate the trim and tilt system through several full UP and DOWN cycles. Record the following:
   a. Note the time required to travel from the full DOWN position to the full trim UP position (trim rams fully extended). Compare your results to **Table 2**.
   b. Note the time required to travel from the full trim UP position to the full DOWN position (point where the swivel bracket first contacts the trim rams [going down], until the rams are fully retracted). Compare your results to **Table 2**.
   c. Note the ammeter reading during a full UP stall and during a full DOWN stall. Compare your results to **Table 1**.

d. Note the ammeter reading as the trim rams are extending (trimming UP). Compare your results to **Table 1**.

e. Note the ammeter reading as the trim rams are retracting (trimming DOWN). Compare your results to **Table 1**.

10. If the cycle times and amperage draw are within specification, and all hydraulic functions are normal, the system is operating correctly and testing is complete.

NOTE
If the tilt tube nut is over-tightened, the amperage draw readings and system cycle times will be excessive.

11A. *Conventional systems*—If the system cycle time (and/or the amperage draw) is excessive in one or both

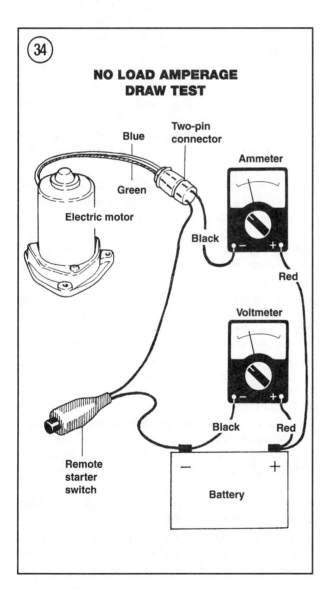

NO LOAD AMPERAGE DRAW TEST

Blue

Green

Two-pin connector

Ammeter

Electric motor

Black

Red

Voltmeter

Black   Red

Remote starter switch

Battery

directions, loosen one tilt (steering) tube nut several turns. Retighten the nut to 50-54 ft.-lb. (67.8-73.2 N•m), then loosen the nut 1/8-1/4 turn. Recheck the system cycle times.

11B. *FasTrak systems*—If the system cycle time (and/or the amperage draw reading) is excessive in one or both directions, loosen the starboard tilt (steering) tube nut several turns. Retighten the nut to 50-54 ft.-lb. (67.8-73.2 N•m), then loosen the nut 1/8-1/4 turn. Recheck the system cycle times.

12. If the amperage draw is excessive, remove the electric motor and perform the *No-Load Amperage Draw Test* as described later in this chapter. If the no-load current draw is within specification, check the hydraulic pump for binding, blocked passages or plugged check valves.

13. If the current draw is below specification, remove the electric motor and perform the *No-Load Amperage Draw Test* as described in this chapter. If the no-load current draw is within specification, check the hydraulic system for a worn or damaged hydraulic pump, valves stuck open, broken valve springs or other internal leakage.

14. Disconnect the negative battery cable from the battery. Remove the ammeter and reconnect the relay bracket red lead to the starter solenoid battery positive terminal. Tighten the nut securely, then coat the connection with OMC Black Neoprene Dip.

15. Reconnect the negative battery cable when finished.

10

No-Load Amperage Draw Test (All Systems)

The trim and tilt motor no-load amperage draw test is an indicator of trim and tilt motor condition. A clamp-on or inductive ammeter, if available, is simplest to use as no electrical connections are required. Make sure that the ammeter used can read higher than the highest anticipated amperage (**Table 1**).

The trim and tilt motor's speed must be measured during the no-load amperage draw test. A vibration tachometer, such as the Frahm Reed Tachometer can be used for this test. Simply hold the tachometer against the motor's frame while the motor is running to measure the speed. A stroboscopic tachometer may also be used, but remember to make a reference mark on the drive end of the armature shaft before beginning the test. Another option is to use a tachometer designed for model airplane engines, available from most hobby shops. This type of tachometer is simply held against the end of the armature shaft to measure the speed.

To perform the no-load amperage draw test, refer to **Figure 34** and proceed as follows:

1. Remove the electric motor from the trim and tilt system as described in this chapter. Securely fasten the motor in a soft-jawed vise or other suitable holding fixture. Do not damage the motor by crushing it in the vise.

2. Obtain a fully charged starting battery with a minimum rating of 360 cold cranking amps (CCA), 465 marine cranking amps (MCA) or 50 ampere-hours. The battery must be in good condition for the test results to be accurate.

3. Connect a suitable voltmeter to the battery terminals as shown in **Figure 34**.

CAUTION
*Make sure the ammeter used in the next step is of sufficient capacity to measure the expected amperage draw (**Table 1**) with an adequate safety margin. For example, if the expected amperage draw is 30 amps, use a 50 amp (or larger) ammeter.*

4A. *Conventional ammeter*—Using heavy gauge (10 gauge minimum) jumper leads or cables, connect a conventional ammeter in series with the positive battery terminal and the trim and tilt motor's blue terminal as shown in **Figure 34**. The ammeter's red lead (or positive terminal) must be connected to the battery's positive terminal and the ammeter's black lead (or negative terminal) must be connected to the electric motor's blue terminal.

4B. *Inductive or clamp-on ammeter*—Using heavy gauge battery cables or jumper cables, connect the positive battery terminal to the electric motor's blue lead. Then install the clamp-on or inductive ammeter over this cable.

NOTE
*A heavy-duty automotive remote starter switch can be used to make the connection between the negative battery terminal and the specified electric motor terminal. Make sure the switch is rated for more than the expected amperage draw (**Table 1**).*

5A. If a heavy duty remote starter switch is available, connect one switch lead to the negative battery terminal and the other switch lead to the electric motor's green lead as shown in **Figure 34**.

WARNING
*Make the last electrical connection to the specified electric motor terminal. Do **not** create any sparks at or near the battery or a serious explosion could occur.*

5B. If a heavy duty remote starter switch is not available, connect a heavy gauge (10 gauge minimum) jumper lead or cable to the negative battery terminal. Do not connect the other end of the jumper lead to the electric motor at this time.

NOTE
*The battery must maintain at least 12.0-12.4 volts during the test. If the voltage falls below this range, yet the current draw does not exceed specification (**Table 1**), the battery is defective or not of sufficient capacity for the test.*

6. When ready to perform the no-load test (in the UP direction), prepare a tachometer for the speed measurement, then depress the remote starter switch button or quickly and firmly connect the remaining cable to the electric motor green lead.
   a. Note the amperage and rpm readings.
   b. Verify the voltage range. The battery must maintain 12.0-12.4 volts during the test.
   c. Make sure the armature shaft rotates in a clockwise direction (as viewed from the drive end).
   d. Release the remote starter switch button or quickly disconnect the jumper lead from the electric motor green lead.

7. If the motor does not perform to specification (**Table 1**), the motor must be repaired (if repairable) or replaced.

8. If the motor rotates in the wrong direction, make sure the motor blue lead is receiving positive voltage and the motor green lead is receiving negative voltage. If polarity is correct and the motor rotates the wrong direction, replace the electric motor.

9. If the motor performs satisfactorily, continue to Step 10.

10. To test the electric motor in the DOWN direction, switch the leads at the electric motor so that the battery positive terminal (and ammeter) is connected to the electric motor *green* lead and the negative battery terminal and remote starter switch (or jumper lead) is connected to the electric motor *blue* lead.

11. When ready to perform the no-load test (in the DOWN direction), prepare a tachometer for the speed measurement, then depress the remote starter switch button or quickly and firmly connect the jumper lead (from the negative battery terminal) to the electric motor blue lead.
   a. Note the amperage and speed readings.
   b. Verify the voltage range. The battery must maintain 12.0-12.4 volts during the test.
   c. Make sure the armature shaft rotates in a counter-clockwise direction (as viewed from the drive end).
   d. Release the remote starter switch button (or quickly disconnect the jumper lead from the electric motor blue lead).

12. If the motor does not perform to specification (**Table 1**), the motor must be repaired or replaced.

13. If the motor rotates in the wrong direction, make sure the motor green lead is receiving positive voltage and the motor blue lead is receiving negative voltage. If polarity is

correct and the motor rotates the wrong direction, replace the electric motor.

Electrical Troubleshooting
(Trim Gauge and Sending Unit)

The trim gauge functions as a simple ohmmeter and reads the varying resistance of the trim gauge sending unit. When the sending unit resistance is high, the gauge indicates DOWN. When the sending unit resistance is low, the gauge indicates UP.

The trim gauge receives switched battery voltage from the ignition (key) switch through the purple lead. The trim gauge is grounded at all times by the black lead. The blue lead is for lighting the gauge for night operation and does not affect gauge operation.

Refer to the back of the manual for specific wiring diagrams for your engine. To troubleshoot the trim gauge and sending unit circuits, refer to **Figure 35** and proceed as follows:

1. Disconnect and ground the spark plug leads to the power head to prevent accidental starting.

2. Verify that the starter system will crank the engine normally. If not, refer to Chapter Three and troubleshoot the starting system. The starting system must be functioning correctly for this procedure to be accurate.

3. Verify that the I (ignition) terminal on the back of the trim gauge (E, **Figure 35**) is receiving within one volt of battery voltage whenever the ignition (key) switch is in the ON or RUN position. If not, repair or replace the purple lead between the ignition switch and the trim gauge, or replace the defective ignition switch.

4. Verify that the G (ground) terminal on the back of the trim gauge (**Figure 35**) is connected to a good ground. Connect a voltmeter's red lead to the positive battery terminal and the voltmeter's black lead to the gauge's *G* terminal. The meter must indicate within one volt of battery voltage. If not, repair or replace the black (ground) lead between the trim gauge and the negative battery terminal.

5. Disconnect the white/tan lead from the S (sending unit) terminal on the back of the gauge (**Figure 35**). Turn the ignition switch to the ON or RUN position and observe the gauge. The gauge must indicate full DOWN. If not, replace the trim gauge.

6. With the ignition switch in the ON or RUN position, connect a suitable jumper lead between the S (sending unit) and G (ground) terminals on the back of the gauge. Observe the gauge. The gauge must indicate full UP. If not, replace the trim gauge.

7. Turn the ignition switch to the OFF or STOP position and reconnect the white/tan lead to the S terminal on the back of the gauge.

NOTE
On 40 and 50 hp (two-cylinder) models equipped with the traditional wiring harness the black/tan leads (pin C) must be connected with a suitable Amphenol jumper lead in Step 8A, or the remainder of this test procedure will produce inaccurate results. The black/tan lead provides the ground circuit for the trim gauge.

8A. *40 and 50 hp (two-cylinder) models*—Disconnect the sending unit tan/white lead from the boat harness by separating the five-pin Amphenol connector (Traditional harness) or three-pin Deutsch connector (MWS harness [**Figure 35**]). On a traditional harness, connect an Amphenol jumper lead between the connector bodies so that the black/tan lead (pin C) is connected, but not any other leads.

8B. *25-70 hp (three-cylinder) models*—Disconnect the sending unit tan/white lead from the sending unit's one or two-pin Amphenol connector (**Figure 35**, typical).

9. Turn the ignition switch to the ON or RUN position. The trim gauge must indicate full DOWN. If not, a short circuit exists between the white/tan lead and engine ground. This can be a direct short to metal anywhere on the power head or an internal short circuit between a black (or black/tan) lead and the white/tan lead. Repair or replace the white/tan lead between the trim sending unit connector and the trim gauge *S* terminal.

10A. *25 and 35 hp (three-cylinder) models*—With the ignition switch in the ON or RUN position, connect the engine harness side of the white/tan lead to a good engine ground using a suitable jumper lead. The trim gauge must indicate full UP. If not, an open circuit is present in the white/tan lead between the trim gauge *S* terminal and the one-pin Amphenol connector. Repair or replace the white/tan lead as necessary.

10B. *40 and 50 hp (two-cylinder) models*—With the ignition switch in the ON or RUN position, connect the boat harness side of the white/tan lead to a good engine ground using a suitable jumper lead. The trim gauge must indicate full UP. If not, an open circuit is present in the white/tan lead between the trim gauge *S* terminal and the five-pin Amphenol or three-pin Deutsch connector. Repair or replace the white/tan lead as necessary.

10

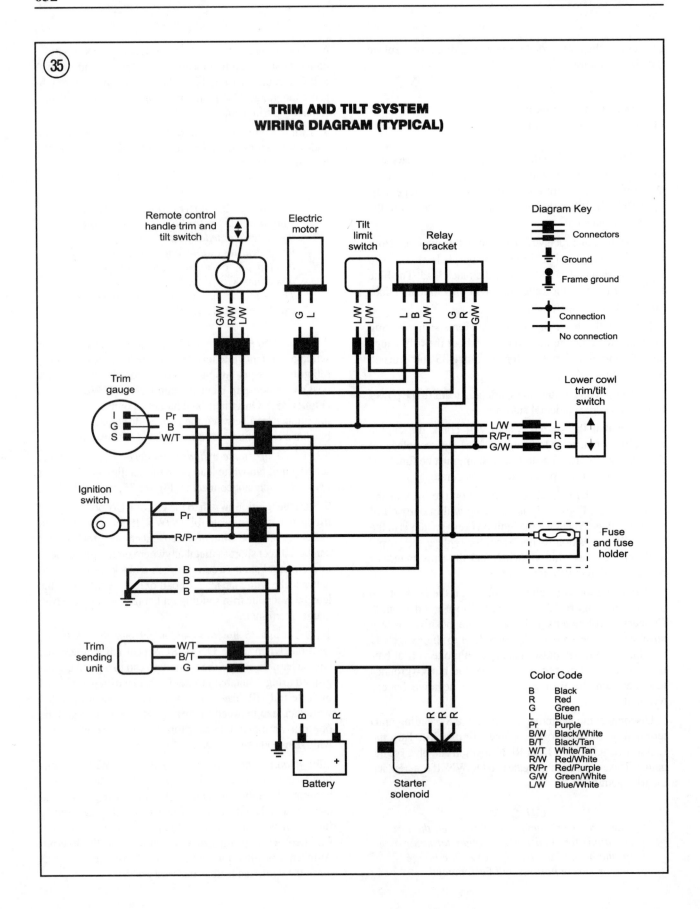

35

TRIM AND TILT SYSTEM
WIRING DIAGRAM (TYPICAL)

Remote control handle trim and tilt switch

Electric motor

Tilt limit switch

Relay bracket

Diagram Key

Connectors

Ground

Frame ground

Connection

No connection

Trim gauge

Lower cowl trim/tilt switch

Ignition switch

Fuse and fuse holder

Trim sending unit

Battery

Starter solenoid

Color Code

B	Black
R	Red
G	Green
L	Blue
Pr	Purple
B/W	Black/White
B/T	Black/Tan
W/T	White/Tan
R/W	Red/White
R/Pr	Red/Purple
G/W	Green/White
L/W	Blue/White

10C. *50-70 hp (three-cylinder) models*—With the ignition switch in the ON or RUN position, proceed as follows:

    a. Using a suitable jumper lead, connect the white/tan lead (pin A) to the black/tan lead (pin B) on the engine harness side of the trim sending unit Amphenol connector (**Figure 35**).

    b. The gauge must indicate full UP. If not, an open circuit is present in the white/tan or black/tan leads. Proceed to substep c.

    c. Connect a suitable jumper lead between the white/tan lead (pin A) and a good engine ground. If the trim gauge now indicates full UP, an open circuit is present in the black/tan lead. Repair or replace the black/tan lead between the trim sending unit two-pin Amphenol connector and its power head ground terminal. If the gauge still does not indicate full UP, proceed to substep d.

    d. If the trim gauge still does not indicate full UP at this time, an open circuit is present in the white/tan lead between the trim gauge *S* terminal and the sending unit two-pin Amphenol connector. Repair or replace the white/tan lead as necessary.

11. If all tests are satisfactory to this point, test the trim sending unit as described in the next section.

12. Reconnect all leads and connectors when finished. Reconnect the spark plug leads last.

Trim Sending Unit Test

The trim sending unit is a variable resistor. The resistance must change smoothly as the engine is tilted and trimmed. If the resistance jumps or is erratic at any point in the tilt or trim range, the sender is defective and must be replaced.

The white/tan lead provides the signal for the trim gauge. All other leads (black, black/tan and/or green) are connected to ground by one of the sending unit mounting screws, a power head ground terminal or an engine harness connector.

1. Tilt the outboard motor to the full UP position. Engage the tilt lock, support the gearcase with a hoist or block the gearcase to eliminate any possibility of it falling during this procedure.

2. Make sure that the ground lead (if equipped) is securely fastened under one of the trim sending unit mounting screws. Make sure the screw and ground lead terminal are not loose, corroded or damaged. Correct any defects noted.

3. Trace the sending unit lead(s) into the motor's lower cowl and to the sending unit connector. Separate the connector and inspect the connector for loose, corroded or damaged pins. Check the connector body for pins that have

backed out of the connector body. Finally, check for broken or damaged leads on both sides of the connector bodies.

4. If equipped with a power head ground lead(s), make sure that each ground lead is securely fastened to the power head and that each lead's ring terminal is not loose, corroded or damaged. Correct any defects noted.

5. Disengage the tilt lock, remove the hoist or blocks and trim the motor to its fully DOWN position.

6. Calibrate an ohmmeter on the appropriate scale to read between 0-100 ohms (typically R × 1).

7A. *25 and 35 hp (three-cylinder) models*—Using suitable jumper leads, connect the meter red lead to the white/tan lead at the trim sending unit one-pin Amphenol connector. Then connect the meter black lead to a good engine ground.

7B. *40 and 50 hp (two-cylinder) models*—Using suitable jumper leads, connect the meter red lead to the sending unit's white/tan lead at the five-pin Amphenol (pin B [traditional harness]) or three-pin Deutsch (pin C [MWS harness]) connector. Then connect the meter black lead to a good engine ground.

7C. *50-70 hp (three-cylinder) models*—Using suitable jumper leads, connect the meter red lead to the white/tan (pin A) lead of the trim sending unit two-pin Amphenol connector and the meter black lead to the black lead (pin B) of the same connector.

8. Note the meter reading. With the motor trimmed fully DOWN, the meter must read a minimum of 80 ohms.

9. Tilt the motor to the fully UP position while noting the meter reading. The meter must indicate a smooth decrease in resistance as the motor is tilting and must read a maximum of 10 ohms when the outboard reaches the full UP position.

NOTE
*If the resistance readings change smoothly, but the readings are too high or too low at the full UP **and** full DOWN positions, loosen the trim sending unit mounting screws and position the sending unit in the middle of its adjustment slots. Retighten the mounting screws securely and repeat Steps 8-9.*

10. Replace the trim sending unit if it does not perform as specified, or if the resistance does not change smoothly as the outboard is tilted (and trimmed) UP and DOWN.

11. Reconnect all leads when finished. Refer to *Trim Sending Unit Adjustment* in this chapter.

POWER TRIM AND
TILT SYSTEM SERVICE

Single Ram System

Removal/installation

1. Tilt the outboard motor to the full UP position. Engage the tilt lock, support the gearcase with a hoist or block the gearcase to eliminate any possibility of it falling during this procedure.

2. Disconnect the electric motor leads as follows:
   a. Separate the large two-pin connector (blue and green leads). Remove and discard the O-ring from the connector body on the electric motor side.
   b. Note the routing of the leads and the position of any clamps and tie-straps. Then remove any clamps and tie-straps securing the leads and pull the leads free from the power head.
   c. Carefully remove the rubber grommet from the rear of the connector body. Note the location of the blue and green leads in the connector body.
   d. Using a pocket screwdriver (or equivalent tool), depress the tab locking each terminal in the connector body, then pull each terminal (and lead) from the connector body.
   e. Pull the leads through the hole in the stern bracket.

3. Remove the locking clip from the upper pivot pin. See **Figure 36**, typical. Install thread adaptor (part No. 340924) into the threaded end of tilt pin. Attach a suitable slide hammer to the thread adaptor and pull the pin from the swivel bracket.

4. Note the position of the lower mounting through-bolt in the stern bracket holes. Then remove the 3/4 in. locknut from one end of the through-bolt. Push the bolt from the stern brackets and power trim and tilt unit. Do not damage the threaded ends of the through-bolt.

5. Pull the trim and tilt unit far enough from the stern brackets to access the ground strap secured under one of the electric motor mounting screws. See 3, **Figure 37**. Remove the ground strap from the electric motor, then reinstall the screw and washer to prevent misplacement.

6. Remove the power trim and tilt unit from the stern brackets and place it on a clean workbench.

7. Remove the two bushings from the cylinder rod eye and the two bushings from the bottom of the cylinder and manifold assembly.

NOTE
Use OMC Triple Guard Grease for all grease applications.

8. To install the power trim and tilt unit, begin by greasing the four bushings. Install the two shorter bushings into the cylinder rod eye and the two longer bushings into the bottom of the cylinder and manifold assembly.

9. Remove the ground strap screw and washer from the electric motor. Position the unit close enough to the stern brackets to connect the ground strap to the electric motor. Secure the ground strap with the screw and washer. Tighten the screw to 35-52 in.-lb. (4.0-5.9 N•m).

10. Position the power trim and tilt unit fully into the stern brackets.

11. Grease the lower mounting bolt. Align the bolt holes (as noted on removal), then install the lower mounting through-bolt into the stern brackets and through the power trim and tilt unit.

12. Coat the threads of the lower mounting bolt with OMC Gasket Sealing Compound. Install the locknut and tighten it to 20-25 ft.-lb. (27.1-33.9 N•m).

13. Grease the upper pivot pin. Align the cylinder rod eye with the swivel bracket bore, then install the pin. Secure the pin by installing the locking clip (**Figure 36**, typical).

14. Route the electric motor leads through the hole in the stern bracket and into the lower cowl. Clamp and/or tie-strap the leads as noted on removal.

15. Insert each terminal (and lead) into the large two-pin connector body. Make sure the leads are reinstalled in their original location. The blue lead must connect to blue and the green lead must connect to green. Make sure each terminal locks into place.

16. Once the terminals are locked in place, push the grommet into the rear of the connector body. Grease a new O-ring and install it into the connector body's groove.

17. Connect the large two-pin connector to its engine harness mate. Make sure the bodies are locked together.

18. Release the tilt lock, remove the hoist or remove the blocks. Refer to *Maintenance* in this chapter, and perform the *Reservoir fluid check*.

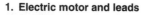

SINGLE RAM SYSTEM

1. Electric motor and leads
2. Screw and washer
3. Ground lead to stern bracket
4. O-ring
5. Pump drive coupler
6. Filter
7. Screw and washer
8. Pump assembly
9. O-rings
10. Upper pivot pin bushing
11. Rod and eye
12. Wiper ring
13. Backup ring
14. Seal
15. End cap
16. O-ring
17. Washer
18. Piston and valve assembly
19. Backup rings
20. Quad ring
21. Rod-to-piston seal
22. Washer
23. Nut
24. Pipe plug
25. Down relief valve spring
26. Down relief valve ball guide
27. Down relief valve check ball
28. Filter
29. Fill plug and O-ring
30. Retaining ring
31. Large O-ring
32. Manual release/thermal expansion valve
33. Small O-ring
34. Valve cap
35. Valve cap O-ring
36. Spring
37. Valve core
38. Valve seat
39. Valve seat O-ring
40. UP check valve assembly
41. Pump control piston
42. DOWN check valve assembly
43. Cylinder and manifold assembly
44. Filter
45. Check ball
46. Filter valve assembly
47. Lower mounting bolt bushing

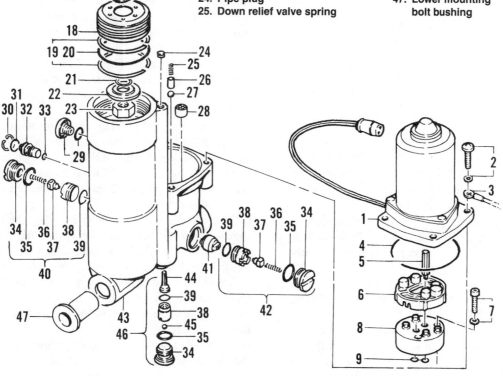

10

Electric motor removal/installation

Refer to **Figure 37** for this procedure. Lubricate all internal components with OMC Power Trim/Tilt and Steering Fluid or Dexron II automatic transmission fluid.

1. Remove the power trim and tilt unit as described in the previous section.

2. Open the manual release valve until it just contacts its retaining ring. If the cylinder ram is not fully extended, pull the ram until it is in the full UP position.

3. Cover the reservoir fill plug with a shop towel and slowly remove the fill plug, allowing any internal pressure (and fluid) to vent before fully removing the plug.

4. Reinstall the fill plug and close the manual release valve to prevent fluid loss and contamination.

NOTE
Use caution during system disassembly, as there still may be residual pressure in the system. During disassembly, cover each component with a shop towel and slowly loosen the component and/or its fasteners, allowing any internal pressure (and fluid) to vent before fully removing the component.

5. Remove the four screws securing the motor to the cylinder and manifold assembly.

6. Remove the motor from the manifold. Remove and discard the motor O-ring (4, **Figure 37**). Locate and secure the pump drive coupler (5).

7. Remove the filter (6, **Figure 37**) from the top of the hydraulic pump. Clean the filter in a mild solvent (such as mineral spirits). If the filter cannot be satisfactorily cleaned, discard it.

8. To install the electric motor, begin by installing the filter over the hydraulic pump. Then insert the pump drive coupler into the hydraulic pump.

9. Prime the hydraulic pump as follows:
   a. Fill the hydraulic pump cavity with the recommended trim and tilt fluid until it is flush with the electric motor mounting deck (the pump is submerged).
   b. Rotate the pump drive coupler back and forth until all air bubbles are eliminated. If no resistance is felt, the pump is air-locked.
   c. If the pump is air-locked, remove the filter and depress the two check balls in the openings in the top of the pump. Then rotate the drive shaft again. A noticeable increase in effort will occur when the pump begins drawing fluid. Reinstall the filter once the pump is primed.
   d. Add fluid as necessary to keep the pump submerged.

10. Once the pump is primed, install a new O-ring onto the electric motor. Lubricate the O-ring with the trim and tilt fluid.

11. Position the motor on the cylinder and manifold assembly. Rotate the motor as necessary to engage the pump drive coupler, then seat the motor on the cylinder and manifold assembly. Make sure the O-ring is not displaced during assembly.

12. Secure the motor with four screws (and washers). Evenly tighten the screws to 35-52 in.-lb. (4.0-5.9 N•m).

13. Install the power trim and tilt unit as described in the previous section.

Hydraulic pump removal/installation

The hydraulic pump is serviced only as an assembly. Do not attempt to disassemble and reassemble the pump. If the pump is to be reused, it must be washed *only* in clean trim and tilt fluid. Replace any O-ring that has been removed.

Refer to **Figure 37** for this procedure. Lubricate all internal components with OMC Power Trim/Tilt and Steering Fluid or Dexron II automatic transmission fluid.

1. Remove the electric motor as described in the previous section.

2. Remove the three Allen head screws (and lockwashers) securing the pump to the cylinder and manifold assembly.

3. Carefully lift the pump from the manifold bore. Remove and discard the two O-rings (9, **Figure 37**) sealing the pump to the manifold.

4. Remove the filter (28, **Figure 37**) from its bore (located under the pump). Clean the filter in a mild solvent (such as mineral spirits). If the filter cannot be satisfactorily cleaned, discard it.

5. Remove the DOWN relief valve components (25-27, **Figure 37**) from their bore (located under the pump). Clean the components in a mild solvent, then inspect the components for damage, wear or debris. Make sure the check ball seat in the manifold bore is free of contamination or other debris.

6. To install the pump, begin by installing the filter (28, **Figure 37**) into its bore. The filter bore is the bore farthest away from the tilt cylinder. Push the filter into its bore until it is flush with the pump mounting surface.

7. Install the DOWN relief valve check ball, ball guide (open end facing up) and check valve spring into their bore (in that order). The relief valve bore is the bore closest to the tilt cylinder.

8. Install two new pump O-rings (9, **Figure 37**) into their recesses in the pump mounting surface.

9. Carefully position the pump into the manifold bore, being careful not to displace either of the O-rings. Make sure the mounting screw holes are aligned, then seat the pump into the bore.

10. Install the three Allen head screws (and washers). Tighten the screws finger-tight, then *evenly* tighten the screws to 25-30 in.-lb. (2.8-3.4 N•m) in a minimum of three progressive stages. The pump must be pulled evenly against the manifold or it will be damaged.

11. Install the electric motor as described in the previous section.

Cylinder and manifold disassembly

Refer to **Figure 37** for this procedure.

1. Remove the manual release valve's retaining ring with a suitable pair of internal snap ring pliers. Then remove the manual release valve from the manifold. Remove and discard the 2 O-rings from the valve body.

2. Remove the UP check valve assembly (40, **Figure 37**) as follows:
    a. Remove the valve cap (next to the manual release valve bore) using a drag link socket (or equivalent). Remove and discard the cap's O-ring.
    b. Carefully remove the spring, valve core and valve seat from the manifold bore. Then remove and discard the valve seat's O-ring.

3. Remove the DOWN check valve assembly (42, **Figure 37**) as follows:
    a. Remove the valve cap (on the opposing end of the UP check valve's bore) using a drag link socket or large screwdriver. Remove and discard the cap's O-ring.
    b. Carefully remove the spring, valve core and valve seat from the manifold bore. Then remove and discard the valve seat's O-ring.

4. Remove the pump control piston (41, **Figure 37**) from either end of the UP and DOWN check valves bore.

5. Remove the filter valve assembly (46, **Figure 37**) as follows:
    a. Remove the valve cap with a suitable Allen wrench. Remove and discard the cap's O-ring.
    b. Remove the check ball, valve seat and filter from the manifold bore. Remove and discard the valve seat's O-ring.
    c. Clean the filter in a mild solvent (such as mineral spirits). If the filter cannot be satisfactorily cleaned, discard it.

6. If the fill plug (29, **Figure 37**) has not yet been removed, remove the fill plug and discard its O-ring.

7. Remove the cylinder end cap (15, **Figure 37**) with a suitable spanner wrench, such as part No. 912084. Once the end cap is completely unthreaded from the cylinder, pull the rod, end cap and piston assembly from the cylinder bore.

8. Clamp the rod eye in a soft-jawed vise with the piston end facing straight up. Then carefully remove the nut (23, **Figure 37**) from the rod.

9. Lift the washer (22, **Figure 37**) off of the piston. Locate the raised mark cast into the piston, then remove the spring and valve from that bore. This is the UP relief valve. It must be reinstalled in its original bore with its original spring. Place the valve components in a plastic bag that is properly marked.

10. Remove the remaining five springs, spring guides and check balls from the piston. These components make up the impact relief valves. The impact relief valves (check balls, guides and springs) must be installed in the five holes not identified by the raised cast mark. Place these valve components in a plastic bag that is properly marked.

11. Slide the piston from the rod. Remove and discard the piston-to-rod seal (21, **Figure 37**), then remove and discard the quad ring (20) and two backup rings (19) from the groove on the piston's outer diameter.

12. Slide the washer (17, **Figure 37**) from the rod. Then slide the end cap from the rod. Remove and discard the end cap's external O-ring (16).

13. Carefully pry the scraper (12, **Figure 37**) from the end cap. Discard the scraper. Then pull the backup ring and seal (13 and 14) from the end cap bore using a suitable hooked tool. Discard the seal and backup ring.

14. Clean and inspect all components as described in the next section.

Cylinder and manifold cleaning and inspection

Use lint-free shop towels to handle all clean components. Even a single strand of lint can cause a check ball or valve not to seat. Leaking valves will cause hydraulic malfunctions.

> *NOTE*
> *Do not attempt to blow dry small components (such as check balls and springs). They are easily lost.*

1. Wash all components in a mild solvent, such as mineral spirits. Blow the larger parts dry with compressed air. Allow the smaller components to air dry on a clean shop towel.

2. Inspect the cylinder bore for corrosion, scoring and grooving. Very light (superficial) scuffing is acceptable. Inspect the cylinder bore threads for corroded, worn, damaged, missing or galled threads.

3. Inspect the manual release valve, filter valve and the UP and DOWN check valve bores for scoring, scratches, nicks, grooves or corrosion damage that will affect their

10

sealing. Make sure the manual release valve threads in the manifold are not damaged, corroded, worn or galled.

4. Inspect all valve cores, check balls and valve seats for wear, corrosion or damage that will affect their sealing. Replace all worn or damaged components.

5. Inspect the UP and DOWN check valve springs. Replace the springs if they are corroded, damaged or collapsed.

6. Inspect the piston (18, **Figure 37**) for wear, scratches or grooves on its outer diameter. Inspect each of the six valve seats in the piston for wear, indentations, debris or any other damage that will affect their sealing ability.

7. Inspect the impact relief valve and UP relief valve components for wear, corrosion, mechanical damage and collapsed or distorted springs.

8. Inspect the cylinder rod for wear, scoring, grooving or any other damage that will affect its ability to seal to the end cap. Remove all threadlocking adhesive from the rod's threads.

9. Inspect the end cap threads for corroded, worn, damaged, missing or galled threads. Inspect the end cap's seal and scraper bores for nicks and gouges that will prevent sealing.

10. Inspect the O-ring groove(s) in all components for nicks, gouges, wear, corrosion or any damage that would prevent sealing.

11. Replace all damaged or worn components.

Cylinder and manifold assembly

Refer to **Figure 37** for this procedure. Install new O-rings and seals during the assembly procedure. Do not make any dry assemblies. Lubricate all internal components with OMC Power Trim/Tilt and Steering Fluid or Dexron II automatic transmission fluid. Do not use any type of grease on any internal components.

NOTE
Cleanliness is the greatest concern during assembly. Do not allow any dirt, debris, lint or any other foreign substance into the cylinder and manifold during the assembly procedure. The system cannot function properly if it is contaminated.

1. Refer to **Figure 38** and assemble the end cap as follows:
   a. Lubricate and install a new backup ring (2, **Figure 38**) into the end cap's internal groove. Install the ring from the upper (outer) side of the end cap. Make sure the ring is fully expanded into the groove.
   b. Lubricate and install a new seal (1, **Figure 38**) into the end cap's internal groove. Install the seal from the lower (inner) side of the end cap. Make sure the seal's lip is facing down (into the cylinder bore) and

that the seal is installed below the backup ring as shown in **Figure 38**.
   c. Lubricate a new scraper (3, **Figure 38**) and install it into the end cap's external bore with the lip facing up (away from the cylinder). Press the scraper into the end cap until it is seated.
   d. Lubricate a new O-ring (4, **Figure 38**) and install it into the end cap's external groove.

2. Clamp the eye end of the rod (11, **Figure 37**) into a soft-jawed vise. The threaded end of the rod must face straight up. Lubricate the rod, then carefully slide the end cap over the rod, being careful not to damage the end cap seals on the rod's threads. The threaded end of the end cap must face the threaded end of the rod.

3. Slide the washer (17, **Figure 37**) over the rod and against the shoulder. Then slide the piston (18, **Figure 37**) over the threaded end of the rod and up against the washer (17, **Figure 37**). The side of the piston with the larger valve openings must face up (toward the threaded end of the rod).

4. Lubricate a new piston-to-rod seal (21, **Figure 37**) and install it over the threaded end of the rod and against the piston.

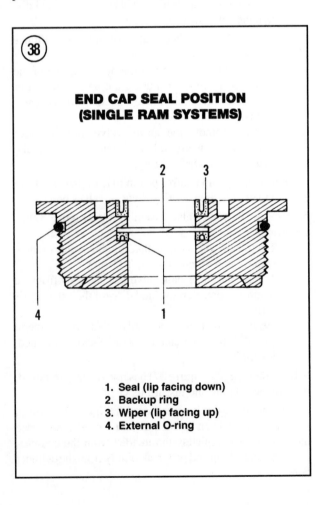

38

**END CAP SEAL POSITION
(SINGLE RAM SYSTEMS)**

1. Seal (lip facing down)
2. Backup ring
3. Wiper (lip facing up)
4. External O-ring

5. Locate the valve opening with the cast raised mark. Install the UP relief valve, then its spring, into this bore. The tip of the relief valve must protrude through the piston.

6. Install the five impact relief check balls, spring guides (small end facing up) and springs (in that order) into the five remaining bores in the piston.

7. Position the washer (22, **Figure 37**) over the threaded end of the rod (with the stepped side facing the piston) and against the springs. Lightly coat the rod threads with OMC Nut Lock threadlocking adhesive, then install and tighten the nut (23, **Figure 37**) to 35-54 ft.-lb. (47.5-73.2 N•m).

8. Lubricate a new quad ring (20, **Figure 37**) and install it into the groove in the outer diameter of the piston. Then position a new backup ring (19, **Figure 37**) on each side of the quad ring. The open ends of the backup rings must be staggered 180° from each other.

NOTE
If the backup rings do not fit tightly against the bottom of the piston groove, hold the ring(s) in your hand and overlap the ends of the ring, temporarily reducing the diameter of the ring. Reduce diameter until the ring is approximately 75 percent of the piston diameter. Hold the ring in this position for a few minutes and allow it to take a set. Then carefully install the ring into the piston groove, being careful not to expand it further than necessary.

9. Carefully clamp the cylinder and manifold assembly in a soft-jawed vise. Do not damage or crush the assembly. The open cylinder bore must face straight up.

10. Lubricate the cylinder bore and piston liberally. Carefully insert the piston and rod assembly into the bore. Be careful not to catch either of the backup rings between the piston and cylinder bore. Once the tapered edge of the cylinder wall is reached, apply a steady downward pressure to the rod eye, while wiggling the eye in a circular motion. Be patient and allow the O-ring and backup rings to work past the taper and into the cylinder bore.

11. Once past the tapered wall, push the piston as far as possible into the bore while still allowing enough space between the end cap and cylinder to fill the cylinder with fluid. Then thread the end cap into the cylinder bore 2-3 turns. Do not tighten the end cap at this time.

12. Install the manual release valve as follows:
  a. Lubricate new O-rings and install them into the grooves in the manual release valve body.
  b. Install the valve into the manifold and tighten it to 45-55 in.-lb. (5.1-6.2 N•m).
  c. Install the retaining ring (30, **Figure 37**) using a suitable pair of internal snap ring pliers. Make sure the ring has fully expanded into its groove.

13. Lubricate the pump control piston (41, **Figure 37**) into the UP or DOWN check valve bore. Center the piston in the bore.

14. Install the DOWN check valve assembly (42, **Figure 37**) as follows:
  a. Lubricate a new O-ring and install it into the valve seat's groove.
  b. Install the valve seat into its bore (on the side of the manifold opposite the manual release valve) with the notched side facing out.
  c. Carefully install the valve core, then the spring into the manifold bore and into the valve seat.
  d. Lubricate a new O-ring and install it into the valve cap's groove.
  e. Install the valve cap into the manifold bore and tighten it to 50-60 in.-lb. (5.7-6.8 N•m).

15. Install the UP check valve assembly (40, **Figure 37**) as follows:
  a. Lubricate a new O-ring and install it into the valve seat's groove.
  b. Install the valve seat into its bore (next to the manual release valve) with the notched side facing out.
  c. Carefully install the valve core, then the spring into the manifold bore and into the valve seat.
  d. Lubricate a new O-ring and install it into the valve cap's groove.
  e. Install the valve cap into the manifold bore and tighten it to 50-60 in.-lb. (5.7-6.8 N•m).

16. Install the filter valve assembly (46, **Figure 37**) as follows:
  a. Position the cylinder and manifold assembly so that the piston rod eye is pointing straight down.
  b. Install the filter into its bore.
  c. Lubricate and install a new O-ring into the valve seat's groove. Then install the valve seat into the bore with the notched side facing out. Drop the check ball into the valve seat.
  d. Lubricate and install a new O-ring into the valve cap. Then install and tighten the valve cap using a suitable Allen wrench to 70-105 in.-lb. (7.9-11.9 N•m).

17. Clamp the cylinder and manifold assembly in a soft-jawed vise so that the rod's eye is pointing straight up. Unthread the end cap (15, **Figure 37**) and fill the cylinder bore with trim and tilt fluid until the fluid is level with the bottom of the threaded area at the top of the cylinder bore.

18. Thread the end cap into the cylinder bore as far as possible by hand, then tighten the end cap to 56-84 ft.-lb. (75.9-113.9 N•m) using a suitable spanner wrench, such as part No. 912084.

19. Install the hydraulic pump, then the electric motor, as described in this chapter.

10

Conventional System

System removal/installation

1. Note the position of the trim limit rod, then remove the rod from the stern brackets.

2. Tilt the outboard motor to the full UP position and engage the tilt lock, support the gearcase with a hoist or block the gearcase to eliminate any possibility of it falling during this procedure.

3. Remove the locking clip from the upper pivot pin. See **Figure 39**, typical. Push the pivot pin from the swivel bracket and tilt cylinder eye.

4. Operate the power trim and tilt unit in the DOWN direction until the tilt cylinder and both trim rams are completely retracted. If the unit will not operate, open the manual release valve (as described in this chapter) and manually retract the tilt cylinder ram. The trim rams cannot be retracted manually.

5. If the unit is to be disassembled, relieve the system's internal pressure as follows:
   a. Briefly bump the trim switch up, then down, then up again. The motor must run briefly in each direction, as specified. This will help relieve internal pressure.
   b. Open the manual release valve until it just contacts its retaining ring.
   c. Cover the reservoir fill plug with a shop towel and carefully and slowly remove the fill plug, allowing any internal pressure (and fluid) to vent before fully removing the plug. It is normal for fluid to vent from the reservoir.
   d. Reinstall the fill plug and close the manual release valve to prevent fluid loss and contamination.

6. Disconnect the electric motor leads as follows:
   a. Separate the large two-pin connector. Remove and discard the O-ring from the connector body on the electric motor side of the connector.
   b. Note the routing of the leads and the position of any clamps and tie-straps. Then remove any clamps and tie-straps securing the leads and pull the leads free from the power head.
   c. Carefully remove the rubber grommet from the rear of the connector body (on the electric motor side). Note the location of the blue and green leads in the connector body.
   d. Using a small screwdriver (or equivalent tool), depress the tab locking each terminal into the connector body, then pull each terminal and lead from the connector body.

7. Remove the six screws (and washers) securing the power trim and tilt unit to the stern brackets. There are three screws on each side of the unit, all located in the lower half of each stern bracket.

8. Pivot the power trim and tilt unit rearward and out of the stern brackets, top first. Pull the electric leads from the hole in the stern brackets as the unit is removed. Place the unit on a clean workbench or mount it in a suitable holding fixture.

9. Remove the two bushings from the tilt cylinder rod eye.

NOTE
Use OMC Triple Guard Grease for all grease applications.

10. To install the power trim and tilt unit, begin by greasing the two rod eye bushings and installing them into the tilt cylinder rod eye.

11. Position the trim and tilt unit into the stern bracket. Insert the bottom of the unit first, then rotate the top of the unit into the stern brackets. Route the electrical leads through the hole in the stern bracket before the unit fully enters the stern brackets.

12. Coat the threads of the six mounting screws with OMC Nut Lock Threadlocking adhesive. Align the screw holes, then install the screws and washers. Evenly tighten the screws to 18-20 ft.-lb. (24.4-27.1 N•m).

13. Install the trim limit rod into the set of stern bracket holes noted on removal.

14. Route the electric motor leads into the lower cowl. Clamp and/or tie-strap the leads as noted on removal. Reconnect the leads as follows:
   a. Insert each terminal into the large two-pin connector body. Make sure the leads are reinstalled in their original location. The blue lead must connect to blue and the green lead must connect to green.
   b. Make sure each terminal locks into place.
   c. Once the terminals are locked in place, push the grommet into the rear of the connector body.
   d. Grease a new O-ring and install it into the connector body's groove.

15. Connect the large two-pin connector to its engine harness mate. Make sure the bodies are locked together.

16. If the manual release valve is open, turn it clockwise until it is closed, then tighten it to 45-55 in.-lb. (5.1-6.2 N•m).

17. Carefully operate the unit in the UP direction until the tilt cylinder rod eye is aligned with its hole in the swivel bracket.

18. Grease the upper pivot pin. Align the cylinder rod eye with the swivel bracket bore, then install the pin. Secure the pin by installing the locking clip (**Figure 39**, typical).

19. Release the tilt lock, remove the hoist, or remove the blocks. Refer to *Maintenance* in this chapter, and perform the *Reservoir fluid check.*

Electric motor removal/installation

Refer to **Figure 40** for this procedure. Lubricate all internal components with OMC Power Trim/Tilt and Steering Fluid or Dexron II automatic transmission fluid.

1. Remove the power trim and tilt unit as described in the previous section.

2. Open the manual release valve until it just contacts its retaining ring.

3. Cover the reservoir fill plug with a shop towel and carefully and slowly remove the fill plug, allowing any internal pressure (and fluid) to vent before fully removing the plug.

4. Reinstall the fill plug and close the manual release valve to prevent fluid loss and contamination.

NOTE
Use caution during system disassembly, as there still may be residual pressure in the system. During disassembly, cover each component with a shop towel and slowly loosen the component and/or its fasteners, allowing any internal pressure (and fluid) to vent before fully removing the component.

5. Remove the three large screws and washers (2, **Figure 40**) securing the motor to the manifold assembly.

6. Remove the motor from the manifold. Remove and discard the motor O-ring (3, **Figure 40**). Locate and secure the pump drive coupler (5).

7. Inspect the rubber ball in the tang of the pump drive coupler. If missing, install a new ball into its bore. The rubber ball helps absorb the shock loads as the motor is started and stopped, preventing the coupler from shearing.

8. Remove the filter (4, **Figure 40**) from the top of the hydraulic pump. Clean the filter in a mild solvent (such as mineral spirits). If the filter cannot be satisfactorily cleaned, discard it.

9. To install the electric motor, begin by installing the filter over the hydraulic pump. Then insert the pump drive coupler into the hydraulic pump.

10. Prime the hydraulic pump as follows:
   a. Fill the hydraulic pump cavity (with the recommended trim and tilt fluid) until it is flush with the electric motor mounting deck (the pump is submerged).
   b. Rotate the pump drive coupler back and forth until all air bubbles are eliminated. If no resistance is felt, the pump is air-locked.
   c. If the pump is air-locked, depress the two check balls in the openings in the top of the pump. Then rotate the drive shaft again. A noticeable increase in effort will occur when the pump begins drawing fluid.
   d. Add fluid as necessary to keep the pump submerged.

11. Once the pump is primed, install a new O-ring onto the electric motor. Lubricate the O-ring with the trim and tilt fluid.

12. Position the motor on the manifold assembly. Rotate the motor as necessary to engage the pump drive coupler, then seat the motor on the cylinder and manifold assembly. Make sure the O-ring is not displaced during the assembly.

13. Secure the motor with three screws (and washers). Tighten the screws evenly and securely.

14. Install the power trim and tilt unit as described in the previous section.

Hydraulic pump removal/installation

The hydraulic pump is serviced only as an assembly. Do not attempt to disassemble and reassemble the pump. If the pump is to be reused, it must be washed *only* in clean trim and tilt fluid. Replace any O-ring that has been removed.

Refer to **Figure 40** for this procedure. Lubricate all internal components with OMC Power Trim/Tilt and Steering Fluid or Dexron II automatic transmission fluid.

1. Remove the electric motor as described in the previous section.

2. Remove the two Allen head screws and lockwashers (6, **Figure 40**) and the single hex head screw, lockwasher and flat washer (7, **Figure 40**) securing the pump to the manifold assembly.

3. Carefully lift the pump from the manifold bore. Remove and discard the O-ring (9, **Figure 40**) sealing the pump to the manifold.

4. Remove the DOWN relief valve components (18, **Figure 40**) from their bore (located under the pump). Remove

10

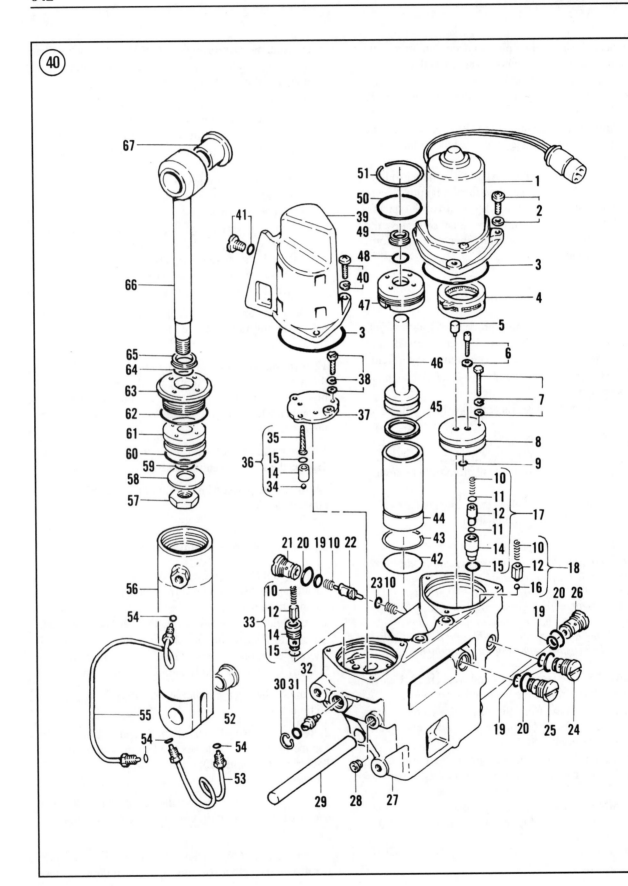

CONVENTIONAL SYSTEM

1. Electric motor
   and lead assembly
2. Screw and lockwasher
3. O-ring
4. Filter
5. Pump drive coupler
6. Socket screw
   and lockwasher
7. Hex screw, lockwasher
   and flat washer
8. Pump assembly
9. O-ring
10. Spring
11. O-ring
12. Valve core
13. Valve core O-rings
14. Valve seat
15. Valve seat O-ring
16. Valve core tip seal
17. Down relief
    valve assembly
18. Thermal expansion
    valve assembly
19. Check valve
    small O-rings
20. Check valve
    large O-rings
21. Reverse lock check
    valve cartridge
22. Pump control piston
23. Pump control
    piston O-ring
24. Trim check
    valve cartridge
25. Tilt check
    valve cartridge
26. Trim/tilt separation
    valve cartridge
27. Manifold assembly
28. Pipe plug
29. Tilt cylinder
    lower pivot pin
30. Retaining ring
31. O-ring
32. Manual release valve
33. Trim UP relief
    valve assembly
34. Check ball
35. Filter
36. Filter valve assembly
37. Plate
38. Screw, lockwasher
    and flat washer
39. Reservoir
40. Screw and lockwasher
41. Level plug and O-ring
42. Sleeve O-ring
43. Sleeve backup ring
44. Trim ram sleeve
45. Trim ram seal
46. Trim ram
47. Trim ram end cap
48. Quad ring
49. Wiper
50. End cap outer O-ring
51. End cap backup ring
52. Lower pivot
    pin bushing
53. Lower (high-volume
    chamber) line
54. Line fitting O-rings
55. Upper (low-volume
    chamber) line
56. Tilt cylinder
57. Nut
58. Washer
59. Rod-to-piston O-ring
60. O-ring
61. Piston assembly
62. End cap O-ring
63. Tilt cylinder end cap
64. O-ring
65. Wiper
66. Rod and eye
67. Upper pivot
    pin bushing

10

and discard the valve core tip seal (16, **Figure 40**) from the valve core.

NOTE
Do not damage the thermal expansion valve
*components (18, **Figure 40**) during removal.*

5. Remove the thermal expansion valve's spring, then pull the valve core from the valve seat with a suitable pair of expanding pliers. Do not distort or damage the valve core. Remove and discard the two O-rings from the valve core.

6. Remove the thermal expansion valve's seat with a suitable pair of expanding pliers. Do not damage or distort the valve seat and do not insert the pliers more than 1/8 in. (3.2 mm) into the seat. Remove and discard the valve seat's O-ring.

7. Clean the valve components in a mild solvent, then inspect the components for damage, wear or debris. Make sure the DOWN relief valve seat (in the manifold bore) is free of contamination or other debris.

8. To install the pump, begin by installing the thermal expansion valve (18, **Figure 40**) as follows:

   a. Lubricate a new O-ring and install it into the valve seat's groove. Insert the valve seat into its manifold bore. Push the seat into the manifold until it is seated.

   b. Lubricate two new O-rings and install them into the valve core grooves. The thicker O-ring goes into the groove at the lower end of the core. Insert the valve core into the valve seat. Push the core into the seat until it is seated.

   c. Insert the spring into the valve core.

9. Install a new valve core tip (16, **Figure 40**) into the DOWN relief valve core's tip. Then lubricate the valve core and install it into its manifold bore. Finally, install the spring into the valve seat.

10. Install a new pump O-ring (9, **Figure 40**) into its recess in the pump mounting surface.

11. Carefully position the pump into the manifold bore, being careful not to displace the O-ring. Make sure the mounting screw holes are aligned, then seat the pump into the bore.

12. Install the two Allen head screws (and washers) and the single hex head screw, lock washer and flat washer. Tighten the screws finger-tight, then *evenly* tighten the screws to 25-30 in.-lb. (2.8-3.4 N•m) in a minimum of three progressive stages. The pump must be pulled evenly against the manifold or it will be damaged.

13. Install the electric motor as described in the previous section.

Manifold and trim ram disassembly

Refer to **Figure 40** for this procedure

1. Remove the hydraulic pump as described in the previous section.

2. Remove the manual release valve's retaining ring with a suitable pair of internal snap ring pliers. Then remove the manual release valve from the manifold. Remove and discard the valve's O-ring.

3. Remove the rigid hydraulic lines (53 and 55, **Figure 40**) from the top and bottom of the tilt cylinder with a line (flarenut) wrench. If the top line fitting on the tilt cylinder has an adaptor fitting (and metal band around the cylinder), use a backup wrench to prevent the adaptor fitting from unscrewing from the tilt cylinder. Discard the 4 line fitting O-rings.

4. Slide the tilt cylinder lower pivot pin (29, **Figure 40**) from the manifold and tilt cylinder. Remove the tilt cylinder from the manifold. Then remove the two lower tilt cylinder bushings (52). Tilt cylinder disassembly is covered in the next section.

5. Remove the three screws and washers (40, **Figure 40**) securing the reservoir to the manifold assembly. Remove the reservoir from the manifold, then discard the reservoir O-ring.

6. Remove the three hex head screws, lockwasher and flat washers securing the plate (37, **Figure 40**) to the manifold. Lift the plate from the manifold, then remove the filter (35) from the plate. Clean the filter in a mild solvent (such as mineral spirits). If the filter cannot be satisfactorily cleaned, discard it.

7. Remove the filter valve assembly (36, **Figure 40**) as follows:

   a. Thread one of the plate screws (38) into the valve seat. Then pull the valve seat from the manifold. Discard the seat and its O-ring.

   b. Remove the check ball from the filter valve bore.

8. Remove the trim UP relief valve assembly (33, **Figure 40**) as follows:

   a. Remove the spring. Then pull the valve core from the manifold. If the valve core tip is damaged, the core must be replaced.

   b. Remove the valve seat with a suitable pair of expanding pliers. Do not damage or distort the seat. Remove and discard the seat's O-ring.

9. Remove the trim/tilt separation valve (26, **Figure 40**) from the port, lower end of the manifold with a drag link socket (or large screwdriver). Remove and discard the valve's two O-rings. This valve is longer than all other check valves. Tag or mark the valve for reassembly purposes.

10. Remove the tilt check valve (25, **Figure 40**), trim check valve (24) and reverse lock check valve (21) cartridges from the manifold with a drag link socket (or large screw-

driver). While the valves are identical, mark or tag each valve so it can be reinstalled in its original position. Then remove and discard the two O-rings from each cartridge.

11. Using a pair of needlenose pliers, pull the pump control piston (22, **Figure 40**) from the reverse lock check valve bore (21). Locate and secure the two piston springs, then remove and discard the piston's O-ring (23, **Figure 40**).

12. If the fill plug (41, **Figure 40**) is not yet removed, remove the fill plug and discard its O-ring.

13. Remove both trim ram end caps (47, **Figure 40**) with the end cap remover (part No. 324598) or an equivalent spanner wrench. Then remove and discard the O-ring and backup ring (50 and 51, **Figure 40**) from each end cap.

14. Carefully pry the wiper (49, **Figure 40**) from each end cap. Discard the scrapers. Then pull the quad ring (48) from each end cap bore using a suitable hooked tool. Do not damage the quad-ring bore during removal. Discard the quad rings.

15. Pull both trim rams from their bores. Remove and discard the seal from the groove of each trim ram's piston.

16. Reach into each trim ram's sleeve (44, **Figure 40**) and pry each sleeve from the manifold with trim sleeve remover (part No. 325065) or an equivalent tool. Wiggle the top of each sleeve while prying (with the remover) to help the sleeve slide out of its bore.

17. Remove and discard the O-ring and backup ring (42 and 43, **Figure 40**) from each sleeve.

18. Clean and inspect all components as described later in this chapter. Make sure each cartridge style check valve (21, 24, 25 and 26, **Figure 40**) is pressure tested as described in this chapter.

Tilt cylinder disassembly

If the tilt cylinder bore is scored or damaged, the tilt cylinder must be replaced as an assembly. To disassemble the tilt cylinder, refer to **Figure 40** and proceed as follows:

1. Clamp the lower end of the tilt cylinder in a soft-jawed vise. Do not clamp above the bushing area or the cylinder will be crushed.

2. Remove the cylinder end cap (63, **Figure 40**) with a suitable spanner wrench, such as part No. 326485 or part No. 912084. Once the end cap is completely unthreaded from the cylinder, pull the rod, end cap and piston assembly from the cylinder bore.

3. If the top of the cylinder is equipped with an adaptor fitting and a steel band, remove the adaptor fitting. Slide the steel band from the cylinder. Then remove and discard the O-ring located between the adaptor and tilt cylinder.

4. Slide the end cap against the rod eye. Using two of the rod holding blocks part No. 983213 (or equivalent aluminum blocks), clamp the cylinder rod in a vise with the piston end facing straight up. Then carefully remove the nut (57, **Figure 40**) from the rod.

5. Lift the washer (58, **Figure 40**) off of the piston. Remove the 4 springs, spring guides and check balls from the piston. These components make up the impact relief valves. Place these valve components in a plastic bag that is properly marked.

6. Slide the piston from the rod. Remove and discard the piston-to-rod O-ring (59, **Figure 40**), then remove and discard the O-ring (60) from the groove on the piston's outer diameter.

7. Slide the end cap from the rod. Remove and discard the end cap's external O-ring (62, **Figure 40**).

8. Carefully pry the wiper (65, **Figure 40**) from the end cap. Discard the scraper. Then pull the O-ring (64) from the end cap bore using a suitable hooked tool. Do not damage the O-ring bore (in the end cap) during removal. Discard the O-ring.

9. Clean and inspect all components as described in this chapter.

Manifold, trim rams and tilt cylinder cleaning and inspection

Use lint-free shop towels to handle all clean components. Even a single strand of lint can cause a check ball (or valve) not to seat. Leaking valves will cause hydraulic malfunctions.

NOTE
Do not attempt to blow dry small components (such as check balls and springs). They are easily lost.

1. Wash all components in a mild solvent, such as mineral spirits. Blow the larger parts dry with compressed air. Allow the smaller components to air dry on a clean shop towel.

2. Inspect the tilt cylinder bore for corrosion, scoring and grooving. Very light (superficial) scuffing is acceptable. Inspect the cylinder bore threads for corroded, worn, damaged, missing or galled threads.

3. Inspect the trim ram sleeve bores for corrosion, scoring and grooving. Very light (superficial) scuffing is acceptable. Inspect the O-ring groove in each sleeve's outer diameter for damage, distortion or any nicks or burrs that wild prevent sealing.

4. Inspect the manual release valve, filter valve and all other check valve bores for scoring, scratches, nicks, grooves or corrosion damage that will affect their sealing. Make sure the manual release valve threads (in the manifold) are not damaged, corroded, worn or galled.

10

5. Inspect all valve cores, check balls and valve seats for wear, corrosion or damage. Replace all worn or damaged components.

6. Inspect the pump control piston springs. Replace the springs if they are corroded, damaged or collapsed.

7. Inspect the tilt piston (61, **Figure 40**) and the trim rams (46) for wear, scratches or grooves on their outer diameters. Inspect each of the tilt piston's four valve seats for wear, indentations, debris or any other damage.

8. Inspect the impact relief valve components for wear, corrosion, mechanical damage and collapsed or distorted springs.

9. Inspect the tilt cylinder rod and trim ram rods for wear, scoring, grooving or any other damage. Remove all thread-locking adhesive from the tilt cylinder rod's threads.

10. Inspect the end cap threads for corroded, worn, damaged, missing or galled threads. Inspect the end cap's seal and scraper bores for nicks and gouges.

11. Inspect the O-ring groove(s) in all components for nicks, gouges, wear, corrosion or any damage.

12. Pressure test each cartridge style check valve (21, 24, 25 and 26, **Figure 40**) to 30 psi (207 kPa) as described in this chapter.

13. Replace all damaged components.

Tilt cylinder assembly

Refer to **Figure 40** for this procedure. Install new O-rings and seals during the assembly procedure. Do not make any dry assemblies. Lubricate all internal components with OMC Power Trim/Tilt and Steering Fluid or Dexron II automatic transmission fluid. Do not use any type of grease on any internal components.

NOTE
Cleanliness is the greatest concern during assembly. Do not allow any dirt, debris, lint or any other foreign substance into the tilt cylinder during the assembly procedure. The system cannot function properly if it is contaminated.

1. Assemble the end cap as follows:
   a. Lubricate and install a new O-ring (64, **Figure 40**) into the end cap's internal groove. Make sure the O-ring is fully expanded into the groove.
   b. Lubricate a new wiper (**Figure 40**) and install it into the end cap's external bore with the lip facing up (away from the cylinder). Press the scraper into the end cap until it is seated.
   c. Lubricate a new O-ring (62, **Figure 40**) and install it into the end cap's external groove.

2. Clamp the eye end of the rod (66, **Figure 40**) into a soft-jawed vise. The threaded end of the rod must face

straight up. Lubricate the rod, then position a seal protector, such as part No. 326005 over the threaded end of the rod.

3. Carefully slide the end cap over the seal protector and onto the rod, being careful not to damage the end cap seals in the process. The threaded end of the end cap must face the threaded end of the rod. Then remove the seal protector.

4. Slide the piston (61, **Figure 40**) over the threaded end of the rod and against the rod's shoulder. The side of the piston with the larger valve openings must face up (toward the threaded end of the rod).

5. Lubricate a new piston-to-rod O-ring (59, **Figure 40**) and install it over the threaded end of the rod and against the piston.

6. Install the four impact relief check balls, spring guides (small end facing up) and springs (in that order) into the piston bores.

7. Position the washer (58, **Figure 40**) over the threaded end of the rod and up against the springs. Lightly coat the rod threads with OMC Nut Lock threadlocking adhesive, then install and tighten the nut (57) to 58-87 ft.-lb. (78.6-118.0 N•m).

8. Lubricate a new O-ring (60, **Figure 40**) and install it into the groove in the outer diameter of the piston.

9. Clamp the lower end of the tilt cylinder in a soft-jawed vise. Do not clamp above the bushing area or the cylinder will be crushed. The open cylinder bore must face straight up.

10. Lubricate the cylinder bore and piston liberally. Carefully insert the piston and rod assembly into the bore. Once the tapered edge of the cylinder wall is reached, apply a steady downward pressure to the rod eye, while wiggling the eye in a circular motion. Be patient and allow the O-ring to work past the taper and into the cylinder bore.

11. Once past the tapered wall, push the piston as far as possible into the bore while still allowing enough space between the end cap and cylinder to fill the cylinder with fluid. Then thread the end cap into the cylinder bore 2-3 turns. Do not tighten the end cap at this time.

12. If equipped with an adaptor fitting and metal band at the top of the tilt cylinder, lubricate a new O-ring and install it into the adaptor fitting. Position the metal band over the top of the cylinder and align it with the hole in the top of the cylinder. Carefully thread the adaptor fitting (and O-ring) through the band and into the cylinder's hole. Tighten the adaptor fitting securely.

Manifold and cylinder assembly

Refer to **Figure 40** for this procedure. Install all new O-rings and seals during the assembly procedure. Do not make any *dry* assemblies. Lubricate all internal components with OMC Power Trim/Tilt and Steering Fluid or

Dexron II automatic transmission fluid. Do not use any type of grease on any internal components.

NOTE
Cleanliness is the greatest concern during assembly. Do not allow any dirt, debris, lint or any other foreign substance into the manifold during the assembly procedure. The system cannot function properly if it is contaminated.

1. Assemble and install both trim ram sleeves as follows:
   a. Lubricate and install a new backup ring into the groove at the bottom of each sleeve. Position the ring at the top of the groove.
   b. Lubricate and install a new O-ring into the groove at the bottom of each sleeve. The O-ring must be below the backup ring (closest to the lower end of the sleeve).

NOTE
If the backup ring does not fit tightly against the bottom of each sleeve's groove, hold the ring(s) in your hand and overlap the ends of the ring, temporarily reducing the diameter of the ring. Reduce diameter until the ring is approximately 75 % of the sleeve's diameter. Hold the ring in this position for a few minutes and allow it to take a set. Then carefully install the ring into the sleeve groove, being careful not to expand it further than necessary.

   c. Lubricate the manifold bores, then install both sleeves into the manifold and seat them in their bores. Be careful not to pinch the O-ring and/or backup ring between the manifold and sleeve. The sleeves must be seated in their bores in order for there to be room for end cap installation.

2. Assemble both trim rams and their end caps as follows:
   a. Lubricate and install a new quad ring (48, **Figure 40**) into each end cap's internal groove. Make sure the ring is fully expanded into the groove.
   b. Lubricate and install a new wiper (49, **Figure 40**) into each end cap's external bore with the lip facing up (away from the end cap). Press each scraper into its end cap until it is seated.
   c. Lubricate and install a new O-ring (50, **Figure 40**) into each end cap's external groove.
   d. Lubricate and install a new backup ring (51, **Figure 40**) into each end cap's external groove. The backup ring must be above the O-ring (furthest from the end cap threads).

   e. Lubricate both trim rams, then slide an end cap over each rod. The threaded end of each cap must face the piston. Seat each end cap against its piston.
   f. Lubricate and install a new seal (45, **Figure 40**) into the groove in the outer diameter of each trim ram piston.

3. Lubricate both trim ram sleeves and both trim ram pistons liberally. Carefully insert each trim ram piston into its respective sleeve. Once each piston has entered its sleeve, thread each end cap 2-3 turns into the manifold, then push both trim rams to the bottom of their bores.

4. Unthread both end caps and remove them from the manifold (but do not remove the trim rams). Fill both trim ram bores with trim and tilt fluid to the top of the sleeves (44, **Figure 40**). This will greatly reduce the bleed time and ensure the system does not air lock.

NOTE
If the backup ring does not fit tightly against the bottom of each end cap groove, hold the ring(s) in your hand and overlap the ends of the ring, temporarily reducing the ring. Reduce diameter until the ring is approximately 75 % of the end cap diameter. Hold the ring in this position for a few minutes and allow it to take a set. Then carefully install the ring into the end cap groove, being careful not to expand it further than necessary.

5. Reinstall both end caps and thread them fully into the manifold. Make sure the backup ring is not pinched between the end cap and manifold. Then tighten both end caps to 55-60 ft.-lb. (74.6-81.3 N•m) using End Cap Remover (part No. 324958) or an equivalent spanner wrench.

6. Install the manual release valve as follows:
   a. Lubricate a new O-ring and install it into the groove in the manual release valve body.
   b. Install the valve into the manifold and tighten it to 45-55 in.-lb. (5.1-6.2 N•m).
   c. Install the retaining ring (30, **Figure 40**) using a suitable pair of internal snap ring pliers. Make sure the ring has fully expanded into its groove.

7. Lubricate two new O-rings and install them onto the trim/tilt separation check valve (26, **Figure 40**). This is the longest check valve cartridge. Install the check valve into the bore at the lower, port corner of the manifold and tighten it to 50-60 in.-lb. (5.7-6.8 N•m).

8. Lubricate a new O-ring and install it into the pump control piston groove. Then install a spring into each end of the pump control piston.

9. Carefully install the pump control piston assembly into the reverse lock check valve bore. This is the check valve bore on the port rear corner of the manifold, right next to

10

the port trim ram. Make sure the springs are not displaced in the process. Seat the piston into the bore.

10. Lubricate two new O-rings and install them onto the reverse lock check valve (21, **Figure 40**). Install the check valve into its bore (over the pump control piston). Tighten the check valve to 50-60 in.-lb. (5.7-6.8 N•m).

11. Lubricate 4 new O-rings and install them onto the tilt and trim check valves. Install the check valves into the bores on the transom side of the manifold. The trim check valve goes into the hole opposing the reverse lock check valve (and pump control piston). Tighten both check valves to 50-60 in.-lb. (5.7-6.8 N•m).

12. Position the manifold so that the reservoir and electric motor mounting pads are pointing straight up.

13. Place the filter valve check ball into its manifold bore. This is the hole closest to the starboard trim ram.

14. Lubricate a new O-ring and install it into the groove of a new filter valve seat. Install the valve seat into its bore (over the check ball). Push the valve seat into the manifold until it is seated.

15. Install the trim UP relief valve (33, **Figure 40**) as follows:

    a. Lubricate a new O-ring and install it into the valve seat's groove.

    b. Install the valve seat into its manifold bore (same side as the filter valve). Push the valve seat into the manifold until it is seated.

    c. Lubricate the valve core and place it into the valve seat.

    d. Install the spring into the valve core.

16. Install the filter (35, **Figure 40**) into the plate (37). Then carefully position the plate (and filter) over the filter valve seat and the trim UP relief valve.

17. Secure the plate (37, **Figure 40**) with three screws, lockwashers and flat washers. Tighten the screws finger-tight, then evenly tighten the screws to 25-30 in.-lb. (2.8-3.4 N•m) in a minimum of three progressive stages. The plate must be pulled evenly against the manifold or it will be damaged.

18. Lubricate a new O-ring and install it on the reservoir (39, **Figure 40**). Carefully position the reservoir to the manifold, being careful not to displace the O-ring. Secure the reservoir with 3 screws and washers. Tighten the screws evenly and securely.

19. Grease the bushings (52, **Figure 40**) and install them into the lower end of the tilt cylinder.

20. Grease the tilt cylinder lower pivot pin (29, **Figure 40**). Position the tilt cylinder into the manifold recess and align the holes, then slide the pivot pin into the manifold and through the tilt cylinder. The top line fitting must point to starboard when the cylinder is installed.

21. Lubricate four new line fitting O-rings and install them onto each line fitting (53 and 55, **Figure 40**). Install both lines and tighten all four fittings hand tight. Once all four fittings are hand tightened, tighten the fittings to 168-216 in.-lb. (19.0-24.4 N•m). If equipped with an adaptor fitting on the top end of the tilt cylinder, hold the adaptor fitting with a backup wrench while tightening the line fitting.

22. Unthread the tilt cylinder end cap (63, **Figure 40**) and fill the cylinder bore with trim and tilt fluid until the fluid is level with the top line's fitting.

23. Thread the end cap into the cylinder bore as far as possible by hand, then tighten the end cap to 18-21 ft.-lb. (24.4-28.5 N•m) using a suitable spanner wrench, such as part No. 326485 or part No. 912084.

24. Install the hydraulic pump, then the electric motor, as described in this chapter.

FasTrak System

Many of the screws on this system are Posidriv screws. These look very similar to *Phillips* screws, but are not the same. Always use the correct screwdriver. The screw and/or screwdriver will be quickly damaged if the incorrect tool is used.

System removal/installation

Refer to **Figure 41** for this procedure.

1. Note the position of the trim limit rod, then remove the rod from the stern brackets.

2. Tilt the outboard motor to the full UP position. Engage the tilt lock, support the gearcase with a hoist or block the gearcase to eliminate any possibility of it falling during this procedure. If necessary, use the manual release valve to accomplish this.

3. Remove the snap rings from both ends of the upper pivot pin (14, **Figure 41**) using a suitable pair of external snap ring pliers. The pin is located in the swivel bracket as shown in **Figure 39**, typical. Push the pivot pin from the swivel bracket and tilt cylinder eye using a suitable punch and hammer.

4. If the unit is to be disassembled, relieve the system's internal pressure as follows:

    a. If the rams are not all completely extended, operate the unit in the UP direction until all three rams are fully extended.

    b. Briefly bump the trim switch in the DOWN direction. The motor must run only *briefly* in the DOWN direction. This will help relieve internal pressure.

    c. Open the manual release valve until it just contacts its retaining ring.

    d. Cover the reservoir fill plug with a shop towel and carefully and slowly remove the fill plug, allowing any internal pressure (and fluid) to vent before fully

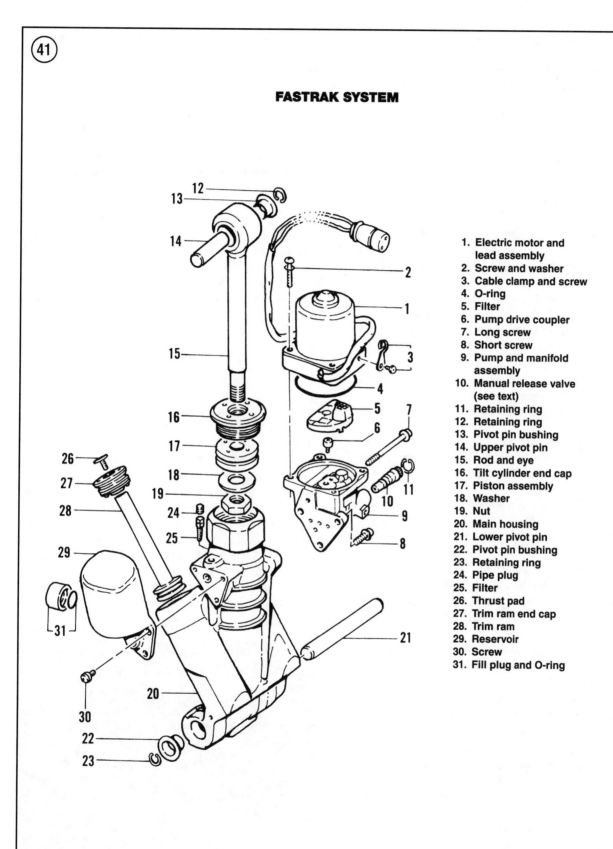

FASTRAK SYSTEM

1. Electric motor and lead assembly
2. Screw and washer
3. Cable clamp and screw
4. O-ring
5. Filter
6. Pump drive coupler
7. Long screw
8. Short screw
9. Pump and manifold assembly
10. Manual release valve (see text)
11. Retaining ring
12. Retaining ring
13. Pivot pin bushing
14. Upper pivot pin
15. Rod and eye
16. Tilt cylinder end cap
17. Piston assembly
18. Washer
19. Nut
20. Main housing
21. Lower pivot pin
22. Pivot pin bushing
23. Retaining ring
24. Pipe plug
25. Filter
26. Thrust pad
27. Trim ram end cap
28. Trim ram
29. Reservoir
30. Screw
31. Fill plug and O-ring

10

removing the plug. It is normal for fluid to vent from the reservoir.

   e. Reinstall the fill plug and close the manual release valve to prevent fluid loss and contamination.

NOTE
Because the electric motor, tilt limit switch, trim sending unit and ground lead are all encapsulated in a braided sleeve, it is necessary to disconnect all of these components from the power head to remove the power trim and tilt unit.

5. Disconnect the tilt limit switch blue/white leads from the engine harness. The connectors are located on the top, port corner of the power head as shown in **Figure 42**.

6. Disconnect the trim sending unit at its two-pin Amphenol connector. The leads are white/tan and black (or black/tan). Then disconnect the ground lead (black or green) at its bullet connector. This connector is very close to the two-pin Amphenol connector.

7. Disconnect the electric motor leads as follows:

   a. Separate the large two-pin connector (blue and green leads [on the power head]). Remove and discard the O-ring from the connector body (on the electric motor side).

   b. Carefully remove the rubber grommet from the rear of the connector body (on the electric motor side). Note the location of the blue and green leads in the connector body.

   c. Using a pocket screwdriver (or equivalent tool), depress the tab locking each terminal into the connector body, then pull each terminal (and lead) from the connector body.

8. Note the routing of the electric motor, tilt limit switch and trim limit switch leads and the position of any clamps and tie-straps. Then remove any clamps and tie-straps securing the leads and pull the leads free from the lower cowl.

9. Pull the electric motor leads free from the braided sleeve and through the hole in the port stern bracket.

10. Remove the screw securing the ground strap to the power trim and tilt unit's electric motor. Remove the ground strap from the electric motor, then reinstall the screw to prevent misplacement.

11. Remove the snap rings from both ends of the lower pivot pin (21, **Figure 41**) using a suitable pair of external snap ring pliers. Push the pivot pin from the swivel bracket and the trim and tilt unit using a suitable punch and hammer.

12. Pivot the power trim and tilt unit rearward and out of the stern brackets, top first. Place the unit on a clean workbench.

13. Remove the two bushings (13, **Figure 41**) from the tilt cylinder's rod eye and the two bushings (22, **Figure 41**) from the lower pivot pin bore (in the main housing).

NOTE
Use OMC Triple Guard Grease for all grease applications.

14. To install the power trim and tilt unit, begin by greasing the four bushings. Install two bushings into the tilt cylinder rod eye and two bushings into the lower pivot pin bore (of the power trim and tilt unit).

15. Position the trim and tilt unit into the stern bracket. Insert the bottom of the unit first, then rotate the top of the unit into the stern brackets. Route the electrical leads through the hole in the stern bracket before the unit fully enters the stern brackets.

16. Grease the lower pivot pin. Align the holes and install the pivot pin through the stern brackets and the power trim and tilt unit. Install a retaining ring onto each end of the pivot pin using a suitable pair of external snap ring pliers. Make sure each ring is fully seated in its groove.

17. Grease the upper pivot pin. Align the tilt cylinder rod eye with the swivel bracket bore, then install the pin. Install a retaining ring onto each end of the pivot pin using a suitable pair of external snap ring pliers. Make sure each ring has fully seated in its groove.

18. Install the trim limit rod into the set of stern bracket holes noted on removal.

19. Insert the electric motor leads into the braided sleeve containing the tilt limit switch and trim sending unit leads.

20. Route the braided sleeve and all electrical leads through the hole in the lower cowl. Clamp and/or tie-strap the leads as noted on removal. Reconnect the tilt limit switch and trim sending unit leads as follows:

   a. Connect the tilt limit switch blue/white leads to their engine harness mates. See **Figure 42**.

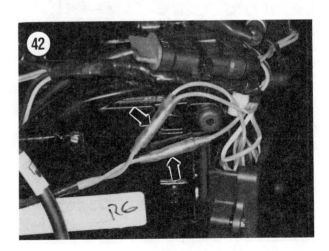

b. Connect the trim sending unit two-pin Amphenol connector to its engine harness mate. Then connect the ground lead (black or green) bullet connector to its engine harness mate.

21. Connect the electric motor leads as follows:

a. Insert each terminal into the large two-pin connector body. Make sure the leads are reinstalled in their original location. The blue lead must connect to blue and the green lead must connect to green.

b. Make sure each terminal locks into place.

c. Once the terminals are locked in place, push the grommet into the rear of the connector body.

d. Grease a new O-ring and install it into the connector body's groove.

e. Connect the large two-pin connector to its engine harness mate. Make sure the bodies are locked together.

22. If the manual release valve is open, turn it clockwise until it is closed, then tighten it to 45-55 in.-lb. (5.1-6.2 N•m).

23. Release the tilt lock, remove the hoist or remove the blocks. Perform the *Reservoir fluid check* as described in this chapter.

Electric motor
removal/installation

Refer to **Figure 41** for this procedure. Lubricate all internal components with OMC Power Trim/Tilt and Steering Fluid or Dexron II automatic transmission fluid.

1. Remove the power trim and tilt unit as described in the previous section.

2. Open the manual release valve until it just contacts its retaining ring.

3. Cover the reservoir fill plug with a shop towel and carefully and slowly remove the fill plug, allowing any internal pressure (and fluid) to vent before fully removing the plug.

4. Reinstall the fill plug and close the manual release valve to prevent fluid loss and contamination.

NOTE
Use caution during system disassembly, as there still may be residual pressure in the system. During disassembly, cover each component with a shop towel and slowly loosen the component and/or its fasteners, allowing any internal pressure (and fluid) to vent before fully removing the component.

5. Remove the 4 screws and washers (2, **Figure 41**) securing the motor to the pump assembly.

6. Remove the motor from the manifold. Remove and discard the motor O-ring (4, **Figure 41**). Locate and secure the pump drive coupler (6).

7. Remove the filter (5, **Figure 41**) from the top of the hydraulic pump. Clean the filter in a mild solvent (such as mineral spirits). If the filter cannot be satisfactorily cleaned, discard it.

8. To install the electric motor, begin by installing the filter over the hydraulic pump. Then insert the pump drive coupler into the hydraulic pump.

9. Prime the hydraulic pump as follows:

a. Fill the hydraulic pump cavity (with the recommended trim and tilt fluid) until it is flush with the electric motor mounting deck (the pump is submerged).

b. Rotate the pump drive coupler back and forth until all air bubbles are eliminated. If no resistance is felt, the pump is air-locked.

c. If the pump is air-locked, remove the filter and depress the two check balls in the openings in the top of the pump. Then rotate the drive shaft again. A noticeable increase in effort will occur when the pump begins drawing fluid. Reinstall the filter once the pump is primed.

d. Add fluid as necessary to keep the pump submerged.

10. Once the pump is primed, install a new O-ring onto the electric motor. Lubricate the O-ring with the trim and tilt fluid.

11. Position the motor on the manifold assembly. Rotate the motor as necessary to engage the pump drive coupler, then seat the motor on the cylinder and manifold assembly. Make sure the O-ring is not displaced during the assembly.

12. Secure the motor with four screws (and washers). Evenly tighten the screws to 35-52 in.-lb. (4.0-5.9 N•m).

13. Install the power trim and tilt unit as described in the previous section.

Pump assembly
removal/installation

The pump and valve body is serviced only as an assembly. Do not attempt to disassemble and reassemble any portion of the pump assembly (9, **Figure 41**) other than the manual release valve (10). If the pump assembly is to be reused, it must be washed *only* in clean trim and tilt fluid.

The manual release valve incorporates the thermal expansion and tilt relief valve functions. Different valves are used on different engine models. On the models covered in this manual, the manual release valve must have a

10

groove in its face as shown in **Figure 43**. If not, replace the manual release valve with the correct one.

Refer to **Figure 41** for this procedure. Lubricate all internal components with OMC Power Trim/Tilt and Steering Fluid or Dexron II automatic transmission fluid.

1. Remove the electric motor as described in the previous section.

NOTE
The white nylon seal rings on the manual release valve are not replaceable. If damaged, replace the manual release valve.

2. Remove the manual release valve's retaining ring (11, **Figure 41**) with a suitable pair of internal snap ring pliers. Then remove the manual release valve from the manifold. Remove and discard the valve's O-ring.

3. Remove the two long screws and lockwashers (7, **Figure 41**) and one short screw and lockwasher (8) securing the pump assembly (9) to the main housing (20).

4. Carefully pull the pump assembly from the main housing. Remove and discard the five O-rings sealing the pump to the housing.

5. To install the pump, begin by lubricating and installing five new O-rings into the grooves on the main housing-to-pump assembly mating surface.

6. Carefully position the pump assembly to the main housing, being careful not to displace any of the O-rings. Make sure the mounting screw holes are aligned, then install the pump mounting screws.

7. Tighten the screws finger-tight, then *evenly* tighten the screws to 60-84 in.-lb. (6.8-9.5 N•m) in a minimum of three progressive stages. The pump must be pulled evenly against the housing or it will be damaged.

8. Verify that the manual release valve has a groove in its face (as shown in **Figure 43**), then lubricate a new O-ring and install it in the valve's O-ring groove (not the identification groove). Lubricate the two nylon seal rings, then install the valve into its bore. Tighten it to 45-55 in.-lb. (5.1-6.2 N•m).

9. Install the retaining ring (11, **Figure 41**) using a suitable pair of internal snap ring pliers. Make sure the ring has fully expanded into its groove.

10. Install the electric motor as described in the previous section.

Main housing disassembly

Refer to **Figure 41** for this procedure.

1. Remove the pump assembly as described in the previous section.

2. Remove the three screws (30, **Figure 41**) securing the reservoir (29) to the main housing. Remove the reservoir from the manifold, then discard the reservoir O-ring.

3. If the fill plug (31, **Figure 41**) is not yet been removed, remove the fill plug and discard its O-ring.

4. Remove the pipe plug (24, **Figure 41**) with a suitable Allen wrench. Remove and discard the O-ring from the groove in the plug.

5. Remove the filter (25, **Figure 41**) from its bore. Clean the filter in a mild solvent (such as mineral spirits). If the filter cannot be satisfactorily cleaned, discard it.

6. Fully unthread both trim ram end caps (27, **Figure 41**) from the main housing with end cap remover (part No. 436710) or an equivalent spanner wrench.

7. Carefully pull each trim ram and end cap assembly from the main housing. Remove the two backup rings and single

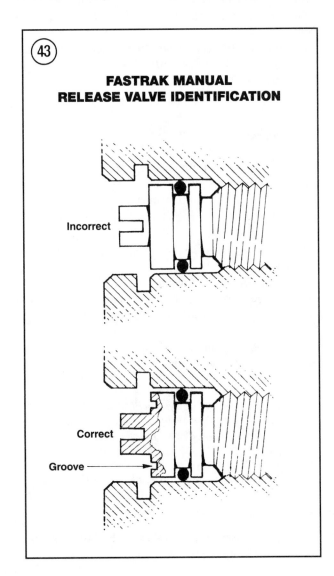

FASTRAK MANUAL RELEASE VALVE IDENTIFICATION

Incorrect

Correct

Groove

O-ring from the groove in the piston end of each trim ram. Discard the backup ring and O-rings.

8. Slide each trim ram's end cap up against the thrust pad (26, **Figure 41**). Using two rod holding blocks part No. 983213 (or equivalent aluminum blocks), clamp a trim ram in a vise. Then carefully unthread (and remove) the thrust pad (26) from the trim ram. Repeat this procedure for the remaining trim ram.

9. Slide the end cap from each trim ram. Remove and discard the external O-ring from each end cap.

10. Carefully pry the scraper from each end cap. Discard the scrapers. Then pull the quad ring from each end cap bore using a suitable hooked tool. Do not damage the quad-ring bore (in each end cap) during removal. Discard the quad rings.

11. Remove the tilt cylinder end cap (16, **Figure 41**) with a suitable spanner wrench. Once the end cap is completely unthreaded from the cylinder, pull the rod, end cap and piston assembly from the cylinder bore.

12. Clamp the tilt cylinder rod eye in a vise with the piston end facing straight up. Then carefully remove the nut (19, **Figure 41**) from the rod.

NOTE
The impact relief valve holes in the top of the tilt cylinder's piston must all measure 0.093 in. (2.36 mm). The four springs must be identical except that one spring, which is slightly shorter than the other three. If not, the wrong piston assembly is installed and it must be replaced with the correct piston.

13. Lift the washer (18, **Figure 41**) off of the piston. Remove the four springs, spring guides and check balls from the piston. These components make up the impact relief valves. Place these valve components in a plastic bag that is properly marked.

14. Slide the piston from the rod. Remove and discard the piston-to-rod O-ring, then remove and discard the O-ring from the groove on the piston's outer diameter.

15. Slide the end cap from the rod. Remove and discard the end cap's external O-ring.

16. Carefully pry the scraper from the end cap. Discard the scraper. Then pull the O-ring from the end cap bore using a suitable hooked tool (such as a dental pick). Do not damage the O-ring bore (in the end cap) during removal. Discard the O-ring.

17. Clean and inspect all components as described in this chapter.

Main housing cleaning and inspection

Use lint-free shop towels to handle all cleaned components. Even a single strand of lint can cause a check ball

(or valve) not to seat. Leaking valves will cause hydraulic malfunctions.

NOTE
Do not attempt to blow dry small components (such as check balls and springs). They are easily lost.

1. Wash all components in a mild solvent, such as mineral spirits. Blow the larger parts dry with compressed air. Allow the smaller components to air dry on a clean shop towel.

2. Inspect the tilt cylinder bore for corrosion, scoring and grooving. Very light (superficial) scuffing is acceptable. Inspect the cylinder bore threads for corroded, worn, damaged, missing or galled threads.

3. Inspect the trim ram bores for corrosion, scoring and grooving. Very light (superficial) scuffing is acceptable.

4. Inspect the manual release valve bore for scoring, scratches, nicks, grooves or corrosion damage. Make sure the manual release valve threads in the manifold are not damaged, corroded, worn or galled.

5. Inspect the tilt piston (17, **Figure 41**) and the trim rams (28) for wear, scratches or grooves on their outer diameters. Inspect each of the tilt piston's 4 valve seats for wear, indentations, debris or any other damage.

6. Inspect the tilt cylinder rod and trim ram rods for wear, scoring, grooving or any other damage. Remove all thread-locking adhesive from the tilt cylinder rod's threads.

7. Inspect the end cap threads for corroded, worn, damaged, missing or galled threads. Inspect the end cap's seal and scraper bores for nicks and gouges.

8. Inspect the O-ring groove(s) in all components for nicks, gouges, wear, corrosion or any damage.

9. Replace any and all damaged components based on the results of this inspection.

Main housing assembly

Refer to **Figure 41** for this procedure. Install all new O-rings and seals during the assembly procedure. Do not make any dry assemblies. Lubricate all internal components with OMC Power Trim/Tilt and Steering Fluid or Dexron II automatic transmission fluid. Do not use any type of grease on any internal components.

NOTE
Cleanliness is the greatest concern during assembly. Do not allow any dirt, debris, lint or any other foreign substance into the main housing during the assembly procedure. The system cannot function properly if it is contaminated.

10

1. Assemble the tilt cylinder end cap as follows:
   a. Lubricate and install a new O-ring into the end cap's internal groove. Make sure the O-ring has fully expanded into the groove.
   b. Lubricate a new scraper and install it into the end cap's external bore with the lip facing up (away from the cylinder). Press the scraper into the end cap until it is seated.
   c. Lubricate a new O-ring and install it into the end cap's external groove.

2. Clamp the eye end of the tilt cylinder rod (15, **Figure 41**) into a soft-jawed vise. The threaded end of the rod must face straight up. Lubricate the rod, then position a seal protector, such as part No. 326005 over the threaded end of the rod.

3. Carefully slide the end cap over the seal protector and onto the rod, being careful not to damage the end cap seals in the process. The threaded end of the end cap must face the threaded end of the rod. Then remove the seal protector.

4. Slide the piston (17, **Figure 41**) over the threaded end of the rod and up against the rod's shoulder. The side of the piston with the larger valve openings must face up (toward the threaded end of the rod).

5. Lubricate a new piston-to-rod O-ring and install it over the threaded end of the rod and against the piston.

6. Install the four impact relief check balls, spring guides (small end facing up), and springs (in that order) into the piston bores. The shorter spring may be installed in any of the four bores.

7. Position the washer (18, **Figure 41**) over the threaded end of the rod and up against the springs. Lightly coat the rod threads with OMC Nut Lock threadlocking adhesive, then install and tighten the nut (18) to 58-87 ft.-lb. (78.6-118.0 N•m).

8. Lubricate a new O-ring and install it into the groove in the outer diameter of the piston.

9. Clamp the main housing (20, **Figure 41**) in a soft-jawed vise. Clamp only across the lower pivot pin bore. The open end of the tilt cylinder bore must face straight up.

10. Lubricate the cylinder bore and piston liberally. Carefully insert the piston and rod assembly into the bore. Once the tapered edge of the cylinder wall is reached, apply a steady downward pressure to the rod eye, while wiggling the eye in a circular motion. Be patient and allow the O-ring to work past the taper and into the cylinder bore.

11. Once past the tapered wall, push the piston as far as possible into the bore while still allowing enough space between the end cap and cylinder to fill the cylinder with fluid. Then thread the end cap into the cylinder bore 2-3 turns. Do not tighten the end cap at this time.

12. Assemble both trim rams and their end caps as follows:

   a. Lubricate and install a new quad ring into each end cap's internal groove. Make sure the ring is fully expanded into the groove.
   b. Lubricate and install a new scraper into each end cap's external bore with the lip facing up (away from the end cap). Press each scraper into its end cap until it is seated.
   c. Lubricate and install a new O-ring into each end cap's external groove.
   d. Lubricate both trim rams, then slide an end cap over each rod. The threaded end of each cap must face the piston. Seat each end cap against its piston.

13. Lubricate and install a new O-ring and two backup rings into the groove in the outer diameter of each trim ram piston. The O-ring must be positioned between the backup rings and the open ends of the backup rings must be positioned 180° from each other.

14. Using 2 of the part No. 983213 Rod Holding Blocks (or equivalent aluminum blocks), clamp a trim ram in a vise. Install a thrust pad (26, **Figure 41**) into the threaded end of the trim ram. Then tighten the thrust pad to 84-108 in.-lb. (9.5-12.2 N•m). Repeat this procedure for the remaining trim ram.

NOTE
If the backup rings do not fit tightly against the bottom of each trim ram piston groove, hold the ring(s) in your hand and overlap the ends of the ring, temporarily reducing the diameter of the ring. Reduce diameter until the ring is approximately 75 % of the piston diameter. Hold the ring in this position for a few minutes and allow it to take a set. Then carefully install the ring into the trim ram piston groove, being careful not to expand it further than necessary.

15. Liberally lubricate both trim ram bores and both trim ram pistons. Carefully insert each trim ram piston into its respective bore. Once each piston has entered its bore, thread each end cap 2-3 turns into the main housing, then push both trim rams to the bottom of their bores.

16. Unthread both trim ram end caps and slide them up their trim ram just far enough to allow fluid to be added into the trim ram bores. Fill both trim ram bores with trim and tilt fluid to the top of their bores. This will greatly reduce the bleed time and ensure the system does not air lock.

17. Rethread both trim ram end caps into the main housing. Then tighten both end caps to 60-70 ft.-lb. (81.3-94.9 N•m) using end cap remover (part No. 436710) or an equivalent spanner wrench.

18. Position the filter (25, **Figure 41**) into its bore near the top of the tilt cylinder. Lubricate a new O-ring and install

it into the groove in the pipe plug (24). Install the pipe plug and tighten it securely.

19. Lubricate a new O-ring and install it in the groove on the reservoir-to-main housing mating surface. Carefully position the reservoir to the main housing, being careful not to displace the O-ring. Secure the reservoir with three screws. Evenly tighten the screws to 35-52 in.-lb. (4.0-5.9 N•m).

20. Lubricate a new O-ring and install it onto the fill plug. Then install the fill plug into the reservoir and tighten it hand tight at this time.

21. Unthread the tilt cylinder end cap (16, **Figure 41**) and fill the cylinder bore with trim and tilt fluid until the fluid is level with the threads at the top of the cylinder bore.

22. Thread the end cap into the cylinder bore as far as possible by hand, then tighten the end cap to 58-87 ft.-lb. (78.6-118.0 N•m) using a suitable spanner wrench, such as part No. 326485 or part No. 912084.

23. Install the pump (and valve body) assembly, then the electric motor, as described previously in this chapter. Make sure the reservoir is refilled with the recommended fluid before attempting operation.

Table 1 AMMETER TEST SPECIFICATIONS

Single ram system	
Full UP stall	7-12 amps
Full DOWN stall	15-20 amps
No load current draw	4.5 amps maximum
No load minimum rpm	5000
Conventional system	
Prestolite 3 in. (76.2 mm) diameter motor	
Full UP stall	30-35 amps
Full DOWN stall	21-25 amps
Trimming or Tilting UP	11-15 amps
No load current draw	7 amps maximum
No load minimum rpm	4700
Bosch 2.5 in. (63.5 mm) diameter motor	
Full UP stall	30-35 amps
Full DOWN stall	18-32 amps
Trimming or Tilting UP	7-10 amps
No load current draw	4.5 amps maximum
No load minimum rpm	5450
Showa 3 in. (76.2 mm) diameter motor	
Full UP stall	19-23 amps
Full DOWN stall	14-18 amps
Trimming UP	5-8 amps
Tilting UP	8-10 amps
No load current draw	4.5 amps maximum
No load minimum rpm	5000
Showa 2.4 in. (61 mm) diameter motor	
Full UP stall	25-29 amps
Full DOWN stall	12-17 amps
Trimming UP	7-9 amps
Tilting UP	9-12 amps
No load current draw	4.5 amps maximum
No load minimum rpm	5000
FasTrak system	
Full UP stall	60-75 amps
Full DOWN stall	35-45 amps
Trimming UP	approximately 22 amps
Trimming DOWN	approximately 16 amps
No load current draw	10 amps maximum
No load minimum rpm	7000

10

Table 2 NORMAL SYSTEM CYCLE TIMES

Single ram system	
Full DOWN to full UP	13-19 seconds
Full UP to full DOWN	10-16 seconds
Conventional system	
Prestolite 3 in. (76.2 mm)	
diameter motor	
Full range UP or DOWN	15-20 seconds
Full TRIM UP range only	7-9 seconds
Full TILT UP range only	7-9 seconds
Bosch 2.5 in. (63.5 mm)	
diameter motor	
Full DOWN to full UP	14-16 seconds
Full UP to full DOWN	15-20 seconds
Full TRIM UP range only	7-9 seconds
Full TILT UP range only	6-9 seconds
Showa 3 in. (76.2 mm)	
diameter motor	
Full range UP or DOWN	16-18 seconds
Full TRIM UP range only	8-10 seconds
Full TILT UP range only	7-9 seconds
Showa 2.4 in. (61 mm)	
diameter motor	
Full DOWN to full UP	14-16 seconds
Full UP to full DOWN	15-17 seconds
Full TRIM UP range only	8-10 seconds
Full TILT UP range only	6-7 seconds
FasTrak system	
Full TRIM range only	approximately 9 seconds

Table 3 HYDRAULIC PRESSURE SPECIFICATIONS

Operational mode	psi (kPa)
Conventional system	
UP running pressure	approximately 200 (1379)
DOWN running pressure	approximately 800 (5516)
Full UP stal	approximately 1500 (10343)
Full DOWN stall	approximately 900 (6206)
Maximum leak-down	200 psi (1379)
FasTrak system	
Running pressure	0-200 (0-1379)
Full UP stall	1400-1600 (9653-11032)
Full DOWN stall	approximately 800 (5516)
Maximum leak-down	200 (1379)

Table 4 TORQUE VALUES

Fastener	in.-lb.	ft.-lb.	N·m
Manual tilt assist cylinder			
Pivot pin set screw	24-26	–	2.7-2.9
Mounting bracket	–	18-20	24.4-27.1
Touch-trim tilt system			
Control cable nut	36-48	–	4.1-5.4
Lower mounting through-bolt	–	20-25	27.1-33.9
(continued)			

Table 4 TORQUE VALUES (continued)

Fastener	in.-lb.	ft.-lb.	N·m
Power trim/tilt systems			
Single ram systems			
Check valve housings	50-60	–	5.7-6.8
Electric motor	35-52	–	4.0-5.9
Fill plug	45-55	–	5.1-6.2
Filter valve plug	70-105	–	7.9-11.9
Lower mounting through-bolt	–	20-25	27.1-33.9
Manual release valve	45-55	–	5.1-6.2
Oil pump	25-30	–	2.8-3.4
Tilt cylinder end cap	–	56-84	75.9-113.9
Tilt cylinder piston nut	–	35-54	47.5-73.2
Tilt tube nut[1]	–	40-45	54.2-61.0
Conventional system			
Check valve cartridges	50-60	–	5.7-6.8
Electric motor	Securely		
Fill plug	45-50	–	5.1-5.7
Hydraulic line fittings	168-216	14-18	19.0-24.4
Manifold plate	25-30	–	2.89-3.4
Manual release valve	45-55	–	5.1-6.2
Oil pump	25-30	–	2.8-3.4
System mounting screws	–	18-20	24.4-27.1
Tilt cylinder end cap	–	18-21	24.4-28.5
Tilt cylinder piston nut	–	58-87	78.6-118.0
Tilt tube nut[2]	–	50-54	67.8-73.2
Trim ram end caps	–	55-60	74.6-81.3
Trim rod thrust plate nuts	–	30-35	40.7-47.5
FasTrak system			
Electric motor	35-52	–	4.0-5.9
Manual release valve	45-55	–	5.1-6.2
Pump-to-main housing	60-84	–	6.8-9.5
Reservoir	35-52	–	4.0-5.9
Starboard tilt tube nut[2]	–	50-54	67.8-73.2
Tilt cylinder end cap	–	58-87	78.6-118.0
Tilt cylinder piston nut	–	58-87	78.6-118.0
Trim ram end caps	–	60-70	81.3-94.9
Trim rod thrust pads	84-108	–	9.5-12.2

1. Loosen 1/4 turn after torquing.
2. Loosen 1/8-1/4 turn after torquing.

10

Table 5 POWER TRIM/TILT TROUBLESHOOTING (SINGLE RAM SYSTEM)

Condition	Probable cause	Solution
No trim up or down (motor runs fast)	Sheared pump coupler	Replace pump coupler.
Outboard leaks down (reverse lock still holds)	Manual release valve	Clean and inspect valve.
	UP check valve	Inspect and/or replace valve.
	Sticking pump control piston	Clean and inspect component.
	Thermal expansion valve	Inspect and/or replace valve.
Outboard leaks down and reverse lock fails	UP relief valve (in piston)	Inspect and/or replace piston.
	Piston O-rings and seals	Replace O-rings and seals.
	Impact relief valves	Inspect and/or replace piston.
	(continued)	

Table 5 POWER TRIM/TILT TROUBLESHOOTING (SINGLE RAM SYSTEM) (continued)

Condition	Probable cause	Solution
No reverse lock (but holds in forward)	Down check valve	Inspect and/or replace valve.
	Manual release valve	Clean and inspect valve.
	Sticking pump control piston	Clean and inspect component.
	Filter valve and seat	Inspect and/or replace valve.
	Broken or weak impact relief	Inspect and/or replace piston or UP relief valve springs.
Unit stuck full UP	Sticking pump control piston	Clean and inspect component.
	Blocked thermal expansion valve	Inspect and/or replace valve.
	Mechanical binding	Inspect midsection.
Sluggish operation	Air in system, low fluid level	Check fluid level and cycle unit to remove air.
	Electric motor binding	Test amperage draw.
	Pump assembly worn or leaking	Replace pump assembly.
Erratic operation (jerky or jumpy motion)	Air in system	Check fluid level and cycle unit to remove air
	Incompatible fluids	Drain system, flush, add correct fluid

Table 6 POWER TRIM/TILT TROUBLESHOOTING (CONVENTIONAL SYSTEM)

Condition	Probable cause	Solution
No trim up or down (motor runs fast)	Sheared pump coupler	Replace pump coupler.
Outboard leaks down in the tilt range only (reverse lock holds)	Trim up relief valve	Inspect and/or replace valve.
Outboard leaks down in the tilt and trim ranges (reverse lock holds)	Trim check valve	Inspect and test valve.
	Sticking pump control piston	Clean and inspect component.
	Expansion relief valve	Clean and inspect valve.
	Trim ram(s) leaking	Replace O-rings and seals.
Outboard leaks down and reverse lock fails	Manual release valve	Clean and inspect valve.
	Impact relief valves or tilt cylinder piston leaking	Clean, inspect and/or replace tilt piston, O-rings and seals.
No reverse lock (but holds in forward)	Reverse lock check valve	Inspect and test valve.
	Sticking pump control piston	Clean and inspect component.
	Filter valve and seat	Inspect and/or replace valve.
	Broken or weak impact relief or UP relief valve springs	Inspect and/or replace tilt cylinder piston.
Will not trim/tilt up (trim/tilts down normally)	Trim UP relief valve	Clean and inspect valve.
	Thermal expansion valve	Clean and inspect valve.
	Pump failure	Replace pump.
Will not trim/tilt down (trim/tilts up normally)	Filter valve and seat	Inspect and/or replace valve.
	DOWN relief valve	Clean and inspect valve.
	Pump failure	Replace pump.

(continued)

Table 6 POWER TRIM/TILT TROUBLESHOOTING (CONVENTIONAL SYSTEM)

Condition	Probable cause	Solution
Unit stuck full UP	Sticking pump control piston	Clean and inspect component.
	Blocked thermal expansion valve	Inspect and/or replace valve.
	Mechanical binding	Inspect midsection.
Sluggish operation	Air in system, low fluid level	Check fluid level and cycle unit to remove air.
	Electric motor binding	Test amperage draw.
	Pump assembly worn or leaking	Replace pump assembly.
Erratic operation (jerky or jumpy motion)	Air in system	Check fluid level and cycle unit to remove air.
	Incompatible fluids	Drain system, flush, add correct fluid.

Table 7 PRESSURE TEST RESULTS (CONVENTIONAL SYSTEM)

Condition	Probable cause	Solution
Low UP stall pressure (DOWN pressure OK)	Trim UP relief valve	Clean and inspect valve.
	Thermal expansion valve	Clean and inspect valve.
	Pump control piston O-ring	Replace O-ring, inspect bore.
	Defective pump assembly	Replace pump assembly.
Low DOWN stall pressure (UP pressure OK)	Down relief valve	Clean and inspect valve.
	Filter valve assembly	Clean and inspect valve.
	Pump control piston O-ring	Replace O-ring, inspect bore.
Low UP and DOWN stall pressure	Leaking tilt cylinder	Replace O-rings and seals. Inspect impact valves and cylinder bore.
	Leaking trim ram(s)	Replace O-rings and seals. Inspect ram bores (sleeves).
	Defective pump assembly	Replace pump assembly.
Excessive UP leak down (DOWN leak down OK)	Trim check valve	Inspect and test valve.
	Thermal expansion valve	Clean and inspect valve.
	Trim UP relief valve	Clean and inspect valve.
Excessive DOWN leak down (UP leak down OK)	Reverse lock check valve	Inspect and test valve.
	Filter valve assembly	Clean and inspect valve.
Excessive UP and DOWN leak down	Leaking tilt cylinder	Replace O-rings and seals. Inspect impact valves and cylinder bore.
	Leaking trim ram(s)	Replace O-rings and seals. Inspect ram bores (sleeves).

10

Table 8 POWER TRIM/TILT TROUBLESHOOTING (FASTRAK SYSTEM)

Condition	Probable cause	Solution
No trim up or down (motor runs fast)	Sheared pump coupler	Replace pump coupler.
Outboard leaks down (reverse lock holds)	Manual release valve	Inspect and/or replace.
	O-rings or internal valve	O-rings and/or valve.
	Defective pump and manifold	Replace pump and manifold.
	Expansion relief valve	Clean and inspect valve.
	(continued)	

Table 8 POWER TRIM/TILT TROUBLESHOOTING (FASTRAK SYSTEM) (continued)

Condition	Probable cause	Solution
Outboard leaks down and reverse lock fails	Manual release valve	Inspect and/or replace.
	O-rings or internal valve	O-rings and/or valve.
	Impact relief valvesor tilt cylinder piston leaking	Clean, inspect and/or replace tilt piston, O-rings and seals.
	Trim ram(s) leaking	Replace O-rings and seals.
	Defective pump and manifold	Replace pump and manifold.
No reverse lock (but holds in forward)	Manual release valve middle O-ring	Inspect and/or replace O-ring.
	Broken or weak impact relief valve springs	Inspect and/or replace tilt cylinder piston.
	Defective pump and manifold	Replace pump and manifold.
Will not trim/tilt up (trim/tilts down normally)	Defective thermal expansion valve (in manual release valve)	Replace manual release valve.
	Pump and manifold failure	Replace pump and manifold
Will not trim/tilt down (trim/tilts up normally)	Manual release valve middle O-ring	Inspect and/or replace O-ring.
	Pump and manifold failure	Replace pump and manifold.
Unit stuck full UP	Defective thermal expansion valve (in manual release valve)	Replace manual release valve.
	Mechanical binding	Inspect midsection.
	Defective pump and manifold	Replace pump and manifold.
Sluggish operation	Air in system, low fluid level	Check fluid level and cycle unit to remove air.
	Electric motor binding	Test amperage draw.
	Pump worn or leaking internally	Replace pump and manifold.
Erratic operation (jerky or jumpy motion)	Air in system	Check fluid level and cycle unit to remove air.
	Incompatible fluids	Drain system, flush, add correct fluid.

Table 9 PRESSURE TEST RESULTS (FASTRAK SYSTEM)

Condition	Probable cause	Solution
Low UP stall pressure (DOWN pressure OK)	Internal pump failure	Replace pump assembly.
	Leaking trim ram(s)	Replace O-rings and seals.
Low DOWN stall pressure (UP pressure OK)	Internal pump failure	Replace pump assembly.
Low UP and DOWN stall pressure	Leaking tilt cylinder	Replace O-rings and seals. Inspect impact valves and cylinder bore.
	Internal pump failure	Replace pump assembly.
Excessive UP leak down (DOWN leak down OK)	Leaking trim ram(s)	Replace O-rings and seals.
	Internal pump failure	Replace pump assembly.
Excessive DOWN leak down (UP leak down OK)	Internal pump failure	Replace pump assembly.
Excessive UP and DOWN leak down	Leaking tilt cylinder	Replace O-rings and seals. Inspect impact valves and cylinder bore.

Chapter Eleven

Oil Injection Systems

The internal power head components are lubricated by mixing oil with the gasoline. On non-oil injected models, the oil and gasoline are premixed in the fuel tank(s) by the boat operator. The recommended fuel/oil mixture ratio for normal operation in all models without oil injection is 50:1.

On oil-injected models, the oil is automatically mixed with the gasoline. Depending on the system, an engine-mounted (or remote) fuel and oil pump (or fuel and oil mixing unit) delivers the correct, premixed fuel and oil mixture to the carburetors.

The various engine components are lubricated as the fuel and oil mixture passes through the crankcases and into the combustion chambers.

The advantage of oil injection is that the operator only has to keep the oil reservoir(s) filled. No calculations are required as to how much oil to add when refueling. Over (and under) oiling from operator miscalculations is eliminated, along with the associated engine problems caused by under or over oiling.

Three different oil injection systems are used on models covered in this chapter:

1. *AccuMix R*—Optional accessory on 4-30 hp (two-cylinder), 18 and 28 jet, 40 hp (rope start) and 48 Special models
2. *Constant ratio oil injection*—The 25 and 35 hp (Three-cylinder) models are equipped with a constant ratio oil injection system as standard equipment.
3. *VRO^2 oil injection*—The VRO^2 oil injection system is standard equipment on the 35 jet, 40 hp (electric start) and all 50-70 hp Models.

Refer to Chapter Four for fuel and oil requirements, engine break-in procedures and oil tank filling procedures.

Table 1 lists oil injection system specifications and **Table 2** special torque values. All tables are located at the end of the chapter.

SERVICE PRECAUTIONS

1998-2003 Model Year Engines

The EPA (Environmental Protection Agency) certifies emission output for all 1998-2003 models. Certified models have an EPA certification plate mounted near the model identification plate on the engine midsection. Refer to *Model Identification* in Chapter Eight for illustrations and additional information on the certification plate.

All repairs or service procedures must be performed exactly as specified to ensure the engine will continue to comply with EPA requirements. For the same reason, all replacement parts must meet or exceed the manufacturer's specifications.

If in doubt as to whether a repair or service procedure will adversely affect the engine's ability to maintain EPA compliance, contact an Evinrude or Johnson dealership, before beginning the repair or procedure.

Fuel And Oil Line Removal/Installation

When removing fuel and/or oil lines from fittings, push the line off of the fitting whenever possible. Pulling on the line only tightens its grip on the fitting. Plastic fittings can be easily damaged or broken from excessive forcing, causing unnecessary component replacement.

If necessary, cut the line with a razor knife and peel the line from the fitting. Replacing the line is always more economical than replacing a fuel or oil injection system component. See *Fuel Lines, Primer Bulbs, Fittings and Connectors*, in Chapter Six, for additional information.

The oil lines on VRO^2 systems must be secured with ratchet (snapper) clamps or the original spring clamps (as equipped). Worm clamps and tie-straps may not be used on VRO^2 system oil lines. See Chapter Six for additional clamp information.

ACCUMIX R OIL INJECTION SYSTEM

System Description

The AccuMix R (remote-mounted) oil and gasoline mixing (injection) system is an optional accessory on 4-30 hp (Two-cylinder), 18 and 28 Jet, 40 hp rope start and 48 Special models. The AccuMix R system (**Figure 1**) is designed to deliver a constant 50:1 fuel/oil mixture to the engine's fuel system at all engine speeds and load conditions.

A bracket-mounted tank with a 2 qt. (1.89 L) oil reservoir is connected between the fuel tank and the engine, providing enough oil capacity for approximately 22 gal. (83 L) of fuel. The diaphragm operated fuel and oil mixing chamber is actuated by the vacuum of the engine's fuel pump drawing fuel to the engine. The AccuMix R system is not equipped with a warning system. Should the oil level fall below the predetermined level, a magnetic float switch (3, **Figure 1**) will pull a fuel piston valve closed, preventing fuel flow to the engine. Refilling the oil reservoir lifts the magnetic float switch, releasing the fuel piston and allowing fuel to flow to the engine.

A serviceable filter (10, **Figure 1**) filters all oil added to the reservoir. Remove and clean the filter anytime debris is evident or if it is difficult to fill the reservoir.

The fuel and oil mixing unit is not serviceable and is replaced as an assembly. Currently, the complete unit is less expensive to purchase than the fuel and oil mixing unit alone.

System Operation

As the fuel and oil mix is pulled from the AccuMix R unit (by the power head mounted fuel pump), the diaphragm in the AccuMix R mixing unit (2, **Figure 1**) is pulled downward, compressing its spring. The downward movement of the diaphragm pulls straight fuel into the mixing unit's upper chamber through the fuel inlet fitting and check valve. The diaphragm also pulls the oil pump piston in the mixing unit downward with it, drawing straight oil from the reservoir into the oil pump portion of the mixing unit.

Once the diaphragm reaches the limit of its downward travel, a poppet valve in the diaphragm opens, equalizing the pressure above and below the diaphragm. At this point the spring below the diaphragm pushes the diaphragm upward (along with the oil pump piston), closing the fuel inlet check valve. The upward movement of the oil pump piston closes the oil pump's inlet check valve, forcing the oil into the mixing chamber, where it mixes with the fuel to create an approximate 50:1 fuel/oil mixture.

As soon as the diaphragm reaches the limit of its upward travel, the poppet valve closes and the fuel/oil mix in the lower chamber is free to be pulled to the power head. The cycle repeats itself as necessary to keep up with the engine's fuel demands. The cycle repeats fastest at wide-open throttle.

Troubleshooting and
Verifying Correct System Operation

The Two failure modes of the AccuMix R system are *no fuel/oil flow* or *insufficient oil flow*. If the system is suspected of malfunctioning, refer to one of the following sections for the troubleshooting procedure.

If you wish to simply verify correct operation of the system, refer to *Insufficient oil flow*.

> *NOTE*
> *If the conventional fuel pump on the power head is malfunctioning, the AccuMix R system cannot operate correctly. If there is any question as to the condition of the conventional fuel pump, refer to Chapter Three and perform the fuel pump pressure and vacuum tests.*

No fuel or oil flow

If the unit will not allow fuel and oil to pass through as the primer bulb is squeezed, the most likely cause of the problem is that the reservoir's oil level is too low or the magnetic float switch is stuck or malfunctioning.

1. Verify that that the reservoir is filled above the point where the float (3, **Figure 1**) is completely submerged.

2. If the oil level is above the float, the float may be stuck. Remove the reservoir from its mounting bracket and briefly invert the unit. Then shake the unit briskly and

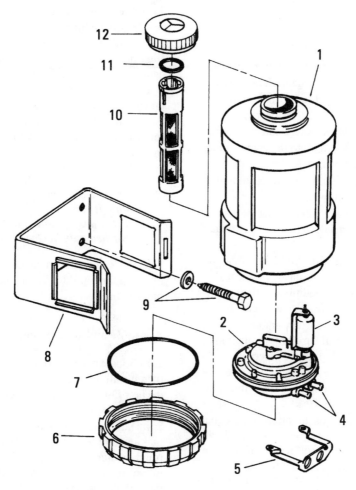

ACCUMIX R UNIT

1. Reservoir
2. Fuel and oil
   mixing unit
3. Magnetic float switch
4. Fuel line fittings
5. Support bracket
6. Retainer ring
7. O-ring
8. Mounting bracket
9. Lag screw
   and washer
10. Filter
11. Seal
12. Cap

11

reinstall it into the mounting bracket. Recheck for fuel flow.

3. If the unit still will not allow fuel and oil to pass through when the primer bulb is squeezed, replace the fuel/oil mixing unit (or the complete AccuMix R unit).

Insufficient oil flow

If the unit does not mix the correct amount of oil with the fuel, the engine will suffer an internal failure or excessive internal wear from the lack of proper lubrication.

If the unit is suspected of not delivering the correct amount of oil with the fuel, *immediately* add the correct amount of recommended outboard oil to the engine's fuel tank to provide a 50:1 fuel/oil premix.

To verify that the system is adding the correct amount of oil with the fuel, proceed as follows:

1. Make sure the boat's fuel tank is full and that the correct amount of outboard oil has been added to the fuel to obtain a 50:1 (fuel/oil) premix.

2. Fill the oil reservoir until it is full. Make sure that you fill the reservoir to a point that can be easily duplicated.

3. Operate the boat under normal conditions until approximately 6 gal. (22.7 L) of fuel has been consumed.

4. Refill the fuel tank, noting the exact amount of fuel required to fill the tank. Then refill the oil reservoir, noting the exact amount of oil required to fill the reservoir.

5A. If no oil was consumed, the AccuMix R system is malfunctioning and the fuel/oil mixing unit (or the complete AccuMix R unit) must be replaced.

5B. If oil was consumed, the consumption must equal approximately 16 fl. oz. (473 mL) of oil for every 6 gal. (22.7 L) of fuel. There are 128 fl. oz. (3785 mL) in a gallon of fuel. Multiply the gallons of fuel used by 128 (3785), then divide the result by the fl. oz. (mL) of oil used. The result must be between 40 and 60 (50 optimum).

    a. If the number is lower than 40, excessive oil is being consumed.

    b. If the number is higher than 60, insufficient oil is being consumed.

    c. In either case, the AccuMix R system is malfunctioning and the fuel/oil mixing unit (or the complete AccuMix R unit) must be replaced.

Removal and Disassembly

1. *Electric start models*—Disconnect the negative battery cable from the battery to eliminate the chance of electrical sparks.

2. Locate the AccuMix R unit in the boat's bilge (or transom), then mark each fuel line so it can be reattached to its original fitting on the AccuMix unit.

3. Remove the tie-straps or clamps securing the lines to the AccuMix R unit. Carefully disconnect each line, then cap the fittings and plug the lines to prevent leakage and contamination.

4. Remove the unit from its mounting bracket (8, **Figure 1**) and set it on a clean workbench.

5. Remove the fill cap and seal (11 and 12, **Figure 1**). Then pull the filter tube (10) from the fill cap opening. Wash the filter in a mild solvent (such as mineral spirits). If the filter cannot be satisfactorily cleaned, replace it.

6. Pour the contents of the reservoir into a suitable container. Dispose of the old oil in an approved manner.

7. Unscrew the large retaining ring (6, **Figure 1**) and remove it from the reservoir. Then separate the fuel/oil mixing unit (2) from the reservoir.

NOTE
*Do not attempt to disassemble the mixing unit. It can only be replaced as an assembly. If the mixing unit is to be reused, it can be washed **only** in clean outboard motor oil.*

8. Remove and discard the O-ring (7, **Figure 1**). Wash the reservoir in a mild solvent, then blow it dry with compressed air.

Assembly and Installation

1. Lubricate a new O-ring (7, **Figure 1**) with outboard oil, then install the fuel/oil mixing unit to the reservoir (using the new O-ring). Install the retaining ring (6, **Figure 1**) and tighten it securely.

2. Install the unit into its mounting bracket (8, **Figure 1**), making sure it snaps into place. If the boat is operated in rough water, use an extra-long tie-strap to clamp the mounting bracket's ears together. Install the tie-strap through the slot in one ear, then pull the tie-strap across the reservoir and engage the slot in the other ear. Tighten the tie-strap until it is snug.

3. Reconnect the fuel lines to the fuel/oil mixing unit's fittings. Make sure each line is reattached to its original fitting. Secure the connections with new tie-straps, ratchet clamps or the original worm clamps. Tighten each clamp securely.

4. Install the filter (10, **Figure 1**) into the reservoir's fill cap opening. Then fill the reservoir with the recommended outboard oil.

5. Install the fill cap using a new seal (11, **Figure 1**). Tighten the fill cap securely.

6. *Electric start models*—Reconnect the negative battery cable. Make sure the connection is tightened securely.

7. Operate the outboard engine on a 50:1 fuel/oil premix until correct operation of the unit is verified as described in *Insufficient oil flow*, located previously in this chapter.

CONSTANT RATIO OIL INJECTION
(25 AND 35 HP [THREE-CYLINDER])

System Description

This oil injection system is used on all 25 and 35 hp (Three-cylinder) models and provides the engine with a constant 50:1 fuel/oil ratio at all engine speeds and load conditions. The fuel and oil mixing unit is externally mounted, near the bottom of the engine-mounted oil reservoir and is driven by pressure pulses from the starboard fuel pump's pressure.

The engine-mounted oil tank's capacity is 1.9 qt (1.8 L). An internal float switch (A, **Figure 2**), provides a low oil signal when the level is low and a separate no oil signal when the oil tank is almost empty. Fill the oil tank as soon as possible after the low oil signal is noted. Fill the tank immediately upon noting the no oil signal.

On tiller handle models, an engine mounted LED (light emitting diode), located near the starter rope handle, will illuminate when the oil tank reaches the *low oil* level. If engine operation is continued, when the oil tank reaches the no oil level, the ignition module will engage the S.L.O.W. (speed limiting operational warning) system. The low oil LED will remain illuminated at both the low oil and no oil levels.

On remote control (1995 [EO]) models an engine mounted LED (light emitting diode) will illuminate when the oil tank reaches the low oil level. If engine operation is continued, when the oil tank reaches the no oil level, the warning horn will sound, and the ignition module will engage the S.L.O.W. (speed limiting operational warning) system. The low oil LED will remain illuminated at both the low oil and no oil levels. The warning system incorporates a self-test function. Refer to Warning Systems in Chapter Three.

Remote control (1996-2003 [ED-ST]) models—The System Check gauge's low oil LED will illuminate and the warning horn will sound for ten seconds when the oil tank

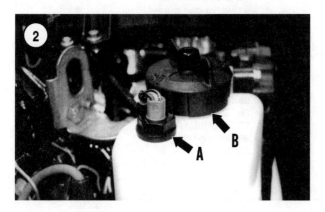

reaches the *low oil level*. If engine operation is continued and the oil tank reaches the *no oil* level, the System Check gauge's no oil LED will illuminate, the ignition module will engage the S.L.O.W. (speed limiting operational warning) system and the warning horn will sound for ten seconds. The low oil LED will remain illuminated at both the low oil and no oil levels. The warning system incorporates a self-test function. Refer to *Warning Systems* in Chapter Three.

> *WARNING*
> *Continued operation of the engine after the* **no oil** *warning has activated will cause power head damage.*

Filling the oil tank requires removing the engine cowl. Remove the fill cap (B, **Figure 2**) and fill the tank with the recommended outboard oil (Chapter Four). Reinstall the fill cap securely.

System Operation

Unlike the AccuMix R system, this unit is operated by fuel pump pressure. Since the unit is under positive pressure at all times, a fuel inlet check valve is not used. Refer to **Figure 3** for this description.

Straight fuel is pushed into the angled fitting (27, **Figure 3**) at the bottom of the fuel/oil mixing unit by the starboard fuel pump. As the fuel is forced into the mixing unit, it pushes the diaphragm (8, **Figure 3**) upward, compressing the large spring (6, **Figure 3**) on top of the diaphragm. The upward movement of the diaphragm pushes the fuel and oil mix from the previous cycle out of the fitting (3, **Figure 3**) at the top of the unit and on to the carburetors. An oil pump piston moves upward along with the diaphragm, drawing oil in from the reservoir through the straight fitting (26, **Figure 3**) on the bottom of the mixing unit.

Once the diaphragm reaches the limit of its upward travel, a poppet valve in the diaphragm opens, equalizing the pressure above and below the diaphragm. At this point the large spring above the diaphragm pushes the diaphragm down along with the oil pump piston. The downward movement of the oil pump piston closes the oil pump's inlet check valve (17, **Figure 3**), forcing the oil through the outlet check valve (18, **Figure 3**) into the mixing chamber, where it mixes with the fuel to create an approximate 50:1 fuel/oil mixture.

As soon as the diaphragm reaches the limit of its downward travel, the poppet spring (7, **Figure 3**) closes the poppet valve and the fuel/oil mixture in the upper chamber is pushed to the carburetors as the diaphragm begins its upward movement. The cycle repeats itself as necessary to

11

③

**FUEL/OIL MIXING UNIT
(25 AND 35 HP [THREE-CYLINDER] MODELS)**

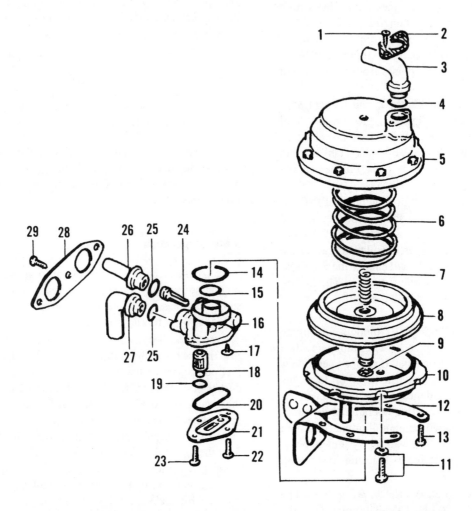

1. Screw
2. Fitting retainer plate
3. Fuel outlet fitting
4. O-ring
5. Main housing
6. Larger spring
7. Poppet spring
8. Diaphragm and oil piston
9. Oil piston seal
10. Intermediate housing
11. Screw and washer
12. Mounting bracket
13. Screw
14. Large O-ring
15. Small O-ring
16. Oil pump housing
17. Oil inlet check valve
18. Oil outlet check
    valve cartridge
19. O-ring
20. Cover seal
21. Oil pump cover
22. Cover screw
23. Mounting screw
24. Oil inlet filter
25. O-rings
26. Oil inlet fitting
27. Fuel inlet fitting
28. Fitting retainer plate
29. Screw

keep up with the engine's fuel demands. The cycle repeats fastest at wide-open throttle.

Troubleshooting

To troubleshoot any problems noted in the warning system, refer to Chapter Three.

If the unit does not mix the correct amount of oil with the fuel, the engine will suffer an internal failure or excessive internal wear from the lack of proper lubrication. Due to the design of the system, it is highly unlikely that the system will mix excessive oil with the fuel.

The system incorporates two oil filters. One filter is located in the reservoir outlet fitting (16, **Figure 4**) and the second filter (24, **Figure 3**) is located inside of the fuel/oil mixing unit.

NOTE
If the conventional fuel pumps on the power head are malfunctioning, the fuel/oil mixing unit cannot operate correctly. If there is any question as to the condition of the conventional fuel pumps, refer to Chapter Three and perform the fuel pump pressure and vacuum tests.

If the unit is suspected of not delivering the correct amount of oil with the fuel, immediately add the correct amount of recommended outboard motor oil to the engine's fuel tank.

NOTE
Electric fuel supply pumps are not recommended by OMC.

To verify that the system is adding the correct amount of oil to the fuel, proceed as follows:

1. Make sure the boat's fuel tank is full and that the correct amount of outboard oil has been added to the fuel (50:1 fuel/oil premix).

2. Fill the oil reservoir until it is full. Make sure that you fill the reservoir to a point that can be easily duplicated.

3. Operate the boat under normal conditions until approximately 6 gal. (22.7 L) of fuel has been consumed.

4. Refill the fuel tank, noting the exact amount of fuel required to fill the tank. Then refill the oil reservoir, noting the exact amount of oil required to fill the reservoir.

5A. If no oil was consumed, disconnect the oil supply line from the reservoir outlet fitting (16, **Figure 4**). Hold a suitable container under the fitting and check for oil flow from the reservoir.

   a. If the oil flows freely, the fuel/oil mixing unit is malfunctioning and must be repaired or replaced as

an assembly. If the unit is to be repaired, make sure the internal oil filter (24, **Figure 3**) is replaced.

   b. If the oil does not flow freely, remove the reservoir and clean (or replace) the filter in the oil outlet fitting (16, **Figure 4**) at the bottom of the reservoir. Make sure the reservoir is thoroughly cleaned with a mild solvent (such as mineral spirits) and dried before reinstalling the filter and refilling the reservoir. Then repeat this procedure.

5B. If oil was consumed, the consumption must equal approximately 16 fl. oz. (473 mL) of oil for every 6 gal. (22.7 L) of fuel. There are 128 fl. oz. (3785 mL) in a gallon of fuel. Multiply the gallons of fuel used by 128 (3785), then divide the result by the fl. oz. (mL) of oil used. The result must be between 40 and 60 (50 optimum).

   a. If the number is lower than 40, excessive oil is being consumed. Proceed to Step 6.

   b. If the number is higher than 60, insufficient oil is being consumed. Proceed to Step 7.

6. If the number determined in Step 5B is lower than 40, the fuel/oil mixing unit is malfunctioning and must be repaired or replaced as an assembly.

7. If the number determined in Step 5B is higher than 60, the oil supply to the mixing unit may be restricted, the internal oil filter may be plugged or the fuel/oil unit may be malfunctioning.

   a. Perform Step 5A to verify that the oil supply is not restricted.

   b. If the oil supply is not restricted, the fuel/oil mixing unit must be repaired or replaced as an assembly. If the unit is to be repaired, make sure the internal oil filter (24, **Figure 3**) is replaced.

Oil Reservoir and Mixing Unit Removal

While the oil reservoir can be removed without removing the fuel/oil mixing unit, removal of the reservoir and mixing unit as an assembly is recommended.

Do not disconnect the fuel and oil lines from the bottom of the fuel/oil mixing unit unless line replacement is necessary or the mixing unit is to be disassembled.

To remove the oil reservoir and fuel/oil mixing unit, refer to **Figure 4** and proceed as follows:

1. *Electric start models*—Disconnect the negative battery cable from the battery).

2. Disconnect the fuel supply line from the quick-disconnect connector.

3. Remove the starboard side of the split lower cowl as follows:

   a. Remove the six screws securing the cowl halves to each other. Access the screws from the starboard side.

11

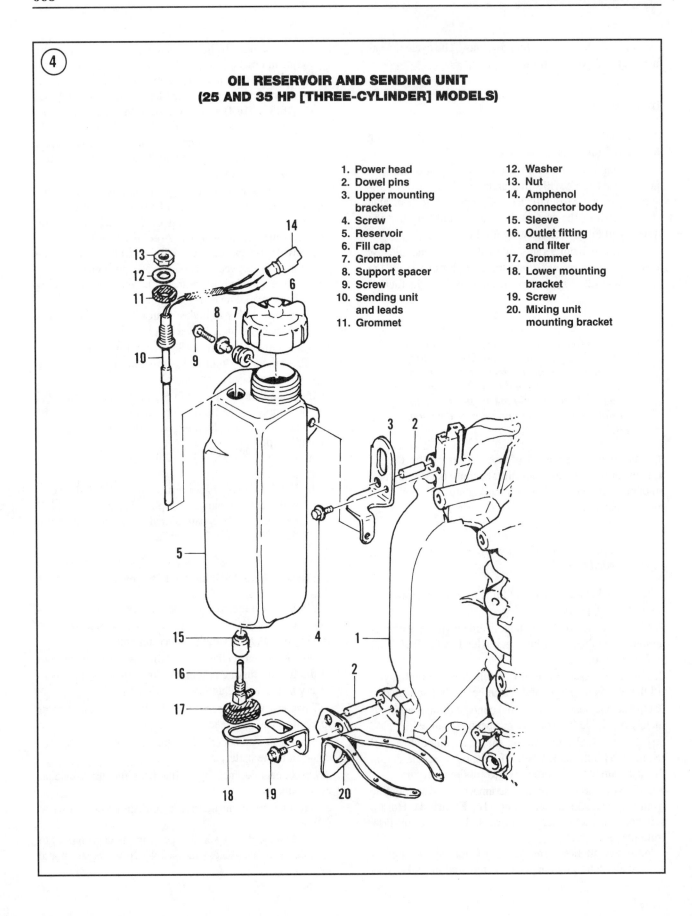

④

**OIL RESERVOIR AND SENDING UNIT
(25 AND 35 HP [THREE-CYLINDER] MODELS)**

1. Power head
2. Dowel pins
3. Upper mounting bracket
4. Screw
5. Reservoir
6. Fill cap
7. Grommet
8. Support spacer
9. Screw
10. Sending unit and leads
11. Grommet
12. Washer
13. Nut
14. Amphenol connector body
15. Sleeve
16. Outlet fitting and filter
17. Grommet
18. Lower mounting bracket
19. Screw
20. Mixing unit mounting bracket

b. Remove the clamp securing the electrical leads to the starboard cowl. Then remove the starboard lower cowl.

4. Disconnect the oil reservoir sending unit from its three-pin Amphenol connector (14, **Figure 4**).

5. Remove the screw (9, **Figure 4**) securing the top of the reservoir to the top mounting bracket (3).

6. Disconnect the fuel supply line coming from the starboard fuel pump from the inline fuel filter. Remove and discard the fuel filter.

7. Remove the screw (19, **Figure 4**) securing the oil reservoir and mixing unit mounting brackets to the bottom of the power head. Support the reservoir as the screw is removed.

CAUTION
*Refer to **Fuel and Oil Line Removal/Installation** at the beginning of this chapter before proceeding.*

8. Carefully pull the reservoir far enough from the power head to access the fuel outlet line at the top of the mixing unit. Carefully disconnect the fuel outlet line from the mixing unit fitting (3, **Figure 3**).

9. Remove the reservoir cap (6, **Figure 4**) and empty the reservoir into a suitable container.

10. To separate the fuel/oil mixing unit from the reservoir, disconnect the oil outlet line from the fitting (16, **Figure 4**) at the bottom of the reservoir. Then pull the mixing unit and bracket from the reservoir.

11. Remove the outlet fitting (16, **Figure 4**) from the bottom of the reservoir. Wash the fitting and its internal filter thoroughly in a mild solvent (such as mineral spirits). Blow the fitting and filter dry with compressed air. If the filter cannot be satisfactorily cleaned, replace the fitting and filter.

12. If the sending unit requires replacement, refer to *Sending unit replacement* in this chapter.

13. Wash the reservoir in a mild solvent, then blow it dry with compressed air.

Oil Reservoir and Mixing Unit Installation

1. Position the reservoir into the grommet (17, **Figure 4**) in the lower mounting bracket (18), then position the mixing unit's mounting bracket (20) over the lower mounting bracket. Connect the oil supply line (coming from the fuel/oil mixing unit) to the fitting at the bottom of the reservoir. Secure the connection with a new tie-strap.

2. Position the reservoir and mixing unit assembly on the starboard side of the power head. Connect the fuel outlet line (coming from the carburetors) to the angle fitting (3, **Figure 3**) at the top of the mixing unit. Secure the connection with a new tie-strap.

3. Position the lower mounting bracket over the roll pin (2, **Figure 4**) at the base of the power head. Apply OMC Nut Lock threadlocking adhesive to the threads of the lower bracket screw (19). Install and tighten the screw to 180-204 in.-lb. (20.3-23.1 N•m).

4. Verify that the rubber grommet and support spacer (7 and 8, **Figure 4**) are installed in the hole at the top of the reservoir. Apply OMC Ultra Lock threadlocking adhesive to the threads of the upper bracket screw (9). Align the holes, then install and tighten the screw to 216-240 in.-lb. (24.4-27.1 N•m).

5. Reconnect the sending unit's three-pin Amphenol connector to its engine harness mate.

6. Install a new fuel filter with its arrow pointing toward the fuel/oil mixing unit. Secure the connections with the original spring clamps or new tie-straps.

7. Fill the reservoir with the recommended outboard oil (Chapter Four) and check for oil leaks. Correct any found.

8. Reattach the fuel supply line from the fuel tank to the quick-disconnect fitting at the front of the engine. Squeeze the primer bulb firmly and check for leaks. Correct any found.

9. Install the split lower cowl as follows:
   a. Position the starboard lower cowl close to the power head and secure the appropriate electrical leads to its clamp. Then seat the starboard lower cowl to the engine.
   b. Install the cowl screws. Install the screws from the starboard side. Tighten all of the screws to 84-106 in.-lb. (9.5-12.0 N•m).

10. *Electric start models*—Reconnect the negative battery cable. Tighten the connection securely.

11. Run the engine on a 50:1 fuel/oil premix until correct operation of the fuel/oil mixing unit is verified as described in *Troubleshooting* in this chapter.

Oil Reservoir Sending Unit Removal/Installation

The sending unit (A, **Figure 2**) can be removed and installed while the reservoir is still attached to the power head. The reservoir does not need to be drained for this procedure. The sending unit is held in its bore by an expanding grommet (11, **Figure 4**).

1. *Electric start models*—Disconnect the negative battery cable from the battery.

2. Disconnect the sending unit electrical leads at the three-pin Amphenol connector (14, **Figure 4**).

3. Hold the top of the sending unit with a suitable wrench, then loosen the sending unit's nut (13, **Figure 4**) with another wrench. Once the nut is loosened, the sending unit may be removed from the oil reservoir.

11

4. If the grommet, washer or plastic nut (11-13, **Figure 4**) require service, the Amphenol connector body (14) must be removed from the sending unit leads. Refer to *Electrical Connector Service* in Chapter Three for service procedures on Amphenol connectors.

5. If necessary, remove the Amphenol connector body and slide the plastic nut, washer and grommet from the electrical leads. Discard the grommet.

6. If removed, install a new grommet over the electrical leads and against the shoulder of the sending unit. The large end of the grommet must face UP. Then slide the washer and plastic nut over the leads and against the grommet.

7. If removed, install the Amphenol connector body to the sending unit leads as described in *Electrical Connector Service* in Chapter Three. The tan/yellow lead must be installed in Pin A, the black lead in Pin B and the tan/black lead in Pin C.

8. Position the sending unit into the oil reservoir. Make sure the grommet is seated in its bore and the sending unit is touching the bottom of the reservoir.

9. Hold the top of the sending unit with a wrench, then tighten the sending unit's nut with another wrench. Tighten the nut securely, keeping in mind that the components are plastic.

10. Reconnect the sending unit's three-pin Amphenol connector to its engine harness mate.

11. *Electric start models*—Reconnect the negative battery cable. Tighten the connection securely.

Fuel/Oil Mixing
Unit Disassembly

A repair kit is available from the manufacturer and contains the O-rings and seals necessary to completely disassemble and reassemble the mixing unit. The diaphragm is not part of the repair kit. Refer to **Figure 5** for this procedure.

1. Remove the oil reservoir and fuel/oil mixing unit, and separate the mixing unit from the reservoir as described in this chapter.

2. Carefully remove the short fuel and oil lines attached to the fittings (26 and 27, **Figure 5**) from the bottom of the mixing unit.

3. Remove the two screws (23, **Figure 5**) securing the oil pump housing (16) to the intermediate housing (10). These are the larger of the four screws on the oil pump cover. Then separate the oil pump housing from the main housing.

4. Remove the two O-rings (14 and 15, **Figure 5**) from the oil pump housing-to-intermediate housing mating surface.

5. Remove the two screws securing the cover (21, **Figure 5**) to the oil pump housing. These are the two remaining

screws in the cover. Separate the cover from the housing. Then remove and discard the molded seal (20) from the cover's groove.

6. Remove the three screws (29, **Figure 5**) securing the line fitting retaining plate (28) to the oil pump housing. Remove the plate, then remove each fitting. Remove and discard each fitting's O-ring (25).

7. Remove and discard the oil filter (24, **Figure 5**) in the oil pump housing. Use a suitable hooked tool to pull the filter from its bore.

8. Remove and discard the inlet check valve (17, **Figure 5**). The valve is located in the oil pump housing (16) and is a simple rubber disc, held in place by a molded stem. Simply pull the valve from the housing and discard it.

9. Push the outlet check valve and O-ring (18 and 19, **Figure 5**) from the oil pump housing. Do not attempt to pull the valve from its bore, as the bore is easily damaged. Discard the O-ring.

10. Note the orientation of the fuel outlet fitting (3, **Figure 5**) to the main housing. Remove the two screws securing the fitting to the housing. Remove the retaining plate, then pull the fitting from the housing. Remove and discard the fitting's O-ring.

11. Carefully remove the seal (9, **Figure 5**) from the tip of the oil piston. Do not damage the piston or its seal groove during removal.

12. Note the orientation of the main and intermediate)housing assembly to the mounting bracket (12, **Figure 5**), then remove the six screws (13) securing the housing to the bracket. Separate the bracket from the housing. Do not remove the two screws and washers (11) that do not pass through the mounting bracket.

13. Mark the main housing and intermediate housing so they can be reassembled in the same orientation, then remove the two remaining screws and washers (11, **Figure 5**) securing the main housing to the intermediate housing.

14. Carefully separate the main and intermediate housings, diaphragm and large and small springs.

15. Wash all components in a mild solvent (such as mineral spirits), then blow them dry with compressed air.

16. Inspect all components for wear and deterioration. Carefully inspect the diaphragm and its piston. Inspect the cylinder in the oil pump housing for scoring, grooves or other damage. Inspect all housings for cracks, distortion, stripped threads or other damage. Replace all parts that are in questionable condition.

Fuel/Oil Mixing
Unit Assembly

Install new O-rings and seals during assembly. A repair kit available from the manufacturer simplifies this process.

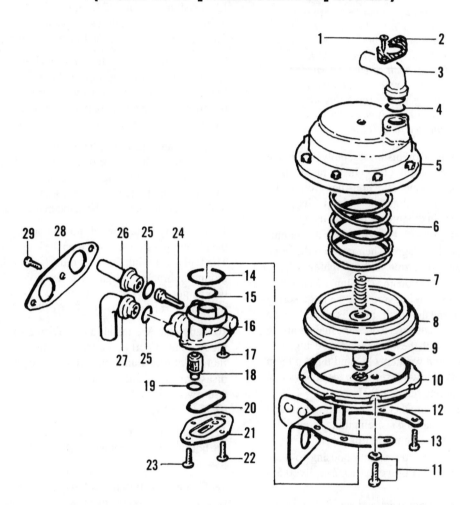

5

**FUEL/OIL MIXING UNIT
(25 AND 35 HP [THREE-CYLINDER] MODELS)**

1. Screw
2. Fitting retainer plate
3. Fuel outlet fitting
4. O-ring
5. Main housing
6. Larger spring
7. Poppet spring
8. Diaphragm and oil piston
9. Oil piston seal
10. Intermediate housing
11. Screw and washer
12. Mounting bracket
13. Screw
14. Large O-ring
15. Small O-ring
16. Oil pump housing
17. Oil inlet check valve
18. Oil outlet check
    valve cartridge
19. O-ring
20. Cover seal
21. Oil pump cover
22. Cover screw
23. Mounting screw
24. Oil inlet filter
25. O-rings
26. Oil inlet fitting
27. Fuel inlet fitting
28. Fitting retainer plate
29. Screw

11

Lubricate all internal components, seals and O-rings with the recommended outboard oil (Chapter Four).

CAUTION
When installing screws into plastic housings, extreme care must be taken to prevent cross-threading the screws. Cross-threading the screws will cause the housing threads to prematurely fail. Install each screw into its bore, then slowly turn each screw backward (counterclockwise) until you feel each screw drop into the housing's preformed threads. Once the threads are properly engaged, each screw may be tightened as specified.

1. Install the diaphragm and oil piston assembly (8, **Figure 5**) into the intermediate housing (10). The oil piston must protrude through the intermediate housing. Rotate the diaphragm as necessary to align the holes in its outer diameter with the holes in the intermediate housing.

2. Position the poppet spring (7, **Figure 5**) over the mounting boss (stub) on the diaphragm. Then position the large spring (6) into the cupped portion of the diaphragm.

3. Carefully install the main housing (5, **Figure 5**) over the large and small springs, making sure that the large spring fits over the raised rib and the small spring is piloted on the raised button of the main housing. Rotate the main housing to align the screw holes with the intermediate housing, then install the two screws and washers (11) and tighten them *lightly* at this time. These two screws are the screws that do not retain the mounting bracket (12).

4. Position the mounting bracket on the mixing unit and align the screw holes. Install the six remaining screws (13, **Figure 5**) and tighten them lightly at this time.

5. Evenly tighten all eight intermediate housing-to-main housing screws (11 and 13, **Figure 5**) to 5-7 in.-lb. (0.56-0.79 N•m).

6. Lubricate a new oil piston seal and install it into the groove at the end of the oil piston. Make sure the seal is seated in its groove and is not pinched or twisted.

7. Begin assembly of the oil pump housing (16, **Figure 5**) by installing the oil outlet check valve (18) into the open bore of the pump housing. Insert the large end of the valve first and gently press it into the bore until it is seated.

8. Lubricate a new O-ring (19, **Figure 5**) and install it over the small end of the outlet check valve (18).

9. Lubricate a new inlet check valve (17, **Figure 5**) and carefully press it into place in the oil pump housing. Do not use your fingernails or any sharp object to install the valve. Simply insert the rubber stem into its bore, then push on the valve with the flat of your finger until it snaps into place.

10. Lubricate a new seal (20, **Figure 5**) and install it into the groove of the oil pump housing's cover (21).

11. Position the cover over the oil pump housing and secure it with the two smaller screws. Make sure the seal is not displaced, then tighten the screws to 5-7 in.-lb. (0.56-0.79 N•m).

12. Install a new filter (24, **Figure 5**) into the oil inlet line fitting's bore. Then lubricate and install new O-rings (25, **Figure 5**) in the oil and fuel inlet line fitting bores.

13. Install the oil line fitting into its bore, then install the angled fuel inlet fitting into its bore. Make sure the fuel fitting is pointing toward the oil pump housing cover. Install the fitting retaining plate and secure it with screws. Evenly tighten the screws to 5-7 in.-lb. (0.56-0.79 N•m).

14. Lubricate and install the small O-ring (15, **Figure 5**) around the cylinder bore of the of the oil pump housing-to-intermediate housing mating surface. Then lubricate and install the large O-ring (14, **Figure 5**) into the recess of the outer diameter of the same mating surface.

15. Carefully install the oil pump housing assembly over the oil pump piston and seat it on the intermediate housing. The fuel and oil inlet fittings must face the bent ear of the mounting bracket. Align the screw holes, then install the two larger screws through the oil pump cover. Evenly tighten the screws to 7-9 in.-lb. (0.79-1.02 N•m).

16. Lubricate and install a new O-ring (4, **Figure 5**) into the fuel outlet port of the main housing. Install the angled fuel outlet fitting and rotate it to the position noted during disassembly. Install the fitting retainer plate and secure it with two screws. Evenly tighten the screws to 5-7 in.-lb. (0.56-0.79 N•m).

17. Install the short fuel and oil inlet lines to the fittings on the bottom of the mixing unit. Secure the connections with new tie-straps.

18. Connect the mixing unit to the reservoir and install the reservoir and mixing unit assembly as described in this chapter.

VRO^2 OIL INJECTION (35 JET, 40 HP [ELECTRIC START] AND 50-70 HP MODELS)

System Description

The VRO^2 combination fuel and oil pump (**Figure 6**) is driven by crankcase pressure and vacuum pulses. The oil is mixed with the fuel in an internal mixing chamber. The output from the pump is approximately 50:1.

A *no-oil* motion sensor located in the pump activates the warning system if a no-oil condition occurs. See *Warning Systems* in Chapter Three for warning signals, warning system operation and warning system troubleshooting. If the *no-oil* signal is noted, the engine must be stopped immediately and the remote oil tank's oil level checked. If the oil tank's level is satisfactory, operate the engine on a 50:1 fuel/oil mixture until the cause of the warning can be determined and corrected.

A 1.8 or 3 gallon (6.8 or 11.4 L) remote oil tank (**Figure 7**) supplies oil directly to the pump. The primer bulb in the oil line is used to purge air and prime the system during rigging, when the oil line has been disconnected, or the oil tank has run dry. Never squeeze the oil tank's primer bulb during normal operation.

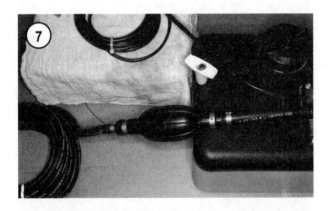

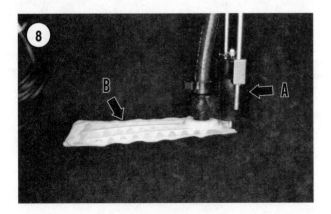

NOTE
Do not squeeze the oil tank's primer bulb before starting the engine. The carburetors will become flooded with oil and starting will be difficult, if not impossible.

A low-oil float switch (A, **Figure 8**) attached to the oil tank's pickup assembly activates the *low oil* warning signal if the oil level in the reservoir becomes low. If this occurs, the engine must be stopped as soon as possible and the reservoir refilled, or power head damage will occur when the oil tank runs dry.

A sock-type filter (B, **Figure 8**) attached to the pickup assembly keeps debris out of the oil lines and the VRO^2 pump. The filter must be changed whenever the oil pickup assembly is removed from the oil tank or when any major service work is performed on the oil injection system.

WARNING
*Continued operation of the engine with the **no oil** warning activated will cause power head damage.*

Filling the oil tank requires first gaining access to the remote oil tank. Then remove the fill cap and fill the tank with the recommended outboard oil. When finished, reinstall the fill cap securely.

System Operation

The VRO^2 combination fuel/oil pump consists of four separate operational sections, each with its unique function. The four sections are the air motor, fuel pump, oil pump and no-oil sensor. See **Figure 9**. The air motor and fuel pump portions of the pump unit are serviceable and may be individually repaired or replaced.

On 1995 (EO) model VRO^2 pump units, the oil pump inlet housing is not available separately, but the no-oil sensor portion is. If the oil pump section malfunctions, the VRO^2 pump unit must be replaced as an assembly.

On 1996-2003 (ED-ST) model VRO^2 pump units, the oil pump inlet housing and no-oil sensor sections are only available as a matched assembly. If either section malfunctions replace both as an assembly.

Refer to **Figures 9-13** for the following descriptions.

NOTE
*All descriptions of right and left movement (in the following sections) are in relation to the operational diagrams shown in **Figures 9-13**.*

11

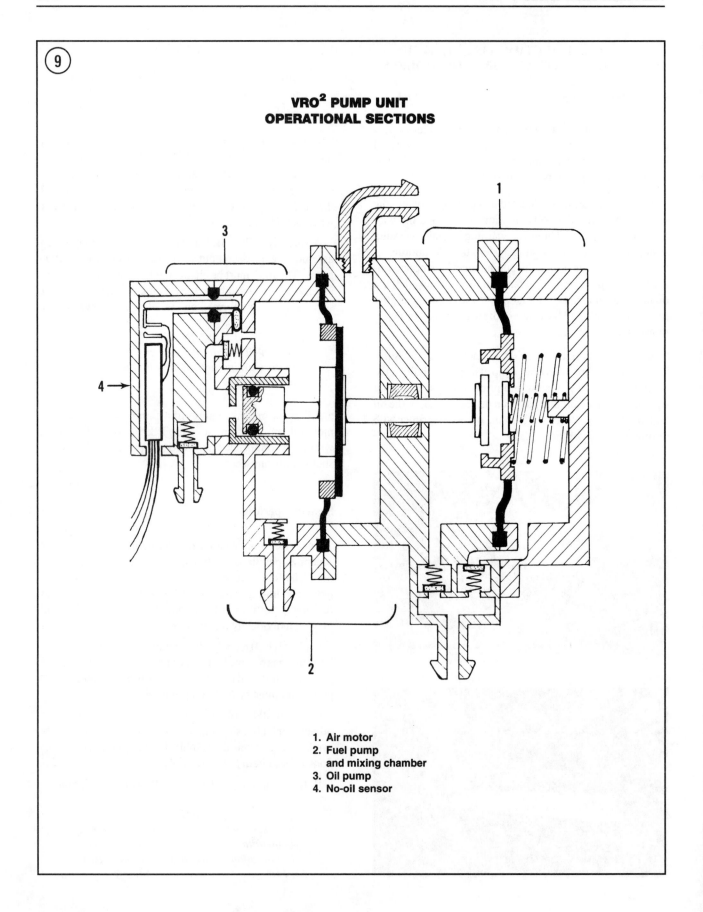

**VRO^2 PUMP UNIT
OPERATIONAL SECTIONS**

1. Air motor
2. Fuel pump
   and mixing chamber
3. Oil pump
4. No-oil sensor

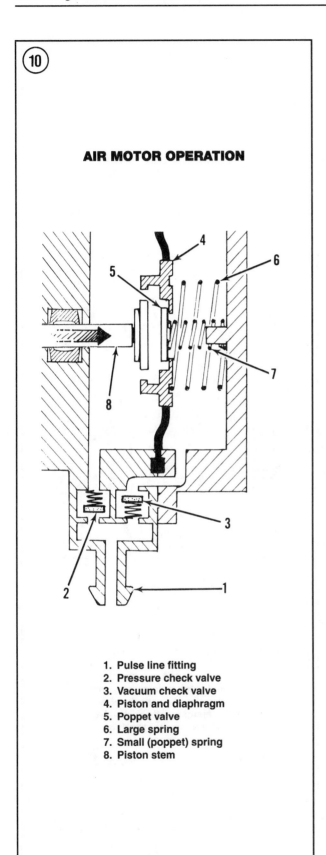

AIR MOTOR OPERATION

1. Pulse line fitting
2. Pressure check valve
3. Vacuum check valve
4. Piston and diaphragm
5. Poppet valve
6. Large spring
7. Small (poppet) spring
8. Piston stem

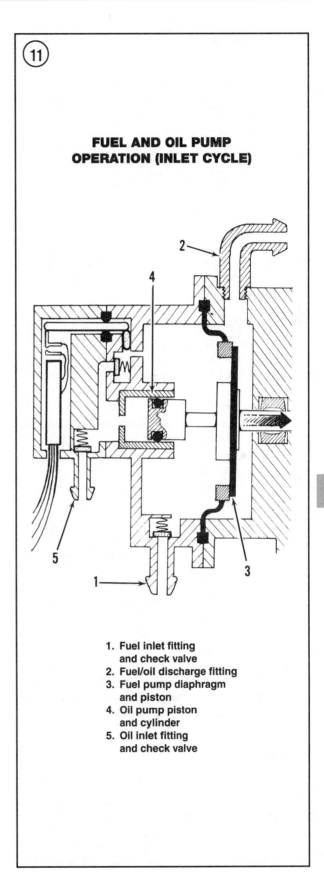

FUEL AND OIL PUMP OPERATION (INLET CYCLE)

1. Fuel inlet fitting
   and check valve
2. Fuel/oil discharge fitting
3. Fuel pump diaphragm
   and piston
4. Oil pump piston
   and cylinder
5. Oil inlet fitting
   and check valve

11

Air motor operation

The air motor supplies the mechanical energy necessary to operate the fuel and oil pump sections of the VRO^2 pump. A shaft (called a piston stem [8, **Figure 10**]) connects the air motor diaphragm to the fuel and oil pump sections of the VRO^2 pump. The air motor receives crankcase pressure and vacuum pulses from a single cylinder's crankcase. On two-cylinder models, the pulses come from cylinder No. 2, while on three-cylinder models, the pulses come from cylinder No. 3.

A special fitting, called a *pulse limiter* is used to protect the air motor from excessive crankcase pressure pulses, such as those caused by a backfire in the induction system. The pulse limiter allows normal air flow in both directions, but blocks high pressure spikes from reaching the air motor.

A pair of one-way check valves (2 and 3, **Figure 10**) are used to direct air flow in the air motor housing. Crankcase pressure pulses are directed to the left side of the air motor diaphragm, while crankcase vacuum pulses are directed to the right (spring) side of the diaphragm. This arrangement causes the air motor to always be pushed (or pulled) to the right during operation.

The air motor continues to move to the right until the poppet valve contacts the raised boss on the air motor cover. This opens the poppet valve (5, **Figure 10**), equalizing the pressure on both sides of the air motor's diaphragm. When the poppet valve opens, the large spring (6, **Figure 10**) forces the air motor to the left. When the air motor has traveled as far as it can (to the left), the poppet valve closes and the cycle of movement repeats itself.

The movement to the left is abrupt and a distinctive click can be heard (or felt) each time the air motor cycles to the left.

The movement of the air motor to the right is limited by the engine's consumption of fuel. The air motor can only move to the right as the fuel in the fuel pump section is consumed by the engine. At idle, when fuel consumption is minimal, the air motor moves very slowly to the right and cycles at its slowest rate. At wide-open throttle, when fuel consumption is maximal, the air motor moves quickly to the right and cycles at its fastest rate.

Fuel pump operation

Refer to **Figure 11** and **Figure 12** for this description.

The fuel pump diaphragm is connected to the air motor by the piston stem (8, **Figure 10**). When the air motor is moving to the right, it is pulling the fuel pump diaphragm (3, **Figure 11**) to the right with it. The fuel/oil mixture on the right side of the fuel pump diaphragm (from the pre-

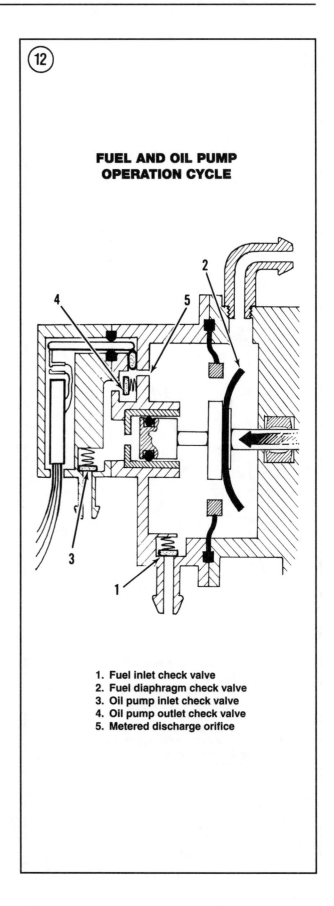

⑫

FUEL AND OIL PUMP OPERATION CYCLE

1. **Fuel inlet check valve**
2. **Fuel diaphragm check valve**
3. **Oil pump inlet check valve**
4. **Oil pump outlet check valve**
5. **Metered discharge orifice**

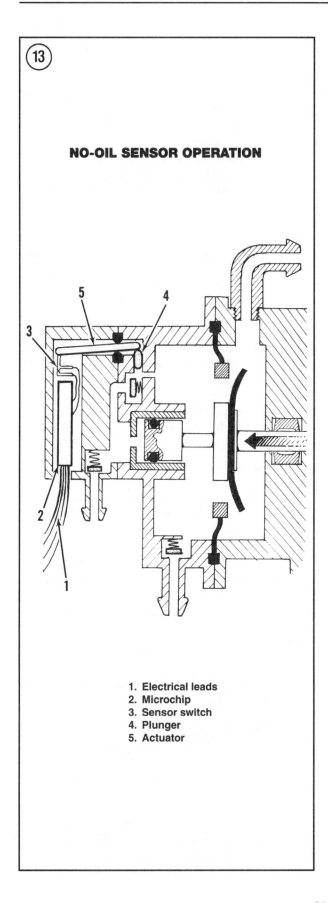

NO-OIL SENSOR OPERATION

1. Electrical leads
2. Microchip
3. Sensor switch
4. Plunger
5. Actuator

vious cycle) is pushed out the fitting (2, **Figure 11**) at the top of the pump and on to the carburetors.

As the fuel diaphragm is pulled to the right, straight fuel is pulled into the left (inlet) side of the fuel pump diaphragm through the fuel inlet check valve and fitting (1, **Figure 11**). When the air motor (and fuel pump diaphragm) cycles back to the left, the fuel inlet check valve closes, trapping the fuel. When this happens, the check valve in the fuel pump diaphragm opens (**2, Figure 12**), allowing the diaphragm to travel to the left, transferring the fuel to the right (discharge) side of the diaphragm. The oil pump adds the correct amount of oil during the cycle to the left.

Once the fuel diaphragm reaches the limit of its travel to the left, the check valve in the diaphragm closes and the fuel/oil mixture (now trapped on the right side of the diaphragm) is pushed out the fitting at the top of the pump as the cycle repeats itself.

Oil pump operation

Refer to **Figure 11** and **Figure 12** for this description.

The oil pump piston (4, **Figure 11**) is connected to the fuel pump diaphragm and the air motor by a shaft. When the air motor and fuel pump diaphragms are moving to the right, the oil pump piston is pulled to the right with them.

As the oil pump piston is pulled to the right, oil is pulled from the oil tank and into the oil pump cylinder through the oil pump inlet fitting and check valve (5, **Figure 11**). When the air motor and fuel pump diaphragms cycle back to the left, the oil pump piston is pushed to the left also. This movement closes the oil pump inlet check valve (3, **Figure 12**) and opens the oil pump outlet check valve (4), discharging the oil into the inlet side of the fuel pump chamber through a metered orifice (5).

Since the oil is being discharged as the fuel pump diaphragm is cycling back to the left, the oil is thoroughly mixed with the fuel by the movement of the diaphragm.

When the air motor and fuel pump diaphragms begin moving to the right, the oil pump piston begins a new cycle.

No-oil sensor operation

An electronic sensing system is incorporated into the oil pump portion of the VRO^2 pump unit. The sensing system requires four leads (1, **Figure 13**) to operate. The four leads are black, purple, gray and tan (or tan/yellow). The leads are connected to the engine harness with a four-pin Amphenol connector. The four leads function as follows:

1. *Black lead*—The black lead provides an electrical ground for the sensing system.

11

2. *Purple lead*—The purple lead provides key-switched battery voltage to operate the microchip and sensor in the no-oil sensing system.

3. *Gray lead*—The gray lead provides a tachometer reference signal so the sensing system can detect that the engine is running and how fast the engine is running. At higher speeds, the system must detect more oil being injected than at lower speeds.

4. *Tan (or tan/yellow) lead*—The tan (or tan/yellow) lead is connected to the warning system. The no-oil sensing system grounds the tan (or tan/yellow) lead to sound the warning horn (or activate the system check engine monitoring system). Refer to Chapter Three, *Warning Systems* for additional information.

A small sensor is installed after the oil pump outlet check valve (4, **Figure 12**) and before the oil discharge metered orifice (5). The sensor functions as a small electrical switch that closes each time it detects the pressure of the oil being discharged into the fuel pump inlet chamber. A small plunger (4, **Figure 13**) moves an actuator (5) to close the switch (3) each time the oil pump piston discharges oil into the mixing chamber.

A microchip (2, **Figure 13**) counts the tachometer pulses (from the gray lead) and determines the engine speed. The microchip is programmed to detect a switch closing signal from the sensor by a predetermined amount of tachometer pulses (based on engine speed). If the microchip does not detect a switch closing signal within the predetermined time frame (tachometer pulses), it grounds the tan (or tan/yellow) lead to activate the warning system.

Disabling the Oil Injection Feature

If you desire to disable the oil injection feature of the VRO^2 pump unit, the following steps must be taken to prevent the warning system from activating *and* to prevent contamination from entering the VRO^2 pump. Contamination will cause premature pump failure.

If the oil injection system is disabled, the engine must be operated with a 50:1 fuel/oil mixture in the fuel tank.

To disable the oil injection feature, proceed as follows:

NOTE
*Cap (part No. 315391) and holder/plug (part No. 329661) are located on a fuel line near the VRO^2 pump unit. The cap and plug (**Figure 14**) are used to plug the oil supply line and cap the oil supply line fitting (on the lower cowl) whenever they are disconnected.*

1. If installed, disconnect the oil supply line (coming from the oil tank) from the fitting on the lower cowl. See **Figure 15**. Then disconnect the oil tank electrical leads at the power head bullet connectors (or 2-pin Deutsch connector). Remove the oil tank, its supply line and its electrical leads.

2. Tape, sleeve or insulate the two bullet connectors (or two-pin Deutsch connector) on the power head.

3. Seal the oil tank mounting holes with 3M Marine sealant 101 or an equivalent polysulfide sealant.

4. Cap the oil inlet fitting on the lower cowl with protective cap (part No. 315391) or an equivalent cap. The seal must be air-tight. Secure the connection with ratchet clamp (part No. 322654). See **Figure 14** and **Figure 15**.

5. Disconnect the VRO^2 pump's four-pin Amphenol connector.

6. Install protective cover (part No. 335655) over the engine harness side of the four pin connector. The engine harness side of the connector must be sealed to prevent any of the four leads from shorting to each other or to the power head.

7. If the protective cover is not available, fill the Amphenol connector body (on the engine harness side) with RTV sealant so that all four pins are completely covered and sealed.

8. Operate the engine on a 50:1 fuel/oil mixture at all times. If the engine is operated on straight gasoline, the power head will be quickly destroyed.

Troubleshooting

To troubleshoot any problems noted in the warning system, refer to Chapter Three.

If the unit does not mix enough oil with the fuel, the engine will suffer an internal failure or excessive internal wear from the lack of proper lubrication. If the unit mixes too much oil with the fuel, the engine will smoke exces-

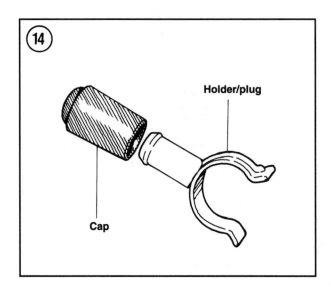

(14)

Holder/plug

Cap

sively, foul the spark plugs and build up carbon in the combustion chambers at an accelerated rate.

If the unit is suspected of not delivering the correct amount of oil with the fuel, *immediately* add the correct amount of recommended outboard motor oil to the engine's fuel tank (to provide a 50:1 fuel/oil mixture).

If the no-oil warning sounds, yet the *Oil consumption test* is satisfactorily completed, check the oil tank and oil supply line for a blocked filter, kinked or blocked lines, or check for air leaks from loose fitting, clamped or damaged lines.

Troubleshooting of the VRO^2 system is divided into the following categories.

1. Verifying that the system is consuming oil. This must be done before beginning operation on straight gasoline.

2. Testing the no-oil warning system and the ability of the pump to prime itself.

3. Testing the integrity of the oil supply line and oil pickup assembly.

4. Testing the fuel pressure output of the pump unit

5. Verifying the correct oil consumption at the pump.

6. Bench testing the pump's internal components with the aid of gearcase vacuum and pressure testers.

7. Determining the cause of excessive oil consumption/excessive exhaust smoke.

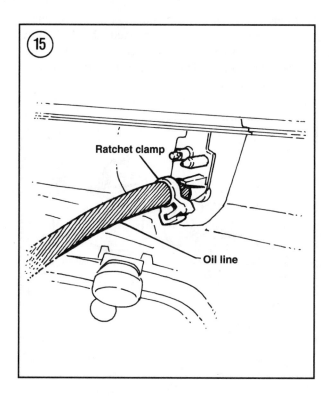

Ratchet clamp

Oil line

Verifying if the system is consuming oil

Perform this test anytime the system is serviced in any manner and before the engine is operated with straight gasoline in the fuel tank.

This test only determines if the system is consuming oil; not that the correct amount of oil is consumed. See *Oil consumption test* in this chapter to determine if the system is consuming the correct amount of oil.

1. Add a 50:1 fuel/oil mixture to the fuel tank. Refer to Chapter Four for additional information.

2. Fill the oil tank until it is full or mark the oil level of the oil tank with a grease pencil. The boat must be resting in a position that can be easily duplicated when the oil level is rechecked.

3. Operate the boat under normal conditions until a minimum of 6 gal. (22.7 L) of fuel has been consumed.

4. Recheck the oil tank level. If the oil level has dropped, the system is consuming oil and the fuel tank may be filled with straight gasoline in the future. If the oil level has not dropped, the system is not consuming oil. Refer to *Oil consumption test* in this chapter to determine if the VRO^2 pump unit is at fault.

Testing the no-oil warning system and the pump's ability to prime itself

The following procedure will determine if the no-oil sensing system is functioning correctly and that the oil pump portion of the VRO^2 pump unit is capable of priming itself.

If the no-oil sensing function is not working correctly, the operator will not receive any warning if the oil pump portion of the VRO^2 pump unit fails.

If the pump cannot prime itself, the system will fail to continue pumping oil if the oil pump pickup is momentarily exposed to air. This can occur under certain conditions, such as a low oil level in the oil tank and when operating in rough water.

1. Disconnect the oil supply line from its fitting on the lower cowl. See **Figure 15**. Plug the oil line to prevent leakage, but do not cap the oil line fitting.

2. Attach a portable fuel tank with a 50:1 fuel/oil mixture to the engine.

> *CAUTION*
> *Do not run the engine without an adequate water supply and do not exceed 3000 rpm without an adequate load. Refer to **Safety Precautions** at the beginning of Chapter Three.*

3. Start the engine and run it in FORWARD gear at approximately 1500 rpm.

11

4. Once the residual oil in the lines between the fitting on the lower cowl and the VRO^2 pump unit has been consumed, the *no-oil* warning must activate. Refer to Chapter Three, *Warning Systems* for an explanation of the warning system signals. It may take several minutes for the residual oil to be consumed.

   a. If the no-oil warning does not activate after 10 minutes, refer to *Warning Systems* in Chapter Three and verify that the warning system is operating correctly. If the warning system is operating correctly, the oil pump and inlet housing assembly (or the VRO^2 pump unit assembly) must be replaced.

   b. If the no-oil warning activates within 10 minutes, proceed to Step 5.

5. Uncap the oil supply line and hold it above the level of the VRO^2 pump unit. Place the open end of the line in a suitable container, then squeeze the oil line's primer bulb until raw oil is flowing from the line. See **Figure 16**. This will purge all air and any contamination from the oil supply line.

6. Connect the oil supply line to the fitting on the lower cowl. Secure the connection with a ratchet clamp. See **Figure 15**. Tighten the ratchet clamp securely. Do NOT squeeze the oil line's primer bulb after the line has been connected to the engine.

7. Start the engine and run it in FORWARD gear at approximately 1500 rpm.

8. The pump must purge the air in the lines between the fitting on the lower cowl and the VRO^2 pump unit (and the no-oil warning signal must cease) within 10 minutes.

   a. If the no-oil warning signal ceases in 10 minutes or less, the VRO^2 pump unit's self priming feature is working satisfactorily. Remove the portable tank within 10 minutes of operation, and reattach the original fuel tank to the engine.

   b. If the no-oil warning signal does not cease operation, check the oil line between the oil fitting on the lower cowl and the VRO^2 pump unit for leaks, loose connections or restrictions. Correct any problems found. If oil line and connections are in satisfactory condition, replace the oil pump and inlet housing assembly (or the VRO^2 pump unit as an assembly).

Excessive oil consumption/excessive exhaust smoke

Due to the design of the VRO^2 unit, a restriction in the fuel supply line or an air leak into the fuel supply line will cause the unit to pump excessive oil to the carburetors. As described under *System Operation*, the speed at which the pump cycles is directly related to the fuel consumption of the engine.

If the fuel supply is restricted or air is leaking into the fuel inlet fitting, the movement of the fuel pump diaphragm will be unrestricted and the air motor will cycle at a rapid rate. Each time the air motor cycles, the oil pump will discharge oil into the inlet side of the fuel pump diaphragm. In extreme conditions, this can result in raw oil being pumped to the carburetors.

> *CAUTION*
> *Do not attempt to run the carburetors dry on an engine equipped with the VRO^2 system. The VRO^2 pump unit will continue to pump oil to the carburetors even though no fuel is entering the pump. This will result in excessive oil flow to the carburetors and starting will be difficult, if not impossible.*

If the pump is suspected of adding too much oil, or the engine smokes excessively, proceed as follows:

1. Clean or replace all fuel filters as described in Chapter Four.

2. Perform the *Fuel supply (vacuum) test* as described in Chapter Three. Do not proceed until this test is satisfactorily completed.

3. Perform the *Oil consumption test* (in this chapter) to verify that the VRO^2 pump unit is mixing the correct amount of oil with the fuel. If the oil consumption is incorrect, replace the oil pump inlet housing or the VRO^2 pump unit as an assembly.

Fuel pressure test

In order for the fuel pump portion of the VRO^2 pump unit to develop the correct fuel pressure, the fuel supply must be unrestricted and free of air leaks. To verify that the fuel portion of the VRO^2 pump unit is functioning correctly, proceed as follows:

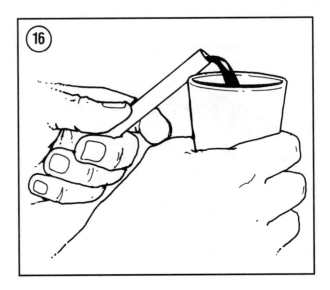

1. Refer to Chapter Three and perform the *Fuel supply (vacuum) tests*. Do not proceed until this test has been satisfactorily completed.

2. Once the fuel supply (vacuum) tests are satisfactorily completed, perform the *Fuel pump output (pressure) tests* as described in Chapter Three.

    a. If the fuel pump output pressure is at least three psi (20.7 kPa) at 800 rpm, the fuel pump portion of the VRO^2 pump unit is working correctly.

    b. If the fuel pressure output is not satisfactory (low or no pressure), proceed to Step 3.

> *NOTE*
> *If the cylinder that drives the VRO^2 pump fails, the pump cannot operate. Check the cranking compression before continuing.*

3. If low or no fuel pressure is observed in Step 2, proceed as follows:

    a. Check the cranking compression as described in Chapter Four. The cylinder that drives the VRO^2 pump must be in good mechanical condition.

    b. Check the pulse line from the crankcase fitting to the VRO^2 pump unit for leaks, kinks, obstructions or loose connections. Correct any problems found.

    c. If the pulse line is in satisfactory condition, replace (or clean) the pulse limiter as described later in this chapter.

    d. Perform the VRO^2 pump unit *Bench tests* as described in this chapter. These tests involve the use of a gearcase vacuum tester to verify the condition of certain internal components in the pump unit. Proceed based on the results of the *Bench tests*.

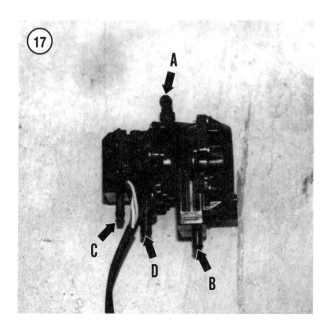

Oil consumption test

This test will determine if the oil injection portion of the VRO^2 pump unit is consuming the correct amount of oil. If the pump is consuming oil, it can be assumed that the pump is mixing the oil with the fuel.

> *NOTE*
> *If the pump unit has been replaced on 1995 (EO) models, the replacement pump will operate to the same specifications as the 1996-1998 (ED-EU) models.*

Oil consumption is referenced to the number of pump cycles. On original 1995 (EO) model VRO^2 pump units, the amount of oil injected (per pump cycle) varies with engine speed and load. On all other models, the pump injects the same amount of oil (per pump cycle), regardless of engine speed and load.

It is imperative that you are able to detect each cycle of the pump. This can be done by listening for the audible click, placing your hand on the air motor housing and feeling the click or installing a fuel pressure gauge to the fuel outlet fitting and observing the fuel pressure fluctuations.

The fuel pressure gauge is the most accurate way to measure pump cycles, as each time the pump cycles, fuel pressure will momentarily drop. Refer to *Fuel System Troubleshooting* in Chapter Three for the fuel pressure gauge installation procedure.

1A. *1995 (EO) models*—Remove the standard propeller and install the recommended test wheel (Chapter Five). A test wheel (propeller) is necessary since the engine must be run at 800 rpm *and* wide-open throttle as part of the oil consumption test.

1B. *1996-2003 (ED-ST) models*—The engine must be operated at 1500 rpm in FORWARD gear for the following procedure. The standard propeller may be used if the boat is backed into the water (on its trailer) or if the boat is securely tied to a sturdy dock. If not, remove the standard propeller and install the recommended test wheel (Chapter Five).

> *CAUTION*
> *Do not run the engine without an adequate water supply and do not exceed 3000 rpm without an adequate load. Refer to **Safety Precautions** at the beginning of Chapter Three.*

2. Start the motor and allow it to warm to operating temperature. Then turn the motor off.

3. Disconnect the oil supply line from the VRO^2 pump unit's fitting (C, **Figure 17**). Plug the line to prevent contamination.

11

4. Obtain a 10 in. (254 mm) length of 1/4 in. (6.35 mm) diameter clear vinyl hose. At one end of the hose, place marks every 1/2 in. (12.7 mm) for at least 3 in. (76.2 mm). Measure carefully and make sure the marks are accurate.

5. Attach the unmarked end of the hose to the injection pump inlet fitting. See **Figure 18**. Secure the connection with a tie-strap. Position the hose so that the marked area (and the open end) are pointing straight up as shown in **Figure 18**. If working alone, tie-strap the hose to the power head to keep it properly positioned.

6. Fill the vinyl hose with the recommended outboard oil (Chapter Four). Start the motor and operate it at idle speed long enough to purge any air from the hose. Then stop the motor and refill the vinyl hose with outboard oil.

7A. *1995 (EO) models*—Proceed as follows:
   a. Start the engine and operate it at 800 rpm in FORWARD gear. Observe the oil level in the vinyl hose *while* monitoring the pump cycles in one of the manners described previously. The oil level must drop 1 in. (25.4 mm) in 4-6 pump cycles.
   b. Stop the engine and refill the vinyl hose with outboard oil.
   c. Start the engine and operate it at wide-open throttle in FORWARD gear. Observe the oil level in the vinyl hose while monitoring the pump cycles. The oil level must drop 1 in. (25.4 mm) in 2-4 pump cycles.

7B. *1996-2003 (ED-ST) models*—Start the engine and operate it at 1500 rpm in FORWARD gear. Observe the oil level in the vinyl hose while monitoring the pump cycles. The oil level must drop 3 in. (76.2 mm) in 6-8 pump cycles.

8A. If the oil consumption is not as specified, proceed as follows:
   a. Check the cranking compression as described in Chapter Four. The cylinder that drives the VRO^2 pump must be in good mechanical condition.
   b. Check the pulse line from the crankcase fitting to the VRO^2 pump unit for leaks, kinks, obstructions or loose connections. Correct any problems found.
   c. If the pulse line is in satisfactory condition, replace (or clean) the pulse limiter as described later in this chapter.
   d. If all checks to this point are satisfactory, yet the oil consumption is incorrect, replace the inlet housing assembly or the VRO^2 pump unit as an assembly.

8B. If the oil consumption is as specified, yet the *no-oil* warning sounds, check the following:
   a. The oil tank pickup filter for debris or blockage.
   b. Kinks or blockages in the oil supply line.
   c. Loose fittings, clamps or other air leaks into the oil supply line.

9. When finished, remove the clear vinyl hose and reconnect the oil supply line. Secure the connection with a ratchet clamp or the original spring clamp (if equipped).

Then verify if the system is consuming oil as described in this chapter.

Bench tests

These bench tests check the condition of the internal check valves and diaphragms in the air motor and fuel pump sections of the VRO^2 pump unit. The test procedure must be performed in the specified order or the test results will not be accurate.

Replacement parts and repair kits vary between the 1995-1997 (EO-EU) models and the 1998-2003 models. In this procedure, all corrective actions not listed in parentheses refer to 1995-1997 (EO-EU) models and all corrective actions listed in parentheses refer to the 1998-2003 models.

The pulse line fitting and the fuel inlet and outlet fittings are replaceable on 1998-2003 models. If any of the fittings leak between the fitting and the pump body, replace the fitting's O-ring and recheck for leakage.

NOTE
External air leaks from or into the pump unit cannot be tolerated. Repair all leaks noted during the testing procedure.

1. Remove the VRO^2 pump unit as described in this chapter.

2. Connect a gearcase pressure tester (such as Stevens part No. S-34) to the pump's pulse hose fitting. Apply 15 psi (103.4 kPa) to the pulse hose fitting (B, **Figure 17**). This

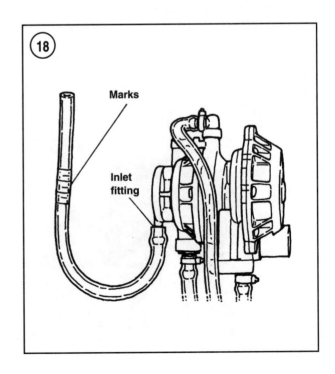

18

Marks

Inlet fitting

will push the air motor to the right until the poppet valve opens, at which point the spring will push the air motor, fuel pump and oil pump components to the left.

3A. *Tester holds pressure*—If the pump holds pressure, hold the pump in its normal operating position, cover the fuel outlet fitting (A, **Figure 17**) with a finger and *quickly* remove the pressure tester from the pulse fitting (to relieve the pressure). The pump must not click.

    a. If the pump clicks, install all components contained in the fuel pump diaphragm kit (or fuel piston and diaphragm kit). Then repeat the bench test.

    b. If the pump does not click, proceed to Step 4.

3B. *Tester leaks down*—If the tester indicates leakage, slowly pump the gearcase tester and inspect for an external air leak and listen for the pump clicking as the pressure tester is pumped.

    a. If the pump unit clicks as the tester is pumped, the air motor is leaking or its housing is cracked. Locate and repair the leak. If necessary, install all components of the air motor housing kit (or replace the air motor cover).

    b. If the pump does not click as the tester is pumped, check for air leakage from the fuel outlet fitting. If air is leaking from the fuel outlet fitting, the shaft seal or intermediate housing has failed. Replace the intermediate housing (or intermediate housing kit).

    c. If the pump does not click as the tester is pumped and air is not leaking from the fuel outlet fitting, an external air leak is present. Locate and repair the external air leak. It may be necessary to replace the air motor and/or intermediate housings.

    d. After repair, repeat the bench test procedure.

4. If the pump does not click in Step 3A, wait five seconds after removing the pressure tester, then remove your finger from the fuel outlet fitting (A, **Figure 17**). The pump must click as your finger is removed from the fitting. Note the results, then proceed to Step 5.

5. Connect a gearcase vacuum tester (such as Stevens part No. V-34) to the pump's pulse fitting (B, **Figure 17**). Apply 15 in.-hg. (50.66 kPa) to the pulse hose fitting. This will pull the air motor to the right until the poppet valve opens, at which point the spring will push the air motor, fuel pump and oil pump components to the left.

6. Hold the pump in its normal operating position, cover the fuel outlet fitting (A, **Figure 17**) with a finger and quickly remove the vacuum tester from the pulse fitting (to relieve the vacuum). Wait five seconds, then remove your finger from the fuel outlet fitting. The pump must click as your finger is removed from the fitting.

    a. If the pump clicks as specified in Step 4 and Step 6, the pump has passed the bench tests. Proceed to Step 8.

    b. If the pump clicks as specified in Step 4, but not Step 6, the pulse line vacuum check valve in the intermediate housing has failed. Replace the intermediate housing (or intermediate housing kit).

    c. If the pump does not click as specified in Step 4, but does click as specified in Step 6, the pulse line pressure check valve in the intermediate housing has failed. Replace the intermediate housing (or intermediate housing kit).

    d. If the pump does not click as specified in Step 4 or Step 6, the air motor diaphragm or poppet valve is leaking. Install the air motor piston kit (or air motor piston and diaphragm kit).

7. Repeat the entire bench test after any repairs are performed, to ensure the correct assembly of the unit.

8. When finished, reinstall the VRO^2 pump unit as described later in this chapter.

VRO^2 Pump Removal/Installation

If a new VRO^2 pump unit is being installed, the pulse limiter must also be replaced.

> *CAUTION*
> *Refer to **Fuel and Oil Line Removal/Installation** at the beginning of this chapter before proceeding.*

1. Disconnect the negative battery cable, then remove and ground the spark plug leads to the power head to prevent accidental starting.

2. Remove the spring clamp (or tie-strap) securing the fuel line to the fuel outlet fitting (A, **Figure 17**). Carefully remove the fuel line from the fitting. Plug the line to prevent contamination.

3. Remove the air intake cover and air intake cover base as described in Chapter Six. Disconnect the pump unit electrical leads at the 4-pin Amphenol connector.

5A. *40 and 50 hp (two-cylinder) and 35 jet*—To provide easier access to the pump unit, remove the electric starter motor (Chapter Seven) and the port side of the split lower cowl as described in Chapter Eight.

5B. *50-70 hp (three-cylinder)*—Remove the two screws securing the VRO^2 pump unit's mounting bracket to the intake manifold.

6. Lift the pump and carefully disconnect the fuel inlet line (D, **Figure 17**), crankcase pulse line (B) and the oil supply line (C) from the pump fittings. Plug each line as it is removed to prevent contamination.

11

7. Once all lines are disconnected, remove the pump from the power head.

8A. *40 and 50 hp (two-cylinder) and 35 jet*—If the pump is to be disassembled, lubricate the three rubber isolation mounts with isopropyl (rubbing) alcohol and pull them from the pump.

8B. *50-70 hp (three-cylinder)*—Remove the three screws and washers securing the pump to its mounting bracket.

9. If a new pump unit is to be installed, remove and replace the pulse limiter as described later in this chapter.

10A. *40 and 50 hp (two-cylinder) and 35 jet*—To install the VRO^2 pump unit, begin by installing the three rubber isolation mounts into the pump body. Lubricate each mount liberally with isopropyl (rubbing) alcohol and install each mount into its bore. Carefully pull and push each mount until it snaps into place. The tapered end of each mount must face away from the air motor.

10B. *50-70 hp (three-cylinder)*—To install the VRO^2 pump unit, begin by assembling the mounting bracket to the pump unit. Secure the pump with three screws and washers. Evenly tighten the screws to 18-24 in.-lb. (2.0-2.7 N•m).

11. Hold the pump unit next to the power head. Connect the oil supply line (C, **Figure 17**), crankcase pulse line (B) and fuel supply line (D) to their respective pump fittings. Secure each connection with a spring clamp or ratchet (snapper) clamp.

12A. *40 and 50 hp (two-cylinder) and 35 jet*—If removed, install the electric starter motor (Chapter Seven) and the port side of the split lower cowl as described in the appropriate *Power head removal/installation* in Chapter Eight.

12B. *50-70 hp (3-cylinder)*—Position the pump mounting bracket to the intake manifold and secure it with two screws. Tighten the screws to 60-84 in.-lb. (6.8-9.5 N•m).

13. Connect the pump unit four-pin Amphenol connector to its engine harness mate. Make sure the wire bail is installed over the assembled connectors to prevent them from vibrating apart.

14. Connect the fuel line to the fuel outlet fitting (A, **Figure 17**) at the top of the pump unit. Secure the connection with the original spring clamp or a new tie-strap.

15. Install the air intake cover base and air intake cover.

16. Connect the spark plug leads, then connect the negative battery cable. Tighten the battery connection securely.

17. Verify if the system is consuming oil as described in this chapter before operating the engine on straight gasoline.

VRO^2 Pump Disassembly

Replacement parts, repair kits and service procedures vary between the 1995-1997 (EO-EU) models and the 1998-2003 models.

The pulse line fitting and the fuel inlet and outlet fittings are replaceable on 1998-2003 models. A rubber disc-type check valve (23, **Figure 19**) is located under the fuel inlet fitting on 1998-2003 models.

NOTE
If the pump unit has been replaced on 1995-1997 (EO-EU) models, the replacement pump will be serviced in the same manner as the 1998-2003 models.

1. Remove the VRO^2 pump unit as described in this chapter.

2. Place the pump onto a clean workbench with the air motor housing facing up. Hold down on the air motor cover and remove the eight cover screws (1, **Figure 19**). After the screws are removed, carefully release the cover (2, **Figure 19**), allowing the internal springs (3 and 4) to relax. Remove the cover, large and small springs and the vacuum passage O-ring (9). Discard the O-ring.

3. Invert the pump so that the oil pump (inlet) housing is facing up. Remove the six screws (17, **Figure 19**) securing the oil pump (inlet) housing assembly to the intermediate (fuel pump) housing (8). Lift the intermediate housing straight up and away from the oil pump inlet housing assembly.

4. *1998-2003 models*—Disconnect the oil piston (15, **Figure 19**) from the stem nut (14) in the fuel piston, then remove the oil piston from the pump unit. Be careful not to damage the seal at the end of the oil piston.

5A. *1995-1997 (EO-EU) models*—Refer to **Figure 19** and disassemble the intermediate housing as follows:

   a. Hold the intermediate housing in one hand. Push the air motor piston and diaphragm toward the intermediate housing and hold it firmly against the housing.

   b. Grasp the fuel pump diaphragm in the other hand and unthread it from the air motor diaphragm and shaft. Then pull the fuel and air motor diaphragms away from each other and out of the intermediate housing.

   c. Grasp the piston stem (7, **Figure 19**) with a pair of needlenose pliers and unthread it from the diaphragm. Locate and secure the fuel check valve (11, **Figure 19**), nylon retainer (10) and oil pump piston (and stem nut) assembly. Discard the piston stem (7, **Figure 19**) and two steel washers (6).

5B. *1998-2003 models*—Refer to **Figure 19** and disassemble the intermediate housing as follows:

   a. Hold the intermediate housing in one hand and push the fuel piston and diaphragm toward the housing. Hold the piston firmly against the housing.

   b. Grasp the air motor diaphragm in the other hand and unthread it from the fuel pump diaphragm and pis-

⑲ **VRO² PUMP UNIT**

1. Screw
2. Air motor cover
3. Small (poppet) spring
4. Larger spring
5. Air motor piston and diaphragm
6. Steel washers
7. Piston stem
8. Intermediate housing
9. O-ring
10. Nylon washer
11. Check valve
12. Fuel piston and diaphragm
13. O-ring (1998 models)
14. Stem nut
15. Oil pump piston and seal
16. Oil pump (inlet) housing
17. Screw
18. Seal
19. Actuator seal

20. No oil sensor assembly
21. Screw
22. Four-pin Amphenol connector
23. Fuel inlet check valve (1998 models)
24. O-rings (1998 models)
25. Fuel inlet fitting (1998 models)
26. Pulse line fitting (1998 models)
27. Fuel outlet fitting (1998 models)
28. Retainer plates (1998 models)
29. Screws

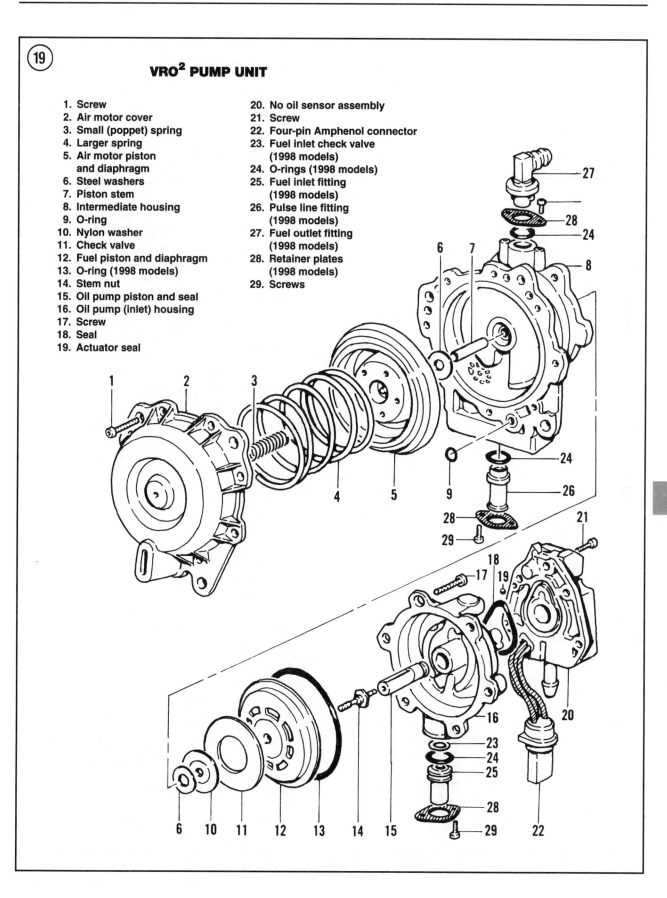

11

ton. The piston stem (7, **Figure 19**) is attached to the air motor diaphragm *or* the fuel piston diaphragm.

c. Pull the fuel and air motor diaphragms away from each other and out of the intermediate housing.

d. Grasp the piston stem (on whichever diaphragm it is still attached to) with a pair of needlenose pliers and unthread it from the diaphragm. Locate and secure the fuel check valve (11, **Figure 19**), nylon retainer (10) and stem screw (14). Discard the piston stem (7, **Figure 19**) and two steel washers (6).

6. If necessary, remove the four screws (21, **Figure 19**) securing the no-oil sensor to the oil pump (inlet) housing. Separate the inlet housing (16, figure 19) from the no-oil sensor assembly (20). Remove and discard the seal (19, **Figure 19**) from the no-oil sensor actuator shaft, then remove and discard the seal (18) between the no oil sensor and inlet housing.

7. *1998-2003 models*—Service the removable fittings as follows:

a. Note the position and orientation of each fitting before removing any of the fittings.

b. Remove the two screws (29, **Figure 19**) securing the retainer plate over each fitting (25, 26 and 27).

c. Remove the retainer plate (28, **Figure 19**), then pull each fitting from its housing. Remove and discard the O-ring (24, **Figure 19**) from each fitting.

d. Remove the fuel inlet check valve (23, **Figure 19**) from the inlet housing. Discard the check valve.

8. Clean all components with OMC Cleaning Solvent. Inspect all parts and components for wear, damage, deterioration or other damage. Replace all parts that are in questionable condition.

VRO^2 Pump Unit Assembly

Lubricate all internal components with the recommended outboard oil (Chapter Four). Make no dry assemblies. Refer to **Figure 19** for this procedure.

> *CAUTION*
> *When installing screws into plastic housings, extreme care must be taken to prevent cross-threading the screws. Cross-threading the screws will cause the housing threads to prematurely fail. Install each screw into its bore, then slowly turn each screw backward (counterclockwise) until you feel each screw drop into the housing's pre-formed threads. Once the threads have been properly engaged, each screw may be tightened as specified.*

1. *1998-2003 (EC-ST) models*—Install the fuel inlet check valve and all three removable fittings as follows:

a. Carefully install a new inlet check valve (16, **Figure 19**) into the fuel inlet fitting port in the oil pump (inlet) housing. Align the hole in the valve with the alignment pin cast into the housing.

b. Lubricate a new O-ring and install it over the fuel inlet fitting. Install the fitting into its bore, being careful not to displace the inlet check valve. Make sure the fitting seats in its bore.

c. Install the retainer plate over the fitting and align the screw holes. Carefully install the 2 screws, making sure the threads are correctly engaged. Tighten the screws until they just contact the retainer plate.

d. If the inlet fitting is angled, rotate the fitting to its original position (as noted during disassembly). Insert a suitable round tool (such as a Phillips screwdriver) into the fitting if extra leverage is needed. Do not damage the fitting with a pair of pliers or similar tool.

e. Once the fitting is correctly aligned, tighten both retainer plate screws *just* until the retainer firmly contacts the housing.

f. Repeat substeps b-e to install the fuel outlet and crankcase pulse line fittings. There are no check valves on these two fittings.

2. If the no-oil sensor was separated from the oil pump (inlet) housing, assemble these components as follows:

a. Lubricate a new actuator shaft seal (19, **Figure 19**) and slide it over the actuator shaft and against the oil pump (inlet) housing (16).

b. Lubricate a new seal (18, **Figure 19**) and install it into the groove on the face of the no-oil sensor housing (20).

c. Position the housings to each other and align the screw holes. Carefully install the four screws (21, **Figure 19**), making sure the threads are correctly engaged.

d. Evenly tighten the four screws in a crossing pattern until the oil sensor housing is *just* held firmly against the oil pump (inlet) housing.

3A. *1995-1997 (EO-EU) models*—Assemble the intermediate housing as follows:

a. Insert the stem nut (connected to the oil pump piston) through the fuel pump piston and diaphragm (from the plastic side).

b. Position the fuel check valve (11, **Figure 19**) over the threads of the stem nut. Then install the nylon retainer (10) over the stem nut threads. The recessed side of the retainer must face away from the diaphragm.

c. Install a new steel washer (6, **Figure 19**) over the stem nut threads, then thread a new piston stem (7, **Figure 19**) onto the stem nut. Tighten the stem using only your fingers. Do not use any tools.

d. Lubricate the stem and fuel piston assembly. Install the assembly into the intermediate housing, making sure the stem fits into the bore in the middle of the intermediate housing.

e. Install a new steel washer over the screw in the air motor diaphragm. Thread the air motor diaphragm onto the stem (protruding through the intermediate housing) in a clockwise direction.

f. Hold the poppet portion of the air motor diaphragm in toward the piston stem to hold the screw in place. Then rotate the diaphragm clockwise to tighten the screw. Tighten the screw 1/4 turn past the point of first contact.

g. Push the outer diameter of the fuel diaphragm into the groove in the intermediate housing.

3B. *1998-2003 (EC-ST) models*—Assemble the intermediate housing as follows:

a. Insert the threaded end of the stem nut (14, **Figure 19**) through the fuel pump diaphragm (from the plastic piston side). Make sure the hex of the nut engages the hex recess in the plastic piston.

b. Position the fuel check valve (11, **Figure 19**) over the threads of the stem nut (14). Then install the nylon retainer (10) over the stem nut threads. The recessed side of the retainer must face away from the diaphragm.

c. Install a new steel washer (6, **Figure 19**) over the stem nut threads, then thread a new piston stem (7) onto the stem nut. Tighten the stem using only your fingers. Do not use any tools.

d. Lubricate the stem and fuel piston assembly. Install the assembly into the intermediate housing, making sure the stem fits into the bore in the middle of the intermediate housing.

NOTE
Do not overtighten the air or fuel diaphragms to the piston stem. By design, these components cannot loosen under operation.

e. Install a new steel washer (6, **Figure 19**) over the screw in the air motor diaphragm. Thread the air motor diaphragm onto the stem (protruding through the intermediate housing) in a clockwise direction until it is barely snug to the stem.

f. Carefully snap the oil piston (15, **Figure 19**) onto the stem screw (14). Lubricate the oil piston seal.

g. Lubricate a new O-ring (13, **Figure 19**) and install it over the oil pump (inlet) housing flange.

4. Install the oil pump and inlet housing assembly to the intermediate housing as follows:

a. Carefully guide the oil pump piston into its bore in the oil pump and inlet housing assembly.

b. Rotate the housings to align the screw holes. On 1998 (EC) models, make sure the O-ring (13, **Figure 19**) is not displaced.

c. Carefully install the six screws, making sure the threads are correctly engaged. Hold the housings firmly together and evenly tighten the screws in a crossing pattern. Tighten the screws 1/8 turn past contact.

5. Make sure the outer diameter of the air motor diaphragm is seated in its groove in the intermediate housing. Then lubricate a new O-ring (9, **Figure 19**) and place it in the vacuum passage relief (in the intermediate housing).

6A. *1995-1997 (EO-EU) models*—Grease one end of the small spring with OMC Triple Guard Grease. Place the spring into the relief at the center of the poppet valve in the air motor diaphragm.

6B. *1998-2003 (EC-ST) models*—Install the small spring over the boss in the center of the air motor cover (2, **Figure 19**). Twist the spring counterclockwise and push it towards the boss until it is firmly attached to the boss.

7. Place the large spring into the large recess in the air motor diaphragm. Then carefully install the air motor cover over the large spring. Push the cover towards the intermediate housing, compressing the large spring. Make sure the small spring fits on both the center boss of the air motor cover and the recess in the center of the air motor diaphragm.

8. Rotate the air motor cover to align the screw holes, then install the eight screws, making sure the threads are correctly engaged. Hold the housings firmly together and evenly tighten the screws in a crossing pattern. Tighten the screws 1/8 turn past contact.

9. Install the VRO^2 pump unit as described previously in this chapter.

Pulse Limiter Service

A pulse limiter is used in the crankcase pulse line on all models equipped with the VRO^2 system. On the 40 and 50 hp (two-cylinder) and 35 jet models, the pulse limiter has nipples on both sides (A, **Figure 20**) and is mounted inline between the power head and the VRO^2 pump unit. On the 50-70 hp (three-cylinder) models, the pulse limiter is threaded (B, **Figure 20**) into the crankcase cover.

The pulse limiter is designed to close the pulse line whenever it detects abnormally high crankcase pressure pulses. The pulse limiter has no control (or effect) over the vacuum pulses. The pulse limiter consists of a disc type valve and spring. The spring holds the valve open under normal conditions. If an abnormally high-pressure pulse attempts to pass through the pulse limiter, the pressure of the pulse against the disc valve will compress the spring,

11

allowing the disc valve to close the pulse limiter. As soon as the high-pressure pulse is gone, the spring will reopen the disc valve, allowing normal operation.

High pressure pulses are created when the engine backfires in the induction system. Typical causes of induction system backfire are: lean air/fuel ratio, improper starting technique, thermostat malfunction, damaged reed valves, crankcase air leaks and incorrect ignition timing.

CAUTION
Do not remove (or bypass) the pulse limiter. The air motor diaphragm in the VRO^2 pump unit can be destroyed the first time the outboard motor experiences an induction system backfire.

Since a malfunctioning pulse limiter can result in restricted crankcase pressure and vacuum pulse to the VRO^2 pump unit (resulting in restricted fuel and oil flow to the power head), the pulse limiter must be cleaned (or replaced) whenever any service is performed on the pump unit. The pulse limiter must be replaced if the air motor fails for any reason or if the VRO^2 pump unit is replaced as an assembly.

To replace (or clean) the pulse limiter, proceed as follows:

1. Disconnect the negative battery cable and disconnect and ground the spark plug leads to the power head to prevent accidental starting.

2A. *40 and 50 hp (two-cylinder) and 35 jet*—Proceed as follows:

    a. Remove the port side of the lower split cowl as described in the appropriate *Power head removal/installation* in Chapter Eight.

    b. Remove the spring (or ratchet) clamps securing the pulse limiter to the crankcase pulse hose.

    c. Carefully remove the pulse limiter from the pulse hose.

NOTE
Depending on the model, it may be necessary to remove the VRO^2 pump unit to access the pulse limiter on 50-70 hp (three-cylinder) models.

2B. *50-70 hp (three-cylinder)*—Remove the spring (or ratchet) clamp securing the crankcase pulse hose to the pulse limiter. Remove the line from the pulse limiter, then unthread the pulse limiter from the crankcase cover. The limiter is located on the bottom, port side of the crankcase cover.

3. Inspect the pulse limiter for carbon buildup, cracks, distortion or evidence of external leakage. Replace the limiter if there is any question regarding its condition. If the limiter passes a visual inspection, clean the limiter by spraying an aerosol carburetor and choke cleaner through it in both directions. On three-cylinder models, clean all old sealant from the limiter's threads.

NOTE
The pulse limiting feature of the pulse limiter must not engage when tested in Step 4. Do not attempt to engage the limiting feature using compressed air.

4. Attach a suitable piece of rubber hose to one end of the pulse limiter. Blow through the hose and limiter. Air must flow freely through the limiter. Then attach the hose to the other end of the limiter and again blow through the hose. Air must flow freely through the limiter. Replace the pulse limiter if air flow is restricted in either direction.

NOTE
On 40 and 50 hp (two-cylinder) and 35 jet models, the pulse limiter (B, Figure 20) can be installed backward. If so, it will not protect the air motor diaphragm from abnormal pressure pulses. The metal (typically brass or aluminum) side of the limiter must face the power head. The plastic (typically blue) side of the limiter must face the VRO^2 pump unit.

5A. *40 and 50 hp (two-cylinder) and 35 jet*—Install the pulse limiter into the crankcase pulse line so that the metal

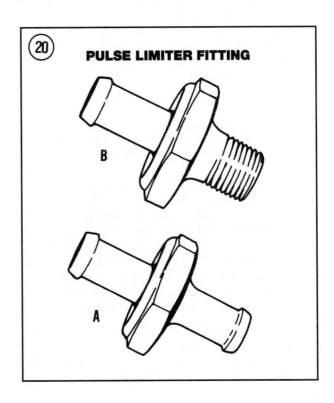

20 **PULSE LIMITER FITTING**

B

A

end of the limiter is facing the power head. Secure the connections with the original spring clamps or new tie-straps. Then reinstall the port side of the lower split cowl as described in the appropriate *Power head removal/installation* section in Chapter Eight.

5B. Lightly coat the threads of the pulse limiter with Loctite Pipe Sealant with Teflon, then install the limiter into the crankcase cover and tighten it securely. Reattach the pulse line to the limiter and secure it with the original (or new) spring (or ratchet) clamp. If it was necessary to remove the VRO^2 pump unit to access the pulse limiter, reinstall the VRO^2 pump unit at this time.

6. Reconnect the spark plug leads and the negative battery cable. Tighten the battery connection securely.

Oil Tank and Oil Supply Line Service

Oil tank service includes changing the filter, checking pickup height, cleaning the reservoir, flushing the oil delivery line and vacuum testing the delivery line and primer bulb. Anytime the oil delivery line is disconnected from the fitting on the engine (**Figure 15**), the oil line must be purged of all air. After performing any service to the oil injection system, run the engine with a 50:1 fuel/oil mixture in the fuel tank, then make sure the system is operating correctly prior to switching to straight gasoline in the fuel tank.

The oil line between the primer bulb (near the oil tank) and the engine *must* be one single piece of 1/4 in. (6.35 mm) braided line. The line is 15 ft. (4.6 m) long from the factory. If desired, the factory line can be removed and a replacement line (up to a maximum of 25 ft. [7.6 m]) may be installed. The replacement line must also be one single piece.

NOTE
While the oil supply line may be up to 25 ft. (7.6 m) long, do not make the line any longer than necessary. Trim the line to the length needed. Avoid excess line that may become kinked or entangled in other systems or components.

To service the oil tank, refer to **Figure 21** and proceed as follows:

1. Locate the oil tank. Lift the two latch handles (5, **Figure 21**) and pivot them away from the oil tank. Then remove the oil tank from its mounting bracket and move it to a more accessible location.
2. Remove the fill cap and pour the reservoir contents into a clean container. Inspect the oil for water, debris or any other contamination. If the oil is contaminated, the tank must be washed and the oil supply line flushed before returning the unit to service.

3. Remove the four oil pickup mounting screws with a No. 25 Torx drive. Lift the pickup assembly from the oil tank and set it into a suitable container to drain. Inspect the pickup seal (**Figure 22**). Discard the seal if it is damaged or deteriorated.
4. Wash the oil tank in a mild solvent (such as mineral spirits), then blow it dry with compressed air.
5. Grasp the filter (11, **Figure 21**) at the bottom of the oil pickup assembly and remove it with a twisting motion. Discard the filter.
6. To flush the oil supply line and vacuum test it for leaks, begin by removing the ratchet clamp (12, **Figure 21**) from the bottom of the oil tank pickup. Then carefully push the oil line from the pickup assembly.
7. Remove the ratchet clamp securing the oil supply line to the fitting on the engine's lower cowl. See **Figure 23**. Then remove the line from the fitting and place it in a suitable container.
8. Apply *low* pressure compressed air to the oil supply line at the oil pickup end. Apply air pressure until all oil (and contamination) is expelled from the engine end of the line.

NOTE
*Cap (part No. 315391) and holder/plug (part No. 329661) are located on a fuel line near the VRO^2 pump unit. The plug (**Figure 24**) can be used to plug the oil supply line.*

9. Insert a suitable plug (such as part No. 329661) into the oil tank end of the oil supply line and secure the connection with the original ratchet clamp.
10. Connect a gearcase vacuum tester (such as Stevens Instruments part No. V-34) to the engine end of the oil supply line. Apply a 7 in.-hg. (23.6 kPa) vacuum to the oil supply line. The line must maintain 7 in.-hg. (23.6 kPa) vacuum for a minimum of 5 minutes.
11. If the line does not maintain vacuum, locate and repair the leak. Do not make splice repairs. Replace the defective line or components (such as the oil primer bulb).
12. Once the oil supply line passes the vacuum test, remove the vacuum tester. Do not reconnect the oil supply line to the engine at this time.
13. Remove the plug from the oil pickup end of the line. Reconnect the line to the pickup. Secure the connection with the original (or new) ratchet clamp.
14. If the pickup seal was removed, install the seal over the pickup and into its groove at the top of the pickup assembly.
15. Install a new oil filter onto the oil pickup with a gentle twisting motion. When correctly installed, the extended end of the filter must point in the same direction as the oil line exiting the top of the pickup assembly.
16. Measure the height of the oil pickup. The measurement is taken from the bottom of the pickup assembly to its oil

11

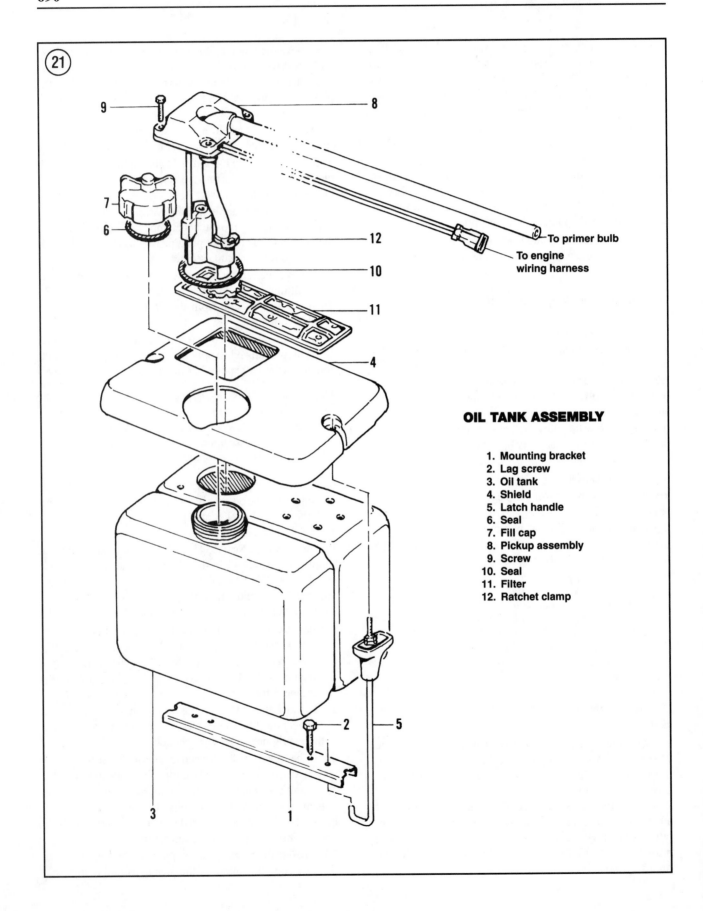

To primer bulb

To engine
wiring harness

OIL TANK ASSEMBLY

1. Mounting bracket
2. Lag screw
3. Oil tank
4. Shield
5. Latch handle
6. Seal
7. Fill cap
8. Pickup assembly
9. Screw
10. Seal
11. Filter
12. Ratchet clamp

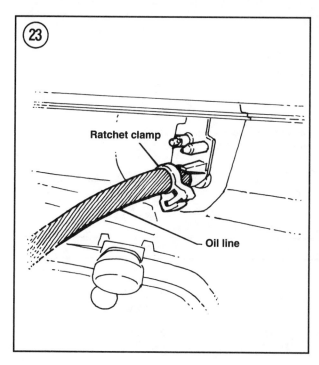

Ratchet clamp

Oil line

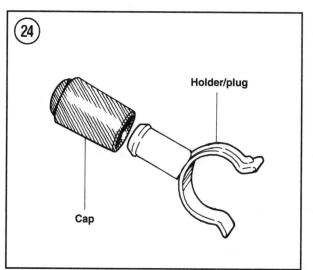

Holder/plug

Cap

tank mating surface. The measurement can be taken with the filter installed.

    a. *1.8 gal. tanks*—The pickup height must be 6.84-6.96 in. (173.7-176.8 mm).

    b. *3.0 gal. tanks*—The pickup height must be 8.74-8.86 in. (222.0-225.0 mm).

    c. If the measurement is not as specified, carefully move the pickup assembly up or down the two metal rods until the measurement is within specification.

17. Install the pickup assembly into the oil tank, making sure the pickup seal is not displaced. Align the screw holes, then install the four screws. Evenly and securely tighten the four screws in a crossing pattern.

18. Fill the oil tank with the recommended outboard oil (Chapter Four).

19. Before connecting the oil supply line to the engine, purge all air from the line as described in the next section.

Purging air from the oil line and oil tank

This procedure must be performed each time the oil supply line is disconnected from the oil line fitting on the lower cowl.

CAUTION
Failure to purge air from the system properly
in Step 9 can result in serious power head
damage from insufficient lubrication.

1. If not already disconnected, remove the oil supply hose from the fitting of the engine's lower cowl. See **Figure 23**.

2. Hold the hose above the level of the VRO² pump unit and place the open end in a suitable container.

3. Squeeze the primer bulb (at the oil tank) until all air has been expelled and only raw oil is discharged from the line. See **Figure 25**.

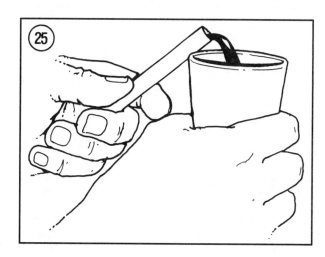

4. Immediately connect the oil line to the fitting on the engine's lower cowl. Secure connection with the original (or new) ratchet clamp. Tighten clamp securely (**Figure 23**).

5. Squeeze the primer bulb (at the oil tank) *ONE* time to push the oil from the fitting to the VRO^2 pump unit. Do not squeeze the bulb repeatedly or the fuel system will become flooded with oil.

6. Operate the engine on a 50:1 fuel/oil mixture until the oil consumption is verified as described in this chapter.

Table 1 OIL INJECTION SYSTEM SPECIFICATIONS

Component	Specification
Oil tank capacity	
AccuMix R models	2 qt. (1.89 L)
25 and 35 hp (three-cylinder)	1.9 qt. (1.8 L)
VRO^2 models	1.8 gal. (6.8 L)
VRO^2 oil tank pickup height	
1.8 gal. tank	6.84-6.96 in. (173.7-176.8 mm)
3.0 gal. tank	8.74-8.86 in. (222.0-225.0 mm)
VRO^2 test specifications	
Minimum fuel pressure	3 psi (20.7 kPa)
Oil consumption test	
1995 (EO) models	
800 rpm	1 in. (25.4 mm) in 5 pump cycles
Wide-open throttle	1 in. (25.4 mm) in 3 pump cycles
1996-2003 (ED-ST) models	
All engine speeds	3 in. (76.2 mm) in 6-8 pump cycles

Table 2 TORQUE VALUES

Fastener	in.-lb.	ft.-lb.	N•m
25 and 35 hp (three-cylinder) models			
Fuel/oil mixing unit			
All small screws	5-7	–	0.56-0.79
Two large screws	7-9	–	0.79-1.02
Oil reservoir			
Lower bracket	180-204	15-17	20.3-23.1
Upper bracket	216-240	18-20	24.4-27.1
VRO^2 models			
Pump to mounting bracket	18-24	–	2.0-2.7
All other screws	See text	–	–

Chapter Twelve

Rope Starters and Remote Controls

ROPE (MANUAL) STARTERS

Manual start models are equipped with a rope-operated rewind starter assembly. The starter assembly is mounted above the flywheel on all models. Pulling the rope handle causes the starter rope pulley to rotate, engage the flywheel (or flywheel cup) and rotate the engine.

Table 1 lists torque values and is located at the end of the chapter. Common engine specifications, recommended lubricants, sealants and adhesives and standard torque values are listed in the Quick Reference Data section, located at the front of this manual.

This section covers starter removal, disassembly, cleaning and inspection, reassembly and installation.

Rope Starter Precautions

Rewind starters are relatively trouble free. A broken or frayed rope is the most common failure. However, the starter is susceptible to failure from two distinct forms of abuse:

1. *Overpulling the rope*—If the rope is repeatedly pulled until it can go no further, the rope will quickly fail and be pulled from the starter pulley. The first time you operate a new motor, pull the starter rope *slowly* until it is fully extended. Mentally note this position. During the starting procedure, make sure that you stop pulling the rope before it reaches full extension.

2. *Jerking the rope*—If the rope is jerked (pulled quickly) from its fully retracted position, the starter pawl(s) will be jammed into the flywheel (or starter cup) with great force. This will result in premature failure of the starter pawl(s) or other starter components. When starting the engine, make sure that you slowly pull the rope until you feel the starter pawl(s) firmly engage, then quickly and smoothly pull the rope with the effort necessary to start the motor.

Rope Starter (2, 3.3 and 3.5 hp)

Starter removal/installation

1. Disconnect and ground the spark plug lead to the power head to prevent accidental starting.

> *NOTE*
> *The rear starter mounting screw also secures the front of the fuel tank. When removing this screw, note the position of the spacer and washers.*

2. Remove the three screws securing the rewind starter assembly to the power head.
3. Loosen the rear fuel tank mounting screw. Lift the front of the fuel tank and remove the starter from the power head.
4. To install the starter, lift the front of the fuel tank and position the starter onto the power head. Make sure the starter's rear mounting flange is positioned underneath the fuel tank.
5. Install the starter mounting screws. Make sure the washers and spacer are correctly positioned on the rear screw. Tighten the screws finger tight at this time.

6. Slowly pull the starter rope to rotate the engine through several revolutions. Then tighten the mounting screws to 60-84 in.-lb. (6.8-9.5 N•m).

7. Tighten the rear fuel tank mounting screw to 60-84 in.-lb. (6.8-9.5 N•m).

8. Reconnect the spark plug lead.

Starter disassembly/reassembly

Refer to **Figure 1** for this procedure.

1. Remove the rope starter as described in this chapter.

CAUTION
Wear leather gloves when holding the rope pulley and releasing the spring tension in the following two steps.

2. Untie the knot securing the rope handle to the rope. While securely holding the rope pulley, remove the handle from the rope.

3. Slowly allow the rope pulley to unwind, releasing the tension on the rewind spring.

4. If necessary, remove the two screws securing the starter handle support to the front of the starter housing. Remove the handle support from the starter housing.

5. Invert the starter and remove the lock clip (10, **Figure 1**), thrust washer (9) and friction plate (8).

6. Remove the return spring (7, **Figure 1**), cover (6) and friction spring (5).

7. Carefully lift the rope pulley approximately 1/2 in. (13 mm) out of the housing, then turn the pulley back and forth to disengage the rewind spring from the pulley. Be careful not to pull the spring from the housing at this time.

8. Remove the pulley from the housing. Then remove the rope from the pulley. Discard the rope.

NOTE
Do not remove the rewind spring from the starter housing unless replacement is necessary. Wear suitable hand and eye protection when removing or installing the rewind spring.

9. If rewind spring replacement is necessary, place the starter housing upright (rewind spring facing down) over a suitable bench. Tap the housing against the bench until the spring falls out and unwinds inside the housing.

10. Clean all components in a mild solvent (such as mineral spirits) and dry with compressed air.

11. Inspect all components for excessive wear, chips, cracks or other damage. Inspect the rope pulley for sharp edges or burrs that could fray the starter rope. If necessary, smooth rough edges with a file or a piece of emery cloth.

12. To reassemble the starter, begin by reinstalling the starter handle support to the starter housing. Secure the support with screws. Tighten both screws securely.

13. Lubricate the rewind spring area of the starter housing with OMC Triple Guard Grease (or Lubriplate 777 grease).

14. If removed, install a new rewind spring. The rewind spring must be installed into the starter housing in a counterclockwise direction, starting from the outer coil as shown in **Figure 2**. Make sure the hook in the outer coil of

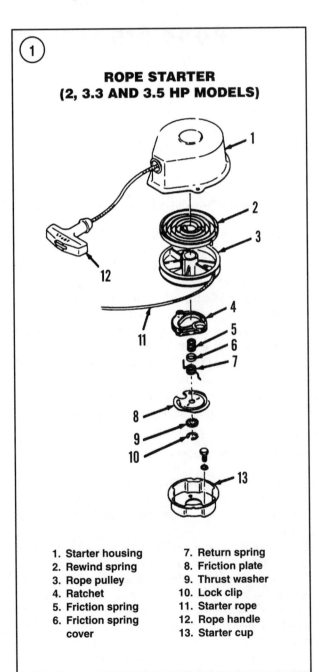

**ROPE STARTER
(2, 3.3 AND 3.5 HP MODELS)**

1. Starter housing	7. Return spring
2. Rewind spring	8. Friction plate
3. Rope pulley	9. Thrust washer
4. Ratchet	10. Lock clip
5. Friction spring	11. Starter rope
6. Friction spring cover	12. Rope handle
	13. Starter cup

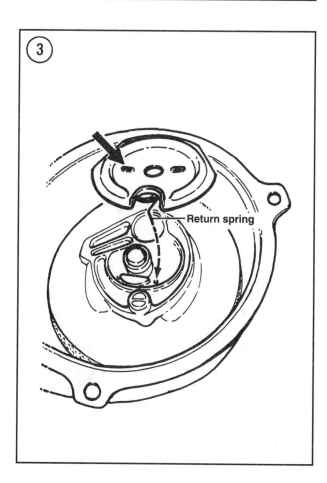

the spring is properly engaged with the catch in the housing as shown in **Figure 2**.

15. Obtain a new starter rope. The starter rope must be 53 in. (134.6 cm) long. If necessary, trim the rope to the specified length. Heat the last 1/2 in. (12.7 mm) of both ends of the rope (with a match or lighter) until the ends are fused. This will prevent the rope from unraveling.

16. Insert one end of the rope through the hole in the rope pulley. Tie a knot in one end of the rope, then push the knot into the recess of the pulley.

17. Wind the starter rope onto the pulley in a clockwise direction as viewed from the rewind spring side of the pulley.

18. Install the pulley and rope assembly into the housing. Make sure the hook on the inner coil of the rewind spring properly engages the slot in the pulley.

19. Install the ratchet (4, **Figure 1**), friction spring (5) and cover (6) onto the starter housing center shaft.

20. Hook one end of the return spring into the friction plate and the other end of the spring into the ratchet. See **Figure 3**. Install the friction plate and return spring onto the center shaft. Install the thrust washer (9, **Figure 1**) and the lock clip (10).

21. Place the rope into the notch (**Figure 4**) in the pulley. While holding the rope in the notch, rotate the rope pulley 3 turns counterclockwise to apply tension on the rewind spring.

22. Hold the rope pulley securely, then pass the rope through the rope guide in the housing. Tie a slip knot to prevent the rope from retracting.

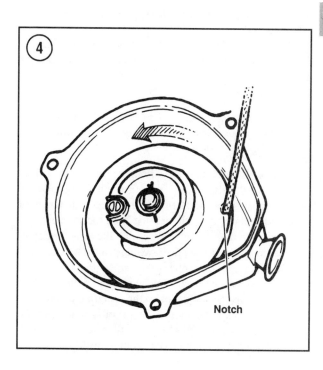

12

23. Pass the rope through the starter handle and secure it with the knot shown in **Figure 5**. Then pull the knot securely into the handle. Untie the slip knot and allow the rope to fully retract.

24. Install the starter assembly onto the power head as described previously in this section.

Rope Starter (3 and 4 hp [Except 4 Deluxe])

Removal/installation

1. Disconnect and ground the spark plug leads to the power head to prevent accidental starting.

2. Remove the three screws securing the starter assembly to the power head. Lift the starter assembly off of the power head.

3. To install the starter, place the starter assembly onto the power head and align the mounting screw holes.

4. Install the starter mounting screws. Tighten the screws *finger tight* at this time.

5. Slowly pull the starter rope to rotate the engine through several revolutions. Then tighten the three mounting screws to 60-84 in.-lb. (6.8-9.5 N•m).

6. Reconnect the spark plug leads when finished.

Starter rope replacement

Refer to **Figure 6** for this procedure.

1. Remove the starter assembly as described in this chapter.

2. Extend the starter rope and tie a slip knot close to the housing. Allow the rope to retract into the housing up to the knot (to relieve the rope tension from the starter handle).

3. Pry the rope anchor (7, **Figure 6**) from the starter handle. Then untie the knot (or cut the rope) and remove the anchor and handle.

CAUTION
Wear leather gloves when holding the rope pulley and releasing the spring tension in the following two steps.

4. Completely extend the rope, hold the rope pulley firmly and remove the slip knot. While firmly holding the rope pulley, grasp the knotted end of the rope with a pair of needlenose pliers and pull the rope from the rope pulley.

5. After removing the rope, carefully allow the pulley to slowly unwind, relieving the rewind spring's tension.

6. Obtain a new starter rope.
   a. The starter rope must be 59 in. (149.9 cm) long. If necessary, trim the rope to the specified length.
   b. Heat the last 1/2 in. (12.7 mm) of both ends of the rope with a match or lighter until the ends are fused. This will prevent the rope from unraveling.

c. Tie a knot in one end of the rope as shown in **Figure 5**.

CAUTION
Wear leather gloves when preloading the rewind spring and holding the rope pulley in the following steps.

7. Preload the rewind spring by turning the rope pulley counterclockwise until it is fully tensioned and binds. Then carefully allow the rope pulley to unwind 1/4 to 1-1/4 turns until the rope hole in the pulley aligns with the rope hole in the starter housing.

8. While firmly holding the pulley in place, insert the rope into the hole in the pulley and pass it through the hole in the starter housing. Pull the rope until the knotted end is seated in the relief in the rope pulley.

9. Tie a slip knot in the rope as close to the starter housing as possible. Then carefully release the rope pulley and allow the slip knot to be pulled up against the starter housing.

10. Pass the rope through the starter handle and secure it with the knot shown in **Figure 5**. Push the knot into the rope anchor, then pull the anchor (and knot) securely into the starter handle.

11. Untie the slip knot and allow the rope to fully retract.

12. Install the starter assembly as described in the previous section.

Disassembly

WARNING
During starter disassembly, the rewind spring may unwind violently. Wear suitable

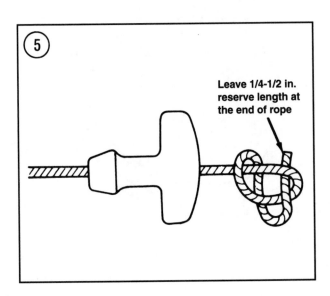

⑤ Leave 1/4-1/2 in. reserve length at the end of rope

hand and eye protection during starter service.

Refer to **Figure 6** for this procedure.

1. Remove the starter as described in this chapter.

2. Remove the rope from the starter as described in Steps 1-5 of *Starter rope replacement in this chapter.*

3. Remove the retainer clip (15, **Figure 6**). Then remove the starter pawl (14), the spring links (13) and the friction spring (12) as an assembly.

4. Remove the spindle screw while firmly holding the rope pulley in the housing. Then invert the starter housing and lift out the spindle.

5. Place the starter housing upright (rewind spring and pulley facing down) over a suitable bench. Tap the housing against the bench until the spring and pulley fall out and the spring unwinds inside the housing's mounting legs.

6. Separate the rewind spring and the rope pulley.

7. Clean all components in a mild solvent (such as mineral spirits) and dry with compressed air. Remove all thread-

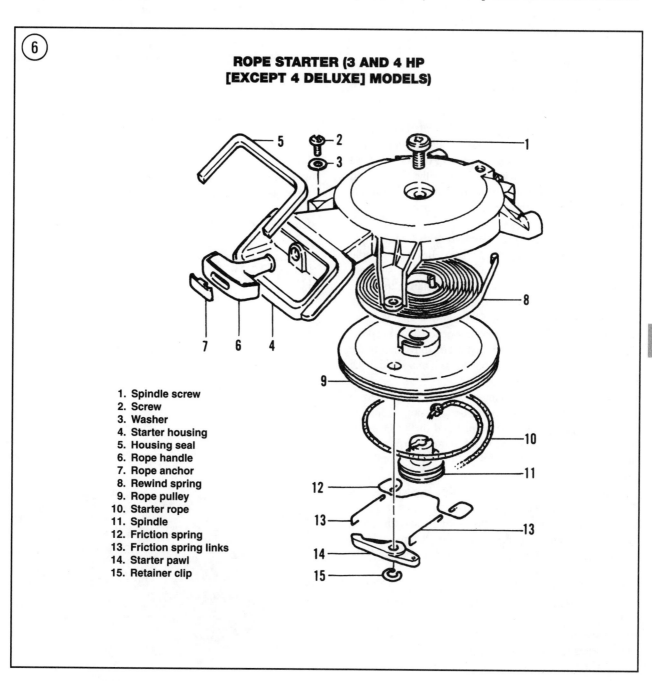

(6)

**ROPE STARTER (3 AND 4 HP
[EXCEPT 4 DELUXE] MODELS)**

1. Spindle screw
2. Screw
3. Washer
4. Starter housing
5. Housing seal
6. Rope handle
7. Rope anchor
8. Rewind spring
9. Rope pulley
10. Starter rope
11. Spindle
12. Friction spring
13. Friction spring links
14. Starter pawl
15. Retainer clip

12

locking adhesive from the spindle screw (and the spindle) threads.

8. Inspect all components for excessive wear, chips, cracks or other damage. Inspect the rope pulley for sharp edges or burrs that could fray the starter rope. If necessary, smooth rough edges with a file or a piece of emery cloth.

Reassembly

> **WARNING**
> *During starter assembly, the rewind spring may unwind violently. Wear suitable hand and eye protection during starter service.*

Refer to **Figure 6** for this procedure.

1. Set the starter housing onto a workbench with the spring cavity facing up.

2. Lubricate the rewind spring area of the starter housing with OMC Triple Guard Grease (or Lubriplate 777 grease).

3. Insert the hooked (inner) end of the rewind spring through the slot in the starter housing. Position the rope pulley over the spring cavity and engage the hooked end of the spring into the slot in the rope pulley (**Figure 7**, typical). Then allow the pulley to rest over the spring cavity.

4. Grease the spindle (11, **Figure 6**) with OMC Triple Guard Grease (or Lubriplate 777 grease). Insert the spindle into the rope pulley. Rotate the spindle until its slots are positioned over the raised ribs cast in the starter housing.

5. Coat the spindle screw's threads with OMC Nut Lock threadlocking adhesive. While holding the spindle slots aligned with the raised ribs in the starter housing, insert the spindle screw into the starter housing and thread it into the spindle. Tighten the spindle screw to 60-84 in.-lb. (6.8-9.5 N•m).

6. Rotate the rope pulley counterclockwise to pull the rest of the rewind spring into the starter housing. Continue rotating the pulley until the looped end of the spring is pulled snugly into its recess in the starter housing. Once the looped end is seated, carefully allow the rope pulley to unwind, releasing all tension on the rewind spring.

7. Install a new starter rope as described in Steps 6-11 of *Starter rope replacement* in this chapter.

8. Install the starter pawl, friction spring and both spring links (as an assembly) as shown in **Figure 8**, typical. Hook the friction spring into the spindle's groove, then push the pawl over its mounting stud.

9. Secure the pawl in place with the retainer clip. Make sure the sharp edge of the clip is facing away from the rope pulley.

10. Check for correct operation of the starter pawl. The pawl must extend when the rope is pulled and retract as the rope rewinds.

11. Install the starter assembly as described in this chapter.

Rope Starter (4 Deluxe Models)

Starter rope replacement

Refer to **Figure 9** for this procedure.

1. Disconnect and ground the spark plug leads to the power head to prevent accidental starting.

2. Extend the starter rope and tie a slip knot close to the housing. Allow the rope to retract into the housing up to the knot (to relieve the rope tension from the starter handle).

3. Pry the cap (1, **Figure 9**) from the starter handle. Then untie the knot (or cut the rope) and remove the rope handle.

> **CAUTION**
> *Wear leather gloves when holding the rope pulley and releasing the spring tension in the following 2 steps.*

4. Remove the slip knot and allow the rope to rewind. Hold the rope pulley firmly and release the starter rope. Then carefully allow the rope pulley to unwind, releasing all tension from the rewind spring.

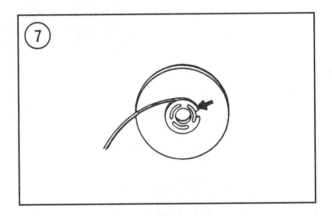

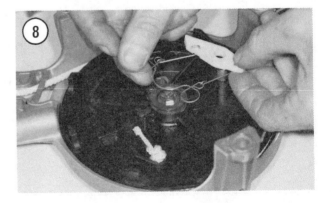

5. Unwind the rope from the rope pulley. Then rotate the rope pulley until the rope knot is visible in the window in the starter cover (**Figure 10**). Grasp the knot with a pair of needlenose pliers and pull the rope from the rope pulley.

6. Make a reference mark on the outer diameter of the rope pulley adjacent to the rope hole (visible in the starter cover's window).

7. Obtain a new starter rope.

   a. The starter rope must be 59.5 in. (151.1 cm) long. If necessary, trim the rope to the specified length.

   b. Heat the last 1/2 in. (12.7 mm) of both ends of the rope (with a match or lighter) until the ends are fused. This will prevent the rope from unraveling.

   c. Tie a knot in one end of the rope as shown in **Figure 11**.

8. Rotate the rope pulley two turns (clockwise) to preliminarily preload the rewind spring. Then continue rotating the pulley until the reference mark on the outer diameter is aligned with the window in the starter cover. Place a small section of the original starter rope between the rope pulley's gear teeth and the idle gear to prevent the rope pulley from unwinding.

9. Insert the unknotted end of the rope through the starter cover's window and through the hole in the rope pulley. Grasp the rope (at the bottom of the rope pulley's groove) with a suitable tool and pull it through the pulley until the knotted end seats in the rope pulley's recess.

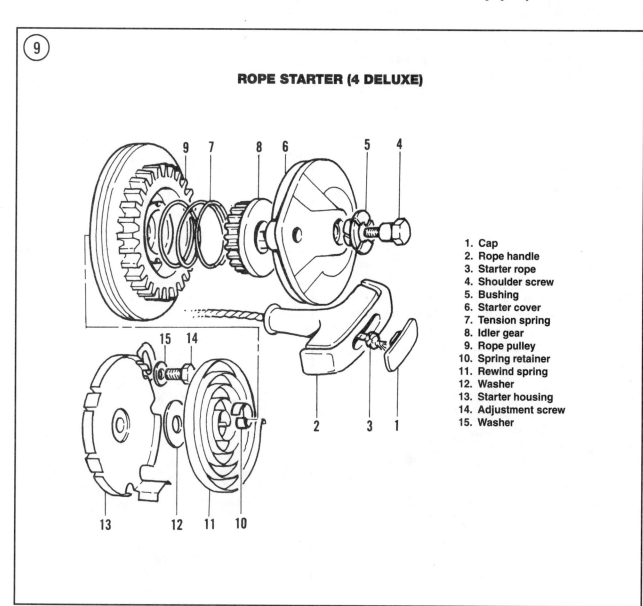

⑨

ROPE STARTER (4 DELUXE)

1. Cap
2. Rope handle
3. Starter rope
4. Shoulder screw
5. Bushing
6. Starter cover
7. Tension spring
8. Idler gear
9. Rope pulley
10. Spring retainer
11. Rewind spring
12. Washer
13. Starter housing
14. Adjustment screw
15. Washer

12

10. Wind the rope around the pulley (in a clockwise direction) making sure that each wrap is routed under the idler gear (at the top) and the rope guard (at the bottom). Pull each wrap snugly into the pulley's groove before continuing with the next wrap.

11. Route the rope out the front of the rope pulley (above the rope guard) and through the eyelet in the lower cowl. Tie a slip knot in the end of the rope to prevent it from being pulled back through the eyelet.

12. Pass the rope through the starter handle and secure it with the knot shown in **Figure 11**. Pull the knot into the handle, then push the cap (1, **Figure 9**) into the starter handle.

13. Untie the slip knot and allow the rope to fully retract.

14. Check the preload on the rewind spring. Pull the starter rope to its full extension and hold it firmly. Then grasp the looped end of the rewind spring (2, **Figure 12**) with a pair of pliers and pull it from the starter assembly until it binds. The spring must extend 8-18 in. (20.3-45.7 cm).

    a. If the spring extends less than 8 in. (20.3 cm), unwind the rope from the pulley one full turn and recheck the preload.

    b. If the spring extends more than 18 in. (45.7 cm), wind the rope onto the pulley one full turn and recheck the preload.

15. When finished, reconnect the spark plug leads.

Removal/installation

1. Disconnect and ground the spark plug leads to the power head to prevent accidental starting.

2. Extend the starter rope and tie a slip knot close to the housing. Allow the rope to retract into the housing up to the knot (to relieve the rope tension from the starter handle).

3. Pry the cap (1, **Figure 9**) from the starter handle. Then untie the knot (or cut the rope) and remove the rope handle.

> *CAUTION*
> *Wear leather gloves when holding the rope pulley and releasing the spring tension in the following steps.*

4. Remove the slip knot and allow the rope to rewind. Hold the rope pulley firmly and release the starter rope. Then carefully allow the rope pulley to unwind, releasing all tension from the rewind spring.

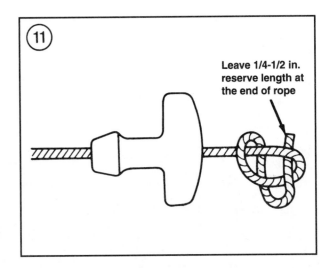

Leave 1/4-1/2 in. reserve length at the end of rope

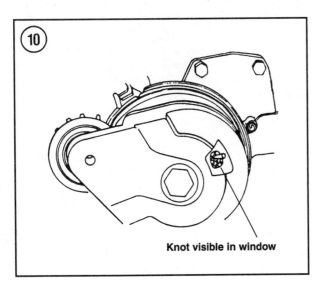

Knot visible in window

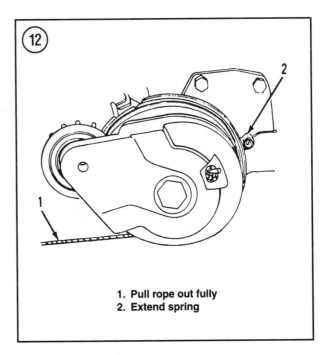

1. Pull rope out fully
2. Extend spring

NOTE
Do not pull the spring from the starter housing unless the starter is going to be disassembled.

5. If the starter is to be disassembled, grasp the looped end of the starter spring (2, **Figure 12**) with a pair of pliers and pull it from the starter assembly until it binds. The rope pulley must be allowed to rotate as the spring is pulled.

6. Remove the port ignition coil as described in Chapter Seven.

7. Remove the adjustment screw (B, **Figure 13**) and washer. Then remove the shoulder screw (A) while firmly holding the starter cover and starter housing (6 and 13, **Figure 9**) together.

8. Remove the starter assembly from the power head. If the starter is not going to be disassembled, install a suitable nut over the shoulder screw's threads and tighten it finger tight. The nut will hold the cover and housing together.

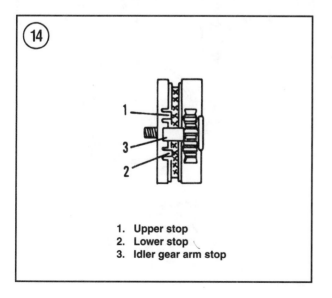

1. Upper stop
2. Lower stop
3. Idler gear arm stop

NOTE
*Firmly hold the starter cover and housing (6 and 13, **Figure 9**) together anytime the nut is removed from the shoulder screw.*

9. To install the starter assembly, begin by cleaning all threadlocking adhesive from the threads of the shoulder and adjustment screws. Then lightly coat the threads of both screws with OMC Screw Lock threadlocking adhesive.

10. Firmly hold the starter cover and housing together and remove the nut from the shoulder screw.

11. Position the starter assembly to the power head and thread the shoulder screw (B, **Figure 13**) into the power head until it is finger-tight. Then install the adjustment screw and washer and tighten it finger-tight at this time.

NOTE
*The upper stop (1, **Figure 14**) controls the engagement of the idler gear to the flywheel teeth. The idler gear arm stop (3, **Figure 14**) must be against the upper stop (1) when adjusting the idler gear position in the next step.*

12. Hold the idler gear arm stop (3, **Figure 14**) against the upper stop (1). Rotate the starter housing to fully engage the idler gear into the flywheel teeth, then tighten the adjustment screw (B, **Figure 13**) securely.

13. Tighten the shoulder screw to 120-144 in.-lb. (13.6-16.3 N•m).

14. Reinstall the port ignition coil as described in Chapter Seven.

15A. *Starter rope removed*—Install the starter rope as described in this chapter.

15B. *Starter rope installed*—Install the starter handle and tension the rewind spring as described in Step 8 and Steps 10-14 of the *Starter rope replacement* section in this chapter.

16. Reconnect the spark plug leads when finished.

Disassembly

Refer to **Figure 9** for this procedure.

1. Remove the starter assembly as described in this chapter. Make sure the looped end of the rewind spring is pulled out from the starter assembly as far as possible (as described in the removal procedure).

2. Remove the nut from the shoulder screw and separate the cover (6, **Figure 9**) from the rope pulley and housing assembly (9-12, **Figure 9**).

3. Remove the idler gear (8, **Figure 9**), tension spring (7) and bushing (5) from the starter cover.

12

4. Lift the rope pulley from the starter housing. Disengage the rewind spring and the spring retainer (10, **Figure 9**) from the pulley.

5. Remove the washer (12, **Figure 9**) from the back of the rope pulley or the face of the starter housing.

6. Remove the starter rope from the rope pulley.

7. Clean all components in a mild solvent (such as mineral spirits) and dry with compressed air.

8. Inspect all components as follows:
   a. Inspect the rope pulley and idler gear teeth for worn, chipped, cracked or missing teeth.
   b. Inspect the rewind spring for wear and distortion. Check both ends of the spring for cracks, chips or missing pieces. Inspect the spring retainer (10, **Figure 9**) for damage or distortion.
   c. Inspect the bushing (5, **Figure 9**) for wear or damage.
   d. Replace all components that are in questionable condition.

Reassembly

Use OMC Triple Guard Grease (or Lubriplate 777 grease) for all grease (lubricant) applications. Refer to **Figure 9** for this procedure.

> *WARNING*
> *During starter reassembly, the rewind spring may unwind violently. Wear suitable hand and eye protection during starter service.*

1. Lubricate the bushing (5, **Figure 9**) and insert it into the starter cover. Insert the bushing from the outside surface of the cover.

2. Set the starter cover (2, **Figure 15**) onto a workbench with the open side facing up. Lubricate the idler gear (3) and spring (1). Install the spring over the raised shoulder at the center of the cover. Then place the idler gear over the idler gear stop arm (4, **Figure 15**).

3. Lubricate the washer (12, **Figure 9**) and position it into its recess in the starter housing.

4. Place the rope pulley onto a workbench with the gear teeth facing down. Install the spring retainer (10, **Figure 9**) over the pin in the pulley. The curved end of the retainer must be pointing in a clockwise direction.

5. Position the hooked end of the rewind spring over the pin in the pulley (and inside of the spring retainer). The spring must lead off into a clockwise direction.

6. Carefully position the starter housing over the rope pulley. Make sure the rewind spring is positioned into the slot in the housing. See **Figure 16**.

7. Firmly hold the rope pulley and starter housing together. Install the shoulder bolt through the rope pulley, washer

and starter housing. Install a suitable nut over the shoulder screw and tighten it finger-tight.

> *CAUTION*
> *Hold the rope pulley firmly against the starter housing during the next step.*

8. Hold the rope pulley firmly against the starter housing and rotate the pulley clockwise (as viewed from the toothed side) until the rewind spring has been fully pulled into the starter housing. Then carefully allow the pulley to unwind, releasing all tension on the rewind spring.

9. Hold the rope pulley firmly against the starter housing and remove the nut from the shoulder screw. Then carefully pull the shoulder screw from the assembly.

10. Carefully install the starter cover assembly over the rope pulley, being careful not to disturb the position of the spring (1, **Figure 15**). The idler gear arm stop must be positioned between the upper and lower stops as shown in **Figure 14**.

11. Lubricate the smooth shank of the shoulder screw and insert the screw through the starter cover, rope pulley, washer and starter housing. Then install a suitable nut over the shoulder screw threads and tighten it finger-tight. This will hold the assembly together until it can be installed.

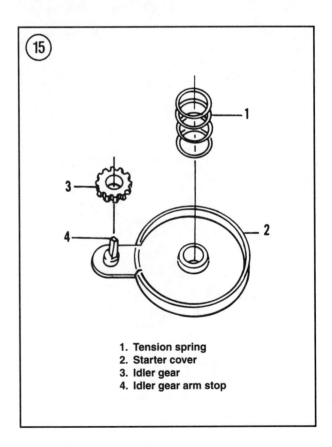

1. **Tension spring**
2. **Starter cover**
3. **Idler gear**
4. **Idler gear arm stop**

12. Install the starter assembly and install a new starter rope as described previously in this chapter.

Rope Starter
(6-15 hp and 25/35 hp [Three-cylinder])

Service procedures for the rope starters used on 6 and 8 hp models, 9.9 and 15 hp models and 25 and 35 hp (three-cylinder) models are all similar (with the exception of the neutral start lockout system).

Neutral start lockout systems prevent the rope starter from operating if the engine is in FORWARD or REVERSE gear. This is to ensure that the engine in only started in NEUTRAL (and cannot be started in gear).

The 6 and 8 hp models use a cable-operated plunger system. See 23-25, **Figure 17**. The cable is operated by a bellcrank on the port side of the power head, just below the carburetor. The cable has a spring-loaded plunger that connects to the rear of the starter housing.

The 9.9 and 15 hp models use a linkage-operated system. The linkage is connected to the port end of the power head-mounted shift lever (located below the port side of the carburetor). The link connects to a spring-loaded plunger at the front of the starter housing. See **Figure 18**.

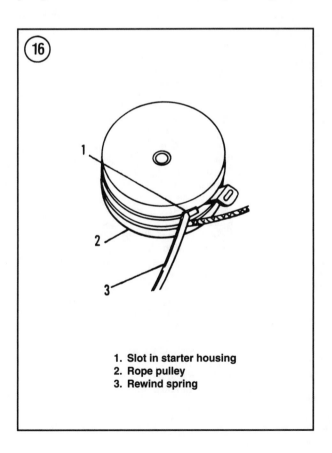

1. Slot in starter housing
2. Rope pulley
3. Rewind spring

The 25 and 35 hp (three-cylinder) models also use a linkage-operated system. The linkage is connected to the shift detent lever on the starboard side of the power head. The link connects to a spring-loaded plunger at the rear of the starter housing. The system is the same as that shown in **Figure 18**, except that all components are located at the rear of the housing.

All neutral start lockout systems use a spring-loaded plunger in the starter housing that engages the rope pulley (16, **Figure 17**), and prevents it from rotating. The plunger must be retracted by the cable (or linkage) for the starter to operate.

Removal

1. Disconnect and ground the spark plug leads to the power head to prevent accidental starting.

2. *25 and 35 hp*—Disconnect the low-oil warning light at its two-pin Amphenol.

3A. *6 and 8 hp*—Remove the three screws securing the starter housing to the power head. Locate and secure the spacer sleeve (2, **Figure 17**) on each screw or in each leg of the starter housing.

3B. *9.9-35 hp*—Remove the three screws and washers securing the starter housing to the power head. Locate and secure the rubber grommet and flanged spacer sleeve (4 and 5, **Figure 17**) on each leg of the starter housing.

4A. *6 and 8 hp*—Lift the starter from the power head and invert it. Using two small screwdrivers, depress the locking tabs and remove the neutral start lockout cable and plunger from the starter housing. **Figure 19** shows the cable and plunger removed with the locking tabs marked.

4B. *9.9 and 15 hp*—Loosen the screw (7, **Figure 18**) several turns to allow the link (8) to be disconnected from the cam (6). Then disconnect the neutral start lockout link (**Figure 20**) from the lockout cam.

4C. *25 and 35 hp*—Disconnect the neutral start lockout link from the lockout cam. The mechanism is located at the rear of the starter housing.

5. Remove the starter from the power head.

Installation

1. *9.9-35 hp*—If removed, install a rubber grommet into each of the starter housing mounting legs, then install a flanged spacer sleeve into each rubber grommet. See 4 and 5, **Figure 17**.

2. Place the starter assembly onto the power head and align the mounting screw holes.

3A. *6 and 8 hp*—If removed, install a spacer sleeve (2, **Figure 17**) into each of the starter housing mounting legs.

12

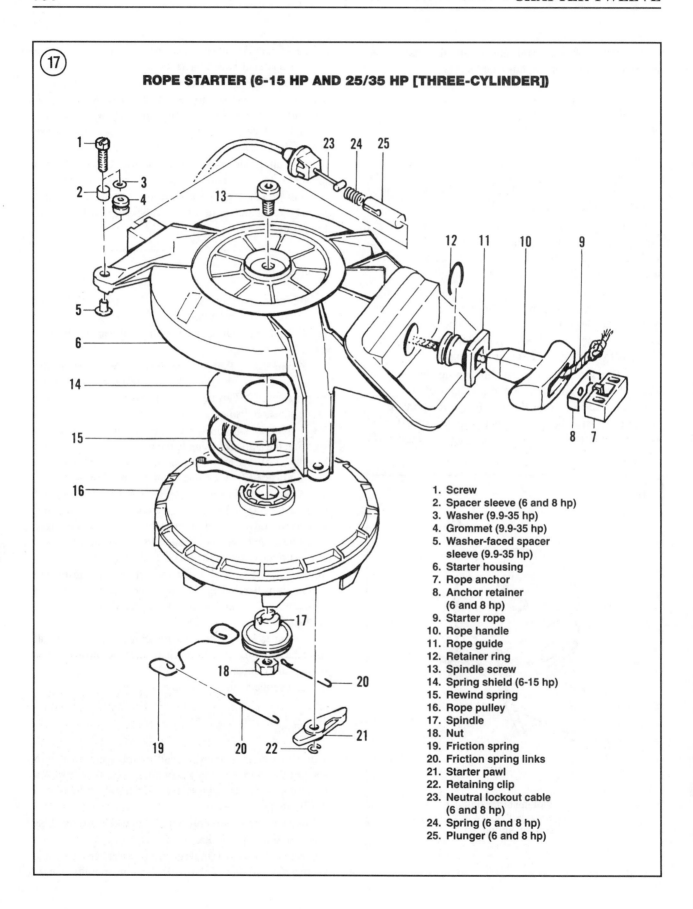

ROPE STARTER (6-15 HP AND 25/35 HP [THREE-CYLINDER])

1. Screw
2. Spacer sleeve (6 and 8 hp)
3. Washer (9.9-35 hp)
4. Grommet (9.9-35 hp)
5. Washer-faced spacer sleeve (9.9-35 hp)
6. Starter housing
7. Rope anchor
8. Anchor retainer (6 and 8 hp)
9. Starter rope
10. Rope handle
11. Rope guide
12. Retainer ring
13. Spindle screw
14. Spring shield (6-15 hp)
15. Rewind spring
16. Rope pulley
17. Spindle
18. Nut
19. Friction spring
20. Friction spring links
21. Starter pawl
22. Retaining clip
23. Neutral lockout cable (6 and 8 hp)
24. Spring (6 and 8 hp)
25. Plunger (6 and 8 hp)

Then install the three starter mounting screws. Tighten the screws finger-tight at this time.

3B. *9.9-35 hp*—Install the three starter mounting screws and washers. Tighten the screws finger-tight at this time.

4A. *6 and 8 hp*—Install the neutral lockout cable. Position the locking tabs on the sides (**Figure 19**) and push the cable into the starter housing until it snaps into place.

4B. *9.9-35 hp*—Connect the neutral start lockout link to the lockout cam. See **Figure 20**, typical. On 9.9 and 15 hp models, tighten the screw (7, **Figure 18**) until it just seats in the cam (6).

5. Slowly pull the starter rope to rotate the engine through several revolutions. Then tighten the three mounting screws to 60-84 in.-lb. (6.8-9.5 N•m).

6. Operate the starter and check neutral start lockout operation. The starter must only operate in NEUTRAL and must not operate in FORWARD or REVERSE gear. If the starter does not perform as specified, repair or replace components of the neutral start lockout system as necessary.

7. *25 and 35 hp*—Reconnect the low-oil warning light's two-pin Amphenol connector to its engine harness mate.

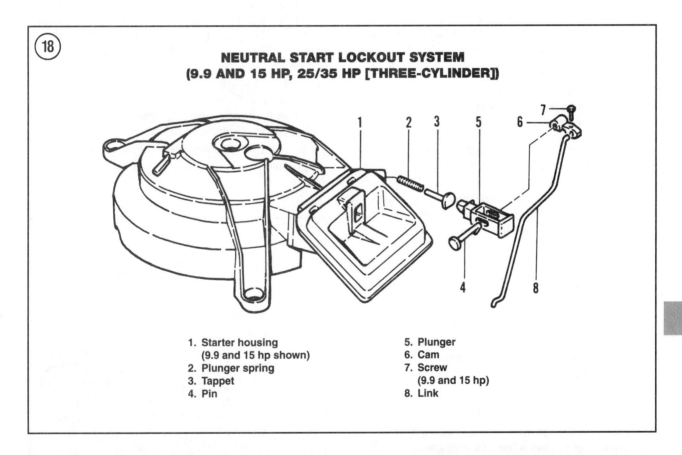

(18)

**NEUTRAL START LOCKOUT SYSTEM
(9.9 AND 15 HP, 25/35 HP [THREE-CYLINDER])**

1. Starter housing
   (9.9 and 15 hp shown)
2. Plunger spring
3. Tappet
4. Pin
5. Plunger
6. Cam
7. Screw
   (9.9 and 15 hp)
8. Link

12

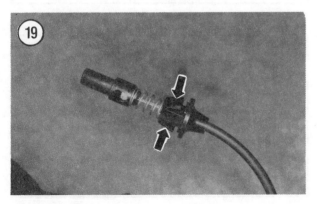

(19)

(20)

Then push the connector into the molded tabs in the ignition module's outer case.

8. Reconnect the spark plug leads when finished.

Starter rope replacement

Refer to **Figure 17** for this procedure.

1. Remove the starter assembly as described in this chapter.

2. Extend the starter rope and tie a slip knot close to the housing. Allow the rope to retract into the housing up to the knot to relieve the rope tension from the starter handle.

3. Pry the rope anchor (7, **Figure 17**) from the starter handle. Then untie the knot (or cut the rope) and remove the anchor, anchor retainer (if equipped) and rope handle.

> *CAUTION*
> *Wear leather gloves when holding the rope pulley and releasing the spring tension in the following two steps.*

4. Completely extend the rope, hold the rope pulley firmly and remove the slip knot. While firmly holding the rope pulley, grasp the knotted end of the rope (with a pair of needlenose pliers) and pull the rope from the rope pulley.

5. After removing the rope, carefully allow the pulley to slowly unwind, relieving the rewind spring's tension.

6. Obtain a new starter rope.
   a. The starter rope must be 59.5 in. (151.1 cm) long for six and eight hp models or 59 in. (149.9 cm) long for 9.9-35 hp models. If necessary, trim the rope to the specified length.
   b. Heat the last 1/2 in. (12.7 mm) of both ends of the rope with a match or lighter until the ends are fused. This will prevent the rope from unraveling.
   c. Tie a knot in one end of the rope as shown in **Figure 21**.

> *CAUTION*
> *Wear leather gloves when preloading the rewind spring and holding the rope pulley in the following steps.*

7. Preload the rewind spring as follows:
   a. Turn the rope pulley counterclockwise until it is fully tensioned and binds.
   b. Carefully allow the rope pulley to unwind 1/4 to 1-1/4 turns (six and eight hp models) or 1/2 to 1-1/2 turns (9.9-35 hp models) until the rope hole in the pulley aligns with the hole in the rope guide (11, **Figure 17**).
   c. Rotate the rope pulley slightly to align the small round hole in the rope pulley with the small round hole in the starter housing. Then insert a No. 2

Phillips screwdriver or a suitable punch through the holes to lock the pulley in place.

8. With the pulley securely locked in place, insert the rope into the hole in the pulley and pass it through the hole in the rope guide (11, **Figure 17**). Pull the rope until the knotted end is firmly seated in the relief in the rope pulley.

9. Tie a slip knot in the rope as close to the starter housing as possible. Then carefully remove the screwdriver (or punch) while holding the rope pulley in place. Carefully release the rope pulley and allow the slip knot to be pulled up against the starter housing.

10A. *6 and 8 hp*—Pass the rope through the starter handle and anchor retainer (8, **Figure 17**). Tie a knot in the end of the rope as shown in **Figure 21**. Push the knot into the rope anchor (7, **Figure 17**), then pull the anchor, anchor retainer and knot into the starter handle.

10B. *9.9-35 hp*—Pass the rope through the starter handle and secure it with the knot shown in **Figure 21**. Push the knot into the rope anchor (7, **Figure 17**), then pull the anchor and knot into the starter handle.

11. Untie the slip knot and allow the rope to fully retract.

12. Install the starter assembly as described in the previous section.

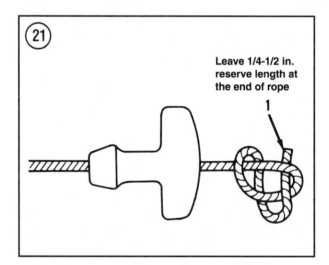

Leave 1/4-1/2 in. reserve length at the end of rope

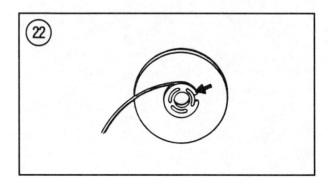

Disassembly

> **WARNING**
> *During starter disassembly, the rewind spring may unwind violently. Wear suitable hand and eye protection during starter service.*

Refer to **Figure 17** for this procedure.

1. Remove the starter as described previously in this chapter.

2. Remove the rope from the starter as described in Steps 1-5 of *Starter rope replacement* located previously in this chapter.

3. *9.9-35 hp*—Disassemble the neutral start lockout as follows:

   a. Depress the locking tab and remove the retaining pin (4, **Figure 18**).

   b. Remove the cam (6, **Figure 18**). On 9.9 and 15 hp models, also remove the screw (7).

   c. Slide the plunger, tappet and spring (2, 3 and 5, **Figure 18**) from the starter housing. Once removed, separate the components.

4. Remove the retainer clip (22, **Figure 17**), then lift the starter pawl (21), spring links (20) and the friction spring from the rope pulley as an assembly.

5. Remove the spindle screw and locknut (13 and 18, **Figure 17**) while firmly holding the rope pulley in the housing. Then invert the starter housing and lift out the spindle. Discard the locknut (18).

6. Place the starter housing upright (rewind spring and pulley facing down) over a suitable bench. Tap the housing against the bench until the spring and pulley fall out and the spring unwinds inside the housing's mounting legs.

7. Separate the rewind spring and the rope pulley. On 6-15 hp models, locate and secure the spring shield (14, **Figure 17**).

8. Clean all components in a mild solvent (such as mineral spirits) and dry with compressed air. Remove all threadlocking adhesive from the spindle screw threads.

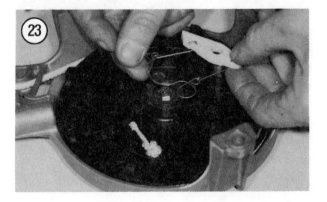

9. Inspect all components for excessive wear, chips, cracks or other damage. Inspect the rope pulley for sharp edges (or burrs) that could fray the starter rope. If necessary, smooth rough edges with a file or a piece of emery cloth.

10. Inspect the neutral start lockout components for wear or damage. Replace components as necessary.

Reassembly

> **WARNING**
> *During starter reassembly, the rewind spring may unwind violently. Wear suitable hand and eye protection during starter service.*

1. Set the starter housing onto a workbench with the spring cavity facing up.

2. *6-15 hp*—Insert the shield (14, **Figure 17**) into the spring cavity.

3. Lubricate the rewind spring area of the starter housing with OMC Triple Guard Grease (or Lubriplate 777 grease).

4. Insert the hooked (inner) end of the rewind spring through the slot in the starter housing. Position the rope pulley over the spring cavity and engage the hooked end of the spring with the slot in the rope pulley (**Figure 22**, typical). Then allow the pulley to rest over the spring cavity.

5. Grease the spindle (17, **Figure 17**) with OMC Triple Guard Grease (or Lubriplate 777 grease). Insert the spindle into the rope pulley. Rotate the spindle until its slots are positioned over the raised ribs cast into the starter housing (or its raised ribs are positioned into the slots cast into the starter housing).

6. Coat the spindle screw's threads with OMC Nut Lock threadlocking adhesive. While holding the spindle aligned with the raised ribs (or cast slots) in the starter housing, insert the spindle screw into the starter housing and through the spindle. Install a new locknut over the spindle screw. Tighten the spindle screw and locknut to 120-144 in.-lb. (13.6-16.3 N•m).

7. Rotate the rope pulley counterclockwise to pull the rest of the rewind spring into the starter housing. Continue rotating the pulley until the looped end of the spring is pulled snugly into its recess in the starter housing. Once the looped end is seated, carefully allow the rope pulley to unwind, releasing all tension on the rewind spring.

8. Install a new starter rope as described in Steps 6-11 of *Starter rope replacement* in this chapter.

9. Install the starter pawl, friction spring and both spring links (as an assembly) as shown in **Figure 23**, typical. Hook the friction spring into the spindle's groove, then push the pawl over its mounting stud.

12

10. Secure the pawl in place with the retainer clip. Make sure the sharp edge of the clip is facing away from the rope pulley.

11. Check for correct operation of the starter pawl. The pawl must extend when the rope is pulled and retract as the rope rewinds.

12. *9.9-35 hp*—Assemble the neutral start lockout components to the starter housing. Make sure the offset side of the cam (6, Figure 18) is facing the retaining plate (under the starter housing), then secure the components in place with the retaining pin (4). Make sure the retaining pin locks in place.

13. *9.9-15 hp*—Install the screw (7, **Figure 18**) into the cam (6) but do not tighten it at this time.

14. Install the starter assembly as described previously in this chapter.

Rewind Starter
(20-30 hp [Two-Cylinder] and 18 Jet)

A neutral start lockout system is used to prevent the rope starter from operating if the engine is in FORWARD or REVERSE gear. The system uses a cable-operated plunger (**Figure 19**). One end of the cable (A, **Figure 24**) is connected to a lever on the starboard side of the power head, just in front of the fuel pump. The other end of the cable (B, **Figure 24**) has a spring-loaded plunger that connects to the rear of the starter housing.

When extended, the plunger (in the starter housing) engages the rope pulley, preventing it from rotating. The plunger must be retracted (by the cable and bellcrank) in order for the starter to operate.

Removal/installation

1. Disconnect and ground the spark plug leads to the power head to prevent accidental starting.

2. Remove the three screws and lockwashers securing the starter housing to the power head.

3. Lift the starter from the power head and invert it. Using two small screwdrivers, depress the locking tabs and remove the neutral start lockout cable and plunger from the starter housing. **Figure 19** shows the cable and plunger removed with the locking tabs marked.

4. Remove the starter from the power head.

5. Remove the metal cup (C, **Figure 24**) from each of the three rubber mounts. Inspect each mount for damage or deterioration. Replace any damaged or deteriorated mounts. Apply OMC Screw Lock threadlocking adhesive to the threads of each new mount. Using a crescent wrench, tighten each mount securely.

6. To install the starter, first make sure that a metal cup is present over each of the three rubber mounts. See C, **Figure 24**.

7. Place the starter assembly onto the power head and align the mounting screw holes.

8. Install the three starter mounting screws and lockwashers. The shorter screw is installed into the hole on the port side of the engine. Tighten the screws finger-tight at this time.

9. Install the neutral lockout cable. Position the locking tabs on the sides (**Figure 19**) and push the cable into the starter housing until it snaps into place.

10. Slowly pull the starter rope to rotate the engine through several revolutions. Then tighten the three mounting screws to 48-72 in.-lb. (5.4-8.1 N•m).

11. Operate the starter and verify correct neutral start lockout operation. The starter must only operate in NEUTRAL and must not operate in FORWARD or REVERSE gear. If the starter does not perform as specified, repair or replace components of the neutral start lockout system as necessary.

12. Reconnect the spark plug leads when finished.

Starter rope replacement

Refer to **Figure 25** for this procedure.

1. Remove the starter assembly as described in the previous section.

2. Extend the starter rope and tie a slip knot close to the handle support plate (8, **Figure 25**). Allow the rope to retract into the housing until the knot is against the support plate (to relieve the rope tension from the starter handle).

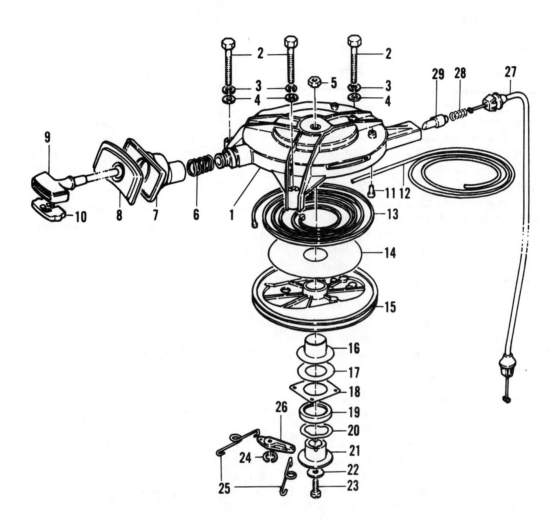

ROPE STARTER (20-30 HP [TWO-CYLINDER] AND 18 JET)

1. Starter housing
2. Screw
3. Lockwasher
4. Washer (not present on all models)
5. Spindle nut
6. Handle support spring
7. Grommet
8. Handle support plate
9. Rope handle
10. Rope anchor
11. Guide pin
12. Starter rope
13. Rewind spring
14. Spring shield
15. Rope pulley
16. Spindle bushing
17. Shim
18. Friction plate
19. Friction spring cover
20. Friction spring(s)
21. Spindle
22. Washer
23. Spindle screw
24. Retaining ring
25. Pawl links
26. Starter pawl
27. Neutral start lockout cable
28. Spring
29. Plunger

12

3. Pry the rope anchor (10, **Figure 25**) from the starter handle. Remove the rope from the anchor, then remove the handle.

> *CAUTION*
> *Wear leather gloves when holding the rope pulley and releasing the spring tension in the following 2 steps.*

4. Completely extend the rope, hold the rope pulley firmly and remove the slip knot. While firmly holding the rope pulley, grasp the knotted end of the rope (with a pair of needlenose pliers) and pull the rope from the rope pulley.

5. After removing the rope, carefully allow the pulley to slowly unwind, relieving the rewind spring's tension.

6. Obtain a new starter rope.
   a. The starter rope must be 73.5 in. (186.7 cm) long. If necessary, trim the rope to the specified length.
   b. Heat the last 1/2 in. (12.7 mm) of both ends of the rope (with a match or lighter) until the ends are fused. This will prevent the rope from unraveling.
   c. Tie a knot in one end of the rope as shown in **Figure 21**.

> *CAUTION*
> *Wear leather gloves when preloading the rewind spring and holding the rope pulley in the following steps.*

7. Preload the rewind spring as follows:
   a. Turn the rope pulley counterclockwise until it is fully tensioned and binds.
   b. Carefully allow the rope pulley to unwind 1/2 to 1 turn until the rope hole in the pulley aligns with the hole in the starter housing.

8. With the pulley securely held in place, insert the rope into the hole in the pulley and pass it behind the roll pin in the pulley. Then pass the rope through the holes in the starter housing, spring, grommet and handle support plate (1 and 6-8, **Figure 25**). Pull the rope until the knotted end is firmly seated in the relief in the rope pulley.

9. Tie a slip knot in the rope as close to the handle support plate as possible. Then carefully release the rope pulley and allow the slip knot to be pulled up against the support plate.

> *NOTE*
> *Starter rope threading tool (part No. 378774) will greatly reduce the effort required to pass the starter rope through the starter handle in the next step.*

10. Grease the end of the rope to ease its installation into the starter handle. Pass the rope through the starter handle and rope anchor (9 and 10, **Figure 25**). Seat the rope into the channel in the rope anchor as shown in **Figure 26**. The

end of the rope must be butted tightly against the end of the channel.

11. Push the rope anchor into the starter handle until it is seated. Then untie the slip knot and allow the rope to fully retract.

12. Install the starter assembly as described in the previous section.

Disassembly

> *WARNING*
> *During starter disassembly, the rewind spring may unwind violently. Wear suitable hand and eye protection during starter service.*

Refer to **Figure 25** for this procedure.

1. Remove the starter as described previously in this chapter.

2. Remove the rope from the starter as described in Steps 1-5 of Starter rope replacement *in this chapter.*

3. Hold the spindle screw and remove the spindle nut.

4. Lay the starter housing on a workbench with the rope pulley facing up.

5. Remove the spindle screw and washer. Hold the rope pulley and lift the spindle from the pulley. Then remove the friction spring(s) and the friction spring cover.

6. Remove the retainer clips securing the starter pawls to the rope pulley. Then lift the friction plate, friction spring links and the starter pawls from the rope pulley as an assembly.

7. Remove the shim (17, **Figure 25**) and the spindle bushing (16).

8. Hold the rope pulley into the starter housing and place the starter housing upright (rope pulley facing down) over a suitable bench. Release the rope pulley and tap the housing against the bench until the spring and pulley fall

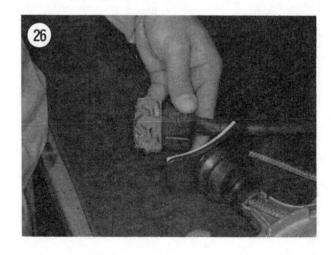

out and the spring unwinds inside the housing's mounting legs.

9. Separate the rewind spring and the rope pulley. Then locate and secure the spring shield (14, **Figure 25**).

10. Clean all components in a mild solvent (such as mineral spirits) and dry with compressed air. Remove all thread-locking adhesive from the spindle screw threads.

11. Inspect all components for excessive wear, chips, cracks or other damage. Inspect the rope pulley for sharp edges or burrs that could fray the starter rope. If necessary, smooth rough edges with a file or a piece of emery cloth.

Reassembly

Use OMC Triple Guard Grease (or Lubriplate 777 grease) for all lubrication applications. Refer to **Figure 25** for this procedure.

WARNING
During starter reassembly, the rewind spring may unwind violently. Wear suitable hand and eye protection during starter service.

1. Set the starter housing onto a workbench with the spring cavity facing up.

2. Lubricate the rewind spring area of the starter housing with grease.

3. Wearing leather gloves, hook the outer end of the rewind spring over the pin in the starter housing. See **Figure 27**. Then carefully wind the spring into the starter housing until it is fully seated in its recess as shown in **Figure 27**.

4. Lightly grease the spring shield (14, **Figure 25**) and position it onto the spring side of the rope pulley. Carefully bend the inner end of the rewind spring to position the spring's loop near the center of the starter housing.

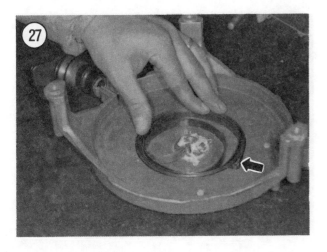

CAUTION
Do not lift the inner end of the rewind spring in the next step or the rewind spring may suddenly and forcefully unwind.

5. Position the rope pulley over the rewind spring and engage the inner end of the spring to the pulley's pin. Then allow the pulley to rest over the spring cavity.

6. Grease the spindle bushing and shim. Install the bushing into the rope pulley, then position the shim on top of the bushing.

7. Install the starter pawls, friction spring links and the friction plate (as an assembly) onto the rope pulley. If disassembled, the looped end of each link must face away from the longer end of each pawl, and the hooked ends of the links must face the rope pulley. Make sure each pawl is seated over its mounting stud.

8. Secure each pawl in place with a retainer clip. Make sure the sharp edge of each clip is facing away from the rope pulley.

9. Grease the friction spring cover and position it over the friction plate with the flat side of the cover against the plate. Then grease the friction spring(s) and place it (them) into the open end of the friction spring cover.

10. Grease the spindle and insert it through the friction spring(s), friction spring cover, friction plate, shim and rope pulley bushing. Rotate the spindle and friction spring cover as necessary to align the flats of each component, allowing the spindle to seat against the cover.

11. Rotate the spindle until its slots are positioned over the raised ribs cast into the starter housing (or its raised ribs are positioned into the slots cast into the starter housing).

12. Coat the spindle screw's threads with OMC Nut Lock threadlocking adhesive. While holding the spindle aligned with the raised ribs (or cast slots) in the starter housing, insert the spindle screw (and washer) into the starter housing (through the spindle). Tighten the spindle screw to 120-144 in.-lb. (13.6-16.3 N•m).

13. Coat the threads of the spindle nut with OMC Nut Lock threadlocking adhesive. Install the nut over the spindle screw threads. Hold the spindle screw in position and tighten the nut to 120-144 in.-lb. (13.6-16.3 N•m).

14. Install a new starter rope as described in Steps 6-11 of *Starter rope replacement* in this chapter.

15. Check for correct operation of the starter pawls. The pawls must extend when the rope is pulled and retract as the rope rewinds.

16. Install the starter assembly as described previously in this chapter.

12

Rewind Starter
(40 hp and 28 Jet)

A neutral start lockout system is used to prevent the rope starter from operating if the engine is in FORWARD or REVERSE gear. The system uses an adjustable cable-operated lever. One end of the cable is connected to the shift lever on the starboard side of the power head. The other end of the cable (C, **Figure 28**) operates a sliding cam (B, **Figure 28**) to move a spring-loaded lever on the port rear corner of the starter housing.

When activated, the lockout lever (in the starter housing) engages the rope pulley, preventing it from rotating. The lever must be retracted (by the cable and slide) in order for the starter to operate.

Removal/installation

1. Disconnect and ground the spark plug leads to the power head to prevent accidental starting.

2. Remove the screw (A, **Figure 28**) securing the lockout cable to the starter housing. Disengage the sliding cam (B) and remove the cable and (sliding cam) from the starter housing.

3. Remove the two screws securing the starter handle bracket (18, **Figure 29**) to the intake manifold. The screws are located at the bottom outer corners of the handle bracket.

> *NOTE*
> *The rear starter housing mounting screw also secures the lifting eye. Note the orientation of the lifting eye before removing the rear screw.*

4. Remove the three screws (12, **Figure 29**) securing the starter housing to the power head. The stack-up of each screw should be: screw, lockwasher, flat washer, rubber grommet, spacer sleeve, starter housing, rubber grommet and flat washer. See **Figure 29**. Be sure to locate and secure all components. The grommets and spacer sleeves will normally remain in the starter housing legs.

5. Remove the starter from the power head.

6. To install the starter, first make sure that two rubber grommets and a spacer sleeve are present in each of the starter housing's mounting legs.

7. Place the starter assembly onto the power head and align the mounting screw holes.

8. Lift the housing slightly and position a flat washer between each leg and the power head.

> *NOTE*
> *Make sure the lifting eye is installed on the rear starter mounting screw as noted during removal.*

9. Install the three starter mounting screws (and washers). The stack-up of each screw must be: screw, lockwasher, flat washer, grommet, spacer sleeve, starter housing, grommet and flat washer. See **Figure 29**. Once the correct stack-up is verified, tighten the three screws finger-tight at this time.

10. Secure the starter handle bracket to the intake manifold with two screws. Tighten the screws finger-tight at this time.

11. Hold the lockout levers (7 and 11, **Figure 29**) away from the starter housing and slowly pull the starter rope to rotate the engine through several revolutions. Then tighten the 3 starter housing mounting screws to 120-144 in.-lb. (13.6-16.3 N•m). Finally, tighten the 2 starter handle bracket screws to 60-84 in.-lb. (6.8-9.5 N•m).

12. Move the shift control lever to the NEUTRAL position. The propeller must rotate freely in both directions.

13. Lubricate the sliding cam (B, **Figure 28**) and the slide area of the starter housing with OMC Triple Guard Grease (or Lubriplate 777 grease). Install the slide and lockout cable. Adjust the lockout cable (A, **Figure 28**) to center the high point of the sliding cam (B, **Figure 28**) against the upper lockout lever (7, **Figure 29**). Then tighten the screw (A, **Figure 28**) securely.

14. Operate the starter and verify correct neutral start lockout operation. The starter must only operate in NEUTRAL and must not operate in FORWARD or REVERSE gear. If the starter does not perform as specified, repeat Steps 12 and 13. If the starter still does not perform as specified, repair or replace components of the neutral start lockout system as necessary.

15. Reconnect the spark plug leads when finished.

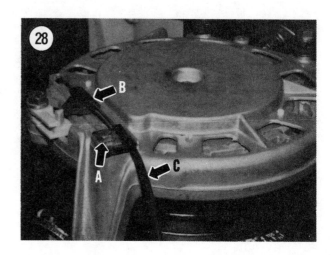

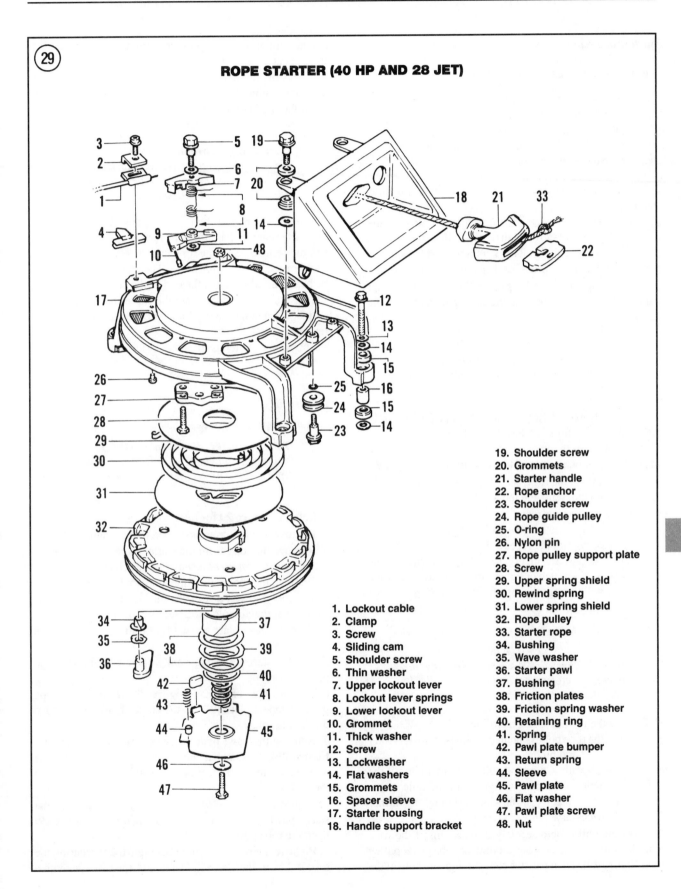

ROPE STARTER (40 HP AND 28 JET)

1. Lockout cable
2. Clamp
3. Screw
4. Sliding cam
5. Shoulder screw
6. Thin washer
7. Upper lockout lever
8. Lockout lever springs
9. Lower lockout lever
10. Grommet
11. Thick washer
12. Screw
13. Lockwasher
14. Flat washers
15. Grommets
16. Spacer sleeve
17. Starter housing
18. Handle support bracket
19. Shoulder screw
20. Grommets
21. Starter handle
22. Rope anchor
23. Shoulder screw
24. Rope guide pulley
25. O-ring
26. Nylon pin
27. Rope pulley support plate
28. Screw
29. Upper spring shield
30. Rewind spring
31. Lower spring shield
32. Rope pulley
33. Starter rope
34. Bushing
35. Wave washer
36. Starter pawl
37. Bushing
38. Friction plates
39. Friction spring washer
40. Retaining ring
41. Spring
42. Pawl plate bumper
43. Return spring
44. Sleeve
45. Pawl plate
46. Flat washer
47. Pawl plate screw
48. Nut

12

Starter rope replacement

Refer to **Figure 29** for this procedure.

> *NOTE*
> *If the lockout lever assembly (5-11, **Figure 29**) is not removed, it will be necessary to manually hold the lower lever away from the rope pulley to allow the rope pulley to rotate.*

1. Remove the starter assembly as described in the previous section.

2. Extend the starter rope and tie a slip knot close to the handle support plate (18, **Figure 29**). Allow the rope to retract into the housing until the knot is against the support plate to relieve the rope tension from the starter handle.

3. Pry the rope anchor (22, **Figure 29**) from the starter handle. Remove the rope from the anchor, then remove the handle.

> *CAUTION*
> *Wear leather gloves when holding the rope pulley and releasing the spring tension in the following 2 steps.*

4. Completely extend the rope, hold the rope pulley firmly and remove the slip knot. Firmly hold the rope pulley in place, then grasp the knotted end of the rope (with a pair of needlenose pliers) and pull the rope from the rope pulley.

5. After removing the rope, carefully allow the rope pulley to slowly unwind, relieving the rewind spring's tension.

6. Obtain a new starter rope.

   a. The starter rope must be 96.5 in. (245.1 cm) long. If necessary, trim the rope to the specified length.

   b. Heat the last 1/2 in. (12.7 mm) of both ends of the rope with a match or lighter until the ends are fused. This will prevent the rope from unraveling.

   c. Tie a knot in one end of the rope as shown in **Figure 21**.

> *CAUTION*
> *Wear leather gloves when preloading the rewind spring and holding the rope pulley in the following steps.*

7. Preload the rewind spring as follows:

   a. Turn the rope pulley counterclockwise until it is fully tensioned and binds.

   b. Carefully allow the rope pulley to unwind until the rope hole in the pulley aligns with the hole in the starter housing. Do not unwind the pulley any further than necessary.

8. With the pulley held securely in place, insert the rope into the hole in the pulley and around the rope guide pulley (24, **Figure 29**). Then pass the rope through the hole in the

handle support plate. Pull the rope until the knotted end is firmly seated in the relief in the rope pulley.

9. Tie a slip knot in the rope as close to the handle support plate as possible. Then carefully release the rope pulley and allow the slip knot to be pulled up against the support plate.

> *NOTE*
> *Starter rope threading tool (part No. 378774) will greatly reduce the effort required to pass the starter rope through the starter handle in the next step.*

10. Grease the end of the rope to ease its installation into the starter handle. Pass the rope through the starter handle and rope anchor. Seat the rope into the channel in the rope anchor as shown in **Figure 26**. The end of the rope must be butted tightly against the end of the channel.

11. Push the rope anchor into the starter handle until it is seated. Then untie the slip knot and allow the rope to fully retract.

12. Install the starter assembly as described in the previous section.

Disassembly

> *WARNING*
> *During starter disassembly, the rewind spring may unwind violently. Wear suitable hand and eye protection during starter service.*

Refer to **Figure 29** for this procedure.

1. Remove the starter as described in this chapter.

2. Remove the rope from the starter as described in Steps 1-5 of *Starter rope replacement* in this chapter.

3. Remove the lockout components (5-11, **Figure 29**) as an assembly. Install a suitable nut over the threads of the shoulder screw to hold the assembly together.

4. Hold the pawl plate screw (47, **Figure 29**) and remove the nut (48).

5. Lay the starter housing on a workbench with the rope pulley facing up.

6. Remove the screw (28, **Figure 29**) securing the rope pulley support plate (27) to the starter housing. Remove the support plate.

7. Remove the pawl plate screw and washer (46 and 47, **Figure 29**). Disconnect the return spring (43) from the rope pulley, then lift the pawl plate and return spring from the pulley.

8. Remove the spring (41, **Figure 29**). Then remove the starter pawl, wave washer and bushing (34-36, **Figure 29**) from the rope pulley.

9. Remove the retaining ring (40, **Figure 29**) securing the rope pulley to the starter housing. Pry the ring free with a

suitable screwdriver. Then remove the friction plates and friction spring washer (38 and 39, **Figure 29**).

10. Hold the rope pulley into the starter housing and place the starter housing upright (rope pulley facing down) over a suitable bench. Release the rope pulley and tap the housing against the bench until the spring and pulley fall out and the spring unwinds inside the housing's mounting legs.

11. Separate the rewind spring and the rope pulley. Then locate and secure the spring shields (29 and 31, **Figure 29**).

12. Remove the bushing (37, **Figure 29**) from the rope pulley.

13. If necessary, remove the guide pulley. Remove the screw (23, **Figure 29**) and guide pulley (24). Discard the O-ring (25).

14. If necessary, separate the handle support plate from the starter housing. Remove the two shoulder screws (19, **Figure 29**). Locate and secure the upper and lower grommets (20) and flat washers (14).

15. Clean all components in a mild solvent (such as mineral spirits) and dry with compressed air. Remove all thread-locking adhesive from the pawl plate screw's threads.

16. Inspect all components for excessive wear, chips, cracks or other damage. Inspect the rope and guide pulleys for sharp edges (or burrs) that could fray the starter rope. If necessary, smooth rough edges with a file or a piece of emery cloth.

17. Inspect the 6 nylon pins (26, **Figure 29**). The pins act as bearings for the rope pulley. If the pins are damaged or worn, install new pins.

Reassembly

Use OMC Triple Guard Grease (or Lubriplate 777 grease) for all lubrication applications. Refer to **Figure 29** for this procedure.

WARNING
During starter reassembly, the rewind spring may unwind violently. Wear suitable hand and eye protection during starter service.

1. Set the starter housing onto a workbench with the spring cavity facing up.

2. Verify that all six nylon pins (26, **Figure 29**) are installed in the starter housing.

3. Lightly grease the upper spring shield (29, **Figure 29**) and position it into the rewind spring cavity.

4. Wearing leather gloves, hook the outer end of the rewind spring over the pin in the starter housing. See **Figure 27**, typical. Then carefully wind the spring into the starter housing until it is fully seated in its recess as shown in **Figure 27**.

5. Lightly grease the lower spring shield (31, **Figure 29**) and position it onto the spring side of the rope pulley. Then grease the bushing (37, **Figure 29**) and install it into the rope pulley.

6. Carefully bend the inner end of the rewind spring to position the spring's loop near the center of the starter housing.

CAUTION
Do not lift the inner end of the rewind spring in the next step or the rewind spring may suddenly and forcefully unwind.

7. Position the rope pulley over the rewind spring and engage the inner (hooked) end of the spring to the notch in the pulley. Then place the pulley over the starter housing's boss and seat it against the rewind spring.

8. Grease the friction plates and friction spring washer (38 and 39, **Figure 29**). Position the spring washer between the two plates, then install the assembly over the starter housing boss.

9. Secure the pulley to the starter housing by installing the retaining ring. Make sure the ring is seated into its groove in the starter housing boss.

10. Lubricate the starter pawl bushing, wave washer and the starter pawl. Insert the bushing into the rope pulley, then position the wave washer over the bushing. Insert the pawl through the washer and into the bushing.

11. Insert the spring (41, **Figure 29**) into the center of the starter housing boss.

12. Make sure the pawl plate bumper and sleeve (42 and 44, **Figure 29**) are installed on the pawl plate. Then position the pawl plate over the starter pawl and rope pulley. Engage the return spring (43) with the small boss next to the starter pawl.

13. Align the hole in the pawl plate with the hole in the starter housing. Install the pawl plate screw and washer (46 and 47, **Figure 29**). Tighten the screw to 120-144 in.-lb. (13.6-16.3 N•m).

14. Coat the threads of the pawl plate screw (protruding through the starter housing) with OMC Nut Lock threadlocking adhesive. Install the nut (48, **Figure 29**) and tighten it securely while holding the pawl plate screw.

15. Install the pulley support plate (27, **Figure 29**). Coat the threads of the screw (28, **Figure 29**) with OMC Nut Lock threadlocking adhesive. Then install and tighten the screw to 60-84 in.-lb. (6.8-9.5 N•m).

16. If removed, install the rope guide pulley. Grease the shoulder screw and position the pulley over the screw. Install a new O-ring over the threaded end of the screw. Install the assembly on the starter housing and tighten the screw securely.

17. If removed, install the handle support bracket on the starter housing. The stack-up on each screw must be:

12

screw, grommet, bracket, grommet, flat washer and starter housing. Tighten both screws securely.

18. Install a new starter rope as described in Steps 6-11 of *Starter rope replacement* in this chapter.

19. Check for correct operation of the starter pawl. The pawl must extend when the rope is pulled and retract as the rope rewinds.

20. Remove the nut (installed during disassembly) from the lockout lever assembly. Position the lockout lever assembly on the starter housing and tighten the shoulder screw securely. The lower tang of the upper spring must contact the starter housing.

21. Install the starter assembly as described previously in this chapter.

REMOTE CONTROLS

This section covers remote control cable removal and installation in a standard OMC side-mount control box. Coverage is also provided for remote control cable removal, installation and adjustment at the engine.

The OMC standard side-mount prewired control box varies slightly in design between the 1995 (EO) model that uses the traditional wiring harness and the 1996-2003 (ED-ST) models that use the modular wiring harness. Refer to *Wiring Harnesses* in Chapter Three for additional information.

The 1995 (EO) control box has a safety lanyard switch and warning horn mounted in the control box.

The control boxes used on 1996-2003 (ED-ST) models do not have a safety lanyard switch or warning horn in the control box. The safety lanyard switch function is incorporated into the ignition switch. The warning horn is mounted underneath the dash panel.

The mechanical function and design of the shift and throttle control mechanisms is identical on both styles of control box.

Control Cable Removal and Installation (at Control Box)

The control box must split to access the control cables. Splitting the control box also allows access to the neutral safety switch and the ignition (key) switch. On 1995 (EO) models, it also allows access to the warning horn and safety lanyard switch.

To remove and install the control cables, proceed as follows:

1. Disconnect the negative battery cable from the battery.

2. Detach the control box from the hull as follows:

   a. Remove the two screws securing the control box to the boat. **Figure 30** shows the location of the mounting screws. The screws usually have a large flat washer, lockwasher and nut located behind the inte-

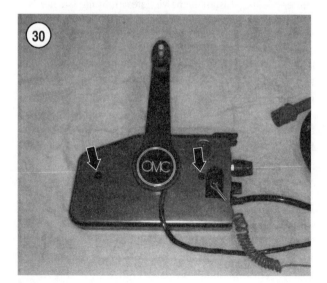

rior panel. However, on some hulls, the screws are threaded directly into a wooden or fiberglass reinforcement panel.

b. Lay a drop cloth over the floor (or driver's seat) and pull the control box away from the interior panel and lay it on the drop cloth. If necessary, remove any tie-straps or clamps preventing the control box from being pulled away from the interior panel. Do not disconnect any electrical leads.

3. The control handle is normally mounted on the port side of the control box. If so, it is not necessary to remove the

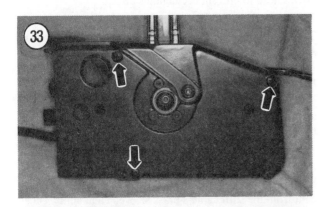

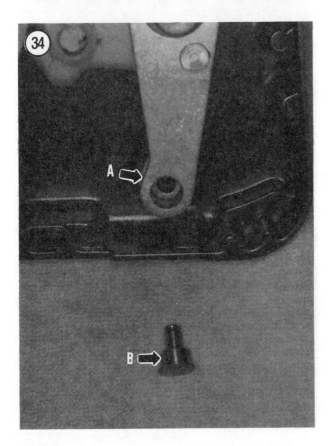

handle to split the control box. If the handle is mounted on the starboard side of the control box, it must be removed as follows:

a. Loosen the Allen screw securing the handle to the control box.

b. Verify that the control handle is in the NEUTRAL detent position. Note the position of the handle.

c. Support the control box with two wooden blocks positioned on each side of the control handle. See **Figure 31**, typical.

d. Drive against the Allen screw with a pin punch that fits into the hex head of the screw. See **Figure 32**, typical. Drive until the handle pops free from the box.

e. Remove the Allen screw and separate the handle from the control box.

4. Make sure the control handle is in the NEUTRAL position (if installed) and that the fast idle lever is latched in the full idle position.

5. Remove the three screws securing the control box halves to each other. See **Figure 33**.

6. Carefully separate the control box halves. The shift cable is mounted to the port half and the throttle cable is mounted to the starboard half.

7. Pull the cable pin from each control lever (shift and throttle). **Figure 34** shows the shift lever (A) and pin (B). It is necessary to manually rotate the throttle lever to the rear of the control box to access its pin.

8. Once the control pins are removed, lift the throttle cable from the starboard half and the shift cable from the port half.

9. To install the control cables, begin by applying OMC Triple Guard Grease to both cable pins and the trunnion pocket in each control box half.

10. Insert the shift cable into the port half of the control box. Seat the cable's trunnion into the control box pocket. Move the cable's casing guide to align it with the shift lever, then install the cable pin. Make sure the pin is seated in the shift lever.

11. Insert the throttle cable into the starboard half of the control box. Seat the cable's trunnion into the control box pocket. Move the cable's casing guide to align it with the throttle lever, then install the cable pin. Make sure the pin is seated in the shift lever. Manually rotate the throttle lever to the front of the control box (position the lever back under the plastic shield).

12. Grease all visible pivot and friction points in both control box halves with OMC Moly Lube (or an equivalent high pressure grease).

13. Apply a light bead of RTV sealant to the top and side mating surfaces of one control box half. This will keep water from dripping into the control box.

12

14. Assemble the control box halves being careful to seat the roller on the throttle lever (A, **Figure 35**) into the channel in the main control gear (B, **Figure 35**). It may be necessary to lift the fast idle lever slightly to align the components. Once the components are aligned, seat the halves to each other.

15. Install the three cover screws. Evenly tighten the screws to 40-50 in.-lb. (4.5-5.7 N•m).

16. If removed, reinstall the control handle in the position noted during removal. Install the Allen head screw and tighten it to 100-120 in.-lb. (11.3-13.6 N•m).

17. Operate the control box and make sure the shift and throttle cables operate smoothly. The control handle must positively lock into the NEUTRAL detent position. Correct any problems found.

18. Position the control box to the interior panel. Secure the box with two screws (and nuts, lockwashers and flat washers [as equipped]). Tighten the fasteners securely.

19. Secure the electrical leads and control cables with the original clamps or new tie-straps.

20. Reconnect the negative battery cable.

Control Cable Removal, Installation and Adjustment (at Engine)

The control cables must always pass under the engine and loop back into the lower cowl. The loop must have a minimum radius of 12 in. (305 mm). Failure to allow an adequate radius or running the cables directly into the lower cowl (with a loop) will cause the cables to bind, kink and fail prematurely.

The control cables must not be clamped (or tie-strapped) together or clamped to the transom or any other cable within 12 in. (305 mm) of the lower engine cowl. Again, failure to follow this recommendation will cause the cables to bind, kink and fail prematurely.

The routing of the cables in **Figure 36** illustrates a correct installation. The cables pass under the engine and make a gentle loop back into the lower cowl. A minimum amount of clamps (or tie-straps) are used.

The throttle control cable must be readjusted each time the idle speed (or idle stop) screw is adjusted. The shift cable must be readjusted each time the gearcase (or shift linkage) is serviced, repaired or replaced.

If adjustment of the engine's throttle and shift linkage (not the control cables) is necessary, refer to Chapter Five and/or Chapter Nine.

Control box requirements

If an aftermarket remote control box is used, it must contain a neutral safety switch and it must provide a shift

stroke of 1.125-1.330 in. (mm), when measured between NEUTRAL and FORWARD gear (full throttle position).

Shift cable removal, installation and adjustment (9.9 and 15 hp)

Use OMC Triple Guard Grease (or an equivalent water-proof grease) for all lubrication applications. The throttle cable must be disconnected when adjusting the shift cable.

1. Disconnect the negative battery cable from the battery. Then disconnect and ground the spark plug leads to the power head to prevent accidental starting.

2. Remove the control cable grommet from the lower cowl.

3. The shift cable is the upper control cable on the starboard side of the power head. Remove the clamp securing the cable's adjustable trunnion into the anchor pocket at the front of the power head.

4. Remove the cotter pin and slide the clevis pin from the shift lever at the top of the shift/throttle lever assembly (at the rear of the power head).

5. Remove the shift cable from the power head.

6. To install the shift cable, begin by shifting the control box into the REVERSE gear position. Clean all old lubricant from the shift cable's brass sleeve. Then apply a coat

of fresh grease to the sleeve (and its threads). Also apply a coat of grease to the anchor pocket on the power head.

7. Shift the control box into the NEUTRAL position. Then manually move the engine's shift lever to the NEUTRAL detent position.

8. Position the shift cable's casing guide into the shift lever. Lubricate the clevis pin and insert it through the shift lever and shift cable. Secure the clevis pin with a new stainless steel cotter pin. Bend both prongs of the cotter pin for a secure attachment.

NOTE
The throttle cable must be disconnected when adjusting the shift cable.

9. Hold the shift cable's adjustable barrel over the anchor pocket on the power head. Gently push and pull the barrel back and forth to determine the slack in the linkage and cable, but do not pull the shift linkage out of the NEU-TRAL detent position. Center all slack, then adjust the barrel as necessary to allow the barrel to slip into the pocket.

10. Install the anchor pocket clamp. Tighten the screw to 60-84 in.-lb. (6.8-9.5 N•m).

11. Install the control cable grommet into the lower cowl.

12. Reconnect the spark plug leads, then reconnect the negative battery cable. Tighten the connection securely.

Shift cable removal, installation and adjustment (20-30 hp [two-cylinder])

Use OMC Triple Guard Grease (or an equivalent water-proof grease) for all lubrication applications. The throttle cable must be disconnected when adjusting the shift cable.

1. Disconnect the negative battery cable from the battery. Then disconnect and ground the spark plug leads to the power head to prevent accidental starting.

2. The shift cable is the control cable on the starboard side of the lower cowl. Remove the clamp screw, washer and

nut securing the cable's adjustable trunnion into the anchor bracket at the front of the lower cowl.

3. Remove the elastic locknut and washer securing the cable to the shift lever near the center of the lower cowl. It may be necessary to use a backup wrench to keep the stud from rotating.

4. Pull the cable through the shift cable anchor bracket and remove the cable from the power head.

5. To install the shift cable, begin by shifting the control box into the REVERSE gear position. Clean all old lubri-cant from the shift cable's brass sleeve. Then apply a coat of fresh grease to the sleeve (and its threads).

6. Shift the control box into the NEUTRAL position. Then manually move the engine's shift lever to the NEUTRAL detent position.

7. Insert the shift cable through the anchor bracket. Then position the shift cable's casing guide over the stud on the shift lever. Secure the cable with the flat washer and elastic locknut. Replace the locknut if it can be threaded on by hand.

8. Tighten the locknut securely. It may be necessary to use a backup wrench to keep the stud from rotating.

NOTE
The throttle cable must be disconnected when adjusting the shift cable.

9. Hold the shift cable's adjustable barrel over the pocket in the anchor bracket. Gently push and pull the barrel back and forth to determine the slack in the linkage and cable, but do not pull the shift linkage out of the NEUTRAL detent position. Center all slack, then adjust the barrel as necessary to allow the barrel to slip into the pocket.

10. Hold the barrel into its pocket in the anchor bracket, then install the screw (and washer). Secure the screw with the elastic locknut. Replace the locknut if it can be threaded on by hand. Tighten the screw and locknut securely.

11. Reconnect the spark plug leads. Then reconnect the negative battery cable. Tighten the connection securely.

Shift cable removal, installation and adjustment (25 and 35 hp [three-cylinder] and 40-70 hp)

Use OMC Triple Guard Grease (or an equivalent water-proof grease) for all lubrication applications. The throttle cable must be disconnected when adjusting the shift cable.

If the neutral detent adjustment is incorrectly set, it may not be possible to correctly adjust the shift cable. If so, refer to Chapter Nine and adjust the neutral detent.

On 40-70 hp models, if the shift shaft height on the lower gearcase is incorrectly set, it may not be possible to cor-rectly adjust the shift cable or the gearcase may not shift correctly even though the adjustment procedure is per-

12

formed correctly. If so, refer to Chapter Nine and adjust the shift shaft height.

NOTE
On the 40-50 hp (two-cylinder) models, it may prove easiest to remove the split lower cowls to better access the control cables. Refer to Power head removal/installation in Chapter Eight.

1. Disconnect the negative battery cable from the battery. Then disconnect and ground the spark plug leads to the power head to prevent accidental starting.

2. The shift cable is the lower control cable on the starboard side of the power head. Remove the screw and clamp (A, **Figure 37**, typical) securing the shift and throttle cables' adjustable trunnions into the anchor bracket near the front of the lower cowl.

3A. *25 and 35 hp (three-cylinder)*—Remove the special stamped-steel locking clip securing the cable to the shift lever. Do not damage the clip during the removal process.

3B. *40-50 hp (two-cylinder)*—Remove the special locking clip (**Figure 38**) securing the cable to the shift lever. Grasp the bent tip (A, **Figure 38**) with a pair of needlenose pliers and gently lift it up and toward the center of the clevis pin to unlock the clip. Then remove the clip and push the clevis pin from the shift lever and cable.

3C. *50-70 hp (three-cylinder)*—Remove the elastic locknut and flat washer securing the cable to the shift lever. See A, **Figure 39**.

NOTE
It is necessary to remove the throttle cable from its anchor pocket and rotate it upward to allow the shift cable to be removed.

4. Pull the cable from the anchor bracket and the control cable grommet (B, **Figure 37**, typical). Then remove the cable from the power head.

5. To install the shift cable, begin by shifting the control box into the REVERSE gear (full throttle) position. Clean all old lubricant from the shift cable's brass sleeve. Then apply a coat of fresh grease to the sleeve.

6. Apply a liberal amount of grease to the anchor bracket's pocket.

NOTE
*When adjusting the shift cable on an OMC side-mount control box (**Figure 30**, typical), the engine and the control box must be in the full FORWARD gear position. When using any other control box, the engine and the control box must be in the NEUTRAL detent position.*

7A. *OMC side-mount control box*—While rotating the propeller, manually move the engine shift linkage into the full FORWARD gear position. The propeller will cease to rotate when the FORWARD gear is engaged. The control box must still be in the FORWARD gear (full throttle) position (from Step 5).

7B. *All other control boxes*—Shift the control box into the NEUTRAL position. Then manually move the engine's shift lever to the NEUTRAL detent position.

8A. *25 and 35 hp (three-cylinder)*—Position the shift cable on the power head. Then connect the shift cable's casing guide to the upper stud on the shift lever. Secure the cable with the special locking clip. Make sure the clip locks in position. Replace the clip if it is damaged or does not lock in position.

8B. *40-50 hp (two-cylinder)*—Position the shift cable on the power head. Then position the shift cable's casing guide into the shift lever. Grease the clevis pin and insert it through the rear of the shift lever and through the shift cable. Grasp the looped end (B, **Figure 38**) of the special locking clip and insert the straight prong through the hole in the clevis pin. Continue pushing the pin until it locks in place. Replace the clip if it does not lock in place. See **Figure 38**.

8C. *50-70 hp (three-cylinder)*—Position the shift cable on the power head. Then position the shift cable's casing guide over the stud on the shift lever. Secure the cable with the flat washer and elastic locknut. Replace the locknut if it can be threaded on by hand. Tighten the locknut securely. See A, **Figure 39**.

NOTE
The throttle cable must be disconnected when adjusting the shift cable.

9A. *OMC side-mount control box*—Hold the shift cable's adjustable barrel over the pocket in the anchor bracket. Pull the cable (barrel) toward the front of the engine (toward the boat) to remove all slack from the control cable and shift linkage. Then adjust the barrel as necessary to allow the barrel to slip into the pocket.

9B. *All other control boxes*—Hold the shift cable's adjustable barrel over the pocket in the anchor bracket. Gently push and pull the barrel back and forth to determine the slack in the linkage and cable, but do not pull the shift linkage out of the NEUTRAL detent position. Center all slack, then adjust the barrel as necessary to allow the barrel to slip into the pocket.

10. Reinstall the control cable grommet into the lower cowl. Then hold the shift and throttle cable barrels into their pockets in the anchor bracket and install the clamp (and screw). Tighten the screw to 60-84 in.-lbs. (6.8-9.5 N•m).

11. Reconnect the spark plug leads. Then reconnect the negative battery cable. Tighten the connection securely.

Throttle cable removal, installation and adjustment (9.9 and 15 hp)

Use OMC Triple Guard Grease (or an equivalent water-proof grease) for all lubrication applications. The shift cable must be installed and adjusted before installing and adjusting the throttle cable.

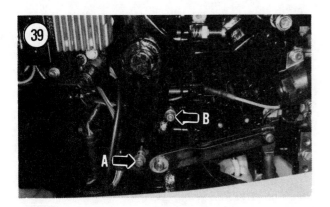

CAUTION
The propeller must be manually rotated when shifting the gearcase into FORWARD or REVERSE gear.

1. Disconnect the negative battery cable from the battery. Then disconnect and ground the spark plug leads to prevent accidental starting.

2. Remove the control cable grommet from the lower cowl.

3. The throttle cable is the lower control cable on the starboard side of the power head. Remove the clamp securing the cable's adjustable trunnion in the anchor pocket.

4. Remove the cotter pin and slide the clevis pin from the throttle lever at the bottom of the shift/throttle lever assembly (at the rear of the power head).

5. Remove the throttle cable from the power head.

6. To install the throttle cable, begin by rotating the propeller and shifting the control box into the FORWARD gear (full throttle) position. Clean all old lubricant from the throttle cable's brass sleeve. Then apply a coat of fresh grease to the sleeve and its threads. Also apply a coat of grease to the anchor pocket on the power head.

7. To correctly position the control lever to adjust the throttle cable, proceed as follows:
   a. Shift the control box into the NEUTRAL position. Note the position of the control lever.
   b. Rotate the propeller and move the control lever into the FORWARD gear (idle detent) position. Note the position of the control lever.
   c. Pull the control lever halfway back to the NEUTRAL position. This is the midpoint of the control lever positions in the preceding substeps.
   d. When correctly positioned, the lever must be halfway between the FORWARD gear idle detent and the NEUTRAL position.

8. Position the throttle cable's casing guide into the throttle lever. Lubricate the clevis pin and insert it through the throttle lever and throttle cable. Secure the clevis pin with a new stainless steel cotter pin. Bend both prongs of the cotter pin for a secure attachment.

9. Hold the throttle cable's adjustable barrel over the anchor pocket on the power head. Firmly pull the barrel to seat the idle speed screw against its power head stop. Then adjust the barrel as necessary to allow the barrel to slip into the pocket.

10. Install the anchor pocket clamp. Tighten the screw to 60-84 in.-lb. (6.8-9.5 N•m).

11. Verify the adjustment as follows:
   a. Raise the fast idle lever on the control box, then return it to its full downward (latched) position. The idle speed stop screw must be seated against its power head stop. If not, readjust the cable's trunnion

12

to pull the stop screw against its stop, then repeat this step.

b. While rotating the propeller, move the control lever (on the control box) into the FORWARD and RE-VERSE gear positions. The lever must not be any more difficult to move than when the throttle cable was disconnected. If the lever is now more difficult to move, the throttle cable is preloaded and the trunnion must be readjusted to relieve the pressure on the idle speed stop screw.

c. If adjustment was necessary, repeat this step to verify correct adjustment.

12. Install the control cable grommet into the lower cowl.

13. Reconnect the spark plug leads. Then reconnect the negative battery cable. Tighten the connection securely.

Throttle cable removal, installation and adjustment (20-30 hp [two-cylinder])

Use OMC Triple Guard Grease (or an equivalent water-proof grease) for all lubrication applications. The shift cable must be installed and adjusted before installing and adjusting the throttle cable.

> *CAUTION*
> *The propeller must be manually rotated when shifting the gearcase into FORWARD or REVERSE gear.*

1. Disconnect the negative battery cable from the battery. Then disconnect and ground the spark plug leads to prevent accidental starting.

2. The throttle cable is the control cable on the port side of the power head.

3. Pull the snap clip (on the throttle cable's casing guide) away from the cable and lift the casing guide from the throttle/spark control arm.

4. Rotate the cable in the anchor bracket until the casing guide is pointing straight down. Then remove the throttle cable from the power head.

5. To install the throttle cable, begin by rotating the propeller and shifting the control box into the FORWARD gear (full throttle) position. Clean all old lubricant from the throttle cable's brass sleeve. Then apply a coat of fresh grease to the sleeve (and its threads). Also apply a coat of grease to the anchor pocket on the power head.

6. To correctly position the control lever to adjust the throttle cable, proceed as follows:

a. Shift the control box into the NEUTRAL position. Note the position of the control lever.

b. Rotate the propeller and move the control lever into the FORWARD gear (idle detent) position. Note the position of the control lever.

c. Pull the control lever halfway back to the NEU-TRAL position. This will be the midpoint of the control lever positions in the preceding substeps.

d. When correctly positioned, the lever must be half-way between the FORWARD gear idle detent and the NEUTRAL position.

7. Insert the throttle cable into its anchor bracket with the casing guide point straight down. Then rotate the cable to lock it in the plate.

8. Lubricate the stud on the throttle/spark control arm. Then adjust the cable as follows:

a. Pull the casing guide firmly to the rear (aft) while holding the throttle/spark control arm against the idle speed stop screw (see Chapter Five).

b. Adjust the cable's barrel to allow the casing guide to slip over the stud on the throttle/spark control arm.

c. Push the snap clip (on the casing guide) over the stud to lock the casing guide to the control arm.

9. Verify the adjustment as follows:

a. Raise the fast idle lever on the control box, then return it to its full downward (latched) position. The throttle/spark control arm must be seated against the idle speed stop screw. If not, readjust the cable's trunnion to pull the control arm against the stop screw, then repeat this step.

b. While rotating the propeller, move the control lever (on the control box) into the FORWARD and RE-VERSE gear positions. The lever must not be any more difficult to move than when the throttle cable was disconnected. If the lever is now more difficult to move, the throttle cable is *preloaded* and the trunnion must be readjusted to relieve the pressure on the idle speed stop screw.

c. If adjustment was necessary, repeat this step to verify correct adjustment.

10. Reconnect the spark plug leads. Then reconnect the negative battery cable. Tighten the connection securely.

Throttle cable removal, installation and adjustment (25 and 35 hp [three-cylinder] and 40-70 hp and 35 jet)

Use OMC Triple Guard Grease (or an equivalent water-proof grease) for all lubrication applications. The shift cable must be installed and adjusted before installing and adjusting the throttle cable.

> *CAUTION*
> *The propeller must be manually rotated when shifting the gearcase into FORWARD or REVERSE gear.*

1. Disconnect the negative battery cable from the battery. Then disconnect and ground the spark plug leads to prevent accidental starting.

NOTE
On the 40-50 hp (two-cylinder) and 35 jet models, it may prove easiest to remove the split lower cowls to better access the control cables. Refer to Power head removal/installation in Chapter Eight.

2. The throttle cable is the upper control cable on the starboard side of the power head. Remove the screw and clamp (A, **Figure 37**, typical) securing the throttle and shift cable adjustable trunnions into the anchor bracket near the front of the lower cowl.

3A. *25 and 35 hp (three-cylinder)*—Remove the special stamped-steel locking clip securing the cable to the throttle/spark control lever. Do not damage the clip during the removal process.

3B. *40-50 hp (two-cylinder) and 35 jet*—Remove the special locking clip (**Figure 40**) securing the cable to the throttle lever. Grasp the bent tip (A, **Figure 40**) with a pair of needlenose pliers and gently lift it up and toward the center of the clevis pin to unlock the clip. Then remove the clip and push the clevis pin from the throttle lever and cable.

3C. *50-70 hp (three-cylinder)*—Remove the elastic locknut and flat washer securing the cable to the throttle/spark control lever. See **Figure B**, **Figure 39**.

4. Pull the cable from the anchor bracket and the control cable grommet (B, **Figure 37**, typical). Then remove the cable from the power head.

5. To install the throttle cable, begin by rotating the propeller and shifting the control box into the FORWARD gear (full throttle) position. Clean all old lubricant from the

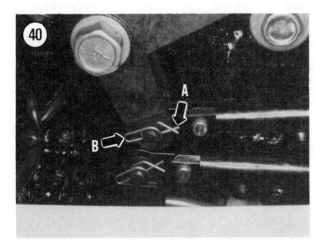

throttle cable's brass sleeve. Then apply a coat of fresh grease to the sleeve and its threads.

6. Apply a liberal amount of grease into the anchor bracket's pocket.

7. To correctly position the control lever to adjust the throttle cable, proceed as follows:
   a. Shift the control box into the NEUTRAL position. Note the position of the control lever.
   b. Rotate the propeller and move the control lever into the FORWARD gear (idle detent) position. Note the position of the control lever.
   c. Pull the control lever halfway back to the NEUTRAL position. This is the midpoint of the control lever positions in the preceding substeps.
   d. When correctly positioned, the lever must be halfway between the FORWARD gear idle detent and the NEUTRAL position.

8A. *25 and 35 hp (three-cylinder)*—Position the throttle cable on the power head. Then connect the throttle cable's casing guide to the stud on the throttle/spark control arm. Secure the cable with the special locking clip. Make sure the clip locks in position. Replace the clip if it is damaged or does not lock in position.

8B. *40-50 hp (two-cylinder) and 35 jet*—Position the throttle cable on the power head. Then position the throttle cable's casing guide into the throttle lever and align the hole in the casing guide with the lower hole in the throttle lever. Grease the clevis pin and insert it through the rear of the throttle lever and through the throttle cable. Grasp the looped end (B, **Figure 40**) of the special locking clip and insert the straight prong through the hole in the clevis pin. Continue pushing the pin until it locks in place. Replace the clip if it does not lock in place. See **Figure 40**.

8C. *50-70 hp (three-cylinder)*—Position the throttle cable on the power head. Then position the throttle cable's casing guide over the stud on the throttle/spark control arm. Secure the cable with the flat washer and elastic locknut (B, **Figure 39**). Replace the locknut if it can be threaded on by hand. Tighten the locknut securely.

9. Hold the throttle cable's adjustable barrel over the anchor pocket on the power head. Firmly pull the barrel to seat the idle speed/stop screw against its power head stop. Then adjust the barrel as necessary to allow the barrel to slip into the pocket.

10. Reinstall the control cable grommet into the lower cowl. Then hold the shift and throttle cables' barrels into their pockets in the anchor bracket and install the clamp (and screw). See A, **Figure 37**, typical. Tighten the screw to 60-84 in.-lbs. (6.8-9.5 N•m).

11. Verify the adjustment as follows:
   a. Raise the fast idle lever on the control box, then return it to its full downward (latched) position. The

12

idle speed/stop screw must be seated against its power head stop. If not, readjust the cable's trunnion to pull the idle speed screw against its stop, then repeat this step.

b. While rotating the propeller, move the control lever (on the control box) into the FORWARD and REVERSE gear positions. The lever must not be any more difficult to move than when the throttle cable

was disconnected. If the lever is now more difficult to move, the throttle cable is preloaded and the trunnion must be readjusted to relieve the pressure on the idle speed/stop screw. Completely repeat Step 10 to verify any readjustment.

12. Reconnect the spark plug leads. Then reconnect the negative battery cable. Then, tighten the connection securely.

Table 1 SPECIAL TORQUE VALUES

Fastener	in.-lb.	ft.-lb.	N•m
Starter handle bracket (40 hp)	60-84	–	6.8-9.5
Starter housing to motor			
2-15 hp (except 4 Deluxe)	60-84	–	6.8-9.5
20-30 hp (two-cylinder) and 18 jet	48-72	–	5.4-8.1
25 and 35 hp (three-cylinder)	60-84	–	6.8-9.5
40 hp	120-144	12-14	13.6-16.3
Starter shoulder (center) screw/locknut			
3 and 4 hp (including 4 Deluxe)	60-84	–	6.8-9.5
6-40 hp and 18 jet	120-144	12-14	13.6-16.3
OMC standard side mount control box			
Control handle mounting screw	100-120	10-12	11.3-13.6
Three cover screws	40-50	–	4.5-5.7
Ignition switch bezel nut	20-25	–	2.3-2.8
Neutral safety switch	15-20	–	1.7-2.3
Warning horn (1995 [EO] models)	15-20	–	1.7-2.3

Table 2 STARTER SPECIFICATIONS

Component	Specification
Starter rope length	
2, 3.3 and 3.5 hp	53 in. (134.6 cm)
3 and 4 hp (except 4 Deluxe)	59 in. (149.9 cm)
6, 8 hp and 4 Deluxe	59.5 in. (151.1 cm)
9.9 and 15 hp	59 in. (149.9 cm)
20-30 hp (two-cylinder) and 18 jet	73.5 in. (186.7 cm)
25 and 35 hp (three-cylinder)	59 in. (149.9 cm)
40 hp	96.5 in. (245.1 cm)
Starter spring pretension	
2, 3.3 and 3.5 hp	3 turns
3 and 4 hp	1/4 to 1-1/4 turns
4 Deluxe (spring pull-out)	8-18 in. (20.3-45.7 cm)
9.9 and 15 hp	Approximately 3-1/2 turns
20-30 hp (two-cylinder) and 18 jet	1/2 to 1 turn

Index

13

13

CD1 IGNITION SYSTEM (2, 3.3 AND 3.5 HP)

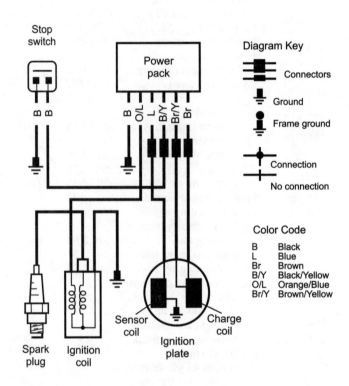

CD IGNITION SYSTEM
(3 AND 4 HP EXCEPT 4 DELUXE)

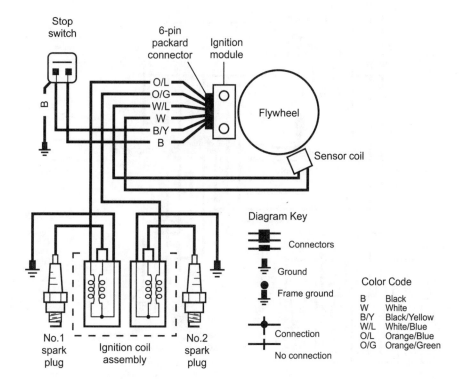

Stop switch

6-pin packard connector

Ignition module

O/L
O/G
W/L
W
B/Y
B

Flywheel

Sensor coil

No.1 spark plug

Ignition coil assembly

No.2 spark plug

Diagram Key

Connectors
Ground
Frame ground
Connection
No connection

Color Code

B   Black
W   White
B/Y   Black/Yellow
W/L   White/Blue
O/L   Orange/Blue
O/G   Orange/Green

14

CD IGNITION SYSTEM
(6, 8, 9.9, 15 AND 40 HP-ROPE START MODELS)

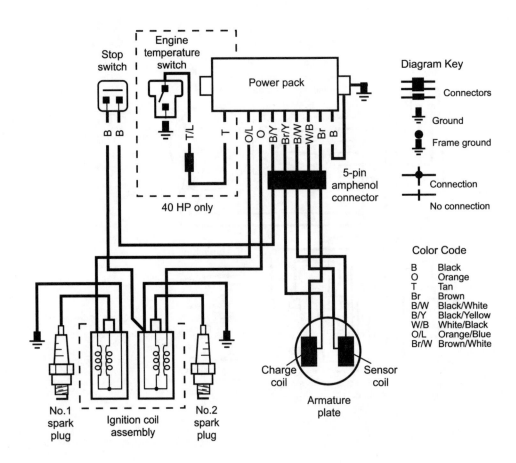

20-40 HP ROPE START

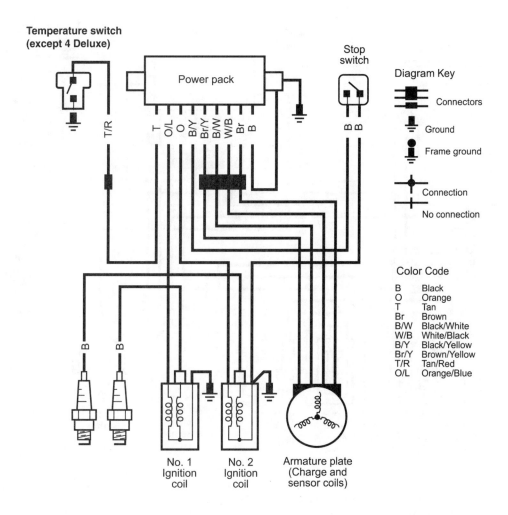

Temperature switch
(except 4 Deluxe)

Power pack

Stop
switch

Diagram Key

Connectors

Ground

Frame ground

Connection

No connection

Color Code

B   Black
O   Orange
T   Tan
Br   Brown
B/W Black/White
W/B White/Black
B/Y Black/Yellow
Br/Y Brown/Yellow
T/R Tan/Red
O/L Orange/Blue

No. 1
Ignition
coil

No. 2
Ignition
coil

Armature plate
(Charge and
sensor coils)

14

CD2 IGNITION SYSTEM
(9.9 AND 15 HP TILLER HANDLE ELECTRIC START)

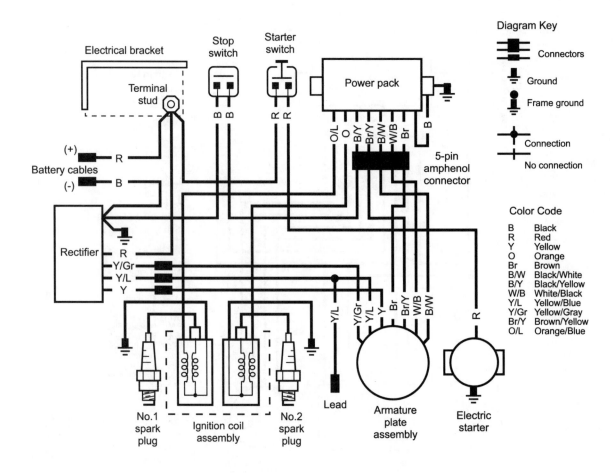

Diagram Key

Connectors
Ground
Frame ground
Connection
No connection

Color Code

B	Black
R	Red
Y	Yellow
O	Orange
Br	Brown
B/W	Black/White
B/Y	Black/Yellow
W/B	White/Black
Y/L	Yellow/Blue
Y/Gr	Yellow/Gray
Br/Y	Brown/Yellow
O/L	Orange/Blue

9.9 AND 15 HP REMOTE CONTROL
(1995 EO MODELS)

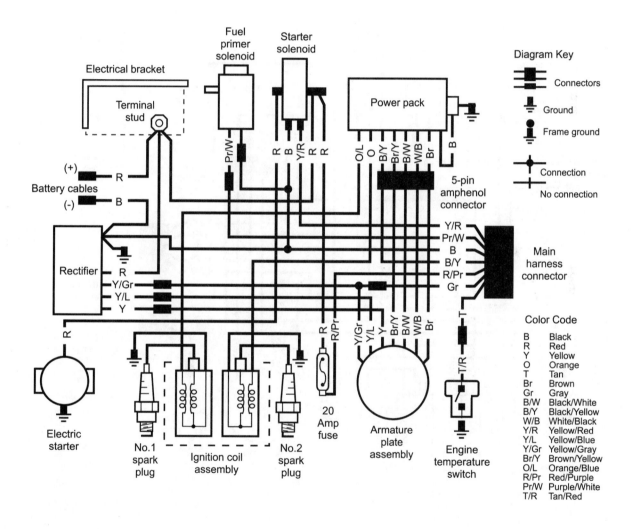

Diagram Key

Connectors

Ground

Frame ground

Connection

No connection

Color Code

B	Black
R	Red
Y	Yellow
O	Orange
T	Tan
Br	Brown
Gr	Gray
B/W	Black/White
B/Y	Black/Yellow
W/B	White/Black
Y/R	Yellow/Red
Y/L	Yellow/Blue
Y/Gr	Yellow/Gray
Br/Y	Brown/Yellow
O/L	Orange/Blue
R/Pr	Red/Purple
Pr/W	Purple/White
T/R	Tan/Red

14

9.9 AND 15 HP REMOTE CONTROL
(1996-2003 ED-ST MODELS)

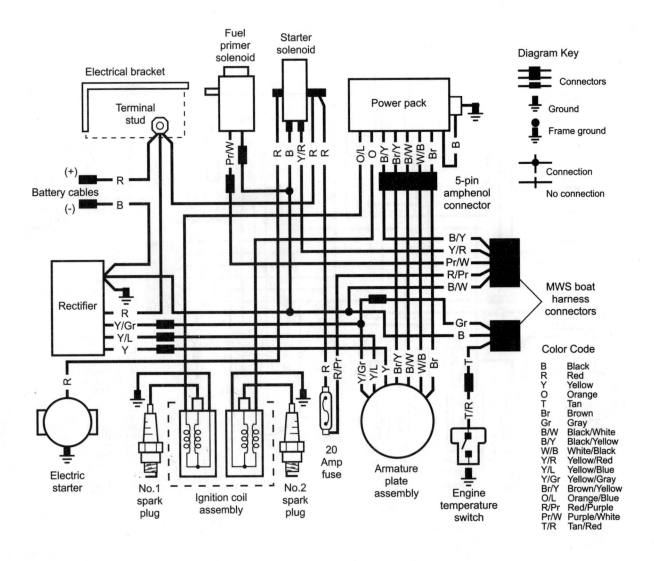

20-30 HP (TWO-CYLINDER)
TILLER HANDLE ELECTRIC START MODELS

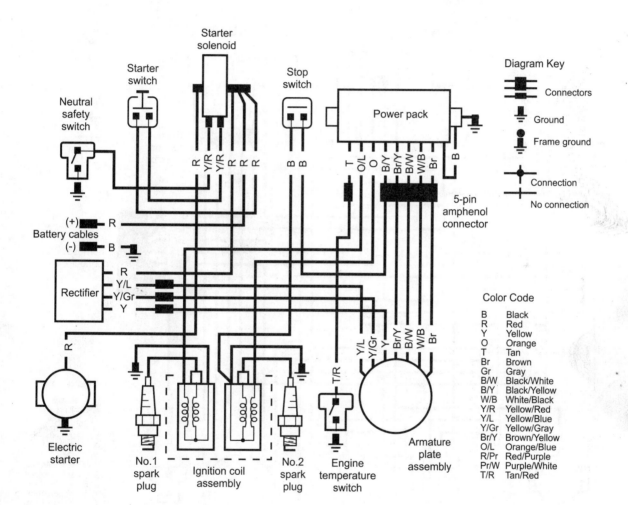

14

20-30 HP (TWO-CYLINDER)
REMOTE CONTROL 1995 EDO MODELS

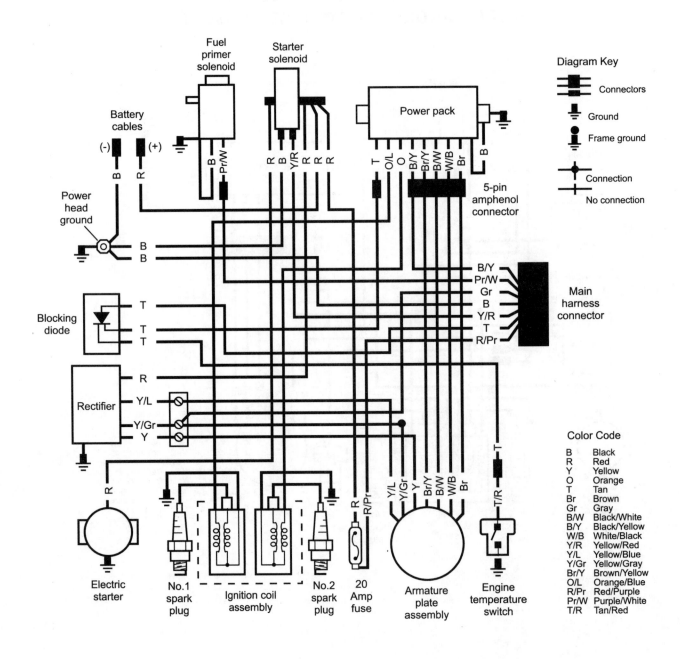

Fuel primer solenoid

Starter solenoid

Power pack

Diagram Key

Connectors

Ground

Frame ground

Connection

No connection

Battery cables

5-pin amphenol connector

Power head ground

Main harness connector

Blocking diode

Rectifier

Electric starter

No.1 spark plug

Ignition coil assembly

No.2 spark plug

20 Amp fuse

Armature plate assembly

Engine temperature switch

Color Code

B	Black
R	Red
Y	Yellow
O	Orange
T	Tan
Br	Brown
Gr	Gray
B/W	Black/White
B/Y	Black/Yellow
W/B	White/Black
Y/R	Yellow/Red
Y/L	Yellow/Blue
Y/Gr	Yellow/Gray
Br/Y	Brown/Yellow
O/L	Orange/Blue
R/Pr	Red/Purple
Pr/W	Purple/White
T/R	Tan/Red

20-30 HP (TWO-CYLINDER)
REMOTE CONTROL 1996-2003 ED-ST MODELS

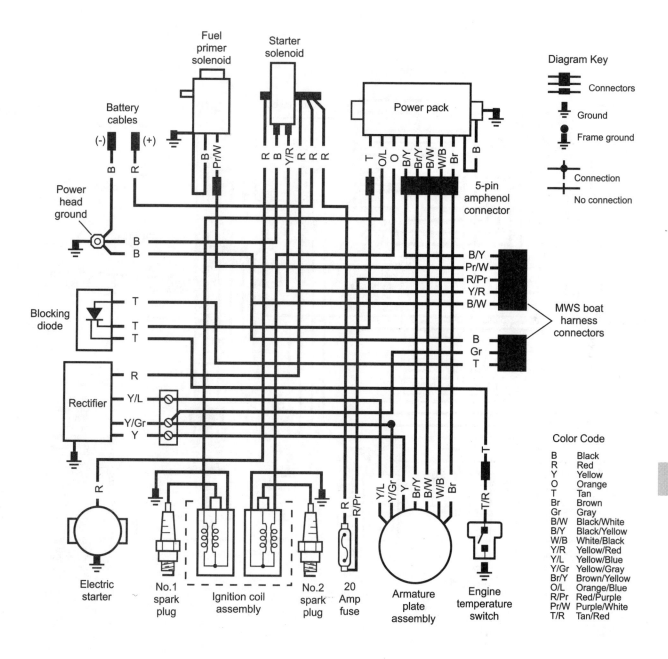

Diagram Key

Connectors

Ground

Frame ground

Connection

No connection

Color Code

B	Black
R	Red
Y	Yellow
O	Orange
T	Tan
Br	Brown
Gr	Gray
B/W	Black/White
B/Y	Black/Yellow
W/B	White/Black
Y/R	Yellow/Red
Y/L	Yellow/Blue
Y/Gr	Yellow/Gray
Br/Y	Brown/Yellow
O/L	Orange/Blue
R/Pr	Red/Purple
Pr/W	Purple/White
T/R	Tan/Red

14

25 AND 35 HP (THREE-CYLINDER) ROPE START

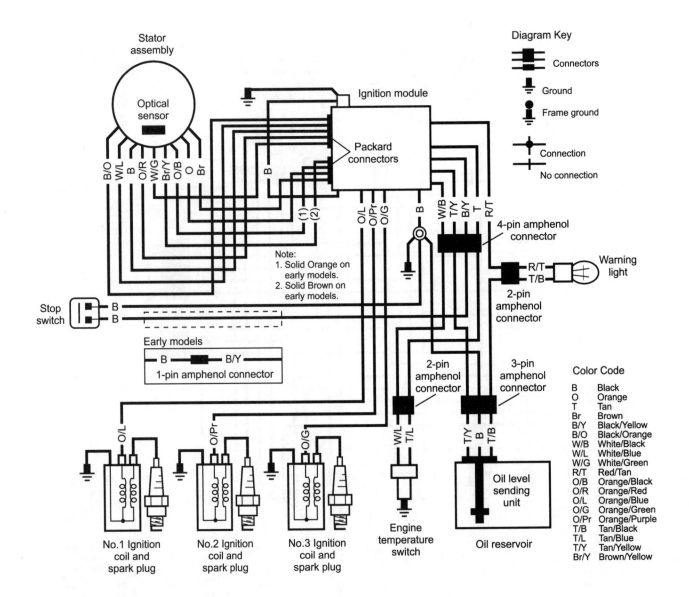

Stator assembly

Optical sensor

Ignition module

Packard connectors

Diagram Key

Connectors

Ground

Frame ground

Connection

No connection

Note:
1. Solid Orange on early models.
2. Solid Brown on early models.

4-pin amphenol connector

Warning light

2-pin amphenol connector

Stop switch

Early models

B — B/Y

1-pin amphenol connector

2-pin amphenol connector

3-pin amphenol connector

No.1 Ignition coil and spark plug

No.2 Ignition coil and spark plug

No.3 Ignition coil and spark plug

Engine temperature switch

Oil level sending unit

Oil reservoir

Color Code

B	Black
O	Orange
T	Tan
Br	Brown
B/Y	Black/Yellow
B/O	Black/Orange
W/B	White/Black
W/L	White/Blue
W/G	White/Green
R/T	Red/Tan
O/B	Orange/Black
O/R	Orange/Red
O/L	Orange/Blue
O/G	Orange/Green
O/Pr	Orange/Purple
T/B	Tan/Black
T/L	Tan/Blue
T/Y	Tan/Yellow
Br/Y	Brown/Yellow

25 AND 35 HP (THREE-CYLINDER) TILLER HANDLE ELECTRIC START

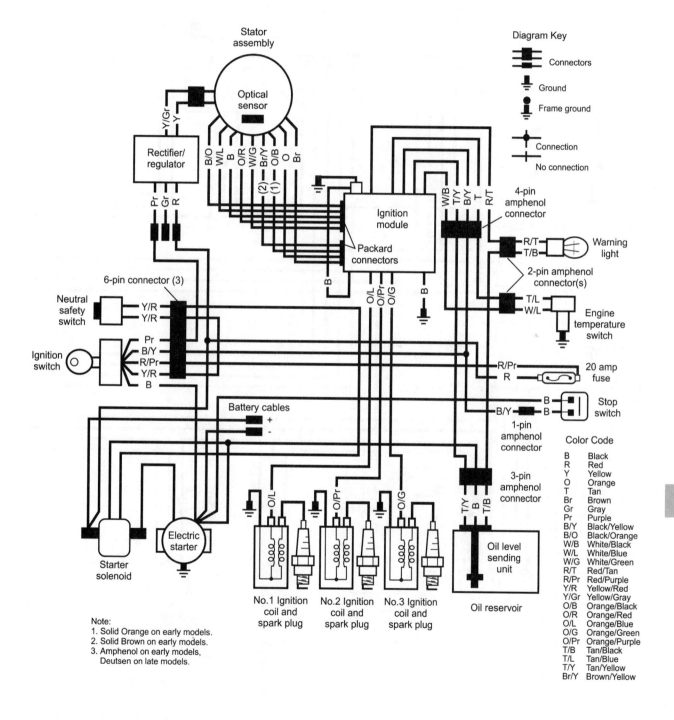

Note:
1. Solid Orange on early models.
2. Solid Brown on early models.
3. Amphenol on early models, Deutsen on late models.

Diagram Key

Connectors

Ground

Frame ground

Connection

No connection

Color Code

B	Black
R	Red
Y	Yellow
O	Orange
T	Tan
Br	Brown
Gr	Gray
Pr	Purple
B/Y	Black/Yellow
B/O	Black/Orange
W/B	White/Black
W/L	White/Blue
W/G	White/Green
R/T	Red/Tan
R/Pr	Red/Purple
Y/R	Yellow/Red
Y/Gr	Yellow/Gray
O/B	Orange/Black
O/R	Orange/Red
O/L	Orange/Blue
O/G	Orange/Green
O/Pr	Orange/Purple
T/B	Tan/Black
T/L	Tan/Blue
T/Y	Tan/Yellow
Br/Y	Brown/Yellow

14

25 AND 35 HP (THREE-CYLINDER) REMOTE CONTROL

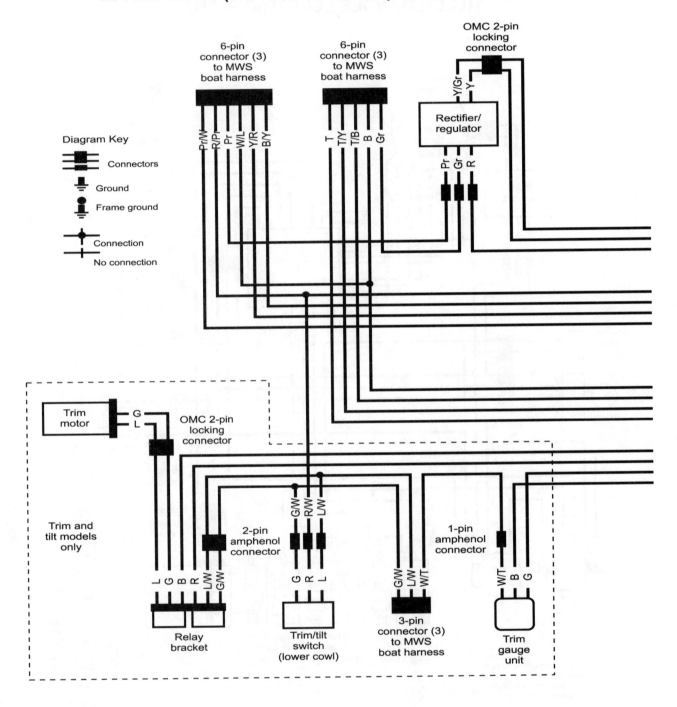

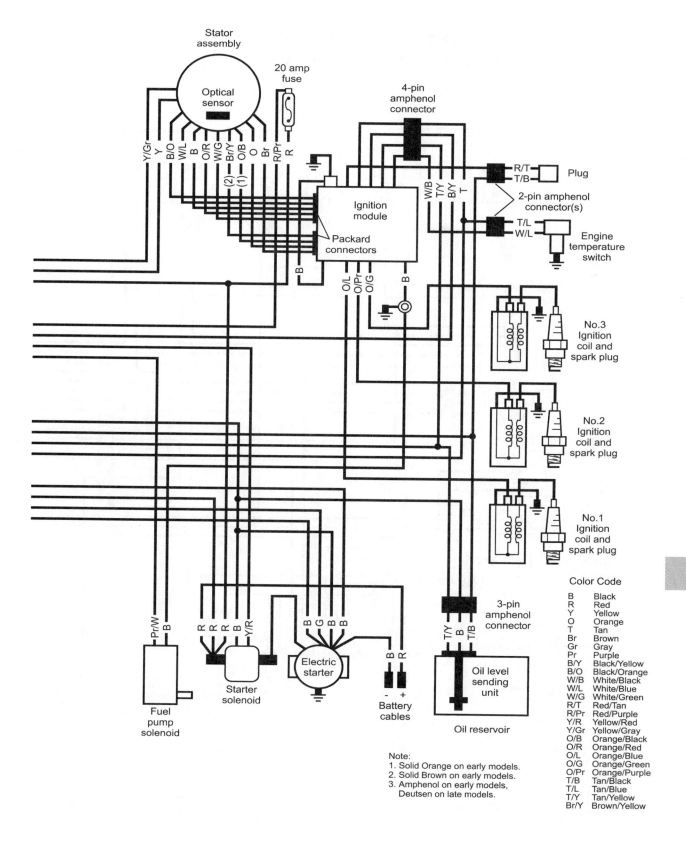

Stator assembly
Optical sensor

20 amp fuse

4-pin amphenol connector

Ignition module

Packard connectors

R/T
T/B
Plug

2-pin amphenol connector(s)

T/L
W/L
Engine temperature switch

No.3 Ignition coil and spark plug

No.2 Ignition coil and spark plug

No.1 Ignition coil and spark plug

Electric starter

Starter solenoid

Battery cables

Fuel pump solenoid

3-pin amphenol connector

Oil level sending unit

Oil reservoir

Color Code
B   Black
R   Red
Y   Yellow
O   Orange
T   Tan
Br   Brown
Gr   Gray
Pr   Purple
B/Y Black/Yellow
B/O Black/Orange
W/B White/Black
W/L White/Blue
W/G White/Green
R/T Red/Tan
R/Pr Red/Purple
Y/R Yellow/Red
Y/Gr Yellow/Gray
O/B Orange/Black
O/R Orange/Red
O/L Orange/Blue
O/G Orange/Green
O/Pr Orange/Purple
T/B Tan/Black
T/L Tan/Blue
T/Y Tan/Yellow
Br/Y Brown/Yellow

Note:
1. Solid Orange on early models.
2. Solid Brown on early models.
3. Amphenol on early models, Deutsen on late models.

14

40 AND 50 HP (TWO-CYLINDER)
TILLER HANDLE ELECTRIC START

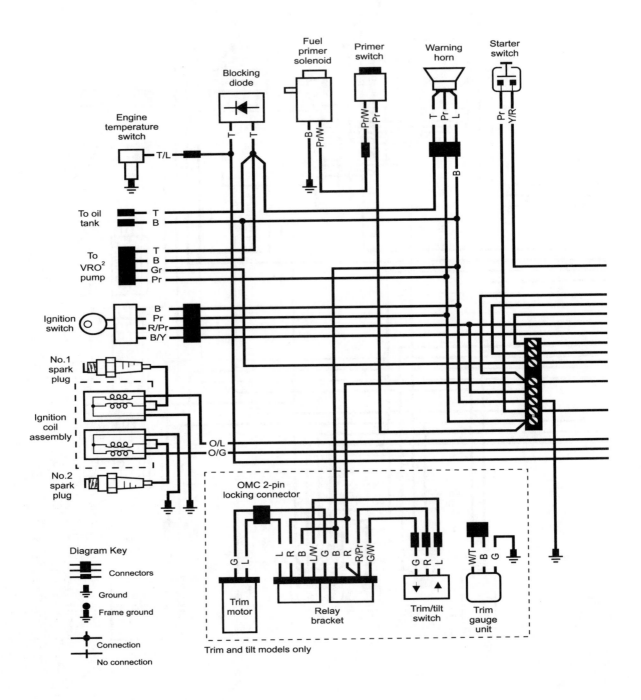

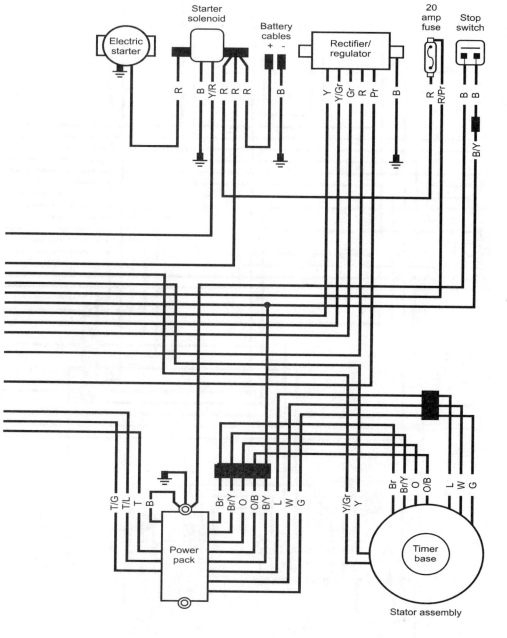

Color Code

B	Black
W	White
R	Red
L	Blue
Y	Yellow
O	Orange
T	Tan
Br	Brown
Gr	Gray
Pr	Purple
B/Y	Black/Yellow
B/O	Black/Orange
W/T	White/Tan
L/W	Blue/White
G/W	Green/White
R/Pr	Red/Purple
Y/R	Yellow/Red
Y/Gr	Yellow/Gray
O/B	Orange/Black
O/R	Orange/Red
O/L	Orange/Blue
O/Gr	Orange/Green
T/B	Tan/Black
T/L	Tan/Blue
T/G	Tan/Green
T/Y	Tan/Yellow
Br/Y	Brown/Yellow

40 AND 50 HP (TWO-CYLINDER)
TILLER HANDLE ELECTRIC START/1995-2003 (ED-ST)

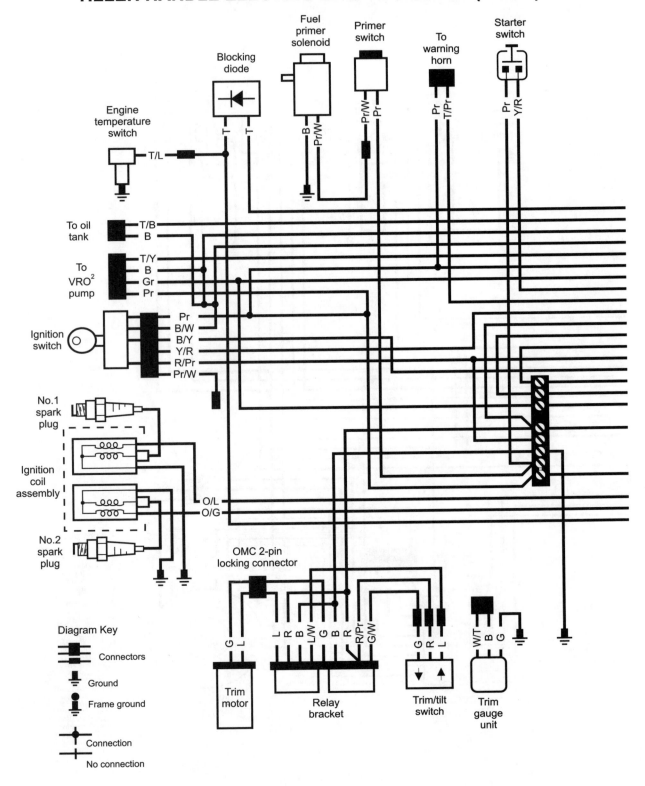

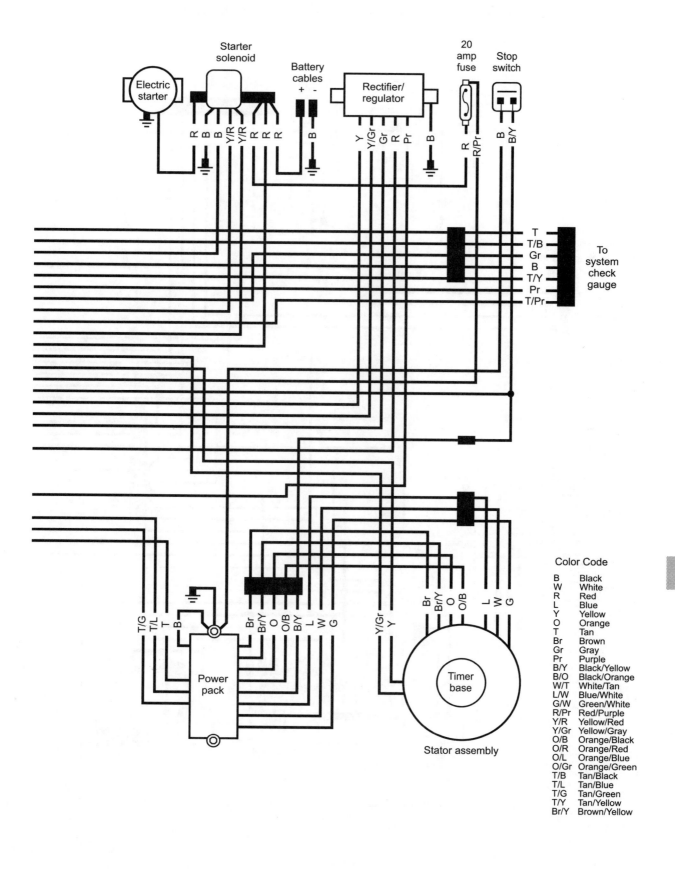

14

40 AND 50 HP (TWO-CYLINDER)
REMOTE CONTROL/1995 (EO) MODELS

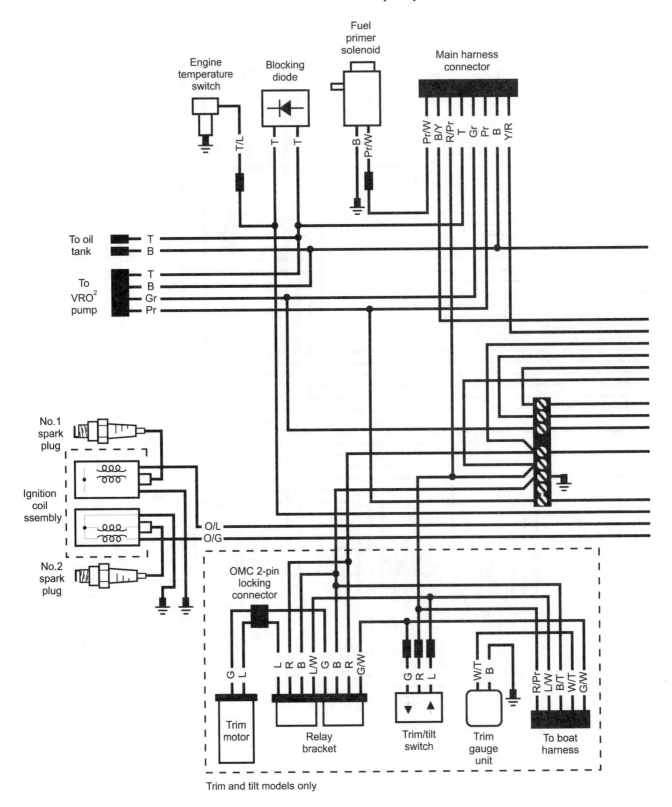

Trim and tilt models only

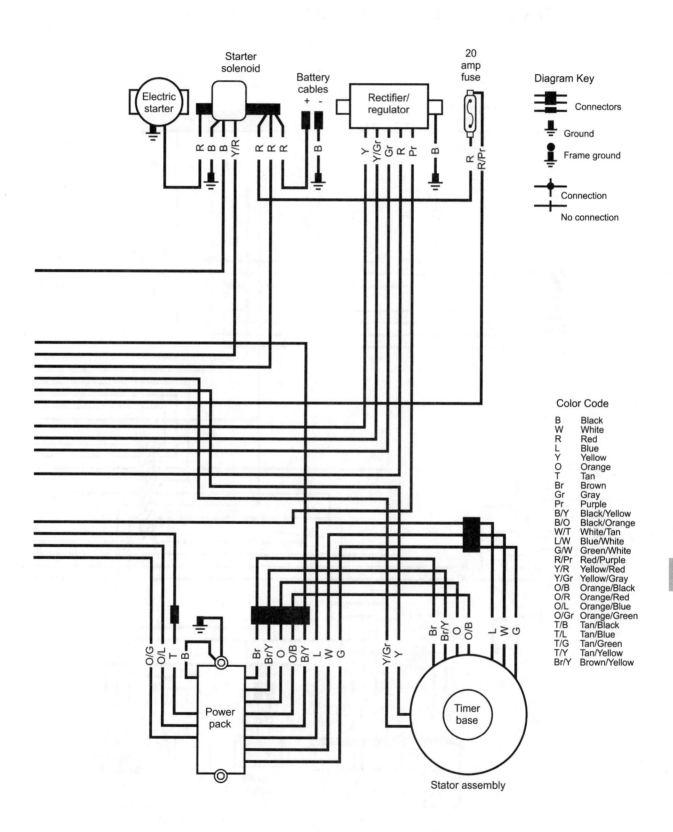

40 AND 50 HP (TWO-CYLINDER)
REMOTE CONTROL/1996-2003 (ED-ST) MODELS

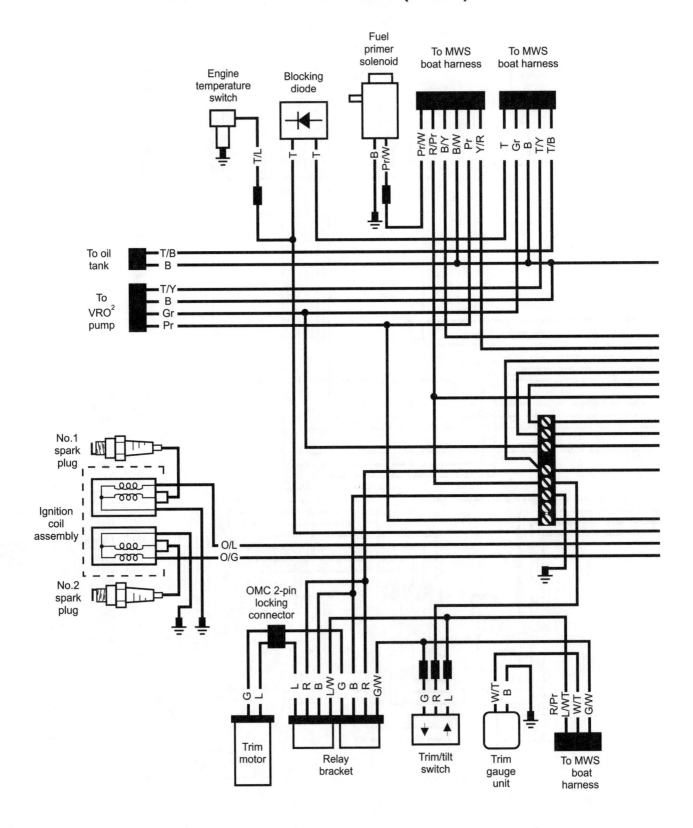

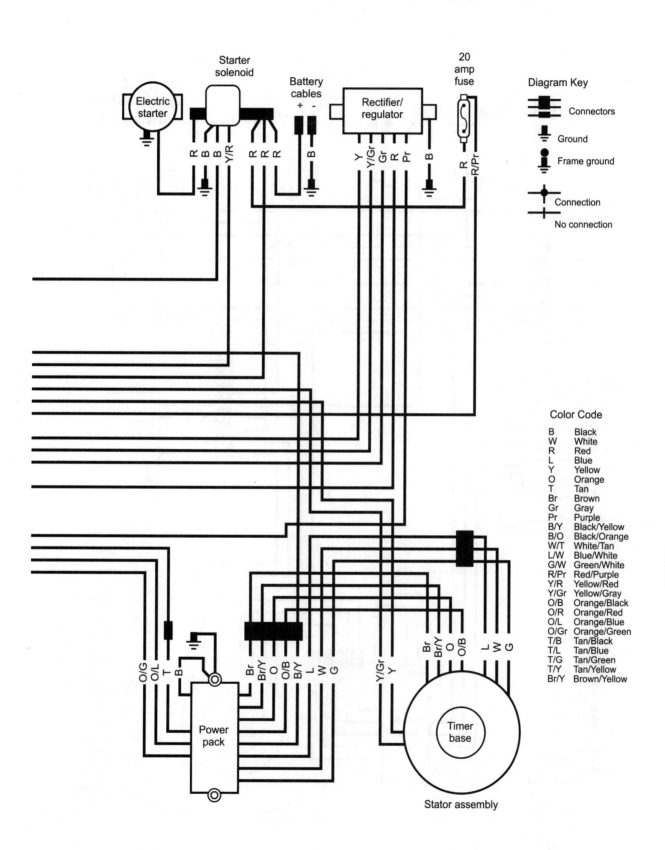

Starter solenoid

Battery cables + -

Rectifier/ regulator

20 amp fuse

Electric starter

Diagram Key

Connectors

Ground

Frame ground

Connection

No connection

Color Code

B   Black
W   White
R   Red
L   Blue
Y   Yellow
O   Orange
T   Tan
Br   Brown
Gr   Gray
Pr   Purple
B/Y   Black/Yellow
B/O   Black/Orange
W/T   White/Tan
L/W   Blue/White
G/W   Green/White
R/Pr   Red/Purple
Y/R   Yellow/Red
Y/Gr   Yellow/Gray
O/B   Orange/Black
O/R   Orange/Red
O/L   Orange/Blue
O/Gr   Orange/Green
T/B   Tan/Black
T/L   Tan/Blue
T/G   Tan/Green
T/Y   Tan/Yellow
Br/Y   Brown/Yellow

14

Power pack

Timer base

Stator assembly

48 SPECIAL 1995 (EO) MODELS

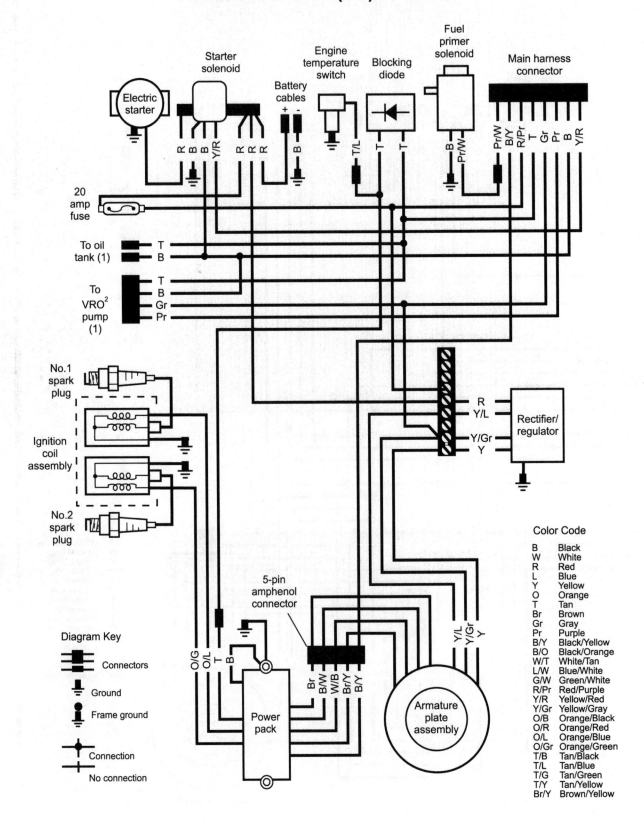

Color Code

B	Black
W	White
R	Red
L	Blue
Y	Yellow
O	Orange
T	Tan
Br	Brown
Gr	Gray
Pr	Purple
B/Y	Black/Yellow
B/O	Black/Orange
W/T	White/Tan
L/W	Blue/White
G/W	Green/White
R/Pr	Red/Purple
Y/R	Yellow/Red
Y/Gr	Yellow/Gray
O/B	Orange/Black
O/R	Orange/Red
O/L	Orange/Blue
O/Gr	Orange/Green
T/B	Tan/Black
T/L	Tan/Blue
T/G	Tan/Green
T/Y	Tan/Yellow
Br/Y	Brown/Yellow

Diagram Key

Connectors

Ground

Frame ground

Connection

No connection

48 SPECIAL 1996 (ED) MODELS

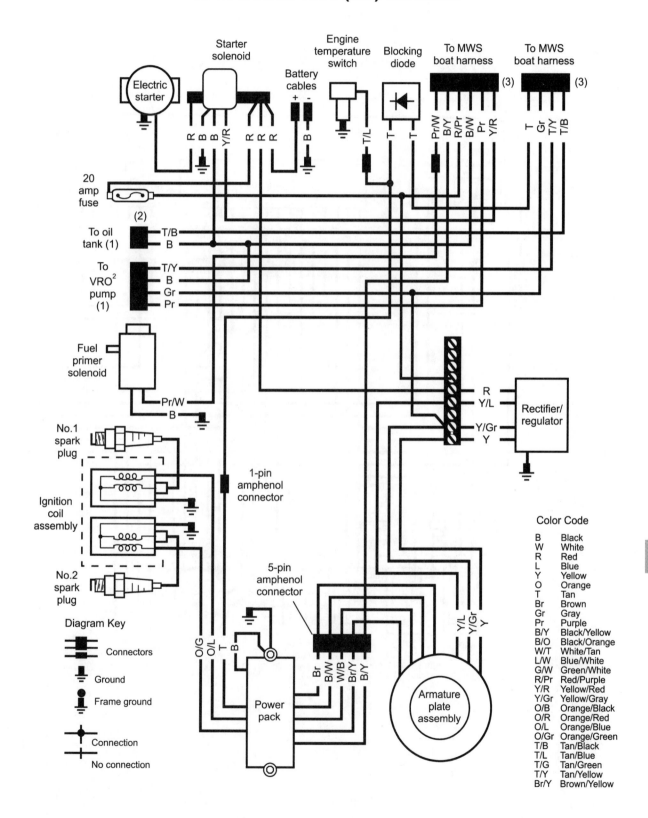

Diagram Key

Connectors

Ground

Frame ground

Connection

No connection

Color Code

B	Black
W	White
R	Red
L	Blue
Y	Yellow
O	Orange
T	Tan
Br	Brown
Gr	Gray
Pr	Purple
B/Y	Black/Yellow
B/O	Black/Orange
W/T	White/Tan
L/W	Blue/White
G/W	Green/White
R/Pr	Red/Purple
Y/R	Yellow/Red
Y/Gr	Yellow/Gray
O/B	Orange/Black
O/R	Orange/Red
O/L	Orange/Blue
O/Gr	Orange/Green
T/B	Tan/Black
T/L	Tan/Blue
T/G	Tan/Green
T/Y	Tan/Yellow
Br/Y	Brown/Yellow

14

60 AND 70 HP TILLER, POWER TRIM/TILT

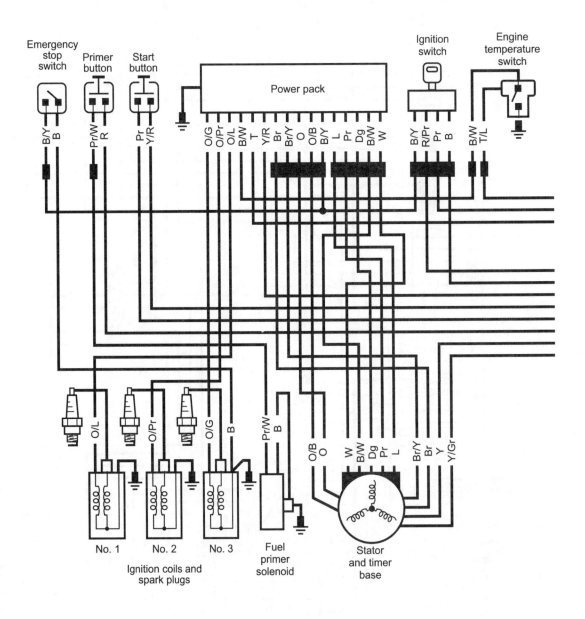

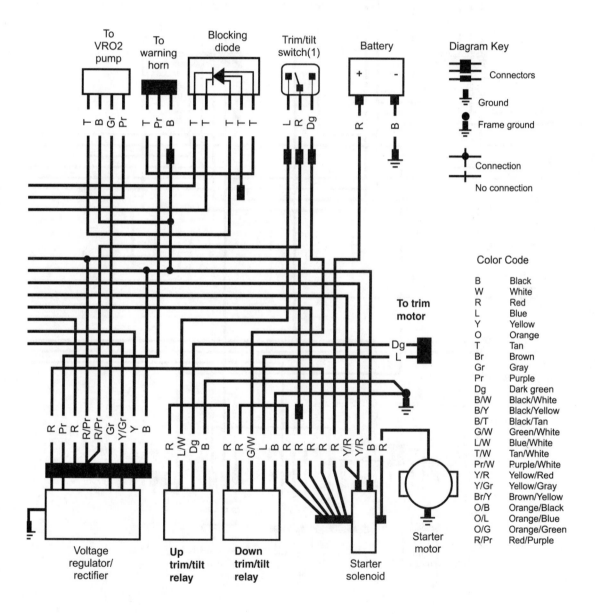

14

50-70 HP (THREE-CYLINDER)
TILLER HANDLE ELECTRIC START/1996-2003 (ED-ST) MODELS

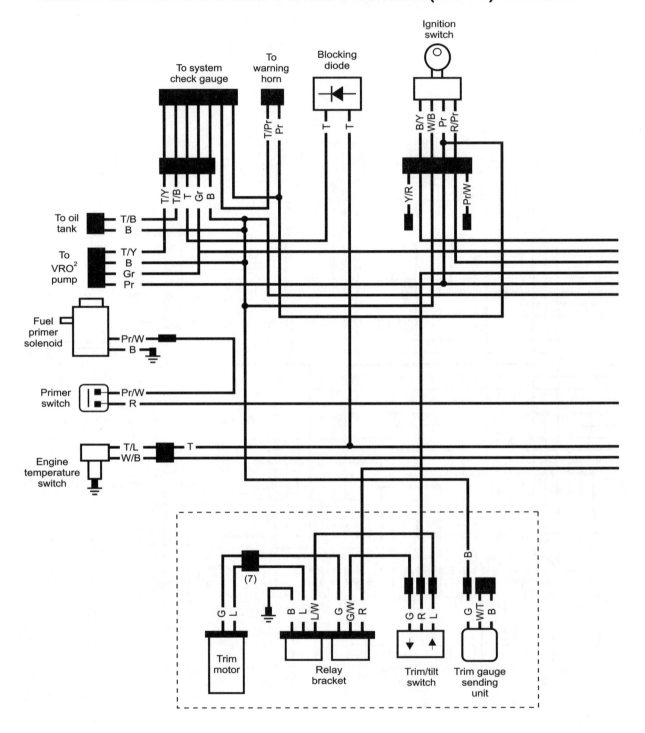

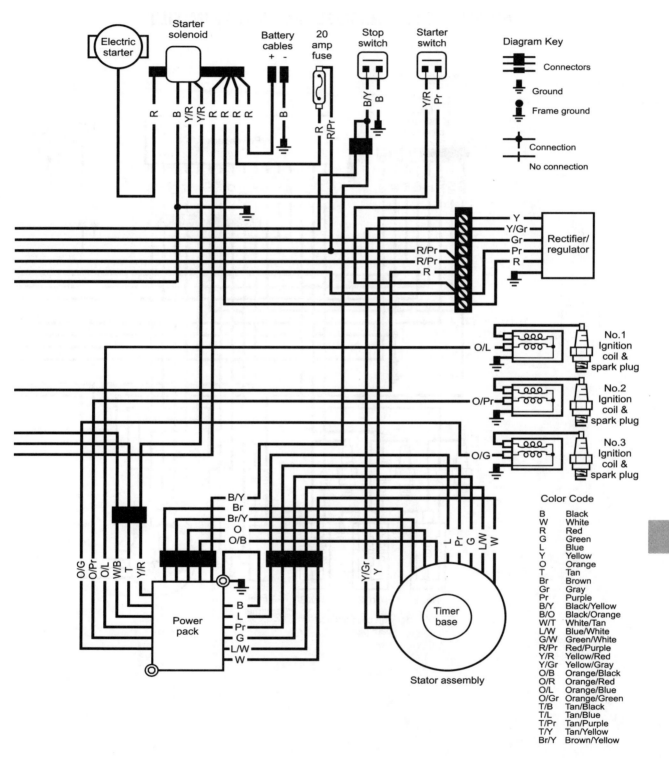

14

60 AND 70 HP REMOTE, POWER TRIM/TILT

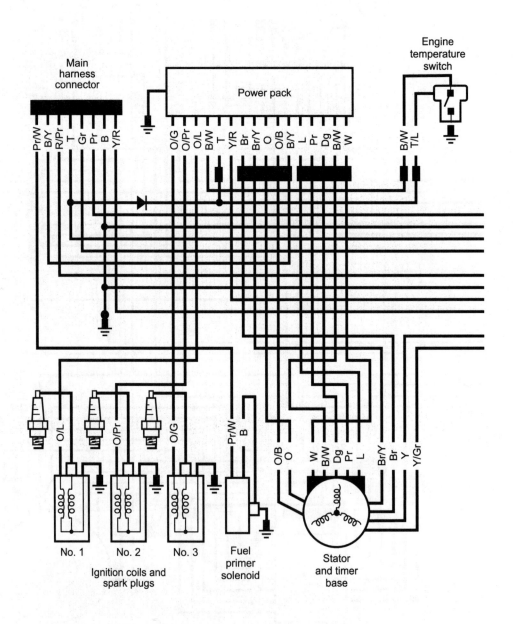

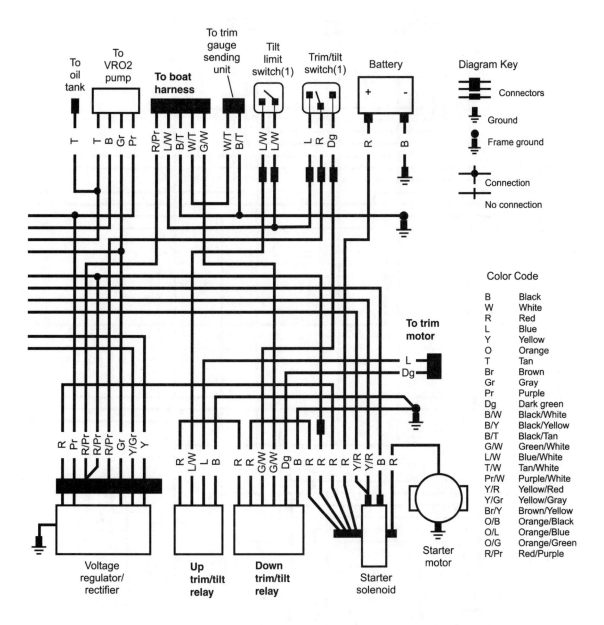

To boat harness

To trim gauge sending unit

Tilt limit switch(1)

Trim/tilt switch(1)

Battery

To oil tank

To VRO2 pump

To trim motor

Diagram Key

Connectors

Ground

Frame ground

Connection

No connection

Color Code

B	Black
W	White
R	Red
L	Blue
Y	Yellow
O	Orange
T	Tan
Br	Brown
Gr	Gray
Pr	Purple
Dg	Dark green
B/W	Black/White
B/Y	Black/Yellow
B/T	Black/Tan
G/W	Green/White
L/W	Blue/White
T/W	Tan/White
Pr/W	Purple/White
Y/R	Yellow/Red
Y/Gr	Yellow/Gray
Br/Y	Brown/Yellow
O/B	Orange/Black
O/L	Orange/Blue
O/G	Orange/Green
R/Pr	Red/Purple

Voltage regulator/rectifier

Up trim/tilt relay

Down trim/tilt relay

Starter solenoid

Starter motor

14

50-70 HP (THREE-CYLINDER)
REMOTE CONTROL/1996-2003 (ED-ST) MODELS

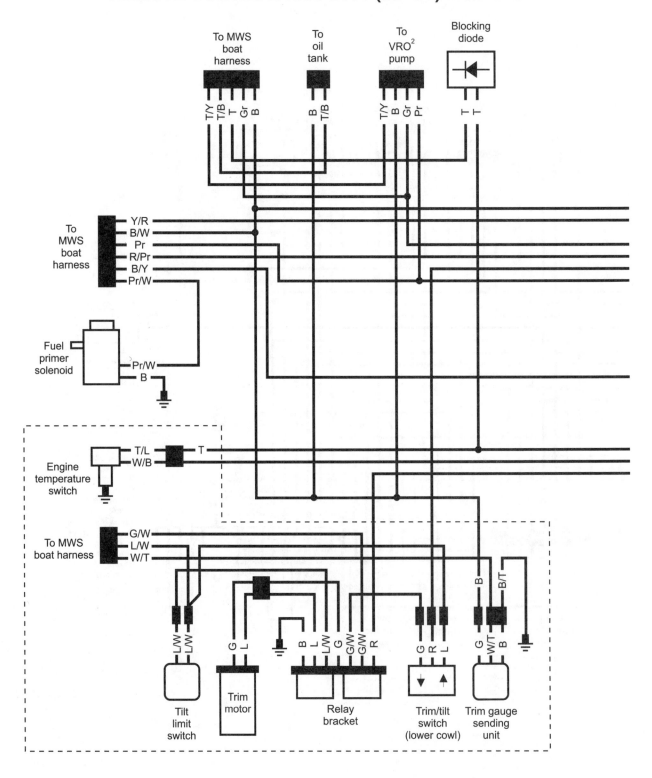

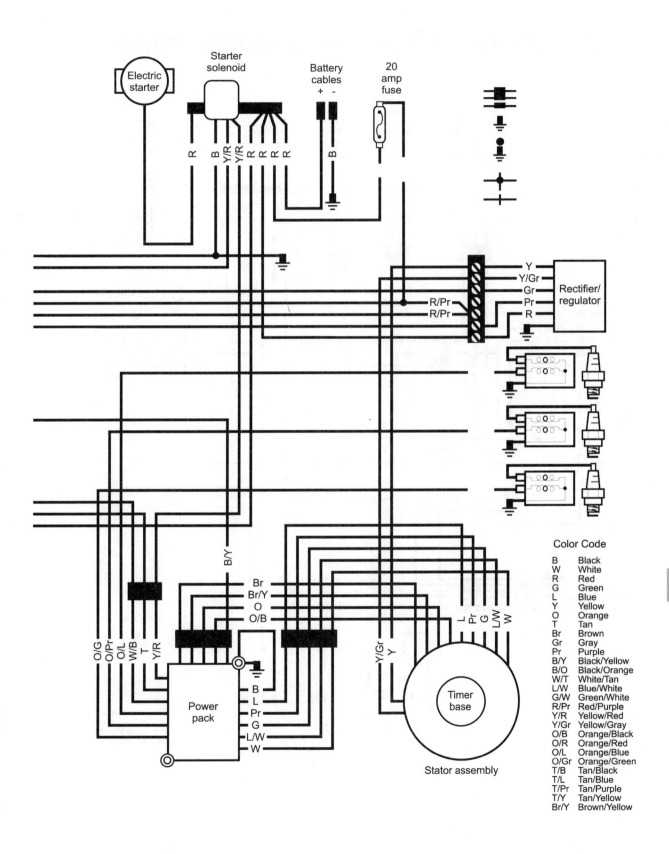

TYPICAL TRIM AND TILT SYSTEM/1996-2003 (ED-ST) MODELS

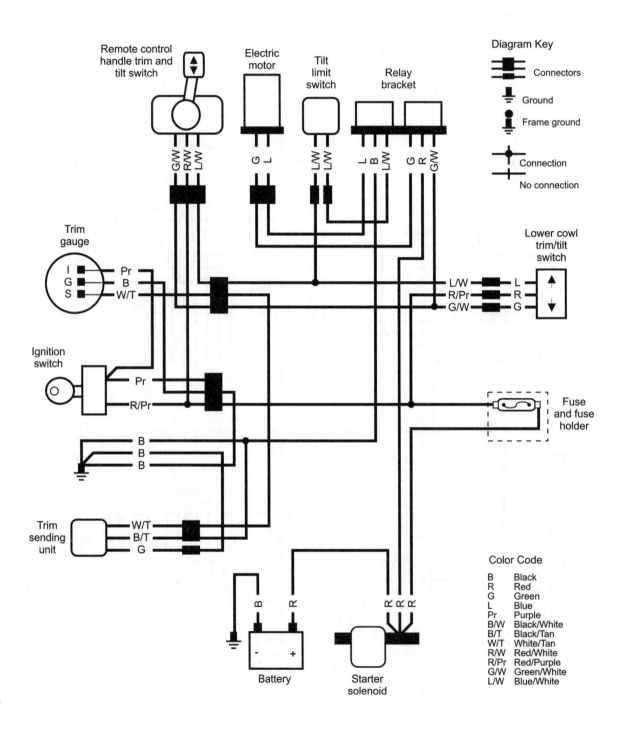

BOAT WIRING HARNESS
(MODULAR WIRING SYSTEM)/1996-2003 (ED-ST) MODELS

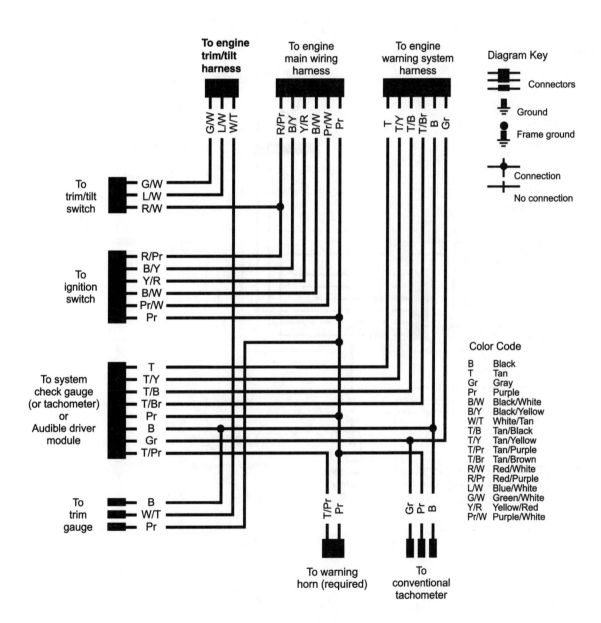

To engine trim/tilt harness — G/W, L/W, W/T

To engine main wiring harness — R/Pr, B/Y, Y/R, B/W, Pr/W, Pr

To engine warning system harness — T, T/Y, T/B, T/Br, B, Gr

Diagram Key
Connectors
Ground
Frame ground
Connection
No connection

To trim/tilt switch — G/W, L/W, R/W

To ignition switch — R/Pr, B/Y, Y/R, B/W, Pr/W, Pr

To system check gauge (or tachometer) or Audible driver module — T, T/Y, T/B, T/Br, Pr, B, Gr, T/Pr

To trim gauge — B, W/T, Pr

To warning horn (required) — T/Pr, Pr

To conventional tachometer — Gr, Pr, B

Color Code

B	Black
T	Tan
Gr	Gray
Pr	Purple
B/W	Black/White
B/Y	Black/Yellow
W/T	White/Tan
T/B	Tan/Black
T/Y	Tan/Yellow
T/Pr	Tan/Purple
T/Br	Tan/Brown
R/W	Red/White
R/Pr	Red/Purple
L/W	Blue/White
G/W	Green/White
Y/R	Yellow/Red
Pr/W	Purple/White

14

CONTROL BOX WIRING HARNESS
(MODULAR WIRING SYSTEM)/1996-2003 (ED-ST) MODELS

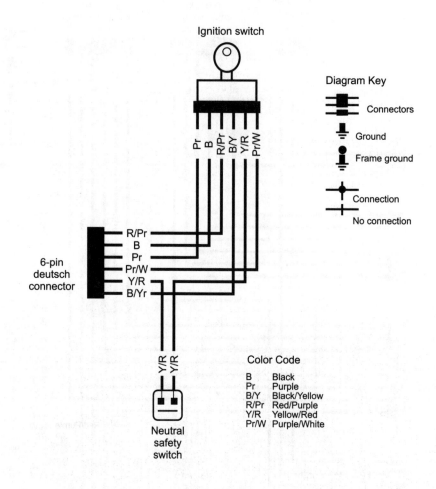

Ignition switch

Diagram Key

Connectors

Ground

Frame ground

Connection

No connection

6-pin
deutsch
connector

R/Pr
B
Pr
Pr/W
Y/R
B/Yr

Pr
B
R/Pr
B/Y
Y/R
Pr/W

Y/R
Y/R

Neutral
safety
switch

Color Code

B	Black
Pr	Purple
B/Y	Black/Yellow
R/Pr	Red/Purple
Y/R	Yellow/Red
Pr/W	Purple/White

CONTROL BOX WIRING HARNESS
(MODULAR WIRING SYSTEM)/1996-2003 (ED-ST) MODELS

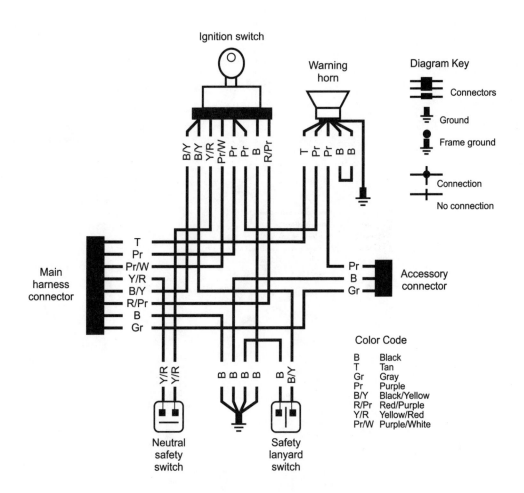

Ignition switch

Warning horn

Diagram Key

Connectors

Ground

Frame ground

Connection

No connection

Main harness connector

T
Pr
Pr/W
Y/R
B/Y
R/Pr
B
Gr

Pr
B
Gr

Accessory connector

Neutral safety switch

Safety lanyard switch

Color Code

B   Black
T   Tan
Gr   Gray
Pr   Purple
B/Y Black/Yellow
R/Pr Red/Purple
Y/R Yellow/Red
Pr/W Purple/White

14

NOTES

NOTES

NOTES

NOTES

MAINTENANCE LOG

Date	Maintenance Performed	Engine Hours